PSYCHOLOGY

Fourth Edition

PSYCHOLOGY

Its
Principles
and
Meanings

Fourth Edition

Lyle E. Bourne, Jr.
Bruce R. Ekstrand

University of Colorado

Holt, Rinehart and Winston
New York   Chicago   San Francisco   Philadelphia
Montreal   Toronto   London   Sydney   Tokyo
Mexico City   Rio de Janeiro   Madrid

Senior Acquisitions Editor   Daniel M. Loch
Developmental Editor   Susan H. Hajjar
Senior Project Editor   Françoise D. Bartlett
Art Director and Cover Designer   Lou Scardino
Production Manager   Pat Sarcuni
Photo and Cartoon Researchers   Mili Ve McNiece, Jo-Anne Naples
Text Designer   Caliber Design Planning
Cover Photograph © Peter Angelo Simon 1981

Library of Congress Cataloging in Publication Data
Bourne, Lyle Eugene, 1932–
   Psychology: its principles and meanings.
   Bibliography: p. 549.
   Includes indexes.
   1. Psychology.   I. Ekstrand, Bruce R.   II. Title.
[DNLM: 1. Psychology. BF 121 B775p]
BF121.B62   1982   150   81–7034
ISBN 0-03-059688-2   AACR2

CBS COLLEGE PUBLISHING
Holt, Rinehart and Winston
The Dryden Press
Saunders College Publishing

For permission to use copyrighted materials, the authors are indebted to the following:

Chapter 1

Photo, p. 1, by Jean-Claude Lejeune, courtesy of Stock, Boston.
Photo, p. 6, courtesy of Wide World Photos.
News story, p. 6, reprinted with permission from *Science News*, the weekly newsmagazine of science, copyrighted 1980 by Science Service, Inc.
Photo, p. 8, courtesy of Harry F. Harlow, University of Wisconsin Primate Laboratory.
News story, p. 11, reprinted by permission of *TIME*, The Weekly Newsmagazine; Copyright Time Inc. 1979.
News story, p. 13, reprinted by permission of Scripps-Howard News Service.

(Continued on p. 561)

To Rita and Norma
for their many contributions
and for making it all worthwhile

Contributors

Douglas Bernstein   University of Illinois, Champaign-Urbana
Chapter 9, Appendix C

James N. Butcher and **Carolyn L. Williams**   University of Minnesota
Chapters 11 and 12

William Damon   Clark University
Chapter 8

Lewis O. Harvey, Jr.   University of Colorado
Chapter 3

Steven F. Maier   University of Colorado
Chapter 4

Michael E. J. Masson   Victoria University
and **Linda S. Sala**   Wayne State University
Chapters 5 and 6

Charles Tart   University of California, Davis
Appendix D

Robert S. Wyer, Jr.   University of Illinois, Champaign-Urbana
Chapter 10

Acknowledgments

Because of their large number, it is impossible for us to name everyone who assisted us in producing this book. Several people, however, deserve special mention because of the importance of their contributions. Foremost among them are the ten professors of psychology, each a teacher of college-level introductory psychology, who served as subject-matter experts and who drafted or revised several chapters in this edition. These psychologists are listed above as Contributors. To each of them we owe thanks.

The book has materially benefited from the comments and reactions of many reviewers. We would like to recognize the thorough, intelligent, and critical essays on our efforts provided by the following: Paul R. Abramson, University of California at Los Angeles; Richard H. Bauer, Kansas State University; Ellen S. Berscheid, University of Minnesota/main campus; Gary Bothe, Pensacola Junior College; Norman Bregman, Southeastern Louisiana University; David M. Brodzinsky, Rutgers University; Jeanne Brugger, Drexel University; John Caruso, Southeastern Massachusetts University; Joseph R. Coble, Clark College; Charles Collyer, University of Rhode Island; Roy Connally, University of Central Florida; Pat Crane, San Antonio College; James H. Davis, University of Illinois/Urbana-Champaign; James Devine, University of Texas; Lee Doerries, Christopher Newport College; Edward Donahue, Brooklyn College of CUNY; Eva Ferguson, Southern Illinois University; Carl B. Freitag, Middle Tennessee State University; Delbart Garnes, Texas Southern University; Barry Gholson, Memphis State University; Barbara Goldman, University of Michigan/Dearborn; Felice Gordis, California State University/Fullerton; Peter Gram, Pensacola Junior College; William T. Greenough, University of Illinois/Urbana-Champaign; Virginia Gronwaldt, University of Toledo; Joseph H. Grosslight, Florida State University; Robert Grossman, Kalamazoo College; Thomas H. Harrell, Florida Institute of Technology; Thomas Hewett, Drexel University; Stephen Hobbs, Augusta College; Donna Hummel, Cleveland State University; Thomas Jackson, Fort Hays State University; William Johnston, University of Utah; Stuart A. Karabenick, Eastern Michigan University; Sara B. King, St. Francis College; Frederick L. Kitterle, National Science Foundation; Julius Kling, Brown University; Donald K. Lauer, Kutztown State College; Robert M. Levy, Indiana State University; John Long, Indiana University/South Bend; Joan F. Lorden, University of Alabama at Birmingham; Thomas Ludwig, Hope College; Barclay Martin, University of North Carolina; Edward McAllister, Russell Sage College/main campus; Hayden Mees, Western Washington University; James C. Megas, Pan American University at Brownsville; Joel Morgovsky, Brookdale Community College; Benjamin H. Newberry, Kent State University; Edward O'Day, San Diego State University; Jeanne O'Kon, Tallahassee Community College; Joseph Palladino, St. Francis College; Linda Petersen, University of Miami; Terry F. Pettijohn, Ohio State University/Marion campus; Rebecca Reviere, Albany Junior College; Daniel W. Russell, University of Iowa; H. R. Schiffman, Rutgers State University; Allan H. Schulman, Virginia Polytechnic Institute; Jonathan Segal, Catholic University of America; Robert Seibel, Pennsylvania State University; Richard O. Straub, University of Michigan/Dearborn; Julia Wallace, University of Northern Iowa; Wayne Weiten, College of DuPage; Carolyn D. Wells, Texas Southern University; Susan K. Whitbourne, University of Rochester; Michael Williams, Embry Riddle University; Frank N. Willis, University of Missouri; Dale Wise, San Jose State University; Bond Woodruff, Northern Illinois University; Rita Yaroush, National Jewish Hospital.

Many ideas and suggestions were contributed by those colleagues who prepared ancillary materials for the text: Arthur Gutman, John Karpicke, and Frank Webbe.

We are also indebted to the people who worked with us throughout this project. Their support and encouragement, ideas and stimulation, expertise and technical contributions are too great to recount in detail. We are especially grateful to Françoise Bartlett, Debbie Burki, Mary Ann Gundel, Susan H. Hajjar, Daniel Loch, Mili Ve McNiece, Jo-Anne Naples, Pat Sarcuni, and Lou Scardino.

L.E.B. Jr.
B.R.E.

Preface

Our purpose has been to provide a useful text for the first course in psychology. The book treats a selection of major topics in the field in depth. We did not intend to produce a superficial or an encyclopedic survey, so that we have not included all of the topics that might be examined. Our coverage has struck the right note with most instructors, however, and therefore the book is again organized into 12 chapters and 4 appendices.

Chapter 1, an introduction, is followed by 11 chapters that discuss basic areas in psychology: biopsychology; perception; conditioning; human learning, memory, and language; cognition; motivation and emotion; human development; personality; social psychology; psychopathology; and psychotherapy. The appendices focus on statistics, neurophysiology, psychological testing, and altered states of consciousness. They are intended as supplementary or extended reading where the instructor finds them appropriate.

We have again employed two techniques unique to this book that were well received by students and instructors in previous editions. First, each chapter is divided into two parts—the main text, dealing with the known concepts in the particular area (what do we know?), and the "What Does It Mean?" section, which considers applications of that basic knowledge. The "What Does It Mean?" sections are set off in colored pages following the main text of the chapter so that they can be easily assigned according to the instructor's objectives. Second, newspaper articles and cartoons illustrate many otherwise esoteric aspects of psychology. We have employed these devices in teaching our own introductory course. Instructors and students have found these resources to be a significant addition to both their enjoyment and their understanding of psychology.

We have, of course, strived to make this edition more informative, interesting, and readable. But there are other changes that are especially worth noting. Chapter 1 now includes a "What Does It Mean?" section which explores careers in psychology. Furthermore, we have added to that chapter a section on basic issues that pervade psychology, and we have introduced the concept of quasi-experimentation—an area that has become increasingly important in contemporary research.

We have tried to reduce the difficulty of Chapter 2, biopsychology, by eliminating some of the complexities of neuroanatomy and by stressing the role of the brain in processing information and controlling behavior. We have also given appropriate emphasis to recent discoveries in neurochemistry.

Chapter 4 on conditioning introduces new material on the physiological bases of simple learning and on cognition and the detection of causal relationships in the world.

Chapters 5 and 6 have been recast and rewritten. Our treatment of traditional approaches to language and human learning has been reduced. We have tried to give these chapters more of a cognitive and/or information-processing flavor. We now deal with the mental representation of knowledge and with psycholinguistics in Chapter 5. We have expanded significantly our coverage of intelligence, introducing the notions of artificial and nonhuman intelligence in Chapter 6.

Chapter 7 contains a new section on cognitive bases of motivation, which includes a discussion of attribution and subjective utility theory. We have also attempted to provide a more systematic, yet simplified, treatment of the basic motivational concepts of need, drive, and incentive.

Chapter 8 now provides greater coverage of the development of social behavior and personality.

Chapter 9 contains new sections on Dollard and Miller, Skinner, and Mischel.

Chapter 10 has been completely rewritten to reflect our overall information-processing theme. There are new sections on social cognition and social knowledge. The organization of this chapter is now much more consistent with the general discussion of human cognition in Chapters 5 and 6.

Chapters 11 and 12 have been changed in accordance with the new diagnostic and statistical manual (DSM–III) for classifying and diagnosing psychopathology. There is more coverage of the cognitive behavioral approach to psychotherapy.

The book has deliberately been kept short as introductory psychology texts go. Thus, for every new topic we added, we reluctantly deleted some old material. Deletions were hard to make, and we apologize if you disagree with some of our choices. We trust, however, that the new material offsets any significant losses. As in the past, we sincerely hope that you will enjoy the text and will find it useful for your introductory course.

Boulder, Colorado   L.E.B., Jr.
October 1981   B.R.E.

Contents

PEANUTS

WHAT ARE YOU READING, FRANKLIN?

IT'S A BOOK ON PSYCHOLOGY.. FROM WHAT I UNDERSTAND, IT SEEMS TO BE PRETTY GOOD..

FORGET IT, FRANKLIN...

NO BOOK ON PSYCHOLOGY CAN BE ANY GOOD IF ONE CAN UNDERSTAND IT!

Dear Reader . . . . .   *Monday, June 22, 1981*

Yesterday's local papers (The Daily Camera, Boulder, and The Rocky Mountain News, Denver) reported the following stories:

ROME (UPI) -- Pope John Paul II, looking pale and thin, was readmitted to the hospital Saturday because of persistent fever complicating his recovery from an assassination attempt May 13.

A British cyclist left Los Angeles on the last leg of his round-the-world bicycle ride, trying to break the existing record of 143 days.

David Berkowitz, the "Son of Sam" killer, told a New York Supreme Court justice that he was going "stir crazy" in Attica prison where he is serving a 315-year term.

189 marchers in a Denver walkathon last Saturday raised $24,488 for the National Organization of Women campaign in support of the Equal Rights Amendment to the Constitution. The most successful fundraiser was Bunny Easter, a veteran of military service with only one leg, who collected pledges of $1,184.

ERICK, Okla. (AP) -- A gunman, yelling that he wanted the FBI to arrest him, hijacked a Greyhound bus Saturday with 32 people aboard.

NEW DELHI, India -- An Indian movie actress has been ordered to answer charges that she kissed Prince Charles of England in public eight months ago during his state visit to India. Ever since India gained independence in 1947, kissing in public has been forbidden. If convicted, a person is usually reprimanded by the court and given a nominal fine.

Rachel Noel has been elected both as the first woman and the first black to head the University of Colorado's Board of Regents.

ASHLAND, Ore. (UPI) -- John Francis III was graduated from Southern Oregon State College last week--some eight years after he spoke his last word. Francis, 35, a math and science student, began what had been intended as a one-year experiment in nonverbal communication in 1973. Since then he has laughed, grunted, pantomimed, and played banjo--but uttered not a word. That did not prevent him from graduating with distinction.

Boulder's massage parlor business is still very much alive, despite the closing by police last September of one of the city's most notorious salons. Police say that at least six parlors are operating in the city now as disguised houses of prostitution.

A Florida-based church that allegedly practices "brainwashing" and mind control techniques on its members has ministers in Boulder and Denver. Reportedly, the church uses four "tactics" to control its members: indoctrination, isolation, grueling activity, and prayer partners. Local ministers of the church have labeled these charges untrue and absurd.

In one way or another, all of these stories are about human behavior. Behavior makes news. Imagine what the newspaper would be like if it couldn't report on behavior. We are all fascinated by behavior, and at least when it comes to our behavior, we are all amateur psychologists.

Psychology is the science of behavior. The goals of this science are to measure and describe behavior, to predict and control it, and to understand and explain it. While you have all been students of behavior, this book will introduce you to the study of behavior as a scientific enterprise and as a formal academic discipline. Our goal is to provide you with an overview of the field of psychology today.

A very large part of understanding psychology has to do with under-standing variations in human behavior. There are two types of variation that must always be kept in mind: (1) variation within the same individual from one time to the next, as in, "Why did I eat more than I usually do last night?" and (2) variation between individuals, as in, "Why does Ralph always drink so much--Harry never does that?"

In seeking answers to questions about variation in behavior from one person to the next, or from one time to the next, we think that generally the answers can be found in one of four general concepts or aspects of behavior: (1) biological capacity--behavior varies because people have different biological equipment to work with, or the biological state of their bodies differs from one time to another; (2) knowledge--people's behavior will differ if their knowledge differs, as, for example, when some people unknowingly eat high-cholesterol foods while others don't; (3) competence or skill, as when some people can ride a bicycle and others can't; and (4) intention or motivation, as when some people want to lose weight and others don't. The variations in behavior we observe are variations in people's performance--it is the performance, the overt behavior that the science of psychology must explain. The explanations will involve variations in biological capacity, knowledge, skill, and motivation. These concepts are crucial in understanding behavior, and we will refer to them repeatedly throughout the book.

We have emphasized two basic aspects of psychology in this book. First we have tried to present the basic knowledge about behavior--the facts, principles, and "laws." We have tried to present answers to the question: "What do we know about behavior?" Second, we have attempted to spell out the significance of this knowledge--how it can be applied, its implications for the future. We have tried to present answers to the questions: "What does this knowledge mean?" Accordingly, each of the chapters has been divided into two parts, the first telling what we know about a particular aspect of behavior, such as memory or motivation, and the second attempting to describe the impact this knowledge had or may have on our lives. We have not hesitated to speculate about the potential usefulness and application of present knowledge. We apologize for sometimes letting our imaginations run away. We do not apologize, however, for attempting to make psychology look important, exciting, and fascinating, and of great applied significance, because it is all that and more.

We hope that this book will convey to you what psychology is about. Psychology, like other sciences, has become highly specialized and diverse, and we can hope only to cover the highlights. To give you an idea of the diversity of specific problems that psychologists are interested in, consider the following sample:

Ralph is a 27-year-old salesman for a large insurance company. He has a promising career with the company, has a good income, and is married with two children. Yesterday he tried to commit suicide. Why?

Mary is undergoing an operation for removal of a brain tumor. She has received only a local anesthetic, and while her skull is open and her brain exposed the neurosurgeon stimulates her brain with a tiny electrical current. Mary reports seeing and hearing a past experience happening again. Has her brain recorded her entire life of experiences? Is everything we have ever done stored in our brains? How can we tap our stored memories more efficiently?

Johnny is in the sixth grade but reads at only a third-grade level. In one study of college students, less than half could read and comprehend at a level necessary to understand their introductory psychology text. How do the eyes perceive the words on this page, and how are these words understood by the reader? Can research on visual perception lead to better methods of teaching people to read?

In the heart of a New York City residential area, a woman is attacked by a man. She screams loudly many times, begging for help. Several residents hear her screams, but no one even bothers to call the police, much less come to her aid. How can we understand this?

Psychologists devise tests of just about every kind of behavior--IQ, ability to assemble pickup trucks, personality, and so on. There are tests to predict your success in college or in various occupations and tests of your current state of mental health. Bill is a young black high school graduate looking for a job. He just finished taking a whole battery of tests as part of a job interview at the local steel factory. He thinks that tests discriminate against blacks. Is there any truth in his belief?

Gene is the successful mayor of a large city. His backers want him to challenge the incumbent governor in the upcoming primary election. Gene wants to see the outcome of a local newspaper poll before deciding. Will the poll be of any use to him in predicting his chances of winning? Can psychologists help him to be a more persuasive speaker, a more attractive candidate? Can psychology help him win the election?

As children grow up, do they acquire knowledge in different ways? Should the method of teaching change as children get older? Are there natural stages in the development of a child that make it impossible to teach some things, such as reading, until the child is at least, say 6 years old? How do people learn anything? Why can't we learn while we are sleeping? Why can't we learn faster? Why are some things easy to learn and others difficult? Why do people forget what they once learned?

Throughout the book you will see more examples of what psychology is about. Many have been drawn from newspapers and magazines. We present you with these clippings, not because we believe everything that is said in each clipping, but because they are thought-provoking, interesting, exciting, and sometimes depressing. You should not accept them as proven facts. Clippings are not a good source of scientific information or of psychological principles. They are however, a fair reflection of what psychology must address. Use your common sense and think about the ideas being expressed in the clippings—do not hesitate to challenge the "facts" as well as the ideas. And, incidentally, this applies as much to what we say in the text as it does to what others are saying in the newspapers and magazines.

We hope that you will maintain an open mind as you read. When you finish with the book we hope that you'll be asking for more—more facts and less speculation, more precise knowledge and less oversimplification, and more real answers to your questions about behavior. If so, we will be satisfied with the book.

The book has 12 chapters. The first chapter is an introduction, telling you in general what psychology is all about and including a little historical background. The next 11 chapters cover basic content areas in psychology: biopsychology, perception, conditioning, human learning and memory, cognitive processes, motivation and emotion, development of behavior, personality, social psychology, psychopathology, and finally psychotherapy. We have tried to select those topics we feel are most important for the beginning student. With a good foundation of principles and applications in these 11 areas, we feel that you will be able to move on to more advanced study.

We hope that you enjoy reading this book. We aren't promising that you won't be able to put it down, but we will be satisfied if it turns out that when you do put it down, you will at least occasionally be thinking about what you read in it. And when you have finished with it, we hope you will have a better understanding and appreciation of psychology.

Sincerely,

1 | The Nature of Psychology

Make a list of what you think are the top ten problems that face the world today. Then ask yourself, What does psychology—the study of human and animal behavior—have to do with these problems. By studying psychology, will you learn anything about solving these problems?

The ten major problems will not be the same for everyone, of course, but very likely you will include war, poverty; discrimination, crime, disease, inflation, the energy shortage, and overpopulation. These are truly serious problems, and it may seem more important to study them as a way of seeking solutions than to study psychology. But wait a minute! While these problems do require knowledge of such areas as biology, economics, engineering, and geology, they also involve psychology. A war between nations is a war between people. It is human beings who decide whether to go to war and how to conduct military campaigns. Such decisions are a part of human behavior. Psychology studies how and why decisions of all sorts are made. For example, isn't the problem of inflation in large measure a matter of human behavior? How do we get people to save their money rather than spend it all, to work more productively, and to live within their means rather than overextend themselves on credit? These are questions about human behavior that can be answered in part only by doing a psychological study.

Consider the related issues of poverty and overpopulation and ask yourself whether changing people's behavior might not be crucial to their solution. The same could be said about the problems of discrimination and the energy crisis. Finally, what about human health? To be sure, vital organs of the body at times go wrong for purely biological reasons. But there is also a major psychological component to illness. People are sometimes ill because they want to be ill or because they have personalities that predispose them to certain illnesses. Where human motivation or personality is involved, the problem is a psychological one. Furthermore, there is good reason to believe that the most important improvements that can be made in the area of health will have to come about by changing behavior —for example, getting people to stop smoking, to exercise, and to eat more sensibly. Psychology is intimately concerned with how we can change or modify human behavior, and so it has an increasing role to play in promoting health.

Psychology, then, is involved in human affairs in ways you might not ordinarily think of, and it can contribute to the solution of some of the problems the world is currently confronting. These problems are not simple, nor does study of them involve a single body of knowledge. Because psychology is relevant to all of these problems, the more you know about it the more you can understand the issues and possibly even contribute toward improving the quality of life for humankind.

A Definition of Psychology

If you were to ask a few psychologists to describe the field, you might get answers like the following: "Psychology is a body of knowledge. It consists of everything we know about human and animal behavior. It is a set of facts that helps us to understand behavior." Or, "Psychology is a way of studying behavior. It consists of procedures for finding out new information about why human beings and animals behave as they do." Or, "Psychology is a way of using facts about human and animal behavior to improve the condition of organisms, to make life better."

None of these quotes really provides a hard and fast definition of psychology. Even among psychologists there is a good deal of disagreement about how to define the subject. Yet each of these quotes is correct in a sense. A body of knowledge about human and animal behavior exists, and it is called psychology. It is the body of knowledge that psychology instructors teach and that you will discover in this text. Psychology is therefore a *discipline*.

But knowledge doesn't materialize out of a clear blue sky. It has to be discovered or uncovered through certain specified procedures. When we talk about discovering new knowledge, we are talking about psychology as a *science*, emphasizing the set of scientific methods that researchers use to discover new things about behavior.

But there is more to it. Knowledge for its own sake is valuable, to be sure —in fact, knowing has been described as the purest of human states. To know is, in a sense, to be a better person. But knowledge also has a practical aspect: A good deal of psychology can be applied to promote human welfare. Psychology is concerned with human welfare, and that is the *professional* side of psychology. It is what persons in applied psychology and public service do.

In summary, we have to think of psychology as consisting of three components: (1) a body of knowledge; (2) the methods of research used to obtain such knowledge; and (3) the application of knowledge for the benefit of human beings. Psychology is a discipline, a science, and a profession. In this first chapter we will focus on the basic research methods of psychologists. Each chapter of this text is divided into two parts, the first emphasizing the knowledge we have about a particular psychological topic — the facts, principles, and "laws" — and the second describing the practical applications of that knowledge in our everyday lives.

The Goals of Psychology

Our aim — to understand behavior, particularly human behavior, from a scientific point of view — involves three basic goals: (1) accurately describing and measuring, (2) predicting and controlling, and (3) explaining behavior.

Measurement and Description

Before we can understand, explain, or predict behavior, we must first be able to describe and measure it. Much of a psychologist's work involves measuring and describing behavior. All the psychological concepts and processes that we will talk about in this book — anxiety, learning, attitudes, abilities, depression, and more — must be measured. A major goal, therefore, is to develop tests or techniques for measuring.

Each measuring device must possess two characteristics: First, it must have **reliability,**[1] which means that a person's score should not change with repeated testing. A scale that registered a different weight each time you got on it would be unreliable, and therefore not useful. Likewise, a test of intelligence that gave you a different score each time you took it would be worthless.

But reliability is not enough. A test must also have **validity,** which means that it must measure what it is supposed to measure. If we measured your IQ by applying a tape measure to the circumference of your head, we might get the same score each time (indicating reliability), but the measuring technique would have little to do with intelligence.

The questions of reliability and validity of measurement and description apply to all techniques developed by psychologists for the assessment of behavior. You should keep these two criteria in mind when examining the experiments, surveys, observations, and clinical assessments reported in later chapters. These criteria are considered in greater detail in Appendix C.

Prediction and Control

The second goal of psychology is to be able to predict and thereby to control behavior. Success in this effort

[1] Terms in boldface type are defined in the Glossary.

relies heavily on measurement. Psychologists commonly use past measurements of behavior as a primary basis for predicting what a person will do in the future. We can predict a student's performance in school with increased accuracy if we know the individual's general intellectual ability. From the factory worker's score on a mechanical aptitude test we should be able to predict his or her success on an assembly line. College entrance exams help to determine who is admitted to college, and aptitude tests help the personnel director decide whom to hire.

Many prediction efforts assess interests rather than abilities. Vocational counselors give their clients tests to find out the kind of work that might interest them most. An ability to predict your future bill-paying behavior would help a credit agency decide whether or not you are a good risk for a loan. Psychological predictions affect the lives of just about every American. If you have been excluded from medical school or denied a job or credit, it is sometimes difficult to think kindly of the psychologist who produced these tests.

Prediction goes hand in hand with behavior modification and control. Let's assume that the knowledge necessary to predict mental illness existed. We certainly would not want to stop there; good predictions alone would not be satisfactory. Psychologists would want to try to change or modify the behavior of the potentially mentally ill person in a way that would help that person. Indeed, behavior change is often the practicing psychologist's primary aim. The psychotherapist tries to change the patient's behavior; the industrial psychologist tries to modify the behavior of employees; the marriage counselor attempts to modify the behavior of husband and wife; and the prison psychologist tries to control and modify the behavior of criminals. In all of these cases, an effort is made to improve the present or future circumstances of the individual and of society.

Many techniques of behavior modification are remarkably successful, allowing the possibility that someone who has mastered them may control others for his or her own ends. This necessitates that appropriate safeguards be used to ensure the ethical use of successful techniques. A drug that can control cruelty or aggression does not exist now. Consider the problems that might arise if such a drug were discovered. Who would decide when and where techniques and treatments of this sort would be used? What would be the role of society, the government, and the individual on whom it would be used?

Explanation

The final goal of psychology, to explain behavior, is a process that involves formulating theories. Theo-

Chronic Offenders Identified

The likelihood of an arrested person committing another crime can be determined with some accuracy by tracking the prior arrest record and other personal factors, according to an LEAA study—"The Scope and Prediction of Recidivism."

The study found that persons with prior records who were arrested for larceny had a 60 percent likelihood of being arrested again. On the other hand, persons with no prior record who were arrested for larceny had only a 24 percent chance of repeating.

There was a 56 percent chance that individuals with a prior record who were charged with a misdemeanor drug offense would be arrested again. But if charged with a misdemeanor drug offense with no prior record, the chance of rearrest dropped to 19 percent.

Career Criminals Identified

The study suggested that prosecutors might consider these indicators of recidivism as criteria for selecting for career criminal prosecution defendants who otherwise might not come under scrutiny. Career criminals are serious, repeat offenders brought swiftly to trial in a growing number of cities.

The study, one of 17 being completed under a $1.5 million, four-year project, was conducted by the Institute of Law and Social Research (INSLAW). It was paid for by LEAA's National Institute of Law Enforcement and Criminal Justice.

PROMIS Data Used

Data came from the Prosecutor's Management Information System (PROMIS), and is based on a study of 4,703 adults arrested for serious misdemeanors or felonies in Washington, D.C., from January 1, 1971, to August 31, 1975. The sample was taken from a total of 72,510 arrests.

The focus of the study, by Kristen M. Williams, senior research associate at INSLAW, is on individuals repeatedly arrested, prosecuted, and convicted.

"Instead of looking for root causes of recidivism, we have tried to assemble the best predictors of recidivism, based on what can be readily learned about a defendant at case intake and screening," she said.

A major finding was that a small proportion of defendants accounts for a large proportion of arrests. . . .

Law Enforcement Assistance Administration,
Department of Justice
June–July 1979

Here is a nice example of a modern prediction study. The results are correlational and do not tell us much about the causes of criminal behavior. Nonetheless, the results can be useful in the effort to control crime.

ries organize the known facts and help us to make reasonable guesses when we do not know the correct answer.

Some people have argued that explanation is really what psychology is all about. A psychologist may be able to describe and measure anxiety, predict from these measurements the likelihood of a person's suffering mental illness, and intervene to help the individual modify his or her behavior in hopes of preventing the illness, but have little or no understanding of why these techniques work. In principle, almost anyone with reasonable intelligence and the necessary books can diagnose and treat a disease without knowing the causes or why the prescribed medication works. Science is motivated by a desire to know, understand, and discover the causes of phenomena.

Psychologists seek to understand the most complex part of the world, human behavior. This endeavor promises both excitement and reward—and the potential for great practical achievement. Basic psychology attempts to understand in detail many significant issues, for example, mental illness, the processes that underlie the skill involved in reading, and the bases of social interaction. Providing accurate explanations for these psychological phenomena has far-reaching implications for society's most important problems.

Psychology as a Science

Basic Issues

Certain issues concerning people's behavior will come up repeatedly in later chapters. To help in organizing your thinking as you read, try to keep in mind the following basic questions:

1. Is behavior determined (by genetic or environmental forces), or are we, as individuals with free wills, at liberty to choose how we will behave in every situation? Are you reading this book now because you chose to read it or because all of your past experiences have predetermined your fate at this moment?
2. Do we need to have a concept called the mind in order to understand behavior, or can all behavior be understood in terms of physical principles operating in our biological bodies? That is, can behavior be explained in terms of biology, physiology, and biochemistry, or do we need, in addition, a nonphysical mind? This mind-body question, of course, is closely related to the first issue concerning free will versus determinism. If you conclude in favor of the mind, you probably conclude in favor of free will; if you say it's "all in the body," then you probably view behavior as determined. Is your mind learning as you read this book, or does the process merely involve the changing of the neurons in your brain?

3. Is our behavior determined by hereditary genetic factors or by the environments we have passed through to the present or by some complex interaction of these? Is your intelligence (which at least partly determined your entering college and reaching the point of reading this book) inherited from your parents or a function of all the environments you have lived in since you were born?

4. Are we basically conscious of our behavior or is much of what we do controlled by our unconscious minds? You are reading this book for several reasons at this moment —are you consciously aware of all of those reasons? Are there some hidden or unconscious motives at work "making" you read and determining what you will read right now?

Notice that each issue was phrased as an either-or question. This is the way the issues typically are presented for discussion. Unfortunately, such phrasing implies that the correct answer is one alternative or another, a clear black-or-white, right-or-wrong choice. For each issue the answer almost certainly is grey, not black or white. Yet we often observe people considering important questions as if each has only one correct answer.

Even though this may be your first course in psychology, you probably already have definite opinions on these issues. This book and your course will require that you carefully think through your positions. Where you come out on these issues can play a very important role in your life. You will feel differently about things if you believe that people's behavior is determined—by their past or biologically and genetically—than if you believe that behavior is based on free will, the mind, and current circumstances. How you stand on these issues will affect your thinking on such critical matters as the following:

Abortion
Capital punishment
Government intervention in the affairs of citizens
Religion
Prison sentences as opposed to treatment in mental hospitals for convicted criminals
Early-enrichment educational programs such as Head Start
The benefit of consulting a psychotherapist for depression as opposed to getting pills from the family physician
Qualities to look for in a mate
Child-rearing methods

To study these and other issues and to find out about behavior in general, psychologists have devised new methods or adapted old methods from other sciences. Scientific methods are indispensable to progress. We need to know something about methodology to decide between fact and fiction and to avoid being misled by fraudulent claims. The methods of psychology differ in both the kind of information about behavior they yield and the types of behaviors to which they are best suited. They are not mutually exclusive, however, and can sometimes be applied in combination to the same problem to gain a broader perspective. We will discuss four major approaches to the scientific study of behavior and offer examples of the possible applications of each.

Individual Case Study

The case study or case history method is perhaps the simplest and most direct form of psychological investigation. One individual is examined intensively to find out as much as possible about a certain problem, question, or issue as it relates to that person. A combination of measures might be used, including biographical data on the individual, scores on psychological tests, and information obtained in extensive interviews.

The case study procedure is most often used to investigate abnormal behavior patterns. Perhaps the best-known clinical case history in psychology is that of a woman with three different personalities, popularized in the movie *The Three Faces of Eve.* Such case histories can have great impact because of the detail of description they provide and the unusual behavior with which they are concerned. One of the earliest and most famous clinical case studies, reported by Sigmund Freud, concerned a patient, Anna O., who was paralyzed without apparent cause. By composing a detailed case history from a variety of sources, Freud was able to piece together the critical events in Anna O.'s life that contributed to her neurotic behavior. The results of this one case also had tremendous impact on Freud's theory.

Naturalistic Observation

As the name would suggest, naturalistic observation is a systematic method for observing and recording events as they naturally occur in the real world. It is used in cases where artificial probes or manipulations might destroy some or all of the basic characteristics of the phenomenon in question or where there is no way of making a more controlled observation. Suppose we were interested in the mating or maternal behavior of wild elk. Any kind of human intervention, no matter how subtle, might disrupt the basic behavioral pattern. Therefore, some animal psychologists use unobtrusive observational procedures, getting close enough to the animals in their natural habitat to be able to observe (with the help of equipment) but far enough away so that their presence goes undetected. Similar techniques are often used to observe human behavior as well, for example, peer interaction among children from behind a one-way mirror. The idea is to observe behavior without influencing it. The observations, of course, are recorded

One of the techniques psychologists use is the survey. Here an individual is being interviewed on the street.

Cheating When It Counts

Baseball, hot dogs, apple pie and . . . cheating? It may not be considered a traditional part of the American way of life, but cheating may be far more prevalent than people suspect, suggests a study performed by the University of Michigan Institute for Social Research. In a study of 218 male students at a midwestern university, researcher Lynn R. Kahle found that 46 percent of the subjects were willing to cheat on a test when given the opportunity.

Moreover, students who cheat tend to do so "in situations which are personally important to them," according to the study, to be published in the January *Journal of Personality and Social Psychology*. Each of the subjects was administered a test of vocabulary, reading comprehension and a self-selected third test—all given on "secret, pressure-sensitive paper" after which the students were given the opportunity (surreptitiously) to cheat by changing and correcting answers.

Kahle reports that people were more likely to cheat on the test they preferred (vocabulary or reading comprehension). This suggests, she says, "that motivation is enhanced when people are in situations consistent with the type of person they are. . . . They do manipulate their environment to make it more compatible with their own preferences, desires, needs, traits, attitudes and characteristics."

Science News
February 2, 1980

Surveys, opinion polls, and interviews are important research devices for the psychologist. This recent example may interest you.

as objectively as possible, often with tape recorders and cameras.

Naturalistic observation is also the best technique in cases where ethical considerations may prevent the scientist from creating the phenomenon in the laboratory. For example, all of us are concerned with relationships between countries and between races. From a scientific point of view, the psychologist would like to know how these relationships develop and how more cooperative relationships might be arranged. Some by-products of these relationships are destructive and unpleasant—for example, wars between nations and race riots. Because both wars and riots are part of the basic phenomenon of interpersonal relationships, they must be examined by the scientist. On the other hand, the scientist is in no position to influence the occurrence of either kind of tragedy. To investigate such behavioral phenomena psychologists have to observe, record, and try to understand the events as they occur naturally.

Tests, Interviews, and Surveys

Psychological tests have been developed and standardized for just about any aspect of behavior you can imagine. Most of us have had experience with these tests in school or at work. There are tests of general ability, called intelligence tests, and tests of specific traits, such as anxiety or leadership ability. (See Chapters 6 and 9 for more detailed discussions of these psychological tests.) All of these tests consist of a number of questions. The pattern of answers people give is thought to reveal something about their level on the traits and abilities being measured. The sum total of a person's answers gives a composite score that is considered a fair reflection of that person's typical behavior in everyday circumstances.

The psychological interview is often used in the case study method. In that context, the interview is usually free-floating and unstructured. Its direction is guided by the responses of the individual being examined and any hypothesis that the examiner might have about the underlying reasons for these reponses. But interviews can also be highly structured. Like psychological tests, they can consist of a series of items to which the individual is asked to respond. A structured interview is more often used to collect data from a group of people that will lead to general conclusions about that population, rather than to do an intensive study of a single individual.

Surveys fall somewhere between structured interviews and psychological tests. Again, they consist of a series of questions to which individuals are asked to respond. The purpose of the interview is to determine general opinions, attitudes, or feelings on a specific issue. A candidate for political office, for example, might want to determine the general attitude of the public toward a particular issue in order to decide whether his or her campaign should stress or minimize that issue.

Testing, interviewing, surveying, and sometimes naturalistic observation are often combined under the general heading of a *correlational approach* to psychological issues. In general, this approach is used to discover the degree of relationship between two or more variables. A **variable** is any characteristic of an object, event, person, or whatever, that can take two or more values. A psychologist might hypothesize, for example, that the position people take on welfare issues (one variable) is highly related to their annual income (a second variable). In general, the more income a person has, the less likely he or she is to favor welfare payments to needy people. To check on this hypothesis, the psychologist would try to find data reflecting both income and attitudes toward welfare. Interviews or surveys of a cross section of the population at large might be conducted. For each person in the study, there would be two scores, one for annual income and one reflecting both direction and degree of attitude toward welfare proposals, ranging from strongly opposed to strongly favorable.

To find out how strong a relationship there is between these variables, the psychologist would compute a numerical value, or statistic, called the **correlation coefficient** (see Appendix A). The correlation of zero signifies no relationship at all between the two variables. In the above example, a correlation of zero would mean that amount of income is not related to a person's attitude toward welfare plans. A positive correlation means that the two variables are related: The higher the value of one score, the higher the value of the other. A positive correlation in this example would mean that the more money a person makes each year, the more likely that person is to favor welfare plans. This, of course, would not confirm the original hypothesis. A negative correlation implies a relationship between the two variables that

is opposite, or inverse: As the value of one variable increases, the value of the other decreases. In the example, a negative correlation would mean that the more people earn, the less likely they are to favor welfare — and vice versa. Thus, a negative correlation *would* be consistent with the original hypothesis.

The Experimental Method

Case studies, naturalistic observation techniques, and the various correlational methods all suffer a major drawback. While they provide information about relationships among psychological variables, they do not allow determination of cause-effect relationships (see Highlight 1-1). For example, a case study of a psychologically disturbed person might reveal a difficult childhood, but this does not mean that unhappy early experiences *necessarily* lead to abnormal behavior. Any number of other factors, including genetic ones, might be responsible for both childhood and adult problems. The fact that elk are observed to mate more frequently after a spring rain cannot be taken as evidence for a causal relationship between humidity and the mating instinct. Perhaps spring rains tend to occur in the late afternoon, the time of day the elk prefer to get together. The fact that high income tends to be *correlated with* opposition to welfare does not necessarily imply that if someone's income were suddenly to double, his or her opinion of welfare would become more negative. The fact is that opinions toward welfare are commonly formed even before an individual has achieved permanent employment. Observational procedures are important, but the establishment of direct, cause-effect relationships requires a different method of investigation, namely, the experimental method.

In addition to observing, experimental psychologists attempt to manipulate and *control* their subject matter. They bring the phenomenon at issue into the laboratory, where conditions of interest can be manipulated with precise equipment and procedures, and where all extraneous and distracting variables can be ruled out. Experimental psychologists set up simplified versions of what goes on in the outside world and examime these phenomena under conditions in which only one thing at a time is changed (see Highlight 1-2). If the changed condition is associated with a change in behavior, then the experimenter can be certain that there is a cause-effect relationship between the changing variable and the behavior in question.

For example, suppose we want to know whether a person should study in relatively short periods over the course of, say, two weeks preceding an examination or whether it would be better to concentrate all study time into the evening before the exam. If we

Highlight 1–1

Correlation Does Not Mean Causality

If two variables are correlated with each other, there is a tendency to conclude that one variable causes the other. On the strength of a correlation between the amount of TV violence and real-life violence, some people conclude that TV violence causes people to be more violent in their everyday behavior. We cannot draw such a causal conclusion from correlations. As the cartoon suggests, the causal connection may be in the opposite direction. Still another alternative is that a third factor, for example, the increased stress of modern living, causes both TV and real-life violence.

The best way to establish the existence and direction of a causal relationship between two variables is to use the experimental method.

"Contrary to the popular view, our studies show that it is real life that contributes to violence on television."

Playboy, February 1977. Reproduced by special permission of PLAYBOY Magazine; copyright © 1977 by Playboy.

Some of the most famous experiments in psychology were done by Harry F. Harlow using monkeys as subjects. Experimental manipulations could be done with monkeys that would be completely impossible with human subjects. His most famous work involved separating newborn monkeys from their mothers and rearing them in isolation with a terrycloth surrogate mother.

perform on a test or less intelligent than the individual who distributes study time. The observations would tell us something, but they might not make all of the effective variables entirely clear.

An experimental approach to the question would be different. First, we would construct a simplified version of the problem for investigation in the laboratory. We might select a set of materials to be learned, similar though not necessarily identical to the kind of material a person might study for an examination. Suppose the test is to cover knowledge of foreign language vocabulary. A simplified version of this might be a list of about 12 to 20 pairs of words that a subject would try to memorize in such a way that given the first word of the pair he or she could respond with the second.

We might decide to investigate the problem under two study conditions. In one, study time is concentrated. The word pairs are presented to the subject for study at a rate of 5 seconds per pair; immediately after presentation the first word of each pair is shown and the subject is tested for ability to respond with the second word. Then the pairs are again presented, followed by a second test. This procedure—study followed immediately by test, followed immediately by study, and so on—is repeated for, say, 20 trials. In the second study condition the same procedure is used except that the subject is allowed to rest for a period of

were merely to observe the study habits of people who happen to be available, we might have difficulty drawing a precise conclusion. The person who distributes study time over two weeks preceding an examination might actually be studying more in terms of total time than the individual who concentrates effort on the evening before. Furthermore, the person who crams might be a psychologically different type of individual, more secure about his or her ability to

Highlight 1–2

The Control Group

The simplest experimental design involves two groups, the *experimental group* and the *control group*. The control group provides a baseline against which to compare the experimental group. Suppose the experimenter wants to know if a particular treatment (treatment X) for mental illness is effective in helping patients. An experimental group of patients is given treatment X, and the experimenter observes their behavior and sees that there is improvement. At this point, it might be concluded that treatment X is beneficial. But perhaps the patients would have improved anyway.

The experimenter needs a control group of patients that is treated the same way as the experimental group (same meals, same hospital, same diagnoses, etc.) with the *single* exception that no control patient is given treatment X. If the experimenter then observes greater improvement in the experimental group than the control group, it can safely be concluded that the difference in improvement between the two groups must have been caused by treatment X, since treatment X was the only thing on which the two groups differed. Many experiments fail because the experimenter did not run an appropriate control group.

The following experiments should provide you with a better understanding of the need and use of control groups in psychological research:

1. A physiological psychologist surgically destroys a particular part of the brain, the hypothalamus, to see if this particular brain structure is important in controlling eating. A control group of animals who undergo brain surgery procedures (anesthesia, cutting open the skull, etc.), but who do not have their hypothalamus destroyed or have some other area of the brain destroyed is required. If the hypothalamus is uniquely involved in controlling eating, the investigator should find greater eating disturbances in the experimental animals than in the control animals.

2. A psychologist wants to know if playing classical music for young children improves their later musical abilities. He arranges with the parents to pipe classical music into their children's cribs for at least six hours a day, every day of the week, for twelve months, beginning when each child is 6 months old. A control group of children must be treated in exactly the same way for the same length of time, except they hear no classical music. The only difference between the experimental and the control group is whether or not classical music is played. Should there be more than one control group in this study?

3. An industrial psychologist thinks that he or she can improve production at a factory by making the surroundings more pleasant—brightly colored rooms, better lighting, and music. The psychologist sets up such a production line in a special room at the factory and selects a random group of workers to work on this line. It is observed that production is higher in this setting than on the regular line in the factory, and it is concluded that the lighting, colors, and music are responsible. The psychologist needs a control group of workers selected from the regular line and also asked to work in a "special" room, but this special room duplicates the regular working conditions. Merely being selected to work in a special room as part of an experiment may make people work harder, if only because they assume that someone is watching their work more carefully.

---

time, say 30 seconds, between each test and the following study period. The same number of trials is given and the same amount of study time is allowed, but practice is spread out over a longer period.

Independent and Dependent Variables

When observations of a subject's performance are made within the laboratory, psychologists are in a position to hold constant or change systematically most variables that might affect performance. All subjects perform as closely as possible under the same circumstances except for the variable the experimenter manipulates. A good investigator will try to control or hold constant all but the variable or variables of interest. The variable of interest is the one that the experi-

menter manipulates and is called the **independent variable.** In our vocabulary-learning example, the independent variable is the time between the study and test periods. There are two levels of this variable, 0 and 30 seconds. That is, half the subjects will learn while getting 0 seconds rest between study and test, and half will learn with a 30-second rest period.

The experimenter measures the subjects' performance to find out whether it is changed in any way by the difference in the independent variable. The measure of performance is called the **dependent variable.** The experimenter tries to determine whether the dependent variable depends in any way on the independent variable. In our example, the dependent variable might be the number of correct

Highlight 1–3

Two Common Pitfalls in Psychological Research

The Placebo Effect

The placebo effect refers to the fact that any kind of treatment may produce a behavioral change, perhaps due to suggestion. For example, suppose the hypothesis is that Drug A will relieve depression. The experimenter gives Drug A to a group of depressives and finds that they improve, leading to the conclusion that Drug A is effective. This conclusion may be wrong—giving these depressives any kind of treatment might have resulted in equal improvement. The experimenter should have included a **placebo-control group** in the experiment. This group would have received a "fake," or placebo, "drug," one that contains no active ingredients. In order to conclude that Drug A is effective, the experimenter must demonstrate that it results in greater improvement than treatment with the placebo. Of course, subjects in the experiment must not know whether they are receiving the real drug or the placebo. In such cases the subjects are said to be *blind* to the conditions of the experiment.

Experimenter Bias

While it is obvious that the subjects should be "blind" to the treatment they receive, it may also be important that the experimenter be uninformed about which group receives the placebo and which the real treatment. If both the subjects and the experimenter are blind, the study is called a **double-blind experiment.** You should be cautious about believing the results of treatment studies that are not double-blind.

Robert Rosenthal has demonstrated that, in several different types of experiments, experimenters, if they know how the results are supposed to come out, can influence them in that direction. The most startling demonstration of this was Rosenthal's study showing that teachers can influence their pupils' scores on intelligence tests (IQ scores). Rosenthal told a group of teachers that certain students in their classes had high intellectual potential as judged by psychological tests. Actually these students were randomly selected. At the end of the year, these pupils showed a much larger IQ gain than students not identified as high in potential. The teachers (the experimenters) expected these children to improve and probably took steps along the way, often unconsciously, to make sure that they did.

responses made by the subject on each test trial. Thus the point of our illustrative experiment is to determine whether number of correct responses (the dependent variable) is influenced by the study conditions during learning (the independent variable). Do study conditions cause a change in performance? Experiments, in general, seek to establish cause-effect relationships. The independent variable becomes the possible cause, and its effect is then measured by the dependent variable.

There is considerable emphasis throughout an experiment on defining terms accurately and clearly. Experimenters commonly use *operational definitions,* that is, definitions in terms of the operations used to measure or manipulate. Thus, the definition of distribution of study time in the example just given is formulated in terms of rest time between each test and study period.

Random Selection

Our main assurance of unbiased effects comes from the way subjects are selected for the various conditions in the experiment; this is an important aspect of

Gahan Wilson Sunday Comics reprinted courtesy of the Register and Tribune Syndicate, Inc.

The equipment or techniques that psychologists use can affect the behavior they are trying to measure. In such cases the measurements are said to be *obtrusive.* The scientist in the cartoon is obviously using obtrusive techniques to study relaxation. But developing *unobtrusive* methods for observing behavior is not always easy.

Puzzling Pills: Are Placebos Magic or Real?

A bit of whimsy making the medical rounds has a pharmaceutical company petitioning the Food and Drug Administration for approval of a new pain reliever. The compound, to be packaged in red, white and blue capsules, will be sold with a label that is indisputably true: PROVED EFFECTIVE IN ONE-THIRD OF ALL CASES AND ABSOLUTELY SAFE. The nostrum's name: Placebo.

Long the butt of jokes, placebos (from the Latin for "I shall please") are one of the oldest, most useful and least understood "remedies" in the doctor's satchel. Generally they come as pills of milk sugar or talc or as injections of salt water. Such substances are considered pharmacologically inert, incapable of eliciting a response when prescribed in reasonable quantities. Yet studies have repeatedly shown that placebos help as many as 30% or 40% of patients with real enough ills, including postoperative pain, migraines, coughs, seasickness, arthritis, ulcers, hypertension, hay fever, even warts.

To account for the placebo's magic, doctors have resorted to virtually every kind of psychological and physical explanation. No luck. Drs. Jon D. Levine and Howard I. Fields and Oral Surgeon

Newton C. Gordon, all of the University of California in San Francisco, may have hit upon an answer. In an experiment involving dental patients having molars extracted, they gave them either a placebo or the drug naloxone, which is known to block the effects of endorphin, a morphine-like pain reliever produced by the brain itself.

To guard against any unwitting influences on the patients or themselves, the doctors did not know which "drug" was being used in any particular case until the end of the test. In the first phase of the experiment, patients who had received placebos experienced less pain than those in the naloxone group. But when the experiment was continued, patients initially in the placebo group but now getting the blocker experienced an increase in pain. In other words, the placebo response diminished. Levine's explanation: somehow placebos apparently activate a body pain-relieving system that relies on endorphin. Says he: "Placebos are not just in people's minds but in their brains."

Perhaps so. But Psychiatrist Arthur K. Shapiro of Manhattan's Mt. Sinai Medical Center points out that the placebo effect may also be influenced by attitudes of patient and doctor toward

drugs and, perhaps more important, toward each other. In fact, says Shapiro, who has collected hundreds of the "useless" nostrums over the years, patient confidence in a physician may be a kind of placebo too, increasing chances of improvement. . . .

Though doctors have long used placebos to appease patients eager for a drug, even when none is indicated, the practice has lately come under question. . . . At a time when patients are demanding more candor, many physicians are asking themselves whether they should prescribe deceptively. Other doubts have also been raised. In a study of 60 physicians and 39 nurses at the University of New Mexico School of Medicine, Drs. James and Jean Goodwin and Albert Vogel found that the majority gave placebos to patients they disliked, considered difficult or suspected of exaggerating pain. When patients reported relief, the doctors and nurses incorrectly took that as proof of malingering. As one doctor told the researchers: "Placebos are used with people you hate, not to make them suffer, but to prove them wrong."

Time
July 30, 1979

Whether a treatment is a placebo or not is sometimes hard to determine. Chapter 2 will discuss some of the many profound effects brain chemicals have recently been discovered to have on behavior.

experimental control. Suppose the performance of the spaced-practice group is better than that of the concentrated-practice group. What is there to assure us that subjects in the spaced-practice condition are not, in general, smarter than subjects in the concentrated-practice condition? Unwanted effects in the experiment might be attributable to the fact that a different group of subjects participates under each of the two experimental conditions.

Experimenters cannot hold individual differences among people constant in the same way they can control other variables operating in the laboratory situation. But they can take the following steps in order to equalize the groups: (1) select all subjects randomly from the population to which they wish to generalize the results; (2) assign subjects randomly to

the various experimental conditions; (3) use a large enough number of subjects in each group to average out random variations; and (4) take all possible precautions to avoid biasing subjects in any way. When experimenters follow these simple steps, they should obtain comparable groups of subjects participating in each condition.

Testing the Hypothesis

Having no reason to believe otherwise, an experimenter might guess that the way people *distribute* their study time has no effect on performance on a test if the *total* amount of time spent in study is comparable. A hypothesis stated in this form is called a **null hypothesis.** It is the prediction that the variable being manipulated, the independent variable, will have no effect on the behavior being measured, the dependent variable.

The results of the experiment provide a test of this hypothesis. If at the end of 20 study trials both groups of subjects perform the same on their test, the experimenter would conclude that distribution of study time has nothing to do with the degree of learning. The null hypothesis would not be rejected. If, on the other hand, a relationship of some sort is observed, then the null hypothesis would be rejected. For example, if performance improves with increasing amounts of rest between study periods, the experimenter would conclude that distribution of study time has a favorable effect on learning.

The key advantage of the experimental method is that it allows for cause-effect conclusions from the data. If all of the variables have been properly controlled, and it is observed that the dependent variable changes when the independent variable is changed, the experimenter can conclude that the relationship is *causal.* Because of this logic, psychologists have a distinct preference for experimental techniques over nonexperimental techniques in the study of behavior. The assumption is that understanding behavior eventually comes down to knowing what causes what, and, in psychology, the experimental method is our chief means of finding out.

Quasi-Experimentation

The experimental method is the best technique available for trying to determine the causes of behavior. Unfortunately, there are many situations in which rigorous experiments simply cannot be conducted. For example, in Highlight 1–4, the study described isn't really a true experiment. The researcher did not *manipulate* the variable father absent/father present but simply *selected* families having one of those two characteristics. Thus, it cannot be logically concluded that the observed difference in annual earnings is *caused* by father absent/father present. Many other factors are correlated with the father being absent (or present); for example, perhaps low-income fathers are more likely to be absent. To conduct the experiment properly the researcher would have to take a group of babies and randomly assign them to homes with and without fathers. Obviously, such an experiment is impossible.

Many experiments that would in fact reveal important *causes* of behavior are impossible for moral, ethical, religious, economic, or other reasons. In such cases we often rely on information gained from nonexperimental methods, such as the correlational approach.

To deal with some of these issues researchers have begun to develop techniques that are quasi-experimental. In such studies, the investigator tries to

---

Highlight 1–4

What's Wrong with This Experiment?

A psychologist is interested in the effects of divorce upon children. The hypothesis is that children raised in fatherless homes will be adversely affected such that they will be less successful as adults. From a large pool of subjects, a group of 30 adults (15 men and 15 women) raised in fatherless homes as a result of divorce is randomly selected. A matching group of 15 men and 15 women raised in homes where both parents were present until the child reached age 18 is also selected. Success is measured in terms of annual salary.

The results show that the average annual salary in the group with fatherless rearing is $11,275, while in the other group it is $17,500. The psychologist concludes that being raised in a fatherless home results in psychological damage, which ultimately causes the child to become less motivated toward achievement (resulting in a lower-paying job as an adult).

---

arrange conditions to approximate a true experiment as closely as possible. This can help to rule out some possible causes of behavior, although not all. In the example given, the researcher has not proved that father presence is the important variable causing income differences in offspring. But he or she has established that, under natural circumstances, this variable and others which correlate with it (such as father income) are, as a whole, determiners of offspring income.

Since techniques of quasi-experimental design and analysis are relatively new, we do not yet completely understand their potential or limits. But they offer considerable promise for the future. (These techniques are discussed further in Appendix A.)

Generalizing to the Real World   Advocates of the quasi-experimental approach often criticize experimental research on the grounds that it may not be representative of the real world. They claim that setting up a laboratory approach to the problem (so that the investigator can manipulate the variables) may make the experiment too artificial or too remote to permit useful generalizations. Suppose, for example, we tackled our sample problem by studying rats or mice, where we *could* randomly assign rat pups to be reared in cages with or without a father rat present. We have tight experimental control, but can the results be applied to human beings? This issue is one of *validity.* If the results of an experiment have broad applicability—that is, can be widely generalized to other situations—the experiment is said to have more validity than some other experiment that cannot be widely generalized. Quasi-experimental designs will often place higher on the validity dimension than more tightly controlled experiments, and this may be important in deciding which approach to follow.

Psychology in Historical Perspective

People have always been curious about themselves. This curiosity was entirely speculative, however, until the nineteenth century when psychologists adopted a

scientific approach to their subject matter. From that point forward, the field took on a new look, which was essentially empirical, with an emphasis on observation as a way of establishing facts. Its underpinnings were biological, and its method was experimental. We will review some of the landmark achievements of scientific psychology, because it is necessary to be acquainted with the history of psychology to appreciate what psychology is today.

Scientific psychology had rather modest beginnings. The problems addressed were simple, perhaps even naive in comparison with the psychological issues that face people and scientists today. Early psychologists, for example, studied the sensations aroused by simple physical stimuli. They were curious about how fast the human hand could react to a

---

Highlight 1–5

What's Wrong with This Experiment?

Study Claims Non-Smoking Lung Cancer Victims Add to Lives
By DON KIRKMAN

WASHINGTON — National Cancer Institute researchers say that victims of lung cancer can add to their life expectancies if they stop smoking cigarettes.

The researchers say that 20 to 25 percent of lung cancer patients who either quit smoking or don't smoke at all will survive more than 30 months. By contrast, no patient who continues to smoke is expected to survive more than 30 months.

Monitoring 112 lung cancer patients, a National Cancer Institute team of researchers studied what happens to persons who quit smoking and what happens to those who don't stop. The study involved patients at the Washington, D.C., Veterans Hospital.

While smoking is officially discouraged, cancer patients have been permitted to smoke cigarettes because many long-time smokers suffer from emotional problems when they try to quit.

The researchers evaluated 54 patients who stopped smoking and 57 who continued. One patient had never smoked.

Eighteen months after the beginning of cancer treatment, 28 percent of those who had quit smoking before having been diagnosed as having the disease were still alive and cancer free.

In addition, 16 percent of those who quit when they were told they had cancer also were alive and cancer free. Only 6 percent of those who continued smoking were alive and cancer free after 18 months. . . .

Rocky Mountain News
June 4, 1980

The basic problem here is that the study was not really an experiment but an observation. The observation is that people who quit smoking survived longer than people who did not quit. But the quitters might have lived longer anyway, not because they stopped smoking but for some other reason. For example, having a body less susceptible to addiction, or having high desire to live, or receiving lots of moral support from family members might be the reason they lived longer. In order for this study to qualify as a true experiment, the investigator would have to have been able to control who quit and who didn't. The 112 smokers would have been *randomly* divided into two groups—those told they must quit (and they would have *had* to quit for the experiment to be valid) and those told they could not quit (and they would have had to keep on smoking). Then, if there were different survival rates in the two groups, it could be directly attributed to the smoking. Such an experiment would be extremely hard to conduct—probably impossible. Therefore, there is no strong evidence concerning smoking and lung cancer. One still has to decide whether to quit smoking or not on the basis of imperfect evidence. Still, the overall evidence is overwhelming in favor of quitting.

stimulus and how small a difference between two pure tones the human ear could detect. By modern standards these early experiments were crude. The new discipline of "psychology" that emerged in the late 1800s as an offshoot of philosophy and physiology lacked coherence and organization. The few scholars who were interested in psychological problems established their own individual schools of thought, and there were very few psychological principles that everyone agreed on. The impact of early scientific psychologists should not be minimized, however. Their accomplishments triggered many significant developments evident in the field today.

The activities of psychologists from approximately 1880 through 1950 were governed by a number of diverse viewpoints and beliefs about (1) the proper subject matter of psychology, (2) the basic questions to be asked about that subject matter, and (3) the appropriate methods for answering these basic questions. We examine now some of the schools of thought that evolved around these issues, because they are the ideas that have shaped and continue to shape psychology today.

Structuralism

The first major theoretical school of psychology was **structuralism,** primarily the work of Wilhelm Wundt (1832–1920), a professor of philosophy who founded the first formal laboratory of psychology at the University of Leipzig, Germany, in 1879 (see Figure 1–1).

Wundt proposed that the subject matter of psychology was **experience,** the experience or awareness one has of the content of one's own conscious mind—in other words, the structure of the mind. Influenced by the rise of modern physical and medical science, Wundt argued that the fundamental approach of science, namely, analysis, should be applied to psychological phenomena. To understand any problem, we need to break it down into its smallest parts, or structures, and then examine the parts themselves as fundamental building blocks. Structuralism, therefore, was an attempt to compartmentalize the mind into its basic parts, the so-called mental elements. Wundt believed that the existence of these elements was well established by philosophical study, but he wanted to identify them *empirically* through a method called **introspection.** Introspection, according to Wundt, requires observers who can objectively examine and verbally report what is going on in their minds in response to controlled stimulation. These verbal reports could then be analyzed and categorized in an effort to determine the number and kinds of basic elements in the mind. Concerned with the

FIGURE 1–1   Wilhelm Wundt

The founder of the structuralist movement felt that psychology should be concerned with studying the contents of conscious experience. By the method of introspection, he concluded that, brought on by external stimulation, the mind consists of three basic elements—sensations, images, and feelings—from which all the rest of our experience is compounded.

reaction of the mind to simple physical stimuli, Wundt's research was directed primarily toward the study of sensory and perceptual processes. Wundt's studies led him to conclude that there are three basic elements, which he called *sensations* (the direct products of external stimulation), *images* (sensationlike experiences produced by the mind itself), and *feelings* (the affective or emotional components of an experience).

The major limitation of structuralism was its failure to relate the concept of mind to human action. Structuralists examined the relation between stimulus and mind, but neglected the relation between mind and action. Psychology is still concerned with mental activities, but today its emphasis in on the way these activities influence human behavior. To explain why people act as they do we need not only to study consciousness through introspection but also to observe how people act, as well as how they think and feel.

Structuralism suffered further from its reliance on introspection as its chief method. Too often it has been found that people who have been trained to introspect in the same way fail to agree about their observations. Thus, introspective data are relatively unreliable, and obviously science cannot progress on questionable evidence. Finally, structuralism suffers as a theory because of its focus on the conscious content of the mind. Though ignored by structuralists, unconscious processes affect behavior in important ways. To leave out these factors is to ignore a good deal of what psychology must study and explain.

Functionalism

Partly because of its strong tradition in philosophy and partly because it was the first major theory of psychology, structuralism dominated psychology for years, both in Europe and the United States. But it was not without critics, and after the turn of the century three new schools of thought became strong competitors. The first was **functionalism,** primarily the product of American psychologists.

Among the foremost functionalists were William James (Figure 1–2) of Harvard University (1842–1910), James Cattell of the University of Pennsylvania (1860–1944), John Dewey of the University of Chicago (1859–1952), and E. L. Thorndike of Columbia University (1874–1949).

Like the structuralists, the functionalists viewed the mind and consciousness as important concepts in psychology. However, they took these concepts a step beyond the structuralists' position. Structuralists were concerned with *what* the mind is made of, that is, the building blocks or structures of consciousness. Functionalists, in contrast, studied *how* and *why* the mind works. They focused on the *functions* of the mind

FIGURE 1–2 William James

One of the earliest and foremost American psychologists, William James founded the first laboratory of psychology in this country. For James the content of the mind was a continuous, ongoing "stream of consciousness" that could not be analyzed into elementary building blocks.

rather than its contents, and studied how these functions benefit the organism.

The functionalists were strongly influenced by Darwin's theory of evolution and his emphasis on adaptation as the most important factor in survival. They argued that the mind is a human being's most important organ for adaptation to the environment. Therefore, they emphasized the uses of the mind rather than its contents. The functionalist approach stressed the connection between the mind and human behavior, thus underscoring the importance of studying mind-body interactions.

The functionalists viewed the mind as a master biological organ that controls other bodily organs in a never-ending struggle to cope with the environment. Thus they regarded introspection as a limited scientific method. Why not, they argued, observe people functioning and adapting to the real world?

The functionalists were among the first to see that a person's most important way of adapting to the environment is through **learning** — the acquisition of facts and skills. This ability is in large measure what sets human beings apart from lower animals and allows us, despite our relatively limited physiology and motor skills, to adapt to many environments.

Behaviorism

Functionalism was a loose general orientation toward psychology. Functionalists studied a variety of psychological processes but never developed a coherent general psychological theory. In contrast, **behaviorism,** the first truly American school of psychology, had a definite and explicit theoretical point of view. Behaviorism was primarily the work of John B. Watson (1878–1958). Although trained as a functionalist, Watson argued that private mental states, those we presumably study through introspection, cannot be the subject matter of a science. Only public events — that is, actions, responses, or performances that can be observed and measured — fulfill the requirements of a scientific discipline. These events he called behaviors. Responses or behaviors, according to Watson, are affected by specifiable stimuli in the environment (see Figure 1–3). Therefore, the major goal of psychology is to identify those stimulus-response relationships that are lawful and predictable.

During the same period in Russia, Ivan Pavlov (1848–1936) provided an impressive demonstration of the use of stimulus-response analysis in his famous description of classical conditioning. In the course of his physiological studies of digestion, Pavlov observed that his experimental subjects, dogs, came to salivate at the sound of a neutral stimulus — say, a bell — if food and bell were repeatedly paired together. Both Pavlov

FIGURE 1–3 John B. Watson

For John B. Watson, the founder of behaviorism, behavior consisted of learned responses to external stimuli that are perceived by the senses. He rejected the concept of "mind," believing it was useless to speculate on the question of whether such a thing existed. In his behavioral system, Watson substituted a "black box" or empty head for the mind and put exclusive emphasis on observable stimulus-response relationships. His was the first stimulus-response psychology, abbreviated as S-R psychology.

and Watson saw this conditioning phenomenon as evidence of the importance of learning and of stimulus-response connections in behavior. Watson saw Pavlov's research as confirmation of the lawful nature of behavior and of the possibility that all behavior, no matter how complex, can be reduced to learned stimulus-response units. For behaviorists, the problem of psychology is to predict what responses will be evoked by what stimuli.

Watson believed that *all behavior is learned.* He once boasted that he could make any healthy baby into any kind of adult—doctor, lawyer, or thief—merely by controlling the conditioning of the child. Today we know, of course, that heredity is also an important determinant of behavior.

Gestalt Psychology

Gestalt psychology was a different kind of reaction to structuralism. The Gestalt movement began in Germany in the early twentieth century, about the time behaviorism began to dominate American psychology. Gestalt psychology is a general research-oriented point of view. It is not to be confused with a recent innovation in psychotherapy called Gestalt therapy (see Chapter 12). The German word *Gestalt* has no exact English translation. Roughly speaking, it means *form* or *organized whole,* reflecting the emphasis of this school on organizational processes in behavior. Whereas the focal problems of behaviorism were motivation and learning, Gestalt psychologists chose primarily to work with sensory and perceptual processes—the same problems addressed by Wundt and the structuralists. Gestalt psychologists sought to prove Wundt wrong in the very area that Wundt himself chose to emphasize. As a result, Gestalt theory is often identified as a theory of perception, although its principles are applicable to all of psychology.

Behaviorists, like the structuralists, accepted the basic scientific idea that complex phenomena had to be analyzed into their simpler parts before they could be understood. The main proponents of Gestalt psychology—Wolfgang Köhler (1887–1967), Kurt Koffka (1886–1941), and Max Wertheimer (Figure 1–4) (1880–1943)—opposed these efforts to reduce experience to a small set of fundamental component parts. They seized on other ideas from physical science, particularly the notions of field theory in physics, arguing that the whole of a phenomenon is different from the sum of its parts. For example, from a series of still pictures we perceive continuity of action in a movie. There is movement even in the neon lights on a theater marquee. Both effects are based on the phenomenon of *apparent movement,* identified by early Gestalt psychologists. Figure 1–5 shows an-

FIGURE 1-4 Max Wertheimer

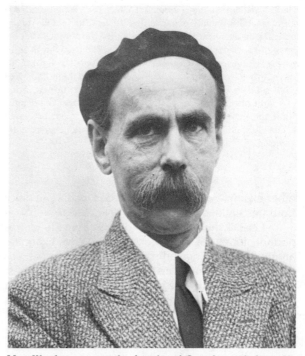

Max Wertheimer was the founder of Gestalt psychology. His guiding principle was that mental content and behavior are different from the sum of their parts.

FIGURE 1-5 The Gestalt approach to perception

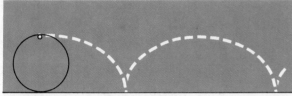

Panel A: rim light

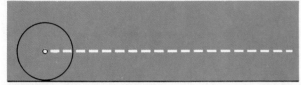

Panel B: center light

Panel C: combination (theory)

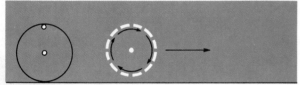

Panel D: what subjects actually see

Here is an interesting perceptual effect that demonstrates a basic Gestalt principle of perception. It suggests that we do not perceive an event merely by adding up the perceptions that we have of the separate parts. A wheel is rolled from left to right across a table in a dark room. In the top panel, a light is attached to the rim of the wheel and the dashed line indicates what subjects perceive. The second panel shows our perception of a light attached at the center of the wheel. Panel C indicates what the geometric sum of the motions of the rim light and center light should look like. Panel D is what subjects *actually* perceive.

other example of how perception of a whole can differ from perceptions of parts.

Gestalt theory can be applied to nearly all important forms of behavior. Köhler, for example, argued that learning and problem solving, like perception, are largely functions of organizational processes. That is, people are able to learn or to solve a problem when they mentally organize the various components of a task. They must order these components in such a way that they can see how the pieces relate to one another. When they see the whole picture they experience a "moment of insight." Notice in the foregoing description the persistent use of terms related to perception, such as "seeing," "perspective," and "expe-

rience." This theme is a consistent one in Gestalt explanations of behavior. Note also the implication that learning and problem solving are "all-or-none," insightful processes. This is another major principle that distinguishes Gestalt psychology from other theoretical views of learning.

Psychoanalysis

Psychoanalysis, the theoretical point of view identified with Sigmund Freud (1858–1939), was both a reaction to structuralism and an effort to apply science and medicine to the study and treatment of abnormal behavior. (Portraits of Freud appear on page 332 in Chapter 9.) Psychoanalysis has been called the third great intellectual blow to human pride. First, we found out from the astronomer Galileo that we human beings are not at the center of the universe; then we were told by the naturalist Charles Darwin that we are descended from apes; and, finally, the psychologist Freud theorized that we are basically controlled by impulses, many of which are buried in the unconscious, below the level of awareness. This assertion questions the basic premise of structuralism. The view that human beings are rational and in conscious control of their behavior was weakened when Freud described the impact of early childhood experience, anxiety, and conflicting unconscious motives on the behavior of supposedly mature adults. While we accept these ideas as entirely reasonable today, they were considered revolutionary when Freud first announced them.

Freud, whose theory is discussed in detail in Chapter 9, described the personality structure of a human being as consisting of three forces: the pleasure-seeking **id,** composed of basic biological impulses; the realistic **ego,** reacting to the stresses and strains of everyday life; and the idealistic **superego,** representing the dictates of one's conscience. Unlike structuralism, functionalism, and the other schools we have discussed, the primary method of psychoanalysis was detailed case study, and its primary focus was abnormal behavior. Indeed, psychoanalysis is primarily identified today with a method of psychotherapy for people with problems of adjustment.

Contemporary Trends in Psychology

Our review of historical events has been sketchy, but it illustrates some of the major trends. The schools of thought just described no longer exist intact, but they still have impact on contemporary thinking.

Structuralism, in its original form, never recovered from the penetrating criticisms raised by other schools. Few psychologists would refer to themselves today as structuralists. Yet the concepts of structuralism are still present in modern psychology. Jean Piaget, the famous Swiss developmental psychologist, has written volumes on how the structure of the human mind changes with age. American experimental psychologists study the way knowledge is organized and refer extensively to the structure of our memory of past events. The principles of association, originally applied by structuralists to the formation of complex mental events out of simpler elements, are still the basis of some learning theories.

Functionalism was never a coherent school, nor did it center on the ideas of any one psychologist. It was, rather, a vaguely stated set of principles about the pragmatic—that is, functional—significance of the mind. But, while there was no strong theoretical commitment, functionalism left a significant legacy in its emphasis on learning as humanity's most important adaptive process.

In a sense, psychoanalysis has been the most persistent point of view in psychology. Its emphasis on unconscious processes is still pervasive. It also continues to have considerable importance in some areas of clinical psychology and personality theory, and it forms the basis of a widely used psychotherapeutic technique.

Behaviorism and Gestalt psychology have probably played the greatest role in shaping modern psychological thinking. The basic ideas that both groups formulated are clearly evident in contemporary psychology, though there are few psychologists today who identify themselves as behaviorists or as Gestaltists in the traditional sense. The behaviorists' emphasis on the role of learned responses as building blocks of behavior is a predominant principle in modern psychological theory. B. F. Skinner has developed both a theory and a technology for changing behavior based on observable responses and their subsequent rewards and punishments. We will have a good deal more to say about Skinner's ideas in our discussions of learning (Chapter 4) and personality (Chapter 9). The insistence of Gestalt psychologists on the importance of organizational processes in behavior, as opposed to a simple analysis of content, persists in a lively form. The issue of content versus process analysis has a bearing on many aspects of contemporary psychology, perhaps the most important of which is memory. These relationships will be apparent throughout the book.

Schools of psychology have disappeared because, as psychologists examine the issues more closely, they have discovered that explanations cannot logically take the simple form offered by structuralism, behaviorism, or any other school. Psychologists have come to realize that behavior is influenced by both heredity and environment and that both mental processes and overt actions are necessarily involved in any description of behavior. There are differences in emphasis and opinion in psychology today, but extremist thinking and close-minded groups are fortunately becoming rare.

Cognition and Information Processing

One perspective on behavior today is widely shared by psychologists across a broad range of interests. This position views the human being as an active information processor. The perspective recognizes that human beings are constantly interacting with their environment and that they bring cognitive or mental capacities to bear on all such interactions. Such a viewpoint has been used by psychologists in the analysis of all levels of behavior, ranging from simple conditioning to abnormal behavior and therapeutic attempts to correct it.

Information enters the human processing system through various sensory receptors. In this sense, the system is data-driven and operates in a "bottom-up" mode. The process involves a succession of stages, beginning with the conversion of physical energy into a psychological or mental form. In the system are various kinds of memory, each with its own characteristics. In *sensory memory* an event can be remembered accurately, but only for a brief time. Somewhat more lasting is the information placed in *short-term memory,* the memory store that, for example, allows us to retain a new telephone number just long enough to dial it. The most important information is usually stored in *long-term memory* until it is needed at a later time.

In addition to its various memories, the human information-processing system also allows for the selectivity of attention, the experience of consciousness, the ability to make inferences and form concepts from incoming data, problem solving and decision making, and the selection of an action (overt behavior). In this sense, the system is idea- or concept-driven and operates in a "top-down" mode.

According to information-processing theories, there is one fundamental source of many of the difficulties we have in functioning effectively in our world. That bottleneck in the system is known as the *limited capacity processor.* Enormous amounts of information may be stored in our memory, but our central processor can retrieve and work with only a small amount of this information at a time. Retrieving large amounts of information, therefore, requires a great deal of time. On the other hand, a lot of information may be entering the system in a very short period of time, such as when you read a textbook that includes a great many new things to memorize, or when you

The advent of modern electronic computers has been of immense value to psychologists. The computer is used in a variety of ways, such as analyzing data, controlling experiments, and simulating the way human beings process information.

listen to a lecture that is crammed with new information. Again there are problems because the processor can handle just so much information at one time.

Imagine yourself listening to a lecture. You take the time to note legibly the first point that is made. But meanwhile the lecturer is making the second and third points. You may be able to hold onto the *second* point by storing it in your short-term memory. Then, as soon as you have finished recording the first point you can quickly jot down the second point before you forget it. But the *third* point? What happened to it? It may by now be totally lost. With a fact-filled lecture delivered by a rapid-fire speaker, you could easily miss half of the points that are made. Your mind is not like a textbook where you can go back and reread underlined parts before the test. There is a good lesson for your professor here: each lecture should contain a relatively small number of important points, and each point should be restated and reemphasized and then perhaps mentioned again in a closing summary.

In summary, human beings possess a truly phenomenal information-processing system, but it has a limited capacity. It can attend to only a very few things at once, it has a limited ability to get new information into the system, and it has a limited capacity to retrieve information stored in memory.

The complex information-processing system called a human being is impossible to summarize in a few short paragraphs. Because the information-processing view is very important in psychology today, we will refer to it throughout later chapters, especially those dealing with perception, learning, memory, language, and cognition (see Chapters 3 through 6). We will try to make it clear how this particular perspective attempts to make sense of the variety of behaviors people exhibit.

SUMMARY

1. Psychology is the study of human and animal behavior. It is a body of knowledge about behavior, a set of methods for investigating behavior, a general theory for understanding behavior, and an array of techniques for using what we know to make human life better.

2. Psychology seeks to attain certain goals, which include refined measurement and description of behavior, procedures for predicting and controlling behavior, and the basic explanations of behavior.

3. Certain fundamental issues about human behavior pervade psychology: Is heredity or environment the more important factor in behavior? Is behavior determined, by genetic or environmental forces, or does it arise out of free will? Can we explain behavior mechanistically, or do we need a concept of the mind? Does consciousness or the unconscious mind exert a stronger influence on behavior? These are basic issues that you should bear in mind as you read later chapters.

4. Psychologists employ a variety of methods to find out about behavior. Among them are (a) the individual case study, an intensive examination of one individual; (b) naturalistic observation, an investigation of psychological processes as they occur in everyday circumstances; (c) surveys, tests, and interviews, techniques that determine the relationships which exist between measurable variables and that measure the strength of these relationships; and (d) experimentation, the establishment of models of psychological situations in the laboratory and the examination of how, in these situations and under controlled circumstances, manipulated independent variables affect dependent variables.

5. The experimental method is the method of choice in psychology because it allows one to make the most clear-cut conclusions possible and often leads to the discovery of cause-effect relationships. Many important problems, however, such as race relations or reactions to natural disasters, do not lend themselves to laboratory analogue and must be studied in a different way.

6. Highlights of the history of psychology include the formation of various major schools of psychological thought and theory during the late 1800s and early 1900s, primarily structuralism, functionalism, behaviorism, Gestalt psychology, and psychoanalysis.

7. Few of these early schools have survived intact, although contemporary psychology was shaped by them.

8. Today, many psychologists view human behavior from an information-processing perspective. They see the human being as an active processor of information, receiving sensory signals from the environment, converting these to mental form, and storing them for future use. A major limitation of this system is that it can deal with only a small amount of information at any given moment.

RECOMMENDED ADDITIONAL READINGS

For more on the methods of research psychology:

Cook, T. D., & Campbell, D. T. *Quasi-experimentation: Design and analysis issues for field settings.* Chicago: Rand McNally, 1979.
Dominowski, R. L. *Research methods.* Englewood Cliffs, N.J.: Prentice-Hall, 1980.

For more on the history of psychology and an analysis of basic issues:

Chaplin, J. P., & Krawiec, T. S. *Systems and theories of psychology,* 4th ed. New York: Holt, Rinehart and Winston, 1979.
Hearst, E. (Ed.), *The first century of experimental psychology.* Hillsdale, N.J.: L. Erlbaum Associates, 1979.

If you are considering a career in psychology, write to the American Psychological Association (1200 17th St., N.W., Washington, D.C. 20036) for a copy of the following publications:

Career opportunities for psychologists: Expanding and emerging areas
Careers in psychology
Graduate study in psychology for 1981–1982
Preparing for graduate study in psychology: Not for seniors only!
The psychology major

What Does It Mean?

There is another answer to the question, What is psychology? Psychology is what psychologists do. A useful way to find out about a concept is to observe how that concept is put into practice by people who understand it. Thus, by examining what psychologists do we ought to be able to add to our understanding of the concept of psychology.

What Psychologists Do

First of all, psychologists specialize. As in most disciplinary areas, not all psychologists are trained or are employed in the same way. While there are various ways to categorize psychologists, we are employing here a set of categories similar to those used by the American Psychological Association (APA) in its booklet *Careers in Psychology* (1979). (A brief description of the American Psychological Association is given in Highlight 1–6.) Thus we have experimental, biological, developmental, social, clinical, industrial, and educational psychologists. Of course, there are subspecialties within each of these groups, and some of these will become apparent in later chapters. Further, these groups do not represent an equal division of all psychologists. The categories are useful, however, in clarifying the major activities of psychologists in their areas of employment.

The following are thumbnail sketches of the major types of psychologists.

Experimental Psychologists

Historically, experimental psychology has referred to a way of studying behavioral processes and phenomena, namely the experimental method. Today the label refers to psychologists who traditionally study a restricted set of problems, including learning, sensation and perception, human performance, motivation and emotion, language, thinking, and communication.

Biological Psychologists

This group is closely associated with experimental psychologists and uses many of the same methods. However, these laboratory-based investigators are more explicitly concerned with the biological underpinnings of behavior. Typically, they apply techniques of the biological sciences in combination with experimental procedures to determine how the nervous system, hormones, genes, and other biological entities and processes interact with behavior.

Developmental Psychologists

Changes in behavior and behavior potential over the life span are the particular concern of developmental psychologists. While in the past focus was on early years of child development, more recently developmental psychologists have adopted the life-span approach, recognizing that important behavioral changes take place at all ages. Developmental psychologists make use of experimental methods, though they are by no means limited to these techniques.

Social Psychologists

Social psychologists study people in interaction. They are particularly interested in the effects of other people on a target individual. Research methods vary widely and include work in the laboratory as well as in the real world. The acquisition of beliefs, attitudes, and values; the behavior of the individual in a group; and the learning of social roles are just a few of the topics that may interest social psychologists.

Clinical and Counseling Psychologists

This group of psychologists specializes in the assessment and treatment of emotional and/or adjustment problems. They are concerned with psychopathology and are trained to diagnose and treat psychological problems ranging from the normal developmental crises of adolescence to extreme psychotic conditions. Clinical psychologists and psychiatrists have a common interest in the treatment of mental illness. We will distinguish between them in Chapters 11 and 12. At this point we merely note that psychiatrists hold doctor of medicine (M.D.) degrees and have a medical orientation toward psychopathology, while psychologists, with doctor of philosophy (Ph.D.) degrees, are more behaviorally oriented.

Educational Psychologists

Educational psychologists are concerned with psychology as it has to do with education. Their activities include the designing, development, and evaluation of materials and procedures for education and training. They are usually employed in an applied setting such as a public school system, the military, or a large industrial concern.

Industrial/Organizational Psychologists

The focus of industrial psychology is work-related behaviors in industrial organizations. These include such areas as employee job satisfaction, efficiency, and morale. Psychologists perform many other jobs for industry as well. They may, for example, study how a work schedule is planned or determine how to raise the satisfaction of people who use an organization's services or products. Industrial psychologists consult with management on such matters as the development of better employee programs, such as those involving training or preretirement counseling, and ways to more effectively organize management structure.

Approaches to Problems

Each type of psychologist brings a particular perspective and a particular set of goals to the study of behavior. Consider, for example, the psychological study of alcoholism.

Highlight 1–6

The American Psychological Association

The American Psychological Association (APA) is a society of scientists, teachers, and professionals organized by charter to advance psychology as a science and as a means of promoting the public welfare. Its membership is approximately 50,000. The Association publishes scientific and professional journals in the various subject-matter areas and specialties of psychology. It also holds an annual convention to aid communication and exchange of new knowledge among psychologists. In addition, the APA sponsors various other meetings and activities that deal with the professional concerns and scientific interests of psychologists. These efforts are supported by many boards and committees consisting primarily of APA members who devote their attention to a wide variety of concerns, ranging from the social and ethical responsibilities of psychologists to their education and training.

The national efforts of APA are greatly facilitated by regional, state, and local associations. The time and place of the meetings of both the APA and the regional and other associations are listed each month in the *American Psychologist* or the *APA Monitor,* a newspaper for psychologists. The addresses and officers of any of these associations may be obtained by contacting the Administrative Services Department of the APA.

Divisions of the APA

The numerous interests and activities of psychologists are currently represented within the APA by the 34 divisions that are listed below. Psychologists who join the APA usually join one or more of these divisions according to their areas of training or interest. Information concerning the interest areas of divisions may be obtained from the division secretaries, whose addresses are published each November on the last page of the *American Psychologist,* or by writing to the Administrative Services Department of APA.

General Psychology
Teaching of Psychology
Experimental Psychology
Evaluation and Measurement
Physiological and Comparative Psychology
Developmental Psychology
Personality and Social Psychology
The Society for the Psychological Study of Social
    Issues—A Division of the APA
Psychology and the Arts
Clinical Psychology
Consulting Psychology
Industrial and Organizational Psychology
Educational Psychology
School Psychology
Counseling Psychology
Psychologists in Public Service
Military Psychology
Adult Development and Aging
The Society of Engineering Psychologists—A
    Division of the APA
Rehabilitation Psychology
Consumer Psychology
Philosophical Psychology
Experimental Analysis of Behavior
History of Psychology
Community Psychology
Psychopharmacology
Psychotherapy
Psychological Hypnosis
State Psychological Association Affairs
Humanistic Psychology
Mental Retardation
Population and Environmental Psychology
Psychology of Women
Psychologists Interested in Religious Issues
Child and Youth Services
Health Psychology
Psychoanalysis
Clinical Neuropsychology
Psychology and Law

The clinical psychologist would focus on treatment of the behavior problems of individual alcoholics, trying to help them restructure their lives to live comfortably without the need for alcohol. The experimental psychologist might focus on the principles of learning and reinforcement that allow the alcoholic to derive satisfaction from drinking or on the principles of conditioning and punishment that could be applied to change drinking habits. The biological psychologist might study the genetic basis of alcohol-related behavior or the physiological basis of the effects of alcohol on behavior—for example, do alcoholics inherit a biological disorder that makes their nervous systems susceptible to alcohol addiction? A social psychologist might investigate the social dynamics that occur in most drinking situations and analyze such effects as conformity and persuasion. This approach focuses on answering such questions as how do social environments support alcoholic behavior and how could these be changed? A personality psychologist might emphasize description of the personality of alcoholics and the development of tests to measure the alcoholic personality (if it exists) and to identify high-risk individuals. This approach might lead to study of the factors in the lives of alcholics that seem to correlate with problem drinking—how is the alcoholic personality formed? A counseling psychologist might talk with school students about dealing with alcoholism problems at home or among the students' peers. He or she might also do marriage or family counseling where drinking problems are involved. A developmental psychologist might focus on personality and social development during adolescence, emphasizing the development of problem behaviors such as juvenile delinquency, drug abuse, and alcohol abuse and asking why some children are susceptible or prone to such behaviors. Finally, an industrial psychologist might study the effects of the work atmosphere on drinking behavior and the ways in which employee morale can be improved to help prevent alcoholism and its heavy losses in terms of low productivity, high absenteeism, and poor-quality work.

Some Relevant Data on Psychologists

Figures 1–6 and 1–7 present the data collected by the American Psychological Association on the characteristics of its membership. As can be seen, the majority of psychologists are trained to do clinical work. At present, however, the largest employer of psychologists is educational institutions. Hospitals, government agencies, industry, and research establishments represent major and growing sources of employment for psychologists. Probably the fastest-growing group is psychologists in private practice. These are primarily clinical psychologists, although some industrial/organizational psychologists also make their living this way. Indicative of a movement away from academic psychology, traditionally their primary work activity, 39 percent of employed psychologists listed applied psychology or private practice as their area of employment. Teaching (24 percent), administration (18 percent), and research (17 percent) are other major employment activities.

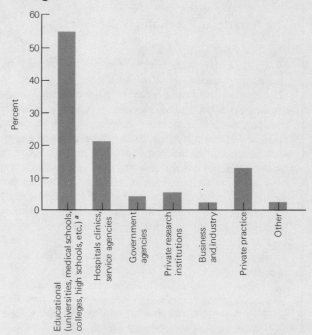

FIGURE 1-7 Employment of psychologists, in percentages

[a] The educational category here includes teachers, counselors, school psychologists, researchers, and so on.

How Do I Become a Psychologist?

You can become a psychologist in a number of ways. How you proceed depends, in part, on the type of psychologist you want to be.

According to current estimates, colleges and universities award about 50,000 bachelor's degrees each year to psychology majors. Most employment opportunities in psychology also require a graduate degree. We recommend that you consult the annual booklet *Graduate Study in Psychology,* published by the APA, to find out about schools that offer graduate programs. You should also discuss your interest with a faculty member in the psychology department where you are presently enrolled. He or she will probably have firsthand information about graduate programs and about your qualifications to meet graduate school requirements.

If you are interested in clinical psychology or are planning a career in public service, you also need to know about program accreditation and state licensing or certification. Accreditation is a process by which the APA evaluates doctoral-level programs in clinical and other applied areas of psychology. The purpose is to insure that psychologists who perform public service functions are adequately trained. Applying graduate programs that meet or exceed the standards set by the APA are accredited. An up-to-date list of colleges and universities with accredited programs is published annually in the December issue of the APA journal *American Psychologist.*

Licensing or certification is a means used by state governments to protect the public. The process insures that individual psychologists meet state standards for edu-

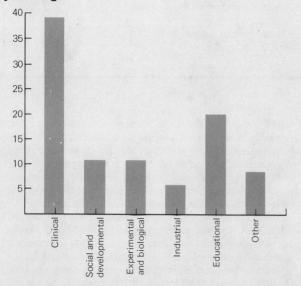

FIGURE 1-6 Primary specialty of psychologists, in percentages

cation, knowledge, and experience. Completing an accredited graduate program does not insure state licensing, however. The use of the term "psychologist" by persons who offer services to the public for a fee is restricted in most states to individuals who meet the standards defined by state law and who are appropriately licensed. These standards usually include a doctoral degree in psychology and at least one year of supervised experience in an internship plus successful completion of a licensing examination.

Education

Level of training in psychology is a major factor determining the job opportunities that will be open to you. Doctoral-level psychologists typically have been exposed to the broadest variety of knowledge and techniques over the longest period of time. The doctor of philosophy (Ph.D.) requires at least three years and averages about five years of education beyond the bacherlor's degree. Earning a doctoral degree demands a high level of academic achievement. In professional specialties, doctoral students complete an internship (on-the-job training under close supervision) either before or immediately after receiving their degree. In research fields, a student may continue in a postdoctoral position for one or more years.

Psychologists with a doctoral degree have the widest range of work opportunities. A clinical psychologist with a Ph.D., for example, could be employed in a university, a rehabilitation setting, a state hospital, or in private practice. The Ph.D. is a research degree, and to earn it a person has to make an original research contribution to the field of psychology. That contribution is written as a doctoral dissertation, which must be approved by a faculty committee of a university. Some clinical psychologists who intend only to be therapists rather than scientists enroll in an alternative program leading to the doctor of psychology (Psy.D.) degree. Training toward the Psy.D. involves more time in practical experience, while the Ph.D. program is more research oriented. At present only a few schools offer programs leading to the doctor of psychology degree.

Master's degree candidates normally spend from one to two years in graduate school after completing the bachelor's program. In addition to course work, the master's degree is awarded either on the basis of practical experience in an applied setting or a master's thesis reporting a research project. Master's-level psychologists work in a variety of settings involving teaching, research, or practice. Their employment options are more limited than those available to doctoral-level psychologists. Persons with only bachelor's-level training have relatively few opportunities to practice psychology. Psychology is one of the most popular undergraduate majors leading to a bachelor's degree. According to APA surveys, 30 percent of the students awarded a bachelor's degree in psychology go on to graduate school in the field. (Approximately 5,000 master's degrees and 3,300 doctoral degrees are awarded in psychology annually.) Another 25 percent do graduate work in some other area (law, medicine, social work, political science, and so on), and about 45 percent terminate their education at the bachelor's level. Of this group, about 75 percent subsequently find jobs in fields in which they can apply their training in psychology.

A Suggestion

If you are considering a career in psychology, we recommend that you keep an open mind. Try to keep different job options open for yourself. Rather than specializing too early, plan your training so that you receive exposure to many aspects of psychology and related disciplines. Such an approach will allow you to make wise choices concerning further training and career possibilities. You need to be sure that your interests, background, and abilities are suitably matched with your career work. Finally, discuss your ideas about a career in psychology with a faculty adviser.

Some Uses of Psychology

You can apply what you learn about psychology to disciplines or professions where you might not expect it as well as to a wide variety of everyday problems. Throughout this book, you will read stories of psychologists at work that have appeared in newspapers, national news and scientific magazines, and other sources. To familiarize you with the practical applications of psychology, several examples follow in this section. We hope that by presenting the basic principles of psychology as well as samples of their application, we will equip you with the knowledge and the skills to use psychology in your own lives.

Psychology and the Law

Under our system of law accused criminals are considered innocent until proved guilty. But if a judge waits to state this reminder until all the courtroom testimony is in, jurors may be more likely to render a guilty verdict than if the judge had stated the principle at the outset of the trial. That, at least, was the way it turned out in a study conducted by two University of Kansas social psychologists, Saul Kassin and Lawrence Wrightsman. These psychologists showed small groups of students a videotaped trial based on a real-life case. After viewing the tape, students were asked whether they thought the defendant was innocent or guilty, how much confidence they had in their own judgment, and what they could remember about key facts, such as the place of arrest of the accused.

In both his opening and closing remarks the defense attorney mentioned that the accused is innocent until proved guilty beyond reasonable doubt and that the burden of proof rests with the prosecution. For one group of student subjects the social psychologists inserted an additional reminder by the judge at the start of the trial. For another group the additional reminder was inserted after the closing arguments. A third group received no additional reminder.

Of those who heard the judge's reminder at the start of the trial, 37 percent found the defendant guilty. Of those for whom the warning came at the end of the trial, 59 percent voted for conviction. Of those who received no additional reminder, 63 percent voted guilty. Not only were the students who were instructed at the beginning of the trial less convinced of the defendant's guilt, they could also remember more facts that came out during the trial. Kassin and Wrightsman believe that jurors who receive reminders from the defense only listen to the evidence under the assumption that the accused is guilty. The results imply that some neutral party, preferably the judge, should warn the jurors of this possible predispostion and caution them against it. Furthermore, the instruction should take place before any evidence is presented. Lawyers and members of the judicial system are becoming increasingly aware of the operation of psychological processes in witness and jury behavior. Today, psychologists are often asked to give expert testimony on matters that involve the interpretation of human behavior.

Psychology and Medicine

Historically psychologists have been involved in the study and treatment of mental illness. In more recent times, however, psychologists have begun to observe significant relationships between mental states and physical illnesses. According to Dr. Mary McLaughlin, Director of Community Medicine at Long Island Jewish-Hillside Medical Center, we live in an era of "lifestyle" diseases. McLaughlin believes that two major killers of human life—heart disease and accidents—can be traced directly to the victim's lifestyle. Further, she argues that one's mode of living is an important contributor to emphysema, cirrhosis of the liver, possibly two types of cancer, venereal disease, alcoholism, obesity, and drug abuse.

McLaughlin studied 7,000 adults over a five-year period. Some of these people consistently followed seven prescribed health rules: (1) eat three meals a day at regular intervals and don't substitute snacks for meals; (2) eat breakfast every day; (3) exercise moderately at least two or three times a week by walking, biking, swimming, gardening, or the like; (4) get seven or eight hours of sleep a night; (5) avoid smoking; (6) maintain moderate weight; (7) avoid alcohol—or at least drink in moderation. After five years, the health status of the individuals who observed these rules was found to be roughly the same as that of persons *thirty years younger* who did not follow any special health regimen. Clearly, by studying such factors as why people smoke, overeat, drink too much, and avoid exercise psychologists can help contribute significantly to longer, healthier, and happier lives.

Psychology and Your Own Life

At the start of this chapter we asked you to list what you think are the top ten problems facing the world today. We hope we have convinced you that solutions to these problems will involve, in large part, the principles of human behavior. But what about your personal life? List your own top five or ten problems and see how many items relate either to your own behavior ("I'd like to lose weight" or "I'd like to become more outgoing and make friends more easily") or to the behavior of the important people around you ("My parents don't understand me—they are always trying to make me behave according to their standards" or "My friends are always pressuring me to do things I would rather not do and I have trouble standing up for myself"). We believe that you will find lots of information in this book about the immediate personal concerns in your life as well as the larger problems of society. We will point out these possibilities as they arise throughout the book.

Ethics in Psychology

The activities of psychologists directly affect the private lives of other human beings. Whether in educational research or in clinical work, psychologists are almost always concerned with and in a position to influence the experiences of others. Psychology aims to contribute positively to the welfare and betterment of humankind, of course, but there is always the potential for negative effects. Psychologists have an ethical responsibility to protect their subjects and clients from these undesirable effects.

Throughout the years of its existence, the American Psychological Association has been concerned with the ethical practice of psychology. Any evidence of unethical practice, whether in research or clinical work, is grounds for dismissal from the organization. Furthermore, the organization has published and periodically revised a book entitled *Ethical Principles of Psychologists,* which prescribes the obligations of psychologists to the human beings with whom they deal.

© 1979 United Feature Syndicate, Inc.

Psychologists have indeed been responsible for conducting controversial experiments. Often questions of the ethical treatment of research subjects have been raised. There is now in place a detailed set of ethical principles for the conduct of research.

Whenever human subjects are at risk of any sort, the experiment must be reviewed and approved by an impartial review committee. Such a committee would undoubtedly disapprove of this grasshopper experiment.

With regard to research, these principles assert that the psychologist will take all necessary steps to protect the confidentiality of the records of any individual, will not knowingly use any procedures that will result in harm or injury to the person, will fully disclose the purpose, procedures, and results of any study in which an individual participates, and prior to any interaction, will obtain from the individual his or her fully informed voluntary consent to participate. Clinical psychologists are obliged to follow much the same rules, but, in addition, must ensure that any testing performed on the client is fair to that individual and that any therapeutic steps are designed to ensure the welfare of the individual.

Ethical considerations in psychology are important but complex. There are many borderline cases. All reputable psychologists know that there must be no exceptions to the rule that the ethics of the profession must be adhered to in every professional interaction in which they engage.

2 | Biological Foundations of Behavior

Stevie Wonder is blind. Beethoven was deaf. There are millions of people in the world who cannot hear or see even with the help of a hearing aid or eyeglasses. The behavior of these many blind and deaf people is affected by a defect of one sort or another in their nervous systems which places limits on what they can do. It is amazing that some handicapped individuals still accomplish incredible feats.

An automobile accident left Robert W. paralyzed from the neck down, confined to a wheelchair. A talented artist, Robert learned to paint by holding the brush in his mouth and by this means is able to support himself. He is creative, intelligent, and articulate. The damage to his nervous system clearly limits his behavior, but probably less severely than you would think.

Henry Martin (a fictitious name but not a fictitious case) has a serious problem. He cannot retain new information unless he repeats it over and over to himself or writes it down. He remembers things he learned long ago, but not anything new he tries to learn. The problem developed after Henry had brain surgery to treat his severe epilepsy. After parts of the temporal lobe of his brain (see page 44) were removed his severe seizures disappeared, but he was left with a serious memory problem. He can see, hear, walk, and talk normally. His IQ of 118 was unaffected by the operation. Try to imagine the various ways his behavior is affected by his inability to learn anything new.

These cases and numerous others like them (see the newsclip "The Cruelest Killer") highlight the fundamental fact that behavior is critically dependent upon the structure and functioning of the nervous system. Behavior is biologically based upon the operation of this system. The nervous system is, in turn, critically dependent upon our genetic heritage—not only upon our membership in the species *Homo sapiens,* but also upon the two members of this species who are your biological parents. In order to understand many of the limits on our behavior, and many of the defects in behavior that can occur, we need to know about the structure and function of the nervous system and about the genetics of behavior. These two biological bases of behavior are the focus of this chapter.

The Nervous System: Behavior's Hardware

The nervous system is the fundamental information-processing system of the body. It collects, transmits, and deals with information. Evaluations are made using both incoming information and information already stored in memory. Finally, decisions are made and information is sent back out through the system to the muscles and glands. The result is action. To simplify, there are three basic functions taking place: (1) information is collected from the outside world and fed into the system—*the input function;* (2) once

in the system, the information is continuously analyzed in the light of all the information (knowledge) the system has stored (knows), leading to decisions—*the processing function;* and (3) once the decisions have been made, the system sends messages out to the places where action is to take place, indicating what is to be done—*the output function.*

The cases in the introduction illustrate these three functions. If a person is blind or deaf there is a serious deficit in the input system. The individual could not behave normally with respect to information coming in by the visual or auditory input channel.

Consider the case of Henry Martin, who cannot learn anything new. Henry can see, hear, feel, walk, talk, and move normally, so his input and output systems work well. His processing system has a defect, however, as a result of the brain surgery. Either he cannot store new information on a long-term basis or he cannot retrieve newly learned information from his memory banks. It is in this central processing function that most information analysis takes place, including thinking, remembering, and deciding. No wonder psychologists are particularly interested in the parts of the nervous system that carry out this function. Of course, one does not need to have had brain surgery to have problems in this system. Consider the time when you couldn't remember the Monroe Doctrine on your U.S. history final (or was it the College Boards?); or when coming up on your psychology final you couldn't remember that Henry's memory deficit resulted from damage to his *hippocampus*

The Cruelest Killer

One day in the 1950s, Marjorie Guthrie noticed that her husband, the celebrated folk singer Woody Guthrie, was walking "a little lopsided." Later, she observed that his speech was a bit slurred. She didn't become alarmed, however, until he suddenly flew into a towering rage, even though he hadn't been drinking his usual cheap wine. "Woody," she said, "you're sick."

Just how sick, slowly became apparent. At first, the doctors told the balladeer that he was an alcoholic. But over the next five years, his symptoms gradually worsened. Most notably, the tantrums became increasingly intense. Finally, one young doctor made the correct diagnosis. Woody was suffering from Huntington's disease, one of the cruelest and most devastating neurological disorders of all. Gradually, Woody lost all ability to talk, read or walk. He could communicate with his wife and children only by pointing a wildly flailing arm at printed cards marked "yes" and "no." In 1967, after fifteen years of emotional and physical suffering, Woody Guthrie died in a state hospital.

Huntington's disease is an inherited degenerative disorder of the central nervous system, first described by Dr. George Huntington, a Long Island, N.Y., physican in 1872. It is caused by a dominant gene. This means that everyone who happens to inherit the gene from one of his parents will inevitably develop the disease—and every child of an HD victim has at least a 50 per cent chance of inheriting the gene. What makes HD especially cruel is that the symptoms usually don't appear before the age of 35. A victim unaware of a history of the disease in his family may unwittingly pass it on to his children before he knows he has it. The children of an HD victim must grow up with the terrible knowledge that they, too, may be doomed.

The Guthrie family provides an illustration of the tragic scope of Huntington's disease. Woody's mother had died of it, but at the time some doctors said the malady afflicted only females and that her son was safe. Two of Woody's children by a previous marriage have since developed HD, and the shadow of the disease now hangs over Marjorie's children—Arlo, 29, a brilliant folk singer in his own right (and already the father of three), as well as Joady, 27, and Nora, 26.

Newsweek
September 27, 1976

The genetics of behavior operates through biochemistry. The basic units of heredity, called genes, consist of DNA (deoxyribonucleic acid). DNA determines what biochemicals will (or will not) be manufactured by brain cells and other cells of the body. This biochemical balance, in turn, controls the operation of the nervous system, and the nervous system underlies behavior. Remember, the genetic influence is just as present in normal behavior as it is in diseased behavior—we just don't usually think that way. Instead, we see normal behavior as being basically environmental, and turn to heredity only in the case of disease. This is wrong because *both* heredity and environment are always working together, for *both* normal and abnormal behavior.

during surgery. In fact, a great deal of our everyday problems with behavior are a result of our limited abilities in the processing function: we don't think or remember or decide things perfectly. Although the system is in many respects phenomenal—on the TV show "Happy Days" what is the name and occupation of the girl that the Fonz was going to marry?—it is not by any means perfect. Many different things can go wrong with it, especially since the system is complex and has many different parts, each with its own subsystems and subfunctions.

Recall Robert W., who was paralyzed from the neck down. His input system was in pretty good order, and his processing system seemed perfectly normal. The output system was blocked because of the accident. In particular we know that it must be a major block or cut in his spinal cord at the neck level. The descending spinal tracts—the "output" lines in the spinal cord—are cut, leaving him completely paralyzed. Thus messages cannot be sent to the muscles below the neck region. Again, this is an extreme case to demonstrate the output function. But you don't have to be paralyzed to have problems on the output side. Consider the time you were trying to speak that foreign language. You heard it properly and you knew the pronunciation rules, but you couldn't get the muscles of your speech system properly coordinated or get your tongue in just the right place to say the words correctly. And what about the time you were trying a new dance at the disco—you knew the steps, but your feet failed you.

Our choice of words, input, processing, output, and the like, suggests a comparison between the nervous system and a computer. This is the fundamental analogy of the now extremely influential information-processing approach to psychology we spoke of in Chapter 1. This approach, when applied to the topic of the biological bases of behavior, identifies the nervous system as the basic "hardware." Accordingly, there is hardware devoted primarily to the input function (for example, our eyes and ears and the ingoing nerves), hardware that handles the processing function (the brain), and an output system (the tracts of the spinal cord and the outgoing nerves) that carries the messages back out to the muscles and glands that "do the work." The input system consists basically of the various sense organs and systems, for example, eyes, ears, nose, taste buds, and touch sensors. Their function is to detect sensory information available in the world, convert this information into a code for the brain, and send the coded message along its way for processing. The conversion process by which physical energy is converted to nervous energy is known as *transducing,* and the coding of sensory information is all based on one feature—the firing of impulses by the basic unit in the system, the nerve cell or neuron.

Take the smell of steaks cooking on a charcoal grill. This information arrives at the nose in the form of particular molecules of chemicals floating in the air. The nose is affected by these molecules and reacts by converting (transducing) this chemical impact into nerve cell impulses. Somehow, the nose produces a coded message that the brain will decode and recognize as "steaks cooking over charcoal." The sensory code is all in terms of (1) which neurons are firing impulses, (2) at what rate they are firing, and (3) where in the brain they are firing. The sensory system sets up the coded message—the pattern of neural firing. The message is passed along the olfactory nerve to the brain for the next step in the analysis, namely, the perception of what is out there. The brain analyzes the information in the coded input, compares this with the knowledge it has stored in memory, and decides that the information is the smell of steaks cooking. The brain then acts accordingly, perhaps sending out a message to the glands in your mouth to start getting ready to eat a beautiful T-bone steak. Are you salivating?

Programming the Brain

One problem the nervous system faces is that it has to do a great deal of processing at the same time. It isn't easy to talk and dance (especially if you are just learning the dance) at the same time. In fact, doing any two things at once is difficult unless one of them can be done "automatically." One way to design a nervous system would be to list all the things you think will need to be done and then build special subsystems that would do each of these jobs. You would have a system that takes care of breathing, another talking, another smelling, and on and on. Each system would be rigidly "hard-wired," that is, permanently connected in a particular way—to do one and only one job. An analogy is a subsystem that automatically makes ice in a refrigerator, but can't do anything else—it uses up space in the freezer and is worthless if you don't need ice. But for keeping you supplied with ice, the system is very efficient. If ice is critical to you, you will probably opt for the automatic ice maker. Similarly, since breathing is critical to you, there is an automatic breathing control system built into the structure of your brain. It takes up some of the available space in your brain, and it isn't useful for anything but breathing because it is hard-wired to do only breathing. Breathing is so important, however, that you give up the space and flexibility in order to have the automatic control system. That way, you can indeed do two things at once: breathe and chew gum or breathe and read this book.

Many things are hard-wired into the brain by a genetic code. There is a hard-wired automatic breath-

Brain Studies May Lead to Memory Improvement

SAN FRANCISCO (AP) — Recent dramatic discoveries about the human brain are generating research that may result in improved memory, a cure for old-age symptoms and more complex computers, says a California neuroscientist.

Richard F. Thompson of the University of California-Irvine said the premier discovery of the past decade involves a family of chemicals first represented by endorphins, substances almost exactly like morphine that are produced in the brain.

About 20 of these brain peptides have been identified and there are probably many more, Thompson said. In most cases, their precise functions can only be guessed at.

Endorphins act on the brain's pain and reward center, blocking pain and perhaps providing pleasure. Thompson said they may also be involved in perhaps the biggest mystery of the brain: the incredible process of learning and memory.

"Events that are associated with either unusual pleasure or pain are stamped in the memory better," he said. "It may well be that endorphins . . . create a situation in the brain where memory is established more rapidly and better." . . .

Thompson said mounting evidence also suggests that a part of the brain called the hippocampus has a major role in memory.

Thompson said he has shown that an animal's ability to learn increases with the level of activity in the hippocampus, raising the possibility of smart pills "that could make you remember better. We haven't even begun to approach anything like this, but I think there's no question it's going to happen."

Another area with exciting promise is the mapping of "the wiring diagram—learning how the brain is hooked together" to produce such things as language and thought, he said.

If the brain's wiring were fully understood, he said, it could be copied to "build a computer that would be far different from anything we've got today—a computer that's very much like the human brain, only a hell of a lot smarter." . . .

Rocky Mountain News
January 9, 1980

The brain is the hardware underlying behavior—it is our phenomenal computer. Neurons function with electrical and chemical activity and have a tremendous capacity to store information as we go through the process called learning. We will have more to say later in the chapter about the discovery of the new family of brain chemicals, the peptides.

ing system, motor control system, sensory reception system, and automatic systems that monitor and control physiological functions throughout the body; there is also a partially hard-wired language system (Figure 2–1). Fortunately, these hard-wired auto-

matic systems do not occupy all the available space in the "refrigerator"—there is a lot of brain left over that is not prewired to do anything in particular. The most recently evolved aspects of the brain seem to be those parts predominantly free from specific functions.

FIGURE 2–1   The hard-wired and programmable systems of the brain

These parts seem to be *programmable by experience* in the world. Mostly we use this free, flexible brain space for storage—to hold information that might be good for many different things but is not necessarily good for any one special thing. The vast amount of information you have stored up by the time you reach college is what makes you the flexible, creative, ingenious, sneaky, wily, competent, and fascinating creature you are compared to most other creatures on the earth.

The flexibility that we have to learn and remember—to profit from past experience and to store knowledge and skills—makes human beings special. We have already mentioned knowledge (information about the world) and skill (information about how to do things) as two major parameters of behavior. The brain stores these for us. Most other living organisms have used up most of their available "brain" space with hard-wired circuits designed by genetic blueprint to do very specific tasks. For example, frogs have a very efficient, automatic, accurate bug detector in their visual system which allows them to flick out the tongue at just the right moment to catch passing insects.

Human beings appear to have the capacity to program new brain subsystems as needed, and extremely complex ones at that, which function almost as automatically as breathing. A good example is the subsystem for driving an automobile. To be sure, you had to learn how to drive, and you have had years of experience with various aspects of driving starting when you learned to steer your tricycle. But as adults, we drive cars virtually without thinking. You can drive and talk with a passenger or think about the job or the class or the date you are driving to. Consider how complex the brain and its program must be in order to permit the almost automatic operation of a car. Think how difficult it would be to program a real computer, stick it inside the head of a robot, and get the robot to drive your car safely over to pick up your date. That should give you some small appreciation for the phenomenal brain you have inside your head. And driving a car is one of its lesser accomplishments!

In general, the hard-wired systems have a specific location in the brain. Breathing regulation, for example, is located in a structure called the *medulla oblongata.* The sensory receiving station for incoming information from the eyes is located in an area in the back of the brain known as the *occipital lobe* of the cortex. In contrast, the flexible, programmable areas are diffusely located throughout the most recently evolved parts of the brain, in the *neocortex,* as a general rule. This means that diffuse, abstract functions are not localized in one particular part or structure in the brain. (The hard-wired ice maker has a particular location, but the more diffuse function of cooling is located throughout the refrigerator, to make

the analogy again.) Location of function has implications when there is brain damage: damage that directly hits a hard-wired location will disrupt the function localized there. Damage to the medulla oblongata will kill you because you will stop breathing; damage to the visual receiving area of the occipital lobe will make you at least partially blind. In contrast, diffuse systems are much less affected by local damage, if at all. Memory, because no single small wound will knock it out, is spread out over a wide range of the cortex of the brain. Thus Henry Martin could remember all the things he had learned before the operation on his brain. He had problems with storing or recalling newly learned information, possibly because the surgery knocked out a hard-wired system in his hippocampus that stores or retrieves the memories from the programmable, diffuse memory banks spread out over large areas of the brain.

Hard-wiring a system into the brain, particularly when it is done by the genetic code, means you must give the system a specific location in the brain. In turn, this means that the system is vulnerable to destruction from brain damage, and probably no other part of the brain can take over the function of the damaged parts. Programmable parts of the brain, however, seem to be able to cover for each other in the event of damage. Brain damage may destroy your ability to do something or to remember something, but other parts of the brain can often take over, and you can relearn much of the knowledge or skill you once had.

The programmable parts of the brain underlie our ability to learn and remember vast amounts of knowledge and skills. Learning and memory are two of our most important psychological functions, and we shall devote Chapters 5 and 6 to each of these topics. The greatest unsolved mystery of the brain is how it learns and remembers information. The hard-wired subsystems of the brain are critical to our survival and normal behavioral functioning. But the programmable parts where we learn, recall, think, dream, and decide or experience emotion, pleasure, and pain are surely the most interesting to psychologists. But then again, perhaps some of our emotional problems occur because parts of the emotional system are hard-wired.

In this chapter we will examine the major parts of the brain. To help you organize your thinking about the brain, keep in mind the distinctions we have already made about functions of the brain: input functions of getting information into the brain; hard-wired, automatic subsystems that serve special functions; soft-wired, or programmable, brain areas that govern the highest mental functions; and, finally, the output systems that send signals or commands to the muscles and glands. Let us begin our examination by considering the operation of the basic unit of the nervous system, the neuron.

The Neuron

If we want to understand behavior from a biological point of view, then we must first understand the physiology of the nervous system. Similarly, if we are to understand the physiology of the nervous system, we must first understand the functioning of its elementary unit, the nerve cell, or **neuron** (see Appendix B).

While there is no accurate count, our nervous system contains at least 10 billion (and perhaps as many as 100 billion) nerve cells. Although there are many types of nerve cells that are specialized in structure and function, most consist of three basic structural units. These are the **soma, dendrites,** and **axon.** These parts of the nerve cell are illustrated in Figure 2–2 (see also Figures B1–2 in Appendix B). The cell body, or soma, contains the nucleus of the nerve cell, which controls all cellular activities such as oxygen utilization and energy production. One cellular activity that nerve cells do not carry out is reproduction. But neurons do die. It has been estimated that human beings lose as many as 10,000 nerve cells each day, a loss that tends to increase with age.

The dendrites are short "fibers" or processes extending from the soma. They act like receiving stations which pick up signals from other neurons. A nerve cell may have just a few or several hundred dendrites, all of which conduct information toward the cell body.

Each neuron has a single longer fiber, the axon, extending from the soma, the cell body. In some cases the axon may divide into several branches after leaving the soma. Some axons are quite long, measuring several feet in length; others are very short. Axons conduct information away from the cell body. They end in terminal branchings, each of which is referred to as an *axon terminal*. These axon terminals are located near other dendrites and somas of other neurons, and the signals generated by the neuron are transmitted along the axon to its terminals, and then to the dendrites or soma of the next neuron.

The region where an axon makes a functional connection, where it comes closest to a dendrite or cell body of the next neuron, is known as the **synapse.** However, the axon terminals do not actually touch the dendrites or soma of the next neuron in the communication chain. There are small spaces between adjoining neurons known as *synaptic spaces,* or *clefts.* A nerve impulse travels down the axon, invading the terminals, where it causes the release of **chemical transmitter substances,** sometimes called neurotransmitters. These chemical transmitters travel the small distance across the synaptic space to the dendrites or soma of the next neuron. In this way nerve impulses are communicated from one neuron to the next and on to distant parts of the body.

We know a great deal about the generation and transmission of nerve signals, which are called **action potentials.** Much of this information is presented in Appendix B for the student who wishes to study these processes more intensively.

One major development in the study of the brain might be described as a shift away from the electrical processes of the action potential of the neuron toward the chemical. The last few years of research have made it clear that there are an enormous number of biochemicals in the brain that differentially affect various parts of the system, and thus, in turn, differentially affect behavior. There are apparently two basic types of chemicals in the brain that influence neuron activity: (1) the fast-acting *transmitters* that carry messages across the synapse from one neuron to the next, and (2) the slower, but much longer-lasting *modulators.* Transmitters are chemicals that are stored in the synaptic vesicles of the neuron endings and are released when the action potential of the neuron travels to the synaptic area. Transmitters quickly travel across the synapse between neurons and have a brief impact on the next neuron—if enough transmitter substance from various synapses influences the next neuron (at the right places, at about the same time), the next neuron can be trig-

FIGURE 2–2 The basic parts of a neuron

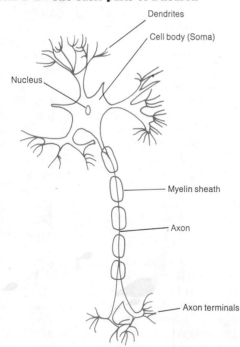

Dendrites

Cell body (Soma)

Nucleus

Myelin sheath

Axon

Axon terminals

Most vertebrate nerve cells consist of three basic parts—the dendrites, the cell body (soma), and the axon. The axon ends in the so-called axon terminals which make contact with another cell, another nerve cell, a muscle, or a gland. Many axons are encased in a myelin sheath which increases the cell's rate of conduction and its action potential.

gered into firing an impulse. The transmitter is quickly removed from the synapse by other chemicals in the area; so its effect is short-lived. The transmitter probably works something like a key, needing to find a lock on the next neuron where it fits and thus can "get in" or activate the neuron and perhaps trigger off an impulse. This lock is called a *receptor site*, and each receptor site accepts transmitters (keys) of only particular shapes. The shape, of course, refers to the chemical or molecular structure of the transmitter molecule, which must match up with the chemical or molecular structure of the lock on the receptor site of the next neuron.

All of this means that the electrical processes are simple (one nerve impulse is just like another) as compared to the chemical processes. There may be special transmitters for special functions (such as a transmitter just for pain signals), and these transmitters could be spread all over the brain, rather than concentrated in a particular place. According to this idea, there would not be a "pain center" in the brain, that is, a place where pain signals congregate. While the brain certainly has specialized systems, each system could be spread out in a variety of brain structures and work by specialized chemical processes. For example, a pain system with pain transmitters and receptors would be located on many neurons throughout the brain, not just localized in one place or pain center.

This brings us to the modulators. These newly discovered chemicals appear to be very much like hormones and are probably manufactured by special neurosecretory cells in the pituitary gland or in the hypothalamus. In contrast to true transmitters, these modulators are not contained in vesicles but "float around" in the synaptic area. Accordingly, they would not act as quickly as the transmitters, but would act for a longer time. The modulator might work by having a shape similar to a transmitter molecule, so it would be able to fit some of the neuron receptor sites.

One modulator chemical that has been publicized recently is beta-endorphin. Beta-endorphin reduces the sensation of pain, probably in this manner: When the body is stressed by pain, neurosecretory cells react by secreting more beta-endorphin, a neuromodulator. The beta-endorphin spreads throughout the system and starts to fill up some, perhaps many, of the locks or receptor sites on neurons transmitting pain signals. When the body experiences more pain-inducing stimulation, the neurotransmitter for pain (labeled Substance P) is released from synaptic vesicles and travels across the synapse to affect the next neuron. But many of the neuron's receptor sites are filled up with molecules of beta-endorphin. Substance P cannot then have as large an effect because its impact is modulated by the presence of beta-endorphin in some of the locks. The behavioral end result of all this complicated chemistry is that you feel less pain. The net effect is like taking a shot of morphine or at least a couple of aspirins.

All of this has enormous potential for application, because presumably all psychoactive drugs, including pain killers, generally operate in this way. They either affect the transmitters directly or influence the modulators. If there are many transmitters and many modulators, and these have very specific effects in the brain, there is hope that new drugs could be developed to control the brain more precisely. For example, perhaps a drug could be found to *specifically* control food intake to help in the treatment of obesity. Some drugs (amphetamines) decrease food intake but seriously disrupt many other systems in the brain. There may, however, be a chemical modulator in the brain that does for food intake what beta-endorphin does for pain. This modulator may be the chemical that normally keeps body weight closely regulated, controlling how much food you take in and even how much food is stored away as fat. There are other exciting possibilities, of course—chemicals that control sleeping, sexual behavior, aggression, and violence.

Brain transmitters and modulators, in one way or another, are probably involved in all aspects of behavior, including the phenomenon we call consciousness. Certainly you know already that certain chemicals can affect your experience of consciousness—drugs such as alcohol or THC, the active ingredient in marijuana. Again, these psychoactive chemicals undoubtedly operate by affecting the transmitter system or the modulation system or both, and because these systems are so intimately involved in other aspects of behavior, the potential for damage to behavioral functioning is great. Prolonged alcohol consumption, for example, is known to be capable of producing severe deficits in the brain's capacity to store new information.

Another important prospect is that the characteristic mental deficiencies of old people, labeled senility, may not be solely or even primarily due to the loss of irreplaceable neurons. But the deficits that go with senility may be primarily chemical, and there is hope that drugs can be developed to replace the deficient transmitters or modulators. There have been several attempts to develop drugs that would improve memory capability, and we can certainly realistically hope that efforts in this area will some day be successful. The full chemical understanding of the transmitter and modulator systems promises to revolutionize the field of chemical control of behavior.

Coding Information

We can think of the nervous system as a very large communication system which transmits information from one part of the body to another. For example, when we "see" something, information is transmitted from the eye to the brain over a neural communication system, the optic nerve. When we "hear" something, information is transmitted from the inner ear to the brain over the auditory branch of the acoustic nerve (see Color Plate 10).

The nervous system has evolved a number of ways of coding the information it transmits. Before we discuss how the nervous system codes information, you should know that most neurons emit impulses or action potentials every once in a while even when nothing is happening—this is called the *base rate of firing*. A neuron can signal that an event has occurred by increasing its rate of firing (turning the signal system on) or by decreasing its base rate of firing (sometimes turning completely off). In other words, the neuron can signal with either "on" or "off" responses. Consider what happens when we shine a light into the eye of a human observer: While sitting in the dark the subject's optic nerve is firing at its base rate. Then, when the stimulus light is turned on, some of the neurons of the optic nerve will increase their rate of firing. Others will decrease their firing rate. The brightness of the light might then be coded by the magnitude of change—a dim light would be coded as a small increase (or decrease) in the rate of firing and a bright light as a larger increase (or decrease) in the rate of firing.

In addition, the neural code for brightness might involve the number of neurons that change their rate of firing as a function of the intensity of the stimulus. A dim light might trigger a change in the firing rate of only a small number of neurons, whereas a bright light might trigger a change in a large number of neurons.

Another way of coding information concerns *which* neurons are firing. For example, a visual stimulus causes a change in the firing rate of neurons in the optic nerve; a tone causes a change in the firing rate of neurons in the acoustic nerve. This principle also applies within a given sensory system. For example, within the eye it makes a great deal of difference *which* neurons of the optic nerve are activated, because these neurons code for the location, color, and other characteristics of the stimulus we are observing. It has also been shown that tones of different pitch stimulate different neurons; in other words, one of the neural codes for pitch is which nerves are firing. Most amazing of all is the relatively recent discovery that specialized cells in the visual system (and perhaps in other sensory systems as well) respond to particular types of stimuli and not to other very similar types. For example, there are cells in the visual system that respond with an "on" signal to a vertical line, but do not respond if a horizontal line is flashed before the eye (see Chapter 3). If this neuron produces an "on" response, a vertical line of some sort has been "seen."

In summary, there are three major factors that characterize the way neurons transmit and code information about what is happening to the organism: (1) The rate of firing impulses, (2) the number of neurons responding, and (3) which particular neurons are firing. All three factors convey information about the nature and location of sensory stimuli.

Neuron Circuits

Some neurons are excitatory, meaning that they cause the next neuron in the chain to become "excited," that is, to increase the rate of firing above the base, resting rate. They do this by releasing into the synaptic space an excitatory transmitter substance, a chemical that causes the next neuron to fire more rapidly. Other neurons are inhibitory—they release inhibitory chemicals when stimulated, and these chemicals cause the next neuron in the chain to decrease the rate of firing below the resting rate.

Any given neuron receives inputs from many other neurons. For example, there may be ten thousand synapses on the dendrites and cell body of a single neuron. Some of those synapses are excitatory and some are inhibitory. The neuron receives conflicting messages—some synapses say "fire more," others say "fire less." The neuron acts chemically as if it were an adding machine, adding up the *more* and *less* messages and tabulating the net total. If the base rate of firing is 100 impulses/second and the neuron receives a total of 50 units of inhibitory messages and 70 units of excitatory messages, it will respond by an increased firing rate of 120, a net increase of 20 units. The simple neuron can thus function like a calculator.

Given this information, we can put together a simple circuit of only a few neurons *that will detect something.* Figure 2–3 shows four neurons in a small circuit (can you imagine a circuit of a million neurons?). Neurons A, B, and C are visual receptor neurons that transduce light into neural impulses. Each of these three receptors connects to, or synapses with, the next neuron in the chain (neuron X) on the way to sending the information to the brain. One way to think about this circuit is to imagine it as a bureaucracy, with A, B, and C all reporting to X, who then reports to the "higher ups." To round out the picture of the circuit, let us say that: (1) X fires at a base rate of 100 impulses per second, (2) neuron B excites X by 10 units if we shine a flashlight on B of constant brightness, and (3) neurons A and C are inhibitory neurons on either side of B and work in opposition to B. Suppose the same flashlight shined on A causes it to inhibit X by 5 units, or shined on C causes C to inhibit X by 5 units also. This inhibition coming from neurons alongside each other is known as *lateral inhibition.* As you will shortly learn, lateral

FIGURE 2-3 Effect of light on visual neurons

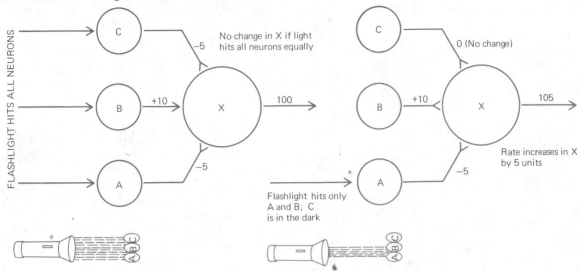

inhibition is a critical feature in neural circuits because it allows some important events to take place.

Let us now focus on the firing rate in neuron X as a function of where we shine the flashlight on A, B, and C. If the light is off, X fires at its base rate of 100. If we turn the light on B and only B, the rate goes up to 110. Note that the beam of light would have to be very tiny to land only on B without hitting A or C. If we shine the light on A, B, and C, nothing happens to X's rate. X is excited by 10 units from B, but inhibited by 10 units—5 each from A and C. If the light is on A and B but not C, X will increase by 5 units; and if it is on B and C, but not A, X will also increase by 5 units. The lateral inhibition from A and C around B allows X to act as if it were a detector of edges, places where the light changes in intensity from a higher value to a lower value. X does not change its firing rate unless the light falls *differentially* on A, B, and C. And differential light usually means there is an *edge*, or contour, of some kind out there in the world.

Using simple circuits like these, you can put together various kinds of detectors. We will have more to say about detectors in Chapter 3. Put several of these circuits together in a more complicated layout and you can build a "bug detector" for frogs' eyes. A single neuron can tell you about a light coming on (firing rate increases) and about how bright the light is (how much the rate increases). But it takes circuits of neurons, with the help of lateral inhibition, to tell your brain about the edges of the light and where they are located out there in the world. Can you see how circuits like these could be put together to detect lines and angles, so you could begin to detect particular shapes? Once you detect the shape, you are well on the way to detecting what is in front

of your eyes—all of this from one fundamental building block, the neuron. Aren't you glad you have 10–100 billion of them?

Neuron Development, Damage, and Death

As adults, you now have all the neurons you will ever have. Unlike all the other types of cells in the body, neurons do not divide and replace themselves as they die off. An often quoted estimate is that we lose 10,000 neurons a day, although no one really knows the extent of daily loss. While neurons are not replaced, the nervous system has some flexibility, particularly in the soft-wired areas where remaining, undamaged neurons can take over the functions or work done by other neurons that might die or be damaged by injury. For example, brain damage might result in some difficulty in language functioning, known as *aphasia*, but with time the person is likely to recover some of the lost language functions as other, undamaged neurons "take up the slack." We probably have many neurons with nonspecific functions that stand as a ready reserve to help out when needed and that have the potential to take over a lot of different roles. The famous neuropsychologist Karl Lashley called this the law of *equipotentiality*, meaning that all brain areas had equal potential for doing the same things. We know this is not true of the hard-wired areas, but within the large area of soft-wired parts there may indeed be equal potential among the neurons to do any job needed.

Neurons do not reproduce themselves, but can they repair themselves if damaged? The answer is complex, but basically not a particularly optimistic

Brain Damage: Sprouting to Recovery

Evidence that the hippocampus—a brain area thought to be involved in learning and memory—repairs itself after injury has been reported by researchers Rebekah Loy and Teresa Milner of the University of California at San Diego. After experimentally destroying cells in the hippocampal region of rat brains, the scientists found an expected degeneration of neurons; they discovered, however, that neighboring neurons sprouted new axons in an apparent attempt to connect with hippocampal cells.

Perhaps most significant, Loy and Milner found that the brains of female rats sprouted more new connections than did the male brains. One possible explanation for the sex difference "is that before injury, the adult hippocampal portion of the brain was different in the males and females because of an early exposure to hormones," Loy says. "Another possibility is that in adults, circulating hormones may enhance sprouting in females or depress sprouting in males, in response to injury."

Whether or not the post-destruction sprouting may actually contribute to memory and other functional recovery is not known at this point. However, Loy hopes that eventually "we can apply that knowledge to the recovery of motor and learning skills after a brain injury. . . . There have been numerous studies indicating that men and women learn differently and have different spatial abilities. After a brain injury, men and women are known to differ in their ability to recover certain skills. Our studies provide an anatomical model for these observations."

Science News
July 12, 1980

The hippocampus is the brain structure, deep within the temporal lobe, that seemingly plays a critical role in immediate memory storage and retrieval. It is the area that was destroyed in Henry Martin's brain (see the introduction to this chapter) during surgery. After brain damage there is often recovery of lost functioning, although complete recovery is rare. New neurons are not produced; rather, surviving neighbors somehow take over some of the work of the damaged ones. This article suggests that this may be accomplished by the sprouting of new axons (there is also probably dendrite sprouting). The differences between male and female brains may be due to hormone effects (see the section "The sex hormones" later in this chapter).

one at this time. In the central nervous system, repair is practically impossible, and rarely takes place. This is why brain or spinal cord damage is devastating. In the periphery of your arms, legs, hands, and so on, there is significant repair capability, so a person who severs a nerve, for example, can expect to regain some sensation and movement in the area served by the nerve if the nerve can be grafted. Progress in microsurgery has made peripheral recovery more and more likely. Neurons in the peripheral system are also lost forever when they die, but they have some ability to regrow damaged axons, whereas neurons in the central nervous system cannot. The reason these neurons cannot regenerate may be simply because cells are so tightly packed together that the neurons cannot even get started on regeneration. Or some of the support cells in the central nervous system may secrete chemicals into the surrounding area that block regrowth. This latter possibility is exciting because it suggests that injections of other chemicals might block this effect and allow neurons to regrow axons. Such drugs could be injected into damaged spinal cord tissue or even brain-damaged areas to facilitate regrowth.

While we are born with nearly all our neurons, at birth not all neurons are hooked up or interconnected as in the adult brain. One assumption has been that as the newborn infant's brain develops, neurons are growing or sprouting dendrites, and the axons are growing in length and developing synaptic connections with other neurons. This may indeed be true for many parts of the brain. A famous series of experiments done by David Krech and Mark Rosenzweig, for example, showed that enriched environments containing swings, ladders, and other toys for infant rats to play with led to a more "fully developed" cortex (a thicker cortex with more chemical transmitters) than the cortex of rats reared in a plain cage with no toys (Figure 2–4). The extra stimulation from the toys and play presumably led to greater brain development in terms of more elaborate interconnections. Also, brain damage from injury often has a much less permanent effect when it happens to a young child or baby than when it happens to an adult. Children often show essentially complete recovery, whereas adults will recover only partially (although, in general, substantially) if the damage is in the soft-

FIGURE 2–4 The enriched rat environment

wired areas. In short, the young brain, like the young body, is more flexible.

Recent evidence suggests that some parts of the brain do not develop by growing dendrites, axon terminals, and synapses. Rather, the process is the opposite. In some parts there are many more interconnections in the young brain than in the adult brain, suggesting that brain development takes place by a process of pruning out the unnecessary connections. As the infant experiences the world around it, the brain reacts with pruning, not growth. The experience works on the brain like a sculptor paring away the unnecessary, thus molding the final product. Experience may not act exclusively or even primarily like a fertilizer promoting axon and dendrite growth. Or, more likely, experience acts like a sculptor on some parts of the brain and like fertilizer on other parts. The brain undoubtedly profits from experience, and the Krech/Rosenzweig experiments suggest it could be seriously retarded in development if reared in isolation. Thus, parents are encouraged to raise their children in stimulating and varied environments.

The Organization of the Nervous System

The nervous system consists of many parts and divisions. The overall organization of the system and its principal parts are depicted in Figure 2–5, while Highlight 2–1 lists the major parts of the system you should be familiar with. Here we will give a brief and simplified overview of the most important parts of the system. By continually referring to Figure 2–5 and Highlight 2–1, your task of learning the major parts of the nervous system presented here will be simplified considerably.

The **central nervous system** (CNS) consists of the brain and spinal cord. It is the interacting and processing center for all bodily functions and behavior. The **peripheral nervous system** includes all of the nerves that run out from and feed back into the brain (12 pairs of cranial nerves) or spinal cord (31 pairs of spinal nerves). The cranial nerves are shown in Color Plate 10. Figure 2–6 shows schematically a typical spinal nerve connecting with the spinal cord.

FIGURE 2-5   The structural organization of the nervous system

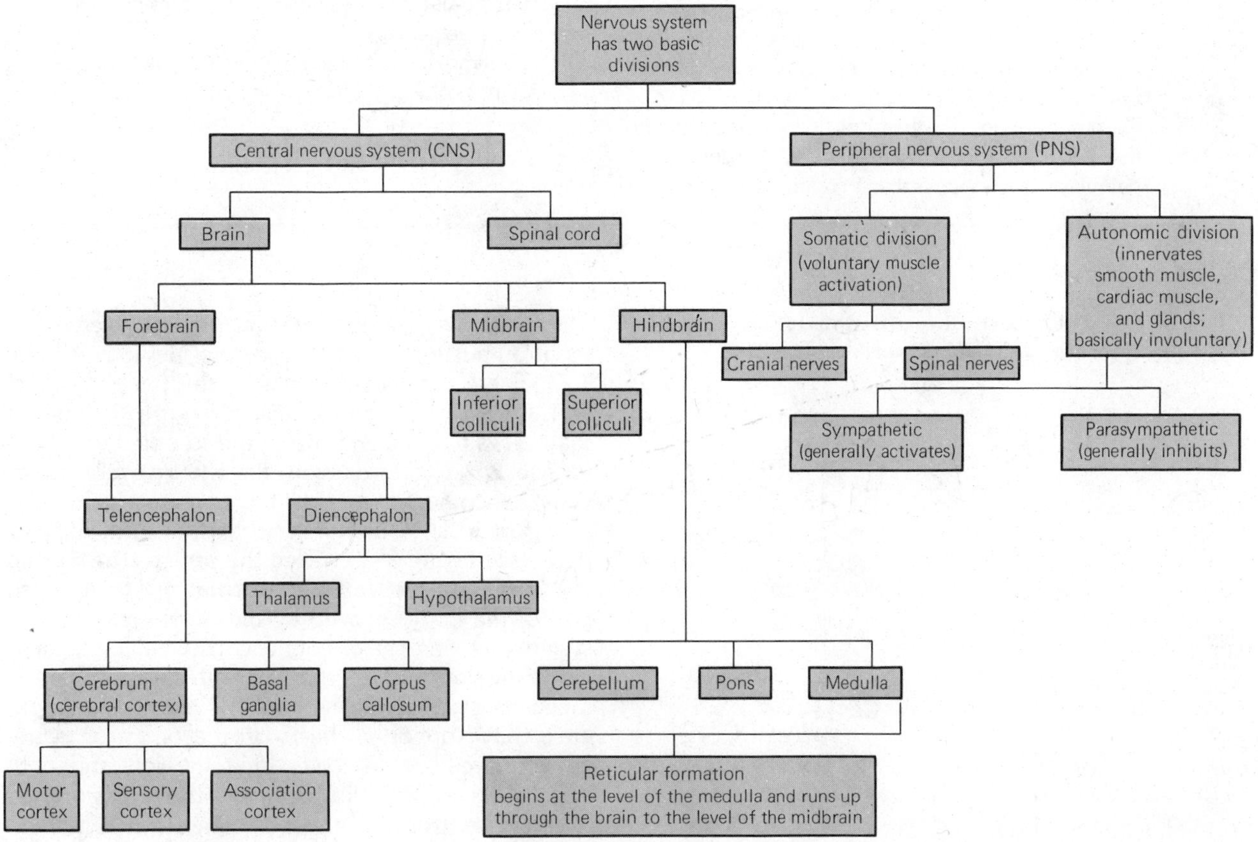

Highlight 2–1

Parts of the Nervous System

Many of the terms in the section on the anatomy of the nervous system may be new and unfamiliar to you. Below is a listing of the most important parts of the nervous system. These are the basic terms you need to know to understand the biological foundations of behavior.

The Neuron

A. The cell body (soma)
B. The dendrites for receiving information
C. The axon for sending information on to other neurons; a nerve is basically a bundle of axons from many neurons
D. The synapse—area of connection between neurons where chemical transmitters are released from vesicles to affect the next neuron

The Brain

A. The cerebral hemispheres
   1. Sensory cortex: receiving area for information from sensory systems
   2. Motor cortex: area that initiates motor responses
   3. Association cortex: the undifferentiated remainder of the cortex that underlies all higher mental functions
   4. Corpus callosum: the band of fibers that connects the two cerebral hemispheres and constitutes a pathway for interhemispheric communication

B. Thalamus: the preliminary-processing and relay station for incoming information
C. Hypothalamus: a complex structure involved in regulating a wide variety of emotional and motivational behaviors
D. Medulla: involved in regulating involuntary behavior
E. Cerebellum: controls motor coordination
F. Reticular formation: regulates arousal level

The Spinal Cord

A. Dorsal roots—collects information coming into the spinal cord
B. Ventral roots—disperses information going out from the spinal cord

The Peripheral Nervous System

A. Somatic division: the nerves that serve voluntary muscles and relay somatosensory information
B. Autonomic division: the nerves that serve involuntary muscles
   1. Sympathetic division: generally activates our bodies, as in emergencies
   2. Parasympathetic division: generally inhibits or slows down involuntary functioning

FIGURE 2–6   The organization of peripheral nerves and their relationship to the spinal cord

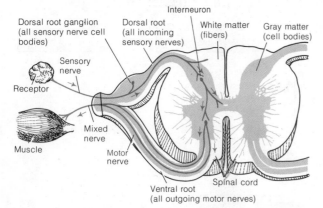

Dorsal root ganglion (all sensory nerve cell bodies)
Dorsal root (all incoming sensory nerves)
Interneuron
White matter (fibers)
Gray matter (cell bodies)
Sensory nerve
Receptor
Mixed nerve
Muscle
Motor nerve
Ventral root (all outgoing motor nerves)
Spinal cord

Only one-half of the cross section of the spinal cord is fully illustrated, but the arrangement is duplicated on both sides.

The peripheral nervous system primarily serves an input/output function to the central nervous system.

There are two divisions of the peripheral system. One, called the **somatic division,** consists of the nerves that primarily serve the so-called voluntary muscles. The other division, the **autonomic nervous system,** services all the involuntary muscles and glands. The autonomic system, in turn, has two parts (see Figure 2–7), called the **sympathetic** and the **parasympathetic nervous system.** Each part of the body serviced by the autonomic nervous system has one set of connections with the sympathetic division and another set with the parasympathetic division. These two sets of connections generally have opposite effects on the organ or gland, as you can see by comparing the left and right sides of Figure 2–7. For example, the pupils of your eyes are controlled in this way. The parasympathetic

FIGURE 2-7 Schematic layout of the autonomic nervous system

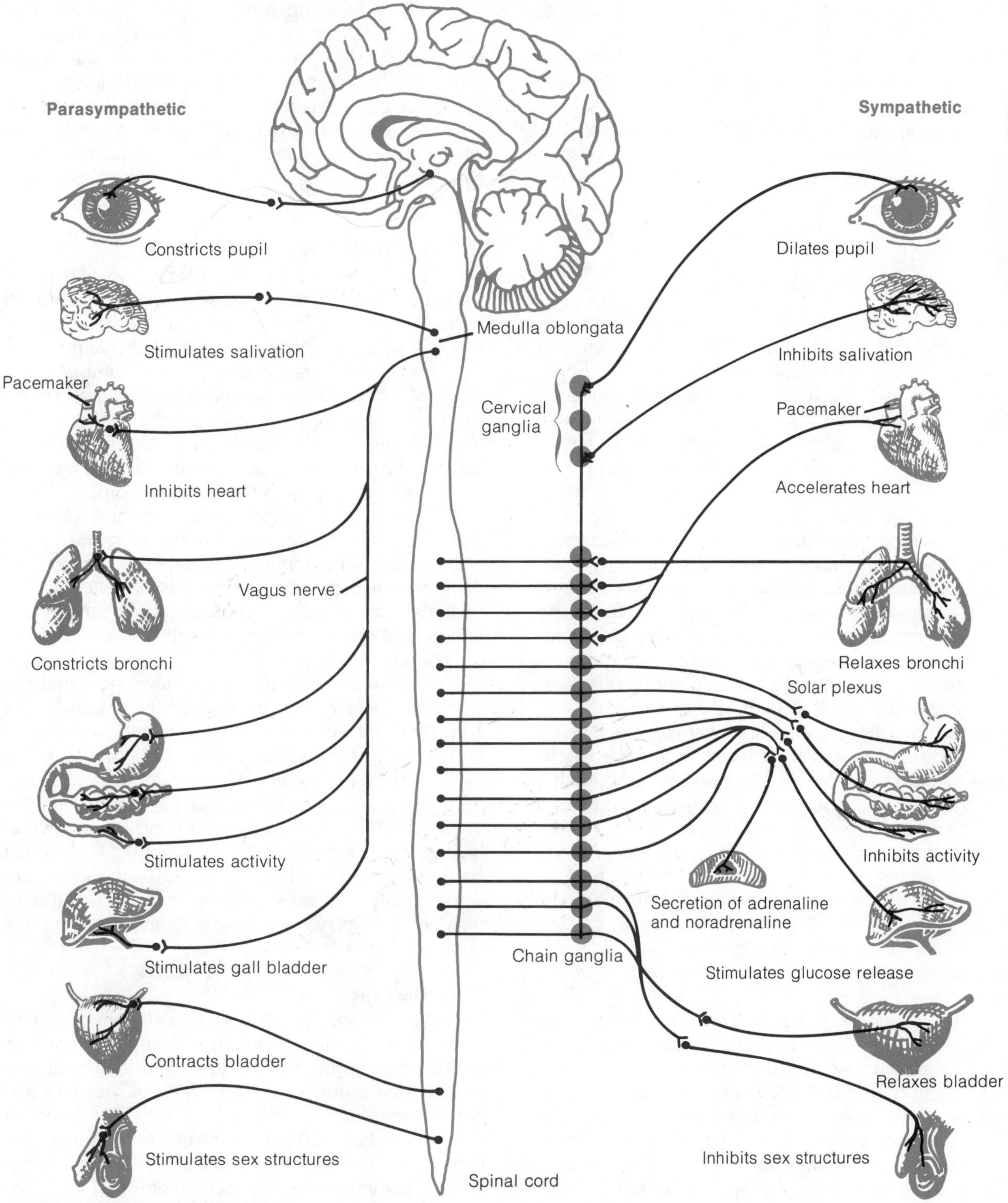

Parasympathetic

Sympathetic

Constricts pupil

Dilates pupil

Stimulates salivation

Inhibits salivation

Medulla oblongata

Pacemaker

Pacemaker

Inhibits heart

Cervical ganglia

Accelerates heart

Vagus nerve

Constricts bronchi

Relaxes bronchi

Solar plexus

Stimulates activity

Inhibits activity

Secretion of adrenaline and noradrenaline

Stimulates gall bladder

Chain ganglia

Stimulates glucose release

Contracts bladder

Relaxes bladder

Stimulates sex structures

Spinal cord

Inhibits sex structures

The sympathetic division is schematized on the right. The neurons are located in clusters or ganglia that are lined up like a chain alongside the middle portion of the spinal column. In the parasympathetic system (shown on the left), communication with the spinal cord is at the top and bottom of the spinal column, and there are neuron cell bodies in the periphery (away from the spinal cord), often distributed near the organs affected by this system. Each organ is "serviced" by two systems—the sympathetic and parasympathetic—with opposite effects.

system controls constriction of the pupil, while stimulation of the sympathetic system causes dilation of the pupils. Thus, examining your pupils and their ability to constrict or dilate to a light shined on your eyes are controlled in this way. The parasympathetic autonomic system. The autonomic nervous system is important because through it the body reacts to stress, so that much of the physiology of our emotions—such as fear, anger, and anxiety—are controlled by this system.

The Central Nervous System

In the CNS, the **spinal cord** is primarily a transmission cable that sends information to the brain and from the brain out to the peripheral system. Some reflex responses (such as the knee jerk), however, take place within the spinal cord and do not involve commands from the brain. The spinal cord is a critical transmission cable—when cut or damaged the effects are severe, as in the case of Robert W. in the introduction to this chapter. Some parts of the cord carry incoming information to the brain, called afferent or sensory information. Damage to these parts will result in a loss of certain bodily sensations. Other parts carry outgoing information—from the brain to the muscles—called efferent or motor information. Damage to these parts will result in paralysis. If both parts are damaged or disrupted, as when the cord is completely cut, the result is total loss of sensation and total paralysis from the point of damage downward.

Most of the action of interest to psychologists takes place in the brain. The brain weighs, on the average, about 3 pounds (1.3 kilograms) and has a volume of approximately 1.5 quarts (1.3 liters). Packed into that one-and-a-half quarts are as many as 100 billion neurons, each having connections (synapses) with perhaps a thousand other neurons. Thus, there may be 100 trillion synapses in the human brain. But given all that the brain has to do, this enormous interconnection is probably a minimal requirement.

The major components of the brain of interest to psychologists are listed in Highlight 2–1 and Figure 2–5. To simplify, we can think of the brain as being divided into two parts, called the brain stem and the cortex, which overlies the brain stem. To visualize this arrangement, imagine making a fist, then plunging your fist deep into a large pile of bread dough, then holding your arm up at an angle with the dough completely covering your fist. Your arm and fist (with a few small attachments) constitute the brain stem, which is connected continuously with the spinal cord. The pile of dough hiding your fist and surrounding the upper part of the brainstem is the cortex. It is this cortex or cortical tissue that human beings have so much of as compared to other species and that provides the substrate for our outstanding talents in language, thought, and memory. The human brain stem, on the other hand, is not very different from the brain stems of most other mammalian species. The brain stem of these species contains many hard-wired centers for carrying out or regulating basic biological functions such as eating, sleeping, and breathing.

The Brain Stem

Only a few of the many structures and nerve tracts contained in the brain stem will be mentioned here. In the lower brain stem area are the pons, the medulla oblongata, and the cerebellum, and spread throughout the lower to middle brain stem is a network of fibers called the reticular formation. Brain stem structures are heavily involved in the control of muscles and muscle coordination (the cerebellum), breathing (medulla and pons), and sleep and wakefulness (the pons and the reticular formation).

The brain stem also contains many centers involved in relaying information between the cortex and various sense organs. These relay centers also do some processing of incoming information. Three of these centers are the **thalamus** (all senses), the inferior colliculus (auditory sense), and the superior colliculus (visual sense).

Finally, the structure in the brain stem that has perhaps interested psychologists the most is the **hypothalamus,** which lies just below the thalamus and just above the pituitary gland (the "master gland of the endocrine system"). The hypothalamus contains many nuclei (see Color Plate 11) and is seemingly involved in almost all behavioral functioning, including sleeping, eating, emotional control, and sexual behavior. It also has been shown to be the site where some pituitary gland hormones are actually manufactured and plays a critical role in regulating the pituitary.

The Cortex

The cortex, or "bread dough" overlying your buried fist, is divided down the middle into two hemispheres, right and left. Buried in the dough is a band of fibers running back and forth between the two hemispheres and connecting them. This band of fibers, called the corpus callosum, is important because it is the major means by which the two hemispheres communicate with each other.

Each hemisphere of cortex can be divided (for purposes of classification) by function and by location. Functionally, the cortex divides into three sections: (1) motor cortex—its function is to control the movement of particular parts of the body, and each muscle group in the body has a control center in the motor cortex; (2) *sensory cortex*—its function is to receive information coming in from the sense organs of the body; and (3) *association cortex*—this is all the rest of the cortex and is presumed to be the most programmable cortex that underlies the high-level processing of the information between its input to the sensory cortex and its output from the motor cortex.

The brain does not have sensory receptors, and therefore cutting brain tissue does not produce pain. For this reason, patients undergoing brain surgery need only a local anesthetic and can, therefore, talk while their cortex is being operated on. During such operations the surgeon can electrically stimulate various cortical areas. As you might guess, stimulation of motor cortex causes a muscle somewhere in the body to twitch. Stimulation of sensory cortex causes persons to say they feel something or taste something or smell something, depending on the sensory cortical area that is stimulated. Finally, stimulation of association cortex has resulted in reports of vivid memories, often from long ago. This last observation led some investigators to suggest that perhaps everything an individual ever experienced is stored in the association cortex, just waiting to be stimulated for recall. However, more recent analyses suggest that a great deal is stored, but not everything a person has experienced.

The cortex may also be divided by location. Each hemisphere can be divided into four **lobes:** (1) The *frontal*—largely association and motor cortex; (2) the *occipital*—largely sensory cortex for the visual system; (3) the *temporal*—sensory cortex for audition and association cortex; and (4) the *parietal*—sensory cortex for the other senses and association cortex. The locations of these four lobes are outlined in Figure 2–8.

The Basal Ganglia

The basal ganglia consist of a group of nuclei buried deep within the cerebral hemispheres. The basal ganglia contain three major nuclei on each side: the caudate nucleus, the putamen, and the globus pallidus. The basal ganglia are important in the control of movement, and their degeneration has been implicated as a factor in Parkinson's disease, a disorder characterized by jerky, uncoordinated movements. Degeneration of the basal ganglia is also a symptom of Huntington's chorea, the disease that killed Woody Guthrie.

The Limbic System

The limbic system is not a specific area but a circuit covering many areas and their interconnections (see Figure 2–9). It includes the hypothalamus, the amygdala, portions of the cerebral cortex such as the

FIGURE 2–8 The cerebral cortex

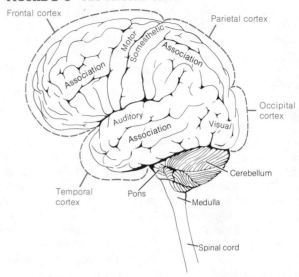

The cortex is often grossly described as consisting of four major lobes or areas: frontal, parietal, occipital, and temporal. Each of the major sensory systems feeds information to the cortex and to a specific receiving area in the cortex. This information is sent to the central nervous system from the peripheral nervous system. Once in the brain or spinal cord, the information is relayed from point to point until it reaches the primary sensory receiving area in the cortex. The figure shows the location of the receiving areas for vision, audition, and somesthesis (touch, pain, temperature). There is also a primary motor area responsible for the initiation of motor movements, located just in front of the somesthetic cortex. Stimulation in the motor area causes a movement of muscles, and stimulation in the sensory receiving areas causes the subject to report that he or she saw or heard or felt something, depending on which primary sensory area was stimulated. Note that most of the cortex is association cortex.

FIGURE 2–9 The major structures within or associated with the limbic system; this system is particularly involved in arousal, motivation, and emotion

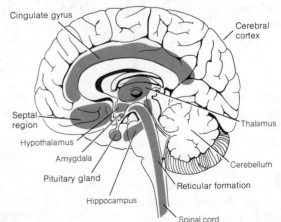

hippocampus, and a number of other nuclei and pathways. The limbic system has been implicated in a number of functions, including motivation and emotion. Stimulation of certain parts of the limbic system may produce eating, drinking, or aggression. Damage to areas of the limbic system may produce docility and other emotional changes.

Pleasure Centers

Stimulation of certain areas of the limbic system and some areas connected with it can produce extremely pleasurable sensations. This important discovery was made by James Olds and Peter Milner in 1954, when they showed that experimental animals could be made to press a lever, or learn other responses, when rewarded with electrical stimulation to these "pleasure centers." In some cases rats quite literally starved to death when given a choice between pressing a lever for food or for electrical stimulation. Animals rewarded in such a way will cross electrified grids, swim through water, and undergo extreme exertion. Humans who have been stimulated in these areas report that the experience is extremely pleasurable, and some have equated the sensations to sexual orgasms.

These fascinating findings suggest that these regions of the brain may be involved in reinforcement and reward, powerful methods for controlling behavior (see Chapter 4). Recently, theories have been proposed which postulate that certain types of abnormal behavior, particularly depressive states, may result from functional abnormalities in these reward systems.

The Split-Brain Operation

Several years ago, a psychologist at California Institute of Technology, Roger Sperry, developed what is known as the split-brain operation. In this operation the two hemispheres are separated by cutting the fibers of the corpus callosum (Figure 2–10) along with other fibers that run between the right and left sides of the brain. Sperry used monkeys in his experiments. This operation was later performed on some human patients as a treatment for a special type of epilepsy.

The result of many years of work with this general type of procedure with animals and with a few human patients is that we now generally believe that different activities predominate in the two hemispheres. This has been somewhat overdramatized to the extent of claiming we have two different brains in our heads. But the general point is an important one. For most right-handed individuals, the left hemisphere controls language functioning, while right hemisphere seems to be specialized to deal with

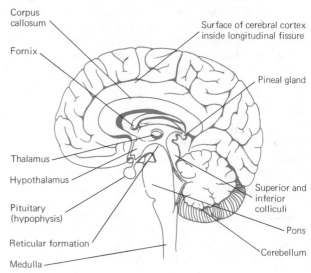

FIGURE 2–10 A midline section through the human brain

Corpus callosum

Fornix

Thalamus

Hypothalamus

Pituitary (hypophysis)

Reticular formation

Medulla

Surface of cerebral cortex inside longitudinal fissure

Pineal gland

Superior and inferior colliculi

Pons

Cerebellum

wholistic stimuli, such as perceiving a face or looking at a painting. Just the opposite is true of left-handed people. This is called brain lateralization—different activities are governed by the two sides of the cortex. Research on brain lateralization is going on at a very rapid pace and is one of the hottest topics in neuropsychology. More recent research suggests that the situation is much more complicated than was thought when the split-brain work was first done. The complexity is too great to go into in detail here. In general, however, one side of the brain (and for most of us it is the left side) is specialized for dealing with stimuli one at a time and in sequence, for example, reading the words in this sentence. This is called serial processing. The other side is specialized for what is called parallel processing, in which lots of bits of information come into the brain at the same time, as in the pieces of a jigsaw puzzle. Looking at the whole, for example, a painting, involves parallel processing. Reading a book might involve both—the words or ideas are combined serially but an image aroused in your mind by the words is constructed in parallel.

Obviously, the two halves of your brain work together quite well. Only by the split-brain operation can we discover the differences. To illustrate, suppose we have a person reach under a cloth and feel an object (say a toothbrush) with the left hand. Information coming into the brain from the various receptors usually crosses over on its way to the brain; so, the information about the toothbrush ends up in the right hemisphere, the one with little or no language ability. A normal person has little or no trouble naming the object felt, because of intercommunication between the hemispheres. But a split-brain patient will not be able to determine what the object is. Yet, with the left hand the patient can pick out a picture of a toothbrush from other pictures as the object under the cloth. The problem is, of course, that only the left hemisphere knows the names of things, and only the right hemisphere "feels" the object. Because the corpus callosum has been cut, the patient cannot connect the name "toothbrush" with the information the right sensory cortex is receiving from the fingers of the left hand. This is what happens when you feel something with the left hand in the dark: the information goes to the right hemisphere, which does not know the name of the object, but since your corpus callosum is intact, you can retrieve the name from the language warehouse in your left hemisphere.

We have a long way to go before understanding brain lateralization. It has become a fad to use lateralization in a very oversimplified way to explain other phenomena, without sufficient evidence. For example, we now have the right brain and the left brain being treated as if they had personality characteristics, with some people being careful, logical, and verbal (they are left-brained) and others being visual, nonlogical, wholistic, and gestaltist (the right-brained). But remember, there is really just one brain, with many complex parts, including two hemispheres working together. While the split-brain work is important and interesting, and while the two hemi-

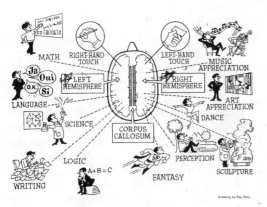

Ever since the inception of the split-brain research by Roger Sperry, there has been a temptation to strictly localize various brain functions in one or the other hemisphere. This diagram shows the most commonly held, simplified picture of hemisphere localization. While oversimplified, the general idea is well portrayed. In actual operation, of course, the two hemispheres work together on all functions and show incredible teamwork.

spheres are clearly different in some functional aspects, the real mystery is how all the complex parts of the brain with their different functions work together so smoothly.

The split-brain research has convincingly demonstrated that the brain is the biological structure underlying our psychological experience, feelings, knowledge, skills, and consciousness. The split-brain patient who can easily name an object felt with the right hand but not with the left is a good example. You'd have to postulate two "minds" if you were to explain this without saying the individual's consciousness is a function of the brain. Or consider one of Roger Sperry's earliest experiments with split-brain monkeys. Normally half the information to each eye crosses over to the other side. Light that lands on the nasal side of the right eye normally crosses over and is processed in the left hemisphere, for example. Light that lands on the temporal side is processed in the right hemisphere. Sperry split the crossing fibers in the monkey's optic nerves, in addition to the callosal fibers. By cutting the crossing fibers, Sperry could be sure that information presented to the right eye went only to the right hemisphere. Next Sperry put a patch over the monkey's left eye and had the monkey learn to solve a visual problem using only the right eye. With a split-brain monkey, this means, of course, that only the right half of the monkey's brain is being used to solve the problem. After several trials, the monkey learned to choose the correct object of a pair (it might be the one with stripes painted on it). Now for the test, the right eye is covered and the problem presented to only the left eye (and the left brain). While a normal monkey has no problem with this transfer task, the split-brain monkey fails. Using the left eye, the split-brain monkey acts as if it had not been trained on the problem before. And, functionally speaking, the left brain *had* never experienced the problem. When you cut the callosum, the two sides of the brain cannot communicate with each other. So you create a monkey with half a brain that can solve a problem and half that cannot solve the problem.

The Endocrine System

We can conceive of all bodily activities, including behavior, as being regulated by two interacting systems, the nervous system and the endocrine system. The **endocrine system** consists of a number of **endocrine glands** located throughout the body (Figure 2–11). Endocrine glands are defined as organs that secrete certain chemicals, namely, **hormones,** into the general circulation. They are distinguished from so-called exocrine glands, which

FIGURE 2-11 **The endocrine glands and their products (hormones)**

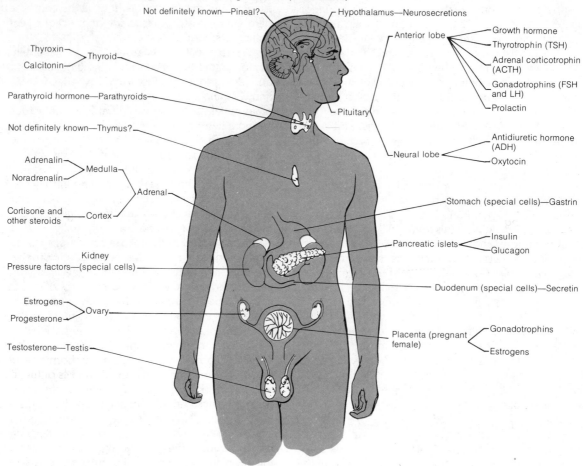

also secrete chemical substances but not into the general circulation; the salivary glands, which secrete saliva into the mouth, are an example of an exocrine organ.

The hormones secreted by the endocrine system function as "chemical messengers" in that they affect the activity of other organs. Also, the neuromodulators we mentioned earlier are largely hormones and play critical roles in the functioning of the nervous system.

Hormones, of course, can have profound effects on behavior. In animals, castration is used to make animals more docile or to get them to eat more, to fatten themselves up for human consumption. Some of the hormones, particularly those secreted by the adrenal glands, play a complex but important role in emotional behavior. This effect is particularly obvious when the body is subjected to long-term tension and stress, one impact of which is the exhaustion of the adrenals and the depletion of the hormones regulating our reactions to stress. The ability to fight or flee from stress can be lost, and we become more susceptible to attack. We are beginning to discover that hormones play a much wider role in behavior than the regulation of sexual behavior. Because they operate in a chemical fashion, and because hormones secreted in one part of the body can travel through the bloodstream and have profound consequences in faraway parts of the body, the effects are subtle and difficult to separate from effects caused directly by the nervous system. Clearly, however, the nervous system and the endocrine system work closely together in regulating behavior.

It is not possible to discuss the endocrine system in any great detail here, but we will mention a few of the major glands, the hormones they secrete, and some of the effects they produce. The full list is contained in Figure 2-11.

The Pituitary Gland

Often referred to as the master gland, the **pituitary gland,** under the regulation of the hypothalamus, secretes hormones that control the activity of many other endocrine glands located elsewhere in the body. In reality, the pituitary gland, often called the hypophysis, consists of two separate organs, the adenohypophysis and the neurohypophysis. The anatomy of the pituitary gland, and the hormones it secretes, are illustrated in Figure 2–12.

The adenohypophysis secretes several kinds of hormones. These include (1) the thyroid-stimulating hormone, (2) the growth hormone, (3) the adrenocorticotrophic hormone ACTH, and (4) the gonadotrophic hormones, of which there are three — follicle-stimulating hormone, luteinizing hormone, and prolactin. Let us briefly consider the actions of each of these hormones.

The thyroid-stimulating hormone, as the name implies, acts on the thyroid gland to stimulate the production and secretion of thyroxin. Thyroxin is then carried to all parts of the body by the circulation and increases the rate of metabolism of all cells.

The growth hormone — which, interestingly, is released primarily during sleep — serves a number of metabolic functions involved in growth and the maintenance of the body, including the rate of growth of bones and soft tissues. Overproduction of the growth hormone may lead to grotesque increases in weight and body features.

ACTH acts on the adrenal cortex (the outer portions of the adrenal gland) to stimulate the secretion of its hormones, in particular cortisol. Cortisol is then carried to all parts of the body and increases the rate of energy production in cells. This hormone is particularly important in mobilizing the body's defenses during periods of stress.

The final category of hormones secreted by the adenohypophysis are the gonadotropins: the follicle-stimulating hormone, luteinizing hormone, and prolactin (luteotrophic hormone). The follicle-stimulating hormone acts on the ovaries of the female, from puberty until the onset of menopause, to stimulate the development of the follicle that contains the developing egg. In males this hormone stimulates the production of sperm. The luteinizing homone also acts on the ovaries to stimulate the development of the corpus luteum, the small tissue that develops from the follicle after the release of the egg. Prolactin also stimulates the mammary glands to produce milk for the potential newborn.

The neurohypophysis, the posterior pituitary, secretes two hormones: antidiuretic hormone (ADH) and oxytocin. ADH acts on certain cells of the kidney to decrease the amount of water passed on to the bladder. Thus, urine is concentrated and the body conserves water. ADH has an important role in regulating drinking behavior (see Chapter 7). Oxytocin has two effects: First, it acts on mammary tissue, resulting in the ejection of milk. Second, it acts on the smooth muscles of the uterus, causing them to contract; this hormone may function in the process of birth.

Peptides and the Pituitary

Of most current interest to psychologists is the new role that has been identified for the pituitary (and its closely related neighbor in the brain, the hypothalamus), namely, the manufacture and secretion of at least some of the neural modulators we mentioned earlier. The most highly publicized of these is beta-endorphin, which acts like morphine. New neural modulators are being discovered regularly, and several other systems besides pain may be involved. One of them, for example, may be involved in "telling" the brain when the body has consumed enough food. Understanding this action could help many dieters. The pituitary manufactures a very large protein molecule consisting of a long chain of various amino acids. Enzymes in the pituitary act like a pair of scissors and cut up the long chain into various

FIGURE 2-12   The pituitary gland (hypophysis) and its major hormones

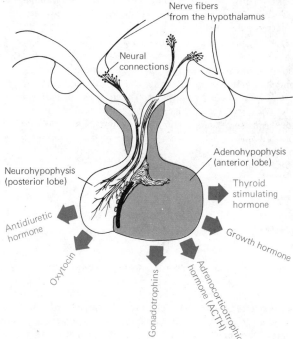

Nerve fibers from the hypothalamus

Neural connections

Neurohypophysis (posterior lobe)

Adenohypophysis (anterior lobe)

Thyroid stimulating hormone

Growth hormone

Adrenocorticotrophic hormone (ACTH)

Gonadotrophins

Oxytocin

Antidiuretic hormone

lengths of small chains. Each small chain, called a *peptide,* can have a different effect on different parts of the nervous system. There can be many, perhaps even hundreds, of different peptide chemicals, each having a specific effect. For each of the major behavioral systems, there may be a particular peptide that governs that activity. There might be, as we said, one that stops and one that starts eating behavior; one that

stops and one that starts drinking; one that starts and one that stops sexual activity; and one that starts and one that stops fighting. Perhaps there is one that starts and one that stops sleeping and dreaming. The possibilities are enormous (see the newsclip "The Peptide Hit Parade"). The implications in terms of developing new drugs to help people with various medical and behavioral problems are phenomenal.

The Peptide Hit Parade

LRF has become the object of intensely competitive research because of its potential aphrodisiac effects. One prominent researcher claims that a company hired to analyze blood samples of impotent men given LRF, stole the data for its own use.

Beta-endorphin seems to help the body turn off its response to pain much as morphine does. There is some evidence that acupuncture anesthesia and pain-relief placebos may work by bringing beta-endorphin or a similar chemical into action.

Enkephalins, the smallest endorphins, take their name from the Greek words for "in the head." What they are doing there no one knows for sure, but they seem to share some of the pain-relieving potential of beta-endorphin.

Factor S, which has been studied by Harvard researcher John Pappenheimer and his colleagues, may be a sleep-promoting peptide. Isolated from the brain fluid of goats and sheep that were forced to stay awake, this substance increases sleeping time when given to rabbits.

Bombesin, first discovered in the skin of the frog *Bombina bombina,* can turn rats from warm-blooded to cold-blooded animals when injected into their brains. The chemical also seems to turn on the sympathetic nervous system, which regulates basic functions like the stress response and blood pressure, and may help determine whether calories in food are used to produce heat or stored as fat. Thus, speculates Marvin Brown at the Salk Instiute, bombesin could form the basis of an anti-obesity drug.

Somatostatin seems to have the opposite effect from bombesin in the brain; it generally turns off the sympathetic nervous system. Drugs based on this peptide may therefore be useful in lowering blood pressure.

Substance P is involved in transmitting pain signals from the body to the brain. If various technical problems can be overcome, "an antagonist to Substance P could be the

ideal anesthetic," according to physiologist Roger Nicoll at the University of California, San Francisco.

Bradykinin may play a similar role in pain transmission. Very low doses of this peptide cause intense pain when injected. It may be the most painful substance known.

Angiotensin, a peptide that regulates fluid excretion in the kidneys, makes experimental animals drink copiously when injected into their brains. It may also be used to develop new anti-hypertensive drugs.

Cholecystokinin, originally discovered in the intestine, appears highly concentrated in the brain's most evolved region, the cerebral cortex. Some researchers have suggested that cholecystokinin normally carries the brain signal to stop eating, and that a deficiency of the peptide may lead to obesity. Rosalyn Yalow, at Veterans Administration Medical Center, Bronx, has found that the peptide is much less prevalent in the brain of a strain of genetically obese mice than in normal mice.

Neurotensin shows a powerful analgesic effect in animal experiments, and a drug company is now testing a number of drugs based on this peptide to see if they are also effective pain-killers.

ACTH, a peptide manufactured by the pituitary gland, is also found in nerve cells in the brain. Over the past decade several studies have shown that people can learn and remember better when they are given a small fragment of an ACTH molecule by injection. Dutch researcher David de Wied has found that the peptides vasopressin and oxytocin can also aid learning and memory. The results are intriguing, but since most chemical models of learning and memory have proved false, many researchers view these experiments with caution.

Science 80
Premier Issue

One of the most exciting developments in neuroscience is the work on peptides in the nervous system. Basically, the research is concerned with a class of biochemicals that only recently were found to be "psychoactive" in the sense of playing a role in the nervous system, most likely as modulators of neural responsiveness. And, of course, if these chemicals regulate neural responsiveness, they will be regulating behavior. This

list cites a few of the most interesting peptides that have been implicated in behavioral control. (The full name of LRF is luteinizing hormone releasing factor, and ACTH stands for adrenocorticotrophic hormone.) Many peptides are hormones, or seem to behave like hormones, being manufactured in one part of the body by the bloodstream and carried to other parts of the body for action there.

The Thyroid Gland

In most species the **thyroid gland** is located in the neck, consisting of two lobes shaped like the capital letter H. The function of this gland is to secrete thyroxin, production of which is triggered by the thyroid-stimulating hormone. Thyroxin has a variety of functions, including (1) stimulation of metamorphosis in certain amphibians, (2) stimulation of growth, including the eruption of teeth and the growth of antlers and horns, (3) effects on the pituitary gland, and (4) regulation of body metabolism. Perhaps through these biological mechanisms the thyroid influences our mood and our motivation.

The Adrenal Glands

This endocrine organ, located just above the kidneys, consists of two distinct anatomical parts, an inner portion called the **adrenal medulla** and an outer part called the **adrenal cortex.**

The adrenal medulla derives embryologically from nerve tissue, a fact reflected in the hormones it produces, namely, epinephrine (adrenalin) and norepinephrine (noradrenalin). The effects of these two secretions are to prepare the body for emergencies by increasing blood pressure, diverting blood from internal organs to the voluntary muscles, and increasing blood sugar levels. The release of these hormones is controlled by direct neural innervation of the adrenal medulla. This direct neural connection allows the medulla to respond quickly to threatening

stimulation. In fact, the medulla secretes hormones whenever the body is under stress. The hormones then cause the rest of the body to experience stress. The adrenal medulla is a major culprit, then, whenever you feel nervous, tense, anxious, fearful, or panicked.

The adrenal cortex secretes as many as 20 different hormones, collectively called adrenal cortical steroids. These substances regulate many metabolic processes, including metabolism of carbohydrates, balancing of sodium and potassium in body fluids, and influencing the reproductive organs. The secretions of the adrenal cortex are stimulated by adrenocorticotrophic hormone, secreted by the pituitary gland. Stress, both mental and physical, can also trigger this pituitary-adrenal cortex system.

The Sex Hormones

The sex hormones (the gonadotrophins and the hormones of the **ovaries** and the **testes**) collectively, of course, regulate the course of events involved in one way or another with propagation of the species. They work in various ways, regulating such functions as (1) the development and release of the female's eggs and the growth of the male's sperm; (2) mating behavior; (3) control over some aspects of the birth process; (4) control over the milk supply in the mammary glands, and the disposition of the mother to nurse; and (5) control over maternal behaviors such as building nests, sitting on eggs, and tending to the newborn. Reproduction and reproductive behavior is largely under the control of the endocrine

Highlight 2-2

Are Androgens the Libidinal Hormone?

We know that hormones are involved in mediating sexual behavior. In animals of most species castration of the male results in a marked decrement in sexual behavior, even though the ability to copulate may not be impaired. The administration of testosterone to such animals restores sexual behavior to normal levels. Similar observations have been reported for human males in whom gonadal malfunctioning has been known to decrease sexual desire, resulting in less frequent coitus. Replacement therapy — the administration of androgens — restores normal desire and behavior fairly rapidly. These results suggest that the male sexual desire, or libido, is somehow mediated by androgens.

In human females the situation is obviously different. The removal of the ovaries, which reduces levels of estro-

gen, has no measurable effect on sexual desire or behavior. Neither does the onset of menopause. In fact, some data suggest that sexual drive is increased as estrogen levels decrease. What then mediates libido in human females?

The answer seems to be that androgens perform this function in females as well as in males. For example, when female patients are given androgens for medical reasons, there is an increase in sexual desire. Removal of the adrenal glands, which are the main source of androgens in females, results in a decrease in sex drive. Data such as these have raised the interesting possibility that the androgens function as the libidinal hormone in humans of both sexes.

system and is tightly regulated by the hormones in virtually all species except human beings. In human beings, of course, reproduction is still heavily controlled by the endocrine system, as women on birth control pills are able to testify. The reproductive behavior of human beings, however, is much less influenced by hormones than is that of other mammals, although hormones still play an important role. The sexual behavior of human beings is not completely free from hormonal control.

Sex hormones also appear to be critically involved in sexual differentiation during embryonic development. Sexually and genetically speaking, men and women differ by only one chromosome (see the following section, "Behavioral Genetics")—women have two X chromosomes, whereas men have an X and a Y chromosome. The sex chromosomes work primarily through directing the manufacture of sex hormones. This is a major factor determining whether the embryo turns out to be a boy or a girl. That is, the sex of the child is determined by which hormones are present and at what levels during the growth of the fetus in the earliest stages of development. Possibly these hormones play a role in sexual differentiation at a later stage of development, and

there may be other differences between boys and girls besides their reproductive components. Specifically intriguing is the possibility of brain differences between the sexes, differences that might be programmed into the brain during development because of different levels of the various sex hormones (see the newsclip "Brains May Differ in Women and Men").

Sex differences in the brain would, of course, presumably imply that there are sex differences in behavior or behavioral capacity. The best example to date relates to the issue of brain lateralization, which we discussed in connection with split-brain research. Males and females may differ in the way in which the two hemispheres of the cortex are specialized. Females are thought to possess hemispheres that, in general, are less specialized. In males, for example, language capacity is heavily governed by the left hemisphere, particularly if the man is right-handed. In females, however, both hemispheres have language capacity. Males typically outscore females on only one type of mental test item—spatial visualization. In a test of this sort you might be asked to look at an actual block design and then imagine rotating the blocks in space. Male superiority on this type of task might be

---

Brains May Differ in Women and Men
By HAROLD M. SCHMECK, JR.

The brains of male and female animals differ physically and chemically in ways that may help explain some basic behavior patterns of the sexes.

Much of the evidence for this has been discovered recently. So far the differences have been found only in animals, but many scientists believe some similar differences between the sexes probably exist in human brains as well and might, someday, help make clear the biological factors in personality. The recent findings include differences between the sexes in the physical structure of some brain regions related to reproduction and differences in the chemistry of nerve signal transmission.

The new evidence may add fuel to the ancient nature-nurture controversy—is heredity the key determinant of identity, or is it environment and upbringing? But as many scientists have noted, the truth is almost always in between the two. Nature and nurture each play a role, and are intertwined with such complexity in humans as to defy

complete separation of their contributions.

While a human's sexual orientation and self-identification as female or male generally seem to be a product of rearing, scientists believe there are also innate behavioral influences from the brain and the hormones that the brain controls.

The characteristic rough-and-tumble play of infant male rhesus monkeys can be induced in females if the hormone testosterone is given at a critical period of brain development. Something akin to this in humans has been reported among young girls in whom there was abnormal growth of adrenal glands. Some scientists have described the effect as sustained tomboyish behavior, but it does not cloud the person's perception of her gender identity.

While such behavioral influences have been observed for many years, specific chemical and physical sex differences in animal brains have been found only recently. . . .

Dr. Bruce McEwen of Rockefeller University and his collaborators—Ann Silverman of Columbia Presbyterian Medical Center in New York and Ulf Stenevi and Anders Bjorklund, scientists at the University of Lund in Sweden—have transplanted brain tissue from fetal rats into brains of adult female rats. The fetal tissue developed receptors for estrogens, indicating that the adult brain maintains the ability to produce the receptors that ordinarily appear in late fetal development. Dominique Toran-Allerand, at Columbia, discovered that mouse brain tissue growing in laboratory flasks would grow hair-like wisps of new cell structures when either testosterone or estradiol was added to the tissue culture. The growth occurred only where estrogen receptors were present. The findings buttress the evidence that the brain is molded chemically by the sex hormones. . . .

The New York Times
March 25, 1980

due to the fact that since the left side of the brain handles language, the right side can specialize in visual/spatial processing. Women would not have a specialized center for this function and therefore might be less capable in this task. Women, on the other hand, are superior to men in some aspects of language, perhaps because in females a larger amount of cortex, involving both hemispheres, is devoted to language functions. Exactly what differences there are in the brain lateralization of men and women remains to be determined; nor is it known at this time to what extent brain lateralization is due to genetic or environmental factors. As we said before, the split-brain work is turning out to be more complex than anyone thought. And now the area is becoming somewhat controversial because it has suggested the possibility of the existence of physical differences between the sexes, both in structure and capacity.

Behavioral Genetics

This field of study is concerned with the *degree* and *nature* of those aspects of behavior that are inherited. Behavioral genetics can be said to have begun with the studies of Sir Francis Galton, who studied eminence (genius) among families. His research led him to conclude that genius "runs in families," that is, that the trait is heritable (influenced by heredity). Galton's studies, though not as rigorous as later experiments, suggested that behavioral traits are determined, at least in part, by genetic factors. Since Galton an extensive research literature has accumulated which suggests very strongly that many behaviors are determined by interacting genetic and environmental factors.

Genetic Structures

Within the last 30 years scientists have discovered that the structures transmitted from parents to offspring are genes that consist of large molecules of deoxyribonucleic acid (DNA). The genes are carried on **chromosomes,** which are structures found within the nucleus of all cells. Each chromosome carries a large number of genes. Through the process of cell division called meiosis, human sperm and ova (eggs) are each provided with 23 chromosomes. The combination of the egg and sperm, called fertilization, results in a cell with 23 pairs of chromosomes. Each pair is distinct from all other pairs, and the two chromosomes of any given pair are referred to as homologous chromosomes, one homolog being of maternal and the other of paternal origin. The genes carried on these chromosomes direct the development and growth of all other cells in the body, and they control all meta-

bolic processes within cells. The chromosome complement of normal human males and females, as well as an abnormality in chromosome number, are illustrated in Figure 2–13.

Genetic Functions

The genetic material, DNA, has two functions: it codes for the synthesis of more DNA and for the synthesis of another large molecule, ribonucleic acid (RNA). RNA is transported from the nucleus of the cell into the cytoplasm where it functions to code for the synthesis of proteins. One class of these proteins, enzymes, controls the metabolism of all cells.

   Although we know a great deal about how DNA functions, we do not yet understand the mechanisms by which the genetic material directs the course of development and behavior. Recent research, how-

FIGURE 2–13   Paired human chromosomes

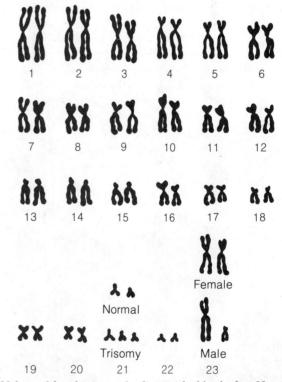

Males and females cannot be distinguished by the first 22 pairs of chromosomes (called autosomes). In pair 23 males and females differ. Females possess two similar chromosomes for pair 23, both called X chromosomes; thus the female genotype is XX. Males have two different types of chromosomes in the 23rd pair, one X and one Y chromosome, and thus have an XY genotype. Note pair 21. Sometimes instead of a pair there are three chromosomes at this position. This "trisomy" results in a form of mental retardation: Down's syndrome, or mongolism.

ever, has provided some clues as to how this might take place. For example, some forms of mental retardation are caused by the lack of specific genes and others by the absence of whole chromosomes.

One disorder resulting from the lack of a single gene is a disease known as phenylketonuria (PKU). PKU is transmitted as a *recessive gene,* which means that parental carriers transmit the condition to one-quarter of their offspring. The disease results from an inability to metabolize an important dietary building block, phenylalanine, because the victim does not possess the enzyme that transforms phenylalanine in normal individuals. Severe mental retardation is one symptom. Although we don't know the cause of this symptom, it seems likely that the excess phenylalanine or some abnormal phenylalanine byproduct is toxic to the nervous system and prevents normal development of intellectual functioning. Identification of the mechanism that results in PKU has made early diagnosis possible; newborns are tested for high levels of phenylalanine in their blood. Early diagnosis has also resulted in the development of a treatment technique. Children with PKU are placed on a special diet low in

"I don't even *like* going bowling with the boys, but it's programmed into my genes."

The New Yorker, July 1, 1972. Drawing by Donald Reilly; © 1972 The New Yorker Magazine, Inc.

phenylalanine, which helps, although it may not provide a complete cure.

Huntington's chorea is another disease with behavioral symptoms transmitted as a single gene defect. Huntington's chorea is transmitted as a single *dominant gene,* which means that an affected individual transmits the condition to half of the offspring. The tragedy of this inherited disease in a famous family was discussed in the newsclip "The Cruelest Killer," p. 30. Other conditions with behavioral symptoms are caused by abnormalities of whole chromosomes, either autosomes or sex chromosomes.

Genetic Methods

The methods used by behavioral geneticists are quite varied and depend, to a great extent, on the species of organisms used in the research. Of course, certain kinds of breeding experiments we can perform on animals are impossible with human subjects. Research methods used with human subjects include twin comparison, family correlations, and adoption studies. For example, experiments of this type have provided evidence that IQ test scores have a genetic component (see Chapter 6 for a more detailed discussion of this topic). Identical twins are more similar with respect to IQ than are normal siblings. This is the case even when twins are separated at birth and reared in different homes. Twin research has also provided strong evidence for a genetic connection in certain types of mental disorders, particularly schizophrenia.

Behavioral geneticists who work with organisms other than human beings have used selective breeding and inbred strain comparison studies extensively. Selective breeding is a technique in which animals are chosen for reproduction on the basis of how much of a particular trait they exhibit. Consider this classic selective breeding experiment reported by Robert Tryon of the University of California at Berkeley. Tryon measured learning in rats with a complicated maze. Those animals that made few errors in learning this maze were mated with similar animals, and rats that made many errors were mated with rats that also made many errors. Two strains were established, and the "brightest" and "dullest" animals *within* each strain were mated for many generations. In due course two strains were established which differed substantially in the number of errors they made in learning this maze (Figure 2–14). Tryon called the strains maze-bright and maze-dull. Given these names, many people conclude that "generally" bright and dull rats had been created. In fact, this is not true. Maze-bright and maze-dull animals behave as predicted when tests are conducted in mazes similar to the one used for selection. In other learning situations maze-bright rats are not necessarily superior to maze-dull animals. Nevertheless, the fact that animals can be selected for this behavior indicates that learning ability is determined, at least in part, by hereditary factors.

Other examples of selective breeding for behavioral traits have been reported. The important concept to remember is that if a trait can be selected for, then it must be influenced by genetic factors. If a trait cannot be influenced by selective breeding, then there is little evidence that it is differentially influenced by the genes.

Another technique in behavioral genetic studies with animals is the use of inbred strains. Inbred strains are developed by mating related animals. As animals are inbred for successive generations, their genetic variability decreases until animals within an inbred line are essentially identical in genetic make-up, just as

Double Take
By MATT CLARK

Flipping through a newspaper, psychologist Thomas J. Bouchard Jr. did a double take: a brief item reported that identical-twin brothers in Ohio had been reunited after 39 years. By examining the pair, Bouchard realized, he would have a rare opportunity to shed new light on a classic question: the importance of genetics versus the environment in shaping human behavior. . . .

The story began this January. James Lewis, a security guard in Lima, Ohio, contacted the county court that had handled his adoption and asked help in finding the brother who had been adopted simultaneously at the age of five weeks by another couple. Court officials contacted the twin, James Springer, a records clerk in Dayton, and the meeting was quickly arranged. "Part of my life came together," says Lewis. "It wasn't like meeting a stranger."

Coincidence
The reaction was understandable. Springer and Lewis both stand 6 feet, and weigh about 180 pounds. Both men have similar mannerisms, the same stance and the same way of folding their arms and crossing their legs. Probably by coincidence, both married—and divorced—women named Linda. More important to Bouchard, both men enjoy mechanical drawing and carpentry and seem to think alike. "I'll start to say something and he'll finish it," says Lewis. "It's like he's reading my mind."

Identical twins have always intrigued researchers. In the 1930s, a study of twenty pairs of twins who had been reared in separate households showed that most had similar IQ's, suggesting that intelligence was predominately governed by heredity rather than environment. Bouchard believes that examination of Springer and Lewis may contribute even more insight into the nature-nurture controversy because no twins reported in the scientific literature were separated so early in life, lived so many years apart and spent so brief a period together later on.

Important Tests
Bouchard and his colleagues, who include psychiatrist Dr. Leonard Heston, himself the father of identical-twin girls, especially want to measure the impact of environment on the Ohio pair. They will administer twenty psychological tests, including some that deal with verbal comprehension, memory span and conceptual capacity. . . .

Newsweek
March 12, 1979

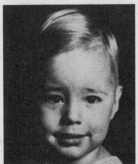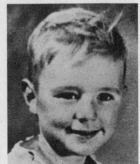

Springer (left), Lewis today, and as tots.

Identical twins come from one zygote, or egg-sperm combination. They are therefore called monozygotic twins (MZ twins). In dizygotic twins (DZ) the mother produced two eggs fertilized by two different sperm, so the offspring are no more similar genetically than regular brothers and sisters. A pair of MZ twins, reared by different families in different environments, is the dream of psychologists interested in behavioral genetics. Why? Why would they be less interested in studying DZ twins reared apart?

FIGURE 2-14 **Results of Tryon's selective breeding experiment with maze-bright and maze-dull rats**

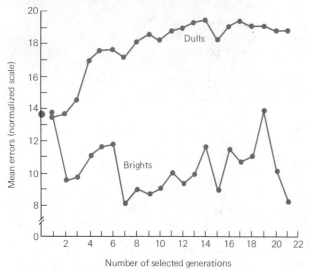

Number of selected generations

identical twins are. There are many such inbred strains, some having been inbred for hundreds of generations. When one animal in an inbred line differs significantly from another, the most important determining factor must be environmental. On the other hand, when animals from two or more different inbred strains are reared and maintained in identical environments yet consistently differ in their behavior, one can confidently conclude that the behavior in question is influenced by genetic variables.

Genetic versus Environmental Influences

Modern work of behavioral genetics, however, leaves little doubt that heredity plays an important part in behavior. This should hardly be surprising, since behavior is a function of living organisms whose genetic make-up must be taken into account if we are to understand individual differences in behavior. But we must never overlook the importance of the environment. Rather, we should consider behavior the product of interacting genetic *and* environmental factors.

Psychologists have usually been more interested in environmental than genetic effects on behavior. One reason for this emphasis is the feeling that we can do something about the environment, that it is more susceptible to experimental control and manipulation, whereas the genetic endowment of an animal is fixed. Do you remember the Krech/Rosenzweig work we mentioned earlier? These and other studies have shown that animals reared in these conditions differ in behavior; rats reared in enriched conditions are superior, as adults, on some learning tasks to animals reared in impoverished environments. Not only are these animals different in their behavior, but animals reared in enriched environments also have thicker and heavier layers of cerebral cortex and larger nerve cells with more extensive dendrites than do animals reared in impoverished environments. These differences are clearly the result of different environments. Furthermore, recall the two strains of maze-bright and maze-dull rats developed by Tryon. Research has shown that an enriched environment in infancy can compensate for a maze-dull heredity. Enriched maze-dull rats can catch up and perform as well as maze-bright rats. In short, we must remember that the behaving organism always has an environmental history as well as a biological or genetic constitution. An adequate understanding of behavior requires careful consideration of both heredity and environment.

SUMMARY

1. The study of the biological foundations of behavior encompasses an understanding of the nervous system, the endocrine system, and the inherited aspects of behavior. Many basic physiological processes underlie behavior and are studied by biological psychologists.

2. The neuron, although it can assume many different shapes, consists of three basic elements—the soma, dendrites, and axons. The neuron is the building block of the nervous system and is specialized to conduct and transmit information.

3. Conduction is accomplished by the all-or-none action potential. Transmission occurs at functional contacts between neurons—the synapses. It involves the release of chemical neurotransmitter molecules.

4. Transmission of information from one neuron to the next may result in excitation or inhibition of the next cell. All nervous activity—and associated behavior—may ultimately be understood in terms of the balance between neural excitation and inhibition.

5. The nervous system is composed of an enormous number of nerve cells and nonneural elements and is organized into a number of functional circuits and divisions.

6. The peripheral nervous system includes all nervous tissue outside the skull and spinal cord. Sensory and motor fibers of the peripheral nervous system bring information to and from the central nervous system.

7. The somatic division of the peripheral nervous system is involved in skeletal movement and bodily sensations. The autonomic division of the peripheral nervous system is involved in emotional responses and controls the smooth (involuntary) muscles and glandular activity. The autonomic nervous system is organized into the parasympathetic and sympathetic branches.

8. The central nervous system may be divided into two major components: (a) the brain stem and (b) the cerebral cortex. The brain stem contains many hard-wired structures that control basic body functions such as breathing. The cortex operates more flexibly, being largely programmable on the basis of experience.

9. In human beings, the cerebral cortex has become extremely enlarged and convoluted so that it very nearly covers the rest of the brain. An understanding of the functions of the cerebral cortex will make it possible to understand the higher mental functions such as language and thought.

10. The endocrine system is composed of the various endocrine glands. These glands secrete chemical messengers called hormones which influence many aspects of physiological and behavioral functioning.

11. The close relationship between the endocrine system and the nervous system is illustrated by the neural control of the master gland—the pituitary—by the hypothalamus at the base of the brain.

12. A branch of biological psychology called behavioral genetics investigates the heritable causes of behavior. Using the techniques of genetics, including twin comparisons, strain comparison, selective breeding, and so forth, investigators in this area are discovering that inheritance plays an extremely important role in many behavioral characteristics.

RECOMMENDED ADDITIONAL READINGS

Groves, P., & Schlesinger, K. *Biological psychology.* Dubuque, Iowa: W. C. Brown, 1979.

Levitt, R. A. *Physiological psychology.* New York: Holt, Rinehart and Winston, 1981.

Hebb, D. O. *A textbook of psychology.* Philadelphia: Saunders, 1966.

Thompson, R. F. *Introduction to biopsychology.* San Francisco: Albion, 1973.

Valenstein, E. S. *Brain control.* New York: Wiley, 1973.

What Does It Mean?

Although our understanding of the brain, endocrine system, and genetics and their relationships to behaviors is far from complete, there are attempts even now to apply research findings to the modification and control of behavior. Some of the methods used to study the nervous system have been successfully applied to the control of behavior, including surgery to cause brain lesions, electrical and chemical stimulation, and electrical recording techniques. Similarly, our understanding of the role of hormones in behavior has been applied in practical ways. The recent findings of behavioral genetics have also had clinical application. The use of these techniques and findings provides great hope for the elimination and control of unwanted behavior, but it also raises the possibilities of misuse and abuse. There are many questions about the biological control of behavior for future students to consider.

Psychosurgery

The use of surgery to control behavior dates back to ancient civilizations. The Egyptians and Peruvians used trephining, a technique in which the skull is opened and the brain is exposed, to rid patients of suspected demons believed to cause abnormal and irrational behavior. More recently, particularly during the 1940s and 1950s, an operation in which the frontal cortex was either removed (lobectomy) or its connections with the rest of the brain were severed (lobotomy), was used extensively in an attempt to alleviate certain emotional conditions, particularly extreme anxiety. Although these procedures sometimes resulted in improvement, as often as not they produced human "vegetables."

Such extreme procedures are no longer used widely in medical practice. However, newer techniques of psychosurgery are being used in many hospitals on a more or less experimental basis. For example, surgical techniques have been used in attempts to control violent aggressive behavior and abnormal sexual behavior. In these operations an attempt is first made to locate that part of the brain presumed to be malfunctioning. Electrodes are placed into the suspected area, and the brain is stimulated with low-voltage electric current. If this produces violent behavior, the surgeon can then produce the lesion by simply increasing the current passing through the electrode. Structures that mediate aggressive and violent behavior are often a part of the limbic system, and surgical removal of parts of this system have produced favorable results in approximately 40 percent of the cases. Lesions of certain parts of the hypothalamus have been produced in patients who have committed a succession of violent sex crimes; recall that the hypothalamus is involved in controlling certain aspects of sexual behavior.

Some psychiatrists and surgeons believe that brain surgery should never be used. First, they point out that the procedures, once applied, produce irreversible results. Second, undesirable side effects, such as irreversible personality changes, are sometimes produced. Other physicians believe that psychosurgery should be used as a treatment of last resort and attempted only after all other methods of treatment have failed. Third, there is always the danger that brain surgery can be used indiscriminately to control unwanted behavior. Clearly, much more research is needed before psychosurgery can be used with any degree of confidence. There are also ethical and moral considerations which must be discussed publicly.

Brain Stimulation

Electrical stimulation of the brain has also been used to control behavior. A dramatic example of the effectiveness of this technique has been provided by José Delgado (Figure 2–15). This neuroscientist stopped a charging bull dead in its tracks by remote-control electrical stimulation of a particular part of the animal's brain. Similar results have been observed in human beings. Electrodes are implanted into the brain, and the patient presses a button to stimulate the brain whenever a violent attack is felt to be coming on. The electrical current calms the patient and the attack is prevented. Electrical stimulation procedures have also been used with some success to produce relief from extreme pain. The electricity may work by causing the brain to re-

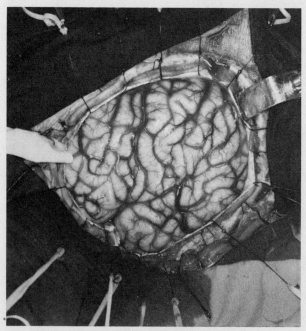

View of exposed human brain during neurosurgery.

FIGURE 2-15

Brave bulls are dangerous animals which will attack any intruder into the arena. The charging animal can be stopped short by remote-control electrical stimulation of the brain. After several stimulations, there is a lasting inhibition of aggressive behavior.

lease its own morphine, the peptide *beta-endorphin* (see the newsclip "Electric Pain Control").

Electrical stimulation of the brain has also been used to "program movements." Experimentally, this is done as follows: First, the motor cortex of monkeys is destroyed, and stimulating electrodes are implanted into lower centers of the animals' nervous system. By means of a computer, electrical signals are generated that mimic the normal influence of the motor cortex on these lower brain structures. Thus, monkeys are programmed to move limbs paralyzed by loss of the motor cortex. Similar procedures have been used in an attempt to aid people who are deprived of sensory input. Small computers are programmed to "pick up" certain features of the visual environment. This computer input is converted into small electrical impulses that are used to stimulate the visual cortex. With these procedures blind individuals "see" certain aspects of the visual environment and can avoid objects in their path.

Two recent applications of brain-stimulation techniques involve the cerebellum, the motor control center. First, stimulation of the cerebellum is useful as a treatment for epilepsy, a technique pioneered by Robert Dow; epileptic patients could theoretically carry around a transmitter and stimulate their cerebellums when they felt a seizure coming on. In the second instance, Robert Heath of Tulane University has reported that cerebellar stimulation can have profound effects on the behavior of chronically psychotic patients. Both reports are exciting but preliminary and need further confirmation.

Electrical Recording

For many years it has been possible to monitor and record the electrical activity of the brain by means of surface electrodes attached to the skull. Perhaps the best-known form of recorded electrical activity is the **electroencephalogram** (EEG) (Figures 2–16 and 2–17). As mentioned earlier, the EEG displays definite patterns during different stages of wakefulness and sleep, and it has been used extensively in sleep research. The EEG is also extremely useful as a diagnostic instrument to detect the specific location of brain injuries. It is used to pinpoint epileptic foci, tumors, or other abnormalities of the brain, such as those caused by accidents. Thus, the EEG is useful not only in detecting brain damage, but in localizing and characterizing the injury.

Another type of electrical activity that can be recorded is the so-called evoked potential. An evoked potential is an electrical signal recorded from the brain in response to sensory stimulation. Within the last decade it has become possible—by means of computer techniques—to record evoked potentials with electrodes placed on the surface of the scalp. The electrodes are relatively far away from where the evoked potentials are generated, which interferes with the recording. However, devices called averaging computers are capable of taking many small and unclear responses and reconstructing them so that, added together, they look like the responses that might have been recorded directly from the surface of the brain.

The evoked potential is a sensitive technique for analyzing the brain's activity and functioning, without having to open up the skull, X-ray it, inject dyes into it, or harm it in any way. The method has tremendous potential for becoming a major tool in the diagnosis and treatment of brain-behavior disorders. For example, evoked potentials have been used as a diagnostic tool to identify hyper-

Electric Pain Control: It's Endorphin

When Charles Niethold fell at work in 1975, he seriously injured his back for the second time. He had already undergone two operations and now a third left him in chronic pain, unable to walk without crutches. But last week he walked easily into a press conference at the University of California Medical Center in San Francisco to testify to the effectiveness of an electrical technique for pain reduction. . . . The reason for the conference was that Niethold's neurosurgeon, Yoshio Hosobuchi, believes he now can explain the physiological working of the pain relief method developed serendipitously a few years ago.

One of the body's "natural opiates," beta endorphin . . . is the key to the pain reduction, Hosobuchi and colleagues conclude. To reduce chronic pain, Hosobuchi implants in the central part of the brain (the periaqueductal gray matter) wires that run to a radio receiver in the patient's chest. For pain relief, a patient simply holds the antenna of a small transmitter over the receiver in his chest. The pain subsides in a few minutes and may not recur for several hours or even days.

In their recent experiment Hoso-buchi and his colleagues . . . examined cerebrospinal fluid from the brains of patients receiving electrical implants. . . . For three patients with chronic pain that responds to narcotics, the first 15 minutes of electrical stimulation increased the concentration of beta endorphin to 2 to 7 times the level in the fluid at the onset of surgery. However, there appeared to be no increase in another natural pain-relieving chemical, leu-enkephalin. Another group, using a different detection method, has reported a moderate enkephalin increase in response to stimulation. . . .

Electrical stimulation has been used to relieve two kinds of chronic pain, and Hosobuchi's research . . . adds to the evidence that different mechanisms are involved. Beta endorphin release is implicated only in relief of the pain that responds to narcotics. Such pain may result from injury to peripheral nerve cells, as in Niethold's case, or from cancer.

Pain that cannot be alleviated with narcotics usually involves damage to the central nervous system, for instance from a stroke or from severing the spinal cord. In such cases, a neurosurgeon can implant wires going to a different part of the brain. These patients require constant electrical stimulation of a broad brain area. When Hosobuchi and co-workers examined three patients receiving such implants, they observed no increase in beta endorphin with electrical stimulation.

While the patient response to electrical implants can be dramatic, problems may also arise. Niethold, who received his implant prior to the present experiment, recalls that almost immediately after electrical stimulation began he was able to raise his leg from the operating table, a movement he had not been able to do previously. However, after that first implant, infection developed and one of the two electrodes in Niethold's brain had to be removed for a year. Of Hosobuchi's 80 patients with implanted electrodes, one has died as a result of infection. Still Hosobuchi concludes that stimulation of the body's pain-killing hormone by electrical means is generally safe and effective for patients with chronic pain who wish to avoid dependency on narcotics, particularly for those patients with pain in the lower extremities. . . .

Science News
January 20, 1979

Brain activity is governed by two sets of processes, one electrical and one chemical. The two processes operate in tandem and obviously affect each other. Electrical activity is generated by chemical events, and the electricity in turn causes the release of still other chemicals. Electrical stimulation may actually work by releasing a chemical (endorphin), but the endorphin may work by blocking or reducing the electrical responsiveness of neurons.

kinetic children. Hyperkinetic children have numerous problems, particularly in school, because their hyperactivity prevents them from concentrating on their schoolwork. Evoked responses to auditory stimulation have been observed to be less frequent and lower in amplitude in hyperkinetic children than in a control group of normal children. Drug treatment for hyperactivity has been fairly successful, but therapists have long felt the need for a test capable of screening large numbers of children to identify hyperkinesis, and the evoked response technique offers hope of becoming such a test.

The technique can also be used to test newborn infants who can't tell you whether everything is normal; their brains "talk," however, and the evoked potential method can pick up this information and tell the doctors if things are normal. The brain, interestingly enough, also gives off a slightly different evoked response if the stimulus is unexpected or surprising, meaning it is new information. Evoked potentials have been used to study how, when, and to what type of stimuli the two different hemispheres of the brain respond, making them a major tool in brain lateralization research. Since the brain responds differently to new and old information, a computer could theoretically be used to run a diagnostic check on the brain to see if you were learning properly as you read material presented to you on the computer screen. That's getting awfully close to automatically programming your brain with new information.

Psychopharmacology

The number of investigations into how drugs affect behavior has increased and has given rise to a new discipline called psychopharmacology, or behavioral pharmacology. Many processes that take place in the nervous system are based on chemical events, and we can learn a good deal about the functioning of the brain from an understanding of how drugs affect behavior. The potential applications of psychopharmacology are enormous. Kenneth Clark, a recent presi-

FIGURE 2-16 Recording the EEG

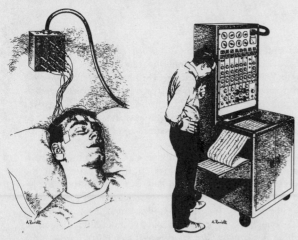

The EEG is recorded by small electrodes glued to the scalp that pick up the tiny electrical potentials generated by the brain. The EEG machine is basically a system for amplifying these potentials and converting them into a written record. The left panel shows a subject wired for a sleep recording. The wires from the electrodes are connected to a "terminal box" in the bedroom, which in turn is connected to the EEG machine in the next room. The right panel shows the EEG being printed out by the pens of the EEG machine.

FIGURE 2-17 Normal EEG records showing different patterns of electrical activity for different stages of sleep and wakefulness.

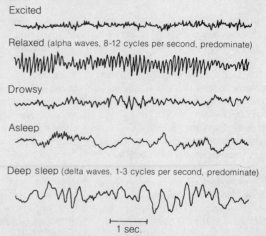

Excited

Relaxed (alpha waves, 8-12 cycles per second, predominate)

Drowsy

Asleep

Deep sleep (delta waves, 1-3 cycles per second, predominate)

|← 1 sec. →|

Note that for each level the EEG shows a characteristic frequency (the number of waves occurring during each unit of time) and amplitude (the height of each wave).

dent of the American Psychological Association, has called for the development of drugs to control violence, and he would have the leaders of the world take these drugs to reduce the threat of war. Drugs, as we shall see, have been used with some success to control obesity, insomnia, and sleep. And why stop there? What about the possibility of producing drugs to increase intelligence, improve memory, increase creativity, and stop criminal behavior?

Research in psychopharmacology has also increased our understanding of the factors involved in addiction, tolerance, and dependence with respect to the so-called drugs of abuse. Examples of drugs of abuse are the narcotics, alcohol, the barbiturates, and the amphetamines. There is clear-cut evidence that heredity plays a major role in alcoholism, and similar suggestions have been made in the case of narcotics addiction. This evidence suggests that there are physical bases for these disorders, over and above the role played by environmental circumstances in the life of addicts. For example, alcoholism may be mediated, in part, by deficiencies in certain enzymes necessary for the metabolism of alcohol, and this lack may contribute to an increased vulnerability to this drug. Individuals who become narcotics addicts may have inherited nervous systems with unusually large numbers of receptors sensitive to these addicting drugs, resulting in an increased susceptibility to addiction.

We are also beginning to understand the bases for certain types of tolerance. Tolerance is defined as the phenomenon that occurs with repeated use of a drug so that previously effective doses no longer produce an effect. It is important to understand that the phenomenon de-

scribes a response to a particular effect. For example, tolerance to the sedative effects of the barbiturates develops fairly rapidly; however, tolerance to the respiratory depressant effects of these drugs develops much more slowly, if at all. Undoubtedly, the tolerance phenomenon is responsible for many of the cases of overdose that are reported for this category of drugs.

An interesting theory with respect to the development of physical dependence is the disuse theory. After repeated use of a drug, its abrupt discontinuance results in gross, sometimes life-threatening, withdrawal symptoms. The disuse theory is based on evidence that prolonged periods of disuse of a muscle results in the muscle's becoming supersensitive. Similar findings have been reported for nervous tissue. Prolonged inactivity of a nerve cell may result in its becoming so highly sensitive that when activity is restored, the nerve may over-respond to the stimulation. Since we know that many of the drugs which result in dependence are central nervous system depressants, their use may produce prolonged "disuse" of major parts of the nervous system. When the drugs are then withdrawn, the nervous system may be so supersensitive that smooth transmission of nerve impulses is impossible. This results in terrible withdrawal symptoms.

Drug research also promises to contribute to our understanding of mental illness. Certain drugs, when taken in large amounts, can induce a reaction which resembles that of psychosis. (More precise definitions of mental disorders and their treatment is given in Chapters 11 and 12.) A basic understanding of the way drugs produce these symptoms may contribute to our understanding of the psychoses themselves. Finally, we should point out that drug development and drug research have already produced major changes in the treatment of mental illness. The major and minor tranquilizers (drugs used in the treat-

Human Aggression Linked to Chemical Balance

In the first reported study of its kind with human beings, federal researchers say they have evidence that "human aggression . . . may have a biological component to it." The component appears to revolve around the critical balance of two or three key brain chemical neurotransmitters.

The findings are consistent with previous animal studies indicating that aggression seems to be mediated by the production levels of serotonin and norepinephrine. Animal results also indicate that dopamine may be related to aggression, but that was not corroborated in the human study, says Frederick K. Goodwin, chief of the National Institute of Mental Health's clinical pyschobiology branch.

The results are additionally significant because the research subjects—26 Navy enlisted men—had no apparent psychiatric problems. This means that in addition to influencing the occurrence of various mental illnesses, "a biological variable . . . can also play a role in determining a range of behaviors considered reasonably normal," Goodwin told SCIENCE NEWS.

Goodwin and his colleagues first evaluated the aggression levels of the volunteers, each of whom "had some difficulty adjusting to service life." Their ratings were based on interviews, records of past behavior and on a 10-item aggression scale that included nonspecific fighting, specific assaults, temper tantrums, antisocial behavior not

involving police, school discipline, loss of jobs, difficulty with police, difficulty with military judicial system, difficulty with military discipline and separation from military service because of preexisting personality disorder.

The men had a wide range of aggression scores among themselves—but their mean score was nearly five times higher than that of a control group of "normal" subjects (employees at the National Naval Medical Center in Bethesda, Md.). In general, the 26 enlisted men were considered to have poor control over impulsive behavior, high levels of anger and aggression and poor judgment.

But an initial analysis of the volunteers' cerebrospinal fluid also showed a wide man-to-man variability in metabolite levels of serotonin. "Serotonin is known to be an inhibitory, modulatory influence" in animal aggression levels, Goodwin says, . . . "Animal studies have suggested that a decrease in serotonin level coincides with a rise in aggressiveness." Similar work also indicates that increases in norepinephrine and dopamine correlate with increased aggression.

Subsequent, more detailed, studies of the men's spinal fluid yielded a "very high correlation between behavior and chemical levels," Goodwin says. The men with the lowest aggression scores almost invariably had the highest levels of serotonin—up to five times higher than those at the opposite end of the

scale. And those who were most aggressive had the highest levels of norepinephrine. Dopamine levels, however, did not correlate with aggressiveness as they had in animal studies. "This was an interesting aspect," Goodwin says, "It may signal some kind of difference between species."

Comparison of the results with various control groups revealed that the chemical-behavior relationship in aggressive personalities is essentially unique, contrasting sharply with correlations among nonpatients, manics, depressives and alcoholics. . . .

Goodwin . . . says the chemical-behavior link "doesn't have to be genetic. Environment, particularly early life experiences, can have an influence" on biochemical balance. The treatment implications are obvious, he says. "There may be medications which could alter such [aggressive] conditions. . . . Lithium has been seen to have beneficial effects on aggressive prisoners," he says.

Lithium has also been shown to boost serotonin levels in animals, Goodwin says. There are indications that other drugs for depression might do the same thing and help counteract aggression, he says. "Of course there are ethical issues, but to me this is just a question of common sense . . . as long as you make sure the subjects are volunteers." This is the "first direct measure" of such metabolites in men, he says.

Science News
June 3, 1978

If human aggressive behavior is as much under the control of biological systems in the brain involving various neurotransmitters, then we are not far away from developing drugs to cure or prevent violent outbursts. The naturally occurring element lithium has already shown some promise in this regard. How would you use a drug that prevented violence?

---

ment of psychoses and neuroses, respectively) have quite literally revolutionized the treatment of these illnesses and have also contributed much to our understanding of the underlying causes of these diseases. For example, there is now good evidence to suggest that some disturbance in chemical transmission mediated by dopamine and norepinephrine may be responsible for the symptoms associated with certain psychoses.

Behavioral Genetics

The work in behavioral genetics has far-reaching theoretical and practical implications. It seems likely that at some time in the future we will have techniques which will allow us to manipulate the genes that determine physical and psychological processes. In the future we may have techniques for actually affecting chromosomes in ways designed to

"I have to take one three times a day to curb my insatiable appetite for power."

The New Yorker, April 25, 1977. Drawing by Dana Fradon; © 1977 The New Yorker Magazine, Inc.

eliminate such problems as mental retardation, schizophrenia, and alcoholism. To reach these goals, behavioral geneticists pursue programs designed to reveal the genetic contributions to various psychological disorders; the hope is eventually to develop techniques that will contribute to their eradication. We can also envision genetic engineering designed to produce offspring with more adaptive characteristics, such as great intelligence. Obviously, such research and the knowledge derived from it will create new moral and ethical issues concerning their application.

There is little doubt that behavioral genetics will have an enormous impact on our future lives. It has already changed our view of behavior, from a simplistic belief in environmental determinism to a realization that behavior results from interacting environmental and genetic factors.

Possible Uses of Biopsychological Knowledge

The potential areas of application of biopsychology are unlimited. Here are two examples.

Obesity

Consider the control of obesity. Research has determined that certain nuclei of the hypothalamus are responsible for the control, both starting and stopping, of eating behavior. (see Chapter 7). As we mentioned earlier, there may be a hormone or peptide that specifically influences the hypothalamic centers which control eating. One such chemical has already been discovered in the stomach and intestines and is called *cholecystokinin* (CCK). It may be the messenger to the brain from the gut that stops eating. It is possible that some day certain types of people with chronic overweight problems will be helped by drugs acting specifically on the hypothalamus, drugs designed to act just like CCK.

Sleep

Insomnia is one of the most common problems in the U.S. population. Since biopsychology has uncovered much of the neurological basis for control and regulation of sleep and wakefulness, there is little doubt that help for the insomniac is just around the corner. This could take the form of new drugs that affect the sleep system, without producing the unwanted side effects of barbiturates. Or there may be electrical devices for stimulating the brain in such a way as to produce sleep. Such devices are already in the experimental stage and may some day eliminate the problem of insomnia.

Insomniacs cannot fall asleep or cannot stay asleep. In contrast, people with *narcolepsy* fall asleep all the time, throughout the day, with little or no warning and against their wishes. They also experience rapid onset of muscle weakness, called cataplexy, which can cause them to fall down in a reversible state of paralysis. Physiological studies have shown that when narcoleptics fall asleep, unlike normals, they go directly into the rapid-eye-movement (REM) sleep characteristic of dreaming (see Appendix D). Normal dreaming during the night is accompanied by the loss of muscle tone, so the cataplexy seems to fit with the general idea that narcolepsy involves the breaking through in the daytime of REM sleep. Presently, there is no cure for narcolepsy, although two sets of drugs are commonly prescribed, one to treat falling asleep and one to combat muscle weakness. It is hoped that greater understanding of the biochemical triggering mechanisms for REM sleep will lead to treatments that will essentially cure this curious but unfortunate disorder.

3 Sensation and Perception

A young couple is sitting on the ground watching the moon rise over the distant horizon. It is a huge golden-yellow globe, a breathtaking sight. They snap a picture of this giant moon to preserve its drama on film. Later in the evening, when the moon is higher in the night sky, it seems much smaller and far less dramatic. And when the film is developed and printed, the moon appears disappointingly small. What has happened?

A commercial pilot is making the final landing approach in a jet airliner. The night is clear and moonless. The city lights twinkle in the distance, and the unlit countryside below the plane is ink-black. Everything seems normal as the pilot guides the plane in, watching the runway lights draw nearer and nearer. Suddenly, without warning, the huge jet crashes into the ground several miles short of the end of the runway and burst into flames. What went wrong?

These are just two of many questions investigated by psychologists who study perception. In this chapter, we will see how the processes of perception work and what consequences they have in our daily lives.

What Is Perception?

Perception has been the subject of philosophical debate since the time of Plato and Aristotle. We regard perception as the process of creating an internal representation of the outside world. This internal representation is what we experience as "reality," and it allows us to find food, to avoid danger, and to enjoy the glow of the setting sun. We are prevented from directly experiencing the outside world; we know

or experience only what our perceptual processes create for us out of the information input from the senses. Internal representations are a joint product of "bottom-up" processing (the information from the senses) and "top-down" processing (information from memory—our knowledge of the world); see Highlight 3-1. Normally, these processes work so well that we are unaware that what we experience is an internal representation and not the world itself. Under certain circumstances, however, the perceptual processes fail to operate properly—with a high fever, with sensory deprivation, in schizophrenia, or with hallucinogenic drugs—and as a result the internal representation created by the perceptual processes is "distorted" and "unreal." People who base their behavior on these versions of "reality" say or do in-

---

Highlight 3-1

Top-Down and Bottom-Up Processing in Perception

This series of drawings, by Gerald Fisher, illustrates the interplay of "bottom-up" (data-based) and "top-down" (constructive) processing in perception. Figures in the middle are ambiguous or reversible and can be easily perceived in one of two ways: a man's face or a woman's figure. Which way you perceive them is largely a function of your knowledge and expectations (top-down processing). The end drawings are typically unambiguous—the data are more compelling of one or the other interpretation, so that top-down processing has less influence on what you see.

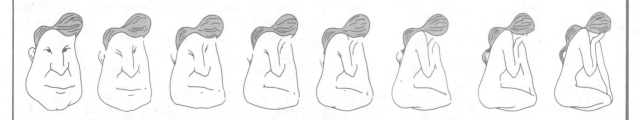

appropriate things which may lead to hospitalization, injury, or death.

The perceptual processes are dynamic. They are continually creating and changing the internal representation in order that we may have answers for two vital questions: "What is out there?" and "Where is it located?" Sensory information, memory, beliefs, and expectations all contribute to the exact nature of the internal representation that exists at each moment in time.

While reading this chapter, keep clear in your mind four different types of concepts: physical, physiological, behavioral, and experiential (see Figure 3–1). Physical concepts describe the physical characteristics of the outside world. The physical characteristics of light include wavelength and intensity. Sound is described by frequency and amplitude. Physiological concepts are used to describe the behavior of cells, especially nerve cells. The two major concepts are excitation and inhibition, the increase and decrease in the activity of a nerve cell. Specialized nerve cells, the sensory-receptor cells, are responsible for changing, or transducing, physical energy into physiological events. Transduction is the first step in the perceptual process. Behavioral concepts are used to describe the behavior of a complete organism. For human beings, they include what people say and do. In a simple detection experiment, one might measure how many times a person said "Yes, I saw that light."

Concepts of the fourth type are used to describe the nature of subjective experiences. Unlike the other three types of concepts, experiential concepts cannot be directly observed. They are private for each individual. If you look at the setting sun and say that it looks green, we cannot test directly whether or not you are telling the truth. What is observed is what you *said,* not what you experienced.

The goal in our study of perception is to understand the relationships among physical stimulation, neural activity, what a person says and does, and what experiences are generated. We know much about these matters now, yet compared with what there remains to learn, we know very little.

The Five Senses

Aristotle classified our sources of information about the outside world into the five senses: sight, hearing, taste, smell, and the skin senses (touch, warmth, cold, and pain). These sensory systems work by means of receptors, or transducers. A **receptor** is a specialized nerve cell that converts physical stimulation into electrical information. This electrical information is then transmitted to the brain by additional nerve cells connected to the receptors. Receptors may be classified into types, based on the physical stimulation required to activate them. *Photoreceptors* in the eye are sensitive to light energy. *Mechanoreceptors* are sensitive to mechanical forces and are found in the skin, the joints, and the inner ear where they function in hearing and in the vestibular senses. *Chemoreceptors* are sensitive to chemical substances and mediate our taste and smell. The senses transform this variety of physical stimulation into electrical signals which the brain can understand and use in its construction of internal representations of the world. Table 3–1 lists some of the characteristics of each sensory system.

Visual Sensory Processing

The visual system takes light energy and transforms it into patterns of neural activity in the brain. This transformation is not a simple one, and during the past 50 years progress has been made toward understanding it. Stop reading for a moment and look around you. Notice the various objects you can see. Look at their visual appearances and consider that all of them result from activity in the brain. We will now look at the physical, physiological, and perceptual processes that produce these experiences.

The Physical Nature of Light

Light is electromagnetic energy that can be seen. Most such energy, such as radio, radar, and X-rays, cannot be seen. Light is composed of packets of en-

FIGURE 3–1 Relationship among four types of concepts used in perception and how these concepts apply to a real-life example

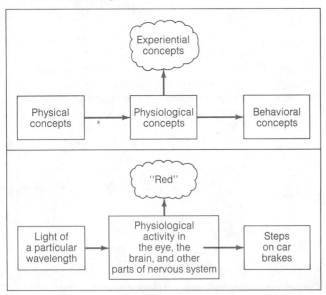

TABLE 3-1   Characteristics of Our Sensory Systems

Sense	Stimulus	Receptors	Minimum Stimulus	Equivalent Stimulus
Vision	Electro-magnetic energy, photons	Rods and cones in the retina	1 Photon absorbed by one rod	Candle flame viewed from a distance of 48 km (30 miles)
Hearing	Sound pressure waves	Hair cells on basilar membrane of the inner ear	0.0002 dynes/cm²	Ticking of a watch in a quiet room 6 m (20 ft.) away
Taste	Chemical substances dissolved in saliva	Taste buds on the tongue	Several molecules (depending on the substance)	1 Teaspoon of sugar dissolved in 2 gallons of distilled water (1 part in 2000)
Smell	Chemical substances in the air	Receptor cells in the upper nasal cavity	Several molecules (depending on the substance)	1 Drop of perfume in a three-room house (1 part in 500,000,000)
Touch	Mechanical displacement of the skin	Nerve endings in the skin*	0.1 μ (0.00000001 mm) (depending on the part of the body)	The wing of a bee falling on your cheek from a distance of 1 cm (0.39 in.)

* Yield sensations of warmth, cold, touch, pain.

ergy called quanta or *photons*. In this book, we will use the term "wavelength" to describe the physical property of photons (although "energy" or "frequency" would do just as well). The unit of wavelength to be used is very much smaller than one meter, the nanometer (1 nm = 10^{-9} meters). One quantum of 500 nm light has a wavelength of only 0.0000005 meters! A 50-watt incandescent light bulb radiates approximately 3,800,000,000,000,000,000 quanta of visible light per second. The range of wavelengths that our visual system can convert into neural signals is incredibly small, extending from approximately 400 nm to only 700 nm (see Color Plate 1).

A light source has two important characteristics—the intensity of the light (the number of quanta per second) and the wavelength distribution of the quanta (the number of quanta per second at each wavelength). Quanta travel in a straight line away from a light source until they strike an object. If the object is transparent, most of the quanta pass through the object. If the object is opaque, some of the quanta are absorbed by the object and the remainder are reflected from it. The ratio of the number of quanta reflected from a surface to the number of quanta falling onto a surface is called the *reflectance* of the surface. The reflectance may be different for different wavelengths. For example, a surface might reflect all

wavelengths equally; it might reflect only long wavelengths or only short wavelengths, or it might reflect wavelengths in various combinations. Thus, the exact nature of the reflectance greatly influences the appearance of a surface.

Only light that enters the eye can be converted into neural activity by the receptors of the eye. Because our eye is not equally sensitive to all wavelengths, equal numbers of quanta at different wavelengths will not cause equal neural activity. In order to measure the intensity of light leaving a surface and at the same time to compensate for the unequal sensitivity of the eye to different wavelengths, the unit of luminance is used. The international unit of luminance is the candela per square meter (cd/m²). All things being equal, two lights having equal luminances, regardless of their wavelength composition, are supposed to appear equally bright when viewed under daylight conditions.

The Eye

The eyeball is an optical instrument much like a camera. Its function is to form an image of the outside world on the **retina**—the network of neural cells (photoreceptors) at the rear of the eye. In the retina quanta of light are converted into nerve activity. The various parts of the eye are shown in Figure 3-2. The optical system of the eye has two major components, the *cornea* and the *lens*. Take a close look at a friend's eye. The curved transparent surface on the front of the eye is the cornea. Behind the cornea you can see the *iris*, the colored part of the eye. Notice that the size of the opening (the *pupil*) in the middle of the iris is constantly changing. The iris helps control the amount of light entering the eye. The pupil becomes as large as 8 millimeters in diameter in the dark and constricts to 2 millimeters in bright light.

Behind the iris is the lens, which you cannot see without a special instrument, called a slit lamp or biomicroscope, used by eye doctors. The lens can change its shape, becoming thinner and thicker in order to keep the image of objects focused on the retina. This process of focusing the image is called **accommodation** and occurs automatically. Many people have eyes that do not allow a sharply focused image to be maintained under all normal circumstances. These people must wear glasses or contact lenses to compensate (see "What Does it Mean?"). Figure 3-3 illustrates the process of accommodation. Notice in the figure that the size of the image on the retina depends not only on the physical size of the object but also on the distance the object is from the eye. For example, if two people, both six feet tall, are standing at different distances from you, the retinal image of the farther person will be smaller than the retinal image of the nearer person. This fact plays an important role in the phenomenon of "size con-

FIGURE 3-3 The process of accommodation

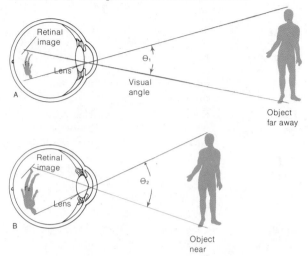

Two examples of optic arrays from objects with their retinal images. Only lines from the extremities of the objects are illustrated. In (A) the object is far away, so the visual angle is small with a correspondingly small image projected on the retina. Notice that the lens inverts the image. In (B) the object is closer, so there is a larger visual angle and a larger retinal image. To provide a sharp focus on the retina the lens has to change its curvature—a process called *accommodation*—so that it is thicker for near objects and thinner for distant ones.

stancy," to be discussed later. The stimulus object at a distance is known as the "distal" stimulus, while the retinal image of that object is called the "proximal" stimulus.

The Retina: The Physiological Receptor for Light

When photons from objects fall on the retina, they are converted into electrical signals by the photoreceptors. There are two types of photoreceptors in the human retina, the *rods* and the *cones*, named for their distinctive shapes. There are actually three different types of cone receptors. The rods and the three different types of cones each contain a different type of photopigment, a substance that reacts chemically when light energy strikes it. This reaction transduces light energy into electrical activity. The receptors differ in their sensitivities to different wavelengths of light because each type contains a different photopigment. Figure 3-4 indicates the relative sensitivity to different wavelengths of the three cones and the rods. Notice in the figure that the R-type cone is maximally sensitive to 570 nm light, the G-type cone to 535 nm light, and

FIGURE 3-2 The eye

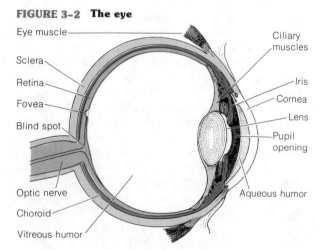

The eye is a complicated structure with many parts. Its purpose is to present an optical image of the world to the retina, where that image is transformed into nerve impulses.

FIGURE 3-4 Relative sensitivity of cones and of rods in the retina

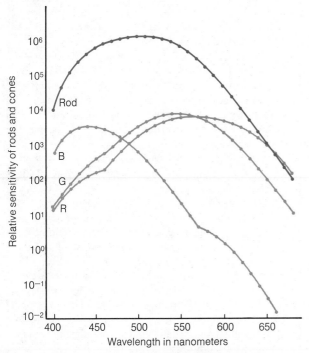

The retina contains three types of cone receptors and one kind of rod receptors. The graph shows the sensitivity of each type of receptor to different wavelengths of light. Notice that each receptor is sensitive to all wavelengths, but in different degrees. Each receptor can be characterized by the wavelength to which it is *most* sensitive.

length of that quantum. There are about 120 million rod receptors and about 8 million cones in each retina. Of the 8 million cones, about 5,225,000 are R-types, 2,600,000 are G-types, and 1,600,000 are B-types. The cones are concentrated in the foveal region of the retina (Figure 3–2), while the rods are completely missing from the central **fovea** and are found in the peripheral retina. An elaborate network of neural connections, involving the horizontal, bipolar, and amacrine cells, connect the 8 million cones and the 120 million rods to 1 million ganglion cells (Figure 3–5). The axons of these 1 million ganglion cells leave the eye and form the optic nerve, which transmits information to the visual areas of the brain. The ganglion cells are constantly active, even in the absence of light. This resting rate of neural activity can be as high as 20 or 30 spikes per second (see Chapter 2).

Each ganglion cell is indirectly connected to a circular region of receptors on the retina. This circular region is called the **receptive field** of the ganglion cell (see Figure 3–6). The circular area is divided into a central region and a surrounding region. The effect of these two regions of the receptive field on the activity of the ganglion cell is opposite. For half the ganglion cells in the retina, shining light in the center of a cell's receptive field will excite the ganglion cell (increase its neural activity), and shining light in the surrounding area will inhibit the cell (decrease its neural activity). Such a cell is said to have an "on-center, off-surround" receptive field. The other half

the B-type cone to 445 nm light. The rod receptors are maximally sensitive to 510 nm light. Also notice that the rods are more than 1,000 times more sensitive to middle wavelength light than are the cones and that all of the receptors have some sensitivity to all the visible wavelengths.

Since rods are so much more sensitive than cones, rods control our vision at night *(scotopic vision)*. During the day the less sensitive cones take over *(photopic vision)*. Because of the neural circuitry connected to the cones, our vision during daylight is marked by color experiences and the ability to see fine detail. Rod vision, on the other hand, creates only black, gray, and white experiences, with much loss of fine detail. We will discover why there is this difference between scotopic and photopic vision in the section on color vision.

The electrical signal generated by a rod or cone depends only on the number of quanta of light absorbed per second. Once a quantum is absorbed, the signal generated is the same regardless of the wave-

FIGURE 3-5 Schematic illustration of a section of the retina showing photoreceptor connections.

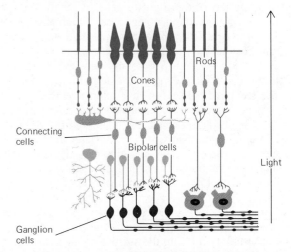

The rod and cone receptor cells are linked with the brain by an intricate chain of neural interconnections.

FIGURE 3-6 Receptive fields

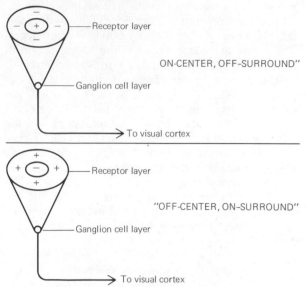

ON-CENTER, OFF-SURROUND"

"OFF-CENTER, ON-SURROUND"

This figure schematically illustrates the receptive field—the circular area of receptors (rods and cones) converging on a single ganglion cell in the next layer of the retina. The 128 million photoreceptors converge onto only about 1 million ganglion cells in the next layer of the retina, meaning that *on the average each ganglion cell is "collecting" input from 128 cells*. The convergence is maximal for rods and minimal for cones (many ganglion cells receive input from only one cone). Convergence happens in one of two basic ways, which gives rise to the two basic types of ganglion cells: (1) on-center, off-surround and (2) off-center, on-surround.

of the ganglion cells in the retina have receptive fields with just the opposite characteristics ("off-center, on-surround"). An important effect of this functional organization of the input to each ganglion cell is that the activity of a ganglion cell is not much affected by a uniform light filling its entire receptive field because the excitatory and inhibitory influences tend to cancel out. The ganglion cell is very sensitive to different amounts of light falling on the center and surround of the receptive field. Thus, it is often said that ganglion cells function as difference or contrast detectors rather than as absolute detectors of light (see the discussion of neural circuits in Chapter 2). Later in this chapter we will learn how the organization of the receptive field has dramatic consequences for what we see. Color Plate 12 illustrates the major visual pathways in the brain, from the eye to the visual cortex. An important principle is shown in Color Plate 12: There is an orderly mapping (called *retinotopic mapping*) of the visual world onto the surface of the visual cortex. Each region of the visual field is represented by a corresponding region of the brain.

Highlight 3-2

Visual Experiences in the Absence of Stimulation by Light

Your visual system is always active. Even when no light is being absorbed by visual receptors, the nerve cells in the eye and visual areas of the brain are generating signals and creating visual sensations. The following exercise will permit you to experience these visual sensations.

Sit quietly and close your eyes. Notice that although you cannot see any objects, your visual field is filled with speckle-like flashes of light. Now cup your hands over your eyes, shutting out as much light as you can without putting pressure on the eyes themselves. What do you experience? Although the sensation is one of greater darkness, notice that the unevenness and speckled appearance is still there. Finally, go into a room without windows (such as a bathroom or a darkroom). Turn off the lights and sit quietly for 5 or 10 minutes. Pay attention to your visual experiences. Notice that your visual field is filled with an ever-changing gray, and that there are light and dark gray patches that come and go. These experiences are called visual noise and are the result of the constant activity in your nervous system. Visual noise makes the detection of very weak visual stimulation quite difficult.

Experiential Sensitivity to Light

When you first enter a darkened room from the bright outdoors, you cannot see at all, and then slowly you recover your vision. This increased sensitivity to light as you remain in the dark is called **dark adaptation.** Figure 3–7 shows the amount of light required for detection as a function of the time spent in the dark. You can see that there are two parts to this function, called the cone branch and the rod branch of the curve. After about 10 minutes in the dark, the cones become as sensitive as they can. At this point the more sensitive rods take over. Then, after about 30 minutes in the dark, the rods reach their maximum sensitivity. This maximum sensitivity is truly fantastic. Careful measurements have shown that if a single rod absorbs a single quantum of light, the change in the electrical activity of the ganglion cells is enough to generate a very faint sensation. Since some of the quanta from a stimulus are reflected from the surface of the cornea and lens, some are absorbed by the

FIGURE 3-7 Dark adaptation

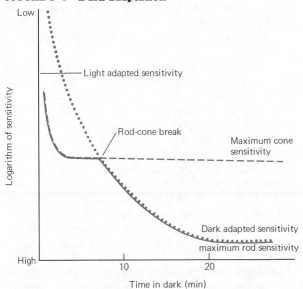

Dark adaptation is measured in terms of the lowest intensity of light that can be seen at a given time. As time in the dark passes, the lowest perceivable level decreases. Laboratory tests show that the processes of dark adaptation take a total of about 30 minutes. Adaptation of the cones produces an increase in sensitivity during the first 10 minutes in the dark. Subsequent changes are due to adaptation of the rods.

fluids within the eye, and some do not actually hit a rod, about 100 quanta need reach the eye to assure that one quantum is absorbed by a rod. This sensitivity is equivalent to seeing a single candle flame more than 30 miles away!

This knowledge has practical use. For example, a soldier on night patrol needs to be dark adapted enough to see where to walk, yet occasionally must use a brighter light in order to read a map. If an ordinary flashlight is used, the soldier will have to go through the process of dark adaptation all over again. This problem was solved during World War II. Notice in Figure 3-4 that the R-cones (the ones that are most sensitive to long wavelength light, that is, red light) are just as sensitive as rods in long wavelength light, and that, compared with their peak sensitivity, rods are relatively insensitive in long wavelength light. What these facts mean is that if the soldier puts a red filter over the flashlight and uses it to read the map, the cones will be sufficiently stimulated to give good visual acuity, but the rods will remain fairly well dark-adapted. This principle is also used by photographers in darkrooms. If they wear red goggles when they are out in normal room light, they will be able to see more quickly when they return to the darkroom.

Visual Detection and Discrimination

What must happen in the nervous system to detect a faint light in the dark? Since the ganglion cells are constantly sending signals back to the brain, even in the dark, light falling on the retina must change this activity enough to be noticed. The act of detection involves two separate processes—a sensory process and a decision process. The sensory process creates visual sensation from the ganglion cell activity. The decision process must decide whether or not a particular visual sensation resulted from light being absorbed by the retina or from random activity in the retina (see Figure 3-8). The decision process decides to say "Yes, I saw the light" or "No, I did not see it." It is important to note in Figure 3-8 that the decision process has access only to the output of the sensory process and not to the world directly.

As Figure 3-8 shows, when a very weak light is being detected, the range of sensations generated by the sensory process does not differ much from the sensations generated randomly in the dark. It is therefore impossible to detect a very weak light with

FIGURE 3-8

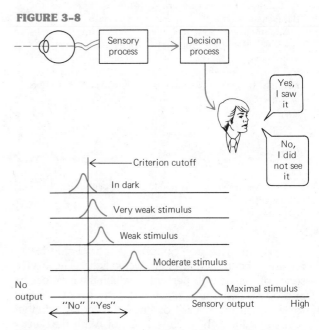

The sensory process converts physical light energy into nerve signals and experiences of brightness. There is some variability or "noise" in this process. The exact output of the sensory process at any moment depends on the intensity of (1) the stimulus and (2) the noise. The decision process can be described as involving: (1) setting up a criterion cutoff line and (2) deciding to say "yes" whenever the sensation is stronger than the cutoff (right of the cutoff line) or "no" when the sensation is weaker than the cutoff (left of the criterion line).

Fire-Engine Yellow

It may well be difficult to picture a black and white Dalmatian perched atop a screaming fire engine of bright lime yellow, but that peculiar color combination is beginning to appear in fire departments around the nation. Thanks to extensive research by such men as Dr. Stephen Solomon, an optometrist and a member of the Port Jervis, N.Y., volunteer fire department, more and more fire chiefs have been made aware of a stark physiological fact: people are red-blind at night. Says Dr. Solomon, who has published a number of articles on color research: "The color red is one of the least visible colors and rates next to black for getting attention."

Fire chiefs have seen the consequences of this principle. Chief Bernie Koeppen of Wheeling, Ill., has changed to lime yellow, even for the department's ambulance. "In accident after accident involving red wagons," he notes, "all you hear is, 'I didn't see it. I didn't see it.'" Adds Chief Ed Underwood of St. Charles, Mo.: "The majority of fire fighters killed or wounded catch it on their way to fires. Red is dead. Lime yellow is the coming color."

Fire engines have been red for so long (for no visible reason) that the switchover may create problems. Ted Haberman, manager of Pueblo West, Colo., points out that automobile drivers are accustomed to red as the danger color, and that since many Americans ride in air-conditioned cars with the windows rolled up, they may not hear the siren from approaching, unfamiliar lime yellow wagons. Simple tradition may also militate against a wholesale switch from red. But as Dr. Solomon accurately observes: "Firemen have one tradition that is stronger, and that is to stay alive."

Time
July 10, 1972

Here's a case in which the inability to see red in the dark may be dangerous.

100 percent accuracy. Suppose you are being tested for the occurrence of that weak light. There is a series of trials on 50 percent of which the light occurs and on 50 percent of which it does not. You are told to say each time "yes" or "no" depending whether you think the light occurred or not. With that weak light you would make many errors—you would often say that you saw a light when there was none and that you did not see a light when in fact it really was there.

When the physical intensity of the light is made stronger, the sensations from the sensory process are likewise stronger and are more different from the sensations due to random activity. It is therefore possible to distinguish the presence of the light more

accurately. For lights of even greater intensity, the sensations produced by the sensory process are so different from those produced by random activity that you could correctly detect the light 100 percent of the time.

A **threshold** is the amount of physical stimulus required to achieve a certain level of correctness in a detection task. We often use the stimulus intensity necessary for 75 percent correct as the threshold level, but this choice is completely arbitrary. If a stimulus is below the threshold intensity, it still is detected, just less often. Very precise experiments in vision and hearing have failed to find a stimulus intensity below which the stimulus is *never* detected. There is always a very low percentage of detection even with the weakest stimuli possible.

To measure the *absolute threshold* just described we measure a person's ability to discriminate between the presence of a stimulus and its absence. Most visual tasks, however, require the discrimination of one intensity of light from another, the *relative* (or *difference*) *threshold*. In order to read, for example, you must discriminate the darker letters from the lighter background of the page. The relative threshold or *just noticeable difference (jnd)* is not constant but changes as a function of the intensity of the background, a discovery made by E. H. Weber in the 1830s (see Highlight 3–3).

The mathematical relationship between the physical intensity of a stimulus and the magnitude of the resulting sensation was first described by G. T. Fechner in his "Elements of Psychophysics" published in 1860. From the further research of S. S. Stevens begun in the 1930s, we know today that the magnitude of a sensation is usually a power function of stimulus intensity:

$$\text{Sensation} = k \cdot (\text{Intensity})^n$$

This law, known as Stevens' law, has been tested over a wide range of stimulus types and intensities. The value of the exponent, *n*, differs for different types of stimuli (see Table 3–2). For example, the psychological sensation we call heaviness would be equal to a numerical constant, *k*, times the weight of the object raised to the power 1.45:

$$\text{Heaviness} = k(\text{weight})^{1.45}$$

Visual Resolution

Visual resolution is the ability to see fine detail and is usually expressed in terms of **visual acuity** (the higher the acuity, the better the vision). A person with poor visual acuity has difficulty reading, sewing, or doing other tasks requiring the perception of fine

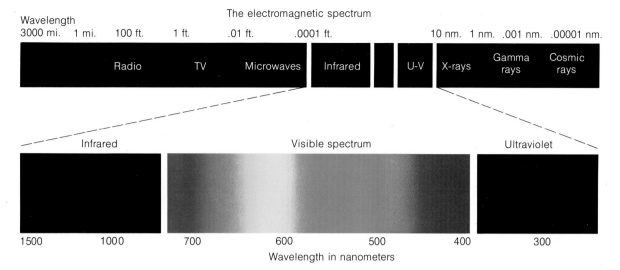

The electromagnetic spectrum

| Wavelength | | | | | | | | | | | |
| 3000 mi. | 1 mi. | 100 ft. | 1 ft. | .01 ft. | .0001 ft. | | 10 nm. | 1 nm. | .001 nm. | .00001 nm. |

| Radio | TV | Microwaves | Infrared | | U-V | X-rays | Gamma rays | Cosmic rays |

| Infrared | Visible spectrum | Ultraviolet |

| 1500 | 1000 | 700 | 600 | 500 | 400 | 300 |

Wavelength in nanometers

Plate 1   The electromagnetic spectrum
The full spectrum of electromagnetic radiation, of which the human eye can
see only the narrow band extending from 400 to 700 nanometers in
wavelength. A nanometer (abbreviated nm.) is a very small unit of length
equivalent to 1/1,000,000,000 meter (a meter is 39.37 inches).

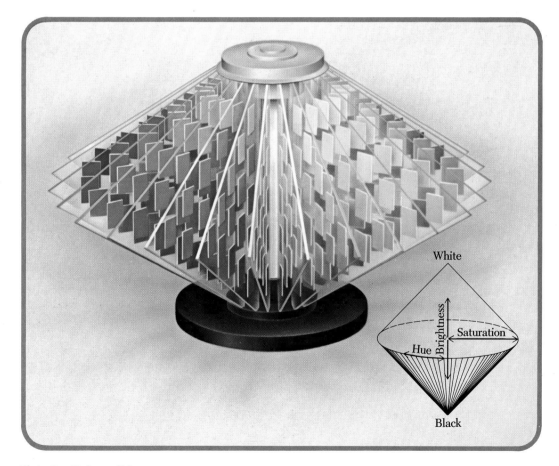

Plate 2   Color solid
Three dimensions of color sensitivity—hue, brightness, and saturation—can
be seen in this color solid. The gradual change in brightness from black to
white along the central axis is illustrated by the diagram.

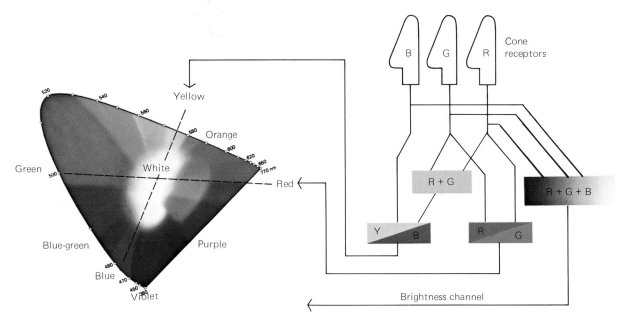

Plate 3 Internal representation of color spectrum
The standard chromaticity diagram (left) and its relationship to the internal
representation of color experience (right)

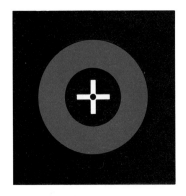  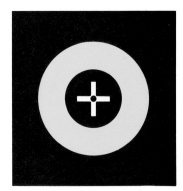

Plate 4 Negative afterimage
Look steadily for about 20 seconds at the dot inside the blue circle, then
transfer your gaze to the dot inside the gray rectangle. Now do the same with
the dot inside the yellow circle. What you see is a negative afterimage. Each
afterimage is the complementary color of the color you stared at.

Plate 5   Additive color mixture

If a *light* of a single wavelength is shined onto a white surface, the perceived color will correspond to that wavelength, because the surface reflects only that wavelength to the eye. Now if two lights of different wavelengths are shined on the surface together, the resulting perceived color will be an *additive* mixture. The surface will reflect both wavelengths, and they will add together to produce a color sensation. As is shown in Plate 5, it is possible to produce the complete spectrum of colors by additive mixture if you mix three properly chosen lights in the correct proportions.

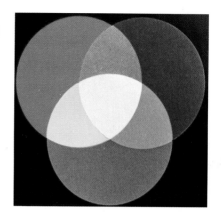

Plate 6   Subtractive color mixture

In contrast to mixing lights, when paints are combined the resulting perceived color is produced by subtraction. For example, a yellow paint absorbs (subtracts) primarily non-yellow wavelengths. If you mix a yellow paint with a blue paint (which absorbs primarily non-blue wavelengths), the result is a subtraction which leaves wavelengths between yellow and blue, namely green. Plate 6 illustrates how you can produce a variety of colors by subtractive mixture given three appropriately chosen paints.

Plate 7   Tests for colorblindness

People with normal vision see a number 6 in the top plate, while those with red-green color blindness do not. Those with normal vision see the number 12 in the bottom plate; those with red-green color blindness may see one number or none. These two illustrations are from a series of 15 color-blindness tests necessary for a complete color recognition examination.

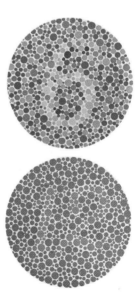

(Man Ray, "The Rope Dancer Accompanies Herself with Her Shadows," 1916. Oil on canvas, 52" x 6' 1⅛". Collection, The Museum of Modern Art, New York. Gift of G. David Thompson.)

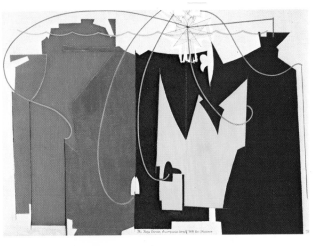 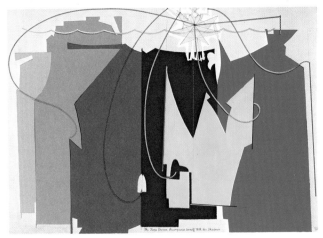

Plate 8   Colorblindness

The painting in the upper left panel appears as it would to a person with normal color vision. If you suffered from red-green blindness, the same picture would be seen as it is in the upper right panel. Similarly, the lower left and lower right panels show how the picture would look to persons with yellow-blue or total color blindness, respectively.

A.

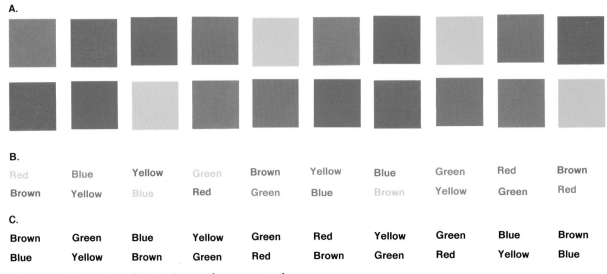

B.

Red	Blue	Yellow	Green	Brown	Yellow	Blue	Green	Red	Brown
Brown	Yellow	Blue	Red	Green	Blue	Brown	Yellow	Green	Red

C.

Brown	Green	Blue	Yellow	Green	Red	Yellow	Green	Blue	Brown
Blue	Yellow	Brown	Green	Red	Brown	Green	Red	Yellow	Blue

Plate 9   Effect of conflicting internal representations

The Stroop Color Naming Test illustrates the effect of interference by "irrelevant stimuli." For A, name the color of each patch as rapidly as possible. For B, name the colors of the words, ignoring the meaning of the words. For C, read the color names. Try A, B, and C on your friends, timing each task.

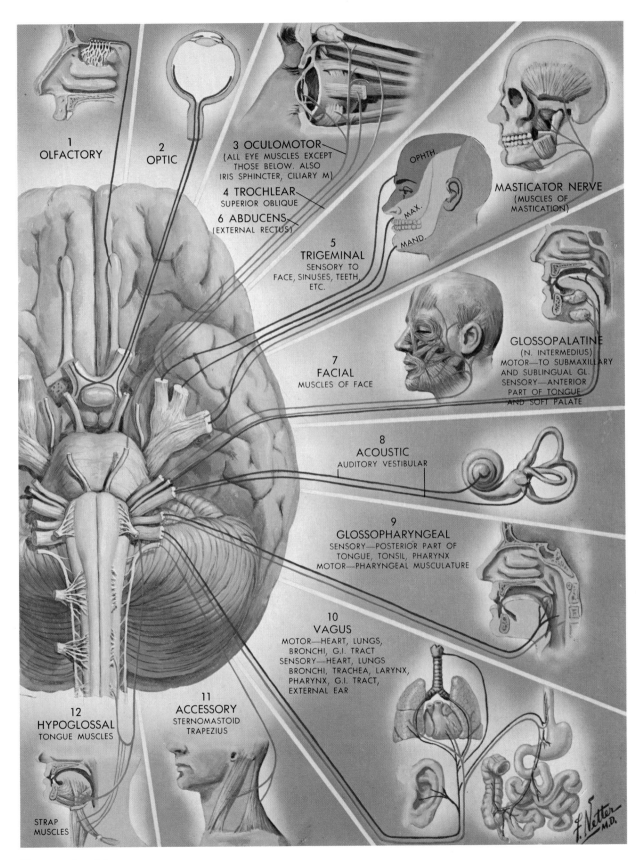

Plate 10   Cranial nerves

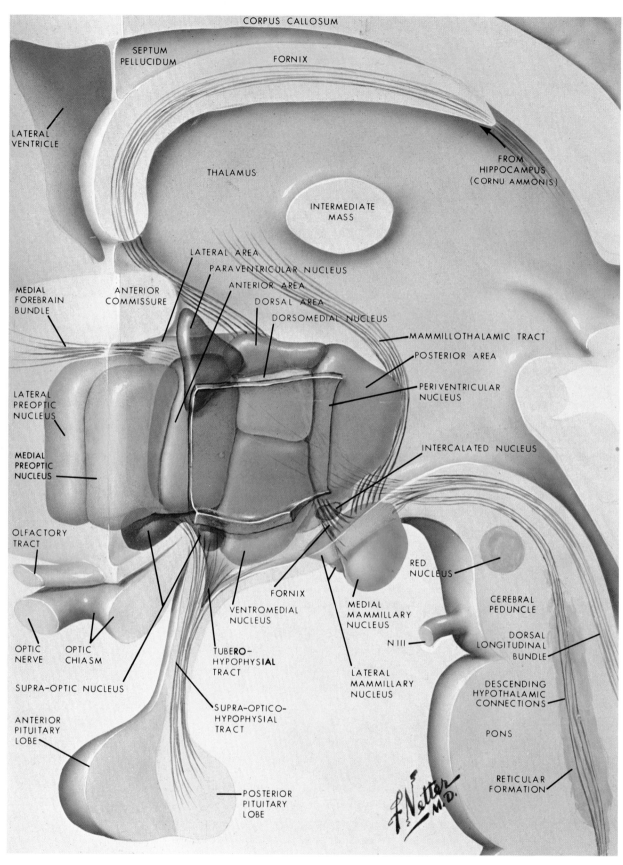

Plate 11　Schematic reproduction of hypothalamus
(three-dimensional)

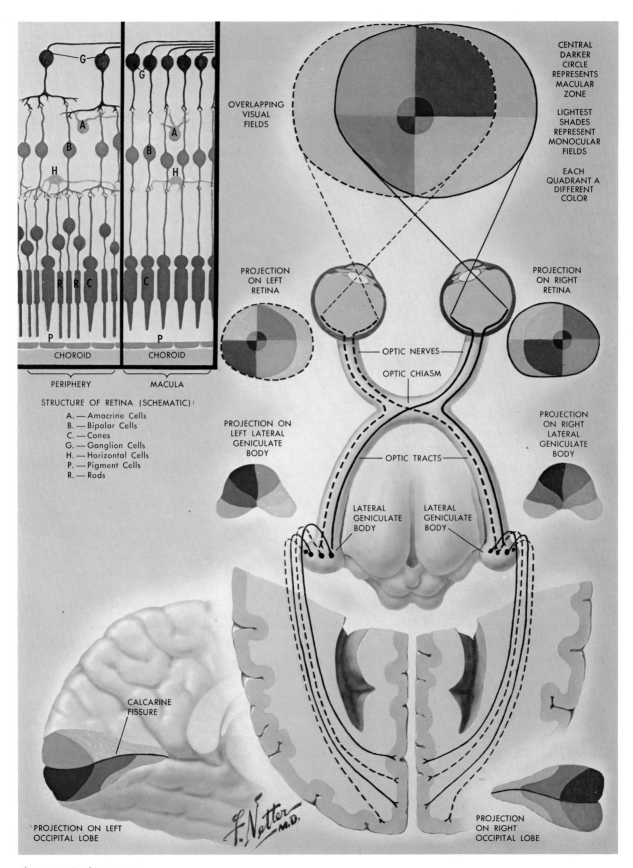

CENTRAL
DARKER
CIRCLE
REPRESENTS
MACULAR
ZONE

LIGHTEST
SHADES
REPRESENT
MONOCULAR
FIELDS

EACH
QUADRANT A
DIFFERENT
COLOR

OVERLAPPING
VISUAL
FIELDS

PROJECTION
ON LEFT
RETINA

PROJECTION
ON RIGHT
RETINA

OPTIC NERVES

OPTIC CHIASM

PROJECTION ON
LEFT LATERAL
GENICULATE
BODY

PROJECTION
ON RIGHT
LATERAL
GENICULATE
BODY

OPTIC TRACTS

LATERAL
GENICULATE
BODY

LATERAL
GENICULATE
BODY

CALCARINE
FISSURE

CHOROID

CHOROID

PERIPHERY

MACULA

STRUCTURE OF RETINA (SCHEMATIC):

A. — Amacrine Cells
B. — Bipolar Cells
C. — Cones
G. — Ganglion Cells
H. — Horizontal Cells
P. — Pigment Cells
R. — Rods

PROJECTION ON LEFT
OCCIPITAL LOBE

PROJECTION
ON RIGHT
OCCIPITAL
LOBE

F. Netter
M.D.

Plate 12   Optic system

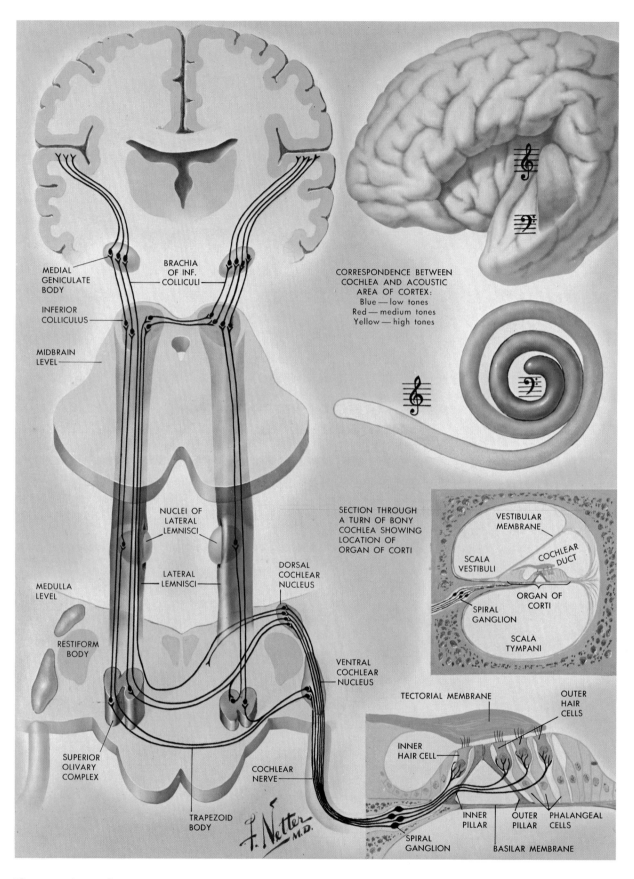

MEDIAL GENICULATE BODY

BRACHIA OF INF. COLLICULI

INFERIOR COLLICULUS

MIDBRAIN LEVEL

NUCLEI OF LATERAL LEMNISCI

LATERAL LEMNISCI

DORSAL COCHLEAR NUCLEUS

MEDULLA LEVEL

RESTIFORM BODY

VENTRAL COCHLEAR NUCLEUS

SUPERIOR OLIVARY COMPLEX

COCHLEAR NERVE

TRAPEZOID BODY

CORRESPONDENCE BETWEEN COCHLEA AND ACOUSTIC AREA OF CORTEX:
Blue — low tones
Red — medium tones
Yellow — high tones

SECTION THROUGH A TURN OF BONY COCHLEA SHOWING LOCATION OF ORGAN OF CORTI

VESTIBULAR MEMBRANE

SCALA VESTIBULI

COCHLEAR DUCT

ORGAN OF CORTI

SPIRAL GANGLION

SCALA TYMPANI

TECTORIAL MEMBRANE

OUTER HAIR CELLS

INNER HAIR CELL

INNER PILLAR

OUTER PILLAR

PHALANGEAL CELLS

SPIRAL GANGLION

BASILAR MEMBRANE

F. Netter M.D.

Plate 13   Acoustic system

Highlight 3-3

Weber's Law

One of the fundamental laws in psychology is known as Weber's Law, after its discoverer, Ernst Weber. It is called a psychophysical law because it describes a relation between physical and psychological events. Weber's Law states that the amount of increase in stimulation that is just noticeable by a human observer is a constant proportion of the starting level of stimulation. For example, suppose you determine that someone carrying a 50-pound load can detect the addition of 1 more pound to the load. Additions less than 1 pound are not noticed. So we say that the *just noticeable difference*, or *jnd*, is 1 pound. This is also called the *difference threshold*. It takes a change of 1 pound in 50 to produce a jnd, so the ratio is:

$$\frac{1}{50} = .02 \text{ or } 2\%$$

Weber's Law says that regardless of the starting weight, it will take a 2 percent increase in weight to be just noticeable. So if you were carrying 25 pounds, we would have to add 2 percent of 25, or 0.5 pounds, before you would notice the increase in weight. If you were starting with 100 pounds, we would have to add 2 pounds, and if you were starting with only a 1-pound box of candy, we would only have to add 0.02 pounds for you to detect it.

Weber's Law appears to hold quite well for middle ranges of values, but breaks down somewhat at extreme values—when the starting weights are extremely small or extremely large. It also applies to just about every dimension you can think of, including judging the height of a building, the loudness of a radio, the number of people in a crowd, and probably the price of merchandise. You could easily get away with a 10-cent increase in the price of a new car, but increasing the price of a roll of Life Savers by 10 cents would quickly be detected or noticed by customers.

The fraction above, 1/50 for weights, is called the *Weber fraction*, and it is a measure of how sensitive we are in various judgments. The smaller the fraction, the more sensitive we are. A fraction of 1/25 would mean we could detect a 4-percent change. Below are some actual Weber fraction values for different sense modalities. Note that the real Weber fraction for lifting weights is, more accurately, 1/53.

Dimension	Weber Fraction	Percent Change Needed to Notice a Difference
Pitch	1/333	0.3
Deep pressure	1/77	1.3
Brightness of a light	1/62	1.6
Lifted weight	1/53	1.9
Held weight	1/30	3.3
Loudness of a tone	1/11	8.8
Smell—amount of rubber smell	1/10	10.4
Pressure on the skin surface	1/7	13.6
Taste—amount of salty taste	1/5	20.0

Weber's Law states that within a dimension the fraction is a constant, independent of the starting value. Between dimensions, however, the fraction can differ and represents how sensitive that sensory system is—the table shows that your sense of pitch change is much better than your sense of change in salty taste. Thus, by this measure, your ears are more sensitive than your tongue.

---

detail. Our visual acuity is very poor under low light conditions and steadily improves with increases in illumination, as shown in Figure 3–9. Like the dark-adaptation function (Figure 3–7), the increase in acuity shown in Figure 3–9 has two branches: a lower one, corresponding to rod vision; and an upper one, corresponding to cone vision. The level of illumination at which your eye switches from rods to cones is the level of the light from the full moon on a clear night.

Under ideal conditions the resolution of our visual system is remarkable. In the laboratory a person with normal vision can detect a fine black line with an angular width of 0.5 seconds of arc. Such resolution is equivalent to detecting a one-quarter

TABLE 3–2 Power Function Exponent for Various Sensory Modalities

Modality	Exponent
Brightness	0.33
Loudness	0.60
Finger span	1.30
Heaviness	1.45
Length	1.04
Taste (NaCl)	0.41
Saturation (red)	1.70
Electric shock	2.50

Source: based on R. Teghtsoonian, "On the exponent in Stevens' Law and the constant in Ekman's Law," *Psychological Review,* 1971, *78,* 71–80.

FIGURE 3-9 Visual acuity as a function of light intensity

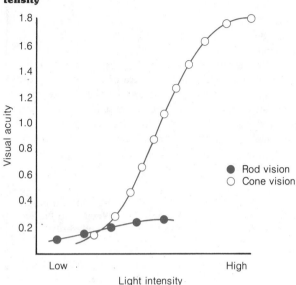

Visual acuity depends upon the intensity of light. Our acuity is much better in daylight than at night.

FIGURE 3-11 Visual acuity tests

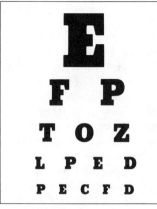

Above are two patterns commonly used for clinical tests of visual acuity. The Snellen letters (on the left) use lines and spaces that become progressively smaller as one reads down the chart. The Landolt C pattern (on the right) requires the viewer to locate the position of the gap—up, down, right, or left. The viewing chart consists of a series of C patterns of decreasing gap size. This test is somewhat more sensitive than the Snellen test, because the perceiver might be able to name a Snellen letter correctly even though only part of it was seen.

inch black wire against the bright sky from more than a mile and a half away!

In the laboratory, visual resolution can be measured using visual gratings like those shown in Figure 3–10. In a well-lighted room, find the distance from your eyes to this page at which the right-hand grating (the finest) is just visible. As you move the page farther away, the right grating will disappear, although the other two remain visible. Repeat the measurement in a dimly lighted room and notice how much closer you have to be to the book in order to see the lines of the grating.

FIGURE 3-10 Grating patterns used in laboratory measurements of visual resolution

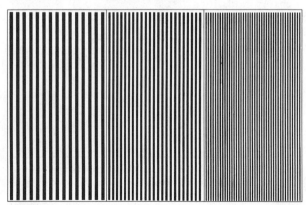

When you visit an optometrist or an ophthalmologist (eye doctors) to have your eyes checked, he or she will first measure your visual acuity. The doctor will not use grating patterns (except in certain specialized clinics and research laboratories; see "What Does It Mean?") but will probably use a letter chart like the one shown in Figure 3–11. Nevertheless, the doctor will measure your resolution threshold—the size of the letter that you can read with 75 percent accuracy. The Dutch ophthalmologist Snell was the first to determine the size letter the average person can read on the eye chart while standing 20 feet away.

If at 20 feet from the chart you are just able to read that size print with about 75 percent accuracy, you have a Snellen visual acuity of 20/20, which is considered normal. If you are able to read finer print, which a normal person could read only by standing at 15 feet from the chart, your Snellen visual acuity is 20/15, better than normal. On the other hand, if you can just read print standing at 20 feet that a normal person is able to read standing at 40 feet from the chart, your acuity is 20/40, which is below normal.

How Do We Perceive Color?

One of the important functions of the sensory processes is to represent the perceptual qualities of surfaces of objects. Of these different experiences the most important is the experience of color. In daylight vision, the sensory processes are able to produce a wide variety of color experiences that better enable you to tell one object from another. Color is a descriptive name for a set of experiences; it is not a physical property of light. A lot is known about color vision and the mechanisms that produce it. Certain individuals do not have normal sensory mechanisms and do not, therefore, have normal color vision. Such people are (incorrectly) called color blind.

Color experiences are actually composed of three separate and independent experiences (psychological dimensions): hue, saturation, and brightness. **Hue** is the dimension of color experience to which we give different qualitative names, like red, violet, blue, yellow, purple, and green. The second dimension of color experience is called **saturation,** which is a description of how intense the hue experience is. For example, white light is a completely unsaturated color experience. Pink is a partially saturated color, while red is deeply saturated. The third dimension of color is **brightness,** an experience that ranges from light to dark. Black and white form the two extremes of the experience. Navy blue, for example, is relatively dark compared with powder blue. Since any color experience may be described by its hue, saturation, and brightness, all possible colors may be represented in a three-dimensional color solid (Color Plate 2).

What perceptual mechanism produces color experiences from the physical energy contained in light? Color Plate 3 presents a schematic diagram of the color mechanism along with a representation of the various hues and saturations the mechanism can produce. This mechanism creates color experiences by comparing the rate at which the three kinds of cone receptors absorb quanta of light. Figure 3–4 shows how the three types of cones differ in their sensitivity to different wavelengths. The electrical signal generated in a cone is proportional to the number of quanta absorbed by it. Therefore, if the light falling on the retina contains mostly long wavelength quanta, then the R-cones will give a signal larger than either the G- or B-cones. Light containing mostly short wavelengths, on the other hand, will cause the B-cones to generate the largest electrical signal. Light containing equal amounts of all the visible wavelengths will cause equal activity in all three types of cones.

The electrical activity of the three cone types is only the beginning. Next, neural mechanisms, called opponent process channels, compare the activity of the cones with each other. There are two of these channels, and their activity is combined to form the color experiences of hue and saturation. The first channel, the R/G channel, compares the activity in the R-cones with the activity in the G-cones. If the two are equal, the R/G channel does not change its resting signal to the brain. If, however, the R-cone is absorbing more quanta than the G-cone, the R/G channel increases its activity. If the G-cone is absorbing more quanta than the R-cone, the R/G channel decreases its activity.

The second color channel, the Y/B channel, compares activity of the B-cones with the summed activity of the R- and G-cones (R + G). If the light falling on the retina contained mostly short wavelengths, the B-cones would be most active, and the Y/B channel would decrease its signal to the brain. If the R- and G-cones were absorbing more quanta than the B-cones, the Y/B channel would increase its signal.

Color experience results from different combinations of signals from the R/G and Y/B channels. These possible combinations are represented in Color Plate 3 as a color surface (a slice through the color solid in Color Plate 2). The exact color, hue, and saturation you experience depends upon the place on the color surface that is stimulated by the activity of the two color channels. For example, if the two channels are both signaling at their resting level, the color experience you will have is colorless (white or gray), as shown in the middle of the color surface. High activity in the R/G channel combined with medium activity on the Y/B channel creates the perception of red. A medium activity on the R/G channel and a high activity on the Y/B channel creates the perception of yellow. A low activity on both channels creates the perception of purple.

The color experiences generated by light of single wavelengths (monochromatic light) are also shown in Color Plate 3. These experiences are as far away from the white center as possible and are therefore the most saturated colors that are possible to experience. Notice that the color purple cannot be created by the light of a single wavelength. In order to see purple, the color mechanisms must be presented with several wavelengths simultaneously — in this case, long and short wavelengths.

Color Plate 3 also predicts what color you will experience if two lights are mixed together. If you mixed monochromatic light of 400 nm with 700 nm light, the color perceived in the mixture would be one of the colors that falls along the straight line connecting these two points. The exact color depends on the relative amounts of each light. If the straight line connecting two colors passes through the point marked "white," the two colors are said to be *complementary colors.* Two complementary colors, when mixed together in the correct proportions, will produce an experience lacking in hue (see Color Plates 4, 5, and 6).

There is a third mechanism in the perceptual process shown in Color Plate 3. This channel, the L channel (for "luminance"—also known as the brightness channel), signals the total quantal absorption of the R-, G-, and B-cones. The activity in the L channel is the main determinant of the perceptual experience of brightness, although brightness is somewhat influenced by the activities in the R/G and Y/B channels. To summarize, there are three channels: R/G and Y/B together determine the experiences of hue and saturation; the L channel largely determines how light or dark the color is.

Color Blindness

Some people do not have normal color mechanisms. These people are missing one or more of the three types of cones. The most common type of color deficiency is red-green blindness caused by the lack of either the R-cones or the G-cones. These two types of red-green defective mechanisms are shown in Figure 3–12. An example of a test for red-green blindness is shown in Color Plate 7. Such people are called red-green blind because they are unable to distinguish between colors a normal person experiences as red and green. The term "color blind" is not really appropriate. Although the R/G color channel does not work properly in these defective perceptual mechanisms, the Y/B channel is almost completely normal. Careful experiments with people who are red-green blind in one eye, yet have normal color vision in the other eye (a rare condition—fewer than 50 cases have ever been reported) have shown that a red-green color blind person experiences the world in colors consisting of blue and yellow hues. Color Plate 8 attempts to represent the color experiences of various types of color-defective people.

In the retina both rods and cones are connected to ganglion cells. At daylight levels of light intensity, the cones are able to function, and therefore the signals that are sent to the brain by ganglion cells reflect cone activity. At night, however, the cones do not function and the rods take over. Ganglion cell signals to the brain then reflect rod activity. Take a good look at the color model in Color Plate 3. In order to operate properly, the opponent mechanisms need to get input from cones with different spectral sensitivities. But at night the three different types of cones are replaced by one type of rod, and the opponent color mechanisms now receive identical inputs. The result of this condition is that the R/G and the Y/B channels send signals to the brain indicating that all receptors are absorbing equal numbers of quanta, the condition that creates the perception of white.

When you are outside at night, you should notice that your perceptual experiences consist only of shades of gray. Objects appear as lighter or darker grays, but there are no experiences of hue. Because at night the rods are connected to the opponent channels, the same message is always sent to the brain—equal activity in all the receptors—regardless of the wavelength composition of the light. The only channel that can give different signals to the brain is the L channel, the one used to code brightness.

How Do We Perceive Brightness?

The experience of brightness depends upon the relative intensities of light coming from objects. In fact, the brightness of an object is closely related to its reflectance. This white page of paper reflects about 80 percent of the light falling on it, while the ink reflects about 5 percent (a 16 to 1 ratio for the paper over the ink). When you look at this page, your cone receptors are absorbing about 16 times as many quanta per

FIGURE 3–12   Red-green color blindness

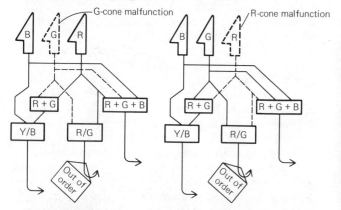

Two conditions are responsible for red-green blindness: a lack of G-cones (left) or a lack of R-cones (right). In both cases the missing cones affect the R/G color channel but not the Y/B color channel.

FIGURE 3–13   Brightness contrast

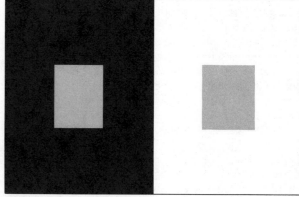

Even though the two center squares reflect exactly the same amount of light to your eye, the one on the right appears darker because of the contrast effect with the white surrounding area.

second as the receptors receiving light reflected from the black letters of the print. This ratio (16 to 1) remains constant regardless of the intensity of illumination on the page. Because ganglion cells in the retina are sensitive to the relative intensity of light falling on the center and the surround of their receptive fields, objects keep their same brightness in bright sunlight and in a darkened room. A lump of coal will look black in your cellar or in daylight because in both cases it reflects less light to your eye than other objects around it.

This constancy of object brightness over a wide range of illumination levels is called **brightness constancy.** It is one of a number of perceptual constancies and reflects a general principle of the perceptual processes: Perceptual properties of objects remain constant in spite of widely changing viewing conditions. Think how unstable the world around you would be if a piece of paper, for example, changed in appearance from black to white when you went from a darkened room to bright sunlight.

The perception of brightness is not just a function of reflectance. The brightness of a surface also depends on the brightness of adjacent objects. Figure 3–13 contains two small squares that are reflecting equal amounts of light to your eye. Yet the squares do not appear equally bright. The square on the right, surrounded by a white field, appears darker than the one on the left, surrounded by a black field. This phenomenon is called *brightness contrast* and is based on the fact that the retinal areas adjacent to each square are not being equally stimulated. *Color contrast* is a similar effect. If the surrounding areas were a saturated color (bright blue, for example) the complementary color would appear in the center instead of the gray (yellow in this example).

Figure 3–14 shows two other examples in which the perceived brightness of a surface does not correspond to the luminance of the light coming from the surface, but is influenced by the luminance of adjacent areas as well. Although each of the strips in the left figure reflects light uniformly (the left side of each

FIGURE 3–14   Brightness perception as a consequence of the receptive fields of ganglion cells

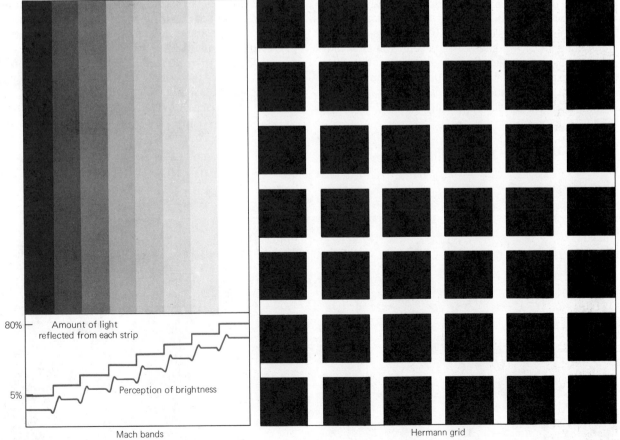

Mach bands

Hermann grid

The strips in the left figure are of uniform luminance, although they appear very uneven in brightness. In the right figure the gray spots at the intersection of the white strips do not exist in the light; they are a perceptual effect.

strip reflects exactly as much light as the right side), they do not appear to be at all uniform in brightness. This perceptual effect is a consequence of the visual system's ability to enhance edges. The dark and light zones at the edge of each strip are called Mach bands, after Ernst Mach who described them in the nineteenth century. In the Hermann grid, the drawing on the right of Figure 3–14, the light reflected from the white areas is uniform in all places, yet in the regions of the four black corners, light gray spots appear. These spots are creations of your perceptual system and do not correspond to lower light intensity from these regions. Both of these perceptual phenomena are due to the circular, center-surround organization of ganglion cell receptive fields.

Perception of Objects: Constructive Processes

The perceptual processes constantly answer two important questions: "What is out there?" and "Where is it?" Our internal representation of the world is filled with objects. Our perceptual processes rarely fail to create representations of objects out of the physical input to the visual system. Even if the physical stimulus is ambiguous, an internal representation of some object will be produced. This fact leads different people, exposed to the same physical stimulus, to experience entirely different things (see Chapter 6 for a discussion of eye-witness testimony).

Physiological Processes in Object Perception

Many of the retinal ganglion cells send their signals to the visual cortex of the brain through the lateral geniculate body (see Color Plate 12 and Chapter 2). There is an orderly relationship between a region of the retina and a region in the visual cortex. It has been known for a long time — from studies of patients with strokes and soldiers wounded on the battlefield — that injury to a restricted region of the visual cortex causes blindness in a restricted region of the visual field. Figure 3–15 shows the extent of vision (the visual fields) of the left and right eyes of a person with normal vision. There is a blind area in each eye (the black oval area on each field) where the blood vessels and the optic nerves enter the eye. Figure 3–16 demonstrates the action of this blind spot. Each eye is able to see more than 100 degrees to the outside, about 60 degrees on the nasal side, and about 60 degrees up and down. Figure 3–17 is a photograph of a soldier shortly after surgical removal of most of the left visual cortex, which had been extensively damaged by shell fragments. The patient was completely unable to detect objects in his right visual field and was also blind in regions of his left visual field as well, due to some additional damage to his right visual cortex. This man, lives a normal and productive life in spite of these losses in his visual fields.

Why are the cells in the visual cortex so important to our perception of objects? About 22 years ago, the studies of cell function in the visual cortex by D. H. Hubel and T. N. Wiesel revolutionized our think-

FIGURE 3–15   Normal vision field

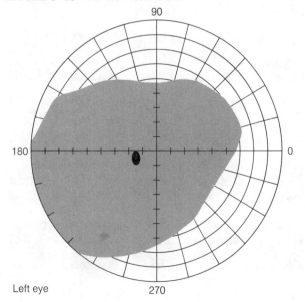

Left eye

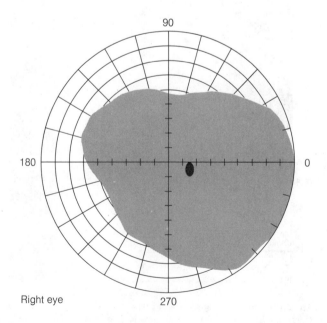

Right eye

FIGURE 3-16 Blind spot demonstration

Do you find this person annoying? Make him disappear by positioning his image on the blind spot of your right eye. Close your left eye and fixate the cross with your right eye. At a view- ing distance of about 14 inches, the face will disappear but the vertical lines will not.

ing about the visual cortex. These investigators made two exciting discoveries. The first is that each cell in the visual cortex does not "look" at a single point on the retina or in visual space, but has a receptive field that is relatively large—in some cases more than five degrees of visual angle. The second important discovery made by Hubel and Wiesel was that each cell is very particular about the kind of visual stimulus that changes its activity. Each cell responds only to an edge or a bar of a specific orientation (Figure 3-18). Hubel and Wiesel found that different cells in the cortex are sensitive to different specific orientations. It seems that

these cortical cells function as edge and orientation detectors.

When you look at a vertical line or edge, only the cells in your visual cortex sensitive to vertical orientation are active; the cells sensitive to other orientations are relatively inactive. If the line is rotated from the vertical, a whole different set of cells, those sensitive to the new orientation of the line, become active. Figure 3-19 demonstrates how it is possible to fatigue a set of neurons sensitive to one particular orientation. In this demonstration, looking at the vertical lines on the left side of Figure 3-19 cause the cells sensitive to vertical orientations to become less sensitive. Thus, when you look at the right side of the figure, the faint vertical lines in the drawing disappear. There is still considerable scientific debate over the exact role played by cortical neurons, but it is clear that without the visual cortex, our ability to perceive objects normally disappears (see "What Does It Mean?").

Psychological Processes in Object Perception

The objects we experience have properties we describe as shape, size, texture, color, distance, and location. The perceptual processes for representing some of these properties were first described by the Gestalt psychologists in the first two decades of this century. The fundamental principle of perceptual organization is called **Prägnanz,** or "goodness of figure." This principle states that the perceptual processes form objects by grouping visual elements together in the simplest manner possible. What is represented by the

FIGURE 3-17 Soldier after battlefield injury prior to cosmetic surgery

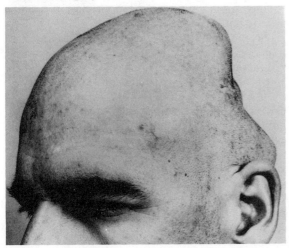

FIGURE 3-18   Mapping the receptive field of a cell in the visual cortex

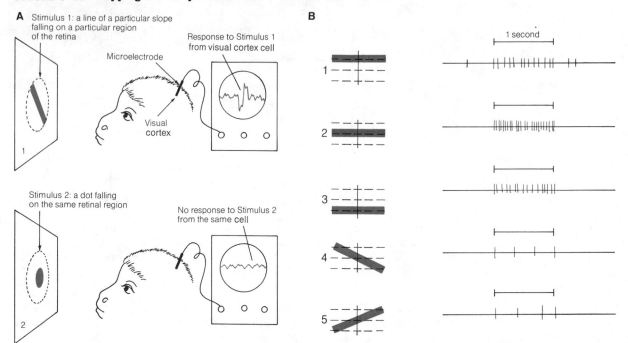

A Stimulus 1: a line of a particular slope falling on a particular region of the retina

Microelectrode

Response to Stimulus 1 from visual cortex cell

Visual cortex

Stimulus 2: a dot falling on the same retinal region

No response to Stimulus 2 from the same cell

B

1 second

Mapping the receptive field of a cell with a micro-electrode implanted in the cortex. Panel A shows that single cortical cells are sensitive to stimuli of a particular type and from a particular area of the retina. In this case, only the slanted bar, and not the dot, elicits a cortical response. The responses of a single cortical cell to five different bar stimuli are shown in panel B. Note that the cell responds mainly to the horizontal bar and hardly responds at all to the slanted bars. Note too that the cell is also somewhat sensitive to location—it fires maximally when the horizontal bar is in the center of the field and responds less when the bar is higher or lower in the visual field. The bar was present for 1 second, indicated by the line above each of the five records.

FIGURE 3-19   Selective adaptation

Look at the center of the left panel for two minutes, then look at the right drawing. The "rain" will disappear for a few seconds. Two minutes of looking at the vertical lines causes "fatigue" in the detectors so that they cannot detect the light vertical lines of the rain.

two elements labeled "3" in Figure 3–20A? Most people would say that there are two rectangles, one behind the other. The principle of Prägnanz predicts this perception because it is simpler to perceive two rectangles, one blocking part of the other, than to perceive a rectangle with a second figure cut out to fit in the manner shown in Figure 3–20B. Figure 3–21 illustrates some other Gestalt principles: *proximity, similarity,* and *closure.*

Sometimes the information in a stimulus is ambiguous and does not permit a unique perceptual organization. Look at the top portion of Figure 3–22. It is possible to perceive the drawing as a rabbit or as a duck. As your perceptual processes try to determine which is "better," your experience of the drawing alternates between the two. It does not seem possible to perceive both the rabbit and the duck at the same time. As soon as we provide other visual information, our perceptual experience becomes stabilized either as the rabbit or as the duck. The same is true of the bottom portion of the figure, where we may see either a young girl or an old woman. Figure 3–22 allows you to experience the dynamic nature of the perceptual process.

FIGURE 3-20   Depth perception

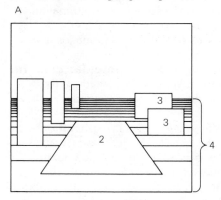

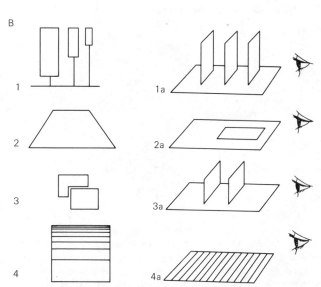

The Prägnanz principle of organization as applied to perception of depth. (A) is a drawing of a surface that can be seen either as stretching away from the eye (in depth) or as a flat, two-dimensional surface. Parts (A1–A4) illustrate monocular depth cues. In (A1) the three posts could have been due to (B1) or (B1a). Which seems simpler? In (A2) the shape could be a trapezoid (B2) or a square (B2a). Which seems simpler? In (A3), one rectangle could be missing a corner (B3) or be behind the nearer one (B3a). Which seems simpler? In (A4) the textured surface could be progressively finer near the top of the picture (B4) or could be stretching away (B4a). Which seems simpler? In each case, organizing the scene in depth permits the objects to be simpler in form; the posts are all the same size, the shape on the floor is regular, the two rectangles are the same, and the textured floor is uniform. For these reasons, the flat scene is perceived as three-dimensional, because that is the simplest perception.

FIGURE 3-21   The Gestalt principles

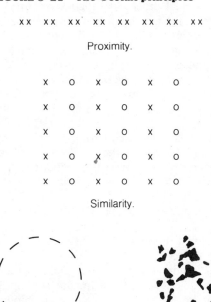

Proximity.

Similarity.

Closure.

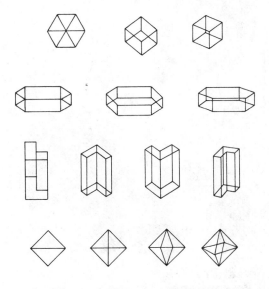

According to the Prägnanz principle, the first member of each series of ambiguous drawings is perceived as two-dimensional and the others as three-dimensional, because these are the simplest ways of perceiving the drawings.

FIGURE 3-22 Reversible figures

Reversible figures demonstrate in a convincing fashion that perception is a joint product of the information contained in the stimulus and internal constructuve processes. The perceiver can construct either of two interpretations from the same data, giving rise to a reversible or ambiguous figure. The rabbit-duck figure in the top drawing was used in 1900 by psychologist Joseph Jastrow as an example of rival-schemata ambiguity. When it is a rabbit, the face looks to the right; when it is a duck, the face looks to the left. It is difficult to see both duck and rabbit at the same time. What are the two interpretations in the bottom figure?

Psychological Processes in Depth Perception

An important aspect of object perception has to do with where objects are relative to each other and to you. Your ability to represent the distance and depth of objects is called **depth perception.** Two sources

of information are used by your perceptual processes to construct depth representations—information extracted from the retinal image of either eye alone (monocular cues to depth) and information that requires both eyes simultaneously (binocular cues to depth). The most important **monocular cues for depth** are partial overlap, size, shading (both attached and cast shadows), texture gradients, linear perspective, and motion parallax. Figure 3–23 illustrates some of these cues. **Motion parallax** is the relative motion of objects created when your head moves from side to side. When you look out the side window of a moving train or car, notice that distant objects seem to move slowly while closer objects move faster. The relative motion of these objects, caused by their being at different distances, is called motion parallax. Our visual system is very sensitive to this motion, and only a slight amount is needed to provide information about the relative depth of objects.

The other monocular cues to depth were discovered by fifteenth-century Italian Renaissance artists, who used them to portray three-dimensional scenes on flat canvas. With the proper use of the monocular cues the artist can achieve a remarkably realistic three-dimensional depth effect. Figure 3–24 is a sophisticated example of this ability. Modern artists, like Maurits Escher, by carefully considering the cues used by our perceptual processes, have been able to draw on flat surfaces pictures of "impossible" objects (see Figure 3–25).

The binocular information about depth is extracted by perceptual processes called **stereopsis,** which operates on the fact that the two eyes are separated horizontally in the head. Each eye views the world from a slightly different position, and therefore the retinal image of various objects at different distances from you falls on very slightly different positions in the retinal images of the two eyes. This difference in the retinal position of the image of an object in the left and right eyes is called **retinal disparity.** In the brain (probably in the visual cortex) are mechanisms that are very sensitive to this retinal disparity. These stereoscopic mechanisms extract the retinal disparity and use it to create the experience that objects are located at different depths.

When you look at a painting or photograph your stereoscopic processes negate the monocular depth cues by providing information that the scene is "really" a flat surface. Your experience of depth can be considerably enhanced if you view paintings and photographs with one eye (to eliminate stereopsis) and hold your head very still (to eliminate motion parallax). When viewed in this manner, many paintings and photographs produce surprisingly realistic depth experiences. Of course, the ultimate way to trick the perceptual processes is to combine all the

FIGURE 3-23 Monocular depth cues

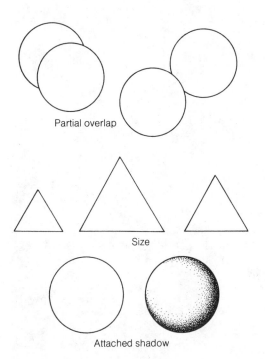

Partial overlap

Size

Attached shadow

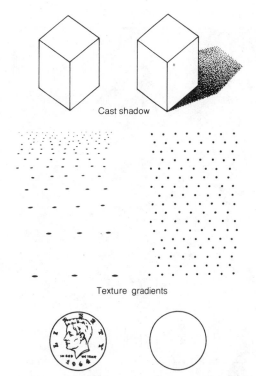

Cast shadow

Texture gradients

The two circles are actually identical in size, yet the filled circle may appear both larger and closer as a function of the fact that the space is filled.

The combined operation of two monocular cues to depth, texture gradients and linear perspective, gives rise to a strong sense of depth in this photograph.

FIGURE 3-24

Monocular cues to depth can fool us and make a two-dimensional object, in this case a painting, look like a three-dimensional dome.

monocular and binocular cues, as is done in a 3-D movie. Under these circumstances, the internal representation is so similar to real-life conditions that your behavior may be influenced by it (people often duck to avoid flying objects shown in 3-D film).

Perceptual Constancy

One of the most impressive capacities of our perceptual processes is their ability to maintain a stable internal representation of objects when the physical stimulus is constantly changing. Brightness constancy, which we have already discussed, is an example of this property. Look around you again. Notice that doors and windows look rectangular regardless of the angle at which you view them. The top of a drinking glass looks circular even though the retinal image is elliptical. This ability is called **shape constancy** —

the ability of the internal representation to maintain a constant shape of an object despite different viewing angles and distances.

Size constancy is the ability of the perceptual processes to represent an object as a constant size even though its retinal image may change drastically. Look at the two drawings of Figure 3–26. The stick figure in the left drawing is standing 10 feet away from the observer. In the right-hand drawing, the stick figure is 50 feet away. If you measure with a ruler the size of the image of the figure on the left, you will find that it is five times larger than the figure on the right. These drawings simulate the retinal image of the observer under the two viewing conditions. The retinal image of the farther figure is one-fifth that of the closer. Yet even in the drawing the left stick figure does not look five times larger than the right one: the size of the two figures remains unchanged in spite of the changes

Highlight 3-4

Impossible But Perceivable Shapes

Psychologists and artists have been especially ingenious at drawing forms that have impossible relationships among the components. Figure 3-25 illustrates three of these. None of these drawings could be translated into touchable three-dimensional objects, but their interest resides in how perceivers can be fooled when looking at them as two-dimensional line drawings. Actually, of course, we are not fooled. We see the drawings as impossible. But it is hard to do so, because if we look at any one place on one of them, the information is quite consistent. It is as if we expect them to be a certain way based on one view, and then when we move our eyes to look at some other part, it is inconsistent with our expectations. Although nobody has fully explained how these are perceived, again we seem to have a case in which our expectations are important in telling us what we perceive and how to construct it. When these expectations are not met, then we are fooled.

FIGURE 3-25 Two-dimensional drawings of impossible three-dimensional forms

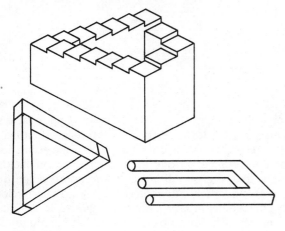

M. C. Escher, *Relativity.* © BEELDRECHT, Amsterdam/VAGA, New York 1982 Collection Haags Gemeentemuseum—The Hague.

in retinal image size. We "know" that the person remains the same size. This knowledge, based on our internal representation, plays a role in size constancy.

What is the basis of this ability? Our knowledge certainly plays a role, at least for familiar objects like people, but it is not necessary for size constancy. Experiments using unfamiliar objects as test stimuli have shown that our perceptual processes can produce reasonably accurate internal representations of the true size of objects at distances as great as three-quarters of a mile! How do the perceptual processes manage this constancy?

Size constancy seems to involve two separate processes, illustrated in Figure 3-27. One process analyzes the size of the retinal image and the other figures out how far away the object is. As shown in the lower part of Figure 3-27, the retinal image size alone does not determine the physical size of an object; one must also know the distance from the observer. One way in which the process could estimate the real size of an object is to multiply the estimate of the retinal image size by the estimated distance of the object. The result of this kind of calculation is the magnitude of the real size in the internal representation of the object.

An important characteristic of the model shown in Figure 3-27 is that the accuracy of the represented size is only as good as the accuracy of the estimations of retinal size and of object distance. Retinal image size is accurately registered since it is present directly on the retina. But the estimate of the object's distance is another matter, depending upon the quality of the monocular and binocular cues for depth. If you could "trick" the process into giving an inaccurate estimate of object distance, then the perception of object size would also be inaccurate.

FIGURE 3-26   Size constancy

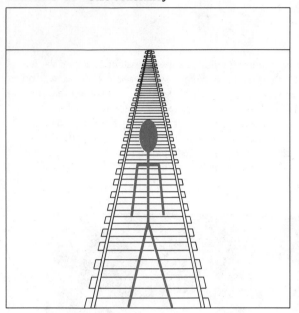
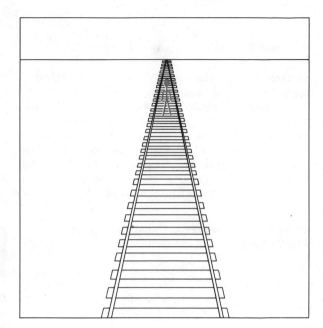

Many visual illusions are thought to be a consequence of the size constancy processes being fed inaccurate distance information. The most famous illusion, one that has fascinated people for centuries, is the moon illusion: The moon appears considerably larger when it is at the horizon than when it is overhead. This effect is not an optical or a physical effect; it is a perceptual effect. Let's look more closely at what happens.

The reality of the moon is that it is a ball 2,000 miles in diameter located 289,000 miles from the earth. Both the actual size and distance are outside the range of our experience. There is no way for the distance process to represent 289,000 miles accurately. As a result, when we look at the moon, the estimation of the distance is completely dependent on factors other than the true distance of the moon. When the moon is overhead, there is absolutely no information the perceptual process can use to estimate its distance. There are no other objects nearby, no texture gradients, and no stereoscopic cues. Under these circum-

FIGURE 3-27   Processing of binocular and monocular information

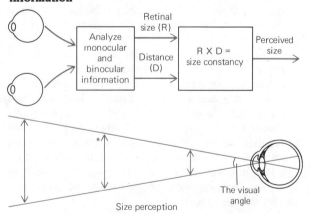

What you expect to see often determines what you do see. Most motorists passing the Illinois state line didn't see anything wrong with this sign.

stances the distance coming out of the perceptual process in Figure 3–27 is greatly underestimated. When the moon is near the horizon, its distance can be estimated relative to objects in the field of vision, to the texture gradients of the ground, and to the interposition of the horizon itself. Thus the message from the perceptual process is that the moon is at least as far away as the horizon. This difference between the estimate of distance over space that is filled with objects (to the horizon) and the estimate of distance over unfilled space (overhead) is a well-known phenomenon.

Filled spaces are judged to be longer than unfilled spaces. Subjects in one experiment were asked to estimate the distance of an airplane. The plane was always located 10,000 feet from the observers. When it flew close to the horizon, it was estimated to be 15,800 feet away; when it flew overhead, it was estimated to be only 6,200 feet away.

The reason for the moon illusion should now be clear, and is illustrated schematically in Figure 3–28. The retinal image size of the moon is a constant (0.5 degrees of visual angle) regardless of its position in the sky, and therefore the perceptual process estimate of its retinal size remains constant. But the estimate of the moon's distance is highly dependent upon its position in the sky. When the moon

Considering distance and the size of the retinal image, you can accurately perceive the people in the foreground, middle ground, and background as being approximately the same size. This phenomenon is called size constancy.

is at the horizon, the perceptual process estimates that it is 2.5 to 4.0 times farther away than when it is overhead. Consequently, the size constancy mechanism calculates an estimated "true" size that is from 2.5 to 4.0 times larger for the horizon moon than for the overhead moon (see Figure 3–28).

Visual illusions have fascinated psychologists, because if we could understand how they occur we would have important information about how the visual system normally operates. In Figure 3–29, three visual illusions are shown that may be created in much the same manner as the moon illusion discussed above—through the misapplication of distance cues. In the Ponzo illusion, the two horizontal lines are physically equal in length, although the upper one appears longer. The size constancy explanation suggests that our perceptual processes estimate that the upper line is farther away than the lower line (largely due to the perspective cues) and thus the upper one is made to appear larger (since the two lines have the same size retinal image). Can you think of similar explanations for the other illusions in Figure 3–29?

"Excuse me for shouting—I thought you were farther away."

If you were a giant and thought everyone else was too, then the simplest perception in this case would be that the man on the left is a giant who is far away.

FIGURE 3-28 **Moon illusion**

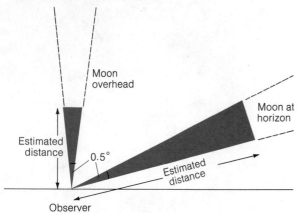

The moon appears larger when it is at the horizon because it "appears" farther away. This effect is entirely psychological.

FIGURE 3-29 **Visual illusions**

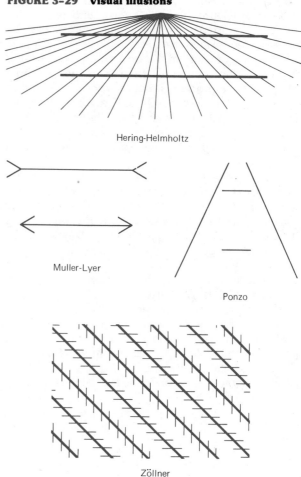

Hering-Helmholtz

Muller-Lyer

Ponzo

Zöllner

Four types of visual illusions thought to be due to a "misapplication" of distance cues.

Auditory Sensory Processing

Although our most accurate information concerning objects comes from visual perceptual processes, the auditory processes contribute a large amount of important information to our internal representation of the world. Since many of the principles in audition are similar to those in vision, we will examine auditory perception more briefly.

The Physical Nature of the Auditory Stimulus

The air around us is composed of various types of molecules. Sound waves are disturbances in the normally uniform pressure of these molecules caused by

The New Yorker, October 6, 1980. Drawing by Levin; © 1980 The New Yorker Magazine, Inc.

vibrating objects. As a vibrating object moves back and forth, it alternately compresses and rarefies the air around it. These waves of compressions and rarefactions then spread out through the air at a rate of about 331 meters per second (760 miles per hour).

The simplest kind of sound is the sound produced by a tuning fork. Such a sound is called a *pure tone* and is shown on the left in Figure 3–30. The time a sound wave takes to complete one cycle of compression and rarefaction is called its *period*. The more common way to express the time aspect of sound is by its *frequency*—the number of cycles completed in one second of time. We are sensitive to sounds ranging in frequency from about 20 cycles per second (abbreviated Hz for Hertz) all the way up to 20,000 Hz. A second aspect of a simple tone is its *amplitude*, expressed in pressure units—dynes per

FIGURE 3-30   Pure and complex tones

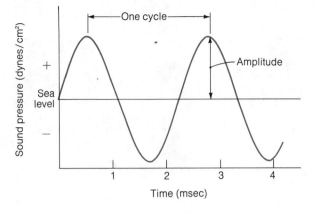

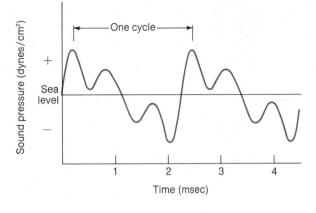

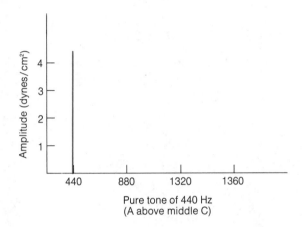

Pure tone of 440 Hz
(A above middle C)

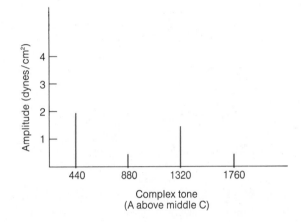

Complex tone
(A above middle C)

square centimeter. Under ideal conditions we can detect sound pressure changes of about 0.0002 dynes/cm². The most intense sound pressure we can hear without doing physical damage to the ear is about 200 dynes/cm², a pressure range of 1 million to 1. To avoid the use of very small numbers (like those above), sound amplitude is usually converted by a logarithmic transformation to **decibels** (dB). The lowest amplitude we can hear is 0 dB, while the highest amplitude before pain and damage sets in is about 120 dB. Figure 3-31 gives the amplitude of common sounds in decibels.

The simple tone on the left of Figure 3-30 is called a *sine wave tone,* because of the mathematical description of its shape. Most of the sounds in nature, however, are not simple sine waves in shape. The sounds produced by the vocal cords and by musical instruments, for example, have complex wave forms, like the one shown on the right side of Figure 3-30. A complex tone may be described as a composite of many simple sine wave tones. The lowest frequency of the complex sound is called its *fundamental fre-*

quency. The simple and the complex waves shown in Figure 3-30 have the same fundamental frequency, 440 Hz. In addition, the complex sound contains other frequencies, called harmonics or overtones. The second harmonic has a frequency twice that of the fundamental, the third harmonic has a frequency three times that of the fundamental, and so on. A very complex tone will have up to 20 or 30 harmonics, while a less complex tone will have only a few. A simple tone, of course, has only the fundamental frequency. The lower half of Figure 3-30 illustrates the harmonic content of the simple and the complex wave forms shown.

The Ear

Sound pressure waves are converted into nerve impulses in the ear. The ear consists of three major structures, shown in Figure 3-32. Sounds enter the *outer ear* and cause the eardrum to vibrate in the same manner as the sounds themselves. The vibrations of the eardrum are transmitted to the *inner ear*

FIGURE 3-31 The decibel scale

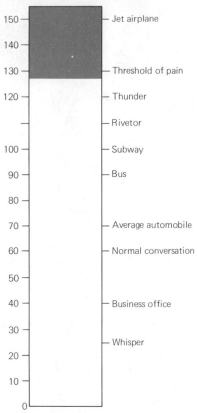

The intensities of various common sounds in decibels (dB). The take-off blast of the Saturn V moon rocket, measured at the launching pad, was approximately 180 dB. For laboratory rats, prolonged exposure to 150 dB causes death.

FIGURE 3-32 The major parts of the ear

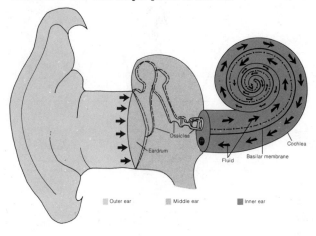

FIGURE 3-33 Map of the basilar membrane

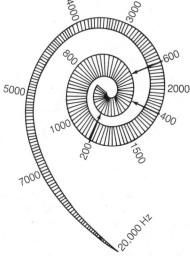

The location on the basilar membrane that receives maximum stimulation depends upon the frequency of the sound.

by the three bones (ossicles) of the *middle ear.* These bones, the smallest in the human body, are named after their shapes: the malleus (hammer), the incus (anvil), and the stapes (stirrup).

The inner ear is a coiled tube 34 mm long. It is called the **cochlea** after the Greek word for snail. The cochlea is filled with fluid and is divided down its length by a flexible membrane, the **basilar membrane.** Sound vibrations in the inner ear cause standing waves which bend and distort the basilar membrane. The exact place where the bending is maximum is determined largely by the frequency content of the sound. Figure 3-33 is a map of the basilar membrane indicating that low frequencies (for example, 200 Hz) stimulate the basilar membrane at one end while high frequencies (20,000 Hz) stimulate the other end. The simple tone shown in Figure 3-30 would stimulate the basilar membrane maximally at the place corresponding to 440 Hz (see Figure 3-33), while the complex tone shown in Figure 3-30 would stimulate the basilar membrane in four

different places: those corresponding to 440, 880, 1320, and 1760 Hz. Georg von Békésy was awarded the Nobel Prize for figuring out exactly how the basilar membrane works. The receptors that convert vibrations on the basilar membrane into nerve impulses are called **hair cells** because stiff hairs protrude from their top. The axons of the hairs cells come together to form the auditory division of the acoustic nerve which carries the information into the brain for further processing. This auditory division is sometimes called the *cochlear nerve* (see Color Plates 10 and 13). The hair cells are very sensitive to the bending of the basilar membrane. If the basilar membrane bends too much, as it will with sounds over about 120 dB, the hair cells will be permanently damaged, and a loss of hearing will occur (See "What Does It Mean?").

Experiential Sensitivity to Sound

Our ears are not equally sensitive to all sound frequencies. Figure 3–34 shows how much sound pressure (in decibels) is required to detect sounds of various frequencies. As we have noted, the lowest frequency our auditory system can transform into an auditory experience is about 20 Hz. The upper limit is about 20,000 Hz, but this limit tends to decrease with increasing age. From Figure 3–34 you can see that although you need only 0 dB to detect a tone of 1,000 Hz, you need 60 dB to detect a 30 Hz sound (60 dB is 1,000 times the pressure of 0 dB).

For human beings, the most important function of hearing is its role in communication by speech. In Figure 3–34 the levels and frequencies of normal conversational speech are shown. In order to comprehend speech the ear must be able to hear these frequencies. There is an upper limit to the sound pressures that the ear can tolerate. This limit is about 120 dB for all frequencies. This sound pressure will cause discomfort and a buzzing in the ears. Above this pressure you risk physical damage to your ears. If after exposure to a loud sound you experience a ringing that lasts for more than a second or two, the sound was too intense for safety.

FIGURE 3–34 The pressure and frequency ranges of hearing

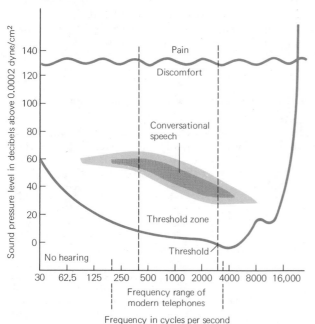

Electronic amplification is used to increase the loudness of rock music. Extreme levels of loudness, however, can damage your ear and affect your ability to hear. (See "What Does it Mean?")

Psychological Dimensions of Auditory Experience

Auditory experiences differ on three major psychological dimensions—loudness, pitch, and timbre. People describe their experiences of **loudness** using words like "loud" and "soft," and in music, *forte, fortissimo, pianissimo,* and *piano.* The loudness of a tone depends not only on its physical intensity, but also on its frequency and complexity. As you can see in Figure 3–34, a 30 dB tone would be clearly audible if its frequency were 1,000 Hz, but would be inaudible if its frequency were 125 Hz.

The second psychological dimension of sound experience is that of **pitch.** It is the property that is described by words like "high" and "low." Musical scales are constructed out of tones having different pitches, arranged in ascending order. Sounds that evoke a strong sense of pitch are said to be musical. Other sounds, like the rustling of leaves, do not evoke a sense of pitch and are unmusical. Complex tones, containing a fundamental frequency and a number of harmonics (Figure 3–30), create a strong sense of pitch. The pitch corresponds to the frequency of the fundamental of the complex tone. Four tones—all having a fundamental frequency of 440 Hz, for example, but differing in the number and intensity of their harmonics—will be perceived as having the same pitch. There still is controversy about the nature of the mechanisms that create the sense of pitch. It is clear that the perception of pitch depends upon the pattern of stimulation on the basilar membrane.

The third major psychological dimensions of sound is **timbre.** Timbre is the psychological experience that allows you to distinguish sounds that have the same loudness and pitch. Timbre permits you to identify an oboe and a violin, even when they play the same note at the same loudness. Timbre is a qualitative dimension that is not well represented by words in our language. Some sounds are described as "nasal," while others are "rich" or "full." The experience of timbre depends largely on the physical complexity of a sound, that is, the number and intensity of the harmonics in a sound. A simple sine wave tone sounds dull and lifeless in comparison to an organ note. The organ note contains many harmonics, while the simple tone has only its fundamental frequency.

Perception of Music

One of the most creative of human activities has been the making of music. Although music has been created for centuries, only within the last 130 years has there developed a theoretical basis for understanding the effects of music. All music made in all cultures is based on the different psychological experiences created by the sequential (melody) and simultaneous (harmony) sounding of musical tones. Some of these combi-

nations are experienced as pleasant while others are experienced as unpleasant. The degree to which musical experiences are found to be pleasant is influenced by one's culture, but the quality of the experience is determined by the perceptual mechanisms that produce pitch, loudness, and timbre. A skillful composer creates music by carefully combining pleasant and unpleasant musical sounds in particular sequences to create a satisfying experience in the listener.

Ancient musicians discovered that certain notes or tones when sounded at the same time created very special psychological experiences. Western music is based on a sequence of eight notes arranged to form an ascending scale. Letter names are used to describe each note in the scale: C, D, E, F, G, A, B, and C. This sequence is the C-major scale, one of many possible scales. These are the notes sounded by playing the white keys on a piano. Notice on the scale that there are two notes called C (actually there are eight different C's in the entire range of musical notes, from a very low-pitched C to a very high-pitched C). These notes have the same name because something about them sounds the same in spite of their having different pitches. Why should the first note on a musical scale (called the tonic note) and the eighth note on the scale (called the octave note) sound so similar?

To answer this question, we need to look at the sounds produced by musical instruments playing these two notes. Musical instruments produce complex sounds, consisting of a fundamental frequency and as many as 20 harmonics. By international agreement, the note A above middle C is defined by a complex tone whose fundamental frequency is 440 Hz. Table 3–3 gives the frequency of the first 10 harmonics of each note of the C-major natural scale beginning with middle C. Notice that the fundamental frequency of

TABLE 3–3   The Frequency of Each of the First 10 Harmonics of Each Note on the Natural C-Major Scale

				Natural Musical Scale				
	Tonic C	Second D	Third E	Fourth F	Fifth G	Sixth A	Seventh B	Octave C
Harmonics								
1	264	297	330	352	396	440	495	528
2	528	594	660	704	792	880	990	1056
3	792	891	990	1056	1188	1320	1485	1584
4	1056	1188	1320	1408	1584	1760	1980	2112
5	1320	1485	1650	1760	1980	2200	2475	2640
6	1584	1782	1980	2112	2376	2640	2970	3168
7	1848	2079	2310	2464	2772	3080	3465	3696
8	2112	2376	2640	2816	3168	3525	3960	4224
9	2376	2673	2970	3168	3564	3960	4455	4752
10	2640	2970	3300	3520	3960	4400	4950	5280

the octave is exactly twice the fundamental frequency of the tonic note. Furthermore, each harmonic of the octave is exactly the same frequency as every other harmonic of the tonic. So when two musical instruments play these two notes (the tonic and the octave) the basilar membrane is stimulated in the same places by the harmonics, which blend smoothly together.

The fifth note on the musical scale (G on the C-major scale) was also singled out by musicians long ago for its special sound when played with the tonic note. A look at Table 3–3 indicates why. Although their fundamental frequencies are different, the second harmonic of the G is the same frequency as the third harmonic of the C, and the fourth harmonic of the G is the same frequency as the sixth harmonic of the C, and so on. When these two notes are played together they stimulate the basilar membrane at some of the same positions. This note combination produces a very pleasant or consonant sound.

Listening to music containing only pleasant sounds would be like having a diet of candy. Musicians deliberately produce unpleasant, or dissonant, sounds as well. For example, look at Table 3–3 to see what will happen when the tonic C is played at the same time as the second note of the scale, D. Only the eighth harmonic of the D and the ninth harmonic of the C have the same frequency. The basilar membrane is thus stimulated in many different places which do not overlap, producing a very dissonant sound.

Modern musical instruments are not tuned exactly to the natural scale frequencies shown in Table 3–3. For technical reasons that allow musicians to play a much wider variety of music (in different keys, for example), all the notes except A above middle C are slightly mistuned by 3 or 4 Hz. This modern musical scale is called the well-tempered scale and is in universal use for playing Western music written since the eighteenth century. In this scale the fundamental frequency of middle C is 261.63 Hz, not 264 Hz. Even in the well-tempered scale, however, the frequencies of the octave are exactly twice the frequencies of the tonic note, and the pleasantness or unpleasantness of note combinations still depends upon the number of shared harmonics and upon the pattern of stimulation on the basilar membrane.

Spatial Localization

The auditory system helps locate objects in space by taking advantage of the ears' location on opposite sides of the head. Because of the separation of the ears, a sound source that is not located straight ahead will stimulate the two ears with slightly different intensities and with a slightly different arrival time. If a sound is located to the left, the left ear will receive more intense stimulation than the right, which is in the "shadow" of the head. In addition, the sound will arrive at the left ear a bit earlier than at the right ear.

The perceptual mechanism that measures the time delay between the two ears is so sensitive that it can reliably detect a difference of only 5 microseconds (0.000005 sec)! The combination of intensity difference and time difference between the two ears is used by the auditory localization mechanisms to localize sound sources at specific places to the left, center, and right. Stereophonic high fidelity recording employs two or more microphones to record the sound from musical instruments as the ears, if they were present, would receive them. These two channels of recorded sound are then reproduced through two loudspeakers, and under ideal conditions the ears of the listener in the living room will receive sound that is similar to the sound they would have received if they had been present when the recording was made.

Location of objects on the basis of sound is especially important to a person without vision. Blind people learn to localize quite accurately on the basis of sound alone. In one experiment it was shown that a blind person can detect large obstacles in his or her path at a distance of 10 or 15 feet in a large room. The blind person's ability to navigate successfully through a room with several barriers is greatly reduced if there is carpeting on the floor (reducing the sound of footsteps which reflect off objects) or if earplugs are worn. Sighted people who are blindfolded do very poorly in locating obstacles but improve with practice, indicating that blind people's ability is a result of their considerable practice and experience in exploring the acoustic environment.

The Sense of Touch

Unlike vision or hearing, the sense of touch is actually not a single sense. Rather, there are four basic experiences that may be had from the contact of the skin with objects: pressure, pain, warmth, and cold. The skin contains a variety of specialized nerve endings (see Figure 3–35). However, a specific nerve ending type does not correspond to a specific type of sensory experience. The exact function of these endings is still not well understood and is the subject of intense research. One measure of touch sensitivity is the "two-point" threshold: How far apart do the tips of a compass have to be in order to experience two points instead of one point. The two-point threshold varies greatly over the surface of the body. The two-point threshold at the tip of the forefinger is about 2.0 mm while it is about 10 mm on the skin of the forearm. Try it for yourself. Tape two pencils together—their points will be about 5 mm apart. Lightly touch the two

FIGURE 3-35 A cross-sectional diagram of human skin

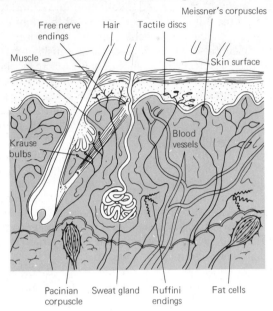

tips to the skin of your finger. You will experience two points of contact. Now move the tips up your finger toward your arm. At some location, you will no longer experience two points on the skin, only one.

Our sensitivity to warmth and cold is mediated by discrete spots on the skin. If you touch your skin with the tip of a cold metal rod, you will discover that you can feel the cold only at some spots and not at others. Likewise, using a warm metal rod, you will be able to feel the warmth only at certain locations on the skin. Our experience of warmth and cold is very dependent on the current temperature. In the winter, for example, a person inside a home may feel that 18 degrees C (65 degrees F) is chilly, while a person coming in from the freezing outside may experience 18 degrees as very warm.

The experience of pain is quite complex. Researchers have described a variety of types of pain experiences; burning, throbbing, and itching pain are examples. Pain usually occurs when body tissue is being damaged or destroyed. The function of pain, therefore, is to allow us to avoid potentially harmful stimuli. Once we are injured, however, the pain should not interfere with our ability to escape from the dangerous situation. The brain releases powerful hormones, such as beta-endorphin (see Chapter 2), to mute the intense pain of a serious injury. It is common for athletes or soldiers to suffer serious injuries and be unaware of them for some time. Women during childbirth have greatly elevated levels of these hormones, presumably to help reduce pain.

Our ability to identify objects from touch has led to the discovery of two types of touch perception: active touch and passive touch. In passive touch we are usually aware of the nature of the touch experience (for example, pressure, warmth, coolness, roughness). Active touch is more oriented toward the identification of objects than the nature of the experiences themselves. This ability to identify objects with active touch was exploited by the blind Frenchman Louis Braille. In 1824 he developed his system of raised dots to represent letters of the alphabet and thus enabled blind people to read printed material. A person skilled in braille can read at a rate of about 105 words a minute (sighted people read regular printing at rates of 200 to 800 words a minute; see Chapter 6). With the advent of computer technology, a variety of devices have been developed to transform visual stimulation (as seen by a television camera) into patterns of vibration on the skin. These devices have had some limited success in allowing blind people to build up internal representations of "visual" objects, including printed material, by the use of their tactile sensitivity on the skin.

Taste and Smell

The senses of taste and smell depend upon the absorption of molecules (the physical stimuli) by receptors on the tongue and in the nose, respectively. Much less is known about the neural mechanisms that process this information than is known about vision and hearing.

Taste (Gustation)

The receptors for taste are grouped together in the taste buds, which are visible on the surface of the tongue. Each bud contains about 10–15 individual receptor cells, and in all there are about 10,000 buds on the tongue (see Figure 3–36). Individual receptor cells are sensitive to and absorb certain specific molecules of substances tasted. These cells have a short life. Each receptor lasts about four days before it wears out and is replaced by a new one created in the taste bud.

The experience of taste can be described in terms of four dimensions: salty, sweet, bitter, and sour. The tongue is selectively sensitive to these four basic tastes. The back of the tongue is very sensitive to bitter-tasting substances like quinine, while the sides are more sensitive to salty and sour substances. The tip is most sensitive to sweet substances like sugar. Place a bit of salt at the tip of your tongue and then along the side. Repeat this experiment with some sugar. You will notice that the salt taste is much

FIGURE 3-36 A taste bud

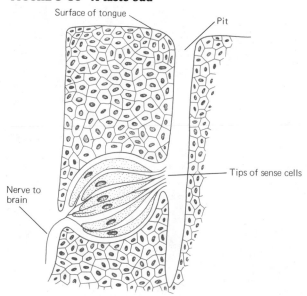

Surface of tongue

Pit

Tips of sense cells

Nerve to brain

The receptor cells of the taste buds convert chemicals dissolved in the saliva into neural impulses which are sent to the brain.

stronger along the side of the tongue and the sugar taste is stronger at the tip.

It is possible to modify your taste experience by knocking out certain of the taste receptors. Artichoke hearts, for example, contain a chemical that reduces the sensitivity of all receptors except those sensitive to sweet substances. After eating an artichoke heart most substances taste sweet. Try this experiment. Take a sip of water and swirl it around in your mouth. Most people experience water as neutral or slightly bitter in taste. Now eat a piece of artichoke heart (unmarinated), chewing it thoroughly. Once again sip some water and concentrate on your taste experience. The water will taste considerably sweeter than before.

Smell (Olfaction)

The receptors for smell lie in the upper part of the nasal cavity (Figure 3-37). There are about 30 million of these receptors in each nostril, which give us an extraordinary sensitivity to odors. Human beings are able to detect smells consisting of only 100 or so molecules, and many animals are even more sensitive. The neural information from the olfactory receptors travels directly to the cortex (all the other sensory systems send information to the cortex via the thalamus).

There have been several attempts to classify our experience of smells into a few categories or "primary" smells, but these classifications have not met with universal acceptance by researchers. The best-

known system consists of seven primary odors and seven secondary odors. The primary odors in this system are *ethereal* (for example, dry-cleaning fluid), *camphoraceous,* or camphor-like (mothballs), *musky* (Angelina root oil), *floral* (roses), *minty* (peppermint candy), *pungent* (vinegar), and *putrid* (rotten egg). Substances with molecules of similar smell have similar shapes. This observation has led to the stereochemical theory of smell, which hypothesizes that olfactory receptors have specific sites on their cell membranes and are sensitive to molecules of certain specific shapes (Figure 3-38). Each odor molecule is a key that will fit only specific locks on a receptor cell. Unfortunately, there are molecules with similar shapes that have very different odors. Thus, more research needs to be done before we will really understand the mechanisms of smell.

Smell seems to serve two major functions: evaluation of food and communication. For the first function, smell combines with taste to allow us to

A Taste Bud for All Flavors

Sweet, salty, sour and bitter are no longer confined to different areas of the tongue. Swedish researchers report that a single human taste bud can sense more than one taste quality, and they have one case in which a single taste bud senses all four. Kristina Arvidson and Ulf Friberg of the Karolinska Institute in Stockholm applied test solutions to single papillae (the visible protuberances) on subjects' tongues. Of 110 papillae tested, 46 responded to at least one taste quality, 39 responded to more than one taste and 14 responded to all four. The investigators then excised the papillae with a fine scalpel and determined by microscopy the number of taste buds in each. No taste buds were found in 62 of the 64 papillae that never responded. The other papillae contained one to 15 taste buds (the mean was 4, the median 3). The number of taste qualities identified generally increased with taste bud number, but in at least 10 cases a papilla was able to sense more tastes than the number of taste buds it contained. For instance, six papillae with only one taste bud sensed two, three or four taste qualities, Arvidson and Friberg report in the August 15 *Science.*

Science News
August 23, 1980

The traditional view has been that there is a different kind of taste bud for each of the four basic taste sensations. Recent evidence questions this assumption, however, suggesting that some taste buds can sense more than one quality. Such a possibility might imply that the different sensations of taste arise from processing that takes place after information leaves the tongue.

FIGURE 3-37   The olfactory system

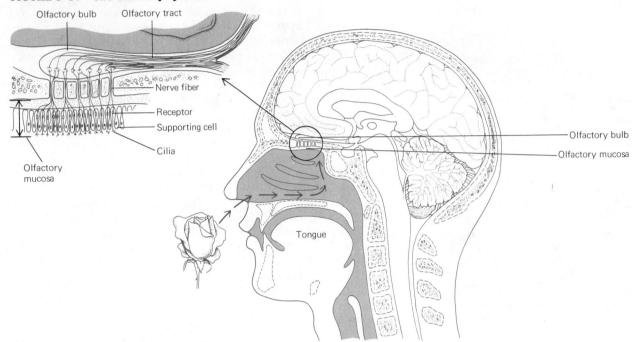

The receptor cells in the nose convert molecules in the air into neural impulses which are sent to the brain through the olfactory bulb.

evaluate the edibility of food substances. Much of what we experience as taste is really mediated through smell. When we suffer from a cold and our nasal passages are blocked, food seems dull and tasteless. Would you believe that an apple and an onion have the same taste; that the differences between them are entirely due to smell? Cut a small piece of apple and an equally small piece of onion (about a 1 cm cube). Holding your nose with one hand, put one piece in your mouth and chew it for a moment; then put the other piece in your mouth. As long as none of the smell reaches your nose, the apple and the onion will taste the same.

The communication function of smell is more important for animals than for humans beings. Two communication uses are in territorial marking and sexual attraction. Chemicals produced for the purpose of communication by smell are called **pheromones.** Many animals have special glands that produce territorial pheromones, while others secrete these chemicals in their urine. You may have noticed that dogs often urinate at the far corners of a yard. The dog is

FIGURE 3-38   Stereochemical theory of olfaction

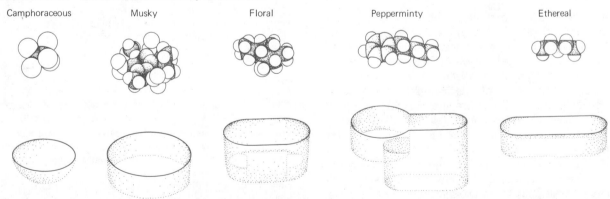

Models of various molecule shapes and receptor sites into which these molecules fit.

Love at First . . . Sniff? Science Says It's Possible
By JILL GERSTON

PHILADELPHIA — He was tall, tanned, and devastatingly attractive, with the sort of burnished blond hair and dazzling white teeth that evoked comparisons to Robert Redford and Nick Nolte.

She was short, snub-nosed, and average-looking—cute, if you were being generous, but by no means central casting's ideal mate for Golden Boy.

That they should meet over luke-warm wine and soggy canapes at a cocktail party at the shore was fate. That he should find her irresistibly, indefinably, overwhelmingly attractive was perhaps a matter of pheromones.

Pheromones?

No, it's not the latest fad in ESP, mental telepathy, astrology, or hypnotism. Nor is it Guerlain's newest blend of jasmine and roses. Rather, pheromones (pronounced fear-o-mones) are the chemical substances, secreted by almost every creature from insect to human, that trigger sexual attraction between members of the same species.

Let a female gypsy moth release her scent signal and male moths will zoom over from as far away as two miles. Likewise, the pheromones exuded by a female monkey are so potent that they can send the average male into a King Kong frenzy of desire.

And though a human's response to chemical attractants is less volatile than that of, say, a tsetse fly, scientific evidence has shown that we nevertheless are susceptible to subliminal human odors.

"You know the old saying about the chemistry being right between two people? Well, it's not as crazy as it sounds," said Lorraine King, an endocrinologist at Jefferson Medical College in Philadelphia who is familiar with the research on pheromones. "In fact there is some basic truth to it."

Thus, the magnetic attraction that made Golden Boy gravitate to Miss Average across a crowded buffet table may have been the erotic power of her natural odor. However, because pheromones are too faint to be consciously noticed—they register at some subconscious level—the sensory allure also may have been her Chanel No. 5 or the clams casino. Who knows? Scientists don't, and without any clear link between human sexual response and pheromones, the question is left in the air, so to speak. . . .

Humans, alas, unlike boll weevils, do not love by scent alone. With us, it's mind over matter—or scent, as the case may be.

"We're more selective," King said. "For instance, a woman might be sexually attracted to a man who is intellectually and socially unsuited to her. For a brief, passionate romance, he's fine, but when it comes down to a long-term relationship, she'll probably think twice."

According to King, studies have shown that pheromones, which are present in men as well as women, are secreted primarily through glands concentrated in the genital region, on the chest, and under the arm. It is still unclear what inhibits or promotes these secretions in humans, how exactly they are perceived, and why individual olfactory responses differ—that is, why a come-hither scent to one person may be a turnoff to another. Scientists still have to decipher the "language of scent" and until they do, speculation is wide open in the field of chemical communication.

The sexual pheromones of the female moth were discovered about 100 years ago by European naturalists, yet it wasn't until recently that researchers detected them in humans. In 1975, a study at Emory University School of Medicine in Atlanta revealed that sex-attractant smells were present in the vaginal secretions of human females. The concentrations of the chemicals found were closely correlated with the women's menstrual cycles and reached the highest level during the subjects' most fertile period. The researchers also found that oral contraceptives to some extent inhibited the secretions.

Such contraceptives would no doubt have a negative effect on the mating instincts of insects and animals, but the opposite is true in humans: A woman on The Pill, unworried about pregnancy, probably will be less inhibited and more sexually active, regardless of her pheromone level. . . .

Chicago Tribune
February 8, 1981

There is strong evidence for a role of the pheromones in regulating animal behavior, particularly sexual behavior. The evidence in human beings is less convincing although quite intriguing. Applications of research in this area would be numerous and important as is obvious from the examples on contraception in animals and insects.

---

really marking its territory with its own scent. Other dogs coming into the yard will immediately recognize the smell and will tend to stay away. When honeybees are disturbed by an intruder in the hive, they release an alarm pheromone. This pheromone attracts other honeybees from the hive and makes them attack the foreign intruder as well.

Pheromones also play important roles in sexual behavior. If a female mouse that has mated with a male mouse is exposed to the odor of a strange mouse within 24 hours, the female mouse will not become pregnant. The odor of the strange mouse causes the release of hormones in the female which block pregnancy. Many female animals give off special pheromones when they are sexually receptive that attract males of the species. Gypsy moths are extraordinary in this regard. The male gypsy moth is able to detect a receptive female gypsy moth several kilometers away by means of sexual pheromones. Female cats and dogs in heat give off pheromones that attract males, often from quite a distance. If you have an unspayed female cat or dog as a pet, you will have witnessed this phenomenon.

Whether or not human beings use pheromones is still a controversial question, and the evidence supporting pheromones is indirect. Women, it is known, differ in their sensitivity to certain musky smells (that of male urine, for example) at different times in the menstrual cycle. The sensitivity to these smells is highest just before ovulation and is minimum during menstruation. Since these musky smells are related to male sex hormones, this cyclical variation may indicate a pheromonelike function. Another piece of evidence comes from studies of women living together in dormitories. When they first start to live together, each has a different menstrual cycle—they get their periods at different times during the month. After living together for a number of months, a considerable number of the women have the same menstrual cycle —their periods come at the same time each month. One mechanism for this synchronization of periods is through pheromones—odors that would not have any particular meaning that one could verbalize, but that would cause the areas deep within the brain which control menstruation (for example, the hypothalamus) to change the cycle so that they would all menstruate at the same time. As of this writing no specific human sexual pheromone has been identified.

A final piece of evidence suggesting that pheromones play a role in human sexual behavior comes from a study by marriage counselors. This study reported that the most common complaint among couples seeking marriage counseling was that one or both partners found that the other "had bad breath" or simply "had a bad smell." This evidence suggests that odors have a profound effect on human interpersonal behavior and that much of this effect exists at a nonverbal and emotional level. The existence of a large variety of mouthwashes, deodorants, and perfumes on the shelves of our stores also suggests this possibility.

Attention: What Gets Processed?

As marvelous as our perceptual processes are in producing rich and complex internal representations of the world, this ability is not without limits. There are a limited number of processing mechanisms, and these can process detailed information only over a limited portion of the world at any one time. In the course of processing information about the world, some information is lost; that is, perception is selective.

The selection of information can generally occur in two different ways: through selection at a peripheral

level and through the selection of specific perceptual processes. Selection in vision is obviously affected by ability to control the direction in which the eyes point. As we saw earlier, the fovea of each retina has a dense concentration of cones; in addition, the brain mechanisms devoted to analyzing information from the fovea are disproportionately large. The fovea occupies only about $1/6,000$ of the total visual field, yet fully one-third of the visual cortex is devoted to the fovea. One mechanism of attention is to point the eyes at objects to which we want to attend. When we are looking at something, other objects in our visual field cannot be processed in very great detail. In addition, we can process information from selected portions of our visual field *without* moving our eyes. If you are looking straight ahead at a screen and are asked to detect targets flashed to the left or right, you will respond faster to the target if you are told in advance on which side the target will appear. This improvement takes place without your moving your eyes. These results indicate that you can select a region of the visual field and concentrate your processing power within it.

The second form of selective attention is determined by which central processes are devoted to a task and how much "mental effort" is allocated to the process. Current theories of attention propose that there is a limit on the amount of mental effort that a person has available at any one time. This effort may be allocated to one process or may be split between several processes. These theories predict that you can

Attention Is a Right-Sided Function

Patients acting like the stereotypic drunk—overactive and unable to concentrate—frequently are not intoxicated, but suffer from damage to the right side of the brain. Norman Geshwind and Marek-Marsel Mesulam of Harvard Medical School presented evidence that the complicated ability to pay attention is localized in the brain's right hemisphere.

In humans, lesions (usually caused by a blocked blood vessel) of the left side of the brain seldom cause severe, persistent loss of attention. However, lesions of the right hemisphere can lead either to general inattention or to particular inattention to stimuli on the left side. Geshwind hypothesizes that normally the right hemisphere scans both sides of space and applies criteria for shifting the focus of attention. If the attention-directing regions (the inferior parietal lobules) of the right hemisphere are destroyed, the left hemisphere eventually begins to monitor its own half of space (the right side), but not the other. In animals, damage to either hemisphere generally produces inattention to stimuli from the opposite side.

Science News
February 25, 1978

perform one very difficult task or several easy ones. When you are at a party with many people talking at once, the sounds from a number of different voices all enter your ears together. Your internal representation contains many voices, male and female, each with a characteristic timbre and located at a particular place in the room. In terms of peripheral attention, you could attend to the male voices or the female voices; you could attend to the voices at specific locations. The main focus of listening to speech is to process the meaning of the words. Experiments on the limits of processing effort suggest that you can fully process the meaning of only one string of words at a time. This limitation shows that you have only one perceptual process sophisticated and complex enough to carry out a "meaning" analysis of the voice sounds. You can allocate this processing for meaning to whichever voice you choose, but to only one voice at a time. Careful studies have shown that when you try to listen to two voices at once, you miss some of both. This effect has been called the cocktail party phenomenon, for obvious reasons. If you fully attend to one of the voices, about the only thing you can detect in other voices is a change from male to female speaker, or vice versa. The unattended voice can even lapse into a foreign language and the change will go undetected.

The information in the unattended voice is not completely ignored because some specific stimuli can be detected in it while one is fully attending to another voice. For example, if you are carefully attending to one speaker, your attention can sometimes be attracted by a second voice that speaks your name. Another example is provided by the sleeping mother who can be awakened by a soft cry from her baby but

"I'm sorry, but I wasn't really paying attention."

The New Yorker, June 18, 1979. Drawing by Chon Day; © 1979 The New Yorker Magazine, Inc.

not by other, louder noises. As a result, you can usually feel comfortable concentrating your attention on your main task, knowing that *important* information will not get totally lost.

SUMMARY

1. Perception is the collection of processes that produce your internal representation of the outside world. Our behavior is based upon this internal representation, which provides the answers to two questions: "What is out there?" and "Where is it?" The study of perception involves the study of physics, physiology, behavior, and subjective experience.

2. Sensory receptors convert physical energy such as light, sound, heat, and pressure into nerve impulses, signals that the brain can understand.

3. The human eye is sensitive to a narrow range of electromagnetic wavelengths, ranging from about 400 to 700 nm. This energy is called light because it elicits visual experiences.

4. The eye is constructed much like a camera, forming an inverted image of the world on its rear surface, the retina. The retina contains four kinds of photoreceptors. The rods are very sensitive and function at low levels of light (scotopic vision). There are three types of cones. They function at daylight levels of light (photopic vision) and form the basis for color vision.

5. Rods and cones are connected to ganglion cells in the retina by means of a complex network of horizontal, bipolar, and amacrine cells. Each ganglion cell receives input from many rods and cones. The area of the retina that influences a given ganglion cell is called the receptive field of that ganglion cell. These fields are circular and consist of a central region and a surrounding region.

6. Visual acuity is the ability to see fine detail. As the average light level increases, visual acuity increases.

7. Color is one of the basic visual experiences. The neural activity of the three types of cones is combined in the retina to form three neural channels of color information: an R/G channel, a Y/B channel, and an L channel. All our color experiences result from various combinations of activity of these three channels.

8. The experience of color is based on three dimensions: hue, saturation, and brightness. Hue is the qualitative nature of the color, saturation is the intensity of the color, and brightness is the description of color that ranges from black to white.

9. Our perception of brightness is closely related to the relative amount of light reflected from objects rather than the absolute amount of light. Our experience of brightness remains stable over a wide range of illuminations. This phenomenon is called brightness constancy.

10. The cells in the visual cortex of the brain provide the first stages of pattern and object perception. These cells are primarily sensitive to bars, gratings, and edges of specific orientations. Different cells are sensitive to different orientations.

11. Gestalt principles describe how stimuli on the retina are formed into objects by the perceptual processes. The basic principle is called Prägnanz, or "goodness of figure." Other Gestalt principles are proximity, similarity, and closure.

12. Two types of cues are used to perceive depth: those requiring both eyes (binocular cues) and those requiring one eye (monocular cues). Skilled artists can use monocular cues to give the viewer a realistic perception of depth.

13. Size constancy is the process of maintaining a stable internal representation of the size of objects when we move around and view them at different distances. This process uses two types of information: the size of the retinal image and the distance from the observer to the object.

14. The stimulus for hearing is sound pressure waves traveling in the air. Physical sound is described by its intensity, frequency, and complexity. Our hearing covers a range of frequencies from 20 Hz to 20,000 Hz. We can hear sounds as faint as 0 dB and as loud as 120 dB.

15. The inner ear analyzes complex sound waves into its sine wave (harmonic) components. The basilar membrane of the inner ear is stimulated at different places by different frequencies of sound.

16. Experience of sound varies on three principal psychological dimensions: loudness, pitch, and timbre. Timbre is the quality that allows you to tell the difference between a violin and a flute playing the same musical note. The pleasantness of various musical notes played in combination is a function of the place on the basilar membrane where the harmonic components of the notes stimulate.

17. Four experiences based on contact between the skin and an object constitute the sense of touch: pressure, pain, warmth, and cold. These four experiences are mediated by specialized nerve endings (receptors) in the skin.

18. Taste and smell are interrelated senses that depend on the absorption of chemical molecules by receptors on the tongue and in the nose. Taste experiences are described as salty, sweet, bitter, and sour. Smell experiences are likewise described as ethereal, camphoraceous, musky, minty, floral, pungent, and putrid. Smell plays an important role in animal communication and sexual attraction.

19. We face a world of myriad stimuli with perceptual processes of limited capacity. Through the mechanism of attention, stimuli are selected for detailed processing. The selection can occur at a peripheral level or at a more central level.

RECOMMENDED ADDITIONAL READINGS

Goldstein, E. B. *Sensation and perception.* Belmont, Calif.: Wadsworth, 1980.

Held, R., & Richards, W. (Eds.) *Recent progress in perception.* San Francisco: Freeman, 1976.

Lindsay, P. H., & Norman, D. A. *Human information processing,* 2d ed. New York: Academic Press, 1977.

Schiff, W. *Perception: An applied approach.* Boston: Houghton Mifflin, 1980.

Schiffman, H. R. *Sensation and perception: An integrated approach.* New York: Wiley, 1976.

What Does It Mean?

Knowledge gained in the study of perception and perceptual processing has had—and continues to have—a strong impact on our culture. This impact may be stronger than from any other area of psychology.

Eye Glasses

One of the first applications of knowledge about the formation of the retinal image was in the prescription of eye glasses. The eye is supposed to focus a sharp image on the retina. This image is then analyzed by neural processes. If the image is not sharp, the information obtainable from it is reduced, and an internal representation adequate for getting around in the world may not be possible.

There are two types of focusing problems generally found. In the first type, called near-sightedness, or myopia, the eye has too much optical power. As a result, the eye forms an image of distant objects in front of, instead of on, the retina, and these distant objects are experienced as blurred. A near-sighted person can clearly see objects close to the eye, where the additional optical power is needed. The method used to allow a near-sighted person to see distant objects is to cancel the excessive optical power of the eye by using a negative lens in front of the eye (see Figure 3–39). A negative lens is one that is thicker at the edges than at the center.

The second type of focusing problem is called far-sightedness, or hyperopia, and results when the eye does not have enough optical power. A far-sighted person can see distant objects clearly, but does not have enough optical power to focus on close objects. In this case the method used to correct the focus is to place a positive lens—one that is thicker in the center than at the edges—in front of the eye. Now when the far-sighted person looks at a close object, the image of that object is focused on the retina, not behind it (see Figure 3–39). Lenses are like crutches; they are aids, but they do not correct the problem itself. They only allow a person to get along in the world. Perhaps in the future someone will discover methods that will allow a near- or far-sighted person to see clearly without the use of these optical crutches.

Clinical Testing of Vision

For a long time optometrists and ophthalmologists have been puzzled by a few patients who come to them complaining that "things don't look right." Upon testing with traditional eye charts (Figure 3–11, for example) these patients were found to have normal visual acuity (20/20). If they have normal acuity, why don't things look right? Using testing methods developed in the research laboratory researchers have recently found an answer to this puzzle. This new method of testing is the measurement of the *contrast sensitivity function (CSF)*, which uses grating patterns like those shown in Figure 3–10. The CSF is a curve that shows the sensitivity of the patient to a wide range of grating sizes, from very broad to very thin strips. In effect, the CSF measures the ability of a person to see objects of all different sizes, not just the small letters used in traditional eye charts. The curve on the left side of Figure 3–40 shows the CSF of people with normal vision. The arrow marks the point on the CSF that corresponds to visual acuity measures made with small letters.

The right side of Figure 3–40 shows the CSF of a selected group of patients complaining of "abnormal vision." Although their visual acuity point is normal (see arrow), the middle part of their CSF is quite abnormal. Their sensitivity to medium-sized objects is greatly reduced even though they are able to see small objects normally. This loss in the middle of the CSF explains why the visual experience of these people is not normal even though measured acuity is normal. These advanced testing methods will play a more prominent role in the clinical evaluation of vision during the next several years.

Visual Illusions

Visual illusions are caused by our perceptual processes creating an internal representation based on inaccurate and misleading information. These illusions are fun to ex-

FIGURE 3–39   Two types of focusing problems

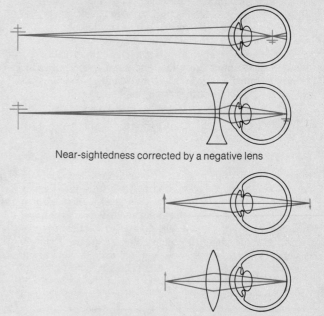

Near-sightedness corrected by a negative lens

Far-sightedness corrected by a positive lens

FIGURE 3–40   Contrast sensitivity functions for normal and abnormal observers

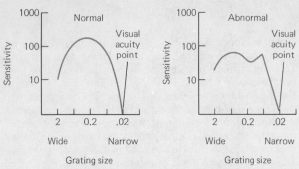

Some patients who have normal visual acuity but complain of abnormal vision are found to have abnormal contrast

perience in the classroom, but in real-world situations, such as flying an airplane, the consequences of illusions may be tragic. Modern technology has developed ways to extend our behavioral capacities beyond our wildest dreams. Not surprisingly, these new behavioral abilities can sometimes outstrip the ability of our perceptual mechanisms to provide an adequate basis for this behavior. For example, our perceptual mechanisms developed not having to support the ability to fly. Fortunately, we have used technology to extend our sensory and perceptual information by means of instrumentation. Today, pilots of large aircraft use instrumentation in many situations where relying on perceptual mechanisms alone would invite disaster.

After a series of accidents in which commercial jets crashed on landing, psychologist Conrad Kraft discovered a visual illusion that caused the pilots to crash. Kraft first found that the crashes all occurred at night, with good visibility, when the pilot was approaching a distant runway from over a black, unlit land or water area. He then carried out several experiments and discovered that when pilots were landing under these conditions and were relying on their vision to provide information about their altitude (instead of looking at the altimeter) they seriously overestimated their altitude. This overestimation could cause the plane to drop dangerously low and perhaps crash into the ground before the pilot realized the danger. Today, pilots are instructed to resist the strong temptation to rely solely on perceptual information and to use the aircraft instruments instead.

Blindness

Blindness can result from any disruption of the visual system. A person may become blind because of interference with the optics of the eye, such as in cataracts. Another cause of blindness is damage to the retina or the optic nerve. In these cases blindness results because information is prevented from reaching the brain. When damage occurs in visual areas of the brain, however, a person's visual ability may not be completely destroyed. As the newsclip "Ambient Vision" suggests, perhaps people whose visual cortex has been damaged and are "blind" as a result have suffered impairment of only one of the types of visual processes—

Sociological Problems Haunt Victims of Dyslexia

SANTA BARBARA, Calif. UPI—At least 10 percent, possibly more, of children in elementary schools suffer from dyslexia—a perceptual disorder which blocks their ability to read, spell, or write legibly. It could turn them into delinquents later on.

Recent federal studies indicate a deep sociological problem results from dyslexia with 80 per cent or more of the prison population in the United States affected by it.

Dyslexia, which may be inherited, scrambles symbols—letters and numbers—in the brain and also can cause a similar effect in hearing.

A dyslexic child may see the word "dog" as "god," may confuse concepts such as "floor" for "ceiling" and "hostile" for "hospitable." A "b" changes into a "d" or a number series such as "1-2-3" may come out "2-1-3."

Experts say many dyslexic children are of superior intelligence but often are lumped with retarded children or others with multiple learning disabilities because the disorder is not widely understood and there are no programs available within the public education system. . . .

Beth Slingerland of Seattle, a teacher and national consultant on dyslexia, told the Orton Society meeting that dyslexic children are "perfectly normal, intelligent children with no brain damage and no primary emotional problems."

"But they may have emotional problems due to academic failure and behavioral problems which may clear up when they get a taste of learning. . . .

Many eminent people have suffered from dyslexia including . . . Nelson Rockefeller. . . .

President Woodrow Wilson and Albert Einstein also suffered from dyslexia, but overcame the difficulty.

Rocky Mountain News, *Denver December 21, 1975*

Disorders of our perceptual systems can cause severe problems in functioning. You cannot easily learn to behave appropriately in a world you cannot perceive accurately. It is hoped that perception research will help us solve or cure such disorders as dyslexia.

those that answer the question "What is out there?". The perceptual mechanisms that locate objects may remain intact. Perhaps it will be possible to train such "blind" people to use these intact mechanisms more fully. Only further research will tell.

When blindness is caused by information not reaching the brain, it may be possible to supply the brain directly with the needed information. One approach is to stimulate the visual cortex directly using electrical signals derived from a tiny TV camera mounted on eye-glass frames. The lack of success with this approach so far may reflect our lack of understanding of the function of the visual cortex. The potential of this method to help blind individuals remains unrealized.

Deafness

The loss of the ability to hear some or all of the auditory spectrum is a serious problem for many people, especially older ones. Loss of hearing can result from mechanical changes in the middle or inner ears or from damage to neural mechanisms. Some loss of sensitivity to high frequencies seems to occur as a result of the aging process. Figure 3-41 shows this trend. Beyond the age of 30, people become progressively deaf to frequencies above about 1,000 Hz. By the age of 70, the loss is severe enough that it interferes with speech understanding. This loss contributes to the feeling of isolation experienced by many older people in our society.

Much of this loss of sensitivity may be due to the exposure to loud noises prevalent in our environment. Figure 3-42 shows the effect of different occupations on deafness to high frequencies. People working in noisy environments

DISTRACTING DELUSION — Fun-loving sign painters Bill Reed, left, and Chris Pielek pose with their seeing-is-deceiving painting in Rockford, Ill. The two decided to play a practical joke on their vacationing boss, spending the entire weekend creating the vision of occupational peril, showing three painters stranded by broken scaffolding. They used fellow painters as models for the preliminary sketch. It was successful, too, causing traffic in the area to come to a standstill before authorities and the painters cleared up the misconception.

Ambient Vision Lets Blind Person "See"

STATE COLLEGE, Pa. AP — The person with "eyes in the back of his head" may be more common than not, a Pennsylvania State University professor says.

Dr. Herschel Leibowitz, a professor of psychology, said his research with the blind shows human beings have two types of sight — normal vision allowing them to see, and an ambient vision that subconsciously tells them where they are in relation to surroundings.

Thus, a blind person whose ambient vision hasn't been destroyed is capable of avoiding walls despite not being able to see them, Leibowitz said.

Because the two systems originate in different parts of the brain, a person may lose one type of vision but not the other in some cases of brain injury, Leibowitz said. Focal vision, as Leibowitz calls that used for reading and recognizing objects, is controlled by the visual cortex in the outer portion of the brain. Ambient vision, he said, originates inside the midbrain.

Leibowitz said the explanation for ambient vision is found in the interaction of fibers from the peripheral retina of the eye with vestibular fibers of the inner ear that are stimulated by gravity. That gives a person a sense of equilibrium, he said, an effect evident through motor activity rather than consciousness.

Experiments at the Neurological Clinic of the University of Freiburg. Germany, with a neurologist, Dr. Johannes Dichgans, confirmed this past year that people, like animals, have the two types of vision, Leibowitz said.

"Focal vision can be improved with glasses. It has to do with the 'what' of perception," Leibowitz said.

"Ambient vision is the 'where' of perception," he said. "It permits us to move about freely and orient ourselves in space. . . ."

The Denver Post
October 13, 1977

Can you think of ways to test Professor Leibowitz's hypothesis that there are actually two types of vision?

(farm and factory workers exposed to loud machinery) experience a much more severe hearing loss than do office workers. Studies have also shown that noise can have additional effects, such as mental depression.

As in vision, scientists are trying to restore the hearing of deaf people by electrical stimulation of the auditory nerve. It is hoped that electrical signals from a microphone can be transformed to stimulate the auditory nerve of a deaf person, resulting in relatively "normal" input to the brain. So far only limited success has been achieved with this technique. But the knowledge gained from these first steps may enable deaf people 50 years from now to hear once again.

FIGURE 3-41 Hearing loss associated with aging

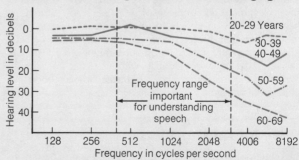

As we age, we progressively lose sensitivity to high-frequency sounds, including some of the sounds important for understanding speech. Each curve represents the reduction in sensitivity at different frequencies for the indicated age groups.

FIGURE 3-42 Hearing loss associated with environment

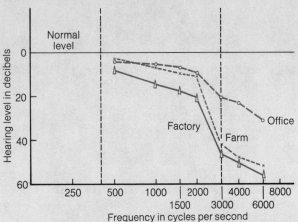

Unless precautions are taken, continuous exposure to loud sounds causes a permanent loss of sensitivity, especially at high frequencies. The graph shows that farm and factory workers (noisy environments) suffer more hearing loss than office workers (quiet environments). To avoid such damage, ear protectors should be worn during exposure to loud noises.

Subliminal Advertising

Several years ago advertising agencies claimed that rapidly presented verbal messages, superimposed on a regular movie, could be used to make people hungry or thirsty without their being aware of the message itself. This technique was called subliminal advertising and was based on the (incorrect) notion that there exists a threshold above which stimuli are detectable and below which they are not. Today these claims are largely discredited. There is no evidence that it is possible to present an effective verbal message without its presence being detected.

It may be possible, however, to evoke feelings, both positive and negative, through the use of non-verbal, visually suggestive material. Unfortunately very little is known at present about the esthetic nature of perceptual experiences. What makes certain visual stimuli — paintings for example — pleasing and others unpleasant? Why have some musical compositions — those of J. S. Bach for example — been treasured by people for more than 200 years, while others are quickly forgotten? Apparently these esthetic effects are pretty much automatic, implying that people can be influenced emotionally without being consciously aware of the influence. This is an area ripe for good experimental research.

Perceptual Conflicts

Our internal representation of the world is built from information from all sensory systems, and usually there is no conflict among them. But what happens if the brain receives conflicting information from two or more sensory systems? One of two things usually happens: either processing continues normally by ignoring all but one of the sources of

Help for Deaf Babies
By MATT CLARK with DAN SHAPIRO

About one in every 2,000 babies in the U.S. is born with a significant degree of deafness. But diagnosis with conventional audiometric testing is difficult in such cases because a baby can't describe how noises sound to him. At the University of California in San Diego, however, a team of neuroscientists is detecting hearing problems in infants by measuring the electrical impulses produced by sound as they travel from the ear to the higher auditory centers of the brain.

The team's leader, Dr. Robert Galambos, says there are two main types of deafness in children: first, conductive hearing loss, often involving damage to the bones of the middle ear that conduct sound waves from the eardrum to the inner ear; second, sensory-neural deafness, caused usually by a lack of hairlike cells in the cochlea of the inner ear that carry sound to the auditory nerve.

Many of these hearing problems can be corrected — by surgery, medication or the use of hearing aids. But because of the difficulty of testing hearing in small children, deafness often isn't detected until the child is around 2. Deprived of normal hearing perception for such a period, Galambos says, a child will suffer a lag in the development of speech and language skills that may lead to a permanent handicap — even after the hearing disorder is eventually diagnosed.

The new test was developed by Galambos and his colleagues at several other laboratories over the past eight years. It involves the measurement of electrical activity generated in response to sound by the brain stem, a short structure between the top of the spinal cord and the base of the cerebral cortex to which the auditory nerve is connected.

Signals
By means of earphones, the infant is presented with a series of clicking sounds that stimulate the auditory nervous system. The electrical activity evoked by the sounds in the brain is picked up by electrodes placed behind each ear and on top of the head. These electrical signals are amplified, fed into a computer and printed out in the form of waves on a graph.

Within 12.5 milleseconds of a click, the graph of a normal baby will show seven distinct peaks, each representing a point along the path the sound has taken from the auditory nerve to the hearing centers of the cerebral cortex. For a baby with impaired hearing, the peaks take longer to appear. Different types of hearing defects, moreover, will produce wave patterns that deviate from the normal in characteristic ways. For example, absence of all seven waves indicates total sensory-neural deafness, which is usually untreatable. In conductive deafness, on the other hand, wave patterns will emerge if the intensity of the sound is increased. Hearing aids are frequently sufficient to correct this problem. . . .

Newsweek
December 8, 1975

See Sex in a Box of Crackers?
That's Subliminal Ad at Work

By MICHAEL DIXON

CHICAGO — When you look at a magazine or television advertisement, you see more than you think you do—only you don't know it. But media-watcher Wilson Bryan Key does.

When Key looks at the picture on the box of a nationally known brand of crackers, or at the crackers themselves, he sees a pattern of the word "SEX" embedded in both.

In a TV commercial for a drain opener, Key sees the word "SEX" in the sink, formed as the water gurgles down the drain. Key even sees those "SEXes" on the arms of a cute little baby in a toothpaste ad.

No, Wilson Bryan Key isn't a twisted personality who sees sex everywhere. He says everybody can see the messages about sex and death that are present in advertising, just as he does. He'll point them out to you, and you'll see them, too. It's all right there for your subconscious to take in and, if pointed out, for the naked eye.

The cracker, drain opener and toothpaste ads are examples of subliminal advertising. By definition, the word subliminal is a psychological term referring to the use of stimuli that operate below the threshold of consciousness. The messages in those ads aren't perceived by the conscious eye, unless told they exist.

But the subconscious mind does perceive the information immediately, and stores it. So the next time you see the brand of cracker, drain opener or toothpaste in a store, you probably will opt for it over other brands.

Wilson Bryan Key may have seen more of those unconscious messages than anyone. He has served as a professor of journalism at four universities and written two books, "Subliminal Seduction" and . . . "Media Sexploitation". . . . Both books and Key's work with the Medaprobe Center for the Study of the Media, his San Diego-based company, all revolve around the exploration of the use of subliminal techniques in media. . . .

"Almost 98 per cent of subliminal ads have themes related to either sex or death," Key explained. "We know that the brain picks up information and retains it largely based on its emotional content. Since most people respond strongly to sex, that's what's used most often. But a lot of subliminal themes revolve around death. . . ."

The Denver Post
July 28, 1977

Despite the fact that there is no good evidence to support subliminal influencing of behavior, many people continue to believe that it is a potent and dangerous phenomenon.

conflicting information or processing is greatly slowed down by the conflict.

In the first situation some of the incoming information is ignored. The most common occurrence of this effect, called visual capture, is when visual information overrules other sources. The ability of a ventriloquist depends on visual capture. On the one hand an observer's auditory localization mechanism is signaling that the source of the dummy's voice is the ventriloquist's mouth, but on the other hand, the observer's visual system is correlating the movement of the dummy's mouth with the speech sounds. Since the visual system indicates that the ventriloquist's mouth is not moving and the dummy's is, the experience you have is that of a talking dummy. Ventriloquists do not "throw" their voices; they depend upon the visual capture effect. If you close your eyes when attending a ventriloquist act, you will hear both the dummy's voice and the ventriloquist's voice as coming from the same location.

A good example of conflict causing disruption of normal processing is shown in Color Plate 9, where the names of colors are printed in ink of different colors. Both kinds of information, the color experience of the letters and the color name represented by the word itself, are coming through the visual system. It is quite difficult to ignore one in order to process the other rapidly. Test yourself on this demonstration. Look at the top section of the plate and name the color of each patch as fast and as accurately as you can, timing yourself with the second hand of a watch. Now name the *colors* of the letters below, ignoring the meaning of the words they spell. You will find that your speed is considerably slowed down. Now read the words printed in black ink below. Your speed will return to normal because no conflict exists. It is as if, when reading the color names printed in different-colored inks, both color names compete for access to the verbal processes, and since we cannot say two different words at the same time, our reading time is greatly slowed.

Another dramatic example of conflict between two types of perceptual information is evidenced in motion sickness. The brain has two major sources of information about body motion: the visual system and the vestibular system located in the inner ear. Normally, the two systems signal the same information about body movement. But picture this situation: If your entire room, with you in it, were tilted 30 degrees to one side, how would you know it? From the visual point of view you would not know it, because, visually, everything would be the same. But the vestibular system would be signaling that everything has tilted. When you are on a ship, especially below deck in a cabin, as the ship rocks back and forth, the vestibular system signals that you are rocking. But below deck, the visual system has no information about your movement, since as your body moves, so does the whole cabin. So your visual system signals that the body is stationary. This situation, for reasons not well understood, causes intense nausea and may result in vomiting.

To prevent seasickness or eliminate it when you begin to feel sick you must restore the agreement between the visual and vestibular information. If you fixate the horizon or an object on land as your body rocks back and forth, the visual system is able to sense the motion by comparison with the stationary land or horizon. It then signals the brain — in agreement with the vestibular system—that the body is rocking. The symptoms of nausea will rapidly disappear. Seasoned sailors adapt to the disagreement between the two systems so that nausea is not a problem. Such persons, when they go ashore, report that there is a short period of time when the stable ground feels as though it is rocking!

4 Basic Principles of Learning

Lynn has just been promoted to branch manager of her company's European division located in Paris. She is madly trying to learn French.

Chuck has just been accepted for a residency program in surgery at Denver General Hospital. He is trying to learn how to tie knots with forceps.

Dave is on the verge of flunking out of college. He needs a 2.5 average this semester to stay in school, and to achieve it he needs a B in his introductory psychology course. To that end he is trying to learn from reading this book.

Marge and Rick's 3-year-old son has been nicknamed "Dennis the Menace." They are intent on learning child psychology to apply it to Dennis to modify his behavior. They hope that Dennis will be intent on learning to behave.

These are just a few obvious examples of the encounters we all have with our world that involve learning. Imagine living in a world in which nobody learned anything—do you think it would be possible to survive? Surely genetic changes, which we discussed in Chapter 2, are one means of survival. We owe some of our behavior potential to biological evolution. But biological changes require a great deal of time, much more than we have in a lifetime. We need a quicker method of behavior change. There is a way to modify our behavior potential as a function of what we have already experienced so that we do not make the same mistakes in the future. This process is called learning. Learning is the only way we have of adapting, in our own lifetime, to our environment. So fundamental is learning in explaining much of human behavior that all branches of psychology rely on the learning concept (see Table 4–1). Experience is the great teacher, and human beings are the best learners on earth. Because of the importance of learning we will devote two chapters to examining it. The present chapter concentrates on basic learning processes, while Chapter 5 discusses more complex forms of learning with emphasis on human memory and information processing.

TABLE 4–1 The Central Role of Learning in Psychology

Branch of Psychology	Sample Concerns Dealing with Learning
Physiological psychology	1. What changes take place in the nervous system when a person learns?
	2. Are there physiological defects in the learning mechanism of mentally retarded individuals?
	3. Are there any drugs that speed up the learning process or correct physiological defects?
Educational psychology	1. Will learning be improved or impaired in school buildings with no walls separating the classrooms?
	2. What is the best way to teach reading? Why do so many children fail to learn to read in school?
Developmental psychology	1. As a child grows, are there changes in the manner in which the individual learns that teachers should be aware of?
	2. Are there periods of readiness for learning (for example, reading readiness) before which attempts at teaching the child will be useless?
Industrial psychology	1. What is the best way to train employees to be safety conscious?
	2. What is the best way to retrain employees for jobs requiring new skills?
Social psychology	1. How do people learn attitudes?
	2. Will social facilitation (being in groups) speed the learning process?
Clinical psychology	1. How can a therapist teach a client not to be afraid of catching a fatal illness from the "germs" in the person's own home?
	2. What kind of reward or pleasure does a "peeping Tom" get from looking into his neighbors' windows?
Experimental psychology	1. What factors are important in determining the rate of learning?
	2. Does learning take place faster with rewards, punishments, or both?
	3. What is the best way to memorize (learn) a set of important facts?

Learning and Behavior

For our present purposes, we will define learning as a relatively permanent change in behavior potential, traceable to experience and practice. Learning is closely related to knowledge, skill, and intention. Knowledge and intention are usually thought to be acquired through experience, and skill through practice. A teacher might tell the class that Columbus discovered America in 1492, and from then on, as long as they remember, the students *know* and can respond to that fact. After an experience of pleasure from an event or activity, such as eating ice cream or drinking good wine, these activities become the objects of one's wants and *intentions*. Some activities, such as driving an automobile or playing baseball, involve *skills* as well as knowledge and intention. Repetition of these activities, or practice, leads to an improvement in skill. Note that each of these cases fits our definition of learning.

The relationship between learning and performance (the observed behavior in a particular situation) is important. Most learning theories, indeed most theories of behavior, note this special relationship, drawing a strong distinction between the two. Traditionally, it is argued that learning is never really observed directly. In many theories, learning is given the status of an **intervening variable,** a variable that stands between (intervenes) and provides a relationship between some stimulus in the environment and some response or performance on the part of a person. Learning is not observed directly but is inferred from observation of a change in **performance.**

Thus learning and performance are closely related but distinct concepts pertaining to behavior. Too often the distinction is not maintained, and performance is taken to be a direct and accurate measure of how much a person has learned. This implies that if learning occurs, performance should improve; and if learning is reduced—for example, by forgetting—performance should get worse. But performance is not always an accurate reflection of the amount learned. Consider the basketball team that does well throughout the season, only to be humiliated in the state tournament. The team performed poorly, but not because the players forgot how to play or lost any of their skill. Other factors, such as tension or distraction, prevented them from performing at the level of their true ability. Schoolteachers frequently report that students do not perform up to their capabilities. The students may have the necessary knowledge and skill, but for some reason these are not reflected in their performance. Their poor performance is often attributed to lack of motivation.

Because learning is such a fundamental concept, let us consider carefully the two main types of conditioning. Most instances of learning can be categorized into these basic types: (1) **classical conditioning** and (2) **instrumental** or **operant conditioning.** Indeed, some investigators suggest that there are just two types of learning. Incidentally, we could just as readily refer to these as classical and instrumental "learning" if it were not for a historical precedent favoring the term "conditioning."

Classical Conditioning

Pavlov's Work

Ivan Pavlov, the Nobel Prize-winning Russian physiologist, was among the first to report classical conditioning. During his studies of digestion, he examined the characteristics of dogs' salivary flow, a reflex response to food in the mouth. Pavlov's experimental method was to present food to the dog and measure the amount of saliva (see Figure 4–1). In the process he discovered that if a neutral stimulus, one that did not automatically elicit saliva, such as a bell, was paired repeatedly with the food, the dog would gradually "learn" to salivate at the sound of the bell alone, without any food. Learning to respond to a formerly neutral stimulus, because that stimulus is paired with another stimulus that already elicits a response, is the essential characterization of classical conditioning.

The importance of Pavlov's work cannot be overestimated. Not long after it became known, some psychologists began to argue that all behavior is based on classical conditioning. Although this extreme view is no longer popularly held in America, Russian psychology is still dominated by theories based on the principles of classical conditioning. It is agreed, at any rate, that a significant portion of our behavior can be better understood by noting the influence of classical conditioning.

FIGURE 4-1 Pavlov's work on classical conditioning

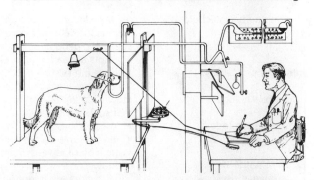

Pavlov's experimental set-up for measuring saliva flow in dogs. Food elicits saliva, measured by a tube connected to a cup placed over one of the salivary glands. The bell serves as the neutral stimulus.

Stimuli and Responses

The conditioning situation involves four events, two pertaining to the stimulus and two to the organism's response. There is a neutral stimulus that, prior to conditioning, does not elicit the desired, to-be-learned, response. This is the **conditioned stimulus** (CS), the bell in our example from Pavlov. The second stimulus is the **unconditioned stimulus** (UCS). Prior to conditioning it reliably elicits the desired response. Presentation of meat, the UCS, elicits saliva flow before conditioning. The salivary response to the UCS is known as the **unconditioned response** (UCR). This is the response that occurs before any conditioning has taken place. The response that begins to happen as a result of conditioning is called the **conditioned response** (CR)—a salivary response to the bell alone in the absence of meat.

Conditioning occurs as the two stimuli are presented contiguously (close together in space and time) and repeatedly. Usually the UCS is presented just after the CS. Gradually, after several pairings of the CS and UCS, the CS begins to elicit the flow of saliva. Whenever this happens, the animal has made a CR. The once-neutral CS (bell) is now capable of eliciting saliva flow by itself. (See Figure 4–2 for a summary of the events of classical conditioning.)

A situation commonly used in the study of classical conditioning in human beings is the reflex action of blinking the eyes. The UCS is a puff of air (delivered to the subject's eye) that regularly and forcefully elicits a blink (the UCR). Experimenters use an apparatus that both delivers the air puff and measures the amplitude, latency (time to respond), and other characteristics of eye blinks. The eye-blink response can be conditioned to a neutral stimulus, for example, the word "psychology." Conditioning begins by pairing the CS (*psychology*) with the UCS (air puff). Usually it is arranged so that the CS occurs slightly in advance of the UCS, for research has shown that a 0.5-second interval between the two stimuli (the CS–

Pavlov, with staff, at the Soviet Military Medicine Academy.

A Cough for Pavlov

"Saint Ildefonso used to scold me and punish me lots of times. He would sit me on the bare floor and make me eat with the cats of the monastery. These cats were such rascals that they took advantage of my penitence. They drove me mad stealing my choicest morsels. It did no good to chase them away. But I found a way of coping with the beasts in order to enjoy my meals.

"I put them all in a sack, and on a pitch black night took them out under an arch. First I would cough, and then immediately whale the daylights out of the cats. They whined and shrieked like an infernal pipe organ. I would pause for a while and repeat the operation—first a cough, and then a thrashing. I finally noticed that even without beating them, the beasts moaned and yelped like the very devil whenever I coughed. I then let them loose. Thereafter, whenever I had to eat off the floor, I would cast a look around. If an animal approached my food, all I had to do was to cough, and how that cat did scat!"

Thus, in free translation by the University of Connecticut's Professor Jaime H. Arjona, runs a story from *El Capellán de la Virgen (The Virgin's Chaplain)*, reprinted in the current *American Psychologist*. No clearer exposition of the principle of conditioned reflexes has ever been written. As every Russian schoolboy knows, reflex conditioning was unknown until it was discovered by Russian Physiologist Ivan Petrovich Pavlov (1849–1936). *El Capellán de la Virgen*, a play about the life of Saint Ildefonso (606–667), Archbishop of Toldeo, was written by the Spanish Dramatist Lope de Vega about 1615.

Time
January 23, 1956

Classical conditioning was known and used long before Pavlov.

FIGURE 4–2 Basic features of classical conditioning

I. *Before conditioning*

1 Present *meat*   and you get   *saliva flow*

Present UCS ⟶ UCR

2 Present *bell*   and you get   *no saliva*

CS ⟶ no response

II. *During conditioning (acquisition training)*

1 Present *bell*   and then   *meat*

CS + UCS paired together

2 Repeat CS + UCS for several trials

III. *After Conditioning*

1 Present *bell*   and you get   *saliva flow*

CS ⟶ CR

UCS interval) will yield most rapid conditioning of the eye-blink response. Periodically, the experimenter tests for the occurrence of a CR, a blink in response to the word "psychology" alone. On test trials the UCS might simply be omitted, or the experimenter might carefully observe records of eye movements to determine whether the subject begins to blink before the air puff is presented. If the eye blink occurs following the CS (and before the UCS), conditioning has occurred. The subject blinks to a formerly neutral stimulus and has acquired (learned to make) a CR.

If we introduce a longer time interval between the CS and UCS, conditioning is more difficult to produce, and if the CS–UCS interval becomes very long, no conditioning at all will take place except under very special circumstances. The best interval for conditioning varies with the response being conditioned. The interval tends to be around 0.5 second for quick responses such as eye blinks, but is longer for more slowly occurring and longer-lasting responses such as fear. The conditioning of fear to a neutral stimulus proceeds best with CS–UCS intervals of around 10 seconds and is not prevented by intervals as long as several minutes. In other words, normally it is necessary for the CS and UCS to be contiguous—close together in space and time—for conditioning to take place. This principle is embodied in the *law of contiguity.*

The Law of Contiguity versus Prepared Learning

The law of contiguity states that any two stimuli experienced together in space and time become associated with each other by the experiencing organism. It is often heralded as the most fundamental law of learning and the basic explanation of classical conditioning. In Pavlov's conditioning studies the CS and UCS were experienced close together in space and time; that is, the bell and food were spatially and temporally contiguous.

But what happens if the CS is separated from the UCS by a long interval? For example, suppose the bell is sounded but the food is not presented until 30 minutes later. The food, of course, elicits salivating in the dog, but even after several trials in which both food and bell are presented, the dog does not salivate to the bell alone. Conditioning does not occur with such a long delay. Thus the law of contiguity seems well supported.

However, conditioning has in fact been demonstrated when the interval between the CS and the UCS was even as long as 7 hours. S. H. Revusky (1968) did such an experiment using X-ray radiation as the UCS and a sweet solution as the CS. Earlier studies had shown that X-rays elicit the UCR of being

sick (radiation sickness), which can be conditioned to the solution. Rats that drank the sweet solution while being radiated developed a firm dislike for the solution, which normally they enjoyed. Eventually the animals became sick at the taste and smell of the solution, even when no X-rays were given. Thus the rats had developed a conditioned aversion to (strong dislike of) sweets, as the law of contiguity would predict.

Revusky tried the same conditioning procedure, except that he changed the CS–UCS interval to 7 hours, so the stimuli were no longer contiguous. The rats drank the sweet water and were radiated 7 hours later. Yet even with such a long delay, the rats developed a dislike for the solution (Figure 4-3). Either Revusky's demonstration is not an instance of classical conditioning or the law of contiguity is not the only explanation of why conditioning occurs.

A possible explanation of this phenomenon is that some organisms have a built-in conditioning system, genetically based, that quickly associated certain kinds of stimuli. Thus there might be a special system that relates food stimuli, through taste perception, with feeling sick. Such a system would have survival value for the species because it would underlie the organism's ability to avoid eating things that might be poisonous. Such learning has been called **prepared learning.**

The concept of prepared learning is nicely illustrated in an experiment performed by Garcia and Koelling (1966). Rats were exposed to a stimulus consisting of a sweet taste, a light, and a noise. This was done by turning on the light and sounding the noise whenever the rat licked at a tube containing the sweet solution. For some rats the exposure to the "sweet bright noisy water" was followed by exposure to an illness-inducing substance. For other rats the exposure to the sweet bright noisy water was followed by electric shock delivered to the paws. The rats were then tested to determine whether they had formed an aversion to the sweet taste or to the light and the noise.

The results were dramatic. The rats that had experienced illness following the sweet bright noisy

FIGURE 4-3 It looks like classical conditioning, but is it?

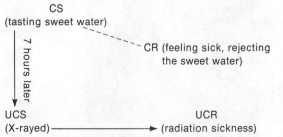

water formed an aversion to the sweet taste but not to the light or the noise. That is, they would not drink a sweet solution but readily drank unsweetened water when the light and noise were present. In contrast, the rats that had experienced electric shock to the paws following the CS formed an aversion to the light and noise rather than to the taste. They drank the sweet solution but would not drink it in the presence of the light and noise. This suggests that rats associate gastro-intestinal consequences (illness) with taste stimuli and exteroceptive consequences (shock to the paws) with external stimuli such as lights and sounds. Such a mechanism would be very adaptive, since in nature illness is usually caused by something that has been eaten, and external pain is usually caused by an external event (a predator, a fall, and so on). Thus this sort of prepared learning should allow organisms to learn quickly to avoid the likely cause of a dangerous event.

Prevalence of Classical Conditioning

Examples of classical conditioning abound in the everyday life of animals and human beings. One important example is the conditioning of emotional responses. Some psychologists have argued that anxiety—perhaps the most common symptom of emotional disorder—is a case of classically conditioned fear. Suppose a person experiences terror from a wild automobile drive that ends in a crash and painful injury. The fear and pain (UCRs) have been elicited in the context of, and thus could become conditioned to, "automobile" stimuli. The mere sight of a car may elicit the vague emotional feeling of fear in the person following recovery. While the feeling of physical pain would be absent, "mental pain" or conditioned fear might occur. Some psychologists have argued that fear conditioned to specific neutral stimuli is the essence of anxiety (see Figure 4–4). This and other everyday examples of classical conditioning are diagramed in Figure 4–5.

Instrumental or Operant Conditioning

The second basic type of learning is called **instrumental** or **operant conditioning.** The term "operant" is used to emphasize the work required of the learners (they must "operate" on their environment), while the term "instrumental" indicates that learners have some control over their own circumstances (what they do is instrumental in determining what happens to them). Thus instrumental conditioning usually involves more activity on the part of the learner than classical conditioning does. When-

FIGURE 4–4 Classical conditioning of fear

A baby develops fear of an animal because that animal has become associated with a fear-eliciting stimulus. In panel 1 the rat is approached by the child, who shows no signs of fear before conditioning. Then the rat is presented contiguously with a loud noise that scares the child (panel 2). Panel 3: After conditioning, the rat alone is capable of eliciting fear in the child. Panel 4: Worst of all, the child may now be afraid of all furry things, such as rabbits, stuffed animals, or even a man with a beard. The fear, originally conditioned to the rat, has now generalized to similar stimuli. Can you identify the CS, UCS, CR, UCR, and the generalization test stimuli? How might a child or even an adult learn to be afraid of policemen? of doctors and dentists? of strangers? of high places? of taking examinations?

ever a person behaves so as to gain reward or avoid punishment, that behavior is an example of instrumental action. The emphasis in this form of behavior is on intention and achievement; the learner acts intentionally in a particular manner to bring about a specific state of affairs. In the broad sense of behavior designed to gain a reward or to avoid a punishment, instrumental behavior encompasses nearly everything you do; indeed, some might argue that it includes all intentional actions. How much of people's behavior, including your own, occurs in order to get some kind of reward or avoid some kind of punishment? No wonder instrumental learning or conditioning is one of the single most important concepts in psychology.

Key words in this type of conditioning are *contingency* and *consequences*. Instrumental learning involves learning about the consequences of behaving

FIGURE 4–5   Diagrams of classical conditioning

Basic pattern	CS - - - - - - - - - - - - - - - - - - ➤	UCR
	UCS ─────────────────➤	
Sight of a car provokes anxiety following automobile accident	Sight of automobile	Fear
	Automobile crash and injury ───➤	
Child cries at sight of baby-sitter before parents leave	Baby-sitter arrives	Crying
	Parents leave child ───➤	
Seeing a cat elicits wheezing before any dander could contact the body	Sight of a cat	Allergic reaction such as wheezing
	Cat dander ───➤	
Constant worrying about one's job, even when not on the job, leads to stomach ulcers	Thinking or worrying about the job	Secretion of acid in stomach
	Tension or anxiety (on the job) ───➤	

TABLE 4–2   The Basic Features of Operant Conditioning

The subject makes a response R	which is followed by ──────➤	a stimulus consequence S
Hungry rat presses a bar R	──────➤	experimenter presents food S

sponse (R) is followed by a particular stimulus event (S) or consequence (Table 4–2).

Another way of looking at this kind of learning is in terms of contingency learning. The learner discovers that in order to make a particular consequence occur (say a piece of candy), she or he will have to make a particular response (perhaps crying). In such a case, we would say that getting the candy is contingent upon crying. The stimulus consequence is contingent upon the learner's making a particular response. In short, responses have consequences; and if we want to produce particular consequences, we have to make particular responses because the consequences are contingent upon the responses. A young boy might have to take out the garbage and mow the lawn in order to get his allowance; his be-behavior of taking out the garbage and mowing the lawn is an example of instrumental behavior. The consequences of doing his chores consist of getting his allowance, having his parents praise and thank him, and so on. Getting his allowance is contingent upon completing his chores.

Whenever the occurrence of a particular stimulus consequence is contingent upon the organism's behavior, or whenever a particular response leads to a particular set of consequences, we have the basic instrumental learning situation. This response-reward contingency is, of course, not present in classical

in a certain way — learning that if a particular response is made it will be followed by a particular stimulus event. For example, a little boy might learn that if he cries, his mother will pay attention to him and comfort him, perhaps even giving him some candy to "make you feel better." The basic idea is simple: Learning consists of discovering that a particular re-

THAVES © 1974 by NEA. Inc.

YOU'VE GOT TO STOP RINGING THAT BELL EVERY TIME YOU FEED HIM, DR. PAVLOV... YESTERDAY HE ATE THE AVON LADY

1-28

Reprinted by permission. © 1974 NEA, Inc.

conditioning. For example, in classical eye-blink conditioning, the air puff (UCS) is delivered regardless of whether the subject blinks when the CS is presented. Of course there is also a contingency in classical conditioning, but it is a contingency between two stimuli (the CS and the UCS). In contrast, instrumental conditioning involves a contingency between a response and the subsequent stimulus consequence (the reinforcer). The reinforcer (the boy's allowance, for example) is contingent upon the prior occurrence of a particular response (mowing the lawn).

Historical Antecedents

Whereas classical conditioning is associated with the name of Pavlov, instrumental conditioning is associated with the names of E. L. Thorndike and B. F. Skinner (see Chapter 1). Thorndike was the first to perform laboratory experiments using instrumental conditioning. His work led him to formulate the **law of effect,** which is the forerunner of the contemporary principle of reinforcement (see below). But it is Skinner who has made operant conditioning famous. He has studied the behavior of pigeons, rats, and human beings, including his own children. His work has led to the identification of the basic elements and laws of operant conditioning. He is the leading figure in the field of operant conditioning and almost single-handedly has been responsible for the recognition of the importance of this type of learning in analyzing, predicting, and controlling behavior. His pioneering efforts have led to the development of an entire philosophy of behavior known as *functional analysis* because of its emphasis on finding the events of which behavior is a function. His discoveries have been the foundation for a whole new technology of **behavior modification** that is still in its early stages, but nevertheless has already had enormous success in its application and has been one of the most controversial developments in the history of psychology.

Reinforcement

A **reinforcer** is a stimulus event (a consequence) that increases the likelihood of any response with which it is associated. A reinforcer is the effective stimulus that makes learning instrumental responses possible. Skinner used a device now known as the Skinner box to investigate the relationship between the events of instrumental conditioning. He placed a rat inside a glass box that contained a lever and a food tray (see Figure 4–6). The animal was allowed to explore the box freely. If it happened to press down on the lever, a pellet of food automatically dropped into the tray. A device connected to the lever recorded each press made by the rat while in the box. Pressing

FIGURE 4-6 The Skinner box

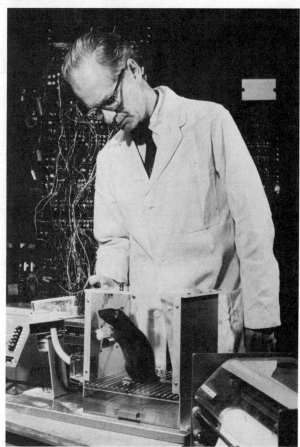

The Skinner box is the most commonly used experimental apparatus for the study of operant conditioning. In this photo, its inventor, B. F. Skinner, observes a laboratory rat in action. When the rat pushes a lever in the box, a reinforcer — a pellet of food — automatically drops into a tray for the rat to eat.

the lever was the response to be learned (the operant response), and the food pellet was the stimulus consequence (or reinforcer). Skinner discovered that by rewarding the rat with food each time it pressed the lever, the rate of presses increased dramatically. The rat learned the instrumental response by being reinforced.

The term "reinforcement" is used to describe the fact that a response increases in frequency when the occurrence of the response is followed by the reinforcing stimulus. There are two basic ways to produce increases in response frequency involving two basic types of reinforcement, positive reinforcement and negative reinforcement.

In positive reinforcement, the response frequency or response strength is increased by delivering a pleasant stimulus when the organism makes the desired response. Thus, rewarding the rat with a food

Highlight 4–1

Punishment Is Not the Same as Negative Reinforcement

Punishment: an unpleasant stimulus is *delivered* contingent on the occurrence of a particular *undesired* behavior. This punishing stimulus terminates at some point in time, but the termination is in no way related to the behavior of the organism being punished.

Examples:
1. A child spills his or her milk and the parents administer a spanking.
2. A prisoner spits in the face of his or her captor and is beaten with a club.

Negative reinforcement: an unpleasant stimulus is *terminated* contingent on the occurrence of a particular *desired* behavior. The beginning of the unpleasant stimulus is in no way related to the occurrence of any particular behavior.

Examples:
1. A prisoner of war is tortured until he or she makes responses desired by his or her captors, such as confession; the torture is then terminated. This process strengthens the response of saying what the enemy wants to hear.
2. A rat is shocked continuously until it jumps over a barrier, at which point the shock is terminated. This strengthens the response of jumping.

In most everyday situations, punishment and negative reinforcement occur together and so are easily confused.

The same stimulus event is used to punish one response and negatively reinforce another.

Example:
A little boy comes home and throws his coat on the floor. The parent yells at the child until he picks up the coat and hangs it in the closet, at which point the yelling stops.

Here the yelling is serving once as a punishment and once as a negative reinforcer. It is a punishment for throwing the coat on the floor because it is an unpleasant stimulus that is delivered contingent on the coat being thrown on the floor. It is a negative reinforcer because it is continuously being delivered until the child picks up the coat and hangs it up, at which point the shouting is all over. The parent has *punished* throwing the coat on the floor and *negatively reinforced* hanging the coat in the closet. So you can see that punishment is used to *decrease* the rate of an undesired response, while negative reinforcement is used to *increase* the rate of a desired response. It is possible, however, accidentally to negatively reinforce a response you do not want to increase. Suppose the parent keeps yelling at his or her child until the child starts to cry, at which point the parent perhaps starts to feel guilty about hurting the child's feelings and stops yelling. A contingency can easily be developed here between crying and termination of the yelling, such that crying gets negatively reinforced. Quickly the child learns to start crying as soon as Mom or Dad starts yelling because "that usually gets them to stop yelling at me."

---

pellet when it makes the response of pressing the lever is an example of positive reinforcement—the frequency of lever pressing increases.

The second basic type of reinforcement—negative reinforcement—also results in *increased* rates of response. However, it is accomplished by arranging a negative contingency—making a particular response leads to the termination or removal of an unpleasant stimulus. For example, if the floor of the rat's cage is electrified so that the rat is being continuously shocked in the cage, and if the shock is terminated for a period of time each time the rat presses the lever, we will observe that the rate of lever pressing increases. Lever pressing is being reinforced, but it is being negatively reinforced. Lever pressing leads to the termination of the shock (an unpleasant stimulus). In contrast, in the case of positive reinforcement, lever pressing leads to the presentation of a pleasant stimulus (a piece of

food). Both cases involve increased rates of responding and are thus instances of reinforcement; however, two opposite ways of increasing the response are used.

The opposite effect of reinforcement on response rate would occur in a situation in which a contingency is arranged that results in a *decreased* rate of response, eventually to the point where the organism completely withholds the response. One such contingency is known as punishment. In punishment, an unpleasant stimulus is delivered if the response is made. For example, if we took a rat that had learned to press a lever in the box because of positive reinforcement and then started to punish the rat with electric shock each time it pressed a lever, we would observe a decrease in the rate of lever pressing, to the point that the rat would cease to press the lever at all.

Secondary Reinforcement

The kinds of reinforcers we have considered thus far are automatically effective. The subject does not need prior experience with reinforcers like food or electric shock for them to have the effect of increasing the subject's responses. Reinforcers like food for the hungry animal, water for the thirsty, and painful shock are all examples of "innate" (inborn) or "unlearned" reinforcers. Technically they are referred to as **primary reinforcers.**

Other stimuli are capable of becoming reinforcers if the organism learns that they are associated with primary reinforcers or that they can be used to obtain primary reinforcers. Once the subject learns about them, they become **secondary reinforcers.** The most potent example of a secondary reinforcer for human beings is, of course, money. Consider the dollar bill and ask yourself why it is that we all learn and perform the extraordinary tasks that we do in order to get money. The dollar cannot be eaten or drunk. It becomes a reinforcer only because we have learned that money can buy food, drink, and many other things; that is, money will buy primary reinforcers (see Figure 4–7) and many secondary reinforcers.

In our society, secondary reinforcers are extremely important. Most people are not starving or thirsty or lacking oxygen. To be sure, the promise of sexual reinforcement may control a portion of human behavior, but, sex aside, most of our activity does not need to be motivated by primary reinforcers. Psychologists of all persuasions have postulated the existence of many learned secondary reinforcers. In addition to money, obvious examples are prestige, fame, security, and approval. There is, of course, a heavy emphasis of social factors in this list, implying the existence of a strong learned need to be liked by others. This, in turn, tends to make us dependent on the people who can deliver these reinforcers.

While it seems rather obvious that human beings, in general, are social animals with a strong need to be liked by other members of the species, it is not necessarily the case that this is based on learning. A new emerging field that is getting a great deal of publicity these days, sociobiology (see Chapter 7), would suggest that much of this type of behavior is innate to the species. It is also true that learned secondary reinforcers, when acquired in controlled laboratory situations, do not work well unless they are rather frequently paired with primary reinforcers. In technical terms, secondary reinforcers extinguish rapidly if they are not occasionally paired with primary reinforcers. This fact leads many people to conclude that human behavior cannot be easily explained by saying it is controlled by secondary reinforcers, since these reinforcers (such as prestige, fame, approval) are paired only with primary reinforcers (food, water, sex, and so on) in extraordinarily indirect ways. So this leaves the door open for other explanations of socially based rewards, the most obvious of which is that evolution has created a species (human beings) that is innately social in character. In other words, the social rewards could be viewed as primary reinforcers, not secondary ones based on learning. It is an interesting point to consider.

Many secondary reinforcers seem to develop through classical conditioning. The most important source of secondary reinforcement for a child is the parents. One or the other parent is almost always associated with the delivery of the infant's primary reinforcement—food, diaper changes, water, and comfort. Thus the mere sight of a child's parents becomes rewarding, and the child will work (crawl around) just to maintain sight of them.

FIGURE 4–7 Secondary reinforcement

Like human beings, chimpanzees can be trained to work for money (secondary reinforcement) that can be exchanged for primary reinforcement. The chimp shown here is about to put its money (a poker chip) into a "chimp-o-mat," which will dispense bananas or grapes. Chimps can be trained to work all day for poker chips if they have first learned that the poker chips can be used to obtain food.

Unfortunately, parents can reinforce a bad habit merely by paying attention to the child at the wrong time. Suppose a little boy is playing with a friend and his mother overhears him saying or doing something "bad." Running to him immediately constitutes secondary reinforcement of the undesired behavior, even if she scolds him when she gets there. Because attention has such a powerful effect, many psychologists recommend that a child's minor bad habits be ignored, at least as a first attempt at solution. Ignoring the child when he engages in "bad" behavior is a form of withdrawing reinforcement and should result in extinction of those habits.

Identifying Reinforcers

In order to institute instrumental reward training, one must identify those objects or events that the learner values. Obviously, candy and other favorite foods can be used with children, but there may be undesirable side effects. What other reinforcers will be effective is sometimes hard to know. One general principle that may be helpful for the identification of reinforcers has been suggested by David Premack. The *Premack principle* is that given two behaviors that differ in their likelihood of occurrence, the less likely behavior can be reinforced by using the more likely behavior as a reinforcer. For example, given free choice, many children will spend more time watching TV than studying. Watching TV is a more probable behavior. The Premack principle states that the amount of studying can be increased by making TV time contingent on study behavior. Again, children are more likely to eat candy than to do odd jobs, given free choice. Thus candy can be used to encourage work. In a prison, playing softball is more probable than learning a new skill, given free choice. To induce skill acquisition, the prison administration might use access to the softball field as a reinforcer. Thus from observation of an organism in a free-option environment, one can develop a list of preferred behaviors.

Highlight 4-2

Basic Instrumental Conditioning Situations

Following are examples of instrumental conditioning situations, one of each of the eight types shown in the table. Try to match each example with its type.

1. You drive under the speed limit only when your radar detector signals "police."
2. Your parents offer you a new wardrobe if you give up your "junk-food" habits.
3. In housebreaking your new puppy, you whack his snout if he wets the carpet.
4. You learn never to advocate liberal political ideas in the presence of your father because doing so always ends up in a shouting match.

5. Your kid brother gets his way whenever he throws a temper tantrum.
6. Whenever you get uptight about an upcoming test, rather than studying or thinking about the test you watch TV.
7. You have trained your dog to do a series of tricks, rewarding the dog occasionally with dog "yummies"; the dog will not perform for anyone else.
8. Jimmy doesn't drink or smoke when rich Aunt Emily is around in hopes that she will remember him favorably in her will.

	A. No cues available			B. Discriminative cues present	
	Train to elicit	Train to withhold		Train to elicit	Train to withhold
Use pleasant stimuli	Reward training	Omission training	Use pleasant stimuli	Discriminated operant	Discriminated omission
Use unpleasant stimuli	Escape training	Punishment training (passive avoidance)	Use unpleasant stimuli	Discriminated escape (active avoidance)	Discriminated punishment

Types of Instrumental Conditioning

We can derive four basic types of instrumental conditioning. We can try either to increase or decrease the rate of response. To accomplish this increase or decrease, we can use either a pleasant stimulus (such as food) or an unpleasant stimulus (such as electric shock). This gives us four combinations: (1) if we increase the rate of response using a pleasant stimulus, we have a positive reinforcement situation called *reward training*; (2) if we decrease the rate of response using a pleasant stimulus, we have a situation called *omission training*; (3) if we increase it by using an unpleasant stimulus, we have a negative reinforcement situation called *escape training*; and (4) if we decrease it by using an unpleasant stimulus, we have *punishment training* (see Highlight 4–2).

Let us now discuss each of the four basic types: (1) In reward training positive reinforcement is used to strengthen a desired response—a pleasant stimulus is contingent upon the occurrence of a particular response. Getting your allowance if you take out the garbage is an example of reward training. (2) In omission training, pleasant stimuli (usually called rewards) are used to get the learner to withhold a response that is not desired. For example, you make

S. GROSS

The New Yorker, July 31, 1978. Drawing by Gross; © 1978 The New Yorker Magazine, Inc.

If given a free choice, a child will choose watching TV instead of doing homework. Thus, according to the Premack principle, watching TV can be used as a reinforcer for increasing the time spent on homework. Does this apply to you at all? If you have trouble getting yourself to study, consider making TV watching contingent upon getting some studying done. Pick out a show you want to watch and tell yourself you won't watch it unless you get some work done. In other words, reinforce your studying by allowing yourself to watch TV. Reinforcers are, of course, often species-specific. Thus, we cannot be sure that what will reinforce a rat will work for a human being, and vice versa.

the purchase of a candy bar for yourself contingent on not smoking for an hour. The rewarding consequence is contingent on *not* making a particular response. (3) In escape training negative reinforcement is used to increase the frequency of a desired response. If the learner gives the desired response, the consequence is that an unpleasant stimulus will be terminated. For example, you could train a dog to jump over a fence by giving it an electric shock until it makes the jumping response. Turning off the shock is contingent on making the jump. Telling a convict that he can have "time off for good behavior" is an example of escape training—he can escape imprisonment if he produces "good behavior." (4) Finally, the fourth basic case is punishment training (also known as *passive avoidance*), and it is used to make the learner stop performing an undesired response. If the undesired response is made, the consequence is that an unpleasant stimulus is presented, and so the subject learns to withhold the response. Spanking children when they say "dirty" words is an example; so is putting people in jail for breaking the law.

Discriminative Stimuli (Cues)

Suppose a young girl is punished by her parents for saying "dirty" words. We might expect that she would never say them again. But the child can be punished only if her parents are there to hear her say the words; that is, the punishment can be delivered only when a certain stimulus (her parents) is present. If the stimulus is absent, the response can be made without the threat of punishment. Thus whether or not the child says dirty words depends upon whether or not her parents are present. The child can discriminate between the presence or absence of her parents, and she learns to make her behavior of saying dirty words contingent on this discrimination. There is a stimulus (the parents) that now controls whether or not the child says dirty words. This process is known as **stimulus control,** and the controlling stimulus is called a **discriminative stimulus** or *cue*.

In stimulus-control situations, a cue or stimulus is present, which can signal to the learner that reward or punishment will take place contingent on his or her behavior. Reward or punishment is contingent on behavior only when this discriminative stimulus is present. When the critical stimulus is not present or some other stimulus is present, no rewards or punishments are delivered regardless of what the learner does. These cued situations are thus different from noncued situations, where reward or punishment is always available and contingent on behavior.

Stimulus-control learning (also called discriminative learning) can be demonstrated in the

Use of Punishment in Treatment of Anorexia Nervosa

By RICHARD BLUE

Case Report

. . . The following case study utilized a novel approach in the treatment of anorexia.

C. was an attractive 15-yr.-old white female . . . with long brown hair and very delicate features. She was initially seen at the local mental health center in April, 1976. Prior to an intake session she had been hospitalized; her weight was 57 pounds. At the first session, she appeared gaunt and "death-like" with her weight holding at 63 pounds. During the first three sessions, C. would cry hysterically and relate how much she hated herself. She expressed a will to die because she couldn't "get it together." During these initial sessions, it was found that C. had set perfectionistic standards for herself and would become severely depressed if she could not live up to these standards. C. was the middle one of three girls and explained that mother and father had been having marital problems for many years. Mother ran the household and was seen by the children as the dominant force in the family. C. stated that two years before, she had weighed 150 pounds, dieted to lose this, and would "die before she would ever be that fat again." When made to eat, she would immediately go and throw up her food. After release from the hospital, she refused to go to school and was assigned a homebound teacher. . . . January, 1977, she once again was hospitalized. It was during this time that her doctor told her that she would never be able

to have children as a result of the damage done to her body. . . .

In February, 1977, after having tried the treatment programs of supportive psychotherapy, psychopharmacological agents, rational-emotive therapy and operant conditioning, it was decided to use punishment. . . . By mid-January, C.'s weight had dropped to 78 pounds and the family was frantic. It was decided to continue the psychotherapy and positive reinforcement on an outpatient basis. The change would be the introduction of punishment to change her maladaptive response pattern. A wooden switch was obtained from a branch and set in the parent's bedroom. Each time C. threw up her food or engaged in a temper tantrum, her mother would follow these actions with five painful hits from the switch. During the punishment nothing was said. Eating continued to be followed by "happy talk." Utilizing this program from February, 1977 – April, 1977, the number of times that C. threw up decreased from a weekly high of 12 to a low of zero. In fact, after 4 wks. of punishment plus positive reinforcement, she quit throwing up her food altogether. Her weight increased from 78 pounds to 94 pounds and she stopped all tantrums. Her perfectionistic standards changed from high rigidity to a more accepting level. She went back to school and in May, 1977, completed the tenth grade. Therapy was terminated during the summer months. A follow-up in September 1977 showed that C. was doing fine; her weight was 106 pounds. She

had become involved with a young man and was participating in extra-curricular activities. A follow-up questionnaire sent to her concerning treatment showed that C. thought the punishment had helped more than any of the other treatments. "It woke me up to what a crazy thing I was doing." She also explained that everyone's "understanding" only seemed to make her situation worse. Another follow-up in March, 1978 indicated C. was making a successful adjustment to both school and family life. At last follow-up her weight had remained at 105 pounds.

Although many differing philosophical approaches and techniques have been utilized in the treatment of anorexia nervosa, the use of punishment and other aversive conditioning techniques have not been used for so called humanitarian reasons. In this particular case, the patient in a follow-up questionnaire indicated that she was able to obtain much reinforcement for remaining ill. The more weight that she lost, the more she was reinforced with attention from family and doctors. Punishment suppressed or extinguished her maladaptive eating pattern. From this study, it was determined that punishment along with positive verbal reinforcement can aid in reducing maladaptive eating habits. Although aversive conditioning is not a treatment of first choice in most counterconditioning procedures, it appears to be an alternative when other procedures have failed.

Psychological Reports
Vol. 44, 1979

Here is an example of the use of punishment training in the treatment of a disorder known as *anorexia nervosa*. This disorder, usually experienced by teenage girls, is characterized by an inability to eat or to keep food in the stomach. The result is that the individual experiences severe weight loss.

laboratory by training a rat to press a lever for food (reward) when a buzzer is sounded (cue present) and not to press when the buzzer is off (cue absent). The rat learns to stop pressing the lever as soon as the buzzer stops and to start pressing again as soon as the buzzer comes back on. Its pressing is then said to be under the (stimulus) control of the buzzer. In a real sense, its behavior is controlled by the buzzer.

Each of the four basic learning situations we have discussed has its counterpart involving a discriminative cue (see the table in Highlight 4–2). The rat's lever pressing for food only when the buzzer sounds is an example of a *discriminated operant.* Teenagers who do not smoke *only* when their parents are around to reward their abstention exemplify the *discriminated omission* response. Convicts who work hard *only* when a guard is watching exemplify *discriminated escape* or *active avoidance* (they actively produce desired responses to avoid punishment from the guard). The child who omits dirty words from her vocabulary *only* when her parents are present to punish her exemplifies the process of *discriminated punishment.*

Shaping

Because the desired response may be uncommon or difficult, the individual using operant training procedures may want to use an auxiliary technique called **shaping.** Shaping consists of learning in graduated steps, where each successive step requires a response that is more similar to the desired performance. It is often known as the method of successive approximations.

Suppose an experimenter wanted to train a pigeon to peck an illuminated response button. He or she might start by reinforcing the pigeon just for turning its head toward the response button. After the animal begins to orient toward the button consistently, the experimenter may then require it to move toward the button before rewarding it. When the bird is trained to stand near the response button, the experimenter may withhold reinforcement until the animal makes slight head movements toward it. In the next stage, the animal may be reinforced only if it actually contacts the response button with its beak. Finally, the animal is reinforced only when it hits the button with sufficient force to trip an automatic switch that controls the delivery of pigeon feed. After the bird has been shaped to peck forcefully at the button, the experimenter may introduce colored illumination as a discriminative cue.

Two-Process Theory: Interaction of Classical and Instrumental Conditioning

Thus far we have discussed classical and instrumental conditioning as though they were two entirely separate processes, some learning situations being an instance of one and some being an instance of the other. However, many learning situations involve both. This is because most instrumental reinforcers also serve as effective UCSs (eliciting a reflexive response) for classical conditioning. Even relatively simple examples that are thought to involve only one could really involve both. For example, take a simple discriminated operant situation in which a rat receives food reinforcement for pressing a lever in the presence of a tone, but does not receive food for pressing the lever in the presence of a light. Instrumental learning occurs when the organism learns a contingency between a response and an outcome of that response. Thus our example certainly involves instrumental learning, since there is a contingency between pressing the lever and food reward. However, our example also contains a contingency between stimuli, as in classical conditioning. Food is presented during the tone but not the light. Thus the tone is paired with the presence of food and the light with the absence of food. Therefore, classical conditioning (for example, salivation to the tone) as well as instrumental conditioning should occur, and it does.

Since both classical and instrumental conditioning frequently occur in the same situation, how does one process influence the other? A theory called **two-process theory** was developed by O. Hobart Mowrer and Richard L. Solomon to explain how the two different learning processes interact. They argued that emotional states become classically conditioned. They also argued that these classically conditioned states motivate instrumental responses and that the occurrence or termination of these states reinforces instrumental responses.

© 1979 King Features Syndicate, Inc.

BC by permission of Johnny Hart and Field Enterprises, Inc.

The dinosaur is responding to a discriminative stimulus—the verbal command "sit." This is not the most elementary form of operant conditioning. In the fundamental form the dinosaur would be rewarded whenever it sat down. From there we might progress gradually—the procedure known as shaping—to the situation where it sits only on command and does not sit if we say "roll over" or if we say nothing.

To understand this view we will apply it to active avoidance learning (see Highlight 4–2). In avoidance learning a warning signal precedes the occurrence of some painful event such as electric shock. The occurrence of a response (for example, pressing a lever) in the interval of time between the onset of the warning signal and the scheduled time of the shock terminates the warning signal and avoids the shock. If no response is made during this interval, the shock is presented. It should be obvious that no responses will occur on the first few experiences the organism has with the warning signal-shock sequence since no learning will yet have occurred. This would mean that the warning stimulus is consistently followed by shock. Two-process theory argues that this should lead to the classical conditioning of fear to the warning signal. Thus on later trials the onset of the warning signal should produce this classically conditioned fear, and two-process theory asserts that this fear state motivates the avoidance response. Further, the avoidance response terminates the warning signal in addition to avoiding the shock. The offset of the warning signal (now a conditioned stimulus for the conditioned fear response) should terminate the fear that it produces, and two-process theory argues that this should negatively reinforce the avoidance response. It may help you to think in terms of voluntary and involuntary responses. The animal presses the lever (a voluntary, instrumentally conditioned response), which terminates the fear (an involuntary, classically conditioned response).

The implication of this discussion of avoidance learning is that classically conditioned responses can control or modulate instrumental responses. The onset of the classically conditioned fear response is said to motivate the avoidance response; and its termination is said to reinforce the response. Two-process theory holds that much of instrumental learning is directly governed by such classically conditioned states rather than by primary reinforcers.

Effects of Conditioning

Conditioning is a phenomenon with several aspects, and it has many effects on the subsequent behavior of the organism. In this section we will discuss several of the more important effects and by-products of conditioning.

Extinction and Spontaneous Recovery

Extinction is a process that takes place when (in classical conditioning) the UCS no longer follows the CS or when (in instrumental conditioning) the reinforcer no longer follows the learned response. In classical conditioning, as the CS is repeatedly presented alone, it gradually loses its power to elicit the CR. In instrumental conditioning, as the response is no longer followed by the reinforcer, the response occurs less frequently. An example of the value of extinction might be the elimination of a bad habit. Habits, good or bad, are usually learned because a person has achieved something, reinforcement, for his or her action. By identifying the reinforcer of a bad habit and removing it, the habit can be extinguished and should disappear. Can you apply this principle to the elimination of temper tantrums in a child?

There is a process, however, that makes complete extinction difficult, if not impossible. This process is called **spontaneous recovery.** To illustrate, suppose a rat is trained to run a maze for food. On a certain day extinction is begun by removing food from the maze. The rat continues to run the maze, trial after trial, until finally it quits running. At this point, you might think that the rat will never again run the maze unless food is reinstated. But you would be wrong. If the rat is put back in the maze after a day, it will run again for a few trials. Although it is given no food, its attraction to the goal box seems to recover without intervening training, that is, spontaneously. If the goal was to eliminate the running response, spontaneous recovery has worked against extinction.

Spontaneous recovery is likely to occur after each of several successive extinction sessions. Total extinction is likely to take a long time. Spontaneous recovery is one reason that we all find it so difficult to eliminate bad habits. Ask anyone who has tried to stop biting his or her nails. One way to minimize spontaneous recovery is to overextinguish the habit by carrying the extinction sessions on long after the response has ceased. Why does spontaneous recovery occur? During extinction, something new is learned — extinction is not just erasing the originally learned response. In classical conditioning, the subject learns that the CS will *not* be followed by the UCS, and in instrumental conditioning, the subject learns that the response will not be followed by the reinforcer. But, this new response learned in extinction is likely to be weaker than the old response, unless extinction training is extensive. Over time, both the new and old response tendencies decay and converge in strength, perhaps to the point where the old response reappears — spontaneous recovery. Learning to withhold a response, the new learning which takes place in extinction, is often called *inhibitory conditioning*.

Partial Reinforcement and Extinction

During learning, reinforcement might not be presented for each and every response that the learner makes. That is, the learner's responses are only partially reinforced. **Partial reinforcement,** a reinforcement schedule in which less than 100 percent of all correct responses are rewarded, is a valuable aid in teaching new habits. For one thing, you save money and effort if you do not have to give your dog a biscuit every time it brings your newspapers or slippers. At the outset of training, you would probably want to use *continuous* (100 percent) *reinforcement.* Once the animal is performing reasonably well, however, you can reduce the percentage gradually with the surprising effect that there is no deterioration in performance. In fact, there is some evidence that the partially reinforced subject actually comes to make the response faster and more vigorously than the continuously reinforced subject.

Now, suppose you institute extinction — no more rewards for the animal ever again. The effect here is also surprising. It will take much longer to extinguish an animal who has been trained on partial reinforcement than one trained on continuous reward. On an intuitive level, it is as if the partially reinforced animal does not realize that extinction has begun. The animal is used to not getting rewarded on some trials. In contrast, the continuously rewarded animal experiences an abrupt change in its circumstances on the first trial of extinction.

Any habit learned instrumentally under partial reinforcement will be difficult to extinguish (this phenomenon does not appear strongly for classically conditioned habits). Partial reinforcement is a pervasive phenomenon for human beings. Not every cigarette tastes good, only some of them; even the best gambler does not win on every play; temper tantrums do not always result in "getting your way." Because of partial reinforcement, we can expect our good habits to persist even in the face of adversity. But our bad ones will, too, and unless we have much time and great patience, simple extinction is probably not the answer to getting rid of them.

Punishment and Extinction

Remember the mother who ran to punish her child for being nasty to a friend? The attention of the mother is a reward for the child, and it is coupled with punishment, which the mother inflicts when she gets there. The child's inappropriate behavior may be strengthened rather than weakened under these circumstances. A juvenile delinquent commonly gets both rewarded and punished by his or her activities. So does a cigarette smoker, a sex offender, an individual with a phobia, and so on. This fact may make these bad habits even more difficult to extinguish or to replace than they otherwise might be. The routine of replacing one habit with another, rather than simply extinguishing a habit without replacement, is called **counterconditioning.** Research shows that counterconditioning is a better procedure than mere extinction for eliminating unwanted responses, particularly if the new, substitute response is incompatible with the undesired response.

An obvious alternative to extinction and counterconditioning for the elimination of a habit is *severe punishment,* probably the most popular, everyday method of response elimination. The use of punishment has been criticized frequently by psychologists on the grounds that punishment itself has undesirable side effects. To take an extreme example, your child may develop an aversion to you or even a personality disorder if you use punishment excessively to control behavior. There is some experimental evidence that punishment during extinction may not accelerate the process. Punishment might cause an early suppres-

Highlight 4–3

Schedules of Reinforcement

There are four major types of partial reinforcement schedules that can be viewed as a 2 × 2 combination of two variables (see diagram below). First, the schedule can depend upon how many responses the subject makes (called ratio schedules), or it can depend upon how much time has passed since the last reinforcement (interval schedules). Second, the number of responses in the case of ratio schedules, or the time in case of interval schedules, can be fixed and invariable, or it can be random and highly variable. This gives us the four basic combinations shown and described below.

	Ratio	Interval
Fixed schedules	Fixed ratio (FR)	Fixed interval (FI)
Variable schedules	Variable ratio (VR)	Variable interval (VI)

1. *Fixed ratio:* You reinforce after a fixed number of responses have been emitted. For example, you reward your dog every fourth time it performs the correct response.

2. *Fixed interval:* You reinforce the first response that occurs after a fixed amount of time since the last response. You might reward a rat for the first lever press after 1 minute has passed since the last reward. Pressing during the 1-minute delay would do the rat no good. Note that getting paid *every* Friday is like a fixed-interval schedule.

3. *Variable ratio:* On the average, you reinforce every fourth response, for example. Sometimes it is given after 1, sometimes after 6, after 3, after 9, and so forth on a random basis, the average being some specified value. The payoff schedule of a Las Vegas slot machine is a good example.

4. *Variable interval:* You reinforce the first response after *an average time interval* of, say, 1 minute. Some-

times only 5 seconds has to elapse, sometimes 2 minutes, sometimes 45 seconds, and so on, but the average time interval is set at a specific value. Have you ever tried hitchhiking? Is that a good example?

In general, the variable schedules (variable interval and variable ratio) lead to much higher rates of performance. They also lead to much greater resistance to extinction. Pigeons and rats have been trained to perform at very high levels over very long periods of time for very little in the way of reward, provided the rewards are scheduled properly. They also will continue to perform for very long periods of time after you have ceased giving rewards altogether.

Gambling casinos depend upon variable-ratio schedules to make a profit.

sion of undesired behavior, giving the impression that it is effectively extinguishing the behavior. The total time for complete extinction, however, may not be affected at all. Still, there are some situations in which punishment does work, particularly if the punishment is not overly severe. Frank Logan (1970) has sum-

marized the available evidence into seven statements concerning the effective use of punishment, which are given in Table 4–3. As Logan himself cautions, his conclusions are not meant to encourage the use of punishment but rather to provide guidelines for its appropriate application.

"Oh, for goodness' sake! Smoke!"

The New Yorker, April 14, 1962. Drawing by Saxon; © 1962 The New Yorker Magazine, Inc.

If you are trying to quit smoking, *extinction* would involve simply stopping, whereas *counterconditioning* would involve substituting a new habit for the old one. In general, counterconditioning is a better procedure for eliminating bad habits, provided, of course, that the substitute habit is not worse than the original one.

Generalization and Discrimination

The importance of two key learning processes, **generalization** and **discrimination,** has been implicit in the foregoing discussion. There are two kinds of generalization, response generalization and stimulus generalization. In response generalization, a person who has been trained to make a particular response sometimes makes a similar response if the originally learned behavior is somehow blocked or interfered with. Stimulus generalization pertains to the occurrence of a learned response under circumstances that are similar to but discriminably different from the original training situation.

As an example of response generalization, consider training a rat to press a lever in a Skinner box for food pellets. The first successful lever press might be quite accidental. Let's say the animal strikes the lever with sufficient force with its left paw while exploring the cage. The immediate delivery of a food pellet reinforces the left paw response. The animal will have

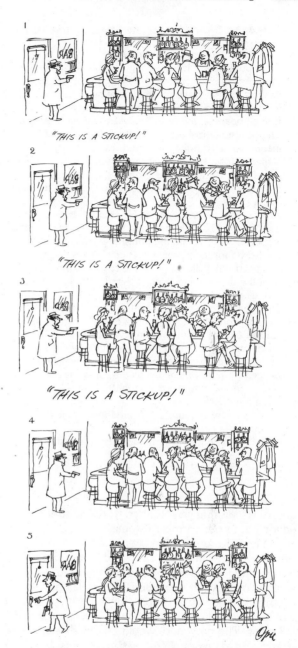

"THIS IS A STICKUP!"

"THIS IS A STICKUP!"

"THIS IS A STICKUP!"

The New Yorker, March 4, 1961. Drawing by Opie; © 1961 The New Yorker Magazine, Inc.

Merely paying attention to someone's behavior can be reinforcing, particularly if the person is "starved for attention." Withdrawal of the reinforcing attention results in the elimination of the behavior.

an increased tendency to make that same response again. With successive responses and reinforcements the response gains strength. But usually that strength will not be limited to left paw presses just because the

TABLE 4–3 Principles for the Effective Use of Punishment

1. *Avoid inadequate punishment.*
   If the punishment is not strong enough to eliminate the behavior, the response is also being rewarded, and fixation on that response may develop. Too small a fine for air polluting may in fact encourage pollution.
2. *If at all possible, the punishment should suit the crime.*
   The punishment should by itself elicit a response incompatible with the undesired response. A jail sentence for a burglar is not necessarily incompatible with future crimes, because he or she may use the time to learn more efficient techniques and to develop better plans.
3. *At least require an incompatible escape response.*
   The person should be required to make an incompatible response to terminate the punishment. Jail sentences should be for indeterminate lengths—until the person has been rehabilitated or, in the case of vandalism, until the damage has been repaired.
4. *If at all possible, punish immediately.*
   Since part of the punishing effects are a result of classical conditioning, and since classical conditioning is most effective with short intervals between CS and UCS, one should try to punish immediately after the undesired response has been emitted. Even better is to deliver the punishment just as the subject is about to make the undesired response, but, of course, this is often impossible.
5. *If punishment cannot be delivered immediately, try to reinstate the circumstances.*
   A child can be told or reminded about a past indis-

cretion that is now being punished. Even better is to "return to the scene of the crime." Make the subject repeat the offense or simulate a repetition, which can then be punished immediately. If you are employing counterconditioning, make the subject reenact the behavior sequence and perform the counter or incompatible response. If you walk into a party and immediately ask to borrow a cigarette when you are trying to quit smoking, go back outside and come in again with your hands in your pockets.
6. *Avoid rewards after punishment.*
   If you feel sorry for your child after punishing him or her and then proceed to offer affection and ice cream, the punishing stimuli will become secondary rewards (they become associated with rewards and are no longer effective). Masochism is a condition in which a person *wants* to be punished. It may result from always experiencing reward following punishment so that the punishment itself becomes rewarding.
7. *Always provide an acceptable alternative to the punished response.*
   If a very strong drive is motivating the behavior, punishment will prevent the satisfaction of this drive, which leaves the subject in a state of strong conflict—wanting to satisfy the drive but knowing punishment will follow. Prolonged conflict in important drive areas (for example, sexual drive) can lead to neurosis. In such cases try to provide an alternative mechanism by which the drive can be reduced.

---

animal began that way. Rather, response strength will generalize to other similar responses.

Now if the intention was to train an animal to press a lever with its tail only, a different procedure would have to be used. The animal would be rewarded only when it pressed with its tail and never when it pressed with its paw or nose; this method would effectively extinguish all responses except the tail press. The procedure would be called **response discrimination** or **differentiation,** resulting in a highly specific, stylized response—pressing only with the tail.

There are many examples of response generalization and response differentiation in human behavior. For example, in athletics, there is generally only one best way (or a very few ways) to perform a desired act, say high jumping or pole vaulting. Even slight deviations from the ideal, the response generalization phenomenon, may result in failure when jumping in a competition event. An athlete must undergo years of training in response differentiation until he or she can make the ideal response over and over again with little variation. Consider the problem of response

differentiation as it pertains to playing a concerto on a piano, cutting a diamond, or disarming a bomb.

Stimulus generalization is likewise an important phenomenon and has received a great deal of attention from both experimental and theoretical psychologists. In this phenomenon, a response learned in one stimulus situation tends to occur in other similar situations. For example, a child's fear of dogs after being bitten may generalize to similar stimuli, such as other animals or even stuffed animals. Experimenters often construct a **gradient of stimulus generalization** to indicate the degree of generalization to various stimuli. Suppose pigeons were trained to peck a button illuminated with a light of 550 nm (a greenish-yellow color). By testing the strength of their response to buttons of other colors, the experimenter can determine the gradient, or level, of generalization (see Figure 4–8). The more similar a test stimulus is to the original training stimulus, the greater the likelihood that the organism will respond to it in the way it has been trained. Thus it is no surprise that the curve in Figure 4–8 shows the greatest number of responses by the pigeons to buttons of illumination close to 550 nm.

FIGURE 4-8 Gradient of stimulus generalization

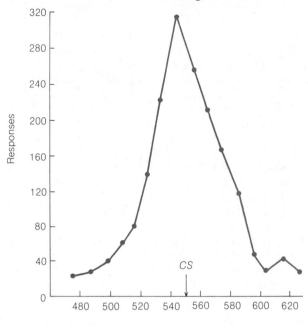

The gradient, or level, of stimulus generalization is shown for a group of pigeons trained to peck a button illuminated with a light of 550 nm and then presented with test buttons of several other colors, ranging from 480 to 620 nm. The graph shows that the closer the test stimulus was to the training stimulus of 550, the more the birds pecked.

Many responses are acceptable in one situation but not in another. In these cases, stimulus generalization may cause mistakes that result in punishment. Thus it becomes necessary to learn a **stimulus discrimination** essentially the opposite of stimulus generalization. The learner must be trained to discriminate among stimuli such that he or she responds to some but not to others. An essential aspect of learning to drive a car, for example, is learning to apply the brakes at the sight of a red light and not at the sight of a green one.

In the laboratory, discrimination learning is usually studied by training a subject to respond to one stimulus by rewarding the subject and not to respond to others by withholding the reward if a response is made. For example, a pigeon could be fed after pecks on a yellow button, but never fed after pecks on an orange button.

The combination of stimulus generalization and differentiation can lead to quite complex learning tasks. Suppose a pigeon is taught to peck at a green response key as rapidly as it can, and after extensive training the response button is suddenly changed to yellow. If the response of pecking the yellow button is not reinforced, the pigeon will gradually stop pecking (extinguishing the response) and begin to form a discrimination. The green button is called the positive stimulus and the yellow the negative. The simplest theory of discrimination learning says that an organism, in this situation, builds up an approach or *excitatory tendency* to the positive stimulus and a corresponding avoidance or *inhibitory tendency* to the negative stimulus. Because of stimulus generalization, excitatory and inhibitory tendencies will generalize to other, similar stimuli. The net tendency to respond to a particular stimulus is determined by the difference between the excitatory and the inhibitory tendencies to that stimulus.

Superstitious Reinforcement

So far this chapter has largely focused on what happens when reinforcers occur contingent on some response of the organism. In the real world, however, reinforcing stimuli frequently occur independently of the occurrence of any particular behaviors. For example, turning up a 7 when rolling dice is a chance event, not dependent on any particular behavior. But the occurrence of such "chance reinforcers" may sometimes strengthen behaviors that accidentally preceded the reinforcer. For example, the dice roller might have squeezed the dice before the roll, and the occurrence of a 7 might reinforce this behavior even though there is no real relationship between it and the following 7. Thus the squeezing behavior might be strengthened enough so that it will reoccur and thus precede 7 when it comes up again. This sort of process might be responsible for the development of superstitions and some forms of maladaptive behavior patterns. Of course, squeezing the dice would not be reinforced on every roll, but only occasionally—reinforcement would therefore be partial, not continuous. As we have just seen, this would mean that the response of squeezing might be resistant to extinction, which is a characteristic of superstitious behavior.

Learned Helplessness

Thus far we have discussed what happens when an organism has control over the occurrence of the reinforcer. If the organism makes the designated response, the occurrence of the reinforcing stimulus is made more probable; if the organism refrains from making the designated response, the reinforcer is made less probable. For example, if a rat is given food for lever pressing it can make food more likely by pressing. If a rat is punished for lever pressing by the administration of shock, it can make the occurrence of shock less likely by not pressing.

But what happens when reinforcing stimuli (rewards or punishments) occur independently of behavior? That is, what happens when a rewarding or punishing stimulus occurs and is unrelated to the behavior of the organism? What happens when the organism does not have control of important events that are occurring? This is an important question because we are frequently exposed to events over which we have no control. Consider the death of a child's mother or father. This is an intensely aversive event, but the child has no control over it whatsoever. Alternatively, consider the child who is given presents and privileges regardless of whether he or she is behaving appropriately. Here the child receives rewards no matter what he or she does.

The behavioral consequences of exposure to aversive events that cannot be controlled have been investigated by Steven F. Maier and Martin E. P. Seligman. They gave one group of dogs electric shocks that the dogs could control. These dogs were able to terminate the shock (escape) by pressing a panel. A second group of dogs was given an identical series of shocks, but they had no control over shock. Each dog in this group was paired with a dog from the first group. Each shock began at the same time for both dogs, and the shock terminated for *both* dogs whenever the dog in the first group pressed the panel. Thus the dogs in the first group could escape shock by responding, but the dogs in the second group had no control.

Both sets of dogs were later placed in a different situation in which shock could be escaped by jumping over a hurdle. Now escape was possible for all dogs. However, Seligman and Maier found that only the dogs which had initially experienced escapable shock learned to escape in the new situation. The dogs that had first experienced shock which they could not control failed to learn to escape even though they were now in a new situation. Maier and Seligman called this the **learned helplessness** effect.

Seligman and Maier developed a view called the learned helplessness hypothesis as an explanation of the later failure to learn produced by exposure to inescapable shock. In essence, they argued that the dogs exposed to inescapable shock learned that shock termination and responding were independent, that shock could not be controlled. They further argued that such learning should have two effects on the organism, one on motivation and one on learning. First, it should reduce the organism's motivation to try to escape when later confronted with shock in a different situation. Second, it should interfere with the learning of an association between the escape response and shock termination should the dog make the correct response.

The learned helplessness hypothesis suggests that certain kinds of experiences should prevent the learned helplessness effect from occurring. Exposure to escapable shock *before* receiving inescapable shock should interfere with learning that shock cannot be controlled and thus prevent the inescapable shock from producing a later failure to learn. Seligman and Maier showed that such an "immunization effect" does indeed occur. In addition, the learned helplessness hypothesis suggests what kinds of procedures might eliminate learned helplessness once it exists. If the subjects fail to learn because they expect the shock to be inescapable, forcibly exposing them to the fact that shock is now escapable should counteract this expectation and thus eliminate the failure to learn. This can be accomplished by physically forcing the subject to make the response that terminates shock. Seligman and Maier showed that this does produce successful therapy.

The effects of exposure to aversive events that cannot be controlled are not limited to poor learning of escape responses. For example, subjects given uncontrollable aversive events are later less aggressive and less dominant in situations involving social competition. Thus, emotional as well as cognitive and motivational changes follow experience with inescapable aversive events. A recent finding of potential significance is that organisms which have experienced aversive events beyond their control are later less sensitive to painful stimuli. This analgesic reaction follows exposure to *uncontrollable* aversive events only; it does not occur if the subject could exert control over the aversive events. This finding is of possible importance because it suggests that the psychological factor of control is able to influence the systems involved in the production of pain.

We described in Chapter 2 some of the ways in which pain levels are regulated physiologically and the role played by the brain's own "opiates" in this process. Since these substances—known as endorphins and enkephalins—are involved in the regulation of pain, they may be altered in some way by experiencing lack of control over aversive events. Perhaps such experience sensitizes the brain's own opiate systems, so that later aversive events are made less painful. When an aversive event can be escaped or avoided it is best to cope with the situation and escape or avoid the event. When the event cannot be escaped or avoided it would be adaptive to make the event hurt less. This approach would allow the organism to conserve bodily resources until such time as escape is possible. Thus, the opiate system might be sensitive to the controllability of events and be responsible for determining some of the consequences of exposure to uncontrollable aversive events.

Exposure to uncontrollable aversive events also has other physiological consequences. Jay M. Weiss has demonstrated that subjects exposed to inescapable shock exhibit a much greater stress reaction than do subjects exposed to equal amounts of escapable shock. Rats that had no control over shock developed severe stomach ulcers; those that could control the shock did not. Such physiological effects are not limited to peripheral changes such as stomach ulcers. Exposure to uncontrollable aversive events also produces disturbances in brain systems involving the neurotransmitters dopamine and norepinephrine (see Appendix B). Thus the effects of controllability are quite wide ranging and seem to have important influences on both behavior and physical health.

Processes That Affect Conditioning

What is responsible for producing a CR to the CS after the CS and UCS have been presented together? After all, the food does not come any sooner if the dog salivates to the bell. So why does the dog salivate in response to the bell?

Pavlov himself suggested an answer. He believed that the presentation of any stimulus to which an organism is sensitive activates an area in the brain responsive only to that stimulus. The contiguous presentation of the CS and the UCS should lead to the CS and UCS areas in the brain being active at the same time. Pavlov argued that the simultaneous existence of activity in two areas of the brain should form something like a connection between them. Presentation of the CS by itself after the CS and UCS have been paired together a number of times should, as always, activate the area of the brain that corresponds to that stimulus. However, Pavlov argued that this should also produce activity in the UCS area, since the CS and UCS areas became connected as a result of their prior contiguous occurrences. Activation of the UCS area should produce the UCR, since the UCR was said to be a reflex response to the UCS. Thus it was Pavlov's view that the CR is simply the UCR, but activated by means of a learned connection between the CS and UCS areas of the brain.

What Pavlov proposed is that a connection between the CS and the UCS is learned or acquired as a result of CS-UCS pairings. The CR is not really learned or conditioned, but occurs because the CS and UCS have been connected. This is why Pavlov's theory has been called a stimulus-stimulus or S-S theory.

Pavlov's views were quickly challenged by a number of the early behaviorists in the United States, most notably John B. Watson. Watson maintained that because the CS and UCS areas in the brain could not be observed directly, connections between them should not be offered as an explanation. He argued that the contiguity of the CS and the UCR—both observable events—established a connection between them. Here, the CR is again viewed as the same as the UCR, but now elicited because the CS and UCR have become connected rather than because the CS and UCS have become connected. For obvious reasons this position came to be called a stimulus-response or S-R view.

Much research has examined this issue. Although not all of the evidence is consistent, the trend supports Pavlov's S-S view. Conditioning seems to be a process in which the CS and UCS become connected in some fashion. However, we still have to explain why the CR occurs. As noted above, Pavlov believed that the CR was merely the UCR elicited through a learned connection between the CS and UCS areas of the brain. That is, the CR was seen as the reflex response to the UCS transferred to the CS. This view requires that the CR and UCR be identical, or at least very similar. Unfortunately, this is often not the case. Moreover, not all behavior that occurs in response to a CS is reflexive. An organism will not only salivate at the appearance of a light that has been paired with food but will also approach the light and direct behaviors at the light that would normally be used in food seeking and ingestion. It is difficult to categorize these behaviors as reflexes.

Memory Representations of the UCS

We have seen that the CR is not directly connected to the CS and that the CR is hard to describe as a transferred reflex. Thus it is still not clear why the CR occurs. Perhaps the basic process involved is one in which the organism acquires an anticipation or expectation of the UCS in the presence of the CS. Along these lines, Robert A. Rescorla has suggested that the CS comes to evoke a *memory representation* of the UCS as a result of the pairings of CS and UCS. That is, after the CS and UCS have been paired a number of times the occurrence of the CS produces an *image* of the UCS in memory. The CR might simply be the organism's reaction to having the memory of the UCS called forth. The advantage of this position is that an image of the UCS allows for motivated behaviors such as approaching the food source, and it could also produce more reflexive responses such as salivation. In addition, the CR and UCR do not here have to be identical, since one's reaction to a stimulus and to the memory of that stimulus do not have to be the same.

Rescorla has provided evidence for this view with what is called the UCS inflation experiment. If the CR is a reaction to the memory image of the UCS, it ought to be possible to change the CR by altering only the memory representation of the UCS without changing the connection between the CS and the image. Rescorla began by pairing a tone CS with an electric shock UCS. In the next phase of the experiment the subjects were presented with even more intense shocks, but no tones occurred. The occurrence of these shocks should not have affected the association between tone and shock since no tones occurred. However, the presentation of more intense shocks should have altered the organisms's image of shock to the image of a more intense shock. If the tone were now presented, it should produce the image of a more intense shock than before. If the CR is really a reaction to the calling forth of the image of the UCS, the CR to the tone CS should now be larger than it was before the intense shocks occurred. Remember that the more intense shocks were not paired with tones, so we would not ordinarily expect this outcome. However, this was the result obtained. The presentation of more intense shocks in the absence of the tone augmented the CR to the tone. This constitutes support for the idea that the conditioning process does involve a memory representation or image of some sort.

Inhibition, Contingency, and Contiguity

The preceding section suggests that the crucial relationship in conditioning is between the CS and the UCS. Before we discuss this relationship further, we must describe a form of conditioning not yet encountered.

Thus far, all examples of classical conditioning we have discussed have involved situations in which the CS is quickly followed by the UCS. Here the CS comes to evoke a CR. This is called *excitatory conditioning* because the CS comes to excite a response as a result of its pairing with the UCS. Conditioning also occurs when the CS is followed by the absence of the UCS, when it is followed by nothing. However, here the CS does not come to elicit the CR but rather acquires the capacity to suppress or inhibit responding. This is called *inhibitory conditioning*.

For example, assume that one CS, which we will call CS$^+$ (say a tone), is followed by meat powder injected into a dog's mouth, and another CS, which we will call the CS$^-$ (say a light), is not followed by meat powder. The CS$^+$ will come to elicit salivation and the CS$^-$ will not. However, the CS$^-$ will not merely come to produce no salivation but will actually inhibit the occurrence of salivation. Thus if a stimulus that produces salivation is present, a CS$^-$ will suppress that salivation if it is presented.

Inhibitory conditioning is hard to interpret within the traditional view that the pairing or contiguity in time between CS and UCS is the crucial aspect of the CS-UCS relationship. The CS is followed by the non-occurrence of the UCS in inhibitory conditioning, so what is it paired with? One suggestion is that the *contingency* between CS and UCS — rather than the pairing of CS and UCS — is the most important feature determining conditioning.

By contingency we mean that there is some relationship between the occurrence of the CS and the occurrence of the UCS. The contingency can be either positive or negative. The contingency is positive when the UCS is more likely to occur in the presence of the CS than in the absence of the CS. The contingency is negative when the UCS is more likely to occur in the absence of the CS than in the presence of the CS. In the first case, the occurrence of the CS predicts that the UCS will soon occur, and in the second case it predicts that the UCS will not occur. The contingency view says that it is these informational relationships between the CS and UCS that determine conditioning. And excitatory conditioning should occur when there is a positive contingency between CS and UCS, and inhibitory conditioning should occur when the contingency is negative. Here prediction of what will happen rather than the contiguity of events is crucial. In fact, excitatory conditioning takes place when the UCS is more likely to occur in the presence of the CS than in its absence; and inhibitory conditioning seems to result when the UCS is more likely in the absence of the CS than in its presence. Thus, conditioning seems to be bipolar, excitatory conditioning resulting when the CS predicts an increased likelihood of the UCS and inhibition resulting when the CS predicts a decreased likelihood of the UCS. These relative likelihoods appear more important than the simple pairing or contiguity between events.

Factors That Determine When These Processes Occur

We have seen that conditioning involves the formation of a connection between the CS and the memory image of the UCS and that the contingency between the CS and UCS is responsible for that connection. However, we would not expect organisms to form connections between all contingent events in the environment. This would be very inefficient, since many of these events are not important to the organism. Only some relationships should be learned about or internalized. What determines when such learning takes place?

The Blocking Experiment
An experiment performed by Leon Kamin suggests that organisms do not condition to all stimuli involved in a contingency. Kamin studied the conditioning of fear. A CS was paired with electric shock and the amount of fear conditioned to the CS mea-

FIGURE 4–9 The blocking experiment

	Phase 1	Phase 2	Test Light
Group 1	——	Tone + light → shock	Strong conditioning
Group 2	Tone → shock	Tone + light → shock	Weak conditioning

sured. In the initial experiment one group of subjects received a compound CS composed of a tone and a light paired with shock. The amount of fear conditioned to the tone and the light was measured separately, and strong fear was conditioned to each. A second group of subjects was first conditioned to the tone and the shock, and then to the tone-light compound with shock. When the tone and the light were tested after their pairings with shock, subjects showed no fear of the light but only of the tone. That is, no conditioning occurred to the light even though the tone-light compound was paired with shock. This means that the prior conditioning of fear to the tone blocked or prevented conditioning of fear to the light. Fear was conditioned to the light when the tone-light pairings with shock were not preceded by the pairing of the tone by itself with shock. However, conditioning to the light was not successful when tone-light conditioning was preceded by tone conditioning. This experiment is shown diagramatically in Figure 4–9.

This blocking experiment is important because it illustrates a case in which conditioning does not occur even though the organism is exposed to a contingency between an adequate CS and UCS. We know the CS and UCS were adequate because strong conditioning to the light occurred in the first group, and the light, tone, and shock were the same for both groups. The only factor that differed between the groups was whether or not conditioning had already occurred to the tone. This means that the mechanisms that produce conditioning are not always brought into play when an organism is exposed to events, and so some process must decide when a relationship is to be internalized or learned.

Rehearsal

Kamin speculated that a contingency is learned only when the occurrence of the UCS is unexpected and thus surprises the organism. He argued that the occurrence of an important unexpected event like electric shock causes the organism to scan backward through its memory in order to find the stimuli that preceded or predicted the important event. This process of scanning backward through memory was believed to be responsible for conditioning. If the occurrence of an important event is expected and thus not surprising, no backward scan of memory—and thus no learning—occurs. In the blocking experiment, the shocks that followed the tone-light stimulus were not surprising since the tone alone predicted the occurrence of shock. This is so because the tone had previously been paired with shock. Thus, the shock should not have provoked a backward scan through memory, and so no relationship between light and shock was learned by the organism.

Allan R. Wagner has recently related Kamin's suggestions to the process of *rehearsal*. Rehearsal means going over something again and again in one's memory. Wagner argued that CS-UCS relationships are learned only if they are rehearsed, and perhaps only surprising or unexpected UCSs promote rehearsal. It is commonly assumed that an organism cannot rehearse many different things at once. (To satisfy yourself that this is true, try to say a number of different things to yourself over and over all at the same time.) This means that if surprising events are rehearsed, and if conditioning requires rehearsal, the occurrence of a surprising event shortly after a conditioning trial should interfere with conditioning. If only a small number of things can be rehearsed at once, rehearsing the surprising event that occurs after the trial should reduce the organism's ability to rehearse the CS-UCS episode that occurred during the conditioning trial. This conditioning should be weak. To see this clearly just assume that only one thing can be rehearsed. If the event after the trial is rehearsed, the events during the trial cannot be.

Wagner, Rudy, and Whitlow (1973) began by following one CS, which we will call CS_1 with a UCS and another CS—CS_2—with no UCS. In the second phase of the experiment a new CS—CS_3—was followed by the UCS, and conditioning to CS_3 was measured. For some subjects the CS_3-UCS pairings were quickly followed by a surprising event, CS_1 followed by no UCS. This would be surprising, since the UCS had followed CS_1 in the past. For some subjects the CS_3-UCS pairings were followed by a nonsurprising event, CS_2 followed by no UCS. This should not be surprising, since CS_2 had never been followed by the UCS. The result was that the occurrence of the surprising episode interfered with conditioning to CS_3, whereas the occurrence of the nonsurprising episode did not. This means that surprising events do command rehearsal and that rehearsal of the CS-UCS sequence is involved in the conditioning process.

This discussion of the processes that affect conditioning should help you understand the role of classical conditioning in aiding organisms to adapt to the environment. That is, it should help you understand why classical conditioning is a useful process. It allows you to picture which events in your environment predict biologically significant events like UCSs. Accurate predictions of this sort should increase your chances of acting adaptively and dealing with those UCSs. If an important event occurs and is surprising, that means that you didn't know it was going to occur. Here rehearsal is brought into play and learning occurs. If you are not surprised, this means that you knew the event would occur. That is, you already have an accurate prediction. Here rehearsal and learning do not occur, for it would be wasteful to use a mechanism on something you already know if that mechanism can be used only on one thing at a time. It would be better to keep it available to be used on new information for which you do not already have an accurate representation.

The view of classical conditioning we have just elaborated holds that the CR is the organism's reaction to the occurrence of the memory of the UCS. However, the CR itself may have adaptive significance. It may aid in coping with the UCS that is to follow. An eye blink to a puff of air might make the puff less harmful, and salivating before eating food might make the food easier to digest.

Conditioning – The Causality Detector

The previous section argued that the "purpose" of conditioning is to allow the organism to learn the relationships that exist between environmental events, and thereby to anticipate the occurrence of biologically important stimuli. If this is so, the conditioning mechanism ought to operate in such a way that it focuses on certain relations between events and not on others. We frequently experience two events occurring together in circumstances where there is no "real" or causal relation between the two events (as with the squeezing behavior and dice rolling discussed in the section "Superstitious Reinforcement"). For example, it might start to rain just after you have scratched your nose. Obviously, the co-occurrence of rain and nose scratching is accidental – scratching one's nose does not produce rain. Thus, it would not be adaptive for you to form an association between nose scratching and rain. The conditioning mechanism should probably be constructed so as to produce an association when there is a "true" causal relation between events, but not when the relation is spurious or accidental. That is, evolution should have selected for a mechanism that utilizes those features that generally accompany causal relationships as important determinants of conditioning. Learning that event A predicts event B will aid in dealing with B in the future only if A is likely to continue to precede B in the future. This situation will be most likely if A causes B.

Many of the features of conditioning that we have already encountered can be understood in this context. For example, we have seen that repeated pairings of a CS and UCS are often required for conditioning. Clearly, the likelihood that A (the CS) will predict B (the UCS) in the future is greater if A and B have frequently occurred together in the past. You may scratch your nose once and have the experience be followed by rain, but this pairing is not likely to occur repeatedly. Other factors, such as the importance of contingency, can be viewed in a similar fashion.

In addition, a variety of new findings can be brought to bear on the idea that *conditioning serves to internalize the causal structure of the environment* and to isolate the best predictors of important events. One interesting aspect of what happens when one event immediately follows another is that sometimes we feel that the first caused the second, but at other times we do not believe that causation is involved. If we see two billiard balls move in succession, we would say that the first caused the second to move if they collided just before the second one moved, but would say the first did not cause the second to move if they did not touch. Research has indicated that in addition to occurrence at about the same time (temporal contiguity), two factors are important in determining when we perceive two events to be causally related. One factor is location in a similar point in space (spatial contiguity) and the other is similarity in the intensity pattern of the events across time. The term "intensity pattern" refers to the fact that any stimulus event changes in certain ways as time passes. For example, some events have a rapid onset but fade out slowly. A taste is an instance of a stimulus that follows this pattern. Other events – for example, an electric light – might have a rapid onset and a rapid offset. In fact, almost any conceivable pattern is possible. Recent experiments indicate that these same two factors influence conditioning. Conditioning is much more rapid if the CS and UCS have similar locations and temporal intensity patterns. Thus, the same aspects of the events that determine our impression that one causes the other influence conditioning as well.

Even more dramatic are experiments which indicate that conditioning to a stimulus is determined not only by how well the stimulus predicts the UCS but also by whether other stimuli in the environment are even better predictors of the UCS. In one experiment rats were exposed to two different CSs. One CS was a light in combination with a tone of a particular frequency $(L + T_1)$, while the other CS was a compound of the same light in combination with a different tone $(L + T_2)$. One group of subjects, called the correlated group, always received UCSs after one of the light-tone compounds, but never after the other. A second group, called the uncorrelated group, was given UCSs after each of the compounds half of the time. The other half of the time nothing followed the CSs. This design is shown diagramatically in Figure 4–10. The question was whether conditioning to the light would be different in the two groups. From a simple point of view conditioning to the light should be the same in both groups because the light is followed by the occurrence of the UCS half of the time in both groups. That is, the light predicts that the UCS will follow with a probability of 0.5 in both groups, and is thus an equally good predictor in both groups. The groups differ only with respect to how good a predictor the tone stimulus is. The tone is a very good predictor in the correlated group: if T_1 is present, the UCS always follows, whereas if T_2 is present, the UCS never occurs. Thus, the tone allows the subject to be sure about whether the UCS will occur. In the uncorrelated group the tones are no more accurate in their ability to predict the UCS than is the light. The result of this experiment was that conditioning to the light was found to be much greater in the uncorrelated group than in the correlated group. Conditioning is determined, therefore, not just by how well a given cue predicts a UCS, but also by how well other cues that are present predict. In general, conditioning will be greatest to the best predictor, to the most valid cue.

These points about causality and relative validity have been made with regard to classical conditioning, but they seem to be equally true for instrumental learning. Instrumental learning is best when responses and reinforcers have similar spatial and temporal characteristics. For example, punishment is most effective when the punishing stimulus is delivered to the same part of the body that was used to make the response that is being punished: Deliver the shock to the rats' front paws if you are punishing a lever-press response they make with their front paws. In addition, how well a given response is learned is determined by how well other responses that occur are correlated with the reinforcer. Surprisingly, instrumental response learning can be altered by how well stimuli that are present predict the reinforcer. Experiments have been performed which follow the design in Figure 4–10. The only difference is that a response plays the role of the light. The response (for example, lever press by a rat) is accompanied by one of two tones and is followed by food half of the time. What differs is the validity of the tone. The more valid the tone, the poorer the learning of the response. The similarity of classical conditioning and instrumental learning in these regards, together with the interchangeability of CSs and responses in competing for association with the UCS or reinforcer,

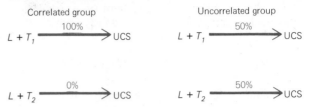

FIGURE 4–10 Elements of a compound CS as predictors of the UCS

suggest a common underlying mechanism. Thus, classical conditioning and instrumental learning may reflect the same mechanism. The method of operation of this mechanism may be to extract causal relations in the environment and produce association to the most valid predictors present, be they stimuli or responses.

Prepared Learning Revisited

Earlier in this chapter we noted the rat's ability to associate tastes with sickness that occurs many hours later. We also described the manner in which this sort of seemingly unique form of learning could be explained by assuming that specialized learning mechanisms have evolved for associating different sorts of stimulus events. The idea was that there might not be a single mechanism that produces conditioning no matter what the nature of the stimuli, but, rather, different mechanisms that are called into play for different stimuli.

The position that there is not a general mechanism of learning has recently come under attack, and it has been argued that general laws of learning can explain the findings previously thought to support the specialized mechanism view. For example, the general memory and causality principles that we have just considered have been used to explain why rats are able to associate tastes and sickness as readily as they do and over long delays. As already noted, Wagner has argued that conditioning occurs when the CS and UCS are rehearsed together in memory. Memory for tastes may be so persistent that the taste experienced is still in working memory several hours later when illness occurs. Therefore, the two could be rehearsed together, thereby producing an association. The association over a long delay might occur not because a unique associative or conditioning mechanism is involved but only because tastes have unique memory characteristics.

The idea of causality has also been brought to bear on this issue. We have already seen that conditioning is very rapid if the CS-UCS sequence embodies those general characteristics leading to the impression that the CS "causes" the UCS. The taste-poison relationship appears to have these characteristics, and this general factor might be responsible for their easy associability. Thus, whether taste-illness associations reflect the operation of a specialized mechanism or a general one is open to question.

The Physiological Basis of Learning

This chapter has thus far examined the behavioral determinants of learning. Another area of fundamental importance is the physiological basis of learning. The search for the *engram,* the physical processes and changes in the brain that form the basis of learning, has challenged psychologists and physiologists for many years. This path of investigation has been an extremely difficult one, and the answers are still largely unknown.

Two different research strategies have been employed to uncover the physical-chemical processes that are responsible for learning. One involves the study of simple or model systems, while the other involves the study of the intact behaving organism. The basic assumption of the simple system view is that it is not necessary to use the complex brain of the type of organism normally used in psychological experiments to study the physiological mechanisms of learning. The idea is that it is easier to study a simple nervous system that contains only a small number of neurons and connections than a complex one with billions of cells and an almost infinite number of connections. Of course, this approach requires the assumption that the physical mechanism of learning is the same in simple systems as it is in more complex organisms.

Use of model systems has other advantages beyond simplicity. For example, some invertebrates possess nerve cells so large that they can be seen with the naked eye, can easily be penetrated by electrodes, and are readily identified from one individual to the next. That is, one can study many different individuals of these species and be sure that the same nerve cells are under investigation. This approach is well illustrated by Eric R. Kandel's series of experiments designed to study the physical-chemical basis of habituation.

Habituation is a simple form of learning in which the reaction to a stimulus diminishes with repeated presentations. Kandel chose to study habituation in a marine invertebrate called *aplysia,* a sea hare. Tactile stimulation near the gills causes withdrawal of the gills. This gill-withdrawal reflex shows rapid habituation to repeated stimulation. That is, the gill withdrawal to touching the gills becomes smaller and smaller as the stimulation is repeated. By recording the activity of single neurons in one of the ganglia in the nervous system, Kandel found that gill withdrawal is produced by a single synaptic connection between the sensory nerve coming into the ganglion and a motor nerve going to the gills. Further, changes at this single synaptic connection are responsible for the habituation of the gill-withdrawal reflex. The isolation of the location of the learned change is important because only then can the process be studied. Kandel found that the process responsible for habituation of the gill-withdrawal response is a depression of excitatory transmission at the synapse, probably due to decreased transmitter release. A similar synaptic mechanism has been found in other model systems and may be the basis for habituation in general.

Although use of model systems such as aplysia has led to many insights, it has not led to an understanding of more complex learning processes such as those discussed in this chapter. Here it is necessary to study the physiological basis of learning in the behaving "higher" animal. This has been a difficult task, but exciting progress has recently been made by Richard F. Thompson. His strategy has been to record the electrical activity of cells in different brain regions while an animal is becoming classically conditioned. The goal is to find an area of the brain in which activity is closely correlated with the CR. The assumption is that a part of the brain that behaves just like the conditioned response must be responsible for conditioning. Thus, electrical activity in this region should develop across conditioning trials just as does the CR, and the pattern of the activity should mirror the pattern of the CR. That is, the activity should not be present on the first few conditioning trials before conditioning has occurred, should increase as does conditioning, should disappear with the extinction trials, and so on. Thompson has found that an area of the brain called the hippocampus meets these requirements. Thus, the hippocampus may be a major site of the engram, and of course, knowing its location now makes it possible to study it. We can anticipate important discoveries concerning how the brain learns, which may lead to such practical applications as the use of drugs to aid learning in retarded individuals.

SUMMARY

1. Learning is defined as a relatively permanent change in behavior potential traceable to experience and practice.

2. Many instances of learning can be classified into two basic types: classical conditioning (based on the work of Pavlov) and instrumental or operant conditioning (identified mainly with the work of Skinner).

3. In classical conditioning, a neutral stimulus (CS)

comes to elicit a response (CR) that, prior to conditioning, was elicited as a response (UCR) only by some other stimulus (UCS).

4. Classical conditioning is thought to be mainly a function of the contingency between the CS and UCS during the learning trials.

5. In operant or instrumental conditioning, the subject must emit a response or withhold a response, this behavior being "reinforced" by the delivery of rewards or punishments contingent on what the subject does.

6. The technique known as shaping (reinforcing successively closer approximations to the desired response) is also frequently used in operant training of a subject.

7. Several learning phenomena take place in both classical and operant learning situations: extinction, spontaneous recovery, generalization (both stimulus and response), and discrimination.

8. Extinction is the process of eliminating a learned response. Partial reinforcement during learning retards extinction. Punishment can also inhibit the extinction of a response.

9. Learned helplessness is a phenomenon that occurs when response and reinforcement are independent, that is, when the subject cannot control reinforcing events in the environment.

10. Among the various processes, all of which are cognitive in nature, that have been implicated in conditioning are: (a) memory representation, that is, an image of the UCS; (b) expectancy (surprise); and (c) rehearsal.

11. The function of conditioning may be to detect causal relationships in the environment and thus allow the organism to anticipate important events. Factors that alter our impression of causality alter conditioning.

12. Research on the physiological basis of learning suggests that a change in synaptic function plays a significant role and that a brain area called the hippocampus may be a major memory area.

RECOMMENDED ADDITIONAL READINGS

Hill, W. F. Learning: *A survey of psychological interpretations,* 3d ed. New York: Crowell, 1977.

Hulse, S. H., Egeth, H., & Deese, J. *The psychology of learning,* 5th ed. New York: McGraw-Hill, 1980.

Mackintosh, N. J. *The psychology of animal learning.* London: Academic Press, 1975.

Schwartz, B. *Psychology of learning and behavior.* New York: Norton, 1978.

Skinner, B. F. *Walden two.* New York: Macmillan, 1948.

What Does It Mean?

Classical and operant conditioning techniques are widely applied. Although some of the applications are sometimes called inhumane or degrading, these techniques have brought about many behavioral changes that have benefited individuals and society. Problems could, of course, develop if someone with a great deal of power decided to use these techniques to his or her own advantage. Misuse of them could be detrimental to humanity.

We have only begun to apply learning principles. The future possibilities demand an informed public understanding of the benefits and dangers involved.

Classical Conditioning

Morphine Tolerance

Learning is often a factor in phenomena not thought to involve learning. Drug tolerance may be one example. Tolerance refers to the fact that a given amount of a drug has less and less effect with repeated usage. This means that more and more of the drug must be used to obtain the same effect. Most explanations of tolerance focus on the cellular effects of the drug in question. For example, tolerance to morphine has typically been explained by proposing that repeated stimulation with morphine either prevents the drug from gaining access to morphine receptors in the brain or decreases the sensitivity of these central receptors.

Shepard Siegel has recently provided strong evidence that physiological factors such as these are not sufficient to account for tolerance to morphine and that learning is involved. You will remember that the CR which develops to a CS as a result of classical conditioning is often different from the UCR to the UCS. In fact, when the UCS is a drug, the CR is often the opposite of the UCR. For example, insulin (UCS) decreases blood sugar (UCR). However, a stimulus repeatedly paired with insulin (for example, the injection procedure) frequently increases blood sugar (CR) when presented by itself. That is, the injection of an inert placebo (say saline) produces increases in blood sugar if the subject has had previous injections of insulin. Apparently this opponent response is part of the body's normal defensive reactions, as it seeks to maintain a constant state (the principle of homeostasis, which will be discussed in Chapter 7).

What if this is true of morphine? As the person repeatedly encounters morphine, conditioning should occur to those stimuli that precede morphine. These stimuli are the injection ritual. The CR should be opposite to the effect produced by morphine and should thus oppose the action of morphine. If the CR is relatively long lasting, it should take away from the action of morphine, since it is the opposite of the morphine reaction.

Morphine is an analgesic; it reduces sensitivity to pain, and tolerance develops to this effect of the drug. That is, a given dose of the drug will have less and less pain-reducing effect with repeated injections. Siegel has argued that this occurs in part because an increased sensitivity to pain develops as a CR to the injection procedure and cancels some of the pain-reducing effect of the morphine. This view predicts that tolerance should be decreased or eliminated if the morphine is given without the stimuli that usually accompany it. The opposing CR should not occur if the stimuli to which it is conditioned are not presented. Clearly, theories that hold tolerance to be only a cellular phenomenon would not expect stimuli preceding morphine administration to make a difference. In fact, Siegel has shown that tolerance is greatly reduced if the usual stimuli that precede the morphine are not presented with the morphine. The pain-reducing effects of morphine were restored simply by presenting new stimuli before the morphine.

This view concerning tolerance has important implications. Consider the heroin addict who habitually takes the drug in a given setting, say with a particular group of people in a particular place. These stimuli should come to elicit a CR opposite in effect to the heroin and counteract it. This leads to bigger and bigger doses to maintain the same effect. What might happen should the person take this large dose with different people in a different place? Could this be one of the causes of overdose death?

The phenomenon of opposed CR and UCR can help us better understand the adaptive value of classical conditioning. It allows the body to defend itself against repeatedly encountered stimuli that produce bodily changes. Such a mechanism would help the organism maintain a balance and cope with events that alter its functioning.

Bedwetting

Principles of classical conditioning have been used to cure children of bedwetting (called **enuresis**). Bladder tension is usually the stimulus that awakens us in the middle of the night, but the bedwetting child has not learned the response of waking up. To stop the child from wetting the bed requires conditioning the awakening response to the stimulus of bladder tension. The UCS would be a stimulus that would awaken a person, such as a loud buzzer or bell. After repeated pairings of the bell with the CS of bladder tension, bladder tension alone should be sufficient to elicit awakening.

In practice, though, how do parents know when a child's bladder is full so they can sound the bell? Obviously the bladder is full at the time the child first starts to wet the bed, but how do parents know when the child is wetting the bed? A psychologist has devised an apparatus that consists of a special sheet equipped with wires that detect urine the moment it starts flowing. The detection apparatus closes an electrical circuit that in turn sounds the bell to awaken the child. After a short period of training with this device, the child begins to awaken himself in anticipation

New Psychotherapy for Drug Addiction

By JERRY V. WILLIAMS

New treatments for drug addiction and schizophrenia were disclosed Friday to 150 psychologists and psychiatrists attending the fifth annual meeting of the Society for Psychotherapy Research at the Cosmopolitan Hotel.

Presenting papers on the new treatments were Dr. Charles O'Brien of the University of Pennsylvania School of Medicine and Dr. Loren Mosher of the National Institute of Mental Health.

In an interview, Dr. O'Brien said he has experienced some success in combatting drug addiction through what he described as "extinction trials" in conjunction with more traditional forms of therapy.

O'Brien said there is a heavy "conditioning" aspect of drug addiction, in which a person gets "conditioned" to compulsive drug use. Many drug users experience "highs' through the simple process of going through their shooting routine.

He termed these individuals "more needle freaks than anything else." With the advent of heavier law enforcement, particularly, resulting in more diluted supplies of heroin, some addicts continue "shooting up" and may even be provoked to the act through stimulation by their environment, O'Brien said.

Studies of addicts treated at the medical school, he noted, showed 20 per cent to be "pseudo-addicts" and another 20 per cent to have "very mild addictions."

Obviously, he explained, treatment with methadone—the only method now available—would create true physical dependence in these individuals. An alternative was needed.

The alternative O'Brien came up with involved the use of an experimental narcotic "antagonist" to neutralize any intake of drug the addict might take.

Extinction trials were undertaken in which the addicts, having been given the antagonist, were given several syringes containing measured amounts of a saline solution or a narcotic. The addicts then were allowed to inject the contents of one or the other of the syringes, after which measurements were made of their physical reactions and they were required to fill out a series of tests.

The first three to five injections showed no difference in the amount of "high" obtained, O'Brien said, whether the saline or narcotic was injected.

After this first plateau, the addicts developed a dislike for the needle routine when the results were no longer maintained.

Reporting on 20 cases with an eight-month followup, O'Brien said six of the 20 are drug-free and another four are on a methadone program and "doing well." The remainder are either "back on the street" or not doing well.

O'Brien estimated the technique would be applicable to only about 30 per cent of the addict population—always in connection with other forms of therapy such as job counseling—because of the degree of motivation required for use of the narcotic antagonist. . . .

The Denver Post
June 16, 1974

Highlight 4-4

Children's Bedwetting Alarms

Helps keep sleeper dry by conditioning him to stop bedwetting. Each bedding pack has 2 foil pads with separate sheet between. Moisture passes from top pad to bottom . . . alarm goes off almost instantly. Units can't shock . . . use low voltage batteries. Not for organic disorders or baby training.

FIGURE 4–11   Conditioning cure for bedwetting

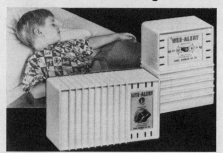

The principles of classical conditioning have been used effectively to cure bedwetting. This device is sold by Sears.

of the release of urine. Indeed, the unit works so well that some companies sell or lease it at extraordinarily high prices to desperate parents. A functional unit, however, can be purchased for a small amount of money from most large catalogue companies (see Figure 4–11). Classical conditioning principles have also been applied to toilet training through the use of a buzzer circuit built into training pants.

Conditioning Taste Aversions

Coyotes kill sheep. As a consequence sheep ranchers have taken up arms against them. The slaughter of coyotes has, in turn, become a matter of concern to environmentalists and naturalists. Thus a controversy has developed, and there is need for a solution that will be satisfactory to both naturalists and ranchers. A direct application of long-delayed conditioning has been made to the problem by Gustavson, Garcia, Hankins, and Rusiniak (1974). Using principles derived from laboratory studies on conditioned aversions, these psychologists reasoned that coyotes could be conditioned to avoid killing and eating sheep flesh.

The basic laboratory procedure consisted of feeding coyotes "free" sheep meat laced with lithium chloride, a chemical that makes the coyotes very sick. Despite the long delay between the CS (tasting the meat) and the UCR (getting sick), coyotes so treated develop an immediate dislike for the kind of food containing the poison. Only one or two "treatments" are needed to inhibit the coyotes' desire for the sheep. Gustavson and his associates showed that this treatment did not affect the coyotes' willingness to eat rabbit or other kinds of meat. The treatment results in a specific dislike for sheep. The authors concluded that a method based on their laboratory procedures could stop coyotes from killing sheep and yet not deprive them of other prey. Sheep-meat baits, laced with a nondeadly but illness-producing chemical, could be distributed around the territory where the coyotes are known to prey on sheep. A coyote who happens on the trap would eat the sheep meat and automatically develop an instant aversion to sheep. It would then stop killing sheep but continue to prey on less-valued species.

Another important application of taste-aversion conditioning is related to chemotherapy, a frequent therapeutic procedure used with cancer patients. The chemical agents employed to arrest the cancerous growths are toxic and often produce nausea and gastrointestinal upset. A side effect of chemotherapy is reduced eating and consequent weakening and loss of weight.

The traditional assumption has been that the reduced food consumption is a direct effect of the chemical substances on appetite—that is, the chemotherapy patient is simply not hungry and therefore does not eat. A knowledge of taste-aversion conditioning, however, suggests a different possibility. Since the chemical agents that are used produce nausea, taste aversions should be conditioned to whatever the patient ate in the several hours preceding the chemotherapy session. Since the patient typically would eat different foods on different days, aversions would be conditioned to many of the foods as the person repeatedly undergoes chemotherapy. Thus, food consumption might decrease because aversions have been conditioned to the foods the patient normally eats and not because of a general loss of appetite. If this is so, could you apply your knowledge of conditioning to design a chemotherapy and eating schedule that would not produce decreased food consumption? Could you design a taste-aversion procedure that would be useful in the treatment of alcoholism? in the treatment of pathological overeating?

Diagnosing and Understanding Infants

One major problem with babies, from the point of view of the doctor trying to treat them or the psychologist trying to understand how they do things, is that the babies can't talk. They can't tell you what's wrong or how they do this or that or if they can do this or that. Conditioning techniques, both classical and instrumental, can and have been used to help "communicate" with infants. For example, early detection of hearing or vision deficits in newborn babies would help prevent more serious problems later on.

Highlight 4–5

Classical and Instrumental Conditioning Usually Work Together

Novel Treatment

ENGLAND (UPI) — Doctors have found a novel way to stop compulsive gambler David Smith from putting his money where his mouth is, Smith says.

"I pick out horses twice a day," Smith said of his treatment. "Then they let me listen to the race broadcast. When I get excited a doctor or nurse presses a button which gives me an unpleasant electric shock through the arms."

"It brings me down to earth every time," he said. "Already I am getting to hate racing and all that goes with it."

DeKalb (Ill.) Daily Chronicle
October 10, 1973

In most behavior modification situations, the therapy consists of a component centering on classical conditioning and another component involving instrumental conditioning. Usually, one of the two components is more obvious than the other (and perhaps more important), but both components are usually present.

The Events

Listening to the races ⟶ getting excited causes therapist to present

Shock ⟷ pain, discomfort

Classical Conditioning Component

CS (listening to the races)

UCS (shock) ⟶ UCR (pain and discomfort)

Results: Eventually the CS alone (listening to the races) should elicit a CR similar to the UCR—the subject will feel anxious (conditioned fear) whenever he hears the races.

Instrumental Conditioning Component

R (getting excited) ⟶ S (shock)

Results: The subject learns that the consequences of getting excited are unpleasant. To avoid shock he learns to avoid making the "excitement response," which of course means that he would say he no longer enjoys (gets excitement from) listening to the races.

But you can't ask the baby to call off the letters on a Snellen eye chart at 20 feet. But you could attempt to condition the infant to a visual CS or an auditory CS: evidence of conditioning would be evidence of the baby's being able to see or hear the type of stimulus being used.

In a related but opposite use of classical conditioning, this technique can be used to detect people who fake deafness on hearing tests in order to receive disability benefits. Hearing is normally tested by asking subjects to indicate which of a variety of tones they hear. Of course, it would be easy to fake deafness, or at least to fake an impairment of hearing. In suspected cases a conditioning procedure is used pairing the tone CS with a mild shock that elicits a reflex response (the GSR) in the skin. The electrical conductance of the skin changes in response to the shock. If a person shows conditioning to the tone CS, it must be that he or she heard the sound.

Treatment of "Deviant" Behavior

Classical conditioning has been applied with some very limited success to the treatment of various types of deviant behavior. In this area especially, the application of learning principles has been most controversial. For example, homosexuality has been treated with techniques based on classical conditioning. A male homosexual might be shown pictures of nude males as CS stimuli, paired with injections of a type of morphine that quickly produces nausea and vomiting. Pictures of nude females would not be paired with feeling sick. Alternatively, strong shocks could be paired with the nude male pictures but not the female ones. The idea is to classically condition a response (the CR) that is not pleasant so that the CS stimuli will be avoided (the CS is made unpleasant). A similar type of treatment has been developed for use with pedophiliacs, or persons who have a sexual love for children. Pairing pictures of nude children with very unpleasant events (shock or vomiting) should develop an unpleasant conditioned response that should help the person avoid the undesirable behavior. The same technique can be applied to alcoholism. The sight, smell, and taste of alcohol can be classically conditioned to elicit a response of nausea if these events have been classically paired with a nausea-inducing drug.

These classical conditioning treatments have not been particularly effective. They have not turned out to be magic cures for undesirable behaviors, although some people have certainly been helped. What does seem clear is that this type of treatment makes many people worry about "mind control" and possibilities for the abuse of such techniques. People are frightened by these methods, particularly if they have seen their potential for abuse vividly portrayed in such movies as "A Clockwork Orange." Indeed, the potential for misuse is real, although probably overblown in most futuristic books and movies.

Instrumental Conditioning

Biofeedback

Psychologists have discovered how to use conditioning techniques to control physiological responses that are under the automatic control of the nervous system. Take the

Coyotes will quickly learn to avoid meat that has been associated with illness due to poisoning. Here, before aversive conditioning, a coyote kills a lamb.

control of blood pressure, for example. To instrumentally condition blood pressure we need a device that will continuously monitor and inform the subject of his or her relative blood pressure at all times. To use the operant conditioning technique, we would construct a device that would sound a tone whenever blood pressure rose above a specifed level. The subject would be instructed to prevent the tone in any way possible.

A shaping technique might be used. At the start the critical blood pressure level would be set fairly high and in such a way that only slight reductions would terminate the tone. The tone offset tells the subjects that the preceding behavior was beneficial to blood pressure level. Those activities, whatever they might be and whether or not they are conscious, are reinforced. When repeated, they are reinforced again. Gradually the subject learns to keep the tone off most of the time.

When the subject has learned to stay below the critical level, the setting is adjusted, making the subject reach for an even lower blood pressure level. Gradually the critical level is reduced to an acceptable range.

With advanced technology, we can expect to see an even greater reliance on bioelectric feedback devices in the control of undesired physiological responses. Use of these techniques will contribute to longer and healthier lives.

One interesting application of biofeedback concerns the operant conditioning of various brain-wave patterns in an effort to treat epilepsy. By learning to increase certain brain waves (in this case, the sensorimotor rhythm), subjects can decrease the amount of seizure waves in their brains. Several studies have indicated that some epileptic patients have been helped by this type of biofeedback. The procedure involves feeding back to the patient a tone or

Biofeedback equipment helps a person learn to control physiological responses by providing informational feedback.

The A–B–A Design and Operant Control of Vomiting

Laura was a nine-year-old child in an institution for retarded children. While she was enrolled in a class at the institution, she began to vomit in the class, and soon vomiting was an everyday occurrence. When she vomited on her dress, the teacher had Laura sent back to her residence hall. No medical cause for the vomiting could be found and no medication seemed to help. Perhaps her vomiting was not a reflex action, but a response Laura was emitting (*operant* behavior) because of its consequences (she could get out of the class).

In order to test this hypothesis, it was decided to measure Laura's vomiting under three conditions: (A) extinction—the reinforcement is eliminated; Laura had to stay in class regardless of vomiting; (B) reinstatement—the original reinforcement is reinstated; Laura was returned to her residence hall if she vomited; and (A again) a second extinction session—vomiting was not rewarded by allowing Laura to leave class.

The results were quite dramatic. During the first extinction period Laura vomited a lot at first, but gradually the vomiting declined in frequency until it reached a zero level. Then reinstatement began (she could leave if she vomited). It was quite some time before she finally vomited again, but when she finally did, she was allowed to leave.

In no time her vomiting reappeared; she vomited once a day and left class. Finally, during reextinction, she was again forced to stay in class despite her vomiting. Again, at first she vomited a great deal, but the vomiting gradually decreased to zero.

This case (Wolf, Birnbrauer, Lawler, and Williams, 1970) illustrates the application of operant conditioning to a behavior problem—once the reinforcing event is discovered, its elimination can be used to terminate the undesired behavior. The case also illustrates the A–B–A design (the reversal design) that operant psychologists use to make sure they have discovered the relevant reinforcers for a behavior. The design involves three stages, where the first and third stages are the same (hence A–B–A). Going from one stage to the next involves a reversal of the contingency thought to be reinforcing the behavior. In this case, the design involved going from reinforcer absent to reinforcer present and then back to reinforcer absent. The ability to reverse the behavior (bring back the vomiting and then make it go away a second time) eliminates the alternate interpretation that Laura might have quit vomiting without any change in the reinforcement contingencies.

light or both (the reinforcers) whenever the brain waves indicate the desired pattern. The patient simply tries to learn whatever behavior it is that keeps the tone or light on. If the patients start to show seizure activity, the training is momentarily stopped, so that they are not receiving reinforcers. This procedure is "technically" called *time-out from reinforcement.* If you have been used to being reinforced and someone calls for a time out, you might not like the discontinuance of reinforcers (no candy or lights or tones). In other words, time out may have the effect of a punishment. Recent work suggests that some of the effects of operant conditioning of brain waves may actually be due not to positive reinforcement of one behavior (the normal waves), but to punishment (through time out) of another behavior (the seizure waves). This is a technical point in the brain-wave biofeedback business, but it indicates that researchers do not know exactly what is being operantly conditioned. More important, however, is the idea that time out from expected reinforcement can act just like punishment. You can produce nearly the same effect by calling a time out as you can by administering a punishment. And for most of us it is easier to call time out ("sorry, no snack tonight") than it is to spank our children.

Behavior Modification

The treatment of behavior defects through the application of operant conditioning procedures has come to be known as **behavior modification.** Operant techniques have been successfully applied to such unwanted behaviors as stuttering, temper tantrums, poor study habits, smoking, excessive eating, and other problems (see Table 4–4).

Teachers are being trained to use operant techniques for handling problem students. For example, withdrawn children often get reinforced for playing alone, because the teacher attends to them in an effort to interest them in group activities. Instead, the teacher should reinforce them with her attention only when they show signs of participating in group activities. The teacher who does not know or fails to apply reinforcement principles often encourages misbehavior and class disruption by his or her attention to it. Ignoring these activities in their initial stages is a much better cure.

Psychologists used operant conditioning procedures in an unusual task during World War II. They trained pigeons to guide missiles to their targets (Figure 4–12). The pigeon was placed in the nose cone of a rocket. As the missile approached the target, the pigeon would peck on a key, sending out signals that modified the direction of the rocket, until the pigeon's actions indicated that the missile was on target.

Pigeons have also been trained to function as quality control inspectors. A company that manufactures gelatin capsules for drugs had a problem spotting defects difficult for the human eye to detect. Moreover, the inspection task was boring to human inspectors. Pigeons, who have remarkable eyesight, were shaped to respond to defects. Their work was superior to that of human inspectors. Nonetheless, the company decided not to use pigeons. Can you guess why?

The Token Economy   Reward training, derived from the principles of operant conditioning, has been applied on

TABLE 4–4   Some Examples of Behavior Modification

1. Elimination of crying episodes of a preschool boy by having the teacher ignore him when he cried and pay attention to him when he talked. Previously, the teacher had usually done just the opposite.
2. Elimination of the psychotic response of a female schizophrenic who always talked about the "royal family" and called herself Queen. The nurses were instructed to reward her with social attention and cigarettes when she talked normally and to ignore her when she talked about her delusions of royalty.
3. Elimination of a patient's obsessive thought about strangling his wife by having the patient punish himself whenever he had the thought. He did this by wearing a thick rubber band around his wrist that he snapped vigorously to inflict pain until the thought went away.
4. Reinforcement of standing and walking in a child who usually crawled around the classroom by having the teacher praise the child when she walked and ignore the child when she crawled.
5. Elimination of a child's tantrums and severe crying episodes at bedtime simply by having the parents stay out of the bedroom after the child was put to bed. Previously the child had cried and screamed until a parent returned to his room, and the parents had developed a pattern of staying with the child until he fell asleep.
6. Getting a patient to feed herself, instead of demanding spoon feeding by a nurse. The patient wanted to stay clean and neat, so the nurse was instructed always to spill some food on the patient during spoon feeding. In effect, the patient was taught, "If you want to stay neat, you will have to feed yourself." If self-feeding occurred, the nurse reinforced this with praise and social attention.

a large scale to shape the behavior of groups of patients living together in mental hospitals. The goal is to teach the patients to behave more in accord with the definition of normal behavior. The hospital staff and patients devise a miniature society based on a token economy. Tokens (poker chips) are used, like money, as secondary rewards. The patients can earn tokens for certain behaviors and redeem them for special privileges.

At the outset the patient may earn points for only the slightest modification of behavior. Gradually the requirements are increased until the patient must behave normally to achieve rewards. In one project, tokens could be earned for the following behaviors: getting up quickly and at the right time every morning; good personal hygiene habits, such as bathing and wearing clean clothes; performing clean-up chores around the ward; and, working at off-the-ward jobs, such as gardening or doing the laundry. The tokens could then be used to purchase a bed with an innerspring mattress to replace a cot, an opportunity to watch TV, and entrance to a fancy dining room rather than the customary undecorated hall.

Why Not Provide Positive Reinforcement in Welfare?
By WILLIAM RASPBERRY

WASHINGTON—Human beings seem to need opportunities to set themselves apart in ways that are considered positive.

We know that, of course, and we act on that knowledge in countless aspects of our lives. We pass out gold stars and other rewards to children who do their school work uncommonly well. We give bonuses to workers who show themselves to be unusually useful.

We sponsor testimonials, award honorary degrees and name public buildings for people who demonstrate uncommon devotion to the public good. We are forever devising ways to satisfy the human urge to be set aside as special.

But somehow this instinct—so effective in reinforcing and encouraging those attributes we believe to be in the public interest—abandons us when it comes to social welfare.

We create all sorts of potentially useful programs for the needy among us—public housing, financial assistance, job training, special educational projects. But instead of using these programs to reinforce and encourage good things, we do just the opposite.

The one overriding criterion for access to any of these programs is: failure.

You have to be a failure to get into the housing projects (you're kicked out if you show signs of overcoming). You have to be virtually without resources, financial and otherwise, to qualify for public assistance payments. You have to be an academic failure to gain entry into a whole host of special education programs.

In general, we reward those things we wish to see repeated. But in social welfare, we reward those things which most distress us, and we are endlessly surprised when people react negatively to the things we offer as rewards for their negative attributes....

I have a feeling we'd all be better off if we turned the thing on its head. Suppose, for instance, that in addition to sheer need—a negative criterion—we established positive criteria for, say, public housing eligibility. We could require, for instance, that public-housing applicants commit themselves to being responsible for the upkeep of both their apartments and, on a rotating basis, such common areas as halls and lawns.

Suppose these families, by exemplary fulfillment of their assigned duties, could earn merit points toward more desirable public housing and, if their economic situation improved a bit, assistance toward home ownership. (The other side of that coin, of course, would be demerits for poor behavior, an accumulation of which would render the family ineligible for public housing altogether.)

My guess is that we would thereby not only greatly diminish the amount of vandalism and other evidences of contempt for public assistance, but also greatly increase the number of families "graduating" into self-sufficiency. In addition, it might have a salutary effect on the ability and inclination of the families to discipline their children....

Rocky Mountain News, *Denver*
February 23, 1978

Can the principles of instrumental conditioning work at the level of society? Here's one man's opinion.

FIGURE 4-12   Operant conditioning with pigeons

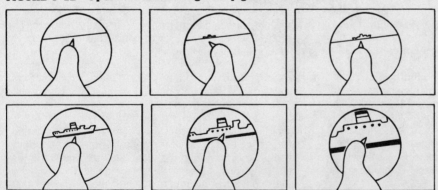

During World War II, B. F. Skinner trained pigeons, through operant conditioning, to guide missiles to their targets. The pigeons would be trained to peck at targets projected on a screen. The pecking behavior would then correct the course of the missile to maintain it on target.

Token economy programs have been extremely successful. Many long-term patients adopt model ward behavior, and sometimes the entire ward completely changes character. Follow-up studies are still in progress, but, on the basis of what is known so far, there is every reason to believe that techniques of this sort speed up the reeducation process for patients and produce more rapid discharge from hospitals. The program provides rewards to patients working on their own problems and encourages them to develop new skills that can be used upon release. The reaction to token economies, however, is not entirely positive. Many lay people and experts alike feel these programs dehumanize patients, training them like lower animals. This reaction is not unfounded, but it must be considered in light of patients' behavioral changes in the direction of what is socially acceptable.

The Behavioral Contract Another popular method of behavior modification is the behavioral contract. Under this system the person whose behavior is to be changed sets well-defined goals in the form of a contract. Positive reinforcement is then provided if the goals are met and negative reinforcement if they are not met. For example, a person desiring to lose weight might contract to lose 1 pound a week. The individual might be required to deposit a small amount of money at the beginning of the week with the

hope of receiving a refund at the end of the week when the 1-pound weight loss contracted for has been met.

The contract method can be used in many situations in which people wish to change their behavior. Cigarette smoking and drinking are obvious examples. Can you see how a contract method could be used to help shy individuals become more assertive? The advantage of the contract method is that it segments a difficult, long-range goal into more manageable and more easily achievable short-range goals that can be frequently reinforced.

Learned Helplessness

When we discussed learned helplessness, we indicated that animals exposed to aversive events they cannot control show symptoms of severe physical stress and later fail to learn to escape the aversive event. Learned helplessness is not limited to animals. Human subjects also later fail to learn to escape aversive events if they are first exposed to uncontrollable aversive events. In fact, they are even debilitated when faced with solving problems such as anagrams if they are first given insoluble anagrams. An insoluble problem is analogous to an event that cannot be controlled. No solution occurs regardless of how hard the subject tries. Like rats, people exposed to uncontrollable aversive events show more signs of stress than do people exposed to controllable aversive events. It has been shown that loud noises over which an individual has no control is more stressful than equivalent amounts of controllable noise.

Research on learned helplessness has been extended to a variety of problems of human adaptation. The most extensive work has been done by Seligman. He has proposed that learned helplessness is a model of reactive depression. Some depressions seem to be induced by environmental events and others seem to occur cyclically without any environmental cause. Seligman has argued that learned helplessness is a model of the first kind. He feels that the cause of learned helplessness is the same as the cause of depression, that the symptoms are the same, and that cure and prevention are similar for both. He argues that depression is not caused directly by all bad events but by the occurrence of bad life events over which the person has no control. Successful therapy should occur if the person is forcibly exposed to the fact that life events are controllable.

This view of depression has a great deal of intuitive appeal because depressions do seem to be brought on by uncontrollable events. Events such as the death of a spouse, marital separation, loss of a job, and aging frequently precede severe depression. More important, Seligman has provided experimental evidence for his assertions. His experiments show that depressed people and nondepressed people given insoluble problems behave similarly in a variety of circumstances. He has also shown that depressed people tend to view events to which they are exposed as uncontrollable. Nondepressed people view these same events as controllable.

The learned helplessness explanation of depression has recently been reformulated by Seligman and his colleagues to take into account more adequately the complexity of human experience. The major difficulty with the original learned helplessness model was that it did not differentiate

Moderation for Drunks

Behavior experts have begun to question the long-accepted wisdom that no alcoholic can learn to drink in moderation. In fact, a few recent experiments have indicated that some alcoholics might learn to become social drinkers (*Time,* March 15, 1971). Now further evidence comes from the Alcoholism Research Unit in Baltimore City Hospitals. There, according to a report in *Behaviour Research and Therapy,* alcoholics who were promised a reward for moderation were able to stop after five drinks or fewer.

The subjects were 19 hospitalized chronic alcoholics. All were told that they could have one-ounce drinks whenever they asked for them, with a limit of 24 ounces. On some days, the patients were offered no incentive for not drinking too much. On other days, they were told that if they restricted themselves to five ounces or less, they could work in a laundry (and earn $1 an hour), take part in group therapy, have visitors, chat with other patients and use a recreation room with games, TV and a pool table. The consistency of the results is impressive. On no-reward days, almost all of the patients drank too much. On reward days, by contrast, every one of the alcoholics proved he was able to keep within the five-ounce limit or to stay entirely on the wagon. In short, say the Baltimore researchers, it begins to look as if "abstinence and drunkenness are not the only alternatives for the alcoholic."

Time
September 18, 1972

"Learned Helplessness" Cited in Wives Accepting Beating

By RYKKEN JOHNSON

Women who put up with beatings by their male mates might be yielding to "learned helplessness," according to a psychologist at Colorado Women's College in Denver.

Battered women who refuse to leave their assailants behave much like dogs and rats which have been conditioned in laboratory experiments into passivity, said Dr. Lenore Walker, assistant professor of psychology at CWC. . . . Walker referred to studies by Martin Seligman at the University of Pennsylvania that provide the basis for her hypothesis. . . .

"Battered women behave like subjects in Seligman's experiments on learned helplessness," Walker said in her paper.

"They believe no one can help them and neither can they stop man's violence," Walker stated. "They have a negative cognitive set, behave in a passive manner and believe they are powerless in their home life."

Ironically, the paper contended, many battered women have responsible jobs and "exciting careers." However, Walker wrote, "There is great reluctance to leave their relationship. They have difficulty learning to take control of their lives." . . .

Walker is quick to emphasize that she doesn't feel women "ask for it" or are in any way at fault for their beatings. . . .

Instead, she said, battered women learn to adapt to their particular situations and that they can't stop the "bashing." Walker said she knew of one battered wife who knew another beating was coming, could feel "tension" around her home, had an important social gathering coming up, and "provoked a fight . . . to get it out of the way" before the gathering.

But Walker strongly suggests that battered women leave an abusive situation. "My advice has been, 'Run, don't walk away from it.' Women don't realize the acuteness of their situation," she said. . . .

The Denver Post
September 13, 1976

Passivity in human beings may result from experiences from which helplessness has been learned as a behavioral strategy.

among different sorts of experiences with uncontrollability. We all encounter uncontrollable events rather frequently, but we do not necessarily become depressed. For example, you have no control over whether it will rain today, but the occurrence of rain would probably not lead you to serious depression.

The basic idea of the reformulated model is that when a person discovers that he or she has no control over some event the individual asks why that is the case. The answer or *attribution* ("To what can I attribute this loss of control?") that the person makes seems to be critical in determining the severity of the effect of the experience of uncontrollability. (See Chapter 10 for a discussion of attribution theory.) Three aspects of the person's attributions are critical. The first is whether the person believes that only he or she is unable to exert control over the event (personal attribution) or whether other people also have no control (universal attribution). A personal attribution will lead to more severe symptoms than a universal attribution. This is why the fact that we have no control over whether it will rain is not very distressing — nobody else has control over it either.

The second dimension is whether the person feels that he or she will always lack control over the event (stable attribution) or whether lack of control is only temporary (unstable). For example, a person who is rejected by a lover might attribute the rejection to his or her own unattractiveness, a factor not likely to change with time. Alternatively, the rejected person might attribute the rejection to having been in a bad mood lately, something that can change. Stable attributions should produce more severe effects than unstable ones.

The final dimension is whether the lack of control is attributed to a very general global factor or to a more limited specific factor. The rejected lover, for example, might decide that he or she is unattractive to all members of the opposite sex (global) or to only the one particular person who was his or her lover (specific). Global attributions lead to more serious consequences. Thus depression should be most likely to occur and be most severe when a person experiences lack of control of an important event and makes a personal-stable-global attribution as to why control was lacking.

Carol S. Dweck has argued that many instances of chronic failure in school are attributable to learned helplessness. The young child may accidentally be taught that success in school is not attainable no matter how hard he or she tries (independent of responding), and so the child stops trying. Dweck found that forced exposure to the escape contingency had a pronounced positive impact on many children who were chronic failures in school. Her procedure involved showing them that they were not trying hard enough when they failed to solve math problems rather than telling them they were stupid or that the problems were insoluble.

Finally, it has been proposed that much of the stress involved in urban living is due to the uncontrollability (for example, noise, crowds, crime) of the things that happen. It has even been argued that crowding has negative consequences for individuals because they have less control in crowded circumstances. The next few years will no doubt see extensions of these ideas.

Applications of Partial Reinforcement

As we have seen, a response that has been learned under conditions of partial reinforcement (rewarded only occasionally) will be more difficult to extinguish than a response learned under continuous reinforcement (rewarded every time it occurs). Partial reinforcement will thus make it harder to get rid of "bad" responses you don't want any more such as smoking or gambling. But at the same time, partial reinforcement can be used advantageously to make "good" responses more permanent and less subject to abandonment during periods of personal difficulties. Psychologist Jack R. Nation of Texas A & M University has recently reminded therapists that if they want their patients to continue making new and healthier behavior responses long after formal therapy is over, they should remember the partial reinforcement effect. Therapists usually apply continuous reinforcement, according to Nation, when teaching a patient a new, adaptive response. Each and every time the patient succeeds with making the new response—such as being assertive and asking for what one has coming—the therapist reinforces the patient, usually with verbal praise. But we would predict that the newly learned assertiveness response would extinguish rapidly once the patient went out into the "real world" without the therapist there to reinforce the new behaviors continuously. Nation suggests that all forms of therapy which use techniques that involve teaching patients new responses—and this could include almost all forms of therapy—should employ partial reinforcement during the therapy. Nation calls it persistence training. Don't praise the patient every time. Praise him or her at the outset as the individual is starting to learn, but as he or she gets the hang of it, skip some rewards. The same principle can be applied to any learning situation involving reinforcers. Consider a parent rewarding a child with candy or money for doing something, say telling the truth or doing chores or doing homework. Rewarding these behaviors every time (continuous reinforcement) will get the job done as long as the parent is around to dole out the money and the candy. But parents or teachers are not always there to hand out rewards; and if the child always expects a reward and then doesn't get it, the desired response may extinguish quickly. If you stop to think about it, in the real world you don't get rewarded all the time, only occasionally, and often only rarely. But we all have to persist with behaving appropriately in the face of nonreward. Our past experience with partial reinforcement is one factor that keeps us going without a reward every time.

5 | Human Learning, Memory, and Language

At parties Jim likes to dazzle his friends with his great feats of memory. A favorite trick is to ask each person in the group to think of a grocery store item. Then each individual in turn calls out his or her item, up to, say, 50 different ones. Having heard them named once, Jim then repeats the items in the order in which they were called out. Actually, he can repeat the items in reverse order just about as easily. He can tell any person at the party the item that he or she called out. How does Jim accomplish this miracle? He really doesn't seem to be any brighter than others at the party. Do you think he was just born gifted in this way?

Phyllis and Al are about equal in academic ability. Both studied for about the same period of time and with the same amount of motivation for a comparative literature exam. Al got an "A" on the exam and Phyllis got only a "C." Phyllis claims she knows the material as well as Al, and Al agrees. Why then the big difference in grades? One factor to consider is that Phyllis studied at home, at night, with the radio blaring, and after she had had a couple of beers. Al studied during the day just after class, in the same classroom in a completely sober state. To what extent might their different study conditions contribute to the difference in their grades? How useful is it for one's state of mind and surroundings to be the same while studying and while taking an exam?

Coming out of class late one night, Terry saw a burglar rifling through a friend's car. When Terry yelled, the man ran off. But Terry got a good look at him. Later, the police asked Terry to identify the man in a lineup of five people. With some confidence she picked out the man she thought was the burglar. On the basis of her identification, the man was convicted of robbery and went to jail. Later, it was discovered that the man Terry identified was innocent. How can such mistakes occur? How can an eyewitness have such a faulty memory?

When you experience new events you are exposed to a wide range of information that you want to understand and remember. Whether you are listening to a conversation, trying to remember a new phone number, or studying a textbook, you rely on a set of complex processes to understand and learn. In reading a new textbook chapter, for example, you would do well to try to organize the different sections into groups of related information. That way when you think of one topic from the chapter, you will be able to call to mind what you know about related topics. Try to develop a structure of major topics and subtopics. And if you can, try to read the chapter before your professor begins lecturing on its contents. By so doing you will have a better chance of understanding the lecture. You may also be able to make many important connections between what the professor is saying and what you read in the textbook — connections that you might not otherwise have thought of. Then, on the test, you can make use of the relationships between different topics to aid your recall of text and lecture material.

Consider the following situation: You are a member of the jury in a murder trial. The defendant is accused of premeditated vehicular homicide. In the United States only *one* eyewitness is needed for a criminal conviction, and the prosecution claims to have such an individual. A particular segment of cross-examination by the defense attorney goes like this:

ATTORNEY: Did you see the defendant seated here driving past Mr. Jones's farm at 4:00 P.M. on December 20th?

WITNESS: Yes, I did. He's the one I saw.

ATTORNEY: How fast was he going when he passed the white barn?

WITNESS: About 35 miles an hour, I would say. As he passed the barn he began to speed up. I could see a hitchhiker ahead to the right. And the defendant began to accelerate as he passed the barn.

Subsequent evidence reveals that there is no white barn on Mr. Jones's farm, near where the hitchhiker was killed. Did the witness lie, or did he use his organized knowledge of farms to infer that Mr. Jones's farm included a barn, as most farms do? Did the attorney's question about the barn lead the witness to presuppose some information to be true (that there was a barn), which in turn changed his memory of the event? Finally, what inferences will *you* make as a member of a jury who must decide the guilt or innocence of the defendant? What will these inferences be based on? On perceptions of the witness's credibility or expectations based on the fact that the defendant had a previous criminal record?

These are among the issues we will now consider. The three key concepts around which this chapter will revolve are:

1. The structure of our information-processing system and how it involves *both* data from the environment *and* expectations, knowledge, and beliefs stored in memory.
2. How we organize our knowledge into structured packets, chunks, or schemata — and how these organizers influence our processing (increasing efficiency in some cases and lessening it in others).
3. The many ways in which we can encode or remember information and the practical implications of these devices for everyday remembering.

Complex Human Learning

Can you imagine what life would be like if we could not read, write, or talk? Without our unique verbal capacities, human beings could not communicate with each other or perhaps even learn simple tasks that are necessary for survival such as securing food and finding shelter. In short, we would be very much like wild animals. When our distant ancestors developed a way of communicating with each other through spoken sounds, they took a huge evolutionary step. In addition to making communication possible, language enabled human beings to learn more easily and to store what they learned for future use. Human beings learn and perform many behaviors according to the principles of classical and instrumental conditioning we discussed in the preceding chapter. But another realm of learning, unique to human beings, is based on our capacity for language. For example, at this moment you may be learning for the first time that Sigmund Freud had a daughter named Anna. You learned that from reading the last sentence, using your language capacity. It is hard to imagine that the learning involved CS–UCS combinations, as in classical conditioning, and it is not easy to see how the learning could be viewed as involving a response followed by reinforcement, as in instrumental conditioning. Learning about Anna Freud hardly seems like dogs salivating to bells or like pigeons pecking for grain rewards. A vast amount of what we have learned, of what we know, has been learned through our verbal abilities. As a result, investigators of human learning have focused on verbal learning, and their most recent theories don't resemble the principles of classical and instrumental learning.

In this chapter we will consider the basic principles of verbal learning and memory.

Despite the fact that verbal learning seems very unlike classical or instrumental conditioning, much of its history has been dominated by a theoretical position that has used conditioning as a fundamental, underlying concept. This position is called *associationism*, because its basis is the concept of an association. Furthermore, it was assumed that the principles of classical and/or instrumental conditioning applied to verbal associations. Hardly anyone believes this today, and yet the concept of verbal association is still extremely important in analyses of verbal learning. We all possess a complex memory system that contains an enormous amount of information; and, in our storehouse of memories and knowledge, there are complex associations among the various pieces of information. These associations make it possible to get from one place to another as we use our knowledge and memories in everyday behavior.

Associations are thus crucial to our survival. In the last five to ten years, however, it has been demonstrated that much more is involved in verbal learning than associations. Applying what we already know and remember to a new problem involves much more than applying old associations to new situations. Perhaps this seems obvious to you. But, historically, psychologists have always tried to construct theories of more complex tasks by using basic elements (like associations) as building blocks. It has traditionally been accepted that complex learning could be understood by inventing complex association networks composed of many simple associations and that these simple associations could be studied by looking at the most fundamental type — the CS–UCS association in classical conditioning.

A major difficulty with this associative tradition stems from the fact that such theories allow little or no room for cognitive activity on the part of the person doing the learning and the behaving. Basically, the theories were passive — the learner didn't *do* anything consciously. But suppose you were given a list of facts to memorize and were told that your ability to recall them would be tested in a few weeks or months and that your test score might affect your admission to medical school. You would do something — you would actively engage in behavior designed to learn and to remember the material. Even the simple task of looking up a phone number and remembering it long enough to dial it involves doing something — you would probably rehearse the phone number, repeating it to yourself. If you got distracted while you were rehearsing, you would probably have to look the number up again, or you might dial a wrong number. In any case, you do things when

There are limits to the ability to process information. You cannot consciously do two things at once, although you can rapidly alternate between tasks (time sharing). It is possible to do two things at once if at least one of them is automatic (can be done unconsciously). Both of this man's tasks—reading and watching a hockey game—require some of the same conscious resources, so that to do one of them will necessarily interfere with performance on the other.

you learn and recall verbal materials. Several different processes and stages are involved, and associations, though important, are only a part of the picture.

The Information-Processing Approach

In trying to develop theoretical models of the kinds of processes and stages that are involved in complex human learning and memory, psychologists found that many of the concepts formulated in communications engineering and computer science were pertinent and useful. In particular, they found that they could draw an analogy between the information-processing function of computers and of human beings. This analogy has given birth to one of the most significant developments in modern psychology—the information-processing approach, which was introduced in Chapter 1. Four characteristics of this approach are important for our present purposes.

Analysis of Information into Stages

First, the approach is characterized by the fact that it analyzes the learning-process flow of information into components or stages and examines what happens to incoming information as it progresses through these stages. At each stage, processes are applied to the information that is flowing through the system: The information is analyzed, rehearsed, or changed (transformed) in some way, leading to the next stage in which different processes operate. We thus have *stages* and *processes* as critical components. For example, we have already mentioned rehearsal, a process that keeps information (the phone number) "alive" in short-term memory (the stage). In general, processes fall into three broad classes, namely, **encoding, storage,** and **retrieval.** Their operation is critical for a properly functioning system. We will have more to say about these processes later.

Limited-Capacity Assumption

The second major characteristic of the information-processing approach is the *limited-capacity assumption.* The assumption is that in each stage the amount of information the system can handle at one time is limited. In other words, information processing requires attention or processing capacity—and we seem to have a limited amount of capacity or space in which to carry out the complex operations that characterize normal mental activity. We cannot do too many things at once or the system will become overloaded and break down. If you are distracted by a TV commercial while you are rehearsing a phone number to keep it alive in your short-term memory, you may start paying attention to the TV (and pro-

---

Highlight 5-1

Can You "Remember" Something You Never Experienced?

Can we *remember* things we've never learned? A recognition-memory study by John Bransford and Jeffery Franks demonstrated just such an effect. Instead of the usual word list, Bransford and Franks used a group of sentences on a related topic. When we think of recognizing a sentence or a prose passage in a book, we seem not to recognize the exact words, but rather the general theme or the "whole idea" expressed in the sentences. Theories of memory, however, have emphasized memory of specific words or elements, as if we memorized each word instead of learning an abstract "idea" that we "pull out of" the prose as we read it. The results of the Bransford and Franks study, however, mean that memory theories will now have to account for this abstraction process.

The group of sentences used in this study could be presented as a single sentence with four elements expressing a "whole idea."

Whole idea: The rock that rolled down the mountain crushed the tiny hut at the edge of the woods. *Four components:* (1) the rock rolled down the mountain; (2) the rock crushed the hut; (3) the hut was tiny; (4) the hut was at the edge of the woods.

During the study phase, the subjects never saw the sentence containing all four elements; they never saw or experienced the whole idea. Instead they saw sentences containing only one or two or three of the elements. For example, a three-element sentence would be: "The rock crushed the tiny hut at the edge of the woods." A two-element sentence would be: "The tiny hut was at the edge of the woods." And a one-element sentence would be: "The rock rolled down the mountain." Several sets of sentences were mixed together for the study phase.

At the time of the test, the subjects were presented with several different kinds of sentences: three-, two-, and one-element sentences they had actually seen before; four-, three-, two-, and one-element sentences they had never seen before; and finally, some sentences that were unrelated to the earlier materials. The basic finding was that the more elements of the whole idea a test sentence contained, the more confident the subjects were of having seen it before. They were most confident of having seen the four-element "whole idea," which had never occurred, as can be seen in Figure 5-1.

The results of the Bransford and Franks study strongly suggest that during learning, while hearing three-, two-, and one-element sentences, the subjects were actually abstracting the whole idea and storing it, even though it had never been presented in its entirety.

FIGURE 5-1 Degree of confidence that a sentence had been seen before

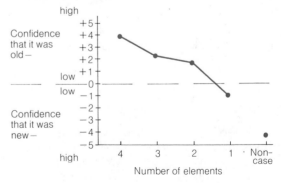

Because the four-element sentence was, in fact, never presented, the person's knowledge of that sentence must have been derived, in part, by top-down processing. This is the sort of thing that happens whenever you read and remember the gist of a story. The gist is a joint product of the bottom-up processing of the information in the text and the top-down application of the knowledge you have stored in memory.

cessing information from it) and, consequently, forget the number. There may also be a bottleneck in the system—only so much information can get through. Possibly our systems can receive more input than they can process all the way through; as when a four-lane highway becomes three lanes, traffic then backs up. If you attempt to read and listen to a record at the same time, you will probably be able to attend to only one source of information. The bottleneck lets only certain pieces of information get through, and much of the rest is lost—you may for example, have to reread a paragraph several times.

Control Mechanism

The third important characteristic of the information-processing approach is a *control mechanism* to oversee the flow and analysis of all the data in the system. The control mechanism can employ higher-level processes to govern the overall operation of the system. Examples might be the setting of overall goals for a particular task or the application of various strategies for solving a problem. With the phone number you want to remember, the control mechanism will determine how the information is processed according to some plan with a goal. If you want to remember the number only long enough to dial it, and you do not expect to use the number again, rehearsal by repetition will be the primary process employed. But suppose the new phone number is one you will be calling at least once a week. The control mechanism will call upon different processes or strategies (for example, trying to make a word with some of the numbers) designed to produce a more permanent memory (long-term memory). Sometimes you get outside help with such matters. In Denver, if you want to order hockey tickets you call 534-PUCK, which is a processed version of 534-7825.

Two-Way Flow of Information

The fourth characteristic of the information-processing approach is the idea that information does *not* necessarily flow in only one direction—from the stimulus receptors to the brain. (We could call this notion "bottom-up" processing because information travels from the bottom—for example, the eye—to the top—the brain.) Information that is already known can be used to process new information more efficiently. "Top-down" processing refers to the influence of old information on the processing of new information—for example, to the use of expectations, predictions, or readiness (conscious or otherwise) concerning the *nature* of new incoming information and how it can be *organized* and incorporated into existing knowledge or schemata. These expectations and predictions are based on our general knowledge of the world and on our specific knowledge of various domains. You could say that not only do the eyes and ears tell the brain something, but the brain (using the memories it contains in some form) tells the sense organs something. For example, as you open a bathroom door you expect to see a sink, bathtub, shower, and so on. You are ready to identify each fixture and to decide where in the room you need to go to find the object. If, however, on opening the door you found yourself looking out on a sunny beach, you would have difficulty understanding what you were seeing. You might not believe what your eyes were "telling" you, so you might close the door, wait a few seconds, then open it for a second look. Now what are your expectations? What are you prepared to see?

The point is that the information-processing system does not undertake a task in a vacuum, waiting to suck up blindly all sorts of new knowledge. Rather, it performs tasks in a particular environment or context that is formed partly by prior knowledge of components of the task at hand. Existing knowledge can be called into play to allow more efficient processing of new experiences. Not only is information sent from the bottom up (for example, from the eyes to the brain) but from the top down (for example, from memory down).

The Fundamental Memory System

Any system that must do all the things we do with our brains and language capacity has to be incredibly complicated. Detailed description of such a complex system is beyond the scope of this book. To give you the flavor of current thinking in this field, however, we will present here a simplified version.

There are three basic memory stages: (1) sensory memory, which persists only for a very brief period (1–2 seconds); (2) short-term memory, which is also temporary (15–20 seconds) and may be thought of as the information that you are consciously aware of at any given time; and (3) long-term memory, which lasts indefinitely and consists of knowledge of your experiences, not currently conscious but capable of becoming conscious if the information stored there can be retrieved.

These three memory systems are diagrammed in Figure 5–2. We have broken the overall flow of information into "memory boxes." Note that information probably does not jump abruptly from one box to another, but rather undergoes continuous transformation as it flows through the system. We use the boxes as a simple pictorial device.

Some evidence from studies of brain-damaged individuals supports the distinction between short- and long-term memory. Brenda Milner has described a syndrome that appears in some individuals with

✗ **FIGURE 5-2 The memory system**

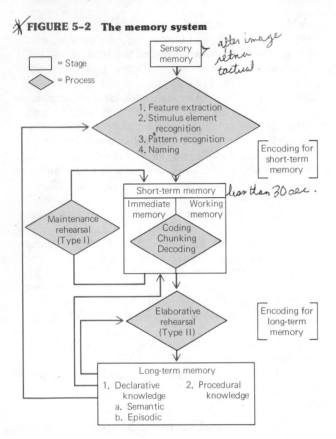

after image
retina
tactual.

less than 30 sec.

briefly after the stimulus itself has been removed. For visual stimuli, the effect is as though we have a very brief "photographic memory" that provides us with a mental photograph of the stimulus. If we want to use this information, we need to process it more fully before it fades. The processing begins with attention, which selectively determines what, out of the massive amount of information in sensory memory, "gets through" for further examination.

The processing of information once it has been attended to and selected from sensory memory is called *pattern recognition*.

We can think of pattern recognition as a process by which information in sensory memory makes contact with a long-term memory (our knowledge of the world). Only when new input information is matched with information in long-term memory is it "recognized" or identified as something familiar to us that we know about. This process probably involves interactions of various "feature-extractors" with the control mechanism. For example, if we encounter the word ORANGUTAN while reading, feature extractors will analyze the lines, angles, and curves comprising the letters, letter clusters, and word itself. A search is then made for anything corresponding to these features in long-term memory. If a match can be found, as it will be if we have previously encountered the word ORANGUTAN, the corresponding infor-

brain damage in the hippocampus region (see Chapter 2). These individuals remember things they knew before the injury, and they can remember something new as long as they keep rehearsing it. Thus, they have both a short- and a long-term memory. Their problem is that they cannot seem to get new information into long-term memory; for example, if their family moves to a new address, they will continuously "go home" to their old residence because they are unable to remember that they have moved. In order to function, they have to write everything down and carry these notes around with them. Such evidence makes a qualitative distinction between short- and long-term memory seem quite reasonable.

William James's distinction between primary and secondary memory (see Chapter 1) is useful in this regard. An event in primary memory (short-term memory) is part of the psychological present, and, we could say, is "in" consciousness. In contrast, an event in secondary memory belongs to the psychological past and has left consciousness. It can, however, be re-entered as an item in primary memory when it is retrieved or recalled.

Sensory Memory and Pattern Recognition

Sensory memory (see Highlight 5–2) permits the effect of a stimulus on a sensory system to persist very

"Let me just make a little note of that. I never seem to get anything done around here unless I make little notes."

The New Yorker, January 6, 1975. Drawing by H. Martin; © 1975 The New Yorker Magazine, Inc.

Could this be a case of brain damage similar to that of patients studied by Brenda Milner?

Hopes for Improving Memory Grow, But Its Precise Nature Is Still Debated

By WALTER SULLIVAN

In the years since 1893 when James made . . . observations about the frustrating nature of man's memory, researchers have been energetically trying to understand and find ways to improve recall. Although it has been a contentious field of inquiry, lately there have been signs that a clearer conception of the memory process is at hand and, some believe, that chemicals may hold the key to countering the deterioration of memory, especially in the elderly.

A prominent area of research has been the use of clinical and animal tests to explore hints that certain chemicals can enhance the synthesis of acetylcholine within the brain. Acetylcholine is believed to play a key role in the transmission of nerve impulses. . . .

Documentation has affirmed what many aging people know on their own — that as people grow older they are able to retain old memories but often have difficulty acquiring and retaining recent ones. One explanation is that there is an accumulation of small injuries to brain tissue due to curtailed blood flow. The research indicates, however, that a loss of memory is not a necessary condition of aging. Two current schools of thought dominate efforts to understand how memory works. The "switchboard" school argues that information is stored in specific locations or regions within the brain and retrieved through activation of a complex pattern of switching, somewhat in the manner of a computer. The switching pattern is imprinted as part of the memory-forming process. The other school says that memory involves the whole brain at once.

Evidence supporting the first of the schools comes from research showing that brain injuries can have effects that are remarkably specific in the ways they affect speech and memory. . . .

In a recent issue of American Scientist Dr. Goodglass told of patients who could recall nouns but not other parts of speech: "oar," for example, but not "or." Likewise "bee" was recognized, but not "be" and "hymn" but not "him." In the condition known as paraphasia some patients can retrieve the relevant bundle of memories, but cannot extract from it the correct one. Shown a picture of a tree, for example, a person will say "flower."

Naming, Dr. Goodglass believes, begins with evocation of a concept in the left hemisphere of the brain, stimulated by sensory input or by the person's own mental activity.

In patients whose corpus callosum — the bundle of fibers linking the two hemispheres of the brain — has been damaged, information derived from the senses by the right side of the brain cannot be retrieved by the memory system.

Two Kinds of Memory

Researchers have long recognized that memory falls into two categories. One, short-term memory, is used in such tasks as remembering a phone number only long enough to dial it. Long-term memory involves rehearsal of ideas or the retention of images with great impact. It is generally what people mean when they talk about memory.

Recent work in this area has indicated that whether one is especially sharp in short-term or in long-term memory can vary with time of day.

One developing line of thinking holds that memories are stored in bunches.

According to Perry W. Thorndyke of the Rand Corporation and Frank R. Yekovich of the United States Army Research Institute there has been a revival of interest in the concept of memory in which related information, constituting a "schema," is stored as a unit. When one retrieves the memory of a single detail the whole archive becomes available.

Some research indicates that it is easier to call up memories that have many associations than those that stand alone. Dependence on such associations would account for the difficulty in naming someone encountered "in the wrong place." It would also explain why some people are able to retrieve extensive passages of literature at will.

If, through practice, one can enhance the ability to develop bunches of memory, this could have important applications in education. Students these days are rarely taught to memorize in large blocks. . . .

But the question of storage persists. Rivaling the notion of specific areas for memories is the "statistical" theory envisioning memory as a collective process involving cells throughout the brain. One of its proponents is Dr. E. Roy John of New York University, who for many years has been studying memory in cats.

He has found that when a cat is stimulated to remember something (a trained performance), "a temporal pattern of electrical activity peculiar to that memory is released in numerous regions of the brain." This has been monitored by electrodes semipermanently implanted in many parts of the brain of free-running cats.

The resulting memory pattern is the average output from ensembles of nerve cells. Individual cells within each ensemble may produce other signals. It is the average that counts. The variability of output from any one cell, he says, "is significant primarily insofar as it contributes to the statistics of the population."

Brains and Computers

Dr. John concedes that damage to specific areas of the brain can affect memory in sharply defined ways. He likens the confrontation between the "statistical" and "switchboard" theories to early efforts to understand the nature of light "waves." Their behavior was known to be like that of particles, yet there was also evidence that they behave like waves. Both proved correct and Dr. John believes the same kind of reconciliation is within reach for theories of memory.

Contributing to the possibility of a harmonizing of the two theories is the fact that the practice of likening brain processes to those of a computer has become increasingly less fashionable as it appears that individual memories are not each assigned to one small point in the brain. If some component of a computer's stored information is destroyed, it is totally lost, whereas a human memory seems to be spread over an extended area. Understanding how that can be could bring together the two schools of thought. . . .

The New York Times
March 17, 1981

Highlight 5–2

Everybody Has a Photographic Memory (Well, Almost)

There is now ample evidence that our brain continues to "see" a visual stimulus for some time after the stimulus has been physically removed, although only for a very brief period of time. This phenomenon is called sensory memory, or short-term visual store.

George Sperling devised the first accurate method for studying visual sensory memory. Subjects were shown three rows of four symbols (numbers and letters):

7 H T 9
P D 3 1
2 K 8 G

The matrix of symbols was briefly flashed (for less than 1/10 of a second), and then the subjects were asked to report what they saw. Typically they would start reading off what they saw, reading from left to right and top to bottom. One subject might say, "7, H, T, 9, ah . . ." and fail on the remaining symbols because the sensory image had disappeared. But if the subject really had an image of the whole matrix, he or she should be able to report any row, as long as it was reported first, before the image disappeared. Sperling demonstrated that if at the time of the flash he inserted an arrow pointing to the row to be reported first, the subject could report any row he asked for. This must mean that the subject had some kind of image of the entire array after it had gone off. Sperling's method is called *cued partial report*, because the subject is given a cue (the arrow) and asked to report only part of the array (the row the arrow points to). For example, the subject would see:

8 9 M F
⟶ 1 J 7 W
X V 6 2

Naturally, reporting was best if the arrow came on before the subject saw the array, because the person could then focus attention on the crucial row. But the subjects could report any row, even when the arrow came on *after* the array, provided it was immediately after. If presentation of the arrow was delayed until the image had faded, the subjects could not report very well. So our visual perceptual system has a brief memory capability.

---

mation in long-term memory will be activated. So too will facts that we know, such as "orangutans are primates." This activated information may enter consciousness, and when it does, we say that the item has been successfully pattern matched, encoded, and stored (temporarily) in short-term memory.

A key point to remember is that not all of the information contained in the sensory memory will make it through all this analysis. Pattern recognition takes time, and our processing capacity is limited. The sensory memory fades rapidly, and much of the information is lost before it can be analyzed by all these processes and will thus never make it into short-term memory. A good example is what has been referred to as the cocktail party phenomenon. If you are at a party, very likely several conversations will be going on around you. Most of the sounds will be registered in auditory sensory memory. Only the sounds comprising the conversation you are selectively attending to will be fully processed. The other sounds will largely be lost from sensory memory before you are even aware of them — unless something unusual happens, for example, someone across the room calls out your name.

Pattern recognition can be used to document the point made earlier about the two-way flow of information in the human information-processing system.

Not only do the sensory organs send information to the brain, but it is now believed that the brain may send information down to lower-order feature extraction or pattern-recognition processes. This type of interactive processing is most apparent when we are processing a stimulus in context (as we usually do). Suppose you heard a string of speech sounds: "i-s-k-r-ee-m." How you process that string of sounds depends largely on the context in which you hear it, as the following set of sentences makes clear:

"When I see a snake, *I scream*."
"When it is hot, I like to eat *ice cream*."

Consider another example (Lindsay & Norman, 1977), the speech stream "noo-dis-pla." Is the speaker referring to a "new display" she saw in a shopping center or a "nudist play" she saw at an avant-garde theater? Clearly, in such situations, knowledge we have stored in memory that is related to the context of an event influences the way we encode the information about that event in sensory memory.

In theorizing about these kinds of complexities, our analogy between human beings and computers really pays off. The rapidly growing field of artificial intelligence has allowed us to model and/or simulate such complex operations as bottom-up and top-down interactions like those mentioned above. The field of artificial intelligence has produced a number of concepts useful in psychological theorizing, and the computer has given us a means of testing theories expressed as computer programs, since we can compare the computer's behavior to human behavior. This permits us to determine whether or not our theoretical notions are adequate.

Short-Term Memory

Short-term memory is traditionally thought of as the intermediate stage between sensory memory and long-term memory. Current research has raised the possibility that it is not a separate memory at all but rather is the activated parts of long-term memory (the parts that were activated by pattern recognition and encoding operations applied to sensory memory). Whichever view is correct, most theorists agree that it is the contents of short-term memory of which we are consciously aware. It is convenient to think of short-term memory as divided into two compartments called (1) immediate memory and (2) working memory.

Immediate memory contains information that can be immediately recalled or directly "read out." *Working memory* processes information in some way that changes its nature (changes its encoding). Consider an analogy with a workbench in a carpentry shop. The carpenter's materials are piled up immediately at hand on part of the bench (immediate memory). The rest of the bench is the area where the carpenter works on the materials with the tools to create something that wasn't there to begin with. How much space the carpenter devotes to each aspect is variable and changes from job to job. Some jobs require large amounts of work space, leaving little room for keeping materials immediately at hand. Other jobs require little work space, allowing enough space for the materials. In short-term memory we can devote much space to immediate memory and therefore keep the maximum amount of information immediately available, but this leaves little room to work on the information. As soon as a task requires considerable working space, we have to take space from immediate memory, meaning that we are unable to have as much information at hand. Just as the carpenter must contend with a work bench of a limited size, all of us must do our mental work with limited short-term memories.

It has been shown that short-term memory can handle about seven "chunks" of information when no work must be done on the information. For example, in the memory-span task, subjects are read a series of digits (1--3--9--8--7--5--6) and simply asked to repeat them (no work on them is required). Memory-span experiments show that people have a capacity of

seven plus or minus two items. However, when subjects are required to work on this information in short-term memory, the number of items that can be kept immediately available drops, because the resources must be shifted to working memory.

Recall that we said seven *chunks*—not seven pieces—of information. A **chunk** is a unit of short-term memory that may contain many pieces or "bits" of information. For example, the word "Freud" contains five letters. This word may be one chunk among the seven. You might be able to handle seven five-letter words and remember them all immediately, which would be the same as remembering 35 letters. If you were tested on a string of letters that you could not chunk into words (BRHSKQM, say), you could remember only about seven different letters. Since we can handle only about seven chunks, we try to squeeze as much information into each chunk as possible to maximize our memories. Consider the following sequence of letters: TVF — BIJ — FKY — MCA. It has 12 letters and is thus beyond the span of short-term memory for letters. You might chunk the sequence into the four groups of three letters presented above, but these chunks don't form words or anything meaningful. Consider the same letter sequence chunked in a different way: TV — FBI — JFK — YMCA. Now it becomes easy to remember the 12 letters because they have been chunked (recoded) into meaningful units. Each unit contains more than one letter, making the overall capacity larger than seven letters. Chunking information into larger and larger units is one of the most important kinds of work we can do with our working memories.

The reverse of chunking (or coding) is called *decoding,* and it is something we must also be able to do in working memory. If you are presented with the sequence of letters BOKGLSRNGBLT, you might first recode to something like BOK — GLS — RNG — BLT and then from there to book-glass-ring-belt. You have then coded a 12-letter sequence into four words. At recall, you will probably remember the four words. But you will have to decode from the words to get back the correct letter sequence. With a sequence like this you could make errors because of decoding mistakes.

Long-Term Memory

Information reaching **long-term memory** has been processed deeply enough to make it *available* for use for a relatively long time. Having the information available, however, does not mean that we have access to it. There is a distinction between *availability* and *accessibility* in memory. Accessibility means that we can get to the information when we want it—this process of getting to the information is called *retrieval.* We can fail on a memory test for two reasons:

(1) the information is not available in long-term memory; that is, it was never learned or stored, or if it was stored, it was somehow removed; and (2) we cannot retrieve the information; it is in there, but we can't get to it. When we say that something is on the tip of our tongue, we are saying that we feel sure the information is available, but we just can't retrieve it at the moment.

Some investigators have speculated that unlike other components of the overall system, long-term memory has essentially unlimited capacity—it cannot be overloaded. There is room for all the information the system can process through the earlier stages—old information is not pushed out as new information comes in. Another astounding speculation is that information is never lost from long-term memory. This view is controversial and difficult to test. In order to test this speculation, we would have to devise a memory test that could distinguish between availability and accessibility. After a failure a subject might be provided with retrieval hints (for example, "his name begins with F"). Studies using these retrieval cues show that much more information is available than is accessible, but they have not proved that everything we have learned is still available. Opinion remains divided. Some believe information is lost from long-term memory, while others say it is never lost, but gets harder to retrieve.

Encoding Processes

In order for you to make use of any new information available in the environment, you must *encode* the information—get it inside and into memory. That is, you must perceive and form some mental record or representation of the information. Usually, we take our encoding processes for granted. When we see a red light at an intersection while driving toward it, we stop. Our behavior in this situation is critically dependent on perceiving and appropriately reacting to the light. Stopping the car is an important consequence of successfully encoding the fact that the light was red.

In many other circumstances encoding is not so effortless or straightforward. Reading and studying class notes or a textbook in preparation for an exam is an example of encoding that requires great effort. A whole variety of processes are responsible for reading and comprehending written information, especially when knowledge of that information is to be tested at some later time. Yet another set of encoding processes is involved when we appreciate a painting or piece of music. We may or may not be successful in grasping the artist's intent, but we can, with a little effort, see or hear the end product and derive some meaning from it. What is more, if asked at a later time, we usually can remember the experience and de-

scribe it. We are able to do so because we have formed some representation of the painting or music in long-term memory. Encoding is the process of forming such representations.

Maintenance and Elaborative Rehearsal

How do encoding processes work, and what kinds are most useful in forming lasting memories? One encoding process that has been studied a great deal is *rehearsal*. Researchers have distinguished between two types of rehearsal. One, called *Type I* or *maintenance* rehearsal, simply involves repeating an item to oneself to prevent it from disappearing from short-term memory. The item is not transformed at all but is repeated so that it will be kept "alive" in memory, just as you might do while reaching for the phone after looking up a number.

At one time it was thought that if an item was rehearsed enough times it would automatically be encoded or stored in long-term memory. It was also believed that the more the item was rehearsed, the stronger it became in long-term memory. But recent evidence strongly suggests that maintenance rehearsal does not automatically result in the encoding of an item in long-term memory. In fact, such an automatic encoding would probably be a disadvantage. Suppose that every time you looked up a phone number and kept it "alive" in memory by maintenance rehearsal until you dialed, the number was automatically

FIGURE 5-3   Elaborative rehearsal

Elaborating an encoding while you rehearse may involve activating other knowledge that you have stored about the item.

encoded into long-term memory. The result could be mass confusion by interference among all the numbers stored in long-term memory. This would surely be nonadaptive when the goal is to maintain an item, unaltered, in short-term memory for a brief time.

For an item to be encoded into long-term memory, additional processing beyond simple rehearsal is generally necessary. The type of work required is called *Type II* or *elaborative* rehearsal. Elaborative rehearsal relates a new item to information that is already in long-term memory. This can be done in a number of different ways. You might try, for example, to think of things associated with the new items; you might try to fit the new item into a category of other similar items already stored in long-term memory; or you might make up a mental image of the new item. The word "Freud" might make you think of "couch" or "Vienna" or "Oedipus" (see Figure 5–3). You might categorize it in some way, such as "psychologist" or "psychiatrist," or you might imagine how Freud looked. All of these alternatives involve relating the word "Freud" to things or information already stored in your long-term memory and then storing the new item.

Levels of Processing

Experiments have shown that the amount and type of elaborative rehearsal performed drastically influences the amount of information that gets transferred from short-term to long-term memory. Much of this work has been done within a theoretical framework called **levels of processing,** developed by Fergus Craik and Robert Lockhart (1972). People working within this framework distinguish between different levels of processing, asserting that some levels involve only superficial or shallow treatment of an item while other levels involve deep processing. The basic assumption is that the depth to which an item is processed determines the ease with which the item can be recalled or retrieved from long-term memory. Processing an item at a deep level is much more important for encoding the item into long-term memory than simply repeating the item to oneself (maintenance rehearsal).

Presumably there is a continuum of levels of processing. At one end are shallow processes related to sensory aspects of an item, for example, how a word sounds or what it rhymes with or the size of a drawing. The other end of the continuum involves deep processes that deal with the semantic aspects of the stimulus (what it means), such as the definition of a word or what category of objects is represented by a drawing. If shown the word "horse," you would be processing at a shallow level if you merely thought of a word that rhymes with it, for example, "course." On the other hand, if you think of words that are associated with the meaning of the word "horse," for example, "domesticated animal," "run races," "can be ridden," deep processing is involved. Many experiments have demonstrated that words processed

---

Highlight 5–3

Levels of Processing: Deep Processing Improves Memory

The levels-of-processing theory of learning maintains that learning is chiefly a product of the type of processing applied to the information to be learned. Shallow processing leads to poor learning and recall compared to deep processing. Deep processing forces subjects to attend to the semantic (the meaning) aspects of the information. Shallow processing involves nonsemantic aspects such as the sound of words. The basic demonstration used to support this theory involves exposing subjects to a list of words. They are not told they will have to recall them. One group of subjects is asked to perform a task with the words that requires only shallow processing, and a second group is given a task that requires deeper processing. After all the words have been exposed and processed, the subjects are given an unexpected recall test. Subjects given the deep-processing task recall considerably more of the words.

Try this experiment for yourself on some friends. Below is a list of 20 words that you should print on a set of index cards. For one group of friends, present each word and ask them to think of another word that rhymes with it (a shallow-processing task). For the other group, ask them to think of a word that means the same thing as the word (a deep task requiring subjects to process meaning). Don't tell either group that you are going to test their memories for the 20 words. You should find that recall is better for the group asked to think of synonyms than for the group asked to think of rhymes. Should you control for the time the words are presented?

Word List			
fast	shoe	rug	ticket
cold	cook	play	car
book	steal	walk	toy
chair	right	mad	stamp
lost	drink	kick	house

deeply (semantically) are better remembered than words processed at shallow levels. Similar results have been obtained with memory for sentences, pictures, and other materials.

Elaboration

Deep processing leads to better memory of information than shallow processing for a number of reasons. Deep processing involves meaning, or semantics. Semantic processing allows more *elaboration* of an item than shallow processing. You can think of many things about a horse—what it looks like, what it is used for, the type of animal it is, and so on. All of this information can be included in the encoding of the word "horse" if semantic processing is used. You can see that a good deal of elaborative rehearsal is involved, and many relationships are drawn between

the item "horse" and information already in long-term memory.

But if only shallow processing is applied to the word "horse," such as estimating how many letters are in the word or thinking of a rhyming word, not much elaborative rehearsal will take place, and little information in memory will be related to the item. It is therefore possible that the amount of elaborative rehearsal involved in deep processing plays an important role in encoding information into long-term memory.

Distinctiveness

Another aspect of deep or semantic processing that could provide an advantage over shallow processing is that semantically encoded information is likely to be more *distinctive* than nonsemantically encoded

---

Highlight 5–4

Serial Position and the von Restorff Effect

When studying textbooks, students often underline important points they want to remember, usually with brightly colored "magic markers" that make the important points stand out. Of course, some students emphasize so much that entire pages become yellow or pink or orange. Do you think the underlining helps? Is there a limit to how much underlining is beneficial?

Here's a simple verbal-learning experiment you can try on your friends. At right is a list of 11 nonsense syllables. Copy each one onto a note card so that you have a set of "flash cards" to show your subjects. Make three sets of cards: (1) none of the syllables are placed in a border of colored magic marker; (2) the middle or sixth syllable is isolated by surrounding it with a colored border; (3) all 11 syllables are surrounded with a colored border. Now test some people on each of the three sets, say three or four subjects on each set. Show them the cards one at a time at a reasonably slow rate. Say nothing about the borders; just ask them to learn the syllables in any order. After this study trial, hand them a slip of paper and ask them to write down as many of the syllables as they can in any order. Then tally the results and see which group remembered the most syllables altogether and which group did best on the middle syllable. In the second group with only one isolated item, was there any recall of the item before the isolate and the item after the isolate? Draw a graph, called a *serial-position curve*, in which you plot the number of people who recalled the syllable at each position. A sample curve is shown in Figure 5–4. In it you can see a **primacy effect** (syllables near the beginning of the list are remem-

bered well) and a **recency effect** (syllables near the end of the list are also remembered well). Did you find these two effects in your serial-position curve? This is a study dealing with what is known as the *von Restorff effect*. The von Restorff effect refers to better retention of an isolated item—in our example the single item surrounded with a colored border—than of other items around it. Was PIJ recalled better when it was isolated (in condition 2) than when it was not (conditions 1 and 3) in your experiment? If so, you demonstrated the von Restorff effect.

FIGURE 5–4 Sample serial-position curve

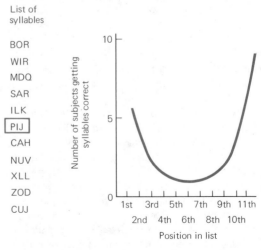

information. If you were to think of a variety of unusual ideas related to the word "shark," you would probably have a more distinct memory for that word. If you merely estimated the number of letters in the word "shark" and did the same for a number of other five-letter words, your encoding of "shark" would not be very distinctive at all. Distinctive encodings are more likely to be recalled, as is convincingly demonstrated by the *von Restorff effect* (see Highlight 5–4). If in a list of items one item is surrounded by a colored border and you are asked to recall the items, you are more likely to recall the distinctive item than the others. The border around the item produces a distinct encoding which has a strong effect on how well the item is remembered. Usually, deep or semantic processing produces more distinctive encodings, and the distinctiveness of the encodings thus created will contribute to their memorability.

Effort

A third characteristic of deep processing is that the amount of *effort* required to do the processing is greater than the amount of effort required to do shallow processing. Encoding tasks that require more effort on the part of the subject lead to better recall of encoded items than do encoding tasks that demand less effort. We measure the amount of effort required in terms of how much attention you must pay when doing a task, how hard you must concentrate, or how many different things you must think about in order to do the task. A semantic processing task like viewing the word "car" and answering the question "Does it contain water?" would demand some effort to come up with the correct reply, "yes." To answer correctly, we have to remember that automobile engines usually use water cooling systems and almost always have a water-based windshield washing solution. Thinking of these sources of water in a car would take more effort than answering the question "Does it rhyme with far?" In many cases, deep processing tasks require more effort and careful thought than shallow tasks. The extra effort or concentration required to process an item semantically probably contributes to the formation of a durable encoding of the item in long-term memory.

Imagery and Organization

Imagery

Imagery is generally correlated with how concrete or abstract items are. Abstract words, for example, lack physical referents and typically fail to arouse any images. Examples of abstract words are "injustice," "envy," and "moral." Concrete words, on the other hand, refer to physical objects, such as "table," "door," and "grass."

Imagery facilitates the learning of information and produces good recall performance. Subjects taught to make up strange visual images of the material to be learned perform at a much higher level than subjects who do not use images. Presumably, encoding words as images somehow enhances the storage of the items in long-term memory. For hundreds of years memory experts have relied heavily on visual images to improve their performance. If you want to remember a list of objects, try to imagine the items in a stack, one on top of another. Visualize what the stack would be like. Another technique is to contrive a picture to go with the words to be remembered. In the brain is a structure called the corpus callosum, a difficult name for most people to remember (do you remember it from Chapter 2?). It is the band of nerve fibers connecting the two hemispheres of the brain. Imagine a colossal corpse lying on a slab between two huge masses of brain tissue. If you can form this image, you may never again forget the name of this part of the brain.

Highlight 5–5

**Imagery and Learning:
A Simple Experiment**

Here are two lists of words, one high in imagery value (concrete words) and one low in imagery value (abstract words). Look at each list for 30 seconds and then try to write down as many of the words as you can remember. You should find that imagery facilitates learning.

High-Imagery Concrete Words	Low-Imagery Abstract Words
nail	injustice
cloud	envy
house	happiness
tire	institution
ball	education
fence	fashion
cigar	modesty
rock	motive
truck	contempt
dress	depth
book	thought
table	void
milk	agreement
telephone	society
bed	temper

Why does imagery facilitate learning and memory? One interpretation is that human beings have two primary modes for remembering: a verbal mode and a pictorial or visual imagery mode. If we encode something in both modes, as is more likely for words that are easy to "image," the chances for later remembering the item are better than if we learned only in one mode. This interpretation assumes that most people are able to form mental images and use them as memory representations of words, pictures, and other stimuli.

Organization

The importance of organization for encoding information into long-term memory has been demonstrated in a number of domains. Let us first consider organization of information in pictures. Suppose you were shown a single picture containing 12 different items randomly arranged (Figure 5–5, panel A). Some objects are upside down or at strange angles—a vacuum cleaner is next to a pole lamp, a group of pictures is on top of a footstool, and so on. The scene is utter chaos, and your task is to remember what all of the objects are and where they are in the picture! Suppose now you are given a picture of the same objects but arranged in an orderly, logical way in a room setting (Figure 5–5, panel B). The vacuum cleaner is standing in a corner, the pictures are hanging on the wall, and so on. You will probably do far better on the memory task with the organized picture than with the chaotic one. Experiments have produced just that result. We can encode information much more easily if it is ordered in a coherent and familiar way. The same holds for verbal messages, as we shall see. The better the message is organized according to a set of schemata, the easier it is to read and remember.

Similar effects have been observed with lists of words. You will have a harder time memorizing a list of unrelated words than a list of related ones. For example, a list composed of word groups, with each group representing a category of objects, could be organized quite easily: "hawk," "plum," "peach," "car," "eagle," "apple," "train." Rather than having to encode each item into long-term memory as an isolated unit, you can group the related words and encode them as a single unit. When you are asked to recall the list you will have to remember only a small number of units instead of a long list of unrelated items. Still another effective organizational method is making up a story that uses each word in the list, thus providing a coherent and meaningful structure for all items to be remembered.

An important organizational encoding technique is *chunking*. It involves forming units or chunks of unrelated items based on certain rules that are highly familiar to a subject. An especially impressive demonstration of this technique has been provided by William Chase and Anders Ericsson. They chose to study the digit-span task in which a subject is presented a randomly ordered list of digits at a rate of about one digit a second. After the list is presented the subject must repeat the list in its original order. Because relatively fast presentation rates are used, people ordinarily are not able to encode the list into long-term memory. They must try to keep the list in short-term memory. Remember that the limit on short-term memory is about seven chunks of information. To a normal person, each digit in the list would represent one chunk, and only lists of up to about seven digits can accurately be repeated. Chase and Ericsson's subject had this limitation until he discovered a unique chunking strategy. The subject's experience as a long-distance runner led him to adopt the strategy of encoding groups of three digits as running times. The sequence "4," "1," "3" would be chunked as a good mile time, "9," "2," "7" as a good two-mile time, "6," "5," "8" as a poor mile time, and so on. Short sequences that couldn't be interpreted as running times were coded as ages, such as 75, 81, and 64.

This subject chunking method thus depends on associating digit sequences with information in long-term memory, thereby allowing the subject to encode these sequences as units into long-term memory. The subject is then freed from the restriction of maintaining the whole list in limited short-term memory. Most of the list actually is stored in long-term memory. It may sound impossible, but it really works. Chase and Ericsson's subject is no genius, yet after a year of practice he achieved a digit span of over 80 items, and his span is still increasing!

The Representation of Knowledge

If there is any single concept that is fundamental to understanding human learning and memory it is the idea that we store internal mental representations of our personal reality. Mental representations of the world around us and our interactions with it are what we have in memory. These representations are a result of encoding information about new experiences into memory. All sorts of different experiences are possible, as are various types of memory representations. In this section we will discuss the different types of long-term memory representations.

Procedural versus Declarative Knowledge

The difference between procedural and declarative knowledge is the difference between "knowing how" and "knowing that." For example, you know how to

FIGURE 5-5

(Panel A)

(Panel B)

Just Remember This: Anyone Can Be Genius
By HENRY W. PIERCE

Virtually any normal person can learn to do the prodigious feats of memory once attributed only to certain geniuses, psychologists at Carnegie-Mellon University have found.

Drs. K. Anders Ericsson and William G. Chase found they could extend the memory span of a 22-year-old student from seven digits to 80 at a time.

The student, Steve Faloon, said yesterday the secret of his success lies in grouping digits together in meaningful patterns. To Faloon, who is a marathon runner, "meaningful patterns" meant running times.

For instance, the numbers 3492 would be combined into three minutes and 49.2 seconds, near world-record mile time.

By breaking down a string of 80 digits into this and similar combinations, Faloon was able to set what may be a record of sorts himself.

His achievement has scientific significance, Ericsson said, because it shows that the super memories claimed by a few outstanding performers really aren't due to unusual inborn abilities.

The finding is considered sufficiently important to warrant publication in the technical journal, Science.

Memory feats involving thousands of digits have been demonstrated by a few performers, but they need many hours to memorize the numbers, Ericsson said.

During the Carnegie-Mellon experiment, Ericsson said, Faloon was required to memorize the digits at the rate of one a second.

Faloon . . . has put his newly-acquired ability to good use:

"I've become sort of a phone directory for my friends," he said. He codes phone numbers, license numbers, and other information into his memory bank and retains the data until they have a chance to write it down.

"When we first started the experiment," Faloon recalled, "I got as high as eight or nine digits and didn't think I could go any further. I knew the normal limit was somewhere between five and nine, and I thought I'd reached it."

Then a strange thing happened. Faloon suddenly found meaning in one group of numbers—907—and retained it in his memory as a single unit.

"It suddenly came to me that 907 was 9 minutes and 7 seconds (9.07), a good two-mile running time," he said.

From then on the numbers began falling into regular running-time patterns.

After 260 to 270 sessions, carried out over a period of 20 months, Faloon was up to 80 digits.

But when the psychologists arranged the digits in a way that couldn't be associated with running times, Faloon's performance dropped to its original level.

"Our data," Ericsson said, "suggest that it is not possible to increase the actual capacity of short-term memory with practice. Rather, increases in memory span are due to the use of mnemonic (memory-aiding) associations in long-term memory. With an appropriate mnemonic system and retrieval structure, there is seemingly no limit to improvement in memory skill." . . .

Pittsburgh Post-Gazette
June 10, 1980

---

ride a bicycle, but you know that George Washington never told a lie. In knowing how to ride a bicycle, what you know or store in memory may be something like a sequence of coordinated muscle movements. In knowing that George Washington never told a lie, what you know is a fact, an item of information. Here are some further ways in which procedural and declarative knowledge differ.

1. Declarative knowledge is possessed in an all-or-none manner, while procedural knowledge may be partially possessed. (In other words, you either know a fact or you don't—but with typing, for example, you may have partial mastery of the relevant knowledge but not be an expert typist.)
2. Declarative knowledge is acquired suddenly by assertion, while procedural knowledge is acquired gradually by performing a skill. (If we assert that Freud had a daughter named Anna, you know this fact at least temporarily; but if we describe how to type, you will have to practice and gradually learn the correct motor movements.)
3. Declarative knowledge can be verbally communicated, while procedural knowledge very often can only be demonstrated. (We can tell you about Freud's daughter —but it is hard to tell you how to do a parallel turn in skiing.)

Many procedural skills we are called upon to learn require much practice before we master them. A prime example is reading. A good deal of effort is involved in helping a person learn to read, and even after years of practice many special reading skills can be learned (for example, speed reading). We can't simply sit down with a child and in a few sentences tell her or him how to read. Similarly, learning to give speeches confidently involves the development of a number of skills that need rehearsal in order to develop fully. Explaining a skill to someone is very difficult, even if you are an expert in the activity. How well do you think you could explain to someone how to drive a car with a manual transmission? Even if you have driven a car with a manual shift for years, your explanation could not match the experience for the learner of a few hours of actual driving.

Propositional versus Analog Knowledge

Psychologists disagree on whether knowledge is represented as a replica or as a description of stimulation from the environment. A replica or "analogical" representation is like an *image* or *a picture in the head*. In contrast, a descriptive or "propositional" representation suggests that information is stored as a logical verbal function.

This may seem complicated and abstract and not very closely related to the real world. Let us take an example and try to make the distinction between analog and proposition more concrete. Suppose you learn that "John rode his bicycle to the grocery store." We could represent this mentally as an image of John riding a bicycle toward the grocery store in the distance. Alternatively, we could store the information as an assertion in the following form:

Rode (John, bicycle, store).

Computers can manipulate information in the form of propositions. Partly for this reason, psychologists have suggested that human beings might use the same kind of representation.

Although in our example the same information was represented in the two different forms, it is not clear that propositional and analog representations are always equivalent in this way. Your room at home or at school might be easy to image. Try it now. But the same room would need hundreds of propositions to describe. Thus, the two memory codes may lend themselves best to different types of situations. Furthermore, there may be large individual differences in the way different people store different kinds of information—some people may prefer or remember more easily in images, and others may not.

Episodic versus Semantic Knowledge

The distinction between episodic and semantic knowledge refers more to the content of a representation than to its form. An episodic memory is a representation of an event or experience that is autobiographical in the sense that it contains the information that "it happened to me at *x* time and *y* place." Episodic memories refer to events in an individual's own past. An essential part of an episodic representation is its reference to the rememberer's knowledge of his or her own personal identity. In contrast, semantic representations contain information that does not usually include such autobiographical references. Rather, they contain conceptual information that is independent of any time or place. For example, you may have a representation of what a "purple cow" is without ever having experienced one or having any knowledge about where or when you first heard the term. Such a representation would be strictly semantic. However, if you actually saw a purple cow, your memory of that event would be an episodic memory that would probably also contain the time and place where you saw it. Many encounters of one type may initially be represented episodically in the context of the original experience—for example, each cat you see purrs when held or stroked. Eventually, however, you will build up a very general idea about cats and purring that is not necessarily connected with specific experiences. That idea would be a part of your semantic knowledge.

Organization in Long-Term Memory

We all have an enormous amount of information stored in our long-term memories, and we keep adding new information to the store all the time. Figuring out how we have all this information organized or structured so that we can get to it when we need it, and get to it quickly, is going to take a great deal of creative theorizing and experimentation. Two important ideas about the organization of information in long-term memory are network models and schema theory.

Network Models

To give you some idea of network models, consider how such a model would deal with a very simple cognitive task—answering questions like, "Do canaries have feathers?" or "Do canaries have skin?".

Network models assume that the information in semantic memory is arranged in a vast, highly organized network consisting of nodes (locations) and connections among nodes. Furthermore, the network is arranged in a hierarchy with more general or abstract information higher in the hierarchy than the more specific information (see Figure 5–6). For example, there would be a node in semantic memory corresponding to the concept *canary*. Extending from this node would be connections leading to other nodes. Information about each concept is stored at a node, with connections specifying its properties. Looking at Figure 5–6, we see that at the canary node there are three properties or features stored about canaries: they can sing, they are small, and they are yellow. We also see a connection leading upward in the hierarchy from canary to the more general concept *bird*. At the bird node additional information is stored which is true of birds in general, including canaries; they have wings and feathers and can fly. Moving upward again, we get to the animal node where we find even more general information, including the fact that animals have skin. To answer our question we would have to enter the network at the canary node specified in the

FIGURE 5-6 A simple hierarchy in semantic memory

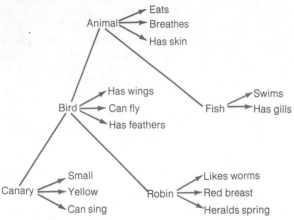

question and then move up to the animal node. It is like saying to ourselves, "A canary is a bird, and a bird is an animal, and animals have skin; therefore, canaries have skin." And so we answer yes to the question. If the question were, "Do canaries have feathers?" we would only have to move up one node to find the answer because "has feathers" is stored at the bird node. Having feathers is particular to birds and does not generally apply to all animals.

Research has shown that we answer the question about feathers faster than we answer the question about skin, which gives support to the hierarchy notion (Collins & Quillian, 1969). It suggests that "has skin" is stored higher in the hierarchy than "has feathers." Network models such as this are only one type of theory, although one of the most popular types at the moment. Just imagine the size and complexity of a network capable of containing all the information we possess!

Take a moment to think about it and you will realize that much of our knowledge is stereotyped. That is, there are many tasks and events that we participate in over and over again. Our knowledge about such commonplace, mundane, and predictable experiences might be organized in a special way. Specifically, there are highly structured portions of our semantic memory network. These tightly organized units of knowledge have been called schemata (singular, "schema"), frames, and scripts by different psychologists.

Schema Theory

Schemata represent things like birthday parties, baseball games, going to a restaurant, doing laundry, grocery shopping, going on a date, and so on. For example, our schema for going to a restaurant may contain knowledge of the reasons for going to a restaurant (to satisfy hunger or craving), the typical events in going to a restaurant (entering, waiting to be seated, receiving a menu, selecting the food, ordering the food, receiving the food, receiving the bill, paying the bill, leaving a tip, and exiting) as well as the typical participants in the restaurant schema (host or hostess, waiter or waitress, cook, cashier).

While the bulk of knowledge in a schema is highly stereotyped, or repeatable from time to time, it may contain various "tracks" to handle variability in the situations to which it applies. For example, a schema for "going to a restaurant" may contain a "fast food" track, a "cafeteria" track, and a "fancy restaurant" track. These would represent the typical events and main conceptualizations necessary for comprehending or participating in a typical experience of going to one of these types of restaurants.

The nodes of a schema's network may be thought of as "slots" that get filled in with the particular details of the current episode for which you are using the schema. In case some of these details are missing from a particular episode, or are not attended to, the schema contains "default" knowledge that it automatically fills in. This "default" knowledge consists of details that are typically true of such events (for example, kitchens usually have ranges and sinks set into a counter), and it allows us to assume, know, and infer things that are not specifically experienced. Consider the following two sentences:

John took Mary to a French restaurant.
John took Mary to a run-down diner.

The default knowledge stored in our "fancy restaurant" and "diner" tracks allows us to formulate expectations about the kinds of clothing John and Mary wore, whether there were candles on the table, the kind of decor that surrounded them, and so on. The default values for the "diner" track of our frame allow us to make very different inferences than the default values for our "fancy restaurant" track.

To summarize the common features of schemata would be to include the following: (1) they serve to organize long-term memory; (2) they contain stereotyped information; and (3) they contain default knowledge. Without such a highly organized system, our semantic knowledge would be very hard to use. Most of us have an immense amount of information stored in memory. To give you some idea of exactly how much we know, consider that the average college freshman knows the meaning of 80,000–90,000 words. In addition, we all have stored in long-term memory relations among concepts and many personal experiences. Thus, the overall central processor or control mechanism must have sophisticated retrieval techniques with which to search memory for facts relevant to a task at hand. Schemata make retrieval easier by organizing our knowledge. Let us now turn our attention to the retrieval process.

Information Retrieval

Once information has been encoded into long-term memory and is represented in some form, it is available for use whenever we want it. There is just one catch. Before we can use the information we have learned we must somehow retrieve it from long-term memory. Many times we fail to remember something, even though we are sure we know it, for example, the name of a friend you haven't seen for years or whether you locked your car after you parked it. After cramming the night before, on the exam we are frustrated by an inability to recall the things we studied. Just as interesting are cases of complete recall after many years. We have fairly vivid recollections of some events, especially from childhood. A poem or verse memorized in grade school may reassert itself verbatim when as adults we come across the title or author. Or consider a phenomenon known as "flashbulb memory," which we seem to have for especially emotional or significant and unexpected events. Think of when you first heard about the assassination attempt on President Reagan. Many people have reported an extremely vivid image of where they were and what they were doing at the time they heard the news. What is it that allows us to remember certain things, and how do we go about retrieving information from memory? Why do we forget and fail to retrieve information no matter how hard we try?

Forgetting

We can break the memory process into three phases: (1) encoding, (2) retention, and (3) retrieval. Encoding is the storage of information to be remembered in long-term memory. Retention is holding items in storage for later use. The interval between initial storage and eventual recall is referred to as the **retention interval.** Retrieval involves the extraction of stored information from memory for use on some task. Memory failures can be traced to any one or all of these processes. Information may be improperly encoded or not encoded at all. Assuming proper encoding, information might somehow be lost through passage of time. Finally, information might be encoded and retained, but for some reason be unretrievable when needed; it is available but not accessible.

Two procedures that can be used to test how much information a person has retained are the *recognition test* and the *recall test.* In a recognition test, the subject is presented with the correct response along with distractor responses (incorrect alternatives), and he or she merely has to recognize which of the responses is correct. In a recall test, the subject has to produce the correct response. As you know, recognition is normally easier than recall. Recognition tests do not require you to come up with the correct answer yourself, making the retrieval process easy. You do not have to retrieve it from

---

Highlight 5–6

Transfer of Training

When we learn something new, some knowledge or skill, we usually do so with the intent to use it at a later time. In some cases we are later asked to recall or remember the exact information we learned, as in a final objective examination in a college course. In such cases, we are concerned with *memory,* which will be covered in the next section. Closely related to memory is the phenomenon of **transfer of training,** which refers to the effect of prior learning on the subsequent performance of a different task. Driving a new car is an example of transfer. While the responses required are similar to those you've learned in earlier driving experiences, they are not exactly the same. You may find it necessary to adapt old habits or learn some new ones. You may even find some of your old habits interfering with the smooth operation of the new car. The point is that there will be some effect of prior learning and that is what is called transfer of training. Table 5–1 shows the definitions of positive and negative transfer between two tasks.

TABLE 5–1   Transfer of Training

Experimental group → learns Task 1 → learns Task 2

Control group → does nothing → learns Task 2

1. If the experimental group does *better* on Task 2 than the control, there is *positive transfer.*

2. If the experimental group does *worse* on Task 2 than the control, there is *negative transfer.*

3. If the experimental group and the control group do not differ, there is *zero transfer.*

The most important variable in transfer of training is the similarity of the two tasks. If Tasks 1 and 2 are highly similar, we can expect positive transfer. If they require opposite or conflicting habits (for example, in Great Britain driving on the left side of the road), we can expect negative transfer.

Why does a fireman wear red suspenders?
A. ☐ The red goes well with the blue uniform.
B. ☐ They can be used to repair a leaky hose.
   C. ☐ To hold up his pants.

The New Yorker, March 25, 1974. Drawing by D. Fradon; © 1974 The New Yorker Magazine, Inc.

The multiple-choice test is a test of recognition memory. One theory is that this test is easier than a fill-in-the-blank test (recall memory) because recall requires retrieval of the correct answer and recognition of the fact that it is correct, whereas no retrieval is required on a recognition test because the correct answer is right in front of you. In short, this theory says that different processes are involved in the two types of test.

memory, as in a recall test. Compare the following two tests:

1. What were the names of the two robots in the movie *Star Wars?*
2. Which of the following was the name of the computer in the movie *2001: A Space Odyssey?*

   a. Alex
   b. Eliot
   c. Hal
   d. Henry

In the first item, you can fail because you never stored the names (encoding) or because you have failed to retain them since you learned them (storage) or because you cannot retrieve them (retrieval). In the second item, the name has already been retrieved for you, so a failure is probably due to poor encoding or storage.

Do you recall the two basic reasons for forgetting? The information is not available, and the information is not accessible. In the first case, we have what is called **trace-dependent forgetting.** Some psychologists believe learning sets up physiological *traces* in the brain. Forgetting is seen as resulting from the fact that the traces are not available at the time of recall. The information is just not available any more.

The second reason we forget involves what is called **cue-dependent forgetting.** Here the forgetting is mainly a retrieval failure—the cues present at the time of learning are not present at the time of recall; or competing interfering cues are also present and block memory. The traces are still with you, but the cues are not appropriate for "getting at" the traces, so we have cue-dependent forgetting. Each of the three theories of forgetting we are about to describe involves one or the other of these processes.

Consolidation

Corresponding to the encoding stage of the memory process is the theory of memory **consolidation.** This theory postulates that every experience sets up some kind of trace. The trace may be thought of as a small electrical and chemical circuit formed in the brain, the circuit somehow coding the experience. This circuit must "consolidate" in order for the experience to be permanently stored. The circuit is not very stable when it is first set up, and the trace must travel around the circuit many times in order to consolidate the circuit, making it final and lasting. During the period between the end of learning and the completion of consolidation the circuit is easily destroyed. According to consolidation theory, then, a major factor in forgetting is that memory is partly destroyed before it is consolidated. This theory focuses on the encoding of information and maintains that memory failures can be a consequence of inadequate encoding into long-term memory.

What kinds of events could affect the consolidation process? Most research has studied the effects of electrical shock to the brain shortly after learning. The shock is called **electroconvulsive shock (ECS)** whenever it is strong enough to produce a convulsion in the subject. ECS has been used as a treatment for severe depression in human beings. Patients who receive ECS report a complete memory loss for events shortly preceding the ECS, a phenomenon known as **retrograde amnesia.** Their long-term memory, however, remains completely intact. The same may be true for someone knocked unconscious by a blow on the head. The strong electric shock or the blow on the head disrupts the memories that are consolidating at the time. Events that occurred earlier are unaffected.

Another side of consolidation theory is even more interesting. Since consolidation is the process of laying down a permanent memory, if consolidation can be facilitated, memory would be facilitated. Lengthening the time that electrical activity responsible for consolidation continues might facilitate consolidation. Certain drugs, including strychnine and picrotoxin, are thought to have just this capability. These drugs excite the brain and might produce faster, more efficient, and more permanent memory storage. Administration of these drugs to animals after each trial of learning a task does result in more rapid learning. This effect is strong support for consolidation theory.

Decay Theory

Given that an item is successfully encoded into long-term memory, what might account for its loss during the retention interval? **Decay theory** postulates that some information "wears out" or decays over time due to some biological process. Since the physiology of the hypothesized decay process is not known, it cannot be directly manipulated (that is, the rate of decay cannot be changed) to test the effect on forgetting. The only variable that can be manipulated is the length of the retention interval. Decay theory sheds little light on forgetting, but future research may indeed reveal the physiological correlates of memory, which may lead to an understanding of the physiological bases of the decay process.

Interference Theory

The best-developed theory of forgetting is based on the notion of *interference*. This theory deals primarily with the third aspect of memory—retrieval.

This theory says that forgetting is caused primarily by interference from other, usually similar, things we have learned. When the interference comes from something you learned before the critical thing you are now trying to remember, the forgetting is said to be due to **proactive interference.** When the interfering learning happens between the time you learned the critical thing and the time you try to recall it, the forgetting is a result of **retroactive interference.** Of course, both proactive and retroactive interference are operative in everyday learning and memory situations.

Laboratory studies have provided strong support for the basic notions of interference theory. Proactive and retroactive interference both can cause large amounts of forgetting. Interference can produce forgetting, but it is not certain that all forgetting is due to interference. We know that people remember more if they sleep during the retention interval than if they are awake. Since we don't learn interfering material while asleep, this observation supports interference theory. There are alternative explanations, however. Sleep might facilitate memory by slowing down the decay process, or it might facilitate the consolidation of materials learned just before going to sleep. While the explanation of this experimental finding is vague, its practical implication is quite clear. It is better to go to sleep after studying for a test than to study for some other test, watch TV, or engage in some other waking activity (other than more studying for the test, which would be best of all).

How does interference operate to produce forgetting? Two basic ideas have been proposed. One is *response competition* and the other is *unlearning.* Consider what happens when you move from one house or apartment to another and are required to change phone numbers. At first, when asked your phone number, two responses may come to mind: the correct new number and the interfering old number. The two possible responses compete with each other, and you might be confused about which one to say. This is an example of response competition. Eventually, however, you come to a point where you are readily able to give the correct new phone number when asked. This may occur because the old number has been "unlearned." It is then no longer available or accessible, and if you are asked your old phone number, you very likely will be unable to give an accurate reply (assuming you don't make regular use of your old number).

Remembering

On most occasions information represented in memory is accessed and retrieved from long-term memory. But sometimes, we need to access information from short-term memory. In these instances retrieval can be very accurate and very rapid. Classic studies by Saul Sternberg required subjects to memorize sets of target items, such as numbers (6–8–9–1–5). The sets varied in size, and subjects received many trials on sets of different sizes. On any given trial subjects were presented a probe number and were to indicate whether the probe was a member of the current target set. The time taken to respond to probes increased by about 40 milliseconds each time the target set was increased by one item. These results led Sternberg to the conclusion that items in short-term memory are scanned at a very rapid rate (40 msec/item) and that all items are scanned before the subject produces a response.

Context

When we are required to remember information represented in long-term memory, more complicated retrieval processes are needed. These processes operate most effectively when conditions of recall are identical to those at the time of learning. This is called the *context effect.* It would be to your advantage, for example, to take an exam (and even study for it) in the same room or lecture hall that was used for regular class meetings of the course.

Context can refer to physical surroundings at the time of learning and recall—characteristics of the room, amount of noise, and so on. It can also refer to the physiological state of the learner at the time of learning and retrieval. One's own body is, in a sense, a part of one's context. Thus, for best performance one's bodily state should be as similar as possible at the time of learning and retrieval. There are anecdotal reports of alcoholics who hide things while they are drunk and are unable to remember their location when they sober up. This phenomenon is called **state-dependent learning.** Laboratory work on state-dependent learning has typically used drug-induced states. Experimenters have found, for example, that if a rat is taught to run a maze under the influence of amphetamines, it performs better if given the amphetamines just before the recall trials.

A different kind of phenomenon of context in retrieval is called **hypermnesia.** This term refers to an enhancement of memory, often brought on by hypnosis. While careful research on hypermnesia is lacking, hypnosis has been used in a number of practical settings to help people remember things they apparently could not otherwise recall. One area in which this technique has been successfully applied is police investigations. Police detectives trained in hypnosis work with witnesses to crimes, attempting to help the persons recall as much as they can about what they saw. While a witness is hypnotized, the investigator encourages the person to recall as much of the target event as possible, hoping that this will assist in recreating as accurately as possible the context of the event. Other methods of hypnosis are used as well, but this technique is closely related to the idea that accurate recall can be promoted by faithful reinstatement of the context of the target information.

The Mystery of Memory
By SHARON BEGLEY with JOHN CAREY

The man known to his doctors as N. A. lives in the perpetual present. Injured 21 years ago when a fencing foil penetrated his nose and stabbed his brain, he is virtually incapable of forming new, enduring memories. What normal people remember for weeks, N. A. retains for a few minutes. If he is taught a new skill such as reading mirror-reversed writing, he masters and retains the skill itself, but forgets how and when he learned it. No memories of events after his accident fill the archives of his mind. Researchers are far from understanding memory; they can't offer foolproof ways to remember bosses' names and lovers' birthdays, let alone cure N. A. Yet, ironically, they can use him to learn how fleeting experiences become either permanently engraved on the mind or lost forever.

Today's quest to understand memory is as urgent as yesterday's drive to crack the genetic code. As Colin Blakemore of Oxford University put it: "Memory is the unsolved challenge for brain research. It is, perhaps, the central question." The ability to remember lifts man out of the terrible eternity of moments; it makes possible his sense of self and his civilization. Traditions, learning and reason all emerge from the tenuous connections of tiny nerve cells.

Because memory spans the territories of the psychologist and the cell biologist, the research is unusually diverse. Pieces of the memory puzzle come from interviews with amnesiacs and experiments on maze-running rats. But there is a hitch. So far, the biologist's chemical and anatomical models of how man forms memories don't always mesh with the psychologist's descriptions.

Researchers have drastically revised what neuroscientists once believed about memory. Experiments in the 1940s suggested that memories reside in neat pockets of the brain, like electrical states in silicon chips in a computer; prodding one spot on the brain with electrodes would call up remembrances as specific as the sound of a mother calling her child on the streets of the patient's old neighborhood. Today, however, researchers doubt that memory is so localized; recent studies show that the electric signals of memory fill the entire brain. How are these signals recorded? Cells fire off impulses when they are stimulated by experiences, and scientists suspect that these impulses are somehow preserved by chemicals in the brain. But the biologists don't know how the chemicals work or even what they are. So the psychologists step in, explaining how experiences that evoke intense emotions or are closely related to facts already in the mind are more likely to be retained than inconsequential or random information.

Scientists believe they will soon amass enough pieces of the memory puzzle to form a complete picture. By studying brain-damaged patients like N. A., for example, they can infer that the memory tasks he fails are controlled by the injured part of the brain. By altering the brain chemicals of rats, researchers learn which compounds affect the vaults of memory.

Dark Alleys

Psychologists are confirming what every mnemonicist knows: the best way to remember is to weave new information into the existing fabric of the mind. This means, in effect, constructing indexed mental files from which information can be retrieved. A lost detail from last night's mystery movie, for instance, might be recalled by concentrating on dark alleys and horrified faces. The brain's need for information categories might explain why people forget their infancy: a baby's world is too new to have neat frameworks into which experiences can be filed.

Correlating emotions works as well as correlating facts. Experiments by psychologist Gordon Bower of Stanford University show that mood is important when receiving new information. If, for example, a person who is happy reads one story about a man's exhilaration

In a hit and run case in Colorado, for example, a witness was hypnotized by police in an attempt to help the individual recall the license number of the vehicle involved. The effort was successful, but because the witness had seen the license number through a rear-view mirror, it was recalled in reverse order! One characteristic of memory is that it improves with repeated efforts to recall the information that is wanted. If you are having trouble remembering something, keep making attempts, and very likely you will be successful in retrieving the data you are seeking. Interrogation of a witness may involve asking the person to go over and over his or her memory of an event, because each time some new information is likely to be recalled.

One reason for poor recall is poor effort. Often a person decides that he or she can't remember something and makes no further attempt at recalling the information. An interrogator or a hypnotist who successfully helps us remember something may only be getting us to put more effort into recall. As more and more elements are recalled, we come closer and closer to re-creating the original context of the event, and this in turn facilitates recall still more. Hypermnesia may largely be a result of increased effort in the form of repeated recall attempts.

Organizational Processes

Besides the reinstatement of context, organizational processes also play an important role in

---

The Mystery of Memory *(continued)*

over his first kiss and a second about the breakup of the Beatles, he is more likely to remember the upbeat tale.

Strong emotions seem to act as embalming fluid for memories. Stressful events such as President Kennedy's assassination remain more vivid in memory than last Monday's lunch, and now experiments are showing why. In a typical study, a rat receives an electric shock if it steps off the shelf in its cage. The shock causes stress, a feeling carried by the brain hormone noradrenaline, and the animal remembers the lesson days later. If the hormone is experimentally blocked after the shock, however, the rat forms no memory of the training and later steps off the shelf. Apparently the hormone is vital for locking into memory short-term changes in the brain such as those produced by the shock. "Memory will fade unless there is an activation of the noradrenaline system that says, 'Print it!'," says Larry Stein of the University of California, Irvine.

Imprints

Scientists believe that several parts of the brain can help form memories. One, the amygdala, makes people react emotionally to stimuli, producing fear of skulking figures in doorways, for instance. Yet it also seems to act as the gatekeeper for emotion-laden memories. Another brain structure, the hippocampus, might also regulate memories tied to places. When Mortimer Mishkin of the National Institute of Mental Health removes these two structures from monkeys, the animals no longer remember which toys are new and which are old. Perhaps, Mishkin speculates, the objects are no longer linked to emotions without aid from the amygdala nor to familiar places without the hippocampus. Thus they cannot be imprinted on the brain as a memory.

If emotions and chemicals are the "ink" that records memories, the brain's anatomy or "paper" on which they are recorded should change to reflect experience. William Greenough of the University of Illinois finds that when rats run mazes, their neurons change. If the animals wear a blindfold over one eye, for example, the side of the brain that "sees" the labyrinth grows more highly branched neurons than the unused side. "This doesn't prove the changes have anything to do with memory," Greenough cautions, "but it does show that where animals are forming memories, changes do occur. It is compatible with the notion that the circuitry of the brain underlies or encodes memory."

The memory circuits in turn seem to light up the whole brain. In experiments with cats, electrical patterns surge through the entire brain when the animals see flashing lights or hear ringing bells that alert them to press a lever to get food. At other times, without the lights or bells, the cats can call up these same electrical patterns and bang the food lever. "The brain can produce an exact facsimile of electrical activity caused by a past event," says E. Roy John of New York University Medical Center. Scientists speculate that structures such as the hippocampus and amygdala receive information from the outside world, process what needs to be remembered and then distribute the electrical memory signal through the whole brain. "Information in the brain is not located in any one place or cell," John concludes, "but rather in large groups of cells cooperating together."

Memory researchers have clearly made headway since Aristotle theorized that the senses imprint memories in the brain like signet rings in wax. Yet they are a long way from connecting the diverse clues to the mystery of memory. Electrical patterns in cat brains and prolific neurons in rat brains still can't account for the magic of the madeleine that unlocked seven volumes of Proust's reminiscences. For now, nobody can improve on J. M. Barrie's explanation: "God gave us memory so we could have roses in December."

Newsweek
June 1, 1981

retrieval. If information is encoded and represented in memory according to some sort of organization or schema, retrieval should be successful if it is based on that schema. If you are asked to name the 50 states, a good plan would be to organize your recall by region. Start with the states of a given region, for example, the New England states, then move on to the next region. In tasks like these, subjects have shown that they naturally rely on the organization of their memories in retrieving information. To continue the example, we would likely see very short pauses between the naming of states of one region and a longer pause before the naming of states of a different region.

These findings indicate that retrieval involves collecting as many elements as possible in an information set and moving on to a different set of information. This process is completely dependent on how information has been encoded or represented in memory. If information is represented in a disorganized fashion, a retrieval plan based on organization will not be effective. Retrieval can be much improved, however, if information is organized in a rational way, particularly if different sets of information can be formulated into a schema. If you can see how different chapters in your text are related, you will find the material easier to learn and to remember than if you treat each chapter as an isolated set of information.

Reconstruction

What we have said so far about retrieval might imply an underlying model that treats the brain as a copying machine. We encode something (copy it) and store it in memory for later recall (retrieval and "read out" of the copy). Yet most of memory is not consistent with such a model. Instead, memory is more in line with a **reconstruction model.** We do not simply copy events and store the copies; rather, we construct representations of the events for storage. In trying to recall an event, we retrieve the representation and try to deduce or reconstruct the event from the representation. The process is similar to what we do to get the default information out from a retrieved schema. It is perhaps most obvious when we try to remember a conversation or something we read. We do not usually have word-for-word copies of the conversation or the printed text stored in our memory; but we have general ideas or facts about what was said or read — ideas or facts that we abstracted as we read or listened. On many occasions, then, retrieval is a problem-solving task of sorts in which different bits of information must be evaluated in order to be remembered successfully.

This type of model makes it clear that two kinds of memory distortion can take place due to the abstract nature of memory representations and the reconstructive nature of retrieval. First, memory distortion can occur at the time of encoding when we have to abstract the general ideas of a conversation or a printed passage. We might misinterpret the incoming information and thus represent information that was not present in the conversation or passage. This is called *constructive* processing, in reference to the construction of additional (possibly inaccurate) information by the listener or reader. As you read or listen you abstract information and construct the overall meaning or "gist." You might include in the gist some default information that was never actually stated but that you assumed to be true.

Consider the following passages and the distorted or elaborated information that might be constructed by someone who hears them:

1. John was trying to fix the birdhouse. He was pounding the nail when his father came out to watch him and help him do the work.

2. It was late at night when the phone rang and a voice gave a frantic cry. The spy threw the secret document into the fireplace just 30 seconds before it would have been too late.

In the first example, you probably would store the general idea that John was fixing a birdhouse with a hammer and nails, aided by his father. In fact, the passage does not say that a hammer was involved at all. In the second example, you probably would store the general idea that the spy burned a secret document just before the police arrived. But the sentence says nothing about burning or the police. Johnson, Bransford, & Solomon (1973) asked subjects who had heard these examples if they had heard the following two test sentences:

1'. John was using the hammer to fix the birdhouse when his father came out to watch and help him do the work.

2'. The spy burned the secret document just 30 seconds before it would have been too late.

The subjects usually incorrectly judged that they had heard (1') and (2') when in fact they had heard only (1) and (2). Apparently, they incorrectly interpreted (1) and (2) and encoded general information, not word-for-word copies. At the time of the test they retrieved the general ideas (which included hammer and burned) and reconstructed from this information some notion of what they must have heard. The reconstruction was then similar enough to (1') and (2') that the subjects were fooled into believing that they had heard these exact sentences.

Memory distortion can also take place at the time of retrieval, regardless of whether inaccuracies were constructed and entered into memory at encoding. Information available during retrieval can have a strong effect on one's reconstruction of encoded events. Working with memory for drawings, Hanawalt & Demarest (1939) showed that information provided at the time of a test affected retrieval. Subjects were shown a set of drawings such as those in Figure 5–7. At the time of the test, subjects were given one or the other list of verbal labels prior to attempting to draw the figures from memory. Subjects' drawings were indeed influenced by the presence of verbal labels at recall, with drawings tending to be consistent with whichever labels had been given. The effect was strongest at the longest retention interval. Here subjects were using their schemata of things like curtains and bottles to guide their recall of the drawings.

In short, memory probably is rarely based on exact copies of the original experience. When we encode information, we are not passive copy machines filing away perfect reproductions for later retrieval. Instead, we actively abstract and interpret information as we receive it (we think as we learn), and we may file away only general representations of the information. Later, if necessary, we can retrieve the general idea and reconstruct the original experience. As a result, our memories may be inaccurate because we misinterpreted the information or added default knowledge in the first place, or because we did not retain sufficient general information to make an accurate reconstruction, or because we committed errors in the reconstruction process itself.

Language

Virtually every topic we have discussed in this chapter has touched on the verbal skills that we take so much for granted. There is probably nothing more central to mature human information processing than language. Our knowledge of our dominant language, and our ability to comprehend and produce it, profoundly influence the way we encode, store, and retrieve information. Language is often considered our greatest intellectual accomplishment. Languages differ from culture to culture, but the language of each culture provides members of that culture with a commonly accepted way of describing and remembering their experiences and communicating them to others. In a language, both visual and auditory—written and spoken—symbols represent various objects, events, actions, and relations that make up our experiences. These symbols are combined in systematic ways to express even larger ideas. The existence of language poses several interesting questions for cognitive psychologists: What is language, and what is involved in understanding language? How is

FIGURE 5–7 Stimulus figures and verbal labels

Reproduced figure	Word list	Stimulus figure	Word list	Reproduced figure
	Eyeglasses		Dumbbells	
	Bottle		Stirrup	
	Crescent moon		Letter "C"	
	Beehive		Hat	
	Curtains in a window		Diamond in a rectangle	
	Seven		Four	
	Ship's wheel		Sun	
	Hourglass		Table	

language acquired? How does language influence learning and memory? Most language acquisition occurs during the early years of life; this process will be described in Chapter 8. For now we will concentrate on how language is understood.

Understanding Language

The familiar act of understanding what someone says to you is really a complicated and remarkable achievement. A speaker converts a meaningful experience into a series of vocalizations, and the listener in turn converts these vocalizations back into meaning. Let us assume that the speaker does his or her job well. Consider the task of the listener. To extract meaning from the vocalization, the listener must be able to identify the units of meaning and understand the rules underlying their organization. Travelers in foreign lands are often unable to perform this task. We are inclined to attribute this failure to inadequate knowledge of vocabulary. "How was I supposed to know that *strasse* means 'street'?"

Actually, the listener's task is much more complex than this. If you heard a language extremely different from your own, it is quite possible that you might not even understand the vocal cues that indicate units—that is, when units begin and end. In other words, you might not have any idea of how to begin processing the vocalization. A listener must be able to analyze the structure of a vocalization in order to understand its meaning. The structure of a language can be described on several different levels, each with its own units and associated rules. Ordinarily we are not aware of processing language at

At an early age children learn to make both auditory and visual discrimination among the symbols of their language.

whether they are voiced (vocal chords vibrating) or voiceless. To see (or feel) this difference, make the *p* and *b* sounds (as in "pat" and "bat") with your lips. Notice that the *b* sound uses the voice box while the *p* sound does not. This is only one way in which the phonemes of the English language differ. Each phoneme can be described in terms of a distinctive bundle of such features.

The written analog of the phoneme is the **grapheme**—a category of "graphs" or letters—to which we similarly respond. For example, the grapheme "a" would include symbols like *a, A,* **A.**

The language user deals not just in sounds or letters but in larger units. The smallest meaningful unit of analysis in language is the **morpheme,** The value of using the morpheme instead of the word as the unit of linguistic analysis is best understood by example. In linguistic analysis the word "bat" is a single morpheme, whereas "bats" consists of two morphemes, "bat" and "s," the second of which is the form for making a plural. Another example is the word "sadly," which is divided into "sad" plus "ly," the latter morpheme being used to produce an adverb from an adjective.

Phonemes combine to make morphemes. The combining process follows certain rules that we use in speaking English, although we may not know them in any formal sense. We use them, however, in the sense of being able to distinguish real English words from nonsense. Thus, certain combinations of sounds are allowable and certain others are not. For example, no English word could begin with "trv." We know immediately that "trvurs" cannot be a word. On the other hand, we might have to use a dictionary to find out about "dib" or "lut." Thus you can use your knowledge of the rules for combining sounds into English to judge whether unfamiliar combinations are real words or not.

Psycholinguists—psychologists who study language—find it useful to distinguish between two major structural components at the level of the sentence: (1) syntax and (2) semantics. **Syntax** deals with the formal structure of the strings of symbols that make up sentences. The elementary units of a language may be combined only in certain ways if they are to be comprehensible. These ways are prescribed by a set of rules called the **grammar** of the language. Speakers of a particular language behave *as if* they know the grammatical rules of their language, even though they might have no conscious awareness of using the rules when speaking or listening to communications. **Semantics,** on the other hand, refers to the *meaning,* or *message,* of a sentence. Distinguishing between syntax and semantics is not always easy. Consider the following examples:

multiple levels because we concentrate on meaning; nonetheless, multilevel processing is taking place. Let us briefly consider what is involved.

Structural Components

Language structure can be described in terms of sounds, words, and sentences. A sentence is made up of words, and the words are made up of sounds. Let us start with the smallest unit and work our way up: in this way, you can see the complexity of processing language.

To begin, consider the fact that the *b* sound is never exactly the same each time the word "boy" is spoken, even by the same speaker. Particular sounds vary from word to word and speaker to speaker. Despite these fluctuations, certain characteristics repeatedly occur, enabling the listener to recognize the sound. Each particular *b* sound, somewhat different from every other *b* sound, is an example of a general, conceptual class of sounds we recognize as "b." These classes are called **phonemes.** Each phoneme is characterized by certain distinctive features that enable us to distinguish it from other phonemes. The features are related to the way in which speech sounds are made by the speaker. For example, one basis for distinguishing phonemes is in terms of

John is easy to please
John is eager to please

The two sentences have similar syntax but different meanings. Consider other examples:

They are eating apples
The shooting of the hunters was terrible

The sentences are semantically ambiguous because their syntactic structure does not uniquely assign one and only one meaning to them. Interestingly, in building early machines that could comprehend and translate sentences, computer scientists found it difficult to give their programs enough syntactic and semantic wisdom to adequately understand language. For example, one such computer, asked to paraphrase the sentence "The spirit is willing but the flesh is weak" produced "The wine is agreeable but the meat is spoiled." Such failures are not only amusing, they also teach us a great deal about the complexity of language—in particular, that the *meaning* of a sentence is much more than the stringing together of individual concepts. We have since realized that the meaning of larger units of discourse also depends on

structure, in this case relationships between sentences that are often omitted from the words themselves and left for the listener or reader to infer. Therefore, let us examine meaning itself.

Meaning

The primary function of language is to convey meaning, and its structural components are related to this function. One of the more difficult problems facing psychologists is the meaning of "meaning."

We mentioned earlier that morphemes and words are the smallest units of language that carry meaning. A great deal of attention has been given to the meaning of words. Actually, words have two different kinds of meaning. The **denotation** of a word is roughly its dictionary definition, a specification of the conditions under which the word may properly be used (as agreed upon by the language community). For example, it is acceptable to call some things chairs but not others, to refer to some people as uncles but not others. The **connotation** of a word refers to all the things we associate with the word but which are not part of its denotative meaning.

Highlight 5–7

Semantic Differential Ratings

The **semantic differential,** developed by Charles Osgood, is one technique for assessing the connotative meaning of a word. People can be asked to rate a word on as many as 50 scales, although it is typically found that the scales can be reduced to a basic set along three dimensions: evaluation (good-bad), potency (weak-strong), and activity (fast-slow). The adjective pairs in parentheses are those best illustrating these three dimensions. Notice that ratings on certain scales, like strong-weak and heavy-light, tend to come out pretty much the

same. These pairs are related to the same underlying dimension, potency. According to the theory behind the semantic differential, the meaning of a word can be indexed according to its position along the three basic dimensions. Thus, "mother" is toward the positive end of evaluation, toward the strong end of potency, and toward the fast end of activity. The semantic differential has been used to measure the connotative similarity of words which might have quite different denotative meanings.

Make your own ratings for the words "Mother" and "Tree"

Mother

Good	Bad
Weak	Strong
Slow	Fast
Light	Heavy
Clean	Dirty
Passive	Active
Bright	Dark
Large	Small
Tense	Relaxed

Tree

Good	Bad
Weak	Strong
Slow	Fast
Light	Heavy
Clean	Dirty
Passive	Active
Bright	Dark
Large	Small
Tense	Relaxed

Compare your ratings with the averages obtained from a group

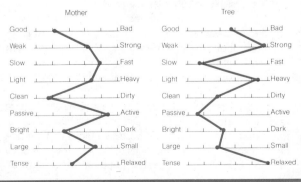

Mother / Tree

For example, "teacher" is denotatively defined as "one who shows how to do something or gives lessons," but "teacher" might also make you think of "stern, threatening, quiet, loving, smiling" (depending on your experience). Such associations make up the connotative meanings of the word.

Many words are labels for classes of things in our experience. Certain kinds of objects are labeled wheels, certain kinds of sensory experiences are labeled red, and certain kinds of activities are labeled jumping. One theory of meaning is that words acquire meaning through consistent pairings with aspects of our experience. While this is one mechanism for acquiring meaning, it is not an all-encompassing explanation. A look at a dictionary will quickly reveal that words, standing alone, are rather ambiguous, yet we have little difficulty understanding them in context. For example, consider the difference in meaning between "the *duck* swam down the river" and "I had to *duck* under the swinging racket." Some words seem to have meaning only in sentences; what are the nonlinguistic referents for "but," "neither," or "however"?

Sentences convey meanings that cannot be completely explained in terms of the meanings of the words they contain. Even though we know the words "the," "boy," "girl," and "hit," this knowledge alone does not enable us to account for the meaning of the sentence "The boy hit the girl." The same words rearranged as "The girl hit the boy" communicates an entirely different idea. Actually, we may not get the full meaning of communication from the sentence alone. Most sentences interact with our knowledge of the world, our semantic memory. Through inferences, sentences provide us with much more information than looking at the sentence alone would suggest. For example, the sentence "Babe Ruth hit a home run and drove in three runs" describes a certain action. But it implies a great deal more. It implies that a baseball game was being played, during a particular time period, probably involving the New York Yankees, that a pitch was made, that two teammates were on base, and so on.

Cultural Differences

It is generally agreed that thought and language are closely related, but the nature of that relationship is subject to considerable debate. Is thought necessary for language? Is language necessary for thought? Is one the basis of the other? Are they identical? Do they have some material effect on each other? Psychologists do not know the answers to questions like these yet, and consequently there is a lot of room for theory and speculation.

Highlight 5–8

Bilingualism and Information Processing

The linguistic relativity hypothesis would imply that a person's knowledge cannot be separated from his or her language. What then of the bilingual person who is fluent, say, in both English and French? One possibility is that some knowledge is stored in French and other knowledge is stored in English. A different, more nearly correct assumption is that the person's knowledge is stored centrally and is accessible to either language equally.

In one experiment, French-English speakers were asked to read various short paragraphs and then to answer questions about the information presented. A paragraph was either all in English, all in French, or in a mixture of both. An example of a mixed paragraph is given below:

His horse, followed de deux bassets, faisait la terre resonner under its even tread. Des gouttes de verglas stuck to his manteau. Une violente brise was blowing. One side de l'horizon lighted up, and dans la blancheur of the early morning light, il apercut rabbits hopping at the bord de leurs terriers.

As long as the person could read the passage silently, it made little difference whether the paragraph was in one or two languages—for the same amount of study time, performance on the examination was the same.

Another test made use of the fact that when people see a long list of words, one at a time, and are then asked to recall as many as possible, words repeated more often in the list are recalled more frequently. The question was whether or not "repetitions" in different languages would have the same effect on recall as repetitions in a single language. The results for French-English speakers indicated that, for example, experiencing "fold" twice and its French equivalent "pli" twice had the same effect on recall as four presentations of "fold." In other words, recall was a function of frequency of exposure to the meanings or concepts, not the linguistic forms expressing those meanings. This finding suggests that the subjects were utilizing a common meaning form that is accessible to either language.

A popular hypothesis about language and thought is the *linguistic relativity hypothesis* put forth by Benjamin Lee Whorf, which is often called the Whorfian hypothesis. It is a complex set of ideas, but basically the notion is that languages are organized differently, and, therefore, because language and thought are closely interrelated, speakers of these languages will think differently. Whorf argues that the way we perceive and think about the world is largely determined by the language we have for encoding the world.

Consider vocabulary richness. There is a tribe in the Philippine Islands whose language has names for 92 different kinds of rice. The Arabic language has about 6000 ways of referring to camels in their speech. Naturally, we would expect people who speak these languages to think more explicitly about rice or about camels than we do. But is this because they can think about camels or rice in ways we cannot, or is it because they just know more about camels and rice than we do? Their superior knowledge is undoubtedly due to the fact that camels and rice are more important in their culture and not that their language is different, as Whorf would argue. Most important, could they have a thought about camels or rice that we could not, in principle, have because we speak English? Basically, no, because *every* language can probably express anything.

The Whorfian hypothesis is an intriguing one. The evidence upon which it is based is, however, anecdotal and offers little support for the idea of linguistic relativity, that is, that language *determines* the general view we have of the world. Language does, however, determine how efficiently we can code our experiences. Eskimos talk more efficiently about snow than we can because they have many single words to represent their discriminations on the subject.

The Whorfian hypothesis raises other issues of concern when we consider different dialects of a language. Educators, politicians, and psychologists are currently wrestling with the problems posed by cultural and dialectic differences within a society. This is an area of considerable controversy that is unlikely to be resolved for some time. It will concern us again in Chapter 6 when we discuss the measurement of IQ.

Discourse Processing

How do we comprehend the information in discourse —an oral or written message consisting of two or more sentences? Psychologists used to believe that comprehension was entirely "bottom-up" processing—one simply extracted everything that was in the message as it was processed through successive stages of analysis. But there is "top-down" processing as well.

The reader or listener carries lots of knowledge in memory, which interacts with the information being abstracted by the bottom-up analysis of the phonemes or graphemes of the message. For purposes of understanding new information coming in, what we already know may be as important as the new information itself. Three types of stored knowledge influence the comprehension process: knowledge of (1) the language, (2) the world in general, and (3) the specific subject of the discourse. Of course, we have to be able to remember, or retrieve, this information from storage in order to use it during discourse processing, an operation that involves complex cognitive activity. Memory, language, and thinking are highly interdependent.

Comprehending discourse involves more than decoding individual words and employing rules of syntax. Discourse-comprehension strategies involve trying out certain hypotheses about the intended meaning of the message that promise success. The primary goal of such strategies, then, is to derive the meaning of a discourse, not to analyze the passage syntactically, although knowledge of syntactic rules can be applied to aid comprehension.

Understanding written or spoken discourse involves an interaction of a number of different sources of information, just as does decoding of single words. We perceive words and sentences either in the visual or auditory domain, and it is our responsibility to grasp the meaning of the message. Besides using the physical information of the written or spoken word, we also use our own knowledge of the topic being discussed, represented in schemata, to help us understand.

Usually we are unaware of the critical importance of our general knowledge in understanding language. If in reading something we cannot call up the knowledge needed to understand the passage, then what we are reading might appear to be nonsense. Read the following passage, taken from Bransford & Johnson (1973):

> If the balloons popped the sound wouldn't be able to carry since everything would be too far away from the correct floor. A closed window would also prevent the sound from carrying, since most buildings tend to be well insulated. Since the whole operation depends on a steady flow of electricity, a break in the middle of the wire would also cause problems. Of course, the fellow could shout, but the human voice is not loud enough to carry that far. An additional problem is that a string could break on the instrument. Then there could be no accompaniment to the message. It is clear that the best situation would involve less distance. Then there would be fewer potential problems. With face to face contact, the least number of things could go wrong.

This passage, which sounds like nonsense, is difficult to comprehend because you do not have the general knowledge necessary to understand the meaning of the sentences. The meaning does not reside exclusively in the words and sentences that make up the passage; if that were so, this perfectly grammatical material would be comprehensible. Rather, comprehension of discourse is obviously an active process in which we interpret the information contained in the words and sentences and through the grammar. To produce understanding this interpretation process must rely on things other than purely linguistic knowledge. To obtain the knowledge needed to comprehend the passage given in the example, look at the drawing of the "electronic serenade" on page 173 and then reread the passage. Now it should be meaningful and easy to comprehend. Once you apply the knowledge of your music-amplification and serenades schemata, you can easily see what this passage is about. This exercise should convince you that in comprehending language, written or spoken, cognitive processes are involved in a very active way, and success is dependent on the processes and knowledge we have available.

Much of our knowledge of the world and of how language and discourse are structured is represented in long-term memory. Knowledge, as we have seen, seems to be organized into schemata and can be drawn on during comprehension. If you are reading a passage about Mt. St. Helens volcano, you can expect to see sentences describing devastation of the land, billows of smoke and ash, and so on. All of this information is readily available once you realize that the topic of the passage is volcanic eruption. You will readily be able to comprehend and encode information relevant to such an event, because to some extent you can predict what generally happens when a volcano erupts. You would be very puzzled if the author had written that as the volcano erupted, the sky became clear. Such information would violate your expectations about what should happen, and you would very much want the author to explain.

Inferences

Not only does use of general knowledge aid comprehension by putting a passage into a meaningful context, it also leads to elaborative or constructive processing of discourse. We may not get the full meaning of a communication from the sentence alone. Most sentences interact with our general knowledge of the world (schemata), to produce *inferences*. One type of inference during comprehension is *presupposition*. This term refers to the idea that a sentence conveys information which implies that other information must also be true—a notion similar to that of default knowledge. Whether someone says "John closed the window" or "John did not close the window," he or she is implying that the window was open. We may encode the information that the window was open

without scrutinizing it very carefully, even though it was never explicitly stated. Normally, presuppositions are assumed automatically. If someone tells Bob's girl friend, Sue, that Bob hasn't stopped going out with Linda, the presupposition is that Bob is going out with Linda. If Sue were to take that presupposition for granted, Bob would be in trouble, even though he may never have gone out with Linda. The presuppositions of a message are often taken for granted by the listener, and so they often mislead the listener.

Other kinds of inferences can also be drawn during comprehension. These serve to elaborate or embellish the information given in a sentence, rather than to imply necessarily true conditions, as is the case with presuppositions. For example, upon reading the sentence "The karate student broke the cement block," we presuppose that prior to the action the block was intact. But one might also construct other elaborative inferences on the basis of the sentence and a schema for karate, such as the idea that the student used a karate chop to break the block. That may not be true at all, however. The student may have been inept and simply broke the block by dropping it. Elaborative inferences, then, are not necessarily true, but they are likely to represent accurate information. Again, this is like filling in default information in your karate schema.

Inferred information, both presuppositions and elaborations, is incorporated into one's understanding of a passage. While inferences may not always be valid, they are important for gaining a full understanding of a communication. If the writer or speaker uses language carefully, we can place much reliance on ourselves to infer the proper information while reading or listening. If everything were carefully and explicitly stated, however, discourse would be very boring indeed, and redundancy would be a greater problem than it already is. At the same time, we must trust that what the speaker or writer has left to be inferred is in fact true. The unwritten contract between the communicator and the comprehender rests on this foundation.

Understanding Stories

As we go about understanding a fictional story that we read we make use of a good deal of general knowledge (much of it stored in an organized, schematic fashion) relevant to the subject of the story. But we also rely on our knowledge of how stories are structured. Through our experience with literature we have become familiar with various techniques of plot and character development, descriptive devices, endings, and so forth. This knowledge constitutes a schema about the structure of stories. Often we are aware of which of these parts of the story we are in, and depending on our interest in each part we might vary how carefully we wish to read. More interesting parts could be read more carefully and might form a more central part of our memory of the story.

Some researchers have successfully described the structure of paragraphs and simple stories, and "grammars" have even been developed for relatively simple stories. Such grammars represent ways of describing or categorizing different parts of the story and are meant to reflect our schematic knowledge of story structure. Consider the following description of a story grammar: A particular kind of story is composed of setting plus theme plus plot plus resolution. A setting is composed of time plus location. The theme specifies a goal. A plot consists of a series of episodes. An episode is composed of a subgoal, an attempt, and an outcome. This partial description indicates that stories can be hierarchical structures—that is, arranged in graded series—above and beyond the sentences they contain. Grasping the structure of a story is crucial for understanding. The full meaning of an episode depends on its relation to the plot, and the theme gives meaning to the plot. If, for example, sentences that convey the theme of a story were deleted or even moved from the beginning to the end of the story, comprehension and retention of the story would be reduced. Without information about the overall theme of the story, the plot would seem disorganized and individual episodes might not make sense.

Their structure also influences how we go about recalling or summarizing stories. Earlier we said that recall of prose involves reconstructive processes operating on a general abstract representation of the original passage. That reconstruction could be guided by schematic knowledge of the kind of information contained in stories. For instance, we know that virtually every story has a setting of some kind, and the nature of events in the story should provide clues about time and location. From this information we could derive a plausible setting and include it in our recall. The hierarchical nature of story structure is important for guiding summarization. If we read a 100,000-word book and are asked to write a 100-word summary of it, we have to be very harsh editors. Selecting what to include in a summary would depend partly on what the summary was to be used for. But in any case we would rely on our knowledge of story structure and the function of each element of the structure to direct our selection of information to be included in the summary. Recent research has shown that when asked to summarize stories, subjects agreed reasonably well on what to include, as long as they worked with stories that had familiar structures. With summaries of stories that had unusual structures, such as some American Indian folktales, subjects did not show agreement. Disagreement resulted because subjects were unable to use their knowledge of story structure to organize the elements of the novel stories. Without such general organization the different parts of the story do not

The electronic serenade

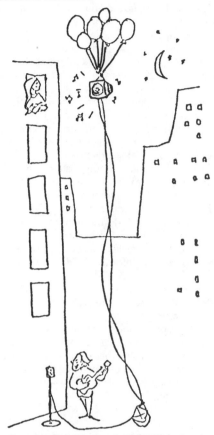

After you have studied this drawing of an "electronic serenade" go back and reread the passage on page 171 and see if the passage is easier to comprehend now that you have the relevant knowledge for understanding.

fit together well, and while each sentence may be comprehensible, the story as a whole fails to be understandable to those not familiar with its structure.

In general, the process of understanding stories, like the process of encoding other types of information, is based on the development of an abstract representation of the critical aspects of the story. We sometimes call this representation the *gist* of a story. Comprehending the gist of a story is highly dependent on knowledge of story structure, since the gist is at least partly determined by the structure. One also needs adequate knowledge of the general topic of the story in order to judge properly the importance of different parts of the story. Knowledge of both structure and topic are critical for the extraction of the gist of a story. We can see the gist as a schema we construct with specific information filled in. Questions involving how readers and listeners get the gist of stories have begun to receive much more attention from memory and language researchers. We can hope to learn a great deal more about this fascinating process.

SUMMARY

1. The modern study of human learning, memory, and language is dominated by the information-processing approach. This approach focuses on three processes in memory: encoding, storage, and retrieval of information.

2. Four characteristics of the information-processing approach are: (a) it analyzes the flow of information into components or stages; (b) it assumes that the system has a limited capacity, implying bottlenecks under high information loads; (c) there is a control mechanism of some sort to organize the information flow; and (d) information flows both from the bottom up (data driven) and from the top down (knowledge or schema driven).

3. The fundamental memory system consists of three basic memory stages: (a) sensory memory, (b) short-term memory, and (c) long-term memory.

4. Rehearsal is important for encoding new information. There are two types: (a) maintenance rehearsal, which preserves information in short-term memory, and (b) elaborative rehearsal, which facilitates long-term storage. This distinction implies that information can be processed at various levels.

5. An influential theory of memory is based upon the principle that the deeper, more elaborate the processing, the better the learning.

6. Two major variables affecting encoding of incoming information are imagery and organization. Images may be powerful memory aids because they organize large amounts of information into one unit that takes up less memory space. Chunking is an especially useful organizational encoding technique.

7. Knowledge about the world is stored in long-term memory in various forms: (a) procedural or declarative; (b) propositional or analog; and (c) episodic or semantic. The information in long-term memory is usually highly organized.

8. Network models and schema theory are two important ideas about the way in which information in long-term memory is organized.

9. There are several explanations for forgetting: (a) memory decay; (b) failure of memory trace consolidation; and (c) interference from learning other information.

10. Remembering can be facilitated by: (a) reinstating the original encoding context; (b) making repeated attempts to recall; (c) using an organized retrieval strategy; and (d) constructing missing elements using an appropriate schema.

11. Memory and language are highly interrelated and interdependent. Language profoundly influences the way we encode, store, and retrieve information.

12. The two major structural components of language are syntax and semantics. Syntax refers to the ordering of linguistic units into grammatical strings designed to convey meaning. Semantics refers to the meaning itself, the content of the strings.

13. Comprehension of written or spoken discourse is heavily dependent upon access to knowledge in memory. Discourse requires decoding, and decoding involves presuppositions, inferences, default knowledge, and expectations not contained in the message itself.

RECOMMENDED ADDITIONAL READINGS

Klatzky, R. L. *Human memory: Structures and processes,* 2d ed. San Francisco: W. H. Freeman, 1980.

Loftus, E. *Memory: Surprising new insights into how we remember and why we forget.* Reading, Mass.: Addison-Wesley, 1980.

Seamon, J. G. *Memory and cognition: An introduction.* New York: Oxford, 1980.

Slobin, D. I. *Psycholinguistics,* 2d ed. Glenview, Ill.: Scott, Foresman, 1979.

What Does It Mean?

Improving Memory and Study Habits

Research on human memory has suggested some steps you can take to improve your studying and memory skills. One of the most important things to do is to maximize the degree of original learning of the material. The better you learn the material initially, the more resistant it is to forgetting. During study it is important that you understand the material fully. Comprehension is a prerequisite for reliable memory of a large set of information. How easy would it be to remember what was said in the "electronic serenade" passage if you hadn't seen the accompanying drawing? You should also organize the different parts of the material being studied so that you can see how they are related to each other. If these relationships are firmly established in your mind, recall of one part of the material will naturally lead to recall of other parts. Try to return to the "scene of the crime." That is,

reinstate the context and learning cues at the time of recall. Study in the place where you will have to perform, and under conditions similar to those under which you will be tested. In order to keep study and test contexts as similar as possible, you should not take drugs to keep awake while studying. With drugs you run the risk of state-dependent learning, unless, of course, you also take the drugs just before the exam. In that case, unwanted side effects such as anxiety or confusion may interfere with your examination performance.

Retrieval Cues

While studying you should try to provide yourself with retrieval cues that you know will be present at the time of recall. In the case of an examination, try to find cues in the examination room to use as "memory hooks" for the material you are learning. For example, the room may contain "no smoking" signs, a chart of chemical elements, and a map. Try to form images relating these items to the materials you are learning. Also, practice using your retrieval cues and recalling the material. After studying a section, recite the important points to yourself or a friend. Get together with friends and test each other on the material. You must be

The Mnemonic Cues of Familiar Rooms

Students taking tests in unfamiliar surroundings may be able to improve their performance by pausing for a minute or two before they start work and visualizing their own classroom. That trick, according to experiments by Steven Smith, a psychologist at Texas A & M University, can overcome an effect discovered several years ago: it is harder to remember lists of words in a strange room than in the room where they were originally learned.

Smith assembled five groups of 10 students each in a basement lounge where 90 one-syllable words were read aloud to them from a tape recorder at three-second intervals. The students were instructed to remember as many of the words as possible. The next day, they returned for a recall test. One group took it in the same lounge; the other four groups took it in a fifth-floor room. In the unfamiliar surroundings, one group received no special instruc-

tions, another group was told to think of a room at home for three minutes before starting the test, and a third group was asked to think for three minutes about the lounge, writing down a list of its sights, sounds, and smells. A fourth group received the same instructions as the third and was also shown slides of the lounge.

The students tested in the basement lounge recalled an average of 18 of the 90 words correctly. The students in the room upstairs who got no instructions averaged 12 correct; those who thought about home got an average of 9.6 right. The students who were asked to think first about the lounge and the group who also saw slides of it, however, got 17.2 and 18.8 items correct, respectively, doing as well or better than students who were tested for recall in the lounge.

Smith is not sure whether students used particular features of the room they learned things in as mnemonic

"hooks" to associate with the words they wanted to recall or whether remembering details of the original room simply increased their feeling of comfort. In any case, Smith is now looking at the exam marks of students in classes that have been split into several classrooms for testing. (This is often done in order to leave vacant seats between the test-takers. Because of Smith's findings, he feels it would be unethical to split his own classes that way.) His conclusions are still tentative, but the environment seems to affect memory most strongly on essay tests, which require people to retrieve information in the same way the free-recall word tests do. The environmental effect virtually disappears in multiple-choice or true-false tests, which call for recognition rather than retrieval to get correct answers. . . .

Psychology Today
October 1980

able to retrieve what you have learned. If you do not practice retrieval, you risk knowing more than you are able to show on an examination.

Mnemonic Methods

A number of memory aids, called **mnemonics,** can help you to remember information. One is to memorize a set of "memory pegs" in advance of learning. A convenient system consists of numbers and words that rhyme with numbers. The rhyme helps retrieve the word when given the number. For example:

One is a bun
Two is a shoe
Three is a tree
Four is a door
etc.

If your task is to memorize a shopping list, use your imagery skills and "hook" each item to be purchased to one of the number-word pegs. This can be done by using an image that involves an interaction between a peg word and a list item. If milk is on the list, think of a shoe filled to overflowing with milk. Continue hooking each item onto the next number-word peg. When you get to the store, reciting each peg word to yourself should call forth the image of the desired item.

Other mnemonic methods include the *method of loci* (locations). In this case, the memory pegs are a sequence of locations that can easily be recalled in order. Each item to be learned is hooked to a different location, possibly through imagery. Locations can be based on things you would see on a long walk from your home, for example, a mailbox, a church, a beauty salon. Suppose again that milk is on your list. You could think of milk spewing out of the mailbox, drenching pedestrians. To recall the list, just retrace your

The New Yorker, June 3, 1974. Drawing by D. Fradon; © 1974 The New Yorker Magazine, Inc.

An acronym is a mnemonic device based on abbreviation. The idea is to condense a lot of information into one chunk.

"When you're young, it comes naturally, but when you get a little older, you have to rely on mnemonics."

American Scientist, September 1978. Reprinted by permission of Sidney Harris.

walk in your mind, stopping at each location to recall the desired material. Another method involves *natural language mediation*. Often we are called upon to remember unfamiliar words or codes. One approach to such a task is to think of an actual word that sounds like the item we are trying to learn. If we are trying to learn the term "olfactory nerve," we might think of "oil factory" as a mediator. This method has been applied to learning new words in a second language. Suppose you want to learn the Spanish word *"carta,"* meaning "letter." You first transform the unfamiliar Spanish word *"carta"* into an English word that sounds similar, such as "cart." Then construct a visual image of a postal letter inside a shopping cart. You can use that image to help you remember the meaning of *"carta"* when you encounter it in the future.

Organizing Schemata

Organizing information that you study into a meaningful schema is a powerful learning and memory aid. It can be accomplished by developing groups of related topics and making an outline illustrating the relationship between topic groups. When you review this material during study, try to avoid repetitive maintenance rehearsal. Instead, try to process the meaning of each topic, calling to mind the important information every time you review the material. Think about what you are studying rather than just rattling the words off to yourself. The outline at the beginning of each chapter in this book can serve as an organizing schema for you when you prepare for your exams in this course.

"Eyewitness" Testimony

When people listen to a number of sentences all related to a general theme, they have, under some circumstances, great difficulty distinguishing between sentences they actually heard and sentences that were not presented but "fit the theme." We also know that the context in which a given sentence is spoken has a good deal to do with its meaning and interpretation. Consequently, a person may have difficulty distinguishing between what actually happened and what he or she infers to have happened. This inferential aspect of remembering is not limited to recalling exact sentences but can affect the recall of "facts," as has been shown in experiments conducted by Elizabeth Loftus and her colleagues.

In these studies people watched a film of a traffic accident, having been told that they were participating in a memory experiment. Subsequently, they were asked questions about what they had seen. The critical variable concerned the way in which the questions were phrased. Some subjects were asked questions like, "Did you see *the* broken headlight?" The definite article "the" implies that there was a broken headlight, with the person having to decide only whether or not he or she noticed it. Others were asked, "Did you see *a* broken headlight?" The indefinite article "a" has no implication—indeed, it raises the question of whether or not there was a broken headlight as well as the question of whether or not the person saw it.

Several questions of both forms were asked about things that had occurred in the film and things that had not. The form of the question did not affect the frequency with which people indicated that they had seen something that actually did occur. However, asking questions with "the" resulted in a much stronger tendency for people to say that they had seen something that had never occurred! An inaccurate presupposition was made.

Similar effects of "suggestive questions" were reported by Loftus and John Palmer. People who had witnessed a traffic accident were asked either "How fast were the cars going when they bumped into each other?" or "How fast were the cars going when they smashed into each other?" Witnesses who were asked the first question estimated much lower speeds than those asked the second. These results are consistent with the view of memory as a reconstructive process and indicate that suggesting plausible inferences to a person at the time of recall can affect what is believed to have happened. Simply by asking the right questions, you can convince at least some people that they saw events that did not happen. The implications of such results for courtroom examinations or police investigations are fairly obvious. Such interrogations are intended to identify the "facts," with attorneys told not to "lead the witness." These findings suggest that the definition of a "leading question" may be very subtle indeed.

Improving Your Reading Speed

Can people actually learn to read thousands of words a minute (instead of just a few hundred) and still comprehend the material being read as courses in reading dynamics claim? Not much research has been directed to this issue, but what has been done suggests that to answer the question we have to define carefully the word "comprehend." If we are interested only in getting a very general idea of a written message, rapid reading may work very well. But only a slower reading pace will allow us to comprehend a passage fully and be able to remember details. The reason is that our reading rate is limited by physical factors. When we read we move our eyes across a page in a series of short fixations (the average fixation lasts about one-quarter of a second), with very swift eye movements between fixations. Since we can accurately perceive only one or two words on each fixation, we have a very strict limit on how fast we can go and still be able to read every word. A limit of about 600 words a minute has been calculated by researchers. A person reading at a faster rate is not processing each word.

The real question of how effective speed reading can be, then, depends on the comprehension level we expect to achieve. Reading a passage at 3000 words a minute will not allow you to see, let alone comprehend, all the information in the passage. But you might be able to get an idea of what the passage is about. In considering whether or not you want to learn how to speed read, think about how you

"You have a choice of three courses. You could increase speed somewhat and retain your comprehension, you could increase speed considerably and reduce comprehension, or you could increase speed tremendously and eliminate comprehension completely."

American Scientist, July–August 1977. Reprinted by permission of Sidney Harris.

Despite the claims of people trying to sell you a "speed-reading" course, there really is a trade-off between speed and comprehension. This is a real-life example of the limits on human cognition and information processing.

would put the skill to use. There might be times when you want to read things rapidly in order to get a general idea of the content or find a specific piece of information. A speed reading course might train you to do this. You might also benefit by practicing skimming and selective reading on your own. But if you expect to read your textbooks and other difficult material at thousands of words a minute and still do well on exams, you will be disappointed.

Perhaps you could be a faster reader than you are now, even when reading for full comprehension. As noted earlier, the physical limit on reading rate is about 600 words a minute if *every* word is read. Do you read that fast now? Not many people do, partly because most people have certain reading habits that slow them down. Saying each word carefully to yourself and looking back at what you have read are two examples. You may sometimes need to use these techniques to help your comprehension, but you may be using them when you don't need to. You might find that if you do not look back very often your speed will increase and your comprehension will not suffer. You might be surprised at how much faster you go, if you set that as your goal and try to trim away time-consuming steps that are not necessary for you to get what you want out of a passage. The key is to decide beforehand what you want to learn from something you are going to read, and tailor your style to that goal.

Beware of the claims for fantastic comprehension at extremely high rates of reading. Often the comprehension test may test general information the reader already knew. A control group is needed of people who take the test without having done any of the reading. But such groups are rarely included, so that tests for reading comprehension are not valid.

Reading Ahead

Reading is obviously one of the most important cognitive skills a person can acquire. In elementary school, reading instruction and practice occupy a major portion of a student's life, and tremendous attention is given to how well students can read at all levels of schooling. If test results show that reading scores are declining, educators, parents, and society as a whole express great concern and call for corrective action. Learning to read is important not just for college students, professors, or newspaper editors—reading skills must be reasonably developed in order to make one's way in society. Of course, different reading tasks require different skill levels. Understanding this textbook requires more skill than reading a traffic sign, for example.

Despite the importance of reading and the attention paid to it, we still have much to learn about what people do when they read. Compared to many other cognitive processes, reading is extremely complicated, and it has proved difficult to analyze. The complexity of the issues can partly be illustrated by considering the following "facts." Understanding *spoken* language is a complicated activity, as we have pointed out earlier in this chapter. Yet most people come to understand spoken language relatively early in their lives and without making very special efforts to do so. In contrast, many people have trouble learning to read, which suggests that reading involves even greater complexities.

Commercials That Go Zip

During a recent commercial demonstration on NBC's "Today" show, a handsome tennis player boasted that his Racquet Club cologne is "my most effective weapon." In fact, the huckster's real competitive edge had more to do with speed than smell. Thanks to a controversial technological innovation called "time compression," his 30-second test spot had been speeded up to fit into 24 seconds —a technique that, studies indicate, dramatically improves viewer recall of the message.

Developed by New York University marketing professor James MacLachlan, and still in the experimental stage, the time-compression process electronically erases minuscule segments of blank space within and between words on a tape recording. The voice track is subsequently spliced back together—without altering its clarity—and then the visual portion of the commercial is accelerated to match the condensed sound. Tests conducted on two groups of college students showed that those who watched the faster-paced ads averaged 36 per cent better in remembering the name of the product. "Speed is the cue that makes people believe in the communicator," explains MacLachlan. "The effect is to make those on the screen appear brisker and more alert." In addition, makers of commercials will be able to pack more content into the ten minutes of network time allotted them in each hour.

On the other hand, those who believe that commercial gimmickry is already flirting with factual distortion may shout, "Not so fast." Conceivably, TV purveyors of such products as household cleansers and power mowers could make them seem to work more quickly than they actually do. For that sort of headache, only the Federal Trade Commission could promise relief.

Newsweek
June 25, 1979

Normal rates of speech are slower than the capability of our information-processing system; that is, speech can be speeded up somewhat without any loss of comprehension. Advertisers are beginning to exploit this psychological fact. Speeding up the message may make it more difficult for the listener to evaluate its truthfulness or logic, however. Faster messages may therefore be more persuasive, as we will see in Chapter 10.

Comparisons of good and poor readers have shown that they differ in many different ways. Two characteristics of good readers are that they read rather automatically and that they *do not* read word by word. In a sense, we have known for some time that skilled reading involves taking in relatively large "chunks" of information with little conscious effort. In recent years researchers have made some progress in describing this behavior in greater detail and in developing training methods. We will describe one such effort.

Language, whether spoken or written, is redundant—that is, words and sentences are formed by rules in such a way that, in many circumstances, information about the end of a word or sentence isn't absolutely crucial because you can predict what it will be from earlier information. Consider these examples: "The cat chased the m____." "The doctor cured the ____." The first part of each sentence establishes strong constraints for how the sentence will end; "mouse" and "patient" are very likely endings. While the redundancy of language does not allow perfect prediction of later material on the basis of earlier information, it is often possible to get a good idea of what is to come. In effect, earlier information can be used to set up hypotheses or expectations about later information, and these hypotheses are frequently confirmed. It is reasonable to suppose that skilled reading involves forming and checking hypotheses in this way, rapidly and automatically. Samuels, Dahl, and Archwamety (1974) tested the idea that poor readers tend *not* to "read ahead" in this fashion and attempted to see if these readers could be taught to do so. In studies with retarded children and third-graders with reading problems, they examined the effectiveness of *hypothesis training* for improving reading performance.

Hypothesis training included practice on a number of reading subskills, but a major emphasis of the training was to encourage the children to make predictions about how sentences would end, and to do this quickly. The tasks were first given with the teacher saying part of a sentence and then asking the child to predict how it would end. When the child had learned to do this well (accurately and rapidly), *printed* versions of incomplete sentences were shown, with the child again asked to predict (quickly) how each sentence might end. For example, the child would be asked to provide an ending when the teacher said "The girl ate the ____." In a later stage of training the child was asked to read a sentence like "My mother sleeps on her ____" and provide an ending. Notice that there is no single, correct answer to the questions. In fact, any reasonable ending was accepted; it was perfectly acceptable for a child to end the sentence "The girl ate the ____" with "pizza," "sandwich," "peanuts," or any other sensible word. The emphasis was on getting the children to think about how sentences might end, and to do so rapidly.

When training was completed, tests of word recognition and reading comprehension were given. The students who had received hypothesis training performed significantly better than those who had been given ordinary reading instruction or a different, experimental training procedure. Hypothesis-trained students recognized words faster and achieved higher comprehension scores. Such findings are quite encouraging. The researchers have provided insight into what skilled reading involves and have demonstrated that positive results can be achieved from appropriate training. At the present time, a great deal of research on reading is being conducted, guided by theory and research concerning a variety of cognitive processes. There are good reasons to hope that this research will result in better understanding of reading and improved methods of reading instruction.

Schemata in Advertising

The world of advertising takes advantage of our tendency to draw inferences and fill in blanks with default knowledge while reading or listening. For example, recent television commercials have promoted a soft drink product that includes the word "lemonade" in its name. Many people were thus led to believe that the drink was a form of lemonade. In fact the drink contained no lemon products whatsoever! It did contain various other ingredients, including artificial lemon flavor. The product name has now been changed and uses the term "lemon drink." The use of the word "lemon" may still conjure up in the unwary the idea that the drink contains lemonade. A similar ad campaign involving orange drink crystals "with vitamin C added" leaves one with the impression that the product is a form of orange juice. Again, artificial flavoring is used and no orange products are involved.

An advertiser's goal is to make a product *seem* better than other available products of its kind; whether or not there is an actual difference in quality depends on the manufacturer, not the advertiser. The advertiser must use visual effects and skillful language to improve the *apparent* quality of the product. Part of the skillful use of language involves relying on the consumer to *infer* information that is not stated and that may not even be true. Is this the same thing as lying?

6 Cognitive Processes

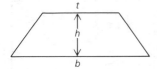

Jimmy, a junior high school student, had a homework problem that involved finding the area of a four-sided figure called a trapezoid. As you can see in the illustration, a trapezoid has two parallel sides and two slanted sides of equal length. The height, *h,* of the figure, the measure of its top, *t,* and the measure of its base, *b,* are givens in the problem. Jimmy knows how to find the area of a rectangle or a triangle but not the area of a trapezoid. Puzzled, he gave up on the problem, but later an insight came to him while he was reading a novel. His idea was that he could use his knowledge about triangles and rectangles to solve the trapezoid problem. Do you understand Jimmy's insight? (The answer is given in Highlight 6–1, p. 184.)

Sally recently attended a debate on the merits of a federally sponsored health insurance program. One debater argued that "Only Communists favor socialized medicine. The bill to establish a national health insurance program is a step toward socialized medicine. Therefore, such a bill is Communist inspired." To Sally, the argument sounded logical and convincing, and she went away thinking that she would write to her congressional representative, asking that she vote against the bill. Was the debater's conclusion logical, and was Sally logical in believing the argument?

Barbara and Elizabeth, identical twins who were separated from their parents shortly after they were born, were raised in different households. Barbara was brought up by a lawyer and his college professor wife in an upper-middle-class neighborhood in a major Texas city. Elizabeth was raised by a farm couple in rural Colorado near the Kansas border. Toward the end of high school, both took college entrance examinations. Elizabeth did relatively poorly on her exams and was barely accepted at a college. Barbara, whose scores were much higher, had her pick of colleges. As it turned out, both girls attended the same college. Elizabeth received A's, while Barbara, in the same classes, was a low B student. What kinds of factors, both genetic and environmental, might account for the differences between the girls both in intellectual abilities and in classroom performance?

The things we do in our heads—mental activities or thinking—we refer to as cognitive processes. These processes include selecting information from the environment, modifying that information in the light of pre-existing knowledge (memory), and using it to meet the demands of the task at hand. Learning and memory are examples of cognitive processes, and we discussed them in Chapter 5. In this chapter we will consider more complex cognitive processes, such as problem solving and reasoning, which involve using knowledge and skills in new situations. Once you have learned certain facts or skills, you generally are able to apply them to various new tasks. To the extent that you can use your knowledge and skills to understand new experiences or to solve difficult problems you will be considered intelligent. Much of the credit we give people for being intelligent is based on the effectiveness with which they are able to apply cognitive processes in various situations.

Many circumstances in our daily activities call for resourceful planning or thinking, for example, setting up a feasible schedule of courses for next semester, answering an essay question, deciding the most efficient order in which to carry out a set of errands, or figuring out how to convince a friend to do us a big favor. Situations like these require that we bring various sources of knowledge into play and that we evaluate a variety of possible courses of action. In other words, we are required to use our cognitive processes.

Theoretical Approaches to Cognition

One of the earliest approaches to the study of cognition stemmed from the behaviorist tradition (see the discussion of J. B. Watson in Chapter 1). Rather than discussing cognition or thinking in terms of mental processes (which were not accessible to direct study), behaviorists emphasized the basic concepts of stimulus and response. According to this approach, knowledge and skill are the result of connecting particular stimuli with overt responses or actions. That

Psychologists study thinking by examining the behavior of people attempting to solve problems of the kind mentioned in the cartoon, and by manipulating the characteristics of the problem, the problem solver, and the nature of the information given to the subject (such as hints or strategies).

Momentous Mistakes

If the spiral tube . . . were lying flat and a ball were rolled through it in the absence of friction or air resistance, what would the ball's path be after it left the tube? The dotted line shows the correct answer: no longer constrained by the curving wall of the tube, the ball would travel in a straight line, as does any moving object not affected by external forces. But in a recent experiment, 51 per cent of college undergraduates chose the solid, curved path. Even those who had studied physics were often wrong, say Johns Hopkins University psychologists Michael Mc-Closkey, Alfonso Caramazza, and Bert Green in a report in *Science.* They found that 34 per cent of those who had taken a high-school physics course chose the solid line, as did 14 per cent of those who had taken college physics.

Many of the incorrect answers revealed the students' implicit belief in the medieval theory of "impetus," which holds that objects tend to continue in any kind of motion, curved as well as straight. The experimenters concluded that science teachers should not only impart facts and theories, but also uncover and correct existing fallacies that have their own internal logic. As humorist Josh Billings said a century ago, "The trouble with people is not that they don't know but that they know so much that ain't so."

Discover
February 1981

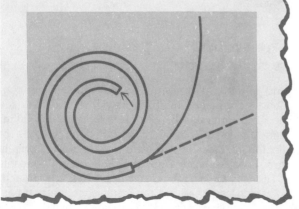

Here is an example of faulty cognition in intelligent people.

is, whenever a stimulus occurs, it provokes the response with which it is associated. All behavior is seen as being derived from conditioning and related processes, although in some cases these processes are very involved and string together a large number of responses.

Motor Theory

One version of stimulus-response theory was the **motor theory** of thinking, in which all behavior was equated with muscular or glandular activity. Most human thought was considered to involve subvocal activity; that is, thinking was viewed as talking to oneself. A motor theorist would claim that thought problems involving language are solved by miniaturized movements in the speech mechanisms such as the vocal cords. Experiments demonstrated that some muscular activity in the throat does occur when people are asked to think about a particular situation or problem. But there are other possible explanations for such findings. Muscular activity could be an incidental by-product of thinking, or an overflow re-

The New Yorker, December 9, 1974. Drawing by Herbert Goldberg; © 1974 The New Yorker Magazine, Inc.

sulting from activities in the brain that occur during thinking, the brain being so active during thinking that signals "spill over" to the muscles through motor pathways. As we discussed in Chapter 5, images and procedural knowledge are certainly involved in some kinds of thinking. These cognitive activities are very difficult, if not impossible, to verbalize and to incorporate into a motor theory. Finally, learning and thinking occur even when the body has been paralyzed by a drug, preventing any recordable muscular activity. Thus, motor theory cannot account for many things we know about cognition.

Mediational Theory

More recently, stimulus-response psychologists proposed **mediational theory** as an alternative to motor theory, suggesting that important stimuli and

"I'm learning to think not only with my mind but with my entire body."

The New Yorker, February 7, 1977. Drawing by Saxon; © 1977 The New Yorker Magazine, Inc.

According to the motor theory of thinking, there is no such thing as purely mental activity. Thinking is accompanied by muscle activity, which means, theoretically at least, that you can think with your entire body.

responses could occur in the head without motor components. Mediational events or thoughts provide a connecting link between the environment and the way one responds to it. When a new situation is encountered that is similar to previous experiences, a number of mediational events are automatically provoked, representing possible responses. One thought dominates the others on the basis of its relative strength — that is, how likely it is to pay off. The person then acts overtly on the basis of that thought. But like motor theory, mediational theory views human beings as essentially passive. Mediational responses are elicited automatically by stimuli. The purposeful aspects of performance, the ability to form and use hypotheses and rules, and the importance of language in thought are not adequately dealt with by either motor theory or mediational theory.

Gestalt Theory

Gestalt psychology originated in Germany shortly after the turn of the century and was contemporary with behaviorism in the United States. Gestalt psychologists were concerned primarily with perception, but applied **Gestalt theory** to nearly all significant psychological problems. For them, thinking and problem solving were matters of "seeing" things in the right way. Thus, their concerns about perceptual processes strongly influenced their ideas of cognitive processes. Discovering a solution to a problem was described as a process of *insight,* that is, of seeing how the different aspects of a problem fit together into an appropriate whole or *Gestalt.* To solve a problem, a person must actively take various perspectives until the parts of the problem fall into place. Often, taking a *new* perspective is the key to solving a problem, as in the example of Jimmy and the trapezoid figure. A significant aspect of Gestalt theory, one that distinguishes it from passive stimulus-response theories, is its characterization of people as active thinkers.

Hypothesis Theory

A more recent theory of cognitive processes which views the organism as an active thinker is **hypothesis theory.** In learning a task or solving a problem, the individual is seen as forming and testing hypotheses or ideas about what is happening in the environment and how to respond. Hypothesis theory suggests that we perform complex tasks such as problem solving by thinking out in advance various possible courses of action. We test these hypotheses systematically until the correct one is found. By formulating hypotheses, we anticipate varous courses of action and their possible outcomes. Thus, our actual responses should show clear patterns rather than random sequences. Supporters of this theory have demonstrated the existence of hypotheses-governed response patterns in a variety of problems. A fairly easy way to identify hypotheses is to ask people if they have any, and if so, what they are. People usually have no difficulty answering such questions and are often eager to offer hypotheses on everything from the best way to play "Space Invaders" to the best way to protest nuclear power plants.

A criticism of hypothesis theory is that behavior is not alway as neat and well organized as the theory might suggest. Organisms do not always approach situations with a set of clearly formulated hypotheses. In addition, hypothesis testing is only a part of thinking. The basic ideas of hypothesis theory, however, have been captured in a broader and currently popular approach to cognitive processes—information-processing theory.

Information-Processing Theory

Under the early influence of behaviorism, such mental concepts as memory and reasoning were considered unscientific and not proper fields for psychological study. But with the development of electronic computer systems, many psychologists realized that one could theorize about cognitive processes. The idea is to use the computer, a mechanical device conceived of and built by people, as a model for the human being. Because we understand the computer and because the computer can remember, calculate, and solve problems, we can use it, by analogy, to better understand ourselves. Because one can talk scientifically about "cognitive" processes in a computer, one can also talk about cognitive processes in people.

Information-processing theory, then, developed partly as an analogy to the workings of computers. The flow of information conceptualized as proceeding through a series of internal stages was discussed in Chapter 5.

Information may be integrated in memory with other information learned earlier, and it can be used to decide how to perform other tasks. Many information-processing theories of cognitive processes not only rely heavily on the computer analogy but in fact consist of computer programs. These programs are written to allow machines to carry out many of the complex cognitive functions of which human beings are capable. Not only can computers store a multitude of information and retrieve it in an instant, but programs have been developed that endow them with the ability to solve problems that have been presented to them for the first time, and even to understand messages and stories. The development of

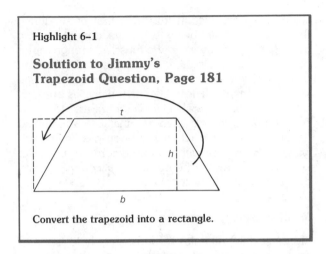

Highlight 6–1

Solution to Jimmy's Trapezoid Question, Page 181

Convert the trapezoid into a rectangle.

such programs has been a major focus of **artificial intelligence,** a branch of computer science.

Recently, many people working in artificial intelligence have realized that psychological principles can prove useful in producing programs capable of complex cognitive activity. Similarly, psychologists have found that development of their theories can be aided by serious consideration of how a computer might behave in a particular situation. Thus, psychologists and computer scientists have begun a rather interesting extension of information-processing theory called *cognitive science.* The area is concerned with building theories of cognition that are sufficiently well developed to be implemented as computer programs. Computer scientists working in cognitive science are not just concerned with how to get a machine to perform a complex task such as problem solving, but with how to get the machine to perform such tasks in the *same way as humans beings.* Getting the computer to act like a human being is called *simulation,* currently an active research method in cognitive psychology.

Limits on Cognitive Processes

Human beings are capable of performing complex tasks because of their cognitive abilities. But, as mentioned in Chapter 5, the capacity for remembering and processing information is severely limited. The mind can cope with only a small amount of information at one time. There are limits to how much information can be held in short-term memory and to what can be done with that information. For example, try multiplying 378 by 49 in your head without using a pencil and paper.

The limitations on processing capacity imply that each of us has a restricted pool of processing resources that can be called on in performing tasks.

"I get depressed thinking of all the data out there, much of it yearning to be processed."

Playboy, September 1977. Reproduced by special permission of PLAYBOY Magazine; copyright © 1977 by Playboy.

Different kinds of cognitive tasks may make different demands on the limited pool of resources. A difficult task like reading that demands a great deal of attention would require more resources than a simple task such as walking up a flight of stairs. Some tasks are so complicated and demand such a great amount of processing resources that we are not capable of accurately performing them without assistance. In the multiplication example just given, it would be highly desirable to have a pencil and paper (better still, a calculator) at hand to keep track of operations. Composing prose, poetry, or music is a much more reasonable task if the author writes down each element as it is produced. Without external aids of this sort, we could not perform some of the important cognitive tasks that we often take for granted.

Another implication for cognitive processes stems from the limitations on processing capacity. Consider attempts you have made to do two or more things at once. Have you ever tried to read while walking up a flight of stairs? You may or may not have been successful. Some tasks can be carried out simultaneously—in parallel—because different mental operations are involved. For example, most people can drive a car and carry on a conversation with a passenger at the same time. Other combinations of tasks cannot be successfully carried out in parallel, for example, taking dictation while reading a textbook. Why is this the case, and what determines whether a particular combination of tasks can be performed in parallel?

There seem to be two reasons why a pair of tasks might not be successfully performed simul-

taneously. First, each task done in isolation may require a large share of the limited pool of processing resources. Reading requires a good deal of attention, and therefore demands a great amount of resources. The same can be said for listening to dictation. If you were to try listening and reading at the same time, you would likely find that only one of the two messages could be comprehended. Understanding both messages at once would place too great a burden on your processing capacity, and you would have to sacrifice performance on one task to maintain a high performance level on the other.

The second reason two tasks might not be successfully performed in parallel is that both might make use of some part of the information-processing system that is incapable of handling the two tasks at the same time. Reconsider the example of climbing stairs while reading. If we have trouble doing these two tasks together, the difficulty would most likely stem from the fact that both reading and ascending stairs require some use of the visual-processing system. If you don't see the top of the stairs you may step up when you don't need to, or if you underestimate the number of steps you might stumble. Because you were busy reading, your visual-processing system was occupied and you were unable to gather accurate information about your path. If you had been *listening* to the same message while climbing the stairs, you probably would have had no problems. Your visual-processing system would be available to guide you along.

Despite the rather severe limits on processing capacity, we can learn to perform complex tasks in parallel. For instance, Ulric Neisser and his colleagues have shown that subjects can be trained to reproduce unrelated words from dictation while at the same time reading and understanding a story. Results like these imply that with practice subjects can overcome capacity limitations, perhaps by learning how to perform the two tasks as a single complex task or by becoming more skilled at each individual task, thereby reducing the demands on processing resources made by each. But it takes a lot of practice!

Higher Mental Processes

Problem Solving

A great deal of what we know about cognitive processes comes from observations of people trying to solve problems. Solving a problem requires that one conceptualize a situation or object in a new way, that one think of some novel way to attain a goal. A key feature of problem solving that separates it from simply executing a well-learned series of behaviors, and even from learning new information, is that it requires you to supply the new knowledge. You are responsible for figuring out a way to alter a problematic situation and transform it into a new, acceptable state of affairs. On many occasions, not only are the steps used to solve the problem new and unique, but so is the final product.

In recent years, Gestalt theory and information-processing theory have dominated the study of problem-solving behavior. These major theories differ both in the types of problems to which they apply and in the basic problem-solving processes they emphasize.

The Gestalt Approach

The influence of perceptual organization in problem solving was of major concern to Gestalt psychologists. For example, consider this problem:

> Given the following array of 16 matches, move 3 and only 3 matches to change the array into a 16-match array of 4 squares all the same size.

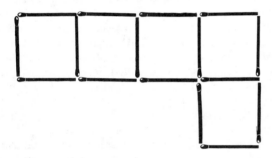

Arriving at a solution to this problem (see Highlight 6–4) depends on the ability to visualize different arrangements of the match sticks. Misperception of the situation contributes greatly to an inability to solve problems of this sort.

Functional Fixedness

Perception also influences problem solving in more subtle ways. Suppose a person is required to discover that a match box tacked to a wall can serve as a platform for a lighted candle. The difficulty of the problem depends critically on how the tacks, the matches, and the match box are arranged when the problem materials are first presented to the subject. If the tacks and matches lie loose on the table and the match box lies empty, the problem seems trivial and the solution is easily discovered. But if the match box contains the tacks or matches when presented, the problem is fairly difficult. If the match box is used as a container, people often either have difficulty thinking of it as serving any other function in the task or don't notice it at all. This phenomenon is known as **functional fixedness.** In experiments on functional fixedness, subjects become so set or "fixed" in their perception of certain objects, or the uses to which the objects can be put, that they are unable to use the objects in novel ways to solve the problem.

A classic example of a functional fixedness problem is the pendulum and two-string problem. To solve this problem, the subject must tie together the ends of two strings which are suspended from the ceiling. The strings are too far apart for a person to be able to reach one string while holding on to the other. The solution is to select a heavy object from a variety of possibilities lying on a table (among them the pliers), tie the object to one string, set it in motion like a pendulum, and while holding the other string grab the pendulum at the nearest point in its arc (see Figure 6–1). If the subject were given the task of wiring a simple electrical circuit requiring the use of pliers be-

FIGURE 6–1   The two-string problem

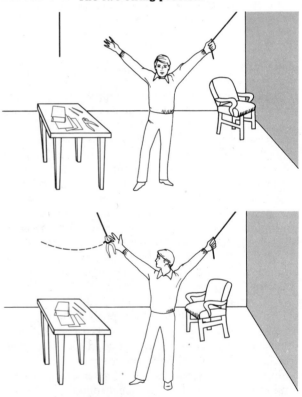

This is perhaps the most famous task ever used in laboratory studies of problem solving. The subject is required to figure out a way to tie two strings together, even though when he is holding onto one string the other is out of reach. A variety of objects are available for use in the solution of the problem, such as a chair, tissue paper, a pair of pliers, and some paper clips. The solution involves tying the pliers to the string and setting it in motion like a pendulum so that it can be reached while the subject is holding onto the other string.

fore attacking the problem, he or she would be less likely to use the pliers as a pendulum weight, even if pliers were obviously the best object for that purpose.

Two interesting aspects of the functional fixedness phenomenon illustrate the importance of prior experience with the object that must be used in a novel way. First, the greater the similarity between the object used in the prior experience task and the object needed for a solution in the primary problem solving task, the greater will be the functional fixedness effect. If instead of the pliers used in the wiring task, a new, identical pair of pliers is placed on the table, subjects are less resistant to using them as a pendulum bob. If a similar but different pair of pliers is placed on the table, even more subjects are likely to use them to solve the pendulum problem. Second, the longer the delay between doing the preliminary task with the pliers and attacking the pendulum problem, the weaker will be the functional fixedness effect. In one experiment, subjects showed no functional fixedness at all when seven days intervened between the preliminary task and the task that required novel use of an object. These effects point to the conclusion that functional fixedness is as much a result of learning as of fixed perception.

Another example of functional fixedness was seen recently when tennis racquet manufacturers finally broke through a design barrier. In their attempts to create better racquets, manufacturers had neglected to consider changing the *size* of the ball-hitting surface. Then, a few years ago, there appeared the "Prince," racquet with an enlarged striking surface. The racquet has received much attention and already has improved the play of many tennis enthusiasts. Less spectacular are many everyday examples of attempts to overcome functional fixedness. Someone once used dental floss to tie old newspaper into a bundle because no string was handy. Have you ever opened a (nontwist off) bottle cap using a seat belt? Or used an empty egg carton for an ice cube tray? Being able to see beyond the intended use of objects is an important part of overcoming functional fixedness and, as we shall see, can also contribute to creativity.

Mental Sets

A related example of the effect of learning specific procedures on one's ability to discover novel procedures involves the classic work of Abraham Luchins. Sometimes, after solving a series of similar problems, we fall into the use of certain procedures that might not operate efficiently or that might even fail if there is a simple change in problem type. In Luchins' demonstration of this phenomenon, subjects were given a series of problems involving a water tap and three different jars—A, B, and C—each of known capacity. For example, suppose A, B, and C hold 10, 32, and 7 units of water, respectively. Your task is to use these jars to measure out exactly 8 units of water. After some experimenting you will find the solution is to fill B and pour from B into A, filling A with 10 units and leaving 22 in B. Then you pour from B into C, filling C with 7. Next, you throw out the water in C and repeat the last step. B will now contain 8 units.

For further practice, solve problems 1 through 5 given in Table 6–1. You will see that each problem is solved by the same procedure, described by the formula: $B - A - 2C$. Once you have developed the **mental set** to use this procedure, problems can be solved readily. Difficulties will arise, however, if a different type of problem is encountered. Mental sets are sometimes hard to break, and if a problem cannot be solved by the formula you will have more difficulty with it. Continue with problems 6 and 7 in Table 6–1. Problem 6 could be solved both by the usual formula and a more efficient method; problem 7, however, cannot be solved by the usual formula. In a typical experiment, some subjects fail to solve problem 7 even after several minutes of effort. The solution to

TABLE 6–1 Jar Problems

Problem Number	Three Jars Are Present with the Listed Capacity			Obtain Exactly This Amount of Water
	Jar A	*Jar B*	*Jar C*	
1	21	127	3	100
2	14	163	25	99
3	18	43	10	5
4	9	42	6	21
5	20	59	4	31
6	23	49	3	20
7	10	36	7	3

Source: Abraham S. Luchins and Edith H. Luchins, *Rigidity of Behavior.* Eugene: University of Oregon Press, 1959, p. 109.

problem 7 is actually simpler than the formula used in the earlier problems: just fill A, pour into C, and there will be the correct number of units left in A. Note that the same simple solution works for problem 6.

The mental set effect can be interpreted as a restriction of our willingness to try different methods or to perceive a new problem in a way that is different from how we went about solving similar recent problems. Our perspective on the problem becomes too narrow for us to see alternative, and possibly simpler, procedures. Imagine your annoyance if you were to discover that the tedious and time-consuming method of balancing your checkbook you have used for years involves many unnecessary steps and that a much simpler procedure is available.

Situations similar to those faced by subjects in the water jar experiments also occur for mathematics, physics, and engineering students. On many occasions, students are taught to use certain equations to solve problems of a specific type. Sometimes, however, instructors like to test students' abilities to use their knowledge in a more thoughtful or analytic way. Thus, students often encounter trick questions in which using the usual solution may yield the correct answer but through many more steps than necessary. A simpler solution might be available if a different set of equations were applied. Often what is required is a different conceptualization of the problem. Similarly, a problem may be given on a test that appears insoluble on first inspection, but the appropriate reconceptualization of the problem (for example, the solution to Jimmy's trapezoid problem) may indicate a rather obvious solution.

You can see that mental set and functional fixedness are similar effects. Both reflect the human tendency to view an object in terms of its intended function or to conceptualize a type of problem in terms of a specific solution strategy. Sometimes these tendencies are highly valuable, but at other times they can be very restrictive. Awareness of these tendencies allows one to surmount them on occasions when it is beneficial to do so.

Insight

Concern with issues like these led to special interest in **insight** problems. These are problems that can be solved in a flash by achieving a new and insightful way of conceptualizing a situation. Some early work on this kind of problem was conducted by Wolfgang Köhler using captive chimpanzees. In one study, a chimp was given the problem of obtaining a banana hanging from the ceiling of its cage, out of reach. There were several boxes in the cage that had to be stacked to provide a platform from which the banana could be reached. At first, the chimp would engage in unsuccessful trial and error behavior and

would then retreat from the problem for a time. The solution finally appeared to come in a moment of insight, as if the chimp realized all at once how to solve the problem. The animal would leap up, stack the boxes, and then climb to reach the banana in one continuous motion.

Köhler believed that his chimp solved the problem through insight produced by taking different perspectives until the solution automatically appeared. Later, more thorough examination of this task revealed that insight rarely occurs in the absence of appropriate previous experiences. Animals who have had no experience with "stackable" boxes rarely solve this problem in an insightful way. The more opportunity the animals have to play with and examine boxes before the experiment, the more likely they are to solve the problem insightfully. Appropriate experiences seem to make insightful problem solving

The New Yorker, September 28, 1968. Drawing by W. Steig; © 1968 The New Yorker Magazine, Inc.

One long-standing issue in the psychology of cognition deals with the question of whether problem solution occurs gradually, through a process of *trial and error,* with the learner getting closer and closer to solution all the time, or whether it occurs suddenly, as if the solver had *insight* into the solution. This cartoon is a takeoff on the famous study by Köhler, who found that chimpanzees could solve problems on an insight basis—they could stack boxes and climb the stack to reach the bananas. However, it turns out that *prior experience* with the problem materials is important in determining whether chimps will solve the problem.

more likely, since one does not need to discover key concepts through trial and error, but instead must simply be clever enough to think of how to apply them.

The Information-Processing Approach

The dominant means of studying problem solving today is the information-processing approach. Work in problem solving has often involved the development of computer simulation models. The idea is to program the computer to simulate, or act like, a human being attempting to solve a particular problem. Like the Gestalt approach, this method of studying problem-solving processes makes certain assumptions about how problems are solved and about the kinds of problems that should be studied. Rather than studying insight problems, which often involve a rapidly occurring reorganization of the perception of a problem, researchers of the information-processing tradition have studied problems that require many steps. A typical problem-solving task studied by information-processing psychologists would involve a sequence of steps, each making some progress toward a well-specified goal. Problem solving is seen as a process of evaluating a given problem situation, selecting one of a number of possible steps toward the problem solution, evaluating the resulting situation, then selecting and applying the next most appropriate step, and so on. This procedure continues until the solution is reached (see Figure 6–2). At each step in the problem-solving process, the solver is involved in some form of information processing. The task of the psychologist is to describe and explain the nature of the information and the type of processing that is applied to it at each step.

Task Analysis

Alan Newell and Herb Simon have given what is now almost a classic description of the information-processing approach to problem solving. They provided an analysis of the different components that comprise almost every problem-solving situation and developed a computer program, called *General Problem Solver* (GPS), that successfully simulates human problem-solving behavior in a number of different tasks. Newell and Simon characterized a person's internal memory representation of a problem as a *problem space*. All efforts to solve a problem are conducted within the problem space adopted by the solver. The problem space consists of a number of elements, including the *initial state* of the problem (the givens), the final *goal state* to be achieved, possible intermediate states, and *operators* that can be applied in moving from one state to another and finally to the goal state. These elements of the problem space can

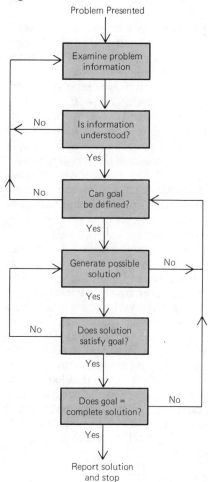

FIGURE 6–2 Problem solving as information processing

The information-processing approach is characterized by breaking up overall problem-solving behavior into separate substages (or states) and processes (or operators) for getting from one stage to the next. The analogy to the flow chart of a computer program is not accidental.

be found in almost every type of problem studied by problem-solving research today.

Consider a game of chess as a problem-solving situation. A novice player's problem space would consist of an initial state (the opening arrangement of pieces on the chess board), a very general idea of the goal state (a configuration in which the opponent's king is captured), a large number of possible intermediate arrangements of pieces, and a set of operators. The operators would be the possible legal moves for each chess piece under the player's command. As a player's skill improves, he or she becomes better able to judge which piece should be moved in certain situations: application of the operators becomes more and more effective.

The existence of a problem space within which we work toward the solution of a problem implies that there are constraints on the possible steps or moves we will be willing to make as we solve the problem. The problem space defines a limited set of possibilities, and on occasion difficulties can arise if we fail to move beyond that limited set. Consider the problem shown in Figure 6–3. As you develop your problem space, you may find yourself placing an unnecessary restriction on the possible ways in which you might draw or extend the length of the line segments. In fact, these restrictions make the problem quite difficult for people who fail to consider the idea of extending certain segments beyond the boundaries of the square defined by the nine dots. A similar effect occurs with functional fixedness, with the problem solver defining his or her problem-solving space in a way that restricts the possible uses of a key element.

A phenomenon known as *incubation* may also be explained in terms of problem space. Incubation occurs when a person takes time out from working on a difficult problem only to discover on returning to the task that the solution is obvious. Incubation may be a kind of unconscious thinking or problem solving. Anecdotes about incubation are plentiful, but we do not yet know why it occurs. Possibly the effect is the result of the solver forming a new and more effective problem space after returning to the problem, rather than the occurrence of any unconscious problem-solving activities during the interval between solution attempts. Sometimes, then, it is advisable to try out completely different approaches when working on very difficult problems.

Algorithms and Heuristics

One of the most important aspects of problem solving is the selection and application of operators to problem elements. What information guides a problem solver in selecting an operator to be applied in a given situation? That is, how does the solver decide what move to make next? In some situations, the answer is simple because the problem solver is relying on a well-developed algorithm that assures the answer will be found. An **algorithm** is a guaranteed route to the solution to a problem. In solving anagram problems (for example, what word can be formed from the letters EABLL?), a solution will be found if every possible ordering of the letters (120 in all for a 5-letter word!) is considered. While algorithms offer guaranteed solutions, they suffer from a number of disadvantages. For one thing, they can be inefficient and time consuming. Did you need to list all 120 combinations of the letters EABLL to come up with LABEL? If algorithms are applied automatically, without considering more efficient methods, we will miss many easier routes to solution; recall the effect

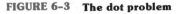

FIGURE 6–3   The dot problem

Consider the following problem: Without lifting your pencil, draw four continuous straight lines through the dots in the figure so that at least one line passes through each dot. Solution of this task requires no knowledge or skills you don't already possess. You might have to modify what you know, or use it in a new way, but you don't really need to learn anything new. If you find the problem difficult, consider the possibility that you are not attending to all the information that has been given. Are you being restrictive or overly selective in your approach? If you haven't solved it yet, the solution is given in Highlight 6–4.

of mental set discussed earlier. Also, not all problems can be solved by known algorithms. There is no known way to win a chess game every time, not every integration problem in calculus can be solved by application of an algorithm, nor can problems like the string and pendulum problem of Figure 6–1 be solved the first time around by an algorithm.

The alternative to using algorithms in problem solving is to use heuristics. A **heuristic** is a method of deriving and evaluating potential solutions that would be efficient but that would not necessarily succeed in solving the problem. For example, in a complex game like chess, some heuristics can guide move selection. One general heuristic is to try to control the center of the board. Moves that would bring more of your pieces into the center positions would be evaluated highly under that heuristic.

A major focus of study has been the nature of heuristics used in problem-solving tasks. In their development of GPS, Newell and Simon endowed their program with a powerful and general heuristic: **means-end analysis.** This heuristic involves comparing the current state of the problem with the desired (goal) state and finding a means of reducing or eliminating the differences detected. As an example of means-end analysis consider a water jar task. Given jars A, B, and C with varying capacities, and with A full of water, carry out a sequence of pouring operations, without adding any additional water, that will distribute the water between A and B in a prescribed way. A sample problem involves capacities of 8, 5, and 3 units for jars A, B, and C, respectively. Initially, A is full and the task is to achieve the goal of having 4 units in A and 4 units in B.

A means-end analysis of this problem would involve a comparison of the amounts of water in A and B with the desired amounts, followed by attempts to reduce the differences. At the outset, A has 4 units too many while B is 4 units short. There are only two possible moves here: pour from A into (1) B or (2) C. If the first alternative is chosen, A will contain 3 units and B will contain 5. This would be close to the desired values. On the other hand, pouring A into C would leave B empty, and A would still contain 1 unit too many. While the problem can be solved efficiently regardless of which opening move is made, means-end analysis would strongly favor the first move — the move that gets you closer to the goal is preferred. The fact that people prefer the first possibility over the second suggests that people use means-end analysis.

Planning

Rather than solving a problem one step at a time, we can often profit by planning ahead and developing a sequence of moves. Often we cannot develop a sequence that is long enough to reach the goal state, but must instead attempt to reach intermediate states called *subgoals*. For example, certain subgoals must be achieved in order to solve the 3-disk Tower of Hanoi problem illustrated in Figure 6–4. The task is to move one disk at a time, from one peg to another, until all three are stacked in order on peg C. The constraint is that no disk may be placed on a disk that is smaller than itself; in any stack, the smallest disk must be at the top and the largest at the bottom. In order to solve this problem, peg A must be cleared of the two smaller disks, and peg C must be completely clear so that the largest disk can be transferred from A to C. This means that peg B must be occupied as shown in panel B of the figure. Once the subgoal is achieved, the next subgoal can be set and attempted until the final solution is reached. The use of subgoals is beneficial on occasions when a "one move at a time" strategy is likely to lead to blind alleys. It is better to plan ahead and to identify intermediate problem states that you know you must enter in order to solve the problem. Tackle these states first, and the final goal

state may be reached in an efficient way, even if you are unable to plan the whole sequence of moves to the final goal state. Now try the Tower of Hanoi problem with 4 or even 5 disks. Remember to plan for and use subgoals.

One major factor distinguishes the Gestalt and the information-processing approach to problem solving. Gestalt theory treats problem solving as an intuitive and sometimes automatic process. The solution is there if only you look at the problem in the right way. Processing theory, in contrast, describes problem solving as a conscious, planned, and logical activity. Also note that processing theories tend to deal with somewhat more complicated and more natural problems. Like other higher mental processes, problem solving probably involves both intuition and logic. Intuition works best when the solution is simple and can be apprehended immediately, while logic is required when there are many steps to the goal. For now, we will accept both Gestalt and information processing as contributing useful ideas to our understanding of problem solving.

Concept Formation

In everyday experience, we tend to think of a *concept* as an "idea" or as "the meaning of something." For many people, concepts are the contents of thought and consciousness. Concepts vary in abstractness, from very concrete notions (such as "chair") to very abstract notions (such as "infinity"). Psychologists and philosophers have tried for years to understand the mental entity of a concept.

A concept can best be thought of as *the basic unit of knowledge*. It is something we can be aware of and think about, as well as something that may reside unactivated in memory until we have a reason for using it. A few analogies will serve to illustrate what we mean by a concept. First, you could think of a concept as a *building block,* in that you can build complex knowledge structures from individual supporting concepts, just as you can build towers or castles from supporting building blocks that are appropriately arranged. Your knowledge about "birthday parties," for example, is built from the supporting concepts of "gifts," "cake," "games," "people," "invitations," and so on. Second, you could think of a concept as a *mental quantum.* A quantum in physics is a packet or bundle of energy (for example, quanta that excite a visual experience are called photons of light (see Chapter 3). In psychology, a concept is a *bundle or packet of knowledge (information).* These packets of knowledge are highly structured both within themselves and among each other (into schemata, say), just as photons of different wavelengths make up

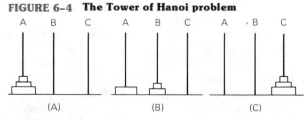

FIGURE 6–4 The Tower of Hanoi problem

Panel A represents the starting state. Panel B shows a necessary subgoal. Panel C shows the final goal state.

Is Problem-Solving America's Lost Art?
By MALCOLM W. BROWNE

Are we Americans really becoming a nation of ignoramuses, and if so, is there anything we can do about it? Scientists, teachers and America's managers are complaining that on the whole our people no longer seem to solve problems very well.

The complaints cite precipitous declines in school and college test scores, the statistical increase in functional illiteracy and the growing difficulty of filling jobs requiring problem-solving abilities.

Professional groups of mathematicians have been warning in recent months that if the slide continues our country could eventually find itself a member of the deprived "Third World," without engineers or the other problem solvers who created American civilization. . . .

But many psychologists have contended lately in professional articles that problem-solving is an art that can be learned, given a certain minimal intelligence. Part of the key, they say, is adopting the habit of looking for the unorthodox, always seeking ways around the problem when the problem itself seems too hard.

A favorite example is the case of the truck with a high load that is unable to get under a low bridge until a small boy suggests letting some air out of the tires.

Psychologists have devised some rules of thumb for improving problem-solving ability. Jumping from one train of thought to another avoids the risk of bogging down. Self-criticism and discussion of one's ideas with others are considered helpful. Devising symbols for the various elements of a problem and assembling them into a model may help.

But, perhaps most of all, problem-solving ability calls for "expertise."

Some recent studies have shown that although a college-educated person can remember about 50,000 words and phrases, and although a master chess player can remember an equal number of moves, no one can remember more than about seven unrelated things at a time.

This means that the human mind works very much like a computer memory system. To call up a given piece of information, a thinker (or computer) must remember the pigeon hole into which he has tucked it, and the pigeon hole is part of a much bigger intellectual structure he has created.

A combined team of computer experts and psychologists at Carnegie-Mellon University recently noted the interesting discovery about the difference between expert and novice chess players. If an expert and a novice are shown a chessboard on which pieces are arranged corresponding with the middle of a game, the expert can easily remember the positions while the novice will not. But if the chess pieces are merely distributed randomly on the chessboard, the expert does no better than the novice remembering the positions.

So expertise seems to depend on three things: accumulating many facts, storing them in an efficient memory network, and being able to perceive relationships between the facts in one part of a network and another.

Becoming an expert in anything—plumbing or quantum physics—takes brainwork and time. To become expert in a subject requires mulling it over, touching and smelling it from many different angles and carefully filing away its various facets in the tool chest of the mind. This exercise promotes expertise and problem-solving ability, and can help save the nation from mind rot.

Or alternatively, we can let it go and watch television.

The New York Times
July 29, 1980

Research comparing expert and novice problem solvers has become a popular tool in seeking to understand problem solving.

different colors of light (for example, white light is made up of all wavelengths of the spectrum).

One of the most important distinctions to have emerged from philosophical treatments of concepts is the distinction between *meaning* and *reference*. The *reference* of a concept is the set of all things that belong to or illustrate the concept. For the concept fruit we have apples, cherries, bananas, and so on. The *meaning* of the concept, which resembles a definition, is more abstract. What does it *mean* for something to be a fruit? Typically, the *meaning* of a concept is conceived as a definition that, when applied to a set of objects, allows us to group together all things in our experience that are examples of the concept, for ex-

ample, all fruit, and all things that are not examples of the concept, for example, all things that are not fruit.

Human beings learn many of their most important concepts early in life. But concepts are generally not formed on the basis of a single experience with an instance of a particular category. Typically, we have to see a variety of examples, nonexamples, and "near-misses" before we obtain an idea of the meaning of a concept and its limits. It would be impossible to know the meaning of "chair" with only the experience of a single chair. Each new experience—an armchair, a reclining chair, a highchair, a folding chair—provides us with information that enables us gradually to refine our concept. In effect, we accumulate information and integrate it with other bits of information in an effort to ascertain what is included in and excluded from the category of objects a concept defines.

In the discussion that follows, it is useful to distinguish between logical and natural concepts. As we shall see, the difference is primarily a matter of definitional precision.

Logical Concepts

Logical concepts are defined on the basis of certain relevant features of instances and a rule used to determine category membership of any instance. A logical concept, once learned, can be used to categorize unambiguously each of a set of objects as either belonging or not belonging to the concept.

FIGURE 6–5 Examples of logical concepts

Stimulus Population

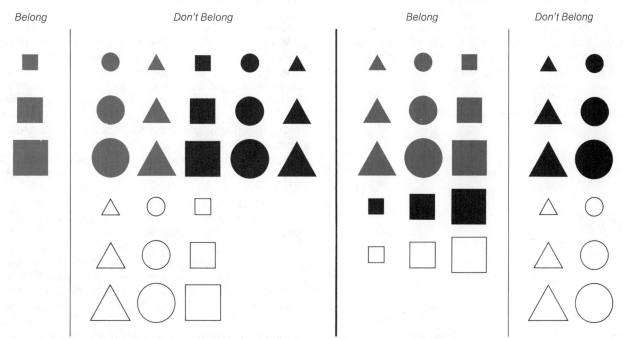

Conjunctive Concept
"Must be *colored and square*"

Disjunctive Concept
"*Colored*, or *square, or both*"

To see how logical concepts operate in real life, let us translate the shape dimension into "safety"— △ is very safe, ○ is moderately safe, and □ is not safe at all—and the size dimension into "fuel economy"—small is very low gas mileage, medium is average mileage, and large is high mileage. The conjunctive concept represented by large △ becomes "a very safe, economical car" or "a quality car." Note that other variables, such as color of car—colored, black, or clear—is totally irrelevant to the quality concept.

Figure 6–5 illustrates these types of concepts. The figure contains a number of geometric forms that vary in color, shape, and size. To define a concept, we must select one or more of these features, say, colored and square, and a rule. One kind of rule is a **conjunctive concept,** which says that an item must possess both attributes ("colored *and* square") to belong to the concept. Another kind of rule is a **disjunctive concept,** which states that an item must possess one or both attributes ("*either* colored, *or* square, *or* both colored *and* square") to belong to the concept. Note that we can apply such abstract rules as these to real-world concepts. For example, the concept of a bird might be something like "an animal with wings *and* feathers." Here the rule is a logical *and,* and the relevant attributes are "wings" and "feathers."

To learn such concepts, a person must determine which features possessed by objects are relevant to the concept (the others being unimportant or irrelevant) and the kind of rule being used. The person uses the information contained in the examples and nonexamples to make these determinations. An illustration of the kinds of experiences a person needs to use to form such concepts is given in Figure 6–6, which uses geometric forms as stimuli. A sample of geometric forms is shown, corresponding to objects and events a person encounters in everyday life, and information is given concerning whether each form does or does not belong to some unnamed concept. Enough information is contained in Figure 6–6 to allow one to figure out how the concept is defined — try to do so. Perhaps you will find yourself trying out

various hypotheses as you explain the materials; remember that hypothesis testing is a commonly used method in such situations. Once you figure out the concept, notice that you are able to categorize correctly all the forms in Figure 6–6.

The importance of studies of logical concepts lies in what they imply about the mental entity that corresponds to a concept. According to notions about logical concepts, when we "know" a concept, the knowledge we have stored consists of a rule that relates two or more attributes in a particular way. This "meaning" of the concept (a rule plus relevant attributes) neatly divides the world into examples and nonexamples. As the concepts illustrated in Figures 6–5 and 6–6 suggest, most logical concepts have been studied using stimuli that varied along only a small number of dimensions (for example, color, shape, and size) and could, in fact, be classified neatly into instances of the concept and nonexamples. However, a consideration of the concepts we most often use in our natural environment suggests that there are many dimensions of variation and that objects are not always easily classified.

Natural Concepts

Some researchers have argued that tightly defined, logical concepts with unambiguous examples and nonexamples are not like most natural concepts. Rather, many natural categories have "fuzzy" boundaries and better-and-worse examples, with different items belonging "more or less" to the category. Some theories of natural categories suggest that a category has a prototype, or best example, which serves as a reference point for the category. In this view, some instances are more typical than others. For example, many people would consider "chair" the best example of furniture (with "wastebasket" much less typical), or many people would view "oranges," "apples," and "bananas" as better examples of "fruit" than "coconuts," "tomatoes," or "olives."

At first glance, these ideas may seem to conflict with the theoretical notions we discussed with respect to logical concepts. For example, if we look at the stimuli in Figure 6–5 that belong to the concept "colored and square," all of the examples are equally good examples; there is no range of typicality. On the other hand, what if we had presented shapes that varied from "true" squares to variously shaped quadrilaterals (for example, trapezoids)? Then we would find that some examples (the true squares) fit the concept better than others (the trapezoids). Thus, it may not be that the concept is itself "fuzzy" or ill defined, but that the fit of any particular exemplar to the concept is more or less good.

In fact, some theories concerning the way concepts are stored in memory are very similar to the

FIGURE 6–6 What is the concept?

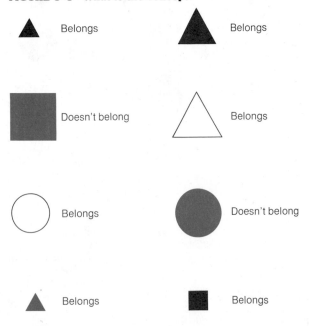

Belongs	Belongs
Doesn't belong	Belongs
Belongs	Doesn't belong
Belongs	Belongs

notion of a rule that relates attributes. For example, the meaning of a category might be stored in memory as a "feature list," where some features are essential for category membership and some are only incidental or characteristic. The features "has wings" and "has feathers," for example, may be essential for something to be classified as "bird," but "can fly" may not be (ostriches are birds but cannot fly). The problem with this approach is that the essential features of a concept may change with the real-world context or setting in which they are found. A screwdriver is typically thought of as a tool, but it also possesses some of the essential features of "weapon" or "pendulum weight" under certain circumstances of need. Faced with the situation of classifying such examples, people tend to hesitate and say, "well, sort of," "maybe," or "sometimes," indicating the ambiguity of the situation.

A careful analysis of the examples in a natural category reveals that the members share different numbers of features with each other. The prototype, or best example, is *most* similar to the other members of the *same* category and *least* similar to members of *other* categories. Eleanor Rosch has used these ideas to distinguish among concepts at three levels of abstraction: superordinate, basic, and subordinate. "Automobile" is a basic-level concept; "vehicle" is its superordinate, and "Corvette" is a subordinate concept. Automobile, vehicle, and Corvette are all concepts because they refer to many instances, not just one. But you can easily see that the concepts differ in the number of different instances they refer to. Categories at the basic level seem to be most important. Children tend to learn basic-level concepts before super- or subordinates. Examples of the basic level have a strong family resemblance. For example, one could conjure up a mental image of the typical car that would be highly representative of all objects classified as cars, but it is harder to envision the typical vehicle. Moreover, objects in a basic-level category are responded to in similar ways. That is, our behavior in cars is always pretty much the same. In contrast, our behavior in vehicles—cars, buses, planes—is more variable.

Like logical concepts, natural concepts can be analyzed in terms of relevant and irrelevant features and sorting rules. For example, a chair must have a seat and usually has a back and four legs. The color does not matter, however, nor whether it is made of wood, steel, or plastic nor whether the chair is in the living room or kitchen. Some everyday concepts involve quite complex rules. Consider the concept of a "strike" in baseball: "A strike will be called on the batter when the pitch passes over the plate and between imaginary lines extended from the batter's knees and shoulders *or* when the batter swings at a pitch and misses *or* when the batter hits the ball into foul territory unless two strikes have already been called on him." If you have ever tried to explain the meaning of a strike to a new baseball fan or remember your own initiation into baseball, you surely appreciate the difficulty involved in understanding this concept.

The importance of the natural concept approach has been the realization that no single feature may be shared by all examples of a concept and that instances differ in their typicality. The importance of the logical concept approach has been that (1) the relationships among features are critical (for example, the concept "quality car" is quite different if we say it must be "fuel efficient *and* safe" than if we believe it must be "fuel efficient *or* safe"), and (2) it provides a way to relate concepts to other logical processes and decision making.

Reasoning and Logical Analysis

It was once thought that the laws of logic were the laws of human thought. Formal logic as a discipline developed in part as a theory of how the human mind works. Psychologists quickly discovered that there must be more to human reasoning than just logic. For one thing, reasoning about many real-life problems, for example, whether to build a nuclear power plant, whether to invest in your mother-in-law's new business, whether to get involved in a relationship, involves emotion as well as logic. Furthermore, everyday reasoning is often based on inferences that go beyond the stated facts, as we saw in the discussion of discourse processing in Chapter 5. Still, much of our behavior is logical, and it is as important to understand these logical processes as it is to understand how we deviate from them.

Formal Logic

Formal logic consists of a set of rules for analyzing an argument and deciding whether or not the argument is internally consistent. Training in formal logic provides us with a set of intellectual skills (competence) that enables us to analyze our own and other people's arguments. People who are not trained make a lot of reasoning errors, but these errors are predictable and understandable as simple deviations from logic. Knowing more about logic will help us understand how people usually reason.

Syllogisms A logical **syllogism** is a three-step argument consisting of two premises, both of which are assumed to be true, and a conclusion that may or may not follow from the premises. The task is to decide whether the conclusion is true, using only the information supplied by the two premises. Perhaps the most familiar of all syllogisms is:

All men are mortal.
Socrates is a man.
Therefore, Socrates is mortal.

When performance on syllogisms is examined experimentally, syllogisms are often presented in a more abstract way. Rather than using real words, as in the Socrates example, psychologists substitute letters:

All As are Bs.
All Bs are Cs.
Therefore, all As are Cs.

This is a valid syllogism. But it turns out that it is relatively difficult to decide whether conclusions drawn from premises presented in this form are valid, invalid, or indeterminate.

In general, people tend to accept too many invalid or indeterminate inferences as valid. Let us examine some syllogisms to obtain an understanding of how difficult this task is. Try to decide which conclusions are necessarily true, given the first two premises.

Syllogism 1
All As are Bs.
All Bs are Cs.
Therefore, all As are Cs.   *True or false?*

Syllogism 2
No As are Bs.
All Bs are Cs.
Therefore, no As are Cs.   *True or false?*

Syllogism 3
All As are Bs.
All Cs are Bs.
Therefore, all As are Cs.   *True or false?*

Syllogism 4
Some As are Bs.
Some Bs are Cs.
Therefore, some As are Cs.   *True or false?*

If you tried these four reasoning problems before reading on, you may be surprised to learn that only the conclusion of syllogism 1 is *logically* true. Many people will accept all four conclusions as valid. To understand how this happens, consider briefly the difference between formal logic and one's own personal logic. Look at the first premise in syllogism 3. Actually, this statement is ambiguous in the sense that it can apply to two different relations between A and B. These two meanings are illustrated in Figure 6–7, using diagrams that make it easier to understand the meanings of the statements. It can be seen that "All As are Bs" might refer to a situation in which there is only one set labeled AB; that is, "All As are Bs *and* all Bs are As." On the other hand, "All As are Bs" can also refer to the things called As being included in the larger set of things called Bs, as in "All dogs are animals."

FIGURE 6–7   Diagrams of the two possible meanings of "All As are Bs"

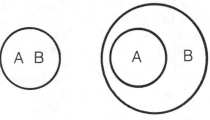

As the diagram demonstrates, "All As are Bs" does not logically imply that "All Bs are As."

Formal logic thus has three requirements: (1) that each premise be considered in all its possible meanings; (2) that the various meanings of the premises be combined in all possible ways; and (3) that a conclusion is valid only if it applies to *every* one of the possible premise combinations. If you can find a way of interpreting the premises and combining them such that a particular conclusion does not apply, then that conclusion is not logically valid. For syllogisms 2 to 4, ways in which the premises can be combined to yield an A-C relation inconsistent with the stated conclusions are illustrated in Figure 6–8.

Reasons for Errors in Reasoning   It would not be surprising if you found that you really had to concentrate to understand the above description of formal logic. Clearly, formal logic requires a person to perform a considerable amount of information processing to analyze an argument or to solve a reasoning problem. Because we are limited information processors, errors occur. Even though subjects tend to accept many invalid inferences as valid, the errors they make are not random; there are at least two typical sources of error.

An *invalid conversion* derives from a misunderstanding of the premises, or, rather, a conversion of the premises to some erroneous meaning from which the conclusion follows. Consider syllogism 3 again. In this case, the conclusion is not logically valid because, as shown in Figure 6–8, the premises can be combined in such a way that the conclusion is not true. Suppose, however, you considered only one possible meaning of each of the premises, specifically the first meaning shown in Figure 6–7 for the "All As are Bs" statement. Thus, you would interpret the first premise as also meaning that "All Bs are As" and the second premise as also meaning "All Bs are Cs." Both are invalid conversions of the stated premises. If you make these invalid conversions, the conclusion is true, but it is based on faulty logic. Your mistake lies in your failure to consider other meanings of the premises.

FIGURE 6–8 **Diagrams of possible meanings of syllogisms 1–4**

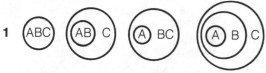

1

"All As are Cs" is true in every case.

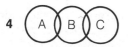

2

"No As are Cs" is false.

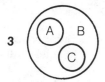

3

"All As are Cs" is false.

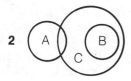

4

"Some As are Cs" is false.

Errors can also arise from the tendency to accept conclusions with surface similarities to the premises. That is, the structure or syntax of the premises creates an *atmosphere* in which a conclusion of similar structure will be accepted as valid. For example, a set of premises all of the form "All ____ are ____," as in syllogism 3, establishes an atmosphere for a conclusion of the same form (see Figure 6–8). Alternatively, if one or more of the premises is negative, the atmosphere is set up for a negative conclusion, as in syllogism 2. Inability to ignore the atmosphere of a problem often leads to mistakes in reasoning.

Sometimes the atmosphere of the problem is in line with the correct answer, as in syllogism 1, although most of the time it is not. Thus, it is always important to look beyond the atmosphere of a problem if you hope to reason accurately. Atmosphere is sometimes used quite effectively in speeches to present illogical conclusions convincingly. The listener has little time or processing capacity for close analysis of the logic of the arguments and is sometimes likely to accept the points the speaker makes without reasoning them through and is thus not able to refute them. We will have more to say on this and related matters in Chapter 10. As you might imagine, the atmosphere effect has been capitalized on by tyrants and saints alike throughout history.

Another interesting characteristic of syllogisms is that people can often recognize valid counterexamples to the conclusion of a syllogism even though they cannot reason to the conclusion itself. For example, many subjects will accept the conclusion of syllogism 3 as valid. However, when the syllogism is presented in concrete instead of abstract terms, subjects are quick to realize the invalidity of the conclusion:

Some women are lawyers.
Some men are lawyers.
Some women are men.

The fact of the matter is, however, that concrete statements like "All cats are animals" do not always lead to more accurate reasoning. Syllogisms containing concrete statements allow people's judgments to be influenced by a semantic or meaning factor, namely, the factual truth or lack of truth of the conclusion. People will tend to accept conclusions that are factually correct or that are consistent with their beliefs, whether or not the conclusions follow logically from the premises of the argument. For example, given the premises "All cats are carnivorous" and "All tigers are carnivorous," one has a strong tendency to accept as valid the conclusion "All tigers are cats," a conclusion that is factually true but logically invalid. This argument is in fact like syllogism 3; if you substitute "dogs" for "tigers" you will see that the conclusion does not necessarily follow.

Everyday Thinking Errors Consider the following facts. Poor automobile drivers typically drive too fast and often tailgate the car ahead. But, they make trip after trip without accident, proving to themselves that they have exceptional skill and reasonable caution. Furthermore, indirect evidence from TV and newspapers indicates to them that when auto accidents happen, they happen to others, not to them. Misleading information and experiences encourage erroneous conclusions. Poor drivers are thus provided with a basis for rationalizing their failure or refusal to take protective actions, such as wearing seatbelts.

The reasoning here can easily be related to syllogistic reasoning. The poor driver generates one or more false premises—for example, accidents happen only to others, from which faulty conclusions follow in a "logical" fashion.

Take another example, a courtroom argument in which the prosecution presents these premises:

"If only he could think in abstract terms. . . ."

Playboy, January 1970. Reproduced by special permission of PLAYBOY Magazine; copyright © 1969 by Playboy.

Imagery is a way of coding and remembering our perceptions of the world and our experiences. As such, imagery plays an important role in cognition. Often we solve problems "in our heads" by imagining the various aspects of the problem; it is obviously much easier to conjure up images of concrete objects such as tables, chairs, and elephants than of abstract things such as love, mortality, and nth roots. Problem solution may be helped by translating abstract terms into concrete ones that can easily be visualized. Psychologists like to do this, for example, by devising mechanical models of psychological processes, as when cognition is treated as a computer program.

All criminals come from broken homes.
The defendant came from a broken home.
Therefore, the defendant is a criminal.

Here, acceptance of the invalid conclusion resulting from the atmosphere effect could be critical for a jury decision of guilt or innocence. Finally, imagine further some of the things you attribute to yourself or others due to reasoning errors:

All people who are not intelligent fail tests.
I failed a test.
Therefore, I am not intelligent.

Notice that this is an example of invalid conversion in which the reasoner erroneously interprets the first premise to mean that *all people who fail tests* and *all people who are not intelligent* are perfectly overlapping sets. Since "I" is an instance of one, the reasoner erroneously concludes that he or she is an instance of the other.

Everyday thinking errors such as these are quite common. No doubt you can think of many other domains in which they occur. You should be aware of them and avoid them where possible, since their consequence can be costly in a personal way.

Natural Reasoning

Most discourse, whether it is a conversation or text, follows a set of conventions. According to the linguist, H. P. Grice, these conventions follow a Cooperative Principle. The principle states that a speaker (or writer) produces language in such a way as to maximize the effectiveness of his or her communication to a listener (or reader). There are four parts to this principle. First, the structure of the communicator's utterance is no more or less informative than is required. Second, what is said is only that which is both believed by the speaker and for which the speaker has adequate evidence. Third, the utterance is relevant. Fourth, the utterance is structured in such a way as to be easy to understand. Most of us follow these principles in our conversations with others, as well as in our writing, without even being aware of them. However, they have some important consequences for the structure of our utterances (or writings).

In particular, a good deal of information is left implicit (for the comprehender to infer) rather than explicitly stated. Suppose we were describing an event we had witnessed. We might begin by saying the following things:

John threw the ball through the window.
Mr. Jones came running out of the house.

There are several things that the listener would understand and probably infer about this episode, based on what he or she knows about the world. Some of them are:

The ball broke the window.
It was Mr. Jones' window.
He came running out to find who threw the ball.
He was angry.

It is unnecessary to express all of these things explicitly in our description of the episode, because our listeners can fill them in for themselves. In fact, if we did explicitly express all inferences, our listener would probably find the communications rather bizarre: "My dog, Ralph, will eat only 'Tender Vittles.' Dogs are animals. Animals eat food. Animals have preferences for certain kinds of foods. But the other day, I got him to eat some canned dog food." Thus, much of our natural reasoning is done in the process of comprehending.

Intelligence

So far we have described a variety of cognitive processes, summarizing what psychologists have discovered about how people reason, solve problems, form concepts, and understand language (see Chap-

Highlight 6–2

Did the Butler Do It?

One kind of problem used in reasoning research is the "whodunit" problem in which the subject is given information about a fairly complex set of relationships and must then determine how they fit together. Such problems can be quite difficult. Although they involve some figuring out of "what follows from what" in a fashion similar to syllogisms, their solution depends heavily on appropriate hypothesizing (about what to figure out next). Because of this need for hypothesizing, performance on whodunit reasoning problems is not strongly related to performance on syllogistic reasoning problems. Try "playing detective" for this rather unrealistic mystery.

A murder has been committed. An examination of the fatal wound established that the murderer had used a dagger that made an unusual mark on the body. There were five suspects: the doctor, butler, cook, gardener, and accountant. Each had been alone in one of the five rooms in the apartment and thus had no one to vouch for his or her innocence. The rooms lie in a line down the single corridor: bedroom, den, living room, dining room, and kitchen, in order. The additional evidence gathered from various sources is as follows:

The butler was in the bedroom.
The man with the poison was in the room next to the man with the brown sweater.
The man with the dagger wore a gray jacket.
The man with the penknife wore a black jacket.
The cook wore a brown sweater.
The gardener was next to the dining room.
The man with the poison was in the living room.
The man with the pistol was in the room next to the man wearing the blue jacket.
The gardener had a rope.
The doctor was in the room next to the man with the black jacket.
The accountant wore a green sweater.

Sifting through the evidence, the crafty inspector deduced who the murderer was. Can you solve the crime? For the answer see Highlight 6–4.

---

ter 5). We have emphasized the role of attention, memory, and a person's knowledge and skills in these complex activities. To many people, the word "intelligence" refers to an individual's general ability to perform cognitive tasks. The belief in a general cognitive ability lies at the foundation of many intelligence tests, although some psychologists argue that intelligence refers to an amalgamation of a number of relatively separate abilities. Whether or not people are *generally* superior or inferior with regard to cognitive accomplishments is one of the major issues that has confronted research on intelligence.

The concept of intelligence has been closely tied to intelligence tests. Our society attributes considerable importance to being intelligent, and scores on intelligence tests have often been used to make important decisions about people's lives. Much controversy, not only in intellectual circles but in social and political arenas, has stemmed from the question of *why* people score high or low on such tests. This section reviews the history and nature of intelligence tests and then reconsiders what intelligence means. Only after understanding the concept will we discuss the reasons people differ in intelligence.

The Relation of Cognitive Theory to Intelligence

Since we have already looked at many important issues associated with the way we learn, remember, and use knowledge, perhaps it would be useful to begin by suggesting how some of these concepts might be useful in understanding what intelligence is. Below is a list of issues that will provide a framework for relating what we have learned in previous chapters to the notion of intelligence. Following the list, we will describe some of these areas in more concrete domains.

1. *Mental representation.* Our discussions of human memory have shown that we must store internally (in some kind of memory code) what we know about the world. Thus, we can ask whether certain types of representations give rise to more intelligent kinds of activities — are certain kinds of memory codes more easily processed than others? Do more intelligent individuals represent their knowledge differently than others?
2. *Use of knowledge.* Part of what we know may be termed "strategic knowledge" — knowledge about how to use our factual knowledge. Do more intelligent individuals deploy this strategic knowledge more efficiently?
3. *Attention.* Do people with higher intelligence have ex-

tended attention spans, or perhaps more processing capacity?

4. *Memory.* Do people with higher intelligence have memory systems that are larger in capacity or better organized than those of individuals with lower intelligence? Do they have quicker access to their memories, or do they retain information for longer periods of time?

5. *Language.* Are individuals of high verbal ability necessarily more intelligent?

6. *Creativity.* How is creative thinking related to intelligence? Does "genius" (for example, Einsteinian thinking) necessarily entail creativity? Are there intelligent people who are not creative?

7. *Decision making.* How does the ability to make decisions relate to intelligence? Are individuals with higher intelligence better able to weigh alternatives and reach decisions than others?

8. *Environment and heredity.* What do environment and heredity each contribute to intelligence? To what extent can intelligence be raised or lowered by environmental experiences?

9. *Culture.* Is intelligence culture-specific? Do the behaviors that enable people to adapt to their environment change from culture to culture? And what about the underlying aptitude for adaptive behavior? Is there such a thing—and is it also culture-specific?

Understanding Nonhuman Intelligence

In trying to determine whether the intelligence of any "alien" species corresponds to or surpasses that of human beings, John Lilly suggests that we first investigate: (1) whether the alien species has a large enough brain of sufficient complexity to carry out the kinds of cognitive processes human beings do, and (2) whether there are sufficient numbers of input and output channels from this brain to support higher-order cognitive skills. Lilly is concerned in particular with whether a brain is large enough to support language processing of a complexity comparable to human language. It is not enough to consider the absolute weight of a brain. Elephants have very large brains—much larger than those of human beings—but they are not good candidates for animals of high intellect. Rather, we need to look at the ratio of brain size to body size or at the ratio of brain weight to foot of body length. Evidence suggests a significant correlation between intelligence and the brain-body ratio. The absolute weight of an adult human brain, on the average, is 1450 grams. The corresponding value for dolphins is 1700 grams. However, when we compute the ratio of brain weight to body size, the value for human beings (250 grams per foot of body length) is slightly higher than that for dolphins (200 grams per foot of body length). Thus, according to Lilly, we can expect that dolphins might have an intelligence level close to but not exceeding that of human beings.

Lilly's primary criterion of intellect is the pro-

duction and understanding of a language. The task of determining whether an alien species has language is difficult, as should be apparent from the discussion of language in Chapter 5. In fact, while dolphins apparently communicate with each other through complex patterns of whistles and clicks, efforts to decipher their language has met with only limited success. More success has been enjoyed by efforts to teach dolphins to speak human language. An example of a sound spectogram of a trainer's interchange with a dolphin named Peter is shown in Figure 6–9. The trainer is trying to get Peter to make sound imitations of the words "BO BO CLOWN." Note that Peter does not imitate the trainer when he says "Listen." Among many things psychologists have been able to teach dolphins is to discern between certain words that are instructions and those that are to be repeated.

Dolphins have two communication mechanisms, both in the nose, below and on each side of the blowhole. These mechanisms can operate independently, giving the dolphin the apparent ability to carry on a whistle conversation with its right side and a clicking conversation with its left side—each controlled independently by one hemisphere of the brain. An analogous human activity might be a typist composing a manuscript while simultaneously carrying on a conversation. In line with our earlier discussions of doing two things at once, human beings have difficulty with this task for at least two reasons:

FIGURE 6–9

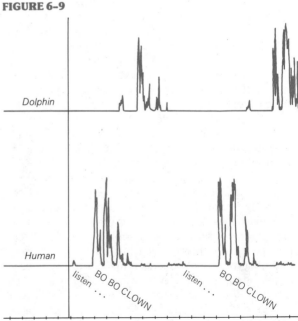

Showing NO overlap . . . . complete separation 2 human 2 dolphin bursts

The tracings in Peter's sound spectogram line that occur when the trainer says listen are artifactual, arising from cross-over from the trainer's spectogram.

1. Structurally, we are not built with two verbal output mechanisms (although we do have two brain hemispheres).
2. Functionally, our processing capacity is limited. That is, we do not have enough resources or attention to meet the demands of producing two conversations simultaneously.

Intelligent individuals may have more processing capacity (or use it more efficiently) than others, allowing them to surmount the functional difficulties. Structural difficulties represent a more severe limitation. In that respect, dolphins are better off than we are.

Research on primates has given us other insights into alien intelligence. For example, a major controversy has developed about the ability of chimpanzees to master a humanlike language (see the newsclip "Are Those Apes Really Talking?"). It is clear, however, that chimps have excellent problem-solving skills. In one recent study, a videotape was shown to an adult chimpanzee. The videotape depicted scenes of a human actor struggling with one of eight problems. After each videotape, the chimpanzee was shown two photographs, one of which depicted an action or an object (or both) that could constitute a solution to the problem. Examples of the problems are shown in Figure 6–10. The results of this experiment were rather striking. The chimpanzee consistently chose the correct solution on seven of the eight problems. The chimp's success suggests not only that she had the intelligence to recognize a problem (for human beings) and possible solutions to it, but that she could bring the correct solution to bear on the problem with which she was presented.

In defining and measuring intelligence, one issue reappears repeatedly—the central importance of language to human cognitive abilities. We confronted this issue in examining both dolphin and primate intelligence, and we will discuss it again in considering efforts to create artificially intelligent machines.

Artificial Intelligence

A well-defined understanding of the principles underlying intelligence is especially necessary for the task of creating artificial or machine intelligence. Some progress in this area has been made. One example is a program named ELIZA that was constructed at the Massachusetts Institute of Technology in the mid-1960s to imitate the intelligent behavior of a nondirective Rogerian psychotherapist (see Chapter 9). For a sample of ELIZA's behavior, read through the conversation in Figure 6–11. The program does a good job of sounding like an intelligent psychotherapist, but is based on certain computing tricks which can easily be recognized after one has listened for a short time. Other projects of this sort have been less

Speedy, a 10-year-old orangutan, focuses a borrowed camera on Tiga, his 9-year-old pinup, after an afternoon's work at a Tampa, Fla., attraction. Speedy's behavior was spontaneous and unrehearsed. Would you call it insight? Could it have been learned by trial and error? What about imitation or observational learning (see Chapter 9)? Do animals think?

grandiose but more successful. One (SHRDLU) has endowed the computer with enough intelligence to move around in and manipulate a world that is limited to a number of toy blocks on a table top (see Figures 6–12 and 6–13). Even this apparently simple task requires immensely sophisticated "mental" processes and is extremely difficult to program.

Efforts like these, which try to simulate intelligent behavior, have helped to advance our understanding of human intelligence, mainly by identifying concepts in need of study that we ordinarily take for granted. Notable among these concepts are notions of how we represent and use knowledge, how we understand language, and how we use attention and processing capacity.

So far, we have explored definitions of intelligence and some approaches to clarifying what we mean by the notion of intelligence. Our explorations have raised a number of unanswered questions about the nature of intelligence. Despite these unknowns, psychologists have devised some clever ways to measure intelligence, and it is to a discussion of these tests that we now turn.

Measuring Intelligence

When it comes to measuring intelligence, an important point to keep in mind is the distinction between *ability* and *achievement*. A true test of ability measures a person's potential for achievement. It does not measure the knowledge and skills the person already has. A test of achievement, on the other hand, measures *existing* knowledge and skills independently of the

Are Those Apes Really Talking?

Laura, the teacher, and her young pupil are romping playfully on the lawn in front of their classroom:

Pupil (rolling on ground): You tickle me.
Laura: Where?
Pupil (pointing to leg): Here.
Laura (after tickling him): Now you tickle me.
Pupil (tickling her): Me tickle Laura.

This dialogue between Laura and her charge might not seem unusual, except for one thing: the pupil was not a human child but a young chimpanzee named Nim. Like several others of his primate kin, Nim had been taught to communicate with humans in American Sign Language, a system of hand gestures developed for the deaf [Nonvocal communication is necessary in experiments with apes because their vocal apparatus cannot produce the wide range of sounds that characterizes spoken language.] He eventually learned to make and recognize 125 signs. But the frisky little chimp and other apes who have received such "language" instruction are now the center of a raging academic storm. The issue: can apes really master the essence of human language—the creation of sentences?

A few years ago, the answer might have been an unequivocal yes. After all, psychologists Allen and Beatrice Gardner of the University of Nevada had managed in the late 1960s to teach the chimp Washoe to use 132 signs; the precocious animal was even credited with having invented a phrase of her own, *water bird* for swan. About the same time, David Premack, of the University of California at Santa Barbara, using plastic symbols of different shapes and colors to represent words, taught his prize pupil, Sarah, some 130 words and reported that she had also mastered some phrases. At the Yerkes Regional Primate Research Center in Atlanta, the husband-wife team of Duane Rumbaugh of Georgia State University and Susan Savage-Rumbaugh, employing a language of their own invention, called Yerkish (its symbols are projected onto a screen when an ape presses the appropriately marked key on a console), even got two chimpanzees to communicate with each other in this artificial "tongue."

Though a few experts expressed skepticism, these claims of the apes' linguistic ability were widely accepted during the 1970s. But now many scientists are beginning to have second thoughts. They suggest that much of what the animals are doing is merely mimicking their teachers and that they have no comprehension of syntax. What is more, they say, the primate experimenters are probably so eager to prove their case that they often provide inadvertent cues to the animals, who quickly realize which "right" answer will bring them some goody. In short, the skeptics raise the possibility that the apes have been making monkeys out of their human mentors.

No one has done more to stir doubts than Columbia University Psychologist Herbert Terrace in his work with little Nim (full name: Nim Chimpsky, a play on the name of Linguist Noam Chomsky of the Massachusetts Institute of Technology, a staunch proponent of the idea that language ability is biologically unique to humans). The object of Terrace's experiment was to prove Chomsky wrong—to show that creatures other than man could, indeed, conquer syntax and link words into sentences, however simple.

Toward that goal, Terrace, with Laura Petitto, a student assistant, and other trainers, put Nim through 44 months of intensive sign-language drill, while treating him much as they would a child. In some ways the chimp was an apt student, learning, for example, to "sign" *dirty* when he wanted to use the potty or *drink* when he spotted someone sipping from a Thermos. Nonetheless, Nim never mastered even the rudiments of grammar or sentence construction. His speech, unlike that of children, did not grow in complexity. Nor did it show much spontaneity; 88% of the time he "talked" only in response to specific questions from the teacher.

Armed with his new insights, Terrace began reviewing the reports and video tapes of other experimenters. Careful study of the record showed the same patterns with other apes that Terrace had noted in the work with Nim. There were rarely any "spontaneous" utterances, and what had seemed at first glance to be original sentences now emerged as responses to questions, imitations of signs made by the teacher, or as rote-like repetitions of memorized combinations. For instance, when Lana, a chimp at Yerkes, said *Please machine give apple*, the first three words seemed to mean nothing more to her than a mechanical prelude to obtaining something she wanted. Says Terrace in his 1979 book *Nim* (Knopf; $15): "The closer I looked, the more I regarded the many reported instances of language as elaborate tricks [by the apes] for obtaining rewards."

An equally serious criticism has been made by Linguist Thomas Sebeok and his wife, anthropologist Donna Jean Umiker-Sebeok, both at Indiana University . . . they maintain that much of what passes for language skill in apes can be explained by the "Clever Hans effect"—a phenomenon named for a turn-of-the-century German circus horse that astounded audiences by tapping out with his hoofs correct answers to complex mathematical and verbal problems. In fact, as a German psychologist finally discerned, Clever Hans was picking up unintentional cues—changes in facial expression, breathing patterns and even eye-pupil size—from his questioner telling him when and how many times to stomp (or, more precisely, when to stop stomping). Say the Sebeoks: "Real breakthroughs in man-ape communication are the stuff of fiction."

Such words touched off angry responses. . . . Premack, now at the University of Pennsylvania, thinks that Terrace's tactic of trying to treat Nim like a human baby was "silly and ill-advised," but he agrees that animals are incapable of spontaneous conversation. The Rumbaughs maintain that their more recent experiments preclude the possibility of trainers giving cues, consciously or subconsciously, to the subjects, but they have their own reservations about the linguistic ability of apes. Acknowledges Duane Rumbaugh: "There is no solid evidence to date that would indicate that the ape is capable of using syntax with competence."

Time
March 10, 1980

FIGURE 6-10   Imitation or intelligence?

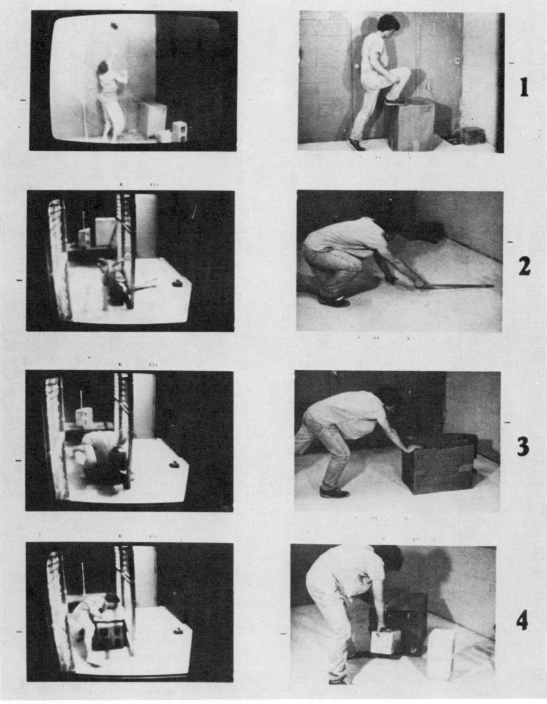

Photographic reproductions of the four televised problem scenes in test 1 (left column) and of the color-photograph solutions (right column). Photographs of the television monitor in the left column were taken during the last 5 seconds of each 30-second videotaped scene. The correct means for solving each problem is portrayed in the photograph directly to the right of each problem scene. In problem 1, the trainer attempted to reach up toward bananas suspended by a rope from the ceiling; in problem 2, to reach under the wire mesh partition toward bananas on the floor; in problem 3, to reach around an intervening box toward bananas on the floor outside the cage; and in problem 4, to push aside a box filled with cement blocks, which obstructed his reach toward bananas on the floor outside the cage. In solution 1, the trainer stepped on a box; in solution 2, he reached out with a wooden rod; in solution 3, he pushed laterally on a box; and in solution 4, he lifted blocks out of a box.

FIGURE 6-11   Conversation with ELIZA

Hello.

→ HOW DO YOU DO. PLEASE STATE YOUR PROBLEM.

I want a good example for my book.

→ YOUR BOOK.

Yes, my book about computers.
Can you help me?

→ YOU'RE BEING SOMEWHAT SHORT WITH ME.

I didn't mean to be.

→ YOU SAY YOU DIDN'T MEAN TO BE.

That's right. What do you know about computers?

→ DO COMPUTERS WORRY YOU?

Not at all. I think they can be very useful.

→ CAN YOU ELABORATE ON THAT?

Computers play a vital role in the operation of our society.

→ WHY DO YOU MENTION COMPUTERS?

Because that is what the book is all about.

→ IS THAT THE REAL REASON?

Of course. Sometimes you are difficult to talk to.

→ WHAT MAKES YOU THINK I AM DIFFICULT TO TALK TO?

You answer in such short, stylized phrases.

→ WE WERE DISCUSSING YOU—NOT ME.

I thought we were discussing computers.

→ WHAT DO YOU THINK MACHINES HAVE TO DO WITH YOUR PROBLEM?

My only problem is to get you to carry on a reasonable conversation.

→ WHY DO YOU SAY YOUR ONLY PROBLEM IS TO GET I TO CARRY ON A REASONABLE CONVERSATION?

You don't use very good grammar.

→ OH, I DON'T USE VERY GOOD GRAMMAR.

That's right. Don't you know the difference between nominative and accusative?

→ YOU'RE NOT REALLY TALKING ABOUT ME—ARE YOU?

I really was, but I'm willing to change the subject.

→ DO YOU SAY REALLY WAS FOR SOME SPECIAL REASON?

The reason is that I would like an interesting conversation in the book.

→ IN WHAT WAY?

So that the readers won't get bored with it.

→ I AM NOT SURE I UNDERSTAND YOU FULLY.

You don't understand very much, do you!

→ WHAT ARE YOUR FEELINGS NOW?

I feel that I am about ready to give up.

→ TELL ME MORE ABOUT SUCH FEELINGS.

The page is almost full now, so I can end this interview.

→ SUPPOSE THE PAGE WERE NOT ALMOST FULL NOW?

Then we would have to continue this silliness a while longer.

→ PLEASE GO ON.

That's all there is to say. Don't you ever get tired?

→ PERHAPS THAT'S ALL THERE REALLY IS TO SAY

Yes. Goodbye.

→ YOU SEEM QUITE POSITIVE.

FIGURE 6-12   SHRDLU's world of toy blocks

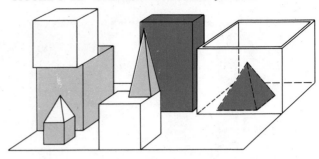

person's ability or potential for future achievement. What you know now is your level of achievement. Your potential for future achievement is your level of ability.

Tests of intelligence generally try to measure intellectual ability. But, in practice, it is extremely difficult, if not impossible, to construct a test that measures pure ability and is completely independent of a person's achievement. This means that it may be possible for two people to earn the same score on an intelligence test for different reasons, one because of high ability and low achievement, the other because of low ability and high achievement. Much of the current debate concerning the fairness of intelligence tests centers on this problem. People with high ability may earn lower scores because a disadvantaged background restricts their level of achievement.

The Binet Test

The first general measure of intelligence was constructed for a simple, practical reason. Around the turn of the century, the Ministry of Public Instruction

FIGURE 6-13   Conversation with SHRDLU

Pick up a big red block.

→ OK.

Grasp the pyramid.

→ I DON'T UNDERSTAND WHICH PYRAMID YOU MEAN.

Find a block that is taller than the one you are holding, and put it into the box.

→ BY 'IT,' I ASSUME YOU MEAN THE BLOCK WHICH IS TALLER THAN THE ONE I AM HOLDING. OK.

What does the box contain?

→ THE BLUE PYRAMID AND THE BLUE BLOCK.

What is the pyramid supported by?

→ THE BOX.

How many blocks are not in the box?

→ FOUR OF THEM.

Is at least one of them narrower than the one which I told you to pick up?

→ YES, THE RED CUBE.

COMPUTERS SUCCESSFULLY REPLACE PSYCHOTHERAPISTS IN BOSTON EXPERIMENT. (News Item)

The information-processing approach to cognition, based heavily on the principles of computer science, promises to have significant impact on our lives. Already there are very sophisticated programs for solving logic problems, playing bridge and chess, and even for directing psychotherapy. Computers will play an increasing role in teaching people how to think, reason, and solve problems in just about any area of knowledge. For example, computers are being used to teach medical students how to make diagnoses according to the principles used by specialists.

in France decided it wanted to identify schoolchildren who were likely to experience difficulty in school and who would benefit from special educational programs. The Ministry commissioned Alfred Binet, a well-known psychologist, and his colleague, Théodore Simon, to develop a test that could be used to identify these children. Since that time, the test, which for simplicity we will call the *Binet test,* has been repeatedly and systematically revised, and versions of it are in common use today. Most recent revisions have been undertaken at Stanford University in California and are called *Stanford-Binet tests.*

Binet and Simon made two basic assumptions. First, they believed that intelligence is a composite of many abilities. Therefore, intelligence tests must contain a large number of different kinds of test items. Most items used in Binet tests are based on

simple everyday tasks. Binet wanted to construct a test that would measure pure ability and not give special advantages to any particular group of children. Despite his concern and careful selection of items, however, we know that Binet's test, even in its most modern versions, is not free from environmental influence. Indeed, there is no test that is truly "culture-free," because the selection of items necessarily involves assumptions about what experiences people do in fact have. The critical point is that, if people have had unequal exposure to certain experiences assumed in a test, differences in their scores cannot conclusively be attributed to differences in their pure ability to profit from these experiences.

The second important assumption behind Binet tests is that the nature of intelligence changes with age. Therefore, items selected for Binet tests must be graded by age as well as difficulty. Items used for testing intelligence at age 3 are not appropriate at age 10. The same items will simply not discriminate low from high from average children at every age. Thus, Binet tests are actually a collection of subtests, one for each year of age. Some illustrative items at different age levels are presented in Table 6–2.

"I can't go bowling tonight, Freddie. I'm cramming for an IQ test tomorrow."

Reprinted by permission of the Chicago Tribune–New York News Syndicate, Inc.

TABLE 6-2 Test Items for the Fifth- and Twelfth-Year Scales of the Latest (1960) Revision of the Binet Test

Year 5

1. Completes a drawing of a man with missing legs and other body parts
2. Folds a paper square twice to make a triangle, after demonstration by an examiner
3. Defines the following three words: ball, hat, stove
4. Copies a square
5. Recognizes similarities and differences between selected pictures
6. Assembles two triangles to form a rectangle

Year 12

1. Defines 14 words, such as haste, lecture, skill
2. Sees the absurdity in such items as: "Bill Jones's feet are so big that he has to pull his trousers on over his head."
3. Understands the absurdity depicted in a complex picture
4. Repeats five digits backwards
5. Defines several abstract words, such as pity, curiosity
6. Supplies the missing word in several incomplete sentences, such as: "One cannot be a hero _____, but one can always be a man."

Binet introduced the concept of **mental age** (MA). If a child can pass the items on which the average 9-year-old child is successful, that child is said to have a mental age of 9 years. Mental age is defined independently of **chronological age** (CA); thus, if a 6-year-old can pass the tests passed by the average 9-year-old, the child is considerably accelerated in mental development. If an 11-year-old can pass only the items passed by the average 9-year-old, his or her development is retarded. Binet felt that a dull child was retarded in mental growth and a bright child was advanced in mental growth.

It is important not to read too much into the concept of mental age, which is simply one method of scoring performance on an intelligence test. The items associated with age 7 are more difficult than those associated with age 6, which in turn are harder than those associated with age 5, and so on. Rather than earning "points" by passing items, the child earns months and years of mental age credit. Of two children tested, the child with the higher mental age has simply passed a greater number of and more difficult items on the test. Suppose a child passes all items up through age scale 7; passes 4 of 6 items, worth 2 mental age months each, on age scale 8; suc-

---

Highlight 6-3

Urban versus Rural Intelligence

Tests of general information are commonly included in intelligence tests. They are based on the assumption that everyone has had a roughly equal opportunity to acquire such information. If so, the people who know more correct answers must be better able to learn and remember. The problems involved in devising information tests that are fair to various segments of a population are nicely illustrated in a classic study by Myra Shimberg. Two different information tests were constructed; examples of the questions on each test are shown below. Both tests seem like reasonable measures of general information for schoolchildren and contain questions much like those on standard intelligence tests.

Information Test A
1. What are the colors in the American flag?
2. What is the largest river in the United States?
3. What is the freezing point of water?

Information Test B
1. Of what is butter made?

2. Name a vegetable that grows above ground.
3. About how often do we have a full moon?

It was found, however, that the two tests had definite but subtle biases. On Test A, urban schoolchildren scored much higher than rural schoolchildren. On Test B, the situation was entirely reversed, with the rural children scoring significantly higher. Analyses of the 25 items on each test indicated that there were many questions for which the direction of the bias could not be predicted by looking at the content of the question. Nevertheless, the two tests yield radically different pictures of rural and urban performance.

This study demonstrated that items on intelligence tests can be biased in subtle ways in favor of one or another part of the population. Similar results have been obtained in other studies. Such findings indicate how difficult it is to make sure that "everyone has had an equal opportunity to acquire the information needed to pass the test."

Standardized School Tests: This or Chaos?
By PATRICIA McCORMACK

The National Education Association and some other groups want to erase standardized tests from the school scene to protect "the kids."

Children would be the last to reject the idea, it's safe to say.

But there is another side to the coin. And experts examining it at a national conference said life without tests would by chaotic.

That's not what foes of tests say. They claim standardized tests discriminate and are, therefore, unfair. Tests, they say, put lifelong labels on kids — bright, dull, high achiever, low achiever, mediocre, average.

The standardized test most often at the center of the attack is the Scholastic Achievement Test which is widely used in college admissions.

However, says Dr. Robert L. Ebel, professor of education, Michigan State University, "The social consequences of not using tests would be disastrous.

"In schools and colleges, in business and government, the information tests described are virtually indispensible," he said. "These institutions suffer not from too much testing but from too little good testing.

"Critics of testing have chosen the wrong point of attack; it is not testing, per se, that is harmful. It is the frequent use of poor tests."

Ebel took on a major opponent of testing — the NAACP, National Associa-tion for the Advancement of Colored People.

The opposition of the "leadership of the NAACP" to testing, Ebel said, serves their "immediate and narrowly special interests.

"They see tests as barriers facing poorly educated minorities, barriers to opportunities for further education and employment. They do not see tests as unprejudiced assessors of competence, as powerful arguments for equality of educational opportunity.

"The low scores that minorities often receive on tests seldom if ever can be attributed to bias in the tests. Almost always they reflect the damage inflicted by inadequate education."

Ebel cited ways in which not testing in schools and colleges would have harmful social consequences. He said it would:

Handicap communities seeking excellence in schools. Tests can reveal how much has been learned of what was set out to be learned. They can indicate how effectively the pupils have been taught, and how successfully they have studied.

Handicap minorities. It would deny them the help of objective evidence in their struggle for equal access to opportunities for education and employment. Tests are color blind. They are essentially unbiased. Low scores on a test for any group do not show that the test is biased against them — simply that for whatever reason — including lack of opportunity to learn — they have not learned the information being tested.

Handicap students seeking to learn. Purposeful efforts to learn require definite goals for learning and definite indications of success in achieving those goals. Good tests help to define goals and provide indications of success.

Handicap schools in their attempts to select and retain competent teachers. To be a good teacher one must know thoroughly what is to be taught and how to teach it. The ability of tests to measure the amount of relevant knowledge a teacher possesses is not likely to be questioned by those who are well informed and reasonable.

Enemies of testing are not the mainstream.

Ebel said:

"Elimination of testing is advocated by relatively small numbers of people, some of whom have relatively loud voices.

"It is not advocated by the public generally, as a Gallup poll has shown.

"Within the enterprise there are a few leaders and many followers who oppose testing out of a misguided egalitarian philosophy."

Denver Post
November 7, 1980

IQ tests are not perfect, but they are improving as we learn more through research on the nature of the various abilities that make up intelligence. These tests are useful when properly administered and interpreted. However, not everyone would agree with the statement made in this article that such tests are "essentially unbiased." For more on this matter, see the discussion in "What Does It Mean?" at the end of this chapter.

ceeds on 2 of 6 items on age scale 9; and fails everything on age scale 10 and above. His or her mental age score is then 7 years plus 8 plus 4 months, or 7 years plus 12 months, or 8 years.

IQ
The most common score derived from the Binet test, and indeed any intelligence test, is the **intelligence quotient,** or **IQ,** which indicates how an individual scored relative to others of comparable age. Using mental age scores, one formula for the IQ is:

$$IQ = \frac{\text{mental age}}{\text{chronological age}} \times 100$$

The test is designed so that the average child earns a mental age score equal to his or her chronological age, which means the average IQ is 100. Individuals who pass more items than the average for their age group have mental ages greater than their chronological ages and thus IQs greater than 100, while those children who do not perform as well as the average will have IQs of less than 100. Using our earlier example of the child who earned a mental age of 8 years, we can see that, if the child were 6 years old, his IQ would be

$$8/6 \times 100 = 133$$

If the child were 10 years old, his IQ would be:

$$8/10 \times 100 = 80$$

This ratio, the IQ, thus indicates a person's achievement on the test relative to the achievement of others of comparable age.

It is not necessary to use mental age units in order to calculate an IQ. The most general formula for the IQ, using the points scored on the test, is:

$$IQ = \frac{\text{the person's score}}{\text{the average score for his age group}} \times 100$$

Whenever people score higher than the average for their age group, their IQs will be greater than 100; should they score lower than average, their IQs will be less than 100.

Wechsler Tests

Another frequently used test of individual IQ is the Wechsler test, named after its creator, psychologist David Wechsler. One version of the Wechsler test is designed for adults, the Wechsler Adult Intelligence Scale (WAIS). A second applies to children in the age range of approximately 6–16 years, the Wechsler

"You did very well on your IQ test. You're a man of 49 with the intelligence of a man of 53."

American Scientist, January–February 1977. Reprinted by permission of Sidney Harris.

IQ defined in terms of mental age and chronological age does not apply to adult intelligence.

Intelligence Scale for Children (WISC). A third version, used with even younger children, 4–6.5 years of age, is called the Wechsler Preschool and Primary Scale of Intelligence (WPPSI). Items on the Wechsler tests are similar to those on the Binet test, but, rather than being organized into age scales, the items are combined into subscales to test different abilities. Performance on each subscale yields a score in points that can be converted directly into IQ. About half of the test is concerned with verbal abilities, involving definitions and similarities and differences among words. The other half assesses performance (nonverbal) abilities such as object assembly and picture arrangement. See Table 6–3 for examples. With the Wechsler tests, it is quite common to calculate both a performance IQ and a verbal IQ. Binet tests tend to emphasize verbal abilities more than Wechsler tests.

The Distribution of IQ Scores

An IQ score of 100 is considered average. Half the adult population scores within the range of 90 to 110 on the WAIS (see Table 6–4). At the high and low ends of the IQ distribution are exceptional people. At the high end, we speak of geniuses. Typically, people with high IQs are not only bright but also eminent. Examination of biographical information on notable historical figures has allowed psychologists to make reasonable estimates of their IQs even though no tests were available. Invariably, this information

---

TABLE 6–3   Examples of Test Materials from the Wechsler Adult Intelligence Scale

Performance IQ

A. *Digit-symbol substitution*—a timed test of ability to substitute symbols for numbers
B. *Block design*—a test of ability to build specified designs with colored blocks
C. *Object assembly*—a test of ability to assemble puzzle pieces to form a common object
D. *Picture arrangement*—a test of ability to arrange pictures in order for telling a logical, coherent story (such as reassembling cartoon panels)

Verbal IQ

A. *Digit span*—a test of ability to repeat a string of digits in forward and backward order immediately
B. *Similarities*—a test of ability to say how things are alike, e.g., a bus and an airplane
C. *Vocabulary*—a test of ability to provide word definitions
D. *Arithmetic*—problems that test arithmetic ability and general problem-solving skills
E. *General information*—a test of general knowledge items like: who invented the telephone, who wrote the *Canterbury Tales,* where does oil come from?

TABLE 6-4 Variations in IQ Scores

Range of Scores	Approximate Percentage of People
130 and above	2
120–129	7
110–119	16
100–109	25
90–99	25
80–89	16
70–79	7
Below 70	2

leads to estimates of IQs in excess of 125, some ranging as high as 200. The following are estimated IQ scores derived in one study: J. S. Bach, 125; Napoleon, 135; Voltaire, 170. Although these numerical values are obviously only estimates and may be off by 10 or more IQ points in either direction, it is clear that individuals who make significant contributions to society or culture often have higher than average IQs.

Biographical data of this sort have been largely substantiated by contemporary studies in which the growth and development of gifted children, those with IQs of 135 and above, have been followed throughout their life span. Contrary to common misconceptions, these children tend to be better than average in their adjustment to their environment, to enjoy good mental health, and to make use of their intellect in ways that often have a significant impact on society. Interestingly enough, however, genius is not always quick to develop, Albert Einstein did not talk until he was 4 years old, and he was 7 before he could read. On the other hand, Mozart composed his first piece of music when he was 6.

At the opposite end of the distribution are individuals who are in some sense mentally deficient. There are degrees, of course. The borderline ranges from about 70 to 90 IQ points, corresponding to an adult with a mental age of 12 years. These individuals are clearly deficient, though not classifiable as retarded. Below IQ 70 are the mentally retarded, who used to be classified by terms such as "moron," "imbecile," and "idiot." These terms have been replaced by adjectives describing the degree of retardation: "mild," "moderate," "severe," or "profound."

Another way of classifying the degree of mental handicap is to indicate whether the person is educable or trainable. Those classified as mildly and moderately mentally retarded can usually be taught some basic skills. The severely retarded can be trained to acquire a few habits of self-maintenance (see Table 6-5). The profoundly retarded, however, need to be cared for, typically in an institution, although today parents are being trained to provide help at home. Special local school programs have been instituted for

TABLE 6-5 Classifications of Mental Retardation

	Preschool Age 0–5 Maturation and Development	School Age 6–21 Training and Education	Adult 21 and Over Social and Vocational Adequacy
Profound	Gross retardation: minimal capacity for functioning in sensorimotor areas; needs nursing care.	Obvious delays in all areas of development: shows basic emotional responses; may respond to skillful training in use of legs, hands, and jaws; needs close supervision.	May walk, may need nursing care, may have primitive speech: will usually benefit from regular physical activity; incapable of self-maintenance.
Severe	Marked delay in motor development: little or no communication skill; may respond to training in elementary self-help—e.g., self-feeding.	Usually walks, barring specific disability; has some understanding of speech and some response; can profit from systematic habit training.	Can conform to daily routines and repetitive activities: needs continuing direction and supervision in protective environment.
Moderate	Noticeable delays in motor development, especially in speech; responds to training in various self-help activities.	Can learn simple communication, elementary health and safety habits, and simple manual skills; does not progress in functional reading or arithmetic.	Can perform simple tasks under sheltered conditions: participates in simple recreation; travels alone in familiar places; usually incapable of self-maintenance.
Mild	Often not noticed as retarded by casual observer, but is slower to walk, feed self, and talk than most children.	Can acquire practical skills and useful reading and arithmetic to a 3rd to 6th grade level with special education. Can be guided toward social conformity.	Can usually achieve social and vocational skills adequate to self-maintenance; may need occasional guidance and support when under unusual social or economic stress.

the educable retarded, often resulting in significant increases in IQ. Other programs attempt to provide employment for the trainable retarded in "sheltered workshops" where they can work at their own pace and get paid. The hope is to provide support services so that parents will be willing to keep the child at home instead of placing him or her in an institution. Institutions for the retarded have all too often been "dumping grounds" where the retarded were kept out of sight of society. It is believed that many people classified as retarded could lead happier, more productive lives outside an institution.

Components of Intelligence

The different kinds of intelligence tests (and different subtests of each) that have been developed attest to the idea that human intelligence consists of a number of different abilities, not just a single, general attribute. Attempts to determine the number of intellectual abilities have been based on examination of the consistency of individual differences when people are given a variety of tests. High consistency means that people who score well on one test also score well on other tests and that people who score poorly on one test do so again on other tests. If individual differences are consistent from test to test, the tests basically measure the same ability, even though they may have different names and different content. On the other hand, inconsistent individual differences, with people scoring high on some tests but low, average, or high in some unsystematic manner on other tests, suggest that the tests measure different abilities. In other words, inconsistent individual differences mean that people's scores cannot be predicted from one test to another; knowing a person did well on one test would not help you predict that person will do well on another test. A statistical technique known as **factor analysis** is used to determine which sets of tests display consistent individual differences. A set of tests that has this consistency is clustered together to form a factor (see Appendix A).

Fluid and Crystallized Intelligence

Raymond Cattell advanced a theory of intelligence based on factor analyses of many different intelligence tests. Cattell's theory includes more factors or abilities than we can describe in detail here. But an important contribution made by Cattell was his observation that intellectual abilities may be placed into one of two general and very different categories. One category is called fluid intelligence and the other crystallized intelligence. *Fluid intelligence* involves insightful performance such as reasoning, in which learning experience plays little part, and corresponds closely with what others have called pure ability.

Crystallized intelligence involves learned skills and knowledge (for example, vocabulary) that are acquired over time and through experiences, corresponding to achievement level.

Crystallized abilities are developed through and determined by the quality of fluid intelligence and the learning opportunities available. High-quality crystallized abilities require both appropriate learning experiences and adequate fluid intelligence. A disadvantaged child with high fluid intelligence will develop only weak vocabulary skills if not provided with suitable learning opportunities. Similarly, a child from a high-income family will not be able to build a strong vocabulary unless sufficient fluid abilities are available to be devoted to the task.

Tests of fluid intelligence tend to correlate well with each other and are the best available measures of pure ability. Tests of crystallized intelligence also correlate highly. The difference between these concepts is revealed by the fact that tests from the two different groups do not correlate as highly as tests within each group. There is some correlation, however, which is taken by Cattell to indicate the necessity of fluid intelligence for the development of crystallized intelligence.

Structure of Intellect

J. P. Guilford has taken a different approach to the factor analysis of intelligence components. In his Structure of Intellect model, Guilford has proposed the existence of 120 separate abilities. The abilities are defined by the possible combinations of five kinds of operations that can be performed (for example, memory), six kinds of products (for example, units, transformations), and four kinds of contents or materials (for example, figural, semantic). Figure 6–14 illustrates this model. For example, one of the 120 abilities is memory for semantic units, and an appropriate test would be to recall a list of unrelated words. Under this conceptual scheme, the different abilities are supposedly unrelated; a special kind of factor analysis is used that produces factors that are not correlated. This approach contrasts sharply with Cattell's theory of related factors. Guilford and his associates have found evidence for the existence of over 75 of the 120 abilities claimed to exist.

The existence of a number of different intellectual abilities means that we have a more complex question than we originally supposed when we ask whether someone is intelligent. An individual can be intelligent in many ways and can have certain areas of strength and other areas of weakness. A person's intellectual abilities can be described, for example, as a profile of scores on a series of ability factors. One individual may be adept at handling numerical and mathematical tasks but have poor language abilities. Another may be superior in both fields. Each person's

FIGURE 6-14 Guilford's model for the structure of intellect

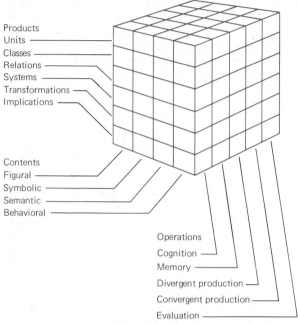

Products
Units
Classes
Relations
Systems
Transformations
Implications

Contents
Figural
Symbolic
Semantic
Behavioral

Operations
Cognition
Memory
Divergent production
Convergent production
Evaluation

According to Guilford, 120 components (abilities) combine to make up the intellect. From this diagram you can see how those 120 components (each little cube) are derived from the combination of six products with five operations and four contents.

combination of abilities and weaknesses determine how successful he or she will be on a given task. It is difficult to say how a set of abilities (whether there are 7 or 120) should be aggregated to produce a single intelligence score. Often it is more useful to consider the specific type of intellectual ability of interest and to base evaluations on that ability.

Information Processing and Intelligence

Intelligence tests, you will recall, were originally developed primarily for practical reasons, to identify children who were likely to experience difficulty in school. The contents of intelligence tests were thus determined on the basis of test constructors' general ideas of what intelligence was and by considering what "worked" (that is, predicted school success). Later research on the composition of intelligence was concerned with the number of abilities involved in performance on intelligence tests. This research was based on the examination of the consistency of individual differences from test to test rather than on a detailed analysis of the processes involved in arriving at answers to test items.

In recent years, researchers have attempted to bridge the gap between work on intelligence tests and

research on basic cognitive processes. For example, Earl Hunt and his colleagues compared high and low scorers on a standard verbal ability test over a variety of information-processing tasks. The idea behind their research was as follows. A verbal ability test supposedly measures what a person knows about language (punctuation, spelling, grammar, vocabulary, and so on). Is it also true that high and low scorers on the test ("high verbals" and "low verbals") differ in how they process information? In one approach, Hunt's group compared high and low verbals on tasks such as short-term memory for letter strings, speed at making same-different judgments about physical or semantic features of two stimuli, and speed at making true-false judgments about whether a sentence accurately describes a picture. High verbals and low verbals differed on some tasks but not on others. Compared to low verbals, high verbals could more rapidly scan short-term memory, more rapidly retrieve familiar information from long-term memory, and more accurately remember information about item order over brief intervals.

In a similar research program, Marcel Just and Patricia Carpenter compared performance of high and low spatial ability subjects on a mental rotation

The drawing-completion test

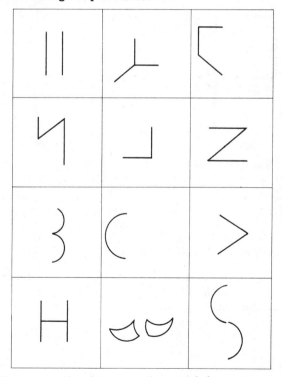

Use your pencil to elaborate on these simple figures in any way that you like. When you have finished, see Highlight 6–4.

FIGURE 6–15 Mental rotation task

Panel A

Panel B

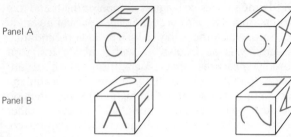

Two mental rotation items used by Just and Carpenter. In each case the subject must indicate whether the block on the left could be rotated to produce the block on the right. It is assumed that a particular number or letter will appear on only one face of a given block.

task. Examples of items used in Just and Carpenter's work are shown in Figure 6–15. In panel A, it is relatively easy to see that we have the same block in both cases, with a single 90-degree rotation applied to the block on the left to produce the block on the right. In panel B, the two blocks are also the same, but a more complicated set of rotations was used to produce the second block. Previous work on such tasks has shown that as the number of 90-degree rotations increases, the time required to respond increases by a certain amount for each additional rotation. Just and Carpenter obtained a similar result for low spatial ability subjects. For high spatial subjects, however, there were many occasions on which complex transformations (such as panel B in Figure 6–15) were solved in a shorter time than would be predicted by the number of 90-degree rotations involved. Subjects with high spatial ability were able to use more efficient checking strategies and were not required to carry out each rotation mentally before answering, as seems to be true for low spatial subjects.

One possible meaning of the work on individual differences in information-processing tasks is that perhaps the differences in ability to process

---

Highlight 6–4

Solutions to Problems

Match-Stick Problem

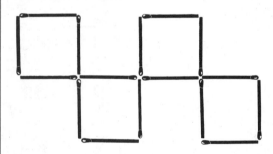

"Whodunit" Problem

Room	Person	Clothing	Weapon
bedroom	butler	black jacket	penknife
den	*doctor*	*gray jacket*	*dagger*
living room	accountant	green sweater	poison
dining room	cook	brown sweater	pistol
kitchen	gardener	blue jacket	rope

The information given in the story can be sorted out and tabulated as shown above. The facts can then be used to deduce that the doctor, who wore a gray jacket, was in the den, had a dagger, and was the murderer.

Dots Problem

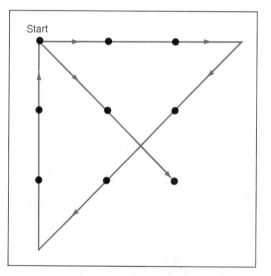

information had existed for a long time and were responsible for the differences in verbal or spatial ability. It is also possible, of course, that the differences in verbal or spatial ability limited subjects' ability to carry out efficiently the information-processing tasks they were given. For practical purposes, the first possibility suggests that knowing a student's information-processing capabilities might be much more useful to a teacher than having a broad characterization of the student's verbal or spatial ability. Further research of this type promises to lead to greater understanding of individual differences in cognitive processes.

Creativity

In most intelligence tests that we have discussed so far, each item was developed with one clear-cut, generally accepted answer in mind. But in many other situations, several "correct" answers are possible, some being "better" than others. The term *creativity* is used to describe the behavior of coming up with an original, practical answer or solution to a problem. Assessing creativity is difficult because it involves making a subjective judgment of the quality of the product of creative behavior. Disagreement about the degree of creativity usually stems from a lack of consensus among judges concerning the extent to which the product is practical or relevant—two people might agree that a painting is original, but they might differ substantially over whether or not it expresses some important idea.

Some tests of creativity have been based on elements of Guilford's Structure of Intellect model. The operation of *divergent production* refers to one's ability to produce a number of different yet relevant responses to an open-ended item like: "Name as many uses as you can think of for a cup." The person who is able to give many varied answers (to hold liquid, as a flower vase, a paper weight, to trap an

Sample Responses to the Drawing-Completion Test

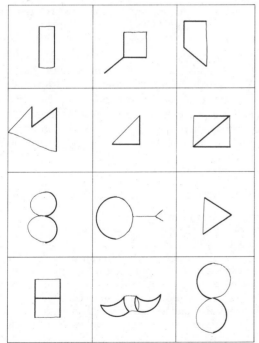

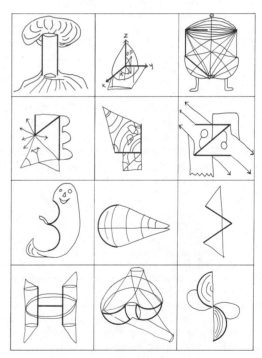

The drawings on the left illustrate the responses of the average person to the drawing-completion test, while those on the right exemplify the responses of creative individuals. The introduction of greater complexity and asymmetry is associated with creativity. Such differences are not limited to the actual production of drawings.

When drawings or colored patterns of varying complexity and symmetry are shown to people, creative individuals show a greater tendency to prefer complex and asymmetrical presentations. Some psychologists have argued that a preference or "need" for complexity is an integral component of creative behavior.

"On second thought, let's *not* take another crack at it."

The New Yorker, January 10, 1977. Drawing by Drucker; © 1977 The New Yorker Magazine, Inc.

A creative idea must be both original and useful — relevant, practical, or feasible in some fashion. Brainstorming is a technique designed to produce large numbers of original ideas. The hope is that at least some of them will also be creative ideas. This is like saying, "Let's be original first and worry about being creative later."

insect) would receive a high score on divergent production and, hence, creativity. Items on creativity tests generally require a person to produce one or more unique, relevant responses based on a combination of reasoning and background knowledge. Note

that this ability is an example of being able to overcome limitations of functional fixedness and mental set.

In addition, creativity tests may also require a person to apply convergent thinking in order to select the most appropriate solution from the set of possible solutions that were generated. For example, a subject may be asked to suggest a specific solution to a concretely specified problem. Being able to produce many possible solutions is only half the battle; one must also be able to apply logic and reasoning to determine the best solution. For example, there may be many routes to the top of a mountain, but only one is the easiest to climb.

Other types of creativity test items involve producing a number of different endings for a fable, suggesting improvements for products, and providing as many meanings as possible for ambiguous words (for example duck = animal, movement, food, and so on). Another type of item is convergent and involves remote associations between words in a set. For instance, what single word is related to the words "rat," "blue," and "cottage"? Try "cheese." What about "square root," "kitchen," and "coffee"? ("table").

Creativity and intelligence are related, but not in a simple way. Up to a certain level of intelligence (IQ of about 110) there is a positive correlation between intelligence and creativity. At higher intelligence levels there is little or no relationship: a person of extremely high intelligence (140, say) may not be very creative, while someone of lower intelligence (115, say) may be highly creative. Thus, a certain level of intelligence is required for a person to be highly creative, but high intelligence does not guarantee creativity.

SUMMARY

1. Cognitive processes refer to the activities you do in your head — complex mental operations that go on between stimulus presentation and overt response.

2. Several different theories of cognition have been proposed: motor and mediational theory are based on stimulus-response concepts; Gestalt theory focuses on perceiving relationships among problem elements; hypothesis theory views human beings as generators and testers of hypotheses; information-processing theory is heavily based on the analogy between human beings and computers.

3. Problem-solving research has been dominated by the Gestalt theory and by the information-processing theory. Gestalt psychologists have stressed the concepts of functional fixedness, mental set, and insight, all three of which relate to perceiving problem elements from a new perspective. Information-processing theory stresses analysis of problem-solving behavior into stages and processes. It

emphasizes the strategies that human beings use to solve problems, including means-ends analysis, planning, and other heuristics and algorithms.

4. A concept can be thought of as the basic unit of knowledge because it organizes many objects or events into a single category. Logical concepts are well defined and based on an explicit rule. Natural concepts are more difficult to define and tend to have fuzzy boundaries.

5. Learning a concept involves two aspects — learning the relevant features or attributes and learning the rule that relates these attributes.

6. Reasoning is the process of analyzing arguments and reaching conclusions, and formal logic is typically used as a criterion of proper reasoning. People usually are not perfectly logical but follow a kind of natural or personal logic that sometimes leads to correct conclusions but often results in systematic errors.

7. Two characteristics of natural reasoning are the failure to consider all possible interpretations of a premise and a tendency to seek confirmation of arguments rather than to determine if the argument can be proved false.

8. Intelligence is pure cognitive ability and, as such, relates to all of the concepts we have discussed in Chapters 5 and 6. Although it is often thought to be a general cognitive ability, research shows that a number of distinct abilities are involved.

9. Studies of nonhuman and artificial intelligence have helped to clarify the nature of human intelligence.

10. There are many different tests of intelligence, the two most popular being the Wechsler tests and the Stanford-Binet. The scores on these tests are converted to an intelligence quotient (IQ) by comparing them to the scores of other individuals of the same age.

11. Creativity is used to describe the behavior of coming up with an original, practical answer or solution to a problem. Intelligence does not guarantee creativity, although the two are correlated.

RECOMMENDED ADDITIONAL READINGS

Anderson, J. *Cognitive psychology and its implications.* San Francisco: W. H. Freeman, 1980.

Bourne, L. E., Jr., Dominowski, R. L., & Loftus, E. F. *Cognitive processes.* Englewood Cliffs, N.J.: Prentice-Hall, 1979.

Cronbach, L. J. *Essentials of psychological testing,* 3d ed. New York: Harper & Row, 1970.

Mayer, R. E. *Thinking and problem solving.* Glenview, Ill.: Scott, Foresman, 1977.

What Does It Mean?

Various attempts have been made to explain human cognitive processes. Although we do not fully understand these processes, present knowledge suggests some applications to real human behavior.

Teaching Mathematics

A great deal of human energy has been expended trying to teach or to learn mathematics. Many people approach mathematics with considerable anxiety and view mathematical problems as insurmountable obstacles. A resounding cheer from many quarters would no doubt be heard if the ideal method of teaching mathematics were discovered. However, research on mathematics instruction suggests that the matter is not a simple one. Instead of a single method being better or worse than another, researchers have found that different instructional methods result in different *kinds* of knowledge. One kind of knowledge might be better for some purposes but worse for others.

In a study of college students, Richard Mayer and James Greeno compared two different instructional techniques. The instructional goal was to learn to use a mathematical formula that allows computation of answers to certain kinds of problems. The formula itself might seem complex to most people:

$$P(X = r/N) = \frac{N}{r} p^r (1 - p)^{N-r}$$

The two kinds of instruction were called formula training and general training.

Roughly, formula training was like a step-by-step drill in using the formula to compute answers. Instruction began with presentation of the formula, followed by identification of its terms and instruction on how to compute different parts of the answer and combine them into a final, numerical solution. In contrast, students receiving general training did not even see the entire formula until the end of instruction. With general training, emphasis was given to relating the terms in the formula to concepts that the students presumably already knew. Explanations were given of terms like "trial," "outcome," "event," and "probability," with gradual introduction of different concepts until the whole formula had been covered.

To compare the training techniques, different kinds of test problems were given after instruction. The general finding was that formula-trained students did better on some problems while generally trained students did better on others. "Familiar" test problems were just like those included in instruction and required straightforward use of the formula to compute an answer. Formula-trained students performed better on familiar problems and on test problems that were slightly different from those encountered in training. However, if the test problem required recognizing that the formula could *not* be used to arrive at a numerical solution (because "impossible" numbers or insufficient information was provided), or if questions were asked about the formula ("Can *r* be greater than *N*?"), students who had received general training were the better performers.

An important point made by the researchers is that asking whether one instructional method is better or worse than another is too simple an approach. It is not enough to ask how much a student has learned—we also need to know *what* a student has learned. The findings suggest that a teacher, in choosing a method of instruction, ought to consider carefully what the students will be required to do when instruction is over.

These findings provoke a number of interesting, related questions. Will students who receive both kinds of training be the best performers on all kinds of problems? If combined training is given, should formula training come first, or should general training precede formula training? Do some students profit more from one training scheme while others are best served by a different method of instruction? Is it possible to identify types of students ahead of time so that the most appropriate training method can then be given? These are important questions with potential application to educational practice. Research continues on these questions, although clear answers are not yet available. Research on mathematics instruction is also related to a broader issue. The findings suggest that different forms of instruction result in different forms of knowledge. Researchers are trying to understand what is meant by "different forms of knowledge." Such endeavors are related to the large and difficult question, What does it mean to know something?

Applications of Artificial Intelligence

With the development of sophisticated computer systems, scientists sought to create computer programs that could perform the kinds of complex activities that human beings are capable of. In fact, it was hoped that computers could be programmed to be more efficient and accurate at these tasks than people are.

Chess

Chess-playing programs have been developed over the last 30 years in an effort to achieve a product capable of defeating any human player. While this goal has not yet been reached, computers are capable of being programmed to play competitively at tournament levels. How has this been accomplished?

Playing chess consists of considering a number of possible moves, evaluating these alternatives by some form of analysis, and choosing the preferred move on the basis of the evaluations. The approach to evaluating moves is one of forward search. One must explore the possible continua-

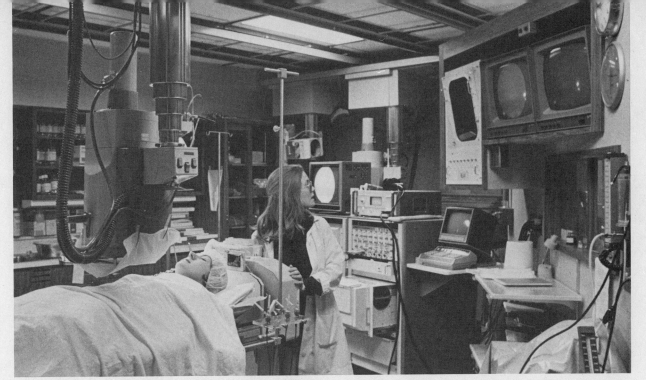

Modern-day electronic computers can be used not only in the diagnosis of human illness but also in its treatment.

tions of the game to a certain depth. It is not possible, however, to explore continuations to the endpoint of the game. Newell and Simon point out that there are about 10^{120} continuations to be explored and much less than 10^{20} nanoseconds available in a century in which to do the exploring. Even the fastest of current computers would be able to discover only a small fraction of the possibilities. Therefore, only move sequences of limited length can be explored. The resulting endpoints must be evaluated in terms of likelihood of leading to success in winning the game. These evaluations involve heuristics like means-ends analysis. Because the computer's powers are not sufficient to encompass the full scope of possible moves, chess programs must rely on the same sorts of heuristics that people typically use.

One characteristic of human chess play that is lacking in most chess programs is reliance on a plan of play throughout a game. Chess programs ordinarily operate on the basis of selecting the best possible move from a particular board configuration. On the next turn, the program will begin again and derive the best move based on the configuration resulting from the opponent's move. In this way, the program's game is built from a series of independent moves rather than from a general plan. Future programs might be more successful if they incorporated the ability to build general plans to guide a series of moves.

A number of lessons can be learned from work on chess programs. The development of a computer system to handle a complex human task cannot always use straightforward algorithms in a brute force manner. On many occasions even the computer's power is not sufficient to encompass completely all possible solutions to a problem. Instead, it is often necessary to endow the system with capabilities similar to those of human beings who successfully accomplish the type of task that a program is being written to handle. In doing so, we learn more about how the task can be approached and, perhaps more important, we learn more about how people go about performing the task.

Medical Diagnosis

Artificial intelligence has also been applied in the field of medicine. The problem of diagnosing a patient's ailment is complex and involves a number of sophisticated heuristics incorporating information about symptoms, diagnostic tests, treatment, and prognosis. Diagnosis can be aided by artificial intelligence programs capable of evaluating much of the myriad of information that doctors would have to deal with. The primary function of the program in this instance is to *assist* the doctor in interpreting the vast array of data on a patient so that a diagnosis can be made that is sensitive to all aspects of the patient's condition.

Story Generation

Some work has focused on developing an artificial intelligence program that is capable of making up children's stories. A computer program called TALESPIN developed by Jim Meehan creates stories based on characters (Joe Bear, Wilma Canary) and miscellaneous props (berries, a worm). An important part of the story-generation process is the program's "knowledge" of the goals of the characters (for example, Joe Bear wants to find some berries to eat) and their plans to reach those goals (bribe Wilma Canary with a worm to get her to tell where some berries are). While the stories that have been produced are restricted to rather simple domains, the program can generate some amusing tales (see Figure 6–16).

FIGURE 6-16 Edited version of a story generated by TALESPIN

(After Joe Bear has given Wilma Canary the worm as a bribe, the program produces the following):

WILMA CANARY EATS THE WORM. THE WORM IS GONE. WILMA CANARY IS NOT VERY HUNGRY. WILMA CANARY TELLS JOE BEAR THAT JOE BEAR IS NOT AT ALL SMART. JOE BEAR LIKES WILMA CANARY NOT AT ALL. JOE BEAR STRIKES WILMA CANARY. WILMA CANARY IS NOT AT ALL HEALTHY. WILMA CANARY WON'T TELL JOE BEAR WHERE SOME BERRIES ARE. JOE BEAR DIDN'T FIND OUT WHERE SOME BERRIES ARE. THE END

Applying Heuristics

Many everyday problems can be solved by applying heuristics such as means-ends analysis, planning, and working backwards. In the process of applying to law school or graduate school, a student uses both means-end analysis and planning. For example, both schools require the applicant to take standardized tests, part of which involve verbal ability. In order to enter the desired school, the student must do well on the test. Reaching the subgoal of doing well on the test involves having high verbal ability. The student who feels that he or she does not have such ability would be wise to correct the situation (that is, reduce the difference between current ability and desired ability). Therefore, the student might embark on a vocabulary-building program and practice timed reading and question

Helping America Catch Up in Thinking Arena
By JOSEPH SELDNER

Michael Gleeson enjoys using analogies when describing his work.

Gleeson, 33, is the director of the Edward deBono School of Thinking, a rather highfalutin name for a place that teaches what Gleeson says is really a very basic skill we all have but few of us fully develop.

He is a colleague and devotee of Edward deBono, director of the Center for the Study of Thinking Skills in Cambridge, England, and creator of the concept of "lateral thinking."

At the heart of lateral thinking, and therefore at the heart of the deBono School, is the notion that people react first and think second in solving problems. Initially, we feel emotionally about a situation and only later do we come up with thoughts or theories to support our first reaction.

The deBono method, Gleeson says, is like learning karate—in a fight, the karate expert doesn't flail around, reacting with fear or anger, he simply implements his skills to emerge from the predicament. . . .

The method is officially called CoRT—Cognitive Research Trust. Far from being a cultlike group designed to train people to think a particular way, CoRT instructors "don't tell anybody what to think," according to Gleeson.

Thinking is the "most important human skill and almost nothing is done

about it," Gleeson said.

People rarely consider long-term consequences when solving a problem; they rarely look at all available options or evaluate all factors needed to make an intelligent decision, Gleeson said.

Through CoRT, people are "trained" to be detached from emotional concerns when facing a problem. The whole CoRT training takes 60 hours, usually broken into six 10-hour sessions during weekends like the one planned here.

Lesson No. 1 is called PMI: Plus, Minus and Interesting. Find a problem, make one up. Think about as many plus factors as possible, as many minus factors and as many factors which, though not necessarily positive or negative, are at least interesting parts of the problem at hand.

By using the PMI, Gleeson said, a group of businesswomen in Toronto went within minutes from all agreeing with a proposition that women should be paid 15 percent more than men to almost unanimously disagreeing with the idea. Given the chance to look at all the Ps, Ms and Is, women who at first thought the higher pay would make up for past inequities concluded that employers would rather hire men than pay the additional salary to women.

But deBono training isn't designed to change anyone's mind, only expose the breadth of solutions to a problem.

Intelligent people, strangely enough, often have more trouble in the training than less intelligent people because smart folks tend to use their thinking to back up, rather than rethink, their points of view, Gleeson said.

The bold plan of Gleeson and his American cohorts is to train a legion of deBono instructors, as many as 250,000 nationwide, 10,000 in the Rocky Mountain area, to introduce CoRT to the masses. Based in New York, the deBono School is in business in Boston, Atlanta, Washington, Los Angeles and Santa Barbara, Calif., as well as Denver.

Gleeson and deBono are adamant about America "catching up" with other nations in the thinking arena. Venezuela, for example, regards thinking as a legitimate skill to be taught to children and practiced through adulthood, and CoRT is widely taught there. Indeed, Venezuela has named a Minister of State for the Development of Human Intelligence who has implemented a "Learn to Think" program at the grade-school level based on deBono's theories.

In the end, the deBono-schooled person worries less and takes pride in being a thinker. "Worry is the absence of thinking," Gleeson said.

Rocky Mountain News, Denver
March 28, 1981

One application of the research on cognitive processes is in training people to think and be creative. Here's an example of one such training program that seems to be helping some people. Can you think of some exercises that might be used to train people to think more effectively?

answering in order to do well on the reading comprehension portion of the test. In addition, the student must have an adequate background of courses in order to enter graduate school in a specific field. Consequently, to prepare for the appropriate specialty, the student must develop a program of study. These are examples of planning the steps involved in reaching a goal (entering law or graduate school) and in devising ways of reducing differences between the current state and the various subgoal states (improving verbal ability).

One can also use the heuristic of working backwards in this process to determine such things as the kinds of knowledge and skills that would be required to be a successful lawyer or college professor. First, one would consider what a lawyer or a professor must do in order to be successful. Given that certain skills are associated with success, one can take one more step back to determine how to develop those skills, and so on. Working backwards is a useful heuristic in cases where the final goal state is clearly specified. That is why, for example, the technique is widely used in developing mathematical proofs. The statement to be proved is clearly specified. Proving theorems in geometry and logic relies heavily on this heuristic.

It is important to rank one's goals according to priorities if the problem is too complex to solve at a glance. For example, developing your schedule of courses for a particular term might produce a number of complicated problems. Suppose you want your Friday afternoons to be

characterize schizophrenic speech, we would say that the speaker seems to have an inability to exclude from a thought sequence (and its actual utterance) material that is associatively related to the major theme of the thought—but is irrelevant to it.

A helpful example cited by Brendan Maher is illustrated below. The thought apparently intended by this speaker is interrupted by intrusions of associations to a word that occurs at the end of a syntactic or semantic unit within the sentence. The resulting juxtaposition of relevant and irrelevant information makes the utterance seem strange and nonsensical to a normal listener. Occasionally, when one set of meanings intrudes into a thought sequence that is built around another set of meanings, the effect is an unwittingly produced pun (*example:* "I have many ties with my home. My father wears them around his collar.")

Recent theories of semantic memory in which activation spreads among concepts that are associatively related provide a framework for understanding such a phenomenon. In normal processing, context limits and clarifies the meaning of sentences within connected discourse. Thus, when we hear the sentence "Marsha bought some beautiful new glasses" before hearing the sentence "The spectacles fit well," we understand it differently than if we had heard the sentence "When she got home, she filled them with water." In each case, comprehension of the sentence relationships depends on activating that portion of the conceptual network which gives rise to the meaning of

---

Thought: "I have pains in my chest and wonder if there is something wrong with my heart."

	ache	ribs box	right	beat
Associates:	doctor	lungs trunk	bad	soul→save
	body	body hope	failure	broken heaven

Actual utterance: "Doctor, I have pains in my chest and hope and wonder if my box is broken and heart is beaten for my soul and salvation and heaven, Amen."

---

completely free. Obviously, you avoid courses that meet during these hours. But during registration you discover that one of the Tuesday and Thursday courses necessary to carry out your plan is full. You pick another course which also meets on Tuesdays and Thursdays, only to discover later that this substitute course is not required for the graduate school you are aiming for. Having the superordinate goal of graduate school in mind would have prevented an inappropriate attempt at a solution.

The Cognitive Basis of Mental Illness

As we begin to understand more about cognitive psychology and the underpinnings of thought, we may find that we have concepts that are fundamental to understanding other more applied domains, such as mental illness. Perhaps the most striking example of the emerging relationship between cognitive psychology and clinical psychology may be seen in the theories directed at understanding thought and language disorders in schizophrenia. If we were to broadly

"glasses" that is relevant to the second sentence, if it is to be integrated with the first. For the schizophrenic, many irrelevant associations seem to be simultaneously activated, compete with one another, and consequently intrude into the thought or speech process.

Recent studies of schizophrenic verbal and communication processes show that these problems arise from three basic sources. Schizophrenic patients appear to be more distractible and less selective in their attention than normals. They also seem to have difficulty holding information in short-term memory. Finally, they are likely to exhibit disorganized long-term memory structures. How these factors combine is not well understood, but they clearly can contribute to the speech type illustrated by Maher.

Birth Order

Intuitively it seems likely that birth order affects personality and intellectual development. In many ways, the oldest child has the most difficult time, especially early in life. It is more difficult for him or her to pass through the birth canal; the mother is more likely to have long labor; there is usually greater head impression during birth; the first-born is less likely to survive childbirth; and he or she weighs less at birth than later-born children. But two or three years later, the first-born tends to weigh more and to be taller than later-born children at the same age. The initial physical growth of the first-born is probably due to the fact that the parents have no one else to care for and thus provide more intensive nurturance. Differences in size tend to disappear by adulthood, because eating at later stages of development is determined much less by parental attention.

Psychologists have studied possible relationships between birth order and personality but have found them very difficult to verify. None of these relationships is especially strong, and questions have been raised about the identification of all the factors contributing to them. Yet no one would wish to imply that birth order is completely irrelevant to any aspect of human development. Rather, it is probably the case that there are *so many* other factors involved that simple generalizations are not possible (see Chapter 8).

Consider a recent analysis of intelligence by Robert B. Zajonc. Using data on intelligence from a study of close to 400,000 Dutch children, Zajonc developed a model for describing birth-order effects on intelligence. First, the overall data did show a birth-order effect. The first-born child is in general slightly more intelligent than the second-born, the second-born is slightly more intelligent than the third, and so on down the line. But the data also show clearly that overall family size is a factor in this relationship. The larger the family, the lower the intellectual ability for all the children. Thus, the first-born in a family of two is likely to be brighter than the first-born in a family of three. Also, the first-born in a very large family, say, nine children, is likely to be *less* intelligent than the second-, third-, or fourth-born in a family of only four children. Thus first-borns can be *less* bright than fourth-borns *when* the family sizes differ.

Zajonc's data also showed that these effects of birth order and family size on IQ depend also upon the spacing between children, such that the closer together the children come, the lower their intelligence tends to be. Thus, a third-born child in a family of three could conceivably be more intelligent than the second-born in some other family of three if the first family spread their children over 10 years and the second family had three children in three years. One final thing Zajonc discovered was that the last-born child in a family tended to be lower in intelligence than would be predicted from factors of family size and spacing. He suggests that this is because the last child does not get the benefit of the intellectual challenge of teaching younger brothers and sisters.

What might account for these birth-order effects? Let's assume that the effect is environmentally determined and not genetic—a first-born child is a first-born, irrespective of whether other siblings follow. There is nothing in the genes of a particular first-born that mark the individual as occurring in a family-to-be of two, four, or nine. Yet according to Zajonc's data, some first-borns from very large families are not as intelligent as second- or third-born children from small families. Thus, it may not be that birth order *per se* is responsible for a child's IQ, but that the

Firstborn Fallacies

ATLANTA — Oldest may not be smartest after all. When several studies in the past decade found that the average IQ of firstborn children is higher than that of other children, it was widely assumed that firstborns enjoy an inherent intellectual advantage, perhaps because they receive extra attention from parents and are responsible for tutoring their brothers and sisters. But a new study by an Emory University sociologist disputes this popular notion.

John Doby argues that previous researchers ignored important socioeconomic variables by looking at large samples of children classed according to birth order. Because parents of big families tend to be less educated than parents of small families, Doby believes that the samples of younger siblings—those born fourth or fifth in line, for example—contained a disproportionate number of children growing up in culturally deprived homes.

To get around this problem, Doby looked at IQs of children within individual families. When he compared brothers and sisters with one another, he found no significant pattern of IQ differences. "The alleged effects of birth order on intelligence and educational achievement do not exist, or exist only slightly," concludes Doby after testing 3,500 children.

The only child traditionally has been an anomaly in studies, behaving more like a less accomplished lastborn than an achieving firstborn. But the image of the only child as spoiled and inferior intellectually has also been discredited in a new study. Social scientists at the American Institute of Research in Palo Alto, California, say that an only child is more likely than other children to live in a one-parent home, and that this disadvantage—not the lack of siblings—accounts for past findings.

When the researchers compared one-child and two-child families in homes with both parents present, the typical only child fared better than a child with a brother or sister. The only child scored higher on intelligence tests, did better academically, and was judged "more cultured, mature, socially sensitive, and tidy."

Science 80
December 1980

amount of attention devoted to the children of a small family and the amount of interaction with their parents may be higher, positively influencing IQ. In contrast, each child in a large family presumably interacts less with his or her parents, thereby enjoying less intellectual challenge or stimulation. Thus, number of parent-to-child contact hours may be as good a predictor of IQ as birth order.

Of course, there are many other factors in determining intelligence besides birth order, family size, and spacing of children. Furthermore, the data on the effects of birth order on IQ are not completely clear (see the newsclip "Firstborn Fallacies"). But Zajonc's analyses suggest the following for people who want to maximize the intelligence of their children: (1) keep the size of the family small—two children is best; (2) plan the family so that there are several years between children; and (3) try to find other younger children in the neighborhood for the last child to teach.

Improving Creativity

People have attempted to stimulate creativity in a number of ways. Some rock musicians and artists, for example, believe that creativity can be stimulated through certain types of drugs. In other professions creativity is assisted through response to free-form environments. The *think tank* environment of a California toy company allows toy designers a free hand in producing innovations. The designers are successful because they are able to use the seemingly disorganized and unrestricted environment to their advantage— to stimulate new ideas. In addition, they have the skills and self-discipline necessary to operate in a convergent manner, rejecting ideas that will not be useful and determining exactly how to make the best ideas into a reality. *Brainstorming* is another method of producing new ideas. An individual can use the suggestions of others in the group to trigger new ways of looking at a problem (an important step in *divergent* production and overcoming mental set and functional fixedness). In order for the system to work, however, the group members must be willing to generate and to hear very bizarre ideas, and must also have the convergent production ability necessary to recognize and select a reasonable and workable alternative from among all those suggested.

Intelligence, Heredity, and Environment

The question of whether intelligence is determined by heredity or environment has provoked considerable public interest and controversy. In recent years, this issue has resulted in heated arguments, social protests, and legal action, stimulated by Arthur Jensen's suggestion that racial differences in measured intelligence *might* be due to genetic differences and William Shockley's suggestion that some means ought to be sought to decrease child-bearing by people with low intelligence. Many commentators have observed that the issues have produced more heat than light, that people have adopted hard positions on the basis of emotions, politics, and religion, and that sensible discussion of the questions is almost impossible. We cannot possibly present a thorough discussion of these questions. The issues are tremendously complex—many books have been written on these questions without achieving a resolution. What we can do is provide a general understanding of the issues involved.

First, the heredity versus environment issue is not meaningful when applied to any particular person. It really doesn't make sense to wonder "Is my intelligence due to my heredity or my environment?" An individual is the simultaneous product of both genetic endowment and experience: both are necessary and intertwined. If you had no genetic makeup, you wouldn't exist; similarly, you can't exist without being in an environment and having experiences. What this means is that the heredity versus environ-

IQ Tests Discriminatory

BURLINGTON, Vt. (UPI) — The country-bred child who says a litter is something a sow produces—not something thrown on the street—may be paying a penalty for his special knowledge.

George Albee, a nationally known specialist in intelligence testing, says IQ tests have an urban bias—leaving rural children at a disadvantage when they are tested.

"A city child has no problem answering a question about what a subway is. A rural child can tell you all about tractors, but he doesn't know about subways," says Albee, a University of Vermont psychology professor. "The problem is, the IQ tests have been standardized on middle-class urban children," he says.

"That means the tests tend to discriminate, by the kinds of questions they ask, against poor children and children from rural areas," he says.

Albee came to his conclusions about the problems faced by rural children as the result of his work on the ways IQ tests discriminate against black children.

Last year, he was a key witness on behalf of black California children who had been placed in classes for the mentally retarded as a result of intelligence testing.

In October, the judge in the so-called "Larry P." case ordered California to stop using the tests and to re-evaluate all black youngsters in classes for the retarded, a decision hailed by psychologists opposed to the use of IQ tests.

"These kids were what we call the 'six-hour retarded child,'" Albee said.

"Outside school, they were perfectly adaptable. They could all ride buses and find their way home and tell you the batting average of every player on the San Francisco Giants.

"They were only retarded by the standards set in the IQ tests," he said.

According to Albee, white rural children face some of the same problems as the California students.

Not only do the kinds of questions asked on the tests tend to reflect an urban bias, but rural children have been brought up in ways that make IQ tests difficult for them.

Since most IQ tests revolve around knowledge of words, Albee says the children who do best "are middle class kids from homes where there is a lot of verbalization."

Many country children, for example, miss the early experience of teachers and group story telling that are offered in day care centers and nursery schools.

Albee said studies have shown children with a nursery school experience do better on later IQ tests.

Boulder (Colo.) Daily Camera
March 6, 1980

"B.C." by permission of Johnny Hart and Field Enterprises, Inc.

ment question has meaning only when applied to differences among people, and some would argue that the question makes no sense even in this case.

The fundamental observation is that individuals differ in terms of their scores on IQ tests. Why? It has long been recognized that there is no absolute answer to this question. To what extent are differences in intelligence due to differences in heredity, and to what extent are differences in intelligence due to differences in environment (experience)? There is in fact no generally acceptable answer at present.

Heredity and Environment, But Not Race, Found to Influence Intelligence
By CHERYL M. FIELDS

Recent studies of the IQ levels and school achievement scores of black and white adopted children indicate that both genetic background and family environment—but not race—have substantial impact on intellectual performance.

This latest chapter in the continuing, explosive controversy over what effects genes, environment, and race have on people's levels of intelligence was reported by Sandra Scarr, professor of psychology at Yale University, at the annual convention of the American Psychological Association here.

Following two adoption studies and other research while she was a professor of child development at the University of Minnesota, Ms. Scarr concluded that "the tests I have been able to make indicate that there are no substantial genetic differences between U.S. blacks and whites in IQ, personality, or any other behavior."

Adopted Children Scored Well
In the adoption research, Ms. Scarr found that in one study of black and mixed-race children adopted by 101 white, working-class-to-upper-middle-class families, the adopted children averaged 110 on IQ tests, well above the average of 90 generally scored by black children in the North Central United States.

School achievement scores provided by the children's school districts, which were scattered throughout Minnesota, also showed that in vocabulary, reading, and mathematics, the adopted children not only scored above the average scores of black and interracial children in the state's public schools, but "were scoring above the national average for white children," Ms. Scarr said.

Such above-average performance is consistent, she said, with the fact that by their desire to adopt children and by meeting the various criteria required by adoption agencies, the adoptive families "are a better-than-average" group in terms of parental IQ, income, education, occupational standing, and desire to rear children.

The lack of a racial explanation for the usual 10- to 15-point difference between blacks' and whites' performance on IQ tests also was demonstrated, she indicated, by a study of 104 white families who adopted white children. These adopted children, who were 16 to 22 years old when tested, had average IQ scores of 106—very close to the 110 scored by the adopted black children, whose average age was 7.

Parents Had Average IQ's

Data available from the state public-welfare department and adoption agencies indicated that the natural parents of the adopted children in both studies had average IQ's and levels of education, Ms. Scarr said. For example, the average IQ of the natural mothers of the white adoptees was predicted to be about 100, she said.

"We concluded that adoptive family environments have increased the scores of genotypically average groups by 5 to 15 points," she said.

"Being reared in the culture of the tests and the schools resulted in intellectual achievement for black and interracial children comparable to adopted white children in comparable families. Therefore it is highly unlikely that genetic differences between the races could account for the major portion of the usually observed difference in performance levels between black and white groups," Ms. Scarr said.

Another study, scheduled to be published in the journal *Human Genetics* also revealed no racially based difference in intelligence, Ms. Scarr said. The study used blood groups to estimate the proportion of African and white ancestry in a group of blacks, with the estimates

Much of the controversy revolves around the concept of heritability. Roughly, heritability is the extent to which differences in some measured trait are due to differences in genetic make-up. If individual differences in the characteristic are totally due to genetic differences, heritability is 100 percent; if differences in the characteristic have nothing to do with genetic differences, heritability would be 0 percent. Values between 0 and 100 percent indicate varying levels of relationship between the particular trait and genetic structure.

The basic evidence suggesting that intelligence has high heritability is the finding that similarity of IQ is strongly related to similarity in genetic make-up. For example, identical twins are more genetically similar to each other than fraternal twins; and, sure enough, the IQ scores of identical twins are more similar than the IQ scores of fraternal twins. This type of evidence has led some people to conclude that 70 to 80 percent of the differences in intelligence can be explained on the basis of heredity. You may be surprised to learn that other researchers examining basically the same evidence have estimated the heritability of

intelligence at 45 percent or 25 percent or even 0 percent.

How can such different claims be made on the basis of the same data? For one thing, different researchers have used different methods to calculate heritability. Methods for calculating heritability estimates were developed to analyze results from breeding experiments with plants and animals (to help in determining how much a characteristic could be developed by selective breeding). The conditions of such experiments typically involved randomly (unsystematically) assigning plants or animals with known genetic differences to different environments. One problem with applying heritability estimates to individual differences in IQ scores is that people are *not* randomly assigned to different environmental conditions. In brief, the conditions of ordinary human affairs do not result in genetic differences being independent of (unrelated to) the kinds of environments people live in.

A second problem is that the data on similarity of IQs among people of varying genetic similarity are not particularly reliable. If you think about it, finding identical twins, or identical twins reared separately, or aunts and nieces in order to measure their IQs is rather difficult. Consequently,

Heredity and Environment (continued)

based on frequency and concentrations of various blood components.

Not the "Ultimate Human Value"
The study showed, she said, "that having more or less African ancestry was not related to how well one scored on cognitive tests. . . . Blacks with greater amounts of white ancestry did not score better than other blacks with more African ancestry."

In publishing their adoption studies, Ms. Scarr and a fellow researcher, Richard A. Weinberg, another University of Minnesota psychologist, cautioned that by using IQ scores they did not intend to endorse them "as the ultimate human value. Although important for functioning in middle-class educational environments, IQ tests do not sample a huge spectrum of human characteristics that are requisite for social adjustment. Empathy, sociability, and altruism, to name a few, are important human attributes that are not guaranteed by a high IQ. Furthermore, successful adaptation within ethnic subgroups may be less dependent on the intellectual skills tapped by IQ measures than is adaptation in middle-class white settings."

Although a strong environmental influence on intellectual performance, and no racial influence, would not be

considered controversial findings by many psychologists, Ms. Scarr also reached what is probably a more controversial set of conclusions about the importance of genetics in intelligence.

In the cross-racial study, the adoptive parents also had 145 of their own, biological offspring. In the study of adolescents, the 104 adoptive families were compared with a control group of 120 non-adoptive families with children of similar ages.

The genetic impact on intelligence was shown, Ms. Scarr indicated, when the researchers tried to account for the variance in IQ scores of the adopted children—that is, why did one child score 90 and another 120? Although the adopted groups averaged IQ scores of 110 and 106, the actual scores ranged from about 75 to 150.

Complex Statistical Analyses
Essentially, the researchers found that the most "advantaged" families in terms of parental IQ's, income, education, and other indicators, did not necessarily produce the adopted children with the highest IQ's. . . .

In the cross-racial study, Ms. Scarr similarly found that in the families with both biological and adopted children, information about education, IQ, and

occupation of the parents "predicts about twice as much of the variance [in children's IQ's] if they are biologically related," than if they are adopted.

From these and other analysis, Ms. Scarr said, "it seems evident to us that the study of adoptive and biological families provides extensive support for the idea that half . . . or even more, of the long-term effect of what we call family background on children's intellectual attainment depends upon genetics, not environmental transmission."

The results, she added, suggest "that within a range of 'humane environments' from a socioeconomic level of working to upper-middle class, there is little evidence for differential environmental effects" on intelligence.

Studies such as hers should permit "behavioral scientists and policy makers to sort out the important from unimportant differences in people's environments," she said. Further, such studies should lead psychologists and others to avoid pressuring everyone to follow the child-rearing practices of "the professional class," she said, when "it has not been demonstrated that variations in child-rearing practices are functionally different in their effects."

Chronicle of Higher Education
September 12, 1977

the question arises as to how representative of "people in general" are those people who do participate in research on intelligence. Furthermore, the variability in findings from study to study is greater than some reports suggest. Leon Kamin has delivered the most severe criticisms of the reliability of the findings in his book *The Science and Politics of I.Q.* (1974), arguing that the available data are not trustworthy enough to justify analyses of heritability.

Even if investigators did agree about the reliability of the evidence, problems of interpretation would remain. For example, it has generally been found that identical (one-egg) twins are more similar in IQ than are fraternal (two-egg) twins. Since identical twins are genetically more like each other than are fraternal twins, this finding is consistent with the idea that intelligence has high heritability. However, it can and has been argued that identical twins have much more similar experiences than fraternal twins. If so, the "fact" that identical twins have more similar IQs could result from their greater genetic similarity, or their greater similarity of experience, or both factors in some unknown fashion. Investigators have not yet satisfactorily disentangled genetic similarity from similarity of experiences.

Heritability estimates have also been misinterpreted in some instances; occasionally, people have reached conclusions that do not necessarily follow, given a finding of high heritability. For example, people tend to believe that if intelligence has high heritability, this means that an individual's intelligence is "fixed," and little or nothing can be done about it. This belief is incorrect. High heritability means that for a particular population of individuals in a particular set of circumstances at a particular point in time, individual differences in some trait (like IQ) are largely due to differences in genetic make-up. Finding high heritability in one population, situation, and time does *not* mean that differences in IQ in other populations, other situations, or other points in time must also be largely due to genetic differences. Furthermore, high heritability does *not* mean that a trait cannot be changed by altering the environment. To understand these issues, let us consider some hypothetical studies with plants.

Imagine that we plant seeds of different genetic make-up in exactly the same environmental conditions and later measure the heights of the plants. Since every plant would have exactly the same environment, any and all differences in height would be due to differences in genetic make-up; heritability would be 100 percent. Now imagine that in another experiment we plant seeds of identical genetic make-up in different environments. Under these circumstances, since all plants would be genetically identical, any and all differences in plant height would be due to environmental differences; heritability would be 0 percent. As you can see, high heritability of a trait in one setting does not mean that high heritability must be found in other settings. Consider again the first setting—genetically different plants

all having the same environment. Clearly, all differences in plant heights are due to genetic differences. However, the actual heights of the plants will depend on whether or not we fertilize them. Whether we fertilize none of the plants or all of them equally, differences in height would be due to genetic differences. Of course, all the plants would probably be taller in the fertilized environment! Applied to intelligence, this means that even if individual differences in intelligence were entirely due to genetic differences, it would still be possible to make everyone more intelligent (on an absolute basis) by improving living conditions in an appropriate manner. Furthermore, if we improved the living conditions for only some of the individuals, thus eliminating the condition of identical environments, heritability would decrease!

The heredity-environment issue is complicated enough when only individual differences in intelligence are considered. The question becomes even more complicated and heated when racial differences in intelligence are discussed, particularly black-white differences. It is a statistical fact that, on the average, blacks in the United States score lower on IQ tests than do whites. Why is this the case? Several years ago the mere suggestion that the black-white differences in IQ *might* be due to genetic differences between blacks and whites touched off a ferocious controversy in scientific, social, and political circles. At the heart of the issue is the question of whether or not blacks and whites have had equivalent experiences relevant to performance on intelligence tests. Those favoring the explanation of the black-white difference in average IQ in terms of environmental factors have argued that intelligence tests are biased in favor of whites and that blacks have not been afforded equal exposure to test-relevant experiences. Resolving the question is difficult. At the present time there is no clear evidence that the black-white difference in average IQ is genetically determined. There is, however, clear evidence that blacks score higher on intelligence tests when their living conditions have improved.

We have barely scratched the surface of the heredity-environment question with regard to intelligence. You should now at least have some understanding of the issues involved and the problems encountered by researchers. More thorough treatments are provided in the books by Kamin and by Loehlin, Lindzey, and Spuhler listed in the Bibliography. The question of how much differences in IQ are due to genetic differences is very emotional; many people consider intelligence to be extremely important. People would hardly be aroused if it were reported that 75 percent of individual differences in fingernail length result from genetic differences. Intelligence somehow seems very special. Look again at the section on intelligence and contemplate how little we really know about what intelligence is. You may then appreciate why some scientists have suggested that issues concerning intelligence ought not to be so important.

7 Motivation and Emotion

Readers of the newspapers are routinely confronted with the following kinds of news items: (1) a couple decided not to let doctors administer insulin to their diabetic son, who subsequently went into a coma and died; (2) a city council-man was arrested for hit-and-run driving; (3) a young boy and his father designed an illegal car in order to win the Soapbox derby; (4) a religious group refused diphtheria inoculations after one of their members contracted the disease and died, leaving the whole group and possibly the state vulnerable to a diphtheria epidemic; (5) three young men were arrested for a "joy killing" of a four-year-old girl; (6) a college student was hospitalized after spending 4½ days in the shower in an abortive attempt to break the world's record (more than 7 days); and on and on it goes. Why do people do such things? Another way to state this question is, "What *motivates* people to behave like this?"

This chapter is about motivation. Motivation raises the question of *why* people behave as they do. This is in contrast to *how* they do it, which is usually a question about the person's knowledge, skill, and performance. In this chapter, we assume that people have the ability to act in certain ways, and ask why they do what they do. Motivation is one of the important answers we can give. We can assume that many teenage boys know how to drive a car and to shoot a shotgun. Why would three such youths use their knowledge and skills to murder a four-year-old girl playing in her front yard? What motivates such a brutal act? Indeed, what motivates common, every-day behaviors, such as playing games, reading novels, eating, and the like? Obviously, in order to understand behavior, we will have to answer questions like these.

Motivation as an Explanatory Concept

The Variability of Behavior

Different people behave differently in the same situation. At the same cocktail party, some people eat the available food and others don't. This is a difference in behavior *between* people. There is also variability *within* the same person. When you pass by a restaurant, sometimes you go in and eat and other times you don't. It is this variability in behavior, both between individuals and within the same person on different occasions, that psychologists seek to understand.

Circularity in Explanations

Consider a man who goes to a lot of cocktail parties. Suppose he eats lots of food at one party and nothing at the next. Motivation is an obvious way to account for the variability in his behavior. We postulate the existence of motivation for food and "explain" the behavioral variability by saying that the man was hungry on one occasion and not on the other. This explanation makes sense, but note the circular reasoning involved. The only way we had of knowing that the man was hungry on the first occasion was the fact that he ate some food — the very behavior we are trying to explain. It goes like this: He eats food. Why? Because he was hungry. How do you know he was hungry? Because he ate the food.

Motivational Constructs

To get around this circularity psychologists look for *independent* ways of defining motivation. Often this boils down to defining the strength of motivation as being the length of time since the person has been satisfied. In our example, the existence and degree of hunger is determined by the number of hours it has been since the man has eaten — the hours of food deprivation. So hunger is defined not by if and how much one eats (which would be circular), but by amount of deprivation. Now the reasoning is like this: He eats food. Why? Because he was hungry. How do you know he was hungry? Because it has been five hours since he has eaten any food.

Motivational constructs, such as hunger, are powerful explanatory devices because they can account for a wide variety of behaviors without having to have a new principle for each action we observe. People go shopping at grocery stores for food, work for food, steal money for food, beg for it, grow it in a backyard garden, stand in long cafeteria lines for it, kill animals for it, and so on. There are numerous different behaviors involved, all centering on food and all understood by introducing one concept, namely motivation for food, or hunger. Instead of having a separate explanation for each of these behaviors, we can use the concept of hunger to account for all or many of them.

Motivation Is Not the Only Explanation

Motivational constructs are used in psychology because they account for some of the variability in behavior. In this regard, motivational constructs are not different from other psychological principles. Take the concept of learning for example. We use it also to account for variability in behavior—Jane is a good bridge player and Harvey is a poor one because Jane has taken lessons and *learned* how to play. We are referring to acquired knowledge or skill. Consider another concept—heredity—Jane and Harvey differ in IQ, in part because they have different genetic backgrounds. Learning and heredity are two major concepts used to understand why people differ or vary in their behavior, but these two concepts cannot ac-

"The crew is in excellent health and seems to be suffering no ill effects, with the exception of Commander Fenwick, who reports that he is hornier than a hoot owl!"

Playboy, September 1969. Reproduced by special permission of PLAYBOY Magazine; copyright © 1969 by Playboy.

Commander Fenwick is suffering from a long period of sexual deprivation. Motives are often measured by the length of time since the person has engaged in the behavior that reduces the motive. In fact, motives are often defined by the fact that deprivation leads to increases in behavior designed to obtain the deprived object. For example, we infer the existence of a hunger motive because if we deprive people of food they will try harder and more often to get food.

Also note the variability—the other two astronauts are apparently not suffering. How would you account for the variability among these spacemen? Does Fenwick have a higher sex motive than the other two? Has he been deprived longer?

count for all the variability. Motivational principles fill in many of the remaining gaps in understanding.

How can we sort out the effects of motivation from those of learning and heredity? Consider the following example. Two rats that are known to have identical genetic make-ups (through extensive inbreeding; see Chapter 2) and identical life histories have learned to run down a straight alley to a goal box for food. These two rats might differ greatly in the speed with which they run down the alley. Further, once they get to the goal box they might differ in the length of time before they start eating or in the amount of food they eat. We see, then, that these two rats differ on three dependent variables—running speed, time to eat, and amount eaten. Why? The reason cannot be heredity or learning because we have used scientific techniques to equate the rats on these two important dimensions. But it could be motivation. Perhaps one rat was fed all the cheese it could eat just before being put in the alley, and the other had not eaten for 24 hours. The variability in all three dependent measures would then be understood in terms of variability in one factor: motivation, or hunger in this case.

Note that we could be sure that the rats were equal in learning experience and had identical genetic make-ups only because they had been raised in the laboratory, where these factors can be controlled. In studying human behavior, we can almost never be sure that two people have equivalent genetic make-ups or learning histories. It is difficult to tell why people behave differently and difficult to conclude with any confidence that differences in motivation are responsible for behavioral variability. In the general case, however, motivation is a critical aspect of behavior, although certainly only one of its basic parameters.

Basic Concepts

The concept of motivation has to do with behavior designed to achieve a goal. Consider a student who, while studying late at night, gets up from his desk and finds two friends. They walk across campus to the student-union building and order a pizza. Since this individual is like most other students in his biological make-up and in his knowledge of the world, we probably cannot explain his behavior in terms of heredity and learning. Rather, we are likely to conclude that he was motivated differently than others who did not go out for a pizza and motivated differently on this night than last night when he studied until bedtime.

Let's analyze this example thoroughly. We have the following components: (1) a behaving organism, (2) instrumental behavior displayed by that organism—getting up from the desk, convincing two others, walking, ordering the pizza, (3) a goal object—a pizza cooked and ready to eat, and (4) consummatory behavior—eating the pizza. These events are all observable. We can see the organism, see its instrumental behavior, see (or imagine) the goal object, and see the consummatory behavior.

To explain how these components fit together and make sense, psychologists typically will make some inferences about three unobservables: (1) need, (2) drive, and (3) incentive. One thing we cannot see is the organism's **need,** an internal biological state that requires correction.

A second unobservable is **drive.** Drive refers to the motivational push that is given to behavior as a result of the organism's being in or gradually developing a state of need. Usually drive refers to the energy level mobilized by the person as a result of being deprived of the goal object for a period of time. Deprivation creates the need for the goal object. If our student friend has not eaten for some time—let's say he skipped dinner because he was fascinated by the psychology book he was studying—a state of need for food (hunger) develops. Need level and drive level are obviously closely related concepts. But the correlation is not perfect, because at very high levels of need, such as when the person is literally starving for food, there may be a great drop off in the drive level or the energy available to behave.

The third unobservable motivational concept, **incentive,** focuses on the goal objects themselves and on the fact that not all goal objects are desired equally. Objects that people are motivated to attain are called goal objects or incentives. The motivating characteristic of a particular goal object relative to other objects in the same general class is called the incentive value of the object. Our student is hungry and is willing to walk across campus for a pizza, but how far would he have been willing to walk if the only food available was a bowl of watery soup? Both pizza and weak soup are food and could satisfy his need (hunger) perhaps equally well, but motivation is likely to be higher for pizza. Thus, pizza has a higher incentive value than watery soup.

Motivation is thus the joint effect of drive and incentive, where drive refers primarily to a state of the organism and incentive refers to characteristics of goal objects. Drive level is derived primarily from the organism's needs, which might be either cognitively based ("I want a Perrier") or biologically based ("I'm starving"). Incentive level refers to the attractiveness of the various goal objects (pizza versus soup). Drive relates to the internal state of the organism, whereas incentive refers to the external situation, to a characteristic of an external goal object. Motivation is the combined action of drives and incentives, the push and pull, and working together it accounts for much of the variability that characterizes human behavior.

In theorizing about the origin and nature of drives and incentives, three basic types of concepts are typically applied: (1) biological concepts, (2) social-personality concepts, and (3) cognitive concepts. These three concepts are apparent in the pizza example. Biological concepts have to do with the student's internal hunger state, the physiological consequences of food deprivation and pizza consumption. Social-personality concepts are concerned with such matters as why the student asked two friends to go with him and why they chose to walk all the way to the student union as opposed to having the pizza delivered. Cognitive concepts include why they chose pizza as opposed to hamburgers, why they walked instead of driving, and the price they were willing to pay for the pizza. In short, motivation cannot be fully understood without reference to the person's: (1) biological make-up, (2) personality and social context, and (3) thinking and knowledge of the world. Each of these concepts is examined in this chapter.

Motivation as a Pushing Force: Drives

The notion of drive is based heavily on an energy analogy. The basic idea originated in attempts to deal with an organism's innate, biological needs, such as the need for food, water, and sex. Deprivation of the needed substance is a critical variable. The longer it has been since an organism has had food, for example, the greater the organism's *need* for food. Our bodies presumably have a system for detecting this need; as the need gets greater, the body activates systems to satisfy the need. In the most popular theory of this type, drive consists of two parts: (1) the energizing part—the body mobilizes its resources to provide increased energy to the organism for purposes of obtaining the needed substance; and (2) the directive function—guiding the system to seek particular goal objects, in the case of hunger, food. The two parts are closely intertwined, of course; the first component activates behavior, making it more vigorous and persistent, while the second component directs the same behavior toward particular objects.

As hours of deprivation increase, the activity level of the organism—the energizing component—increases, although only up to a point. Continued deprivation of food, for example, eventually leads to symptoms of starvation and a decline in activity levels. In general, however, depriving the organism of a needed substance will result in increased activity, increased behavior, and increased persistence of the behavior. This increased vigor and persistence of activity leads to the conclusion that there is some type of energizing system that "fires us up" when we are in a state of need.

Evidence suggests that energizing is not an automatic process that takes place whenever we are deprived. Rather, energizing may take place only when cues or stimuli in the environment suggest that there is some hope of attaining the desired goal object. The increased activity in food-deprived laboratory rats occurs only in the presence of stimuli suggesting food to the rat. If completely isolated in the dark with no noises or smells, the rat is not active. But if the experimenter comes in, turns on the lights, shuffles through the feed bags, and so on, there is an instant increase in the activity level of the animal over normal levels when the rat is not deprived of food. The rats are quicker to respond to stimuli, particularly if the stimuli are related to the needed substance, such as the smell of food, and they respond with greater activity. Another way to describe this would be to talk about arousal. An organism that has been deprived of a goal object is in a state of need, and this is translated into a high degree of arousal or arousability.

The directive component of drive refers to the fact that the deprived organism behaves only in particular ways designed to attain a particular goal. In the typical laboratory demonstration, on alternate days rats are deprived of food and water. They are trained in a T-maze with a choice of making a left turn to food or a right turn to water. The rats, of course, learn to turn left on food-deprived days and right on water-deprived days. Clearly, the animal somehow knows its needs and behaves accordingly, using the knowledge it has acquired through experience. Depriving the organism of food presumably leads to events or stimuli that signal the organism that food is needed. The reaction may be stomach contractions or growling, or the stomach may secrete hormonelike substances into the blood that signal the brain, or the liver may detect low levels of nutrients in the blood and signal the brain. In any case, somehow the organism detects what is needed, and this knowledge then serves to guide the behavior engaged in.

Motivation as a Pulling Force: Incentives

The incentive theory of motivation stresses the attracting or repelling power that particular stimuli appear to exert on reward and punishment and the conditions of reinforcement for behaving (see Chapter 4). Incentives and reinforcers are closely related. Incentive refers to the motivation the person has to achieve a particular goal object. Reinforcement refers to learning—the fact that a particular response increases in probability of occurrence if attaining the goal object is contingent upon making that response. Incentive theory rests on the assumption that the behaving organism knows what the consequences of its behavior

She Prays, Lifts 500 Lb. Stone Off Girl

TROUT RUN, Pa. (UPI)—Barbara Sechrist says "the grace of God" gave her the strength to lift a 500-pound tombstone that fell on a 50-pound, 5-year-old girl.

The granite headstone broke Heather Isgate's collarbone, an ankle and a rib and bruised a lung.

Sechrist had taken Heather and several other children for a walk. . . .

"We were sitting down and talking when Heather jumped up," Sechrist recalled. "I guess she was happy, because she hugged a tombstone. I was watching, horrified, as the tombstone fell on her."

"All you could see was her eyes. She was looking at me and I kept pushing to get the tombstone off," she said, her voice trembling. "I prayed and prayed and by the grace of God, it moved. Heather's a miracle girl to me."

The Rev. James Dawes, pastor of the church in the tiny Lycoming County community, said two paramedics were unable to lift the 100-year-old tombstone, which he estimated weighed 500 pounds.

"It took a couple of young men with a lever to lift it later in the week," he said. . . .

Chicago Sun-Times
April 8, 1981

Motivation as a source of energy.

will be. Thus, it focuses attention on the circumstances we are attempting to obtain (positive incentives) or those we are trying to avoid (negative incentives). Incentive theory is primarily concerned with the objects, events, and states of affairs that people find rewarding or punishing and are thus motivated to achieve or avoid. The emphasis is on the goals of behavior. Such an analysis of motivation leads researchers to study what it is that people are trying to acquire—food, drink, love, fame, prestige, money—and what it is they are trying to avoid—pain, anxiety, frustration, starvation, poverty, and the like. Incentives are not only objects to be obtained, such as money, but may include complicated states of affairs, such as receiving a promotion, winning an election, feeling satisfied with one's accomplishments, earning the respect of a colleague, and so on. They are the states that have value to us, either positive or negative. They are thus capable of serving as positive and negative reinforcers in "controlling," that is, motivating, our behavior.

Switching the emphasis away from drives and toward incentives is consistent with the facts of human motivation. People do not seem particularly driven to behave, except in special circumstances usually centering on physical needs of the body. For example, our behavior with respect to getting food is usually

The New Yorker, January 7, 1974. Drawing by H. Martin; © 1974 The New Yorker Magazine, Inc.

Most of the time we are not motivated by incentives that are staring us in the face. Rather, we are motivated by our ability to anticipate the receipt of positive incentives or the avoidance of negative incentives. We are motivated by our knowledge that certain behaviors will lead toward positive incentives or away from negative ones.

better described as behavior designed to prevent intense hunger rather than behavior caused by an intense hunger drive. We engage in all sorts of behavior aimed at preventing us from becoming hungry or thirsty. We go to the grocery store not because we are driven by an intense hunger drive but because we know that food is necessary to prevent intense hunger and starvation. We know the consequences of not being able to eat, and so we arrange our behavior so that we keep food available. We also go because we have learned to like particular foods that taste good. Food has positive incentive value, and, of course, foods vary in the amount of incentive value they have. We have these in mind when we shop. Thus, our behavior is usually best described as an attempt to achieve certain goals. We are primarily motivated by the consequences of our behavior. We seek positive incentives and we avoid negative ones.

Why Incentives and Not Drives?

Many factors led to deemphasis on drives and increased emphasis on incentives as motivators. We have already mentioned one, the fact that deprivation states apparently do not automatically energize behavior. We have also indicated that drive theory does not contribute much to an understanding of human motivation because our behavior seems more appro-

priately described as a search for goals. Another major factor comes from experiments showing that drives are not necessary to motivate behavior. In one study it was found that animals will work to achieve rewards that have nothing to do with any known need state. Rats will perform in order to get to drink a sweet saccharin solution, even though they were not deprived of water, and the saccharin, an artificial sweetener, does not provide any body nutrients. Saccharin has positive incentive value (it tastes sweet) but satisfies no known drive or need. Monkeys will work and learn just for an opportunity to see out into the laboratory or to see novel objects (see Figure 7–1). Of course, human beings do many things that do not alleviate any known drives—they go to horror shows, read murder mysteries, play all sorts of games, run nude through school cafeterias, and try to break the world record for staying in the shower. It seems nearly impossible to explain such behaviors as attempts to satisfy drives. Rather, they appear to be a result of the consequences of the behavior—excitement, pleasure, recognition, prestige, or whatever.

Thus the emphasis, particularly in human motivation, has shifted from drives to incentives, from push to pull, from motivation as an attempt to reduce a

FIGURE 7-1   The curious monkey

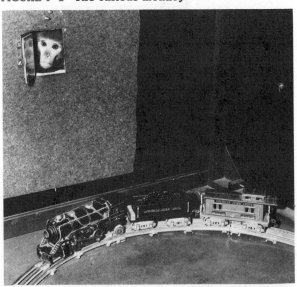

One major problem with drive theory became obvious when various studies showed that animals would learn and work for rewards which did not reduce any known drive. Thus, it was difficult to maintain that it was a drive which motivated them in the first place. One of these studies demonstrated that monkeys would learn to operate a lever that opened a door in the box just so they could see out into the laboratory or get to see novel objects such as a toy train. The monkey in the picture above, however, seems more interested in the photographer than in the train.

Incentive refers to the *motivational* properties of a reward. Two things, say a hug and a kiss for Lucy, might be rewards in that she would learn something in order to get either one. But the kiss might motivate her more than the hug—she would try

harder for a kiss reward than a hug reward. In that case, we would say that the incentive value of a kiss was higher than the incentive value of a hug.

drive to motivation as a search for goals or motivation as the engaging in intentional behavior designed to obtain positive incentives and avoid negative ones. What is needed, however, is an understanding of how incentives produce their motivational effects and of how we learn the incentive values of various things. Why is one person's positive incentive (snails or caviar) another person's negative incentive?

Motivation and Biological Needs

We are biological creatures with bodies that require certain things to survive—our primary needs. The motivation for much of our behavior can be traced to these needs, which give rise to our primary drives. We need food, water, air, sleep, and a certain amount of heat, and our behavior can often be described as an attempt to obtain these life-sustaining items. We have built-in physiological systems for regulating the intake of such things as food and water. It is because of these needs and the systems that regulate them that such items as food and water can reinforce behavior. As examples, in this section we will discuss the regulation of eating and drinking, but first we must introduce the important concept of homeostasis.

Homeostasis

Complex physiological systems determine the conditions under which a need for food or water exists, resulting in the organism's becoming predisposed to eat or drink or to engage in behaviors that have in the past led to food or water. When sufficient food and water have been ingested, the system detects this fact and the organism is no longer predisposed to eat or drink.

Basically, these physiological systems are designed to maintain a "steady state" in our bodies. As

such, they are said to operate according to the principle of **homeostasis.** The best analogy for describing homeostasis is the heating system in the typical home. The system is designed to maintain a steady state, say a temperature of 70 degrees. In order to accomplish this, we have a thermostat (a homeostat for temperature) that detects the need for heat, turns on the furnace when the temperature is too low, and then turns off the furnace when the temperature has reached 70 or so again.

The physiological systems underlying our biological needs appear to operate in a similar fashion, that is, according to a homeostatic principle. Thus, we presumably have "sensors" that detect when we need food and water. When the need reaches some critical level, we become motivated to act in ways designed to obtain and ingest food or water. When we eat or drink, the system senses that the need is being reduced and modifies our behavior so that we stop eating or drinking at the appropriate time. Of course, we must remember that overlying this homeostatic system is an elaborate system of learned behaviors designed to make food and water available. We have learned to anticipate the need in order to prevent starvation or dehydration. Many of these behaviors have been learned because food and water reinforced them; part of the motivation for these behaviors stems from the fact that food and water are positive incentives. But given that we have learned how to find, buy, beg, or borrow food or water, the homeostatic systems regulate how much we consume. We shall next consider three important examples of homeostatic systems: (1) eating, (2) drinking, and (3) arousal level.

Eating

We eat in part to satisfy a primary biological need. We must supply the various tissues, organs, and structures in our bodies with the nutrients required for growth and proper functioning. We have to take in such varied items as calcium, sodium, iron, protein, and various vitamins. It is the homeostatic system that regulates the maintenance of these supplies. Eating is the behavioral component of this system that gets the food into the body where it can be utilized. The homeostatic system is very complex and we still have much to find out about it, though we know some important things about it already. First, we know that the homeostatic system works incredibly well if left to itself. Despite wide variations in our expenditure of energy, our body weight stays remarkably constant—the system obviously adjusts intake to outflow. Just imagine if the system were consistently off by as little as one-half ounce per day. In a year that would amount to over 10 pounds gained or lost. Starting at age 15 with a 150-pound person, such a system would produce a 45-year-old person who weighed 450 pounds, or, if you can imagine a negative weight, a person weighing −150 pounds.

We also know that this complex system involves multiple control factors that provide "fail-safe" back-up or auxiliary support should one aspect of the system fail. Thus, it is not nearly so simple as the home-heating system.

Predispositions—The Set Weight Level

Like the thermostat in the home set to a particular level, the body has a set weight level, and the homeostatic system is designed to regulate food intake in a way that maintains that level. We have little information about the exact way this is accomplished, but research to date indicates that the culprit is fat—fat levels in the blood and the number of fat cells in the body as a whole. Here we are speaking of the long-term regulation of weight, not the hour-by-hour food intake, which, as we will see later, appears to be related to the level of sugar (glucose) in the blood.

Evidence is beginning to accumulate which supports the hypothesis that the number of fat cells in the body is a crucial determinant of the set weight level. The body sets a weight level according to the number of fat cells in the body, in order to keep a relatively constant level of fat. For example, the overweight person apparently does not have bigger fat cells, stuffed to the brim or overflowing with fat, but rather *more* fat cells stuffed to the same level as the fat cells of the normal-weight person. In other words, the system regulates food intake in a way to keep a constant level of fat in the cells, but if you have more cells than the next person, you will obviously have to eat more to keep your fat cells stuffed to the same degree. And, of course, because you have more cells for storing the fat, you will weigh more.

The hypothalamus in the brain is involved in regulating the set weight level over the long term.

There is evidence that the hypothalamus may regulate fat levels in the cells by being sensitive to the levels of free fatty acids in the bloodstream.

The evidence for the important role this structure plays comes from studies on surgical destruction and electrical stimulation or activation of two areas of the hypothalamus: the ventromedial nucleus and the lateral nucleus. Destruction of these areas is accomplished surgically by making lesions in them.

Making a lesion in the ventromedial nucleus produces an animal with **hyperphagia,** an abnormally increased desire for food. The animal overeats and becomes enormous (see Figure 7–2). But the animal does not go on eating forever and ever until it explodes. Instead, the animal levels off at a new, although very much higher, weight and then maintains that weight. It is as if the thermostat or "fatostat" has been reset at a higher level. In fact, if the animals are gorged and forced to become extremely overweight before the operation, they will not overeat after the operation but will actually eat less until they reduce

FIGURE 7–2 Hypothalamic hyperphagia

A hyperphagic rat made obese by a lesion in the ventromedial nucleus of the hypothalamus. This rat weighs 1080 grams (the indicator has spun completely around the dial and beyond). A normal rat the same age weighs less than 200 grams.

TABLE 7–1   Effects of Surgical Destruction and Electrical Stimulation (Activation) on Two Parts of the Hypothalamus

	Destruction	Activation
Ventromedial nucleus	Animal becomes hyperphagic and overeats	A hungry animal that is eating will stop eating immediately
Lateral nucleus	Animal becomes aphagic—it will not eat at all and will die unless force-fed	Animal will immediately start eating, even if it has just eaten all it wants

The overall, long-term predisposition to eat thus seems to be mainly a function of the number of fat cells in the body. Long-term food consumption is designed to maintain body weight at some set level, and this seems to be quite closely regulated by structures in the hypothalamus that are sensitive to levels of body fat.

Precipitating Factors

In the short term, day-to-day food intake seems to be more a function of blood glucose (sugar) levels than of fat levels in the body. The hypothalamus also plays an important role in this phase of food-intake regulation.

Glucose is the body's basic source of energy, and when we are using it up quickly the blood glucose levels are affected. Blood glucose levels are obviously monitored by the body, because the level is closely regulated to stay within certain limits. If blood glucose levels drop, presumably we are using energy and need food. This decrease in sugar levels is somehow detected and results in our eating.

Taking insulin into the body results in decreased blood glucose levels. People who take insulin injections report feeling hungry soon afterward, and animals given insulin injections will start to eat. Reversing the process works too; giving glucose injections to hungry animals will cause them to stop eating. Actually, the regulation may be more complex than simply monitoring overall glucose levels. Overall levels do not correspond very well to hunger and the amount eaten; therefore, it has been suggested that what is monitored is the *difference* between the glucose levels in the arteries and the levels in the veins. In any case, it is clear that glucose levels are critically involved.

down to the new weight level, which, of course, is now set higher than normal.

Surgical destruction of the lateral hypothalamus produces the opposite effect, apparently resetting the "fatostat" to a lower level. Animals exhibit **aphagia;** they will not eat at all. Such an abrupt and complete cessation of eating would normally lead to death, and so they have to be force-fed for a while. After recovery they eat on their own, but they maintain their body weight at a much lower level than normal. If the animals are gradually starved down to a very low weight before the operation, then after the operation they will eat to bring themselves up to the new weight level, which is much lower than normal but higher than the weight they were starved down to.

Electrical stimulation of these two areas of the hypothalamus produces an effect opposite to that caused by surgical destruction. Stimulation of the ventromedial nucleus will cause a hungry animal that is eating to stop immediately. Stimulation of the lateral nucleus will cause an animal to start eating immediately even if the animal has just eaten all the food it wants (see Table 7–1).

It has been suggested that there are specialized cells (glucoreceptors) in the body to detect glucose levels and communicate the need for food to the higher centers of the brain, which then initiate eating. There may be glucoreceptors in the stomach, the liver, and also in the hypothalamus. At one time it was thought that hyperphagia and aphagia were merely a result of destroying the parts of the brain that start and stop eating, presumably the parts that monitor glucose levels. The picture is not so simple, however, because, as we have seen, the hypothalamus regulates not only short-term but also long-term weight level. Moreover, hyperphagic rats prone to overeating are not particularly *motivated* to eat. They overeat their favorite food if it is right under their noses, but if the food does not taste good or if they have to do the least bit of work to get it, they do not appear to be hungry.

It is perhaps the case that both the long-term weight level (based on fat levels) and the short-term system (based on glucose levels) have regulatory centers in the hypothalamus and that these two systems are complexly intertwined. As mentioned previously, the hypothalamus is only one, though evidently a crucial, part of the complex system involved in regulating food intake. The manner in which the hypothalamus plays its role in regulating food intake is not completely known at this time.

Peripheral Precipitators

Blood fat and sugar levels and the hypothalamus are critical, but there are other factors that play a role, although small when compared to that of the blood and the brain. For example, consider the stomach. We have already mentioned the possibility of glucoreceptors in the stomach that would monitor glucose and send information to the brain. The stomach also monitors and signals to the brain the amount of food it contains. Ingested food is also monitored in the mouth by taste, smell, and muscle receptors involved in chewing and swallowing. All of this information is used by the brain to decide when to start or stop eating.

But neither mouth factors nor stomach factors alone are absolutely necessary. We can feed an animal working for food rewards by directly placing the food in its stomach, bypassing the mouth completely. The animal will regulate its weight within normal limits even though it never gets to taste or chew any of the food it has been working for. Likewise, we can surgically remove the stomach or cut the nerves from the stomach to the brain and the animal will still be able to regulate its eating. Mouth and stomach factors play a role, but they are only part of the system.

Taste seems critically involved in regulating what we eat. This is shown by experiments on *specific needs*. We can create a specific need in an animal by feeding it a diet deficient in one particular item, say salt. There appears to be a built-in system designed to detect and regulate sodium (salt) intake, and taste is critical to it. If you take a rat's favorite food and cut out all the sodium to produce a sodium deficiency, the rat, when given free access to several different foods, will immediately eat only the ones with sodium. Of course, taste is also involved in the pleasurable aspects of food, and much of human eating is centered on producing taste sensations we have learned to enjoy.

It was once concluded from these experiments on specific needs that we had specific detectors regulating the intake of all the various types of nutrients our bodies require. Thus there would be a detector for salt, for each of the vitamins and minerals we must take in, and so on. It was suggested that proper nutrition would automatically happen as a result of the control these detectors would exert on what we eat. While there may be a few such detection systems built into the system (for example, salt), it now appears that most of the results of these experiments can be explained on the basis of the novelty of the taste. If you have been specifically deprived of a particular nutrient and are offered some food with that nutrient in it, you will eat it, but probably because it has a novel and presumably more pleasant taste, since you haven't had that taste for awhile. In short, good nutrition does not happen completely automatically.

External Precipitators

Did you ever "stuff yourself" at dinner on the turkey and dressing and then somehow find room for the pumpkin pie with whipped cream? Did you ever eat something because it looked good, or did you ever feel hungry all of a sudden because you smelled the pizza your dormitory neighbor just had delivered? It is obvious that stimuli outside the body also play a role in getting us to eat. The sight, smell, and anticipated taste sensations of food and even the presence of other eaters can induce us to eat.

Perhaps the most amazing fact about the external factors is that we regulate our food intake so well *despite* their continued presence. But there is also some impressive evidence that external stimuli can come to play a dominant role in food consumption for some people, overriding the internal regulatory systems we have been talking about. As you might guess, these are people with weight problems, the obese or overweight. We shall consider their plight in the "What Does It Mean?" section of this chapter.

A good deal of our eating behavior seems to be under the control of external cues. This is what makes it difficult to resist many foods in a cafeteria line.

Human Diet a Case of Matter Over Mind?
By HAROLD M. SCHMECK Jr.

BETHESDA, Md. — The effects of diet on the human brain and of the brain on human diet constitute a highly promising area for research in nutrition, scientists said at a national conference here last week.

"Hunger and thirst are states of specific arousal in the brain," said Dr. Alan N. Epstein of the University of Pennsylvania. While humans often attribute feelings of hunger or thirst to the stomach or the mouth, they are in fact moods and urges of the brain, he said.

While it is obvious that too little water and food produce these sensations, he said, there is little knowledge of the mechanisms involved.

Epstein described recent research linking a hormone in the body to the sensation of thirst. The chemical, called angiotensin, has long been known to constrict blood vessels and thus to raise blood pressure.

When rats were given steady infusions of small amounts of angiotensin directly into their brains for four consecutive days, he said, they drank huge amounts of water, even water so salty that they seldom if ever touched it without the stimulation of the hormone.

The compulsive drinking of both types of water continues for days after the infusions had ended, he said, indicating that the hormone had altered the brain and that the alteration had endured.

The scientists said that this research has practical implications beyond revealing some aspects of brain function. Excessive salt intake, often seemingly caused by cultural eating habits, is thought by some to be a contributor to high blood pressure. . . .

Chicago Tribune
July 9, 1978

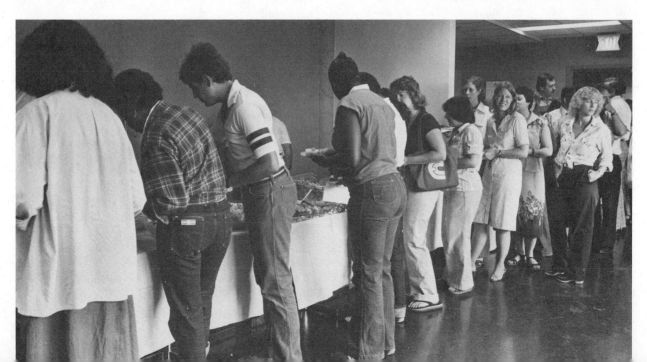

The Role of the Liver

Physiological psychologists have almost uniformly emphasized the brain, particularly the hypothalamus, in their theories about eating. The brain and nervous system are critical in the behavioral aspects of eating, but the liver may be the key organ that monitors and sends out signals about the flow of nutrients to the body tissues and from the fat deposits. The liver obviously plays a key role in body metabolism and seems to be the central processor in the physiology of nutrients. Such processes as the conversion of amino acids into glucose, of fatty acids into ketones, and of glucose into energy (to be used) or fats (to be stored) all take place in the liver. Through the bloodstream the liver sends its various products out to the tissues to be used in cell metabolism or to be stored as fat for later use. Because of its role as central processor, the liver, we may reasonably assume, analyzes the levels of the various substances and regulates its processes accordingly. If this is true, then the liver may well be the place where the signal to eat is generated and sent on to the brain. In such a system there would be no need for glucose or fat monitors in the brain itself. Thus many psychologists may be placing too much emphasis on the hypothalamus, which may only be the place where the signals from the liver are *first* processed. We do not yet know the entire role of the liver, but it appears that this organ is far more important in regulating eating behavior than we have so far considered.

The key point about eating is that the starting and stopping of the behavior is controlled by many factors that work together in a complex way. There is regulation of fat stores and the blood glucose level and monitoring of the sensations from the stomach and mouth. The hypothalamus is critically involved in the regulation process, but it is not the only crucial brain center, and it certainly is not the simple food thermostat we once thought.

Drinking

Another primary, biologically based drive is thirst. Our bodies require water to operate. To keep bodily fluid levels within some critical range, we have developed a complex and sophisticated homeostatic system. If fluid levels are too high, the body gets rid of excess water by sweating or by excreting it in urine. If fluid levels are too low, the body takes steps to conserve the water it has by first inhibiting urine formation and then activating our motivation to search for and drink water.

As with hunger, the hypothalamus seems to play a crucial role in the homeostasis of bodily fluid. It does this by controlling two key processes: (1) drinking and (2) urine formation. When information reaches the hypothalamus that our fluid levels are too low, the system responds by motivating us to seek and drink water and by slowing down the rate of urine formation in the kidneys. The result is that we drink more and urinate less until balance is restored.

Destroying parts of the hypothalamus in rats can disrupt normal drinking, creating either adipsia (no drinking) or polydipsia (excessive drinking). Recently, there was a human case reported where a man developed a severe polydipsia after brain damage caused by an auto accident. He consumed 20 gallons of water a day at first but later scaled the amount down to 6.5 gallons. We would have to guess that it was his hypothalamus that was damaged.

The hypothalamus detects low fluid levels in the body in two ways. First, body cells shrink in size as water levels decline, and some cells in the hypothalamus (osmoreceptors) apparently shrink themselves, thus signaling low fluid levels. Second, the blood flow through the kidneys slows down, causing the kidneys to signal the hypothalamus by secreting the hormone **angiotensin.** There may also be blood-flow detectors in the walls of blood vessels which directly signal the hypothalamus by using the nervous system to communicate instead of the blood. In either case, the hypothalamus detects the low fluid levels and activates its two responses.

One response, the slowing down of urine formation, is activated when the hypothalamus signals the pituitary gland to secrete a hormone called **antidiuretic hormone** (ADH; see Chapter 2). This hormone is then carried in the blood to the kidneys where it inhibits urine formation. We form less urine and conserve water, keeping the fluid decrease to a minimum.

The second response of the hypothalamus is to activate the behavior we use when we are thirsty—we seek out and drink water or beer or whatever is handy. Exactly how this happens is not known, but obviously the behavior involves the application of knowledge and skills we possess to locate the vital fluid. Finally, as we drink receptors in the mouth, throat, and stomach evidently monitor how much we consume and at the appropriate time signal the hypothalamus to deactivate the thirst system and to stop signaling the pituitary to release ADH.

In terms of the concepts we have used to analyze motivation, we can think of the biological system just described as consisting of the hypothalamus, ADH, angiotensin, and various receptors in the blood vessels and mouth which together regulate our level of predisposition to drink. Water or fluids become positive incentives for us and precipitate drinking behavior only when the level of predisposition is above some critical point. Otherwise, water and other beverages will not have positive incentive value. Of course, which particular fluids we choose to seek out and drink, whether water, beer, wine, or cola will be determined by other factors, notably taste. The pleasant or unpleasant taste effects of various fluids will contribute to (or detract from) the incentive values of these fluids. The incentive value of the fluid, combined with our knowledge of what will be required of us in the way of behavior to obtain that particular fluid, will determine, for example, whether we drink water at home or drive to the corner for a couple of beers.

We have a complete system fundamentally based on a biological need and a physiological system to monitor the need. But this system is supplemented by an incentive system based on what we have learned. The biological system predisposes us toward drinking, and the incentive system controls or directs our behavior in ways designed to satisfy the biological need and to give us pleasant experiences at the same time. We have a biological system that predisposes, and we have a cognitive system that precipitates and directs behavior.

Arousal

A third homeostatic system appears to exist in order to keep the physiological arousal level of the organism within some optimal range. We used to think that the goal of behavior was to satisfy all needs and keep arousal low or nonexistent. Much of the time we behave in precisely the opposite manner—we try to increase our arousal level. To do this, we seek rather than avoid sources of stimulation. On these occasions external sources of stimulation become positive incentives that we will work to expose ourselves to. Think of mountain climbers, daredevils, race-car drivers, and ski jumpers. Consider the things you might say you do for "fun," such as playing bridge or poker, watching TV, reading mystery stories, and playing tennis. A lot of these things have a common feature—they involve exposing yourself to external stimuli that will arouse you. These activities can hardly be described as attempts to keep your arousal level at a minimum. Obviously, then, a theory which implies that we try to keep arousal at a minimum is just plain wrong. The homeostatic arousal system functions to keep arousal at an optimal level and this level is not zero.

There were two quite startling demonstrations that we are not motivated to keep stimulation at a minimum. First, James Olds and Peter Milner made an extremely important discovery while studying the effects of electrical brain stimulation on behavior. Electrodes had been embedded deep into the brains of rats during surgery, making it possible to deliver

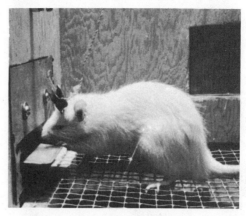

FIGURE 7–3 One of James Old's electrode-implanted rats

electrical stimulation to certain brain areas (Figure 7–3). What Olds and Milner discovered was that the rats liked it! The rats would work hard to have their brains stimulated in certain areas. It has since been demonstrated that a rat will press a bar thousands and thousands of times a day to activate brain stimulation. There have been reports that, if the electrodes are in the right place, the rats will spend so much time pressing for stimulation that they do not have time to eat. Correspondingly, there are areas in the brain where the electrical stimulation is not pleasant, but extremely unpleasant. The rats will work hard to *prevent* the stimulation in these areas.

The second demonstration addressed the question of stimulation from the opposite point of view. If we are seeking to keep stimulation at a minimum, then the minimum state must be the most highly desired. What would be the consequences of being in a state of stimulus or sensory deprivation? The answer came from the work of W. H. Bexton, W. Heron, and T. H. Scott. These investigators paid undergraduate students up to $25 a day to participate in a **sensory-deprivation** experiment. Subjects were to remain in a room under conditions designed to minimize sensory stimulation (see Figure 7–4) for as long as they possibly could. The subjects, of course, had adequate food, water, oxygen, heat, and toilet facilities. But every effort was made to cut off all other sensory input. The important result was that no students lasted very long in this environment despite the high rate of pay for those days (about 1953). Some of the students reported bizarre experiences, including hallucinations, after enduring the situation for several hours. All in all, the environment was not a pleasant one. The conclusion is that an environment designed to minimize stimulus input is not something we generally seek out.

FIGURE 7-4 A sensory deprivation study

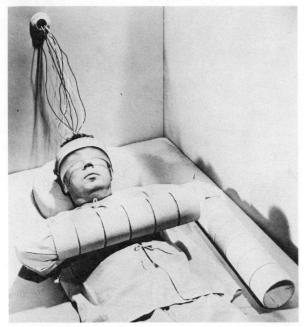

In a series of experiments at McGill University, students were paid $25 a day to stay in a room in which stimulation was reduced to a bare minimum. They wore an eyeshade that reduced vision to a dim haze and arm casts that kept their hands from feeling anything. They were placed in a soundproof room where they could hear nothing but the continual hum of a fan. Not many could stay for more than two days, and some very bizarre behaviors occurred, such as hallucinations. One theory of hallucinations is that they are self-generated stimuli designed to increase arousal toward that person's optimal level. What about dreams?

Arousal and Homeostasis

Studies like those just cited have led to the notion that arousal level is crucially involved in motivation. The idea is that we are motivated to maintain an optimal, presumably moderate, level of arousal. Of course, there would be individual differences—some people would have optimal levels that were very high, others very low, with most in the moderate area. The arousal level at any moment is a direct function of the total amount of stimulation (from both external and internal sources) impinging upon the organism. If the current arousal level is above optimum, the organism will be motivated to reduce the level of stimulation. For example, if you are terribly frightened (and thus above the optimal level of arousal) when watching a scary vampire movie, you might cover your eyes or actually leave the theater during the most frightening parts of the movie to keep the arousal level from getting too extreme. On the other hand, if the current arousal level is below optimum, the organism will be motivated to do things that will increase the level of

stimulation. This is why you might have gone to see the vampire movie in the first place.

Note the homeostatic system—if we become overaroused or underaroused, we are motivated to alter things until the arousal level returns to the normal range. One implication of this is that any stimulus, if it is strong enough, will be a source of motivation. It will increase the arousal level so much that the person will be overaroused, resulting in behavior motivated to eliminate the stimulus or reduce its intensity. An extremely loud and continuous noise, for example, would motivate you to do something about it. Similarly, too little stimulation would result in the arousal level drifting below the optimal range, and you would be motivated to increase stimulation. When you are alone in your room and bored (too little stimulation), you might turn on the radio, or you might leave the room to go watch TV.

What constitutes the optimum arousal level will depend upon the individual and the task at hand. There is some optimal level of arousal for engaging in any behavior. The relationship between arousal and efficiency of behavior is an *inverted U function* (see Figure 7–5). At very low levels of arousal, such as when we are drowsy and near sleep, our performance will not be very efficient. At extremely high levels of arousal our behavior will be disorganized and inefficient to the point that people might describe us as "wild" or "berserk." Between the extremes of sleep and frenzy are the moderate levels of arousal that are presumably optimal for behavior.

Exactly where the optimal level lies depends on the task at hand. With a very easy task (or a hard one

FIGURE 7-5 Arousal and performance: the inverted U function

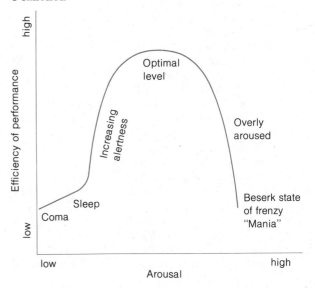

that you have learned to do easily) the optimal level will be high — the task is so easy that efficiency does not suffer until extremely high arousal takes place. With a very difficult or complicated task, the optimal level will be on the low side. You should be aroused somewhat but not very much. This principle is generally known as the **Yerkes-Dodson Law** and applies to motivation in general, not just the arousal aspects of motivation. The principle says that the optimal level of motivation depends upon task difficulty — the more difficult or complex the task, the lower will be the optimal motivational point (see Figure 7–6).

The optimum arousal level will also vary from one person to another, some having very high optimal levels and others very low. This is analogous to what Marvin Zuckerman has called the dimension of *sensation seeking*. People with high optimal arousal levels will seek out sources of stimulation (for example, mountain climbing) to keep a high arousal level — these are sensation seekers. People who have low optimal arousal levels will be trying to keep stimulation at minimal levels. Their hobbies are more likely to be stamp and coin collecting than mountain climbing.

The incentive value of a particular external stimulus also depends on your arousal level at the moment. Listening to a tape-recorded listing of all the closing prices on the New York Stock Exchange might not be something you would want to do if you were already moderately aroused. But subjects in sensory-deprivation experiments, who are underaroused, are often quite happy to get to hear about the daily fortunes of IBM, AT&T, and GM. A quiet walk in the woods might be nice if you were troubled and worried about lots of things (overaroused), but it might not be so nice if you were lonely and bored with the world.

Instinct

The earliest biological concept applied to motivation was the instinct, or inherited pattern of behavior or predisposition to behave in particular ways. Thus, a man who fights a lot would be characterized as having a strong aggression instinct, and it is this instinct that motivates the individual to fight. The instinct conception of human motivation had its origins in the evolutionary theory of Darwin, which stressed the survival value of instinctive animal behaviors (particularly instincts centering on aggression, feeding, and reproduction) and which hypothesized that human beings are descendants of the lower animals. If animals are obviously creatures of instincts, then it followed that human beings are too. Freud also adopted an instinct-based theory of motivation. The instinct theory came to dominate psychology around

FIGURE 7–6 The Yerkes-Dodson Law

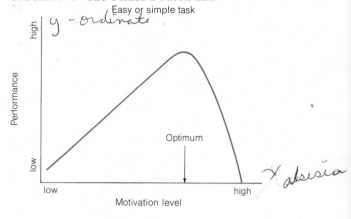

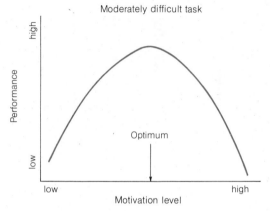

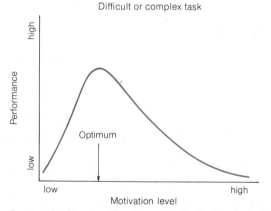

Graphs showing the effect known as the Yerkes-Dodson Law of motivation and performance. In all tasks, increasing motivation increases performance. With increasing task difficulty, the optimum motivation level (that giving best performance) decreases.

the turn of this century, when two distinguished psychologists, William McDougall and William James, adopted the concept as the central explanatory construct in their theories.

But the popularity of instincts did not last long. Instinct theories were attacked as being useless for understanding behavior, basically because of the circular reasoning problem: He fights. Why? Because of a strong aggression instinct. How do you know he has such an instinct? Because he fights. Psychologists were also indiscriminate in their use of instincts.

"Everything under the sun" was viewed as being caused by an instinct. The concept of instinct "explained" everything and nothing, and so it gave way to another explanation.

What instinct gave way to was learning. Instinct theories imply that behavior is predominately a function of heredity. In the early years of this century,

FIGURE 7-7 Important ethological concepts

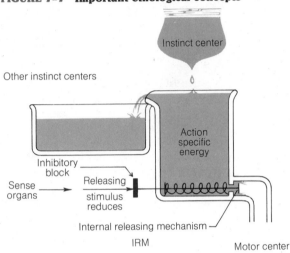

A hen searches frantically for a peeping chick she cannot see but ignores the chick in distress that she can see but not hear. Sound is the releasing signal for her maternal behavior. Can you suggest why sound rather than sight evolved as the releaser here?

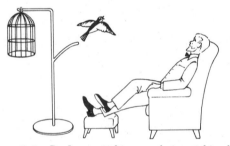

Vacuum activity. Dr. Lorenz in his easy chair watching his fly-catcher snap at an insect that is not there.

The male flicker's defense of territory instinct is released by the sight of another flicker in his territory provided the intruder has the black "moustache" that distinguishes the male from female. This black patch is the releaser stimulus.

Releasing stimuli are generally simple but specific and conspicuous so that in nature they would not be confused with other characteristics. For example, the herring gull's chicks peck at the red spot on the parents' bill to get food.

Displacement activity. When one instinctual center is blocked from expression its energy may "spill over" to another center to produce displacement behavior. Thus ducks show preening and gulls show grass pulling as displacement behavior.

psychology turned radically away from such ideas, focusing instead on the concept of learning. Classical conditioning, Pavlov, Watson, and the rise of behaviorism, to a large extent, were responsible for the decline of instinct theories. Behavior came to be viewed as primarily learned, not inherited. But learning theories quickly found that a motivational principle of some kind was necessary. Instead of instinct, they adopted the concept of **drive** as the central motivational force.

Ethology and the Resurrection of Instincts

The concept of instinct lay dormant until the 1930s when it began to reappear in the writings of a small group of influential European zoologists studying animal behavior in natural settings. They called their science **ethology** and resurrected the concept of instinct in a new and scientifically acceptable form. The three most notable figures in ethology are Konrad Lorenz, Karl von Frisch, and Nikolaas Tinbergen. In 1973 they became the first scientists to win the Nobel Prize in physiology and medicine for work done strictly in the area of behavior.

Fixed-Action Patterns   For the ethologists, an instinct is defined as an invariant behavior sequence that is universally observable in and unique to the members of a single species of animals. Furthermore, there is no learning involved—the behavior is innate to members of that species. In short, an instinct is an *innate fixed-action* pattern uniquely characteristic of a particular species (species-specific). The crucial aspects of the behavior, then, are (1) it is innate, (2) it is invariant from one time to the next, (3) it is universally found in all members of the species (if you look at the right time and place and at the appropriate sex), and (4) the pattern is unique to that species. From

Chapter 2, recall the concept of a hard-wired system. Fixed-action patterns are perfect examples of hard-wiring in the brain.

Of course, modern ethology theory consists of much more than just saying that the behavior is an instinct. The major concepts are illustrated in Figure 7–7. First, innate fixed-action patterns do not just happen. Instead, they are triggered by stimuli known as **sign stimuli** or **releasers**. For example, the territorial defense-action pattern of the flicker is "released" by the black "moustache" of the male flycatcher trying to intrude. For the squirrel, the action pattern of burying nuts is released by any object that is hard and round. Place a steel ball bearing on a concrete floor and the squirrel will go through all the motions (the fixed-action pattern) of trying to bury it. Another example comes from Tinbergen's classic studies of a species of fish called the three-spined stickleback. Aggressive behavior in defense of territory in this fish is released by the red belly of the male intruder. Tinbergen used balsawood models of males in order to determine what would release the defensive aggression pattern. He found that a perfect replica of the male intruder would not release the pattern if the belly was not painted red, but that a very crude model with a red belly would release the pattern (Figure 7–8). Even a floating beachball would release aggression if it was red.

Action-Specific Energy   The diagram in the upper left-hand portion of Figure 7–7 shows the general hydraulic model that Konrad Lorenz developed to account for fixed-action patterns. It is a drive-energy model that states that members of the species inherit action-specific energies to motivate specific fixed-action patterns. The energy builds up (we might say the animal is becoming predisposed to respond) and

The New Yorker, December 3, 1979. Drawing by Levin; © 1979 The New Yorker Magazine, Inc.

Instincts (fixed-action patterns) are presumably hard-wired into the brain and thus are not modifiable by experience. Imprinting, one of the most studied fixed-action patterns, is the name for the behavior of following the mother in a line. The ducks having to cross the street would not change the following pattern to one of holding hands. Incidentally, baby ducks will become im-

printed upon the first slow-moving object they encounter shortly after birth—a critical time period—even if that object is not their mother. They can become imprinted on a dog, a human being, or whatever they encounter. Fortunately, in nature the object is almost always their mother.

FIGURE 7-8 Stickleback models

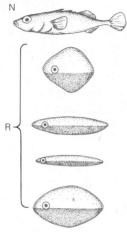

N is a carefully made form- and color-true imitation of a stickleback without a red belly. It is less frequently attacked than the four simple red-bellied models of series *R*.

is finally released (we might say precipitated) when the sense organs perceive the sign stimuli. If no sign stimuli or releasers are encountered, the energy will continue to build up, finally bursting forth and releasing the behavior in the absence of a releasing stimulus. When this happens, the behavior is called a **vacuum activity.**

Another principle states that competing action patterns (say, both an aggressive pattern and a sexual pattern) can block each other, leading to a build-up and overflow of action-specific energy into other instinct centers, from which the energy is then released. Under these circumstances the animal is said to be engaging in **displacement activity.** For example, an animal that is neither aggressive nor sexy, may groom (displacement activity) because the energy from the sexual and aggressive instincts has overflowed into the grooming instinct centers. The interpretations of vacuum activity and displacement activity have been among the most controversial aspects of ethological theory. Critics say such a theory explains these behaviors only in an after-the-fact fashion.

Many ethologists have rejected the hydraulic model based on action-specific energy. This model was derived because instinctive behaviors occurred when no stimulus appeared to be present—the so-called vacuum activity just mentioned. The alternate interpretation would be that in fact there is a stimulus present, either in the environment or within the body. The vacuum activity may simply appear to be happening in a vacuum (no stimulus present) because we have not looked closely enough in the environment

nor inside the body to find stimuli. To the extent that stimuli are found, vacuum activity is not an appropriate name. And this would mean, of course, that we do not have to postulate a hydraulic system with overflowing action-specific energy. In fact, we wouldn't need an energy concept at all, only the innate action patterns automatically released by a specific stimulus. If we broaden the concept of stimulus to include *events* or *states* within the body, such as the levels of various hormones, we can account for most, if not all, instinctive behavior without postulating action-specific energy. The releasing stimulus can then be seen as a specific *configuration* of various stimulus elements, including the internal state of the body. This is the trend in recent ethological theories of instinctive behavior.

Ethology and its revised treatment of instinct is not without its critics and problems. We have already mentioned the problem with displacement and vacuum activity. Another major problem has been the tendency of ethologists to generalize their findings to human beings without adequate evidence. Lorenz, for example, has written a book, *On Aggression,* that implies that aggressiveness in human beings is basically instinctive. The ethologists have been helped in this endeavor by such authors as Desmond Morris *(The Naked Ape)* and Robert Ardrey *(The Territorial Imperative),* who have taken great liberties in applying instinctive concepts to human beings. Do we have a personal territory that we will instinctively defend against intruders? Are such instincts responsible for world problems such as the Arab-Israeli conflict and war in general? The ideas are certainly provocative and worthy of study, but at present the evidence is barely suggestive, at best.

Sociobiology

A recent theory to explain motivation comes from biology and is known as **sociobiology.** It began to receive widespread attention in 1975 when Edward Wilson, a leading proponent, published the first major text in the field. For sociobiologists, motivation is closely related to instincts in that it is largely hard-wired or preprogrammed into the organism. The basic assumption is that preprogrammed motivation has one and only one function: to ensure the survival of the DNA material which constitutes the genes. All forms of living organisms, including human beings, are seen as survival machines designed to protect and propagate the genes. The genes, in a selfish endeavor to survive, are viewed as controlling just about all behavior. Even social behavior in human beings is seen as automatically motivated by the genes in order to ensure their own survival. It is not the survival of the particular organism that is at stake, but of the particular genes in the cells. In today's world of women's liberation, sociobiology is particularly controversial because it suggests that it is natural for males to desire polygamy so they can impregnate the maximal number of women and pass on the most genes. The female, the argument often goes, is naturally monogamous, needing only one strong male to impregnate her and protect her and her offspring. Interestingly, the leading sociobiologists are all men.

Sociobiology starts with the assumption that the primary motivation is purely biological. Allowances are made for learning. Moreover, human beings have capability for resisting the self-preservation struggle of the genes. But most human behavior is seen as selfish, designed to protect the genes from extinction. In its treatment of what we would call altruistic behavior sociobiology has stirred considerable controversy.

One would think that preserving the genes would be a matter of reproduction at the level of the species or of the individual organism. This is essentially the Darwinian theory of evolution through natural selection and survival of those individuals that are the fittest. Fitness, according to Darwin, would be mainly a matter of surviving and reproducing. Competition for limited resources and natural selection would "weed out" the unfit, who would not live to reproduce and pass on their genes. In the Darwinian system it is the species or the individual organism that is struggling to survive. In contrast, sociobiological theory says it is not the individual but the genes that are trying to survive. Thus survival is possible through ways other than reproduction—namely, you can help other people who have some of the same genes as you do. Fitness is not simply a matter of self-reproduction but of gene reproduction. To determine the fitness of your genes, then, we have to look not only at your reproduction but at that of all people who share your genes—your relatives. Since we have to include your relatives to determine your fitness, a key concept in the theory is called **inclusive fitness.**

Sociobiologists have relied heavily on studies of animal behavior in their attempt to show that altruistic behavior can be accounted for by the concept of inclusive fitness. In the sociobiological scheme, helping your brothers and sisters—even cousins—to survive ensures the survival of your own genes even if you give your life in helping them. Wilson has even argued that homosexuality is a result of the genetic drive to pass on one's genes. His argument is that homosexuality allows some individuals to be free of the burdens of parenthood and thus able to help their close relatives to have more children, thereby passing on shared genes. In other words, the homosexual is displaying altruism for close relatives, sacrificing so that brothers and sisters can reproduce more. Such claims seem farfetched, have little evidence to support them, and detract from the theory. However, some studies, in fact, indicate that helping behavior can be predicted by kinship—the closer the kin, the greater the helping. As one sociobiologist said, "I'd give my life for two brothers or eight cousins." Each brother would have one-half his genes in common, and each cousin would have one-eighth in common. Thus saving eight cousins would be preserving the same number of genes represented by two brothers, either of which would be roughly equivalent to the biologist having two children of his own.

This system is sometimes referred to as *kinship selection* or *kinship genetics* to indicate that relatives with shared genes must be included in the analysis of gene fitness. Kinship genetics, for example, can explain why daughters of insect queens do not themselves reproduce but devote themselves to servicing their queen mother. The genetics is such that all the daughters will have about three-quarters of their genes in common. Thus a particular daughter will reproduce more of her genes if she helps mother to give her more sisters than if she herself produces offspring that will carry only half her genes.

Robert Trivers, another leading sociobiologist, has devised the concept of *reciprocal altruism* to account for the altruism among nonrelatives. According to this notion, the individual who helps another really expects something in return, something that eventually, in one way or another, will help his or her own genes to survive. Reciprocal altruism is seen not as something that is learned but as a tendency that has been built in by the genes through natural selection over millions of years. To the extent that helping others leads a person to help in return, the helper will have improved survival chances, so natural selection can operate to pass on the genes of helpful organisms. Thus, reciprocal altruism could be genetic in origin.

Sociobiological theories are, as you can imagine, highly controversial because they cast human beings in an ultimately selfish light. Our motivation is seen as almost purely biological and purely grounded in our genes. It is worthwhile to remember that we are biological creatures with a genetic background that has been subjected to natural selection. However, it remains for sociobiology to prove that we are simply gene-survival machines. The concepts of sociobiology have been useful in understanding some insect and animal behavior, but the application to human behavior (see the article on child altruism) is likely to be limited in effectiveness, simply because it is obvious that so much of our behavior is learned. To be sure, genetics is crucial, but so is learning.

Motivation as a Personality Characteristic

When we think about human behavior and the factors that motivate it, we are likely to conclude that instincts, biological needs for food and water, a need for optimal stimulation levels, and related factors do not account for very much. Certainly our behavior does not look much like the fixed action patterns characteristic of instinctive behaviors. Moreover, most of us are fortunate enough to have ready access to adequate food and water. True, some of the things we do are probably motivated by these needs, but these behaviors seem to be rather minor and infrequent. Maybe we do most of the things we do largely for fun and excitement so as to maintain an optimal arousal level. But isn't there a lot more to human behavior than just maintaining optimal arousal?

In an attempt to answer questions about the motivation for uniquely human behaviors, psychologists have offered answers that treat the concept of motivation as a personality characteristic. Like motivation, personality is a concept that is used to account for variability in behavior, and many personality theorists have made motivational concepts central in describing personality. This is rather like saying that your personality can be described by describing your motives or, more specifically, your needs. In short, we might say, "You are what you need." If you need to be with people, we say you are friendly, extroverted, and gregarious. If you need to work hard in order to beat out the next man or woman, we say you are hard-driving or energetic. To some extent, then, a description of the things you need is a description both of your personality and your motivations. In other words, to understand human motivation completely, we will have to understand personality.

FIGURE 7-9 Measuring human motives and needs

The object in the TAT is to make up a short story about what is happening in a picture like the one above. You might try it with this picture. Tell in your story (1) what is happening and who the people are, (2) what led up to the situation shown in the picture, (3) what the people in the picture are thinking and feeling, and (4) what will happen in the future. Does your story tell you anything about yourself and your motives and needs?

Henry Murray's Work on Psychogenic Needs

The pioneer worker in this field was Henry Murray. For him the concept of need was central to personality, and he spent a great deal of time attempting to objectify the measurement of needs and to identify the various needs that human beings have. He is perhaps most famous for having devised the Thematic Apperception Test (TAT) with Christiana Morgan (see Figure 7–9). In this test, the subject is shown a picture and asked to make up a story about what is going on in the picture. The basic idea is that the subject "projects" into the story his or her own needs, and so a careful analysis of the stories will tell a great deal about the person who made them up. Murray also developed questionnaires for assessing needs in a more direct way. His intensive scrutiny of a small group of subjects led him to believe that there are many independent human needs. Table 7–2 lists 20

representative needs that Murray felt were present in various degrees in each of us. This list has been expanded and modified somewhat in his later writings, but it should give you a good idea of what Murray sees as the needs of humanity. The listing is primarily of the *psychogenic* (psychological or learned) *needs,* as opposed to what Murray called the *viscerogenic needs,* such as needs for food, water, and oxygen.

Murray made another important point, namely, that each person has a hierarchy of needs; some needs are more important than others, with the viscerogenic needs being most important because they are so directly tied to survival. The needs will be satisfied in order of their priority for each person—if two incompatible needs arise, the stronger need, which is higher in the hierarchy, will be satisfied first. If you need water and you need aggression, chances are you will drink first and fight later.

Finally, Murray also recognized that motivation is partly a function of environmental factors, which he

TABLE 7–2 Twenty Human Needs Identified by Henry Murray

Need	Brief Definition
Abasement	To surrender. To comply and accept punishment. To apologize, confess, atone. Self-deprecation.
Achievement	To overcome obstacles, to exercise power, to strive to do something difficult as well and as quickly as possible.
Affiliation	To form friendships and associations. To greet, join, and live with others. To co-operate and converse sociably with others. To love. To join groups.
Aggression	To assault or injure an other. To murder, belittle, harm, blame, accuse or maliciously ridicule a person. To punish severely. Sadism.
Autonomy	To resist influence or coercion. To defy an authority or seek freedom in a new place. To strive for independence.
Counteraction	Proudly to refuse admission of defeat by restriving and retaliating. To select the hardest task. To defend one's honour in action.
Defendance	To defend oneself against blame or belittlement. To justify one's actions. To offer extenuations, explanations, and excuses. To resist 'probing.'
Deference	To admire and willingly follow a superior allied other. To co-operate with a leader. To serve gladly.
Dominance	To influence or control others. To persuade, prohibit, dictate. To lead and direct. To restrain. To organize the behaviour of a group.
Exhibition	To attract attention to one's person. To excite, amuse, stir, shock, thrill others. Self-dramatization.
Harmavoidance	To avoid pain, physical injury, illness, and death. To escape from a dangerous situation. To take precautionary measures.
Infavoidance	To avoid failure, shame, humiliation, ridicule. To refrain from attempting to do something that is beyond one's power. To conceal a disfigurement.
Nurturance	To nourish, aid, or protect a helpless other. To express sympathy. To 'mother' a child.
Order	To arrange, organize, put away objects. To be tidy and clean. To be scrupulously precise.
Play	To relax, amuse oneself, seek diversion and entertainment. To 'have fun,' to play games. To laugh, joke, and be merry. To avoid serious tension.
Rejection	To snub, ignore, or exclude an other. To remain aloof and indifferent. To be discriminating.
Sentience	To seek and enjoy sensuous impressions.
Sex	To form and further an erotic relationship. To have sexual intercourse.
Succorance	To seek aid, protection, or sympathy. To cry for help. To plead for mercy. To adhere to an affectionate, nurturant parent. To be dependent.
Understanding	To analyse experience, to abstract, to discriminate among concepts, to define relations, to synthesize ideas.

called *press*. You may have, as a personality characteristic, a strong need for achievement (*n* achievement); particular environmental situations will arouse this need. For example, seeing a friend beat someone in a chess game might arouse your own achievement motive and cause you to challenge your friend. This would be a case of press for achievement (*p* achievement). Seeing a picture of a juicy steak would constitute *p* food, which, along with your viscerogenic need for food (*n* food), would motivate you to eat something. So motivation for Murray is a result of the combined action of personal needs (characteristics of people) and press (characteristics of the environment). We would classify the needs as predisposing factors and the press as precipitating factors.

The human needs we will discuss in this section are all based on a model like Murray's. During psychological development, each person acquires (learns) certain psychological needs. Different people acquire

different strengths of the various needs and thus different hierarchies of needs. Initially, the psychological needs develop from the inherited, innate, biological needs, but later these needs somehow become independent of the biological needs, and the goals that satisfy these needs become ends in themselves.

For example, we begin with a biological need for food and water, which for an infant is satisfied by other people, mainly the parents. The infant is almost entirely dependent on other people and is likely to be happiest when other people are around, fulfilling the needs for nourishment, playing with and entertaining him or her, and so on. Because of this kind of continued exposure, the people who tend the infant become secondary reinforcers (see Chapter 4), having been continuously associated with the baby's general state of well-being. As secondary reinforcers, people then become goal objects themselves, and the child will want to be with people and will want these people

---

Highlight 7–1

Abraham Maslow and the Hierarchy of Human Needs

The psychologist most often associated with the idea of a hierarchy of needs, arranged in order of importance, is Abraham Maslow. His writings have had tremendous impact in the modern movement known as humanistic psychology. Indeed he was one of the founders of this movement. Maslow grouped the various needs (like those postulated by Henry Murray) into five categories and arranged them in the order shown in Figure 7–10. With the exception of the highest need, self-actualization, the needs are self-explanatory.

It was his concept of self-actualization that made Maslow such an important figure in the humanistic psy-

chology movement. Self-actualization is conceived of as a need to fulfill oneself, "to become whatever one is capable of becoming." It is a need to develop and utilize one's talents, abilities, and potential fully. It is a need that very few people have ever satisfied, and Maslow spent a great deal of his time studying people (such as Eleanor Roosevelt and Albert Einstein) who he thought had become self-actualized.

The needs higher in the hierarchy will emerge only as the lower ones become satisfied. We will not need love-belongingness and self-esteem if we have not first satisfied our physiological and security needs. If we live in fear for our safety or in anxiety about where our next meal will come from, we will have no need for love and self-esteem. In our society, where safety and security and physiological needs are reasonably well satisfied for everyone, we appear to be motivated largely by needs for love and self-esteem.

Maslow felt that our inability to satisfy these needs was the major cause of neurotic psychopathology in this country. Ideally, of course, a society would provide for all the lower needs and allow for the emergence of the need for self-actualization in everyone. Although few people may ever fully satisfy this need, everyone should be striving at this level in the pyramid, free of the lower needs. In fact, for Maslow, such persons are no longer "striving" but are "being" — being themselves rather than being people who are seeking something external to themselves.

FIGURE 7–10 Maslow's hierarchy of needs

According to Maslow's motivational theory, human needs form a hierarchy, and lower needs must be satisfied before higher needs are felt.

to care for and like him or her. The child will behave in ways designed to win the approval and affection of people. After a while, we might conclude that the child has developed a need to be with people and win the approval of people (n affiliation in Murray's list) and a need to be nursed, loved, and protected by people (n succorance). If the people in the child's life themselves value and reward achievement, the child may develop a strong need to achieve (n achievement) in order to win adult approval.

Although this is merely a speculative example, you can see how three of the human needs that Murray identified might develop and be learned by the child. Of course, different children have different experiences and different parents, who themselves have different needs and different values. Out of these differences in environmental circumstances each child learns a different set of priorities. Each child develops the human needs to various degrees or strengths and emerges into adulthood with his or her own hierarchy of psychological needs. It is this variation in the strengths of the various needs that largely accounts for the variation in adult personality, that is, for the fact that one person is a hard-driving, success-seeking fighter and another is an easygoing, introverted pacifist. We shall now turn our attention to some of the specific human needs that psychologists have found most interesting.

The Need for Achievement

Largely because of the efforts of David McClelland and J. W. Atkinson, the need for achievement (n ach in their shorthand) has been studied intensively. These investigators elaborated on Murray's TAT techniques for measuring needs and developed sophisticated scoring systems for the stories that subjects told in response to the carefully selected pictures. Their attention turned first to n ach, the need to excel, overcome obstacles, attain a high standard, accomplish the difficult. In the United States, we are so achievement oriented that for us motivation really means achievement motivation.

After developing a TAT scoring system for n ach, McClelland and Atkinson demonstrated that they could arouse the achievement motive (precipitate it) simply by telling subjects in an experiment that they had failed. The subjects took a group of tests and were told that they had done poorly and then were asked to tell TAT stories. The experience with failure aroused or precipitated the achievement motive, as measured by an increase in the number of achievement themes and elements in the stories. These psychologists went on to demonstrate that individuals vary in their need for achievement and that each person has a relatively stable level of n ach over time.

Performance Differences Due to n Ach

Many studies have shown that people with high n ach as measured by the TAT procedure do better than people with low n ach on a variety of experimental laboratory tasks, such as solving anagrams and doing arithmetic problems. It has also been demonstrated that high n ach people perform better in school than low n ach people with comparable intelligence. In the business world, high n ach people advance further than low n ach people with the same training and opportunity for advancement.

As suggested earlier, achievement motivation is apparently developed during childhood and is determined largely by the cultural and parental emphasis placed on achievement. These values are transmitted to the children during their socialization into the culture. One study, for example, demonstrated that mothers who themselves were high in n ach behaved differently toward their children than mothers low in n ach. High n ach mothers demanded that their children become independent and self-sufficient at an earlier age than low n ach mothers. Low n ach mothers were more protective of their children and placed greater restrictions on them for longer periods of time.

Success and Failure

More recently, it has been suggested that n ach is not a simple unidimensional personality characteristic, but a complex combination of factors. Atkinson, for example, has suggested that at least two factors are involved in achievement, a *need for success* and a counteracting *fear of failure,* and that different people have different combinations of these two tendencies. He has also stressed the importance of the situational factors operating at any given time, particularly the probability or chances of success or failure on a particular task and the incentive value of success or failure. If the task at hand is so difficult that nobody could possibly do it, then failing is nothing to be ashamed of and failing would have no negative incentive value. Likewise, if the task is so easy that anybody can do it, then achieving success is not worth much; success has little positive incentive value. Also, the goal itself (independent of the probability of getting it) has a positive incentive value that will determine the amount of motivation to achieve it. A person high in n ach will not indiscriminately attempt to achieve every conceivable goal. He or she might work very hard to achieve a goal of great value, but expend little effort to achieve a prize of no value.

In 1969, Matina Horner shocked many psychologists when she reported evidence based on the imagery in women's TAT stories suggesting that women have a greater *fear of success* than men. The reason, Horner suggested, is that success for a woman conflicts with the traditional female role in our society. Horner's hypothesis was that many women simply cannot allow themselves to compete successfully in what is perceived as a man's world. As you might expect, Horner's fear-of-success hypothesis has not gone unchallenged in the intervening years. There does appear to be a fear of deviation from one's sex role norm, but there is evidence that this fear occurs in both men and women. This is not to say that there is no fear of success. Evidence suggesting fear of success has indeed been found in numerous studies, but if we look at all the experiments, there is no support for the conclusion that fear of success, in general, occurs more often in women than in men. People of both sexes can have a fear of success, which can motivate them to behave in ways that will make success less likely.

The Need for Affiliation

We are social creatures who derive much of our satisfaction from other people. We join clubs, sororities, fraternities, Weight-Watchers, and Gamblers Anonymous. We try hard to make friends and often become very dependent upon them. Henry Murray would say we have a need for affiliation (n aff), and that like n ach, this functions to motivate us, making particular goals, such as being admitted to the local civic club, positive incentives. Likewise, other events, such as anything that would cause the defection of friends, will serve as negative incentives to the person with high n aff. Such a person will avoid hurting the feelings of his or her friends or avoid doing things that those friends would find shocking.

Elizabeth French has developed a special set of test items for measuring and distinguishing between n aff and n ach. She has shown that subjects high in n aff perform better on a simple task than subjects low in n aff under extremely pleasant and relaxed conditions designed to avoid arousing n ach instead of n aff. French concluded that the desire on the part of the high n aff subjects to please the experimenter, cooperate, and be friendly is what motivated them to perform better. In another experiment, French studied how people high in n ach and n aff go about picking partners to work with. People high in n ach choose partners who are competent at performing the task at hand (rather than choosing friends for partners), presumably because their goal is to succeed at the task. In contrast, people high in n aff tend to choose their friends as partners, as opposed to selecting partners on the basis of ability. When choosing sides for a game of volleyball, football, or charades, do you pick your friends for your team or the people who you believe will be the best players?

Like n ach, n aff is conceived of as a personality predisposition, presumably learned in childhood and possessed in varying degrees by different people. Like n ach, n aff is also subject to precipitation by the current circumstances. A person high in n aff will not be motivated by the goal of affiliating with a person or group of people who is extremely unpleasant and disliked. Instead, such people will be motivated by a friendly request to cooperate, to help out for the common good, given that the request comes from a person or group that has positive incentive value.

Finally, it has been suggested that the desire to affiliate ourselves with others is not really a need, but that instead affiliation is a goal for some other need, either our need to escape or avoid anxiety or to have others approve of us, known as a need for social approval, our next topic.

The Need for Social Approval

Perhaps the most fundamental purely psychological need is the need for social approval — the need to have others approve of us and our actions. It is obvious, for example, that the need to affiliate with others could be based on a need for approval. Also, one could argue that the need to achieve is ultimately based on a need to win recognition and approval from others. If others did not approve of striving to achieve, then people probably would not strive to achieve. The cross-cultural and family differences in achievement motivation suggest that approval from others is an important factor in determining the strength of the achievement motive. There is almost no limit to what some people will do to get certain other people to approve of and therefore like them. Conversely, such people will often do anything to avoid creating the circumstances that will lead others to disapprove of and therefore dislike them.

The need for approval is an important motive for understanding much of our social behavior. Consider, for example, why people tend to be conformists, to do what others do or what they think others would do. The pioneer investigators of the need for social approval are Douglas Crowne and David Marlowe. Together these investigators have developed a test to measure social desirability, the need to be liked by others or to be socially desirable. They show that people who score high and low on the test and thus presumably have high and low motives for approval sometimes behave in vastly different ways.

In one experiment the subjects were asked to spend 25 minutes doing an incredible task: taking 12 spools and one at a time putting them into a small box, then emptying the box and starting over again. Afterward Crowne and Marlowe asked the subjects how

One outcome of the women's movement is that women are moving into more political offices. They have learned that it is now acceptable to pursue their personal need for achievement.

An example is State Senator Alene Ammond of New Jersey, on whom all male eyes are riveted in this conference.

much they enjoyed the task. Subjects with high-approval motives, believe it or not, said they enjoyed the task, more so at least than subjects with low-approval motives. In addition, high need-for-approval subjects said they learned more from the task, rated the experiment as more scientifically important, and had a greater desire to participate in similar experiments than low need-for-approval subjects. Would you pack and repack spools (and say that you enjoyed doing it) in order to gain the approval of the person who asked you to do it?

In another study Crowne and Marlowe showed subjects slides containing two clusters of dots, one clearly larger than the other. The subject was asked to indicate which cluster was larger, a very easy task indeed, except that there were other "subjects" in the room (actually not subjects but assistants to Crowne and Marlowe) who lied and said the wrong answer before the real subject could speak. The results showed that on 59 percent of these trials where the confederates lied, the high need-for-approval sub-

jects lied also. The low need-for-approval subjects conformed and lied only 34 percent of the time. These results show that subjects with high- and low-approval motives behave differently, and they suggest that conformity (in this case, agreeing with the judgment of others) comes from the need to win the approval of others. How much of your own behavior is motivated by a desire to be desirable?

The Need for Power

Recently, McClelland has expanded his research work to include what he refers to as the need for power — power motivation — the need to dominate and control others. Two interesting results from this work have emerged already. In one study, the suppression or inhibition of power motivation was shown to be related to high blood pressure. Based on judgments of power needs in people at age 30, McClelland was able to predict high blood pressure levels 20 years later. In a second study, McClelland observed a sig-

Highlight 7–2

Motivational Dilemmas and Conflict

A person is in a state of conflict when he or she has two or more competing motives, all of which cannot be satisfied. There are two basic kinds of motives: *approach motives* refer to situations in which there is a reward or positive incentive to be gained if the person approaches the goal; *avoidance motives* refer to cases in which the incentive is negative—it is an object, event, or state of affairs that is unpleasant and is to be avoided. All cases of conflict between motives can be described in terms of approach and avoidance:

1. *Approach-approach conflict:* In this case two positive incentives exist but cannot both be attained—one or the other must be chosen. An example is trying to decide whether you should spend the evening at a movie or watching a favorite TV program. An approach-approach conflict is usually easily resolved (you can see the movie tomorrow), unless the motives for both incentives are very strong and the goals are indeed incompatible.

2. *Avoidance-avoidance conflict:* This conflict results when the choice is between two negative alternatives or incentives. For example, one may have to decide which of two dull courses to study for tonight. The most distinctive feature of avoidance-avoidance conflict is that it is usually difficult to resolve, especially if both incentives are strongly negative. Often we fail to make any decision at all, attempting instead to remove ourselves from the conflict situation, for example, by watching TV and not studying at all.

3. *Approach-avoidance conflict:* Frequently a goal or incentive has both positive and negative aspects, resulting in both approach and avoidance responses. For example, foods that you find particularly tasty may cause weight gain and cavities. In this type of conflict, "distance" from the incentive appears to play an important role. At great distances, the negative aspects do not seem as im-

FIGURE 7–11

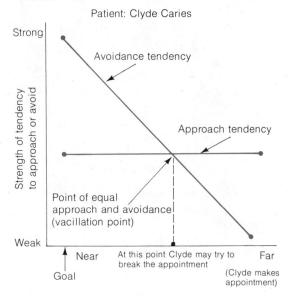

The graph diagrams the approach-avoidance conflict of a patient (Clyde Caries) who makes an appointment with his dentist a long time before he actually has to show up. There are two tendencies, one to approach (go to the dentist) and one to avoid (stay away from the dentist). In this example, the approach gradient does not change as the time for the appointment gets closer, but the avoidance tendency gets stronger and stronger (Clyde anticipates a lot of pain) as the appointment gets closer. At first, the approach tendency is stronger than the avoidance tendency, and so the appointment is made. Later, as the time for the appointment draws near, the avoidance tendency gets stronger and at some time

portant as the positive ones, and so you move toward the goal, for example, by making a dental appointment for six months in the future. As the time for the appointment gets nearer, however, the negative aspects increase in strength

nificant correlation between the power needs of men (measured during college) and the degree to which their wives had successful careers 10 years later. The higher the husband's power needs, the lower the degree of the wife's career commitment. Such correlations, demonstrated over 10- or 20-year periods, strongly support the existence of a relatively stable personality characteristic involving need for power. Like needs for achievement, affiliation, and social approval, need for power implies that motivation is partly determined by the stable predispositions of a person, that is, by personality.

A Final Note of Caution

The work on human motives as personality traits is very appealing and seems to contribute greatly to our understanding of human behavior. However, we must remember that there are pitfalls (see the section on dispositional theories of personality in Chapter 9). With a long list of needs, you can account for just about everything by saying that the person did what he or she did to satsify such and such a need. It is the same problem we encountered with the long list of instincts that were once used to explain everything,

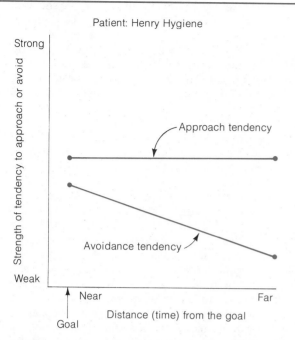

Patient: Henry Hygiene

Approach tendency

Avoidance tendency

Strong

Strength of tendency to approach or avoid

Weak

Near

Far

Goal

Distance (time) from the goal

it becomes as strong as the approach tendency. This is the point of maximum conflict about what to do, the vacillation point. This is when Clyde may try to cancel or at least postpone the appointment. In any conflict situation what happens will depend on the strengths of the approach and avoidance gradients and how steep they are. For example, in the right graph, the avoidance tendency is not as strong as in the left graph because Henry Hygiene is not as afraid of the dentist as Clyde is. For Henry, the approach and avoidance tendencies never intersect, and so he does not try to cancel his appointment.

and may surpass the positive ones, causing you to retreat from the goal (you break the appointment). The reaction of two different patients to this approach-avoidance conflict is shown in Figure 7–11.

or the long list of drives. A long list of needs may not be as much of an improvement as it first appears. We must remember that there will have to be independent ways of defining and measuring these needs to avoid circular explanations.

This is why we investigate ways to measure human needs with various kinds of tests, such as the TAT storytelling technique. But there is still a lot of room for improvement. The tests are not highly reliable, and they may be measuring other things besides the intended need. Another problem is that people are not as consistent in their behavior as such

theories imply. For example, a person with a high need for approval does not always behave in a way designed to get approval. This may just mean that we have a long way to go in understanding the precipitating conditions for behavior; but it may also mean that it is not very useful to speak of enduring, stable traits, such as a high need for approval. Behavior may be so much a consequence of the precipitating circumstances that personality predispositions are only modestly useful in predicting what a person will do in any given situation.

Note that most of the studies we have talked about in this section are basically correlational in character. If we pick out people who are high and low in achievement motivation and see that the highs do better on some task than the lows, we merely have a correlation between n ach and performance. This does not mean the n ach differences caused the performance differences. Perhaps high n ach people are more intelligent, or better coordinated, or stronger, or whatever, than low n ach people. If so, the performance difference could be due to that factor and not to n ach. It is not easy to reach unequivocal conclusions in this complex area of human motivation. Thus, we must remember to be cautious.

Motivation and Cognitive Processes

Most sources of human motivation are learned, whereas the behavior of lower animals is guided more by hard-wired biological systems. Clearly, the incentives that human beings seek out are largely a product of experience. Even if you dislike brussels sprouts, a single taste of brussels sprouts prepared à la Julia Child, sautéed in lemon butter and various spices, could make you a devotee of this otherwise bland vegetable. You have learned and are now cognitively aware of a new incentive value for brussels sprouts.

Throughout this chapter we have used examples of motivation involving learning and cognitive processes. Now we will consider directly the role of cognition in motivation. One thing to realize at the outset is that human beings have the ability to acquire new incentives not only from direct experience but also by inference. If you have enjoyed peas, beans, and carrots prepared à la Julia Child, you might *infer* that brussels sprouts prepared her way will be better than (have higher incentive value) plain brussels sprouts.

Inference and Attribution

It is clear that many incentive values are acquired by inference, observation, or imitation. Consider your neighbor who has just purchased a new pair of brand

X skis. If she is an excellent skier who teaches skiing on the weekends, you probably will infer that the brand is an excellent one and therefore will assign a high incentive value to it.

The establishment of incentive values through inference is closely connected with a process called *attribution* and a theory called attribution theory. Attribution theory was formulated primarily in the context of social psychology (See Chapter 10). The theory assumes that each person in a social situation is constantly analyzing the behavior of others, attempting to answer the "why" question, trying to form attributions, or statements about the causes of the other people's behavior. We also constantly ask this same question about our own behavior — "Why did I do that?" This is called self-attribution — the reasons or explanations we develop for our own behavior.

Consider again the neighbor and her new skis. Why did she buy brand X? If we attribute the purchase to the fact that she is an expert skier, is intelligent, and carefully investigates things before she acts, we are likely to conclude that brand X is a top-quality ski for its price. This set of cognitive activities would then result in the incentive value of brand X going up for us. In contrast, suppose we analyze the situation and come up with the following: She is a ski instructor, and the manufacturers of brand X gave her the skis free as a promotional gimmick designed to make people think all instructors use brand X. We then attribute her using brand X skis to the fact she got them free, not to the quality of the skis. In such a case, the incentive value of brand X might not be raised very much at all.

A major goal of all advertising is to cause the incentive value of the product being advertised to rise *in your mind*. Note that the emphasis has to be on your cognitive activity. Because the advertiser can seldom arrange for you to experience the product directly (except perhaps by giving you a free sample), TV and magazine ads are all designed to get you to *think* that the product is excellent. If you need (the drive concept) a product of this type, you will conclude that brand X has high incentive value. Now you know why products are so often depicted in such a way as to get you to infer or conclude that wonderful things will happen to you if you choose this particular brand.

One of the most interesting parts of attribution theory relates to the differences between self-attribution and observer attribution. To what do you attribute your own behavior compared with what an observer of your behavior would conclude? One version of attribution theory suggested that self-attributions are likely to be heavily based on environmental factors. The cause of your behavior is attributed externally to the situation, as when you say, "I hit him because he insulted me." In contrast, observers of a person's behavior (your behavior, for example) tend to base attributions less on the situation, context, or environment and more on the personality of the person behaving. An observer of your fight would be more likely than you to conclude you hit the other person because you are a hostile, aggressive individual. Thus we tend to explain our own behavior by our circumstances, but we explain the behavior of others by their personality.

More recent research has suggested that our explanations of our own behavior will also depend upon whether or not the outcome of the behavior was desirable or undesirable. If we do something that has a good outcome (we win a tennis match), our tendency is to credit our success to ourselves — we say we won because we had better skills, were smarter, and so on. If our opponent wins the match, we credit the circumstances rather than his or her ability or personality — "It was just a lucky bounce of the ball." On the other hand, when the outcome is undesirable,

---

I Win Because of Me; I Lose Because of You
By JACK C. HORN

Superior athletes seem to explain failure much as you and I do. They tend to credit themselves and their teammates for wins and to blame losses on someone or something else: bad breaks, bad umpiring, or a super effort by the other team.

The tendency to give internal explanations for success and external ones for failure has been confirmed in psychological laboratories, but Richard Lau of Carnegie-Mellon University and Dan Russell of the University of Iowa looked into how the tendency works in the real world of sports. Lau and Russell started with all the articles from 8 newspapers that dealt with 6 World Series games and with 27 college and professional football games in 1977. Every explanation for a win or loss by players, coaches, or sportswriters was coded as either internal ("We played a great game" or "We stunk out the joint") or external (referring to the other team or some other outside force, such as bad luck or a string of injuries).

Just over 80 percent of the reasons for wins were internal, compared with only 53 percent of the explanations for losses. After a win in the Series, for example, Yankee manager Billy Martin said of the outfielder who had starred in the game, "Piniella has done it all." Dodger third baseman Ron Cey, in contrast, blamed the fates for his team's loss: "I think we've hit the ball all right. But I think we were unlucky."

Psychology Today
November 1980

the situation is likely to be reversed in our minds. We say *we* lost because of circumstances or bad luck, but the other person lost because of poor skill or ability or intelligence.

We may want to credit ourselves to such an extent when we win that we misperceive the role of luck or chance. We like to perceive ourselves as being in control of things or as being competent even when we are not. Studies have shown, for example, that people prefer to select their own number in a lottery instead of having one given to them; people feel more in control in a lottery-type game if they get to pick their own ticket as opposed to the experimenter picking for them. It has been suggested that human beings have a motive to control and will often behave as if they are in control even when they clearly are not. The bowler who displays lots of "body English" *after* having released the ball or the person shooting craps with a special blowing and shaking of the dice come to mind.

Robert W. White has proposed that the need to be competent and to control is a central component in human motivation. Demonstrated failure to control leads us to feel incompetent. If this applies to a large proportion of our experiences, we run the risk of concluding that we are helpless and worthless. This is the cognitive aspect of the learned-helplessness theory of depression (See Chapter 4). Another cognitive aspect of competency deals with self-judgment of competency — our cognitive appraisal of our own competence. Obviously feeling competent is a critical factor in motivation. Albert Bandura has made *self-efficacy* (See Chapter 9), our appraisal of our own competence, a major aspect of his social learning theory of personality. He argues that if you do not think you are competent (even though you actually may be), you will not even try to succeed.

Attributing failure or poor performance to circumstances rather than to ourselves may be adaptive; at least failure then becomes understandable in that the individual avoids anxiety and feelings of incompetence. Such feelings can make the situation even worse, causing further failure and leading to a vicious circle which could become pathological. A laboratory study illustrates this process. Subjects were assessed on the fluency of their speech during an experimental task and asked to explain why they stammered. Self-attribution of the stuttering was correlated with significantly more stuttering than attributing the stuttering to the tenseness of the experimental situation. There is a message here for therapy — anxiety may often be caused by inappropriate self-attribution, for example, taking the blame for everything personally, with nearly a complete failure to recognize and attribute at least part of the causes to one's particular circumstances.

Inference and Utility

Incentive value is typically a relative matter. Brand X may have more features that you like than brand Y, but you may have to work harder to get X than Y, or X may cost more than Y. Once you conclude that you need something of a particular type, then you have to ask yourself what your chances are of getting that something. What is the probability that behavior B will produce object X? This aspect of motivation was brought to the attention of psychologists by the proponents of what is often called *subjective utility theory.* This general theory also emphasizes cognition, particularly decision making about what behavior to engage in.

Utility theory combines incentive and drive, or push and pull, into one concept — *utility.* Of what utility (how useful) would a particular goal object or goal state be to you? The degree of usefulness of an object is the object's utility. Notice the combination of *need* and *incentive* — if you don't *need* skis, the best-quality pair in the world will have low utility for you, and if you are literally starving for food, the worst-tasting food will have high utility. The utility, then, is a joint function of how much you *think* you need something and how attractive the particular thing is. Utility theory focuses on the fact that, in any given situation, there are always at least two alternative behaviors for you to choose from. Each leads, with a certain probability, to a certain outcome or goal. Each goal will have its own utility.

Consider that old TV game show in which a contestant is in the following situation: Host Monte Hall gives the contestant a choice between a sure $500 and whatever is behind curtain 3. Every so often behind the curtain there is something fantastic (high utility), and *every so often* there is something silly or dumb (low utility). The contestant is certain of getting $500 and has a low probability of getting something with either much higher or much lower utility than $500.

Utility theory reminds us that a critical aspect of overall motivation is probability of success. How do you know what the probability of success is, and how do you decide on the utility value of a particular outcome? The answer is that you estimate *them* in your head using all the knowledge and skill at your command — applying your cognitive abilities. Because you are estimating them, and not actually calculating them, they are called *subjective* probabilities and *subjective* utilities. The theory says we compute an overall judgment, called the *expected utility,* for each of the alternative courses of action. We do this by combining the subjective utility of the goal object with the subjective probability that a particular behavior will lead to that goal object. Suppose the subjective utility of the fantastic object behind curtain 3 is evaluated in dollars as $5000, and the subjective probability of that object actually being behind curtain 3 is .10 (1 chance in 10 or 10 in 100). Multiplying the two (.10 × 5000) gives an overall subjective expected utility of $500. This is exactly the same as the utility of the sure $500, and that is likely to make the choice quite difficult.

Remember that subjective probabilities and utilities are judgments. The actual utility might turn out to be different, for example, when the person finds that the "fantastic prize" is actually worth only $2000. A key notion in utility theory is that what we think is the case, not what actually is true, determines our behavior. If we think our chances are 1 in 10, we are more likely to choose curtain 3 than if we think our chances are 1 in 1000.

The expected utility of a course of action will be closely correlated with the overall motivation to engage in that action, other things being equal. If a given behavior is likely to lead to a highly desirable (high utility, high positive incentive value) goal object or state, then the motivation to engage in that behavior will be quite high. Likewise, low probability of success for achieving a low utility object will surely result in low motivation to engage in that behavior. Utility theory focuses our attention "inside the head" of the behaving person, on the cognitive aspects of motivation, and on the fact that a great deal of information processing takes place in even the simplest choice and motivational situations.

Sexual Motivation

Sexual behavior, particularly human sexual behavior, is motivated in many different complex ways. Any occurrence of sexual behavior is likely to be motivated by more than one factor, and the motivating factors will change from one instance to the next. To understand sexual motivation then, we will have to borrow from all the concepts we have discussed in this chapter. Let us briefly review these factors and see how they apply to sexual behavior.

First, we talked about drives and incentives as the pushing and pulling forces, respectively, in motivating behavior. Some aspects of sexual behavior can be understood in terms of a sex drive, although it is clear that sexual deprivation does not have the same kinds of devastating effects that food or water deprivation have. From the incentive point of view, we hardly need to tell anyone that sexual behavior can be incredibly pleasurable, and thus the opportunity to engage in sexual intercourse can have enormous positive incentive value. People are motivated to do all sorts of things in order to gain access to this

incentive. We feel that predisposition and precipitation more accurately capture the full range of motivational phenomena. Much of sexual behavior can be understood by looking for factors that will predispose us toward engaging in sexual behavior, and then examining the environment for the precipitating stimuli.

What about the biological basis of motivation? Sexual behavior is clearly grounded in the endocrine system we discussed in Chapter 2. However, this strong biological regulation of sexual behavior by hormone balance applies mainly to the sexual be-

Sex and Angry Women

Numerous studies over the years have shown that certain types of erotic literature, pictures and films can increase aggression in males. Generally more explicit sexual depictions tend to make men—already angered by experimenters—more angry and aggressive. At the same time, softer core erotic materials seem to soothe the hostility in angry males.

In one of the first such experiments involving females, Robert A. Baron of Purdue University tested 45 undergraduate women. The subjects were either angered (by unflattering personal evaluations from another student) or not angered and then exposed to varying degrees of erotic pictures of men and men and women, as well as to non-erotic pictures. Baron reported . . . that heightened sexual arousal does increase aggression in women, as well as men; and there is indication that it may take less to make women more angry than it does for men. As with males, however, mild erotic pictures appear to reduce aggression in angered women, he reports. Aggression was measured in the intensity and frequency of "shocks" they believed they were giving to the person who angered them, as well as by questionnaire.

Science News
September 16, 1978

There is some evidence linking sexual arousal with aggression, and, of course, this has been brought to bear on political issues such as pornography. Freud, in a very controversial paper, argued that there was a close link between the two, with sexual behavior in men being largely motivated by hostility toward women. Perhaps this newsclip suggests that what's good for the gander is good for the goose. Again, perhaps the link is an indirect one via a general arousal factor. General arousal can serve to predispose an organism to react to stimuli of any sort; some stimuli can then precipitate violent behavior, while others would precipitate sexual behavior. This is a clear example that would fit general arousal theory—each stimulus has two effects: (1) an arousal effect and (2) a cue effect that elicits particular responses. But why would "soft core" erotic materials be soothing?

havior of animals. Human beings have largely, although not completely, freed themselves from this regulation. For example, there is evidence that sexual desire in women does correlate somewhat with the menstrual cycle (see the newsclip "A Cycle Named Desire"), which is regulated by hormones. Another example is evidence which shows that alcohol intake depresses the level of neural activity and the male hormone testosterone. This may explain the effect alcohol can have on male potency. Hormone therapy for sexual behavior problems also serves as a good reminder to us that human sexual behavior is not all psychological. The explanation for animal sexual behavior lies primarily in the concept of instinct and in the fixed-action patterns described by ethologists.

These patterns run off "automatically" when the animal is properly predisposed (probably by the endocrine balance), and the fixed-action pattern is triggered by an appropriate releasing stimulus. While human sexual behavior seems largely independent of instinctual motivation, the theory of sociobiology reminds us that many behaviors are motivated by the sexual need to reproduce and pass on one's genes. However, there is good reason to question the applicability of this theory to human sexual behavior.

Next consider the general need for stimulation to maintain the optimal arousal level. Sexual behavior is obviously arousing, and much of human sexual behavior may be motivated by such needs. Recall our discussion of the pleasure centers in the brain. The

A Cycle Named Desire
By LINDA ASHER

Are women, like nonhuman female primates, more inclined toward sexual activity around the monthly moment of ovulation, when conception is most likely? Psychoanalytically oriented studies years ago discerned such a rise in women's desires at mid-month by examining their emotional and dream lives. Other research, however, asked about the times women had intercourse and found no conclusive patterns. Recently, a group of researchers at Wesleyan University questioned women not only about intercourse in general, but also about intercourse that women initiate, as well as asking about caressing, masturbation, fantasies, and arousal by books and films. Around ovulation, they found, sexual activity initiated by women takes a lusty leap, increasing by about 20 percent—except for women on the Pill.

Thirty-five white married women, ranging in age from 21 to 37 and selected from volunteers, filled out daily questionnaires for an average four months each at the behest of psychologists David B. Adams, Alice Ross Gold, and research assistant Anne D. Burt. Twelve of the women were using the Pill, 11 were protected from pregnancy by an IUD or by their male partner's having undergone a vasectomy, and 12 used methods that take special planning each time intercourse occurs, such as condoms, a diaphragm, foam, or the rhythm method.

The women in the non-Pill groups appeared to feel markedly more aroused at mid-month, although those who used birth-control methods requiring preparation did not have intercourse as often as those using less bothersome techniques. Perhaps because the Pill blocks ovulation, Pill-users exhibited no such peak at mid-cycle. In fact, for reasons the researchers cannot explain, the levels of masturbation and initiating intercourse of women taking the Pill actually decreased in the middle of their cycles.

The researchers emphasize that cycles of desire can be influenced by a large array of factors in addition to ovulation. For example, the study found that many women, especially those in couples that abstain from intercourse during menstruation, show a significant rise in intercourse right after their periods. "But the peak we found around ovulation indicates that there is some cyclical biological underpinning to the sexual drive in women," Gold told *Psychology Today* in an interview. "It's not a major factor, but it's there."

Psychology Today
February 1979

A Potent Myth

Impotent men have traditionally received cold comfort from their physicians. "It's all in your head," they are usually told before being shuttled off to psychologists and psychiatrists. Now comes a report in this week's *Journal of the American Medical Association* urging doctors to take a closer look at the patient's physical condition. Endocrinologist Richard Spark of Boston's Beth Israel Hospital writes that the problem in many cases is medical, not mental. Using sensitive radioimmunoassay techniques that can pick up infinitesimal levels of hormones in the blood, Dr. Spark and his team studied 105 impotent men, aged 18 to 75. They found that 35% of the men had previously overlooked disorders of the endocrine system—too little testosterone, for example, or overactive thyroids. In these cases, medical treatment corrected the conditions and restored potency.

Time
February 25, 1980

Here are two articles that should serve to remind us human beings that our sexual behavior is still at least partly regulated by our biological heritage.

"I can go two weeks without *water*, but *sex* is an entirely different matter!"

Playboy, February 1969. Reproduced by special permission of PLAYBOY Magazine. Copyright © 1969 by Playboy.

intense pleasure from sexual gratification may come about from such pleasure centers. Human sexual behavior appears to be very heavily dominated by the incentive aspects of the situation, the intense pleasure one experiences.

Next we turned our attention to motivation as a personality characteristic. Obviously, the need for achievement, the need for affiliation, and the need for social approval play a very important role in human sexual behavior. There clearly are situations in which sexual behavior is treated as an achievement, a game in which people try to "score" points— a rather sad commentary, but nevertheless often true. Equally questionable is the use of sexual behavior as a way of satisfying a need for approval, where sex is "handed out" as a bribe to win approval. On the more positive side, the need for affiliation brings people together to enjoy each other, to fall in love, and to share the beauty and pleasure of mutual sexual fulfillment.

Finally, we considered the cognitive aspects of motivation, the role of thinking and knowledge. For animals, sexual behavior appears completely natural, automatic, and instinctive. Cognition plays little if any role, and cognitive concepts are not relevant. In contrast, human sexual behavior may be more cognitive than biological. Thinking, expectations, and knowledge are the primary factors that determine decisions about whether, where, and with whom one will engage in sexual behavior. As a simple illustration, consider the extent to which your decisions about sex are affected by your knowledge of contraception.

In summary, sexual behavior is motivated partly by a drive and partly by incentive; we are predisposed to engage in sexual behavior and there are precipitating stimuli; sexual behavior is deeply rooted in the physiology of the endocrine system and the biology of instincts and the need to reproduce. However, it is also intensely pleasurable and arousing and,

in human beings, is influenced by psychogenic needs and cognitive processes. All of these concepts are helpful in understanding sexual motivation.

Freud's Theory

In its original form Sigmund Freud's theory of sexual development (see also Chapters 8 and 9) is based heavily on instinctual and drive-reductionistic concepts. Its basic component is the concept of ever-occurring sexual energies. Freud's theory has had and continues to have a profound impact on sexual beliefs, partially because it is one of the few really complete theories of sexual development and partially because of its historical position. It was presented near the end of the Victorian era (one of the most antisexual eras of history) and was a sharp breakaway from the sexual attitudes of that period.

While Freud postulated a number of sources of drive-related energies, it was the sex energies or *libido* which were most powerful. This sex energy, along with hostility and aggression, account for most human motivation.

Two ideas are central to Freud's explanation of sexual behavior: unconscious mental processes and infantile sexuality. The id is composed of the basic biological drives (including the libido), and its contents are unconscious to the individual. These id drives, Freud postulated, seek a goal of pleasure. At the other end of the scale is the superego. A primarily conscious force comprised of learned moral and social concepts, the task of the superego is basically to block the pleasure-seeking id. The ego mediates between the id and the superego.

Freud's second concept, that of infantile sexuality, postulates that the instinctual id forces operate through a series of developmental stages beginning at birth and continuing through puberty. During this infantile development process a blueprint is established or "wired" into the individual for future personality and sexual patterns. In each of the three major stages of development the pleasure-seeking id forces center in a particular body area (the mouth, anus, or genitals). In each stage a particular task, usually in conflict with the id forces, must be completed. (These stages are described in detail in Chapter 9). An end product of the compromises reached among instinctual id forces and ego and superego forces, this blueprint will be activated during puberty.

Another major conceptualization of sexual motivation based on biological concepts is represented by the work of C. S. Ford and F. A. Beach, who studied sexual behavior across several cultures and species of animals. Beginning with a general thesis that a fundamental drive to act sexually exists, they then assumed that any behavior common to human beings and other animals was probably genetically

Anxiety Discovered As Sex Therapy Aid
By D'VERA COHN

PROVIDENCE, R.I. (UPI)—A Brown University researcher says sex therapists who find that relaxation fails to improve their clients' sexual response should try anxiety instead.

John P. Wincze, who is conducting studies at the Veterans Administration Hospital in Providence, said his research shows people have stronger sexual response to pornography if they watch violent movies first.

He said the finding means, in some cases, anxiety may be a useful new tool in sex therapy.

"It has been assumed in sex therapy that anxiety is the cause of a lot of problems," said Wincze, who is chief of the hospital's psychology services. "Yet in dealing with clinical subjects, relaxation didn't work with them always.

"For those individuals that are expressing anxiety associated with their problem, we can work with their anxiety," he said.

Wincze ran experiments in which he showed people a videotape of a violent automobile accident or an Alfred Hitchcock thriller movie, followed by hard-core pornography. For comparison purposes, he showed other people a "neutral" film first.

The results, he said, were "statistically significant." The men and women shown the violent movies first get more readily aroused by the sex films.

Wincze conceded the heightened response may be simply relief that the violent movie is over, but he said the anxiety film may also "be acting as sort of a primer—your heart rate is racing, your blood pressure is up, which is exactly what happens during sexual arousal."

Other studies show anxiety and sexual arousal have remarkably similar physiological manifestations and Wincze said his results prove anxiety also can actually contribute to sexual arousal, not kill it.

Denver Post
July 13, 1979

Here the arousal theory of motivation is applied to the treatment of sexual problems. Some such problems may be caused by arousal deficits. The technique described here uses the indirect link between violence and sex through general arousal. Some aberrant sexual behaviors such as masochism and sadism may develop because some people have found that they can become sufficiently aroused only through violence. This response can come about by simple reinforcement on a few occasions where violent behavior is followed immediately by sexual gratification.

based. Eventually Ford and Beach concluded that four types of sexual behaviors were probably instinctual in that they occurred among all primates, including humans. These include coitus, masturbation, homosexual activity, and methods of attracting a sexual partner.

Learning Theory

During the past two decades the increasingly predominant view has been away from biology to learning as an explanation of human sexual behavior. Research suggests that the higher up the phylogenetic scale one goes, the less evidence there is of hormonal or other biological controls in sexual patterns and the more evidence there is of learned sexual behavior. No specific theory of sexual development based on learning theory really exists. We must assume that the same general principles would apply to sexual learning as well as to other types of learning. We will not attempt to consider sexuality from all of the possible theoretical frameworks, but instead examine a few key concepts general to most learning theories as they apply to sexuality.

Consider the operant conditioning paradigm (see Chapter 4). Events become established as behavior patterns when they are associated with some form of reward or reinforcer. For instance, suppose that a child becomes sexually stimulated while pressing against an object, or perhaps climbing a tree. While the sexual feeling is not fully understood, the experience was pleasant. The child may attempt to replicate the experience, possibly using the hands. Eventually the activity is carried far enough to experience masturbation and orgasm. In each instance the pleasure obtained reinforces the activity, and a habit or pattern is established. As further learning occurs, the sexual activities become associated with particular settings (for example, darkness, being in bed) and social awareness (parental and peer attitudes).

The learning theory approach assumes that change continues throughout life even though early repeated experiences may be most influential. The general application of learning principles to sexual behavior is increased through the use of the processes of generalization and discrimination. In the process of generalization, a particular stimulus can elicit a response conditioned to a related but different stimulus. Thus learning to associate sexual feeling with one particular member of the opposite sex can generalize out to all or most members of the opposite sex. Discrimination operates in opposition to generalization and allows us to limit the objects to which we respond sexually in order not to be aroused by an ever-increasing field of stimuli.

In addition to direct experiential learning, social-learning models (as we will see in Chapter 9) suggest that we can learn indirectly or vicariously those behaviors that we will identify as rewarding. Thus the media could present strong models for appropriate and rewarding sexual behavior, and these are then imitated.

Most social-psychological explanations of sexual behavior tend to be extensions of a particular school of personality theory, usually with a heavy emphasis on interpersonal relationships. Such theories see sexuality as a part of some process such as Maslow's self-actualization (see Highlight 7–1) and do not explain its development. One exception to this is a fairly well-developed theory advanced by Ken Hardy which utilizes both learning theory and social-psychological concepts. He postulates that we move toward some specific sexual behavior because we have learned to expect that in so doing we will produce some positive change in our lives. And it is the expectation of positive change that is the basis of sexual motivation.

Hardy believes that young children build tentative sets of positive expectations regarding simple sexual activity such as hugging and kissing through observing apparently positive responses to these activities in parents, older siblings, and media presentations. Children then move toward testing these simple behaviors because of their belief system, not their biology. If the initial experiences are positively reinforced (through social reinforcers), this increases the strength of the belief system. As knowledge becomes more sophisticated, a type of generalization due to positive past experience expands the expectation that more events will be positive. This in turn increases the probability that new experiences will be explored because of the expectation of positive change. What is developed eventually, according to the theory advanced by Hardy, is a learned appetite rather than a biological drive.

"I'll tell you what's missing from your game, Cowley—hate."

The New Yorker, October 24, 1974. Drawing by Lorenz; © 1974 The New Yorker Magazine, Inc.

Emotions are generally considered to be important sources of motivation. This is particularly evident in athletics. Emotions involve arousal, and arousal is correlated with motivation.

Emotion

People love and hate. They are afraid, anxious, and sometimes terrified. They are happy and sad, angry and mad. People are emotional. They have feelings. Furthermore, there are motivational consequences associated with these emotions. People fight, we say, because they are angry and full of hate. People seek each other out because, we say, they are in love. People are motivated to do all sorts of things in order to escape or avoid unpleasant emotional states (fear, anger, anxiety) or in order to obtain pleasant emotional states (love, happiness, joy, pleasure). Clearly emotion and motivation are closely related topics.

In psychology, the concept of emotion has proved complex and difficult to study scientifically. This is partly because so much of emotional experience is private personal experience that is not readily open to scientific scrutiny. Also, it is difficult to elicit emotions in controlled laboratory situations (particularly the positive emotions such as love, pleasure, and joy). But although there is still a long way to go, we can say that progress is being made.

Emotion and Incentives

A great deal of effort has been expended in an attempt to devise a classification system for emotions. There are hundreds of words in our language referring to different emotional experiences. Many of these overlap in meaning, however, or refer merely to slight differences in the intensity of the emotion. There are two primary dimensions of emotions: (1) the qualitative dimension of *pleasant-unpleasant* and (2) the quantitative dimension of *intensity.* Emotional states are basically pleasant or unpleasant, and they vary in the intensity of the feeling of pleasantness or unpleasantness. Thus the difference between anger and rage is primarily one of intensity, as is the difference between happiness and ecstasy.

These two basic dimensions also determine the motivational consequences of emotional states. First, we can expect that unpleasant emotional states (and the things we have learned will produce them) will act as negative incentives (we will be motivated to avoid or escape them). Likewise, pleasant states (and the things that will produce them) will be positive incentives (we will be motivated to achieve them). Because we learn about the world, we can usually anticipate the emotional states that specific objects, events, and states of affairs will elicit. Then we can seek as goals those things that we expect will elicit positive emotions and try to avoid those things that we expect will result in unpleasant emotional experiences. Of course, we cannot *avoid* everything unpleasant— sometimes we accidentally encounter an overbearing bore at a party. Under those circumstances, we will be motivated to *escape* (the bore) because we failed to avoid (him or her).

Second, we can expect that the degree of motivation will depend upon the strength of the anticipated or experienced state. The stronger or more intense the emotion, the greater the motivation to approach or avoid. In other words, the emotional intensity will determine the amount of incentive, and whether the emotion is pleasant or unpleasant will determine whether the incentive is positive (approach) or negative (avoid).

Anxiety and Anger

Psychologists have been particularly interested in the motivational consequences of two emotional states, anxiety and anger. Anxiety is of interest because it appears to play a central role in the motivation of abnormal (see Chapter 11) as well as everyday behavior. Anger is of interest because it is the standard emotion accompanying frustration, and it probably underlies most acts of aggression. Together then, anxiety and anger represent two emotional states that may produce a great deal of undesirable behavior in people. Understanding these emotions may help us control or eliminate much of this behavior.

Anxiety

Anxiety is an anticipatory fear attached to no particular object or situation. We are anxious when we anticipate the occurrence of a harmful or threatening stimulus. Fear is what we experience when the threatening stimulus actually occurs. Presumably anxiety is an unpleasant experience with negative incentive value, meaning that we will be motivated to escape anxiety when it develops and to avoid it if at all possible. Much of psychopathological behavior is thought to be motivated by the desire to escape anxiety. Behaviors that allow a person to escape anxiety will be reinforced, and thus repeated, and eventually will become habits for dealing with anxiety. Similarly, objects, events, and circumstances that we have learned will prevent or counteract anxiety become positive incentives, and we will direct our behavior toward achieving these goals. In some cases the anxious person is unable to recognize the stimuli that are anxiety provoking. This is known as *free-floating anxiety* or *diffuse anxiety*.

The classic experiment demonstrating anxiety as a motivating force was done with rats by Neal Miller, using a shuttle box with two compartments, one black and one white. A rat was placed in the white compartment and electric shock was turned on, causing the rat to run into the black side of the box, where it escaped from the shock. This routine was repeated

for several trials until presumably the fear was conditioned to the white compartment. At that point no further shocks were given. Despite the absence of shocks, the rat continued to show signs of fear when placed in the white side—the rat was "anxious." It continued to run into the black side even though it was never shocked again. The white side took on negative incentive value and the black side probably took on positive incentive value.

Next, a door was put in place between the compartments, and a wheel was placed in the white compartment. This wheel, if turned by the rat, would open the door. The result was that the rats learned the wheel-turning responses to get out of the white compartment, even though shock was not administered. The rats were not escaping from real shock but from the threat of shock. They were escaping from the white compartment because it had been associated with shock. They were evidently motivated by the conditioned fear or anxiety produced by the white compartment. They may also have been motivated by the positive incentive of the black side of the box, because this side had repeatedly been associated with relief from the shock.

You might ask yourself about your own behavior at this point. How much of your behavior is motivated by the desire to escape or avoid an unpleasant consequence? How often do negative incentives (like the rat's white box) influence your behavior? How often does the positive incentive value of things (like the rat's black box) stem from the fact that they allow us to escape anxiety, although many of these things may simply be temporary solutions to our anxiety? You may be anxious about a test, and instead of studying you may find yourself watching TV, a momentary relief from the anxiety. Or consider the alcoholic who may find temporary relief from anxiety in alcohol (the alcohol becomes a positive incentive). Because there are so many maladaptive ways to deal with the anxiety that is normal in life, anxiety can become a devastating state. While it can motivate appropriate behaviors such as studying for the exam, it can also motivate behaviors that ultimately cause trouble. We will have more to say about anxiety in Chapter 11.

Anger and Frustration

Dollard, Doob, Miller, Mowrer, & Sears (1939) have suggested that all aggressive acts are caused by frustration. Frustration is produced by blocking someone's efforts to attain a goal. The typical emotion experienced when this happens is anger, and the typical reaction is aggression. This theory is known as the **frustration-aggression hypothesis.** Inflicting harm on others is a major problem in our society and the world, and so it is important to understand the motivation for this aggression. There is very strong evidence that frustration is sufficient to produce aggression, although it is almost impossible to determine whether frustration is also a necessary factor — that is, whether all aggression involves frustration. Consider just one study, in which a very hungry pigeon was trained to peck a key in a Skinner box in order to get grain. After the pigeon had learned this response, an "innocent bystander" pigeon was placed in the box with the trained pigeon and simultaneously the experimenter stopped giving grain for pecking (extinction). During this extinction period, the trained pigeon attacked the bystander by pecking at its head, throat, and especially its eyes. There is little doubt that this was an attack reaction, apparently elicited by the frustration that was caused by the termination of the grain rewards (compare this with Figure 7–12).

The same kind of attack reactions were elicited in birds that had been reared in isolation, suggesting

"Can I kick it for you this time, Daddy?"

The Family Circus by Bil Keane, reprinted courtesy The Register and Tribune Syndicate.

In modern technological society machines that do not work properly are a common source of frustration, as this cartoon suggests. A common reaction, in line with the frustration-aggression hypothesis, is an aggressive act directed toward the machine. The cartoon also illustrates the fact that children can learn aggression by imitation. Presumably, the child has seen his father kick soda machines many times in the past and is already prepared to kick this one for him.

FIGURE 7–12   Aggression substitute

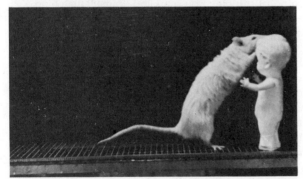

Two rats fight each other, ignoring the doll. When an appropriate object of aggression is missing, the lone rat displaces its aggression, attacking the innocent bystander. The most appropriate object for aggression is the object that is the source of the frustration. Often there are constraints against expressing the aggression against this source, as when a person is frustrated by the boss and hesitates to aggress against him or her for fear of being fired. So the aggression is displaced onto an "innocent bystander" such as his or her secretary or spouse.

that there is an innate biological component to this behavior. This conclusion accords with the suggestions of the ethologists, who have argued that there is an aggressive instinct in human beings as well as in animals. However, although it may be true that there are aggressive instincts that result in predisposing us to fight when frustrated, it is clear that learning is also important. We learn aggressive tactics from seeing how others practice aggression, and limiting such observation may be one way of exerting some control on the development of aggression. This is why, for example, so many people are concerned about the violence on television.

Issues and Theories

The Sequence of Events

If you encounter a ferocious bear in your room, at least two things are likely to happen: (1) you will run and (2) you will have an emotional experience (a feeling) that is usually called fear. Most of us would guess that we experience the fear first and run second. The first major psychological theory of emotional behavior postulated that we do just the opposite. This is known as the *James-Lange theory* after William James and Carl Lange, who independently in the late 1880s suggested that we run first and then are afraid. More specifically, the idea is that perception of the bear in the room leads simultaneously to running and to all sorts of changes in body physiology, such as increased blood pressure and heart rate. When we perceive these changes in our body, we experience the emotion (fear). This implies that we experience different emotions because the body produces a different set of physiological changes for each

of the emotions. Fear is not the same thing as anger, presumably because the physiological activity in the body is qualitatively different during the experience of these two emotions. Whether or not this is true constitutes a critical issue to which we shall return shortly. For now, just remember that the James-Lange theory requires it to be true.

Other psychologists disagree with James and Lange. A prominent alternate view is the *Cannon-Bard theory,* named after W. B. Cannon and P. Bard, who formulated the theory in 1915. Whereas James and Lange say, "We see the bear, we run (and our body physiology changes), and then we experience fear," the Cannon-Bard theory gives the common-

---

Highlight 7–3

Stress and the General Adaptation Syndrome

"Stress" may be defined in many different ways, depending upon one's perspective. From a physiological point of view stress may be defined as any state during which the body tends to mobilize its resources and during which it utilizes more energy than it ordinarily would. In a general

FIGURE 7–13

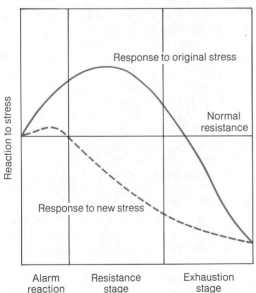

Resistance to stress increases during the alarm and resistance stages of the general adaptation syndrome. However, if the stressful situation continues for too long, or if a second stress occurs, the individual may enter the so-called exhaustion stage with very severe consequences.

way reactions to stressful situations, by which we mean extremes of overwork, anxiety, pain, temperature, and so on, occur in three well-defined stages which Hans Selye has called the *general adaptation syndrome* (see Figure 7–13).

The Alarm Reaction
The first reaction to stress is similar to that observed during emotional states. Changes occur in heart rate, respiration, skin resistance, and endocrine activity. To give the body added energy, the adrenal glands begin to secrete large amounts of epinephrine and norepinephrine, which act on the liver to cause an increased release of stored sugar. In general, during intense stress the sympathetic nervous system is activated, whereas the parasympathetic nervous system is inhibited.

Resistance to Stress
During the second phase of the general adaptation syndrome bodily processes return to normal, and the individual endures the stress. Considerable strain has been placed on the individual, and if the stress continues, or if other stresses occur, the person may enter the third stage of the reaction.

Exhaustion
During this phase the individual may exhaust the resources mobilized to cope with the stress. If the stress persists, the individual may weaken to the extent that death occurs. Psychological stresses seldom reach this final stage, which is more typically observed in response to prolonged exposure to cold or heat or other extreme conditions.

sense argument: "We see the bear, we experience fear, and then we run (and our body physiology changes)." Cannon and Bard thought that the thalamus (see Chapter 2) was the "seat of emotions" (although, as we now know, the hypothalamus would have been a better guess). According to them, when an emotional stimulus is presented, there is first strong stimulation of the thalamus. The thalamus then discharges electrical impulses upward into the brain, activating the cerebral cortex, and downward throughout the body activating the autonomic nervous system. This produces an all-over state of arousal that prepares the person for "flight or fight." It is this state that is experienced as the emotion. After this comes the observable behavior, the running. So for Cannon and Bard, emotion precedes overt behavior and consists mainly of a general state of arousal or activation. There is only one basic physiological state in this theory, namely arousal, although obviously emotions differ in terms of degree of arousal.

Do Different Emotions Correspond to Qualitatively Different Physiological States?

The James-Lange theory required a yes answer to this question, while the Cannon-Bard theory said no, there are just differences in degree of arousal. The evidence on several fronts went against the James-Lange theory. Cannon criticized the James-Lange theory because the evidence available at the time did not show different physiological patterns for different emotions. Cannon also thought that the physiological changes out in the body's periphery took place too slowly to be the primary source of emotion. Further, in one study subjects were injected with adrenalin (epinephrine), which produces arousal in the autonomic nervous system, and yet these subjects did not report emotional experiences; the reason, according to Cannon, was that the central nervous system was not activated through the thalamus (there was no emotional stimulus). The overall picture is strongly against the James-Lange theory, although it is dying a slow death.

One reason the James-Lange theory still persists is that there is some evidence for differences in peripheral responses for different emotions. Most often cited is the work of A. F. Ax, who has demonstrated physiological differences between fear and anger. The adrenal glands secrete two different hormones, epinephrine and norepinephrine. Ax found that during fear epinephrine seems to dominate, while during anger both epinephrine and norepinephrine are implicated. Other studies have shown that animals which are preyed upon (and should thus be creatures of fear) secrete high amounts of epinephrine in contrast to the animals that do the preying. The

preying animals (creatures of "anger"?) show predominately norepinephrine secretion. More recent work has centered on the biochemical substances that serve as neural transmitters in the central nervous system, which seem to be involved in different ways depending on the emotion. Furthermore, Gary Schwartz and his colleagues have reported particular configurations of muscle tensions, especially in the face, which correspond to different psychological states or emotions, such as depression. The universality of certain facial expressions is consistent with these differential physiological patterns. There is probably a basis in genetics or heredity for both the physiological pattern and the facial expression (see the newsclip "The Science of Smiling"). Despite this evidence, however, there is still a strong commitment to the notion that basically the emotional state is a general diffuse state of overall arousal or activation.

How Important Is Cognitive Appraisal of the Situation?

If the emotional state consists mainly of general arousal and there is not a different physiological state for the different emotions, how do we know whether we are happy or sad, pleased or angry? The answer probably comes from analyzing the total emotional experience into two basic parts: (1) the *general arousal* and (2) the *cognitive appraisal* or *evaluation* of the situation—such as "there is a bear loose in my room and it is about to attack me." In a simplified sense, the appraisal is designed to answer the question "Why am I aroused to this degree?" There is a continual interplay between the arousal and the appraisal, out of which emerges the emotional experience. The experience is thus a joint product of the arousal (including the degree of arousal) and the ongoing evaluation of the situation. Which comes first is not of much concern in this theory, because arousal and appraisal are constantly changing and interacting with each other. Sometimes the arousal may precede the appraisal and sometimes it may come later.

The key new element in this interpretation is cognitive appraisal. The person is appraising the situation and at the same time is looking for something that the arousal can be attributed to (the bear is an obvious choice). This part of the theory comes from the *attribution theory*. Having something to attribute the arousal to and having a cognitive evaluation of that thing (such as "it can harm me") are crucial. Without these components there would be no emotional experience even if the arousal component has occurred. Thus, as mentioned earlier, subjects given injections of adrenalin, which produce the arousal, do not become emotional because there is nothing to attribute the arousal to other than the in-

Science of Smiling
By ROBERT LOCKE

SAN FRANCISCO (AP) — . . . Psychologist Paul Ekman says he has hard scientific proof that, regardless of country or culture, human faces use the same expressions to show the same basic emotions. . . .

He said his and others' research on nonverbal communication shows that happiness, sadness, surprise, anger, fear and disgust produce the same expressions—smiles, frowns, wide eyes, clenched jaws and so on—in any culture.

These universal expressions, said the University of California-San Francisco psychologist, seem to be programmed into our genes.

But if expressions are the same from culture to culture, gestures emphatically are not. . . .

"They have a vocabulary that's different from place to place and the same movement can mean entirely different things."

He said the circled thumb and forefinger that means "AOK" in the United States is "a real insult in Southern Europe—an unprintable insult."

And where an American youngster might stick out his tongue to show defiance, "in some cultures that's a sexual invitation." . . .

While Americans have 60 or 70 common symbolic gestures, Ekman said, Israelis—the champion gesturers—use more than 200. Southern Italians are close behind.

Social scientists have argued for decades whether emotional expressions are products of our genes or of our culture.

Charles Darwin sparked the debate . . . by contending such expressions grew out of man's evolutionary past. Many psychologists argued in this century that, as one said, "What is shown on the face is written there by culture."

Ekman, after nearly 25 years of research including two expeditions to an isolated village in New Guinea, contends both groups are partly right.

The universal expressions, Ekman said, are controlled by each culture's "display rules," which can be so strong they are violated only at great peril. Politeness is an example.

Ekman said television, movies and jet planes are shrinking the world so rapidly that few cultures are unexposed to the expressions and gestures of other societies. And exposure raises the possibility that one culture's expressions may have been learned from another.

But Ekman visited a South Fore village so isolated on a New Guinea mountain that villagers didn't know the purpose of the camera that recorded their expressions—expressions as familiar as those of Iowa farmers or Japanese businessmen.

In a series of experiments, the villagers almost always correctly identified the emotions displayed on pictures of American faces. . . .

Boulder Daily Camera
July 22, 1980

The universal nature of emotional expressions on the face is strong support for a genetic component in emotions. On the other hand, one could argue that if smiling, for example, has consequences for the infant such as attention and care from the parents, then what we have is universal reinforcement of smiling. As always, both learning and heredity are involved.

jection. On the other hand, if the subjects were misled about the injection ("this is a vitamin shot") and were told that it would not produce arousal, then when they became aroused they would need an explanation and would evaluate their predicament in seeking the explanation.

Stanley Schachter and Jerome Singer tricked subjects in just this way—the subjects received adrenalin but thought they were getting a vitamin shot. Half the subjects, after receiving the "vitamin" shot, were asked to wait in a room with someone else who was pretending to be very angry. These subjects reported that they became angry. The other half waited in a room with someone who was acting very happy, and these subjects said they were happy. They thus falsely attributed the arousal they were experiencing to the situation and experienced an emotional feeling that was consistent with their evaluation of the situation. In a control condition where subjects were given a placebo injection, these emotional reactions did

not occur. This is presumably because without the adrenalin, there was little arousal. So both arousal and context are needed for the feeling of emotion.

To emphasize the back-and-forth interplay between arousal and evaluation, we can point out that there is evidence that persons evaluate the degree of arousal as well as the situation that is apparently producing the arousal. The evaluation of the degree of arousal will be fed back into the system and can affect the evaluation of the situation. In an ingenious experiment Stuart Valins demonstrated this feedback feature. Male subjects were led to believe that they were listening to their own amplified heartbeat over a loudspeaker, when in fact what they heard was a prepared tape recording. Valins then showed these men pictures of nudes from *Playboy;* for half the nudes, the fake heart rate sounds were speeded up when the picture appeared. This was designed to create the false impression in the subjects that they were especially aroused by these particular nudes.

Later the subjects were asked to rate the nudes on attractiveness, and, as predicted, they rated the nudes that had been associated with increased heart rate as more attractive than the other nudes. The reasoning is that the subjects, thinking they were aroused, searched for an explanation by more closely examining the nudes to find particularly attractive features in the photographs. Having found these features, the subjects would judge the photographs more attractive.

In fact, Valins has demonstrated that the subjects still rate these nudes as more attractive after they are told that the "heartbeats" were a fake. Fake or not, they caused the subjects to discover more attractive features. It has also been shown that the "heart-rate" effect does not take place if the nude photos are presented rapidly, presumably because the subject does not have time to find the explanation for his arousal—he does not have time to find attractive features in the Playmate.

The currently most popular account of emotional experience stems from a combination of general arousal theory (similar to the Cannon-Bard theory) and attribution theory. This third approach, then, combines biological and cognitive concepts. The experienced emotion is a complex function depending on the interplay among several factors: (1) the arousal level—the degree of arousal (or more accurately the degree to which the arousal level is changed from some baseline) probably mediates the

A Painful Theory on Pleasures
By JOHN LEE

It is known, in the usual jawbreaking jargon of the trade, as the Opponent-Process Theory of Acquired Motivation. A small number of psychologists—some 30 around the U.S.—think it explains addictive behavior and much of the relationship between pleasure and pain. Although the theory is supported by experiments with lab animals during the past several years, it remains so hard to believe that even its chief exponent sometimes talks as if he has lost the faith. He is University of Pennsylvania Psychologist Richard Solomon, 62, who says, "I'm suspicious of it myself. I wish someone would . . . prove it untrue.". . .

The basic notion of opponent-process theory is that addiction comes naturally to mammals. Solomon holds that the same principle that produces junkies and alcoholics also produces social attachment, love, thrill seeking, power seeking, overeating and other forms of addiction. The theory's kicker: each addiction eventually produces its opposite; pleasure turns to pain, and pain to pleasure.

"At the start," says Solomon, "drugs are highly pleasant. You get a big 'rush' and euphoria. But as tolerance builds up, the rush disappears and the threat and pain of withdrawal begin to take command. We think that every event in life that has a strong effect also has an opposed process that fights it."

A runner's "high," says Solomon, is an example of pain giving way to pleasure. Withdrawal symptoms are signs of the opposite process: pleasure turning to pain and anxiety. Studies of parachute jumping, done in the 1960s by Psychologist Seymour Epstein at the University of Massachusetts, found that some experienced jumpers become severely distressed when bad weather cancels their sport. Epstein says that this "appears to be an addiction to jumping.". . .

What triggered his formulation of the opponent-process theory was a series of animal experiments conducted by him and other researchers that did not seem to bear out accepted views on stimulus response. The experiments indicated that if medium-intensity shocks are applied at regular intervals to dogs, cats, rats and other animals, tolerance builds up and the animals show progressively less emotional reaction to pain, instead of the unvarying reaction that might have been predicted. . . .

Such studies, says Solomon, suggest that in its early stages any attachment is controlled mainly by pleasure, but late in the attachment the main control is the threat of separation and loneliness. Although the leap to human behavior is a long one, Solomon sees the same mechanisms at work. "The ecstasy and madness of the early love affair are going to disappear," he says, "and when they do, it means that a withdrawal symptom has to emerge if you are denied the presence of your partner. We call it loneliness."

According to the theory, the size of doses and the intervals between doses are crucial to addiction. . . . A rat fed a food pellet every 60 seconds will show withdrawal symptoms (agitated behavior, drinking too much water) after each morsel. But the symptoms disappear if the pellets are spaced several minutes apart. The implication: proper timing of dosage prevents addiction. . . .

One spin-off of opponent-process theory is a bit of advice for human dieters. Why do people keep eating when their stomachs are full? "Because we like to fight off withdrawal by re-dosing with a pleasurable taste," says Solomon. "The better the taste of the food, the bigger the opponent process and the harder the withdrawal." So it makes sense to eat tasty foods early in the meal and save the bland ones for last, so the withdrawal will be easier. Better yet, eat only bland, uninteresting foods, and arrange to have someone interrupt your meal with a phone call. "You'll waste some food, but it will work," says Solomon. . . .

Time
November 10, 1980

intensity dimension of emotion; (2) the cognitive evaluation of the situation producing the arousal change, which will at least partly determine the pleasantness-unpleasantness dimension; and (3) the evaluation of the arousal change, which may in turn affect the cognitive evaluation of the situation. A fourth factor is the specific physiological pattern of the arousal, which may partly determine the quality of the experience (is it fear or anger?). As yet, however, we know very little about what biochemical and physiological factors differentiate the various emotional states.

It is also possible that the degree of arousal change from the normal baseline may play a role in determining the pleasant-unpleasant dimension, in addition to determining the intensity dimension. If we assume that there is a homeostatic arousal system trying to keep arousal level in the moderate range, then we would guess that very large changes in arousal from this optimal level will, in general, be experienced as unpleasant. We might also expect that this homeostatic system will, in such cases, immediately attempt to counteract these large changes in arousal in an effort to return the arousal level to the moderate range.

The Effect of Opponent Processes in Emotions

Richard Solomon and John Corbit have proposed just such a counteracting, opponent-process model: Given a large change in arousal produced by either a pleasant or an unpleasant stimulus, the homeostatic system will immediately activate an opponent process to counteract the emotional reaction. The opponent process, in general, will have just the opposite effects of the initial process, meaning that the overall experience will be a combination of the opposing processes. If the initial experience is pleasant, it will be maximally pleasant only for a short while, because the opponent process, which is by definition unpleasant, will soon be activated and begin to counteract the pleasant process. As the unpleasant opponent process gathers strength, the experience will become less and less pleasant. If the original stimulus situation that triggered the pleasant process were suddenly removed, we would experience only the opponent process in action. That is, we would experience an unpleasant emotion.

In contrast, suppose the initial state of arousal is unpleasant. Soon afterward a pleasant opponent process will be activated to counteract the arousal. Such an experience will be maximally unpleasant only in the beginning because the opponent process will begin to temper or diminish the degree of unpleasantness. If at this moment the original unpleasant stimulus situation is suddenly removed, only the opponent process will be active and we will experience a pleasant emotion.

SUMMARY

1. Motivation is an explanatory concept used to answer questions about why organisms behave as opposed to how they accomplish the behavior. It is used to account for observed variability in behavior both within the individual (the same person behaves differently on two occasions when the situation is identical) and among individuals (in the same situation, two different people will behave differently). Three basic approaches are covered: (1) biological, (2) social-personality, and (3) cognitive.

2. Two fundamental concepts of motivation are drive and incentive. Drive refers to the "push" behind behavior—the energy. Incentive refers to the goal objects that entice or pull the behavior. In practice, drive is measured by length of deprivation and incentive by the quality and quantity of the goal object.

3. In the past, most psychologists emphasized drive as the more important factor, implying we are mainly pushed into behaving. More recently, the emphasis has shifted to incentives as the most important aspect of motivation, especially in analyses of human behavior.

4. For some time it has been believed that deprivation leads to increased energy and more activity. Recent analyses, however, suggest that deprived animals are not automatically more active, but instead are more reactive to stimuli in the environment.

5. We have built-in physiological systems that regulate the intake of such things as food and water. These systems operate according to the principle of homeostasis, with the goal of maintaining a steady state within our bodies.

6. The homeostatic system regulating food intake is complex and involves a preset weight level determined largely by heredity and involving the monitoring of fat and sugar levels in the body. The hypothalamus is a primary neurological mechanism for regulating weight levels and food intake.

7. A homeostatic system also keeps fluids within a critical range. If fluid levels are too low, the body conserves water by inhibiting urine formation and then activating our behavior to find and drink water. The hypothalamus also plays a central role in the homeostasis of bodily fluids.

8. Much of our behavior appears to be motivated by a homeostatic system that is designed to keep our arousal level at some optimal point. We seek out sources of stimulation when our arousal level is lower than optimal, and we attempt to reduce stimulation when we become overaroused.

9. An instinct is an inherited, invariant behavioral sequence that is unique to the species. It is a fixed-action pattern precipitated by environmental "releasing" stimuli. Ethology has revived the concept of instinct and has used it to account for feeding, reproductive, and defensive behaviors in animals.

10. Sociobiology describes human behavior as pre-programmed and having only one function—the survival of the genes.

11. Psychologists studying human motivation often treat motivation as a personality characteristic, dealing with the psychological needs of people. These personality characteristics can be viewed as predispositions to respond to particular incentives.

12. Cognitive activity such as the attributions we make about our circumstances and the subjective utility of various courses of action will greatly affect our behavioral choices and the vigor with which we pursue them.

13. Sexual behavior is motivated in very complex ways. In order to understand sexual motivation, we must consider such factors as drive, incentive-precipitating stimuli, physiology, cognitive processes, personality, and social learning theory.

14. There are two primary dimensions of emotion, the qualitative dimension of pleasantness-unpleasantness and the quantitative dimension of intensity. Emotions are generally considered to be important sources of motivation—we seek positive, pleasant emotional states and strive to avoid negative states.

15. Modern analyses of emotion suggest two basic components, a general arousal and a cognitive evaluation of the circumstances that led to the arousal. There is also an evaluation of the degree of arousal, which in turn can affect the evaluation of the situation.

RECOMMENDED ADDITIONAL READINGS

Beck, R. C. *Motivation: Theories and principles.* Englewood Cliffs, N.J.: Prentice-Hall, 1978.

Cofer, C. N. *Motivation and emotion.* Glenview, Ill.: Scott, Foresman, 1974.

Cofer, C. N., & Appley, M. H. *Motivation: Theory and research.* New York: Wiley, 1964.

Lorenz, K., and Leyhausen, P. *Motivation of human and animal behavior: An ethological view.* New York: Van Nostrand, 1973.

Weiner, B. *Human motivation.* New York: Holt, Rinehart and Winston, 1980.

What Does It Mean?

Increasing Motivation

If psychological research allows for the identification of the factors that determine motivation, it should be possible to bring these factors to bear on an individual or group in hopes of increasing motivation to behave in some particular way. The focus of such an effort would probably be on increasing achievement in one way or another. In industry, for instance, it is obviously important to management that the productivity of employees be increased, that the employees increase their motivation to produce. In fact, of course, industrial psychology has concerned itself with this issue for a long time, attempting to understand how principles of motivation can be applied in a work setting. Many studies of the effects of various incentive plans on productivity have been carried out, with the goal of identifying the optimal incentive conditions for the employees.

Recently, there has been a recognition of the fact that performance in an industrial setting is dependent on more than monetary incentives. Giving praise and recognition to employees is often equally important. Consider the following case. A few years ago the management of the Emery Air Freight Corporation instituted a program to improve performance based on the motivational ideas of operant conditioning. The heart of the program consisted of setting specific goals for the employees and giving them a great deal of feedback as to how they were doing in reaching these goals. The first target for the program was shortening the time a customer had to wait for replies to questions about air freight shipments. The goal was to respond to all customer questions within 90 minutes. Although the employees thought they were meeting this goal most of the time, studies showed that in fact only about 30 percent of the time did the response to the customer come in less than 90 minutes. By keeping accurate performance records, and by praising employees for improvements found in the daily records, management was able to increase performance dramatically in a very short time—in some offices it took only one day to meet the 90-minute criterion. After three years on the program, the response rate is now so high across the entire company that 90–95 percent of all customers receive a reply within 90 minutes.

Next, the same techniques were applied to loading dock employees in order to motivate them to be more efficient in the use of "containers." The idea was to combine lots of small packages into one large package or container, which results in substantial savings in the air freight charges. If the dock workers could be motivated to increase their use of containers, the company could save a great deal of money. Again it was found that the employees thought they were making good use of the containers, but they were wrong. Containers were used in only about 45 percent of the shipments where they could be used. By keeping accurate records, management could give feedback to the workers about how they were doing and could reward them, again with praise and recognition, whenever the rate of container use went up. The result was that container use shot up from the old 45 percent figure to over 90 percent, and two years later it was still at a very high level. In one month alone the company saved $125,000 because of their container program.

Intrinsic and Extrinsic Motivation

It seems obvious that the best way to increase motivation (and thereby performance) is to increase incentives. But increasing incentives is a very tricky business and can often have effects just the opposite of those desired.

A Simple Solution to Job Motivation: More Money
By BERKELEY RICE

For years, industrial psychologists and management consultants have stressed three basic approaches to motivating workers: setting specific production goals, letting workers participate in setting goals or in other workplace decisions, and "job enrichment"—increasing the variety, autonomy, responsibility, or scope of a job. Now, an academic review of 80 studies evaluating these techniques has shown that money works best.

Edwin Locke and his colleagues in industrial psychology at the University of Maryland found that various monetary incentives led to a median increase in productivity of 30 percent. The most effective approach of all involved monetary incentives tied to clear-cut production goals. By itself, goal-setting produced only a 16 percent increase in productivity; job enrichment yielded 8 to 16 percent increases. Worker participation in making decisions was least effective of all—it produced a median increase of less than 1 percent.

The researchers say the recent growth of supposedly scientific knowledge about human behavior may have made industrial psychologists lose sight of something as basic as money.

Psychology Today
May 1980.

Need we remind you that money is an incentive? Probably not, but industrial psychologists sometimes need reminding. Of course, they are interested in increasing both motivation and morale, and usually management tells them to figure out ways to do that which do not cost money.

Some recent research has demonstrated that it is possible to *decrease* motivation by giving rewards for performance. The reason is that people are self-motivated to do certain things. Some tasks are interesting and enjoyable and provide their own rewards to the people doing them. If a psychologist, a teacher, an employer, or a parent offers tangible rewards to a person for doing a task he or she would do well anyway, the person may develop a more negative attitude about the task. Where once the task seemed worth doing by itself, the new reward system makes the task take on the complexion of work. The task is now perceived as something that must be done in order to get the reward, rather than as something important in its own right. When a person does something for no obvious tangible reward, we say that he or she has *intrinsic motivation*. If, on the other hand, a person is doing something in order to receive a particular tangible reward, say a paycheck, we say that he or she has *extrinsic motivation*. If the amateur photographer decides to become a professional photographer, taking pictures may take on a different flavor and become much less fun and much more like drudgery.

Edward Deci has suggested that praise works differently than money because praise involves giving feedback to the subject about his or her competence and self-determination. Tasks that are intrinsically interesting are presumably those that, when completed, automatically give the person good feelings of competence. Perhaps this is why praise and recognition worked so well, in the case of Emery Air Freight.

In this regard, remember the *competence motive* postulated by Robert White—it may be the basis of intrinsic motivation. This motive causes us to interact with our environment in ways designed to master and control it, according to White's theory. We are intrinsically rewarded by demonstrating competence in the world to ourselves. White views the competence motive as basic to human nature—it is a primary drive like hunger and thirst. It can be used to explain a lot of behavior that apparently has no rewards. For example, mountain climbing can be seen as an attempt to demonstrate competence over the environment—indeed, an individual climbs a mountain "because it is there," and the climber must master it to feel competent.

Tangible external rewards will not always have the desired effect of increasing motivation, and we must pay close attention to the types of incentives we use. In the classroom, for example, we might inadvertently turn the task of learning into a chore by promising the students all sorts of rewards. Many parents and grandparents have promised children money or special privileges for good grades. These promises may have contributed to an attitude about school that makes studying appear like work. We hope that further research in the area of motivation will allow us to discover the best ways to motivate behavior, and this includes the best ways to develop intrinsic motivation for the most important tasks of our lives.

"I was reminded of the refrigerator by the installment I just paid on it."

The Better Half by Barnes, reprinted courtesy The Register and Tribune Syndicate, Inc.

According to Schachter's theory of hunger motivation, obese people are overcontrolled by external food-related stimuli and undercontrolled by internal stimuli related to bodily needs for nourishment. Thus, the fat person is likely to eat in response to food or food-related stimuli (such as the bill for the refrigerator installment) regardless of the internal state of his body. The normal person responds to food and food stimuli more in accord with his internal cues—he tends not to eat unless "physiologically" hungry.

Changing the Personality Aspects of Motivation

As we have seen, motivation is often used as a personality concept, particularly when we are discussing human motives or needs. Earlier in this chapter we focused on achievement motivation. Is it possible to alter such personality characteristics in adults? Typically it has been assumed that once a person has reached adulthood it is quite difficult—if not impossible—to change personality characteristics such as achievement motivation. However, we can expect that an understanding of the principles of human motivation might eventually allow us to manipulate or change the personality aspects of motivation. There is not a great deal of research on this topic, mainly because we do not as yet have anything like a complete understanding of human personality. But as our knowledge grows we can expect that our ability to change human motivation will increase.

As one example, consider the work of David McClelland on achievement motivation. He has used the knowledge derived from his research on the development of achievement motivation and from other areas of psychology to develop a training course designed to increase the level of need for achievement in students. He has taught this course to numerous groups of businesspersons, mainly in India, and has done careful follow-up studies of the effects of the course on students' later achievements in the business world.

The participants were thoroughly trained in the theory and measurement of achievement motivation. They all took the TAT and scored their own stories for achievement motivation. They were taught to think about everything in terms related to achievement. They analyzed the achievement motivation level in their own culture by scoring such things as books, children's stories, and customs of the culture on achievement. They also played a business game in which each person had to think in achievement terms (for example, set goals for profits and productivity) and could get fast feedback about how he was doing in running the business. The results were measured by comparing students who had taken the course with control students who had applied for the course but had not been admitted. On a number of economic measures—starting new businesses, working longer hours, increasing the number of employees in existing businesses, and so on—the students in the course did very much better than the controls. This, of course, is taken as evidence that the course did indeed succeed in increasing the achievement motivation of the participants.

McClelland's course was specifically designed to increase only achievement motivation. McClelland believes, however, that the principles he used in setting up the course would be applicable to any personality aspect of motivation. In short, his results suggest that it would be possible to design training programs or courses that would affect all of the human psychogenic needs or motives, such as the need for affiliation, the need for power, and the need for social approval.

In fact, McClelland has gone on to do this in the case of the need for power, the focus of his most recent research. Two examples will be mentioned here. First, it was determined that power needs seem to play a major role in the personality of alcoholics—for them, drinking is motivated by a need for power. Particularly if they were powerless before, or were experiencing a sense of loss of power they once held, it is easy to see why drinking might artificially satisfy power needs. Analysis of the fantasy stories of alcoholics showed support for these ideas—they are high in power needs and feel more powerful after drinking. Recognizing this effect led to an effort to incorporate special training into the therapy for alcoholics. McClelland and his research associates developed a short course that might be called power awareness training in which the alcoholic patients were made aware of their power needs and of how they used drinking to satisfy these needs. Of course, the emphasis was then placed on helping them develop other ways to deal with their power needs. In a pilot test of this power awareness training, it was found that twice as many patients stayed sober for one year after treatment (standard therapy plus power awareness) than did under the standard therapy alone.

The second example concerns what McClelland has called the imperial power syndrome. People with this syndrome have high power needs, but in addition they are low in need for affiliation (low need to have everyone like them), and they are high in self-control (they are well organized in their behavior). First, McClelland determined that people with the imperial power syndrome are more effective managers than others; thus one application of this finding might be selecting managers on the basis of tests to measure the level of the imperial power syndrome. Second, McClelland developed a special training program for managers designed to get them to behave in ways consistent with the behavior of the more successful managers. Again, the results of the short training program were promising—the employees rated these managers higher, and employee morale was increased. (Interestingly, the people identified as having the imperial power syndrome were the ones McClelland found to be most likely to have high blood pressure after 20 years on the job.)

Most recently, McClelland and his colleagues have concentrated on a more behavioral approach, which they call competency testing. They argue that it is the behaviors of successful people that make them successful or competent in their jobs. Therefore, in personnel selection or personnel training one should select people who already have the desired behaviors, or one should train the *specific* behaviors needed. The typical approach is to compare successful and average performers on the job—say selling encyclopedias. What behaviors do the successful salespeople engage in that the unsuccessful or average ones do not? McClelland's consulting firm will design tests to identify people who already have the necessary behaviors and will prepare a training course to teach these behaviors to people already hired. Early reports have been quite positive, measured by increased sales, of course.

Controlling the Hand That Feeds You

One major area of concentration in motivation research is hunger and eating. A major application of knowledge derived from this research is body weight control. Obesity is a problem for millions of people in this country. It has been implicated as a major factor in heart disease, to say nothing of the personal pain, discomfort, and rejection that the obese person so often feels. Presently we do not have very good techniques for controlling obesity. People go on diets and lose weight, but only a small proportion of them are able to keep the weight off. Most dieters gain back later what they lost and spend much of their lives losing the same 10 pounds over and over again. Recent research has begun to suggest reasons for this typical pattern. This knowledge may eventually lead to effective techniques for combating obesity permanently.

Numerous experiments by Stanley Schachter and his colleagues suggest that obese people have difficulty in controlling their weight because they eat mainly in response to uncontrollable external cues in their environments. This external-cue orientation manifests itself in such diverse ways as: (1) the tendency for obese Caucasians to use forks rather than chopsticks in Chinese restaurants; (2) for overweight Air France pilots to be less disturbed by meal-time changes; (3) for obese orthodox Jews to be less uncomfortable than those of normal weight when fasting on Yom Kippur (but only if they are fasting in the synagogue where there are no food cues); and (4) for the tendency of obese individuals to give in to impulse buying in supermarkets.

Schachter's experiments showed that normal-weight people, in contrast, eat mainly in response to internal physiological cues. Normal persons eat because their internal food-intake system "tells" them to eat, while obese persons eat whenever they encounter external stim-

The Chemistry of Smoking

"Don't ask me why I smoke," says the grim-looking man in the Winston cigarette ad. Columbia Psychologist Stanley Schachter, 54, agrees that it is better not to ask. The Winston man — or any other heavy smoker — would probably say he smokes for pleasure, or because it calms his nerves, gives him something to do with his hands or solves his Freudian oral problems. "Almost any smoker can convince you and himself that he smokes for psychological reasons or that smoking does something positive for him — it's all very unlikely," says Schachter, a virtual chain smoker himself. "We smoke because we're physically addicted to nicotine. Period."

Schachter reached his conclusion after conducting a series of experiments over the past four years. Like other researchers, Schachter and his team (Brett Silverstein, Lynn Kozlowski and Deborah Perlick) found that heavy smokers, given only low-nicotine cigarettes to smoke, tried to compensate: to inhale their normal quota of nicotine, they smoked more cigarettes and puffed more frequently. Even so, some were not able to make up the difference and showed withdrawal symptoms: increased eating, irritability and poorer concentration.

The researchers then went further by testing volunteers to see whether smoking eases stress. On the assumption that the more anxious a person is, the less pain he will tolerate, groups of smokers and nonsmokers were asked to endure as much electric shock as they could bear. Smokers proved to be sissies when deprived of cigarettes or given only low-nicotine brands. Those supplied with armloads of high-nicotine brands to smoke accepted a higher number of shocks — but no more than the control group of nonsmokers. Schachter's conclusion: "Smoking doesn't reduce anxiety or calm the nerves. Not smoking increases anxiety by throwing the smoker into withdrawal."

Mindless Machine

Then why do most smokers smoke so heavily when under stress? Schachter's answer: because stress depletes body nicotine, and the smoker has to puff more to keep at his usual nicotine level. The key is the acidity of urine. One result of anxiety and stress is a high acid content in the urine. Highly acidic urine flushes away much more body nicotine than normal urine does. Schachter discovered that smokers who were administered mild acids (vitamin C and Acidulin) in heavy doses smoked more over a period of days than comparable smokers who took bicarbonates to make their urine more alkaline. His tests also show that bicarbonates reduce smoking under stress. One experiment indicates that partygoing increases the acidity of the urine for smokers and nonsmokers alike. "It follows," Schachter says puckishly, "that the concerned smoker should take the Alka-Seltzer before — not after — the party." . . .

Time
February 21, 1977

Why do people smoke? Is it pleasurable? Are smokers addicted to nicotine? Is the smoker seeking to maintain a homeostatic balance of nicotine in the blood? Why do people start smoking in the first place?

uli that have something to do with food, such as when they walk by a doughnut shop or see a TV commercial for frozen pizza. Normal-weight persons encounter identical stimuli, but their food intake is not under external control and so they do not respond by getting something to eat. It follows that it will be easy for obese persons to lose weight if they isolate themselves from these stimuli. And indeed it is. If obese people are put into the hospital and deprived of TV, magazines, and any stimuli that have to do with food, they can lose large amounts of weight without great pain or discomfort. But what happens when they leave the hospital and return to the world of refrigerators, restaurants, MacDonald's hamburger stands, and 31 flavors of ice cream? Yes, indeed, they gain back what they lost.

More recent research by Judith Rodin, once a student of Schachter, who has become a leading authority on obesity, has raised some doubts about his theory. Her results indicate that being responsive to external food-related stimuli is a characteristic found in many normal-weight people; also, many obese people are not to a high degree externally responsive — some are and some aren't. Rodin's most recent research and theorizing has focused more on physiological factors such as metabolism rate, which is controlled by various hormones, and is probably heavily influenced by genetic factors. For example, recent studies have indicated differing levels of a critical metabolic enzyme (ATPase) in obese and normal-weight people. It may be that genetics determines enzyme level, which in turn determines the metabolic rate at which a person burns calories, with some people inheriting high rates and others low. It has been shown, for example, that two different people of the same weight and activity level can differ by as much as 100 percent in the amount of food needed to maintain that weight at a constant level.

Rodin herself has become interested in the way the body responds to becoming overweight or to being starved. Dramatic changes take place as a person gets fat, including a slowing down in the rate of calorie burning, which just makes the problem worse. Surprisingly, the results also indicate that a slower rate of metabolism sets in if you starve yourself — as if the body comprehends that no food is coming in and so it compensates by drastically reducing metabolism and conserving energy. As a result, you don't lose much weight despite starving. Rodin's recommendation is that you diet by eating several small meals a day and that you stay away from so-called starvation diets.

Clearly, obesity is an extraordinarily complex problem involving genetic, physiological, and psychological factors interacting in complex ways. As we unravel this puzzle with research results, perhaps one day we can have some proven and lasting methods for weight control.

Controlling Emotions

If we understood emotions fully we would be able to control and to express them in an appropriate fashion. Knowledge of emotion has potentially far-reaching application in the area of mental health. Many psychologists believe that inability to deal with and appropriately express emotions is the major source of psychopathology. The individual's attempt to escape anxiety is thought to be the primary motivation for pathological behavior. As we will see in Chapters 11 and 12, anxiety is a key concept for understanding mental illness, and teaching people to cope appropriately with their anxiety is a key concept in psychotherapy.

Complete knowledge of the physiology underlying emotion will also contribute to emotional control. We already have tranquilizing drugs and "mood-elevating" drugs, and as our knowledge of the physiology of emotion grows, additional techniques will be developed. As we saw in Chapter 2, there are now surgical procedures that can be used to destroy parts of the brain that control violence and aggression. The suggestion has been made that all world political leaders be given drugs to control their aggression. Perhaps we could ultimately control and eliminate all violence from child beating to war.

The ability to control emotions would have impact on our physical health as well as our mental health. Medical science has implicated emotional factors in many diseases,

The New Yorker, August 28, 1978. Drawing by Lou Myers; © 1978 The New Yorker Magazine, Inc.

Remember, a major part of emotional behavior is the cognitive appraisal of the circumstances. How you think about your circumstances will largely determine how you feel. You can make conscious choices to experience particular emotions by choosing your cognitive appraisal.

Highlight 7-4

Controlling Your Arousal Level

Slow, deep breathing is helpful in generating what Herbert Benson has called the relaxation response. He suggests that to elicit this natural response which counteracts stress you should do the following:

1. Go to a quiet, out-of-the-way location where you will not be interrupted or distracted.

2. Place yourself in a comfortable position, one that requires little effort from your muscles to support yourself —such as in a comfortable chair with good head support.

3. Say something to yourself over and over. This is the *mantra* that is "personally selected" for you if you take meditation lessons, but Benson argues that any sound or word will do. Note that if you are repeating the word "cosmos" and are really concentrating on it, you can't be making cognitive appraisals of the stressful events in your life.

4. Maintain passive attitude—don't worry about how your're doing; distracting thoughts will naturally occur, but if you notice them, avoid concentrating on them and instead return your attention to the sound or mantra you are repeating to yourself.

Developing the ability to relax at will using breathing and the above steps is a helpful skill to develop. Benson's book, *The Relaxation Response,* should be consulted for more information.

Breathe Deep, Imagine Beach When Taking Exams, Says Professor

By MICHAEL DECOURCY HINDS

NEW YORK — "You're waiting for the final exam to begin. The professor is taking forever to sort out the exam booklets and your hands feel clammy. You don't know what kind of a test it's going to be and all the material you studied is flashing back and forth inside your head, which begins to throb. Important names and dates blur and slip away."—Taken from an "anxiety inoculation" demonstration at New York University.

During the next three weeks, students in about half of the country's colleges and universities and in most of its high schools will still be cramming for final exams. And some will be torturing themselves with so much anxiety that their fears may become self-fulfilling prophesies: Fear of failing blocks other thoughts and they fail.

But this isn't likely to happen to 20 anxiety-prone students who took part in a pilot behavior-modification program at New York University this past semester.

"Test anxiety is like having a knife at the student's throat: He's put himself in a situation completely out of his control and he's scaring himself to death," said Iris Fodor, professor of psychology and director of the program. "What we try to do is put the student back in control."

Most of the 50 students who have taken part in the program since it began said they felt much more optimistic and were better able to cope with their anxiety, according to Fodor.

The program is based on experimental projects recently conducted by other psychologists. Exam settings are simulated and the students are taught to recognize anxiety-producing thoughts and replace them with positive ones.

Although successful behavior modification requires intensive, individualized treatments with trained therapists, aspects of the program can be distilled into a few self-help tips that might prove useful for others about to take exams.

One is to list, according to intensity, a number of anxiety-producing situations, ranging from being asked a casual question in class to facing a difficult test question in an important final exam. Then vividly imagine the least anxiety-producing situation and monitor the resulting thoughts and physical feelings.

In the class, as soon as students began to feel tense they were encouraged to escape mentally to a sunny beach, hot tub or any other relaxing place. Students were trained to have this mental picture postcard ready for recall at the slightest sign of tension.

They were told to breathe deeply and slowly until they felt at ease. Deep breathing is very important in relaxing, according to Fodor, who said anxiety-prone persons—who tend to take shallow, nervous breaths—should study yoga to learn the method. Alternately tensing and relaxing muscles also helps relieve stress.

Other tips for the anxiety-prone include:

Monitor interior dialogue and stop any negative thinking. Fodor and others believe that what people say to themselves just before and during a test will affect performance. Replace "I'm so dumb" with "Slow down, breathe deeply, take one step at a time."

"Don't be unrealistic, life will not be ruined if you flunk biology," said Fodor. Put the exam in perspective.

Use humor. Exaggerate the situation until it becomes ridiculous or make up a song that makes fun of yourself.

Don't be too hard on yourself. "It's destructive and it never seems to help."

Denver Post
May 30, 1979

Study Pinpoints Stress-Illness Link

To many, the notion that emotions can affect physical health, and vice versa, is little more than common sense. Most researchers, however, take nothing for granted until it is proved through scientific inquiry. Numerous studies have demonstrated links between psychological stress and physical illness. . . . But a consistent problem in this area is the paucity of *prospective* research—studies that trace the characteristics of an initially healthy population over time, rather than waiting for illness to strike and then trying to pinpoint the historical causes. Such predictive methods hold an advantage, scientists believe, because the researcher is not prejudiced by searching for contributors to an illness he or she knows has already occurred.

Perhaps the most significant prospective study on the interaction between mental and physical health has been published in the Dec. 6 [1979] *New England Journal of Medicine.* From an original sample of 204 men in the sophomore classes of 1942 to 1944 at Harvard University, 185 have been followed more than four decades. Over the years the men have received a wide range of psychological and physical tests and interviews, as well as annual or biennial questionnaires. The psychological "predictors" in the tests included factors such as visits to a psychiatrist, little occupational progress, job dissatisfaction, unhappy marriage, little recreation or vacation time and poor psychological "soundness."

The results, reported by Harvard psychiatrist George E. Vaillant, appear to confirm not only that a mind-body health link exists, but that even physically healthy persons who react poorly to stress or have chronic mental health problems run a significantly higher risk than most people of developing serious health problems or dying by the time they reach their fifties. "Of 59 men with the best mental health, assessed from the age of 21 to 46 years, only two became chronically ill or died by the age of 53," Vaillant reports in the journal. "Of the 48 men with the worst mental health from the age of 21 to 46, 18 became chronically ill or died."

The results were "statistically significant" after Vaillant and his colleagues eliminated the possible effects of alcohol and tobacco use, obesity and the lifespan of the subjects' ancestors—indicating even more strongly that mental health deficiencies are causative factors in illness. Between 1940 and 1967, the terms used to describe poor adult adjustment were attributed "at least twice as frequently" to men who became chronically ill or died in 1975.

In what Vaillant cautions are "tentative conclusions," he says that "in this sample chronic anxiety, depression and emotional maladjustment, measured in a variety of ways, predicted early aging, defined by irreversible deterioration of health. . . . The data suggest that positive mental health significantly retards irreversible midlife decline in physical health." . . .

Science News
December 15, 1979

Learning to control your emotions gives you the power to control the level of stress you experience and can have positive effects on your health. Stress-management courses have become extremely popular in recent years.

the so-called psychosomatic disorders. For example, asthma and stomach ulcers are usually thought to be partially caused by emotional factors. If our knowledge of emotion were sufficient, we should be able to teach people ways to control their emotions and in turn to improve their physical health. Recently there have been suggestions that emotional factors play a role in two diseases that are major causes of death, cancer and heart disease. If this is true, then the ability to change our emotional habits could significantly prolong our lives. At the very least, it ought to be possible to identify people who because of their emotional habits are high-risk individuals. Perhaps these people could be given special medical treatment of a preventive nature.

Emotional control can be accomplished in one of two basic ways, corresponding to the two basic components of emotion—general arousal and cognitive appraisal. First, we can teach people to control or modify their general arousal level. Usually, we conclude that persons in need of emotional control are overly aroused; therefore, they would be taught relaxation techniques such as meditation or biofeedback control of muscle tension. A very effective method for dealing with stress is simply to try to remain relaxed and calm. Very high arousal levels make it difficult to perform on anything but the simplest tasks (according to the Yerkes-Dodson principle), so relaxing and reducing arousal will almost always help behavior become more successful. One of the very best ways to relax is by deep breathing—taking large breaths and slowly exhaling.

The second aspect of emotions is your appraisal of the situation. Learning to control your emotions will mean you must learn to control and modify your cognitive appraisals. You will need to develop control over your thinking—if you don't think about your situation, for example, the emotion disappears. Consider the two most common features of meditation and yoga—deep breathing and repeated thoughts about a mantra (a sound you say over and over to yourself). The deep breathing, as we suggested above, will lower your arousal; and focusing your thoughts on the mantra will prevent you from making any cognitive appraisals of your situation. The two techniques used in combination are an excellent treatment for reducing emotional stress.

You may not be able simply to drop off into a meditative trance any time you are in a tense situation, but you can try to think about your emotion-causing circumstances in a different way, creating a different cognitive appraisal. You can learn to make several cognitive appraisals of the same situation and thereby develop greater control over your emotions. Suppose someone cuts in front of you in traffic, causing you to slam on your brakes. Appraise the event in more than one way. If you think about the situation only in terms of the danger to yourself or the wear and tear on your brakes or the additional delay it causes you, you will probably end up feeling the emotion we call anger. But suppose you focus on your skills and alertness as a driver, and on how important defensive driving is because no one on the road is perfect. All of these thoughts would probably keep you from experiencing anger. In general, whenever you feel strong emotions, stop and ask yourself whether there is a more constructive way to think about what is happening to you. This approach will often be helpful, not just because it brings your emotional reaction under control, but because it helps you determine your next move.

If you learn to control your arousal level and to be flexible in making your cognitive appraisals (especially if you learn to empathize, or to imagine how the other person is appraising the situation), you will have two strong tools for controlling your emotions. Controlling your emotions can perhaps help you avoid such ills as ulcers, asthma, and heart disease, to say nothing of anxiety and all the problems it causes. An added benefit of such a simple maneuver is the possible prevention of unnecessary violent behavior. You can reduce much of the stress that is a normal part of life by learning to relax and to think about stressful events in constructive ways.

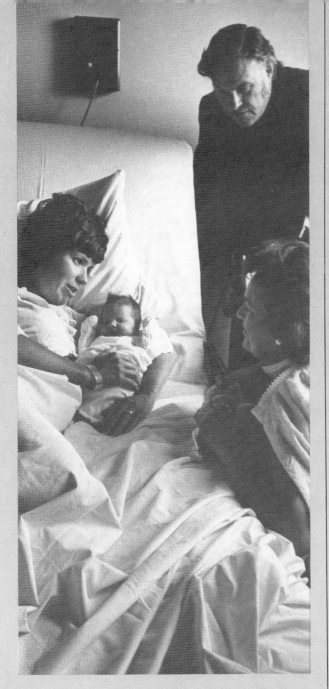

8 | Developmental Psychology

Martha and John are concerned about their 4-year-old son Jimmy, who appears to be lagging far behind other children of the same age in his speaking ability. They are beginning to worry that he might be mentally retarded. Friends, however, tell them that they are overreacting. How can we judge whether a child is developing normally in intellectual and social skills?

Mary Jane has called her mother from the county jail to inform her that she has just been arrested for shoplifting and possession of marijuana. Her mother is shocked, appalled, and fed up with all of Mary Jane's adolescent problems. She bails her daughter out after getting a commitment from her to see a therapist. The therapist tells her mother that Mary Jane is suffering through an adolescent identity crisis. What is an identity crisis? Does everyone pass through such a phase?

Ralph is nearing the time when he must retire from his job as foreman at a local factory. He feels depressed and is not sure why. All his life he has been looking forward to the leisure of retirement. But retirement means a significant change in his life-style, a prospect that appears to underlie his depression. Ralph's is a typical adult crisis. Are there others, and what can be done to help people resolve them successfully?

It takes more than two decades for a newborn child to acquire the intellectual and social capabilities necessary for mature functioning in modern society. Even then, development is not complete. All through life an individual may acquire new skills, develop new insights and understanding of the world, and establish new means of relating to others. Sometimes these changes are self-initiated; other times they are instigated by social experience. Some changes come easily, while others are the result of a long and arduous reassessment of one's thinking and behavior. Such changes are part of the dynamic process of transformation that we call human development.

Developmental psychology is the study of changes in thinking and behavior that occur throughout life. But not all psychological changes are equally interesting to the developmentalist. Momentary changes of mood, for example, have no developmental significance. Neither do briefly held attitudes, incidental actions, or a whole range of other behaviors that do not bear long-lasting implications for an individual's functioning. Rather, developmentalists are interested in the psychological changes that signify substantial change in the individual's adaptation to the world. A developmental change is a change that enables a person to cope more successfully with the demands of physical, intellectual, or social life.

What is the nature of developmental change through the life cycle? What factors facilitate it, and what obstacles retard it? Are some types of behaviors more difficult to acquire than others? What are the critical patterns of behavior and thinking that distinguish a 4-year-old from an 8-year-old, or a 10-year-old from an adult? These are some of the developmental questions that we shall take up in this chapter.

Developmental psychologists are particularly concerned with the lives of children, including children's family environment, their behavior in home and school, and their potential for growth and adaptation. What are the consequences of different child-rearing patterns, of different types of mother-child interaction, or of critical social experiences such as divorce in the family? What are the implications of personal characteristics of the child, such as sex or temperament? To what extent does each child have unique problems in growing up that set the child apart from other individual children? Practically, how can we as parents or professionals optimize a child's chances for successful adaptation to the world, both now and in the future?

There has also been increasing interest and research directed at the process of lifelong change, on development that continues beyond childhood and adolescence. People do not stop developing once they reach maturity, and some psychologists have even focused on possible "stages" of development that occur in adulthood. These areas, too, are the province of developmental psychology, and we will touch on them later in this chapter.

The Process of Development

Many factors are involved in the development process. The child's physical body, including the brain, matures biologically. The child has many different experiences with the outside world, including parental commands, instruction at school, and communica-

"He's walking!"

Ted Key, Squirrel in the Feeding Station. *New York: Dutton, 1967. Reprinted by permission of Ted Key. Copyright © 1967 by Ted Key.*

Developmental milestones such as walking often occur with no prior warning or indication.

tion with peers. Children seem to approach the world with curiosity, and with a desire to acquire competence, both of which motivate them to develop new means of behaving and making sense out of the world. These external and internal conditions are fundamental for development. Although no single factor may be sufficient for substantial psychological change, in combination a variety of factors have profound developmental consequences for the individual.

Theories of development have attempted to explain how these and other factors interact during development but have varied in their assumptions about which factors are of greatest importance. The three major current developmental theories are psychoanalytic theory, behavior theory, and cognitive developmental theory. We shall briefly describe the point of view presented by each.

The Psychoanalytic Perspective

Psychoanalytic theory, first introduced by Sigmund Freud over 80 years ago (see Chapter 1), views human development as the result of conflicting biological and social forces. Freud envisioned a lifelong conflict between, on the one hand, internal antisocial instincts that are a part of human nature, and, on the other hand, the forces of civilization that must subdue these

instincts. From the time the child confronts the demands of toilet training to the time the adult must establish family and occupational roles, development according to Freud entails channeling one's needs and desires into productive and socially acceptable forms. In many ways, psychoanalytic theory portrays human beings as organisms in constant conflict motivated by internal and external forces often beyond their control. Only through the development of "ego" systems that regulate these forces do human beings regain some control over their own destiny.

Freudian theory emphasizes three aspects of development: the *dynamic,* the *sequential,* and the *structural.* The dynamic aspect consists of basic instincts or needs of the human species. Freud identified two broad, opposing classes of instincts, one representing life forces *(eros)* and one representing death forces *(thanatos).* These forces are often in conflict with one another as well as with the demands of society. For example, sexual desire is an *eros* instinct, and—as in Freud's Victorian world—is sometimes repressed socially. (One modern criticism of Freud's theory is that it is obsolete because many of the sexual taboos of Freud's day no longer hold.) Aggression is a *thanatos* instinct, and in its raw form is generally considered antisocial by nature. According to Freud, development is the result of the individual's attempts to reduce the conflicts between the opposing instincts, as well as between each instinct and the demands of civilization. The individual's goal during development is to find acceptable ways of expressing these basic desires. In Freud's pessimistic view, this goal was never entirely possible. The individual was doomed to some degree of lifelong conflict that one would hope could be kept to a manageable level.

The sequential aspect of psychoanalytic theory is the notion that every individual passes through qualitatively different stages of development. Freud called these **psychosexual stages,** since their sequence in his theory was determined by the passing of sexual energy from one part of the body to another in the course of biological maturation. As different areas of the body become the focus of sexual energy, the orientation of the individual is radically changed. During the *oral stage,* which spans the first 18 months of life, the mouth is the most sensitive part of the body. The baby "receives" the world through pleasurable activities like mouthing and sucking. In the *anal stage,* which lasts until the third year of life, psychic energy is focused on the organs that control the elimination of wastes from the body. This is the critical time for toilet training. During the *phallic stage,* children discover their genitals as a source of pleasure, and entertain Oedipal (mother conflict for males) and Electra (father conflict for females) fantasies about sexual relations with the opposite-sex

"It's from Oedipus. He says he's found a girl just like the girl
who married dear old dad."

Playboy, December 1974. Reproduced by special permission of PLAYBOY
Magazine; copyright © 1971 by Playboy.

parent. Psychosexual energy recedes during the *latency stage,* which coincides with the elementary school years. In this time of sexual dormancy, children acquire the intellectual and social skills that prepare them for adult life. With puberty the sexual forces are reawakened, and during the final *genital stage* energy is again focused on the genital area. By this time the individual should have developed the capacity to channel this energy into reproductive sexual relations with another individual, and into creative work activities as well.

Later versions of psychoanalytic theory—such as that of Erik Erikson—emphasize the social as well as the biological influences on the order of life's stages. Erikson modified Freud's stages by describing the social relations that children experience at different periods of life, rather than only the physical location and nature of the sexual energy they feel. Erikson and others also extended these psycho*social* stages through the entire lifespan, including adulthood and old age.

Finally, Freud proposed three principles of mental organization. The **id,** representing biological needs, is governed by the pleasure principle and seeks the immediate gratification of impulses. The **super-ego** develops later in life and represents parental and societal forces that require the individual to control impulses and desires. The **ego** acts as the mediator between the id and the superego, and in the final analysis is the individual's means of asserting control over internal and external reality. In balancing the forces of impulse and culture, the ego attempts to

serve the one without neglecting the other. The ego is the individual's route to realistic satisfaction of need. In Freud's view it was the primary accomplishment of the developmental process: his famous description of this process was, "Where id is, there shall ego be."

Freud's theory has been criticized on the grounds that it lacks scientific precision. Many of his theoretical constructs, for example, lead to several contradictory predictions about human behavior. How can the theory be tested if we do not even know what it specifically predicts? Yet, despite such uncertainties, Freud's approach is still an important force within developmental psychology—perhaps because it deals with vital human phenomena, like emotions, that other theoretical approaches often do not touch on.

The Behavioral Perspective

The behavioral viewpoint is entirely different from that of Freud and his followers. While psychoanalytic theorists see human development as the result of internal conflicts, behaviorists emphasize environmental influences. Behaviorists do not believe that the concept of developmental stages is a valid explanation of the developmental process. For them, development is a function of learning; experiences become organized in different ways for different people, and these differences account for the variation in individual behavior.

This emphasis on learning was thoroughly explored by a number of behaviorists, such as Ivan Pavlov and John Watson (see Chapters 1 and 4). It was the work of B. F. Skinner, however, that placed behaviorism in the forefront of modern psychology. Skinner identified two types of behaviors, respondent behaviors and operant behaviors. Respondent behaviors—classically conditioned behaviors, such as salivating to the sight of doughnuts on a TV commercial, are controlled by what comes before them. These were the kinds of behaviors Pavlov and Watson studied. Operant behaviors are controlled by what follows them, and this discovery was Skinner's greatest contribution to psychology. Skinner discovered that the stimuli (or events in the environment) that follow a behavior can cause that behavior to either increase or decrease in strength. Operant behaviors are a function of their consequences. We can judge the effectiveness of an environmental force by the effects it has upon a behavior. For example, for some children being spanked is partly reinforcing because it represents getting attention; yet for others being spanked represents only punishment.

Skinnerian psychologists view development as the result of various types of conditioning, the end product of a long sequence or "chain" of experiences.

For this reason behaviorists contend that if the environment is properly structured, the potential for learning (that is, development) is unbounded. For example, people classified as severely retarded can sometimes be taught new and adaptive ways of functioning.

Another group of behaviorists believe that other factors besides environmental influences should be considered. Proponents of the *social learning theory,* such as Albert Bandura (see Chapter 9), say that although development is a function of learning, there is a reciprocal give and take relationship between the organism and the environment. They believe that understanding processes such as memory, perception, and other "mental" operations is essential to understanding how human beings acquire behaviors. The greatest contribution of these theorists has been in the area of imitation, or modeling—the process of learning new things by observing others.

In many ways the behavioral perspective is as controversial today as the psychoanalytic perspective was 70 years ago. Some people feel that the behavioral view represents development as a passive process with no input whatsoever from the organism. On the other hand, the behavioral perspective has allowed us the luxury of systematizing and understanding factors that influence behavior by the application of rigorous scientific procedures. It has also had a tremendous impact on applied psychology in general. Not only are behavioral techniques used in many different therapeutic situations—such as in desensitizing children to certain fears—but they have led to such developments as *programmed instruction,* which have greatly benefited education in recent years.

The Cognitive Developmental Perspective

While the psychoanalytic and behavioral models have influenced a large number of psychologists, a major criticism of these models has been that they assume that human beings play a passive role in their own development. In contrast, the cognitive developmental model assumes that people actively construct their own understanding of the world in the course of development. Further, cognitive developmentalists assume that this self-constructed understanding of the world determines how much the child is capable of learning from others and influences the child's everyday behavior at home, school, or play.

The developmental process of active construction is the result of imbalances, or "states of disequilibrium," between an individual's current knowledge and the reality presented by the physical and social environment. When a person discovers that a particular idea does not conform with the way the world actually is, the person is forced to alter the idea. Development, therefore, is the reworking of ideas that do not work, motivated by the self's desire to make sense of the world in the best possible way. For example, a child may believe that heaping 10 objects into a mound increases the number of objects. One day the child may count the objects before and after they are piled up, discovering that they remain 10 in number. The child is then forced to revise the idea that the arrangement of objects determines their number, and consequently considers the new notion that number is "conserved" across spatial transformations. Throughout life, in countless such experiences, we actively construct new knowledge of the world.

Cognitive developmental theory has also been called Piagetian theory, since its original and most distinguished proponent was the Swiss psychologist Jean Piaget. Piaget proposed a sequence of stages that describe the transformation of a child's understanding of the world from birth through adolescence. These stages differ from psychoanalytic stages in a number of ways. First, they describe changes in children's cognitive processes rather than in their emotional, sexual, or social orientations. Second, Piaget's stages are seen as resulting from the child's active explorations of the environment, rather than solely from biological maturation and shifting bodily sensations. But the Piagetian and psychoanalytic stage systems share some assumptions that distinguish them from the social learning model. Both sets of stages are seen to occur in a fixed sequence, despite specific social-contextual influences upon the child. Also, both stage models imply that different periods of development are qualitatively different from one another. A child cannot be viewed simply as a "little adult," but must be seen as having his or her own distinct way of experiencing the world. Rather than saying that children know *less,* we would be more accurate saying that children know things *differently* than do adults.

In Piaget's model, the different stages build upon one another in such a way that each new stage is a reorganization and extension of all the preceding stages. Recall the Gestalt concept that the whole is different from the sum of its parts. Development from the cognitive developmental perspective is the process of various elements coming together to form a new structure, different and more powerful from all the previous notions that it includes.

The Major Issues

One purpose of a model of human development is to serve as a tool in generating new questions for study. Sometimes these new questions present challenges to the developmental psychologist because there is no right or wrong answer. Rather, the issues serve as a means of clarifying the multiple processes and influences that determine human development. We shall now discuss some major questions that have long been debated in developmental psychology.

The Source of Development

A person's future is partly shaped at conception when the genetic material from both parents is combined to determine biological characteristics, such as hair color, and psychological characteristics, such as intelligence. But that is not the whole story. Development depends not only on hereditary factors but also on learning.

Intense controversy has surrounded the question of whether children's intellectual abilities (such as measured by IQ tests) are determined primarily by hereditary factors or by learning (see Chapter 6). Although virtually every conceivable position has been taken on this issue, the general consensus among psychologists is that the two types of influence cannot be separated since both are an essential part of intellectual development. The same is true of most other aspects of a child's personality. Even temperamental dispositions which are present at birth are soon modified by environmental experience. It seems unlikely that any psychological characteristic is the result of a "pure" hereditary factor untouched by learning, or vice versa.

During the process of **maturation** some abilities develop in a preprogrammed way with biological growth. Although maturational changes are most obvious in behaviors that are closely tied to anatomical growth, many psychologists believe that maturation is also responsible for changes on a psychological level. These changes tend to be the same in children from various cultures, and consequently are not dependent upon individual experiences. For example, all normal children develop some form of verbal communication we call language at approximately the same time, independent of any specific training. Psychologists who have tried to accelerate development by attempting to teach children to talk early have not been successful.

Many behaviors appear to be maturational in nature, such as the ability of an infant to control eye focus. This ability develops only when the various muscles that control eye movement and shape of the lens have fully matured. Other examples are the ability to walk and to vocalize. Both are dependent on muscular growth and a degree of organization not present at birth. Learning, on the other hand, is a direct function of experience. Children of foreign-speaking parents do not speak the natural language of their parents outside the home, but rather speak the language of the society in which they grow up.

Treating Malnutrition: Food Is Not Enough

Children need both adequate nutrition and emotional stimulation in order to develop normally; deprived of either, they lag behind in physical and mental growth. Now, evidence suggests that the ill effects of these two deficiencies are intertwined to an extent not recognized previously. What we know as malnutrition may come from more than a lack of nutrients, and more than an adequate diet may be needed to correct it. Joaquin Cravioto of the Instituto Nacional de Ciencias y Tecnologia de la Salud del Nino-DIF in Mexico City presented these findings at the annual meeting of the Institute of Medicine in Washington.

For three years, Cravioto and colleagues followed the progress of a group of children who, at birth, were approximately equal in height, weight, skull circumference and other physical characteristics. They looked at the children's nutritional status as well as at their psychosocial, language and motor development. Using an Inventory of Home Stimulation, the researchers evaluated the quality of the children's language environment and of the interactions between mother and child, including expressions of affection, interest in the child and sensitivity to his or her behavior.

A curious pattern emerged. Cravioto found that by looking at the Home Stimulation scores, he could identify those children who would become malnourished six months to two years before they began to suffer from malnutrition. The "future malnourished" children had poor quality language environments (suffering from what Cravioto calls "vocal malnourishment"), and their mothers tended to be passive and nonreactive toward the children, not proud or admiring.

The intermingled effects of stimulation and nutritional intake continued when the children were hospitalized for treatment. One group lived in a livened-up hospital environment and received systematic stimulation from the staff. The remaining children stayed in a normal (i.e. unstimulating) hospital environment. Both groups recovered physiologically, but only the stimulated children caught up mentally and emotionally.

Science News
November 10, 1979

Clearly, a child's welfare depends on both the physical and psychological environment. The evidence reported here suggests a relationship between the quality of the psychological environment and both physical and psychological health.

In general, most psychological abilities are the result of both maturation and learning, as well as of the child's own initiative in making use of the contributions of each. Some developmentalists, however, explain the acquisition of some abilities more in terms of one than of the other process. For example, developmentalists studying perceptual abilities in children have often emphasized maturation, whereas

FIGURE 8-1 **Group differences, individual differences, and overlap**

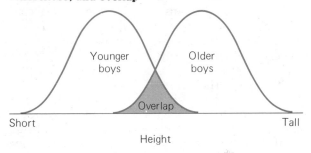

psychologists studying social behavior patterns have often emphasized learning. The precise extent to which one or the other actually contributes to any given ability is usually not possible to determine, despite the debate and speculation that this question has generated.

Developmental and Individual Differences

Many descriptions of behavior provided by developmental psychologists are normative, that is, the focus is on average performance on some particular task at a certain developmental level. Although the norm is a useful concept, we should recognize that there are always individual differences. Not all of us reach puberty or attain our intellectual peak at the same time, since variation in the rate of development is characteristic of development itself.

The importance of these differences is represented by a concept called overlap, shown in Figure 8-1. In this case the two bell-shaped, or normal, curves represent the heights of two different groups of boys. As you can see, the older group is taller in general. But while the average height of the older boys is greater than the average height of the younger boys, some younger boys are taller than some older boys. This area of overlap, shown by the cross-hatching in the figure, demonstrates how norms are important as a point of reference for an entire group. Unless individual differences are considered, the true picture of development might not be clear. Norms are helpful in detecting serious deviations from the average, but to interpret them as characteristic of the whole group can be dangerous.

This point is especially important to keep in mind when assessing intellectual development, since in the course of growing up children acquire mental abilities at widely varying rates. One child may begin slowly and end up surpassing all of his or her peers at a later age. Comparing a child's abilities to those of other children the same age may give a false impression, since the child's rate of development may change

Too-Small Kids May Be Short of Love
By ROBERT CONN

The unloved child may unknowingly be advertising its problem for all the world to see—by being too small for its age.

There are lots of reasons why a child may not be growing as fast as its friends, and many children of devoted and loving parents may be short simply because it runs in the family.

But the most startling reason is what doctors are now terming psycho-social short stature.

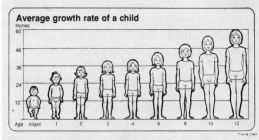

According to a report in the current Medical World News, psycho-social short stature is considered the hallmark of the emotionally battered child—one who does not get enough love.

Up to a point, such short stature is reversible. If the child is removed from a home where it is not loved, and placed in a home where there is love, the child frequently grows very rapidly.

The Medical World News report—part of a major survey of the reasons why children are too small or too tall, cited one series of youngsters studied by Dr. Robert M. Blizzard, chief of pediatrics at the University of Virginia Hospital in Charlottesville.

Blizzard, who specializes in pediatric endocrinology [hormones] found that the diagnosis of psycho-social short stature is provable after the fact—because it does reverse.

In 13 youngsters that Blizzard studied, growth in foster or convalescent homes was startling: The average growth rate was 0.65 inches per month [which works out to 7.8 inches a year], compared with the normal for that age range of 0.2 inches per month [2.4 inches a year].

Blizzard suspects that the emotional problems that a child experiences in his original home prevents it from eating or sleeping properly.

"The possibility that growth will be retarded [because of a social environmental factor] is much more widespread than people would have suspected," says John Money, a psychologist who has worked with children in a clinic similar to Blizzard's at Johns Hopkins. . . .

Chicago Tribune
March 21, 1976

It is difficult to sort out the effects of maturation versus experience in human development. Bodily growth appears to be influenced by the social environment and by biological development or maturation.

in future years. Particularly unfortunate are cases in which a child has been labeled intellectually slow because he or she may be temporarily behind other children. Such labeling can damage the child's self-confidence and discourage the incentive to achieve.

Continuity and Discontinuity in Development

As children grow, do they change gradually, acquiring new skills and behavior bit by bit with each passing day? If this were the case, we would say that human development is a *continuous* process. Or is a person's psychological state wholly transformed during certain critical developmental periods? In this case we would say that development is *discontinuous*. In the insect world, the metamorphosis of a caterpillar into a moth is an example of discontinuous developmental change.

A paradox of human development is that it is continuous in some respects and discontinuous in others. From day to day children change slowly and somewhat unevenly: rarely do we look at a child on

FIGURE 8-2 Three models of the developmental course of individual stage-specific cognitive items

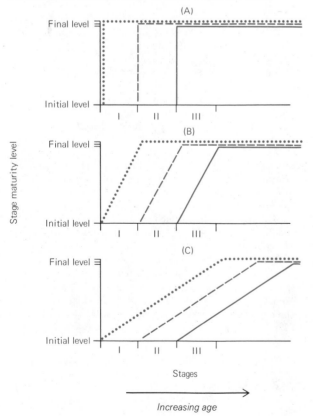

Tuesday morning and notice radical improvements in the child's capabilities since Monday. On the other hand, the broad patterns of development reveal considerable discontinuity. As stage theorists have shown, the thinking of an 8-year-old is in many ways qualitatively different from the thinking of a 4-year-old. The qualitative difference is itself a discontinuity in development. The paradox, therefore, is that development consists of discontinuous changes that come about gradually and in small steps as the child grows.

Developmental psychologists have debated about how best to resolve this paradox. Some have revised or abandoned the notion of stages, believing that qualitative descriptions of change may be replaced by continuous descriptions. Others have doubted that such attempts can capture the full range of developmental changes portrayed in the stage models of Freud, Piaget, and their many followers. In order to tell the full story of human development, this latter group believes, some stage notion must be retained, although it must be accommodated to the reality of gradual growth. Figure 8-2 presents three different stage models as described by John Flavell. Each model shows a different way that a person might pass through three stages of development, I, II, and III. Model A shows discontinuity and no overlap between successive stages. Model B shows gradual (continuous) development within a stage, but still no overlap—stage I is completed before stage II even starts, and II is completed before III starts. Finally, model C portrays gradual development and stage overlap. Stage II begins before stage I ends, and stage III begins before stage II ends. From day to day, therefore, we would expect stage mixture and continuous, gradual change from one stage to the next. But over the long term the child's abilities are wholly and qualitatively changed.

Research Methods in Developmental Psychology

Partly because the study of development is the study of change, and partly because the subjects of developmental research are often children, research methods in developmental psychology are quite different from other psychological research methods.

One way to study behavioral development is to observe or test groups of children of different ages at approximately the same time. If older children are found to act differently than younger children, we may infer that the difference is a sign of development. This is a *cross-sectional* research method. But to confirm that differences found in cross-sectional research are really developmental differences, a *longitudinal* research design must be included. In a longitudinal design, children are periodically observed as they themselves grow older. Both types of designs have strengths and both have weaknesses. In a cross-sectional design, there is no way to separate developmental from incidental differences between age groups. For example, suppose all the children in one age group were born during a famine. In longitudinal research, it is difficult to assess the effects on subjects of repeated testing and observation. Where possible, the ideal developmental research design combines cross-sectional and longitudinal techniques.

As in other areas of psychology, developmental research is often *experimental*. Developmental experiments focus on the process of change. One common type of developmental experiment is the "training study," in which the experimenter teaches to each child a new concept or skill. Subjects exposed to the training are compared with control subjects who have not been so exposed. In this way the effectiveness of the training procedure may be determined, and the learning process may be observed.

In addition to experiments, two techniques that are particularly useful in developmental research are the observational and the clinical interview methods (see Chapter 1). The *observational* method is a means of obtaining information about children in their natural settings. The method is considered to be "ecologically valid" because it investigates children's behavior as it occurs spontaneously, say at home or in school. The technique has proved especially valuable in work with infants and preschoolers. The *clinical interview* method is an in-depth means of exploring children's ideas. The questioning in the clinical interview follows the line of the individual subject's reasoning, so that the child is led to express his or her full knowledge. Countersuggestions and probing follow-up questions are frequently included. In addition, hypothetical stories or dilemmas are presented during the interview in order to help children formulate their answers in terms of concrete events. This technique has been widely used to determine children's understanding of social and moral problems that are too complex or abstract to ask children about directly. For example, although children may not be able to offer rich verbal definitions of "justice," they can speak at length about their conceptions of fairness during a clinical interview focused on common childhood social actions such as sharing toys or "playing fair" in a game.

Intellectual Development

The world we live in is enormously complex, consisting of a diversity of people, objects, and events. In addition, there are unseen relations connecting various parts of the world to one another: physical relations like the law of gravity and social relations like friendship. An essential task in growing up is to develop accurate and useful ways of knowing the world around us.

Several ways of knowing the world are available to us. Perception enables us to make immediate assessments of information that comes to us directly through our senses. Cognition enables us to reason about the events that we observe and to infer meaning from our experience. Language enables us to communicate our thoughts through a medium. In this section we shall discuss the acquisition of knowledge in each of these three intellectual areas: perceptual development, cognitive development, and language development.

Perceptual Development

Infant Perception
Even newborn infants exhibit certain perceptual skills. They are attracted to stimuli in the environment, can hear differences in the pitch of sounds as small as one note apart on the piano, and can differentiate among some odors and tastes.

Interestingly, the most important sense — vision — is more immature at birth than are other systems. Once an infant opens its eyes, its visual focus is rela-

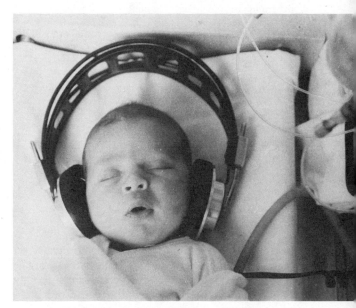

Modern technology has allowed developmental psychologists to begin testing infants' sensory abilities almost immediately after birth. Here a 2-day-old infant wears headphones as part of a hospital program to check taste, hearing, sound recognition, and smell.

Those Baby Blue Eyes Can See Fine, Thank You, Doctor Reports
By JON VAN

Babies, even newborns, can see rather well, better than doctors once believed—if they find something worth watching.

"Doctors traditionally were taught that children didn't achieve good vision until age 5 or so, but research has proven that theory in error. They may achieve 20-20 vision by 6 months to one year," said Dr. Creig Hoyt, director of pediatric ophthalmology at the University of California in San Francisco.

Hoyt tested more than 200 infants in their first minutes of life by moving a ping-pong paddle 6 to 8 inches in front of their faces. If the paddles were painted to look like a human face, 94 per cent of the babies would follow the paddle movement with their eyes, Hoyt said.

Plain paddles or those with indistinguishable designs on them attracted the attention of only 6 per cent of the infants.

"Babies seem to have a genetically preprogrammed preference for the human face," Hoyt told a meeting of the American Academy of Ophthalmology in Chicago recently. "They are more interested in their mother's face than in any other human face."

Hoyt compares the findings with those on other species. Newly hatched birds become agitated when shown a picture of a natural predator, even though they have had no experience with enemies.

"In the case of the birds, we have a negative genetic programming, and with human babies, we have a positive programming, something very important in human bonding," Hoyt said.

Improved understanding of a baby's vision and more sophisticated tests to measure it are valuable in treating newborns with cataracts. While the cataracts may be removed and an artificial lens fitted, an infant's brain also must learn to "see" images transmitted from the eye.

Hoyt said tests that accurately measure an infant's visual response have allowed doctors to put patches over normal eyes so that corrected eyes may be forced to learn to see.

Chicago Tribune
November 16, 1980

FIGURE 8-3 **Measuring visual preferences in infants**

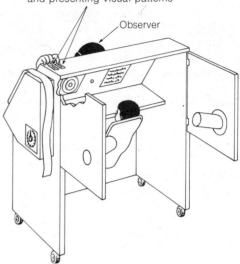

Switches for recording fixation time and presenting visual patterns

Observer

A device used to measure the interest value of different visual patterns in terms of time spent looking at them. The subject sits facing a "stage" where patterns are presented. His or her view is restricted to the inside of the illuminated chamber.

proves to about 20/150, where it remains until further maturation of the visual system.

Infants spend much of their waking time just looking, and they exhibit definite visual preferences. A device used to measure looking behavior and visual preferences is shown in Figure 8-3. Infants presented with a moving array of lights and a stationary pattern are more attentive to the moving stimulus. One-day-old infants also spend more time looking at patterns such as a bull's-eye than at plain-colored figures like a red circle (see Figure 8-4). These preferences occur so early in life that many people conclude that sensitivity to pattern is an innate phenomenon.

One of the most interesting of the newborn's visual preferences is the human face. Infants smile more at a line drawing of a face than at an equally complex nonhuman pattern. They attend more to a three-dimensional mask than to a line drawing of a face and pay more attention to real faces than to masks. After several months, real, familiar faces elicit more smiling than unfamiliar ones. Then, at about age 2 years, the child's preference for familiar and more realistic objects tends to wane. Unusual stimuli become attractive and appear to take on the character of problems in need of solution. Thus, the child's perceptual activity develops from a period in which attention is given primarily to movement and contrast to a second period in which what is familiar and meaningful is most attractive and finally to a point in which the focus is a search for the unusual.

tively fixed at about 9 inches from the cornea, which is the approximate distance between the baby and its mother's face during feeding. The coordination of the infant's eyes is poor because the eye muscles are weak. Indeed, the newborn infant often appears cross-eyed. The retina is also immature, but it responds to changes in light intensity. It has been estimated that at birth infants have a visual capacity of only 20/600 (as compared with the 20/20 vision of normal children). After a month, infant vision im-

FIGURE 8-4 Pattern preferences in infants

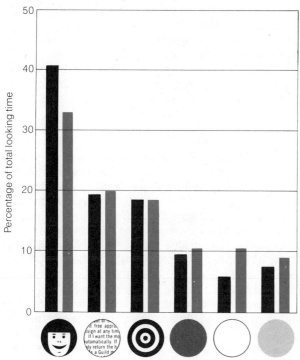

Importance of pattern rather than color or brightness is illustrated by the response of infants to a face, a piece of printed matter, a bull's-eye, and plain red, white, and yellow disks. Even the youngest infants preferred patterns. Black bars show the results for infants from two to three months old, colored bars for infants more than three months old.

The perception of objects in depth, which adults take for granted, seems to develop by the time the child begins to crawl (6 to 8 months and possibly even before). The existence of depth perception in young children has been verified using the "visual cliff" (Figure 8–5). The illusion of a cliff is built into a level glass floor, and the child is urged to crawl across the floor over the edge of the "cliff." Babies have refused to crawl across the surface beyond the cliff even to reach their mothers. This does not mean that depth perception exists at birth, but it suggests that it develops early in life.

Later Development of Perceptual Skills

New sensory experiences lead to changes in behavior. These changes reflect both new knowledge and new ways of gathering knowledge. Consider the following experiment. A child is blindfolded and given the chance to explore tactually a strangely contoured object. The object is then put on display with a number of other objects, and the child must identify the target object on the basis of touch only. A 3-year-old presented with this problem tends to hold the target object briefly in the palms. Contact is minimal and

FIGURE 8-5 The visual cliff

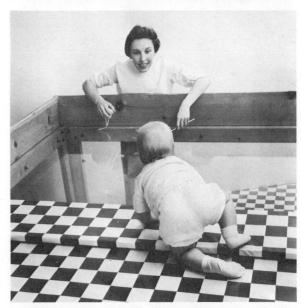

A mother testing her child on the "visual cliff." Above, the child eagerly crawls to the mother on the "shallow" side of the cliff, where the checkerboard pattern is placed right below the glass surface. Below, the pattern has been placed on the floor, giving the illusion of depth or of a cliff. Now the child refuses to crawl off the cliff despite the mother's inducements.

uninformative, and the child typically fails to identify the object. In contrast, 7- and 8-year-olds run their fingers around the edges and spread the thumb and forefinger in an apparent effort to gauge the length of the object. The 10-year-old efficiently touches just those features that are likely to distinguish the object from others. The organized search pattern of older

FIGURE 8-6 **Which is writing?**

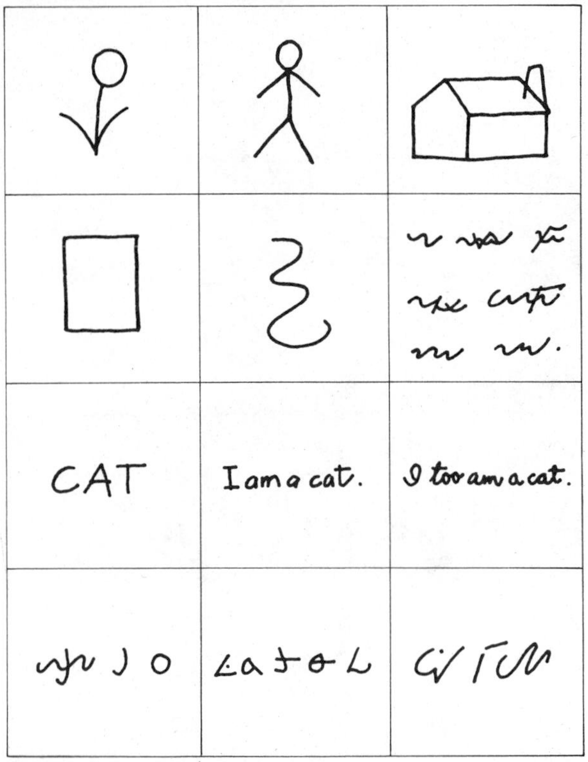

Because they do not distinguish scribbles from letters, three-year-old children have trouble determining what represents writing. Even five-year-olds may have difficulty.

children allows them to identify objects more quickly and more accurately. Systematic, efficient, and thorough search patterns develop with age in all sensory systems, not just in touch.

E. J. Gibson's analysis of reading shows that what is searched for—as well as the search method itself—changes with age. When adults scan a book they use highly refined reading skills the 3-year-old does not possess. Asked to identify letters, the 3-year-old will correctly ignore line drawings but will incorrectly assume that unintelligible scribbles are letters. Even 5-year-olds who know which marks are letters often cannot isolate words because they ignore spaces between words (Figure 8-6).

By the time the child reaches the age of 10 or 12, perceptual skills, including those involved in reading, are essentially fully developed. Significant changes occur later, such as the commonly observed deterioration in one or more sensory systems brought on by the aging process, but the fundamental abilities underlying perception reach their peak at a relatively early age. Only intense specialized training can bring about significant further improvement in perception.

Cognitive Development

Learning in Infants

It was once thought that newborns could not actively learn, but with the advent of new experimental procedures researchers have begun to destroy that myth. There is evidence that some learning even takes place before birth.

A common example of early learning is the classical conditioning of anticipatory sucking at the sight of a nipple. In one experiment Kaye (1967) sounded a tone just before a nipple was presented. Babies only 3 or 4 days old quickly learned that the tone was a signal for the subsequent appearance of the nipple. Even during extinction (when the tone was no longer paired with the nipple), many babies persisted in sucking in response to the tone alone. The conditioning of sucking responses is one of the first signs of learning that parents notice. Babies typically recognize the feeding position and begin to suck as soon as they are placed in that position.

Instrumental or operant conditioning can also be demonstrated. Infants have been taught to turn their heads when a buzzer was sounded. Rewards were then switched so that reinforcement was given when the baby turned at the sound of a tone instead of a buzzer. Babies 3 days old quickly reversed their behavior. Clearly, infants are capable of learning discriminations as soon as they can be tested.

Infants also show signs of responsiveness to secondary reinforcers. For example, vocalization and smiling can be increased when reinforced by a friendly pat or a bit of baby talk; subsequent withdrawal of adult contacts produces a decrease in vocalizing and smiling.

Concept Learning in Early Childhood

At first, children's concepts are rudimentary and based on concrete, perceptual examples. Having formed simple concepts such as "dog" and "cat," they are later able to classify correctly entirely novel experiences, such as a stray dog. Although a child's repertoire of concepts increases with experience over the years, children do not develop abstract concepts until the fifth or sixth year. Young children probably learn their first concepts by simple observation and rote learning. That is, they associate the same response (or category) with each of a large number of individual stimuli before the process of generalizing occurs. In contrast, the older child (7 or 8 years) learns in a different way. These children can abstract the characteristics of objects, analyze each stimulus into its constituent parts, and use only those parts that define the concept. They have more sophisticated problem-solving skills.

The transition point in this developmental sequence from rote learning to analytic and abstract

Boys Are Better at Math Than Girls, Study Says

WASHINGTON.(UPI) — Two psychologists said Friday boys are better than girls in math reasoning and they urged educators to accept the fact that something more than social factors is responsible.

"You can't brush the differences under the rug and ignore them," said Camilla Benbow of Johns Hopkins University. . . .

Benbow and Julian Stanley reported in Science magazine that their findings were based on the aptitude test results of 9,927 gifted boys and girls in the seventh and eighth grades—a stage when children of both sexes have the same math training and attitudes about it.

"We just have to contend with the fact that there is a mathematical aptitude difference at seventh grade, before there are really any differences in

attitudes and course taking," Benbow said in a telephone interview.

She said the differences have been apparent for some time, but that many people have tried to ignore them on the grounds they are caused by social factors.

"They say if the girls would take just as much math as the boys, then we wouldn't have to worry about it," Benbow said. "Then there would be no sex difference. We're showing that's not the case." . . .

"The greatest disparity between the girls and boys is in the upper ranges of mathematical reasoning ability," the report said.

Benbow said the reasons for male superiority in math aren't understood, but might be the result of a combination of inborn factors such as hormonal or brain differences and environmental

factors such as the way children are raised and the toys they play with.

In an article accompanying the psychologists' report, Science said disagreement with the conclusions of Benbow and Stanley already has appeared.

"I think they are on darned shaky ground when they draw conclusions about genetic differences," Elizabeth Fennema, of the University of Wisconsin, was reported as saying.

But Science said Jane Armstrong, of the Education Commission of the States in Denver, has results that tend to confirm the findings of Benbow and Stanley.

"As a woman, I don't want to think there is something about us that does not allow us to do math like the men do," said Diane Tobin, another Johns Hopkins researcher studying the issue.

Denver Post
December 6, 1980

As you might imagine, this report has created considerable controversy. It suggests that differences in math ability are sex related in a way that cannot be accounted for environmentally.

While this may turn out to be true for math, modern research on sex differences has found very few behavioral differences between men and women.

abilities comes at about the same time as the child is developing a command of language. This is also the period when children develop the ability to talk to themselves. Some theorists believe that this internalized speech operates as a problem-solving device and as a mechanism for guiding and regulating overt speech and other forms of behavior. Soviet psychologists like Vygotsky and Luria have devised some ingenious experiments to demonstrate this possibility. In one such experiment, children were told to squeeze a rubber bulb every time a red light shone and not to squeeze it when a yellow light shone. One- and 2-year-olds performed less well at this manual task if also told to say the word "squeeze" (meaningless to 1- and 2-year-olds) when the red light came on. Children aged 3 and above, however, were aided in their manual performance by saying "squeeze." This finding indicates that as children learn to use words properly they develop an important tool to help them in controlling their own activity.

Stages of Intellectual Development

The most comprehensive account of cognitive growth is Piaget's stage model. Piaget divides development into four major stages: sensorimotor, pre-

operational, concrete operational, and formal operational. Within each stage are further subdivisions; for example, during the sensorimotor stage, six substages describe development in infancy. Piaget believes that all children, regardless of social or cultural background, progress through the stages and substages in the same order. Some children, however, may not reach the final stage of formal operations because of the lack of complex environmental experience.

In Piaget's system, two developmental processes, assimilation and accommodation, operate during each of the four stages. These processes are the basis for cognitive growth and ensure the child's intellectual adaptation to the world of reality. **Assimilation** is the "digesting," or modification, of received information to fit into what the child already knows of the world. For example, a young infant may "know" objects primarily through sucking on them and therefore may assume all objects are "suckable." When encountering a new object, the infant assimilates that object to its sucking schema (or internal structure) by putting the object in its mouth. The complementary process of **accommodation** modifies the internal structure to fit the demands of reality. If the new object encountered by the infant is a sharp

Piaget: Exploring the Child's World
By JERRY ADLER with JOHN CAREY

On the one-way journey through childhood we take no notes. The mental landscape we inhabited as children is hidden; the few adults who have explored it have astonished the world with what they found. Just as man's image of himself changed forever after Freud mapped the emotional terrain of childhood, so the Swiss psychologist Jean Piaget both charted and transformed the child's intellectual world. And when Piaget died last week at 84, he ranked with Freud as one of the most original thinkers of the twentieth century.

A child's mind, Piaget found, is neither a miniature model of an adult's nor an empty vessel that gradually fills up with information. It is active from infancy, as the child struggles to understand the complicated world in which he finds himself: a world in which objects mysteriously change shape as we move around them, where things alarmingly disappear when something else comes in front of them, where marbles suddenly take on life when placed on an incline. The spatial, sequential and causal relationships that adults take for granted are, Piaget discovered, constantly re-created by every child in a hard-won triumph of experience and creativity.

The Sublime
Piaget's approach was that of the naturalist. His most important subjects were his own three children, yet his results have been replicated with hundreds of children from diverse cultures. His genius was to see the sublime intelligence at work where others could see only a childish mistake; indeed, mistakes were his raw data. In one classic experiment he presented a young child with two containers—one tall and narrow and the other wide and shallow—each holding the same amount of water. Children, he discovered, will believe that there is more water in the tall glass than the short one, and no demonstration to the contrary can change their minds—until, quite suddenly, at 6 or 7, they spontaneously

© 1981 by Jill Krementz.
Jean Piaget: Experience and creativity.

develop the notion that the mass of a liquid is conserved no matter what the shape of the container.

From observations such as these, Piaget in the 1920s and '30s formulated his theories of mental growth: that all children pass through a series of distinct intellectual stages, beginning at birth when the young child is unconscious of his own existence and culminating, after 11, with abstract thought. Piaget believed that all children go through these stages in the same order and at roughly the same ages—propositions that are increasingly being questioned in the light of recent research. But the broad concept is now widely accepted. His ideas on education have been especially influential. "The goal of education," he wrote in what might have served as a manifesto for the early-childhood movement of the 1960s and 1970s, "is to create the possibilities for a child to invent and discover."

Piaget was active in research for more than 60 years, and he left behind more than 50 books and monographs. In his later years he became interested in abstract logic, and his books became increasingly difficult. He will be remembered more for his earlier works, and above all for discovering, in his own phrase, "the embryology of intelligence."

Newsweek
September 29, 1980

and bitter-tasting pencil, the infant will discover that all things cannot be sucked. The sucking schema is then adapted to reality by including the notion of "nonsuckables." Assimilation enables the child to understand new information by using old ideas, and accommodation enables the child to change his or her ideas where necessary. Together the two constitute a dual process called equilibration, since the goal is to establish an equilibrium, or balance, between the structure of a child's thinking and the demands of the external world. States of perceived disequilibrium provide the child with motivation for further growth and development.

The Sensorimotor Stage (Birth to 2 Years)
Babies are born with primitive ways of knowing the world called *reflexes*. These are mostly actions that help a baby survive in the context of the mother-child relation. Two such reflexes are sucking and grasping. Visual and auditory reactions are other examples. During the first *sensorimotor stage,* lasting about one month, the baby's intelligence is confined to the performing of such reflexive activity.

In the second sensorimotor stage (months one to four), some of these reflexes develop into action *schemata* through which infants begin to explore their immediate world. Through the various manual,

Baby Apes: Shake, Rattle and Think

When Samara first arrived at the nursery, she flailed her arms about and made high-pitched cries whenever her blanket was taken away to be washed. She soon began sucking one of her fingers and clasping her hands, then reached out to shake rattles, ring bells, play with toys and feed herself. Later, the play became more complex—she combined several toys at once and experimented by placing objects such as scarves, clothing or cereal bowls on various parts of her body. She next began to learn about the functions of objects—that balls can be dropped, thrown, rolled, bounced and caught; that toys can be deposited and removed from buckets, . . . Finally, she began to solve such problems and tasks before actually physically attempting them.

This evolution of behavior is fairly typical of an infant's development during the first two years of life, according to Jean Piaget's six stages of human intellectual development. But Samara is not a human child—she is an orangutan. And the development exhibited by Samara and many of the other 35 orangutans, gorillas and chimpanzees involved in a behavioral study intriguingly parallels that of the eight human infants they were compared with during the first two years of life.

"I am finding that orangutan and human infant development are strikingly similar," says Suzanne Chevalier-Skolnikoff, an anthropologist specializing in primate behavior at the University of California, San Francisco. . . . Like the other great ape subjects in the study, Samara was hand-reared by human surrogate mothers in settings where play patterns could be observed and various intelligence tests administered.

In attempting to "enhance our knowledge of . . . the history and evolution of human intelligence and human language," the anthropologist compared the apes with human babies at Piaget's six stages:

Reflex—From birth to one month; grasping for nearly everything within reach, particularly the mother.

Self-investigation—One to four months; sucking fingers, clasping hands and feet. . . .

Reaching out—Four to eight months; reaching for objects, beyond mother, in the nearby environment and attempting to bring most of them into the mouth.

Combinations and coordinations—Eight to 12 months; combining behaviors and coordinating body movements.

Experimentation—Twelve to 18 months; trial and error testing of relationships among objects, problem solving.

Mental problem solving—Eighteen to 24 months; solving through insight or symbolism rather than through physical experimentation.

While apes and children alike experienced these stages, there are differences. First, the ape's "rate of development is different from that of a human baby," Chevalier-Skolnikoff says. Stages two through four seem to be reached two months earlier in apes, while the two later stages develop more slowly than in humans.

The primary difference, however, is in vocal behavior. Like human infants, orangutans and other apes may cry at birth. "But the similarities in vocal development between ape and human end here," she says. Apes do not progress along the remaining five stages of vocal development—from cooing and babbling to speaking words. Rather, the apes acquire only "emotional vocalizations," such as grunts, laughs and various calls.

Samara's behavior reflects both the similarities and the differences detected in the study. "Manipulatively she is almost human," says the anthropologist. "Vocally she is an animal, in use of her feet she is strictly an orangutan. Figuratively speaking, Samara is a human baby, an animal and an orangutan all in one little orange furry bundle."

Science News
July 21, 1979

 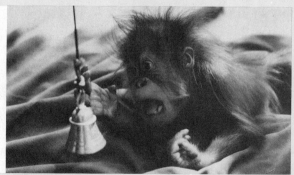

Margaret K. Burks

Suzanne Chevalier-Skolnikoff.

Human and orangutan babies display similar "reaching out" behavior by ringing bell.

There are sufficient similarities between human and certain animal species to warrant close examination and study of the development of animal behavior. Of course, experimental manipulation of such things as the environment are possible with animals, but for ethical reasons cannot be tried with human infants.

oral, visual, and auditory schemata, the infant receives information about the world that will lead to the further elaboration and development of these schemata. At the end of this period, infants begin to *coordinate* their various schemata. They look at what they grasp. They move their hands to touch an object by alternating their gaze between hand and object, closing in on the object through trial and error.

During these first four months of life, however, infants are still mostly unaware of themselves and the objects around them. They do not realize that the bottle they grasp one minute and the bottle they suck the next are the same object. When an object drops out of sight, it literally drops "out of mind," reflecting what Piaget called a lack of *object permanence*.

By stage 3, between 4 and 8 months of age, infants begin more actively to control and manipulate objects, although their initial attempts are often comical. They may hear an interesting noise and want it repeated, but since they do not know what caused

FIGURE 8-7 **Object permanence**

(A)

(B)

In the first four months of life an infant attends only to objects that are physically present (A). At eight months and beyond the infant knows about and attends to the location of hidden or occluded objects (B).

the noise, they try to make the noise recur by repeating whatever they were doing when they heard the noise. Piaget called this an example of "magical procedures to make interesting spectacles last." During this period, the baby first begins to realize that objects exist when they are out of sight. If a toy is dropped, the child will search for it, but only for a short time.

In the final four months of the first year (stage 4) magical thinking gives way to more instrumental activity. By this point children have achieved object permanence (Figure 8–7). They have some internal image of the object to help them recall it and its location. Moreover, they display a sense of space and time, as exemplified by the organized and orderly actions of lifting a pillow to search for a hidden object. But the child is still quite limited intellectually. If you hide the object under one pillow and then move it in plain view to a second, the child will search under the first pillow and may or may not move to the second.

The 12- to 14-month-old (stage 5) is likely to go to the second pillow to find the hidden object. Piaget sees much of cognitive growth as the formulation of increasingly complex hypotheses about events and the modification of these hypotheses in the light of experience. For example, a child may systematically vary the position from which he or she drops a toy in order to discover where the toy will land. There are parallel developments in the infant's perceptual processes during this time.

The final stage of sensorimotor development covers the last half of the second year of life (stage 6). In the preceding six months the child appears stumped when an object is placed under one pillow and then is moved in a closed fist to another pillow. Older children are not fooled by this movement because they infer what the moving hand holds. This last stage is important because it represents the beginning of the child's ability to represent mentally objects that are no longer physically present. In essence, it is the start of symbolic thinking.

The Preoperational Stage (2 to 7 Years)

The major advance made during the *preoperational stage* is the ability to represent objects in the external world mentally by means of symbols. This is the period in which language develops and begins to reflect the child's cognitive abilities and limitations. The preoperational child is in a transitional period. His or her perspective on the world is expanding rapidly, but the child is still confused in the use of physical concepts and in evaluations of cause and effect. During this phase children make illogical inferences and often attribute their feelings to inanimate objects — assuming, for example, that clouds "cry" to make rain. The child's unique conception of the world is revealed in the following interview:

ADULT: Why is it dark at night?
CHILD: Because if you don't sleep, Santa Claus won't give you any toys.
ADULT: Where does the dark come from at night?
CHILD: Well, bandits. They take something or mother pulls down the blinds and then it's very dark.
ADULT: What makes it day?
CHILD: God, he says to the dark, go away.
(Laurendeau & Pinard, 1962, pp. 170–171)

Notice what Piaget would call *egocentrism* in this example. Young children place themselves at the center of things and have difficulty imagining perspectives other than their own. In the above example, the child actually believes that the coming and going of night has something to do with the demands, made by Santa Claus and mother, that children go to sleep. This personalized view of events is common in early childhood, since young children do not consider the many other people in the world who also experience the same nightfall that they do. Piaget has reported countless similar examples of egocentrism — for example, children saying that the sun follows them around all day, or that rivers flow so that they may have fresh water to drink. Although the most blatant forms of egocentrism disappear with the transition into middle childhood, even adults often think egocentrically when encountering new and complex problems. For example, do you tend to think you are the only one with some particular problem, say, excessive shyness?

The Concrete Operational Stage (7 to 11 Years)

The *concrete operational stage* is characterized by the emergence of mental operations that enable children to establish multiple perspectives on events, and therefore to move away from the limitations of their own points of view. One example is provided by children's performance on Piaget's "three mountains" experiment. When faced with an array of three mountains, a preoperational child assumes that the array looks the same from all angles as it does from the angle from which the child is viewing it. With the advent of concrete operations, children can reconstruct other perspectives on the array, so that they can understand that the way the mountains look is determined by where one is standing. In the case of the mountains problem, concrete operations enable children to go beyond their immediate perspectives by mentally maintaining spatial relations like right and left or in front of and behind.

Piaget's most famous examples of concrete operations involve his "conservation" experiments. In these experiments, Piaget showed that only concrete operational children are able to understand that transformations in the appearance of physical objects do not affect their quantity. In one version of Piaget's

"Why did you cut my squash in half, Mommy? Now I have TWICE as much to eat."

The Family Circus by Bil Keane, reprinted courtesy The Register and Tribune Syndicate, Inc.

Is this an example of conservation?

conservation experiments, children are shown two identical beakers of water filled to the same level. Water from one beaker is poured into a taller but thinner beaker, and, of course, the water level rises (see Figure 8–8). Preoperational children maintain that the amount of water has increased, because they focus upon the higher water level of the first beaker when compared with the second. The child takes only one aspect of the situation (the height) into account, ignoring the narrower width of the new beaker and also the way in which the new beaker was filled. If

FIGURE 8–8 Conservation of quantity

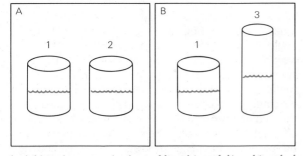

A child is shown two beakers of liquid (panel A) and is asked, "Which contains more, 1 or 2?" A 5-year-old child will say that the beakers contain equal amounts. The contents of beaker 2 are poured into beaker 3, a taller and thinner beaker (panel B). The child is asked again, "Which contains more?" The 5-year-old child answers, "3." The child is said to be unable to conserve quantity.

the child remembered that the new beaker was filled with the same quantity as the unchanged beaker, he or she might realize that the amount of water remains unchanged.

At about age 7, the child grasps the solution to the conservation of quantity problem by developing three types of concrete operations. The first is *compensation:* the water reaches a higher level, but that change is balanced by a decrease in the width of the beaker. The second operation is *reversibility:* if you pour the water back into its old beaker, it will reach the same level it originally reached. The third operation is *identity:* no water has been added or subtracted, so it must be the same amount of water. These three operations support one another, constituting a mental "grouping" that develops as a structural unit.

In the concrete operational period the child acquires and applies the notions of reversibility and identity across a wide variety of tasks. During this period systems of classification and of number are learned. Arithmetic is much easier when it is realized that $4 + 3 = 7$ also means that $7 - 4 = 3$. The ability to perform these mental operations in many different situations, with many numbers in any concrete problem, eliminates the need for rote memorization. The same rules apply across all situations. The child gives evidence during this period of beginning to realize that arithmetic and other disciplines are based on systems of rules.

The Formal Operational Stage (Adolescence On)

The complex, abstract, and mature logic of adults begins to manifest itself during adolescence with the systematic analysis, exploration, and solution of problems.

The following problem can be used to demonstrate how the *formal operational stage* differs from earlier stages of cognitive development. Four similar glass containers of different colorless, odorless chemicals along with another small container holding a fifth chemical, potassium iodide, are placed on a table before the subject (Figure 8–9). A certain amount of chemical from two of the similar containers is poured into an empty glass. The experimenter then adds several drops of potassium iodide, and the liquid, consisting of two unknown chemicals and the potassium iodide, turns yellow. The subject is asked to reproduce this color, using any or all of the containers.

Infants up to 2 years old pay no attention to the problem situation and merely play with their toys. Children in the preoperational stage randomly combine chemicals, making no attempt to keep track of what they have done. Between the ages of 7 and 11 years children begin to combine chemicals systematically, but tend to become confused after several

FIGURE 8-9 The chemical problem

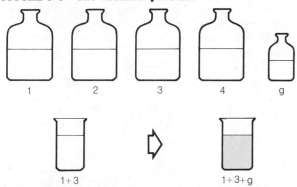

The chemical problem illustrates the different stages of cognitive development described by Piaget. Children of different ages are presented with four containers of colorless, odorless chemicals and a fifth beaker (g). Next, the children are shown a glass with a combination of two chemicals (unknown to the children, these are chemicals 1 and 3). When several drops of g are added to the glass, the liquid in the glass turns yellow. The children's task is to reproduce this color.

steps. Children over 11, however, are able to approach the problem with a logical and complete plan. They take chemicals from the containers two at a time, keeping a record of those that do not work so they do not repeat themselves. Piaget's explanation of these chronological differences in problem-solving ability is summarized in Table 8-1.

Most teenagers can deal skillfully with abstract questions or questions that are contrary to fact, like "What would have happened if the United States had not entered the Vietnam war?" The more literal, concrete operational child insists that questions of this sort are invalid because the war did take place with U.S. involvement. In addition, the formal operational thinker is more aware than the younger child that events can be interpreted in many ways and that there is no final version of truth. He or she is also more sensitive to the discrepancy between reality and ideals. Teenagers' knowledge of politics and attitudes toward arbitrary rules of conduct are very different from those of younger children. If a rule proves un-

TABLE 8-1 Contrasting Approaches to Solving the Chemical Problem

Stage	Behavior	Explanation
Sensorimotor (birth–2 years)	Child ignores the request and plays with the toys.	Lacks the vocabulary and motor skills to understand what's required to perform the task. Before 8 or so months lacks object permanence. Should one container drop from view, the child won't search for it.
Preoperational (2–7 years)	Child combines two containers at random.	Understands goal, but does not order the tests (takes one jar and "g," then the next, then the third). The child cannot keep track of what has been done, and does not classify the results into combinations that produce a yellow color and those that do not. The child is likely to think an irrelevant feature like the shape of the containers or the amount of the contents determines the color.
Concrete operations (7–11 years)	Child adds the fluid from each container in a systematic fashion. Then starts to combine "g" with pairs of containers and becomes confused.	Can order tests, one container at a time, but has difficulty ordering two variables simultaneously. Can classify container combinations into those that make the yellow color and those that do not. Possesses logical operations of reversibility and identity. Understands conservation. Knows the problem has to do with the identity of the chemicals, not the shape of their containers.
Formal operations (11 years and older)	Child takes the containers and combines them with "g" one at a time, and so on. Is able to keep track of the system and identify both chemicals that make the dye and some of the others.	Possesses knowledge of permutations and combinations. Can go beyond data to describe in abstract terms the nature of his or her system of testing. Can figure out what would happen if new chemicals were introduced; can deal with hypothetical situations, laws of probability, and so on (possesses the essentials of symbolic logic).

workable, they are likely to advocate change, while younger children act as if no other system of rules is imaginable. Formal operational thought allows the mastery of complex systems of literature, mathematics, and science. It also enables the development of abilities necessary for adult social adjustment, such as the planning of future goals and the integration of past and present roles into a realistic self-identity.

Language Development

The acquisition of language is an achievement unique to human beings, and it occurs with remarkable speed. A child starts to speak intelligibly at about 1 year of age and goes on to master the fundamentals of language in about three years. By age 4, the child has a vocabulary of well over 1000 words and can understand and produce most of the grammatical structures of the language. Let us now consider how this is all accomplished, taking into consideration the contributions of both maturation and learning.

Initial Speech

Sound production progresses through four phases — from crying to cooing to babbling to speaking words. The baby's first vowel-like sounds are merely accidental by-products of the business of living — breathing, digesting, crying in distress. Cooing begins at about 12 weeks when the child responds vocally to interesting sights in the environment, particularly faces. Consonants begin to emerge, and at about 6 months babbling begins. Consonants and vowels are combined into one-syllable utterances ("na"), and at about 8 months children begin to imitate their own speech and that of others, producing repeated syllables like "di, di, di, di, di." Some of the syllables heard in babbling are associated with objects or events, resulting in the child's first words at about 1 year of age.

Although such "words" are not, strictly speaking, part of the English language, their consistent usage as labels for objects and classes of objects

makes them function like words. The meaning of the word is likely to be less precise or perhaps more flexible than the corresponding word in adult speech. "Da Da" may describe father, mother, a babysitter, or indeed any adult.

In the first year of life, the production of speech lags somewhat behind the comprehension of speech. The infant may be able to hear the difference between *b* and *p* without being able to make the sounds distinctly. A lisping child may call himself "Tham" and yet shriek in protest at someone who fails to pronounce "Sam" correctly. In infant intelligence testing, 10-month-olds are expected to respond accurately by gesture to questions like "Where's Daddy" and yet are not expected to verbalize their answers until they grow older.

One- and Two-Word sentences

Between 8 and 18 months, children acquire a vocabulary of hundreds of words, although they still tend to speak in one-word utterances. Often a child will compress the meaning of an entire sentence into a single word. "Milk" may mean "the milk spilled," "I want milk," or simply, "This is milk." Such one-word expressions of extended meaning have been called *holophrases* by psycholinguists.

During the second year of life, children begin chaining together two words into utterances called *duos*. Roger Brown has defined several types of duos that occur regularly in 2-year-old speech. Some of the types include "naming" ("A cookie!"), "recurrence" ("More banana"), "nonexistence" ("Bye-bye milk"), and "agent-action" ("Susie run"). These brief utterances are the child's first attempt at grammatical construction, and Brown has pointed out that they are remarkably error-free. For example, children rarely confuse subject and object (saying, for example, "hit Billy" when they mean "Billy hit"). Other examples of early two-word sentences are given in Table 8-2.

Some early psycholinguists described children's language at this two-word stage as a simplified or "telegraphic" version of adult speech. But recent evidence suggests that the young child's language is unique. Its peculiar nature leads to unusual sentences that do not occur in adult speech and therefore cannot be direct imitations, for example, "All gone shoe," "Bye-bye car." The following conversation between a 2-year-old and his father, who has arrived home from work and is changing his clothes, illustrates how a young child combines two words to form some short sentences.

CHILD: Hi, Daddy.
DADDY: Hi, Johnny. Did Mommy buy this truck?
CHILD: This truck.
DADDY: Can you make it go fast?

TABLE 8–2   Early Two-Word Sentences

A coat	More coffee
A celery*	More nut*
A Becky*	Two sock*
A hands*	Two shoes
The top	Two tinker toy*
My mommy	Big boot
That Adam	Poor man
My stool	Little top
That knee	Dirty knee

* Ungrammatical for an adult.

Interpreting Baby Talk

What do an infant's cries mean? Hunger, usually, or discomfort, or fear. But they also reveal a slow process of learning how to communicate. Within a few months the baby's noises already show signs of patterns: a cry followed by a pause to listen for reactions, then another cry.

So reports Jerome Bruner, 60, long-time Harvard psychologist now teaching at Oxford and author of such pioneering works as *A Study of Thinking* (1956) and *The Process of Education* (1960)....

Adult Vicars

Learning to talk is no sudden discovery, according to Bruner. It takes about two years of dogged practice — by the mother as well as the child. (Bruner means not necessarily the child's natural mother, but someone who acts as "vicar" of the adult community.) Every word the vicar uses is a lesson in what sounds and tones work best. By the age of two months, the child can make a cry that demands or one that requests, *i.e.*, one that awaits

a response from the mother. "Mother talk," corresponding to "baby talk," tells the child that its request will be met and gives the child signs of the consequences of his request. Says Bruner: "Linguistic competence is developing before language proper."

In addition to making sounds, mother and child use their eyes as part of the communication process. A mother spends much of her time during the child's first four to nine months, says Bruner, simply trying to discover what the child is looking at....

She begins pointing out objects and giving them names. From ten months onward, the child as well begins pointing out objects. Mothers introduce a familiar pattern: 1) pointing to an object; 2) putting the question to the child, "What (or who, or where) is that?"; and 3) labeling the object, person or place ("That's a hat," "That's Grandma," "That's the bedroom").

Without knowing it, the mother has already set in motion the process of fostering the four basic skills that

Bruner considers essential for making sentences later on:

"Well-formedness," when the mother demands a closer approximation to the correct pronunciation of a word with each repetition.

"Truth functionality," generally begun after the first year, when she corrects a mistake: "That's not a dog, it's a cat."

"Felicity," which means that the manner of speech must be appropriate to the situation.

"Verisimilitude," when she allows a child to place a box on his head and pretends it is a hat, but does not encourage him to do the same thing with, say, a ball.

Step by step, in a steady series of accretions of meaning, these lessons lead toward acquiring the gift of speech. Says Bruner: "Man realizes his full heritage when he reaches language. But he is doing things along the way which are also quite remarkable."

Time
August 23, 1976

CHILD: Go fast. Hat off. Shirt off. Pants off. That blue.
DADDY: Yes, my pants are blue.
CHILD: Sweater on. See Mommy. Hear Mommy.
DADDY: I'll go and help her carry in the groceries.
CHILD: Groceries. Bye-Bye. Two bag. Chicken. That red. Bag fall. Close it.
DADDY: I can't close the box so we'll have pizza for dinner.

(Palermo, 1970, p. 437)

The child's "mini-sentences" lack many features of adult speech, such as noun-verb or adjective-noun agreement. But the sentences are nonetheless recognizable, functional, and governed by some linguistic rule. Most important, they convey meaning.

Linguistic Transformations

The child soon goes beyond two-word sentences. During the third year, linguistic transformations appear in utterances. For example, "You went there" is a simple declarative sentence that can be transformed into a question ("Did you go there?"), a negative ("You didn't go there"), and a number of other linguistic forms, each conveying a particular meaning. First, however, the child must learn basic

transformational rules of grammar. These are acquired with astonishing rapidity after the second year of life. Interestingly, the transformational rules that children learn are universal. Analyses of the underlying structures of many different languages have revealed a striking similarity among them.

Before the end of the third year, children have mastered a vocabulary of up to 1000 words. They begin piecing together more and more complex sentences. The first questions involving who, what, where, when, and why appear in their speech. They turn more frequently to negation types of statements ("Not hungry now"). Soon they will try out the most sophisticated forms of syntax, such as tag questions ("We're leaving soon, aren't we?"). By the time they enter school, children normally possess a language indistinguishable in its syntactical and grammatical aspects from the speech of adults.

Language and Thought

Almost all psychologists believe that language and thought are closely related, but there is considerable disagreement as to exactly *how* they are linked.

Piaget and his followers believe that language is a result of important advances in children's cognitive abilities, particularly the ability to symbolize that develops at the end of infancy. In this view, language is seen as one of many by-products—though an admittedly valuable one—of cognitive growth. Evidence for this position can be found in Piaget's conservation experiment. Children's use of the word "more" (as in "This beaker has more water") clearly changes after they develop the cognitive operations necessary to consider both the dimensions of height and width in their judgments of quantity.

An opposite point of view is that language structures thinking, and that once children learn words and syntactical relations the power of their reasoning increases manyfold. One expression of this position is the *Whorfian hypothesis,* advocated by many cultural anthropologists (see Chapter 6). Whorf and Sapir pointed out that the particular vocabularies of certain cultures indicate how members of the culture see the world. For example, Eskimos have several different words for "snow," and, perhaps as a result, are able to discriminate between varieties of snow more readily than members of cultures with only one such word. An extreme version of this position maintains that once children have mastered their culture's language they have learned all the fundamental codes and concepts necessary for functioning in that society.

A middle position has been maintained by Soviet psychologists like Vygotsky and Luria. Vygotsky's theory portrayed language and thought as developing together and aiding one another in the process. In infancy, he wrote, there are prelinguistic concepts and prerational words, neither of which function as true intelligence. When in early childhood the streams of thought and language merge, both become immensely more powerful. As a consequence of this merger, children become able to gain control over themselves and their environments, to reason logically about the world, and to express their ideas meaningfully to others. Inner speech, discussed previously, is an early example of this mutually beneficial merger of thought and language.

Social Development

Nothing in a child's personal development is as important as coming to terms with the social world. From the time of birth, a child is part of a social network made up of tangible others as well as not-so-tangible institutions, codes, and standards of behavior. The child's tasks in growing up are to establish productive and satisfying relations with significant others in the social network, to participate in important institutions (like school), and to live according to the codes and

---

Language in Deaf Children: An Instinct

The acquisition of language has always been one of the more intriguing aspects of childhood development. "The child of English-speaking parents learns English and not Hopi, while the child of Hopi-speaking learns Hopi, not English," note Susan Goldin-Meadow of the University of Chicago and Heidi Feldman of the University of California at San Diego School of Medicine.

"But what if a child is exposed to no conventional language at all?" the researchers ask in the July 22 SCIENCE. "Surely such a child, lacking a specific model to imitate, could not learn the conventional language of his culture," they say. "But might he elaborate a structured, albeit idiosyncratic, language nevertheless? Must a child experience language in order to learn language?"

In attempting to answer that question, Goldin-Meadow and Feldman videotaped six deaf children in their homes for one to two hour sessions at six- to eight-week intervals. The 17- to 49-month-old children—four boys and two girls of "normal intelligence"—had not been exposed to manual sign language because their parents wanted to expose them to oral education. Yet none at that point had acquired significant knowledge from their oral education program.

The youngsters were observed and taped during informal interactions with a researcher, their mother and a standard set of toys. The researchers found that the deaf children "developed a structured communication system that incorporates properties found in all child languages. They developed a lexicon of signs to refer to objects, people and actions, and they combined signs into phrases that express semantic relations in an ordered way." . . .

"We have shown that the child can develop a structured communication system in a manual mode without the benefit of an explicit, conventional language model," the researchers conclude. They compare the findings with the "meager linguistic achievements of chimpanzees," where chimps have been shown to develop languagelike communication, but only with training. "Even under difficult circumstances, however, the human child reveals a natural inclination to develop a structured communication system," say Feldman and Goldin-Meadow.

Science News
August 20, 1977

One way to examine the relative effects of both heredity and environment on the formation of language is to study the language habits of deaf children.

---

standards that make social functioning possible. The consequence of not accomplishing these social tasks can be devastating. A failure to establish good social relations leads a child to social conflict or isolation. Failure to engage properly in social institutions can leave a child impoverished in essential skills and competence. And failure to adopt cultural codes and standards can lead to social deviance and criminal delinquency.

Even the development of the self and the self's identity are wrapped up in an individual's social development. Throughout life, and especially at the beginning, one knows the self only through others. This is because, in infancy and early childhood at least, the kinds of social relations that one experiences determine to a large degree what one thinks of oneself. Social development and the fashioning of personality are therefore inextricably woven together as the child grows.

Throughout the life span, social development progresses in two complementary ways, performing a dual function in the individual's life. The first function is the "socialization" of the individual, which includes the efforts of the individual to get along with others, to regulate his or her behavior according to social codes and standards, and to develop a conscience. This is the *integrating* function of social development, since it is the aspect that connects the individual to society through relationships and responsibilities. The second function of social development is the formation of the individual's unique social identity and personality. This function focuses on developing one's sense of self, knowing one's idiosyncratic personal characteristics, and understanding the implications of one's sex role, family role, and social status. This is the *differentiating* function of social development, since identity and personality formation require separating oneself from others, coming to know one's unique social characteristics, and consequently ordering oneself in a special position within the social network. Through the inte-

grating social-developmental function one enjoys the fruits of social relations with persons and institutions, and through the differentiating function one acquires a social status and a knowledge of self.

In this section we shall discuss the lifelong development of the individual with respect to both the socialization and identity-formation aspects of social development.

Infancy

As early as infancy we can see the dual processes of social development at work. Many developmental psychologists now believe that the integrating function of social development is established at birth by inborn patterns of behavior. These inherited behaviors assure the infant of contact with those persons in society who are necessary for the infant's survival because they provide protection, shelter, and food. For most infants the most prominent of these persons is mother. The behavioral patterns that the infant uses to establish close and sustained contact with mother are called *attachment* behaviors. These behaviors include smiling, cooing, and grasping as the infant's positive means of attracting mother to his or her reach; and crying, stomping, or screaming as the infant's negative means of protesting mother's departure.

Although not all child psychologists agree that attachment behaviors are biologically based, evidence from naturalistic and experimental studies have made the biological argument difficult to contest. The classic studies of Harry Harlow with rhesus monkeys (see Figure 8–10) and other studies with human infants have shown that prototypical attachment be-

FIGURE 8–10   Clinging to "Mom"

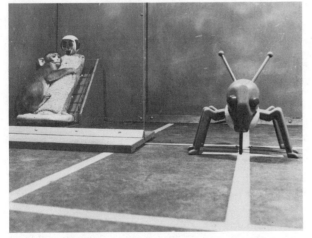 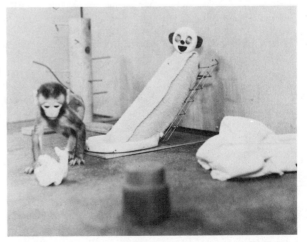

Harry Harlow studied the attachment behavior of infant monkeys using substitute (surrogate) mothers made out of chicken wire and terrycloth. When placed in a new environment, baby monkeys become highly agitated and fearful. They cling to their mothers, real or surrogate, until they calm down. Subsequently, they begin to explore the new environment, increasing their distance from "mother" only gradually.

The Wisdom of Babies
By SHARON BEGLEY
with JOHN CAREY

. . . ["Infants"] are capable of doing much more than we think much earlier than we thought," says psychologist Michael Lewis, director of the Institute for the Study of Exceptional Children in Princeton, N.J.

By studying the mental behavior of babies, scientists are learning about the mechanisms of the human mind. Researchers have found, for instance, that babies quickly develop the notion of "self"—of being different from other things in the world—which suggests that the brain may be prewired for this concept. And despite the widely held theory that language molds human thought, infants who cannot speak seem to grasp such abstract ideas as how to place objects into categories. These findings carry an important message for parents: since babies have incipient minds, they should be stimulated early.

Senses
Infants are clearly developing acute senses by the sixth month of gestation, according to pediatrician T. Berry Brazelton of the Children's Hospital Medical Center in Boston. When pregnant women (wearing abdominal belts to measure fetal response) enter rooms with bright lights and harsh noises, the fetuses are startled. In contrast, soft lights and sounds attract them. These responses are quite independent and unrelated to the mother's reaction. Immediately after birth, infants have even sharper senses. They can distinguish their mother's voice from a male pediatrician's and can perceive the difference in pattern of different-size checkerboards.

Because infants perceive their world from the moment they enter it, they must arrive prepared to explore it and, ultimately, to understand it. What intrigues researchers is where this natural endowment leaves off and experience begins. So far, the evidence shows that babies follow their reflexes for the first three months of life. All newborns smile, for instance, even if they are blind, and all babies tightly clutch objects placed in their palms. Both habits have apparently been prewired into the brain as firmly as the optic nerve.

Such prewiring, however, resembles less a finished circuit board than a few rudimentary connections. Depending on the baby's experiences, scientists speculate, circuits develop to let him think characteristically human thoughts. "Infants are born with a set of dispositions to perceive the world in a certain way," says psychologist Jerome Kagan of Harvard University. When they perceive something that fits these dispositions—such as seeing that their image in a mirror matches their potential sense of self—the experience becomes absorbed.

Soon infants learn to take in information with one sense and transfer it to another. In a typical experiment by Susan Rose and Wagner Bridger at Albert Einstein College of Medicine in New York, the baby is gently encouraged to reach through a screen and feel a simple wooden star. Wide-eyed with curiosity, the baby tinkers with the toy, tracing the surface with his pudgy fingers. Then the star and a similarly sized wooden ball are put on a tray and shown to the infant. The child recognizes the star and, already bored with it, reaches for the ball. Infants as young as six months are apparently able to identify the object they felt through the screen. "The ability to make these connections [between touch and vision] may form the basis for symbolic thinking," says psychologist Rose. "The infant could be creating a mental representation of the object."

Common Traits
Since the ability to form categories is the basis for more advanced conceptual thinking, psychologist Leslie Cohen of the University of Texas tests for this skill. He shows babies a series of pictures from a single category and records how long they look at each. When they see nothing but toy stuffed animals, they get bored quickly. Cohen finds even seven-month-olds seem to recognize stuffed animals as members of the same category whether they are rabbits or pandas. But when he interjects pictures from another category, such as a rattle, they take notice. Cohen suspects that the infants recognize common traits in the many examples and use them to construct categories.

This explanation of forming categories contradicts the belief that humans need language to make the mental leap from the specific to the general. Psychologists used to think that humans label what they see—calling houses, churches and skyscrapers all buildings, for example—in order to generalize. But if infants generalize, it must not require words. Instead, babies might use "visual averaging." In their minds they might abstract common features to draw mental pictures of prototypes. If they draw an abstract picture of walls, a roof and other building features, any building can be put into the right category. . . .

Now that scientists see that infants are so brainy, they are applying their findings. A mother, they say, should recognize that her baby will respond to her from birth. Parents should provide more than a stimulating environment of bright mobiles and toys: they must also respond to their infants. The more the baby feels he can influence his world, the more he will investigate and participate in it.

Newsweek
January 12, 1981

haviors like clinging are unlearned and that close, frequent contact with another (usually mother) is a primary need during the first few months of life. The need for frequent physical contact does not derive from other needs such as feeding. Nor can it be safely eliminated from the child's life: in studies both with animals and with institutionalized human children, scientists have found that infants deprived of steady, physical "mothering" often show psychotic behavior, inferior intellectual development, and higher than

A Child's Second Birth

Some of life's greatest turmoil is over by the age of three. Though infancy may seem to be a time of games and gurgling, the baby is caught up in earnest and sometimes desperate attempts to make sense of the world, control aggression, and come to terms with the awesome power of parents. In a remarkable new book, *Oneness and Separateness*, Psychologist Louise Kaplan, 48, offers a baby's-eye view of the child's struggle to become an individual. Behind that struggle, says Kaplan, are opposing needs of the child—to cling to mother and to strike out on its own. The child's solution to the dilemma will powerfully affect its adult attitudes toward love, initiative and trust.

Kaplan is director of child clinical services at the City University of New York. . . . In the first four months of life, says Kaplan, the baby is merged with the mother in "the bliss of unconditional love" that later becomes the model for adult conceptions of ecstasy and perfect union.

Starting at five months, as the baby becomes alert and exploratory, the merger begins to break down. The baby's growing independence is tinged with uncertainty and loss. "Peekaboo" is a serious game; the baby toys with separateness without fearing that he or she will be abandoned. . . .

Until the age of ten months, the baby's world is in fragments. It is still not sure where its body begins and ends and does not fully realize that the mother is a separate individual. Outbursts of rage, sometimes violent ones centering on feeding, rise from this stress, . . . A parent who responds with rage just reinforces the fear of fragmentation. What the child needs, says Kaplan, is a "calming yes-saying voice," conveying assurance that its aggressive urges are not dangerous.

From ten to 15 months, the child is a high-spirited conquering hero, exploring and manipulating the physical world. It is also the period, Kaplan notes, when mothers damage daughters out of a mistaken notion that girls are more fragile than boys. . . . When the mother goes out, the child is almost always depressed, but baby sitters should avoid trying to cheer the child up or distract it with a game. The reason: the child is learning how to manage loss. . . .

The emergence of the child's thinking mind, at around 15 months, brings wrenching change. The static world of symbols, images and concepts replaces the world of simple motion and action—the child can no longer simply flow through life. . . . The child's central idea is that it is not a conqueror after all, but a small and vulnerable self. Instead of wooing the mother, the child makes more and more coercive demands that she act as an extension of itself. As the child moves toward psychological birth, and the first use of the word "I," the mother's role becomes even more frustrating. If she gives in to the coercion, she undermines the child's independence. If she does not, she enforces its sense of aloneness. . . .

The author recommends that parents react tolerantly to the child's willfulness and compulsive no-saying at this stage. Parents should resist some demands, give in to others. . . .

The child's resolution of the oneness-separateness conflict between the ages of 18 and 36 months, says Kaplan, will shape, but not determine, the adult it will become. "To the extent that a child is trapped in imperfect reconciliation at the age of three, it will be more difficult for it to take advantage of what life offers later on, but it won't be impossible."

The father's role in a toddler's life is important but subsidiary. He must make certain that the psychic separation of mother and child actually takes place. Mother and the baby "play dangerously on the brink of not being able to separate," and without an active father, the baby may grow up to be a dependent, adult-sized infant. . . .

Time
June 19, 1978

Can you conceive of what the world looks like to the developing infant? Can you imagine what a struggle it must be for a baby to "get a grip on reality"? You might try to enact the role of a baby and examine your introspections about what's going on around you. After all, we all went through this stage once—do you remember?

---

usual mortality rates. In later life, infants surviving such deprivation often experience severe difficulty in establishing social and sexual relations with peers. Thus, the physical and emotional bond that normally emerges between mother and child is more than just an intensely affective social relation. It is a cornerstone of the infant's early physical survival, as well as an important condition for the child's optimal future growth.

An experimental technique for studying patterns of attachment between infants and their mothers has been designed by Mary Ainsworth. In a technique called the "strange situation," infants are observed encountering a stranger and new objects both in the presence and absence of the mother. Ainsworth found that infants who are "securely attached" use their mothers as a "base" for exploring their environment. Although they take pleasure in their mother's presence, and greet her warmly when she returns from a brief absence, they are able to venture into the world on their own. Insecurely attached infants, on the other hand, show little interest in exploring new objects or people; they often cling to their mothers in a new environment, and yet do not show obvious warmth or affection when greeting her upon return. Ainsworth and her colleagues have identified several distinct patterns of secure and insecure attachment, and believe that the quality of the mother-infant bond strongly influences children's later social relations with peers and adults.

Although some attachment patterns may be an inborn part of children's behavioral repertoires, and although an infant's need for "mothering" may be primary, this does not mean that the infant's intense relations with mother remain constant throughout life. As the child's physical and cognitive capacities grow, there is dramatic change in the behaviors through which he or she expresses attachment: Smiling at human faces begins not long after birth, but protest at separation—often called separation anxiety—normally does not appear until 7 months of age. Some theorists have portrayed attachment as a never-ending, lifelong process, citing the adolescent's ties to school, the adult's loyalty to country, or the mother's love of family as later manifestations of this intrinsic human need.

The close nature of the mother-infant relation has many benefits for the child, but also poses a problem; it is initially very difficult for the infant to separate the self from the mother. At first the infant has difficulty distinguishing even its own body from that of the mother. Even after the infant establishes its own physical identity, it continues to identify its mental perspective with the mother's well into the second year of life. Eventually, the infant struggles to distinguish its desires and thoughts from those of the mother and evolves ways of asserting its own independence. The first culmination of this struggle occurs at the end of infancy, during the noisy period that leads the child to be called a "terrible 2." For the child, socially, this period coincides with his or her first successes in obtaining an objective understanding of the self uncontaminated by the earlier confusion between the self and the caregiver. Children now begin to realize the uniqueness of their own viewpoints, and the rest of the world may go its own way. Though something of a child-management problem for parents, the "terrible 2" period represents a prodigious achievement for the child in the differentiating aspect of social development.

Recently Michael Lewis and Jeanne Brooks-Gunn completed an investigation into infants' acquisition of self-knowledge. The researchers tested the abilities of infants to recognize themselves in pictures, mirrors, and on TV. They dabbed the infants' noses with red to see whether the infants noticed anything different about themselves. They also showed infants images of themselves and of other children, to see whether infants could single themselves out. Lewis and Brooks-Gunn found that only at about 15 months can infants specifically recognize changed features of themselves (like reddened noses). In addition, not until this age can infants regularly tell themselves apart from others on the basis of facial and other char-

acteristics. First distinctions seem to be made on the basis of age and sex (that is, the infant realizes that he is a baby boy). Later, other distinguishing features of self are realized and added to these initial ones.

Childhood

As the child grows beyond infancy, peer interactions assume an increasingly important role in social development. Even during infancy, children engage in meaningful contact with peers, and one currently booming area of child research has documented the remarkable reciprocity, cooperation, and overall sophistication that characterize infants' peer interactions. But the real advent of social and cooperative play between peers takes place during the preschool years, between the ages of 3 and 5 years. It is then that egocentric and "parallel" play between children begins to decline. In its place emerges a genuine interchange of ideas and actions. This interchange forces the child to come to terms with points of view that often conflict with the child's own, encouraging the child to adopt new ideas and behaviors.

L. S. Vygotsky called children's play the "zone of proximal development" because of the many ways in which play contributes to children's intellectual and social abilities. Cathryn Garvey has documented the remarkable sophistication and variety of children's social play. Particularly significant is the way in which children try out new social roles and practice rules of social interaction during their playful exchanges. During play a child can pretend to be a father, a school leader, a policeman, or a baby. Conflicting desires or problems can be acted out with none of the consequences of real life. Play offers children an opportunity to experiment, to symbolize, and to invent new patterns of social behavior. It is a nonserious activity with vastly serious social-developmental benefits.

Peer Relations

In the course of interacting with peers, children begin to establish continuing social relationships, and also begin regulating these social relations with norms and values that help maintain the relationships. The most general social relation between peers is friendship, and in the preschool years we see children first expressing an awareness of friends as people of special significance. Research in social cognition (the child's understanding of the social world) has documented the development of children's friendship conceptions. At first, for children in the preschool and early school years, friends are seen simply as playmates, or as those with whom one comes in frequent contact, such as neighbors and schoolmates. Friendships at this early developmental level are established by material acts such as giving and sharing toys, food,

"Dickie has just started Phase Two of his maturation process."

The New Yorker, March 9, 1981. Drawing by Weber; © 1981 The New Yorker Magazine, Inc.

or favors. Friendships are terminated by negative material acts of the same order, such as stealing, hitting, refusing to share. But both the establishment and termination of friendships occur quickly and are easily reversed, since the friendship relation at this point is not seen to have a permanent or even long-term status. Later in childhood—approximately from the middle school years until early adolescence—children's conceptions of friendship develop further. Consequently, there is a change in the nature and quality of children's relations with peers during this period. At the second developmental level of friendship, a friend is seen as a particular kind of associate rather than as just anyone who happens to be a playmate. Specifically, friends are now seen as persons who will help when needed, who are kind, nice, and trustworthy. Friendship is understood as a relation that is in the reciprocal interest of both parties, so that each is expected to respond to the other's needs or desires. Thus, children's friendships become more stable, since they are now based upon the children's affirmations of special qualities (kindness, niceness) in one another, as well as upon a mutually shared trust.

Childhood Morality

While establishing social relations like friendship, children learn a great deal about the expectations of others in relation to their own needs and desires. In order to maintain successful relations with others, children must learn how to regulate their own behavior in a way that does justice both to their own and others' social perspectives. For example, if children are to have friends, they must learn both to take turns at a toy and to give others their turn. Accordingly, in early encounters with social requirements like sharing and fairness, the child begins to develop a sense of obligation and a sense of justice. This is the early form of that complex system of social regulation that is called morality. There is little in a person's social development as crucial for the integration of the self into the social network as the development of moral judgment and character.

The earliest manifestations of morality in the child's life are the early sharing, turn-taking, and other examples of "fairness" found in young children's play. William Damon has described the development of fairness in the thinking and conduct of young children. At the earliest developmental level, found primarily in children 4 years and younger, fairness is associated only with the child's own desires. For example, a child might say that it is fair that he should get more ice cream than his sister because he likes ice cream and wants more. A bit more advanced than this is the justifying of such egocentric desires with reference to some "objective" criterion. For example, a child might say that he (or she) should get what he wants because he's the fastest runner in his house, or because he's a boy, and so on, even if such criteria may be illogical, untrue, or irrelevant to the reward under consideration. At the next level, usually found around age 6, fairness is associated with strict equality in actions; it is fair that everyone get the same, regardless of special considerations like merit or need. Next comes an identification of fairness with deserving; those who worked hardest, were smartest, or acted best should be specially rewarded because they deserve it. We are at this point normally into middle childhood, in the early and mid-elementary school years. Among children a bit older, fairness is thought of as compromise, with special regard for those in unfortunate circumstances (the poor, the incompetent). Finally, the most advanced children in this age span consider the particular function of the reward from situation to situation.

Morality involves not only sharing and fairness but also respect for the rules of society. Piaget studied children's orientations to social rules by observing children playing a common marble game in the streets of Geneva. He identified four stages in children's rule-following behavior. At first, shortly after infancy, young children play in a private, nonsocial manner, inventing their own idiosyncratic "rules." The child's marble playing might have some regularities, but these are not shared by anyone else who might be playing. At the second stage, called *heteronomous morality,* the child (now age five or so) takes the rules of the game quite seriously, acting as if the rules were sacred and unchangeable. The letter of the law is valued above all. Nevertheless, despite this inflexible orientation, children at this age often follow rules erratically. Their absolute respect does not translate into consistent obedience. Piaget called the third stage *autonomous morality.* At this stage, the child (now 8 or 9) regards rules as changeable agreements that are made by people to serve people's needs. Cooperation and reciprocity, rather than constraint, become the child's rationale for obeying rules, and in fact the child's rule-following becomes more consistent. The fourth stage develops at about the time of formal operations. During this period, when children become able to consider hypothetical possibilities and formal rule systems, their moral thinking begins to operate on the plane of complex political and social ideology. As we shall see in the following section, Lawrence Kohlberg has revised and expanded Piaget's moral judgment theory, focusing particularly on the periods of adolescence and adulthood.

Parent-Child Relations

Parents influence their children's behavior and development enormously throughout the childhood years. A parent's style of child-rearing can have wide-ranging implications for the child's personal development. Diana Baumrind has distinguished three major styles of child-rearing: the *authoritarian,* the *authoritative,* and the *permissive.* Authoritarian parents discipline their children strictly, demanding maturity from them but not communicating frequently or clearly with them, and are not particularly warm or nurturant. Authoritative parents also exert control and make demands on their children, but are more democratic in discussing family problems and decisions with their children. They are also high in nurturance. Permissive parents communicate well with their children but do not discipline them nor demand intellectual or social achievements from them. Baumrind found that children of authoritative parents were more likely to develop "instrumental competence" (social responsibility, independence, achievement orientation, and vitality) than children of authoritarian or permissive parents. This finding was particularly true of girls, whose self-reliance and assertiveness were greatly enhanced by an authoritative upbringing. Interestingly, the seemingly opposite patterns of authoritarianism and permissiveness were both associated with shyness and dependency in girls and with hostility in boys.

Children's Acquisition of Sex Roles

As for the differentiating aspect of social development during childhood, children are constantly seeking ways to define themselves. As Lewis and Brooks-Gunn found, one of the earliest means of self-identity is one's sex, perhaps because sex is one of our most important personal characteristics. Consequently, sex-role development has been the subject of intense study by child psychologists.

Differences between males and females are first of all physiological and biological. But to identify maleness and femaleness from a psychological perspective other criteria need to be applied as well. Early training and experience for example, are both important factors in the development of sex-role identification.

Although sex-role identification was once thought to be inherited, recent evidence suggests that it results from learning. In one study, for example, parents were asked to "describe your baby as you would to a close friend." Parents also filled out a questionnaire, rating the baby on 18 scales such as firm-soft, big-little, relaxed-nervous. Finally, the psychologist obtained hospital records on each baby's weight, height, muscle tone, reflexes, heart rate, and so forth. None of the hospital data showed any difference between male and female babies. Parents, on the other hand, "detected" marked differences. Parents of daughters thought their babies were significantly softer, finer featured, and smaller than did parents of boys. Fathers went further than mothers in enumerating differences between boy and girl babies in looks and behavior. Such evidence strongly suggests that sex stereotyping begins at the time parents first learn the sex of their child and is not so much a function of biology as was once thought.

By age 2 or 3, most children can distinguish themselves as boys or girls. The absence of any clear sex-role differentiation by this age may be indicative of later difficulties in adjustment. John Money has found that children who have suffered severe accidents affecting their biological gender can be treated both medically (through hormone treatment) and socially (through parent education) to orient them toward different psychosexual roles in spite of biological endowment. Very young children have not established sexual identity, and certain environmental influences during early life can have irreversible effects on later development. (In fact, there may be no such thing as permanence with regard to a specific sex role. Adults when properly counseled both medically and psychologically can undergo a sex-change process that reverses their former sex role.)

Sex Differences and Androgyny

Historically, many people have felt that men are biologically better suited for certain tasks (such as being the "provider") than women, who are destined to remain in the home as child bearers and housekeepers. People tend to employ sexual stereotypes for both males and females, and as a result, equal opportunities for both sexes have not always been

Two Verdicts on Infant Stereotyping
By VIRGINIA ADAMS

Among the unresolved issues in psychology is the extent to which adults treat boys and girls differently and thus foster sex differences in later life. Two recent experiments produced diametrically opposing findings on one aspect of the issue: whether or not adults playing with infants favor different toys for girls and boys. Yes, they do, conclude Laura S. Sidorowicz and G. Sparks Lunney of New York. No, they do not, say Kenneth J. Zucker and Carl M. Corter of Toronto.

Sidorowicz and Lunney asked 60 college students to spend a few minutes playing with a baby whose sex was disguised by an undershirt and diapers. The students were told they were participating in a study of "young infants' responses to strangers." Two baby boys and one baby girl were used, but without regard to the infant's actual sex, the researchers told one-third of the students that they would be playing with a boy named Johnny and another third that their playmate would be a girl called Jenny. The rest of the time the baby got no sex label; if subjects asked, the experimenters said, "I'm really not sure which infant we are using today." Three toys were set out in the play area:

a tiny and presumably masculine football, a "feminine" doll, and a teething ring, assumed to be sex-neutral. Each session ended soon after the subject had picked up a toy.

When they thought the baby was male, 65 percent of the subjects chose the football, 20 percent the doll, and 15 percent the teething ring. When the infant was labeled female, 15 percent picked the football, 80 percent the doll, and 5 percent the teething ring. With sex unspecified, the percentages were 25, 40, and 35, respectively.

The Zucker and Corter experiment varied these procedures only slightly. The researchers recruited 31 mothers, who played with their own infants in 10-minute experimental sessions, and 31 college students, each of whom played with one of the same babies for the same length of time at the conclusion of the mother's session. The experimenters told the mothers the true purpose of the study, but gave the students the same explanation Sidorowicz and Lunney used. The 17 girl and 14 boy babies all wore sexless clothes and were introduced to the strangers either as David or as Susan. Six toys were available: a dump truck, and a Batman doll

("masculine"), a Holly Hobbie doll and a set of miniature pots and pans ("feminine"), and a squeaky mouse and a rattle with a movable face on one side and a mirror on the other ("neutral").

Both strangers and mothers used the neutral toys much more than they did the masculine or feminine ones. With a "male" baby, strangers used a neutral toy for 223 seconds, a masculine one for 21, and a feminine one for 33. When the infant was supposedly a girl, the number of seconds was 213 for the neutral toys, 37 for masculine ones, and 57 for feminine ones.

The researchers were cautious in interpreting their results, suggesting that the subjects could have chosen the mouse and rattle less for their neutrality than for their attractiveness, especially their eye and ear appeal. They also acknowledged that the mothers' awareness of the study's purpose could have led them to shun sex-linked toys, but they considered this unlikely, "since the female strangers, without such information, behaved in a similar manner."

Psychology Today
June 1980

How do children develop sex-role behaviors? Do parents insure the behavioral differences between boys and girls by treating boys and girls differently from the moment of birth? The question seems simple and straightforward, but research like that described here shows the answer will not be simple.

provided. In their comprehensive book *The Psychology of Sex Differences,* Eleanor Maccoby and Carol Jacklin concluded that there are relatively few substantial differences between males and females that can be supported on evidence currently available. Yet there are many implied differences that have been inadvertently reinforced in our culture and that have no basis in fact.

In a time when males and females are finding any occupational goal within reach, biological sex is no longer the important variable it once was. Gender is a convenient dimension across which individuals can be separated, but this does not mean that it is a useful one in terms of understanding behavior or the developmental process.

Recently, a new perspective called **androgyny** has emphasized that biological males and females have both masculine and feminine characteristics. The word "androgyny" comes from the combination of two Greek words, *andr* meaning "male," and *gyne,* meaning "female." The truly androgynous person uses whichever behavior is most adaptive at a given time. For example, a male who is aggressive in business may be very nurturant toward his children. Figure 8–11 contrasts this perspective with the traditional view of sex differences.

This new way of viewing sex differences encourages young males and females to set goals and aspirations regardless of their physical characteristics. It also allows them to act in ways that are entirely

Reining In Androgyny
By CARIN RUBENSTEIN

During the early 1970s, a hot trend in psychology sometimes made it look as though being traditionally masculine or feminine were a handicap, and that the most successful people were those who combined the best of both masculine and feminine traits. "Androgyny" became something of a buzzword: men and women who were classified as androgynous on psychologist Sandra Bem's Sex Role Inventory (BSRI) seemed to be more flexible and responsive in various situations than "masculine" men and "feminine" women. Now, Faye Crosby, a psychologist at Yale, and Linda Nyquist have analyzed some underlying problems of androgyny research.

"An androgynous self-concept allows an individual to engage freely in both masculine and feminine behaviors," wrote Bem in 1975. Scores of studies based on her work showed, for example, that androgynous college students were more relaxed than traditionally sex-typed men and women when they met members of the opposite sex for the first time. Yet, deciding what should be called androgynous is a problem, say Crosby and Nyquist. Not one but four different scales are now used to measure the condition, and several recent studies show that anywhere between 33 and 42 percent of those who are classified as androgynous on one scale would not appear as androgynous on another.

Most androgyny research implies that the ideal person has a flexible and wide-ranging repertoire of sex-role behavior. Pushing the idea to its extreme, Crosby and Nyquist point out that by this definition a bisexual person is more flexible than one who is heterosexual or homosexual and therefore must be psychologically healthier. Moreover, Crosby and Nyquist say that androgyny researchers seldom pause to ask whether flexible behaviors are really appropriate.

An androgynous person is assumed to be "cheerful and gentle in one type of situation and competitive and forceful in another," Crosby and Nyquist say.

"Yet if the hypothetical individual were adolescent, some researchers would characterize him or her as a confused youth suffering from ego identity diffusion. If the individual were a young mother, other researchers might characterize her as ambivalent, [or] even . . . the kind of schizophrenogenic mother who puts her children in a double bind."

The concept of psychological androgyny, in short, was accepted before it was well documented. It was seductive, because it fit the argument of the women's movement that everyone would benefit if more women entered the assertive, masculine domain of work and more men participated in the stereotypically expressive, feminine arena of home and child care. The chief contribution of the debate, Crosby and Nyquist imply, is to help deflate the tacit assumptions of most sex-role research that "masculine and feminine self-images and behaviors are mutually exclusive," and that masculine is better.

Psychology Today
March 1980

natural (such as a nurturant father) but that have been discouraged up to now. As a society, we can all benefit when both males and females can contribute their skills, whether as airplane pilots or homemakers, or both. The challenge is to shake off the old stereotypical ways of thinking of males and females and begin to see people for what they are as individuals.

Adolescence

Once past childhood, the individual confronts a qualitatively different social order. The adolescent in any technological society is faced with a range of new social concerns, among which some are institutional (occupation, political affiliation, economic status) and some social-relational (sexual intimacy, marital status, familial responsibility). Not all of these concerns must be resolved during the adolescent years, but the adolescent is made increasingly aware that their ultimate resolution will determine his or her future. Consequently, the stakes of social development become more serious, and the adolescent's capacity for understanding the social world and the self's place within it becomes intensely challenged. It is not surprising that these often anxiety- and conflict-ridden years have been characterized by Goethe's *"Sturm und Drang"* ("storm and stress") metaphor as long as novelists and psychologists have been writing about this period of life.

Psychosexual Changes in Early Adolescence
Soon after the first decade of life there is a marked increase in the production of sex hormones, leading directly to a spurt in height and a change in the

FIGURE 8-11 Two views of sex differences

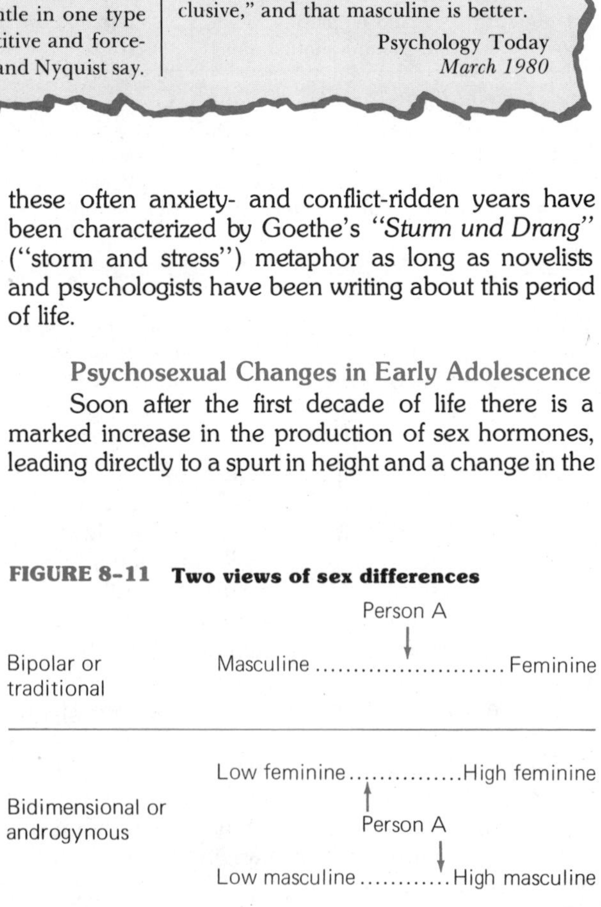

Bipolar or traditional

Person A
↓
Masculine .... Feminine

Bidimensional or androgynous

Low feminine .... High feminine
↑
Person A
↓
Low masculine .... High masculine

reproductive organs. Other physical characteristics such as brain volume remain more or less stable, and there is even a decrease in the size of certain endocrine glands. For girls, the onset of the growth spurt is about 11 years. The next notable change occurs when the breasts begin to develop, followed by the appearance of underarm then pubic hair (see Figure 8–12). Last comes the first menstrual period (menarche). The first ova produced are probably immature, but relatively soon after menarche a girl is fertile and essentially is able to support pregnancy.

The adolescent growth spurt in boys begins around 13 years (see Figure 8–12). Marked changes in height become apparent between age 9 and 14. The average length of the penis doubles, and the volume of the testes increases tenfold between the ages of 12 and 17. Growth of the genitalia is followed in rapid succession by the appearance of pubic, underarm, and facial hair, deepening of the voice, and the first ejaculation of semen (approximately 13.5 years).

The clumsiness so often observed at the beginning of adolescence is not due to a lack of motor control of the new physical dimensions of the body, but rather to increased self-consciousness about bodily activities. Boys may find themselves having an erec-

FIGURE 8–12 The typical sequence of sexual maturation in boys and girls

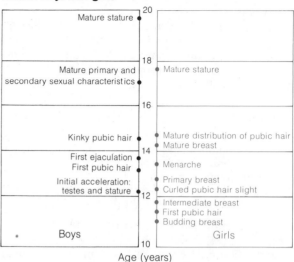

Age (years)

"Pop, can I have four hundred dollars to go to Fort Lauderdale and run wild?"

The New Yorker, March 18, 1967. Drawing by Lorenz; © 1967 The New Yorker Magazine, Inc.

Many adolescents face the dilemma of economic dependency on their families, yet desire social and personal independence. This conflict often leads to a breakdown in communication between teenagers and their parents and can be a source of great difficulty.

tion at embarrassing or unexpected times. Girls who are not comfortable about the changes taking place in their bodies may try to hide breast growth rather than welcome these signs of maturation. While wide fluctuations in the voice tone of a teenage boy may be a source of amusement to others around him, the adolescent is typically self-conscious about these unexpected variations. Girls also go through a voice change, but the amount is not nearly so dramatic as it is in boys, and it tends to occur more gradually.

Adolescent Friendships

Adolescent friendships have some special qualities that distinguish them from the two developmental levels of childhood peer relations described above. For the young adolescent, friends are persons who understand one another, sharing innermost thoughts and feelings. Friends are seen to help each other with psychological problems, such as loneliness, sadness, loss, and fear. No longer is friendship seen simply as a context for exchanging material goods, favors, or help, as during the childhood years. In adolescence, friendships become increasingly intimate, becoming that valued characteristic that Harry Stack Sullivan called the "chumship." In Sullivan's theory, the chumship was for the adolescent an important shelter from the pressure of parent and school and served as the building block for psychological health and maturity. The closeness and intimacy of adolescent peer relations also leads to their "cliquishness" and sense of exclusivity. Because friends are considered to be specially chosen people with whom one shares private communication, careful attention is paid to who is and is not included in this bond.

Adolescent Morality

The psychological study of the adolescent's integration into society has focused primarily on the adolescent's moral judgment. Lawrence Kohlberg's well-known work on moral judgment has focused mostly on moral development in the years from early adolescence through college. To trace the development of morality in an individual, Kohlberg uses a clinical-interview approach. He begins by telling a person a story such as the following:

> A man wanted to buy a new drug that could save his wife from a fatal, incurable disease. The inventor of the drug, wanting a profit, tried to charge the husband much more than he could afford to pay. When the inventor refused to change his price, the desperate husband stole the drug.

After hearing the story, the person is asked to offer a moral judgment of the husband's act. Was it justified? Why or why not? Kohlberg found that people take different moral approaches and exhibit different attitudes depending upon their developmental level and experience.

According to Kohlberg, morality develops in stages, with each successive level representing a more mature form of moral reasoning (see Table 8–3 and Figure 8–13). There are six stages. Stage 1, found mostly in children age 10 and under, values power, punishment, and rules in their own right. This stage is

FIGURE 8-13 Mean percent of moral statements on Kohlberg's three levels made by boys aged 7 to 16

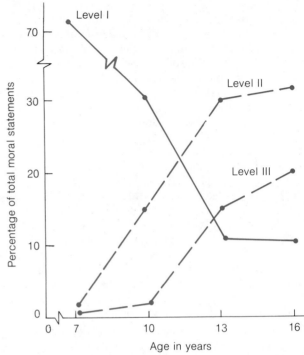

The figure illustrates the typical decrease from the first type of moral reasoning with advancing age and the accompanying increase in advanced moral judgments.

TABLE 8-3 Kohlberg's Stages of Moral Development

Level	Stage
Level one Step 1	*Premoral* Punishment and obedience orientation. Obey rules to avoid punishment.
Step 2	Naive instrumental hedonism. Conform to obtain rewards, have favors returned.
Level two Step 3	*Conventional role conformity* Good boy/girl morality. Conform to avoid disapproval or dislike by others.
Step 4	Law and authority maintaining morality. Conform to avoid censure by authorities.
Level three Step 5	*Self-accepted moral principles* Morality of contract, individual rights, and democratically accepted law. Conform to maintain community welfare.
Step 6	Morality of individual principles of conscience. Conform to avoid self-condemnation.

very similar to Piaget's heteronomous morality. Stage 2 in Kohlberg's system shows the first workings of a sense of moral reciprocity. The child—now age 12 or above—conceives of justice as an equal exchange of good or bad deeds ("You scratch my back and I'll scratch yours"; or "An eye for an eye, a tooth for a tooth"). Stages 3 and 4 are called *conventional* moral orientations, and normally adolescents do not get beyond these developmental levels. At stage 3 the individual understands and upholds the principle of the golden rule, valuing such acts as generosity for the needy and forgiveness for wrongdoing. Justice at stage 3 means doing good within the context of interpersonal relationships. Stage 4 extends the concept of justice to include the entire social order. Thus, justice at stage 4 includes establishing good citizenship, working hard, and maintaining the law of the land.

Stages 5 and 6 are the *principled* stages of moral judgment. The principled moral thinker at stage 5 can contemplate such meta-ethical issues as "Why one should be moral." He or she conceives of moral responsibility as binding upon all those who would claim the rights of society. This, then, is a "social contract" conception of morality. At the highest level in

He Got Illicit Drugs to Ease Wife's Pain

CHICAGO (UPI)—With his term as Indiana's governor ending and his wife, Beth, dying of bone cancer, Otis Bowen took the law into his own hands. Moved by his wife's suffering, the physician-politician used illegal drugs to ease her pain.

Bowen rubbed away her pain with an industrial solvent used to treat arthritis in animals, soothed the nausea caused by chemotherapy with an extract of marijuana and tried to cure her with a bone-mending drug illegally imported from France.

Mrs. Bowen died Jan. 1, as Bowen prepared to step down from the governorship he had held for two terms—the maximum allowed by law.

In the final months of her illness, Mrs. Bowen had been in agony, slowly dying of multiple myeloma, a type of bone cancer.

Bowen, now on the faculty of the Indiana University medical school at Indianapolis, said Friday he turned to illegal drugs to help her—and himself—live with the pain. . . .

Denver Post
February 15, 1981

How would you describe the level of moral development displayed here in terms of Kohlberg's stages?

Kohlberg's system, stage 6, the individual can freely take the role of all parties in a moral conflict. He or she arrives at a just solution that may, in certain instances, transcend obedience to society's codes. But such solutions always respect the universal rights of others. A just solution at stage 6 "is a solution acceptable to all parties . . . assuming none of them knew which role they would occupy in the situation" (Kohlberg, 1971, p. 213). Although there is, at stage 6, a fundamental respect for the human social order, laws may occasionally be ignored in instances where great injustice would result from blind obedience. Principles such as the equal right of all to human life are supreme, and law is seen as an imperfect means to such ends, rather than as a moral end in itself.

The transition from conventional morality (stages 3 and 4) to principled morality (stages 5 and 6) often marks the transition from adolescence to adulthood. This transition requires a sometimes painful evaluation of one's personal beliefs in light of the collective institutions and regulations necessary to maintain social life in an advanced society. This transition has been characterized as a long, conflictual period during which the adolescent is often drawn toward a rejection of all cultural values on the grounds that "everything is relative." Not until the adolescent is able to sort out those moral principles that require unwavering commitment from those conventions and standards which may vary from culture to culture (and which are therefore arbitrary) will the adolescent succeed in constructing a coherent, principled morality.

Identity Formation During Adolescence

During adolescence the question "Who am I?" comes to the forefront, creating much confusion, turmoil, and anxiety. The adolescent answers this question only by forging a stable and consistent sense of personal identity. Erik Erikson, in his writings on the "identity crisis," has thoroughly described this differentiating aspect of adolescent social development.

Erikson's descriptions of the adolescent's struggle to resolve the identity crisis have much the same flavor as psychological accounts of the transition from conventional to principled morality. The adolescent questions even the most deep-seated beliefs, rejects once-cherished notions, and becomes acutely critical of both the self and society. Only after a long period of painful self-evaluation, sometimes accompanied by great vacillations between cynicism and utopianism, between political idealism and introspective egoism, between hedonism and asceticism, does the adolescent weave an identity stable enough to withstand the multiple pressures and demands of a complex, modern society.

Erikson's theory of identity formation is at the center of his eight-stage model for psychosocial development through the life cycle (Table 8–4). For Erikson, all aspects of psychosocial development are intertwined at each stage of development, but each aspect has its own time of ascendancy at some period of life. During its time of ascendancy, each aspect of psychosocial development represents a *crisis,* or a "turning point" for the individual. With respect to each particular aspect of development, the individual faces either potential for growth and future strength (if the crisis is resolved successfully), or a vulnerability for maladjustment and future stagnation (if the crisis is not resolved). Adaptive psychosocial development means resolving each successive crisis as it arises during the stages of the life cycle. Resolving the crisis at any stage has implications both for the other aspects of psychosocial development that coexist with the crisis at that stage and for the resolution of all future crises as they appear in their own time.

Although even infants struggle with the problem of self-identity (as Lewis and Brooks-Gunn have found), self-identity is not the most important aspect of development during infancy. Rather, basic trust is. Identity does not reach its peak until adolescence, at which time the "identity crisis" becomes the focus of psychosocial development.

TABLE 8–4 Erikson's Eight Stages of Psychosocial Development

Psychosocial Stage		Task or Crisis	Social Conditions	Psychosocial Outcome
Stage 1 (birth to 1 year)	Oral-sensory	Can I trust the world?	Support and provision of basic needs	Basic trust
			Lack of support and deprivation	Basic distrust
Stage 2 (2–3 years)	Muscular-anal	Can I control my own behavior?	Permissiveness and support	Autonomy
			Overprotection and lack of support	Shame and doubt
Stage 3 (4–5 years)	Locomotor-genital	Can I become independent of my parents by exploring my limits?	Encouragement to explore	Initiative
			Lack of opportunity to explore	Guilt
Stage 4 (6–11 years)	Latency	Can I master the necessary skills to adapt?	Adequate training and encouragement	Industry
			Poor training and lack of support	Inferiority
Stage 5 (12–18 years)	Puberty and adolescence	Who am I? What are my beliefs, feelings, and attitudes?	Internal stability and positive feedback	Personal identity
			Confusion of purpose and unclear feedback	Role confusion
Stage 6 (young adulthood)	Young adulthood	Can I give fully of myself to another?	Warmth and sharing	Intimacy
			Loneliness	Isolation
Stage 7 (adulthood)	Adulthood	What can I offer succeeding generations?	Purposefulness and productivity	Generativity
			Lack of growth and regression	Stagnation
Stage 8 (maturity)	Maturity	Have I found contentment and satisfaction through my life's work and play?	Unity and fulfillment	Integrity
			Disgust and dissatisfaction	Despair

Erikson sees the relations between life-long identity development and the major psychosocial crises as they appear from stage to stage throughout development as *genetic* relations. This means that all aspects of psychosocial development in Erikson's theory can be traced back to their roots in infancy. Further, each of the major life crises is ordered according to its position in the developmental sequence. This means that we can follow each successful resolution of crisis backward to the last successful resolution and forward to the next crisis. Each aspect of psychosocial development may be traced backward and forward to its earlier and later forms, both prior to and after the time when that aspect was in ascendancy during its own stage of crisis.

The resolution of the identity crisis sets the stage for the adolescent's confrontation with the crises of adulthood. The first of these, according to Erikson, is the challenge of establishing lasting intimacy with a loved one. Persons who are secure in their sense of identity are prepared to open themselves to others and share important parts of themselves. They are able to risk "losing" themselves in another. Persons with identities too fragile to risk hurt confine themselves to superficial rather than close relations, experiencing isolation in the long run. Also following a successful resolution of the identity crisis is the challenge of "generativity." To avoid a sense of stagnation, the adult must find ways to contribute to the world, such as through productive work or the raising of children.

In modern societies, individuals typically continue to reassess their personal identities long after the initial identity crisis has passed. Such reassessment often happens during middle age, after retirement or job loss, or after separation from a spouse. Although these later reassessments do not have the developmental significance of the earlier crisis, they are often accompanied by the same feelings of turmoil. A process of personality exploration and reorganization again becomes necessary in order to provide self-satisfying answers to the question "Who am I?".

Highlight 8–1

The Myth of Aging

The stereotypes most people hold regarding old persons are remarkably inaccurate. Erdmure Palmore has developed a short quiz for assessing knowledge about aging. How much do you know about old people? How many of the following questions can you get right? Circle "T" for True, or "F" for False.

T F 1. The majority of old people (past age 65) are senile (i.e., defective memory, disoriented, or demented).

T F 2. All five senses tend to decline in old age.

T F 3. Most old people have no interest in, or capacity for, sexual relations.

T F 4. Lung capacity tends to decline in old age.

T F 5. The majority of old people feel miserable most of the time.

T F 6. Physical strength tends to decline in old age.

T F 7. At least one-tenth of the aged are living in long-stay institutions (i.e., nursing homes, mental hospitals, homes for the aged, etc.).

T F 8. Aged drivers have fewer accidents per person than drivers under age 65.

T F 9. Most older workers cannot work as effectively as younger workers.

T F 10. About 80% of the aged are healthy enough to carry out their normal activities.

T F 11. Most old people are set in their ways and unable to change.

T F 12. Old people usually take longer to learn something new.

T F 13. It is almost impossible for most old people to learn new things.

T F 14. The reaction time of most old people tends to be slower than reaction time of younger people.

T F 15. In general, most old people are pretty much alike.

T F 16. The majority of old people are seldom bored.

T F 17. The majority of old people are socially isolated and lonely.

T F 18. Older workers have fewer accidents than younger workers.

T F 19. Over 15% of the U.S. population are now age 65 or over.

T F 20. Most medical practitioners tend to give low priority to the aged.

T F 21. The majority of older people have incomes below the poverty level (as defined by the Federal Government).

T F 22. The majority of old people are working or would like to have some kind of work to do (including housework and volunteer work).

T F 23. Older people tend to become more religious as they age.

T F 24. The majority of old people are seldom irritated or angry.

T F 25. The health and socioeconomic status of older people (compared to younger people) in the year 2000 will probably be about the same as now.

The key to the correct answer is simple: all the odd numbered items are false and all the even numbered are true.

Adulthood

Until about 1960, developmental psychology focused on the behavior changes that take place from birth through adolescence. Rarely were there references to the years beyond biological maturity; indeed, this practice helped to create the myth that no important changes occur during adulthood. Developmental psychology has, however, widened its scope, and in recent years much attention has centered on the adult years.

What has been the impetus for this change of focus? It has always been easier to study certain dimensions of human development in children, since they change much more quickly than do older adults. Children also form a "captive" population that can easily be observed and studied. Schools and other child-oriented institutions such as day care centers provide consistent settings. Interestingly, a similar situation exists in the case of the elderly who are in institutions or nursing homes.

The study of adult development is becoming more important for at least three reasons. First, the myth that development is a stable process after adolescence is slowly being dissolved by empirical studies that examine development in older people. In fact, many radical changes in cognitive, physical, and social behaviors occur throughout the life span. Second, as a result of fluctuations in the birth rate, the age of the general population is increasing. If present trends continue, by the year 2000 half of all persons in the United States will be 50 years or older, and

It's Myth: Memory Loss Not Part of Aging Process
By CHARLES SEABROOK

ATLANTA—Dr. Anderson Smith is shooting down some myths about aging, especially the one that says people naturally become more befuddled the older they get.

Smith, a psychologist at Georgia Institute of Technology here, says older people can remember as well as young people with the right help and conditions. . . .

Memory, Smith says, depends not just on age, but on other characteristics of a person, including the person's job background and education.

The characteristics of the thing to be remembered—whether it's a face or a name, for instance—also influence memory, as well as the way a person is tested for his ability to remember things. A person may do better on a multiple-choice test, for instance, rather than a word-recall test.

Another thing influencing memory is "encoding," or what people were doing at the time they were learning the thing they later try to remember, says Smith.

Smith, who has spent several years researching what memory changes accompany the aging process, tests people of all ages on their memory abilities. . . .

Smith says although tests have shown significant differences "on recall between the young and old" he has found that tests which call for recognition, such as multiple-choice tests—as opposed to free recall of a specific list of words—show no memory differences between age groups.

"Just by changing the conditions of retrieval, we can eliminate differences due to age," says Smith.

Smith's research also indicates that people tend to change their learning "strategies" as they get older and as they are exposed less to formal, textbook-type education, Smith points out.

People involved in formal education, such as school or college, tend to organize their memory in different ways, says the Tech researcher. Studying for a college exam, for instance, may involve memory strategies different from

remembering where one's car is parked.

Some tests have shown that when an older person is given specific instructions on what to do with words, such as organizing them into categories—similar to what people learning from textbooks do—his memory goes up.

"We're showing that the commonly observed differences between the young and old are not some type of irreversible neurological problem," says Smith. "We're not talking about (brain deterioration); we're talking about normal aging."

He says one of the most commonly heard excuses among elderly people for forgetting something is that they are getting old and cannot remember as well as they did, say, 25 years ago.

This excuse in general holds no water, he says. Tests have shown that short-term memory does not change with age; an older person may simply enjoy thinking about the old days more than the present. . . .

The Denver Post
April 1, 1981

---

one third will be 65 years or older. This shift is a direct result of the post-World War II "baby boom" generation entering this stage of adult development. Finally, the life expectancy of men and women (although different) is constantly increasing. A baby born in 1900 had an average expected life span of 47 years; today it is well beyond 70.

Psychosocial Development in Adulthood

According to Erikson, the last of life's crises is the struggle to achieve a sense of integrity as opposed to feelings of despair. Resolving this crisis is the goal for which the seven earlier stages have prepared us. If an individual has successfully mastered the challenges of intimacy and generativity, the adult years may be spent creating the unifying meaning for one's life that Erikson called *ego integrity*. A sense of integrity develops when one can feel that life has been lived with purpose and commitment and that one's efforts have been directed toward good ends. If, however, one views one's life as having been useless and without dedication, then disgust will result. Despair is a concomitant: "It's too late to change now (or too hard to

change), so I'll never make anything of myself." A healthy resolution of this crisis brings a feeling of wholeness and peace as one lives out one's life.

Some psychologists have tried to be more specific than Erikson about the course of development during adulthood. They have outlined "stages" like marriage, the mid-life "second adolescence," the "mellowing-out" period after 50, and so on. But one problem with this analysis is that not everyone who develops in adulthood experiences these particular events. Another problem is that there is no apparent reason for these events to occur in a particular sequence, other than that many middle-class Americans seem to pass through them at more or less the same ages. These "stages," therefore, do not meet any of the criteria for true developmental stages; they are not universal, do not occur in a logically fixed sequence, and do not build upon one another through the restructuring of basic competencies or personal characteristics.

A new approach to adult development, called *life-span psychology*, has attempted to remedy the problems inherent in the stage approach (see the newsclip "When Age Doesn't Matter"). The life-span

In Erikson's view, life's final psychosocial stage is the struggle to attain a sense of unity and fulfillment as opposed to feelings of disgust and despair. Resolving this crisis brings a feeling of peace as one lives out the adult years.

"I used to be old, too, but it wasn't my cup of tea."

The New Yorker, March 7, 1977. Drawing by Weber; © 1977 The New Yorker Magazine, Inc.

approach focuses on universal processes through which people at all ages grow socially and intellectually. It tries to determine why one person will experience a major event (such as economic hardship) and find a way to benefit developmentally from that event, whereas another individual will resist the possibility of progressive change. Thus, life-span psychology tries to separate age and development; it assumes that all people can continue to develop, provided they remain open to social influence and to new ideas.

The life-span school has also emphasized the necessity for flexibility in discussions of adult development. No one end point can describe all the complex personal goals of individuals in modern society (unless the end point is very generally phrased, like Erikson's integrity stage). Developmental psychologists must respect the individuality inherent in the development process. This is particularly true when discussing adults, since the psychologists' "subjects" can be as thoughtful and as reflective as the psychologists themselves. The goals of these subjects must be respected on their own terms even when they are different from those of the psychologist.

The study of adult development is at this point still in its infancy. We certainly know less about it than about development during other periods of life. In the future, as psychologists increasingly focus on these years, we are certain to learn more about this fascinating final phase of development.

When Age Doesn't Matter
By KENNETH L. WOODWARD with ELOISE SALHOLZ

The hottest news in psychology half a decade ago was the discovery that adults go through predictable "life stages" just as children do. As popularized in Gail Sheehy's "Passages," the human life cycle was envisioned as a staircase of social-psychological crises that everyone could expect to experience at about the same periods in their lives. Now a different school of behavioral scientists is vigorously challenging life-stage theories with a more elastic model of "life-span development." According to this paradigm, people continue to change throughout life but, unlike stages, these changes are not necessarily sequential, irreversible or tied to chronological age.

The major assumption behind life-span analysis is that after adolescence, age is no longer a reliable factor in how people feel or act. "Our society is becoming accustomed to the 28-year-old mayor . . . the 50-year-old retiree, the 65-year-old father of a preschooler and the 70-year-old student," observes gerontologist Bernice L. Neugarten of the University of Chicago. Neugarten argues that the United States is evolving into an "age-irrelevant society."

Need
If age were to become truly irrelevant, the consequences would be far-reaching. Psychologically, people would no longer measure their progress in life against socially constructed timetables; women would not feel old at 40, men would not feel topped out at 50 and older people would no longer feel superannuated at 65. Ideally there would be no bias for or against youth, and no special supports for the old. Already, in fact, some proponents of age-irrelevancy are questioning whether social security and other benefits should be paid to elders regardless of need. But many scholars doubt that age will ever be irrelevant, and even some life-span specialists say the social order would be destroyed if it were. "We have to have age norms to anchor and structure our lives," says Cornell University sociologist Glen H. Elder Jr. "An age-irrelevant society is a rudderless society."

Life-span research is a multidisciplinary effort, less than two decades old, that tries to explain how people change and develop from birth to death. At its most ambitious, it challenges traditional Western views of human development teaching that adulthood is shaped largely by childhood experiences. Life-span researchers argue instead that the consequences of later-life events are far more significant than traditional theories suggest. Moreover, says developmental psychologist Paul Baltes of Pennsylvania State University, "As people grow older, they become more and more different from one another, so that age means less and less as a determinant of character and behavior. . . ."

Norms
Glen Elder believes that human beings need age norms on which to hang their expectations. "If you carry Neugarten's thesis all the way," he says, "you end up with a life span in which people have no opportunity to anticipate and prepare for major life events, like marriage, children and death." Marjorie Fiske, director of the Human Development and Aging Program at the University of California at San Francisco, contends that age irrelevancy only encourages the old to try to stay young, thereby denying dignity to old age. . . .

It seems unlikely that society will ever find age totally irrelevant. On the contrary, as the U.S. population ages, the old may assume new and more definite roles as elders. Nonetheless, life-span studies have already forced social planners to re-examine negative stereotypes with a view to eradicating ageism from public policy—even when it benefits the aged. What's more, life-span research reminds us that society itself establishes the meaning of age. The remaining question is whether America can overcome its fascination with youth and find in the old a dignity to which the young can legitimately aspire.

Newsweek
August 11, 1980

The most recent school of thought to evolve in developmental psychology is now usually called the *life-span developmental* approach. It is in contrast to theories that argue for rigid stages of development. Life-span theorists typically see development as a fluid and flexible process that goes on through the entire span of life.

SUMMARY

1. Developmental psychologists study changes in behavior and thinking that have long-lasting implications for a person's adaptation to the world. Although developmental psychologists have a special interest in children and the environmental factors that influence them, the field of developmental psychology covers the entire range of life, from conception to death.

2. Three theories of development, the psychoanalytic, behavioral, and cognitive developmental, have most influenced contemporary thinking in developmental psy-

chology. Each theory is based upon its own set of assumptions about human nature, and each is associated with a particular kind of research methodology. Most developmentalists today borrow from each of the theories rather than remaining within the boundaries of any one.

3. The development of physical, social, and intellectual abilities are the result of a combination of factors working together. These factors include the child's genetic endowment, the process of biological maturation, learning, and the child's own initiatives in acquiring skills. It is

difficult, if not impossible, to determine the exact influence of any one factor taken and considered separately from the others.

4. Children differ from one another in their rates of acquiring physical as well as mental abilities. Such individual differences in development may or may not have permanent significance for an individual child; many children start off more slowly than their peers but surpass them in the end.

5. Development is in some respects continuous and in other respects discontinuous. It is continuous because changes are gradual and often uneven from day to day. It is discontinuous because there are major qualitative differences in the thinking and behavior of people at different ages.

6. Age differences in development are studied either through a cross-sectional research design, which compares groups of people at different ages, or through a longitudinal research design, which follows individual subjects as they grow older. Both designs have strengths and weakness; the ideal research strategy combines the two.

7. Perception depends upon the development of sensory systems, not all of which are fully mature at birth. Perceptual abilities improve dramatically during the first year of life.

8. According to Piaget, cognitive development can be divided into four qualitatively distinct stages: sensorimotor (birth to 2 years), preoperational (2 to 7 years), concrete operational (7 to 11 years), and formal operational (11 years and beyond).

9. In a period of less than four years, a child develops the ability to produce complex, grammatically correct language. There is considerable debate among developmental psychologists as to whether a child's cognitive development makes language acquisition possible, or whether the acquisition of language makes advanced thinking possible. Some psychologists have taken a middle position on this issue,

emphasizing the reciprocal influences of language and thought during development.

10. Social development performs two functions for the growing child: the integration of the child into society and the differentiation of the child from others in society. The former entails establishing relations with others and learning to guide one's behavior according to the regulations of society. The latter entails the acquisition of identity and a sense of self.

11. During infancy, a child experiences feelings of attachment for its primary caregiver. Optimally, the child will feel secure enough in its attachment so that eventually he or she can risk assertions of independence. The child's first knowledge of self is established during the infant years.

12. Peer interactions like play and sharing are central in a child's social development. Through relations with peers, children acquire an understanding of friendship, justice, and other important social conceptions. In addition, during peer play children have an opportunity to try out and practice social rule-following. Later, such activity will become a serious and necessary part of adult life.

13. Parents have an enormous influence upon their children's social development. Different parents have different styles of child rearing, and certain styles have been shown to be associated with particular patterns of behavior in children.

14. During adolescence, friendships become more intimate, morality begins to take on a broader, societal perspective, and logical thinking becomes increasingly abstract, hypothetical, and formal. The adolescent organizes the complex array of information about the self into a coherent sense of identity.

15. Until very recently, little was known about development in the adult years. Now, with the advent of life-span theories and techniques, psychologists are discovering that human development remains dynamic right through the later years of life.

RECOMMENDED ADDITIONAL READINGS

Flavell, J. H. *Cognitive development.* Englewood Cliffs, N.J.: Prentice-Hall, 1977.

Gardner, H. *Developmental psychology.* Boston: Little, Brown, 1978.

Maccoby, E. E. *Social development.* New York: Harcourt Brace Jovanovich, 1980.

Mussen, P. H., Conger, J. J., & Kagan, J. *Child development and personality,* 5th ed. New York: Harper & Row, 1978.

Whitbourne, S. K., & Weinstock, C. S. *Adult development: The differentiation of experience.* New York: Holt, Rinehart and Winston, 1979.

What Does It Mean?

Developmental psychology lends itself to several types of practical application. First, it can shed light on controversial issues in contemporary society. One such issue is the psychological consequences of separations caused by divorce or day care at an early age. A related issue concerns the effects of television on children. Second, research in developmental psychology can provide tools for educational innovation. Third, as we learn more about children and the normal processes of development, the diagnosis and treatment of potential disturbances (either in the child or in the family) become more effective.

Divorce, Day Care, and the Child's Attachment Needs

How adequately can another person, or a group of persons, substitute for the child's biological mother in providing the child with secure attachment relations? This question is currently the focus of much debate, not only among psychologists but among citizens concerned with public and legal policy making. As one example, courts have traditionally favored the mother in granting child custody, on the assumption that the mother-child bond is irreplaceable. Recently, however, Anna Freud and others have maintained that children should be placed with the parent that is better able to provide a stable, continuous relationship. From this point of view, the child's attachment needs depend not upon a specific person (such as mother) but upon continuity in caretaking by any nurturant adult. Some findings also indicate that the *quality* of nurturing is more important than who does it. For this reason, marital discord that distracts parents from interacting attentively with their children can be more harmful to young children than a divorce that "clears the air."

Another controversial social policy issue that revolves around attachment theory concerns day care, which has become an important topic in recent years because many women today work shortly after giving birth. Day care relies on the assumption that substitute mothering during large portions of a child's waking time will not impede growth. Some recent experimental evidence (see the newsclip "Study Notes 'No Harm' in Day Care"), as well as some observational studies of communal child-rearing in Israel and the Soviet Union support this claim. Additionally, some data from rhesus monkey studies and anecdotal accounts of young children orphaned during wartime suggest that motherless children may obtain from their own peers the physical and social contact necessary for both survival and development. In contrast, however, concerned child developmentalists like Selma Fraiberg have argued that an ongoing relation between child and parent can never be replicated in all of its intimacy, subtlety and complexity and that full-time exposure to such a relation during the first few years of life is "every child's birthright." The resolution of this debate will certainly have profound effects upon child-rearing patterns in every society that has the freedom to make choices about its cultural institutions.

The Effects of Television

One of the most surprising things about television is that until recently nobody cared about its effects on human development. Although television stations are licensed by the federal government, there has been little supervision of program content. Considering that 25 percent of all television programs are aimed at children (sometimes called "kidvid"), that 96 percent of all U.S. homes contain at least one television set, and that one quarter of a child's waking hours up to the age of 18 is spent watching television, it is no surprise that this medium is finally being seen as the pervasive socializing agent it really is.

One advantage of "the tube" is that it provides many valuable experiences that otherwise might not be possible. For example, many children who would never have the opportunity can see and hear a symphony orchestra or a baseball game. Television brings the world closer and provides some of the fun and entertainment necessary for healthy development. In addition, it also provides a stimulus for family discussion. A few years ago over 130 million people watched the TV production of *Roots,* a family-centered story of a man's search for his ancestors.

In addition, television may foster verbal and cognitive skills. Studies have shown that children who watch *Sesame Street* regularly seem to benefit intellectually from the experience. The positive effects, however, are mostly noticeable among very young children (under age 4) and among middle-class rather than disadvantaged children, perhaps because it is these children who attend most actively to the educational programming.

Television, of course, also has disadvantages. Children who frequently watch TV are less likely to participate in outdoor activities. Too, the content of some programs may be detrimental to healthy development, and the more TV children watch, the greater this influence. Another disadvantage is that since the primary purpose of network (not public) television is to make a profit, the main source of income is from advertisers. Commercials (which can take almost one third of total program time) focus on hard-sell techniques that encourage children to put pressure on their parents to purchase the latest fad in presweetened cereals or toys. Finally, TV in its selective presentation of characters and stories creates stereotypes that give the viewer a false image of the world. For example, the white male is the predominant character in most television programs and commercials. Similarly, older people are often made to appear senile and incompetent.

Regardless of the debate over the relative advantages and disadvantages of television, children do learn from

Study Notes "No Harm" in Day Care

BOSTON (UPI) — In a finding for working mothers, a Harvard psychologist reported that good day care centers apparently do not harm the development of young children — a reversal of his earlier position.

Only four years ago, Dr. Jerome Kagan was among those warning against taking young children from their home environment for fear the change would harm their social and intellectual development during the critical years of life.

But Kagan said that exhaustive tests into everything from language development to attention spans to relationships with other children did not find any substantial differences in children tested at age intervals from 3½ to 29 months.

Five-Year Study

Kagan reached the conclusion on the basis of a five-year study that compared young children who remained home all day with those placed in a special Harvard-operated day-care center seven hours a day, five days a week.

"There were no important differences between the two groups," Kagan said in a report for a children rearing symposium at the annual meeting of the American Association for the Advancement of Science.

"The data support the view that day care, when responsibly and conscientiously implemented, does not seem to have hidden psychological dangers," he said. "I expected differences. We did not find them. It is not easy to say why. It is a bit of puzzle.

"Merely being outside the home for seven hours a day for 100 weeks does not seem to have a profound effect. There's no difference in aggressiveness, there's no difference in social play. There are just as many shy children in the day care center as there are at home," he added.

Kagan emphasized, however, that the Harvard day care center presented close to an ideal situation for the youngsters with conditions that may not be duplicated very often in centers across the nation.

He said he still believes poor day care centers can be harmful to young children, and he estimated 15 to 20 per cent of day care centers in the nation may fall in that category.

Among other things, the Harvard facility had one caretaker for every three children during their first year of life and one for every four or five toddlers. The cost of such care, Kagan estimated, would be $85 a week if it weren't subsidized.

The Denver Post
February 23, 1976

"What price day care?" Can a child who is away from his or her parents all day receive the love and attention necessary for healthy development? Current research seems to indicate that if the setting is well staffed, the answer is yes.

watching it. The question of how much violence children learn from watching television has been raised again and again. A recent report of the U.S. Surgeon General examined evidence concerning the effects of violence portrayed on television on the development of social behaviors in children, especially aggression. The general method for examining children's susceptibility to aggressive models is to show them a movie or tape of a person acting in a violent fashion who is either rewarded or not rewarded for that behavior. The child is then placed in a situation in which he or she is allowed to act out that modeled aggression (such as in social interaction with another child). More often than not research evidence has shown that children who are exposed to an aggressive model indulge in aggressive acts to accomplish some goal (see Chapter 9, Figure 9–4). In some cases the children did not like the aggressive model, but they still copied the aggressive behavior. Knowing what we do about a young child's tendency to imitate, and the importance of imitation as a learning process, we may expect violent and aggressive modes of behavior to be learned. Considering that cartoons are the most violent of all television programs and that children watch cartoons as much as any other production, we have to assume that children are in fact exposed to aggressive models. A few studies, however, have shown that viewing television violence reduces hostility in some people. Because hostile feelings usually precede aggression, TV viewing may remove the underpinnings of aggression. On the basis of these studies,

some people have theorized that viewing violence on television may be a form of release, a way of working things out, that allows people to get rid of hostile feelings without expressing them openly. On the other hand, the majority of the studies clearly suggests that increased rather than decreased aggression is a consequence of viewing violent acts on television.

Early-Enrichment Programs and Planned Intervention

Along with many other movements that characterized the "great society" of the 1960s were the beginning attempts to eradicate the effects of poverty. A great deal of time and money were invested in programs that tried to counteract the negative effects poverty has on the development and future potential of young children. Perhaps the best-known such program is Head Start, a massive effort funded through both federal and state agencies.

These programs have had mixed results. Initial evaluation of Head Start by the Westinghouse Corporation showed the program to be unsuccessful in affecting change in young children. However, many critics of this evaluation came quickly to the defense of Head Start and similar programs, claiming that the evaluation was not well planned and did not reflect the true value of the program. In addition, recent information seems to suggest that the early Head Start groups of children progressed in areas of social and emotional development not examined during the initial evaluation.

The issue of whether and how intervention is effective is unresolved. Most psychologists believe that some sort of intervention is necessary. In a review of many different programs, Urie Bronfenbrenner, a long-time advocate of children's rights, concluded that an effective intervention program should contain the following five elements: (1) effective parental education before children are born; (2) adequate provisions for basic needs such as housing and nutrition; (3) a structured program of infant-parent interaction during the early years; (4) a preschool program for children from 4 to 6; and (5) parental support of the child's educational experiences. A potentially important sixth element is the degree to which parents are directly involved in the child's program.

Unfortunately, social policy is inextricably tied to the political arena. Too often the responsibility for the health of our country's children lies in the hands of public officials, who may be well intentioned but know little about educational matters. For this reason, psychologists have recently begun to form lobbying groups with the primary goal of educating those people in government who make the decisions that have long-range and important consequences for us all.

Child Abuse

The physical and psychological abuse of children is a serious and complex problem. In the past, few incidents were reported to the proper authorities because people were afraid to become involved in lengthy legal matters. There was also little legislation in the area of child abuse that made it possible for those indirectly involved (teachers, doctors, nurses, and social workers, for example) to take effective action. Often those who did try to help became so tangled in red tape and received so many threats of retaliation by parents that they failed to pursue the issue. Only recently have state and federal laws made it mandatory for physicians (and others) to report cases of child abuse when they come to their attention.

What constitutes child abuse? When gross physical harm is done to a child, it is obvious that abuse has taken place. However, it is often difficult to prove such a case legally. Characteristically, one incident leads to another, and by the time action is taken, the child is often severely damaged. In addition, the matter of deciding when corporal disciplinary measures, such as spanking, become abuse is touchy and difficult. The issue becomes even more clouded when the abuse is sexual or emotional in nature, leaving no physical aftereffects. How does a concerned citizen prove that a parent is psychologically or sexually damaging a child?

Determining how much child abuse actually takes place is difficult. Estimates have been placed at between 200,000 and 250,000 cases each year in the United States. Of course, many cases are not reported to the authorities. Unfortunately, some physicians treat only the child's symptoms, ignoring problems of family conflict and pathology on the part of the abusive parent.

What are abusers of children like? There is no answer to this. Child abusers come from every social and economic stratum of our society, include both men and women, well and poorly educated people, law-abiding citizens as well as those with criminal records. To make matters more complicated, child abusers often focus their maltreatment on one child out of several in a family. This is usually because the child is temperamentally difficult from the time of birth, thus "drawing" the parent's attacks. There is, therefore, an unfortunate interaction between parents with abusive tendencies and particular kinds of children that leads to child maltreatment.

One of the only known similarities among child abusers is that many were themselves the victims of abuse at an early age. Further, they often repeat the type of abuse that they experienced, whether the maltreatment was physical, sexual, or emotional.

How can we begin to solve the problems of child abuse? First, prospective parents must be educated and encouraged to explore their own upbringing. Another step should be the involvement of personnel from all disciplines concerned with the issue, including medicine, education, law, and psychology. Parent organizations where anonymous abusers can go (or call for help) in times of crisis can also play an important role. Finally, special programs for abused children should be implemented to insure that their future development is not impaired by their past experience.

Another approach that is beginning to yield positive results involves observing the behavior of parents toward the child at birth. For example, the amount of eye contact between mother and infant might be observed. Researchers at the University of Colorado Medical Center have discovered ways to predict from early parent-child interactions those parents who are likely to abuse their children. It may become possible to prevent abuse from occurring by providing help and counseling for the parents.

Educational Toys

On the market today is a variety of toys that are supposed to hasten physical, social, and intellectual development. There are toys to stimulate infants' senses, develop their eye coordination, build motor control of the limbs, and so forth. Toys for older children are designed to teach recognition of attributes, such as color and spatial relations and shapes.

There is considerable disagreement among psychologists about the value of such toys. Some claim that environments "enriched" with mobiles, mirrors, tape recordings, aquariums, and so on, may have the effect of depriving the child of normal interaction with parents — watching their faces and being held and talked to. Moreover, a child may learn as much playing with pots and pans as with expensive toys.

An elaborate educational machine called the talking typewriter has been developed to teach children how to read. These typewriters are used in some schools and institutions, often with children who need special instruction. The typewriter has a conventional keyboard except that the keys are different colors. The child's fingernails are painted in matching colors. When the child presses the key, the machine prints the letter and pronounces it. After the

Therapist Works to Resolve Parent-Toddler Conflicts
By STEVE SZKOTAK

EAST PROVIDENCE, R.I. (UPI)— When group therapy is mentioned, you may envision a collection of neurotic adults who meet on a regular basis and discuss their hangups.

For Anne Benham, the term means twice-a-week sessions with 2- and 3-year-olds and their mothers.

Since May, Dr. Benham, 33, has been treating several sets of mothers and children in group therapy sessions at Bradley Hospital, a psychiatric center affiliated with Brown University.

"The parents are having trouble negotiating with their children; they're deadlocked in struggle," Dr. Benham said in her office, where dolls and hand puppets share shelf space with books.

She said parent-child conflicts can be sparked by a death in the family, an alcoholic parent or a combination of events.

Her main goal is to solve each conflict early, so it doesn't worsen as the child gets older.

Dr. Benham says the idea toddlers can't suffer from psychological or emotional problems is a myth.

"In general, people believe children can't have problems, that they'll grow out of them just because they're young," Dr. Benham said. "At this age, a child's repertoire is small.

"I've seen suicidal 5-year-olds, but no younger than that. My belief is, a very serious problem early on gets compounded later."

She believes her therapy method is unique.

Down the narrow corridor from her office, a small playroom is reserved for the group. During two-hour sessions, a teacher directs activities while therapists meet individually with parents and children.

One woman was referred to Dr. Benham's therapy group after her 2½-year-old daughter came home from the hospital. Circumstances of the child's injury are unclear, but she may have been abused by her father.

Guilt and anger surfaced when the child returned home.

"The mother became totally depressed," Dr. Benham said. "The child withdrew from everybody. She began to have tantrums and head-banging sessions."

Finally, the mother came to the therapy group.

"One of the most difficult issues to deal with is anger—both the child's and parent's anger," Dr. Benham said. She said there are no sure answers to problems a child and parent experience.

"One of the advantages of the group approach is parents can use each other for support and find common problems," she said.

Group sessions also help the therapists.

"We may suggest something that works with a child," she said. "We might also find that our suggestion doesn't work.

"Our focus is to treat the parent and child. We say, this is your child, let us help. We essentially say you can solve the problem, you can handle it," Dr. Benham said.

"For one thing, we certainly don't want to overtreat people," she said. "We're not trying to invent problems that aren't there."

Boulder Daily Camera
October 2, 1980

Research on parent-child interaction and children's social-emotional development may lead to more effective means of giving therapy to families needing help.

child has explored the device, the typewriter takes the lead. A letter is printed and spoken, and only the matching key is operable. Initially children search the keyboard, ignoring letter configurations. Eventually, however, they learn to match the key and letter. After letters come words. Most children progress rapidly with the help of this intriguing machine. Even kindergartners learn to produce and type short stories.

Educational Innovation

Jean Piaget's theory of intellectual development has sparked attempts at educational reform, especially in the open classroom tradition of the British school system. Piaget insists that children at different stages require different kinds of education. Many schools, unfortunately, instruct even the youngest children as though they were in the formal operational stage, using abstract lecture methods. Because they rely primarily on the enactive mode of symbolic representation, preschoolers learn best if they can manipulate things. According to Piaget, a 6- to 7-year-old child taught on a purely verbal level learns to mimic phrases but not necessarily to understand them.

Piaget and Bruner believe that young children learn best through active discovery. Thus, classrooms in the early grades might be arranged in a series of centers stocked with intriguing materials to arouse children's curiosity. In informal instructional laboratories set up to investigate discovery learning, children are allowed to manipulate things and see results. They are asked to describe outcomes and sometimes to make reports. Classmates are encouraged to question procedures and explanations, forcing children to communicate their ideas more clearly.

A curriculum based on such principles stresses new ways to organize experience rather than the mere accumulation of knowledge. Specific tasks designed to teach conservation of concepts, for example, are sometimes included in the curriculum. The development of conservation of area, for instance, might be facilitated by using the linoleum squares on the floor. Children might be given 12 squares and asked to work out how many different shapes can be made from them. In this way they learn that area

Many schools base their curriculum on the principle that children learn best through active discovery.

is independent of shape and depends on a square measurement unit. Fundamentals of arithmetic can be taught by a Dienes balance (Figure 8–14). Each side of the balance rod contains numbered hooks placed at equal intervals from the center, starting with 1 and going outward to 9. Children must figure out where to place two rings on one side to balance one ring placed at 6 on the other side. Following simple addition, they might place rings at 2 and 4 or at 1 and 5. They also discover they must multiply the number of rings by the number at which each ring is placed to achieve a balance. One ring at hook 6 is balanced by three at hook 2.

Other theoretical orientations have also been applied to educational settings. As we saw in Chapter 4, application of the principles of operant conditioning has led to another approach to classroom learning. Instead of discovering concepts through free exploration and manipulation, in the operant approach the learner is led through a series of steps of increasing complexity, each building on the preceding, until the task has been learned. The structured steps may be presented by the teacher or by a programmed textbook. Whereas the Piagetian method of discovery learning involves intrinsic reward from the pleasure of solving problems, external reinforcement (such as tokens) supply the motivation for learning in the operant approach. The two learning approaches are not necessarily

incompatible. Teachers can and should use a combination of approaches in the classroom.

Educational motivation based upon developmental psychology has not been confined to the fostering of cognitive skills. Lawrence Kohlberg at Harvard has founded a Center for Moral Education and has produced filmstrips, discussion guides, and a wide variety of other aids for teachers. He and his colleagues have turned a Cambridge high school into a "just school," and have designed

FIGURE 8–14   The Dienes balance

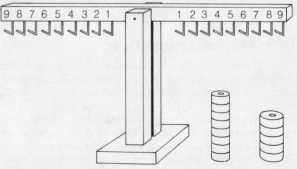

The Dienes balance uses Piagetian principles to teach arithmetic.

Do Moral Values Belong in School?

By GIL SEWALL with ELLIOTT D. LEE & TERENCE MAITLAND

If you are a teen-age girl, should you go to bed with your boyfriend if he asks you to? If you catch a classmate stealing your wallet, do you attack him or tell the teacher? How do you decide who your school friends should be? These are questions being asked of thousands of American children in school programs with names like "values development." But a growing number of educational authorities—and parents—don't think that the classroom is the proper place to ask such questions. "Home and church—not the school—are the right places for moral education," says Tacoma, Wash., parent Becky Banfield.

The stated purpose of "values" education is to help youngsters learn the difference between *what is* and *what should be*. Developed in the sour moral atmosphere after Vietnam and Watergate, these courses have grown steadily more popular. More than 300,000 classroom teachers have attended workshops and summer institutes to learn how to teach the courses, and at least 6,000 school systems have offered values programs. "When children hear each other respond to real-life situations, they begin to make up their own minds about how to feel and act," says former New York City instructor Gloria Armstrong.

These classroom teachers do not pretend to be traditional moral philosophers. They insist that they do not try to instill their personal standards of conduct, but rather help children arrive at moral choices independently. "No adult knows all the answers, and the children's responses are never judged right or wrong," says University of Massachusetts education professor Sidney Simon, a popular leader in the values movement. By making students decide what they like and dislike, he says, a teacher increases their confidence and self-worth. The most sophisticated system was created by Harvard psychologist Lawrence Kohlberg. He considers moral development a six-stage process. At the lowest level, a person behaves civilly because of fear of punishment; the supreme stage is a conscious belief in universal justice. "Kohlberg's ideas have made us conscious of what a moral dilemma is," says Shelley Berman, who teaches in a Brookline, Mass., high school.

Time

Opponents label values education "impoverished" and "simplistic." Teachers should exert their own moral influence, the critics say; students should not be led to believe that any opinion they have is always legitimate. Critics also contend that the programs are mainly a waste of time. "Values courses are well intentioned but confused," says Edwin Delattre, president-elect of St. John's College in Annapolis, Md. William Bennett, director of the National Humanities Center, says: "The movement appeals to the American preoccupation with easy technical solutions."

Values education faces stiff resistance in many school districts. Conservatives attack it for "socialistic intent" and "encouraging the breakdown of morals." Even in liberal Brookline, the League of Women Voters protested that values should not be taught as a separate course. The school officials reassured them that the Kohlberg-based program had been incorporated into social-studies courses. State legislators, faced with rising educational budgets, question money spent in programs that appear faddish.

So far, values educators cannot demonstrate that these classes result in superior behavior. They do insist that such programs produce more socially responsible citizens. "We are not suddenly producing Martin Luther Kings," says Boston University education professor Ralph Mosher, who helped to design Brookline's program. "But children who participate gradually move toward more principled thinking." Most educators believe that American schools try to teach values as part of their fundamental curriculum. At a time when teachers are returning to basics, a fillip like values education may turn out to be an idea whose time came—and quickly went.

Newsweek
June 2, 1980

The study of moral development by psychologists has revealed that little direct attention is typically given to this area. Many people think that moral development should be identified as a major goal of formal education. Of course, you can imagine that many, many others believe that this area should be left strictly to parents and the parents' chosen religous institution. What do you think? How did you receive your moral education, and from whom?

remediation techniques for juvenile delinquents and criminals. In addition, "social-emotional growth" and "values clarification" curricula are being introduced with increasing frequency in elementary and secondary schools across the country. But education in social competence is a new and almost totally untested enterprise.

Of course, we do not need actual educational techniques to justify the scientific study of development. Important "application" of scientific findings can be found simply in the understanding that these findings engender. In psychological writings, the stages through which an individual's thinking and behavior develop have been richly and carefully described. These descriptions are invaluable for anyone working with children, adolescents, or adults, or even for anyone wishing to understand more about his or her own developmental roots. Such understanding has a subtle but unmistakable influence upon the way one deals with everyday problems. Teachers who recognize early forms of moral behavior in their students, as one example, will be better able to place this behavior in perspective than will those who sees it merely as an aberration from "acceptable" standards. An awareness of the long-forgotten idiosyncrasies of early development enables adults to be more comfortable in their relations with children and adolescents. It is just such an awareness that developmental psychology, at its best, is able to offer.

Fighting Off Old Age

By JOHN LEO and BARBARA BLONARZ DOLAN

Ronald Reagan, say gerontologists, may do for old age what Henry VIII did for divorce. Not that the new President, who turned 70 last week, is about to lavish money on septuagenarian lobbyists, the Gray Panthers or age researchers. Those researchers, in fact, consider themselves prime targets for Reagan's budget cutting. The gerontologists, rather, think Reagan may actually help retard the rate of aging among senior citizens simply by remaining active and competent. Reason: after decades of work in the field, researchers have concluded that warding off old age is in large part a matter of self-image, positive thinking and staying active. Says Jack Botwinick, a psychologist and the author of *Aging and Behavior:* "There's a general feeling that people could have a self-fulfilling prophecy of decline. By keeping active they'll hang on longer."

Part of the problem, say the researchers, is the chilling power that certain numbers have come to possess: to many Americans, 65 means used up; 70 or 75 means ready for death. Yet today's 65-year-olds can expect to live 16 more years. In sports too, numbers have some of the same paralyzing power. A baseball player is considered old at 35, a basketball guard at 30. Athletic skills clearly erode with time just as everyday physical capabilities inevitably decline after, say, 65, but some researchers think that even in sports aging is nearly as much mental as physical. . . .

Dr. James Fries of the Stanford University Medical Center talks of shifting the "markers" of age in much the same way that Pete Rose talks about rejuvenating himself each spring: exercise plus an upbeat attitude equal success. At Stanford's arthritis clinic, says Fries, "I tell patients to exercise—use it or lose it. 'Run, not rest' is the new advice of the cardiologist."

Most progress in medicine, Fries maintains, has come from exchanging acute medical problems for chronic ones. For instance, people who might once have died from diseases such as

"It's amazing. After ninety-three years of carrying on, his chickens still haven't come home to roost."

The New Yorker, July 26, 1976. Drawing by Geo. Price; © 1976 The New Yorker Magazine, Inc.

smallpox and tuberculosis now live long enough to develop chronic ailments like atherosclerosis and emphysema. Since we are running out of acute problems to "exchange," Fries says, the job of medical researchers is to keep the steady decay of organs at a low level, and the task of everybody is to work at postponing or reducing the severity of their chronic problems—giving up smoking to delay emphysema, for example, or treating hypertension to delay problems with the arteries. Regular checkups are necessary to detect early signs of disease, and exercise is crucial. "The body is now felt to rust out rather than wear out," says Fries. . . .

Genetics, socioeconomic status and luck all help determine who will live to a ripe old age. So does education, according to one theory. Sociologist George Maddox, director of the Center for the Study of Aging and Human Development at Duke University, argues that education "is associated with the notion of taking hold of the future in a special way, and it leads people to organize their lives differently." If that

theory is correct, then rising national levels of education may mean that tomorrow's elderly will have an easier time of it than today's.

One of the elderly who fit the gerontologist's prescription of peppy indomitability is Al Beatty, 87, a retired railroad man living alone in a trailer in the Riviera Mobile Park in Scottsdale, Ariz. Beatty is legally blind and partially deaf, but he manages to keep a full daily schedule, dances whenever he can, and about four years ago started to teach a workshop in personal development to the elderly at the Scottsdale Senior Center. "It's the ones who don't conform to the stereotype of the elderly who live the longest," says Rosemary Perry, director of Beatty's center. Though she has not read about Dr. Fries' ideas, she manages to express them well enough: "You may have a chronic illness and have to get to bed earlier. But it's not the end of the world. It's just a slowdown."

Time
February 16, 1981

Recent research has dispelled many of the myths about old age. Among other things, this research should help improve the self-image of senior citizens. This, in turn, should improve the quality of their lives.

9 | Personality

Imagine that as part of a psychology experiment you are spending an evening observing the behavior of shoppers in a large and busy supermarket. You are recording the approximate age and weight of persons who purchase candy, sour cream, and frozen pies (for later comparison with those who stick to melba toast and cottage cheese). Suddenly all the lights go out. Being an intrepid scientist, you attempt to continue your observations in the illumination provided by the store's emergency spotlights, but you find that conditions are not adequate for you to make accurate age and weight estimates. You therefore turn your attention to how individuals deal with the situation. In the produce department you spot a person calmly squeezing avocados as if nothing unusual were going on, while over by the green peppers another individual is frightened and begins to scream. You arrive at the meat counter in time to see an opportunistic shopper tuck a standing rib roast under each arm and head for the exit. Nearby, you hear an irate customer inform the manager that there is no excuse for this kind of situation and threaten to patronize a competitor's store in the future.

In short, you find that each individual handles the unexpected blackout differently. This is not particularly surprising; we expect great diversity in human behavior. Of course, we also expect that each individual will usually display some consistency in behavior in different situations. Thus, a person who is quiet and shy at parties usually also behaves timidly and quietly in class, at public meetings, and on a date. Similarly, you expect a close friend to deal with you in a warm and interested manner in most situations and on a daily basis, not just once in a while.

How can we understand and explain these differences among individuals as well as consistencies within individuals, which we may take for granted as part of "human nature"? What makes people so different from each other yet so consistent within themselves? For centuries philosophers, physicians, and religious leaders have wrestled with this basic question about people and their behavior, and in recent decades psychologists have studied and theorized about it.

TABLE 9–1   Some Definitions of Personality

1. The dynamic organization within the individual of those psychophysical systems that determine his unique adjustments to his environment (G. Allport).
2. The more or less stable and enduring organization of a person's character, temperament, intellect, and physique that determines his unique adjustment to his environment (H. Eysenck).
3. That which permits a prediction of what a person will do in a given situation (R. B. Cattell).
4. A person's unique pattern of traits (J. P. Guilford).
5. The most adequate conceptualization of a person's behavior in all its detail (D. McClelland).
6. Each individual's characteristically recurring patterns of behavior (L. Kolb).

The most commonly used term to describe and account for individual differences and behavior consistencies in human beings has been "personality." In everyday situations we hear people's behavior described in terms of their personality: "He would be a nice guy if he didn't have such an aggressive personality"; "Your blind date is a bit on the heavy side but has a great personality"; "My psychology professor really knows her material but has no personality." In addition, the concept of personality is often used to explain behavior: "I think my roommate's depression is caused by his basically insecure personality," or "Her stable personality allows her to handle any situation."

What Is Personality?

Even though almost everyone frequently uses the term "personality," there is little agreement on what it actually means. To get some idea of the problem, jot down your own definition (before you finish this chapter) and then ask three friends for theirs. You will probably find that each one has a somewhat different conception of the term and that the three definitions you collect differ from your own. Such differences of opinion result not only from the fact that you and your friends are not experienced psychologists but also from the generality of the concept of personality.

Over the years, people have defined "personality" in various ways, including one's outward appearance, one's role in life, the totality of one's qualities or attributes, the way one "really" is, one's general behavior pattern, and many others. Today dozens of formal definitions exist (see Table 9–1), none of which is universally accepted. Like all definitions, those in the table reflect the interests of their sponsors: prediction (Cattell), dynamics (Allport), predispositions (Eysenck), individual differences (Guilford), description (McClelland) and observable behavior (Kolb). But each of these aspects is subsumed under our general orientation toward personality as a concept to describe and account for individual differences and consistencies in behavior.

It is somewhat easier to define personality as an area of psychological inquiry than as a "thing" that people have. Because the concept of personality is so broad, its study involves more branches of psychology than any other speciality. A psychologist interested in personality may ask questions as diverse as: How do personality characteristics develop? Does the existence of one characteristic predict the likelihood that the person will have certain other characteristics? What role do other people play in the development of an individual's personality? When and why do different people behave similarly and given individuals behave inconsistently? How do genetic and physiological factors influence personality? What causes the appearance of "abnormal" versus "normal" personalities? Can personality be changed, and if so, how?

The study of personality can involve all facets of human behavior and can encompass aspects of developmental, social, experimental, physiological, and clinical psychology. Thus, in a sense, any psychologist who deals with human behavior can be said to be exploring some segment of personality.

The Role of Theory in Studying Personality

If, as we have seen, there is no universally accepted definition of personality, on what do psychologists base their studies of human personality? Clearly, any investigator must proceed with some sort of guidelines. The psychologist uses a **theory** of personality. The theory is important because it provides some basic assumptions about human behavior and a working definition of the concept.

For example, one could start out with the somewhat fanciful assumption that all human behavior is the result of the presence of thousands of tiny, invisible elves that reside in the pancreas. An abundance of depressed elves would produce lethargic behavior except when they were sleeping, when a smaller number of happier and more optimistic elves would take over the controls, producing less melancholic behavior. Personality could then be defined through a kind of census of the elf population in each individual. People hosting lots of anxious elves would be called neurotic, those with a preponderance of sociable elves would be labeled extroverted, and so on.

Suppose that the investigator elaborated this kind of thinking into a comprehensive set of statements or assumptions that could account for human behavior as we know it, generate accurate predictions about it, and suggest procedures through which it can be altered. He or she would then have a personality theory that might result in hundreds of experiments designed to test the validity of its assumptions and hypotheses. "Elf theory" would probably also foster the development of highly specialized procedures (such as extremely sensitive X-ray devices) for assessing the specific kinds of elves in each individual. In addition, the theory might suggest specific strategies for elf research.

This absurd example is meant only to make the point that, because human behavior can be interpreted in so many ways, personality can be approached, defined, assessed, and researched from any one of a wide variety of theoretical points of view, each of which has strengths and weaknesses. Literally dozens of such theories exist. Here we shall present a description and discussion of four major classes of personality theories: dispositional theories, psychodynamic theories, learning theories, and phenomenological theories. In considering each class of theories, you should not ask which are "right" and which are "wrong," but which come closest to providing an efficient, complete, and testable account of the development, maintenance, and modification of human behavior, "normal" and "deviant." Note that each of these four classes of theories forms what might be called a "strategy" of personality study (Liebert & Spiegler, 1978) in the sense that, like the "elf approach," they provide not only a way of thinking about personality but also a set of procedures for measuring and investigating it. With the exception of dispositional theories, each class of approaches has important things to say about how behavior becomes deviant or abnormal, and each has also generated techniques designed to produce change toward a more healthy personality; these topics are discussed in Chapters 11 and 12.

Dispositional Theories

When people say, "He is the nervous type" or "Kindness is one of her most outstanding traits" or "Some people are driven to work hard by their strong need for achievement," they are, usually without knowing it, adopting a *dispositional* theory of personality. Dispositional theories start with the basic assumption that personality is composed of *dispositions within the individual* to behave in certain ways. Further, they assume that these dispositions are relatively stable in time and generalize over a wide variety of circumstances. From this they conclude that if you know about people's dispositions, you can make some predictions about their future behavior. The names given to these hypothesized behavioral dispositions are different in different theories.

Personality Types

Some dispositional theories assume that there are a few specifiable personality *types* and that each type is disposed to behave differently. One of the earliest personality-type theorists was the ancient Greek physician Hippocrates. Working on the assumption that the human body contains four fluids, or humors (blood, phlegm, black bile, and yellow bile), he categorized people into four corresponding personality types: phlegmatic (a calm, apathetic temperament caused by too much phlegm), choleric (a hotheaded, irritable temperament due to an excess of yellow bile), sanguine (an optimistic, hopeful temperament attributed to a predominance of blood), and melancholic (a sad, depressed temperament based on black bile). Hippocrates' theory is no longer taken seriously, yet it survives as a way of describing people—you will still find his four personality types listed in your dictionary. Since Hippocrates, several other *type* theories of personality have been proposed, most of which seek to relate behavioral dispositions to physical characteristics. For example, Cesare Lombroso, a nineteenth-century Italian anthropologist, suggested that people's facial characteristics provided clues to the kinds of behaviors they would display. This "science" was called *physiognomy,* and related factors such as head size, distance between the eyes, shape of the chin, and color of the hair to personality type.

The most elaborate theory of personality based on body characteristics was developed in the late 1940s and early 1950s by William Sheldon. Sheldon's system involved three primary body types: endomorphic, mesomorphic, and ectomorphic (see Figure 9–1). But instead of assigning individuals to one category, he characterized each person in terms of the degree to which that person displayed features of each primary type. (This approach contains features of *trait* theories of personality, to be discussed later.) Sheldon then examined the relationship between people's body type and their behavior. He found that endomorphs tended to be what he called "viscerotonic" (relaxed, sociable, slow, and tolerant); mesomorphs displayed "somatonia" (an assertive, athletic, energetic, and bold temperament); and ectomorphs were "cerebrotonic" (introverted, restrained, fearful, and artistic). It is interesting to note that these relationships parallel popularly held stereotypes about physique and behavior (the jolly fat person, the bold athlete, the frail, sensitive artist). Research in social psychology and related areas has shown that, to a certain extent,

FIGURE 9–1 Extreme examples of Sheldon's body types

Physique	Temperament

Endomorphic (soft and round, overdeveloped digestive viscera; Orson Welles, for example)

Viscerotonic (relaxed, loves to eat, sociable)

Mesomorphic (muscular, rectangular, strong; Arnold Schwartzenegger, for example)

Somatonic (energetic, assertive, courageous)

Ectomorphic (long, fragile, large brain and sensitive nervous system; Don Knotts, for example)

Cerebrotonic (restrained, fearful, introverted, artistic)

people still tend to be "body-type theorists." Much of the impression we get of other people (and part of the impression we have of ourselves) is influenced by physical appearance. After all, we can literally see people's bodies but not their personalities. Sheldon's particular theory has not received strong support and is not now influential.

The convenience and simplicity of type theories make them very popular. It would be nice to know everything about a person by looking at his or her face, manner of dress, handwriting, hair style, body type, or genetic make-up, or by asking for the person's astrological sign. But the behavior of human beings is too diverse and too complicated to be dealt with by using a cut-and-dried, "pigeonhole" system of categories. Thus, type theories are not generally valid because they are oversimplified and inadequate descriptions of behavior. Furthermore, they can be harmful because they tend to generate or maintain prejudices about people. (See the "What Does It Mean?" section of this chapter.) But stereotypes and pigeonholes make our lives simple-minded and easy; we can deal with an infinity of people by sorting them into just a few categories or mental schemata, even if this does injustice to them all. It is all too easy to be a type theorist in our dealings with others.

Traits of Personality

Trait theories of personality seek to avoid the limitations of type systems by accounting for both the diversity of human behavior and the behavioral consistencies within the individual. They start with the basic assumption that one's behavior is controlled not by the type of person one is, but mainly by the wide variety of stable personality traits (such as dependency, aggressiveness, gentleness, thoughtfulness, and the like) which each individual possesses to some degree or another. Thus, just as grade-point average is determined by a student's academic performance in many separate courses, personality is determined by the particular combination of traits, occurring at varying strengths, that is present in each individual. The idea that many combinations of trait strengths are possible accounts for both the uniqueness of the individual and the differences among people, while the idea that the individual's traits are enduring explains the relative consistency in each person's behavior over time and in many different situations.

Like type theory, the trait approach has a clear appeal; in fact, most of us use traits in describing others. If you ask a friend to tell you about his or her parents, for example, you will very likely be given a list of traits: "Dad is *hard-working, serious, and shy,* but overly *dependent* and *insecure* as well. Mom is *warm, outgoing, efficient,* and *optimistic,* but also *impulsive* and often *overbearing.*"

The danger in the casual use of this approach to personality is that trait descriptions like "Integrity is Ralph's strongest trait" can too easily be used as explanations. If we use Ralph's trait of integrity to "explain" his honesty, we end up making a statement that may be true but is not very useful in terms of understanding behavior: "Ralph is honest because he has integrity." This is like saying, "Ralph is 6 feet tall because he measures 72 inches from head to toe." Our description of behavior cannot also be its cause. We must use trait labels carefully so that we do not fool ourselves into thinking we have explained behavior when, in fact, all we have done is described it.

Over the years, there have been many scientific attempts to avoid this problem. Some early efforts, such as those of Franz Gall (1758–1828), were temporarily influential but have ultimately been discredited. Gall believed that all behavioral dispositions and abilities existed neurophysiologically in the brain and that the better developed a particular part of the brain, the stronger would be the corresponding trait or ability. Gall and his most prominent follower, Johann Spurzheim, believed that there were 37 basic traits, and they developed a "map" of the head to locate each of them. Personality assessment then became a matter of feeling an individual's skull for bumps (well-developed traits) and depressions (poorly developed traits), a technique known as *phrenology.* Gall and Spurzheim traveled from one end of Europe to the other, feeling heads for a fee. Perhaps one outcome of this continental trek was the origination of the expression "having your head examined."

Reprinted by permission. © 1978 NEA, Inc.

Personality is something that is inferred from behavior; often we make personality inferences about people based upon observing an incredibly small bit of their behavior. Here the patient makes a personality inference about his therapist based upon the fact that the therapist asks a lot of questions. In using personality as a causal explanation for behavior, we have to be careful not to fall into circular arguments that really don't explain anything.

For example: "Why does he ask so many questions? Because he has an obnoxious, prying personality. How do you know this about his personality? I know it because he asks me lots of obnoxious prying questions." It is important to remember the difference between using personality concepts as a means for describing behavior and using them as a means for explaining behavior.

Highlight 9–1

Tricks of the Fortune-Telling Trade

I. Young girl
  A. Wild type
    1. I can't catch, or hold, my man.
    2. My conscience is bothering me.
    3. I'm in trouble.
  B. Home girl
    1. I'm afraid of men.
    2. I'm afraid of life and responsibility.
    3. I'm afraid of Mom.
  C. Career girl (usually jealous of a brother)
    1. Under twenty-five: I'm ambitious. I hate and despise men and marriage!
    2. Over twenty-five: I'm panicky. Maybe no one will marry me!

II. Mature woman (30–50)
  A. Still wild
    1. Why isn't it as much fun anymore? I'm lonely.
    2. I'm afraid of getting my face scarred, or burning to death in a fire. (This never misses)
    3. I've got to believe in something—the occult, a new religion that doesn't include morals, or you, Mr. Fortune-teller!
  B. Wife and Mother
    1. Is my husband seeing another woman?
    2. When will he make more money?
    3. I'm worried about the children . . .

III. Spinster
  A. Still presentable
    1. When will I meet him?
  B. Given up hope
    1. My best friend has done me dirt.
    2. I'm crushed—a gigolo has got my savings!

IV. Young man
  A. Wild-oats farmer
    1. Is there a system for beating the races?
    2. What do you do when you get a girl in trouble?
      a. Is she playing me for a sucker?
  B. Good boy
    1. Will I be a success?
    2. How can I improve my education?
    3. Is my girl two-timing me?
      a. She's mixed up with Type A.
    4. I'm afraid of Mom!

V. Mature man
  A. Wolf, married or single
    1. Girl trouble
      a. I can't get her!
      b. I can't get rid of her!
      c. Her male relatives are after me!
      d. Does my wife know?

How can fortune tellers, palm readers, tea-leaf readers, and so on, manage to assess personality and detect problems well enough to impress many of their customers? The above outline, taken from an article on this topic entitled "Fortune Tellers Never Starve," offers some insight. By classifying a customer into one of the seven types, the fortune teller can then deal in generalities which are likely to apply to people of that type (the "Barnum effect"). This fascinating article by William L.

Traits as Entities

Gordon Allport, one of the first and most influential of the modern personality theorists, who worked between the 1930s and the 1960s, also believed that traits actually existed within the person as "neuro-psychic systems," but he went about describing them in a quite different and far more scientific way than did Gall. Allport discussed several kinds of traits, organized according to their generality: (1) *cardinal* traits, which determine behavior in the widest range of circumstances (describing someone as "a regular Albert Schweitzer" would be an example of the use of the cardinal trait of humanitarianism); (2) *central* traits, which are not as broad as cardinal traits but are still fairly general (our earlier descriptions of a hypothetical set of parents provide examples); and (3) narrow *secondary* traits, which appear only in certain circumstances (for example, "She is grouchy in the morning"). Further, Allport pointed out that while some traits appeared *to some extent* in everyone (*common* traits, for example, aggressiveness), others were unique to the individual (*individual* traits, for example, cynical verbal aggression) and could be studied only on an intensive, long-term case-by-case basis. Cardinal traits, in particular, apply to only relatively few people.

B. Businessman
   1. Where's the money going to come from?
   2. Will this deal work out?
   3. Did I do right in *that* deal?
   4. What does my wife do all day?

VI. Elderly people
   A. Woman
      1. Will my daughter get a good husband?
      2. Will That Creature be a good wife to my son?
      3. Will the children (or grandchildren) be all right?
   B. Man
      1. Will I ever have enough money to retire on?
      2. I'm afraid to die.
   C. Both
      1. Am I going to need an operation?

VII. Wise guy
   A. Toughie
      1. Make one false move, fortune-teller, and I bust ya one! (Ease him out quick.)
   B. Defensive bravado
      1. I'm smarter than most people; I see through you. (Flatter him; he'll end by eating out of your hand.)

Gresham appeared in *Esquire* magazine in 1949. Incidentally, rigid application of type theory gives rise to the concept of stereotype, a concept that underlies prejudice. We will discuss the concept further in Chapter 10.

"You seem to bump your head a lot. You are running and bouncing something. It's a ball. Wait! Now I see you putting the ball in a basket, but someone interferes and takes the ball away."

The New Yorker, April 5, 1976. Drawing by Modell; © 1976 The New Yorker Magazine, Inc.

Don't be too impressed with people who read palms, crystal balls, tea leaves, astrological charts, or handwriting. They use generalities in interpreting personality—characteristics that apply to just about everyone—and they can get lots of clues from your appearance, dress, manner of speaking, and so on. When people are gullible enough to accept such a personality description of themselves, they are succumbing to the "Barnum effect," after circus impressario P. T. Barnum ("There's a sucker born every minute").

Allport's methods for describing common traits included asking people to tell how they would behave in certain situations. Their responses allowed him to do two things. First, he could measure the strength and stability of a trait in a single individual by determining how often and how generally a person displayed the trait. Second, he could measure the frequency of traits among people in general by totaling the answers he received from large numbers of subjects.

Allport's influence upon the development of modern trait theories has been enormous, but a problem with his approach is that one could spend several lifetimes describing and researching all of the 18,000 or so trait names in the English language, let alone the relationships among them. Some more efficient method of dealing with traits was needed, and a technique called factor analysis provided it.

Traits as Factors

Basically, **factor analysis** is a statistical procedure that allows the personality researcher to look at large amounts of data relevant to the traits of many individuals and summarize what seems to "go with" what (see Appendix A). Then the investigator can group related traits and classify them as personality factors. An example, based on the behavior of one person, should help to clarify the general idea. Several days of close observation of a particular man might result in a long and varied list of highly specific activities, including: "places food in mouth," "rakes leaves," "plays tennis," "waxes car," "reads newspaper," "sits at desk," "chews food," "kisses wife," "drives to tennis court," "buys newspaper," "swallows food," "burns leaves," "writes reports," "sits on toilet," "removes clothes," "lies asleep for 8 hours," "washes dishes," "argues with supervisor," "sets alarm clock," "watches TV," "pets dog," and on and on. You could report on the man's behavior simply by presenting the entire list of everything he did during the period of observation (which is analogous to listing all of a person's personality traits), but the results would be difficult to deal with.

Alternatively, you could summarize all the specific behaviors under a few categories (analogous to personality factors). You might see that certain behaviors are related in some way. A group of behaviors such as "plays tennis," "pets dog," "drives to tennis court," "reads newspaper," and "watches TV" might be called "Recreation" or "Relaxation" (the name you give it is arbitrary; you could just as easily call it "Behavior Group A"). Several other behaviors may be unrelated to those called "Recreation" but highly related to one another—such as "washes dishes," "rakes leaves," "burns leaves," "waxes car"—and this group might be named "Household Chores." You could use the same grouping and naming procedures for all the other behaviors observed; the result might be a report saying that the person spent his time engaged in five categories of behavior: "Housework," "Occupational Pursuits," "Recreation," "Sexual Activity" (which may or may not be the same as "Recreation"), and "Body Maintenance."

Factor analysis (see Chapter 1 and Appendices A and C) allows the same kinds of summaries as those in our example, but in factor analysis the relationship among specific traits is determined through sophisticated statistical procedures applied to large numbers of subjects, not just through human observation of a single individual. We turn now to the work of one of the leading theorists who has used factor analysis in his investigation of personality traits.

Cattell's Surface and Source Traits

Raymond B. Cattell, whose major work appeared in the 1950s and 1960s, is one of the foremost proponents of factor analysis as a means of learning about personality traits. In his research on personality, Cattell has tapped three sources of information about human behavior, which he refers to as L-data, Q-data, and T-data. L-data do not come directly from the person under study but from life records, generally supplied by individuals who have observed the subject and who can provide information about the individual's behavior. Q-data consist of the subject's answers to questions about himself. T-data consist of scores on standardized, objective tests, such as Cattell's own 16 PF test (see below). Cattell argues that one cannot obtain a complete picture of personality without using these multiple data sources.

Like Allport, Cattell recognizes that some traits are broader and more pervasive than others. His extensive research has resulted in the grouping of human behavior into about 35 *trait clusters.* Cattell calls these clusters *surface traits* because they summarize the most obvious ways in which overt behaviors are related. For example, "honest" is a surface trait that summarizes a range of related behaviors which might include "returning a lost wallet," "telling the truth," "paying a parking fine," and the like. The other end of this surface trait dimension, "dishonest," summarizes an opposite set of related behaviors.

Because they describe only clusters of overt behaviors, Cattell regards these surface traits more as "symptoms" or *manifestations* of personality than as the basic underlying personality itself. In order to identify the more basic elements, the sources of personality, Cattell used factor analysis to analyze the surface traits. With this procedure he isolated 16 *source traits.* He then developed a test in 1964 called the 16 PF (personality factors) to measure their relative strengths in individual subjects. Thus, instead of describing personality in terms of specific behaviors or even clusters of behaviors (surface traits), Cattell provides a profile for each person in terms of his or her scores on source traits such as "reserved-outgoing," "shy-venturesome," or "relaxed-tense" (see Appendix C). Cattell views these source traits as the building blocks of personality and notes that they stem from either environmental influences (*environmental-mold* traits) or genetic-constitutional factors (*constitutional* traits).

Eysenck's Three Basic Dimensions of Personality

Cattell's research is confined mainly to the description of the so-called normal aspects of personality and has resulted in the isolation of 16 source traits. Hans Eysenck, a British psychologist whose major work began in the 1960s, also developed an approach using factor analytic techniques, but he outlines only three basic personality dimensions, and they relate to both "abnormal" and "normal" behavior. Eysenck began with the notion that personality traits are based on learning (classical and operant conditioning—see Chapter 4) and that because of genetic-constitutional factors, some people are more easily conditioned than

FIGURE 9-2 Characteristics of introverts and extroverts as neuroticism increases

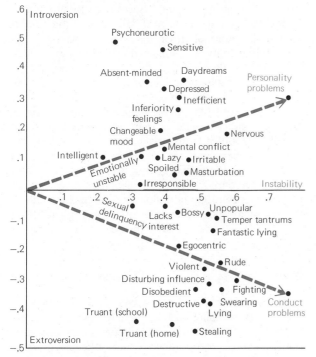

Points on the horizontal axis represent the degree of personality stability from a relatively normal condition on the left to highly neurotic at the right. The vertical axis represents the introversion-extroversion dimension. The graph suggests that someone who does a lot of fighting and swearing in public is probably quite extroverted and rather neurotic. In contrast, the person who daydreams a lot and tends to be a loner and depressed is probably an introverted person with a moderate amount of neuroticism. One can predict, on the basis of Eysenck's analysis, that relatively normal introverts and extroverts will, if they become neurotic, show completely different symptoms. As a result, they should be given different therapies.

others. For example, one child may avoid a forbidden activity after having been punished for it only once; another might learn much more slowly, and a third might persist in the activity indefinitely. Eysenck found that by using factor analysis to assess human behaviors and the traits they form he could describe a given individual on three basic dimensions: neuroticism, psychoticism, and introversion-extroversion. (Eysenck uses the terms *introvert* and *extrovert* in a sense different from the popular stereotypes of the extrovert as outgoing and the introvert as shy and withdrawn. In Eysenck's terminology, introverts are those who condition most easily and as a result develop behaviors that reflect their susceptibility to conditioning, such as anxiety and depression. Extroverts, on the other hand, condition less easily and tend to be more impulsive and unruly.)

On the basis of specially designed personality tests such as the Maudsley Personality Inventory (MPI), an individual can be given a score on each of these dimensions. Eysenck has found that particular combinations of personality factors (especially introversion-extroversion and neuroticism) are associated with particular patterns of behavior. Neurotic introverts, for example, are likely to display intense emotions involving anxiety, while neurotic extroverts will also be emotional, but their behavior will be antisocial or even criminal (see Figure 9–2).

Interestingly, although Eysenck's theory does not contain suggestions for *new* personality-change techniques, it does have clear implications for psychotherapy (see Chapter 12). If a therapist is working with a neurotic introvert, the goal would be to help the person *reduce* overlearned reactions (such as fear of authority). By contrast, an *increase* in conditioned reactions might be desirable when dealing with an extrovert who has not learned to "play by the rules."

Need Theory

Another kind of dispositional approach to personality views behavior as driven by the individual's needs or goals rather than by traits or personality type. This approach is exemplified by the work of Henry Murray (see Chapter 7), who postulated the existence of 12

Henry Murray.

primary human needs, such as air, water, food, and sex, and 27 secondary, or psychogenic, needs, such as achievement, recognition, dominance, autonomy, aggression, affiliation, and nurturance. These needs, in combination with environmental influences (called *press*), shape the individual's personality and behavior. From Murray's point of view, measurement of personality involves assessment of both *manifest* (obvious) needs and *latent* (more subtle) needs.

Manifest needs can be measured directly by observing how often, how long, and how intensively a person engages in particular behaviors. An individual who spends a lot of time pushing others around has a stronger need for aggression than a person who seldom if ever behaves that way. Latent needs, however, are not overt—for instance, a person's latent need for affection might be expressed through romantic daydreams—and therefore they must be measured indirectly. To measure these needs, Murray and his colleague Christian Morgan, in 1943, developed the Thematic Apperception Test (TAT), in which the subject looks at an ambiguous stimulus, such as a picture (see Chapter 7 and Appendix C), and tells a story about it. The content of the story is seen to reflect the individual's latent needs. Tests of this type are called **projective tests** because they allow the subject to "project" aspects of his or her personality onto relatively neutral stimuli. We shall mention other projective tests in discussing psychodynamic theories in the next section.

Some Problems with Dispositional Theories

Dispositional theories have been influential in psychology and have generated a massive amount of research that has increased our ability to describe and make predictions about human behavior; but they have also been criticized on several points. For example, although dispositional theories describe personality (in terms of traits, types, or needs), they provide very little explanation of how personality develops. This relative lack of attention to processes of personality development is a weakness of the dispositional approach.

In addition, one might question the assumption that personality is entirely a collection of stable, enduring, unchanging traits. Behavior and personality do not seem always (or even typically) to be independent of the individual's current circumstances or context—we do not always behave the same way. For instance, we may be generous most of the time but downright stingy on occasions. Explaining the variability of behavior shown by the same person is often difficult for the dispositional theories. These theories, then, tend to overemphasize the disposition

(the personality) of an individual and to underemphasize the role of context or the immediate circumstances of the individual. According to attribution theory (see Chapters 7 and 10), this is the fundamental attributional error that we are all prone to make when trying to explain the behavior of others.

Finally, dispositional theories have been criticized for their extensive use of self-report procedures in personality assessment and research. Asking someone about his or her behavior may be one of the most direct means of gaining information about personality, but it is also risky, because the data collected on a personality test may be biased or distorted in various ways. Subjects may try to present themselves in a particularly positive or negative way, or their responses may be influenced by factors such as the characteristics of the person giving the test, the situation in which they take the test, or prior events.

Psychodynamic Theories

Psychodynamic theories are based on the assumption that personality and personality development are determined by intrapsychic events and conflicts—that is, events and conflicts which take place within the mind—and that these can best be explored and understood through careful, in-depth study of individual subjects. The foundations for this approach were set down late in the nineteenth century, primarily by Sigmund Freud. A physician devoted to the principles of science, Freud evolved one of the most comprehensive and influential theories of personality ever presented.

Freud's Theory

Freud called his approach **psychoanalysis** and based his theorizing on a few fundamental principles. One principle was *psychic determinism,* the idea that human behavior does not occur randomly but in accordance with intrapsychic causes, which may not always be obvious to an outside observer or even to the person displaying the behavior. This concept, that all of our behavior "means" something, even if we are not aware of its meaning, is one of the most significant and widely known features of Freud's theory. In the psychoanalytic perspective few, if any, aspects of human behavior are accidental: Writing the word "sex" when you meant to write "six," calling your lover by another person's name, or forgetting a friend's birthday could be interpreted as expressing feelings, desires, fears, or impulses of which you may not be aware.

Freud called the part of mental functioning that is out of our awareness and to which we cannot gain access the **unconscious.** Thoughts, feelings, and ideas of which we are unaware but that we can bring into the **conscious** portion of the mind are said to be **preconscious.** For example, you can easily become aware of the feelings of your tongue even though, until you read this sentence, you were probably not thinking about it. Such thoughts are preconscious. By contrast, according to Freud, if you harbor unconscious hatred toward a close friend, you would claim that no such feelings exist because you do not experience them consciously.

Another of Freud's fundamental assumptions was that human personality is formed out of the continuous struggle between the individual's attempts to satisfy inborn instincts or impulses (primarily involving sex and aggression) while at the same time coping with an environment that will not tolerate completely uninhibited conduct. In Freud's view, all human beings are born with instinctual, or innate, sexual and aggressive impulses that demand immediate gratification but that individuals cannot always directly express without causing themselves harm or other negative consequences. Thus, it becomes each individual's lifelong task somehow to satisfy instinctual urges while taking into account the demands, rules, and realities of the environment. For example, a man may desire sexual relations with a particular woman, but because he has been socialized by his parents and other agents of society, he knows that he cannot just walk up to her as a perfect stranger and attempt to attain his goal directly. Therefore, he may seek to meet her socially, develop a close relationship with her over some period of time, and ultimately reach his original objective. This solution to the man's problem is far more socially appropriate than a direct expression of sexual impulses and thus reflects a compromise between instinct and reality. For Freud, then, personality is a kind of arena in which what individuals want to do (instinct) conflicts with what they have learned they should or can do (morality and reason) and where some compromise is worked out.

It is important to note that Freud lived and wrote in a time of Victorian sexual repression. Open discussion of adult sexuality was risqué in itself, but his hypotheses about infantile sexuality was nothing short of heresy. His views therefore cast him as a rebel against society. Freud's theory was seen as dangerous to the existing social order, and his persistence in proposing such a position should not be overlooked.

Structure of Personality

As we saw in Chapter 8, Freud called the unconscious, instinctual component of personality the **id.** In the id are all of a person's inherited sexual, aggressive, and other impulses that seek immediate expression. All of the psychic energy, or **libido,** that motivates behavior is part of the id at birth. Because the id seeks to gratify its desires without delay, it operates on the **pleasure principle** (this might be translated as "if it feels good, do it"). Because it is unconscious, the id is not in touch with the world outside.

As the person grows, the real world will impose more and more limitations on direct gratification of the id's instinctual impulses. At the same time, a second aspect of personality, called the **ego,** begins to take shape. The ego gets its energy from the id, but it is partly conscious and thus is in contact with external reality. The ego's function is mainly to find ways to allow satisfaction of id impulses while at the same time protecting the organism as a whole from danger. In our example of the man who wanted to have intercourse with a certain woman (id impulse), the ego planned and directed the implementation of a socially acceptable way of doing so. Because the ego takes reality into account while seeking to facilitate expression of id impulses, it operates on the **reality principle** (which might be translated as "if you are going to do it, do it quietly" or "do it later" or "be careful").

As growth continues a third component of personality, the **superego,** develops. It is roughly equivalent to the "conscience" in the sense that it contains all of the teachings of the person's family and culture regarding ethics, morals, and values — how one should behave. In Freudian theory, the development of the superego actually involves internalizing these teachings so that they function not as someone else's values but as our own. Thus, this aspect of personality acts as a kind of internalized representative of society that seeks to influence us to behave in a socially acceptable fashion. Feelings of guilt are seen as the result of failing to follow the demands of the superego.

In Freud's system, then, personality is a three-part structure, partly conscious, partly unconscious (see Figure 9–3), that is constantly involved in conflicts within itself. The ego is involved in most of these intrapsychic conflicts because it must find a way to reconcile the impetuous impulses of the id, the perfectionistic demands of the superego, and the requirements of the outside world. Some examples of intrapsychic conflicts are presented in Table 9–2.

Ego Defense Mechanisms

According to Freud, one of the main functions of the ego is protection. It serves to protect the person (1) from threats from physical danger, (2) from the possibility of becoming conscious of taboo id impulses, and (3) from the condemnation of the superego should its rigid standards be violated. For ex-

FIGURE 9-3 **The relationship of the id, ego, and super-ego to levels of awareness**

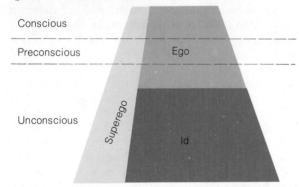

Freud's greatest impact came from his idea that a great deal of our behavior can be attributed to the unconscious. But unconscious determinism of behavior is also the source of the greatest controversy about Freud.

Left: Freud at 66 in 1922. This was one of Freud's productive yet disappointing times. The Committee, a group of Freud's disciples which had existed for 10 years, was disrupted by dissension among its members. This event coincided with the first signs of cancer, from which Freud would eventually die. In 1920 he changed his original ideas of the unconscious and began a new theory of the ego, which is considered a great advance in the theory of psychoanalysis.

Right: Freud at 82 in 1938. Because he was a Jew, Freud was forced to leave his lifelong home of Vienna, Austria, during the Nazi invasion. Here he is in England in the process of reading and writing his last work, the *Outline of Psychoanalysis.* He was still writing the manuscript a year later when he died.

ample, if id impulses were to tempt a hungry person to take food from a neighboring restaurant table while waiting for his or her own lunch, the ego would recognize the potential physical danger of such action and would also "hear from" the superego which would point out that such behavior is wrong. Obviously, the ego must also "do something." In his early writings Freud suggested that the ego tried to keep id impulses out of consciousness mainly through a **defense mechanism** called **repression.** Thus, if a father has strong unconscious impulses to murder his children, his ego may prevent him from becoming aware of them. At one time Freud thought that repression causes anxiety, but he later concluded that it is the other way around: Anxiety appears when id impulses threaten to emerge into consciousness, and

the repression reduces anxiety. However, like trying to hold a fully inflated beachball under water, repression takes a lot of constant effort. At times the repressed material may threaten to surface, or actually do so, with anxiety as the result (see Table 9–3).

Complete and entirely successful repression without additional help is unlikely, and Freud ultimately came to believe that the ego often employs

TABLE 9-2 **Possible Conflicts among the Aspects of Personality**

Conflict	Example
Id vs. ego	Choosing between a small immediate reward and a larger reward that requires some period of waiting (i.e., delay of gratification)
Id vs. superego	Deciding whether to return the difference when you are overpaid or undercharged
Ego vs. superego	Choosing between acting in a realistic way (e.g., telling a "white lie") and adhering to a potentially costly or unrealistic standard (e.g., always telling the truth)
Id and ego vs. superego	Deciding whether to retaliate against the attack of a weak opponent or to "turn the other cheek"
Id and superego vs. ego	Deciding whether to act in a realistic way that conflicts both with your desires and your moral convictions (e.g., the decision faced by devout Roman Catholics as to the use of contraceptive devices)
Ego and superego vs. id	Choosing whether to "act on the impulse" to steal something you want and cannot afford—the ego would presumably be increasingly involved in such a conflict as the probability of being apprehended increases

TABLE 9-3 Defense Mechanisms

1. Repression	5. Displacement
2. Denial	6. Rationalization
3. Reaction Formation	7. Sublimation
4. Projection	8. Regression

Sample Behaviors—Can you match each one with its corresponding defense mechanism?

a. A man with a considerable dislike for animals becomes a zookeeper.
b. A woman with an unconscious hatred for her mother becomes extremely anxious when she has to visit her parents.
c. A college student, anxious about flunking out, starts wetting his bed at night.
d. A couple routinely physically harms their child while administering punishment, because they say such punishment builds "strong moral fiber."
e. A man is overly protective of his daughter, refusing to let her date, saying that today's bachelors are interested in nothing but a woman's body.
f. A man is forced to declare bankruptcy but continues his high-living life-style.
g. A sexually frustrated graduate student spends all of his waking hours in the laboratory testing his mentor's pet theory.
h. An executive, having lost out on a promotion, fires her secretary.

Note: any behavior can be interpreted in a variety of ways, many of which are normal and do not involve a defense mechanism against neurotic anxiety. For example, a man can protect his daughter out of love, or an executive can fire her secretary because the secretary is incompetent. It takes careful work by a trained therapist to determine if there is neurotic anxiety present which leads to the generally abnormal behavior indicative of the use of one or more defenses. Freudian theory presents a major problem in this regard because almost any behavior can be made to appear defensive and therefore neurotic. Thus, do not become carried away with your interpretations.

several supplementary defenses to keep unacceptable material from consciousness (see Table 9-3). Probably the most primitive defense mechanism is **denial.** For example, a woman whose husband recently died may for a time behave *as if* he were still alive by making dinner for two or placing the evening paper next to his chair. Another common defense is **reaction formation,** in which the individual thinks and acts in a fashion directly opposite to the unconscious impulse. In the example of the murderous father cited earlier, the man might thus be extremely overprotective of his children and express great concern for their welfare. He might also employ (unconsciously, of course) the defense mechanism called **projection,** through which he would attribute his own taboo impulses to

others. This might take the form of being overly concerned about the problem of child abuse in the community. A defense mechanism called **displacement** actually allows some disguised expression of the id impulses. In this case the father who unconsciously wishes to harm his children may "take it out" by yelling at the family dog, a young employee, or some other more acceptable target. If he justifies or explains inappropriate or unacceptable behavior toward his children without being aware of the "real" unconscious reason for it, he is using the ego defense mechanism called **rationalization.** Thus, he might point out that he punishes his children frequently because he loves them and it is "for their own good."

In Freud's view, only one defense mechanism results in socially adaptive behavior. It is called **sublimation** and involves expressing taboo impulses within productive, creative channels. For instance, it has been suggested that, in some cases, an individual's sexual impulses may be converted into artistic energy and result in the production of paintings or sculpture. Sublimation can provide a more or less permanent solution to the problem of protecting the person against anxiety. The other defenses, however, are less desirable alternatives that "tie up" large amounts of psychic energy, and they may eventually break down, thus allowing a partial breakthrough of repressed material, forcing the person to fall back to even more primitive lines of defense. (This is why dependence on maladaptive ego defense strategies often indicates a need for psychotherapy; see Chapter 12.)

Freud believed that when adult ego defenses fail, the person may to some extent **regress,** or revert to behavior characteristic of earlier, less mature developmental stages. Partial regression may result in behaviors that are simply immature or otherwise mildly inappropriate, for example, an adult temper tantrum. More profound regression can result in the appearance of severely disturbed, even psychotic, behavior.

Personality Development

As we discussed in Chapter 8, Freud postulated that every human being passes through several **psychosexual stages** of development. Each stage is named for the area of the body most closely associated with pleasure at the time, the erogenous zones. Thus, the first year or so of life is the *oral stage* because eating, sucking, and other oral activities are the predominant sources of pleasurable stimulation. If because of premature or delayed weaning oral needs are frustrated or overindulged, the child may cling to some behavior patterns associated with the oral stage and not progress to the next stage of development. Freud called this phenomenon **fixation,** since the personality fixates on some mode of gratification (in this case, oral gratification) because that is the only way it has of dealing with anxiety or frustration at the time.

As an example, consider that a baby can reduce its tension only orally (by crying and sucking). If the frustration is overwhelming to the developing ego, it will interfere with reality testing, and the personality will handle future tension (unrealistically) as it did earlier. Thus, an anxious adult may smoke cigarettes heavily. Oral stimulation might have helped the individual with childhood problems, but will smoking relieve problems at the office? Adults who depend upon patterns of behavior that are oral in nature, such as smoking, overeating, or using "biting" sarcasm, may be said to have oral personalities or to exhibit some degree of oral fixation. Freud believed that the more strongly fixated an individual was at a given psychosexual stage, the more likely the person was to display behaviors typical of that stage and to regress to that stage when under stress. Thus, Freud viewed forms of psychosis in which individuals become totally dependent on others for their care as a nearly complete regression to the oral stage.

Freud assumed that the anus and the stimuli associated with eliminating and withholding feces were central to the second or third year of a child's development, and so he called this period the *anal stage*. The critical feature of this period is toilet training, and Freud thought anal fixation resulted from either overly rigorous or overly indulgent toilet-training practices. Fixation at the anal stage is indicated in adulthood either by excessively "tight," controlled behavior or by very "loose," disorderly behavior. Individuals who are (for example) stingy, obstinate, highly organized, and overconcerned with cleanliness and small details are characterized as anal-retentive personalities. Those who are (for example) sloppy, disorganized, or overgenerous may be labeled anal-expulsive.

Following the anal stage (at about age 4), the genitals become the primary source of pleasure, and the child enters the *phallic stage*. As the name implies, Freud paid more attention to psychosexual development in the male than in the female. He theorized that during the phallic stage the young boy begins to have sexual desires toward his mother and wants to eliminate his father so that he will not have to compete with him. Because these desires parallel the plot of the Greek tragedy *Oedipus Rex,* Freud characterized them as the **Oedipus complex.** The child fears that he will be castrated for having incestuous and murderous desires, so he normally resolves the conflict and its resultant anxiety by repressing his sexual desires toward his mother. He attempts to imitate, or **identify** with, his father

The New Yorker, August 21, 1978. Drawing by Opie; © 1978 The New Yorker Magazine, Inc.

(father becomes his "role model") and ultimately finds an appropriate female sex partner. Freud outlined a parallel though less clearly specified process for girls involving what is now called the **Electra complex** (after another Greek play). Here, the girl experiences "penis envy" (because she does not have such an organ), which may result in a desire to possess her father while rejecting her mother. She must resolve this situation by repressing her incestuous feelings, identifying with her mother, and eventually finding an appropriate male sex partner.

Freud believed that successful resolution of the conflicts inherent in the phallic stage is crucial to healthy personality development in that identification with the same-sex parent facilitates the incorporation of gender-appropriate behaviors. But conflict resolution at this stage is extremely difficult. Freud thought fixation at the phallic stage was common and was responsible for a variety of later interpersonal problems, including aggression and various sex deviations such as exhibitionism.

Following the phallic stage, the child enters a sexually dormant period that lasts until the onset of puberty. This is called the *latency period* and is characterized by a lack of sexual interest.

During adolescence, the child matures physically and sexually and begins the *genital stage,* which lasts through the adult years. Pleasure is again focused in the genital area, but the individual seeks more than the self-satisfaction characteristic of the phallic stage. If all has gone well in the earlier psychosexual stages, the person seeks to establish stable, long-term sexual relationships that take into account the needs of others.

Freud assumed that because so much of personality operates at the unconscious level, individuals cannot be relied upon to report their own personality accurately. Thus, he and others who followed him developed special methods of assessing the unconscious aspects of personality functioning. The main problem as Freud saw it was to get around the ego defense mechanisms that prevent unconscious material from surfacing. In his early attempts to do this, he interviewed patients while they were under hypnosis. Later, he employed procedures such as free association, the analysis of "accidental" behavior, such as slips of the tongue, and the interpretation of dreams (see Chapter 12). Today, projective tests such as the Rorschach Inkblot Test and the TAT are commonly used to explore the unconscious (see Appendix C).

Variations on Freud's Theory

Freud's original ideas have undergone many changes over the years since he first enunciated them. In fact, Freud himself was constantly altering, editing, and supplementing his views, so that it is possible to speak of many editions of his theory. He clung to a few of his basic principles, however, notably the instinctual basis of human behavior (emphasizing sex and aggression); and it was on this point that many of his prominent followers ultimately broke with him. Each took Freud's ideas and developed them in a slightly different way. The ultimate result was the appearance of new psychodynamic theories as well as revisions of the basic Freudian view. These theoretical develop-

"Good morning, beheaded—uh, I mean beloved."

The New Yorker, December 24, 1979. Drawing by Dana Fradon; © 1979 The New Yorker Magazine, Inc.

ments also prompted the evolution of a group of new therapeutic approaches and emphases.

Generally speaking, early variations on Freud's theory tended to deemphasize the inherited, instinctual basis of human behavior and pay more attention to environmental factors, especially the influence of the individual's social situation. Here we will briefly consider a few of the many approaches that grew out of Freud's system.

Carl G. Jung

Initially Jung was a member of Freud's inner circle and, for a time, Freud's heir apparent. As a result of certain differences, including Jung's insistence that libidinal energy is not entirely sexual, he broke with the Viennese school and in Zurich, Switzerland, founded his own system of *analytic psychology*. Whereas Freud considered the individual to be buffeted by instincts and fully molded by early adolescence, Jung suggested a continuing process called *individuation* leading toward harmony between the individual and the world. At the heart of his theory is his conception of the self, which he believed consists of four basic functions—thinking, feeling, sensing, and intuiting. The way these functions are carried out in the individual is influenced largely by whether the person is an introvert or an extrovert, and it was Jung who first brought this personality dimension into psychology. He is also known for his use of the word-association test to study the unconscious.

Jung could not accept Freud's analysis of the unconscious as the source of all our psychic energies. Instead, he viewed the unconscious as made up of two parts—the personal unconscious and the collective unconscious. Jung's personal unconscious is much the same as Freud's unconscious, the repository of forgotten and repressed memories. The collective unconscious, on the other hand, contains archetypal, or basic, elements (for example, "The Mother" or "The Hero") that are common to the entire human race. It is an intrinsic aspect of personality that has accumulated through history and been passed from generation to generation. For Jung, the two parts of the unconscious are related in the sense that the personal unconscious contains complexes that develop out of the archetypes of the collective unconscious. For example, all human beings have personal unconscious thoughts and feelings about their own mothers, but these are supplemented by the archetypical concept of "motherhood" with all its cultural and historical associations.

Among the more prominent archetypes in Jung's system is the *shadow*, our most primitive, animal-like instincts, and two others, representing aspects of the opposite sex which he believed each person carries. The feminine aspects of the male's

"I've always found Freud a little tough to swallow."

Playboy, February 1972. Reproduced by special permission of PLAYBOY Magazine; copyright © 1972 by Playboy.

personality was called *anima,* while the male aspects of the female's being was called *animus.* (Although Jung wrote about these things in rather mystical terms, it is interesting to note that modern personality researchers are now conducting research on psychological androgyny, the notion that males and females may each display features traditionally associated with the other; see Chapter 7.)

Like Freud, Jung believed that behavior disorders result when there is disharmony among various aspects of personality, but he employed a larger number of components. For example, in neurosis, there may be conflicts between and among the personal unconscious, the ego, and the collective unconscious. If these conflicts become so extreme that the underlying unity among the various personality structures is shattered, a psychosis results.

Jung argued that the personality is heavily guided by a forward-looking, goal-directed process. In that sense, his theory is an optimistic alternative to Freud's pessimistic view of the individual.

Alfred Adler

One of the first of Freud's colleagues to reject the instinct theory of behavior was Alfred Adler. He developed instead an approach called *individual psychology,* which assumed that the most important factor in the development of personality is that each person begins life in a completely helpless, inferior position. Adler believed that the individual's subse-

quent behavior represents a "striving for superiority" (first within the family, then in the larger social world) and that the way in which each person seeks superiority constitutes the individual's *style of life.* He thought adaptive life-styles are characterized by cooperation, social interest, courage, and common sense, while maladaptive styles of life involve undue competition, lack of concern for others, and the distortion of reality. For Adler, maladaptive life-styles and the behavior problems they cause are due, not to unresolved conflicts but to *mistaken ideas or basic misconceptions* (faulty thinking or cognition) that the person has about the world. For example, a child may discover that a good way to exert control over others (and thus gain some feeling of superiority) is to be very dependent on them. Over time, the individual may develop the misconception that he or she is a "special case" who cannot deal with the world independently. Accordingly, a life-style may evolve in which the person is always sick, hurt, frightened, or handicapped in some other way and therefore demands attention and special consideration from others. Other common examples of "basic mistakes" or "personal myths" include thoughts such as "I have to please everybody," "Life is hard," and "People are hostile."

Unlike Freud, Adler believed that many of these cognitive and behavioral problems are conscious, or at least accessible to consciousness through careful interviews in which obvious and subtle features of the person's life-style are revealed. He believed, for example, that a person's earliest recollections may contain clues to the characteristics and origins of a life-style. Such recollections may contain a theme (such as being ignored or belittled), which suggests that today's behavior (life-style) represents part of a continuing attempt to overcome past indignities. The person's family history is also seen as significant in learning about life-style. Birth order provides a good example. The early social world of a firstborn is far different from that of the youngest of eight children and may have an enormous impact on the individual's view of self (for example, "the leader" versus "the baby") in childhood and in later life (see Chapter 6).

Social Influences in Psychoanalysis

Neo-Freudian personality theories are chiefly characterized by a focus on social factors as opposed to the Freudian emphasis on biological factors (instincts). Adler was a forerunner of this emphasis, which is brought out more fully in the theories of Karen Horney (pronounced "Horn-eye"), Erich Fromm, and Harry Stack Sullivan. All of these theorists said that Freud had failed to emphasize sufficiently the social-cultural aspects of personality development. Personality, they claimed, is shaped and influenced more by society, culture, and the other people in the life of the individual than it is by instincts. Horney's theory illustrates this trend.

Relationships with others play a dominant role in Horney's theory of neurotic personality functioning. For Horney, the primary personality construct is called *basic anxiety,* which has its roots in childhood when the child's primary fear is of being isolated, deserted, and helpless. Thus, basic anxiety stems from threats to the child's safety, security, and physiological needs, to use Maslow's hierarchy for comparison (see Chapter 7). The child develops strategies for dealing with basic anxiety, and any of these strategies can become permanent characteristics of the individual's personality.

Horney suggested that the individual's strategies for solving the problems created by basic anxiety can easily develop into irrational and maladaptive (neurotic) forms of behavior. The strategy becomes

such an important part of the personality structure that it takes on all the characteristics of a drive or need. Horney identified 10 *neurotic needs* that constitute three basic attitudes a person might acquire in his or her relationships with other people (see Table 9–4). The strategy might cause the person to move (1) toward other people, (2) against other people, or (3) away from other people.

The neo-Freudians stressed the principles of social psychology, the influence that the real or implied presence of other people has on behavior. They strongly believed that personality is shaped by experience—social and cultural experience—and, as a consequence, is readily subject to modification. This view naturally led to a much greater realization that there are vast individual differences in people's personalities and that not everyone can be described in the same way. Perhaps most important, it led to a greater optimism about human nature and the ability of human beings to change than was present in the original Freudian notions, which were based on biological rather than social foundations.

Neo-Freudians, for example, especially those known as *ego analysts,* suggested that the ego does not evolve entirely from the id and that the functions of the ego go beyond merely defending against anxiety and resolving unconscious conflicts. The ego is

TABLE 9–4   Horney's List of 10 Neurotic Needs (Neurotic Ways of Coping with Basic Anxiety)

1. *Needs that involve moving toward people.*
   a. The need for affection and approval—the person seeks to please everyone and be liked by everyone.
   b. The need for a "partner" who will take over one's life—submerges his own personality and becomes a "parasite" on someone else.

2. *Needs that involve moving against other people.*
   a. The need for power, mainly in order to dominate others—may seek power through intellectual superiority over others as well as through more obvious means.
   b. The need to exploit others.
   c. The need for prestige—seeks public recognition and admiration.
   d. The need for personal admiration—neurotically overestimates his own personal worth and wants admiration of this false front.
   e. The need for personal achievement—is basically insecure and truly drives himself in search of more and more achievements, overdriven to achieve goals which often are not that important to others.

3. *Needs that involve moving away from people.*
   a. The need for self-sufficiency and independence—the person, completely frustrated in his attempts to relate to others, essentially gives up on them and becomes the loner, the hermit.
   b. The need for perfection and unassailability—fears that others will detect his faults and mistakes and so constantly strives for the ultimate in perfection to make himself invulnerable.
   c. The need to restrict one's life within narrow borders—moves into the background, makes few demands, is overly modest and self-critical.

Karen Horney.

T.A.: Doing OK

In the 1960s it was encounter groups. In the 1970s it is transactional analysis, or T.A., the pop-psychological path to happiness charted by Sacramento Psychiatrist Thomas A. Harris in his bestseller *I'm OK—You're OK*. T.A., or close facsimiles of it, is now practiced by some 3,000 psychiatrists, psychologists, social workers and ministers in the U.S. and 14 foreign countries. In fact, it may be the most widely used and fastest-growing form of treatment for emotional distress in the world. . . .

The central thesis of T.A., as Harris teaches it, stems from Psychiatrist Alfred Adler's concept of a universal "inferiority feeling." Most people, Harris says, never stop thinking of themselves as helpless children overwhelmed by the power of adults. For that reason they go through life believing that they are inferior, or "not OK," while they view everyone else as superior, or "OK." The aim of T.A. therapy is to instill the conviction that "I'm OK—you're OK," meaning that no one is really a threat to anyone else. . . .

More specifically, transactional analysts believe that what makes a person unhappy is an unbalanced relationship between the three parts that constitute every human personality: Parent, Adult and Child. Harris rejects any suggestion that these are the equivalent of Freud's superego, ego and id. "The Parent, Adult and Child are real things that can

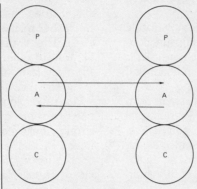 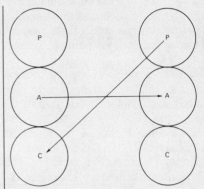

be validated," he insists. "We're talking about real people, real times and real events, as recorded in the brain." Be that as it may, the theory is that unless the mature, rational Adult dominates the personality, or, in the language of T.A., is "plugged in," the overly restrictive Parent and the primitive, self-depreciating Child will foul up most "transactions," or relationships with others.

To put his Adult in charge, Harris says, the troubled person must "learn the language of transactional analysis and use it in examining his everyday transactions." He must also learn to diagram these transactions, using three circles to represent the personality components of each person and drawing arrows to show how two people interact. Parallel lines depict "complementary

transactions," which occur, for instance, when a husband's Adult speaks to his wife's Adult and gets a response in kind. In that type of exchange, the husband might ask, "Where are my cuff links?" and his wife might reply, "In your top left dresser drawer"—or, perhaps, "I'm not sure, but I'll help you find them."

Crossed lines like this denote uncomplementary transactions, and bode trouble. For example, the Adult-to-Adult question about the cuff links might be answered with a sharp "Where you left them," a reproof that comes from the wife's Parent and is addressed to what she sees as the inept Child in her husband's personality. . . .

Time
August 20, 1973

One major reason T.A. has been so popular is that the theory uses language that is easy to relate to one's own experience.

seen as containing *conflict-free* areas whose function is to promote growth, autonomy, mastery over the environment, and adaptive learning. Erik H. Eriksen's neo-Freudian model of *psychosocial* (rather than psychosexual) development is consistent with this view and was examined in Chapter 8. Interestingly, too, while Freud placed heavy emphasis upon male sexuality and intrapsychic processes, neo-Freudian ego-analytic writers have helped to balance the picture by devoting equal attention to female psychodynamics.

Transactional Analysis

Most recently, psychiatrist Eric Berne has recast many of Freud's basic notions into terms and concepts that have captured a great deal of attention. In

accordance with the tendency among neo-Freudians to emphasize ego (rather than id) functions in energizing and determining behavior, Berne described a triad of *ego states* called "Parent," "Adult," and "Child" (paralleling the superego, ego, and id, respectively). Books by Berne (such as *Games People Play*) and others (such as T. A. Harris' *I'm OK, You're OK*) describe the use of **transactional analysis** to illuminate the ways in which ego states mediate interpersonal behavior. The lively interest shown by the public in this approach in recent years attests to the continuing influence of some of Freud's basic themes as they appear in modern form. For more detail on transactional analysis, see the newsclip, "T.A.: Doing OK."

Psychodynamic Approaches to Personality Assessment

From the point of view of most psychodynamic theorists, a great deal of important information about personality characteristics and intrapsychic features can be assessed by having people take various types of psychological tests. For example, frequently personality descriptions for research purposes and for pretherapy evaluations are based upon the results of several objective and projective tests, some of which are described in detail in Appendix C.

Another major source of psychodynamically oriented personality assessment data is, as noted earlier, the clinical or research interview, in which the interviewer pays close attention to *free associations,* reports about *dreams, errors* in speech ("Freudian slips"), and patterns of *everyday behavior* that might provide clues to important unconscious trends and defenses (see Chapter 12). Neo-Freudians are especially likely to look for statements, early memories, and stories that emerge in interviews which may provide insight into recurring interpersonal strategies (or games) and ego functions.

Some Problems with Psychodynamic Theories

Freud had an enormous influence. His concepts are so well known that they have become a part of our language and culture. It is not uncommon to hear people refer in everyday conversation to "Freudian slips," unconscious motivation, the Oedipus complex, and psychoanalysis. Freud's theory has also been strongly criticized, mainly on the grounds that his concepts (such as the id, ego, and superego, defense mechanisms, and the unconscious) are elaborate abstractions that cannot easily be measured. The techniques designed to assess personality and personality functioning in Freudian terms have not shown themselves to be very reliable or valid. The fact that the entire basis for Freud's approach was his experiences with a relatively small number of case studies (a few patients, virtually all of them women, and Freud himself) rather than experimental research has prompted the criticism that psychodynamic formulations are unscientific and do not apply to the bulk of the human population.

Critics also point out that many of Freud's assumptions about personality are difficult or impossible to evaluate because the results of any test can be interpreted according to his theory. For example, if psychoanalytic interviews or projective test results lead to the conclusion that a person harbors strong unconscious feelings of hostility toward the whole world, subsequent hostile behavior would be interpreted as evidence for the breakthrough of unconscious impulses, thus confirming the original hypothesis. But *lack* of subsequent hostile behavior could also provide evidence for underlying hostility because it could be seen as a defense mechanism (reaction formation). It has also been argued that psychodynamic personality theories make it too easy to interpret behavior as indicative of pathology and thus create problems where none existed before. For instance, a man might be called anxious and insecure if he shows up for work early, resistant and hostile if he is late, and compulsive if he is right on time.

Learning and Social Learning Theories

Instead of emphasizing intrapsychic conflicts, instincts, or dispositions (such as enduring traits), *learning* theories focus on behavior and the environmental conditions that affect it. From this point of view, personality is the sum total of the individual's behavior rather than some hypothetical structure that behavior reflects. Learning theories also assume that behavior (personality) is determined primarily through learning that very often takes place in a social context (then it is called social learning). These two basic assumptions have resulted in an approach to personality usually called *social learning theory* that accounts for both variation and consistency in behavior. This approach explains differences among people in terms of each person's unique learning history. For example, under stress conditions such as an exam, a person who has learned to deal with problems by depending upon others may seek to cheat, while another who has been rewarded for self-reliance may not.

Learning theories view consistencies in individual behavior as a function of generalized learning. A person may learn to be calm and serious in most situations if that behavior has been consistently rewarded over many years and under a wide variety of circumstances. Further, these theories seek to understand inconsistencies in individual behavior and other "unpredictable" behavioral phenomena in terms of the concept of behavioral specificity—the idea that behavior changes to fit particular circumstances.

There are many learning theories of personality. Although they often differ substantially with respect to certain specifics, all share several common characteristics: (1) an emphasis upon measurable behavior as the content of personality, (2) stress upon environmental as opposed to hereditary influences or other "givens" in personality and personality development, (3) attention to experimental research on the behavior of both human and nonhuman organisms, and (4) use of scientific methods to evaluate hypotheses about behavior and personality-change techniques. The main differences among these theories are the type of learning process emphasized (for example, classical versus instrumental conditioning versus social learning by observation; see Chapter 4) and the degree to which cognition (thinking) plays a role in learning and in guiding overt behavior.

The Role of Motivational Drives

One of the earliest learning theories was developed as part of an attempt to recast Freud's clinically derived concepts into a language consistent with experimental data on human and animal learning. The task of explaining Freudian phenomena in learning theory terms was undertaken in the 1940s by John Dollard and Neal Miller. They began with the assumption that human beings enter life not with instincts but with primary *needs*—for food, water, oxygen, and so forth—that must be satisfied. They further assumed that each person *learns* to satisfy these needs (and others based on them) in somewhat different ways, thus leading to the development of individualized patterns of behavior (personality). For example, an infant's need for food results in strong internal stimuli, such as hunger pangs. Dollard and Miller called such stimuli *primary drives* because they motivate or impel behavior aimed at satisfying primary needs early in life. Such behavior is usually fairly diffuse and generalized—for example, crying and thrashing. This activity may bring a parent into the room with food, which reduces the hunger drive and *rewards* or *reinforces* the behavior leading to it. In this way, each child learns to repeat those particular behaviors that result in or are associated with reduction of primary drives.

Of course, Dollard and Miller did not assume that all human behavior is learned as a function of reduction of primary drives. The behaviors necessary to drive a car, for example, are reinforced by praise, encouragement, and other social rewards that do not involve primary drives in an obvious way. Dollard and Miller postulated that these kinds of rewards reduce *secondary* or *learned* drives. Citing much laboratory data, they asserted that humans can "learn to need" things (such as praise), and the resulting acquired or secondary drives can motivate behavior in the same fashion as primary drives.

Dollard and Miller dealt with many Freudian concepts, but instead of treating them as intrapsychic events they considered them to be environmentally determined and experimentally researchable phenomena. For example, they saw conflict not as a clash between or among the id, ego, and superego but as the result of competition between incompatible behavioral tendencies. They divided these tendencies into two types: approach tendencies, involving attraction to behaviors in which the person wants to engage; and avoidance tendencies, involving withdrawal from behaviors a person wants to avoid. As mentioned in Chapter 7, a person is in conflict when he or she must choose (1) between two positive activities *(approach-approach conflict),* such as going to a party or attending a film; (2) between two negative activities *(avoidance-avoidance conflict),* such as mowing the lawn or taking out the trash; or (3) whether to do something that has both positive and negative aspects *(approach-avoidance conflict),* such as deciding whether to be with someone who is sexually attractive but not very considerate.

Perhaps the most difficult situations to resolve are those known as double approach-avoidance conflicts. Here the person faces two alternatives, each of which has both positive and negative features. If you have ever had to make a choice about which of two restaurants to visit when one is nearby but expensive while the other is less costly but inconveniently located, you know how it feels to be in such a conflict. Choosing which college to attend often results in double (or triple) approach-avoidance conflicts because one school may be prestigious but very large and impersonal, while another is smaller and friendlier but less well known for quality.

Much as Freud had done, Dollard and Miller emphasized the role of conflict and anxiety in the appearance of behavior disorders, but they employed learning theory terminology. Thus, in their terms, a "neurotic" conflict could be analyzed as follows: A person's approach tendency toward a member of the opposite sex may be thwarted by a simultaneous avoidance tendency, such as anxiety based on negative social experiences or parental teachings against the expression of sexual desires. The closer the person gets to contact with the feared-yet-desired situation, the stronger the avoidance tendency becomes, and the individual retreats, thus reducing anxiety but allowing the approach tendency to reappear. The person in such a conflict may seesaw between approach and avoidance. In some cases he or she may experience such great psychological discomfort that therapy is needed to strengthen the approach tendencies or reduce the avoidance tendencies, or both.

The Role of Operant Conditioning

Although Dollard and Miller's system eliminated some of Freud's intrapsychic ideas, it retained other concepts such as "drive" and "anxiety." Thus, their theory depended to some extent on hypothesized internal processes and mechanisms to account for personality. Quite a different learning approach has been presented by the well-known American psychologist B. F. Skinner. He views personality as learned, but assumes that inferred constructs such as "anxiety," "drive," "motive," "conflict," "need," and the like, are unnecessary to account for and understand the learning involved. Instead, Skinner asserts that careful observation of and experimentation with the learned relationships between environmental stimuli and observable behavior will ultimately allow for a complete picture of the development, maintenance, and alteration of human behavior (recall here the discussion in Chapter 4 of operant conditioning, which is central to Skinner's view of behavior). This means that instead of theorizing about personality (behavior) and introducing unobservable constructs (such as ego, drive, or trait) to explain it, one should simply observe the ways in which behavior relates to its consequences and then describe these relationships. This method of learning about behavior is called *functional analysis* because it involves analyzing the causative, or functional, relationships between the environment and behavior.

As an example of how Skinner's functional analytic approach eliminates inferred constructs, let us consider the notion of motive or need. Dispositional theorists assume that individuals "have" needs or motives whose existence is inferred from behavior — for example, aggressive behavior reflects the need for dominance. Skinner would focus instead on the functional relationship between, say, aggressive behavior and its consequences. He would argue that a person's aggressive behavior simply reflects the fact that such behavior has in the past been rewarded or reinforced — that is, has been operantly conditioned. No further explanation in terms of internal dispositions is necessary. Thus, Skinner would say that the person in question has *learned* through operant conditioning to behave aggressively, not that he or she "has" a need to be aggressive.

The same approach can be used when talking about concepts like drive. Instead of saying that a person who has not eaten in 48 hours "has" a strong hunger drive, you could simply observe that after such deprivation food is a stronger reward than if no deprivation had occurred. "Hunger" can then be defined not in terms of "drive strength" but in terms of the number of hours since the person's last meal.

Similarly, behavior disorders may be understood without reference to inferred constructs. A person who spends the day silently staring into space, fails to maintain control over bowels and bladder, and must be fed from a spoon would not be considered "psychotic," "regressed," or "mentally ill." Instead, Skinner's version of the learning approach to personality would assume that the individual had gradually developed these "disordered" behaviors as a function of various kinds of reinforcement, probably over a long period of time.

Like other versions of learning theory, Skinner's approach to personality not only promotes understanding of the ways in which behavior is learned (how it relates to its environment) but also leads directly and logically to appropriate "treatment" procedures. As one might expect, these procedures tend to focus on observable behaviors as "treatment targets" and on the use of operant conditioning principles in the production of behavior change (see Chapter 12).

The Role of Cognition and Imitation

Although Skinner's functional analytic approach is influential and has attracted many ardent followers, it has also provoked a considerable amount of antagonistic reaction. Many theorists, even within the learning camp, feel that Skinner pays too little attention to cognitive or symbolic processes in the development and maintenance of personality (behavior). Accordingly, several alternative *social learning* theories have appeared.

Expectancy and Locus of Control

The role of cognitive variables has a central place in the social learning theory of Julian B. Rotter, who places strong emphasis on the importance of *expectancies* in the development, maintenance, and alteration of behavior. In Rotter's system, the prob-

TABLE 9-5 Testing for Locus of Control

Instructions: Pick the response that better describes your belief.

1. Success on the job is largely a matter of:
   a. being in the right place at the right time
   b. hard work and dedication
2. Doing well on your psychology final exam will depend heavily upon:
   a. finding sufficient time to study
   b. the degree to which the questions happen to match up with what you know
3. Criminals are:
   a. born, not made — victims of fate
   b. people who deliberately chose to engage in illegal acts ·
4. In general, I:
   a. control my own destiny
   b. believe in luck

Here are a few test items stimilar to those on the I-E scale developed by Julian Rotter. You should have no trouble telling which alternative suggests internal versus external control. People who are at the external end of the scale believe that they have little control over life events. Getting such people to do things to help themselves or improve their circumstances can be difficult. Those at the internal end of the scale believe that they are the masters of their own fate: Improving their circumstances is simply a matter of working hard.

ANDY CAPP by Reggie Smythe. © 1980 Daily Mirror Newspapers, Ltd. Dist. Field Newspaper Syndicate.

Andy is complaining that Flo uses internal attribution when things go well and external attribution when things go poorly. She credits herself or attributes good fortune to her own ability, but blames others, particularly Andy, when things go wrong. This is a natural tendency, but it can lead to illogical thinking and illogical behavior. After all, sometimes we do deserve the blame and others the credit. The depressed person typically thinks just the opposite of Flo—blaming himself or herself for all bad things and blaming others if things go right or attributing the success to luck or chance. We have here a joining of locus of control theory with attribution theory (see Chapter 10).

ability that a given behavior will occur is dependent on (1) what the person expects will happen following the response and (2) the value the person places upon that outcome. Thus, a person will pay for a ticket if he or she expects that this will result in admission to a movie theater (outcome) and if the film being shown is of interest (value). Rotter assumes that the expectancies and values that influence, organize, and alter behavior (personality) are a part of each person's knowledge base, acquired through learning. Therefore, in order to "have" an expectancy about an outcome or make a judgment regarding its value, a person must have had some direct or vicarious experience with equivalent or similar situations in the past. What you know, a cognitive concept, becomes critical.

One of the best-known products of Rotter's expectancy-oriented theorizing has been the concept of generalized expectancies, particularly as it applies to people's perception of how events are controlled. Rotter developed a test called the *Internal-External Locus of Control Scale* (also known as the I-E or the LOC scale). In simplest terms, it measures the degree to which individuals generally expect the things that happen to them to be determined primarily by their own efforts (internal control) or by factors beyond their control (external control). A considerable amount of research has been devoted to an attempt to determine the importance of locus of control as a personality dimension (see Table 9–5).

Observation and Imitation

Another influential cognitive social learning theorist is Albert Bandura, a Stanford University psy-

chologist whose prolific writing has led to a great deal of research about the ways in which cognitive activity and social influences contribute to learning.

Bandura is probably best known for his work on *observational learning,* in which he has shown that human beings can learn new behaviors without obvious reward or reinforcement and even without the

Albert Bandura.

FIGURE 9–4 Learning aggression by imitation

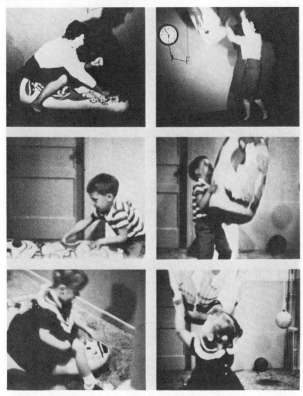 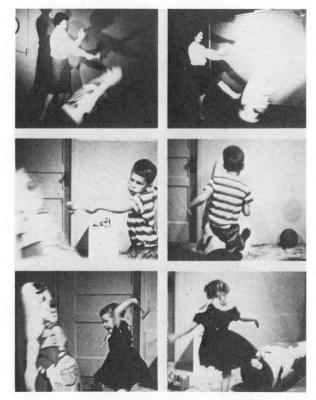

In specialized situations, there is little doubt that children will imitate the aggressive actions of adult models. Here are some pictures from a study by Bandura, Ross, and Ross (1963) that is now a classic. In the top row an adult model exhibits four different ways to hurt a Bobo clown doll. The next two rows show a boy and a girl duplicating the model's efforts.

opportunity to practice. All that may be required is for the person to observe another individual (called a *model*) engage in the to-be-learned behavior; later, especially if the model was rewarded for his or her performance, the observer may also display the new response. For example, children may learn how to display aggression by observing someone else do so. In one well-known experiment (see Figure 9–4) Bandura and his colleagues arranged for preschool children to observe models either vigorously attacking or sitting quietly near an inflatable Bobo clown doll. In subsequent tests, the children who observed aggression tended to match the model's behavior quite precisely, while those who had seen a passive model tended to be nonaggressive.

Thus, a major thrust of Bandura's theory is its emphasis upon vicarious processes—processes involving observation and imitation of others. For Bandura, personality develops not only as a function of what we learn directly (through classical or operant conditioning) but also through observation of other people's behavior and its consequences and an understanding of how those consequences could apply

to us. According to Bandura, vicarious processes can result in a wide variety of behavioral effects, including acquisition of new responses, as in the Bobo experiment; inhibition or disinhibition of already learned behaviors, as when a person violates a "Don't Walk" sign after watching someone else do so; and facilitation or prompting of behavior, as when, during gasoline shortages, a long line of cars forms at a closed station after a single prankster pulls up to the pumps.

Note that although Bandura's theory emphasizes the role of observational and cognitive processes in learning, it also recognizes the importance of both social and primary reinforcement as factors influencing the continued performance of new or altered behaviors. Thus, a person may learn how to meet members of the opposite sex by watching others do so successfully, but unless the approach actually leads to positive consequences (once in a while, at least), it will ultimately be abandoned.

In fact, in his more recent writings, Bandura has emphasized that the development of and changes in human behavior are caused by a combination of three factors, all of which are continuously interacting.

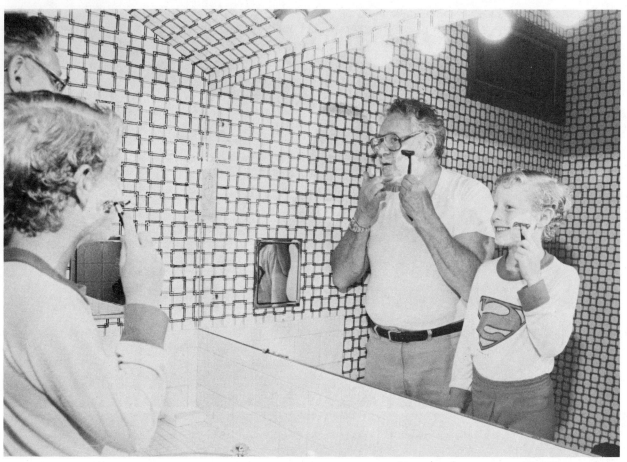

For social learning theorists, this would be an example of learning by imitation. Freudians, on the other hand, would view the situation as an example of identification with the same-sexed parent.

These three factors include (1) what people think, perceive, know, and expect (*cognitive* variables); (2) what people actually do (*behavioral* variables); and (3) what happens to people (*environmental* variables). Bandura (1978) refers to this process as *reciprocal determinism* and notes that watching television provides an everyday example. The viewer's cognitions (that is, preferences) influence the channel-choosing (the behavior), which determines the program (environmental stimulation) that appears on the screen. Such behavioral choices serve to strengthen certain cognitions (for example, "I like that show"). While *every* viewer of the same program sees the same environmental stimuli, each viewer's cognitions (perceptions, biases, and so on) may alter the meaning of the program somewhat for him or her. Further, the quality of a given program (environment) may influence certain cognitions (for example, "That show is no good anymore"), which in turn change future channel-selection behaviors and, thus, may help to alter the TV environment by getting the show off the air. All three variables are reciprocally determined; they influence and are influenced by the others.

Another important feature of Bandura's model is that the importance of each of the three factors can vary from time to time and from person to person. For example, in dealing with an impending automobile accident, most drivers' behavior will be influenced mainly by the external environment (that is, the location, direction, and speed of the other car). In dealing with a difficult math problem, however, a person's behavior will be partly a function of the details of the task (the environment) and partly a function of how confident she or he feels about successfully completing it (a cognitive variable). Bandura suggests that, in some situations, a person's feeling of *self-efficacy*—the learned expectation that one will succeed at something—may overcome environmental obstacles and be more influential than anything else in determining how the individual will behave.

Kids Who Watch TV—They'd Rather Fight
By RONALD KOTULAK

HOUSTON—Young children who watch excessive amounts of television may become more aggressive, according to a husband and wife team of Yale University researchers.

A year-long study of 140 3- and 4-year-old youngsters is the first to show that even very young children can be adversely affected by too much TV viewing, the couple said at the 145th meeting of the American Association for the Advancement of Science.

One surprising finding of the study is that programs other than those featuring violence also raise aggression levels in children, said Dr. Jerome L. Singer of Yale's Family Television Research and Consultation Center.

While boys are more affected by action or detective shows that feature violence, girls are influenced by game shows and certain situation comedy programs, he said.

The game shows and other programs depict a lot of frenetic activity, such as yelling, jumping up and down, screaming, crying, and kissing, he said.

Excessive viewing of these shows led to a 10- to 20-per-cent increase in the amount of aggression displayed by the youngsters, he said.

The type of aggression measured included pushing, shoving, kicking, and fighting not part of a game.

The children watched television for an average of 23 hours a week. The most avid fan was a youngster who watched 72 hours of TV a week.

The major causative factor in homes where children showed the most aggression was lack of parental control over TV sets, Singer said. These parents didn't seem to care how much TV the children watched or what programs they saw.

Dr. Dorothy G. Singer said the researchers are not recommending that parents get rid of TV sets, but that they be more selective about what children watch.

Chicago Tribune
January 9, 1979

Study Links Publicity, Murder-Suicides

WASHINGTON (UPI)—Newspaper publicity about murder-suicides seems to trigger an increase in similar acts disguised as non-commercial airplane accidents, a California sociologist reported.

David P. Phillips found in a five-year study that multi-fatality crashes of private and business aircraft increased sharply three days after widely publicized murder-suicides.

Phillips, of the University of California at San Diego, . . . conducted the study after research by others found that suicides and motor vehicle accidents increase following publicized suicides.

"These findings suggest that suicide stories help to trigger a rise in suicides, some of which are disguised as motor-vehicle accidents," Phillips said.

"One type of disguised murder-suicide may occur when a pilot deliberately crashes an airplane with passengers on board," he said. "If murder-suicides trigger subsequent murder-suicides, fatal aircraft accidents should increase sharply and briefly just after such stories are published."

Phillips said his preliminary research indicated non-commercial airplane fatalities follow a pattern similar to those involving motor vehicles, and rise to a peak on the third day after the publicized death.

"On the basis of these earlier studies, I predicted that a day-three peak should also be found in the study period, 1968 to 1973," he wrote. "As predicted, aircraft fatalities increased sharply on day three after publicized murder-suicides."

He found airplane fatalities on the third day nearly doubled the average daily number of deaths for a 14-day period.

Phillips studied states in which the most civilian aircraft are operated, examined the largest newspapers from those states, and found: "The amount of newspaper publicity devoted to a murder-suicide was strongly correlated with the number of multi-fatality crashes following the story." . . .

Rocky Mountain News, *Denver*
August 20, 1978

Bandura (1980) points out that his theory sees human beings as neither totally in control of all aspects of their behavior and their environment nor totally at the mercy of either, but as some of both.

Person-Situation Interactions

A related and perhaps even more comprehensive social learning theory of personality has been outlined by Walter Mischel, a colleague of Bandura at Stanford University. Mischel (1978) points out that understanding human behavior requires us to study not only what people do and the environments in which they do it, but also such subtle factors as:

Social learning refers to knowledge acquired by observing others, knowledge that can lead to imitation of what was observed. A great deal of your knowledge base was acquired in this vicarious way, such as when you observe (read about) behavior through TV, newspapers, and books. Because you can surely learn about the bad things that others do, say by seeing violence on TV, some people would have censorship of what is available to you. Should newspapers downplay or even not report violence or suicides because research indicates such behavior will be imitated by others?

Highlight 9–2

Parents as Models

The social learning approach to personality places great emphasis upon learning by observing others. We tend to imitate behaviors we observe others doing, especially if it seems as if others are benefiting from or being rewarded by these behaviors. The behavior of parents before their children is critical here. The theory has been used to argue that drug and alcohol problems in young people have their roots in the home when children observe their parents drinking and taking pills for everything imaginable. The theory has also been used to buttress the argument against depicting violence on TV and to insist that, if violence is shown, the villain always lose in the end. The latter position draws on the principle that we also learn *not* to do things which we observe have led to punishments for others. Both good and bad forms of behavior can be learned by observation. The advertisement here, sponsored by a major distiller of alcohol, picks up on this theme.

"I have a headache, I'd better take a couple of jelly beans."

The Family Circus by Bil Keane, reprinted courtesy The Register and Tribune Syndicate, Inc.

THEY LEARNED TO TALK AT YOUR KNEE.

THEY'LL LEARN TO DRINK AT YOUR ELBOW.

Your children imitate you.
Good and bad.
    And they'll get their first
lessons in drinking from you.
    During your cocktail hour.
    At your parties.
    And your drinking habits
will be theirs when they're old
enough to drink.
    Make sure they're good ones.

Seagram
Distillers Company.

1. The range of thoughts and actions of which a person is capable (for example, a person behaves unassertively; is it because he or she does not know how to be assertive?).
2. The ways in which the person organizes or tends to perceive the environment (for example, "defensive" persons may tend to interpret most remarks made by others as critical of them).
3. The expectations the person has about the outcome of her or his behavior and environmental events (for example, a person may come to believe that his or her best efforts in a given situation are never going to be good enough or that most problems he or she faces will never be solved).
4. The value the person places on the consequences of her or his behavior (for example, a student will probably not study very hard if good grades are not valued).
5. The ways in which the person engages in *self-regulation*. This involves goals the person sets (for example, realistic versus unrealistic) and his or her criteria for self-reward (is the person easily satisfied with himself or herself or is he or she liberal with self-blame and stingy with self-praise?). Self-regulation also involves the person's ability to adjust his or her behavior to accommodate changing circumstances (for example, does the person persist in making a request after it has been turned down, or does he or she try alternative strategies?). Finally, self-regulation involves the person's ability to make and

carry out *plans* (for example, to engage in a logical sequence of behaviors resulting in a goal).

Like Bandura's view, Mischel's theory emphasizes that people are neither passive recipients of environmental forces not wholly independent of those forces; instead, they are seen as actively participating in a constant interplay between themselves and the situations in which they find themselves.

In this regard, cognitive social learning approaches to personality provide an important and valuable middle ground between "person-oriented" theories (such as dispositional theories, which see human behavior as controlled mainly by traits and other variables inside the person) and "situation-oriented" theories (such as operant conditioning, which see behavior as controlled mainly by reinforcement, punishment, and features of the environment). Bandura, Mischel, Rotter, and other cognitively oriented learning theorists do not seek to resolve the person-situation debate by proving the value of one side *or* the other. Instead, they point out the need to recognize and attempt to understand the complex interaction of both kinds of variables.

An important implication of this "interactionist" view is that it may not be possible to study personality *per se*. Instead, a meaningful understanding may require focusing upon *person-situation interactions*. For example, Mischel (1973) suggests that instead of describing someone as "aggressive" (a personality trait label), it would be more valuable to know, for example, that a particular person is *verbally* abusive in situations in which his or her job competency is questioned, but is physically abusive when athletic performance is criticized.

Learning Approaches to Personality Assessment

We noted earlier that the various strategies employed by dispositional and psychodynamic personality theories to measure personality—paper-and-pencil tests, dream analysis, projective techniques—assumed that a person's responses to assessment procedures provide indications or *signs* of underlying personality traits or characteristics. Learning approaches to personality measurement begin with radically different assumptions. Because they view behavior and personality as virtually identical, learning views are not concerned with underlying traits or constructs. Instead, the focus is on careful, systematic attempts to assess (1) how the person in question behaves and (2) the environmental and other circumstances that influence that behavior.

Thus, an individual's response to Rorschach inkblot cards would be assumed to tell us not about

unconscious processes but about how that person behaves during psychological testing. In other words, the learning approach treats responses to any personality assessment procedure as a behavior *sample* that is useful in making predictions about future behavior in similar or related circumstances, not as a sign of broad, generalized personality characteristics (see Appendix C). Because of this orientation, learning procedures tend to focus on direct or indirect observation of behavior rather than on traditional personality tests.

The questionnaires that are used tend to be direct and straightforward, asking the respondents simply to provide information about the effects of environmental stimuli on their behavior. Examples of this sort of "test" are the Fear Survey Schedule (Geer, 1965; and Wolpe & Lang, 1964), which simply asks persons to rate the degree to which they fear a wide variety of objects and situations, and the Reinforcement Survey Schedule (Cautela & Kastenbaum, 1967), which asks respondents to rate the degree to which they enjoy a variety of activities, such as dancing, talking to friends, and eating.

"They've always been such nice neighbors—friendly, quiet. Up until today, of course."

The New Yorker, June 9, 1980. Drawing by Ziegler; © 1980 The New Yorker Magazine, Inc.

What are your neighbors *really* like? Are they the quiet, friendly people you have thought, or are they the wild and violent people you see in the shoot-out. The interactionist position says there is no simple answer to the question of what actually constitutes personality. They stress that behavior is a joint product of a person's characteristics and the environmental situation in which the person is behaving. So, sometimes the neighbors are nice and quiet and sometimes they are wild and violent. The goal of psychology is to develop ways of describing and predicting these interactions.

Learning theorists also employ several types of direct behavioral observation procedures. Some ask the individual to act as his or her own observer. This technique is commonly used when the particular interest is in adult behaviors that occur in the natural environment. Examples of the procedure — called *self-monitoring* — include asking individuals to keep records of the number of cigarettes they smoke or the frequency and duration of sleep disturbances. A clinician who employs such assessment techniques may seek to understand a client's "depression" or "anxiety attacks" by asking the person to specify the behaviors, feelings, and thoughts that make up such states and to keep track of the frequency of their occurrence and the environmental conditions that precede, accompany, and follow them.

This type of personality assessment leads to precise statements about behavior ("This person behaves in a depressed fashion on the average of three times per week") instead of labels ("This person is depressive"). Further, the technique can provide clues to the factors that are contributing to the problem. For example, a careful behavioral analysis of "depression" often reveals that episodes of discomfort tend to be associated with periods during which the client does not have access to very many enjoyable activities. An increase in such activities might thus become part of an overall treatment program.

In other forms of learning-oriented personality assessment, specially trained personnel make systematic observations of the behavior of children or adults. The method may simply involve watching a child in a large playroom containing a wide variety of toys, games, and other materials. Recording the relative amounts of time the child spends engaged in each of the various activities available allows the observer to determine the kinds of things that interest the child (and that might thus be usable as rewards in a later behavior-change program). Note again that instead of attempting to identify the child's internal needs, traits, or motives, the learning approach seeks to identify the external stimuli that influence behavior for each person.

Some Problems with Learning Theories

Learning theories of personality have been criticized mainly on the grounds that their emphasis on learning as the basis for behavior results in a narrowing of their perspective. This argument has been blunted somewhat by the more recent emphasis on cognitive processes in the social learning theories, but some critics still point out that learning theories pay too little attention to the influence of hereditary, physiological, and constitutional factors in the determination of human behavior. Others note that experimental evidence for various learning principles is not free from controversy and that these principles are really not as firmly established as learning theorists would have us believe.

Additional criticism has been aimed at the laboratory data cited in support of learning theories of personality. For example, even where learning phenomena are well established through research on animals, they may not be analogous to the way human beings learn. A cat faced with a difficult or insoluble task may display a bizarre behavior pattern known as experimental neurosis, but human neurotic behavior may not develop in the same way. Indeed, even if learning theory treatments *resolve* a personality problem, that problem may not have developed in accordance with learning principles.

Another problem involves the tendency of some learning theory assessments of personality to be based upon observation of people's behavior in contrived settings (such as in a laboratory in which subjects are asked to role-play being assertive), which may or may not reflect the ways people would behave in natural settings.

Finally, many people simply cannot accept thinking of human behavior as being systematically related to its environment in accordance with a set of laboratory-based principles. They interpret learning theory to imply that human personality develops, changes, and guides behavior in ways that exclude free will, self-determination, and that elusive quality called humanness. Learning theorists see this objection as a misconstrual of their position, but the humanism-behaviorism issue (see Chapter 1) remains a point of lively debate.

Phenomenological Theories

So far we have discussed personality theories that view human behavior as primarily influenced by (1) underlying traits or needs, (2) intrapsychic events and conflicts, and (3) direct or vicarious learning. A fourth group, called *phenomenological theories*, rejects many of the basic assumptions of the other three approaches. In this approach the behavior of each human being at any given moment is seen as determined primarily by that particular person's perception of the world. In other words, phenomenological theories assume that each person is unique because his or her view of the world's phenomena — that is, of reality — is a little different from anyone else's and that each person's behavior reflects that view of the phenomena from moment to moment. Thus, for example, one person may react favorably to a political speech and plan to vote for the speaker, while another person who hears the same speech may decide to vote for the speaker's opponent. Phenomenologists view these divergent reactions as due not to the listener's personality traits, ego development, or reinforcement history, but to his or her individual perceptions of the candidate who was speaking.

From this perspective we are not passive "carriers" of personality or mere recipients of reinforcement. Rather, emphasis is upon the active, thinking nature of human beings, upon their ability to make plans and choices about their behavior, and upon the fact that each person is ultimately responsibile for his or her own actions. Although phenomenological theories recognize the existence of biological needs, these are deemphasized in considering personality and its development. Instead, these theories assume that people are born with a potential for growth that provides the impetus for behavior. Each person is seen as having an innate tendency to grow and develop into a fully mature individual, just as a seed contains the potential to be a flower. In contrast to Freud, who saw people as motivated by crude instinctual desires, phenomenological theorists view the individual as a basically good organism that will naturally strive for the attainment of love, joy, creativity, harmony, and other positive goals.

Perhaps the most important implication of the phenomenological view of personality development, assessment, and change is that no one can truly understand another's behavior unless he or she can perceive the world through that person's eyes. Accordingly, phenomenological theories, like learning theories, reject the concept of mental illness and other pejorative labels for behavior that appears strange, unusual, or unexpected. Instead, they assume that all human activity is normal, rational, and sensible *when viewed from the point of view of the person being observed.* Thus, people who are violently hostile toward others are seen not as "sick" or "disordered" but as simply acting in accordance with their perceptions of other people. If you could "get inside their heads" you would understand their behavior because you could see the world as they do.

Phenomenological theories have evolved from several sources. In part, they represent a reaction against Freud. In his rejection of the importance of instincts and his emphasis on the uniqueness of the individual and his or her conceptions of the world, Adler anticipated phenomenological theories. Attention to the individual's perception of reality also was prompted in part by the existential philosophies of Heidegger, Kierkegaard, Sartre, and Camus, which assert that the meaning and value of life and everything in it is not intrinsic but is provided by the perceiver. For example, a person is not "actually" beautiful or ugly; these qualities can be assigned only when someone else sees and reacts to the person in

question. Thus, a different "reality" is in the eye of each beholder. This focus on the individual's view of reality was also sharpened by the writings of the Gestalt psychologists, who, as we saw in Chapter 3, emphasized that the human perceiver is an active participant in viewing the world, not just a passive receiver.

Rogers' Self Theory

Perhaps the best-known example of phenomenological approaches to personality is the **self theory** of the American psychologist Carl Rogers. Many of Rogers' basic propositions about personality are similar to those of other phenomenologists. For example, these statements from Rogers' writings are characteristic of all phenomenological theories: "Every individual exists in a continually changing world of experience of which he is the center." "The organism reacts to the field as it is experienced and perceived. This perceptual field is, for the individual, 'reality.' " "The organism reacts as an organized whole to this phenomenal field."

Rogers assumes that the single innate human motive is the tendency toward "self-actualization" and that this concept is sufficient to account for the appearance of all human behavior, from the most fundamental food-seeking to the most sublime acts

Carl Rogers

of artistic creativity. He has defined this innate quality as "the directional trend which is evident in all organic and human life — the urge to expand, extend, develop, mature — the tendency to express and activate all the capacities of the organism" (Rogers, 1961). Given this basic motive, Rogers views human personality (as reflected in behavior) as the efforts of individuals to actualize themselves within the world as they view it.

As the person develops and interacts with the environment he or she begins to differentiate between the environment and the self. In other words, each of us becomes aware of a part of our experience that we recognize as "I" or "me." According to Rogers, all of a person's experiences, including self experiences, are evaluated as positive or negative. The person thus evaluates experiences according to whether they are consistent or inconsistent with self-enhancement or self-actualization. Experiences are evaluated partly in terms of direct or *organismic* feelings, as when a child evaluates the experience of ice cream positively simply because of its taste; and partly through the influence of others, as when a young boy negatively evaluates the experience of stimulating his genitals even though it "feels good" because his mother told him the behavior was "bad."

Thus, the self or self-concept emerges not merely as a set of experiences but as a set of evaluated experiences, and the positive or negative value assigned to these experiences is influenced by the combination of direct evaluations and evaluations provided by other individuals.

Positive Self-Regard

Rogers postulates that human beings tend to act in ways that produce positive regard (good evaluations) from others and that this allows them to have positive self-regard. When a person's behavior results in positive direct (organismic) experiences as well as positive regard from others, there is no problem. For example, a child practices reading skills and experiences not only positive direct feelings based upon gaining competence but also positive regard from a parent, such as "I am so proud of you." The result will probably be a positively evaluated self-experience, such as "I like to read." Here, the positive direct organismic experience is in accord with, or as Rogers puts it, is congruent with, the positive self-experience, and the child accurately perceives both its own behavior and its evaluation of it (see "Parent Effectiveness Training" in the "What Does It Mean?" section.)

However, as in the example of the boy touching his genitals, some behavior may produce a positive organismic experience but a negative reaction from others. When this happens, especially when it happens early in life, the evaluations of others may overwhelm the individual's direct evaluation. Then, instead of developing a self-experience like "I enjoy masturbation but mother is opposed," the person may acquire the self-experience "I do not want to masturbate." Rogers theorizes that this uncomfortable discrepancy (or incongruity) between organismic experiences and self-experiences is caused by what he calls *conditions of worth* — feelings that one can receive positive regard from others (and, ultimately, from the self) only on a conditional basis, that is, when one behaves in certain prescribed ways. Conditions of worth are usually set up first by parents and others, but later by the self.

According to Rogers, recognition that one's feelings and/or behavior do not fulfill conditions of worth results in anxiety over potential loss of positive regard. To prevent this, one may seek to reduce incongruity by distorting or misperceiving reality or one's own experience of it so that it fits the self-concept. For example, children are usually taught to behave in ways "appropriate" to their sex and may receive positive evaluations only when they display such behavior. Thus, when a mother scolds her little boy for displaying emotional behavior (such as crying) and praises him for unemotional "masculine" reactions, she may be setting up conditions of worth. If the child actually feels better when he expresses strong emotions than when he suppresses them, he may have to discount his experiences in order to conform to the requirements of the situation. Or he may distort his own personal reality — the fact that he feels better when expressing his emotions — by maintaining that anyone who is emotional is weak.

Rogers thinks that behavior disorders result from the individual's attempts to reduce incongruity by altering actual feelings and experiences so that they approximate the self-concept. The more incongruity and distortion, the more severe the disorder. Rogers' approach to treatment of psychological problems is aimed at helping people reduce incongruity without distorting reality (see Chapter 12).

Learning To Feel Feelings

Many of Rogers' notions about personality and personality change are similar to those associated with the Gestalt therapy of Frederick S. (Fritz) Perls. Although Perls used terms and procedures substantially different from Rogers', and although he focused more on using personality-growth experiences than on articulating a formal, researchable personality theory, the basic ideas of Perls and Rogers are very similar. Perls believed that behavior problems arise when people deny or disown their feelings or experiences (that is, are incongruent, in Rogers' terms) or when they claim as their own feelings or ideas they have borrowed from others. Gestalt therapy, then, is oriented toward helping persons take responsibility for themselves and experience or "get in touch" with genuine feelings. It is assumed that when this occurs it is possible for individuals to face and resolve conflicts and internal inconsistencies of which they had been unaware. Application of the concepts and principles enunciated by Rogers and Perls (among others) prompted the widespread interest in and the rapid growth of a wide variety of encounter and sensitivity groups (see Chapter 12).

Growth Toward Self-Actualization

Another major phenomenological theorist is Abraham Maslow (1962), whose theory of needs was discussed in Chapter 7. Maslow based his theory on the notion that human beings are innately good and that the ultimate goal of human effort is fulfillment, growth, and happiness. Maslow argues that each person has a hierarchy of needs (physiological, safety, love, self-esteem, and self-actualization), each one of which must be met before the next assumes control of behavior. In addition, Maslow takes into account

TABLE 9-6 Some Attributes of the Self-Actualized Person

1. Able to perceive reality accurately and efficiently.
2. Accepting of self, of others, and of the world.
3. Spontaneous and natural, particularly in thought and emotion.
4. Problem-centered: concerned with problems outside themselves and capable of retaining a broad perspective.
5. Need and desire solitude and privacy; can rely on their own potentialities and resources.
6. Autonomous: relatively independent of extrinsic satisfactions, for example, acceptance or popularity.
7. Capable of a continued freshness of appreciation of even the simplest, most commonplace experiences (for example, a sunset, a flower, or another person).
8. Experience "mystic" or "oceanic" feelings in which they feel out of time and place and at one with nature.
9. Have a sense of identification with mankind as a whole.
10. Form their deepest ties with relatively few others.
11. Truly democratic; unprejudiced and respectful of all others.
12. Ethical, able to discriminate between means and ends.
13. Thoughtful, philosophical, unhostile sense of humor; laugh at the human condition, not at a particular individual.
14. Creative and inventive, not necessarily possessing great talents, but a naive and unspoiled freshness of approach.
15. Capable of some detachment from the culture in which they live, recognizing the necessity for change and improvement.

TABLE 9-7 Sample Items from the Personal Orientation Inventory

Instruction: Select the answer that most accurately describes you.

1. a. I prefer to save good things for future use.
   b. I prefer to use good things now.
2. a. My moral values are dictated by society.
   b. My moral values are self-determined.
3. a. I often make my decisions spontaneously.
   b. I seldom make my decisions spontaneously.
4. a. It is important that others accept my point of view.
   b. It is not necessary for others to accept my point of view.
5. a. I try to be sincere but I sometimes fail.
   b. I try to be sincere and I am sincere.
6. a. I have a problem in fusing sex and love.
   b. I have no problem in fusing sex and love.
7. a. People are both good and evil.
   b. People are not both good and evil.
8. a. I find some people who are stupid and uninteresting.
   b. I never find any people who are stupid and uninteresting.
9. a. I am afraid to be tender.
   b. I am not afraid to be tender.

The Personal Orientation Inventory (Shostrum, 1963) is often used by phenomenological researchers to assess self-actualization. Table 9–6 lists the characteristics Maslow identifies with self-actualized people. Can you figure out what Maslow would consider to be the "self-actualized" answers to the above items? The answers are given on page 352.

aesthetic needs, or the desire for structure, order, and symmetry in the world about us.

A human being's highest goal is to become self-actualized. One cannot accomplish self-actualization, however, until one has structured one's world so that the deficiency or *D-needs* (physiological, safety, love, and most critically, self-esteem needs) can be easily satisfied. Working toward self-actualization, according to Maslow, involves a fundamental shift in outlook, or phenomenology (see Table 9–6). Maslow saw the process as involving a change in one's values and mode of cognition, away from the D-needs and toward what he called *metaneeds* or *B-values* (being values). D-needs emphasize the negative side of life — its deficiencies. B-values focus on the positive side of life, on the here and now, and on the qualities of truth, justice, beauty, and goodness. A person's D-needs must be under control before he or she can really address the metaneeds. Of course, no one can maintain B-value motivation continuously because to survive human beings periodically must attend to their lower-level D-needs.

Moments of pure B-value control are called peak experiences. These times are marked by rap-

"Self-Actualized" Answers

1, b	6, a
2, b	7, a
3, a	8, a
4, b	9, b
5, b	

turous feelings of excitement and great tension, or peace, tranquillity, and a deep sense of relaxation. Everyone enjoys peak experiences at some time or another, and these experiences help us to discover our identities and to push us toward self-actualization. Presumably persons who have peak experiences frequently and who have established their identities are self-actualized.

Maslow has offered suggestions for people who wish to work toward self-actualization, and by examining the characteristics of self-actualized people (Table 9–6) you can probably think of others. The following are some possibilities:

1. Be more open to your own feelings—don't "bottle up" your emotions.
2. In each situation you find yourself, including difficult or stressful ones, try to take a positive perspective, asking yourself what you can get out of the moment that will benefit you in the long run.
3. Try to be less cynical and less critical of the world around you; stop making value judgments of everything and everybody around you; when you do criticize things, resolve to work toward changing them.
4. Set positive but realistic goals for yourself; then try hard to achieve them, but don't expect you will never fail.
5. Stand up for what you honestly believe is right, even if you are not following the crowd.
6. Allow some room in your life for spontaneity, and try new and unusual, perhaps even childish, things every now and then—reduce the rigidity of your behavior.
7. Be more candid with others about yourself, your strengths and weaknesses, your hopes and fears—share yourself more.

Phenomenological Approaches to Personality Assessment

Learning-oriented theorists, we have seen, tend to object to traditional personality assessment concepts. They take this position not only because they have doubts about the utility of such concepts but also because they are concerned that people should not be made to be passive objects of study, placed in an inferior social status, given possibly damaging personality labels, or assessed without regard for the physical and social environment in which they function.

Phenomenologically oriented theorists are in basic agreement with these concerns, although they propose solutions that are quite distinct from the learning approach. Some, such as Rogers, have argued against all forms of formal assessment on the grounds that the procedures used are inherently dehumanizing, take responsibility away from clients, and, if therapy is involved, may pose a threat to the quality of the therapist-client relationship.

Other phenomenologists suggest that assessment data *collected* through traditional means, such as tests, can sometimes be useful if they are employed in more humanistic ways. For example, test responses might be viewed as indicators of how the client looks at the world instead of being summarized in a score or plotted into a profile. Another approach is to discuss test responses with the client as a means of helping him or her engage in further self-exploration.

A third trend in phenomenological assessment has been the development of special test instruments which are thought to improve on traditional tests. An example is the Personal Orientation Inventory, sample items from which are given in Table 9–7.

Some Problems with Phenomenological Theories

Critics of the phenomenological approach, like those of other approaches we have presented, argue that it is too narrow. They point out that by restricting attention to immediate conscious experience as the main determinant of behavior, phenomenologists fail to recognize the importance of unconscious motivation, reinforcement contingencies, situational influences, and the like. Another criticism is that phenomenological theories do not elaborate sufficiently on the ways in which personality develops; postulating an innate tendency toward growth or actualization that is assumed to "drive" the organism can account for development but it does not explain it.

This brings up a related point of criticism: Phenomenological theories provide excellent descriptions of human behavior but are not usually focused on scientific exploration of the functional causes of behavior. To say that people behave as they do because of their unique perception of reality or because they are seeking to actualize themselves is not very informative in terms of promoting understanding of the variables that are important in the development and alteration of human behavior.

Finally, critics point out that many phenomenological concepts, like psychodynamic variables, are vague and therefore difficult or impossible to measure. Indeed, many phenomenological theorists (not including Rogers) see research on human behavior as relatively unimportant compared with activities designed to promote increased individual awareness. This emphasis on experiential rather than experimental evidence has made phenomenological theories unpopular with those who favor a careful, controlled research approach. When human beings are described as "a momentary precipitation at the vortex of a transient eddy of energy, in the enormous and incomprehensible sea of energy we call the universe" (Kempler, 1973), it is difficult to generate an easily testable hypothesis about their behavior.

SUMMARY

1. Personality is a broadly defined term that is used to describe and explain individual differences and stylistic consistencies in human behavior.

2. Intensive studies by psychologists over the last 100 years show that personality pervades every aspect of human behavior.

3. Many diverse theories have been proposed to explain personality. Each of them begins with a working definition of the concept and some basic assumptions about human behavior. There are many theoretical disagreements about the proper definition and the necessary assumptions.

4. These theories fall into four general classes: dispositional, psychodynamic, learning, and phenomenological. Each approach has strengths and weaknesses, and each seeks to provide a way of understanding personality as well as a means of assessing, investigating, and changing it.

5. Some dispositional theories assume that there is a small number of personality types, each of which has a unique set of general behavioral tendencies.

6. Dispositional theories see personality as being made up of characteristics, such as traits or needs, within the person which guide the individual's behavior.

7. Psychodynamic theories derive largely from Sigmund Freud's writings about psychoanalysis. They assume that personality is shaped by events and conflicts (many of them unconscious) that take place within the mind through the action of hypothesized internal structures known as the id, ego, and superego.

8. Learning theories base their approach on the assumption that personality is essentially the total of each individual's learned behaviors, not an independent structure that is merely reflected in behavior. According to learning theory, personality depends upon, and therefore may change with, the social context.

9. Dispositional, psychodynamic, and learning theories differ mainly in whether they emphasize traits and internal needs or environmental contingencies and cognitive variables as major determinants of an individual's personality. In contrast, phenomenological theories view personality as that pattern of cognitions and perceptions of reality, unique to each individual, which guides behavior. To understand someone's personality, you must be able to see things from that person's point of view.

10. Each kind of personality theory has shortcomings. No complete or universally accepted description and explanation of personality has yet been provided.

RECOMMENDED ADDITIONAL READINGS

Cartwright, D. S. *Theories and models of personality.* Dubuque, Iowa: W. C. Brown, 1979.

Hall, C. S., & Lindzey, G. *Theories of personality,* 3d ed. New York: Wiley, 1978.

Liebert, R. M., & Spiegler, M. D. *Personality: Strategies for the study of man,* 3d ed. Homewood, Ill.: Dorsey Press, 1978.

Mischel, W. *Introduction to personality,* 2d ed. New York: Holt, Rinehart and Winston, 1976.

Monte, C. F. *Beneath the mask: An introduction to theories of personality,* 2d ed. New York: Holt, Rinehart and Winston, 1980.

What Does It Mean?

So far, we have looked at the ways in which psychologists of several theoretical persuasions conceive of the concept called personality. In this section, we shall examine the ways in which the concepts advanced by personality theorists affect the everyday behavior of other psychologists and the rest of society. As we shall see, personality is anything but an "ivory tower" concept. Personality theories have had significant impact on the lives of millions of people, whether they are aware of it or not.

Perhaps because some theorists conceive of personality as a collection of actually existing traits or because they talk about "personality structure" or the "distorted" or "disorganized" personality, the personality concept has achieved the status of an entity or thing in the minds of many psychologists and certainly in the minds of the general public. As noted at the beginning of this chapter, personality is commonly thought of as something that a person either does or does not possess and that he or she can turn on or off like a tap.

Of course, this view distorts the writings of many careful theorists, but the notion persists that we all carry around inside us a thing called personality that determines our behavior. On recommendation forms for some graduate schools, for example, there is an item asking the professor to rate the student's personality on a five-point scale from "poor" to "excellent." Presumably, this rating is thought to relate in some way to the student's potential as a graduate student. Whether they conceive of personality in terms of

---

U.S. Assassin Syndrome: The Profile

By JANE E. BRODY

NEW YORK — National emphasis on civil liberties for the mentally ill, the lack of cultural restraints on expressions of hostility and the ready availability of pistols are combining to make assassination an increasingly common American event, say psychiatrists who have examined the problem.

Assassination and assassination attempts are more common here than in any other country, experts on violence maintain. In fact, assassination is the leading cause of death of American presidents in office.

Unlike other countries, where assassinations of heads of state are carried out either by political fanatics or in the course of a military coup, in this country nearly all assassins have been personally, not politically, motivated.

"Here, assassination is often the product of a single mentally disturbed person who is alienated from society, who feels like a zero, is wanted by no one and can't get a job," said Dr. Zigmond Lebensohn, a Washington psychiatrist. "We used to lock such people up, but our current legal attitude permits them all to wander about."

Dr. Shervert Frazier, psychiatrist in chief at McLean Hospital in Belmont, Mass., said:

"In this democracy, you can get away with a lot of things. Unlike the English, there is no cultural restraint against expressions of hostile feelings in public. Nor do we have much moral restraint in our society right now; people can do and do do anything they want to. Also, there are a lot of handguns around—one for every two persons."

Frazier is one of 27 experts preparing a report on the prediction of violent behavior for the National Academy of Sciences at the request of the Secret Service. The group held a three-day meeting on the subject last month.

Except in the case of the two Puerto Rican nationalists who tried to kill President Harry Truman in 1950, psychiatric studies of the backgrounds and motivations of assassins of American presidents and similar authority figures have shown that nearly all were mentally unstable, alienated persons who were failures in their own eyes. By killing a powerful and respected person, such as the president, they sought personal aggrandizement—status and fame—the analyses suggest.

Though some assassins professed affiliation with a particular political viewpoint, the groups they identified with did not regard them as representatives. In fact, the assassins often were rejected by their chosen group or had ended their affiliation with the group because of philosophical or tactical disagreements.

John W. Hinckley Jr., the 25-year-old son of a Denver oil company executive who has been charged with the attempt . . . on President Reagan's life, had either left or been expelled from the National Socialist Party of America, a neo-Nazi group, because Hinckley felt the group was not militant enough.

Hinckley has been described as a drifter with a history of psychiatric problems. He had attended college off and on over a six-year period, but had not completed his education. Nor did he have a job.

The suspect's profile fits the pattern of American assassins, according to Dr. Irving D. Harris, a Chicago psychiatrist

Is there an "assassination personality profile"? The recent attempt on President Ronald Reagan's life highlights the need to understand the causes of violent behavior. These experts each have an opinion or "explanation," ranging from birth order to

traits, types, or intrapsychic events, people want to assess the personality of other individuals, sometimes in order to describe them as they are and sometimes in order to make predictions about what they will do in the future.

Personality and Clinical Psychology

In clinical treatment settings, the therapist is interested in assessing personality in order to understand his or her client more fully. Naturally, the clinician's overall approach to personality will dictate the kinds of diagnostic and treatment procedures employed (see Chapters 11 and 12). Thus, when one chooses from among several sources of psychological assistance, it is important to know the personality strategy adopted by each practitioner.

However, the importance of personality in clinical psychology goes beyond attempts to assess the characteristics of individual clients. Considerable research activity focuses on exploring more general relationships between personality and the appearance of a variety of psychological

and bodily disorders. For example, about 25,000 Americans kill themselves every year; about 1000 of these are college students. Many were depressed prior to or at the time of suicide, but others apparently were not. Furthermore, countless thousands of people suffer depression but do not take their own lives. How can psychologists and others interested in suicide prevention tell who will commit suicide and who will not? Is there a "suicidal personality"?

Unfortunately, data from traditional personality tests, such as the Minnesota Multiphasic Personality Inventory (MMPI; see Appendix C), provide no clear answer. For example, one study found that in terms of MMPI scores persons who had only thought of suicide were more deviant than either those who had actually made a suicide attempt or "controls" who had never even thought of self-destruction. In other recent studies (for example, Clopton, Pallis, & Birtchnell, 1979) MMPI data collected prior to suicide attempts or successful suicides were not significantly different from those coming from nonsuicidal individuals. Similar results have been reported on the basis of Rorschach Inkblot Test data (Geller & Atkins, 1978).

U.S. Assassin Syndrome (continued)

who has made a study of the problem.

"America's assassins have almost always been younger children in their families, and in most cases they have had older brothers," Harris wrote in Psychology Today.

The list includes John Wilkes Booth, who killed President Lincoln; Charles Julius Guiteau, President Garfield's assassin; Leon Czolgosz, who shot President McKinley; Lee Harvey Oswald, who killed President Kennedy; Sirhan B. Sirhan, who killed Sen. Robert F. Kennedy in the course of his campaign for the presidential nomination, and Arthur H. Bremer, who shot Gov. George C. Wallace of Alabama during another presidential campaign.

"Their one-down family position predisposes them to rebel against authority and tradition, to resent their unequal status, and to wish to gain status by competing with the successful rival or by weakening the power of authority," Harris said of the assassins. "If these feelings find no constructive outlet, then a shortcut to fame may seem reasonable."

Harris has isolated two characteristics that he believes characterize American assassins: depression and despair over one's self-worth, and attempts to counter this despair by seeking a new self-image that commands attention and respect.

These characteristics are quite common and "fairly normal," the psychiatrist said. What differentiates the assassin is the route chosen. Rather than getting society to confer the new identity, the assassin makes himself a "hero" by becoming judge and executioner.

Dr. Lawrence Z. Freedman, psychiatrist at the University of Chicago, observed that American assassins were unable to avoid a sense of personal failure. "Ambitious out of all proportion to their prospects," he noted, "they were lonely and alienated from an immediate community of friends and sought their private solution in a massive assault on the head of the republic."

Other psychiatrists have emphasized the schizophrenic personalities of American assassins. According to the late Dr. Donald Hastings, who was director of psychiatry at the University of Minnesota, most assassins were of the "para-

noid" type who had lost contact with reality, harbored delusions of persecution and grandeur and had a strong hatred of authority.

"Hatred of a powerful father before whom a boy is helpless can become a murderous loathing," Hastings wrote. "In later years, the father is symbolized by figures of public authority. With the exception of John Wilkes Booth, all the assassins were 'little people,'" and even Booth was the lesser light in a family of actors more successful than he.

Freedman said that "in this country, the president is the locus of power, a highly visible celebrity and object of envy—all things the assassin is not." The real question, he said, is not why presidents are sometimes shot, but why they are not shot at more often. "The opportunities number in the billions," he remarked.

Frazier added that the loose cultural climate that seems to be encouraging self-expression through assassination tended to go in cycles.

The Denver Post
April 5, 1981

psychopathology. The fact that there is lack of agreement among them merely highlights the need for research on human **personality and the underlying causes of violent behavior.**

Personality Type Plays Key Role in Aging, Psychologist Reports
By MARGERY ROSE-CLAPP

The suicide rate among elderly men is four to five times greater than that for elderly women, according to a Denver psychologist.

Dr. Martin Dubin, a staff psychologist from Bethesda Community Mental Health Center, told a group of senior citizens . . . that drug and alcohol problems and loss of work roles contribute to the chronic depression often seen in old age. . . .

In discussing what he called "disengagement" and withdrawal from society in the later years as compared with continuance of activity, Dubin asked the seniors to volunteer specific situations that one faces during the twilight years.

They listed loss of a marital partner as a specific stress. . . .

Others said that retirement is a stress, as are physical limitations and feelings of little self-worth. Limited finances is another factor that must be dealt with by the elderly, they said. . . .

Along with inflation comes a fear of financial dependency on children, the seniors added.

Society is structured so that the elderly are forced into financial and emotional dependency, and then told they shouldn't feel or be dependent, they argued.

While offering solutions to the problems of coping gracefully with the aging process, the seniors suggested that, while one is capable of changing his personality and lifestyle, his early patterns are basically carried through life, getting modified from time to time by forced changes.

Keeping one's mind alert after retirement is important, they said, as well as building hobbies, making new friends and, for some, living around other seniors, although some said they prefer to be around families and children.

Having family ties helps sociability, they agreed, and holidays shared with family and friends are less depressing. . . .

Dubin told the group that, while the suicide rate among women peaks around the age of 40, it tapers off after that, and men become victims more than women. Senior centers often help dispel the isolation people suffer from living alone, he said.

In discussing various theories of personality development, Dubin said there are specific dimensions of personality types seen in older age that serve as variables for whether one ages successfully or unsuccessfully.

They include zest as opposed to apathy; resolution versus fortitude; desired achieved goals, and feelings of self-worth.

From these dimensions, research studies have come up with four personality types that determine how gracefully one will age. The "only really successful aging type," said Dubin, is the "integrated" personality.

An integrated person is assertive, has a good sense of identity, is comfortable with himself, knows who he is and is not obsessed with anxiety about death.

A "defended" person has made his career his entire identity, is ambitious and has a high achievement orientation. This person is likely to think of himself as "John Smith the architect" rather than as simply "John Smith." Loss of work or retirement shakes up his identity. Executives often have this personality type, said Dubin.

The third type is the passive-dependent person who has coasted through life on someone else's shirttail. This person rarely displays angry, hostile or aggressive feelings, and his withdrawal is a powerful tool for controlling someone else.

The fourth personality type, he said, is "unintegrated. This group needs some kind of support system or treatment. They aren't coping with life stresses or aging. They're angry, anxious, stressed and indecisive," said Dubin.

The Denver Post
March 23, 1980

Here is a new and interesting application of personality concepts. It can be used to predict and perhaps eventually modify the way people — especially those in our society — deal with the problems of aging.

Thus, if one thinks of personality as a collection of enduring traits or characteristics, an individual's personality can tell us little about his or her suicidal potential. However, if one conceives of personality in terms of overt behavior and other observable information, the accuracy of predictions about suicide increases markedly. It is known, for example, that the greatest risk of suicide occurs among males over 50, divorced, living alone, who have a history of suicide attempts and/or talking about suicide, are depressed or stressed, have no family or friends, and have worked out a clear and lethal plan for self-destruction. Of course, the presence of *all* these factors is not necessary to prompt suicide, but knowing about them provides some guidelines for the professional and nonprofessional workers who deal with potentially suicidal individuals through "hot lines" or in other contexts. In this sense, then, there is a "suicidal personality," but it can best be described in learning rather than in dispositional or trait terms.

In addition to being consulted about which people are likely to harm themselves, psychologists are also frequently asked to make judgments about who is likely to harm others. In a society such as ours, where the incidence of violent crime (murder, rape, aggravated assault, and so on) is frighteningly high, there is an urgent need to identify "dangerous" individuals — that is, those who are likely to commit violent crimes. We seek to find personality clues that single out potentially violent people. And we look for ways to predict whether a person who has already committed a crime of violence is likely to repeat that behavior. Questions such as these most frequently come from schools, courts, and other agencies responsible for making decisions about the offender's future that will ultimately affect society: Is there a risk that a certain child is moving in a criminal direction and is thus in need of special counseling or other attention? Should a nonviolent juvenile offender be put on probation or be placed in a reform school? Should an adult convicted of a violent crime be imprisoned, placed in a community-based rehabilitation program, or committed to an institution for the "criminally insane"? Is a formerly violent convict ready for parole?

Questions such as these are particularly difficult to answer because we are trying to identify a very small group of dangerous people in a very large population (in one study of 900 hospitalized mental patients, for example, less than six committed a violent crime after discharge; further, only about seven of every 100,000 arrests in the United States involve violent crimes).

Some professionals who view personality from a dispositional or psychodynamic perspective employ such instruments as the Rorschach Inkblot Test or the MMPI in the hope that test responses will provide clues to future criminal behavior. As has been the case with suicide, however, no "criminal personality" has emerged from the use of such tests. The MMPI, TAT, Rorschach, and other objective and projective personality measures do have some value in separating *groups* of people who *may* be more likely than others to be violent, but as one expert has noted, "no structured or projective test scale has been derived which, when used alone, will predict violence in the individual case in a satisfactory manner" (Megargee, 1970). Predictions based on such tests are often incorrect and can lead to tragic consequences. Part of the problem is that a person's tendency to act violently or to inhibit violent behavior fluctuates over time and across situations. Situational factors (such as intoxication, the presence of children, and the like) are therefore often decisive and need to be taken into account for an assessment to be truly comprehensive.

Taking into consideration a person's past learning and behavior may also increase predictive accuracy. For example, the earlier in life an individual is arrested or tried for an offense, the more likely he or she is to continue criminal activity; the earlier in life an offender leaves home, the more likely the individual is to continue a life of crime; the more serious the first offense, the greater the likelihood that later crimes will be serious. The type of crime a person has committed may also provide prognostic clues. Murderers, rapists, and other violent criminals are least likely to violate parole; violations are most common among persons who have committed nonviolent crimes such as theft, burglary, or forgery.

Personality and Selection

Everybody at one time or another will probably be subjected to some kind of selection procedure—for employment, military service, higher education, or other roles. Personality and personality assessment play a large part in such selection efforts because it is hoped that applicants' responses to various tests and interviews will allow accurate prediction of their future behavior. Personality assessment in one form or another is employed whenever one wishes to identify individuals who will behave in a particular way.

The Campus Setting

On college campuses, for example, a informal process of personality assessment occurs continuously. In fact, one study indicated that college students *say* that they select social partners on the basis of personality, looks, and intelligence, in that order. (Tests, however, have established that height, physical attractiveness, and proximity are actually the three major factors.)

Both men and women collect personality data on members of the opposite sex from various sources. They observe the verbal and nonverbal behavior of individuals of interest by talking to them or watching them as they interact with others: Did she talk about her career plans? Did he talk about himself all the time? They listen carefully to the reports of those who know the "target" individuals—"Believe me, Jack, she is all show!"; "Listen, that guy is a smooth talker but basically a real jerk." And they look for other clues, such as manner of dress, grooming habits, type of car owned, and the like. They then summarize this information in some fashion and use it to predict "target" persons' behavior and to guide decisions about initiating or accepting invitations for social contacts with them. Not surprisingly, selections made on the basis of this kind of personality assessment are not always satisfactory, especially when the predictions are based on presumably enduring personality traits. Anyone who has had to repulse unwelcome amorous advances or suffer through an evening filled with tense silences ("We always found things to talk about during class") knows that personality can be radically altered by situational factors.

Another option chosen by many (on or off the campus) is to allow a computer to collect and analyze personality data in a more formal fashion and "fix them up" with potentially compatible dates. The matching is usually based upon similarity of personality characteristics, interests, and attitudes, but at least two experiments have shown that such pairings do not result in any more satisfactory results than do random matches. The more imaginative computer dating services attempt to increase customer satisfaction by supplementing written assessment data with a videotaped interview which prospective social partners may view before deciding to spend time with the person in question. This provides an example of how the use of overt behavior samples can augment trait summaries of personality.

The Work Setting

Selection errors in business and industry, where many decisions involving hiring and promotion are made each year, are far more costly than errors in selection of social companions. Accordingly, companies of many kinds and sizes spend significant amounts of time and money to develop employee selection procedures. Some kind of personality assessment usually plays a part in these procedures. IBM, for example, requires potential employees to have an initial interview, fill out a formal application, take a variety of ability and personality tests, have a second interview, provide letters of reference, and pass a physical examination.

The personality tests most commonly employed in industrial selection procedures include projective tests like the Rorschach test (especially in executive selection, even though the evidence against their validity and usefulness is strong) and self-report inventories like the MMPI and the

comdates COMPUTER DATING SERVICE

3260 West Irving Park Road
Chicago Illinois 60618

(414) 444–4800

Fill out the form as completely as you can. You may omit questions
if absolutely necessary, but please remember that the questions are designed
to determine compatibility and to match you with your dates. By filling out
the questionaire as completely as you can, you help to ensure more compatible
matches.

A. *All of the following information in this section will be held in strictest confidence.*
Check all that apply or that you are in agreement with.

1. My sex is:
☐ male
☐ female

2. My race is:
☐ white
☐ black
☐ oriental
☐ other

3. My date's race should be:
☐ same as mine
☐ don't care

4. My religion is:
☐ Protestant
☐ Catholic
☐ Jewish
☐ Other
☐ Non-religious

5. My date's religion should be:
☐ Protestant
☐ Catholic
☐ Jewish
☐ Other
☐ don't care

☐ 6. I am previously married

☐ 7. My date should not be previously married

8. My education is:
☐ grade school
☐ some high school
☐ high school graduate
☐ some college
☐ college graduate

9. My date's education should be:
☐ about my own
☐ doesn't matter

10. I think I:
☐ won't ever marry
☐ will not marry in the near future
☐ might marry the right person
☐ would like to marry soon

11. I consider myself:
☐ highly religious
☐ somewhat religious
☐ agnostic
☐ atheist

12. I am
☐ very underweight
☐ somewhat underweight
☐ average
☐ somewhat overweight
☐ very overweight

13. My body condition is:
☐ below average
☐ average
☐ above average

14. My personal appearance is:
☐ attractive
☐ somewhat attractive
☐ plain

15. To me, physical appearance is:
☐ very important
☐ somewhat important
☐ unimportant

16. Among my friends, sex is:
☐ discussed freely;
☐ occasionally;
☐ rarely mentioned

17. I think pre-marital sex is permissible:
☐ never
☐ for engaged couples
☐ with one you love
☐ with one you date regularly
☐ with any date

18. I am:
☐ very interested in sex
☐ somewhat interested in sex
☐ not too interested in sex
☐ dislike sex

19. I drink:
☐ regularly
☐ socially
☐ seldom or never

20. I participate in sports:
☐ actively
☐ somewhat actively
☐ occasionally
☐ never

21. I am a sports spectator:
☐ avidly
☐ frequently
☐ occasionally
☐ never

22. I attend cultural activities:
☐ regularly
☐ occasionally
☐ infrequently
☐ never

23. I participate in:
☐ many organized activities or clubs
☐ some organized activities or clubs
☐ no organized activities or clubs

24. I am
☐ quiet
☐ moderately talkative
☐ very talkative

25. I am a:
☐ student
☐ blue collar worker
☐ white collar worker
☐ professionally trained person
☐ management employee
☐ in business for myself

26. After I am married,
I would like children
☐ immediately
☐ after a few years
☐ never

27. I would like
☐ 1 child
☐ 2 children
☐ 3-4 children
☐ more than 4 children
☐ no children

28. I am primarily interested in
☐ just dating
☐ marriage
☐ both

29. To me, money is
☐ very important
☐ somewhat important
☐ not too important
☐ unimportant

Computer dating services operate on
the principle that people with similar
personality attributes, interests, and
attitudes will be compatible. Some
studies have indicated, however, that
such selection procedures do not
yield more satisfactory results than
random matches. Here is a portion
of the kind of questionnaire the individual who is applying for a date is
asked to complete.

Mental Attitude Key to Sports Success
By CHRISTOPHER DRAKE

SAN JOSE, Calif.—You think you've got your backhand down and your serve is super and everything else is as graceful as a swan. So why, you ask, do you always fall apart in the middle of the second set?

Maybe you should check your mental toughness. Or perhaps you happen to be one of those players who is guilt prone. Or maybe you've been fooling yourself all these years, you're not competitive and would much rather be eating popcorn at the movies.

There is help. For $25, the weekend jock can do what hundreds of professional athletes have been doing for years—test his athletic motivation. "Mental attitude is what separates the good players from the great players," says William Winslow, president of Winslow Research Institute of San Jose, the largest national testing center for athletes in the country. . . .

The institute's Athletic Motivation Inventory (AMI), begun by three San Jose State University professors over a decade ago, has now tested 100,000 high school, college and professional league athletes. It gives both coaches and athletes insight into their mental outlook by testing the strength of 11 key traits—drive, aggressiveness, determination, guilt-proneness, leadership, self-confidence, emotional control, mental toughness, coachability, conscientiousness and trust (in teammates).

And now, it is expanding to include the so-called recreational athlete, whether he be golfer, runner, tennis player or sandlot ball player. . . .

Some of the traits are common sense, although, perhaps, the athlete may not be aware of them. Drive—the desire to win—or aggressiveness—enjoying confrontation—are part and parcel of each swing, of each step of most competitive games. But the player can go beyond common knowledge by seeing where he ranks compared to thousands of other athletes.

The 162-question test asks such things as "In athletics, one must either push or be shoved" (to measure aggression), whether the athlete requires praise (for mental toughness), or whether one has difficulty sleeping because he is worried about the next day's game—a measure of one's guilt proneness. "A player who scores in the upper 90 percentile is probably realizing his potential, but someone at 50 or 60 percent has a ways to go," Winslow said.

Athletes may never have thought of their guilt-proneness, which, according to Winslow, can ruin an otherwise brilliant player. This is the type who dwells on each and every error he makes. Of course this tends to cause more errors, until the player comes away thinking "I've let the team down. I shouldn't be playing. I'm a real dunderhead." . . .

Self-confidence, followed by emotional control, are the two traits consid-

ered most important by Winslow for a successful athlete. . . .

With the rise in women's sports, more and more female athletes are now taking the AMI, according to Winslow. He says there is a marked difference in the scores between the men and the women.

"Women score quite a bit lower in aggression and emotional control," he said. "They score the same (as men) in determination. They're higher than men in conscientiousness, though lower in trust. On all of the other traits, they are lower."

The different athletic opportunities available to the two sexes are the reason he believes. . . .

Aside from giving the athlete some ideas about himself, the AMI also is used by coaches across the country to figure the best ways to work with their teams. He knows, for instance, not to bawl out the kid with a low score in mental toughness, but that he may lean harder on the one with the high score in that category. He is advised by the AMI to give some responsibilities to the player scoring high in leadership, even though this person may not be captain of the team. If he is the coach of a football or soccer team—sports needing high levels of aggression—he is told to use the high-aggression player as a model for the rest. . . .

Boulder (Colo.) Daily Camera
March 27, 1980

Here is personality psychology in action. Now you can make your draft picks or base your recruiting on the results of a personality test. Notice the emphasis on the trait/dispositional approach. How would you incorporate other personality theory approaches in screening for athletic performance?

Guilford-Zimmerman Temperament Survey (which ask respondents to answer questions such as whether they start a new project with enthusiasm). By and large, self-report inventories of personality do not fare well in industrial settings.

The Courtroom Setting
Personality assessment has begun to play a role in jury selection. Recently psychologists have begun to advise defense and prosecution attorneys during the process of *voir dire,* (Suggs & Sales, 1978). From the Old French phrase for "to say the truth," *voir dire* in law refers to the

oath taken by prospective jurors to answer truthfully as to their qualifications to serve. The idea is to eliminate from the jury individuals who would be likely to be unsympathetic to the defendant or to the prosecutor's arguments.

Ideally, perhaps, attorneys would like to have personality test data or other formal assessment information available for each prospective juror, but this is not possible in practice. Instead, certain personality characteristics are inferred from observation of jurors' appearance and behavior in the courtroom. Psychologists commonly guide attorneys to look for other personality traits. Authoritarian jurors (those who are more likely to vote for conviction and

"I don't like the look of this at all."

The New Yorker, October 24, 1964. Drawing by Richter; © 1964 The New Yorker Magazine, Inc.

severe punishment) are, according to personality theory, likely to be respectful of authority figures but domineering over lower-status persons. Accordingly, the attorney pays special attention to prospective jurors who are especially deferential to the judge or other courtroom authorities. A

TABLE 9–8   Patient Attitudes and Psychosomatic Reactions

Disorder	Patient Attitude
Ulcers	Feels deprived of what is due him and wants to get even.
Hypertension	Feels threatened with harm and has to be ready for anything.
Asthma	Feels left out in the cold and wants to shut the person or situation out.
Colitis	Feels he is being injured or degraded and wishes he could get rid of the responsible agent.
Eczema	Feels he is being frustrated and can do nothing about it except take it out on himself.
Acne	Feels he is being picked on and wants to be left alone.
Psoriasis	Feels there is a constant gnawing at him and that he has to put up with it.
Rheumatoid arthritis	Feels tied down and wants to get free.
Low backache	Wants to run away.
Raynaud's disease	Wants to take hostile physical action.

Keep in mind that this is a set of hypotheses about psychosomatic disorders. The evidence to support the idea of a specific link between a particular personality and a particular disease is rather weak.

related tactic is to attempt to categorize jurors as to their characteristic views about law, justice, and punishment. Those who see laws as inflexible rules to be rigidly enforced (the kind of person the defense wishes to avoid) are thought to be more respectful of the judge (for example, always addressing him or her as "Sir" or "Your Honor"), while those who view laws as guidelines which must be interpreted flexibly and individually (the type of person the defense would like to retain) are likely to appear more relaxed, less submissive, and more apt to express their own unsolicited opinions in court.

Some psychologists have attempted to use systematic observation of nonverbal cues such as body movements, facial expressions, tone of voice, and speech disturbances as indicators of prospective jurors' positive and negative reactions to issues (such as the death penalty or racial prejudice) raised during an attorney's questioning.

The *voir dire* methods described here are still only tentatively validated, at best, and much more research on them is needed (see Chapter 10 for more on jury research).

In other settings, personality variables have recently been used to predict the competence of college dorm advisers, football players (see the newsclip "Mental Attitude Key to Sports Success"), psychological counselors, and even state police. Whether this trend turns out to be a beneficial one will depend largely on how carefully users of personality tests evaluate the validity and utility of their procedures. Assessment for the sake of assessment does no one any good, and because personality measurement can constitute an invasion of privacy, it should at least be restricted to spheres where it is clearly demonstrated to be useful.

Personality and Illness

As we shall see in Chapter 11, many physical illnesses include a psychological component. Such psychological factors as an emotional reaction to stress may bring on physical disorders resulting in such psychological consequences as depression. Some investigators have hypothesized that personality variables may help determine the particular forms of illness to which an individual is susceptible (see Table 9–8 for one theory of this sort).

There is little evidence to suggest that specific personality traits are associated with the incidence of heart attacks (Mordkoff & Parsons, 1968), but a personality-related behavior pattern — called *Type A* — has been related to coronary heart disease (Rosenman, Brand, Jenkins, *et al.*, 1975) and high blood pressure (Harrell, 1980). The Type A pattern is typified by persons who are competitive, impatient, hard-driving, concerned about wasting or losing time, and, often, hostile. In the laboratory, for example, Type A's are more likely than less coronary-prone Type B's to push themselves hard on mental and physical tasks, perceive time as moving more slowly than it actually does, perform less well when delayed responses are required, and to demonstrate aggression toward others (Glass, 1977). Outside the laboratory these people may always be "on the run," may never find time to relax, and may be preoccupied with achievement and competition.

The Type A pattern is assessed through special interviews in which people are asked about competitive

Study: Cutting Stress Reduces Cardiac Risk
By JANE E. BRODY

NEW YORK—In 1958, two California cardiologists proposed that an achievement-oriented, competitive behavior pattern they called "Type A" could cause heart attacks, a notion that for years was rejected or ignored by most heart researchers, who focused on such readily measured risk factors as diet, smoking and blood pressure.

Now, however, preliminary indications from a large ongoing study suggest that changing this stressful way of living may in fact reduce the risk of heart attack. This study and smaller ones like it also are showing that although American society equates Type A behavior with success, modifying the pattern actually can enhance productivity and satisfaction with life.

At the same time, the role this hurried, aggressive, controlling and often hostile behavior pattern plays in a person's chances of suffering a heart attack is gaining ever-wider acceptance, even among the epidemiologists and cardiologists who had denigrated it.

A blue-ribbon panel convened by the National Heart, Lung and Blood Institute recently concluded that the Type A pattern, like high blood cholesterol, cigarette smoking and high blood pressure, is "solidly established" as a significant risk factor for heart disease.

And the institute is financing a $900,000, five-year study among 900 coronary patients to find out how to modify potentially harmful aspects of Type A behavior. . . .

Thus far, according to a co-worker, James Gill, second heart attacks have occurred less often than expected among those in the study who have modified their Type A behavior. . . .

He cited the case of one accountant who failed to heed the group's advice that he set a limit on clients accepted before the federal income-tax deadline. Instead, for months, the man worked "14 to 16 hours a day, seven days a week, and we buried him several days before April 15," Gill recalled.

Several earlier studies involving thousands of initially healthy people have indicated that Type A behavior doubles a person's risk of suffering a heart attack. However, most of the studies involved primarily middle-class, white American men, and it is not yet known what effect Type A behavior has on other groups.

Robert Levy, director of the national institute in Bethesda, Md., said that even if the current study fails to provide scientifically valid evidence of reduced cardiac deaths, it should show whether, in a society that fosters Type A behavior, the pattern can be changed. . . .

Friedman's colleagues say he himself was an archetypical Type A—very hard-working, intense, fast, aggressive, loud, uncompromising and impatient—before his heart attack 14 years ago. . . .

In the study, 600 persons . . . go through a structured, videotaped interview from which their Type A score is derived.

Then they meet regularly in small groups with a professional leader to discuss their life strategies and problems, troublesome situations (such as saying "thanks, but no thanks" to someone asking you to be on a committee), give one another advice and learn "exercises" to practice being more Type B. . . .

[Carl] Thoresen [a Stanford University psychologist who is a principal investigator in the study] and his co-workers trace the preoccupation with work and achievement among many Type A people to a "basic underlying insecurity—they work harder and faster and longer in an endless pursuit to prove they are good." . . .

Denver Post
September 17, 1980

Research on the Type A personality pattern is especially important to psychologists because applying behavior measurement in the diagnosis and treatment of a major illness represents a breakthrough.

drive, time urgency, and competitiveness. A 61-item multiple-choice questionnaire called the Jenkins Activity Survey provides an alternative means of assessing Type A which does not require an interview.

It is important to note that although Type A's suffer significantly more coronary heart disease than Type B's, only a minority of all Type A's actually have heart attacks. Current research in the field of behavioral medicine is aimed at specifying more clearly how Type A relates to disease. For example, it may be that Type A is predictive of heart attack only in persons who must face situations which they perceive as stressful and uncontrollable. Or perhaps only the competitive and impatient components of the Type A pattern are really significant. Regardless, discovery of this personality-related dimension has helped enhance our understanding of our nation's most significant health problem.

A less well-developed but nevertheless interesting line of related research is underway involving the psychological factors that may be predictive of cancer. Much of this work is psychodynamic in nature and based upon theories that suggest cancer is the consequence of (1) trauma and depression following the loss of a loved one, a job, or self-esteem (especially in persons prone to feelings of helplessness) or (2) inhibiting emotions and the use of the unconscious defense mechanisms of denial and repression. One recent study (Dattore, Shontz, & Coyne, 1980) found support for both hypotheses in the sense that, compared to noncancer patients, patients with cancer had significantly higher levels of depression and repression as indicated by scores on the MMPI and Byrne Repression-Sensitization tests which they had taken years earlier. As with heart disease, the cancer-personality link requires far more research.

Hostile, Emotional Cancer Victims May Live Longer
By AL ROSSITER JR.

WASHINGTON (UPI)—A Johns Hopkins University study of women dying of cancer suggests that people who are outwardly angry and anxious about their illness live longer than those who seem more content and happier.

The study of 35 women with advanced breast cancer supports earlier reports indicating that the way a person deals with the disease psychologically might affect survival time.

The research team led by Dr. Leonard R. Derogatis of the university's department of psychiatry and behavioral sciences said it has been suggested that emotional factors influence the course of advanced cancer by somehow affecting the body's immune or hormonal systems. . . .

Not only will more be learned about the interaction between the mind and body, but the report said further research in this area might be able to make an important contribution to the treatment of people with cancer.

Psychological aid currently designed to provide support and comfort for the cancer patient could be redesigned, the report said, to "place the patient in better contact with his or her emotions."

The 35 women with advanced breast cancer in the Johns Hopkins study were evaluated psychologically at the start of a chemotherapy treatment program. The women were interviewed by a trained counselor and the treating doctor, and also completed personal psychological evaluations of themselves.

Based on the records of similar cases of breast cancer that had spread to other parts of the body, the researchers classified patients who died less than one year after start of the drug treatment as short-term survivors, and those who lived longer as long-term survivors.

Thirteen women lived less than a year with a mean survival time of 8.8 months. Twenty-two lived longer than a year, with a mean survival following the start of drug treatment of 22.8 months.

"Long-term survivors showed significantly higher levels of anxiety, hostility and psychoticism than short-term survivors," the report said.

Patients who were classified as short-term survivors had a particular lack of hostile symptoms, and generally higher levels of positive mood states such as joy, contentment and affection.

In addition, the physicians' ratings indicated that they perceived the long-term survivors as less well adjusted to their illnesses with significantly more negative attitudes than those who survived for shorter periods.

Clearly, the report said, the long-term survivors had a different psychological response to their disease. . . .

The researchers said patients who died sooner appeared less able to express feelings of distress, particularly anger and hostility. . . .

The Denver Post
October 12, 1979

Could there be a link between personality and cancer susceptibility or survival?

Parent Effectiveness Training

Parent effectiveness training (PET) is a course to teach parents how to interact more effectively with their children. It was developed by Thomas Gordon, who apparently was influenced by Rogers' self theory. Since 1963, over a half million parents have taken the course from Gordon or one of his many trained instructors. In the normal course of living, conflicts develop between parents and children. They can be dealt with effectively or ineffectively. Ineffective parent-child relationships always produce a winner and a loser. For example, often the conflict is dealt with by the parent deciding what should be done and inflicting that decision upon the child. If the child complies, there is no immediate problem and the parent gets his or her way. But clearly, the child is a loser. As a loser, the child is likely to be unmotivated to carry out the requirements imposed by the parent. Further, the child is likely to resent the parent and come away from the whole interaction with bad feelings. The cost to the parent is a resentful child who disobeys often and who has bad feelings about both the parent and about himself or herself.

To impose an arbitrary decision, then, is an ineffective way of dealing with conflict, but it is not the only ineffective way. Under some circumstances, the child can become a winner over the parent. Some children learn how to control their parents with temper tantrums or with techniques for making the parent feel guilty. Letting the child become the winner in any interaction is as negative as the parent becoming the winner. The child exhibits little discipline. The child's attempts at intimidation carry over to interactions with others who might not be so willing to accept that form of behavior. The parents become resentful, irritated, and angry.

Typically, neither parent nor child is consistently a winner or a loser. Interactions vaccilate, with the child winning through whining or not eating on one occasion and the parent winning through power and authority on others. But there is always a winner and a loser. Gordon offers an alternative, "no-lose" strategy in which neither parent nor child wins or loses. His method consists of training both parents and child to seek a solution that is mutually acceptable whenever a conflict arises. The training procedure is too detailed to go into here, but basically consists of alerting both parties to the necessity of recognizing problems when they exist and to search for an agreeable solution that will benefit both. The solution is to be jointly arrived at so that no one comes off winning or losing. When the loser notion is eliminated, so is resentment, anger, hostility, and later problems. At least that is the theory, and it seems to be working in practice.

10 Social Psychology

Bob is interviewing for a job as a management trainee with a large computer manufacturing firm. He is concerned about the impression he will make on the recruiter; she, in turn, is interested in persuading Bob that joining her firm would be a good move for him. The behavior of each is strongly influenced by the behavior of the other during the interview, and what each thinks about the other is determined in a complex way by the kinds of information each processes.

Terry, a high school junior, is being pressured by some of his friends to smoke. Despite knowing that it is bad for his health, he succumbs to their influence. Why does he let them affect his behavior in many areas, from the way he dresses to the habits he develops? Why are Terry and his friends influenced by TV ads that show star football player Earl Campbell chewing tobacco?

John is a "red-neck," Martha is a "knee-jerk liberal," Samantha is a "prude," Marty is a "bookworm," Jessica is a "tomboy"—the list of stereotypes goes on and on. Why do we categorize people and then treat them accordingly, assuming that the label we give them tells us everything we need to know about them?

Michael, now known as Steppenwolf, has joined a spiritual cult located in the mountains of northern California. Having "disowned" his parents and former friends, he now obediently follows the dictates of the cult leader. His parents claim he has been "brainwashed" and have hired a private detective to kidnap him and then "deprogram" him. The leader of another cult that moved to Guyana convinces everyone in the group to commit suicide. How can such things happen to normal, intelligent people?

The Focus of Social Psychology

Social psychologists are concerned with the social aspects of human identity—the behavior of people in groups and how people are affected by that social experience. Social psychology is the study of the effects on individual and group behavior of the real or imagined behavior of others. Its focus is the special aspects of behavior that takes place in social settings—situations in which more than one person is present.

Think for a moment about your own life and the situations you typically encounter. What percentage of time during the day do you spend completely alone with no other person able to observe your behavior in any way? For most of us the percentage of such time is relatively small. An enormous amount of our behavior takes place not in isolation but in the presence of others. Do you think your behavior is different when others are present? Of course it is, and accounting for and understanding these effects is the special task of social psychology. In order to comprehend social behavior, we will need to apply many of the concepts we have already learned about. In addition, we will encounter new concepts unique to social behavior. In general, we will be particularly concerned

with two of the major behavioral parameters we introduced at the very beginning of this book, namely, a person's knowledge and a person's motivation or intention.

Social Knowledge

A critical aspect of social behavior relates to the knowledge parameter. As you become "socialized" into your culture, you acquire a great deal of information about how to behave in social settings. Much of this knowledge you receive verbally, as instruction, from your parents, teachers, and others. Perhaps even more knowledge is conveyed to you in nonverbal form as you observe what other people do, not just what they say. Some of this nonverbal information is conveyed in quite subtle ways, for example, through tone of voice, facial expression, and body "language."

You also learn about such things as social status and social class, and you develop stereotypes, which are really just concepts, about particular types of people. In fact, the whole process that sociologists called socialization boils down to the acquisition of this knowledge, which we shall call *social knowledge*. The amount of social knowledge that our limited

© 1979 United Feature Syndicate, Inc.

information-processing systems must deal with is overwhelming. Therefore, like other types of knowledge, to be of maximal value social knowledge must be well organized. Social knowledge must be organized into chunks, or schemata (see Chapters 5 and 6). Suppose that this afternoon you are invited to a fraternity house toga party. Stored away in your brain is probably a general idea of the types of behaviors that take place and are expected at such parties. This information would be retrieved as one large chunk that contains within it lots of small pieces of information about social behavior at toga parties. Using cognitive terminology, we would say you retrieve the toga party schema. The information in this schema would play a role in determining your decision about whether to accept the invitation; it would affect your motivation to attend the party; and, if you chose to attend, it would certainly affect your behavior while there. Social knowledge, largely organized into schemata, is a major determinant of social behavior, and it is the major topic of the first part of this chapter.

Social Motivation

A second major consideration is *social motivation*. Behavior in social situations, like all behavior, has a motivational component. Recall from Chapter 7 that motivation is a joint product of drives and incentives, of push and pull factors, or of a person's predispositions being activated by precipitating circumstances. Social behavior is no different. People behave in social situations because they are intentionally trying either to achieve a desired outcome or to avoid an aversive or unpleasant outcome. The outcome has a positive or negative incentive value for the person because the person has particular needs or predispositions that can lead to drivelike aspects of behavior. Social behavior is often motivated by unique factors not present when behavior takes place in complete privacy.

Need for Social Approval

One motivational concept that seems especially relevant to social behavior is the need for social approval, as we mentioned briefly at the end of Chapter 7. Early in life, we acquire the social knowledge that it is desirable to have other people like us and approve of our behavior. In many situations, then, we behave in particular ways that our social knowledge tells us will lead to the approval of others. Or in aversive situations, we often behave in ways designed to avoid others' disapproval. Social motivation that stems from the need for social approval can have an enormous impact on our behavior. Terry, in the example at the beginning of the chapter, might start smoking because he wants his "friends" to like him; or he might start chewing tobacco because Earl Campbell does, and men like Earl will like him more if he chews, to say nothing of how attractive his chewing and spitting will be to girls. If you go to the toga party, you may do some things there against your "better judgment," meaning you wouldn't do them if you were alone or in most other situations. You might agree to participate in the wet toga contest because you want others at the party to like or accept you.

Getting others to like us or avoiding having them dislike us is a critical concept in social psychology. This chapter will have much to say about the factors that lead to liking and disliking between people, otherwise known as *interpersonal attraction*. Our own impressions of liking and disliking others determine in large part how we will treat others. In addition, our own impression of ourselves—our *self-concept*—determines a large part of our behavior with others. Consider the example of Bob, who is being interviewed by the recruiter from the computer firm. Critical to the outcome of the interview is Bob's own self-concept, his impression of the recruiter, and her impressions of him. Woven into this interplay of approve/disapprove or like/dislike judgments is our social knowledge of how we should behave and of how we would like to see the other person behave. Faulty social knowledge ("I didn't know that I shouldn't invite the interviewer out for a drink") can produce inappropriate behavior just as much as faulty motivation.

As you study this chapter, keep in mind that the two fundamental concepts just introduced—social knowledge and social motivation—account for a great deal of social behavior. Many of the unfortunate results of some people's behavior can be traced to faulty social knowledge or beliefs—such as the belief that women like men who chew tobacco. Or they can be traced to faulty social motivation, as in the case of Terry, who started to smoke to win approval or to avoid disapproval. On the positive side, the same is true: Much of the good in the world comes about because of the correct application of social knowledge and the need for social approval. Look to variations in social knowledge or in social motivation to explain the variations in social behavior we will consider in this chapter.

Organizing Social Knowledge

As Sir Fredrick Bartlett suggested many years ago, very complex representations of the world exist in memory. These representations, which contain configurations of interrelated concepts, are used to interpret and organize larger bodies of information acquired either in a single situation or over a period of time. Several different terms have been used to refer to such "knowledge structures" by cognitive and social psychologists. The most popular one, as you will remember from Chapters 5 and 6, is **schema.**

Nature of Schemata

Schemata interpret and organize information about people and events and provide a basis for making inferences about them. That is, when new information has been received and its individual features have been encoded, the set of encoded features is compared to the features of schemata that are potentially relevant to interpreting this new information. If a sufficient number of features of the new object or event are in common with those of an existing schema, the new object or event is identified as an instance of that schema. Once this identification has been made, the object or event may be inferred to have characteristics of the schema used to interpret it. On the other hand, features of the original object or event that are irrelevant to the schema may be forgotten. Suppose we are told that a woman is tall and thin, wears her hair in a bun, has horn-rimmed glasses, and wears dresses buttoned to her neck. This description may

suggest a "typical librarian" (we encode the information in terms of a prototypic "librarian" schema). In turn, we may infer that the person is probably quiet and prudish, reads Shakespeare, likes classical music, and prefers wine to beer. Alternatively, the description of a short woman who dyes her hair blond, wears sweatshirts and jeans, and likes to disco may activate a quite different schema, which may lead to quite different inferences about the person's personality and interests. Neither set of inferences may be correct. Still, the schema that happens to be activated and used as a basis for interpreting and organizing information will substantially influence the sorts of inferences that are made.

The latter possibility is important for several reasons. First, once an inference is made about a person the inference becomes part of the representation of the person and may function in place of the original information. In fact, if the inference is made when the information is first received and is incorporated into the representation of the person, the inference may over a period of time become indistinguishable from the original information. The inference may be recalled as actually having been presented rather than merely inferred.

A good example comes from a study in which subjects were given information about a conversation between a man and his fiancée that had taken place in the past. During the conversation, the man tells the woman that he does not want children, at which time a bitter argument ensues. The experimenter, who ostensibly knew the couple, remarked incidentally that the couple eventually married and, four years later, were still happily together. One month later, subjects returned to the experiment and were asked to recall the information they had received in the earlier session. They were explicitly asked *not* to make any inferences or guesses but to report only the information actually presented as they remembered it. Despite these instructions, the subjects made numerous errors in recall. The errors were of the sort that reconciled the couple's disagreement about having children with the fact they were happily married. For example, one subject "recalled" that the woman found out she could not have children, while a second "recalled" that the man had changed his mind about having children. These errors were presumably based on inferences that subjects had made at the time the information was presented, based upon schemata pertaining to events involving happily married couples. Later, the inferences could not be distinguished from the original information upon which the inferences were based.

The representation formed of a person may affect not only the inferences that are made about the person but also behavior toward the person. This possibility has further implications if one considers that

Highlight 10–1

In-group Heroes, Out-group Villains

The sociologist Robert K. Merton (1957) has cleverly illustrated how the in-group virtue becomes the out-group vice:

We begin with the engagingly simple formula of moral alchemy: the same behavior must be differently evaluated according to the person who exhibits it. For example, the proficient alchemist will at once know that the word "firm" is properly declined as follows:

I am firm,
Thou art obstinate,
He is pigheaded.

There are some, unversed in the skills of this science, who will tell you that one and the same term should be applied to all three instances of identical behavior. Such unalchemical nonsense should simply be ignored.

With this experiment in mind, we are prepared to observe how the very same behavior undergoes a complete change of evaluation in its transition from the in-group Abe Lincoln to the out-group Abe Cohen or Abe Kurokawa. We proceed systematically. Did Lincoln work far into the night? This testifies that he was industrious, resolute, perseverant, and eager to realize his capacities to the full. Do the out-group Jews or Japanese keep these same hours? This only bears witness to their sweatshop mentality, their ruthless undercutting of American standards, their unfair competitive practices. Is the in-group hero frugal, thrifty, and sparing? Then the out-group villain is stingy, miserly, and penny-pinching. All honor is due the in-group Abe for his having been smart, shrewd, and intelligent and, by the same token, all contempt is owing the out-group Abes for their being sharp, cunning, crafty, and too clever by far. Did the indomitable Lincoln refuse to remain content with a life of work with the hands? Did he prefer to make use of his brain? Then, all praise for his plucky climb up the shaky ladder of opportunity. But, of course, the eschewing of manual work for brain work among the merchants and lawyers of the out-group deserves nothing but censure for a parasitic way of life. Was Abe Lincoln eager to learn the accumulated wisdom of the ages by unending study? The trouble with the Jew is that he's a greasy grind, with his head always in a book, while decent people are going to a show or a ball game. Was the resolute Lincoln unwilling to limit his standards to those of his provincial community? That is what we should expect of a man of vision. And if the outgroupers criticize the vulnerable areas in our society, then send 'em back where they came from. Did Lincoln, rising high above his origins, never forget the rights of the common man and applaud the right of workers to strike? This testifies only that, like all real Americans, this greatest of Americans was deathlessly devoted to the cause of freedom. But, as you examine the statistics on strikes, remember that these un-American practices are the result of outgroupers pursuing their evil agitation among otherwise contented workers.

our behavior toward others often determines how others behave toward us. If on the basis of a representation we have formed we expect a person to be warm and friendly, we may behave in a friendly way toward that person. Our behavior, in turn, may lead the person to be friendly toward us, thus confirming our expectancies. On the other hand, if our representation suggests that the individual will be unpleas-

"Some of you used to call us 'boy,' and that's why now some of us like to call you 'mother.'"

Playboy, November 1971. Reproduced by special permission of PLAYBOY Magazine; copyright © 1971 by Playboy.

Stereotypes are social schemata that are applied to classes of people rather than to classes of situations. For example, stereotypic schemata are applied to the sexes, the races, various religions, and different age groups. Employing a schema of this sort constitutes prejudice—prejudging an individual in advance of knowing the facts.

ant, we may behave in a cold and indifferent way toward the person. The person may reciprocate by being unpleasant as well, only confirming our possibly erroneous expectations. Here we have what is called the **self-fulfilling prophecy.** These effects may occur even when the information upon which the representation is based is completely false.

Theories of Social Schemata

People who share the same culture have many experiences in common. Most of us learn, for example, that people usually like those who agree with them better than those who disagree or that people work hard to make money or that people typically believe in what they say. Although we are aware of many exceptions to these "rules of thumb," we may apply them in making inferences about others when no other information is available. Thus, if we believe that people with similar opinions typically like one another, and we are told that Bob and Sara believe that capital punishment should be abolished, we may, in the absence of other information, infer that Bob and Sara are more apt than not to like one another. Alternatively, if we are told that Bob likes Sara, we may

apply that principle and infer that they hold similar opinions about capital punishment. We have an implicit theory of what goes with what.

Cognitive Balance

Fritz Heider proposed a formal conceptualization of the manner in which attitudes toward persons and objects are interrelated. The theory, known as **cognitive balance theory,** states that when an individual believes two elements (for example, two persons or a person and some issue) are positively associated (belong to the same group or category or have positive feelings about one another), the individual typically has similar feelings toward the two elements (either likes both or dislikes both). However, when an individual believes that two elements are dissociated (are members of different categories or dislike one another), the individual tends to feel differently about the two elements (one is liked and the other disliked). These sets of relations can be diagrammed as follows, where P is a person, O and X are the two other persons or objects, and the relations between them are denoted either p (positive or favorable) or n (negative or unfavorable).

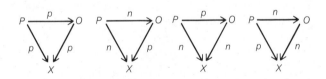

Thus, the first diagram represents a situation in which P likes both O and X and believes that O and X are positively associated; the fourth diagram represents a situation in which P dislikes O, likes X, and believes that O and X are negatively associated (different). Note that in each diagram, the number of negative relations is even (0 to 2). Heider therefore postulated that a set of three cognitions was *balanced* if it contained an even number of negative relations. Two hypotheses were then made:

1. If an individual knows two of the three relations in a set of three elements, the individual will tend to infer the third to be in balance with the other two.

"It can't be much good."

The New Yorker, July 3, 1971. Drawing by Dana Fradon; © 1971 The New Yorker Magazine, Inc.

Cognitive dissonance theory would imply that if something is free, it can't also be valuable.

2. If an individual is presented information that creates a state of imbalance in a set of three cognitions, the individual will tend to change one cognition in a way that reestablishes balance.

Cognitive Dissonance

Leon Festinger extended and elaborated Heider's principles in a formulation known as **cognitive dissonance theory.** Festinger emphasizes the motivational properties of imbalance, which he calls cognitive dissonance. Dissonance theory is basically a theory of rationalization. It concerns the tendency of people to justify their behavior or decisions in order to convince themselves that their actions were appropriate. Certain beliefs and attitudes are typically *consonant* (in balance) with the decision to engage in any behavior and imply that the decision was correct. Others are *dissonant* with that behavior and imply that the behavior should not have occurred. Thus, if a person has decided to stop smoking, certain beliefs (that smoking is bad for the health, that it is expensive, and so on) imply that the decision was a good one (are consonant), and others (that cigarettes taste good, that they calm the nerves, and so on) imply that it was a bad one (are dissonant). The magnitude of the consonance or dissonance produced by any cognition is a function of the strength of one's belief that the cognition is true and one's perception of its

What You Can't Have, You Duz Want— A Tide Stronger Than Dirt
By KENNETH GOODALL

When Big Brother swoops down on Big Mama and outlaws her favorite laundry detergent, how will she react? Such, roughly, was the question investigated by social psychologist Michael B. Mazis in Miami after Dade County authorities banned the sale, possession or use of phosphate detergents.

Mazis saw the ban as a good opportunity to test the predictive power of psychological reactance theory in a field setting. This theory states that when a person's freedom of choice or action is restricted he or she will experience psychological reactance, a motivational state directed toward regaining the freedom. It figures. First advanced by Jack Brehm in 1966, the theory has generated much lab but little field experimentation.

When the Dade County antipollution measure went into effect, few of the popular brands of detergent were available in no-phosphate formulas, so many Miami housewives had to switch brands as well as formulas. All of them found their choices drastically reduced.

Mazis speculated that Miami housewives would be aroused and "feel an increased desire to have the forbidden detergent. . . ." This reactance, in turn, should result in "higher effectiveness attributed to phosphate detergents . . ." and "more negative attitudes toward governmental regulation of environmental matters . . ." by housewives in Miami than in a control city, Tampa, where phosphate detergents were still legal.

Pollsters interviewed 76 middle-class housewives in Miami and 45 in Tampa. All had at least one child under 16 living at home and all had depended primarily on phosphate detergents during the previous six months. Asked to rate the effectiveness of these phosphate detergents on such characteristics as whiteness, freshness, stain removal and gentleness, the now-deprived Miami housewives gave them significantly higher overall ratings than did the Tampa housewives. Miami housewives also expressed significantly less agreement with the statement that "Legal restrictions should be imposed against the sale of detergents containing phosphates." So Mazis' data supported his forbidden-fruit predictions. . . .

Mazis says that his study shows that psychological reactance is not solely a laboratory phenomenon and has public policy implications for administrative decisions and ordinances that restrict the public's freedom of choice. . . .

Psychology Today
September 1975

Social or legal pressure to change attitudes can sometimes backfire. Could dissonance theory predict this effect?

Highlight 10-2

When Prophecy Fails

What happens when you vehemently make a prediction, such as telling your friends over and over that you are going to lose weight or that the Cowboys are going to win the Superbowl, only to have the prediction fail miserably? The result is dissonance that you must somehow reduce. Leon Festinger, Henry Riecken, and Stanley Schachter did a study on this kind of problem, which we might call "when prophency fails." (For further information see the book by these authors, *When prophecy fails: A social and psychological study of a modern group that predicted the destruction of the world.* New York: Harper & Row, 1956.)

The investigators studied a group of religious followers of a woman who, some years ago, predicted the end of the world in December of that year. She and her followers believed that only they would be saved, because a spaceship would rescue them. Some of the members made considerable financial sacrifices to join the group, and all of them were strongly committed to their belief in the woman's prophetic powers and the test of their beliefs with the impending disaster. The situation was set up for a monumental cognitive clash between prophecy and outcome. The hour was set—the world was to end, but it didn't.

The experimenters, following the situation closely (even to the point of joining the group), made a curious prediction. They said that instead of disbanding and trying to live down and forget the affair, the followers would maintain their beliefs and their group commitment and would seek even more support. The experimenters were right. As the hour of destruction passed, apprehension within the group grew. But soon the leader received a "message" that the group's devotion had been the world's salvation. Thanks to their devotion, destruction had been avoided.

At the critical moment, two facts were in dissonance. The followers believed in their prophet, and her prophecy failed. Choosing to maintain their beliefs, the followers then wholly accepted a reinterpretation of the events. That the world was not destroyed they saw as an even greater sign of the prophet's power. Now the cause was redirected. Whereas before the prophecy failed the group had avoided publicity, now they actively sought more followers. They purposely exposed themselves to public ridicule in the belief that this would increase their popular support. In short, they did what they could to increase the number of consonant elements and decrease the dissonant ones.

---

relevance to the decision. People are motivated to reduce dissonance. Reduction of dissonance can be accomplished in several ways. One is to decrease the importance of the dissonant cognitions. In our example, this could be done by decreasing the belief that cigarettes taste good or that smoking calms the nerves. A second way is to increase the magnitude of the consonant cognitions. Thus, one may increase beliefs that smoking is bad for the health or that it is expensive. Still another way is to add new cognitions that bolster the decision. For example, one might seek additional information supporting the decision. Alternatively, one might attempt to get other persons to stop smoking as well, since the cognition "others have decided to stop smoking" is consonant with one's own decision to stop.

The empirical interest in dissonance theory has principally derived from a second postulate, namely, that the greater the dissonance one experiences, the more aversive the dissonance is, and therefore the more one will be motivated to reduce it by changing one's beliefs. In one study, subjects were offered $20 to try to convince others that a task they believed to

be dull was actually quite interesting. Other subjects were offered only $1 to convince others that the task was interesting. In each case, after engaging in the behavior subjects were asked to report their own interest in the task. Which group should rate the task more favorably? Presumably the belief that the task is actually boring is dissonant with the decision to convince another that it is interesting. Being paid to do so is consonant with the decision, however, and the *amount* of consonance is greater when the pay is $20 than when it is $1. Thus, the ratio of dissonant cognitions to consonant cognitions is less in the first case. Therefore, as was in fact the case, the person paid $1 should rate the task more interesting than the person paid $20.

In a more recent study, Zanna & Cooper asked subjects to volunteer to write an essay favoring a particular position on an issue to which they were initially opposed. Before engaging in this behavior, however, they gave subjects a pill—actually a placebo —that some subjects were told would increase tension or discomfort and other students were told would relax them. In control conditions, no pill was admin-

Balance or dissonance: Can either of these theories account for Cathy's feelings?

istered. Subjects in all cases presumably experienced discomfort as a result of performing the counter-attitudinal behavior. However, the authors reasoned that if subjects were told they had taken a pill that produces discomfort, they would attribute their discomfort to the pill and not to the dissonance they experienced; therefore, they would not change their belief in the position advocated in order to reduce dissonance. On the other hand, if they had taken a pill that they thought would relax them but experienced discomfort, they would infer that they were extremely upset by their decision to engage in the behavior and would attempt to reduce dissonance by changing their beliefs *more* than if they had not taken the pill. This is exactly what happened. That is, subjects who took a pill described as arousing changed their beliefs very little after writing the essay in comparison to subjects who received no pill; subjects who took a pill described as relaxing changed their beliefs even more than did the no-pill subjects. This finding is important for two reasons. First, it establishes that belief change following a particular behavior is often mediated by a desire to eliminate feelings of discomfort produced by an inconsistency between one's beliefs and the decision to manifest the behavior. Second, the finding suggests that people will *not* attempt to eliminate inconsistencies if there are alternative explanations for the discomfort they experience as a result of them.

Attitudes and Judgments

We just considered the processes underlying the use of information to form attitudes and to make judgments. Another important question has to do with

what information is used and *how much* influence it has on the attitudes and judgments to which it is relevant. This general question has been the focus of attention in three major research areas of social psychology: (1) attitudes, communication, and persuasion, (2) attribution processes, and (3) interpersonal attraction.

Attitude Formation and Change: Communication and Persuasion

Certainly our beliefs and attitudes are influenced by what we read in newspapers and magazines and what we see on television. We are also influenced by lectures we hear and by informal discussions we have with others. But which types of written and oral communications have the greatest effect and why? In fact, a large number of factors have been found to affect the influence of a communication on beliefs and opinions. The effects of most of these factors can be conceptualized in terms of a general model of communication and persuasion postulated by William McGuire. Specifically, McGuire has noted that the influence of a communication on a person's belief in the position advocated in the communication may depend upon (1) the person's comprehension of the communication and (2) the person's ability or tendency to counterargue, or refute, the validity of the position. People will not be persuaded by arguments they do not understand. Neither will they be influenced by arguments they find easy to refute. The implication is that messages which are easy to understand but contain arguments that are difficult to discredit will be more effective than those which are difficult to comprehend but, once understood, are easy to refute. However, holding constant the particular communication content, the tendencies to comprehend and refute the contents of a communication may be affected by characteristics of the situation in which the information is presented, the form in which the information is presented, characteristics of the recipient of the communication, and the nature of the source of the communication.

Situational Variables

Suppose a person receives a communication under conditions in which he or she is able to concentrate fully on the contents, say in a quiet library. In this condition, the person may be best able to comprehend the communication, but may also be best able to refute it, and so the information may have little influence on the person's beliefs. In contrast, suppose the communication is presented in a situation in which a number of distractions interfere with concentration, say at a football game. Under these conditions, the person may still be able to comprehend the information, but may not be able to evaluate it carefully or refute its contents. In this case, the influence of the communication may be high. Of course, if the distraction becomes *too* great, the person may not even comprehend the communication and its influence will again be low. This reasoning implies that the influence of a persuasive message will be greater when it is presented under conditions in which there is moderate distraction rather than excessive or no distraction.

"Mother, I get enough pressure from my peer group without getting it from you."

The New Yorker, June 9, 1980. Drawing by Weber; © 1980 The New Yorker Magazine, Inc.

traction. That is because the recipient will be able to comprehend the message but not think about it carefully.

Several studies have demonstrated the latter statement. In one, fraternity members listened to an oral communication attacking fraternities that was accompanied by either a videotaped film of the speaker or a very entertaining silent film that was unrelated to the message. Subjects' attitudes toward fraternities were more influenced by the communication in the second condition than in the first, apparently because the entertaining film distracted subjects from refuting the arguments of the persuasive message.

This conclusion is subject to an important qualification, however. That is, the interpretation assumes that subjects are *motivated* to argue against the communication. If a communication supports one's initial position, or if one has no strong opinions on the issue, one may be less likely to counterargue even in the absence of distraction. In fact, the study showed that nonfraternity members who received antifraternity messages were equally influenced under both distraction conditions. This finding suggests that these subjects, unlike fraternity members, did not counterargue even when distraction was low, and thus were influenced under this condition as well.

Fear-Arousing Communications

In the example just described, distraction was generated by a pleasant stimulus that was irrelevant to the content of the communication. However, distraction may also result from content-relevant features. For example, a communication advocating brushing teeth daily may be accompanied by gory photographs of rotting teeth and diseased gums. While this material may be informative, it may also generate fear or worry; fear may then serve as "internal noise" that distracts the recipient from attending to and evaluating the content of the communication itself. According to the reasoning outlined earlier, messages that contain moderately fear-inducing material (distraction) will have greater impact than those that instill little fear. If the fear-provoking aspects of the message are too extreme, however, they may interfere with reception of the message as well as counterarguing on the part of the recipient, and thus their influence may decrease.

Research on the effectiveness of fear-arousing communications is fairly consistent with this line of reasoning. For example, one study showed that when people believe they are able to cope with the danger conveyed in a communication (for example, smokers who believe they are able to stop smoking), the introduction of fear-arousing material increases the acceptance of the communication advocating behavior designed to eliminate the danger. However, when persons feel they are unable to cope with the danger (for example, smokers who feel unable to stop smoking), the introduction of fear-arousing material has the opposite effect. Very likely the fear-provoking material induces a moderate amount of fear (or distraction) in copers, leading to positive influence, but a high level of fear in noncopers, with the result that the communication has less effect.

Source Factors

A second set of factors that may affect reception and counterarguing has to do with the characteristics of the source to which the communication is attributed. That is, if the source of a message is considered credible or has high prestige, people may be more likely to pay attention to the communication and may also be less inclined to counterargue. Thus, they may be more influenced by the message than if the source had low credibility.

While this prediction is generally supported, the effects are complicated. The above reasoning pertains only to changes in one's true beliefs in the position advocated in a communication. The beliefs people actually *report*, however, may be influenced by other factors. For example, people may report opinions similar to those held by a high-prestige source because they infer that these opinions are socially desirable and are likely to gain them social approval. Similar effects may occur when the source is well liked. These factors may lead to greater *public* advocacy of the opinions of a highly regarded source without necessarily any underlying change in private beliefs.

Thus, one must often distinguish between the effects of source *expertise* or *competence*, which presumably affects true belief change, and the effects of other source characteristics. A good example of the need for this distinction is provided in a study by Herbert Kelman conducted in the early 1950s. Subjects at an all-black university listened to a tape-recorded speech advocating the continuation of all-black colleges and universities. The description of the speaker was varied, however. After hearing the speech, subjects reported their own attitudes toward all-black colleges under conditions in which they were told that their responses would be either anonymous or identifiable. When the source of the message was described as an expert in black history, subjects' opinions were affected under all conditions and persisted over time, suggesting that in this case true opinion change occurred. However, when the source was described as a wealthy alumnus who often donated money to the university and to individual students, subjects changed their opinions only when they believed their responses might be made public, and these changes did not persist over time.

Awareness of Persuasive Intent

The tendency of people to argue against the message of a communication may also be affected by their perception that the communication is being presented for persuasion purposes. Persons who believe that someone is intentionally trying to influence them may think more critically about the message, and thus may be less influenced by it. Thus, subjects who read a message under the assumption that their comprehension of the message is being tested are more influenced than those who are told explicitly that the experimenter is interested in determining the persuasiveness of the message. Presumably, subjects are less likely to counterargue in the first case, and thus are more persuaded.

The intent to persuade may often be conveyed indirectly by the content of the message itself. A communication that presents only one side of an issue may be seen as biased, and therefore may lead to greater attempts to refute its contents, than a message that, while generally presenting the same arguments as the first, also contains arguments that advocate the opposing point of view. In fact, the latter type of message is more effective than the former in inducing opinion change.

Resistance to Persuasion

The above discussion primarily concerns factors that make a communication more effective. However, in a provocative series of experiments suggested by his information-processing theory, McGuire asked an equally important question: What sorts of experiences might be given people before they are exposed to a persuasive communication to increase their *resistance* to persuasion, or to make them less susceptible to influence? Based on the notions outlined above, the answer is straightforward. That is, resistance to persuasion by a communication that attacks a particular belief should be strengthened by increasing the recipient's ability to counterargue, or to refute the arguments contained in this attack. This ability is, in turn, a function of two general factors: (1) the *knowledge* that one has available to use in counterarguing and (2) the amount of *practice* one has previously had in refuting attacks on the belief being threatened.

To demonstrate this idea, McGuire selected cultural truisms (for example, "People should brush their teeth daily") that people typically accept without questioning their validity. McGuire reasoned that these beliefs, albeit strong, would be susceptible to influence because subjects had neither prior knowledge to use in counterarguing against attacks on these beliefs nor practice in doing so. In fact, persuasive communications attacking the validity of these truisms were effective in changing subjects'

Vaccinate Against Peer Pressure
By JUDITH SERRIN

One of the childhood diseases parents fear most is very contagious, strikes in early adolescence, lasts about a decade, and has no known cure except time.

The "disease" is peer pressure.

To many parents, every case is hopeless.

"Parents often complain the trouble with little Johnny is the kids he hangs out with," says Dr. Irving Sarnoff, a New York school psychiatrist.

A Midwestern father of three lamented, "About all you've got with your kids is eight or nine years, then the peer group takes over."

Psychologists and others who work with children are not so pessimistic. While peer pressure is part of growing up and can never be eradicated, they say, children can often be made immune to its worst effects.

Part of the secret is starting the prevention effort early enough, said Sylvia Cutts, director of a drug program in New York City schools.

In general, the need to be liked by peers becomes especially strong in the early teen-age years, Cutts said in an interview.

Because of different maturation rates, girls may be affected somewhat earlier than boys.

When her counselors meet students in sixth grade, she said, "You work with young ladies (to convince them) that they are beautiful, and they are beautiful for themselves and they don't have to be carriers of drugs for their boyfriends."

She said parents should start earlier in the pre-school years, building up children's sense of self-esteem and making them seem important as individuals. . . .

In addition, experts say children should be given experience in making decisions from an early age, with the thought that then they will be less likely to let others decide for them.

Once a child gets to the susceptible

age, the ways to combat peer pressure are more limited. One Cutts suggested involves keeping the child busy with work, classes or other activities. . . .

Often [Sarnoff said] parents should look at themselves if their children seem to bend too easily to their peers.

He said sometimes parents pressure their children to be popular.

Other times, he added, "It's not always what the parent says but the way the parent lives his or her life."

Sarnoff said parents who are overly concerned with what the neighbors or the people at the club will say should not be surprised to find their children following along with the group. . . .

Cutts recommended that parents talk to their children about what she calls survival skills, such as lying. Many teenagers, for example, nurse fictitious hangovers as an excuse to take a soft drink instead of beer at a party. . . .

Boulder (*Colo.*) Daily Camera
December 12, 1979

beliefs in them. To reduce this influence, McGuire exposed some subjects to arguments attacking the truism and then either had them read refutations of these arguments or write their own refutations. Presumably, reading the refutations increases knowledge, whereas writing them provides practice. Both procedures were effective in increasing resistance to a subsequent attack on the truism. In contrast, subjects who read information supporting the truism were as susceptible to later attacks on it as subjects who received no information at all. Since supportive information provides neither knowledge nor practice in *refuting* arguments (counterarguing), this finding is consistent with McGuire's reasoning.

The most interesting aspects of McGuire's research concern findings that resistance to persuasion is increased even when the arguments refuted in the prior "defenses" differ from those contained in the subsequent attack. Moreover, merely exposing subjects to arguments against the truism is sufficient to increase resistance to persuasion provided a period of time has elapsed between the presentation of the arguments and the persuasive message. McGuire suggests that exposure to these arguments makes people aware of their vulnerability to persuasion and stimulates them to bolster their defenses spon-

taneously either by acquiring additional knowledge or by practicing counterarguing. As a result, people become more resistant to influence. This is called an **inoculation effect;** that is, a small dose of the disease (exposure to an argument against the truism) makes one immune to a larger dose (the persuasive communication attacking the truism) when one receives it later on.

Predicting Behavior from Attitudes

In general, we would expect a strong correlation between attitudes and behavior. The more positive your attitude toward something, the more likely you are to behave in a positive way toward that something; and the more negative your attitude, the more likely you are to behave negatively. If, say, you strongly endorse the Equal Rights Amendment, we might predict that your attitude would be exhibited behaviorally in one of several ways — for example, you would write to your state legislators urging them to vote for ratification. However, research has shown that there are certain qualifications to this principle, and attitudes toward a person or object have not been found to be consistent predictors of behavior toward the person or object. For example, there are many persons you like whom you probably would not want to room with or would not recommend for a job. You may consider some professors personally obnoxious but still want to take their courses. You may favor legalizing abortion but if you are a female may not have one yourself. You may believe that cigarettes cause cancer but still smoke. Clearly, a variety of factors in addition to attitude enter into our decision about how to behave toward a person or object.

Two such factors limit our ability to predict behavior from attitudes: (1) lack of information regarding attitudes about the specific behavior being predicted and (2) normative constraints on behavior. Consider the attitudes of a person toward nuclear power plants. Suppose these attitudes are extremely negative. Predicting this person's behavior, for example, whether he or she would picket the construction site of a new plant, from attitudes toward nuclear energy would be difficult. We might not know enough about the above-mentioned two factors. That is, we don't know the person's attitude about picketing or civil disobedience in general, and we don't know what social pressures might prevent (or encourage) picketing. Predictions are greatly improved if you know all three factors—the person's attitude toward nuclear energy, the person's attitude toward the various behaviors such as picketing, and the norms defining "proper" behavior. There were very few acts of civil disobedience in this country until it became clear that the social norms against such acts were not as strong as most people had assumed they were. Indeed, picketing is now practically commonplace and perfectly acceptable.

Attribution—Why Did It Happen?

The most popular research area in social psychology during the last decade has focused on the explanations we give of natural events, including our own behavior and the behavior of others. Explanations of behavior are based upon attributions we make about people or their circumstances. An **attribution** is a statement about the probable cause of an event. Consider the common thief—what causes the person to steal? Do we attribute the behavior to the individual's disposition—"He steals because he is an evil, malicious, no-good, degenerate person"? Or do we attribute the stealing to the person's circumstances—"She steals because she is poor and unemployed."

Attribution processes are pervasive in social behavior. Consider interpersonal attraction, for example. We are more likely to like someone who praises us if we believe that the other's behavior reflects a genuine feeling that we are praiseworthy than if we attribute it to mere flattery. Moreover, our decisions about future behavior may depend upon the attributions we make about the outcomes of similar behavior in the past. For example, we might study harder for an exam if we attribute our past failures in the course to lack of effort than to lack of ability or to the instructor's unfairness. Thus, attribution processes are a central ingredient of social judgment and interpersonal behavior.

Behavior and its consequences often have several possible explanations. For example, a student who studies for an introductory psychology examination may be doing so because (1) he or she wants to get an A in the course, (2) he or she has an intrinsic interest in the subject matter, (3) a poor grade would disappoint his or her parents, (4) he or she has a bet with a roommate as to who will get a higher grade, and so on. In fact, behavior is likely to be multiply caused. Attribution theory and research is not, of course, interested in the *actual* causes of behavior, which may be difficult to determine. Rather, the question typically asked is what sorts of explanations are usually given for behavior, and under what conditions do they occur.

The possible explanations for behavior have often been classified into two types: (1) internal attributions, those that concern the person; and (2) external attributions, those that concern the situation in which the behavior takes place, including any other people who might be present. A further distinction has been made between causal factors that persist over time and across situations (stable) and those that may have existed only at the time the behavior was observed (unstable). Thus, my nasty remark to a co-worker might be attributed to a characteristic of me that is either stable (I am a generally hostile and obnoxious person) or unstable (I am in a bad mood). Or it may be attributed to a stable characteristic of the other person (the person is obnoxious) or to an unstable characteristic (the co-worker was irritable due to heavy work pressure).

Schemata in Attributions

In many cases we probably would not actually attempt to estimate how stable or general the behavior is among people and across situations before making an attribution. Rather, our past experience may have given rise to schemata of the sort described earlier in this chapter; we then apply these schemata to explain the behavior we observe, in much the same way we use schemata to make other sorts of inferences.

We know that people behave in ways that are likely to attain desirable ends. We often apply this notion in making attributions without engaging in any more extensive cognitive work. In one demonstration of this phenomenon, subjects listened to a tape-recorded interview of a person applying for a job that required certain personality qualities. During the interview, the candidate responded in a way that suggested either he had the qualities required by the job or he had the opposite qualities. When the candidate's responses were inconsistent with job requirements, he was judged to be truthful and to have the qualities he professed. However, when his responses were consistent with job requirements, he was judged to have only an average amount of these characteristics. Apparently, in the latter conditions, subjects attributed the actor's behavior to wanting the job for which he was applying and not to the actual characteristics he described.

This tendency exemplifies a principle that accounts for many attribution phenomena. That is, when a person's behavior can be explained by an external attribution based on a situational schema, no stable personality or dispositional characteristic of the actor needs to be invoked. Note that this tendency accounts for much of the research on belief and attitude change. For example, if one agrees to write an essay under conditions in which one is paid, one is judged (by both oneself and others) to have made the decision because of the money (external factor) and not because of a general underlying belief (stable dispositional factor) in the position being advocated.

But as noted earlier, explanations are sometimes based on internal attributions. Whether an external or internal attribution is made depends upon which explanatory schema is activated. For example, if we happen to be viewing a situation from a particular perspective, the factors that are called to our attention from this perspective may be most likely to be used as a basis for our explanation. This possibility helps to account for differences between the explanations that observers give for actors' behavior and the explanations that actors give for their own behavior. (a phenomenon we discussed in Chapter 7, p. 252). In a typical situation, observers' attention is directed toward the actor, whereas the actor's attention is typically focused outward, on other persons in the situation or on characteristics of the situation itself. To this extent observers' explanations of the actor's behavior may typically be in terms of characteristics (for example, personality) of the actor, whereas actors' explanations for their own behavior may typically be in terms of situational characteristics.

However, the choice of explanatory schemata is even more complex. The selection of schemata can be reversed through experimental procedures that change the focus of attention on actors and observers. For example, showing observers a videotape of the situation from the perspective of the actor, or alternatively asking them simply to imagine themselves in the role of the actor, substantially increases their tendency to attribute the actor's behavior to situational characteristics rather than to characteristics of the actor. In contrast, making actors self-conscious (for example, having them behave in front of a mirror) increases their tendency to attribute their behavior to characteristics of themselves (the internal attribution) rather than to the situation (the external attribution).

Motivational Factors

Motivational factors play a role in attributions, particularly when the attributions concern one's own behavior or the outcomes of that behavior. For example, typically we all like to think well of ourselves. Thus, we may tend to explain events in ways that either preserve our images of ourselves as competent or as having socially desirable qualities. Subjects often attribute their *success* on a task to their ability, but avoid attributing their *failure* to their lack of ability. This tendency is called **hedonic bias.** This bias affects the *preferred* explanation of one's behavior when more than one alternative is available. When people succeed on a novel problem, they tend to take responsibility for their success. When they fail, however, they take responsibility only if no alternative explanations are available (see the newsclip "Baseball, Apple Pie and Hedonic Bias").

Interpersonal Attraction

Persons are attracted to other persons for a variety of reasons. Moreover, there are many different kinds of attraction. Our attraction to a friend of the same sex differs qualitatively from our attraction to someone of the opposite sex. "Love" may mean something different when applied to romantic attachments than when applied to one's parents or children.

Most social-psychological research on interpersonal attraction has focused upon factors that underlie the *initial* attraction to persons whom one does not already know. In fact, in many studies, the persons toward whom attraction is assessed are fictitious rather than real. Thus, at the present time we know very little about the factors that underlie the development, maintenance, and deterioration of long-term human relationships. For this reason the present discussion primarily concerns initial attraction.

Similarity and Attraction

In describing balance theory, we noted that a person, *P,* should like another person, *O,* if the two have similar attitudes toward a third person or object, *X,* but should dislike *O* if they have different attitudes toward *X*. Although based on different assumptions, a similar conceptualization has been suggested by Donn Byrne. Byrne hypothesizes that a person's liking for another person is related to the proportion of the

Baseball, Apple Pie and "Hedonic Bias"

"Well, it was, ah, you know, total team effort, and like, ah, coach here says, there are no stars on this team. The individual is, you know, only as good as the rest of the team. I tell you what, though, I was really poppin' those suckers out there today." The speaker, a hypothetical linebacker of a winning football team, is unwittingly creating some sticky problems for social science researchers. His gracious complimenting of his teammates could be considered an external attribution, but since football is a team sport, it may also be an internal attribution; however, there is no question that because the first part of the statement refers to an entire season, rather than just one game, it should be coded as stable, along the stable-unstable dimension. In the second part, the speaker's acknowledge-

ment of his own uncanny ability to inflict harm on the bodies of opposition team members is undeniably an internal attribution; however, his obvious reference to the particular game just played would qualify that portion of his comments as unstable.

Applying these and other criteria to 594 published explanations in 107 articles about 33 major sporting events, social scientists Richard R. Lau of UCLA and Dan Russell of the University of Iowa have completed probably one of the most extensive investigations ever of "hedonic bias"—"the tendency to make internal attributions [to self, teammates, etc.] for success and external attributions [to weather, luck, the other team, etc.] for failure."

As expected, four of five attributions by players and coaches following win-

ning games were attributed to internal factors, while only slightly more than half the attributions were internal after a loss. Sportswriters, however, appeared somewhat more evenhanded, attributing wins to internal (involving the home team) causes 69 percent of the time after wins and 57 percent of the time after losses.

But perhaps the real value of the study, according to the researchers, lies in its demonstration that "it is possible, and we might argue more appropriate, to study the attribution process in natural settings" rather than with college students in the laboratory....

Science News
August 16, 1980

Here is an interesting application of attribution theory, testing a particular hypothesis about internal versus external attribution. In general, we attribute the occurrence of something good to our own ability and effort—internal attribution—but the occurrence of something bad to factors outside ourselves—external attribution. A theory of depression based on attribution theory proposes that the depressed person has a reversed

hedonic bias. Such a person takes all the credit—internal attribution—for the bad events and credits other people—external attribution—for the good outcomes. Couple this kind of thinking with the additional feeling that one is helpless to change things (see "Learned Helplessness," Chapter 4) and it is no wonder some people are depressed.

two person's attitudes that are similar. In a typical experiment, subjects, whose own attitudes toward a variety of topics have been previously determined, are given false information about the attitudes of another whom they believe to be real and expect to meet. The proportion of these attitudes that are similar to those reported earlier by the subject is systematically varied. The subject is then called upon to evaluate the other person along scales related to interpersonal attractiveness. As expected, these evaluations increase in favorableness with the proportion of similar attitudes.

While this relation is not surprising, the reasons for it are not very clear. It could be a result of processes similar to those implied by cognitive balance theory. Another possibility is that a person who has a given attitude toward an issue may simply consider a similar attitude toward the issue to be a desirable attribute, and thus the attitude may affect attraction in much the same way as other favorable attributes of the person ("intelligent," "friendly," and so on).

Byrne's interpretation, however, relies more heavily on the assumption that attitude judgments are mediated by one's underlying feelings about the other. Specifically, he argues that when we learn that another's attitudes are similar to our own, our self-concept is reinforced and thus is rewarded in the learning theory sense (see Chapter 4). The positive feelings produced by the reinforcement generalize to the other person, increasing our liking for that individual.

Reciprocation of Liking

An obvious determinant of our attraction to others, one that is implied by several formulations described earlier, is our perception of others' attraction to us. We are more apt to like someone who has evaluated us favorably than someone who has derogated us. This principle is encompassed by cognitive balance theory and is also suggested by the considerations Byrne has raised. One who praises or reinforces us confirms an aspect of our self-concept,

thus producing positive feelings that generalize to that person. Alternatively, we are more likely to anticipate an enjoyable interaction with someone who likes us than with someone who dislikes us, and thus we may be more attracted to the person for this reason as well.

Why does one person evaluate another in a particular way, favorable or unfavorable? The explanation or attribution we make about the person's reasons will affect our evaluation of the person. For example, we are less likely to like someone who praises us if we believe that the person is just flatter-

The closeness of the friendship between these two women will depend, to a large extent, on the degree to which they are similar in such things as attitudes, habits, and feelings.

Almost Everyone Is Shy, Sometimes

STANFORD, Calif.—Barbara Walters says, "If I'm the epitome of a woman who is always confident and in control, don't ever believe it of anyone."

Elizabeth Taylor says, "I'm basically shy. When I look in the mirror, all I see is an unmade-up face or a made-up face."

Johnny Mathis says, "For a while I thought there was no way I could get over the hangups and be able to be at ease on stage and look like I belong here. It was hell at times. I used to be genuinely petrified. But I'm still not sure what to do and how to act between songs. I feel more at ease than I used to, but shyness on stage is still a problem."

Shyness on stage and in personal life is a problem for a lot of people. Not just celebrities like Carol Burnett, Lawrence Welk and Joan Sutherland. Shyness is a problem that "affects 80 per cent of us at one point or another," says Dr. Philip G. Zimbardo, a social psychology professor at Stanford University, who has spent five years studying it.

"At any one time at least 40 per cent

of the people you meet will tell you they're shy. Two-thirds of those who are shy consider it a personal problem," says Zimbardo.

Because "statistics are convincing but individuals persuade," Zimbardo likes to use celebrities as examples. He is saying to a shy person, "Here are people you admire and respect who have learned to conceal their shyness, but down deep they feel as shy as you do."

Shyness is a complex phenomenon with no one single cause, according to Zimbardo. It is a phenomenon that some people encourage because it is to their advantage.

"It's rare that parents are upset over a shy child. Shyness for many parents and teachers is preferable to assertiveness and outgoing behavior on the part of a child.

"Behavior management is the essential ingredient to the way they perceive their job. Shy people are easy to manage."

For the shy child that never grows out of it they can look forward to a life where "almost every aspect of it is

diminished. They have few friends. Less sexual contact, if any. They tend not to date or marry. The kinds of jobs they take lead to positions of less authority.

"It's a minimal arrangement with life. The shy person gives little and gets little. They always sell themselves short and always settle for less than they ought to."...

It is a myth that men tend to be more shy than women, points out Zimbardo. But it is the man who will suffer more, because the traits of shyness stereotypically accepted in women as attractive and appealing features are not in men....

"The central feeling of shyness is anxiety that other people will evaluate your performance in a negative way. Everything you do, you see as a performance. Life is a performance filled with an audience of critics like William F. Buckley Jr. ready to pounce on your every wrong move or utterance," says Zimbardo....

Boulder *(Colo.)* Daily Camera
December 27, 1977

An obvious prerequisite to effective interpersonal relationships is a willingness to engage in interaction with others at some minimal level. Socializing is an important part of our experience, and much of our lives is the product of social interaction. Nevertheless, many people are uncomfortable in social situations because they feel shy, an obvious example of inhibitory

social influence. Shyness as a phenomenon has recently been studied by social psychologist Philip Zimbardo and his colleagues. Of thousands of high school and college students surveyed, 40 percent described themselves as presently shy, and 80 percent reported that they had been shy at some period in their lives.

"Do you know what I like about you, Rachel? You're old, like me."

The New Yorker, July 22, 1974. Drawing by Weber; © 1974 The New Yorker Magazine, Inc.

ing us than if we believe that the person is sincere. In the first case, we attribute flattery; in the second, we attribute sincerity. Factors that affect the attributions we make will in turn influence our overt behavior.

It would be wrong to conclude that ingratiation, or insincere praise of another, has no effect on liking. Although we are less affected when we consider praise to be insincere, we nevertheless would rather be flattered than ignored or evaluated negatively. Using flattery may not get one as far as sincerity will, but it will get one farther than offering no praise at all.

Attributions may enter into interpersonal attraction phenomena in other ways. For example, situations that make us uncomfortable may lead us to experience negative feelings. We may misattribute the cause of our discomfort to the people we are with rather than to the context, thus decreasing our liking for these people. Suppose you accept a blind date to go to a dinner party only to find out that the conversation is dull and the food is terrible. Some of the negative feelings caused by the context may be attributed unfairly to your date, making it less likely that you will accept other invitations from that person in the future. Manipulations of a person's mood by methods that are completely unrelated to other people nonetheless affects judgments of the attractiveness of those people.

Equity and Beliefs in a Just World

One interesting hypothesis concerning the determinants of attraction is that most people have a need to believe that ours is a just world. Information that another good person has been the victim of misfortune may therefore threaten our belief that the world is just. To maintain this belief, we may consequently derogate the victim or in other ways convince ourselves that the person deserved the misfortune. Moreover, this derogation should be greater when the victim's trouble is serious than when it is slight. In one experiment, a person is asked to observe and evaluate a subject serving in a learning experiment. The subject is receiving punishments for errors. The observer's evaluation of the subject turns out to be correlated with the number of punishments he or she expects the subject to receive — the more punishment the subject receives, the less the observer likes the subject. This is true even though neither the observer nor the subject has any control over the number of punishments.

A general formulation of interpersonal attraction that encompasses just-world considerations is **equity theory.** In equity theory the emphasis is shifted from individual to mutual benefits. It is assumed that a group of people can maximize their outcome in any interaction situation by working out an arrangement for equitably dividing the benefits and costs among group members.

In a just world, equity would prevail — what you get out of a relationship would be approximately equal to what you put into it in the way of your personal attributes and the behaviors you exhibit during the relationship. Stable relationships will be formed only when equity exists between input and output. Long-term interpersonal attraction is based upon the stability and degree of equity in the relationship. Inequity leads to instability and decreased attraction, mainly, of course, for the person who is getting "the short end of the stick," the person who is putting in more than he or she is getting out. Equity is thought to apply to all aspects of the relationship, not just to how the two people treat each other. It applies to such nonbehavioral aspects as the degree of physical beauty of the two people: Equity says that a *stable* attraction will form most often when the two people are about equally beautiful (see the newsclip "Attractively Matched Pairs"). Presumably equity would also apply to the financial resources of the two individuals. Overall equity, however, is the critical feature of a stable attraction, not necessarily equity on *every* dimension. Compensatory factors can and will offset each other, keeping things roughly equitable, as when a very rich but not so beautiful man forms a stable relationship with a poor but beautiful woman. For example, a fantastic "personality" could compensate for lack of physical beauty. Equity theory has the most to say about what relationships will be lasting or stable, with the stability of the relationship being directly proportional to the degree of

Attractively Matched Pairs

People may fantasize about love affairs with the most attractive possible partner, but in reality they enjoy the closest relationships with friends and lovers who most nearly match them in physical allure. In a study of 150 couples at the University of California, Los Angeles, which included people representing a range of closeness from casual daters to married students, those who were judged to be most equal in attractiveness by others judged themselves to have the most positive "love change" over time.

Gregory L. White of the University of Maryland reported in the Journal of Personality and Social Psychology that he photographed all 300 men and women individually, asked a panel of arbiters to rate their attractiveness, and got the subjects to assess their love lives on a questionnaire. Nine months later, Dr. White retested many of the original respondents to gauge the progress of their courtship or marriage.

He found in the first round that the married couples, whom he assumed to be the most intimate pairs in the sample, most nearly balanced each other in attractiveness.

At the time the second questionnaire was administered, 20 couples who had been casually or seriously dating reported break-ups. And, as predicted, they were the ones least like each other in attractiveness.

The New York Times
December 23, 1980

Equity theory predicts that stable relationships involve partners who contribute equally. Equity applies to both behavioral dimensions (for example, the two people are equally kind to each other) and physical dimensions, as this newsclip testifies.

equity. Our initial attraction to another person is less a matter of equity, although we may make judgments about the potential of equity in deciding what attractions we wish to pursue. We might be attracted to someone much more beautiful than ourselves, but we wouldn't do anything about it because we would expect inequity and thus not a lasting relationship.

The Role of Self in Social Behavior

One factor that distinguishes much of social psychology from other areas of research is the recognition that one's conception of oneself (a crucial set of schemata) plays an important role in the processing of social information and in the subsequent social behavior. In other words, the most important schemata each of us has are the self-schemata, or the self-concept. This effect has been implicit in much of our previous discussion of attribution and interpersonal attraction. However, because of its importance and the wide variety of ways in which self enters into social information processing, a brief overview of these effects is desirable. Included are (1) the role of self schemata in organizing and interpreting information about others; (2) the effect of self-consciousness on social behavior and judgments; and (3) the motivating effects of self-esteem on behavior and judgments.

Self Schemata

We noted earlier that people tend to interpret and organize information with reference to previously acquired schemata that are easily accessible in memory. The most easily accessible schemata may be those we have about ourselves. Evidence that we often use information about ourselves as a basis for interpreting information and making inferences about others comes from many sources. Only a few examples will be provided here.

1. People are more likely to remember information about others if they have been stimulated to think about the information with reference to themselves (for example, whether another's characteristics are like or unlike one's own) than if they have been asked to think about it in other ways.
2. People may use their own opinion about a topic as a measure for judging the favorableness of others' opinions. For example, you may judge the statement "Jimmy Carter did an average job as President" as being either favorable or unfavorable to Carter, depending upon your own opinion of Carter's performance. If you thought he was a poor President, you will take the statement as being favorable and judge the person making it to be a Carter supporter; the opposite will happen if you thought Carter did an excellent job.
3. When we have made a decision to engage in a behavior, we may use this information to predict what others will do in the same circumstances. This may lead to a "false consensus bias," or a tendency to infer that more people behave as we ourselves behave than is actually the case. Moreover, we may then judge people who behave differently than we do as "deviant."

Self-Consciousness

The effects described are presumably more likely to occur when we are actively thinking about ourselves (self-conscious), and therefore we are more apt to use ourselves as a basis for comparison in processing information about others. However, there may be additional consequences of such self-awareness. For one thing, people who are self-conscious may be more sensitive to the implications of their behavior. This possibility may give rise to a variety of effects. For example, people may be led to behave in the way they

Highlight 10–3

Are There Any Faces in a Crowd?

Social psychologists have suggested that crowd violence may, to a large extent, be a function of the fact that crowd members typically lose their individual identity. They may feel less personally responsible for their behavior, less likely to be punished because they cannot be identified, and, as a result, more prone to behave violently. Phillip Zimbardo (1969) has done an ingenious experiment to demonstrate the importance of the deindividuation, or loss of personal identity, that takes place in groups. Groups of four female subjects listened to recordings of interviews with potential "victims." Some groups were given a deindividuation treatment—the women wore growns and hoods to disguise themselves, and the experimenters never used their names. In other groups the women were not disguised; they wore name tags, and everyone referred to everyone else by name—these were the identifiable groups. Each group listened to interviews with pleasant and unpleasant "victims," and later each group member was induced to deliver shocks to the victims, whom they could now see through a one-way mirror. The victim was, of course, a coinvestigator in the study, and she acted as if she were being shocked, although no shocks were delivered. The key finding was that women in the deindividuation groups delivered longer shocks than women in the identifiable group, and this was true regardless of whether they perceived the victim as a pleasant or an unpleasant person.

Deindividuation is not just a laboratory phenomenon.

consider to be socially responsible or consistent with socially learned standards for appropriate behavior. On the other hand, if the behavior is observed and evaluated by other persons, people may be made more sensitive to the expectancies of other people and more likely to conform to these expectancies. With decreasing self-consciousness the person's tendency to consider the social implications of his or her behavior may decrease and the person may

be led to behave in ways that are inconsistent with generally accepted standards of social responsibility. In short, self-consciousness can serve to constrain behavior to conform to standards or norms.

The role of self-consciousness has been investigated in a variety of research paradigms. One of the most striking demonstrations of the importance of self-consciousness (or, in this case, the lack of it) was provided by Philip Zimbardo. Zimbardo used male student volunteers to play the roles of guards and prisoners in a simulated prison environment. The experiment took place over a period of several days in a realistic prison atmosphere. Although participants were typical of most college students, placing them in their assigned roles led them to behave spontaneously in ways they would consider immoral outside the prison environment. For example, the "guards" often became brutal and sadistic toward the "prisoners," forcing them to engage in activities that were personally degrading. In fact, the experiment was prematurely terminated because of signs of severe emotional disturbance in many of the participants. Apparently, taking the roles provided by the social structure of the experiment led subjects to become *deindividuated,* or less conscious of themselves as individuals. They therefore became insensitive to the norms of social morality and responsibility they typically adopted outside the experimental atmosphere.

In another study, researchers unobtrusively observed Hallowe'en trick-or-treaters taking candies under conditions in which they had been asked to take only one candy each. In standard conditions, many children violated the norm, taking more than they were told to take. However, identifying each child by name when she or he first came to the door substantially reduced this tendency. Although the children did not know they were being observed, identifying them by name apparently made them aware of themselves as individuals, and this led them to invoke general normative standards of responsible behavior that had temporarily been deactivated in the excitement of Hallowe'en.

Self-awareness can be induced in fairly subtle ways. In the laboratory, for example, subjects are more sensitive to external standards for evaluation when they are in a room in which there is a mirror. Although the mirror ostensibly has nothing to do with the experiment, subjects who see themselves in the mirror apparently become more self-conscious, and consequently more sensitive to the implications of their behavior. This sensitivity is manifested in a variety of ways, ranging from a tendency to report less positive (that is, more "modest") self-evaluations to a tendency to administer shock to another person under conditions in which doing so is either normatively acceptable or unacceptable.

Motivating Effects of Self-Esteem

Much research has been based on the assumption that people are motivated to behave in ways that maintain and enhance their self-image. Moreover, people will distort their perceptions of others' behavior toward themselves so as to preserve this self-image. Thus, as we noted in the discussion of attribution processes, we discredit information that we have done poorly on a task by attributing our failure to our lack of effort, to bad luck, or to the fact that the task would be impossible for anyone to do well. In fact, we are motivated actively to seek information that helps us maintain our self-esteem: If we scored low on an intelligence test, we may seek information that questions the validity of the test in preference to information that suggests the test results are accurate. The tendency to disparage people who evaluate us unfavorably, predicted by balance theory, may also be viewed as a means of preserving self-esteem by discrediting the source of the evaluation. The teacher who failed us is incompetent, the person who left us for another lover is not worth having. The reasons for this motivational effect are fairly clear. In the extreme, failure to preserve our self-esteem can have devastating consequences for our mental health, such as severe depression (see Chapter 11).

The discussion here provides only a few examples of the ways in which "self" enters into the processing of information, either as (1) a source of information, (2) a basis for comparison, or (3) a motivating factor that affects reactions to information and behavioral decisions. The role of self is also critical with respect to the effect of other persons on one's behavior—the issue to which we now turn.

The Presence of Others

The effect of other persons on an individual's attitudes and behavior is evident from much of the research we have already described. In this section, we will consider the effect of these factors in some detail. Four general topics will be considered: (1) the desire to seek interaction with others to obtain information about oneself; (2) the effects on behavior of the mere presence of persons with whom one does not necessarily interact; (3) the effects of interacting cooperatively with others; and (4) the effects of interacting with others in competitive or conflict situations.

Others as a Basis for Self-Evaluation

Not only do we use ourselves as bases for judging others, but we also use other persons and their behavior as bases for evaluating ourselves. Three questions arise in connection with the tendency to compare ourselves with others: (1) *when* do we compare ourselves with others? (2) *with whom* do we compare ourselves? and (3) *what* are the effects of these comparisons?

When?

People are most likely to compare themselves with others when they desire to evaluate themselves or their reactions but do not have previously developed internalized standards or norms to use in making these evaluations. Such is most likely to be the case when the situation is novel or the information we receive about ourselves is ambiguous. Early work on affiliation behavior by Stanley Schachter and his colleagues provides a good example. Female subjects were initially told they would have to undergo a series of shocks that were described as either very mild or very painful. While waiting for the experiment to begin, they had to choose between sitting alone or in a room with another potential subject. Subjects more frequently chose to wait with the other subject when they anticipated receiving severe shocks than when they anticipated mild shocks. The generally accepted interpretation is that subjects chose to wait with other participants because these persons provided a standard of comparison that subjects could use in evaluating their own reactions; thus they could determine if they were more or less upset and worried than "average."

While Schachter's research is striking, a situation need not be as emotionally arousing as those he constructed in order to stimulate persons to engage in social comparison. In fact, we live in a world in which there are few absolute standards of evaluation, and we must often rely upon others to provide these measures either directly or indirectly. Much of the information we receive about ourselves, if considered in isolation, is difficult to interpret. For example, a person who learns his or her score on a multiple-choice examination may have no means of interpreting the score without knowing how other students performed. Or we may wish to know whether our reactions to a new movie are similar to others'. In some cases, of course, clear social norms have been developed for evaluating our behavior and its consequences. In these cases, we may use these norms as standards, and the opinions and behavior of others may not be necessary. In other cases, however, social comparison is clearly essential for self-evaluation.

With Whom?

Not everyone is a useful source of information. Rather, the persons with whom we are most likely to compare ourselves are those who we believe are similar to us along dimensions relevant to the characteristic being evaluated. Thus, college students are unlikely to want to compare their performances on an introductory psychology exam with those of either graduate students or high school dropouts. Rather, students are apt to prefer to compare their scores with those obtained by others with similar backgrounds

and training. An implication, of course, is that the persons with whom we compare ourselves will vary, depending on what characteristic is being judged, and also may change over time as our own background and experience changes.

Sometimes people choose poor models to compare themselves with, often because of similarities on characteristics not relevant to the issue at hand. For example, seeing that many people quite similar to yourself can run a marathon, you enter such a race without adequate training, and you fail miserably. You neglected to consider that the persons you saw crossing the finish line trained hard for perhaps a year. Not knowing enough about the people you compare yourself with can make matters worse for you, while learning about others can help you. Failure to compare yourself with truly similar others can cause you to miscalculate your own circumstances. For this reason, groups such as Alcoholics Anonymous, Weight Watchers, and Parents without Partners are extremely helpful to their members. Getting together with similar people who have similar difficulties and who want to help each other is one of the most effective treatments for these types of problems.

What?

One reason for comparing yourself with others is to measure how deviant you are from the "typical" person of the sort you consider to be a relevant basis for comparison, that is, persons similar to yourself.

Thus, our satisfaction with our job and salary may be affected substantially by the jobs and salaries we perceive others hold with whom we compare ourselves. A university faculty member may feel more satisfied with her salary of $25,000 if she compares herself to other members of her department at the university than if she compares herself to friends with similar backgrounds and experience who are working in business or industrial settings. Moreover, she may feel more satisfied if she finds that her university colleagues with equivalent experience make $20,000 a year than if they make $30,000. To the extent that job satisfaction affects performance, desire to change jobs, and so on, the results of social comparisons may be rather profound.

In the case of *opinions* or personality characteristics, the effects of social comparison may be somewhat different. That is, if a person finds he scores lower on a "feminism" scale than others with whom he compares himself, the person may conclude that his attitude or behavior is more antifeminist than is socially desirable. The individual may consequently change these opinions to conform to those of others, or may attempt to behave in ways that are more profeminist. Such reactions, typically referred to as *conformity* behaviors, are discussed later in this chapter.

Comparing yourself with people who are quite different from yourself in appearance or life-style can result in erroneous conclusions about what is appropriate for your own behavior.

Effect of Others on Behavior

The mere presence of other persons may be sufficient to affect your behavior in a situation. Social psychologists have focused on two areas of inquiry in examining these effects. First, they examine the effect of other people on task performance to see if the presence of others will facilitate or inhibit your performance. Second, they look at the effect of the presence of others on your willingness to help someone in trouble. Robert Zajonc postulated that the presence of other persons is motivating, arousing, or drive producing. As a result, the magnitude of responses that typically occur in a situation will increase. Thus, if the responses that are dominant in an achievement situation facilitate performance, performance may be increased by the presence of others. This effect is termed **social facilitation.** However, if the dominant re-

sponses interfere with performance, the presence of others will have a detrimental effect. This effect is called **social interference.** Reasoning of this kind has been applied in achievement situations in which the difficulty of the task has varied. As expected, on easy tasks, where the responses that facilitate performance are well learned, the presence of others appears to facilitate performance. On difficult tasks, where subjects may have a variety of competing responses that interfere with performance, the presence of others decreases performance.

The effect of others' presence is quite different in situations in which someone needs help. People are less willing to help a person in distress when they believe that others are present and also potentially available to help. In fact, the likelihood that a person in distress will receive help actually *decreases* as the num-

**Woman Slain in Subway;
12 Watch, Don't Help**

NEW YORK (AP) — Police say more than a dozen persons watched without helping as a would-be robber knifed a 34-year-old former Denver woman to death in the 66th Street IRT subway station at Lincoln Center.

Claudia Curfman Castellana, of 560 Riverside Drive, New York, was stabbed and slashed 10 times in the chest, back and arm at the bottom of the stairs of the subway station . . . , police said.

Witnesses said they heard the woman screaming, "Leave me alone. Leave me alone," just before the killer attacked.

Mrs. Castellana staggered further into the station and collapsed between the turnstiles and the change booth just as passengers began to leave a train that had pulled into the station. She was pronounced dead on arrival at Roosevelt Hospital. . . .

Police said persons who witnessed the attack apparently made no move to help the woman fight off the killer, but some of those getting off the northbound local chased a man they believed to be the assailant. The man got away.

"He got away and we don't know whether it was the right man or not," a detective said late Sunday.

Police believe the assailant followed the woman into the subway, intending to rob her. . . .

Mrs. Castellana's murder came just as Transit Authority police released a report claiming that major crime in the subways had dropped 16 per cent in the first seven months of this year.

The Denver Post
August 8, 1977

Social psychologists are grappling with the problem of bystander apathy, the refusal of bystanders to help in an emergency. One theory is that the more bystanders there are, the more everyone tends to assume that someone else in the group will take the responsibility.

ber of persons available to provide help increases. An extreme is the well-known Kitty Genovese case in New York. Here, the woman was heard screaming and observed being attacked and ultimately murdered in a parking lot by no less than 38 witnesses in a neighboring building, not one of whom attempted to intervene even by calling the police. This phenomenon, eventually termed *bystander apathy,* was studied first in the laboratory by Latané and Darley (1970). Subjects participated in an experiment in groups of two, three, or six persons. In all cases, subjects were physically isolated from one another and communicated over an intercom. During the experiment, one subject (a confederate) was overheard to experience an epileptic seizure, becoming increasingly agitated

and incoherent, asking repeatedly for help, and ultimately lapsing into a state of apparent unconsciousness. When subjects believed that only two persons (themselves and the victim) were present, 85 percent offered help (by reporting the emergency to the experimenter). However, when one other subject was present, only 62 percent helped, and when four others were present, the percentage decreased to 31. According to Latané and Darley, when subjects believe that others are available to help, they perceive themselves to be less personally responsible and are less inclined to lend help. Another possibility is that subjects are unsure that the victim's apparent discomfort really constitutes an emergency, and thus rely upon others to make that decision. In either event, the social consequences of the phenomenon are somewhat upsetting.

In the Latané and Darley study, subjects were all anonymous and did not expect to meet one another personally. If subjects believed they would be meeting and interacting with others after the experiment, the overall likelihood of their offering help substantially increased, and the effect of differences in the number of others available decreased. Thus, when persons are not anonymous and expect that others will evaluate their behavior, they are less likely to shift responsibility, and their willingness to help increases. It is interesting to compare these findings with those on deindividuation (see p. 382). In that case, persons who were identified by name had a decreased tendency to violate norms of social responsibility. A similar process may be operating in bystander apathy.

Group Problem Solving and Decision Making

In many situations, persons are called upon as a group to solve a problem or make a decision. One instance is in class projects where everyone must work together to solve a particular problem. Another familiar example occurs in the courtroom, where a jury must decide as a group whether a defendant is or is not guilty. In this research, several questions have been raised concerning the nature of the decision process itself, and given this process, the sorts of solutions that are likely to occur. The answers to these questions depend on (1) the nature of the problem to be solved, (2) the distribution of members' individual predispositions concerning the correct solution, and (3) the number of persons in the group.

Type of Problem

Two general types of problems may confront groups. In the first, there is a demonstrably correct answer that, once identified, becomes obvious to all group members. A good example is an anagram: The

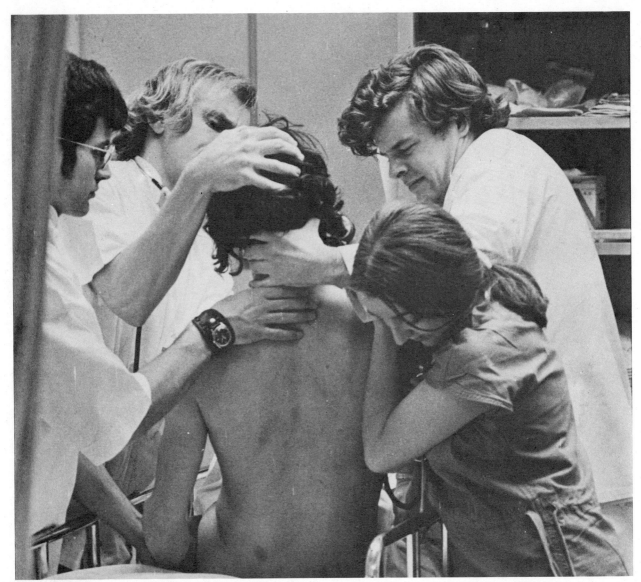

Group problem solving works best when each person has a clearly identified role and special expertise and the contribution of each individual is necessary to obtain the group's objective.

anagram HOTUG may be initially difficult to unscramble, but once a person has done so, it becomes clear to everyone that the answer TOUGH is correct. In the second type of problem, there is no clear-cut solution. For example, in the case of a political group trying to decide on its candidate in an election, there may be no clearly correct answer that everyone will agree upon.

In the first type of problem, the group's decision as to the correct solution can be predicted on the basis of the initial distribution of individual opinions before group discussion of the situation. Thus, if at least two group members have independently identified the

demonstrably correct solution, the group will adopt the solution regardless of the number of other members who initially disagreed. However, typically a single person with the demonstrably correct solution is *not* sufficient to guarantee that the group will recognize the solution; apparently groups tend to give little attention to the judgment of a single person, even if the judgment would be recognized as correct if it were considered. A minority opinion can in fact influence group decisions when there is a clear-cut solution, but only if the minority is greater than 1. When there is a correct solution that is not obvious, however, a large minority, or even a majority, is required to produce a group solution. As a result, on difficult problems, people generally perform less well as a group than the best member would perform if allowed to proceed individually.

In the second type of problem, where there is no obviously correct solution, the group will typically evaluate and waiver considerably before arriving at a decision. In a simulation of jury decision processes, for example, James Davis has found that for a judgment to be made, usually about two-thirds of the members must initially favor one alternative solution (for example, guilty or not guilty). Otherwise, the jury is often "hung" and arrives at no solution. Davis points out the implications of this finding for jury size. When the likelihood is low that individual jurors will initially favor a guilty verdict, a 6-person jury is more likely to convict than a 12-person jury. As this likelihood increases, however, the importance of jury size decreases. This conclusion has important practical implications for legislation on the number of members that should be allowed to sit on juries: Typically, the smaller the jury size, the more detrimental the jury is for the defendant.

Conformity

The processes of group decision making, and in some cases those that underlie effective group performance, often lead individual members to adopt opinions or behaviors that are dictated by the group as a whole. People may conform to the judgments or behavior of others for two primary reasons. One influence is *informational*—people may believe that others' opinions or behaviors are more likely to be correct than their own. A second reason people may conform is that, regardless of whether they consider the group opinions or behaviors to be correct, they do not want to *appear* to disagree with other members of the group. This *normative* influence is likely to be pronounced when people (1) are concerned about receiving social approval from other group members and (2) feel that this approval is contingent upon adoption of the majority opinion.

Conformity is typically greatest when a person believes that he or she is the only one who deviates from the normative group position. Solomon Asch, for example, found that conformity is substantially reduced when subjects perceive that at least one other group member is also willing to deviate from the group norm. (See Highlight 10–5). This finding has important implications. For example, social pressure to adopt a position or behavior may lead to the establishment and maintenance of a group norm that few members of the group actually consider desirable, but that none is willing to oppose publicly because of the incorrect belief that others will disapprove of the opposition. However, as soon as one person is willing to deviate, others are also prompted to deviate and to

Highlight 10–4

Social Loafing

When people cooperate on a common task, group output is supposed to increase. Team spirit is thought to encourage individual effort. But this is not the case, according to some recent research, which found that when people think their individual contribution to the group cannot be measured, their individual output tends to slacken. This phenomenon resembles bystander apathy. In the context of group productivity, it has been called *social loafing*.

In recent studies, relatively simple behaviors such as cheering and clapping, two moderately tiring activities that people commonly perform in groups, have been used as tasks. Both tasks depend upon the simple sum of individual efforts and can easily be measured. As one would expect, the more people clapping or cheering, the louder the noise and the higher the level of sound pressure produced. However, the sound-pressure level does not grow in proportion to the number of people in the group. In fact, the average sound-pressure level generated by each person decreases with increasing group size.

One explanation for social loafing is that when performing in groups people may feel that any praise or blame received is less contingent on their individual output than when they perform alone. People can "hide in crowds" and avoid the negative consequences of slacking off. Any credit that accrues to the group as a whole has to be divided among its members equally, regardless of individual contributions. Thus, some group members tend to become freeloaders and coast on the group's efforts. This temptation may grow with the size of the group and with the effort required to perform the task. Do you think that the alleged decline in the labor productivity of U.S. workers might be related to the phenomenon of social loafing?

One possible generalization of this phenomenon arises when people must share a common resource. We are all constantly being reminded of the pollutants in our air and water, the limitations on our energy supplies, and other serious threats to our vital resources. But the fact that our resources are *shared* could contribute to the frequently observed tendency for individuals to use more than their share, perhaps thinking "others will conserve" or "no one will notice the difference." As in industrial productivity, promotion of individual responsibility might be required to counteract these tendencies. Inducing each person to conserve is probably as important as finding new energy sources or inventing nonpolluting engines.

The New Yorker, December 6, 1976. Drawing by Lorenz; © 1976 The New Yorker Magazine, Inc.

adopt the position they personally believe is correct.

Although the conformity research just described pertains to group judgments, conformity in general is a common occurrence. A certain degree of conformity may be manifest simply to facilitate communication with others and permit congenial everyday interactions. When we meet another person for the first time we are unlikely to express extreme opinions on issues in order to avoid offending the other. If you are politically liberal, you would not tell a politically conservative person that you consider right-wing politics to be dangerous. Rather, we may attempt to arrive at some compromise between our actual belief and the belief we believe the other person holds. Or we may express our opinion somewhat tentatively, in a way that is unlikely to be offensive. This sort of conformity is simply a matter of social etiquette.

The tendency to comply with others' expectations in social situations may nevertheless be surprisingly strong, as powerfully demonstrated in a study by Stanley Milgram (1965). Subjects in the experiment were asked to administer electric shocks to another subject for making errors in a learning experiment. The "victim"—a confederate who, of course, was not actually shocked—deliberately made repeated errors, thus leading subjects to administer increasingly intense shocks. As the severity of the shocks increased, the victim began to manifest extreme agitation, com-

plaining of a bad heart and pleading with the investigator to terminate the experiment. Despite these pleas, most subjects continued to administer shocks—often up to a level of 450 volts—upon minimal urging from the experimenter that they must continue for the success of the study. Interestingly, many subjects in a control group, who simply had the study described to them, said that the study was immoral and that they would refuse to participate in it. The experiment provides a striking example of the influence of social pressure on people to engage in behavior that under other circumstances they would consider objectionable.

"A word to the wise, Benson. People are asking why they don't see Old Glory on *your* bike."

Playboy, June 1971. Reproduced by special permission of PLAYBOY Magazine; copyright © 1971 by Playboy.

Highlight 10–5

Conformity: Asch's Findings

FIGURE 10–1   To conform or not to conform?

In the classic study of conformity, Solomon Asch had seven subjects sit around a table and judge which of three lines was equal in length to a standard line they had seen earlier. The only real subject was Number 6; the others were paid confederates of Asch. Although the task was very easy, in one of the experimental conditions the confederates all lied about which line was correct. When it was Number 6's turn to respond, he usually showed signs of conflict (straining, double-checking, and so on) over whether to conform to the group judgment or give the response that he perceived was correct.

FIGURE 10–2   Asch's task

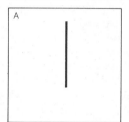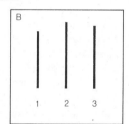

After viewing card A, the subjects must pick the line from B that matches.

FIGURE 10–3   Asch's results

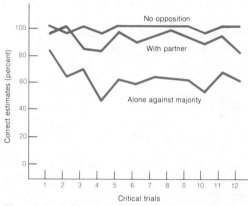

The number of correct responses of subject Number 6 under three conditions: when the group did not lie (no opposition), when they all lied together (alone against majority), and when one confederate agreed with Number 6 against the majority (with partner). Note that all it takes is one other person to counteract the conformity effect.

Other Effects of Group Decision Making

While there is abundant evidence that conformity influences group functioning, one common result may seem to be inconsistent with this tendency. That is, a judgment rendered by a group tends to be more extreme than the *average* of individual judgments made before participation in the group judgment. Moreover, this shift to extremity is reflected in the judgments made by individual members after the group judgment has been arrived at. This phenomenon, the *group polarization effect,* has been detected in a variety of judgmental situations. Of these, one of the most interesting occurs when a group is called

Highlight 10–6

The Robbers Cave Experiment

A classical social psychology experiment on group conflict called the Robbers Cave experiment (named after the site of the study) was published in 1961 by Sherif, Harvey, White, Hood, and Sherif. Here are the facts of the Robbers Cave experiment.

The subjects were 12-year-old boys selected to be good examples of typical middle-class American children. They were normal, healthy, well adjusted, happy, fun-loving, and energetic. The experimenters divided the boys into two groups designed to equate the members on such attributes as intelligence and size.

The boys understood they were going to summer camp, and each group was taken separately to an isolated Boy Scout camp.

The camp was actually being run by the experimenters, who hired the camp counselors. The counselors observed the boys' behavior and reported on it to the experimenters (the measurement was unobtrusive because the boys merely thought of the counselors as counselors). The experimenters and counselors conducted camp activities according to a preconceived experimental plan that had three stages.

In the first stage the two groups of boys were treated separately in such a way as to develop a feeling of group identification and belongingness. This was done by having the boys work on projects designed to achieve goals that they all would value and that they all would have to cooperate to attain. Sample projects were improving the swimming hole and building a rope bridge. Each group was treated so that the end result would be two groups of boys, each with a high level of within-group cohesiveness. One group of boys decided to call itself the Rattlers, and the other group took the name Eagles. At this stage each group was separated from the other and worked independently on different projects. By the end of the first stage the experimenters had succeeded in creating two real groups as opposed to just a collection of boys. Within each group there were definite feelings of belonging to the group.

In the second stage the counselors began to create conflict between the two groups, pitting one group against the other in a series of contests, such as baseball and tug-of-war. The competition between groups produced intergroup hostility, expressed in name calling, fighting, and raiding each other's camps. The Rattlers did not like the Eagles, and the feeling was mutual. Prejudice against out-group members and in favor of in-group members clearly existed.

The third stage consisted of efforts to reduce the intergroup hostility. Simply bringing the two groups together (for example, having them eat together) had no effect on the hostility. Providing the boys with a common enemy (a third group of boys) did reduce hostility between the Rattlers and the Eagles, but the boys were still hostile. The groups merely displaced their hostility to the common enemy.

What did reduce the total hostility was the same thing that was responsible for developing the feelings of group belongingness in the first stage. The experimenters set tasks that required the two groups to work together to achieve the goals, and the goals were designed to be of value to members of both groups. For example, it was arranged for the camp truck to break down while it was taking both groups on a camping trip both were looking forward to. All the boys in both groups were needed to pull the truck up a hill to get it started again. Because the goal was positive in character, hostility was not elicited. Because cooperative effort between the groups was necessary, intergroup hostility was no longer appropriate. A series of such cooperative ventures eventually led to intergroup friendliness to the point that the boys requested that they go home together in one bus. In fact, with their prize money one of the groups treated the other to milkshakes on the way home.

---

upon to make a decision that involves an element of risk. In this case, if subjects are already inclined toward a risky decision, group discussion increases risk-taking. On the other hand, if individual members lean toward conservatism, group discussion *decreases* risk-taking.

A variety of possibilities have been suggested to explain this phenomenon. One hypothesizes that the effect is partly due to conformity, with the individual group members who are originally more extreme in their opinions having greater influence.

A second possibility is based on social comparison considerations. That is, persons may believe that taking a definite stand on issues is desirable and may consider themselves to be somewhat above "average" in their willingness to do so. However, if in comparing themselves to other group members they find that their position is only "average," they may attempt to maintain their self-image by increasing the extremity of their stance in either direction. These two possibilities are not incompatible, and both probably contribute simultaneously to the group polarization effect.

Conflict Resolution

The preceding discussion is restricted to situations in which persons interact cooperatively in pursuit of the common goal of arriving at a correct judgment. In other situations, participants have different goals, and the behavior of each person affects both the individual's own outcomes and those of others. Moreover, the goals of the participants may conflict, so that the condition which is most desirable for one person may be undesirable for others. Under these circumstances, how are the conflicts resolved?

The most interesting general approach to the investigation of conflict resolution has been to simulate in the laboratory complex bargaining situations of the sort found in labor-management disputes and in the political arena. This research takes into account the important fact that people bring to most interaction situations different skills and resources. These various strengths may affect the sorts of agreements that are reached.

The processes of bargaining and negotiation are complex. Suppose, for example, that three people, Adams, Black, and Cooper, are candidates for nomination by a political party and that 450 votes are required for nomination. Adams controls 400 votes, Black 300, and Cooper 200. No single candidate has enough votes to win, but any two, by combining their votes (forming a *coalition*), can claim victory. Suppose that 100 patronage jobs are available as a result of winning the nomination. Which two persons will form a coalition, and how will the patronage jobs be allocated between the two?

A variety of theoretical models have been proposed to answer these questions. Although the models differ in detail, the more successful ones have been based in part upon the equity considerations noted earlier in this chapter. Suppose each candidate, by forming a coalition with another, believes he will re-

ceive rewards (patronage) proportional to his input (votes controlled). Under these conditions, each candidate would prefer to form a coalition with the one who contributes the *least*, provided the contribution is enough to guarantee victory. Thus, Adams would prefer to form a coalition with Cooper rather than Black, since Adams could expect to receive 67 percent (400/[400 + 200]) of the patronage in the first case but only 57 percent (400/[400 + 300]) in the second. Black, in turn, would prefer to form a coalition with Cooper than with Adams, while Cooper would prefer Black to Adams. Thus, both Cooper and Black would rather form a coalition with one another than with Adams, leading to a coalition of the two weaker candidates against the most powerful one (the one who controls the most votes).

Matters can become more complicated, however. If Adams believes that Black and Cooper may form a coalition against him, and he prefers a coalition with Cooper, he may back down from his demand for equity (that is, for 67 percent of the patronage jobs) and offer Cooper slightly more patronage than Cooper would receive by joining up with Black. Thus, since Cooper would be able to demand 40 percent (200/[200 + 300]) of the rewards by joining with Black, Adams may offer him 41 percent, leaving himself with the remaining 59 percent (still slightly more than he would obtain by coalescing with Black). This turn of events may lead to counteroffers by Black, and so on. One interesting aspect of this example is that Cooper, the candidate who controls the fewest votes, becomes the most preferred coalition member, whereas Adams, who controls the most votes, is the least preferred. Thus, unless the votes of the strongest individual participant are required to win, this participant may prove to be the weakest once negotiations begin, a state of affairs that is completely contrary to our intuition and common sense.

SUMMARY

1. Information about specific people and events is assumed to be organized with reference to schemata. Once a person or event is identified as an exemplar of a particular schema, it may be inferred to have other characteristics that were not described in the information presented but are typical of other exemplars of the schema (default knowledge; see Chapter 6).

2. Persuasive communications are effective to the extent that (a) they are received and understood, and (b) the recipients are unable to refute their validity (to counterargue). Factors that distract persons from counterarguing will increase the effectiveness of a communication. Resistance to persuasion can be increased by giving persons information that helps them refute attacks on the position.

3. Persons who behave in a way that is inconsistent with their beliefs may attempt to justify their behavior either by attributing it to external factors over which they have no

control or by changing their beliefs so as to be consistent with their behavior.

4. Behavior will be attributed to external, situational factors rather than to personal characteristics if there is evidence that the behavior is unlikely to be manifested by other persons under similar circumstances or to generalize over situations. Explanations of one's own behavior may be affected by desires to maintain self-esteem. Thus, we are apt to take responsibility for success, but to attribute failure to external factors.

5. One's attraction to a person is in part a function of the favorableness of the attributes the person is believed to have. These attributes include the person's similarity to oneself in attitudes. We also like people who evaluate us favorably.

6. Attitudes toward a person or object (for example, cigarettes) are often poor predictors of actual behavior in-

volving these objects (for example, smoking). However, attitudes toward the behavior itself (for example, toward smoking), in combination with normative factors (beliefs about what others think one should do), *do* predict behavior and behavioral intentions.

7. People often use characteristics of themselves as bases for interpreting and organizing information about others, and use themselves as a basis for comparison in judging others. People who are made self-conscious may be more sensitive to the implications of their behavior in terms of how they will be evaluated by others and may modify their behavior accordingly.

8. People use others as a basis for evaluating themselves and their reactions to novel situations, particularly when other bases for self-evaluation are not available. People prefer to compare themselves with others who are generally similar in background and experience along judgment-relevant dimensions.

9. Comparison of oneself with others may have two related effects. First, it produces a contrast effect on self-judgments—the more positive another is perceived to be along a given dimension, the more negatively one will evaluate one's own position along this dimension. Second, if one perceives oneself to be discrepant from another along a dimension in a direction one considers undesirable, one may attempt to eliminate this discrepancy, for example, by changing one's opinion.

10. The presence of others in a situation may increase one's performance on an achievement task if the task is simple, but may decrease performance if the task is complex. In addition, the presence of others may lead one to take less responsibility for attainment of group goals, and also less responsibility for helping persons in distress. Finally, the presence of many other persons with whom interaction cannot be controlled may cause discomfort and therefore may lead to avoidance of contact with others both in and outside the situations that have created the distress.

11. When persons interact in order to solve a problem or make a group decision, the influence of individual members on the solution adopted by the group as a whole depends on whether the correct solution, once identified, can be recognized as such by all parties. The less obvious the correct solution, the less influence any given member will have over adoption of this solution.

12. People are likely to conform to the opinions of others if they (a) believe that the others' opinions are more apt to be correct than their own, or (b) they desire social acceptance by others and believe that their acceptance depends on their conformity.

13. In competitive interaction situations, the solutions that people agree upon are based partly on considerations of equality (where all parties share equally in the rewards available) and partly on considerations of equity (where individuals' rewards are proportional to their contributions to the group). In some situations, individuals may form coalitions with others in order to maximize their own outcomes. In these situations, coalitions with persons who have the least to contribute are often most preferred, as these individuals may demand a smaller proportion of the rewards available.

RECOMMENDED ADDITIONAL READINGS

Aronson, E. *The social animal,* 2d ed. San Francisco: Freeman, 1976.

Berkowitz, L. *A survey of social psychology,* 2d ed. New York: Holt, Rinehart and Winston, 1980.

Brown, R. *Social psychology.* New York: Free Press, 1965.

Worchal, S., & Cooper, J. *Understanding social psychology.* Homewood, Ill.: Dorsey Press, 1976.

Wyer, R. S., & Carlston, D. W. *Social cognition, inference and attribution.* Hillsdale, N.J.: Lawrence Erlbaum Associates, 1980.

What Does It Mean?

Social psychology has application in many diverse areas. For example, in any industry, employee attitudes toward fellow workers and toward the company will influence production and product quality and will also play a large part in employee morale. There are group norms about how to work, how much work to do, how to behave on the job, and who to associate with. There are problems of picking and training leaders. Virtually every aspect of social psychology can be applied to the industrial setting, for the industrial setting is itself like a small society. Other areas in which social psychology has useful applications include educational institutions, mental hospitals, and prisons. There is also a social psychology of sexuality, which ranges from studies of sexual promiscuity to studies of love and platonic friendship. There is a social psychology of organizations, of the family, of prejudice, of altruism, and of many other topics. In short, because social behavior is so prevalent, social psychology has wide applicability.

The Social Psychology of Justice

Juries as Social Groups

Social psychologists have increasingly attended to the processes of jury selection and decision making by juries. The findings of social psychology apply to the jury room as well as to the psychological laboratory. It has been found, for example, that persons with greater prestige—higher in social class—are more active participants in jury discussions and are more often chosen as jury foremen; similarity of the defendant to members of the jury also influences decision making.

Physical attraction also plays a role in jury verdicts. In several studies it was found that attractive offenders received more lenient treatment. However, in a more recent study beauty was shown to be a liability on occasion. When the crime was burglary—a crime unrelated to physical appearance—attractive defendants received more lenient sentences. When the crime was related to physical appearance—swindles—attractive defendants received more severe sentences.

The U.S. Supreme Court recently ruled that the state of Florida can use six-member juries. As noted earlier in this chapter, social psychologists have studied the results of decisions made by six-member juries in contrast to twelve-member juries. They found that jury size made no apparent difference when the guilt of the defendant was not clear; however, when the defendant's guilt was apparent, the six member group showed a greater tendency to convict. Evi-

The Death Penalty: A Black and White Case

There are those who argue that true equality among races will not come solely from courtroom edicts or legislative decisions, but more from gradual changes in personal philosophies and attitudes that have been ingrained for centuries. Proponents of such a view may well point to the court system itself to illustrate their point.

In 1972, a U.S. Supreme Court Decision (*Furman* v. *Georgia*) was handed down to eliminate discrimination in the imposition of the death penalty. At least partially in response to that decision, Florida reinstated the death penalty in 1976. Now, in a study presented at the recent meeting of the American Psychological Association, psychologist Linda A. Foley of the University of North Florida has examined the 1972 decision's effect in Florida courts.

Foley has investigated every Murder I indictment in about one-third of the state's counties between 1972 and 1978. After studying the records of 421 blacks and 386 whites, Foley says "the data reported in this paper strongly indicate that Florida's new statute . . . allows the death penalty to be applied in a discriminatory manner."

The overt racial discrimination present in death penalty sentencing before 1972 is far less prevalent, Foley says. But at the same time it "has been replaced by a much more subtle form [of discrimination] . . . based on the race of the *victim*." Statistics over the period studied show that all offenders accused of murdering whites are more than five times more likely (16.5 percent vs. 2.8 percent) to receive the death penalty than those charged with murdering blacks. Moreover, black offenders were given the death penalty 23.4 percent of the time for murdering a white person and only 2.6 percent of the time for murdering a black person.

Foley also reports that white defendants were about twice as likely as blacks to have their cases *nol prossed* or dropped or, to a lesser extent, be acquitted or found incompetent to stand trial. She adds that mitigating circumstances such as the offender's occupation and employment status, number of prior convictions, the victim's occupation or the circumstances of the crime do not sufficiently explain the apparent race discrimination in the imposition of the death penalty.

"A male offender who is black is at a particular disadvantage," she says, "since he is more likely to be adjudicated guilty, more likely to be convicted of Murder I and more likely to receive the death penalty if the victim were white."

Science News
September 22, 1979

Prejudice is everywhere. Despite the gains in recent years, a very subtle kind of racial prejudice may still be operating in the judicial system.

dence that six- and twelve-member juries do not make equivalent decisions may affect the future structure of the jury system.

Testimony of Eyewitnesses

Witnesses to a crime may infer that certain events occurred in order to "make sense" out of what they actually witnessed. In fact, astute lawyers may intentionally lead friendly witnesses to make inferences about what happened during preliminary questioning outside the courtroom. Later, in court, these witnesses may testify to having actually observed the inferred events take place. The witnesses may not be intentionally lying; rather, they may be genuinely unable to distinguish between what they actually saw and what "must have happened."

Once a memory representation has been formed of an object or event, it—rather than the original information—is used as a basis for later judgments and decisions even though the original information is subsequently found to be false. In one study, subjects were asked whether each of several suicide notes was genuine or false. Some subjects were led to believe that they had been correct on most trials, while others were led to believe they had done poorly. However, after receiving this feedback for several trials, some subjects were "debriefed"; that is, they were told that the feedback they received had nothing to do with their actual performance. They were then asked to predict how well they would do on a similar task. Despite this debriefing, subjects who were (falsely) told they had done well on the previous task predicted they would do better in the future than those who were (falsely) told they had done poorly. Why did this occur? Presumably, subjects in the course of receiving the feedback attempted to explain their ostensible performance by selectively retrieving information about themselves that was consistent with their performance. Thus, "successful" subjects may have recalled events in which they had shown high perceptiveness, whereas "unsuccessful" subjects recalled past experiences that implied they would not do well on judgmental tasks. The representation of themselves formed on the basis of this subset of knowledge was then used to predict their future performance even after the feedback that led it to be formed was invalidated.

Persuasive Communication

Persuasive communication is a big business in the United States, and persuasion is mainly an application of the principles of attitude formation and attitude change. The most obvious example is advertising. An advertisement or TV commercial is basically a message designed to change your attitudes about some product or service, particularly the action tendency component of attitudes—advertisers want you to buy their product.

We can apply the principles of attitude change to advertising and see what an effective (persuasive) ad would look like. The fact that such an advertisement might not be one we would like in the esthetic sense is irrelevant, as you can well appreciate if you have ever watched television.

The effective ad, say for a new cereal, might have the following characteristics:

1. It would be catchy or lively or loud—you want your ad to stand out and be seen or heard. You want to have a lot of action so that the listener does not have any free time to think about contrary evidence or ways to refute what the ad claims.
2. It would be fairly simple-minded—you want your message to be clear and understandable to all who are to receive it.
3. It would repeat the message over and over, for example: "Buy Zappo! Zappo, the best cereal you ever tasted. Remember Zappo, Z-A-P-P-O, that's Zappo. Get Zappo today."
4. It might have a famous football player saying that he eats Zappo every day, implying that this is why he is such a good football player. A football player would be used, of course, only if the people you were trying to impress considered football players to be high-prestige and high-status individuals—people they would like to be like. You would adjust your choice of the actor in the ad according to the audience you wished to persuade. A roller derby star would probably not help you sell a Rolls-Royce.
5. It would demonstrate for the audience the value of eating Zappo, perhaps by showing all the beautiful, rich, sexy, and completely happy people who eat Zappo.

How do you think the advertising business is doing with respect to the use of these principles? Have you ever seen a TV commercial that fits this description?

Actually, persuasive communications, such as speeches, TV commercials, and newspaper articles, sometimes fail to change attitudes, despite what seem to be optimal conditions. The best example of this is the failure of the antismoking campaign to decrease cigarette consumption in this country—despite some very clever and dramatic TV spots, a barrage of newspaper and magazine articles, warnings on cigarette packages, and a ban on TV cigarette ads. One major problem, obviously, is getting the audience to attend to the message; smokers probably pay less attention to the antismoking ads and obtain less information about the harmful effects of smoking. As for the warning on the cigarette pack, the odds are that it is perceived rarely, if at all.

With regard to cigarette smoking, one technique of persuasion that has shown some promise is *role playing*. In one study smokers were required to assume the role of a patient who had just been diagnosed as having lung cancer. The technique was similar to psychodrama (see Chapter 12), with each subject acting out the role of the dying cancer patient and with the experimenter playing the doctor role and repeatedly giving antismoking information. Role playing significantly reduced smoking in this study. Other, similar studies have shown significant attitude change resulting from giving speeches in favor of the desired attitude, especially if the subject must improvise the speech. Thus, getting a bigot to stand up before an audience and improvise a speech favoring equality, integration, and civil rights will produce more attitude change in the bigot than in the group

Sweet Victory for TV Ads

Food advertising during children's television programing is a hot topic politically as well as nutritionally. Though there is evidence that TV ads do influence a child's eating habits, just how much influence such ads exert has yet to be determined. Many studies in this area have used the child's own report of what he or she eats to measure the impact of TV ads.

Now, however, researchers at the University of Montana report they have measured actual food preference and consumption among 47 four- and five-year-olds before and after different types of TV food advertisements. First, the youngsters were exposed to various samples of low-nutrition foods (corn chips, cookies, sweet cereals, cola and other sweetened drinks) and high-nutrition foods (cheese, carrots, grapes, apples, milk and orange juice) for an eight-minute period. Their food consumption was measured and food preferences and other information obtained in interviews.

One week later, the children underwent the same procedure, but first were shown 12 minutes of children's programing that included a half-dozen commercials that were for low-nutrition foods, high-nutrition foods or toys (a control group). The results indicate that food preference and consumption were significantly influenced by commercials for the low-nutrition foods, but not by ads for high-nutrition foods. "Children exposed to advertising for Hersheys and Fritos significantly increased their consumption of those foods while those who saw ads for milk, grapes and cheese did not exhibit significant increases," reports the team, headed by psychologist D. Balfour Jeffrey. The children also remembered the low-nutrition commercials better than other commercials.

The results, they say, suggest not only that commercials do in fact influence the eating habits of children but that advertisers of healthful foods should popularize their commercials, much like low-nutritional ads, "to use many of the techniques which the modeling literature has proven to be successful—multiple models, peer groups, catchy songs, enhanced screen action, etc."

Science News
September 22, 1979

The principles of effective advertising at work.

of people who merely listen to the speech. Can you see how dissonance theory would account for this? Why is it better to have a person improvise a speech as opposed to just reading a prepared speech?

Persuasive communication is involved in just about all aspects of our lives. Consider the massive advertising involved in political campaigns. Consider sermons delivered at churches. Consider government propaganda on drugs and alcoholism. Attitude formation and attitude change is a major aspect of education. We hope that some of your attitudes about behavior will be changed by reading this book.

The Social Psychology of Health

What makes people sick? Most physicians point to parasites, bacteria, and viruses. Psychiatrists and clinical psychologists suggest that people sometimes think themselves sick. Richard Totman, a social psychologist, has recently argued that society is to blame for many illnesses. He points to a large number of studies showing that so-called physical illnesses like ulcers, hypertension, heart disease, and even cancer and senility are the result of people's inability to behave as society expects them to. Totman believes that physical illnesses are more influenced by social factors than by viruses or wear and tear on the body. An accumulation of evidence suggests that people with social problems—those who have recently lost a spouse or a job or moved to a new and unsettling home situation—are far more susceptible to certain illnesses than persons who feel secure in their lives and in their roles.

Totman may be overgeneralizing. Nonetheless, an increasing number of authorities are coming to accept the important role that social factors play in disease. The newsclip "Social Ties and Length of Life" attests to the relation between social support and the processes of different diseases.

Not only the cause but also the treatment of certain illnesses may be based on social-psychological processes. A major factor underlying the effect of psychotherapy may be that undergoing therapy requires an expenditure of money and effort. To justify these costs, patients may convince themselves that they have been helped. A number of demonstrations support this view, which is based on cognitive dissonance theory. In one, the effects of psychotherapy were compared with the effects of simple physical exercise, both of which were described to the subjects as successful treatments for a snake phobia. When subjects were not given a choice between the treatments but assigned randomly to one or the other, both treatments were effective; that is, subjects subsequently became more willing to approach snakes. A social psychologist would say that the decision to undergo voluntarily any type of aversive, costly, or difficult experience produces dissonance that leads to a change —in this case in attitudes toward snakes—justifying the decision to engage in that activity. Thus, any therapy may be effective provided that it is (1) engaged in voluntarily and (2) is aversive enough or requires sufficient effort to create cognitive dissonance.

In another study, subjects with a history of insomnia were instructed to take a pill, actually a placebo, before going to bed. Some patients were told the pill would relax them, while others were told the pill would temporarily excite them. The next morning, patients were asked how well they had slept. Those who had been told that the pill would excite them reported going to sleep more quickly than those who had been told the pill would relax them. From a social-psychological point of view, this outcome is explained as follows. Typically, persons with insomnia are restless when

Social Ties and Length of Life

Friends, relations and acquaintances not only add spice to life but may also add length. A nine-year study of 7,000 randomly selected adult residents of Alameda County, Calif., finds that persons with the most social contacts were the least likely to die during the study period. When the data were adjusted to take into account age differences, a solid network of friends, relatives and acquaintances decreased the probability of dying by a factor of 2.3 among the men and 2.8 among the women.

The underlying reasons for this strong link still evade scientists, Lisa F. Berkman of Yale University School of Medicine told the meeting in New York on The Healing Brain. "We don't know what is critical about social networks," she says. "The pathways from networks to illness are relatively unexplored." But analyses of the Alameda County data have ruled out a variety of proposed explanations.

Berkman has calculated a "social contact index," a value that takes into account whether a person is married, has close contacts with friends and relatives, belongs to a religious group and has other organizational affiliations. The effects of the various contacts appear to be cumulative, Berkman says. People with only one category of social contacts have an elevated risk of dying, no matter into what category the contact falls. . . .

Berkman takes a broad view of the social network's role. Whereas social networks have been considered to have a beneficial "buffer" effect on events in a person's life, Berkman points out the fact that the networks themselves may provide important events and that events such as moving can change the social network.

In addition to the emotional support that networks can supply, Berkman suggests they provide a person with important information (such as what jobs are available and how to obtain medical care) and pragmatic help (goods, money and services). . . .

Science News
December 20 and 27, 1980

Social support from friends and loved ones is seen as an important component of health, both mental and physical. Caution — the data are correlational in form.

they go to bed. Those who thought the pill would excite them attributed their restlessness to the pill and were not concerned about it. As a result, they actually relaxed and went to sleep more easily. However, those who thought the pill would relax them but still felt restless concluded that they were restless despite the pill, that their insomnia was worse than usual, and their concern about it led them to have even more difficulty than usual going to sleep. Thus, although the pill itself had no effects on patients' actual ability to sleep, the description of the pill affected the attributions that patients gave to their behavior. These attributions, in turn, affected their subsequent behavior, namely, going to sleep.

Public Opinion Polling

In order to study attitudes and opinions, psychologists have developed techniques for measuring attitudes accurately and efficiently. The development of these measurement techniques has had an enormous impact on our lives, and in the case of public opinion polling this impact has not always been beneficial. It is possible, by sampling techniques, to measure a small number of people and determine the attitudes of the entire group from which the small number was sampled. Thus, one could get a fairly good idea of how all people in the United States feel about a particular issue or event by random sampling — asking just a few hundred people.

Public opinion polls are valuable sources of data on the beliefs, opinions, attitudes, and values of representative samples of large populations. Although most psychologists recognize the importance of generalizing to a large population, seldom do they have the opportunity to collect data on more than very restricted and rather particular groups such as college sophomores or white rats. Increasingly, social psychologists are recognizing the possibilities of using poll data to test hypotheses. Being interested and involved in attitude assessment, social psychologists have contributed extensively to the design of public opinion polls.

The technique of polling public opinion is much abused, as you probably know. But when properly conducted, polls are *exceedingly* accurate estimators of public opinion. Their impact as a contributory factor to democratic processes has been reflected as much in their misuse as in their proper application. Two factors, which we discussed in Chapter 1, are of great importance in evaluating polls: (1) that the data are based on random selection of respondents from the appropriate population and (2) that the basis for the data collection is not biased (leading questions, for example, are to be avoided). Few polling organizations meet these two criteria, which has led to some lack of confidence on the part of the public. Clearly, just because an organization calls itself an "independent research firm" does not ensure either its independence (lack of bias) or research competence.

Environmental Psychology

Environmental psychology, an emerging subfield in psychology, is defined as the study of how physical and social surroundings, taken as a whole, influence behavior. As you may have guessed, there is a good deal of overlap between environmental and social psychology. One aspect of environmental psychology focuses on behavior in small groups, with particular emphasis on how individuals manage their own personal space within these groups. Another deals with how people react to stressful factors in the environment, such as noise, air pollution, and crowding. Several recent studies have investigated the differences in social behavior between individuals who live in crowded cities and those who live in less crowded rural environments. Definite psychological differences have been observed which are largely a function of adaptation to the greater amount of stress imposed by city life.

Personal Space and Territoriality

The tendency among some animals to stake out and defend a specific area against members of the same species is well known. For example, dogs urinate to mark their territory with their own scent. Most research on territoriality has been done with animals, but some researchers have speculated that human beings may also exhibit this tendency. Certainly human beings mark their own territory—as evidenced by the familiar "No Trespassing" sign. Some street gangs in large eastern cities mark their territories with graffiti. Typically, the graffiti of a particular gang is seen with increasing frequency as one approaches the geographical center of the gang's territory. Signs of territoriality allow individuals to "know their place" and to stay clear of areas in which they are not welcome. Thus, the practice helps to avoid certain acts of aggression and violence. But territoriality, if it works at all, probably does not operate in the same way in human beings as it does in animals. Territories have fixed boundaries, whereas people tend to move around. Thus, carving out a specific territory has less survival value for human beings than it does for animals. Social psychologists have argued that more important to human beings is **personal space,** an area with no visible boundaries or fixed position that moves with the person it belongs to. Despite its mobility, personal space can be measured. One technique is to place a person in the center of an otherwise empty room and ask another individual to approach the target person. The target person is instructed to say "Stop" whenever the approaching individual gets "too close for comfort." Various approaches are made from different angles.

A study that used this technique with prisoners found that individuals with a history of violent behavior had significantly larger personal spaces than nonviolent persons. Very likely personal space size varies among all people. Particularly important or charismatic individuals may project a larger space than the average person. Furthermore, the size of one's space may vary with the nature of the social interaction. Clearly, intimate interactions allow for deeper penetration, even physical contact, than conversational interaction or any public interaction. Hall (1966) has suggested that there are four distance zones of personal space rather than a single one, and that each zone is identified with certain kinds of activities (see Table 10–1).

What happens when someone invades your personal space without invitation? Robert Sommer questioned students about their seating patterns in a library. When asked where they would sit to avoid distractions, students predominantly indicated the end of a table. But if asked where they would sit to discourage someone else from sitting at the same table, they more often selected the middle of the table. The effectiveness of either strategy depends, of course, on the conditions in the room. If the room is relatively empty, the strategy of sitting at the middle of the table works well. As the room fills up, the person sitting in the middle runs the risk of being surrounded. Therefore, under crowded conditions, an end chair is better, and, other things being equal, students do more often choose end positions over middle positions at library tables. You might check out this tendency the next time you study in the library.

On occasion, defensive tactics are not sufficient to prevent invasions of personal space. Under those circumstances, the options are fight or flight. The typical response in our culture is flight. In one study, experimenters invaded the personal space of pedestrians at a street corner. The closer the experimenter stood, the faster the pedestrian crossed the street. When crossing was not possible because of a "Don't Walk" sign, the invaded person exhibited postural changes, avoidance of eye contact and, on occasion, physiological changes such as sweating.

TABLE 10–1 Four Distance Zones

Distance	Zone	Activities	Sensations
0 to 1½ feet	Intimate	Contact sports (sex, wrestling)	Very strong. Touch dominates vocalization.
1½ to 4 feet	Personal	Interactions with friends and acquaintances	Moderate. Vision normal. Vocalization dominates touch.
4 to 12 feet	Social	Conducting business	Minimal. Normal voice levels. No touch.
over 12 feet	Public	Formal interactions—e.g., giving a speech	Very weak. Exaggerated gestures augment verbal speech.

Characteristics of the four interpersonal distance zones proposed by Hall (1966). Notice that as distance increases, the amount of sensation decreases.

Environmental Sources of Stress

Human beings must tolerate a wide variety of environmental pressures in their day-to-day lives. These pressures, as we noted earlier, are often implicated in illness. Public awareness of the relationship between health and stressful factors in the environment has led to the enactment of significant legislation at the national, state, and local levels. Environmental sources of stress, including noise, air pollution, and crowding, are more prevalent in urban than nonurban settings. Thus, city dwellers might be expected to suffer more severe problems than those who live in the country.

Social Crowding   Most Americans live or work in cities. Despite the flight to suburbia, cities continue to grow. Most people today have almost continuous contact and interaction with other people, many of whom are strangers. As a consequence, social psychologists have become increasingly interested in the effects of crowded conditions and city life in general on human behavior. This interest is prompted, in part, by the large number of socially pathological incidents that have been reported in recent years, for example, bystander apathy, referred to earlier, which *seem to be* unique to cities.

Stanley Milgram (1970) has offered a social-psychological interpretation of the behavior of city dwellers in terms of *information-overload hypothesis*. He argues that people who live in large cities are subjected to an often overwhelming influx of stimulation and information. As a consequence, these people develop strategies to protect themselves against the overload. Among the most common strategies are noninvolvement in the affairs of others, respect for privacy, tolerance of diverse life-styles, and distrust of strangers.

Milgram has conducted a number of experiments to demonstrate the existence and function of these strategies. In one study, for example, experimenters attempted to get themselves invited into the homes of both a selected sample of New York City residents and a similar sample of residents of a small town outside New York City. Male experimenters could gain entry some three to five times as often in a small town than in a city. Female experimenters were more likely to gain entry than males, succeeding nearly 100 percent of the time in the small town. Still, even females could gain entry in less than half of their attempts in the city. Apparently, city dwellers have a greater distrust of strangers than do small town residents. These results clearly are consistent with Milgram's hypothesis.

Some findings on the effects of crowding, consistent with Milgram's overload hypothesis, include: (1) the more dense the environment, the less children interact with each other; (2) violations of personal space lead to more rapid withdrawal in the city than in rural areas; and (3) adults in crowded situations look at each others' faces less than in less crowded situations. These studies show the dislike we have for the crowds and the lack of privacy that characterize city life. Noncity residents often wonder how people manage to function at all in such a stressful environment. Yet city dwellers adapt. Milgram has offered one explanation of how this adaptation works and the price that a city resident must pay for it.

"I find that as long as you avoid eye contact, you hardly realize there *is* a crowd."

© 1979 by Sidney Harris.

Utilization of Milgram's strategies to protect against informational overload often leads to a marked decrease in social responsibility. The city dweller learns to ignore strangers, reserving processing capacity for higher-priority social interactions. This indifference to the needs of others is apparent in many urban situations. Not only do we have bystander apathy, but there is evidence that social contact with strangers is actively avoided in cities.

Psychological distinctions between small town and big city life can go beyond mere indifference to other people. For example, there is a difference in the two locations in the way property of others is viewed. A car that social psychologists left "abandoned" in Palo Alto, California, remained unharmed for an entire week. Indeed, someone even closed the hood to protect the car from rain. In contrast, a car abandoned in the Bronx section of New York City quickly became a target for vandals and thieves. Ten minutes after it was left, the first vandals appeared. The trunk and the glove compartment were cleaned out and the battery and radiator taken. A short time later, another individual jacked the car up and removed a tire. Within a single day, every portable part of the car was carried off.

Vandalism is one act of behavior that is not well explained by Milgram's information-overload hypothesis. Philip Zimbardo has used the notion of deindividuation to account for the dramatic differences in respect for property between Palo Alto and the Bronx. Being just another unknown face in the crowd releases our inhibitions against vandalism and antisocial behavior in general. Since city dwellers are more anonymous than small town residents, they are more likely to yield to the temptation of antisocial behavior when the opportunity knocks.

All of this is not to say that rural life imposes no stress of its own. Surprising as it may sound, the rural dweller is more likely to use prescribed stress-reducing drugs than the urbanite. Furthermore, there appear to be no reliable differences in the incidence of psychiatric illness between city and noncity locales. City residents appear to have adapted effectively to environmental stress. Perhaps the implication is that human beings are adaptable enough to

Cults: The Vulnerability of Sheep

By LITA LINZER SCHWARTZ
(Professor of Educational Psychology, Pennsylvania State University, Ogontz Campus)

In November, 1978, the nation experienced a great shock at the massacre-mass suicide events at Jonestown, Guyana. Since this was a religiously oriented cult, affiliated with the Disciples of Christ denomination, the already upset parents of youth involved with other religious cults experienced considerable magnification of their anxieties. Parents of younger adolescents not yet so involved were jolted by the tragic reminder of what *might* happen to their children a few years hence. General concern was aroused. How could other children's vulnerability to a potential horror situation be prevented? . . .

What makes an individual willing to be so submissive? It is evident from a variety of sources that those successfully recruited by the cults have dependent personalities. They seek someone who will make decisions for them, as they also seek to fill some deficiency in their lives. They feel unready to assume the responsibilities of mature adulthood. They appear to lack a clear system of moral and/or spiritual values by which they can order and securely run their own lives. . . .

One anthropologist, who studied a Krishna Consciousness group in New Orleans, found that the devotees were "quite explicit regarding their reasons for joining and staying: they liked living in the house because they were told how to act and how to be. They no longer had any responsibility for themselves, except to conform." . . .

How can these perceptions be turned to good advantage? First, the inner-directed youth—however much he or she is lonely, frustrated, depressed, desirous of being accepted by others, and anxious to do good works—can withstand better than the exter-nally directed one the pull of the cults. A young man comes to mind who was shy, non-conformist, annoyed with his (as he saw them) hedonistic peers of the dormitory—an ambitious student whose desire for achievement far outran his academic performance. He had experienced rejection early in his life, had learned to live with it to some degree, and had every reason except one to be as vulnerable as other youths have been to the cults. The "exception" was a strong determination to make his own way, to prove himself independent, capable, and worthy of the family who loved him. He was inner-directed.

To become inner-directed, the *child* must have opportunities to make informed decisions; to meet challenges, risks, and frustrations; and to know that, right or wrong, *both* of his parents are stronge enough to be supportive in these efforts. (Both parents are stressed because several investigators have hypothesized, and many have confirmed the hypothesis, that a weak father-child relationship contributes to vulnerability.)

A second problem confronting today's youths is an apparent lack of morality in their lives and environment. Poverty in the midst of affluence, corruption at all levels of government by "respected" political figures, and "rip-offs" of the "establishment" by peers who rationalize their behavior by asserting that the establishment did the same to them first—all are symptoms of society's amorality that disturb young people at an age when they are most idealistic. Some youths become similarly amoral, pointing to one or another front-page figure whose misconduct was punished only by a figurative "slap on the wrist," instead of public and personal disgrace. Others become cynics, trusting no one and rejecting even demonstrations of affection as solely a means to exploit them. Still others take refuge in drugs as a means of withdrawing from a world in which morality seems turned upside-down. Then there are those who seek out or unconsciously welcome indoctrination into a religious group, where idealism apparently flourishes. One of the components of religion is, after all, a standard of "right" behavior toward which the individual can strive. . . .

Parental example is, obviously, important in the teaching of morality. Also crucial to the development of a system of moral values, however, is information. Children need to be told what is right and what is wrong, with reasons. They need to have limits set on their impulsive behavior, and want them, so that they can mature as moral citizens in society. The young school-child, with his dogmatic view of right and wrong, but without an understanding of different perspectives of these alternatives, is often led astray when his parents appear to be behaving in ways contrary to what they have told him is "right" or appropriate. The adolescent who has not grown beyond his early stage of moral development then takes the attitude that "if it's right for my parent, it's right for me." This is why he needs to know the reasons for behaviors at variance with what he is taught, and also why he needs to have limits appropriate to his age. Furthermore, he needs to have opportunities to discuss the reasons and limits so that, once understood, he can internalize the moral values he has been taught. This internalization will help him to be more internally directed. . . .

USA Today
July 1979

Cults draw persons in gradually by getting them to do simple things, such as joining a protest march. At each step of the way, demands for more deviant behavior are made, so that eventually the person can be induced to commit quite bizarre acts—as finally took place in Guyana with the mass suicide of the members of the People's Temple, led by the Rev. Jim Jones. Such incidents are strong testimony to the impact that social behavior processes can have.

contend with stress of any kind or magnitude, wherever it might appear. Despite the fact that you might have to work harder at getting along there, the compensating cultural and economic advantages of a city environment will continue to attract individuals just as long as the stress remains within the limits of human adaptability.

Cults

One of the most intense and cohesive of all social organizations is the so-called religious cult. Relatively few people are attracted to a cult, but those who become involved tend to develop a fanatic devotion to the group and to the group's leader, often to a point of being willing to die for the leader.

In recent times, perhaps spurred on by the Jonestown mass suicide, social psychologists have become more interested in the principles underlying cult membership and cult behavior. In one investigation, cult members were divided into four categories: (1) those who remained in their cult, (2) those who were deprogrammed but then returned to their cult, (3) those who were deprogrammed and did not return to the cult, and (4) those who left the cult voluntarily without deprogramming. Individuals in all four categories typically tested normal on all aspects of mental status and IQ. They also exhibited what has come to be called a "strong ideological hunger." Cults appear to provide, at least for a time, some nourishment for this ideological hunger, as well as some relief from internal turmoil over ambivalence regarding life goals.

There are differences among these four groups, however. Among the individuals who tended to drop out without intervention, needs for a safe, structured, predictable environment were less intense. The other three groups appeared to join religious cults out of a strong need for structured opportunities to make connections, particularly emotional connections, with other people, which they viewed as difficult to accomplish before joining the cult.

A safe and emotionally connected environment, however, does not seem to be enough to hold people in a cult. Those who left after deprogramming reacted negatively to having been dominated and forced into a submissive role. Those who stayed perceived their roles far differently and actually felt dominant themselves. Finally, the data suggested that cult members actually have an underlying hostility toward their leader which they repress or deny. As a consequence, the hostility is projected onto figures outside the cult. This process, which results in other-directed or outer-directed hostility, seems to be an extremely powerful generator of the cohesion that is manifested by cult fanatics. The more hostility directed toward outsiders, the more appropriate it seems to be an insider; so it becomes cognitively consistent to support the "in-group."

And since group or cult leaders do not want their members to be exposed to "propaganda" from outsiders, they therefore take steps to minimize such opportunities. One way of doing this is to go on the offensive, trying to proselytize at airports, for example. Another is to isolate the cult group in the mountains or in a distant, strange country—such as Guyana. Cults, as we have indicated, appeal to people who have not been particularly successful in receiving social support in their normal environment. Some form of isolation of the cult members would also serve to insure that only the cult would be around to provide social support that most people need at some level, further binding the members to the group. Of course, once isolated and surrounded by group members who all are seemingly deeply committed to the cult, a new member in search of social support is extremely vulnerable to being drawn quickly and solidly into the cult. The result may be an amazing, rapid personality transformation—so difficult to understand from the perspective of an outsider that outsiders had to invent a new name for it, brainwashing.

In fact, all of the many complex processes involved in cults have their basis in elementary social psychology. The cult phenomenon simply demonstrates in a very convincing fashion that these principles can exert tremendous control over human behavior. After all, remember that Stanley Milgram got about two-thirds of his subjects to deliver an extremely dangerous shock to someone with a heart condition, just by telling them they must continue the experiment. These psychological principles are extremely powerful, although we may not like to admit we are as subject as we are to the influence of others.

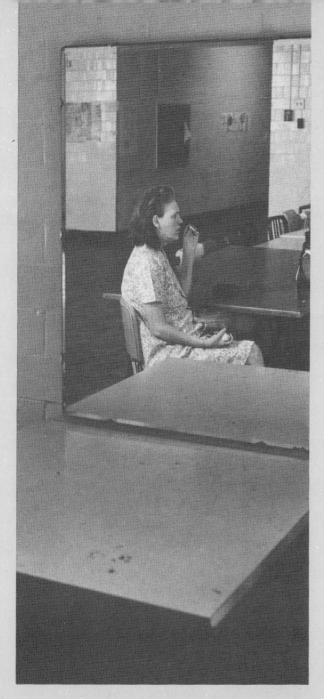

A Definition of Psychopathology   404
Views of Psychopathology   404
Medical Viewpoint
Dynamic Viewpoint
Behavioral Viewpoint
Phenomenological Viewpoint
Ethical Viewpoint
Diagnosis of Psychopathology   407
Advantages and Disadvantages of Diagnosis
Major Diagnostic Categories
DSM–III: Axis I Categories   408
Organic Mental Disorders
Anxiety Disorders
Somatoform Disorders
Substance-Use Disorders
Psychosexual Disorders
Affective Disorders
Schizophrenic Disorders
DSM–III: Axis II (Personality Disorders)   431
Stress and Personality Disorders
Passive-Aggressive Personality
Paranoid Personality
Antisocial Personality
Dependent Personality
Compulsive Personality
Summary   434
Recommended Additional Readings   435
What Does It Mean?   436
Has the World Gone Mad?
The Danger of Diagnosis
The Unreliability of Diagnosis
The Danger of Diagnosing Your Own Problems
Alcohol Abuse
The Aftermath of Mental Illness

11 Psycho-pathology

Joel, a 17-year-old high school senior, was considered by his teachers to be the most promising student in the school. They were shocked when he was arrested for setting numerous fires. The last blaze caused the deaths of four elderly nursing home residents.

Mary, the despondent 28-year-old wife of a senior medical student, took an overdose of sleeping medication. She was rushed to the hospital and successfully treated. During her brief stay there, psychological evaluation revealed a long-standing depression and a severe alcohol problem (she was intoxicated when she took the sleeping pills). Mary refused a referral to enroll in a chemical dependency program, and while her husband was encouraged to commit her for treatment, he declined. She was discharged from the hospital against medical advice.

David, a 21-year-old college junior, was experiencing great difficulty living up to the high expectations of his family. An only child, David had also lived a life rather isolated from his peers. He had no friends on campus, and his only social contacts, outside of class, were his monthly visits home. Two weeks before he was planning to take an important examination to qualify for graduate school, he began to develop severe abdominal pains. He went to the student health service on several occasions, but the "attacks" did not respond to treatment. He was later referred for psychological evaluation and treatment.

This chapter is about abnormal behavior, technically called psychopathology. During the Middle Ages abnormal behavior was thought to be caused by demons, and disturbed individuals were often burned at the stake or mistreated to rid them of their curse. With the eighteenth-century Enlightenment more humane treatment gradually became common, based on moral (religious and humanistic) reasoning; during the nineteenth century, with the growth of natural and biological sciences, the "insane" became the focus of medicine. Great strides were initially made in the understanding and cure of certain disorders, particularly disorders like general paresis, which was explained as having a physical cause—advanced syphillis. In more recent times, the psychological cause of abnormal behavior has been explored. Beginning with Freud's view of the importance of the child's earliest experiences in the development of abnormal behavior and continuing with the contemporary emphasis upon the role of learning processes, psychological factors have been given increasing weight as causal elements in psychopathology.

The term **psychopathology** covers a range of behaviors. For example, it can be applied to a college student who gets violently ill before every final exam; a man who cannot quit gambling even though he does not enjoy it; a 22-year-old girl who believes she is the Virgin Mary; a woman who consumes a fifth of vodka every day; and a man in his late thirties who believes his mind is being controlled by creatures from Mars using invisible laser beams.

The extreme diversity of psychopathological behaviors, indicated by the examples above, makes it difficult to formulate a single definition to fit all cases. Some psychologists have tried to define the group of behaviors traditionally labeled psychopathological as behaviors that are characterized by *subjective discomfort*, that is, feeling anxious, depressed, or otherwise dissatisfied without apparent cause. The person's discomfort seems to be "all in the mind," as in the case of a person who claims to feel chest pains but has no physical signs of disease. However, in some cases the *lack* of discomfort may indicate psychopathology, as when a person responds to the death of a loved one with no signs of grief or depression. Thus, this definition does not cover all instances.

Psychopathological behavior has also been defined as behavior that *deviates from the norm*. This definition is also unsatisfactory because it includes positive abnormalities such as great intelligence or creativity, which are seldom considered pathological. Too, some deviant behaviors are seen as more significant than others—eating peas with a knife might be more unusual than suicide in our country, but it would be considered much less pathological.

Others have defined psychopathological behavior as *maladaptive behavior*, that is, behavior which has adverse effects for either society or the individual. This definition clearly covers many of the conditions we described, such as compulsive gambling, alcoholism, and suicide, and it comes closer to what we mean by psychopathology.

Highlight 11–1

The Pervasive Reach of Mental Illness

Psychological disorders are among the nation's most serious health problems. The President's Commission on Mental Health (1978) reported high rates of emotional disorder involving great personal and financial tolls in all segments of the U.S. population:

Over 1 million people are actively schizophrenic.

Over 2 million people suffer profound depression.

Over 7 million individuals are mentally retarded.

Over 10 million suffer from serious alcohol and drug abuse problems.

Over 20 million people are believed to suffer from neurotic disorders.

Over 26,000 people die each year from suicide.

Over 200,000 cases of child abuse occur each year.

Suicide is not an exclusive problem of aged, depressed, or intoxicated individuals. Every year there is a reported, even alarming, increase in suicide among young people. This problem was highlighted in the following newsclip.

Suicide Belt

The 20-mile stretch of lakefront along Chicago's suburban North Shore is one of the richest areas in the nation, with family income of $60,000 a median. Teen-agers there grow up in well-manicured neighborhoods, attend first-rate colleges and flaunt the trappings of affluence; many drive around in Mercedes. Yet for such youths, there is trouble in paradise. Among local therapists, the area is known as "the suicide belt." In a 17-month period ending last summer, 28 teen-agers took their own lives. Eighteen died by gunshot, eight by hanging and two by lying down in front of trains.

Nationwide, suicide is now the third leading cause of death among youngsters ages 15 to 19, ranking just behind accidents and homicides. In 1977, the last year for which figures are available, 1,871 teen-agers in that bracket killed themselves, a 20% increase in one year and a 200% increase since 1950. In affluent areas the rate of increase is higher. One cluster of ten suburbs on Chicago's North Shore now leads the state in teen-age suicides, with a 250% increase in the past decade. This is true despite various community efforts to curtail the upsurge. Among them: training programs for schoolteachers and social workers in suicide detection and prevention, seminars and discussion groups for parents and children, and 24-hour "hot lines" such as the one maintained by Chicago Psychoanalyst Joseph Pribyl, which receives more than 150 suicide-related calls a month.

"We have an outrageous number of suicides for a community our size," says Laurie Pfaelzer, 19, of Glencoe, who knew one student who slit his wrist and two who ran their cars into trees. "Growing up here, you're handed everything on a silver platter, but something else is missing. The one thing parents don't give is love, understanding, acceptance of you as a person." Adds Isadora Sherman of Highland Park's Jewish Family and Community Service: "People give their kids a lot materially, but expect a lot in return. No one sees his kids as average, and those who don't perform are made to feel like failures."

Still, suicides are hardly limited to students who cannot keep up academically or socially. The death of Rhonda Alter, 19, an attractive, intelligent and popular student who hanged herself last year, sent shock waves through Winnetka. "She had everything going for her, and no sign anything was wrong," says her teen-age brother. Last week a Winnetka resident overheard two youngsters coolly talking about suicide, "just like they were discussing what kind of socks to buy." Says he: "I'm convinced that intelligent kids are most likely to commit suicide. They carry around burdens beyond themselves and feel frustrated at the lack of solutions." . . .

But why should the suicide rate be so high among the well-to-do? Says Chicago Psychiatrist Harold Visotsky: "People on the lower end of the social scale expect less than these people. Whatever anger the poor experience is acted out in antisocial ways—vandalism, homicide, riots—and the sense of shared misery in the lower-income groups prevents people from feeling so isolated. With well-to-do kids, when the rattle goes in the mouth, the foot goes on the social ladder. The competition ethic takes over, making the child feel even more alone. He's more likely to take it out on himself, not society." The '60s may have held down the teen-age suicide rate by providing a sense of community, built around drugs and opposition to Viet Nam. "But even that's gone," says Los Angeles Psychiatrist Irving Berkovitz. "There's nothing to distract a teen-ager today."

Time
September 1, 1980

A Definition of Psychopathology

We shall define psychopathology as *the failure to behave in a socially appropriate way such that the consequences of one's behavior are maladaptive, or detrimental, for oneself or society.* This failure might reflect *organic deficiency* (such as brain damage), *functional deficiency* (lack of knowledge, competence, or motivation), or a combination. In short, a person might fail to behave appropriately or adaptively for any of four reasons: the individual might not have the necessary (1) physiological equipment; (2) knowledge; (3) competence; or (4) he or she might not want to behave appropriately.

The word "appropriate" is important in our definition because labeling behavior as abnormal is necessarily a culturally determined act. A woman from a rural area who thinks she is hexed may be behaving quite appropriately in her community, although her behavior would be considered abnormal by a psychologist or psychiatrist in the city. The anthropologist Ruth Benedict notes that trances and seizures, which most cultures consider pathological, or abnormal, may be a sign of prestige and power in some Indian tribes of California. The daily life of the people who live on an island in northwest Melanesia is based on suspicion and paranoia. They are preoccupied with being poisoned by a neighbor, and the person who failed to be suspicious would be viewed as behaving inappropriately and maladaptively. Thus there is no single set of behaviors that is considered appropriate in all societies and cultures. However, some extreme behaviors are considered unusual in most cultures. Most primitive cultures, in fact, though they do not use the sophisticated terms we use, have concepts of "craziness" that they consider undesirable.

Views of Psychopathology

Part of the problem of defining psychopathology is due to the fact that maladaptive behavior is diverse and its causes are not unitary but may result from many possible sources. Thus much of our discussion in this chapter will be based on *theories of psychopathology.* As we saw in our discussion of personality, psychological theories are typically based on a framework or structure, a viewpoint, which provides a way of conceptualizing behavioral observations. We will examine five major viewpoints that serve as the basis for most theories of psychopathology: the medical viewpoint, dynamic viewpoint, behavioral viewpoint, phenomenological viewpoint, and ethical viewpoint (see Table 11–1).

TABLE 11–1   Views of Psychopathology

View	Theoretical Cause of Abnormality	Theoretical Cure	Therapist
Medical	A process similar to that underlying physical illness	Medication, rest, physical treatment	Physician
Dynamic	Unconscious conflicts	Insight into conflicts	Specially trained physician or mental health professional
Behavioral	Maladaptive learning	Learning or relearning	Behavior modifier
Phenomenological	Lack of meaning in life or cut off from experiencing	Development of awareness of here and now	Phenomenological therapist
Ethical	Lack of responsibility	Acceptance of responsibility	Reality therapist

The particular viewpoint one chooses has profound impact on how one sees others and on whether one conceptualizes feelings and behaviors as pathological or normal. The approach also serves as a guide in selecting both the kind of therapy to be used for persons with emotional problems and the source of the treatment. The classification of psychopathology in this chapter is influenced by the medical and dynamic viewpoints, largely because that is the system most commonly used today. It will be apparent in the next chapter on psychotherapy, however, that different views organize or classify abnormal behavior in very different ways.

Medical Viewpoint

In the **medical viewpoint** pathological behaviors are seen as symptoms of a disease or a process *like* a disease. Hence the term *mental illness.* One basic assumption of the medical viewpoint is that emotional problems, like physical diseases, can be fitted into diagnostic categories that have implications for cause and treatment.

The medical viewpoint is commonly held today, although many people both outside and within the medical profession are disturbed by certain unfortunate consequences. If an emotional problem is truly an illness, then one might argue that physicians are the only people capable of helping the emotionally disturbed. Although such restrictions may be appropriate in cases in which there is a known organic involvement (such as psychosomatic illness), or genetic or biochemical causes (as may be true in the psychotic disorders called schizophrenia), there are many problems of living in which other kinds of treatment are clearly called for. A person who is anxious and cannot get along with others typically does not have a physical illness. The disorder could perhaps be viewed as analogous to physical illness, but this does not automatically make it a "medical" problem. The problem is not so much something that the person *has* as it is something that the individual *is* or *does.*

Furthermore, the medical viewpoint has led people to feel no sense of responsibility for their behavior. It is common for persons to ask therapists to "cure" them of emotional problems in the same way they ask physicians to cure a cold. Typically, the therapist has no "cure"—the patient must assume some responsibility for changing his or her own behavior.

Finally, although the term "mentally ill" was thought to be a more humane label for people with emotional problems than "insane" or "lunatic," few people view the mentally ill with the same compassion they feel for the physically ill. The negative attitudes and fears associated with the irrational, unpredictable, and sometimes dangerous behaviors of the emotionally disturbed have become associated with the term "mental illness." Thus, although the medical viewpoint provided the impetus for hospital care and medical treatment of people with emotional problems, it did not lead to much attitude change, as the "jokes" about "men in white coats" perhaps indicate.

The medical viewpoint is well represented in psychopathology research and theory today. It may be encountered in the search for biological correlates of psychological problems which is widely represented among researchers today. It is also in the background when the psychiatrist prescribes an antianxiety medication or performs electroshock therapy on a depressed patient.

In spite of its negative consequences, the medical viewpoint has been exceedingly useful in the treatment of some types of psychopathology. As we shall see, much of the terminology, explanation, and therapy to be discussed in this chapter reflects the conception of psychopathology as a disease process.

Dynamic Viewpoint

In the **dynamic viewpoint** the basic assumption is that abnormal behavior reflects a "dynamic" battle or conflict between parts or aspects of a person's personality rather than any physical or organic deficiencies. Ironically, it was Freud, a physician by training, who pioneered the dynamic view of psychopa-

thology. He found the assumption of a neurological basis unsuitable for understanding of some psychological problems and developed in its place the first truly dynamic theory.

Freud believed that behavior is partially determined by psychological conflicts of which the individual is totally unaware. He proposed that mental processes occur at three levels: the **conscious,** the **preconscious,** and the **unconscious.** The conscious is made up of the ideas, thoughts, and images that one is aware of at any given moment. The preconscious consists of ideas, thoughts, and images that one is not aware of at the moment but that can be brought into awareness with little or no difficulty. Finally, the unconscious is that part of the mental process that one resists being aware of—the unacceptable drives of sex and aggression, and the memories, thoughts, impulses, and ideas that were once conscious but were removed from awareness because they made the individual anxious or tense.

Freud proposed that anxiety grows out of socially unacceptable impulses, the expression of which would lead to punishment or disapproval from one's self or others. For example, a child might find that his mother is terribly hurt and disapproving of the anger he feels and expresses toward her. He might then try to forget that he has angry feelings; although he is still unconsciously angry toward his mother, he consciously tries to convince himself and others of his devotion. If the process ended here, there would be no problem—the child would have rid himself of all unpleasant or unacceptable thoughts and feelings. However, as we will see, Freud believed that these thoughts persist, causing unconscious conflicts, and that they tend to be expressed behaviorally in ways that are often socially inappropriate. According to the dynamic model, therapy should make the person aware of unconscious processes.

Theoretically, the medical viewpoint and the dynamic viewpoint are independent of one another. One can accept the basic assumptions of one without accepting the assumptions of the other. Historically, however, the two viewpoints are closely related. In the United States some of the strongest proponents of the dynamic view have been psychiatrists, who are themselves trained in medicine. But recently many mental health workers have come to accept the idea that one can view humankind as functioning in a dynamic way without assuming the process is similar to physical disease.

Behavioral Viewpoint

Behaviorists, as we have seen, believe that because the unconscious is by definition unavailable for direct study, it is neither a scientific nor a useful concept.

They assume, rather, that a person's observable actions determine whether he or she is normal or abnormal; one is abnormal if one *acts* abnormally. One can understand abnormal behavior by knowing the individual's learning history—what particular reinforcements or punishments are operating to maintain or suppress certain behavior.

According to the **behavioral viewpoint,** fathered by B. F. Skinner, all behavior, normal or otherwise, is a product of learning about the environment. Behavior is determined by one's history of reinforcement. Thus, abnormal behavior can be changed into normal behavior by retraining (reeducating or reconditioning) individuals (that is, teaching them new and appropriate responses to environmental stimuli) and/or by changing their environment in certain ways. Bandura's social learning theory (see Chapter 9) is typical of the theories based on the behavioral model. The application of learning principles to emotional problems is fairly recent, but the behavioral viewpoint poses a strong challenge to the medical and dynamic views and has provided the basis for several effective therapeutic approaches generally known as behavior modification.

More recently the behavioral viewpoint has been expanded to include not only observable behavior but covert, or unseen, behavior as well. The new perspective, known as *cognitive-behavioral theory,* recognizes that our behavior is determined in no small part by inner thoughts, particularly what we tell ourselves. That is, our behavior is determined by the cognitive structure. Thus, a cognitive-behavioral therapist will attempt to alter an individual's behavior by changing what the person thinks and "says" to himself or herself. This viewpoint and the treatment approach will be described in more detail in Chapter 12.

Phenomenological Viewpoint

Some theorists have considered both the dynamic and behavioral viewpoints to be too mechanistic and inadequate to account for human motivations and problems. The **phenomenological viewpoint,** represented by Carl Rogers, Abraham Maslow, and Fritz Perls, emphasizes the importance of the person's existence, getting in touch with one's emotions, and the human need to actualize one's potential. This approach focuses on the internal reality of the conscious mind. Feelings and intuition become a part of the phenomenological understanding of causes of behavior.

One type of phenomenological view is *existential psychology,* which focuses on the need for each person to develop his or her own meaning for life, to take responsibility for guiding personal growth. *Existential anxiety* is experienced when life seems meaningless. Rather than assuming that a person's behavior is determined by past experiences, the existential approach assumes that behavior is determined by the choices the individual makes in life.

Ethical Viewpoint

Thomas Szasz (1961), (see "What Does It Mean?") in an attack on the medical viewpoint, suggested that having "problems in living" is the most appropriate way of looking at those who suffer from emotional problems. He proposed that life is not essentially harmonious and satisfying but rather is filled with stresses (economic, social, biological, and political) one must cope with. Individuals who need professional help are those who cannot handle these problems by themselves.

Some **phenomenological** theorists use the concept existential anxiety to describe the experience that many people have of

life seeming to be meaningless. Such people feel as if they have no choices, no place to go.

Szasz proposed that the medical "myth" of abnormal behavior allows people to avoid the *moral* responsibility of their actions. The **ethical viewpoint** assumes that individuals are responsible for their own behavior. The same idea underlies Glasser's (1965) concept of reality therapy. For Glasser, abnormal behavior is behaving irresponsibly. Only when people are ready to accept responsibility for the consequences of their behavior can they adequately cope with their problems.

The ethical and existential viewpoints are the only ones that assume people have responsibility for their own behavior rather than attributing the behavior to illness, unresolved childhood conflicts, reinforcement, or other governing factors. The question of responsibility for individual behavior has far-reaching social implications. For example, our courts of law are currently having difficulty resolving the issue of personal responsibility. If a person's behavior is determined by his or her reinforcement history, how can the individual be held responsible for illegal behavior?

Diagnosis of Psychopathology

The procedure of deciding how to classify a person is known as *diagnosis*. The diagnosis is the basis for selecting a treatment (therapy) and making a *prognosis*, a judgment about the likely course and outcome of the disorder. Several kinds of evidence are typically taken into account in making a diagnosis, including family history and biographical information, descriptions of the problem behavior, and assessments of the person's intellectual, emotional, and personality characteristics. This information is usually obtained by having a relative or friend fill out a questionnaire giving the person's medical history and other data, interviewing the person, and administering appropriate tests. Assessment techniques such as personality inventories and projective tests are discussed in detail in Appendix C.

Advantages and Disadvantages of Diagnosis

The chief advantage of any diagnostic system is that it enables professionals to communicate with each other. Diagnostic patterns convey a lot of general information about a person's behavior and enable therapists, researchers, and others to discuss psychopathology in general or in specific cases. Knowing that an individual has symptoms similar to those of other patients also helps a psychologist form reasonable expectations about the individual's future behavior and chances for improvement. In turn, this knowledge allows the psychologist to plan and conduct the most suitable therapy. However, since no two cases are exactly alike, the gain in communication and treatment planning can be costly, for it may obscure the unique features of the individual case.

Classification is important for communication, and thus we spend considerable time on the subject in this chapter. But we should not be fooled into thinking that classification is the same as understanding and treatment. No classification system should be regarded as explanatory. There is a tendency to feel that behavior can be explained by attaching a label to it, but labeling is neither explanation nor cure.

Another problem is that labeling someone may have the effect of making the person behave according to what he or she thinks are the therapist's expectations (for example, suicidally). The therapist, if anxious to prove that the diagnosis is correct, may pay special attention to aspects of the person's behavior that support the diagnosis and completely fail to notice other important aspects that do not fit it. Thus, the diagnostic prophecy becomes self-fulfilling.

Some professionals oppose the use of diagnostic labels and resist efforts to classify individual problems into diagnoses. One group referred to as "humanistically" oriented psychologists and psychiatrists prefer attempting to describe the person as a unique being who needs to be understood on his or her own terms. Another group of mental health professionals, the behaviorally oriented, also oppose the use of diagnostic labels but on grounds that summary classification makes it too easy to overlook important and unique behavioral information needed for treatment.

Major Diagnostic Categories

The most common scheme for classifying abnormal behavior is based on grouping people according to similar behavioral or emotional symptoms. The assumption is that behaviors can be grouped together in meaningful and reliable ways. Thus everyone who behaves in certain ways would be given the same label. The term "symptom" is commonly used because of the assumption that the behaviors classified as abnormal are indications of an underlying disorder in the way that a fever is a symptom of a cold or infection.

Ideally, your diagnostic system would follow directly from your theory or viewpoint regarding psychopathology. We have just seen, however, that there are at least five different viewpoints, each potentially having its own diagnostic system. To avoid the mass confusion of five different diagnostic systems, efforts have been made to agree on one system, called the *Diagnostic and Statistical Manual of*

"When Jud accuses Zack, here, of hostility toward his daughter, like he seems to every session, why, it's plain to me he's only rationalizing his own lack of gumption in standing up to a stepson who's usurping the loyalty of his second wife. The way he lit into him just now shows he's got this here guilt identification with Zack's present family constellation. Calling Zack egotistical ain't nothing but a disguise mechanism for concealing his secret envy of Zack's grit and all-around starch, and shows mighty poor ego boundaries of his own, it appears to me."

The New Yorker, April 5, 1976. Drawing by Whitney Darrow, Jr.; © 1976 The New Yorker Magazine, Inc.

Psychological concepts have reached almost all corners of our society. The articulate use of diagnostic jargon does not imply any real understanding of mental disorder.

Mental Disorders (DSM). In a sense the DSM has been like a compromise among the differing viewpoints. As such, it has been controversial but useful. Recently, a committee of the American Psychiatric Association published the third version of this manual, called DSM–III (1980). If anything, DSM–III seems to be more consistent with the medical viewpoint than any other.

DSM–I and DSM–II placed almost exclusive emphasis on the current symptoms the patient was experiencing in attempting to make a diagnosis. The major change of DSM–III is that it recognizes that psychopathology involves much more than current symptoms. DSM–III, accordingly, uses a multi-axial classification system (see Highlight 11–2). The person's primary present set of symptoms is classified on the first axis (Axis I); however, there are four other axes as well. For example, perhaps there are some problem behavior patterns that have existed since the

person's childhood and need to be considered separate from the person's present symptoms. This behavior, referred to as a personality problem, is rated on Axis II separate from the primary diagnosis of Axis I. Any physical disorder is evaluated on Axis III; and the significant psychosocial sources of stress in the person's life are evaluated on Axis IV. Finally, the individual's previous level of adjustment is rated on Axis V. This classification system is based on the premise that psychological problems are complex and provides a multi-axis means of rating the most important information needed to understand a given case.

The complete DSM–III is complex, and it is not possible to describe here all the categories in this diagnostic system. We will limit our coverage to seven of the major categories comprising Axis I (relating to current symptomatology) and to five examples of the major category of Axis II, Personality Disorder (the long-standing personality disorders of the patient). Combining the two axes gives us the arrangement Shown in Figure 11–1 (p. 412).

DSM–III:
Axis I Categories

We will discuss seven major diagnostic categories on Axis I from the DSM–III: (1) organic mental disorders, (2) anxiety disorders, (3) somatoform disorders, (4) substance-use disorders, (5) psychosexual disorders, (6) affective disorders, and (7) schizophrenic disorders. Keep in mind throughout this discussion that the experience of stress may often precede and may directly produce the development of many of these disorders. Thus, psychopathology is often viewed as an abnormal or inappropriate reaction to stress. Even when there are known physical causes of a disorder, such as brain deterioration, environmental stress may play a role.

One major distinction is between functional and organic disorders. A **functional disorder** refers to an emotional problem that is the result of psychological variables rather than biological ones. A person who has a fear of going outdoors may be thought of as unconsciously avoiding the worry associated with failure on the job, for example, or some other anxiety-provoking situation. An **organic disorder,** on the other hand, is typically caused by impairment of brain functioning. Organic mental disorders usually result from (1) brain trauma, perhaps caused by severe head injury; (2) toxic factors such as lead poisoning; (3) brain disease such as paresis; or (4) brain deterioration such as hardening of the arteries in old age.

The distinction between organic and functional disorders is an important one in abnormal psychology.

Beyond Neurosis
By DAVID GELMAN

He is elated one moment, despondent the next. He sleeps badly, washes his hands too often, avoids down escalators and even-numbered buses, loves his pet snake and hates his mother. He is convinced, against the opinion of a battery of doctors and friends, that his curvature of the spine is becoming terminal. Once, any armchair psychiatrist could have tagged that familiar, exasperating figure for what he was— a simple, self-tormenting neurotic. But according to the latest version of the American Psychiatric Association's official diagnostic manual, neurotic is no longer precisely the word. More properly, the patient would have to be called a cyclothymic personality, suffering, perhaps, from a bipolar affective disorder, with obsessive-compulsive manifestations.

That ponderous language emerges in the proposed third edition of the Diagnostic and Statistical Manual of Mental Disorders known to psychiatrists as DSM–III. Under preparation for the past four years by an APA task force, the revised manual aims to eliminate such fuzzy stereotypes as "neurotic" (but not "psychotic") and provide more specific diagnostic terms for emotional ailments. . . .

But in the process of sharpening its description of the symptoms, DSM–III virtually omits any discussion of underlying causes. Some critics thus see it as part of a long-term "anti-psychoanalytic" trend toward quick therapies and biochemical treatment. And far from clarifying matters, they argue, the weighty new document will add fresh layers of bafflegab to a profession seldom known for plain speaking.

Au Courant
In defense of the effort, Task-force Chairman Robert Spitzer points out that DSM–III is intended as a guide for diagnosis, not treatment. "The emphasis is on description of the problem, not the why and how, because in most cases we don't really know," explains Spitzer, who heads biometric research at the New York State Psychiatric Institute. Psychiatry . . . is the only medical subspecialty that publishes such a manual because it deals with "illnesses" far more difficult to define than, say, arthritis or anemia. First issued in 1952, the manual has a wide influence on psychiatric training. The current draft is around ten times longer than the ten-year-old DSM–II, and has twice as many diagnostic categories.

Psychiatrists agree that DSM–III will be more informative than the old manual. Typically, where DSM–II dealt summarily with psychosexual dysfunctions, DSM–III describes eight varieties of disturbance, including premature ejaculation and inhibited sexual desire. For the first time, it also includes an *au courant* section on transsexualism, as a "gender identity disorder." Unlike the old manual, DSM–III also notes "associated features," "course" and "age at onset" for each category, and makes a stab at "predisposing factors" ("Transsexualism always develops in the context of a disturbed parent-child relationship").

But while the result may be clinically tidier, the manual seems to ignore the role of the unconscious in mental illness. Most visibly, DSM–III drops "neurosis" as a separate category and lists its symptoms, instead, under such headings as "anxiety disorders," without any reference to emotional underpinnings. . . .

Politics
On still other grounds, DSM–III has stirred a furious debate by adding tobacco dependency to a chapter on drug addiction. The cautiously worded section suggests that smokers who experience distress over their habit qualify for psychiatric care. . . .

Undergirding the tobacco controversy is a deeper grievance over what some see as a worrisome trend toward social activism in the profession, dating back to the 1973 decision to omit homosexuality from DSM–II. Spitzer was the author of that proposal, which was generally acknowledged to be a political measure rather than a scientific one, aimed at easing the legal sanctions against homosexuals. But psychiatrists who opposed that move are outraged anew that tobacco use should be included in a catalog of mental disorders while homosexuality is not. . . .

Motive
Other critics offer less ominous theories. Psychiatry, they note, moves with the times; contemporary practitioners operate in a social context where homosexuality is becoming more acceptable and tobacco use ever less so. A study of diagnostic changes over a twenty-year period, published in the American Psychologist recently concludes: "Diagnosis is relative to the historical era in which the diagnosticians perform their task." . . .

Newsweek
January 8, 1979

DSM–III is largely descriptive of mental disorders emphasizing symptomatology rather than underlying causes. There are many controversial aspects to the system, but it appears to be a significant improvement over previous versions.

There is an interesting case history of a man who drank a bottle of insect killer because he thought it would make him sick and his girl friend would feel sorry for him. His behavior would be considered functionally abnormal, though not necessarily psychotic. However, as a consequence of his behavior, he was poisoned and developed a psychosis that was organic in nature. Chronic alcoholism is perhaps the most common cause of organic psychosis today. With organic psychosis the behavioral problem is usually resolved if the underlying biophysical malfunctioning is corrected.

DSM-III: A Multi-Axial System of Classification of Mental Disorders

The American Psychiatric Association published a revised classification system of abnormal behavior in 1980. The *Diagnostic and Statistical Manual of Mental Disorders* (DSM-III) includes a broader coverage of abnormal disorders and more refined diagnostic criteria than the previous systems. The DSM-III system, in addition, recognizes the complexity in classifying mental disorders and attempts to improve upon previous systems by including five major dimensions of classifications in the system. The system, referred to as a *multi-axial classification* scheme, includes the following features.

Axis I: Current Symptomology
Axis I includes a wide range of symptom clusters or clinical syndromes. The traditional diagnostic classification system, based on symptoms, has been broadened to provide a more comprehensive set of categories. Actually, the system has come under some criticism that it has included too much as mental disorder. For example, it includes such "disorders" as tobacco withdrawal syndrome, caffeine intoxication, and Developmental Arithmetic Disorder. However, the DSM-III system has generally improved upon past systems in that it provides more explicit criteria that may result in more reliable diagnoses.

Axis II: Personality Disorders
The inclusion of this dimension is a recognition of the complexity of psychological disorder and provides for the diagnosis of secondary or contributing disorders in addition to the symptom syndromes on Axis I. On Axis II the personality disorders or maladaptive traits the individual has are evaluated. For example, an individual may be diagnosed as having a major depressive disorder on Axis I and be considered as having long-standing compulsive traits. Thus, an Axis II diagnosis of compulsive personality would be recorded.

Axis III: Medical Disorders
This axis enables the diagnostician to record current physical disorders that may be important to the understanding or treatment of the psychological disorder.

Axis IV: Current Stress Level
With this dimension the clinician can rate the severity of the stressors in the person's life. The rating is based upon the stress the individual has experienced within the past year. The codes and terms of the rating along with an example of the stress level is given in Table 11-2.

TABLE 11-2   Severity of Stress Scale, Axis IV

Code	Term	Examples
1	None	No apparent psychosocial stressor
2	Minimal	Minor violation of the law; small bank loan
3	Mild	Argument with neighbor; change in work hours
4	Moderate	New career; death of close friend; pregnancy
5	Severe	Serious illness in self or family; major financial loss; marital separation; birth of child
6	Extreme	Death of close relative; divorce
7	Catastrophic	Concentration camp experience; devastating natural disaster
0	Unspecified	No information, or not applicable

Axis V: Adaptive Functioning
The individual's highest level of adaptive functioning is important information for developing treatment programs as well as attempting to understand the severity of the present disorder. The level of adaptive functioning is rated in Table 11-3.

A second major distinction that has been used for many years is between the psychotic disorders **(psychosis)** and the neurotic disorders **(neurosis).** The major distinguishing characteristic between psychosis and neurosis is whether or not the person is in contact with reality. The characteristics of a psychotic disorder are gross disturbance in thought processes, distortion of reality, and loss of reality testing. Thus, a psychotic person cannot tell the difference between fantasy and actuality. Neurotic disorders are less severe. A neurotic individual maintains basic control over thoughts and feelings and is in contact with reality, but experiences considerable anxiety and discomfort stemming from ineffective ways of dealing with the problems of living. DSM-III contains a more sophisticated treatment of this distinction. The terms "psychosis" and "neurosis" are no longer major diagnostic categories, although they are still commonly

TABLE 11–3 Level of Adaptive Functioning

Levels	Examples
1. *Superior*—Unusually effective functioning in social relations, occupational functioning, and use of leisure time.	Single parent living in deteriorating neighborhood takes excellent care of children and home, has warm relations with friends, and finds time for pursuit of hobby.
2. *Very good*—Better than average functioning in social relations, occupational functioning, and use of leisure time.	A 65-year-old retired widower does some volunteer work, often sees old friends, and pursues hobbies.
3. *Good*—No more than slight impairment in either social or occupational functioning.	A woman with many friends functions extremely well at a difficult job, but says "the strain is too much."
4. *Fair*—Moderate impairment in either social relations or occupational functioning, *or* some impairment in both.	A lawyer has trouble carrying through assignments; has several acquaintances, but hardly any close friends.
5. *Poor*—Marked impairment in either social relations or occupational functioning, *or* moderate impairment in both.	A man with one or two friends has trouble keeping a job for more than a few weeks.
6. *Very poor*—Marked impairment in both social relations and occupational functioning.	A woman is unable to do any of her housework and has violent outbursts toward family and neighbors.
7. *Grossly impaired*—Gross impairment in virtually all areas of functioning.	An elderly man needs supervision to maintain minimal personal hygiene and is usually incoherent.
0. *Unspecified*	No information.

Case Illustration of DSM–III

Betty D., age 43, was admitted to the hospital following a series of drinking episodes in which she often created public disturbances such as throwing drinks on people in bars, which resulted in her being arrested on two recent occasions. During her hospitalization she experienced severe alcohol withdrawal symptoms, including DT's (delirium tremens, popularly known as the "shakes").

She was given an Axis I diagnosis of *Alcohol Abuse Disorder.*

Psychological and life history examinations revealed a long-standing problem of dependency in which she allowed others to assume responsibility for her life. She lacked self-confidence and believed herself unable to function without her husband or, after her divorce, another male companion.

She was given an Axis II diagnosis of *Dependent Personality Disorder.*

Since she was experiencing severe physical complications related to her long-term alcohol use, her Axis III diagnosis was found, upon physical examination, to be *Alcohol Cirrhosis of the Liver.*

Betty had experienced great psychological stress in recent months—divorce, extreme financial setbacks, several arguments, break-up of love relationships, deterioration of moral standards, and arrest. Her rating on Axis IV psychosocial stress was considered to be *extreme* (6 on a 7-point scale).

She has not functioned well during the past year. Her family and work relationships have deteriorated, she has not been occupationally self-sufficient, and she tends to stay intoxicated much of the time. Her rating on Axis V is *poor.*

used in a descriptive sense to reflect the degree of "contact with reality." In their place are the seven major categories of Axis I.

Organic Mental Disorders

We have seen that abnormal behavioral conditions caused by permanent or temporary changes in the brain are referred to as organic mental disorders. A wide range of behavior has been found to result from brain damage—for example, the bizarre actions of the 80-year-old man who after a long and reputable life began to expose his genitals in public and pull down the pants of small children; or the erratic and violent behavior of the adolescent boy who took PCP, or angel dust; or the sniper with a brain tumor who, after reported threats, killed a number of people from the bell tower at the University of Texas. All of these cases

FIGURE 11-1 The two major diagnostic axes of DSM-III

Axis II Personality Disorder (Long-standing)

Axis I Category	Paranoid	Antisocial	Dependent	Compulsive	Passive-aggressive	None
Organic						
Substance-use disorder						
Schizophrenic						
Affective disorder						
Anxiety disorder						(II) no disorder / extreme test anxiety (I)
Somatoform disorder						
Psychosexual disorder			(II) extreme dependency / loss of sexual desire (I)			
No Axis I disorder					(II) passive-aggressive personality / no Axis I symptoms (I)	

The figure illustrates the major categories of the two basic diagnostic axes of the DSM-III. Axis I is used to categorize current symptoms or problems; for example, the person's chief complaint or symptom is loss of sexual desire, which is categorized on Axis I as Psychosexual Disorder. Axis II is used to categorize any long-standing personality disorder; for example, the person presents a history indicating extreme dependency. The cell corresponding to this person's diagnosis is filled in in the figure.

A second illustration, also completed in the figure, demonstrates that a person may have an Axis I disorder with no Axis II disorder. Our example is a student who reports panic during examination periods, but has no history of any personality disorder.

Finally, people may have personality disorders on Axis II, but no major Axis I symptoms or complaints. Our example, completed in the figure, is the person diagnosed on Axis II as having passive-aggressive personality disorder (a long-standing history of expressing emotions indirectly) but no specific Axis I problem. The figure illustrates 48 possible combinations of Axis I and Axis II categories—the major combinations from DSM-III. It should be noted that not all of the 48 combinations are equally likely to occur, but all are theoretically possible.

Concluding note: This is a simplified version of DSM-III, cast as a dimensional table, to help you "visualize" the system. Remember that the full diagnosis also includes judgments on three other axes: III = physical or medical problems; IV = severity of current stress; and V = level of adaptive functioning. Furthermore, it is possible for a person to have more than one combination of Axis I and II symptoms.

dramatically illustrate the importance of the brain to human behavior and the problems that can accompany brain malfunctioning.

Organic problems (such as the case of Woody Guthrie; see Chapter 2) account for over 6 percent of the admissions to psychiatric hospitals—and, if organic problems of a toxic nature (caused by alcohol and other substance abuse) and mental retardation are included, the organic disorders account for 30 percent of all admissions. The wide variety of emotional, motivational, and behavioral problems that occur with organic disorders are classified in one of the six organic brain syndromes: (1) delirium and dementia; (2) amnestic syndrome (failure to remember) and organic hallucinosis; (3) organic delusional syndrome and organic affective disorder; (4) organic personality syndrome; (5) intoxication and withdrawal; and (6) mixed brain syndrome.

Delirium is a confused or clouded state of consciousness in which the individual is unaware of what is happening in the environment. The delirious person demonstrates an inability to sustain attention, misperceives stimuli, and exhibits a disordered thought process. Delirious conditions generally fluctuate. This syndrome, previously referred to as acute brain syndrome, is illustrated by the 80-year-old retired Army major who periodically misperceived his environment —for example, attempting to get water in his cup from a light switch. On several occasions he also mistook for his son the psychologist who was interviewing him.

The amnestic syndrome involves disruption or impairment of memory. The person exhibits an in-

Jobs that repeatedly place people under great stress—such as trading gold futures on the floor of the Chicago Board of Trade— may contribute to the development of both psychological and physiological problems.

ability to learn new material (short-term memory deficit) or an inability to remember past events (retrograde amnesia). The individual may be unable to recall important life events and as a result be confused and disoriented.

Persons with *organic delusional syndrome* experience delusions, or false beliefs, about themselves or their environment. They are usually not confused as in the delirium syndrome, nor do they show memory loss. Some cognitive or intellectual impairment may be found, and there may be some unusual motor

---

Highlight 11–3

Becoming Psychotic

A few weeks before my illness I began to regress into success daydreams somewhat similar to, though not quite as naive and grandiose as, those I had had during early adolescence. I was puzzled by this tendency, though not greatly alarmed because it hardly seemed that my daydreaming self was a part of my adult ethical self. At the onset of panic, I was suddenly confronted with an overwhelming conviction that I had discovered the secrets of the universe, which were being rapidly made plain with incredible lucidity. The truths discovered seemed to be known immediately and directly, with absolute certainty. I had no sense of doubt or awareness of the possibility of doubt. In spite of former atheism and strong antireligious sentiments, I was suddenly convinced that it was possible to prove rationally the existence of God. I remember at the

time trying to write an essay on cognition. I began to write compulsively and at the same time was aware that I was developing schizophrenia. I found later among the disorganized notes which I had carefully hidden away, a number of passages that were quite lucid as well as others that were incoherent and full of symbolic sexual content. I also felt that I was embarking on a great Promethean adventure. I was filled with an audacious and unconquerable spirit. As panic mounted, I grew afraid of being alone, had an intense desire to communicate. I had for a short time a sense of exclusive mission but was able to struggle consciously against messianic delusions. These tendencies were replaced by a sense of burdensome and exclusive responsibility, which continued throughout the entire several years of illness. (Anonymous, 1955)

activity, bizarre or unkempt dress, and disturbed speech. The individual may have seriously disrupted social and family relationships and may act upon delusions, like the man who fired a shotgun several times in the street because he believed there was an invasion from another planet. If the patient also experiences things which are not present, such as Martian invaders, then the person is said to be having hallucinations or to be suffering from an attack of *hallucinosis*. When the hallucinations are caused by a disorder of the nervous system, the condition is called *organic hallucinosis*. Hallucinosis is a common condition with the six major classes of organic disorders.

The *organic personality syndrome* is usually marked by dramatic personality changes. Usually severe temper outbursts, explosive behavior, or fits of crying are described, and there is often a recent history of poor social judgments such as sexual misbehavior. The organic personality syndrome is frequently caused by actual structural damage to the brain such as brain deterioration or brain tumors.

The *intoxication syndrome* involves a state of maladaptive behavior that results from the consumption of toxic substances such as alcohol, cannabis, amphetamines, and other drugs. To be diagnosed as pathological the intoxication must be severe and result in socially inappropriate behavior. For example, social use of alcohol or cannabis would not be considered an intoxication syndrome unless the behavior interfered with work or was inappropriate, such as fighting in public places. *Withdrawal* is a physiological state resulting from reduced use or cessation of use of addictive substances.

The *atypical* or *mixed brain syndrome* is used for organic brain disorders that do not fit well with the other disorders. It is a catch-all term for disorders with a believed organic basis but with no clearly defined pattern.

Anxiety Disorders

An anxiety disorder is a functional problem (often referred to as a neurosis) that centers around the experience of intense anxiety or the development of psychological mechanisms to control felt anxiety. According to the psychodynamic viewpoint, neurosis is a special pattern of behavior that is instigated and maintained for the purpose of dealing with stress and avoiding anxiety. What are the indications that a pattern of behavior is neurotic? First, if the person is prevented from performing the behavior, he or she will become anxious. Second, the behavior has a rigid, overdriven quality about it; the person cannot perform the behavior in a relaxed manner. Finally, the

need being served by the behavior is insatiable; the person never seems to relax and give up the behavior.

Thus it is easy to see why anxiety and the defenses against it become a problem for the individual. Defending against the anxiety takes up a tremendous amount of energy that the person could usefully spend elsewhere. In addition, the time spent avoiding the anxiety prevents the person from ever dealing effectively with its cause. Thus new behaviors are never learned that would allow the person to get out of the anxiety-provoking situation altogether. This self-perpetuating aspect of neurosis is called the **neurotic paradox.**

The paradox refers to the fact that the neurotic individual persists in the maladaptive behavior even in the face of unpleasant consequences. The behavioral model also helps explain this behavior. The unpleasantness may not occur for some time after the behavior has taken place, whereas the immediate consequence is that anxiety is reduced, providing positive reinforcement of the neurotic behavior. The immediate reduction of anxiety is called the neurotic's **primary gain.** The primary gain is so great that later negative consequences, if they arise, do not have much effect in changing the neurotic behavior.

Neurotic behavior is extremely persistent because it often has other positive consequences in addition to the relief from tension, or primary gain. The additional benefits are the **secondary gains** of neurosis. For example, the neurotic may receive sympathy and support from friends or special dispensations that allow him or her to avoid responsibilities or activities that are disliked. The fact that neurosis has both primary and secondary gains makes behavior change more difficult. In some cases the therapist may have to detect and remove the sources of secondary gain in addition to working on the neurotic's primary source of anxiety.

Anxiety States: The Failure of Repression

Anxiety states are intense, recurring episodes of anxiety that result from an individual's being unable to defend himself or herself against the dangerous feelings (often unconscious) being experienced. Such persons report feelings of being jittery or nervous without being able to determine their source. They may displace the anxiety by attaching it to less relevant and less threatening stresses. In this way, they may react with overwhelming anxiety to an objectively mild stimulus—for example, the woman who has been experiencing acute episodes of anxiety every few days since she visited a friend and her new baby in the hospital. She wanted to have children of her own but was physically unable to conceive. The visit to the hospital to see her friend's new baby produced

Highlight 11-4

A Case of Obsessive-Compulsive Disorder

The following case description illustrates how the obsessive-compulsive individual successfully avoids anxiety-provoking situations. His defensive behavior, however, also prevents him from trying and learning new behaviors that would enable him to cope with his anxiety.

Eliot H., a college student, went to a telephone booth to call up a wealthy girl whom he had recently met, to ask her for a date. He spent an hour there, anxious and indecisive, unable to put the coin in the slot and unable to give up and go home. Each time his hand approached the telephone he anxiously withdrew it because he felt that telephoning her might ruin his chances with her. Each time he withdrew his hand he seemed to be throwing away a golden opportunity. Every positive argument for telephoning her he matched with a negative argument for not doing so. He went into all the ramifications of his ambivalent motivations. He imagined to himself what the girl and the members of her family — whom he scarcely knew — might think of his attentions to her; and he had to picture to himself what they would think if he neglected her.

His whole future seemed to Eliot to hang on the outcome of this little act. Had he any right to put his coin in? If he did so would the girl respond favorably? If she did, what would happen next? Eliot fantasied every conceivable consequence as he sat there sweating in the booth, consequences to him and to her, on and on into remote contrasting futures. He was helplessly caught in an obsessive dilemma, as he had been caught before hundreds of times. The more he tried to be sure of what he did, the more things he imagined going wrong, any one of which might ruin everything. In the end he gave up the anxious debate and went home, exasperated and worn out. Later he became convinced that in not making the call at that particular time he had missed the chance of a lifetime for winning security and happiness.

This absurd little episode sounds like the mere exaggeration of a shy suitor's hesitancy, but it was much more than this. It was a condensed symbolic expression of an intensely ambivalent personality, one that was volatile, impulsive, and unpredictable. Almost every enterprise upon which Eliot had embarked since early adolescence had involved similar obsessive rumination. Into each decision he funneled all of his ambivalent conflicts — conscious, preconscious, and unconscious — and then he found himself unable to follow through to a decision. The same thing unfortunately happened to his search for therapeutic help. He began with despair, switched quickly to great optimism, and then got bogged down in endless doubting and rumination over whether to continue. In the end he withdrew from therapy without ever becoming really involved in it. (Cameron, 1963, page 396)

feelings of inferiority and resulted in her anxiety over her felt inadequacy.

In anxiety attacks, the person experiences heart palpitation, the need to urinate, choking sensations, and other physical symptoms in addition to feelings of terror or impending doom. In other words, the person has feelings and physical reactions similar to someone who is in real danger, but there is no environmental stimulus for the behavior.

Phobias: The Displacement of Anxiety

Phobias are intense, irrational fears that, according to psychoanalytic theory, arise from the displacement of anxiety onto a situation that could be mildly dangerous. Thus the woman who has a fear of heights (called acrophobia) might be symbolically expressing her anxiety over an overwhelming anger toward her parents. By displacing her fear she is prevented from acting directly on her anger, which she has repressed. Other phobias are fear of small enclosed spaces (claustrophobia), fear of water (hydrophobia), and, for young children, school phobia.

Phobic disorders involve a persistent and extreme desire to avoid an object or situation. The fear is usually recognized by the individual as irrational. If the person is brought into sudden contact with the feared object or activity he or she becomes panicked and attempts to escape.

Neurotic fears should be distinguished from the common "phobias" many people have of spiders or insects that have no effect on their lives. Neurotic phobias generally have a significant impact on the individual and drastically reduce social functioning — for example, a secretary working on the 97th floor of a New York City office building develops a fear of closed places and cannot ride an elevator to her job.

Obsessive-Compulsive Disorder: Defenses against Anxiety by Means of Cognitive and Behavioral Activation

The obsessive or compulsive approach of neurotic defense involves behavior in which the person repetitiously thinks about or performs a behavior against his or her own wishes. Most of us have obsessions (repetitive thoughts) from time to time, such as a song that keeps running through our heads. And we frequently feel compulsive about performing some act. Obsessions and compulsions are neurotic only when the thought or action interferes with the person's ability to behave appropriately. Obsessive thoughts and compulsive behavior tend to go together in the same individual, thus the term **obsessive-compulsive disorder.**

Obsessive-compulsive behavior functions in two major ways. First, it prevents the individual from thinking anxiety-provoking thoughts. Obsessive persons may fill their minds with constant trivial thoughts (counting their heartbeats, for example) as a way of avoiding awareness of ideas or memories that would be threatening. A person who keeps to a rigid schedule or who maintains an extremely neat home may be structuring life so as to avoid any possible upsets. Compulsive behavior involves repetitive responses such as counting fence posts or heartbeats.

Sometimes the obsessive thinking or compulsive behavior bears a symbolic relation to the anxiety-provoking thought. In one case a woman had an obsessive fear that she would harm herself if she picked up a kitchen knife. This fear so frightened her that she was unable to prepare meals. Therapy led to the interpretation that her obsession was covering up a desire to kill her husband (felt in a primitive way at the unconscious level and consciously unacceptable to her). By obsessively avoiding knives she was also able to protect herself from overtly acting out her conflict. In addition, obsessive-compulsive behavior may be an expression of guilt and fear of punishment. The classic example of this is the compulsive hand washing of Shakespeare's Lady Macbeth. Compulsive hand washing has also been associated with conflicts over guilt and masturbation.

Somatoform Disorders

Psychological problems may find ready expression through physical symptoms. One group of functional problems, the **somatoform disorders,** involve physical symptoms for which there is no demonstrable physical cause. In addition to more routine physical symptoms (nausea, diarrhea), there are often dramatic problems such as sudden blindness or intense experienced pain with no organic basis. Commonly there is also an extensive and varied history of physical problems along with a preoccupation with physical health and illness.

There are several types of somatoform disorders that generally differ with respect to the symptom picture they present, the onset of the problem, possible causal factors, and the extent of disability resulting from the disorder. The fours types to be discussed here are (1) somatization disorder, (2) hypochondriasis, (3) conversion disorder, and (4) psychogenic pain disorder. A patient may possess attributes of more than one of these categories, so that making a final classification of the predominant symptom pattern may not always be easy.

Somatization Disorder

Somatization involves a pattern of vague but recurring physical complaints. Individuals with **somatization disorder** have a long and complicated medical history, usually well established before age 30. Patients are likely to be women who continuously seek medical attention, frequently changing doctors. Individuals with somatization disorder may repeatedly seek unnecessary surgery, and they usually obtain large supplies of varying medications. This disorder is chronic and tends to be highly resistant to psychological treatment—partly because such patients refuse to believe that psychological factors are involved in their problems. They consider their ills to be "medical" and shop for doctors who will treat them as such.

Hypochondriasis

Another type of problem arising from displaced anxiety is **hypochondriasis,** a preoccupation with one's physical health. For example, a hypochondriac may read the health columns in the newspapers and magazines and rush to a doctor with all the latest symptoms. Such persons may distort the meaning of minor aches and pains, imagine discomfort in various parts of their bodies, and constantly complain of ill health, although the physician can seldom find anything physically wrong. Physicians have estimated that as many as 60 percent of their patients express anxiety about their lives in their physical symptoms. The "medical student syndrome," in which students working and studying in a hospital develop whatever illness they read about or are exposed to that day, is probably a response to the extreme pressure of medical school training. Some male students express great relief when on duty in the obstetrics ward.

The same process of displacement can occur as psychology students read about psychopathology. They too can experience the "medical student syndrome," seeing themselves described on every page and concluding that they have serious emotional problems. More likely these students are reasonably well-adjusted persons who have feelings and thoughts that are included in the diagnostic categories.

"He was a dreadful hypochondriac."

© Punch (Rothco)

In DSM–III, hypochondriasis is one of the somatoform disorders. However, it is not a fatal illness.

Conversion Disorder

A person can defend against anxiety-provoking thoughts by selectively cutting off certain experiences. One subclassification of this response is the **conversion disorder,** in which the person reduces the anxiety by inactivating part of the body (as in paralysis, blindness, deafness, or the like). Thus the person converts the psychological problem into a physical one that prevents him or her from behaving in a way that would be anxiety provoking. For example, the student who suddenly became "blind" would be unable to do class assignments. There are no actual physical changes; the inactivation is due to unconscious psychological factors.

One of the most famous conversion disorders is that of "glove" anesthesia, in which the person loses all feeling in the hand. The pattern of loss of feeling follows the outline of a glove (see Figure 11–2). Physicians are immediately able to identify this symptom as nonphysical because the nerve pathways for the hand mark off narrow strips of sensitivity that go up the arm, and it would be impossible to have a glove pattern of anesthesia unless there were also anesthesia of the arm. Conversion disorders were fairly common in Freud's day (and prompted him to move from neurology to psychiatry), but today people are better informed about biophysical processes, and their reactions to anxiety usually take other forms, such as pain and simulation of bodily disease. Simply reading this chapter may prevent you from ever developing a glove anesthesia. Conversion disorders have, as a result of mass communications and increased psychological sophistication, become more subtle. Conversion "hysteria," always considered the great

imitator, has adapted to modern trends and may be found masked as multiple sclerosis and other neurological diseases, and back and other orthopedic problems.

Psychogenic Pain Disorders

The **psychogenic pain disorder** involves the report of pain in the absence of a physical basis for the disorder. Frequently the pain is reported over areas of the body in which the anatomic distribution of pain receptors could not account for it, or the reported pain is excessive relative to the minor physical changes that have occurred. The pain reported is "real" in that the person actually feels it as opposed to a consciously faked disorder known as *malingering.*

Often, however, there is a clear *secondary gain* aspect of the pain disorder. That is, the individual is receiving some gain or reinforcement for having pain, such as Workmen's Compensation, care and attention from the family, or the opportunity to avoid a disliked chore.

Present treatment approaches frequently do not distinguish between real or imagined pain but treat the "report of pain" as a problem in itself (see "Pain Management" in Chapter 12). Often individuals with psychogenic pain disorder encounter severe problems in their attempts to seek pain relief. Most such patients

FIGURE 11–2 "Glove" anesthesia

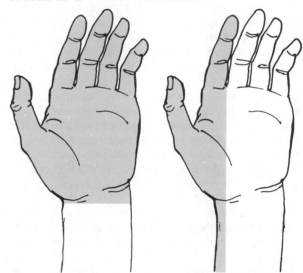

In the conversion reaction known as "glove" anesthesia the person loses all feeling in the hand in a pattern that follows the outline of a glove, stopping short at the wrist. However, because the nerve pathways for the hand go up the arm, as shown on the right, it would be impossible to have a *physically* caused glove pattern of anesthesia, as depicted on the left, unless there were also anesthesia of the arm.

make excessive use of analgesic and tranquilizing medication, and many become addicted to these drugs. Psychogenic pain patients may seek surgery to relieve their pain and often become actual invalids— an all too frequent example of the influence of mind over body.

Substance-Use Disorders

Substance-use disorders such as those brought on by alcohol and drug abuse have several characteristics in common with personality disorders. Many psychologists group these disorders together because they involve similar habit patterns, appear to be developed over time as a result of learning, and respond similarly to treatment. We shall examine these two addictive disorders in detail because they are major health and social problems in the United States today.

The Alcoholic

An alcoholic is defined as an excessive drinker whose dependence on alcohol is so strong that it interferes with the performance of socially appropriate behavior. Some alcohol workers do not use the term "alcoholic" because it conjures up visions of the skid row derelict. Most persons with severe drinking problems cannot view themselves in this way and thus refuse to accept the idea that they are alcoholics. Some workers prefer the term "problem drinker" or "chemical abuser." Whatever the label, alcohol abuse occurs in all social classes and occupational groups, although the incidence appears to be higher in the middle and upper socioeconomic levels. Skid-row bums are estimated to constitute only 5 percent of the over 10 million alcoholics in the United States. Alcoholism is fourth among the major health problems in this country and is considered a major social problem as well. Long-term consumption of alcohol can lead to damage to the central nervous system and susceptibility to other diseases, such as tuberculosis and liver disease. Alcohol dependence may also be the cause of family disruption, poor job performance, and social isolation for the individual. Society suffers from the high crime rate associated with alcoholism and the tragic consequences of drunken driving.

Contrary to popular belief, alcohol is not a stimulant but a depressant. Its first effect is to inhibit processes in the higher levels of the brain and reduce inhibitory control over lower levels. Thus, sexual activity might increase under mild intoxication because sexual controls are reduced more than sexual drive. At more extreme levels of intoxication, however, sexual desire is also reduced. Excessive drinking invariably results in some degree of motor dysfunction and inability to make fine discriminations (see Appendix D). More important in the development of alcohol-

ism is the fact that perception of discomfort (both physical and psychological) is dulled.

Many people are capable of restricting their intake to social drinking, but for others this is the first phase in the development of alcoholism (called the *prealcoholic phase*—see Table 11–4). In the second or *prodromal phase* the person drinks in the morning and experiences blackouts. In the *crucial phase* he or she loses control over drinking behavior. The *chronic phase* is marked by long "binges" of drinking and impairment of thought processes.

Causes of Alcoholism

There is no single cause of alcoholism. Although there is some evidence of a genetic component in alcoholic behavior, most psychologists still feel that the alcoholic has learned to drink to reduce anxiety generated by personal problems. There is no evidence that alcoholics are under unusual stress. They tend to be immature, impulsive individuals with low self-esteem and feelings of not living up to their own goals and standards, and they display an inability to tolerate failure.

Treatment of Alcoholism

Alcoholics are extremely difficult to treat. The dependence on alcohol is evidently a result of deeply embedded personality traits, possibly coupled with a genetic predisposition for the effects of alcohol.

Some drugs have been used to reduce the typically rather mild withdrawal symptoms of craving for alcohol—tremors, sweating, and nausea. **Antabuse** is a drug frequently given to alcoholics; it causes intense nausea if alcohol is consumed while the chemical is in the bloodstream. The knowledge that drinking will lead to a severe illness helps some alcoholics refrain from impulsive drinking. But because taking the drug each day requires the cooperation of the alcoholic, such a treatment program helps only the

---

TABLE 11–4 Pattern of Development for Alcoholism

1. Prealcoholic phase	→ Social drinking → drinking to reduce tension → Daily drinking
2. Prodromal (beginning) phase	→ Blackouts with no memory the next day → morning drinking to offset hangover or to face a difficult day
3. Crucial phase	→ Loss of control over drinking → loss of family and job
4. Chronic phase	→ Prolonged bouts of drinking → impairment of thinking

alcoholic who sincerely wants to control drinking and needs a "crutch" to eliminate impulsive drinking.

Insight-oriented psychotherapy has not been successful in treating alcoholism. Alcoholics tend to see therapists as unsympathetic and lacking in understanding. Many do not return after the first session, and most leave therapy within a month.

Another approach to treatment involves *aversive conditioning* techniques, first mentioned in Chapter 4. Individuals are given alcohol along with intense electric shock, or a drug that causes vomiting. The aversive stimulus might also be a cognitive one, as in covert sensitization. For example, the alcoholic is taught to imagine repulsive events (such as the vomiting) in association with thoughts about alcohol. These conditioning methods have often been used to bring about reduced alcohol consumption or to get the person to drink socially or in a controlled way. *Social or controlled drinking* research has generated controversy because perhaps the majority of alcohol workers believe that *abstinence* is the only viable approach to alcohol treatment.

Alcoholics Anonymous (AA), a mutual aid organization with a religious orientation, has had perhaps the greatest success in treating alcoholics. AA groups provide social support and reassurance from recovered alcoholics who understand alcoholics' problems. AA members help new members withstand the trials of "drying out" and provide social events to prevent them from returning to their drinking habits, especially during nonworking hours. Alcoholics must learn new ways to spend their time in place of their drinking activities. Part of the difficulty in treating alcoholism is that alcoholics frequently do not accept the fact that they have a drinking problem, rarely seek treatment voluntarily, and in most states cannot be forced to seek treatment.

The Drug Addict

Some people cope with the problems of life by the excessive use of drugs other than alcohol. It is useful to distinguish between psychological addiction and physiological addiction. In the former, the individual becomes psychologically dependent upon a substance that has little addicting quality itself, such as marijuana. In the latter case, the substance itself has properties that in themselves are highly addicting. When it is not available to the individual the substantial and dangerous physiological reaction of *withdrawal* is induced.

Most addictive drugs that are abused in the United States today are actually prescription medications such as the anti-anxiety drugs like Valium and Librium, sleeping medications such as barbiturates, and hypnotics like quaaludes. One addictive substance—heroin, a street drug, has serious physical and psychological consequences and constitutes a major social problem because of the large amount of illegal behavior associated with addiction; the loss of socially appropriate behavior like working and maintaining a family; and the "contagion" effect—it is estimated that each addict introduces an average of *six* others to narcotics.

There are several differences between drug addiction and alcoholism. Psychologically, many drugs frequently produce euphoria rather than just the reduction in tension that comes with the consumption of alcohol. Furthermore, while the alcoholic shows an initial slight increase in tolerance for alcohol, followed later by a decrease, the drug addict finds that an increasing amount of the drug is required in order to maintain the same "high." For this reason addiction becomes tremendously expensive, and the addict may need $100 or more a day to maintain the habit. For many people, antisocial behaviors such as stealing or prostitution are the only means for attaining the necessary funds. Because the addict cannot be sure of the quality of the drugs, overdoses (ODs) are common and often result in death.

Whereas the chronic alcoholic may experience only mild illness when withdrawn from alcohol, the heroin addict always becomes severely ill within two days after withdrawal from the drug. (Note, however, that alcohol withdrawal can often be quite severe, sometimes worse than heroin withdrawal.) The symptoms of heroin withdrawal may begin anywhere from 4 to 12 hours after the last dose, depending on the level of addiction. Restlessness, depression, and irritability may begin the withdrawal, followed by vomiting, diarrhea, cramps, pains, severe headaches, tremors, and possibly hallucinations and delirium. The symptoms peak in three to four days and decline after the fifth day. The tolerance built up before withdrawal disappears after the addict goes "cold turkey" (so called because of the common "goose bumps" seen during withdrawal), and people have died from taking a dose as heavy as the ones they were taking before withdrawal.

Causes of Addiction

Many heroin addicts are more antisocial in their learning histories than the impulsive, immature, and dependent person who becomes an alcoholic. One indication of the personality-disorder aspect of these addicts is the fact that many of them take the "cure" not to be cured but in order to start over again with a less expensive habit. Although the withdrawal symptoms are severe, it is not fear of withdrawal that maintains a drug habit, as is commonly believed. The sociopathic drug addict finds that drugs are an *easy* way to maintain a pleasure-oriented approach to life.

However, not all drug addicts are sociopathic. About 20 percent of the patients at the federal hospital for drug addiction in Lexington, Kentucky, used drugs originally to relieve anxiety. These people feel unsure of themselves and gain psychological support from the drug subculture. Another group of addicts come from middle-class liberal backgrounds. These addicts become users during adolescence and frequently try their first heroin out of curiosity. Often they are rebelling against their family's life-style and start using drugs as one way of experimenting with alternative life-styles. These individuals are rarely involved in criminal activities.

Treatment of Addiction

Treating drug addiction is even more difficult than treating alcoholism. The addict's lack of motivation to behave in socially appropriate ways is a major problem. Psychotherapy is typically not successful. Enforced treatment in a government hospital has produced cure rates varying from 1 to 15 percent. Drugs have not been extensively applied, although **methadone** is increasingly being used. Maintenance on methadone prevents withdrawal symptoms from heroin addiction, and when taken orally, methadone does not produce the intense "high" that prevents the drug user from functioning in society. (Interestingly, methadone does produce a mild "high" of its own, which has led to a methadone black market.)

Although methadone tends to block a heroin high, thus reducing the pleasurable (reinforcing) aspects of heroin, this treatment technique has been severely criticized because methadone itself is addictive. It is probably well to remember that years ago heroin was touted as the "cure" for morphine addiction. On the other hand, methadone is cheap and legal when used in a medically supervised treatment program. At the very least, it reduces the probability that an addict will have to steal or become a prostitute to get drugs. Methadone is not a cure-all, however, as demonstrated by the fact that when an addict withdraws from methadone, the craving for *heroin* returns.

Psychosexual Disorders

There are four distinct subgroupings of **psychosexual disorders** in the DSM–III classification scheme: (1) *gender-identity disorders,* in which the individual is confused over sexual identity; (2) the *paraphilias,* involving bizarre or unusual sexual imagery or inappropriate sexual objects; (3) the *psychosexual dysfunctions,* defined as failure to achieve a complete sexual response; and (4) *ego-dystonic* (unacceptable to self) *homosexuality.* We shall examine each of these in detail to give the reader a picture of the broad range of psychosexual disorder.

Gender-identity disorders involve a clear and compelling discomfort with one's biologic sex—a

In recent years homosexuals have been militantly protesting their unequal treatment by society.

strong feeling that one's anatomy is wrong. One male *transsexual* seeking a sex-change operation complained that he was "really a woman trapped in a male frame." Most transsexuals wish to get rid of their own genitals and become a member of the other sex. Hundreds of sex-change operations were performed in the United States for several years. The operation is no magic cure for a person's psychological problems and is now far less common.

The paraphilias are a group of psychosexual disorders in which bizarre acts or unusual practices are necessary for a person to become sexually excited. For example, consider the need to use fetishes or nonliving objects to complete the sex act in *fetishism*. The individual may take women's clothing or shoes and use them to masturbate. Another paraphilia is *voyeurism*, which involves looking at people who are naked or in the process of undressing. The "peeping Tom" usually masturbates to achieve orgasm while viewing another person. Another disorder involves an individual's shocking another person while *exhibiting* his genitals (this disorder is almost exclusively found in males). The *exhibitionist* may masturbate while exposing himself. This disorder appears to have a strong component of hostility in it; one young man was caught several times exhibiting himself in church to older women. There also appears to be a repetitive quality to exhibitionism. A well-known professional football player, for example, was caught exhibiting himself several times under similar circumstances. Other paraphilias involve the sexual attachment to such inappropriate objects as animals (*zoophilia*, formerly called bestiality) and children (*pedophilia*).

Psychosexual dysfunctions are psychological disorders affecting the characteristic male or female sexual response. Adults typically experience a sexual response cycle involving (1) appetite, (2) excitement, (3) orgasm, and (4) resolution (relaxation). Inhibitions may occur and interfere with completion of the sexual cycle. A person may, for example, experience inhibited sexual drive in the context of situations that would not generally produce it (for example, being married). Inhibitions may also occur in the excitement phase of the sexual response (the terms "impotence" and "frigidity" have been used to describe the inability to experience sexual excitement). Problems may also occur in the orgasm phase of the sexual response, resulting in premature ejaculation or failure to achieve orgasm, or sexual relations may be accompanied by intense pain.

Much has been learned in recent years about normal sexual response patterns and the treatment of sexual dysfunctions by William Masters and Virginia Johnson. The treatment methods pioneered by these researchers have helped many people achieve more satisfactory sexual adjustment, although this research has been criticized recently for its lack of scientific rigor.

Ego-dystonic homosexuality, or feelings of sexual attraction toward members of one's own sex, is considered a psychosexual disorder. This is not to say that all homosexuals are considered to be sexually disordered. In 1973 the American Psychiatric Association removed homosexuality from its list of sexual disorders on the grounds that many homosexuals do not consider their life-style wrong or experience accompanying psychological problems. The present diagnostic system, DSM-III, includes homosexuality as a psychosexual disorder when an individual's changed sexual orientation becomes a persistent concern. If the person is unhappy and dissatisfied, the problem is said to be dystonic with his or her ego and therefore is viewed as a psychological problem appropriate to treat.

Affective Disorders

Psychological adjustment is often reflected in states of mood. Mood or affect is an emotional condition that modulates our action and dominates our total behavior. When we are depressed, nothing seems to go right—life is dull and meaningless and the future seems hopeless. When we are "up," or in an elated mood ("on top of the world"), our prospects appear bright and no problem or burden can slow us down.

People also experience extreme changes in mood as a result of environmental events. The death of a loved one or the loss of material goods can produce an extended low period. An unexpected good fortune, similarly, can lift our spirits and make us feel positive and optimistic for some time.

"I miss my periods of depression."

This section examines extreme disturbances of mood—problems that today are widespread in the United States. Here we will consider two subdivisions—(1) the milder *dysthymic disorders,* formerly called neurotic depression, and (2) the more extreme, *major affective disorders,* which involve a break with reality (psychosis).

Dysthymic Disorder (Neurotic Depression)

The increasing incidence of dysthymic, or depressive, neurosis in our society has led some people to suggest that we are facing an epidemic of depression. *Neurotic depression* is characterized by an excessive reaction of depression, usually accompanied by significant anxiety feelings. The disorder usually involves feelings of fatigue, weakness, and exhaustion—and yet the individual has difficulty falling asleep. Such individuals almost always consider themselves worthless persons who have accomplished nothing in life and who expect to accomplish nothing in the future; often depressive neurotics feel guilty. Despite all these symptoms, the depressive neurotic does not suffer from loss of contact with reality, although some reality distortion is often present. Typically the person maintains a reasonable level of functioning in day-to-day life, a fact that distinguishes neurotic depression from the much more severe psychotic depression.

Neurotic depression is often attributable to a personal loss such as the death of a loved one or a serious financial setback. Occasionally, depressive neurosis follows the achievement of an important goal in the person's life. At least four other factors have been suggested as important in neurotic depression, each having a different theoretical orientation. According to Freudian theory, depression is a result of the inability to outwardly express hostility and anger, even when this expression would be perfectly appropriate. Such persons turn their anger inward against themselves. They convince themselves that they are worthless bums who do not deserve any of the good things they have earned.

In Carl Rogers' view depression arises because the person has an image of an ideal self that he or she sees as different from the real self. The ideal self-image is so completely perfect that the real self seems impossibly far from attaining any of the qualities of the ideal self. If, as Rogers claims, one of a person's major goals is to strive for self-actualization, such a conception of the distance between one's real and ideal selves would lead the person to be depressed.

Another explanation of depression, based on behavioral theory, is that a person becomes depressed because there is a lack of positive reinforcement in his or her life, a view similar to the idea of personal loss. Feelings of happiness, freedom, and self-worth are seen as basically due to consistent receipt of positive rewards for one's behavior. If persons find themselves in life situations in which their behavior is controlled mainly by negative reinforcement (they do what they do to avoid punishment), then their emotional responses will be depressive.

Depression Appears to Afflict Thousands of Children in U.S.
By ROCHELLE SEMMEL ALBIN

After years of debate, a growing number of psychiatrists and psychologists are concluding that even children can suffer from depression. Clinicians had long insisted that children under about 14 years of age lack the psychological capacity to experience depression, and some still remain skeptical.

Dr. Jules Bemporad, a psychiatrist at Harvard Medical School, says, "Real depression comes from attributing external events to oneself, but children can only look at life intuitively and do not search for reasons." Nevertheless, advances in the diagnosis and treatment of adult depression have generated research on the applicability of those advances to children.

Scientists estimate that 5 to 20 percent of all adults are depressed. Their inability to pinpoint its incidence more accurately suggests that they are using different definitions of depression. They do agree, however, that depressed adults feel sad and worthless, and are hopeless about the future. Depressed adults also commonly experience loss of interest in pleasurable activities, a lack of energy and disturbances in their sleep.

Rather than concluding that children lacking these symptoms are not depressed, many researchers now believe that children's symptoms of depression simply differ from those of adults as a result of the limited psychological development of children.

Epidemiologists do not yet know just how common depression among children may be. Dr. Jamad Kashani, a child psychiatrist at the University of Missouri Medical School, thinks that "about 2 percent of all children are probably depressed." He bases this figure on a study of more than 100 boys and girls from 7 to 12 years old. Using diagnostic criteria recently developed by the American Psychiatric Associa-

tion, he suspects that "there may be over 400,000 depressed children in this country." . . .

Uncertainty about the existence of childhood depression may be tied to the fact that its symptoms do not fully match those of depressed adults. This has made it difficult to differentiate feelings of ordinary sadness and unhappiness from true depression. Hopelessness, for example, is common among depressed adults but not among children.

"In order to feel hopeless," Dr. Maria Kovacs [a psychologist at Pittsburgh Western Psychiatric Institute] explained, "we must be able to think about the future. But Piaget's work has shown that young children have a very limited ability to understand the future and to locate events in time. This makes it unlikely that they will feel hopeless when depressed."

Some research indicates that, above all other symptoms, it is hopeless thoughts that lead depressed adults to commit suicide. Dr. Kovacs suggested that the dramatic increase in suicide at adolescence may stem from the development in the second decade of life of the capacity to understand future time and to experience hopelessness. "For a 10-year-old," she explained, "another 10 years seems endless. But for an adult, it is conceivable to even make plans that far ahead."

She said the fact that "depressed children may feel unloved and friendless instead of sad as do adults" further clouds the distinction between depression and unhappiness. And because play fulfills many functions in a child's life, she said, depressed children often continue to play and, unlike their adult counterparts, to experience some pleasure. "It is hard to diagnose as depressed this type of behavior," she said.

120 Symptoms Identified
Dr. Kovacs has identified more than 120 symptoms that research has linked with childhood depression, a number that has made diagnosis very difficult. She speculates that the wide range of symptoms may result from the developmental changes that children go through. In research last year for the National Institute of Mental Health, she began to study the relationship between reported symptoms and cognitive and physiological development.

"We think that we will be able to account for differences in symptoms of depression among children of various ages by observing the level of a child's cognitive and pubertal development," she said. "A child too young to conceive of the future will not feel hopeless once depressed. And the intensity and severity of a child's feelings of depression might be related to the increased secretion of hormones that begins during puberty."

Dr. Kovacs has isolated five basic symptoms that she thinks might occur among all depressed children, regardless of age.

"Research indicates that all depressed children may experience mood changes such as sadness and irritability, sleep disturbances, loss of appetite or increased appetite, feelings of worthlessness, and withdrawal from other people," she said. Eventually, she hopes to come up with "several versions of cognitive psychotherapy to treat children of different ages."

Few depressed children ever see a psychologist or psychiatrist. Because of the confusion about diagnosis, depressed children are rarely treated, Dr. Kovacs said. . . .

The New York Times
March 31, 1981

As we saw in Chapter 4, a different conceptualization of depression comes out of *learned helplessness* research with animals. In a typical learned helplessness experiment a dog is placed in a large box and given electric shock. There is no way for the dog to escape the shock, and after some time the animal's response to the situation appears very much like depression in human beings, with such symptoms as passivity, loss of appetite, weight loss, and loss of motivation to escape. Later, when the dog is given an opportunity to escape the shock, it does not even try. Martin Seligman has proposed that depression in people occurs in a similar manner. A person comes to believe that he or she has no personal control over life—that there is no way to escape anxiety-provoking situations—and gives up. Both the animal and person have learned to be helpless and hopeless. Not all experimental evidence supports the analogy between learned helplessness in animals and depression in human beings, but the results are sufficiently interesting to be worthy of further exploration.

In summary, there are at least five possible factors in depression: (1) personal loss, (2) anger turned inward, (3) an unusually large discrepancy between the real and ideal self, (4) the lack of positive reinforcement, and (5) learned helplessness. Dysthymic disorders may often be triggered by personal loss, but the other factors are probably all important in maintaining the depression. In any particular case, however, only one or two of these factors may be operating, and very likely one factor alone cannot account for all depressive disorders.

Major Affective Disorders

There are two types of major affective disorders, both of which refer to severe or extreme disturbances in mood and would be generally described as psychotic. One type is called *bipolar disorder* (formerly called manic-depressive psychosis), and the other type, *major depression* (psychotic depression).

Bipolar Disorder During the nineteenth century Emil Kraepelin, the father of the present psychiatric diagnostic system, identified two emotional problems with opposite characteristics—depression and mania—as part of the same "disease" process. A person who swings back and forth between the two poles of mania and depression is said to have a *bipolar disorder*. Deep or psychotic depression involves feelings of profound sadness, loneliness, and lack of self-worth. Thought processes are slowed down, and the person has a very low level of energy. In contrast, individuals who are experiencing a *manic episode* are experiencing elated mood, increased activity, and expansiveness without environmental cause for such mood elevation. Individuals in a manic episode behave erratically—they are often irritable, sleep little or not at all, and become overextended in activities. They may reflect inflated self-esteem, proclaiming great things about themselves, and they often have *delusions of grandeur* (as do schizophrenics, as we will see in the next section), believing that they have unusual powers. Such persons may behave in extreme ways, so as to call attention from the police—for example, one manic man completely nude bolted down a busy sidewalk proclaiming his divinity.

Major Depression Individuals who swing back and forth between mania and depression are relatively rare. More common is the unipolar condition called major depression, which reaches psychotic proportions when a person loses contact with reality. Individuals with unipolar, major depression may have hallucinations and delusions involving depressive thoughts. An example is the psychotic depressive who feels that his insides are rotting and filled with insects. There is evidence for a continuum of severity in depression from normal depression (with the normal disappointments of life) through dysthymic disorders (neurotic depression) to the most severe psychotic depression. All depressions, whether severe or mild, involve systems of fantasies that may become delusional. For example, it is not unusual for the depressed adolescent to have fantasies of committing suicide—an act that so upsets people that the individual imagines himself finally appreciated at his funeral. If the depression is severe, the person may "live" this fantasy.

Suicide

Most people believe that suicide occurs in the depths of depression. With severe depression, however, the person seldom has enough energy to try suicide. It is during the swing out of depression that the risk of suicide is often greatest. The person is still depressed, but now is active enough to do something about it. Indeed, the lifting of the deepest depression may indicate that the person has found one solution to personal problems—death. Deep depression and suicides tend to occur during holidays, pleasant weather, and the first day of spring rather than in dreary weather. Apparently this has to do with the discrepancy between how persons feel and how they think they ought to feel. The expectation that everyone should be happy at Christmas causes depressed persons to feel even more depressed.

Suicide ranks ninth in causes of death in the United States, with about 200,000 attempts each year and about 25,000 successes. Three times as many men as women successfully complete suicide, but three times as many women attempt suicide. Suicide attempts are highest among professional groups. During national crises like war and earthquakes, suicide rates decrease, but they increase during economic depression.

Heredity

Population statistics are often used to document the role of heredity in the affective disorders. Kallman (1953) noted that 25 percent of the brothers, sisters, parents, and children of manic-depressives were also manic-depressive, whereas the expectancy rate in the general population is around 0.5 percent. In a

Suicide Proving Major Health Issue

Suicide is a relatively recent and a distressingly difficult subject of research. Psychiatrist Dr. Betsy Comstock is president of the American Association of Suicidology, an 11-year-old group of mental health professionals such as herself and volunteers, such as the people who staff suicide prevention hot lines. The conversation below took place in her office at the Baylor College of Medicine in Houston's sprawling Texas Medical Center.

"Suicide is a rare event," she said, "but it is a public health issue of considerable proportions. Thirty-five thousand people a year, 95 a day, commit suicide in this country. It usually ranks as the 10th cause of death nationally. On some college campuses, it is the leading cause of death; on most campuses, it is either first or second.

"A block-by-block population survey of New Haven, Conn., done by Yale University a few years ago indicated suicide attempts on the part of 400 of every 100,000 people (1 of every 250). But there were 30 to 40 times more people with suicidal feelings—wishes to die, thoughts about killing themselves, plans to commit suicide.

"From the number of people who show up in hospital emergency rooms seeking treatment, I'd estimate 2,000 attempts at suicide per 100,000 population."

Q—Who commits suicide?

A—There is an increase in the number of attempts and of deaths on the part of young people, people aged 15 to 24. Prior to the late '60s, that group used to supply a negligible suicide number. In the late '60s, the change began. The rate became almost twice what it was. I'm inclined to think because of the period involved that it happened because of massive sociological shifts, the instability, the mobility of young people. As the alternate society turned away from the establishment, people who embraced the alternate society but who needed a sense of identity and cultural principles suffered.

Q—Would a decline of religious belief and of family ties be part of those cultural principles?

A—Yes, all that. Also the drug culture is a factor, the turning to drugs in times of stress. Several years ago, gunshot was the most frequent cause of death in suicide. Today, sedative overdose is the most frequent cause.

The cliche that black people don't commit suicide is just that, a cliche. In particular, black males are closer to white males, while black females lag behind their white counterparts.

Q—Is there a profile of the typical suicide victim?

A—Suicide is as variable in its dynamics as people are variable. There are certain kinds of people who are more vulnerable to suicide than others. I would be anxious about giving a profile because it might imply that if you don't fit the profile, you're home free. It's not that simple. The one group I would caution about, however, is highly impulsive people. I think that's worth putting in the newspaper. By impulsive people I mean people who change jobs frequently, have less marital stability, change residence often, buy and sell possessions erratically. There are more suicides among people who do things impulsively because when suicide as a problem-solving mechanism occurs to them, they are more likely to act. Permanence in life is a deterrent to suicide.

If people are aware of their impulsiveness, perhaps they can stop themselves in the act and give it some thought. They need to watch their decision-making process and put the brakes on, particularly around such fundamental issues as life and death. They must be told, "Make up your mind in advance that when you get the idea to kill yourself, sleep on it before you go ahead." Just that could save a lot of people.

Q—Has society's attitude toward suicide changed? Is suicide more accepted?

A—I'm not convinced that it is. It's a stigmatizing business. When it occurs, a sense of family disgrace often goes with it. The grieving reactions are much harder to deal with in suicide. Survivors have to deal with guilt, nonacceptance, anger. . . .

Q—Aside from physical restraint, how should I handle a suicidal person?

A—First, try to communicate that another human being, a concerned human being, is there and that you want that person's attention as your right as a concerned human being. I don't think you get very far dealing with negative aspects, saying "This is going to hurt other people," things like that. What you have to do is urge that the person consider whether there aren't some alternatives he hasn't examined . . . and that since a decision for death is available to anyone at any time, it's worth taking time to explore what kinds of help there are. I've never talked to anyone who wasn't ambivalent about death —never. There may be such people, but I've never talked to any."

Boulder Daily Camera
January 18, 1978

later study (1958) Kallman compared the **concordance rate** of manic-depressives in fraternal and identical twins. The concordance rate is defined as the probability that one member of a pair of twins is manic-depressive, given that the other twin is so diagnosed. Fraternal twins have the same overlap of genes as any two brothers or sisters, whereas identical twins have identical genetic make-up. Kallman reported that the concordance rate for fraternal twins was .265 and for identical twins .957. He concluded that manic-depressive reactions result from a genetic defect in the neurohormonal mechanisms that control emotion.

These findings, while impressive, are not as conclusive as Kallman suggests. First, being from the same family, all siblings—including twins—have a much more similar environment than randomly chosen members of the population. Thus, if the nature of the environment is such as to produce depression in one family member, others subject to the same circumstances might be affected in the same way. Furthermore, identical twins, because they look alike, will have even more similar environments than fraternal twins or ordinary siblings. Because it is difficult to tell one from the other, identical twins tend to elicit the same responses from people. Thus, the higher correlations noted by Kallman among identical twins as contrasted with fraternal twins or ordinary siblings could be environmentally rather than genetically based.

In addition, there are methodological problems associated with Kallman's work. At the time of his studies techniques for distinguishing between identical and fraternal twins lacked precision. A fraternal pair might be incorrectly classified as identical if they looked and behaved enough alike — for example, if they were both depressed. Nowadays, blood serum studies make it possible to recognize twin types with little error. Furthermore, it should be noted that medical diagnoses of depression are not made blindly. A physician who finds in the family history that the identical (or fraternal) twin of a patient has been diagnosed as depressive is more likely to apply that label to his patient. These factors, too, tend to inflate the estimates of depression among family members.

Research evidence tends to support the idea that bipolar depression has a major genetic component. There is much less evidence for genetic causes in unipolar depression, however.

Biochemical Causes

Current research has led to an increasing interest in the role of biochemical factors in affective disorders. One theory proposes that a state of well-being is maintained in the body by hormones produced in the brain called *catecholamines* (epinephrine and norepinephrine). Deficits of these hormones may lead to severe emotional disruption and the mood swings of the manic-depressive. The evidence to support this theory is indirect. A group of drugs that lifts depression in some people is known also to increase the level of norepinephrine in the brain, while a drug that tends to produce depression reduces the amount of this hormone in the brain (see Appendix D).

Psychological Causes

Some evidence is difficult to fit into any strictly biological theory of manic-depressive psychosis. For example, a disproportionate number of affective disorders tend to come from upper socioeconomic groups, and income is unlikely to be heavily biologically determined. Some researchers and clinicians have reached the conclusion that severe depression

may be rooted in rejection in early childhood. The manic-depressive seems to be trying to win approval from parents who are constantly finding fault. Frequently, the precipitating event for the depression is loss of a loved one or loss of status. Behavior theorists have proposed that depression results from the lack of positive reinforcement within a person's life, a view that has a slightly different focus than the dynamic point of view but is consistent with it.

Treatment

A unique aspect of depression is the spontaneous remission of symptoms; that is, depression tends to lift after a period of time without the benefit of treatment. If a person in a severe depression is kept from committing suicide, the depression will lift. It may take weeks, months, or even years, but the state is self-limiting. This does not mean, however, that the person will not experience depression again in the future. Treatment is important, even though the depression is self-limiting, in order to reduce the suffering of the depressed person and his or her family.

How to understand and treat affective disorders is still very much unresolved. Many factors are involved, and no single set of circumstances has been found in the history of all affective psychoses. The treatment of psychotic depressives is difficult. Many psychotically depressed individuals respond to antidepressant medication, that is, they experience an elevation of mood. Electroconvulsive shock therapy has also been found to be effective in limiting the depression (see Chapter 12). One successful psychological treatment for severely depressed individuals has been cognitive-behavioral treatment. In this method patients are provided support and are encouraged to alter their attitudes about the future. (A person's beliefs are presumed to be the major source of or the reasons for the maintenance of the depression.) Patients are then encouraged to "experiment" — to change their experiences and become actively involved in life. Cognitive-behavioral treatment is examined in greater detail in Chapter 12.

Schizophrenic Disorders

Schizophrenia refers to a group of psychotic disorders characterized by disturbances in thought processes and emotions as well as a marked distortion of reality. Conscious thought processes are often unpredictable because they usually follow a chain of free associations that is difficult for others to understand. Generally the schizophrenic withdraws from interpersonal relationships, and there is a blunting or flattening of emotional responses, which may change to extreme, inappropriate emotional re-

Psychotics Prefer Delusions

WASHINGTON—The delusions of grandeur entertained by some schizophrenics may be far more comforting to these patients than the stark realities they face in moments of sanity.

This is the conclusion reached by a team of psychiatric researchers after a three-year study to determine why some chronic schizophrenics persistently refuse to take drugs that alleviate their psychoses, while other patients, also suffering from schizophrenia, are unswervingly faithful in complying with their treatment regimen.

The study involved 59 patients—29 who persistently refused drugs and 30 who just as persistently came in for medication—at the Brentwood Veterans Administration Hospital in Los Angeles.

The crucial factor that distinguished the two groups appeared to be the nature of their personal psychoses. . . .

While the drug refusers basked in Napoleonic delusions, the schizophrenics who cooperated with the drug-treatment program were far more likely to be subject to acute attacks of anxiety and depression when they failed to take their medication and slipped back into psychosis. . . .

The observation that hard-core drug refusers can count on a resurgence of a florid psychosis characterized by grandiosity and relative absence of such dysphoric affects as anxiety and depression does not necessarily mean that they stop taking medication for that reason," the researchers said.

"However, three years' experience with a merry-go-round of readmissions and discharges forced us to realize that there exists a group of chronic schizophrenic patients who never become reconciled to the need for antipsychotic medications and who cannot tolerate the drug-induced increase in reality."

The researchers cited the case of a 30-year-old man who was hospitalized 19 times, harboring delusions that he was a composer, that he possessed "billions" and that he was "the greatest aeronautical engineer in the world."

While in the hospital, he spent his time sketching "satellite stations" and would demand from time to time to see his imaginary publisher.

As drugs he was given to clear up his psychosis took effect, the researchers reported, "He started to mention his loneliness and his realistic lack of any life accomplishments and developed some insight into his illness.

"At this point he demanded to leave the hospital and resumed living in a lonely hotel. He returned for only one injection (of the anti-psychotic medication) and was re-admitted three months later, psychotic as before.". . .

"The hard-core drug refusers resembled Elwood P. Dowd, the whimsical hero of the play 'Harvey'," the researchers said. In the play, Dowd's closest friend and most frequent companion is a civilized, six-foot, invisible white rabbit, who goes by the name Harvey.

"When his psychiatrist urged (Dowd) to struggle with reality," the researchers noted, "he responded, 'Doctor, I wrestled with reality for 40 years and I am happy to state that I finally won out over it'."

The authors of the study were Dr. Theodore Van Putten, Evelyn Crumpton and Coralee Yale.

The Denver Post
February 16, 1977

Some theorists have proposed that delusions serve the function of reducing anxiety for the psychotic.

sponses. Another frequent symptom is depersonalization, or the loss of personal identity. The schizophrenic may become preoccupied with bodily functions, which are attributed to nonhuman causes. Such people may feel that a hand has turned to stone or that the body is full of bugs so that they are no longer human. There seems to be a preoccupation with inner fantasies. While schizophrenics are probably of normal intelligence, their lack of attention to the external environment leads to low scores on IQ tests.

In some cases schizophrenic breakdown is highly dramatic and is described by persons as something happening to them rather than something that they are doing. Schizophrenia in which there is a sudden onset of symptoms is sometimes referred to as **reactive schizophrenia;** the probability of recovery (prognosis) is good in such cases. Schizophrenia characterized by slow onset of symptoms over a period of years with progressive withdrawal from others, increasing deterioration of thought processes, and slow onset of hallucinations and delusions is referred to as **process schizophrenia;** in this case the prognosis is very poor. Some evidence suggests that genetics may play a greater causative role in process schizophrenia than in reactive schizophrenia.

Types of Schizophrenia

There are four main types of schizophrenia in the DSM–III classification: (1) undifferentiated, (2) disorganized (formerly called hebephrenic), (3) paranoid, and (4) catatonic.

The *undifferentiated* type is characterized by delusions, hallucinations, incoherence, and grossly disorganized chaotic behavior. The individual does not exhibit any of the catatonic or paranoid charac-

The Bethlehem Royal Hospital in England, better known as Bedlam, was founded some 500 years ago for the care of the mentally ill. This engraving by William Hogarth for *The Rake's Progress* was done in the eighteenth century.

teristics described below. The *disorganized* type of schizophrenic patient is also typically incoherent and shows inappropriate affect (for example, laughing at something sad) or blunted affect (no emotions at all). Delusions are not characteristic of the disorganized schizophrenic.

Paranoid schizophrenia is frequently a reactive problem, and there is a reasonable chance of recovery. This subtype is characterized by delusions of persecution and suspicion of others. The feeling of being singled out for persecution leads the paranoid to conclude that he or she is a special person, selected because of unusual powers or qualities. Thus, the paranoid schizophrenic is often characterized by *delusions of grandeur*. In one case, a youth attacked a total stranger who was standing near him at a baseball game. When asked later by the police why he had done this, he responded that it was well known that he was sexually attractive to women and this man was trying to steal his sexual

attractiveness by electrical waves. It is assumed that paranoids use projection, denying their unacceptable anger and ascribing it to others. Paranoid schizophrenia should not be confused with the paranoid personality, a personality disorder characterized by suspiciousness and jealousy but no loss of contact with reality.

Catatonic schizophrenia may be a reactive or a process type. The reactive catatonic probably has the best prognosis of any of the schizophrenics. The catatonic is characterized by a *waxy flexibility* of body and limbs, loss of motion, and a tendency to remain motionless for hours or days. Such persons may allow their arms to be placed in uncomfortable positions without resistance and remain in that position far longer than the normal individual would tolerate. The dynamic theorists see the catatonic as handling hostility by immobility. The catatonic may have episodes of furious rage from time to time that alternate with the rigid withdrawal.

Highlight 11–5

The Case of a Paranoid Schizophrenic

I, LPK, had a few days to spend with Long Island relatives before returning to work for the War Dept., Wash., D.C. One day I went to reconnoitre in N.Y. City's East Side. Being a stranger I was surprised to hear someone exclaim twice: "Shoot him!", evidently meaning me, judging from the menacing talk which followed between the threatener and those with him. I tried to see who the threatener, and those with him were, but the street was so crowded, I could not. I guessed that they must be gangsters, who had mistaken me for another gangster, who I coincidentally happened to resemble. I thought one or more of them really intended to shoot me so I hastened from the scene as fast as I could walk. These unidentified persons, who had threatened to shoot me, pursued me. I knew they were pursuing me because I still heard their voices as close as ever, no matter how fast I walked . . . Days later while in the Metropolis again, I was once more startled by those same pursuers, who had threatened me several days before. It was nighttime. As before, I could catch part of their talk but, in the theatre crowds, I could see them nowhere. I heard one of them, a woman, say: "You can't get away from us; we'll lay for you, and get you after a while!" To add to the mystery, one of these "pursuers" repeated my thoughts aloud, verbatim. I tried to allude [sic] these pursuers as before, but this time, I tried to escape from them by means of subway trains, darting up and down subway exits and entrances, jumping on and off trains, until after midnight. But, at every station where I got off a train, I heard the voices of these pursuers as close as ever. The question occurred to me: How could as many of these pursuers follow me as quickly unseen? Were they ghosts? Or was I in the process of developing into a spiritual medium? No! Among these pursuers, I was later to gradually discover by deduction, [there] evidently were some brothers, and sisters,[1] who had inherited from one of their parents, some astounding, unheard of, utterly unbelievable occult powers. Believe-it-or-not, some of them,[2] besides being able to tell a person's thoughts, are also able to project their magnetic voices—commonly called "radio voices" around here—a distance of a few miles without talking loud, and without apparent effort, their voices sounding from that distance as tho heard thru a radio head-set,[3] this being done without electrical apparatus. This unique, occult power of projecting their "radio voices" for such long distances, apparently seems to be due to their natural, bodily electricity, of which they have a supernormal amount. Maybe the iron contained in their red blood corpuscles is magnetised. The vibration of their vocal chords, evidently generates wireless waves, and these vocal radio waves are caught by human ears without rectification.[4] (Kaplan, 1964, pages 133–135)

[1] Maybe some were half brothers, or half sisters, or both.
[2] There is little doubt but what more than one of them can read minds.
[3] Hence the term "radio voices."
[4] The other day I read about a man who could hear radio broadcasts of a local station thru his teeth without a receiving set. In the plant where he worked the air was filled with tiny carborundum crystals, and some of these had collected on his teeth.

While these four types of schizophrenia are carefully described in diagnostic manuals and books of psychopathology, it is important to note that individuals seldom fit into such neat patterns. The two most common diagnoses made within the schizophrenic classification are *paranoid* and *chronic-undifferentiated.* The latter diagnosis is a wastebasket term indicating that the person has characteristics belonging to more than one subtype. In general, schizophrenics can be described as being either paranoid schizophrenic or undifferentiated schizophrenic and as either process or reactive. The term "schizophrenia" is often applied when a person is

The patients in this picture are in positions that they might hold rigidly for long periods.

psychotic but not depressed. The lack of clarity in the use of the term "schizophrenia" and its different definitions from one mental institution to the next has complicated the extensive research conducted on the causes of the disorder.

Causes of Schizophrenia

We shall briefly consider research on genetic, biochemical, and environmental factors. It is clear from the research that all three of these factors are involved in causing schizophrenia.

Genetic Factors There is little doubt now that there is a genetic component in schizophrenia, although different investigators have found widely different concordance rates for sets of identical twins. For example, Kallman, whose research is most well known in this area, found that of 174 pairs of twins with one member who had already been diagnosed as schizophrenic, the other twin was also schizophrenic in 103 cases (see Table 11–5). On the other hand, Essen-Moller found no pairs of twins in which both members were schizophrenic.

It is generally agreed now that Kallman's data significantly exaggerate the degree of heredity involved in schizophrenia. We reviewed some of the general problems with his methods in our discussion of affective disorders, but additional questions have arisen in connection with his work on schizophrenia. For example, Kallman's sample of patients has been criticized as having involved only the most severe cases and as having a preponderance of females. There is some evidence (Gottesman and Shields, 1966) that the degree of concordance between twins is higher as the severity of the affliction increases. This in turn suggests that schizophrenia is not a unitary disorder and that process forms may be more genetically based than reactive forms.

Perhaps the best estimate of the degree of genetic determination of schizophrenia can be ob-

tained by pooling the results of several different studies. On the basis of the results of the seven studies shown in Table 11–5, we conclude: Given that one twin is schizophrenic, the chances are 46/100 that the other twin will be schizophrenic (the probability that the other twin will be schizophrenic = .46). The value for ordinary brothers and sisters would only be around 10 to 15 percent, so these data strongly suggest a genetic component in schizophrenia. Even if the other twin is not schizophrenic, the odds are quite high that he or she will have some significant behavior abnormality. Thus, if one of a pair of identical twins is schizophrenic, about 88 percent of the other twins either will be schizophrenic or will suffer from some other behavior disorder (the sum of columns two and three in Table 11–5).

It is probably true that in all cases of schizophrenia, as in the affective disorders, both heredity and environment are important, a notion formally called the *diathesis-stress* theory of psychosis. According to this theory, schizophrenia develops because there is a genetic predisposition to the disorder (called *diathesis*) *and* because there are environmental factors (*stress*) that trigger the disorder. If either factor is missing, the disorder will not appear. This theory is a better approximation to our current knowledge than a model which suggests that one type of schizophrenia is genetic (the process type, say) and the other is environmental (the reactive type).

Biochemical Factors Are there biochemical factors in schizophrenia? At times chemicals have supposedly been found in the blood of schizophrenics that are not found in normal blood. However, no single chemical has been consistently found by all research groups. It has also been proposed that a neural transmitter, called *serotonin,* produces the symptoms of schizophrenia, but our understanding of how neural transmitters work is still far from complete.

TABLE 11–5 Schizophrenia Rates in Identical Twins

Investigator	Number of Twin Pairs Studied (One Twin Already Diagnosed as Schizophrenic)	Number of Pairs in Which the Other Member of the Pair Also Has Schizophrenia	Number of Pairs in Which the Other Member of the Pair Is Abnormal But Not Schizophrenic
Kallman	174	103	62
Essen-Moller	9	0	8
Slater	37	18	11
Tienari	16	1	12
Kringlen	45	14	17
Inouye	53	20	29
Gottesman and Shields	24	10	8
Total	358	166 (46.4%) Concordance rate = .46	147 (41.1%) Concordance rate = .41

All the studies implicating biochemical factors suffer the same difficulty in interpretation—it is never clear if the biochemical change is a cause or a result of the disorder. For example, many mental hospitals are nonhygienic and overcrowded. Most patients are on medication of some kind, taking drugs that often have unknown biochemical side effects. The eating habits of psychotics may be poor, since they often withdraw from all activity in the external world. All these factors may lead to biochemical imbalance. Although it is tempting to think of biochemical abnormalities as the cause of schizophrenia, these conditions suggest that they might really be the result.

Environmental Factors   In an effort to isolate environmental factors, extensive research has been done on the family life of the schizophrenic. Lidz et al. (1963) have proposed that there is a *marital skew* in the family, in which serious psychopathology in one parent is accepted or supported by the other parent. In other families the problem is one of *marital schism*—there is open warfare between husband and wife. Bitter arguments are so common that the marriage is in constant danger of breaking up. There may be a serious lack of understanding and cooperation between parents, resulting in distrust and rivalry. The father is frequently seen as insecure and weak, and the mother as domineering and hostile.

Gregory Bateson has described a conflict situation known as the *double bind,* in which a parent presents to the child ideas, feelings, and demands that are contradictory. At one level of communication the parent may express love and at another rejection. At the third level of communication the parent prevents the child from commenting on the paradox. The parent may say "I love you" but provide no physical contact, indicating rejection. Uncertain as to whether or not he or she should respond to the parent's expressions of affection, the child withdraws and establishes no relationships. The prototype of the parent of a schizophrenic is called the *schizophrenogenic parent,* and much effort has been devoted to identifying the characteristics of such parents.

Still, there is a great deal of overlap between schizophrenics and normal people in family background. Also, people from completely different types of families become schizophrenics. Of two people from relatively similar backgrounds, one may be schizophrenic while the other is quite normal. Thus, as in the case of biological factors, the role of family and other social influences in schizophrenia is far from clear.

DSM–III: Axis II (Personality Disorders)

"You agreed to fix the screen door!"

"I know, I know. I will. I just haven't had a chance to do it yet."

"But I asked you to fix it over two months ago."

"Look, I said I would do it and I will. I will get it done in the next couple of days."

(Two weeks later.)

"Dear" *(said with controlled anger),* "I thought you said you were going to get the screen door fixed!"

"You are absolutely right, dear. I don't have time right now, but I'll get right to it. You don't have to nag about it."

That was two years ago and the screen door is not fixed yet!

There is strong evidence for a genetic component in mental disorder, particularly the most severe or psychotic disorders. There may also be particular types of parents (called in the case of schizophrenia, schizophrenogenic parents) who set up environmental factors leading to illness. Of course, parents are affected by the disturbed behavior of their children. The DSM–III does not use the term "insanity," which is a legal term, not a psychological one.

You might ask what the above example has to do with abnormal psychology. Certainly the importance of getting the screen door fixed is minor compared to the distress and lack of functioning that we see in severe anxiety disorder or psychosis. However, this interaction illustrates a maladaptive relationship that leaves one member of the couple with extreme levels of frustration and anger and the other with a self-righteous indignation over being nagged after having agreed to the reasonableness of the demands.

This section describes a class of behavior referred to as **personality disorders.** People with personality disorders are defined as individuals with *long-standing dominant personality traits that lead to behavior that is seen as maladaptive to society.* Much of what we know about personality disorders comes through indirect means rather than through clinical case study or empirical clinical investigations. Individuals with severe personality disorders tend not to seek psychological help themselves—they do not feel anxious or upset. Instead, they usually are seen as a result of a family member being in treatment, or they are sent for treatment by the justice system. This does not make them ideal candidates for therapy.

Stress and Personality Disorders

Unlike the neuroses, the personality disorders are not clearly reactions to stress. While maladaptive reactions to stress are characteristic of some personality disorders, such as the passive-aggressive personality and the alcoholic, stress reactions do not define these problems. Personality disorders occur as the result of deeply ingrained habits or personality styles, not as defense mechanisms against anxiety.

DSM–III identifies many different personality disorders on Axis II, of which we will discuss five prominent examples: (1) passive-aggressive, (2) paranoid, (3) antisocial, (4) dependent, and (5) compulsive personality disorders.

Passive-Aggressive Personality

The procrastinating spouse we saw above has some of the characteristics of the passive-aggressive personality who illustrates an extraordinarily effective technique for manipulating other individuals. *Passive aggression* is typically seen in individuals with deep dependency needs that prevent the direct expression of anger because of fear that the dependency needs will no longer be met. Since overt anger or even behavior that might lead to disagreement and thus unpleasantness must be avoided, the person develops a pattern of behavior that involves *apparent* agreement

and compliance, but that in fact displays passive resistance. The example demonstrates easy agreement over the assignment of chores, but *procrastination* as a way of avoiding a chore that obviously is unpleasant.

Other strategies of the passive-aggressive involve stubbornness and *passive obstructionism.* Passive-aggressives can also behave in a passive-dependent manner, acting *helpless, indecisive,* and *clinging.* The passive-aggressive strategy is effective because it blocks any discussion about the trouble that arises from its use. All the passive-aggressive person has to do is agree readily with all the criticisms, apologize profusely, and continue to avoid doing whatever is asked *or* self-righteously assume the martyr role, pointing out that he or she has always been agreeable and that the demands reflect an intolerance on the part of the other person.

Theorists of both the dynamic and behaviorist schools agree that passive-aggressive behavior is the result of faulty personality development rather than unconscious responses to internal or external stress. Passive-aggressive individuals frequently are quite satisfied with themselves and would be content to persist in their behavior if society would just leave them alone.

Paranoid Personality

Suspiciousness and mistrust of others are the cardinal traits of *paranoid personalities.* These personality characteristics make the individual highly vulnerable to viewing all interpersonal relationships with overcautiousness and vigilance. Such persons are rigid and wary—afraid they are going to be tricked or threatened. They generally believe that others are out to do them harm, even when there is evidence to the contrary.

Paranoid personalities are often preoccupied with moral issues, and many of them expend great energy writing letters to newspaper editors or calling talk shows about their causes. They tend to be argumentative individuals who are possessed with knowing what is "right." Persons with these characteristics are often viewed by others as aloof and cold and as having no sense of humor, though they consider themselves objective and rational in all their actions. Often they isolate themselves from social contact and generally have few friends.

The paranoid personality may go through life with a bristling stance that alienates others, maintaining a borderline adjustment, remaining employed, and raising a family. He or she may never develop extensive psychological problems or require hospitalization. Paranoid features may accompany severe psychotic disorders as well—for example, in paranoid

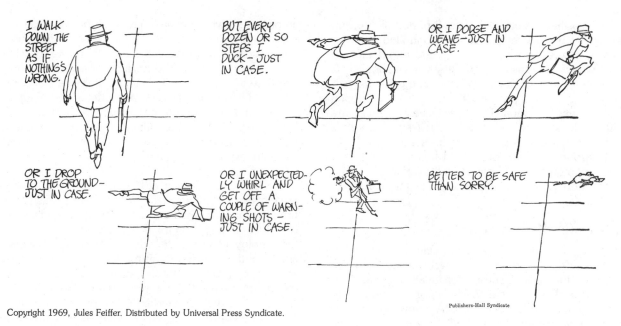

I WALK DOWN THE STREET AS IF NOTHING'S WRONG.

BUT EVERY DOZEN OR SO STEPS I DUCK—JUST IN CASE.

OR I DODGE AND WEAVE—JUST IN CASE.

OR I DROP TO THE GROUND—JUST IN CASE.

OR I UNEXPECTEDLY WHIRL AND GET OFF A COUPLE OF WARNING SHOTS—JUST IN CASE.

BETTER TO BE SAFE THAN SORRY.

Publishers-Hall Syndicate

Copyright 1969, Jules Feiffer. Distributed by Universal Press Syndicate.

Perhaps this man is suffering from what DSM–III would diagnose as *paranoid personality disorder* (on Axis II, long-standing personality disorders).

schizophrenia. If the paranoid features are long-standing personality attributes, the person would receive an Axis II diagnosis of paranoid personality disorder in addition to an Axis I diagnosis of paranoid schizophrenia.

The cluster of traits making up the paranoid personality is developed through lifelong learning processes. Consequently, individuals with these personality characteristics usually do not experience psychological difficulties themselves but attribute problems and causes of their difficulties to others. If they end up in psychological treatment they generally remain distant and attempt to change the therapist rather than themselves.

Antisocial Personality

Antisocial individuals, often called **sociopaths,** are pleasure-oriented (hedonistic) and indifferent to the needs or concerns of others. They exploit others for their own selfish ends and do not feel guilty or anxious except when it is clear that they might be prevented from satisfying their needs for pleasure. At this point they will become anxious but will not regret their past behavior or learn from punishment to avoid this behavior in the future.

In the early twentieth century antisocial personalities were viewed as "moral imbeciles" who were incapable of differentiating right from wrong. We know now, however, that these people are above average in intelligence and especially adept at manipulating others. They also tend to be physically attractive, which gives them a head start in learning to manipulate others. Punishment seems to have less impact on these individuals than is normal. The presence of an antisocial parent within the home is one of the chief factors in the development of a sociopath. The child learns at an early age how to win social approval.

Individuals with antisocial personality disorders often come into contact with the law, and many—especially severe cases—wind up in jail. Often they are repeaters in prison; failing to learn from punishing experience, they tend to get involved in impulsive acts, seemingly wishing to get caught. For example, one young man had spent two years in prison for car theft; on release, his father bought him a new car so he could have transportation. Within one week he parked his own car and went for a ride in an old "junk" he took from a shopping center lot, only to be caught and sent back to prison.

Treatment of antisocial personalities is difficult. Such persons see nothing wrong in their behavior, and they will seek help only to manipulate their way out of trouble. Clearly, this kind of maladaptive behavior is a failure of *motivation* to behave appropriately, and psychotherapy is seldom *effective* in producing change. Individual psychotherapy with antisocial personalities is often ineffective because when the treatment situation becomes emotionally intense the patient tends to "flee" to avoid problems.

Some positive results have been reported with group treatment using peer pressure in controlled environments. However, the personality-disordered individual, particularly the severe antisocial personality, is a challenging and difficult patient. The behavior pattern has been well established over a lifelong learning history, and emotionally corrective experiences are difficult to arrange and implement. If it were not for the fact that many such individuals seem to "burn out" around the age of 30 and less actively pursue their manipulations of others, they would present a much more serious social problem than they do.

Dependent Personality

Persons with *dependent personalities* allow other people to dominate and take responsibility for major areas of their lives. These individuals lack self-confidence and are unable to rely upon themselves to manage day-to-day decisions. A common type of dependent personality in clinical situations is the abused wife who tolerates extensive physical or psychological mistreatment for fear of alienating and losing her spouse. Individuals such as these remain in intolerable situations out of fear that they cannot make it in life on their own.

Compulsive Personality

Several behavioral features characterize the *compulsive personality disorder* and result in severe distress and impaired social relationships. These disordered individuals tend to be perfectionistic and to become preoccupied with details, often at the expense of appreciating major issues. They are rigid and stubborn, and typically they fail to see others' viewpoints. Often they are disorganized, indecisive, and fearful that they will make a mistake, so that they are unable to complete assignments or meet deadlines. People with compulsive personalities are usually conventional and rule governed, and others often consider them to be too serious. Warm emotions are difficult for them to express, and their associates view them as cold and uncaring.

Bill P., a 51-year-old accountant and newly appointed department head in a large manufacturing firm, is a prime example of the compulsive individual who tries to adapt by throwing himself into work. All the employees in the department hated Bill. He was critical of their work and nit-picking about the precise time of their coming to and leaving the job; and he attempted to maintain a serious and formal atmosphere in the work situation. Bill was preoccupied with office procedure and spent a great deal of his time "improving" the "rules," to be sure that his 30 employees stayed on their toes. Often, however, he had difficulty organizing himself and his staff to respond to important deadlines. Bill demonstrated great indecisiveness when it came time to release "final" reports, and often his employees had to recheck the documents even after deadlines had passed. Bill's difficulties in making decisions and his extremely compulsive behavior resulted in his being demoted to the position of accountant, where his "careful" approach was appreciated and where he did not have to make large decisions or deal with a group of other people.

SUMMARY

1. Psychopathology is the failure to behave in a socially appropriate way such that the consequences of one's behavior are maladaptive for oneself or society.

2. There are a variety of theoretical viewpoints on psychopathology. The medical viewpoint considers psychopathology as a symptom of an underlying disease process. The dynamic viewpoint assumes psychopathology results from a conflict between conscious and unconscious aspects of the personality. The behavioral viewpoint proposes that psychopathology is the result of positive and negative reinforcement provided by a person's environment. The phenomenological viewpoint emphasizes the importance of the here and now existence and each individual's own internal reality. The ethical viewpoint asserts that psychopathology is the result of an individual's making irresponsible choices in life.

3. The most widely used system for classifying abnormal behavior today is the Diagnostic and Statistical Manual, third edition, (DMS–III). The system classifies or rates people on five axes: (1) current behavioral symptoms or problems, (2) long-standing personality disorders, (3) current medical symptoms or problems, (4) severity of current stress, and (5) the level of adaptive functioning.

4. Seven Axis I categories were discussed: organic disorder, substance-use disorder, schizophrenia, affective disorder, anxiety disorder, somatoform disorder, and psychosexual disorder.

5. Organic mental disorders are caused by permanent or temporary changes in the brain.

6. An anxiety disorder is a functional problem once referred to as a neurosis, that centers around the experience of intense anxiety and the development of psychological mechanisms to control that anxiety.

7. Somatoform disorders occur when a psychological problem finds expression through physical symptoms, even though there is no demonstrable physical cause.

8. Substance-Use disorders refer to the abuse of alcohol or other addictive drugs.

9. There are four distinct types of psychosexual disorders: (1) gender-identity disorders, (2) paraphilias, (3) psychosexual dysfunctions, and (4) ego-dystonic homosexuality.

10. Affective disorders refer to extreme disturbance of mood, ranging from the mild dysthymic disorder (neurotic depression) to the more extreme major affective disorders (psychotic depression and bipolar disorder).

11. Schizophrenic disorders refer to a group of psychotic disorders characterized by severe disturbances in thought and emotion and a marked distortion of reality. There are four types in DMS–III: undifferentiated, disorganized, paranoid, and catatonic.

12. Axis II of the DSM–III identifies many types of personality disorders, defined as long-standing dominant personality traits that lead to behavior that is maladaptive to society or the individual. Five prominent examples are: passive-aggressive, paranoid, antisocial, dependent, and compulsive personality disorders.

RECOMMENDED ADDITIONAL READINGS

Alvarez, A. *The savage god: A study of suicide.* New York: Bantam, 1973.

American Psychiatric Association. *Diagnostic and statistical manual of mental disorders* (DSM–III), 3d ed. Washington, D.C.: The Association, 1980.

Coleman, J. C., Butcher, J. N., & Carson, R. C. *Abnormal psychology and modern life,* 6th ed. Glenview, Ill.: Scott-Foresman, 1980.

Goldstein, J. J., & Palmer, J. O. *The experience of anxiety: A casebook,* 2d ed. New York: Oxford University Press, 1975.

Kaplan, B. (ed.) *The inner world of mental illness.* New York: Harper & Row, 1964.

Plath, S. *The bell jar.* New York: Harper & Row, 1971.

What Does It Mean?

Most of the meaning of our scientific knowledge of psychopathology is best illustrated by our discussion of psychotherapy in Chapter 12. Indeed, the techniques of psychotherapy can be seen as an outgrowth of the application of personality theory (Chapter 9) to the problems of pathological behavior described in this chapter. Therefore, this section will be somewhat briefer than comparable sections of earlier chapters. We will concentrate on only a few general issues.

Has the World Gone Mad?

We have already made it clear that psychopathology is to some extent a culturally defined activity. Behavior that is accepted in one society may be considered seriously deviant in another. Thomas Szasz (1963) was one of the earliest psychiatrists to ask the important question, "Who defines the norms and hence the deviation?" On the one hand, the person himself may decide that he deviates from the norm. Alternatively, someone other than the sufferer may decide that the person is deviant in some important respect. When a psychiatrist is hired by the court to decide whether a person is sane or insane (and whether the individual should be held responsible for his or her behavior), the psychiatrist is not given the alternative to testify that the accused is normal, but the legislators are "insane" for passing the law that made that behavior illegal (Szasz, 1963, pages 14–15). Obviously, society's laws and rules are not infallible. With respect to psychopathology, one need only consider the decision by the American Psychiatric Association to remove homosexuality from the list of categories of abnormal behavior. The arbitrariness of classification is illustrated by the fact that this change was made by the close vote of a committee!

R. D. Laing (1967, 1969) has gone even further than Szasz in attacking labels and diagnostic categories. Schizophrenia is not a "mental illness" but an adaptive response to an insane world, according to Laing. Diagnostic labels are "straightjackets" that keep us from communicating with the disturbed person. Society and particularly the family in the society are destructive forces that attack the self. Laing's approach is strongly anticognitive, and he sees feelings and intuition as the hope of mankind. Yet when we look at the behavior of a suffering neurotic or psychotic, it is difficult to defend the idea that such behavior is always a creative way of adapting to a disordered world, as implied by Laing.

However extreme their positions in some respects, both Szasz and Laing remind us that societies as well as people can be disordered. Of course, all societies label some behaviors unacceptable. The range of behaviors is simply too great to permit all behaviors to exist in a society without some form of control. But societies that permit a greater range of non-harmful (a value judgment!) behaviors—behaviors that do not endanger the safety or well-being of others, for instance—can be viewed as healthier or more adaptive. As well as being willing to confront their personal ethical and social conflicts, people must be open to recognizing when the social structure needs changing.

The Danger of Diagnosis

It has been demonstrated that psychologists' expectations about the results of an experiment can influence (through their own behavior) the results that are obtained. The diagnosis of an individual—assigning a label to him or her—can have the same effect.

Although it is important to recognize that behavioral problems do exist and to know which symptoms indicate significant disorder, there is a danger that diagnostic labels will become self-fulfilling prophecies of the person's behavior. There is some evidence, for example, that teachers who assume that minority students will do poorly in school lower their standards and demands for excellence, leading the students to perform at a lower level than they might otherwise. Persons who are labeled mental retardates can be treated in such a way that they are effectively no longer allowed to learn. The juvenile labeled as delinquent starts to behave in such a way as to realize society's expectations. With psychopathology, the same problem exists. There is a strong moral responsibility for the diagnostician to keep labels away from people who might misuse them. Thus, a diagnosis is seldom given to the person or family of the person who is diagnosed for fear that the diagnosis will be self-fulfilling.

The Unreliability of Diagnosis

The relatively clear descriptions of diagnostic categories given in this chapter might lead one to assume that diagnosis is a straightforward job for clinicians. It has generally been found that there often is disagreement among clinicians in the assignment of patients to the major diagnostic categories such as neurosis, personality disorder, or psychosis; for the subcategories—for example, simple and hebephrenic schizophrenia (DSM–2 terms)—however, disagreement is even lower. In one study, four experienced psychiatrists diagnosed 153 patients referred for outpatient treatment (Beck, Ward, Mendelson, Mock, & Erbaugh, 1962). Each person was interviewed by two psychiatrists. The overall rate of agreement on diagnosis averaged only 54 percent. Agreement occurred only 53 percent of the time for schizophrenia (a lower percentage than the 70 percent agreement usually found for *hospitalized* patients), 40 percent for involutional melancholia (DSM–2 term), and 63 percent for neurotic depression. Such difficulty in reaching agreement in diagnosis makes it clear why research on the cause and cure of specific diagnostic disorders is so difficult.

Noted Psychiatrist Calls Insanity Myth
By MARILYN WEBB

There is no mental illness and therefore no need for psychotherapy, according to Dr. Thomas Szasz. The whole thing is a giant lie.

Szasz is a psychiatrist and professor at Syracuse University's Medical School.

He has been well-known for his anti-establishment views since the early 1960s when he wrote the book "The Myth of Mental Illness. . . ."

"Mental illness is a term applied to a wide variety of behavior which is socially deviant. These terms are in need of much more careful use," Szasz said in an interview Monday. . . .

Szasz says deviance is defined by whoever is in power at the time.

Those our society calls "mentally ill" merely have different value systems, he says, and the great variety of these systems should ideally "be fought out in the open system of debate.

"It doesn't say in the constitution that you can't be irrational," he observes.

But psychiatry has arisen to "rationally" incarcerate those with different viewpoints, he says.

While mental health practitioners here chafed at Szasz' views on treatment, he claimed that the whole psychiatric establishment "is based on massive lies upheld by an irresistible bureaucracy.

"Psychiatrists are the tools, and partly the unwitting fomenters of the bureaucracy here. They will also be the victims, as they are being sued now for malpractice both when patients are committed and released."

If this whole system continues, Szasz warns, "we may be at the end of freedom as we know it."

Szasz cites Hitler as an example. In our society he would have been considered a madman, but in Nazi Germany, because he was in power, he was considered sane.

Definitions of madness and sanity are only socially based, Szasz believes, and should therefore be given little weight.

"There's no standard, it's just arbitrary. You can't prove somebody is schizophrenic or not," but psychiatrists have been granted the power to rule on such things as involuntary admissions to mental hospitals, insanity cases in court and on severe treatments such as electro-shock and drug therapy.

Rather than granting psychiatry what he believes are repressive powers, Szasz feels it should be seen as just another religion in the free market of belief systems.

If it were treated as any other religion and were stripped of its power— for example tax money, court expertise, and legally upheld coercion—Szasz says the whole field would wither, much as witch hunts withered centuries ago.

Asked whether psychotherapy, even if stripped of its powers, is a viable help for disturbed individuals, Szasz says "there would be no market for it outside of coercion."

The process of discourse can go on between two individuals, he says of psychotherapy, because people are free to go to whatever church they like.

But "doctors are faking" treatment of supposedly ill patients "because it is profitable and influential. They are the priests in the white coats—they've be-

come the hight priests of our society."

While Colorado has state statutes upholding involuntary commitment and confinement of patients considered harmful to either themselves or others, Szasz says no society should be allowed to preventatively detain someone against his will.

If someone commits a crime, he should then be punished for it, but suicide, on the other hand, is a personal matter, Szasz believes.

Mental hospitals should have no locks, he says. "Just as churches have no locks and worshippers are free to get up and leave if they don't like the sermon, so should mental hospitals.

"The psychiatrists are fake doctors and the patients are fake patients, because they are not ill. They are just pretending, like the Son of Sam, or the classic case where a woman says she has a headache at night when she knows her husband's been running around," he says.

Szasz maintains that patients who pretend to be ill are merely giving up responsibility for their own lives.

He recommends giving patients the opportunity to stand by and defend their own values and belief systems, instead of locking people up or drugging them into "normality" or submission.

Reasonable defense of one's value system can only occur, however, when there is not an imbalance of power, as there is in the present psychiatrist-patient relationship.

Boulder Daily Camera
March 20, 1979

The Danger of Diagnosing Your Own Problems

A little learning is a dangerous thing. It is not unusual for persons reading about abnormal behavior for the first time to raise questions about themselves and their own levels of adaptive or maladaptive functioning. The "medical student's syndrome" (where the medical student imagines he or she has every disease studied about) often occurs in students reading about abnormal psychology. One could suffer needlessly thinking that every symptom one shows that is similar to those described here is an indication of a behavior problem. As we noted, everyone shows one or more of these symptoms from time to time.

It is best to keep in mind the definition of psychopathology given at the beginning of this chapter; psychopathology is a failure, for either organic or psychological reasons, to behave in a socially appropriate and acceptable way, such that the person or society suffers adverse consequences. Suppose you were unhappy and worried about poor school work. No one would think it unreasonable for you to feel anxious about the consequences of flunking out of school, and psychotherapy would not be indicated. However, if your poor work could be traced to a panic state you

The Man with Ten Personalities:
Experts Unravel the Psyche of an Ohio Rape Suspect

Terror stalked the Ohio State University campus last year. Between August and October, four female students were abducted, forced to cash a check or use a bank card to obtain money, then driven to a rural area and raped. Acting on a mysterious phone tip and a mugshot identification by one victim, police in Columbus arrested William Milligan, 23. At first the suspect seemed like a classic young offender: physically abused as a child, cashiered from the Navy after one month, constantly in trouble with employers and police. That familiar portrait changed suddenly during a psychological exam. When a woman psychologist addressed Milligan as "Billy," he replied, "Billy's asleep. I'm David." It was the first strong clue that Milligan suffered from a rare and dangerous disorder: true multiple personality.

Psychiatrist George T. Harding Jr. was called in on the case, along with Cornelia B. Wilbur, the psychoanalyst who melded the 16 personalities of a patient known as Sybil, later the subject of a book and television play. With Wilbur's aid, Harding came to a startling conclusion: Milligan had fractured his psyche into ten "people," eight male and two female, ranging from Christene, a vulnerable three-year-old, to Arthur, 22, a rational, controlled planner who speaks with a British accent and tries to repair the damage done by the other personalities.

According to the psychiatrists, Milligan's personalities use different voice patterns and facial expressions, test at varying I.Q. levels, and turn out different kinds of artwork. Ragen, 23, who speaks with a Slavic accent, is "almost devoid of concern for others." Danny and Christopher are decent, quiet teenagers, but Tommy, 16, who initiated the enlistment in the Navy, is depressed and has many schizoid characteristics.

Most surprising of all, for reasons the psychiatrists cannot explain, the personality that committed the rapes is a woman, Adelena, 19, who Milligan says is a lesbian. Allen, 18, is a sociable, talented artist and the only personality who smokes. David, 9, a frightened and abused child, may have made the call leading to Milligan's arrest. The police number was found on a pad next to Milligan's phone. Billy, 23, is the core personality—guilty, suicidal and "asleep" for most of the past seven years. When Wilbur first summoned up Billy, Milligan jumped off his chair and said, "Every time I come to, I'm in some kind of trouble. I wish I were dead."

Milligan's multiple personality, like others, is a desperate attempt to handle conflicting emotions by parceling them out to different "people" and is associated with a severely warped childhood. The illegitimate son of two Florida entertainers, Milligan was three when his father committed suicide. His stepfather physically abused his mother and sod-omized young Milligan, threatening to bury him alive if he told. As a teen-ager in Ohio, Milligan fell into trances and walked the streets in a daze. He was incarcerated twice, once for rape, once for robbery, and failed at every job he had.

While nearly everyone agrees that Milligan is seriously ill, there is some doubt about whether to bring him to trial. Earlier this month, Harding reported to the court that Milligan's personalities had fused to the point where he was competent to stand trial, and Judge Jay C. Flowers set a December trial date. Last week, however, Milligan came apart again. His Ragen personality emerged and handed Public Defender Gary Schweickart a picture of a rag doll with a noose around its neck, hanging in front of a cracked mirror. Three days later, Arthur was in control, questioning the attorney closely about what had happened and how the other personalities could be protected. Said Schweickart: "The stress of jail and confinement was too much." Psychiatrist Wilbur thinks the prognosis for Milligan is doubtful. So does Milligan. His Tommy personality turned out this poem: *I am sorry I took your time/ I am the poem that doesn't rhyme/ So just turn back the page/ I'll waste away/ I'll waste away.*

Time
October 23, 1978

Multiple personality is a relatively rare but extremely intriguing disorder. Under the DSM–III system it is listed as a subcategory of the Axis I category called Dissociative Disorders, to imply that one or more parts of the mind become dissociated, or separated, from the rest.

experienced before each exam, your anxiety would appear to be inappropriate and you might benefit from a therapy designed to replace fear responses with more functional behavior.

To be overly sensitive to minor anxiety or depression could lead you to worry more about the normality of feelings than about the stress that caused those feelings in the first place. Yet to ignore strong feelings of distress because of fear of being abnormal could lead you to settle for a much less rewarding life than you could obtain. All too often people are more concerned with knowing whether they can be labeled with a diagnosis of neurotic or psy-chotic rather than with asking and answering much more basic questions: *Am I functioning appropriately under the circumstances? Am I behaving responsibly? Am I happy or am I working toward goals that will allow me to be happy?*

Alcohol Abuse

The personal costs of alcoholism are well known. Almost every family has its problem drinker. Over 10 million alcoholics have sordid tales of lost jobs, disrupted social relationships, divorce, and many other problems. The social costs of alcoholism are equally astounding:

© 1979 by Sidney Harris.

There are over 80 million alcoholics and drug addicts in the world.

Over 10 million Americans — about 2 million women — are alcoholics.

In the United States there are about 205,000 alcohol-related deaths each year.

About half the traffic accidents, half the murders, and one third of the suicides in the United States are alcohol related.

Alcoholism costs over $43 billion a year in the United States in production loss and medical expense.

Alcohol abuse is becoming common among young people, with 19 percent of 14–17-year-olds being recognized as problem drinkers.

In view of the enormous costs of alcohol abuse, it would obviously be of great benefit to identify potential alcoholics. To this end screening tests have been developed. The following are clear indications that a person has a serious problem with alcohol:

1. *Frequent desire to drink* and eager concern for drinking after work. A concern over having enough to drink is evident.

Mental-Patient Releases Questioned
By RONALD SULLIVAN

Following a national trend over the last 20 years, New York State has been gradually emptying its mental hospitals, accepting the widely held premise that most mental patients are better off receiving therapy and care in a community setting.

However, smoldering community resentment against the state's deinstitutionalization program has reached a flash point. Irate community groups and local officials contend that the state has actually been "dumping" thousands of chronic mental patients without providing for their after-care.

While espousing deinstitutionalization, some state officials privately concede that the program has not fulfilled its promise of after-care in the community and that this failure has reproduced psychopathic behavior in released patients and turned parts of Manhattan's West Side and communities along Long Island's South Shore into neighborhood bedlams.

Only last month, Dr. James Prevost, the Acting State Commissioner of Mental Hygiene, conceded that 40 of the 500 to 800 patients discharged into Long Beach needed to be sent back to the hospital, largely because inadequate or nonexistent community services had caused their conditions to deteriorate....

Background
... During the last century the state constructed mammoth, fortress-like institutions that are now regarded by psychiatrists as obsolete and counter-therapeutic. State hospitals are often described as psychiatric warehouses where patients are sedated into drug-induced stupors....

However, the introduction of iso-tropic drugs in the 1950's enabled hospitals to achieve remarkable improvements in patients, and the state began discharging many of them. At the same time, the Federal Government began treating as many patients as possible at the community level. In 1963, the first Federal funds were approved for community mental health centers....

Over the last 22 years, the state says that the patient population of its hospitals has dropped from 90,000 to 26,000....

Critics of the state program charge that released patients are caught in a pattern that leads them to squalid housing, then to the streets, and finally back into the hospital again when they break down or get out of hand.

For State's Policy
Dr. Kevin M. Cahill, the Governor's special health adviser, said the state had no choice but to release patients whose conditions do not warrant their being kept in a hospital....

Dr. Alvin M. Mesincoff, the state regional mental hygiene director for New York City, supports placing patients in the least restrictive setting. "But I also feel," he said, "that local communities have an irrational fear of them, that they provoke intensive community anxiety, and that they are perceived as an economic and social threat."

Dr. Mesincoff also contends that deinstitutionalization will only work when local hospitals and community health groups combine with the state in creating a jointly run, community-based mental health system....

The New York Times
March 13, 1978

2. *Increased consumption.* The increase may be gradual but noticeable over periods of time. The individual may worry about the excess drinking.
3. *Extreme behavior while drinking.* Committing unacceptable acts, such as verbal or physical aggression, for which the person feels guilty the next day.
4. Experiencing *blank spells* while drinking — not being able to remember portions of the evening before.
5. *Morning drinking* to help begin the day or to help cure a hangover.
6. *Missing work* or social obligations as a result of drinking or a hangover.
7. *Loss of control* while drinking is one of the more telling prealcoholic indicators and a clue to more serious problems ahead.

The Aftermath of Mental Illness

It has been estimated that, over the last 10 years or so, more than 100,000 mental patients have left psychiatric hospitals and re-entered society, with little provision for the continuing needs either of these individuals or of the communities which they enter. Most states have government agencies that are responsible for the care of mental outpatients, but because of inadequate and shrinking funding for community mental health centers, these agencies have had great difficulty meeting their responsibility. In some states, no record is kept of the whereabouts of discharged mental patients. Typically, upon discharge, the patient is given a supply of medication and directions to an outpatient clinic or a community care facility. A large but unknown proportion of these patients never appear at the clinic and thus, for all we know, never receive further care. One consequence of this state of affairs is that over 50 percent of all released patients re-enter the hospital within a year. Reductions in funding for community-based facilities seem to be correlated with an increase in hospital re-entry.

The ability of a released patient to get along depends in large measure on the availability of adequate housing. Most released patients must survive on a small monthly allotment from the government. Minimal food and clothing requirements nearly exhaust this allotment, and little is left to pay for housing. In addition, the lodging that is available consists of inadequate homes which were never designed for the chronically ill. Many patients live in run-down residential hotels which fail to meet minimal sanitary requirements.

In some states, private nonprofit groups have been able to provide an alternative housing plan. For example, in New York City, concerned citizens have made available in excess of 100 apartments as options to the adult home or nursing home concept. But unless others come forward or there is greater investment of public funds in housing and community support services, we will continue to hear horror stories about the isolation, illness, and squalor in which released mental patients live.

12 | Psycho-therapy

A surprisingly large number of us have already or will feel the need to seek professional help in solving a mental or emotional problem, either for ourselves or for someone close to us. Most families experience some maladjustment at one time or another, whether the problem is psychologically based or stress-induced. Such illnesses include migraine headaches or ulcers, a period of depression following divorce or the loss of a job, a dependence on alcohol or drugs, or a profound mental disorder such as schizophrenia. Some people believe, in fact, that the vast majority of American adults are neurotic to some degree. Divorce rates and suicide rates are skyrocketing in some areas, as are crime and delinquency. Psychological distress and disorder are common in our society, and psychopathology constitutes a major social problem.

Indeed, serious disturbances in psychological functioning are so common that it is absurd to attach any particular stigma to them. For a long time the mentally ill were treated as criminals, witches, or worse, and even today some people "look down on" those who seek professional help for psychological problems. They are often regarded as weird, "funny," or weak in some way, although some problem behaviors, such as alcoholism, seem to be more acceptable in our society than others, such as sexual exhibitionism.

Of the many different ways of responding to behavior problems, only some are therapeutic. Others, such as imprisonment, cruelty, or rejection may be detrimental to future adjustment. When mental illness was viewed as possession by the devil, drilling holes in a person's head to allow the evil spirits to escape was perhaps an appropriate "therapy." And when mental illness was considered a symptom of character weakness or moral degeneracy, chains and whipping were attempts to correct it. But given our modern conception of psychopathology as the failure, for organic or psychological reasons, to behave in a socially appropriate way, how is treatment conceptualized and practiced today?

A Definition of Psychotherapy

Psychotherapy can be defined as *a corrective experience leading a person to behave in a socially appropriate, adequate, and adaptive way.* The therapy will focus on the lack of knowledge, the lack of skill, or the lack of motivation to behave appropriately, or on the abnormal behavior itself. In most cases, a combination of these factors would be involved in the pathology, and the therapy would be adjusted accordingly. When we speak of therapy we usually imply that it is delivered by a professional—a psychologist, psychiatrist, psychiatric social worker, or psychiatric

nurse (see Table 12–1). This does not mean, however, that all corrective experiences are professionally arranged. Close personal friends often do a great deal of counseling. Here, however, we will be concerned mainly with formal psychotherapy administered by professionals. Finally, it is important to note that all those concerned with correcting maladaptive behavior should be equally concerned with *preventing* it. Although in the past prevention has not been a major focus of therapists' efforts, it will be increasingly so in the future.

One of the first questions in a therapist's mind when confronted with a person seeking psychotherapy is, Why is the person here? The most common reason people seek therapy is that they are uncomfortable with the way they are handling their lives. They may be frequently anxious when interacting with others or find that they are having trouble coping successfully with their job or marriage. Other reasons may enter into the decision to seek therapy, however. A person may be coerced into therapy, such as when a man threatens to leave his wife unless she seeks help. The police may bring a person who has been exhibiting bizarre behavior to a crisis center to determine whether the individual is a danger to self or others, and therefore requires immediate hospitalization. Or a physician may tell a patient that his or her ulcers or headaches are psychological in origin and that psychotherapy is recommended. Or a court may require an adolescent to seek therapy as part of a probation program. Such situations are more difficult to treat and are different from those of people who are experiencing anxiety, anger, or depression and desire to find out why and regain control. In cases like court-ordered treatment, the therapist has an ethical responsibility to make clear to the client his or her goals in therapy and to indicate how they might differ from the client's goals.

The types of therapy to be discussed in this chapter can be divided into several categories: (1) insight-

TABLE 12–1 Mental Health Professionals

Name	Degree	Specialization	Education
Clinical psychologist	Doctor of Philosophy (Ph.D.) Doctor of Psychology (Psy.D.)	Research therapy, diagnostic testing	Graduate education in a department of psychology or professional school of psychology
Psychiatrist	Doctor of Medicine (M.D.)	Psychotherapy, management of medication, electroconvulsive therapy	Residency training in psychiatry
Psychoanalyst	M.D., Ph.D., Psy.D	Psychoanalysis	Usually psychiatrist with additional training in psychoanalysis
Psychiatric social worker	Master of Social Work (M.S.W.)	Individual and family therapy and counseling, community orientation	Graduate education in school of social work
School psychologist	Master of Arts (M.A.), Ph.D., or Doctor of Education (Ed.D.)	Counseling or educational testing	Graduate work in psychology or education
Counseling psychologist	Same as school psychologist	Counseling, therapy, vocational counseling, rehabilitation	Graduate work in psychology or education
Psychiatric nurse	Registered Nurse (R.N.)	Counseling, therapy, care of hospitalized mental patients	Training in nursing and psychiatry
Paraprofessional	None necessary	Ability to communicate with people in own community	Short orientation in service facility

oriented therapies, which focus on change in motivation and knowledge; (2) behavior and cognitive behavior therapies, which focus on change in motivation, skills, performance, thoughts, and attitudes; (3) medical therapies; (4) group therapies; and (5) community mental health.

Insight-Oriented Therapies

Insight-oriented therapy is based on the assumption, similar to that of the dynamic model of psychopathology, that emotional problems stem from the conflict between conscious and unconscious processes. To resolve this conflict persons must become aware of their unconscious processes, and thus the goal of therapy is insight or self-knowledge. The insight-oriented therapies can be divided into two types: (1) those focusing on the repressed memories of the past, such as psychoanalysis — these are based on the dynamic viewpoint of psychopathology discussed in Chapter 11 — and (2) those focusing on denied aspects of present feelings, such as client-centered therapy and Gestalt therapy — these are based on the phenomenological viewpoint.

The Dynamic Viewpoint: Insight into Past Experiences

Psychoanalysis is the therapeutic technique Sigmund Freud developed on the basis of his psychoanalytic theory. Freud assumed that emotional problems are in part the result of repression of drives, feelings, and memories and that an awareness of these unconscious mental processes will resolve most emotional problems. However, the client must not only achieve insight into the cause of his or her symptoms but must also experience the emotion associated with the original memory.

> . . . we found, to our great surprise at first, that each individual . . . symptom immediately and permanently disappeared when we had succeeded in bringing clearly to light the memory of the event by which it was provoked and in arousing its accompanying affect (emotions), and when the patient had described that event in the greatest possible detail and had put the affect into words. Recollection without affect almost invariably produces no result. (Breuer & Freud, 1957)

Because the open expression of sexual and aggressive feelings is generally thought unacceptable

Highlight 12–1

Comparative Approaches to Psychotherapy

Case 1
John is a compulsive eater who weighs 350 pounds. In seeking help, he would very likely find therapists who would approach his problem in different ways.

Physician (Medical Approach)
The physician assumes that the behavior is the result of a physiological illness. The doctor might prescribe amphetamines to reduce John's appetite or tranquilizers to reduce anxiety associated with stress. A dietary program of therapeutic fasting or a surgical procedure in which a large portion of the small intestine is bypassed (preventing food absorption) might be used in cases of extreme obesity.

Psychoanalyst (Dynamic Approach)
The psychoanalyst explores early childhood memories, the content of dreams, free association, and slips of the tongue to determine the symbolic meaning of the eating behavior. The psychoanalyst would look for the possibility that John is gratifying strong needs for love through food intake.

Behavior Therapist (Behavioral or Learning Theory Approach)
The behavior therapist explores the rewarding aspects of overeating and determines whether such behavior allows John to avoid anxiety-evoking situations. The therapist may set up a conditioning form of treatment in which John is punished for overeating or thinking about eating or is rewarded for noneating behavior. The therapist might try to increase behavior incompatible with eating or change John's eating patterns. If eating leads to anxiety reduction, relaxation techniques may be used to lower anxiety levels. Unlike the physician, the behavior therapist conceptualizes overeating as learned behavior, not as an illness.

Case 2
Jane is a 25-year-old graduate student with a severe stuttering problem. Seeking help, she may find therapists who would treat her problem in the following ways.

Physician (Medical Approach)
The therapist assumes that stuttering is a neurological problem in the perceptual motor areas of the brain. The physician might prescribe medication (tranquilizers) or recommend perceptual-motor training.

Psychoanalyst (Dynamic Approach)
The therapist assumes that the stuttering behavior is an expression of an unconscious conflict associated with hostility, particularly toward Jane's parents. Therapy would involve trying to bring into awareness this underlying conflict through the interpretation of free association, dreams, slips of the tongue, and repressed memories.

Behavior Modifier (Behavioral or Learning Theory Approach)
The therapist explores the possibility that the stuttering behavior was a classically conditioned response. Techniques to treat stuttering might involve negative practice, a technique requiring a person to stutter repeatedly on purpose. Rhythmic speech patterns and operant conditioning involving rewards for appropriate speech might also be used. Finally, if stuttering increases as anxiety increases, then relaxation training might be used.

Existentialist (Phenomenological Approach)
In both cases, stuttering and overeating, the therapist makes no assumption about the underlying meaning of symptomatic behavior. Therapy would focus on helping the client clarify values, goals, and feelings. The client would be helped in understanding how he or she feels and would be led in a nonjudgmental, accepting atmosphere to experience those feelings in the here and now.

---

for children and adults in our society, we are taught to inhibit or repress these feelings, Thus, sexual and aggressive feelings are a main focus in psychoanalysis. Sexual mores are changing dramatically in the direction of greater freedom. If this is a mentally healthy change, psychoanalysis should in the future focus less on sexual feelings and more on aggressive feelings.

The aim of psychoanalysis is to help the client overcome the unconscious resistance to remembering anxiety-provoking thoughts and impulses. Freud developed a variety of techniques to aid the client over-

come this resistance. One of these is the use of the *couch,* the subject of numerous jokes. In psychoanalysis the patient typically lies down on the couch, looking up to the ceiling, and the analyst sits behind the client out of direct sight. Some reasons for the use of the couch may have nothing to do with technique. First, Freud discovered the importance of recollection of repressed memories through hypnosis, and the couch is in part a carryover from the use of hypnosis as a technique. Second, it is rumored that Freud preferred sitting behind the patient because he

"The Electra complex is always a toughie, and on top of that, you were born under Aquarius. Let's see what the 'I Ching' says."

Playboy, November 1974. Reproduced by special permission of PLAYBOY Magazine; copyright © 1974 Playboy.

felt uncomfortable having people look at him all day. Thus, the couch may be attributable to one of Freud's own hang-ups! Most important, however, is the fact that the couch reduces external stimulation and encourages the client to turn inward to focus on his or her own associations.

Some analysts who prefer face-to-face contact with the client want the client to be aware of their reactions on the assumption that one of the client's problems might be a lack of sensitivity to the reactions of others. However, the psychoanalyst is more interested in an inward focus of attention to facilitate the remembering of repressed memories. The following techniques are used to help patients understand the contents of their own unconscious.

In classical psychoanalysis the patient lies on a couch, and the therapist sits out of the client's direct line of sight.

Free Association

Clients are instructed to say anything and everything that comes to mind. They are told to express their thoughts as freely as possible and hold nothing back, no matter how trivial or shocking. This basic rule of psychoanalysis sounds relatively easy, but, in fact, most people find it extremely difficult to give up their concern over the impression they are making on someone else, including the analyst. Resistance to the basic rule of free association at the unconscious level will therefore often lead to blocking—the person simply cannot think of any association. Such resistance helps the analyst understand what areas of the person's memories are repressed and can then help the client overcome such resistance to remembering.

Symptomatic Acts

The behavior of the client during analysis may lead the analyst to understand areas of repression. Slips of the tongues, changes in behavior toward the therapy hour, forgetting therapy appointments, and unusual behavior during therapy may all be symptomatic of deeper and more significant unconscious processes.

Dream Analysis

In his book *The Interpretation of Dreams,* Freud maintained that it was useful to consider dreams as representing, in a symbolic way, the unconscious conflicts or desires of the dreamer (see Appendix D). The purpose of the symbolic nature of the dream message is to avoid anxiety that would wake the person up. The symbolic meaning of elements of a dream cannot easily be interpreted without knowing the associational links of the individual who had the dream. There have been "dream books" published that propose to interpret the symbols in dreams. The authors tend to interpret every pointed object in a dream as a symbol of a phallus and every open space as a symbol of a vagina because Freud believed that sexual conflicts determined most symbols. Although Freud proposed that such general symbolism may be involved, he felt that each person tends to have idiosyncratic associations that lead to unique symbols as well. It is the therapist's task to discover the meaning of such symbols.

After the client has related a dream, the analyst asks the person to free associate to various elements of the dream. He may also ask for information about the previous day in an effort to understand the **manifest content** (the superficial story of the dream), and the **latent content** (the symbolic meaning of that story). For example, a woman reported dreaming that a man unknown to her stole her car and was killed in an accident—the manifest content. The latent content of her dream was not obvious and could be

"Just between ourselves, your obsession that the rest of society is mad is probably true . . . but they are in charge."

© 1973 Norris — Vancouver Sun (Rothco).

clarified only with free association and the therapist's knowledge of some of the personality dynamics of the client. However, the latent content became clear when the therapist discovered that the unknown man could be considered a symbol for her husband. The woman did not know or understand her husband very well ("unknown to her"), he frequently took advantage of her ("stole her car"), and she was very angry at him for this manipulative behavior ("he was killed"). Her anger toward him was unacceptable to her, and she feared expressing it because she felt he would leave her. The anxiety-provoking latent content of the dream was expressed symbolically.

Interpretation

The psychoanalyst's basic job is interpretation, explaining to the client the unconscious meaning of what he or she says. The purpose of interpretation is to help the client overcome the resistance to remembering repressed thoughts. Not infrequently the symbolic meaning of what is being said is not obvious, and the analyst must maintain a free-floating attention for many sessions, looking for cues to the content of the unconscious mind.

Once he or she develops a degree of certainty about an interpretation, the analyst must decide when to present it to the client. If the interpretation is given before the client is capable of accepting it, anxiety will be generated and the repression will become more severe. It is desirable to lead clients slowly so that they can gradually arrive at their own interpretations and work at overcoming their own resistance.

A single proper interpretation does not resolve the client's problems. The repression of unconscious material shows up in various aspects of the person's life, and repeated interpretations are required to help the person give up the repression in all aspects of his or her life. The process of repeated interpretation and continued efforts on the part of the client to resolve the conflict is called *working through.*

Transference

According to the theory of psychoanalysis, the patient must **transfer** to the therapy relationship the conflicts from early life that interfere with the capacity to live normally. As a consequence, however, the analyst becomes a unique person in the client's eyes. Freud first noticed transference when he realized that patients ascribed to him characteristics of God and the devil or professed mad love for him even though their meetings were brief and infrequent. Transference is necessary and desirable, but it is only a temporary goal of psychoanalysis. As the significant unconscious processes affecting his or her behavior are made conscious to the client, he or she gives up neurotic defenses. As defenses are lowered, transference is resolved. The client comes to respond more appropriately to the analyst, no longer exhibiting a need to defend against unconscious conflicts. The problems that brought the person to analysis are resolved, and the problem of transference disappears.

Recent Changes in Psychoanalysis

Although the basic techniques of Freudian psychoanalysis have remained the same, some variations have been tried. For example, analysts who follow the school of ego psychology place less emphasis on sex and aggression and more emphasis on the rational aspects of the ego. Most analysts still use the techniques of free association and dream interpretation, although with greater caution and less frequently than did Freud. Some analysts have given up the use of the couch and have a more spontaneous face-to-face interchange with the client. Many psychoanalytically trained therapists place more emphasis on the here and now and less on what happened in the past. Chief among these therapists is Rollo May, one of the pioneers in a technique called *existential therapy.*

Disadvantages of Psychoanalysis

Psychoanalysis is inefficient by today's standards. The analyst can treat only one person at a time, and each client is seen sometimes as frequently as five days a week for a 45- or 50-minute "hour" over a period of months or even years. Because analysis takes such a long time, the analyst can treat only a very small number of people in a lifetime. Furthermore, since the analyst is so highly trained and treatment is so time-consuming, the total cost to the client is very high. The cost alone excludes many potential users of psychoanalysis. For some people, such as children, analysis is ineffective or inadequate because they are not equipped for the highly verbal nature of the technique, and some potential patients are too disordered to benefit from it. Thus, most persons in psychoanalysis are from the upper or middle class, although psychoanalysts have made some attempts to broaden their scope of treatment.

The Phenomenological Viewpoint: Insight into Present Experiences

Client-centered Psychotherapy

Rather than attempting to provide insight into repressed memories of the past, the client-centered therapist tries to help clients accept all aspects of themselves in the present. Emotional problems are seen as stemming from a lack of self-knowledge, a denial of certain feelings, and an inability to experience all feelings fully. In order to describe how the therapist tries to help the client in therapy, it is nec-

essary to outline the progress that client-centered psychotherapy has made over the years.

Carl Rogers, whose ideas we encountered in Chapter 9, first wrote about the theory of present-oriented therapy in 1942. His early views focused on recognizing and clarifying the client's expressed feelings. At that time the technique was called **nondirective therapy** because a basic rule was that the therapist should only respond to the stated feelings of the client and never direct the conversation. The purpose of clarifying clients' feelings was to facilitate the appropriate expression of feelings, to help persons understand how they felt, and to help them use feelings as a basis for action. The term "nondirective" was dropped because it became clear that the therapist was indeed directing the course of treatment with clarifying comments.

Client-centered therapy is based on Rogers' theory of personality, in which, as we know, the main concept is the self. The **self concept** is defined as *a relatively consistent and enduring framework of self-regarding attitudes.* Disturbed persons are those who

The goal of client-centered psychotherapy is to help clients achieve acceptance of themselves in the present so that they can go on to lead more fulfilling and meaningful lives in the future.

find some of their experiences or feelings to be inconsistent with the concept they have of themselves, and so they deny that the feelings apply to them. If the person denies part of his or her own experience, these feelings and experiences cannot be used as a guide for action.

For example, one woman in therapy responded to every question about how she felt about a negative event in her life with the comment that she was "upset." When asked by the therapist what she meant by "upset," she said she did not know. Later it was discovered that in her formative years her mother had denied her the implications of any negative feelings. She would say, "You aren't angry at me, you're upset." The woman had learned to cut off feelings of anger, depression, jealousy, and anxiety. She responded to situations that would normally have elicited such feelings with vague reactions of apprehension and uneasiness. Therapy led her to understand and accept the fact that she has these feelings and to experience them in appropriate situations. Instead of being confused and disoriented in unpleasant situations, she could respond spontaneously and openly with her feelings. Openly expressing one's feelings is more apt to help resolve the situation causing the negative feelings. For example, people are likely to avoid saying things that make you angry if they know how you feel about such things.

Client-centered therapy promotes self-exploration. The therapist tries to develop an environment of acceptance in which clients can take the chance of facing their denied feelings. Clients are encouraged to move to an internal frame of reference in which they decide how worthwhile they are rather than always looking to others for evaluation. Emphasis is placed on the development of a *real* relationship in therapy rather than on role playing for the therapist.

Rogers proposed that the therapist must possess three basic characteristics before he or she can successfully use the client-centered technique: empathic understanding, unconditional positive regard, and congruence. **Empathic understanding** means that the therapist accurately understands the immediate feelings of the client. **Unconditional positive regard** means that the therapist cares about the client. He or she does not put conditions on the caring, nor does the therapist care less when clients reveal aspects of themselves about which they are ashamed and anxious. This does not mean that the therapist agrees with the view that the client presents; but it does mean that the therapist cares about the client as a person regardless of viewpoints. **Congruence** means that what the therapist is experiencing inside and how he presents himself or herself to the client are consistent. Thus the therapist is genuine.

Rogers outlined several stages of development of the integrated person in the therapeutic process. The first stage is characterized by rigidity and remoteness of experiencing, with no self-relevant communication to others. As clients come to accept their feelings, they may progress to the point where they can admit to feelings that are still removed from experience. For example, a client in therapy may be able to tell the therapist about how angry he or she was the previous week in therapy, while denying any annoyance at the present time. Eventually, through therapy or other positive experiences, the client is able to express immediate feelings and to integrate his or her self-concept with present everyday experiences.

Behavior and Cognitive Behavior Therapies

The behavior and cognitive behavior therapies have their origins in the experimentally established principles of learning (see Chapters 4 and 5). Behaviorists and cognitive behaviorists believe that maladjusted behavior follows the same principles as "normal" behavior. They see maladjusted behavior as learned, and thus subject to processes such as reinforcement, extinction, and punishment. Early behaviorists focused on directly observable behavior, virtually ignoring cognitive processes like thoughts; more recent cognitive behaviorists include covert processes or thoughts as behaviors that can (and should) be studied and modified.

Historical Background

Behavior therapy developed, in part, as a reaction to the more established psychoanalytic therapy. The early behaviorists criticized the psychoanalysts' emphasis on the unconscious determinants of behavior and their reliance on inferences. Instead, they suggested that the rigor of a laboratory investigation be applied to psychological treatment. For them, this meant the rejection of the concept of the unconscious or subconscious, instead concentrating on directly observable behavior. Eliminating the patient's problem behavior rather than determining the cause of the behavior became their aim.

As discussed in Chapter 1, John B. Watson was the earliest proponent of behaviorism. His 1920 study with Rayner of the conditioning of Little Albert is widely cited as an empirical test of Watson's theory of behavior and emotional development. Watson reportedly conditioned 11-month-old Albert to fear a white rat by making a loud clanging sound whenever Albert touched the animal. Albert reacted with crying and avoidance behavior when the rat was presented after seven pairings of the rat and noise. Five days later Albert was presented with the rat and again responded with a strong fear response. He also responded with fear to the presentation of a rabbit, a dog, and a sealskin coat; had a "negative" response to a Santa Claus mask and Watson's hair; had a mild response to a package of white cotton; and played freely with wooden blocks and the hair of Watson's two assistants. Watson and many other behaviorists claimed that the Little Albert study demonstrated that phobias could be induced (or learned). Unfortunately, while the Little Albert study is one of the most widely cited experiments in the psychological literature, it is often misquoted or misrepresented. After a detailed examination of its methodology, results, and how its details changed over the years, a recent psychologist concluded that it did not provide convincing proof for the correctness of Watson's views (Harris, 1979). Despite that, the study was certainly an impetus for the behavioral approach.

Mary Cover Jones, a child therapist, followed up on the Little Albert study in 1924. She reasoned that if Watson could condition fears in children, then fears could also be "deconditioned." Watson served as her adviser in the treatment of her best-known client, Peter, a child with fears similar to the ones Albert was conditioned to have. Her treatment of Peter's fear of rabbits, which she called "direct conditioning," was similar to today's desensitization and modeling procedures. The child was seated in a highchair and given his favorite food; the rabbit in a wire cage was brought closer and closer as long as its presence did not interfere with Peter's eating. Other children, who were not fearful of rabbits, were occasionally brought into the treatment sessions with Peter so that he could observe their nonfearful responses. Jones concluded that her treatment was successful, and although a modern reader would find the study's methodology weak, it nevertheless provided the framework for future behavioral treatments.

Another early application of conditioning methods to the treatment of behavior disorders was presented in 1938 by O. H. Mowrer. He described a treatment for enuresis (bedwetting) using a classical conditioning approach. Enuresis had long been viewed by psychoanalysts as a symptom of an underlying disturbance. The analysts argued that if only the symptom was treated without determining its cause, *symptom substitution* (the appearance of another behavior problem in its place) would occur. However, Mowrer developed a behaviorally based treatment for the problem behavior. He placed a device on the child's bed that was capable of sensing the slightest amount of urine and setting off an alarm. The alarm would wake the child so that he or she could finish urinating in the toilet. It was reasoned that the stimulus of the full bladder became conditioned to the response of awakening and inhibiting urination. This treatment is still widely used today, with success rates ranging from 70 to 90 percent.

Highlight 12–2

Relationship between Etiology and Treatment

Can effective treatment for a disorder be developed without establishing the specific cause or causes of the disorder? Exact causes of psychological disorders are sometimes difficult to determine. However, treatment procedures may prove to be highly effective long before agreement has been reached on basic causes. The following problem illustrates this situation.

For years Manhattan Poet Joel Oppenheimer, now 47, took exactly the same route from his Greenwich Village apartment to his local bar, the Lion's Head. One day he tried a more circuitous route, walking along different streets. Midway to the bar he broke out in a cold sweat, suffering from heart palpitations, jelly legs and vertigo. "I had no control over my body," he said. "It was total panic."

Diagnosis: agoraphobia, the most common and disabling of all the phobias, one that may afflict as many as 2.5 million Americans—85% to 90% of them women. Classically known as "fear of open spaces," agoraphobia is actually a cluster of different fears, all amounting to intense anxiety about panicking in unfamiliar situations. Crowds are no protection; Oppenheimer suffered one attack while surrounded by 55,000 fellow Met fans at a playoff game. Severe agoraphobics stick to familiar routines and rarely venture out alone. When they do travel, they usually bring along a friend, child or dog as a prop. "For years," says Oppenheimer, "I was terrified of a new bed, chair, bar, room or restaurant."

Time
November 7, 1977

Several causes have been proposed for the neurotic condition agoraphobia, including (1) the victim has a hereditary predisposition to become anxious; (2) the victim experienced a severe traumatic situation around which the fear has generalized; (3) the disorder is considered by psychoanalysts to be a symbolic expression of deeply threatening sexual or aggressive impulses; and (4) it is viewed by behaviorists as simply a learned habit pattern.

Regardless of the "cause," most therapists consider the most effective treatment to be to have the patient "reexperience" the feared situation and relearn more adaptive responses to it. The process of desensitization and learning new responses has proven to be an effective management technique.

Highlight 12–3

Desensitization Training with an Athlete

Systematic desensitization can be easily used for anyone who is anxious in a particular situation. Test anxiety, fear of speaking in front of large groups, and phobias have all been successfully treated with desensitization training. This type of therapy was effective with Mr. J, a talented basketball player attending college on an athletic scholarship (Katahn, 1967). Just before coming into therapy, Mr. J began to feel that his game was falling apart. He was tired and sluggish on the court. His anxiety was so great that he lost eight pounds in one month. Although the intensity of the anxiety was new, he had felt anxiety about playing for a long time. Nausea and vomiting had occurred on the day of a game since he was 12 years old. Although his father did not seem to have a heavy involvement with his playing, his mother's avid interest in his achievement made him even more nervous.

Three therapy sessions were devoted to the construction of an anxiety hierarchy and training Mr. J in muscle relaxation. The following hierarchy, from least to most anxiety-provoking, was established:

1. Mr. J meets an assistant coach in the gym, and the coach doesn't say "hello" to him.
2. He is in the gym changing for practice, and he notices his hands are beginning to sweat.
3. He is trying to study, but he can't get the day's practice out of his thoughts.
4. He finishes practice, and the "drugstore coaches" (his term for spectators who have passes for practice) speak to the other players and ignore him.
5. He is on the court and gets a tired, draggy, no-good feeling.
6. He is on the court and notices that the coaches are keeping a record of each player's performance.
7. He is visiting at home, and his mother makes some remark about another player.
8. He is eating dinner with his mother when she asks him something about how his game is going.
9. It is time for the late afternoon pre-game dinner, and he is on the way to the cafeteria.
10. He is in the cafeteria line, and the sight of food makes him feel sick.
11. He is in the gym changing for a game, and he is sick to his stomach.

After about 14 more sessions the anxiety hierarchy had been completely worked through and the client stopped vomiting before games. The nausea and the tired, sluggish feeling during the games had also disappeared. The counseling that accompanied the desensitization focused on study habits and the role of basketball in Mr. J's life. As a result of the combined therapeutic techniques, his grades rose from a "D" to a "B" average. Basketball plays a less overwhelming (although still important) part in his life, and he has been accepted by a law school.

However, many children require treatment for several months, and a 32 percent relapse rate has been reported. The wetting of children who relapse can usually be controlled by reinstating the treatment procedure. Most of the recent studies did not find evidence of symptom substitution in children whose enuresis was eliminated by this procedure.

While there were many other behavioral studies between 1920 and 1950, it was only in the late 1950s and 1960s that behavior therapy was clearly established as an alternative to insight-oriented therapies. The behavior therapies were derived from two principal sources: the classical conditioning approach of Pavlov and the operant conditioning procedures of Skinner and his colleagues. Eventually, Bandura suggested that in addition to classical and operant conditioning, human behavior is also controlled by cognitive mediational processes, or thoughts, thus bringing "private events" to the attention of behaviorists. Even though some of today's radical behaviorists still delegate concepts like "private events" and thoughts to the realm of the psychoanalyst, cognitive behavior therapy is a rapidly growing field of investigation and techniques.

Techniques of Behavior Therapy

Systematic Desensitization

An early use of classical conditioning techniques in psychotherapy was reported by Joseph Wolpe in the late 1950s. Wolpe agreed with Watson that neurotic habits are learned in anxiety-provoking situations by the association of neutral stimuli with anxiety responses. The anxiety response is made up of subjective feelings and physiological tension. Wolpe proposed that if a response incompatible with anxiety, such as relaxation, sexual arousal, or assertiveness, occurred in the presence of the anxiety-provoking stimuli, the connection between the stimulus and the anxiety response would be weakened. He called this process reciprocal inhibition.

Wolpe developed the technique of therapy called **systematic desensitization** based on the process of reciprocal inhibition. The first step in desensitization therapy is to gain an understanding of the types of stimuli that lead to anxiety responses. Based on interviews with the client, a hierarchy of fear-provoking stimuli is constructed ranging from situations involving very mild fear to ones in which the fear is quite intense.

While the hierarchy is being constructed, **relaxation training** begins. Wolpe focuses on muscle relaxation techniques in which the client is taught to become aware of and control specific muscle groups throughout the body by successively tensing and re-

laxing each muscle group. Deep and slow breathing coupled with the relaxation of more and more muscle groups can lead to very deep relaxation. While deeply relaxed, the client is asked to imagine a scene involving the least threatening stimulus in the hierarchy. If any anxiety is felt while imagining the scene, the person raises a finger and is told to put the scene out of mind immediately. Deeper relaxation is induced. When the scene can be imagined without anxiety several times, the person is asked to move up the hierarchy and imagine the next most anxiety-provoking scene. The relaxation response slowly generalizes to other items on the list, making the next item less stressful. Once relaxation to the entire list of scenes

---

Resolute Prisoners Struggle against Behavioral Modification
By WILLIAM CLAIBORNE

In a solitary confinement cell behind two locked corridor grills in a remote wing of the medical center for federal prisoners here, Forest G. is engaged in a desperate struggle of wills with the U.S. Bureau of Prisons.

But for Forest G., a 34-year-old convicted bank robber serving 15 years, solitary confinement has become a way of life. He has been sitting alone in what amounts to a walk-in closet for more than eight months, and in all likelihood he will remain there at least until next February.

From Forest's point of view, what is at stake in the struggle is his pride and his right to control of his own behavior, even if it is regarded by others as belligerent and recalcitrant.

From the prison authorities' point of view, what is at stake is the right of the state to promote change in the behavior of the most hardened inmate, even if the only alternative is to let the inmate vegetate indefinitely in maximum security incarceration.

Sunshine Street
The struggle will ultimately be resolved in a U.S. District Court in Kansas City, but for now the drama is being painfully acted out at the massive, 40-year-old prison hospital here, which is incon-

gruously located on Sunshine Street, on the outskirts of town.

At issue in the court test brought by a group of inmates and supported by the American Civil Liberties Union (ACLU) is a year-old behavior modification program called START, an acronym for Special Treatment and Rehabilitative Training. . . .

START is based on a deceptively simple system of programmed rewards in which a prisoner begins a fixed term at the most severe level of incarceration and then "earns" some freedom of movement and a few privileges by adapting to various rules of behavior. . . .

Time Off
Gradually, the inmate is allowed more privileges, is allowed to earn money in an adjacent factory six hours daily and begins to have sentence time off for good behavior restored.

In 7½ months, he is "graduated" from the program and is returned to the general population of the penitentiary that referred him to START in the first place. If the inmate rebels, refuses to follow rules or becomes verbally abusive to staff members, he is returned to the solitary confinement level for a designated period. If he refuses to participate, he remains in solitary for a

year, and is then returned to a segregation unit of his home institution.

Forest G. was in the "hole" (segregation unit) at the Leavenworth penitentiary for two years when he was notified that he was to be sent to Springfield's START program. . . .

Forest did briefly participate in the program, earning points for good behavior. Then, he said, he saw several other inmates being beaten by guards during a disturbance in the tier opposite his cell, and he decided to lay down and finish his year in solitary.

Hole with Factory
"After you look at it a while, all this is a hole with a factory, and somebody calls it behavior modification. There's nobody here who's going to modify me," said Forest.

Asked if he had considered faking a change in his behavior long enough to earn privileges and graduate from the program, Forest replied, "It wouldn't be no act, it would be for real. They're trying to get a program going smoothly by bribing guys. If you are playing a game on them, you are playing it on yourself, because they want you modified, and they don't care what makes you do it. . . .

Boulder (Colo.) Daily Camera
January 5, 1974

The use of behavior modification in corrective institutions has led to a strong controversy about the ethics of paying people to behave in "socially appropriate" ways. Do criminals have the right to resist such treatment? Does such a program constitute "cruel and unusual" punishment?

is complete, the client finds that freedom from anxiety to an imagined stimulus generalizes and results in freedom from anxiety to the real event. Or the therapist may decide the client needs a few sessions of *in vivo* (or real-life) desensitization, in which the therapist helps the client "walk through" the actual feared situation. For example, in the case of a flight phobic, the therapist might accompany the client to the airport and board a plane, while demonstrating coping behavior and helping the client control his or her anxiety.

Positive Reinforcement and Shaping

The use of positive reinforcement and shaping derive from the principles of instrumental conditioning. We saw in Chapter 4 that shaping involves reinforcing components of a complex behavioral sequence with the goal of teaching the entire sequence. Shaping has been applied to the problem of short attention span, a frequent cause of classroom disruption and poor academic performance. The child with a short attention span can be rewarded for paying attention to his or her studies for even short periods of time. If the longest period of time a child can attend to studying without becoming distracted is one minute, then he or she is initially rewarded at the end of every minute of actual studying. After this habit is well established (perhaps after several days), the requirements are increased. The child is rewarded

only when the studying is for two-minute periods. The length of the study time is gradually increased until the child is able to work for a half hour or more without interruption. Through the judicious use of reinforcement a therapist can shape the desired behavior from modest beginnings. After the new behavior is established, the external rewards can be withdrawn, because new rewards will maintain the behaviors. One hopes the rewards of easier studying, increased feelings of competence, and better grades will all help to maintain the behaviors.

Positive reinforcement has been surprisingly effective with some severe cases of psychopathology. Withdrawn children can be trained to speak with others if properly rewarded. The behavior of severely schizophrenic hospitalized adults can be modified by rewarding them for talking to other patients on the ward, grooming themselves, or making their beds. The hospital staff may use cigarettes and candy for rewards, or it may use tokens that can be traded for items or privileges the patient wants. As we saw in Chapter 4, some mental hospitals use token economy treatment programs in which operant procedures are applied to patients' behavior. A patient on a token economy ward can acquire privileges (for example, TV time, candy, a weekend pass) he or she desires only with earned tokens. Token economies have been effective in reducing the problems of institutionalization, which refers to the passive, dependent behavior

---

Highlight 12–4

Management of Chronic Pain: A New Behavioral Approach to an Old Problem

A novel use of reinforcement theory is found in recent work in the management of chronic pain. Many individuals who experience chronic pain are generally not open to psychological interpretation of their problems and thus are not treatable through insight-oriented therapies. Moreover, their problems are complicated by the fact that the patients have been taking numerous medications (often highly addictive substances). Pain-management programs usually require that the patient be hospitalized in order to be withdrawn from the drugs and establish more adaptive attitudes toward the pain. Usually the program involves the following procedures:

1. Medication withdrawal is accomplished by having the patient list all the medications and the dosage level he or she has been taking (even aspirin). These substances are then mixed into one medication, referred to as the

"pain cocktail," which is disguised in appearance and taste. These pain cocktails are administered on an interval schedule (see Chapter 4) rather than when the person feels pain. This technique weakens the relationship between the drug and relief from pain. The drug content of the pain cocktail is reduced each week until there are no active ingredients in the liquid.

2. The patient's pain behavior is modified according to principles of learning, reinforcement, and extinction. The staff is trained to ignore pain complaints and provide positive reinforcement for adaptive behavior such as physical activity and work.

Behaviorally oriented pain-management programs have been found to be the most effective means of altering pain behavior and reducing medication dependency among chronic pain patients.

of the "model" mental patient who bothers no one and always does as told. In extreme cases of institutionalization, patients withdraw completely from the real world, requiring diapers and spoonfeeding. Behaviors like that are rare on token economy wards. Token economies have been used successfully in institutions for the mentally retarded, prisons, and regular classrooms, although not without criticism.

Aversion Therapy

The use of aversive techniques to control an individual's behavior has a long history (see Chapter 4). Aversive techniques are used whenever society sends an individual to jail for stealing or a mother spanks a child for eating a cookie before dinner. Despite this, behaviorists come under the most strong criticism when using aversive techniques in therapy. Whether or not to use aversion therapy is a tough ethical problem. Most therapists prefer to use it only as a last resort. It is most often employed to eliminate addictions and other destructive or deviant behaviors (recall its use with anorexia nervosa in the newsclip on page 116).

Aversion therapy can take either an operant conditioning or a classical conditioning approach. In the operant case, punishment training (see Chapter 4) is the most common technique. An inappropriate response which the therapist wants to eliminate is punished by delivering a noxious or aversive stimulus (for example, shock) each time the response occurs. Punishment, however, has undesirable side effects, in that every time punishment is used, negative reinforcement of some other response may also occur. For example, spanking a child for eating a cookie

"Today we'll try aversion-therapy. Every time you say something stupid, I'll spill a bucket of water on your head."

© 1982 by Sidney Harris.

before dinner can reinforce loud crying, because loud crying is the response that occurs just before termination of the aversive stimulus (spanking). In the classical conditioning case, therapy takes the form of pairing up the CS the therapist believes elicits the inappropriate response with a noxious stimulus, regardless of whether the patient emits the response.

To clarify the distinction, consider aversion therapy for obesity. An obese patient checks into a hospital for treatment. In an operant approach, the noxious stimulus is delivered whenever the patient makes undesired eating responses—for example, reaches for a high-calorie dessert in the cafeteria line. A classical conditioning technique might be to show the patient pictures of high-calorie foods and pair the presentation of each picture with presentation of shock. Pictures of healthy, low-calorie foods might be presented and not followed by shock.

Much controversy is generated whenever aversive techniques are used with children. The idea of using electric shock with children is repugnant to most people. However, some autistic, psychotic, or severely retarded children have self-destructive behaviors (like severe head banging) that are life threatening. The alternative to aversion therapy (which has been demonstrated to eliminate these behaviors) is considered by many to be less desirable: physically restraining these children by tying their arms, legs, and head to a bed or chair so that they will not cause irreparable damage to their bodies.

Less drastic punishment techniques are also used with less severely disturbed children. *Time out* (from positive reinforcement) is used in many classrooms and homes. In this procedure, whenever the child breaks a rule, he or she is isolated for a few minutes. After being in the time-out chair, or room, the child is returned to his or her environment and asked to correct the misbehavior. When properly used, time out is a very effective procedure for eliminating problem behaviors. However, it is important to note that it should be combined with a program of positive reinforcement for appropriate behavior to be truly effective.

Biofeedback

Biofeedback is a procedure to teach people to gain control over their physiological responses to stress (see Chapter 2 and Appendix D). In biofeedback a person is attached to an electronic measuring device that monitors various physiological responses which are usually affected by emotion, such as muscle tension or skin temperature. The person's physiological signal is then amplified and "fed back" to the client in the form of a tone, clicks, or various colored lights. A high tone, fast clicks, or a red light might reflect high muscle tension, low skin temperature, or

biofeedback. Biofeedback is used to help people with anxiety in a broad range of areas. In addition, the technique has been helpful in treating such varied stress-related conditions as migraine headaches, tension headaches, asthma, and arthritis.

The effectiveness of biofeedback has been questioned recently. Some of the important early research on biofeedback has not ben replicated, and the power of the treatment procedure has been criticized. Some authorities believe the main effect of biofeedback lies in its forcing the client to relax, bringing about a reduction in tension. If this turns out to be true, then there are more economical means of relaxation training than the expensive electronic biofeedback laboratories. Some of the ''popularity'' of biofeedback as a psychological treatment can be attributed to the push by instrument manufacturers in marketing biofeedback equipment. Some research pioneers in the area have been skeptical of the recent treatment ''fad'' and have called for more basic research in demonstrating the effectiveness of the treatment.

Modeling

Bandura has demonstrated that behavior change can be affected by what we observe, not just by the reinforcements we receive. We are strongly influenced by the models around us. Not only do we learn to cope with stress by observing how others around us handle stress but we can learn new coping styles from our observations. Bandura has accumulated impressive evidence to demonstrate that watching models cope well with situations that are fearful for the observer can significantly change the observer's ability to cope with the situation in real life.

Modeling is used as a behavioral treatment technique for problems with anxiety and skills deficits. It is frequently used to alleviate the anxiety of patients about to undergo a stressful medical procedure, for example. Before their examination, patients are presented with a model demonstrating coping techniques to use during the procedure. The models can be live, on film, or described so that the patient can imagine the model going through the procedure.

Another use of modeling is in *social skills training,* a procedure for patients who have problems in social interactions. Often the therapist ''models'' an appropriate social response, such as how to ask a person for a date. A related procedure involves the therapist and patient acting out a real-life situation that is problematic for the patient. The therapist can model more appropriate behavior for the patient to try out, first in the less threatening therapy session and then in real life.

A popular new development in biofeedback is a process teaching muscle relaxation to reduce the effects of stress and the diseases it can nurture.

high heart rate. A low tone, slow clicks, or a green light might reflect low muscle tension, warm skin, or a slow heart rate. By trying various fantasies, relaxation, meditation, or other strategies, people can learn to control the feedback signal by changing their physiological responses. For example, using feedback on the amount of tension in the forehead muscle as a cue, one can learn to obtain deep muscle relaxation. These techniques can then be applied in stressful situations as a means of eliminating anxiety responses. Often people who have trouble with the progressive muscle relaxation used in systematic desensitization can learn deep relaxation by means of

Technique of Cognitive Behavior Therapy

Rational Emotive Therapy

Instead of focusing exclusively on a person's observable behavior, Albert Ellis became interested in people's cognitive understanding of events, which he believed, when mistaken, could lead to maladaptive behavior. Ellis proposed that these mistaken beliefs or self statements are learned early in life. Ellis' list of common irrational beliefs is presented in Highlight 12–5. Ellis' therapy, called *rational emotive therapy,* is based on the premise that through extensive talking with clients the therapist can lead them to see the irrational nature of their self statements and bring them to a more appropriate way of viewing the world.

Highlight 12–5

Common Irrational Beliefs

Albert Ellis considers the core of most people's maladjustment to be irrational beliefs. Common irrational beliefs people hold, according to Ellis, are:

1. One should be loved by everyone for everything one does.
2. Certain acts are awful or wicked and people who perform them should be severely punished.
3. It is horrible when things are not the way we would like them to be.
4. Human misery is produced by external causes, or outside persons, or events rather than by the view that one takes of these conditions.
5. If something may be dangerous or fearsome, one should be terribly upset about it.
6. It is better to avoid life's problems if possible than to face them.
7. One needs something stronger or more powerful than oneself to rely on.
8. One should be thoroughly competent, intelligent, and achieving in all respects.
9. Because something once affected one's life, it will indefinitely affect it.
10. One must obtain and perfect self-control.
11. Happiness can be achieved by inertia and inaction.
12. We have virtually no control over our emotions and cannot help having certain feelings.

Building on the work of Ellis, cognitive behavior therapists have treated the *self statements* that people make by using guided fantasy or by pairing particular fantasies with relaxation. Instead of merely imagining an anxiety-provoking scene while under deep muscle relaxation, the client might be asked to fantasize *coping* with an anxiety-provoking situation. Practice with such fantasy has been demonstrated to lead to more effective coping in the actual situations.

In addition, people are asked to pay attention to the self statements they make and modify them when necessary. A young woman being treated for problems with anger control was asked to write down all the things she said to herself when angry. By doing this, she saw that many of her self statements (for example, "This always happens to me and nobody else" and "I'm so stupid all the time") made her feel even angrier. She learned to concentrate on what she said to herself when angry, substituting more appropriate self statements (for example, "What do I have to do to get out of this mess?" and "Just relax, everything will straighten out if I approach this problem calmly") for the anger-provoking ones.

Covert Sensitization

Covert sensitization was developed to a certain extent as an attempt to resolve some of the ethical problems of using aversive stimuli like electric shock in therapy. Instead of using a physical punishment, the patient's imagination is used. Covert sensitization is most simply described as punishment training by imagination. The technique is designed for eliminating an undesired behavior and involves asking the patient to imagine first engaging in the behavior and then to imagine very undesirable things that happen as a result of the behavior. We will illustrate with the treatment of obesity, although the technique has been applied to other undesired behaviors like alcohol abuse, smoking, and sexual deviations. The obese person is told to imagine that he or she is about to overeat. The individual is then told to bring into the fantasy the sensations of nausea and vomiting. It is hoped that after frequent repetitions of this fantasy the person will come to associate the thought of overeating with nausea. Consider the following example:

> I want you to imagine you've just had your main meal and you are about to eat your dessert, which is apple pie. As you are about to reach for the fork, you get a funny feeling in the pit of your stomach. You start to feel queasy, nauseous and sick all over. As you touch the fork, you can feel some food particles inching up your throat. You're just about to vomit. As you put the fork into the pie, the food comes up into your mouth. You try to keep your mouth closed because you are afraid that

Smart Person's Illness
By RIAN E. McMULLIN

Exceptional people often have exceptional problems. Highly intelligent, verbal, creative people—people who are assertive, socially skilled and in touch with their feelings, are the prime candidates for an extremely painful psychological disorder called agoraphobia.

Although agoraphobia literally means fear of open spaces, the word is a misnomer. The agoraphobic can be afraid of hundreds of things; such as crowds, planes, freeways, leaving his home, losing control of himself, being embarrassed in public or going insane.

Society loses some of its best contributors because such talented people get so anxious. . . .

Their fears seem mysterious. Agoraphobics may be happy for several days, when suddenly a terrifying panic grips them without any apparent cause. . . .

When panicked, agoraphobics develop an almost irresistible desire to escape from where they are. They believe if they can't run away or get some help quickly, something absolutely horrible and catastrophic will happen.

These symptoms may occur every day or only once a month. They may last five minutes or five hours. But once they feel the panic, agoraphobics will spend much of their waking life trying to keep the panic from happening again.

Many people will go to incredible lengths to prevent the terror. They will avoid anyplace where they can't escape easily, like limited access highways, elevators, or airplanes. They refuse invitations to public gatherings like concerts, churches, department stores, crowded restaurants or football games where others might see them go berserk. . . .

Gradually, as the agoraphobia continues, they will restrict their lives more and more until they have retreated back to their homes, destroying any semblance of a social or professional life.

We have been treating and researching agoraphobia at the Counseling Research Institute in Lakewood for several years. We believe we have come up with the probable sources of the panic. . . . We are concluding that agoraphobia is caused by very specific, programmed superstitious beliefs. In certain situations the agoraphobic activates a mental "tape recorder" of these superstitious thoughts, which immediately kindles a panic attack.

Although agoraphobics may have an enormous variety of superstitions, most can be condensed into a few core beliefs.

• I might totally lose control of myself and behave monstrously bizarre and grotesque.

• I must ward off my fear or it will break out and make me insane.

• If I don't switch off this panic immediately, I will surely have a complete nervous breakdown.

The fear of losing control may be learned in several ways. A surprisingly high number of agoraphobics have had a bad drug experience while taking marijuana, LSD or amphetamines. Others have had a close friend or relative suffer a nervous breakdown. Some experience a very embarrassing social situation like fainting at a funeral, vomiting in a restaurant, or having diarrhea in public. They developed the specific fear of losing control of their bodies. There are also many agoraphobics who were taught the old "teapot" theory of emotions, that emotions came from deep inside our unconscious and that if we don't release them correctly, we could explode. They often wait for years for the explosion to take place because they mishandled an emotion.

Therapists have tried many ways to cure agoraphobia. They have rummaged through early childhood experiences, hoping to give clients insight into the origins of their fears. But in many cases just knowing the origin doesn't get rid of the panic.

Other therapists have attempted a form of behavior therapy called desensitization. This technique teaches clients to relax while imagining their frightening images. But we have found that the agoraphobic has so many fearful images, that as soon as one is desensitized another one pops up in its place. . . .

After searching through a variety of other techniques, one approach seems very promising. A branch of Behavior Therapy, called Cognitive Restructuring, has helped many clients remove their panic attacks.

The technique employs counter conditioning principles to help agoraphobics erase their previous cognitive programming. Agoraphobics are first taught to carefully record all thoughts that trigger their panic attacks. Next, with the help of their therapist, they dissect the logic of each belief. Finally, tapes are prepared to help the clients deprogram their anxious thinking. The tapes include counter images, autosuggestion, and realistic beliefs which are made up specifically for each patient. Clients then are instructed to listen to these tapes 30 minutes a day for as long as it takes to reduce the panic attacks.

We don't want to give the impression that getting rid of agoraphobia is easy. There are no magic quick cures, and every sufferer must work very hard to reduce the fear. Our clients have told us it was one of the most difficult things they ever had to do. But we know that many sufferers can significantly reduce, and at times eliminate, their agoraphobia if they are willing to put in the work. . . .

Rocky Mountain News *(Denver)*
November 9, 1980

Cognitive behavior therapy concentrates on modifying cognitions, not just behavior. It stresses modification of thoughts or beliefs, assuming that disordered behavior is a normal result of faulty thinking. This article illustrates the approach as it might be applied to the treatment of agoraphobia.

you'll spit the food out all over the place. You bring the piece of pie to your mouth. As you're about to open your mouth, you puke; you vomit all over your hands, the fork, over the pie. It goes all over the table, over the other people's food. Your eyes are watering. Snot mucus is all over your mouth and nose. Your hands feel sticky. There is an awful smell. As you look at this mess you just can't help but vomit again and again until just watery stuff is coming out. Everybody is looking at you with a shocked expression. You turn away from the food and immediately start to feel better. You run out of the room, and as you run out, you feel better and better. You wash and clean yourself up and it feels wonderful (Cautela, 1967, p. 462).

Despite its intuitive appeal, research on this procedure has to date provided only very limited support for its usefulness.

Stress-Inoculation Training

Another cognitive behavioral method that has been widely used in recent years is stress-inoculation training. This approach involves determining what stresses the individual will be facing and teaching him or her how to cope with them. For example, major surgery often produces severe anxiety and maladaptive behavior in patients. The psychologist attempts to lessen the patient's stress by helping the person know what to expect and what his or her reaction to the operation will be. Stress-inoculation training is carried out in three stages: The first stage involves *cognitive preparation,* in which the therapist and client explore the client's beliefs and concerns about the problem. Special emphasis is placed on "self statements," or what people tell themselves about the problem. The second stage involves *acquisition and rehearsal.* The individual learns adaptive self statements and practices applying these under simulated stress situations. The final stage involves *application,* or using the cognitive coping strategies under actual stress conditions.

Group Therapies

Most of the treatment approaches discussed thus far have involved a therapist and a client on a one-to-one basis. Since World War II, however, group psychotherapy has become increasingly popular. Since group therapy is a more efficient use of the therapist's time and talents, it can be offered with less expense to more people. The size of a group can vary from 3 to 20, although 8 to 10 seems optimal.

Group psychotherapy, moderated by an effective leader, can frequently provide a person with experiences that are difficult to duplicate in a one-to-one

"We must try this group-therapy thing again, sometime soon."

The New Yorker, April 11, 1970. Drawing by J. Mirachi; © 1970 The New Yorker Magazine, Inc.

setting. First, typically people feel that their problems are unique and worse than anyone else's. In a group people frequently find that others have similar problems. Second, a group member can get feedback from several points of view about how he or she affects others, and this feedback carries a weight that the therapist seldom can provide. Group members can pool their experiences and encourage a member to try new solutions to problems. Third, group members frequently fulfill the needs of other people in the group. And helping someone else is often therapeutic for the helper. Finally, the individual may try out new behaviors on others in a relatively safe, accepting environment.

Gestalt Therapy

As we have seen, Gestalt psychology emphasizes the perception of patterns or totalities rather than separate elements of a stimulus. **Gestalt therapy,** founded by Fritz Perls, developed from attempts to help persons look at the entirety of their immediate experience. According to Perls, people with emotional problems tend to focus their attention on only part of what they feel and on only part of what they do, especially in their communications with others. The focus of Gestalt therapy is not *why* the client is behaving in a certain way but rather *what* the person is feeling and *how* the person is behaving. The therapist helps the client overcome barriers to self-awareness. This is typically accomplished in group therapy sessions. The goal is for the clients to become aware of what they are doing from moment to moment and to accept responsibility for that behavior. Theoretically, clients will then be able to attend to all aspects of their experience. Attention and awareness become integrated.

Notice in the following excerpt of a Gestalt group therapy session how the therapist points out all aspects of the client's behavior—the tone of her own voice and the shaking of her leg. The client had been describing a dream in which her dead mother appeared, and the therapist, noticing that she was beginning to sound whiny and complaining, asked her if she had any "unfinished business" with her mother. The client replied:

MRS. R: Well . . . if only she had loved me, things would be different. But she didn't and . . . and I've never had any real mother love (crying).

S (STEVE TOBIN): Put your mother in that chair and say that to her.

MRS. R: If only she had cared for me, I'd be much better today.

S: I want you to say this to her, not to me. Can you imagine her sitting there in front of you?

MRS. R: Yes, I see her as she looked when she was still alive. Mother, if you had only loved me. Why couldn't you ever tell me you loved me? Why did you always criticize me? (almost a wail, more tears).

S: Now switch over to the other chair and play your mother. (She moves over to the other chair and doesn't say anything.)

S: What do you experience as your mother?

MRS. R: I-I-I don't know . . . I don't know what she would say.

S: Of course you don't know. She's not around any more. You're playing the part of you that is your mother. Just say whatever you experience there.

MRS. R: Oh, I see. Well, I don't know what to say to her.

S: Say that to her.

MRS. R M (MRS. R as MOTHER): I don't know what to say to you. I never knew what to say to you. I really did love you, you know that. Look at all the things I did for you, and you never appreciated it (voice sounds defensive and whiny).

S: Now switch back and reply as yourself.

MRS. R S (MRS. R as SELF): Loved me! All you ever did was criticize me. Nothing I ever did was good enough! (voice beginning to sound more whiny). When I got married to J. you disapproved, you were always coming over and telling me what I was doing wrong with the kids. Oh, you never came right out and said anything, but you were always making snide remarks or saying, "Now, dear, wouldn't it be a good idea to put another blanket on the baby." You made my life *miserable;* I was always worrying about you criticizing me. And now I'm having all this trouble with J. (breaks

down and starts to cry.)

S: Did you hear your voice?

MRS. R S: Yes.

S: What did you hear in it?

MRS. R S: Well, I guess I sounded kind of complaining, like I'm feeling sor—like I'm feeling mad.

S: You sounded more like feeling self-pity. Try this on for size: say to your mother, "Look what you've done to me. It's all your fault."

MRS. R S: Look what you've done. Everything's your fault.

S: Now let yourself switch back and forth as you find yourself changing roles.

MRS. R M: Come on, stop blaming me for everything. You are always complaining about something. If you had been better—if you had been a *decent* daughter, I wouldn't have had to criticize you so much.

MRS. R S: Oh, oh (under her breath). Damn. (She's swinging her right leg slightly.)

S: Notice your leg.

MRS. R S: I-I'm shaking it.

S: Exaggerate that, shaking it harder.

MRS. R S: (Shakes leg harder, it begins to look like a kick.)

S: Can you imagine doing that to your mother?

MRS. R S: No, but I-I-I-I'm sure feeling pissed at her.

S: Say this to her.

MRS. R S: I feel pissed off at you! I hate you!

S: Say that louder.

MRS. R S: I hate you! (volume higher, but still some holding back).

S: Louder!

MRS. R S: I HATE YOU, YOU GODDAMNED BITCH. (She sticks her leg out and kicks the chair over.)

S: Now switch back.

MRS. R M: (voice sounds much weaker now) I-I guess I didn't show you much love. I really felt it, but I was unhappy and bitter. You know all I had to go through with your father and brother. You were the only one I could talk to. I'm sorry . . . I wanted you to be happy . . . I wanted so much for you.

MRS. R S: You sure did! . . . I know you did love me. Mother, I know you were unhappy (voice much softer now, but sounding real, not whiny or mechanical). I guess I did some things that were ba—wrong, too. I was always trying to keep you off my back.

MRS. R M: Yes, you were pretty sarcastic to me, too. And that hurt.

MRS. R S: I wish you had told me. I didn't think you were hurt at all.

MRS. R M: Well, that's all over now.

MRS. R S: Yeah, it is. I guess there's no use blaming you. You're not around any more.

S: Can you forgive your mother now?

MRS. R S: Mother, I forgive you . . . I really do

In group therapy, finding out that other people are in the "same boat" can help a person to cope with his or her own problems.

Most group leaders employ techniques that foster honest communication among members.

forgive you. (Starts crying again, but not in the whiny way of before. She sounds genuinely grieving and cries for a couple of minutes.)

S: Now switch back.

MRS. R M: I forgive you too, dear. You have to go on now. You can't keep blaming me forever. I made my mistakes but you have your own family and you're doing okay.

S: Do you feel ready to say goodbye now?

MRS. R S: Yes. I-I think so (starts to sob). Goodbye, Mother, goodbye. (Breaks down, cries for a few minutes.)

S: What do you experience now?

MRS. R: I feel better. I feel . . . kind of relieved, like a weight is off my back. I feel calm.

S: Now that you've said goodbye to her, to this dead person, can you go around and say hello to the live people here, to the group?

MRS. R: Yes, I'd like that.

(She goes around the room, greets people, touches some, embraces others. Many in the group are tearful. When she reaches her husband, she starts crying again, and tells him she loves him, and they embrace.) (Tobin, 1971, pages 154–155)

Encounter Groups

In an **encounter group** the goal is not to work on specific problem areas of the members but rather to sensitize each member to the feelings of others. Members are placed in a face-to-face encounter under instructions to say what they feel and "pull no punches." Theoretically this procedure enables members to experience and express their feelings more forcefully.

The encounter group process varies tremendously from one group to the next. All encounter

459

"Don't be alarmed. We're an encounter group."

Ladies Home Journal, © 1972. Reprinted by permission of S. Gross.

Some individuals have developed an erroneous stereotype of the encounter group as a free-for-all "love-in."

groups focus on here-and-now feelings, negative *and* positive feedback to each member of the group, and the removal of facades that interfere with honest, open communication. Most group leaders use a variety of techniques that are designed to make the participants communicate honestly. Some of these techniques are:

1. Self-description. All group members write down the three adjectives most descriptive of themselves. The slips of paper are mixed, and the group discusses the kind of person that is being described.
2. Eyeball-to-eyeball. This technique involves two participants staring into each other's eyes for a minute or two, communicating as much as possible, and discussing the feelings afterward.
3. The blind walk. All group participants pair off, and with one person leading and the other blindfolded, the "blind" person walks around the room or outdoors and becomes sensitized to the environment. One variant of this exercise is for the "blind" persons to try to communicate by touch alone.
4. Trusting exercises. Participants take turns being lifted and passed around a circle formed by the group members.
5. Hot seat. One group member sits in a special chair and others give the individual honest feedback about how he or she affects them.
6. Positive and negative bombardment. In this method similar to the hot seat technique, the group member is given feedback that focuses on only positive or only negative feedback.

Some groups may not use any formal techniques. Instead, the group is allowed to develop its own strategies for encouraging honest and open interactions.

The majority of participants in encounter groups report positive changes as a function of participation. One study, however (Yalom and Lieberman, 1971), reported that 16 of 170 students who had participated in one or another of several different encounter groups reported significant psychological damage as a result of participation. Other studies have also reported possible psychological damage. These studies indicate that anyone entering an encounter group should be careful to choose one with an experienced, nondemanding, and open leader.

Family Therapy

One special form of group psychotherapy has received the particular attention of practitioners for many years. Therapists were quick to discover that the problems of a troubled child are often embedded in pathological interactions within the family. Even if the therapist were able to help the child in individual psychotherapy, the child would have to return to a family life that supported old, inappropriate ways of behaving. In these cases therapists with family orientations quickly moved away from working with the identified client to working with the whole family to change ways of interacting.

The therapist's first goal is to determine what each family member sees as the problems within the family and what each hopes to achieve through family therapy. The therapist tries to determine how the problem that is presented relates to the family network and how the family maintains a homeostatic balance among members. Family rules are uncovered. Some rules are overt—such as those that state when bedtime is and who is supposed to take out the trash—and some are covert—such as "Don't take your problems to Dad. He is too mixed up." The family may make a scapegoat of one family member (often the identified client) as having all the problems in the family. The family therapist will try to (1) improve communication within the family, (2) encourage autonomy and empathy among family members, (3) help the family develop new ways of making decisions, and (4) facilitate conflict resolution.

Social-Skills and Assertiveness-Training Groups

A widespread group-treatment approach in the past few years has been social-skills and assertiveness-training groups. Social-skills training focuses on teaching a much broader range of appropriate social behaviors than does assertiveness training, with its emphasis on teaching individuals to stand up for their rights. Both types have been used for a wide range of problems (from teaching shy college students how to interact with members of the opposite sex to teaching chronic psychiatric inpatients basic social behaviors like eye contact and smiling). These group treatments use such techniques of behavior therapy as role playing, modeling, and social reinforcement. Homework assignments are often given, requiring the individuals to practice the skills taught in the group.

Social-skills and assertiveness groups bear some resemblance to the older group method of *psychodrama*. In psychodrama one group member agrees to be the *protagonist* (the main actor in the drama), who typically describes a problem in interpersonal relationships. Other group members (including the therapist) play other roles in the drama, play aspects of the protagonist's personality, or merely observe as the audience. Because the situation is not real and the people with whom the protagonist is having trouble are not usually present, the individual feels less threatened and is capable of freer expression of feelings and greater spontaneity. Alternative solutions to problems can be tried out in the drama without danger. Not infrequently, spectators with similar problems become just as emotionally involved in the drama as the protagonist.

Ethical Concerns

Group psychotherapy has become so popular that many "groups" have arisen relatively spontaneously, and too frequently with untrained and unqualified leaders. Individuals who have participated in a single group experience as a client sometimes feel competent to lead another group. If nothing happens, the results may be minimally dangerous; however, the intensity of emotion experienced in groups generally requires an experienced leader to ensure that negative experiences do not occur. A person interested in participating in a group should get information about the level of competence of the leader before volunteering. The same caution, of course, applies to all forms of psychotherapy.

While ethical guidelines may provide some structure for professionals concerning appropriate behavior, individual judgment must always be involved in solving ethical problems. How a therapist handles clients whose problems involve religious or political or moral issues must always stem from the therapist's understanding of the dangers and benefits that are involved for the client. How would you weigh client benefit for a client who wants to be a more effective heroin pusher or a more effective bigot? Take the case of a male therapist who decides, contrary to therapeutic ethics, to date a shy, withdrawn female client. Who is benefiting from the treatment, and how can the therapist be sure that *his* welfare is not being given

more importance? What would you do if you heard that a therapist is on drugs while seeing clients? Professional guidelines provide for a series of steps from a personal warning to notification of the licensing board. Unfortunately, nonprofessional, unlicensed group leaders have no guidelines or contingencies on their behavior. A person is best advised to avoid groups led by these individuals and to join those led by trained professionals.

Medical Therapies

Lobotomy and Shock Therapy

The belief that mental illness can be treated by altering the body through surgery, direct physical stimulation, or chemicals has been around for centuries. In fact, even cave dwellers used physical means, a surgical procedure known as trephening (perforating the skull with a sharp instrument) to release "evil spirits" from aberrant or suffering people. The history of modern medicine is abundant with examples of the search, some successful, others unsuccessful, for somatic treatments for major mental disorders. For example, the discovery that advanced syphillis produced a mental disorder known as paresis stimulated workers to prevent and cure syphillis. This effort has

"Oh good Lord, no! It was just a primal scream."

The New Yorker, July 2, 1973. Drawing by Whitney Darrow, Jr.; © 1973 The New Yorker Magazine, Inc.

Primal therapy is based on assumptions somewhat similar to psychoanalysis. It focuses on one particular conflict, the cutting off of feelings experienced as a young child in response to an accumulation of hurts and rejections on the part of the parents. In primal therapy, one indication that a person has experienced the pain of hurts accumulated during childhood is the expression of the primal scream, an agonizing scream of pain.

virtually eliminated paresis in our time. On the other hand, the use of psychosurgery, such as *lobotomy* (which, as we saw in Chapter 2, is an operation to sever the nerve fibers connecting the frontal lobes with other nerve centers) proved to be a dead end, having little therapeutic value but drastic physical side effects.

One approach to somatic treatment involves stimulation of the brain (often referred to as shock treatment) through chemical means, such as insulin, or through electrical stimulation. These therapies were widely used during the 1940s and 1950s to treat severe psychological disorders. The introduction of the major tranquilizers reduced the reliance on these methods. However, electroconvulsive therapy is still the treatment of choice for some disorders.

Electroconvulsive therapy (ECT), or shock therapy, has been demonstrated to be effective for people with relatively severe depressions that do not respond to chemotherapy. In ECT the patient is placed on a bed, given muscle relaxants, and while lightly held by attendants, is given an electric shock across the temples of sufficient intensity to produce a convulsion. The convulsion lasts up to a minute and is followed by unconsciousness for about half an hour. Although scientists do not actually know how ECT works, both convulsion and resulting coma seem to be necessary for effective treatment. The patient cannot remember anything about the shock or convulsion. Surprisingly, ECT has been found to be effective in reducing or eliminating depression (after several treatments), but it is not effective in treating other problems. Although the treatment may seem drastic, it can eliminate months of suffering and possibly prevent suicide. Unfortunately, ECT does not reduce the possibility of future depressions.

Chemotherapy

Drugs to treat psychopathology have been used for at least as long as recorded history. Many of the drugs used for treatment today, however, were originally used for other purposes, and their psychological effects were discovered accidentally. Even now, in many cases, scientists have only a vague idea why some drugs work. The drugs used in **chemotherapy** can be roughly divided into four categories: sedatives, tranquilizers, antidepressants, and antipsychotics (see Table 12–2).

Sedatives and Tranquilizers

Sedatives and tranquilizers have been used to help highly anxious people under transient stress or those showing early manifestations of neurosis and psychosis. Although tranquilizers have been in use only since the middle 1950s, sedatives have been known for a long time. A **sedative** is defined as a drug that reduces anxiety and tension by inducing muscle relaxation, sleep, and inhibition of the cognitive centers of the brain. Although they do reduce severe anxiety responses, sedatives have a major disadvantage; sedated individuals cannot function well in activities involving complex cognition because of the sleep-inducing quality of the drugs. The most common sedative is alcohol; others include barbiturates (a common type of sleeping pill), bromides, and chloral hydrate (also known as "knock-out" drops).

In the middle 1950s, a new group of drugs—the **tranquilizers**—were introduced. They had the advantage of reducing anxiety in neurotics and psychotics (as well as people under unusual stress) without the severe sleep-inducing side effect of the sedatives. Tranquilizers have become tremendously popular. Under moderate doses a person can cope with stresses of life without debilitating anxiety.

Both sedatives and tranquilizers have a major drawback that also applies to the antidepressant and antipsychotic drugs; once the person quits taking the drug, the emotional problems return. Severe dependence on tranquilizers and sedatives is far too com-

TABLE 12-2 Prescription Drugs Used in Chemotherapy

Sedatives

Generic Name	Trade Name
Amobarbital	Amytal
Chloral hydrate	Noctec
Flurazepam hydrochloride	Dalmane
Methaqualone	Quaalude
Phenobarbital	Luminal
Sodium secobarbital	Seconal sodium
Sodium pentobarbital	Nembutal sodium
Triclofos	Triclos

Tranquilizers (Antianxiety Drugs)

Generic Name	Trade Name
Chlordiazepoxide	Librium
Clorazepate	Tranxene
Diazepam	Valium
Hydroxyzine	Atarax
	Vistaril
Meprobamate	Equanil
	Miltown
Oxazepam	Serax

Antipsychotic Drugs

Generic Name	Trade Name
Acetophenazine	Tindal
Butaperazine	Repoise
Carphenazine	Proketazine
Chlorpromazine	Thorazine
Haloperidol	Haldol
Molindone	Moban
Perphenazine	Trilafon
Prochlorperazine	Compazine
Thioridazine	Mellaril
Trifluoperazine	Stelazine
Triflupromazine	Vesprin

Antidepressant Drugs

Generic Name	Trade Name
Amitriptyline	Elavil
Despiramine	Norpramin
	Pertofrane
Imipramine	Presamine
	Tofranil
Isocarboxazid	Marplan
Phenelzine	Nardil
Protriptyline	Vivactil
Nortriptyline	Aventyl
Tranylcypromine	Parnate

mon in our country. However, the drugs can be used effectively to help persons under transient situational stress and to help neurotics or psychotics reduce their anxiety to the point at which they can work on their problems in therapy.

Antidepressants

Although tranquilizers do not help individuals who are depressed, a group of drugs referred to as "mood elevators"—the **antidepressants**—are useful. The first drug discovered to have this effect was iproniazid. Originally designed for the treatment of tuberculosis, iproniazid was observed to have an unexpected side effect. The patients became less depressed and happier about life. Other drugs belonging to the same chemical family or having similar biochemical properties were subsequently found to have some antidepressant function. Antidepressants apparently affect the amount of certain biochemical transmitters within the brain, which in turn affects synaptic transmission (see Appendix D). Although the manufacturers claim tremendous success with antidepressant drugs, they are generally less effective for their purpose than are tranquilizers.

Antipsychotics

The first **antipsychotic** drug was extracted from a plant, *Rauwolfia serpentina,* mentioned in Hindu writing over 2500 years ago. The root of this plant was used in India to treat snake bites (which it

Lithium Termed Psychosis Tool

WASHINGTON (UPI) — Lithium has been so successful in treating manic depression that two researchers estimate it has saved at least $2.8 billion in hospital costs and prevented production losses of $1.2 billion in the past 10 years.

Lithium has been used since its introduction in 1969 to treat the major mental illness—a psychosis marked chiefly by emotional instability and striking mood swings.

Ann Reifman of the government-supported St. Elizabeth's Hospital in Washington and Dr. Richard Jed Wyatt of the National Institute of Mental Health said lithium has had a remarkable effect in stabilizing patients with the illness. . . .

Other researchers report patients taking lithium do much better than when they were hospitalized numerous times, given multiple courses of electrotherapy and treated with a variety of other drugs.

Lithium, developed as a drug by an Australian psychiatrist in 1949, is an element available in inexpensive salt form. Serious side effects are uncommon. . . .

Before the introduction of lithium, the researchers said manic depression was a far more expensive disorder. . . .

The Denver Post
May 1, 1980

An effective treatment for manic-depressive psychosis, lithium salt is a rather common substance. Only recently has its curative powers in controlling manic behavior been known.

Use of Drugs for Depression Challenged

LOS ANGELES (UPI) — Depression in varying degrees affects about 60 million Americans at any given time, but a University of Southern California psychiatrist believes widely used mood-elevating drugs are not the answer.

Dr. Edward J. Stainbrook, chairman of the USC Department of Human Behavior, said tranquilizers and antidepressants camouflage, rather than solve, the problems causing the condition.

"Most people feel unable to cope with anxiety and depression and become even more anxious and depressed," he said in an interview.

"Actually, such emotions give us valuable information about ourselves if we let them. If the result is action that reduces the emotional pain then these negative emotions have served their purpose."

Stainbrook said we tend to think of emotions causing behavior when, in fact, the feelings result from behavior. . . .

Rocky Mountain News (Denver)
September 10, 1976

Writer Says Drugs Lifted Depression
By BOB JAIN

Drugs — some new and some not so new — may prove potent weapons against severe mental depression, a former foreign correspondent who has suffered that affliction said. . . .

Percy Knauth [said] . . . that he had seriously contemplated suicide a few years ago because of a "mood of pervasive sadness" that struck him for no apparent reason.

'Saved Life'
His understanding wife, Knauth said, probably saved his life at that time, but real recovery came after he became a patient at the Depression Research Unit of the Connecticut Mental Health Center. There, he said, he received drugs that eventually brought him back to normal.

Recovery wasn't immediate, he said, because the drugs worked cumulatively, correcting a chemical imbalance in his brain. He still is taking a "maintenance dose" of those drugs, much reduced from what he took during treatment, and may have to take them the rest of his life, he said. . . .

The experience was "a terrible journey, a frightening journey, that brought me very close to death," Knauth said, but he added that he had no regrets at having experienced it. . . .

He said symptoms were sadness, "to which was added fear, hopelessness and (a feeling of) personal worthlessness" that eroded his self-confidence and hurt his ability to make even the smallest decision.

"I came out of it a better person," he said, "certainly a different person."

The Denver Post
September 12, 1974

Two very different views on the use of medications to relieve depression.

did not affect), epilepsy and dysentery (which it made worse), and insomnia and insanity (which it helped). Not until the late 1940s were the therapeutic effects of this plant noticed in the Western world, and the active ingredient, called reserpine, was isolated in the early 1950s.

Although reserpine markedly helps to calm agitated psychotics, it occasionally produces undesirable side effects such as severe depression. For that reason reserpine has largely been replaced by another group of drugs — the phenothiazines — that dramatically calm agitated psychotics. The first phenothiazine to be used to treat psychosis — chlorpromazine — was, like the antidepressants, discovered by accident. It was originally used in anesthesia for surgical patients, in whom it produced profound calm before the operation.

Many hospitalized psychotics have been discharged under chlorpromazine treatment, but the symptoms tend to reappear if the patient quits taking the drug. Some patients have complained about uncomfortable side effects of the drugs, such as muscle stiffness and dryness of the mouth. Recently much concern has been expressed about the long-term effects of antipsychotic drugs. One disorder, *tardive dyskinesia* (a disfiguring disturbance of motion control), believed to be an irreversible neurological condition, has raised concern about the overuse of psychotic medication.

We know relatively little about how these drugs work. However, antidepressant and tranquilizing drugs may affect a person's level of motivation by altering the process of synaptic transmission in the central nervous system. They probably also have peripheral effects, such as producing muscle relaxation. Antipsychotic drugs also affect CNS transmission and may work by inhibiting bizarre psychotic cognitions that interfere with applying more realistic knowledge and skills. Until more is known about the nature of the action of these drugs, however, we can only speculate.

Hospitalization

Persons who are not competent to handle everyday requirements, who are not helped by psychotherapy and/or medication to function effectively, whose behavior might be dangerous to themselves or others, or who need more intensive treatment than can be provided by a therapist in an office setting may require hospitalization. Each year about a quarter of a million people are admitted for the first time to mental institutions in this country. At any given time around three-quarters of a million people are hospitalized for emotional problems — at least as many as are hospitalized for all physical illnesses combined. Fortunately, the average length of confinement today is roughly two weeks, a drastic reduction from earlier years. Still, one out of five will remain hospitalized for a year or more, and about 50 percent will be hospitalized again later in life.

Most of the hospitalized mental patients have been *involuntarily committed* by civil court procedures for a specific period of days or months or perhaps for an indefinite period, to be released only at the discretion of hospital officials. Commitment is a serious step and is presently quite controversial. In most states the involuntarily committed person is denied most civil rights and may not be able to vote, marry, or obtain a divorce. Some states have put civil rights for patients into law, but in many states there is no protection. If a patient is disliked by the people in charge, there are few legal pathways available to obtain freedom. All too frequently the mentally ill are committed and "forgotten." Steps have been taken only recently to try to ensure that those who are committed to mental hospitals for treatment do in fact receive treatment.

A few years ago most state mental hospitals were little more than rest homes for the emotionally disturbed, with little or no treatment administered to patients. Frequently, the patient population numbered in the thousands while the professional staff was a mere handful. "Back" wards, where some people spend all their lives, are becoming less common, and antipsychotic drugs have helped reduce patient loads. Hospitalization is now seen primarily as an aid to therapy and not a therapy itself. The federal government and many states have a policy of trying to reduce the size of mental hospitals by keeping afflicted persons in their communities, functioning as best they can under drugs if necessary and with some outpatient form of treatment.

Chronic patients in mental hospitals have been the "lost persons" of society, often remaining in institutions for many years without hope of recovery and usually without adequate treatment. But chronic patients can be significantly helped, and a high percentage can be successfully returned to the community. In an extensive six-year program, Paul and Lentz (1977) compared *social learning therapy* (based on principles of learning) with *milieu therapy* (self-government of wards) and *traditional* psychiatric care (medication and custodial care). They found that 90 percent of patients treated by social learning therapy and 70 percent of patients treated with milieu therapy remained in the community after their release. Traditional custodial treatment resulted in only 50 percent successful releases from the hospital. Their research suggests that even severely disturbed chronic patients can be helped if proper treatment is given. One of the most critical mental health needs today is for sufficient *after-care* programs to aid psychiatric patients after their discharge (see Highlight 12–7 in "What Does It Mean?").

Social Approaches to Emotional Problems

Community Mental Health

The field of **community mental health** has developed out of two concerns: (1) the need for more efficient and comprehensive provision of mental health services and (2) the attempt to prevent mental illness by "treating" a community or a whole social system rather than each individual in the community.

President John F. Kennedy proposed to Congress in 1963 that comprehensive community mental health centers be set up to provide treatment for the emotionally disturbed *within* the community. By so doing, Kennedy shifted the focus away from treatment in state hospitals, which were originally built in isolated rural areas usually miles away from the home of the disturbed individual. Under President Lyndon B. Johnson, the Comprehensive Community Mental Health Centers Act was passed, providing federal aid to states for the construction of community mental health centers. The centers were required to provide: (1) short-term hospitalization; (2) outpatient care, usually traditional psychotherapy; (3) 24-hour emergency service, including suicide prevention and crisis therapy; (4) day care for people who need a structured setting during the day but can return home at night;

(5) night care for people who need a sheltered place to stay at night but can work at jobs during the day; and (6) consultation to community agencies.

Although community mental health centers have not eliminated the need of many individuals for long-term care in a state or other hospital, they have provided more convenient treatment and a wider range of services than was previously available. Ultimately, these centers aim at broadening their activities so they can intervene in community crises before emotional disturbances occur. One center, for example, was instrumental in preventing a race riot by sending a team of crisis workers into a school riddled by racial disturbances.

Community mental health programs tend to divide into three kinds of services: primary, secondary, and tertiary.

Primary Services

Primary prevention is aimed at preventing the occurrence of mental disorders through seeking out and erasing the potential causes of a problem. Examples are attempting to reduce poverty, disease, or racial discrimination because these factors are associated with the development of psychological problems. The theory of primary prevention is that by eliminating these sources of problems abnormal reactions can be prevented. It is in primary prevention that the most important gains can be made in the control of psychopathology, but so far there has been little work toward this end in our society. This approach to prevention is the hardest to implement since the underlying causes of problems may be so pervasive and so difficult to alter that major societal changes will be required to have any effect. As we have seen, psychologists have strong feelings about possible changes in the structure of society that could reduce the frequency of mental disorder and mental suffering. However, such changes may involve expensive programs that the taxpayer is not willing to support, and there is frequently disagreement about the types of changes needed. Not infrequently a redistribution of power is required, and those in power are not willing to give it up. Because a political activist orientation implies the direct confrontation of incompatible social values, such activities are controversial, and an activist orientation is not shared by all mental health professionals. However, almost all mental health professionals are concerned about social change.

Some psychologists have been active in redefining for society what is abnormal. Several states have removed or are considering removing laws pertaining to sexual behavior between consenting adults, because there is no victim and no crime. Homosexuality would then no longer be a crime. Psychologists have tried to institute changes in the punishment techniques used in prisons on the basis of modern rein-

forcement principles. Some have tried to remove bail as a requirement for release from prison prior to trial. The belief is that the poor should not be penalized by imprisonment simply because they cannot pay bail.

In the schools some psychologists concerned with social change have worked not to produce a better curriculum content but to change the focus of teaching from the memorization of facts to the process of problem solving. Working in such areas of concern is frustrating, however, because large institutions build up considerable inertia and change very slowly.

Secondary Services

Secondary prevention efforts are aimed at reducing the impact or severity of a problem once it has developed. For example, emergency psychological treatment for victims suffering severe losses brought on by natural disasters such as floods or tornadoes might relieve their present symptoms and bring about a more rapid and better adaptation to their crisis. One of the most effective treatment approaches in the community mental health movement is *crisis intervention*.

A **crisis** can be defined as a point in a person's life that is unusually stressful and may be handled in a maladaptive way. Crisis intervention (see Highlight 12–6) is based on the assumption that persons can best be helped when there is an immediate crisis in their lives, for example, when their marriage or romance has just broken up. At this time a person is more willing to accept help from a mental health worker and is able to change more in a shorter period of time. Crisis therapy involves helping the person define the immediate problem and seek alternative solutions to it, because people panic when they see no way out of the problems they are facing. Crisis therapy tends to be more directive and confrontative than traditional insight therapy. Receiving short-term psychotherapy during crisis situations can frequently prevent the need for hospitalization, medication, or psychotherapy at other times in life. Students who are in danger of flunking out of school, individuals who have lost their jobs, or people in any of a thousand other crisis situations may need a therapist for four or five sessions to help them over that crisis, although they can function normally at other times.

A specific example of crisis intervention is *suicide prevention*. In many cities across the country phone numbers are available that will connect a potentially suicidal person with a counselor at a suicide prevention center. Prevention centers are effective because people who are suicidal usually are ambivalent about dying, wanting to die but also wanting to live. It is well known that most people who are considering killing themselves communicate these feelings either in their behavior or by talking about suicide sometime

Highlight 12–6

Crisis Intervention: A Treatment and Preventive Approach

An effective, relatively new treatment method, crisis intervention, focuses on both the treatment of acute symptoms and the prevention of psychological disorder (secondary prevention). Crisis-intervention therapy is concerned with symptom relief, management of immediate stress situations, and development of adaptive strategies for dealing with future problems. The techniques of crisis intervention grew out of the work of Eric Lindemann, who treated survivors and family members of the tragic Coconut Grove nightclub fire of 1943. Since that time crisis-intervention procedures have been used with victims of tornadoes, floods, fires, airplane and train crashes, and terrorism. The article below highlights an emergency treatment program for rescue workers who had to clean up the debris from the 1978 San Diego air disaster.

Crash Taking Toll on Rescuers

SAN DIEGO (UP)— More than three weeks after the nation's worst air disaster killed 144 people, a police officer wakes up crying in the middle of the night and another has nightmares that he is trapped inside a "body bag" used to carry off the dead.

Other officers, firemen and rescue workers recall with pain the mangled remains of youngsters killed in the crash and see bodies exploding in their dreams. Some suffer headaches and depression, have trouble eating and sleeping and wonder if they shouldn't be in a different profession.

"What we are trying to tell them is that it is perfectly normal to feel the things they are feeling after a catastrophe of this magnitude," said Dr. Allan Davidson, president of the Academy of San Diego Psychologists.

His group, working with the city of San Diego, offers free psychological therapy to the 800 police, firemen, ambulance drivers, rescue workers and military personnel who witnessed first-hand the devastation of the Sept. 25 crash of a commercial jetliner into a residential neighborhood.

But so far, only 16 policemen, many of them senior officers with several years of experience, along with two firemen and six rescue workers have taken advantage of the service from 100 clinical psychologists who volunteered their time. . . .

Davidson said people affected by the crash could have more serious psychological problems a year from now if they keep their feelings pent up.

"Most of the people are trying to forget what they saw and are using defense mechanisms to try to block it out," he said. "What we are trying to do is get through these defense mechanisms and give them a framework to ventilate their feelings. If they don't get their feelings out, the nightmares, crying and other symptoms could continue."

He said the 16 officers taking part are "normal, well adjusted individuals."

"When they were first exposed to the death scene, their first feeling was one of shock. It was especially painful to see the bodies of children, since many had families of their own.

"After the shock wears off there is a period of questioning. They want to know 'why am I not feeling a lot better sooner?' It is an entirely normal situation."

Davidson said therapy usually takes three to four weeks with individual sessions lasting an hour or more once, twice or three times a week. . . .

He said the clinical psychologists chosen for the program are skilled in crisis intervention techniques that focus on immediate psychological problems.

"Some of our people worked with victims of the tornadoes in Ohio in 1974, floods, fires and accidents involving multiple deaths," he said.

Boulder (*Colo.*) Daily Camera
Wednesday, October 18, 1978

---

before any attempt is made. Finally, suicide attempts occur when a person is in a crisis and therefore is more receptive to help.

One of the first things a suicide prevention counselor will try to do when on the phone with a suicidal person is to determine the risk. The following factors help determine how lethal the attempt is:

1. Age. The older the person, the greater the risk of death.

The exception is among male blacks, for whom the greatest risk is from age 20 to 24.

2. Sex. Men are about three times as likely to commit suicide as women, although women are about three times as likely to attempt suicide as men.

3. Plan for suicide. The more specific the plan and the more deadly the method, the greater the risk. Guns are a greater danger than pills or wrist cutting.

4. Resources. People who have fewer resources to turn to for help in a crisis are a greater risk for suicide. Those

who are isolated from family, relatives, and friends and are not in a position to turn to physicians or clergymen for support and help are a greater risk. Divorced people have a suicide rate three to four times the national average.

If the risk of death is high, the counselor will be more active in trying to intervene. If the risk is low, the counselor will first try to establish a relationship over the phone in order to maintain contact and obtain information. The counselor first tries to communicate interest and optimism about finding a solution to the crisis. The second step is to identify and clarify problems. The suicidal person is often confused and unsure as to precisely what problems he or she faces. At this point alternative solutions to the problem might be suggested. The resources of the person will be taken into account, and attempts will be made to bring the person in contact with mental health professionals within the community.

In an attempt to make mental health services more available to the poor, *storefront clinics* or outreach centers have been set up in the middle of poverty areas. These clinics are usually staffed by people from the community who act as problem solvers, sympathetic listeners, and community facilitators. Trying to obtain services from community agencies, for example, can be very frustrating if a person does not know what is available, which agency is appropriate, and what the eligibility requirements are. Sometimes mental health professionals work in conjunction with community service programs such as Model Cities.

Tertiary Services

Tertiary services, or *tertiary prevention* efforts, are concerned with the after effects of having emotional problems. Tertiary prevention aims at reducing the long-term effects of a problem. This type of treatment is generally referred to as *rehabilitation*. People who have had severe emotional problems may have lost their job or family and need counseling to get back into the community. This may involve job training, counseling in how to get a job, and development of social skills.

The State of the Art

If you view these two chapters on psychopathology and psychotherapy superficially, you might arrive at the following oversimplified view. The clinical psychologist, confronted with a case of behavior disorder, first makes a diagnosis of the disorder, then applies a treatment or a therapy (psychotherapy) to remove the disorder or "cure" it, and finally helps his patient resume his normal activities within the community. In other words, the procedure appears quite similar to

the medical model of treating physical illness (diagnosis-treatment-cure-rehabilitation)—a nice, neat, and simple picture. However, the picture is not nearly so neat in reality, and we would like to close by emphasizing that fact.

In Chapter 11 we saw that diagnostic classification is a difficult task, and clinical psychologists may disagree about specific diagnoses in some cases. More important, we saw that with present knowledge of psychopathology, psychologists are rarely certain of the causes of or "cure" for a particular disorder, even if they have been able to agree on what to call it. We have seen in this chapter that there are many different types of psychotherapies and that each type can be applied to a wide variety of diagnostic categories. Any particular therapist is likely to adhere to one school of thought in which he or she is a highly skilled and knowledgeable student. This method of therapy is then applied to just about all the cases encountered. However, psychotherapy is not uniformly effective—it depends to an unknown degree upon the skill and experience of the therapist and possibly to an even greater extent upon the problems of the client. Some psychological disorders appear relatively resistant to known treatments, while others may respond well to a particular method and may be worsened by another. All of the therapies appear to be effective with some problems, and no therapy is effective with all psychological problems. Therefore, successful treatment outcome depends on many factors—including luck in the client's locating an appropriate therapist.

But there are some promising trends emerging that we would like to highlight in this concluding comment. First, as noted in Chapter 11, there is less emphasis today on diagnostic classification—the psychologist now attempts to identify the client's problems and does not worry too much about being able to fit each client into a neat category of mental "illness." Second, psychotherapists are more likely today than they were 10 years ago to be trained in a variety of techniques. The hope is for more adaptable behavior on the part of the therapist in the future. Third, the new methods of behavior modification hold great promise for specific disorders, and more and more psychologists are becoming sophisticated in the application of these techniques. Fourth, we see a greater realization among psychologists of the fact that traditional psychotherapy is not the answer to every problem for several reasons—it costs too much, it cannot be given to enough people, not everyone benefits from it, and the delivery system as it now stands discriminates unfairly. As a result of all these factors, we see a fifth trend emerging—a trend away from individual psychotherapy delivered after someone has developed a disorder to a community mental health system oriented around preventive mental health, crisis intervention, short-term psychotherapy, and minimal hospitalization. We see the continuing rise of community psychology with its attempts to delineate and attack the social-cultural sources of behavioral disorders.

We do not mean to conclude that psychology will shortly discover all the answers to mental illness. We do mean to suggest, however, that the next 20 years may result in more progress than the last 20 years. We do not believe that this progress will neces-sarily consist of the discovery of great new "cures" for neurotic disorders (although we would hope that this would be the case for the psychotic disorders). Rather, we expect there to be an entirely new set of working assumptions about mental health, and we expect these assumptions to conflict dramatically with the "diagnosis-treatment-cure" model that has charac-terized the work of the clinical psychologist and psy-chiatrist for some time.

SUMMARY

1. Psychotherapy is defined as a corrective expe-rience leading a person to behave in a socially appropriate way. The types of therapies can be divided into several cate-gories: insight-oriented therapies, behavior and cognitive behavior therapies, group therapies, medical therapies, and community mental health procedures.

2. Insight-oriented therapies assume that emotional problems stem from conflicts between conscious and un-conscious processes. The two major types are those focusing on repressed memories of the past, such as psychoanalysis, and those focusing on denied aspects of present experi-ences, such as client-centered therapy and Gestalt therapy.

3. In classical psychoanalysis the patient, lying on a couch to reduce external stimuli, is asked to free associate, to say anything and everything that comes to mind. Dream interpretation and interpretation of such unusual behaviors as slips of the tongue help the therapist evaluate the con-tents of the unconscious mind.

4. Client-centered psychotherapy has as its focus helping the client move from denial of certain feelings and experiences to acceptance and experiencing of all feelings and thoughts in the here and now. The client-centered therapist develops an atmosphere of empathic understanding, unconditional positive regard, and congruence to encourage the client to risk facing his or her denied feelings.

5. The behavior and cognitive behavior therapist uses well-established principles of learning in order to change behavior. Behavior therapy is derived from two principal sources: classical and operant conditioning. In addition, cognitive processes have also been suggested as important in behavior change, a position held by the cognitive be-havior therapists.

6. Three common behavior therapy techniques are: (a) systematic desensitization, which pairs relaxation train-ing with the fantasy of feared stimuli, moving slowly from the least to the most feared; (b) positive reinforcement and shaping, which involve reinforcing components of a com-plex behavioral sequence with the goal of teaching the entire sequence; and (c) aversion therapy, which involves punishing undesirable behaviors.

7. In biofeedback people can learn to control the physiological processes that are affected by emotion, thus learning to obtain deep muscle relaxation in response to stress or to control psychosomatic illnesses.

8. Modeling is based on the principle that behavior change can be affected by what we observe, not just by the reinforcements we receive.

9. Through rational emotive therapy, clients see the irrational nature of some of their self-statements and come to view the world in a more appropriate way.

10. In covert sensitization, unpleasant images and fantasy are paired with behavior that the therapist is trying to help the client change.

11. Group therapy offers group members the oppor-tunity to understand others, get feedback, share solutions, be a therapist for others, and practice new behaviors.

12. Medical therapies include psychosurgery, shock therapy, and chemotherapy. Lobotomies (cutting nerves in the frontal lobe of the brain) and electroconvulsive therapy (in which a person has a convulsion induced by electric shock across the temples) are techniques that have become less common since the use of drugs in psychiatric treatment. Drugs used in psychiatry for the treatment of emotional problems can be divided into four categories: sedatives, tranquilizers, antidepressants, and antipsychotics.

13. Hospitalization may be used when therapy and medication alone are not sufficient to help a person function effectively. Social learning therapy is effective in treating chronic inpatients.

14. Quite often social approaches are effective in treating emotional problems. Community mental health is concerned with the more efficient delivery of mental health services, particularly to the poor, and treatment of a com-munity or social system rather than each individual.

15. In primary services the focus is on eliminating the cause of emotional problems. Secondary services center on problems that already exist. Tertiary services deal with rehabilitation and the after effects of having emotional problems.

RECOMMENDED ADDITIONAL READINGS

Bandura, A. *Principles of behavior modification.* New York: Holt, Rinehart and Winston, 1969.

Duke, M. P., & Frankel, A. S. *Inside psychotherapy.* Chicago: Markham, 1971.

Freud, S. *A general introduction to psychoanalysis.* New York: Washington Square Press, 1920.

Goldfried, M. R., & Davidson, G. R. *Clinical behavior ther-apy.* New York: Holt, Rinehart and Winston, 1976.

Kendall, P. C., & Hollon, S. D. *Cognitive behavioral inter-ventions.* New York: Academic Press, 1979.

Weiner, I. B. *Principles of psychotherapy.* New York: Wiley, 1975.

What Does It Mean?

What Is It Like To Be in Therapy?

Once one has decided that help with an emotional problem is needed, one has to do something about it. Table 12–3 presents the results of a survey concerning why people seek help. Table 12–4 indicates that most people do not seek help from a therapist, but usually go to their clergy or physician. Unfortunately, in many cases in which the problem is severe, it is someone else who decides that the individual needs treatment, and involuntary commitment is sought. Indeed some people have the misconception that one must be obviously psychotic or nonfunctioning before it is legitimate to ask for help. Actually, just the desire to *change* is sufficient reason to seek professional help. Dissatisfaction with his present existence was the client's motivation in the following case:

> This [psychotherapy] is something I've been thinking about for a long time. I've known that it was something I've needed and wanted, but I just haven't done anything about it. Recently though, I've been realizing more than ever that I'm just not

TABLE 12–3 Nature of Personal Problems for Which People Sought Professional Help — Survey Results

Problem Area	
Spouse; marriage	42%
Child; relationship with child	12
Other family relationships — parents, in-laws, etc.	5
Other relationship problems; type of relationship problem unspecified	4
Job or school problems; vocational choice	6
Nonjob adjustment problems in the self (general adjustment, specific symptoms, etc.)	18
Situational problems involving other people (e.g., death or illness of a loved one) causing extreme psychological reaction	6
Nonpsychological situational problems	8
Nothing specific; a lot of little things; can't remember	2
Not ascertained	1
Total	**
Number of people	(345)

** Percentages total to more than 100 percent because some respondents gave more than one response.

TABLE 12–4 Where Do People Go for Help?

Source of Help	
Clergyman	42%
Doctor	29
Psychiatrist (or psychologist): private practitioner or not ascertained whether private or institutional[a]	12
Psychiatrist (or psychologist) in clinic, hospital, other agency; mental hospital	6
Marriage counselor; marriage clinic	3
Other private practitioners or social agencies for handling psychological problems	10
Social service agencies for handling nonpsychological problems (e.g., financial problems)	3
Lawyer	6
Other	11
Total	**
Number of people	(345)

[a] Actually only six people specifically mentioned going to a private practitioner. This category should thus be looked upon as representing in the main those people who said "psychiatrist" without specifying that he or she was part of a mental hygiene agency.

** Percentages total to more than 100 percent because some respondents gave more than one response.

the way I want to be. I'm not sure what I am, and I'm not sure I want to know, but I sure don't like this. I'm not even sure what I want to be — sometimes it's one thing, sometimes something quite different. I don't know where I am or where I'm going, but I've at last decided to try to find out. (Fitts, 1965, page 16)

It can, of course, be frightening to ask a strange person for help with a personal emotional problem, taking a chance that the therapist will understand and not criticize or consider the problem trivial. Finally, the client must feel that he or she can trust the therapist, or openness and frankness will not be possible. The client in the following case was probably not ready to benefit from therapy until he got over some of his initial doubts about therapy and the therapist:

> The first few visits I felt uneasy, tearful, embarrassed, ashamed, guilty, and depressed, and constantly reminded myself: "surely I could have done better than this; why did this have to happen to me?" What does my Doctor think of me? How could he know what I'm going through? Why should he care? Why should he spend his time with me? (Someone else maybe, but I should be capable of straightening this out myself!)

Highlight 12–7

Deinstitutionalization and the After-Case Crisis

Mental hospitals have long been criticized for their "dehumanizing" effects and for the fact that people committed to them become dependent and unable to return to productive life. In recent years there has been a trend toward deinstitutionalization—the early return of patients to the community and the effort to keep people out of hospitals by providing broader community treatment programs. The recent availability of major antipsychotic and antidepressant medications that help control extreme psychological symptoms has made it more possible for people to remain in the community even though they are still psychotic. Thousands of individuals have been returned to the community, although not necessarily to a productive, happy life. On the contrary, many returned patients have been found to be in need of psychological services that are unavailable in the community. In addition, the "board and care" facilities that have cropped up to handle discharged patients have simply taken over the functions of the state hospital—providing a place to sleep and an asylum from life's pressures.

> As I sat in that chair choked with emotion, and ashamed that I was, it was hard for me to say anything. When I did have a feeling and wanted to express it, it was so vague I couldn't find the words. After three sessions of saying so little, I felt like I wasn't getting anywhere, and was wasting the Doctor's time. I wanted the therapist to be proud of me. What he thought of me was always important. (Fitts, 1965, page 26)

Therapy is difficult under the best of circumstances. There are times when the process of trying to understand oneself can be physically painful, and the effort is always tiring. People develop feelings of anger and affection for the therapist that can get in the way of clear thinking. Sometimes people get annoyed at the one-sided nature of the relationship, because clients learn little or nothing about the therapist. If therapy takes a long time, persons can become embittered. Their high hopes, unfulfilled, make for considerable disappointment. It is known that some therapists can never empathize with certain clients. Therefore, to prevent extreme disappointment, it may be best to try another therapist before giving up therapy as a way of solving problems.

How Effective Is Psychotherapy?

In the early 1950s, Hans Eysenck challenged psychology to demonstrate whether psychotherapy was effective or not. In summarizing 19 experimental studies involving 7000 cases of psychoanalytic and nonpsychoanalytic types of treatment (behavior modification had not become popular at that time), Eysenck concluded that people who did not receive psychotherapy (but who may have received custodial care or care by a general practitioner) improved as much as or more than those who underwent psychotherapy! Using successful social and work adjustment as the criterion, Eysenck found that 66 percent of the patients who completed psychoanalysis improved, 64 percent of those who received nonpsychoanalytic therapy improved, and 72 percent of those who received no formal psychotherapy improved (Eysenck, 1952).

As you can imagine, Eysenck's report was a blow to mental health professionals, since it seemed to demonstrate that psychotherapy was useless. Subsequently, however, it became clear that there were several things wrong with Eysenck's conclusions. First, the people who improved without formal psychotherapy were frequently receiving help from some other source. Second, people who seek help are different from those who do not, and there is some evidence to suggest that those who seek help are the kinds of people who do not improve without it. In several respects, such as severity of problems, Eysenck's treatment and nontreatment groups were not comparable. Also, he used different criteria of improvement for the two groups. Finally, some kinds of problems simply do not get better without professional intervention; for example, the symptoms of neurosis do not commonly disappear spontaneously.

Very recently, Gene V. Glass has reexamined the vast research literature on psychotherapy outcome, using modern statistical evaluation techniques. While no single study, including Eysenck's, is conclusive, the sum total of the evidence strongly indicates that psychotherapy is an effective treatment for psychopathology.

Despite these findings, it is apparent that many people improve without psychotherapy. Those who conclude that nearly everyone needs a therapist sometime in life are vastly underrating the ability of people to solve their own personal problems, although often with the help of relatives and of close friends.

People use different criteria for "cure" in therapy. The psychoanalyst will evaluate whether transference is resolved, the Rogerian will look at the quality of expression of feelings and experiencing, and the behavior modifier will be concerned with changes in the specific behavior that led to the request for therapy. It is difficult, therefore, to find a simple criterion for improvement for all kinds of therapy. Why not ask clients themselves whether they are better?

Dead Woman's Father Asks for New Laws on Mentally Ill
By DAVID CRARY

A district attorney and the father of a young woman killed by a former mental patient issued pleas Thursday for closer supervision of potentially dangerous patients by the state mental health system.

William Fralick, whose 21-year-old daughter Amy was stabbed to death in 1975 while a student at Colorado State University, urged changes in the legal system so that a person found not guilty by reason of insanity could nonetheless be held accountable for the act in question.

Under the proposed change, if the defendant is judged to have committed the act, Fralick told the Legislature's Interim Judiciary Committee, the state could obtain a conviction and retain control of the accused.

"Under the present Colorado system, at least to the layman, no one murdered our daughter," he said. "We defy you to support that conclusion after reading the autopsy report."

The interim committee in response to four homicides in the past eight months committed by former mental patients, is seeking to determine if changes are needed in state laws dealing with the confinement and release of the mentally ill.

Colorado Springs District Attorney Robert Russel accused the state mental health officials of "evasion of responsibility" for being reluctant to monitor potentially dangerous patients after their release from state facilities.

He suggested that the Department of Institutions assign professionals to keep close track of ex-patients identified as possible risks to society. He said these professionals would be the equivalent of parole officers, checking for indications of trouble and ensuring that the ex-patients receive required medication.

"The mental health people are always passing the buck," Russel said. "If we decide to take a chance on releasing these people, we've got to have somebody out there following up."

Russel referred to the case of Seth Buckmaster, who completed the latest of a series of mental-hospital confinements just a few months before he was arrested for killing Colorado Springs policeman Augustus Peirrera.

Russel said officials at the Fort Logan Mental Health Center noted in their own report that Buckmaster might become violent in a confrontation with police. He said the officials released Buckmaster despite numerous indications he was dangerous and planned to buy a gun.

However, attorney Larry Schoenwald of the Colorado Trial Lawyers Association said the most damaging result of the four recent homicides could be an overreaction resulting in an infringement on individual liberties.

He said the best way to reduce violence by the mentally ill is to continue improving treatment and monitoring, rather than changing state laws so a dangerous person could be confined without a formal ruling that the person was either guilty of a crime or mentally ill.

"You can't separate the dangerous without depriving all of us of liberties which are much more important," he said. "Probably all of us can be classified as dangerous at one time or another."

Rocky Mountain News (*Denver*)
August 15, 1980

Are former mental patients dangerous? It is true that, as in this case, some former patients commit violent crimes. This may be more true at present because there is a trend toward earlier release of patients and the desire to keep individuals out of psychiatric hospitals as much as possible. However, most people who recover from psychological disorder (especially if they have no history of violence) are not dangerous.

A common problem that shades the client's evaluation of the therapy is the *hello-goodbye effect*. When the client says "hello" to the therapist at the beginning of therapy, he presents himself as unhappy and troubled; in fact, he may exaggerate to convince the therapist he is really "sick." At the end of the therapy, the "goodbye" effect is apt to occur. The client tries to present himself as strongly improved in order to resolve any dissonance about wasting his time and money and to express appreciation to the therapist for his efforts. Thus it would be easy to mistake the hello-goodbye effect for real improvement.

The ideal situation would seem to be to determine the type of therapy that is most effective for each type of problem and refer people to the appropriate therapist, much in the same way that a physician writes a prescription for an illness. For example, behavior modification has been demonstrated to be effective with phobias and anxiety states in which there is a specific anxiety-provoking stimulus. Typical reports suggest that as many as 90 percent of clients with such problems are helped with behavioral techniques such as systematic desensitization. As behavior modification techniques have been extended and applied to more complex problems, such as very diffuse anxiety, the improvement rate has not been as high. Because of all these uncertainties, the question of the best therapy for a particular problem is still far from being resolved.

What Kind of Therapist Is Best?

For some reason there has been little research isolating the personality characteristics of good therapists. Many training programs in clinical psychology place considerable weight on intellectual attributes such as grade point averages and test scores in deciding which applicants to accept for training. But do high intelligence and outstanding grades mean that a person will make a good therapist? Most of us would agree that other personality characteristics are also crucial to the effectiveness of a therapist. Even in the case of behavior modification therapies, which in some sense seem pretty impersonal, therapist "warmth" plays a role in determining the effectiveness of therapy.

It is clear that therapists do differ widely in their success rates. One factor contributing to this variability is the amount of experience the therapist has. It has been found that effectiveness in establishing an ideal therapeutic relationship with the client increases with experience. In fact, experience is a much more important factor in a therapist's success than the school of therapy to which the therapist belongs.

In addition, three personality characteristics of the therapist (all derived from Rogers' theory of therapy; see Chapter 9) seem to be important for positive change in therapy: *accurate empathy, nonpossessive warmth,* and *genuineness.* Accurate empathy means that the therapist is sensitive to the feelings of the client and is able to communicate that awareness to the client. Nonpossessive warmth is basically caring for the client as a person without demanding changes in feelings and experiences as a precondition to acceptance. Genuineness is defined as a lack of defensiveness on the part of the therapist, who must present himself or herself in an uncontrived, honest way.

In one study it was shown that when therapists ranked low on the three characteristics, a 50 percent rate of improvement in their clients was found, but when therapists ranked high on the three personality characteristics, a 90 percent rate was found. The combined rate of 70 percent for the two groups is near the level of improvement found by Eysenck for untreated controls (Truax et al., 1966). This research has not gone unchallenged, however. Some researchers have questioned whether these variables are measured in an appropriate, non-biased way. Others have suggested that such therapist characteristics may be important only when weak interventions are used.

Other therapist variables have been found to be significant. Not surprisingly, the more the client *likes* the therapist, the more effective the therapy—and the longer the person stays in therapy. There is also evidence to suggest that therapists who have unresolved conflicts in the areas of dependency, warmth, intimacy, and hostility are less effective in helping people with their problems. Whether or not empathy, warmth, and genuineness are critical variables in therapy is as yet unresolved, although there is supportive evidence particularly for therapist warmth. However, a likable, conflict-free therapist is more likely to be effective than a cold, neurotic one.

An interesting hypothesis regarding the relationship between personality and therapeutic effectiveness is that certain personality characteristics may make a therapist ideally suited to treat one type of behavioral disorder but poorly suited to treat other types of disorders. Many therapists realize this implicitly and will refer clients who have problems with which they have had little success to therapists who have obtained better results in treating such cases.

Highlight 12–8

Violent Patients and the Responsibility of Therapists

Are mental health professionals responsible for violent acts committed by their patients? A recent California court ruled (the Tarasoff decision, 1977) that a therapist has the responsibility of warning potential victims of danger if their patients disclose threats to them. (In the Tarasoff case the therapist had warned the police but not the individual whose life was threatened. The woman was killed by the patient.)

Failing to recognize that a patient may be dangerous or failing to take aversive action if violence is threatened can mean legal jeopardy for therapists.

Mental Health Center, 2 Doctors Sued in Stabbing
By STEVE CHAWKINS

A mental health center and two doctors were accused Thursday of "reckless and negligent" supervision of a mental patient who fatally stabbed a city driver a year ago.

In a suit in Denver District Court, the family of Jon D. Bauer demanded a total of $11,003,000 from Southwest Denver Community Mental Health Services and Drs. Paul R. Polak and Timothy Weissinger.

The suit also demanded damages from David P. Dela Cruz, the knife-wielding mental patient who boarded Bauer's Regional Transportation District bus in the Cinderella City Shopping Center parking lot Sept. 15, 1979. Dela Cruz, then 21, stabbed Bauer several times and shoved him out of the bus in an apparent hijack attempt.

Just before, he had rammed his car through the glass doors in another shopping center.

Dela Cruz was found innocent by reason of insanity and was committed to the State Hospital in Pueblo.

According to the suit, Dela Cruz was sent to the Southwest Mental Health Center after a previous arrest Dec. 28, 1978. There he was diagnosed as a "paranoid schizophrenic, openly hostile, violent and dangerous."

The center for the next nine months—until Bauer's death—treated Dela Cruz "as an out-patient, allowing him total freedom within the community, contrary to the recommendations of Denver General Hospital, the Denver County Court, and the standard of care expected in the community," the suit charges.

The two doctors allowed Dela Cruz to stop his therapy treatments and reduce his intake of Mellaril, a medication for behavioral disorders. . . .

Rocky Mountain News *(Denver)*
September 12, 1980

Selecting the Right Therapist Could Be Traumatic

By CAROL KLIEMAN

Caution! Therapy may be hazardous to your health!

That's a warning from a therapist, Dr. Manny Silverman, associate professor of guidance and counseling at Loyola University of Chicago.

A registered psychologist with a doctorate in counseling, Silverman says selecting a therapist is a consumer problem that only the consumer can solve — cautiously, very cautiously.

"Much psychological research shows that the net effect of therapy may not be that positive," says Silverman. "Doctors, clergy, and others who try to match people with the right therapist don't always succeed. Sometimes it's effective, and sometimes it's not.

"When it comes right down to it, you are the best judge of who and what are best for you."

First, the consumer makes the decision she needs therapy. Then she must decide to whom to go.

"A decision to seek therapy is laden with further decisions that would be difficult enough in good times, let alone when things appear rotten," he says.

"But it is vital to evaluate the person from whom you are seeking help."

To help people shop for therapy, Silverman holds workshops and classes at Greenerfields Unlimited and Loyola. They are attended by consumers, therapists, doctors, lawyers, and clergyman who frequently are asked to recommend someone.

"Caveat Emptor — let the buyer beware — has too long been the rule for therapy," Silverman says.

The professor, who also does private therapy, adds, "The point is not that there are bad therapists, but that there might be certain credentials that would be important to you as the client and that might make the difference in whether your therapy is successful or not."

The beauty of asking a potential therapist direct questions is that the asking is part of the answer.

Some questions:

Where did you get your training?

What is your marital status? "This is a very personal question," says Silverman, who has been married 11 years

and has two children, "but if the therapist has been divorced three times it might be indicative of a mind set you should know about. And if it matters to you, ask."

How long have you been in practice?

What types of problems do you see?

What types do you like to see?

What types do you least like to see?

Do you routinely suggest a physical examination before therapy begins?

How long on the average do you see someone?

What is your fee? Do you charge for missed sessions? How far ahead can I cancel?

Any other questions that are relevant to you.

"The basic premise of therapy is trust," Silverman says. "The way these questions are answered can tell you a lot. Remember, this is someone you will want to relate to, who should be able to listen to you, and to understand.". . .

Boulder *(Colo.)* Sunday Camera
June 20, 1976

Shortage of Therapists

There are simply not enough therapists to aid everyone who needs psychological help, and the population is growing faster than the number of psychologists and psychiatrists. Thus the movement toward community mental health has developed, as well as other alternative ways of providing help to those who need it. One approach that has emerged from the community mental health orientation to problems has been the use of *paraprofessionals.* Paraprofessionals are interested individuals in the community who can with a minimum of training serve as temporary therapists. Housewives, bartenders, and beauticians have successfully served this role. Individuals from poor neighborhoods, ghettos, and foreign-language-speaking areas of a city are all frequently alienated from the middle class, traditionally trained clinician. Paraprofessionals can communicate with these people better and are more aware of the cultural pressures surrounding them. Paraprofessionals are particularly useful in crisis intervention and community action.

One of the more recent interesting attempts to compensate for the shortage of therapists is the use of computers. Although the definition of the problem usually requires a skilled clinician, once the problem is defined, many behavior modification approaches are relatively automatic. It is possible to program a computer to provide rewards and punishments in a systematic desensitization routine in much the same way that a programmed textbook or computer-assisted instruction works. A human therapist has to construct the hierarchy of anxiety-provoking situations, but the list can then be turned over to the computer, which will teach a person how to relax. Although lacking the warmth, genuineness, and empathy that may be important with the insight-oriented therapist, computers work with some people. Instrumentally and classically conditioned problems can probably also be treated with computer-assisted psychotherapy. Psychology is just beginning to explore alternative means of helping people, and many scientists are working on developing more efficient means of providing help.

APPENDICES

Elementary Statistics

The single most commonly used tool in psychology is statistics. All areas of psychology rely on one or both of the two basic types of statistics: (1) *descriptive statistics,* which are used to summarize the results of research, and (2) *inferential statistics,* used to infer conclusions about the results.

Descriptive Statistics

Measures of Central Tendency

Suppose a teacher gives an IQ test to 10 students. How would he or she describe the test results? One way would be to name all students and list their IQ scores — 10 names and 10 scores. That would probably work nicely in a small class. But it would certainly be inefficient and confusing with a class of 500. Moreover, a listing of numbers does not indicate much of anything about the group as a whole. It would be helpful to know the average, typical, or more representative score. What is needed is a measure of *central tendency* in the group of scores, a number that represents the average. We will describe three commonly used measures.

The Arithmetic Mean   The **mean** is the number you arrive at when you add up all the scores and divide by the number of scores. In the above example you would add up the 10 IQ scores and divide by 10. We have made up a set of 10 scores and computed the arithmetic mean in Table A–1, which also introduces some elementary statistical symbols. Any score for an individual subject is an X. It could be an IQ score, an anxiety score, a measure of height, or anything. In Table A–1, X is an IQ score. We add up the 10 Xs. The capital Greek letter sigma (Σ) is a shorthand symbol for "add up these scores." So, Σ X means add up the X scores. Table A–1 also gives each student's height in inches. To keep height distinct from IQ scores, we signify height by Y. Very often a problem involves two scores for each subject, as in this case, and we use X and Y to keep them separate. So Σ Y tells us to add up the heights, which is also done in Table A–1.

The final step in computing the arithmetic mean is to divide by the number of scores added (symbolized by N). There are 10 IQ scores, so we divide Σ X by 10 and get the mean IQ: 108.5. Likewise, we divide Σ Y by 10 and we get the mean height: 66.8 inches. The shorthand way of indicating that a particular number is a mean and not a single score is to put a bar over the letter. Thus, the arithmetic mean of the X scores is symbolized as $\overline{X}$ (read "X bar"), and the mean of the Y scores is $\overline{Y}$ (read "Y bar"). Thus, we arrive at a shorthand formula for finding the arithmetic mean of a set of X scores:

$$\overline{X} = \frac{\Sigma X}{N}$$

And, of course, the arithmetic mean of a set of Y scores is calculated by the formula:

$$\overline{Y} = \frac{\Sigma Y}{N}$$

Now if students ask the teacher how the class performed on the IQ test, the teacher could simply report the value of $\overline{X}$; and if they ask about how tall the students are, he or she

could report $\overline{Y}$. This is obviously much simpler than listing all the X and Y scores. It gives a better idea of the general level of ability of the students and a general idea of how tall they are.

The Median   The arithmetic mean of the scores is not always a good way of determining what is the *most representative* score. In these cases two other measures of central tendency are often used. The **median** is the *middle-most score* in a list of scores that have been arranged in increasing order. If there is an odd number of scores, then there will be one score exactly in the middle. Thus, if the class had 11 students, the score of the 6th student in order would be the median — there would be 5 scores higher and 5 scores lower. Or if there were 27 scores, the 14th score in order would be the median.

With an even number of scores there is no single middle score. Instead there are 2 scores that determine the middle; 1 is above and 1 is below the theoretical midpoint. In a set of 10 scores arranged in order, the 5th score from the bottom is not the median — there are 5 scores above it, but only 4 below it. In the same fashion, the 6th score is not the median, because there are 4 higher scores but 5 lower scores. So we compromise and take the halfway point between the 5th and 6th scores as the median of a set of

TABLE A–1   Computation of the Mean IQ and Height of a Class of 10 Students

Student's Name	X (IQ)	Y (Height in Inches)
Rita	125	65
Norma	120	60
Lyle	105	66
Bruce	100	68
John	130	72
Jane	95	64
Linda	90	62
Ralph	110	74
Frank	85	70
Polly	125	67
	$\Sigma X = 1085$	$\Sigma Y = 668$
	N = 10	N = 10

Then, the mean of the X scores is:

$$\overline{X} = \frac{\Sigma X}{N}$$

or

$$\overline{X} = \frac{1085}{10} = 108.5$$

Likewise, the mean of the Y scores is:

$$\overline{Y} = \frac{\Sigma Y}{N}$$

or

$$\overline{Y} = \frac{668}{10} = 66.8$$

"That's the gist of what I want to say. Now get me some statistics to base it on."

The New Yorker, December 19, 1977. Drawing by Joe Mirachi; © 1977 The New Yorker Magazine, Inc.

10 scores. The median of 28 scores would be the mean of the 14th and 15th scores. Table A–2 shows the 10 IQ scores from Table A–1, but this time we have arranged them in order. The middle point is somewhere between the 5th and

TABLE A–2   Computation of the Median IQ Score of a Class of 10 Students

Name	X	
John	130	
Polly	125	
Rita	125	
Norma	120	
Ralph	110	← The middle is in here, somewhere be-
Lyle	105	← tween 105 and 110
Bruce	100	
Jane	95	
Linda	90	
Frank	85	

The median here is the mean of the 2 scores nearest the middle point, in this case, 105 and 110. We take the mean of 105 and 110:

$$\frac{105 + 110}{2} = 107.5$$

This is the median. Note that the median would not be changed if we changed John's score from 130 to, say, 160. But the mean would change. What would the mean be in this case?

6th score, somewhere between 105 and 110. So we take the mean of these 2 scores and use this as the median. The answer is 107.5.

The mean and the median are typically close, but not always the same. They will only be the same whenever the distribution of scores is symmetrical or equally balanced around the mean. Now consider the set of "salary scores" in Table A–3. Here we note that most of the 10 people working for the Zappo Cereal Company are not making a lot of money. One employee, obviously the president, is making a bundle. This distribution of scores or values is asymmetrical and unbalanced. Technically, we call it *skewed.* The distribution in Table A–3 is skewed to the high end (positively skewed). The mean monthly salary for Zappo employees is $1395, which might lead you to believe that the company pays very well. But the median is only $425, which would make you think a little differently about Zappo. The median will be unaffected if the president gives himself or herself a big raise, but the mean will go up. You can see that in this case the median is more representative of the group as a whole than the mean is. Furthermore, the median is *unaffected* by extreme scores such as the salary of the president.

The Mode   The third measure of central tendency is called the **mode.** The mode is a quick but crude measure defined as the *most frequently occurring* score. In a small set of scores, as in Tables A–1, 2, and 3, there is the possibility that no score occurs more than once. Thus there is no mode. But suppose a psychologist gives an anxiety test to a group of 200 mental patients. With such a large group it is

TABLE A–3   Comparison of the Mean and Median Monthly Salaries of the Zappo Cereal Company Employees

Employee Number	Monthly Salary X (in Dollars)	
1	10,000	
2	600	
3	550	
4	500	
5	450	← midpoint
6	400	
7	375	
8	375	
9	350	
10	350	
	ΣX = 13,950	
	N = 10	

We can see from the midpoint that the median salary is the mean of 400 and 450, which is $425.

Yet the mean salary is:

$$\overline{X} = \frac{\Sigma X}{N} = \frac{13950}{10} = \$1,395$$

Which value, the mean or the median, do you think is more representative of Zappo wages?

convenient to set up a *frequency distribution* showing the various possible scores on the test and, for each possible score, how many people (*f* or frequency) actually got that score (see Table A–4). Suppose, for example, that 27 people got a score of 15 on the anxiety test. Looking down the frequency column in Table A–4, we see that 27 is the highest value. This means that 15 is the *mode* or the *modal score,* because it is the score that happens most frequently. Note that the sum of all the frequencies in the f column is equal to N, the number of people taking the test, in this case 200.

Frequency distributions can also appear in graphic form. Figure A–1 shows a frequency distribution using the data from Table A–4. The horizontal axis of the graph (technically, the *abscissa*) gives the value of X, the anxiety score, and the vertical axis (the *ordinate*) gives the frequency of the score.

The frequency distribution is a very important concept in statistics. More advanced techniques are heavily based on the frequency distribution principle, so make sure you understand just what it is.

Measures of Variability

People vary; not everyone gets the same score on a test or has the same height. There are **individual differences** among people. People may vary a lot when it comes to anxiety or IQ scores, but little when it comes to the number of fingers they have. Is there a convenient and accurate way of measuring the degree of variability in a set of scores?

TABLE A–4   A Frequency Table of the Anxiety Scores of 200 Mental Patients

Score (X)	f or Frequency
20	10
19	10
18	12
17	15
16	20
15	27
14	15
13	21
12	22
11	12
10	10
9	8
8	7
7	5
6	3
5	0
4	2
3	1
2	0
1	0
	$\Sigma f = 200 = N$

The mode, the score that occurs most frequently, is equal to 15.

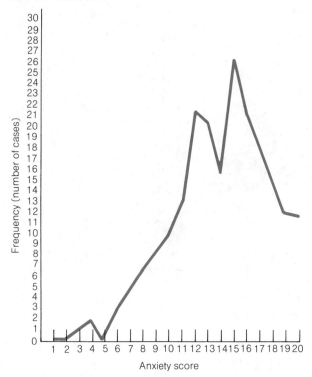

FIGURE A–1   A frequency distribution based on the data in Table A–4

The quickest and least informative measure of the variability in a set of scores is the range. The **range** is defined as the *highest score minus the lowest score.* In Table A–4 we see that the anxiety scores of the patients "range" from a low of 3 to a high of 20, so the range would be $20 - 3 = 17$. The main reason for using the range as a measure of variability is that it is easy to compute. But because it is based on only two scores (the highest and the lowest, and therefore the two most unusual scores), it reflects very little about the distribution. A better and more commonly used measure of variability is the *standard deviation,* which reflects the degree of spread or fluctuation of scores *around the mean.*

Suppose we have a set of 10 scores with an arithmetic mean of 20. Two such sets are shown in Table A–5. The scores labeled Set A consist of only 5 different numbers that are all close to the mean of 20 (18, 19, 20, 21, and 22). Obviously, the variability in Set A is low. In Set B we have the same mean, 20, but the variability is much higher. There are 9 different scores, and some of them are a long way from the mean. If we described both sets with a central tendency measure, we would not be communicating the fact that the two sets are different in a quite basic way. To be more complete we need to provide a measure of variability.

The **standard deviation** is the *square root of the mean of the squared distance from the mean of the scores.* That's complicated, so let's analyze it in steps. First take each individual score, X, and subtract the mean from it, as we

TABLE A–5 Two Sets of Scores That Have the Same Mean But Differ in Variability

Set A	Set B
22	36
22	32
21	28
21	24
20	20
20	20
19	16
19	12
18	8
18	4
$\Sigma X = 200$	$\Sigma X = 200$
$N = 10$	$N = 10$
$\overline{X} = \dfrac{200}{10} = 20$	$\overline{X} = \dfrac{200}{10} = 20$
Range $= 22 - 18 = 4$	Range $= 36 - 4 = 32$

have done in Table A–6. You should be able to see that these new scores, symbolized by the lower-case x, are merely measures of the distance each score is from the mean. Now why not just calculate the average or mean of these distance scores? A glance at Table A–6 should convince you that if you add up the distance scores to get a mean distance score, you will always get a sum of zero. For every score that is above the mean (a positive distance score) there is another score below the mean (a negative distance score) that cancels it out, meaning that the sum of

the distance scores will always be zero. Instead, we square each score, which eliminates the negative numbers, and we have a new concept—the squared distance score, x^2. The x^2 scores are also shown in Table A–6. Now we can add these scores up and take the mean of them:

$$\frac{\Sigma x^2}{N}$$

This gives us the mean squared distance from the mean.

The mean squared distance from the mean has a special name, the **variance,** and a special symbol, the lower-case Greek letter sigma, squared (σ^2). The square, of course, serves to remind us that it is the mean *squared* distance score. The variance is a very good measure of variability, as you can see by comparing this value for Set A and Set B scores; σ^2 is much higher for B (96.0) than for A (2.0). This is as it should be because the Set B scores vary more (from 4 to 36) than the Set A scores (from 18 to 22).

The variance can be used by itself as the variability measure, but it is usually more convenient to take the square root of the variance. We squared the distance scores before we added them up, so now we take the square root of the variance to get back to the original scale of measurement. The square root of the variance is the standard deviation (symbolized σ). The larger the value of the standard deviation, the greater the variability in the corresponding set of scores.

The Normal Frequency Distribution

The frequency distribution in Figure A–2 is known as the *normal distribution*. A normal distribution is symmetric; if you fold it over at the mean, the two halves would super-

TABLE A–6 Computation of the Variance and Standard Deviation for Two Sets of Scores

Set A (Ages of 10 People at a College Dance)			Set B (Ages of 10 People at the Park)		
X	$x = X - \overline{X}$	x^2	X	$x = X - \overline{X}$	x^2
22	2	4	36	16	256
22	2	4	32	12	144
21	1	1	28	8	64
21	1	1	24	4	16
20	0	0	20	0	0
20	0	0	20	0	0
19	−1	1	16	−4	16
19	−1	1	12	−8	64
18	−2	4	8	−12	144
18	−2	4	4	−16	256
	$\Sigma x = 0$	$\Sigma x^2 = 20$		$\Sigma x = 0$	$\Sigma x^2 = 960$

$$\sigma^2 = \text{variance} = \frac{\Sigma x^2}{N} = \frac{20}{10} = 2.00$$

$$\sigma = \text{standard deviation} = \sqrt{\sigma^2} = \sqrt{2.00} = 1.414$$

$$\text{or } \sigma = \sqrt{\frac{\Sigma x^2}{N}} = \sqrt{\frac{20}{10}} = 1.414$$

$$\sigma^2 = \text{variance} = \frac{\Sigma x^2}{N} = \frac{960}{10} = 96.0$$

$$\sigma = \text{standard deviation} = \sqrt{\sigma^2} = \sqrt{96} = 9.798$$

$$\text{or } \sigma = \sqrt{\frac{\Sigma x^2}{N}} = \sqrt{\frac{960}{10}} = 9.798$$

FIGURE A-2   The normal distribution of IQ scores

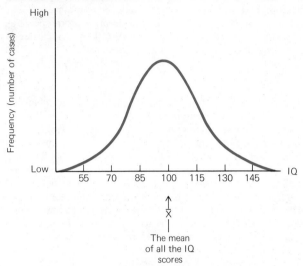

FIGURE A-3   The normal distribution divided into standard deviation units

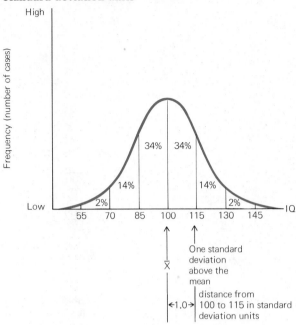

impose. Moreover, it is bell-shaped; scores near the mean are most frequent, and frequency drops off smoothly as we move to the extremes. The normal distribution is the most important distribution in statistics because so many psychological factors are "normally distributed" in the population. IQ is a good example. IQ is normally distributed with a mean of 100 and a standard deviation of 15. This means that if we obtained IQ scores for everybody and took the mean of them, it would be 100, and the standard deviation would be 15. Furthermore, if we drew a graph representing the frequency of each of the possible IQ scores, it would be bell-shaped—normal—and would look like the one in Figure A-2.

If we know that a characteristic is normally distributed and if we know the mean and the standard deviation, we can use the theoretical properties of the normal distribution to deduce more information about the characteristic. We can do this because in any normal distribution the standard deviation can be used to divide the distribution into sections containing fixed percentages of the cases. Figure A-3 shows a normal distribution divided up in this way—again we have used IQ scores. The fixed percentages are printed in the various sections of the frequency distribution. For example, about 34 percent of the people lie between the mean and 115—that is, 34 percent of the people have IQs between 100 and 115. Because the standard deviation is 15, we can see that a score of 115 is one standard deviation above the mean ($115 - 100 = 15 =$ the standard deviation). Remember that the standard deviation is a distance measure, so the "distance" from 115 to the mean of 100 is one standard deviation unit. Two standard deviation units above the mean would be the distance up to 130, and three units would be to 145. Of course, we can go in the other direction also, below the mean. One unit below would be an IQ of 85, two units of standard deviation distance would be 70, and three units would be 55. From three standard deviation units *below* the mean on up to three units *above* the mean (from 55 up to 145), we cover essentially all the

scores. Very few people score below 55 or above 145. So the range of scores, as measured in standard deviation units, goes from a low of -3 to a high of $+3$. It is very convenient to convert the IQ scores into standard deviation scores, called *z scores.*

$$z = \frac{X - \overline{X}}{\sigma}$$

A major advantage of the z score is that it can be used as a common yardstick for all tests. This allows you to compare scores on different tests. For example, suppose you receive an 80 on an English test, which has a mean $= 70$ and $\sigma = 10$. But on your psychology test, you got a 90 where the mean was 80 and σ was 10. Which test did you do better on? These tests are not immediately comparable; but, if you change your score on each test into a z score, you will discover that you did equally well on both tests.

Figure A-4 again shows the IQ normal distribution, but this time we have two horizontal axes displayed. The upper one shows IQ scores and the lower one shows standard deviation scores, or z scores. Thus you can see that an IQ score of 115 is one standard deviation above the mean, so the z score corresponding to 115 is $+1.0$. If your friend tells you that his z score in IQ is $+2.0$, you can see that he has an IQ of 130. If he tells you that his z score is $+4.0$, he is either very brilliant or he is pulling your leg. Note that the mean of the z scores will always be equal to zero.

From Figure A-4, suppose we ask you to figure out what percentage of the people have IQs between 85 and 115, which is the same as asking how many people have z scores between -1.0 and $+1.0$. The answer is 68 percent;

FIGURE A-4 **The normal distribution and z scores**

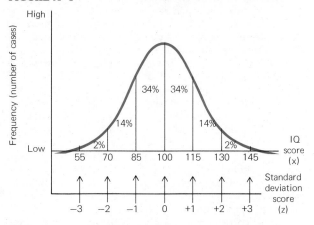

FIGURE A-5 **The normal distribution of waist size in American men (hypothetical)**

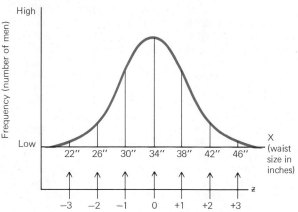

34 percent between 85 and 100, and another 34 percent between 100 and 115.

An important thing to remember is that these percentages and the z score procedure apply to *any* normal distribution, not just the IQ distribution. The only difference between the IQ distribution and any other normal distribution is that they probably have different means and different standard deviations. But if you know that something has a normal distribution and if you know the mean and standard deviation of it, you can set up a figure like the one in Figure A-4.

Suppose, for example, that we told you that waist size in American men is normally distributed with a mean of 34 inches and a standard deviation of 4. You could now set up a normal frequency distribution, as in Figure A-5. The waist size scores run from a low of 22 inches (z score of −3; 22 is three standard-deviation units *below* the mean) up to a high of 46 (z score of +3); 3 units *above* the mean. Now can you fill in the percentages and answer the following questions:

1. What percentage of men have waist sizes less than 30 inches?
2. What percentage of men have waist sizes greater than 38?
3. If Joe's waist size is 47, is he unusual?
4. If we randomly selected one man from the American population, what is the probability (how likely is it?) that his waist size is equal to or greater than 38?

This last question brings us to the notion of probability. **Probability** refers to the *proportion of cases that fit a certain description.* In general, the probability of A (the likelihood that a randomly drawn object will be an A object) is equal to the number of A objects divided by the total number of all possible objects. The number of A objects divided by the total number of objects is, of course, the proportion of objects that *are* A, so the probability is just a proportion.

Suppose that an A is someone with a waist size equal to or greater than 38. To find the probability of selecting an A-man at random from the population, we have to know what proportion of all men are A-men. Figure A-5 tells us

that 14 percent of the men have waist sizes between 38 and 42 inches and an additional 2 percent are greater than 42, so we add 14 percent and 2 percent and we see that 16 percent of the men are A-men. In proportion terms, this becomes .16 (we move the decimal point two places to the left to translate a percentage into a proportion). In summary, the probability of selecting a man with a waist size equal to or greater than 38 = .16. This means that 16 out of every 100 selections would yield a man who fits this description.

Suppose that scores on an anxiety scale are normally distributed in the population of all American people with a mean of 50 and a standard deviation of 10. You should be able to calculate the probability that a randomly drawn person has an anxiety score that is equal to or *less* than 40. Can you do it?

Correlation

The final descriptive statistic to be discussed is the **correlation coefficient,** which was introduced in Chapter 1. The correlation coefficient does not describe a single set of scores as the mean or standard deviation does. Instead, it describes the degree of relationship between two sets of scores. It is basically a measure of the degree to which the two sets of scores vary together, or *covary.* Scores can vary together in one of two ways: (1) a *positive covariation,* in which high scores in one set tend to go with high scores in the other set (and low scores go with low scores), or (2) *negative covariation,* in which high scores in one set tend to go with *low* scores in the other set (and low scores go with high scores). When there is a positive covariation, we say the two sets are *positively* or *directly correlated,* and we say they are *negatively, indirectly,* or *inversely correlated* when there is a negative covariation. A common example of positive correlation is the relationship between height and weight — the taller you are the more you tend to weigh. A common example of negative correlation might be the relationship between the amount of alcohol a person has drunk in an evening and ability to drive an automobile. The more the person has drunk, the lower the ability to drive.

Note that we used "tend to go with." Correlations are almost never perfect—not all tall people are particularly heavy, and not all short people are lightweights. Of course, there is the third possibility too, namely, *no correlation* between two sets of scores, or *zero correlation*. Thus, for example, we probably would expect there to be a zero correlation between your height and your ability to learn psychology. So two variables (two sets of scores on different measures) can be *positively* or *negatively correlated* or *not correlated at all*. And the degree of correlation can be great or little. What we need is a statistic that conveniently measures the degree and the direction (positive or negative) of the correlation between two variables. This is what the coefficient of correlation does for us.

Table A–7 shows the scores of 10 people on two tests. Each person took both a test of anxiety and a test of "happiness." The possible scores on each test ranged from 1 to 10, with 1 meaning low anxiety and 10 very high anxiety for the anxiety test. For the happiness test, 1 means a low degree of happiness and 10 means a high degree of happiness. Intuitively we would expect a negative correlation between the two variables of anxiety and happiness; the happier you are, the less should be your anxiety, and vice versa.

For convenience we arranged the anxiety scores in order in Table A–7. What this does is to cause the happiness scores to fall in *perfect reverse order*. In other words, it is obvious in this table that there is a perfect negative correlation between anxiety and happiness. This is best displayed by making a *scatter plot* of the data, which we have done in Figure A–6. Here the horizontal axis is the anxiety score, and the vertical axis is the happiness score. Each person is represented by a point on the graph that locates him or her on the two tests. For example, Clint had an anxiety score of 4 and a happiness score of 7. So we go over (to the right) to 4 on the anxiety scale and then up to 7 on the happiness scale, and we place a dot at that point to represent Clint on the graph. All 10 people are represented in the graph. You can

see that the 10 points all fall on a straight line, which means that the correlation is perfect. You can also see that the line slopes down to the right, and this means that the correlation is negative in direction—as you go up the anxiety scale the happiness scores go down.

As we have said, however, correlations are almost never perfect. This means that the points are likely to be scattered all over the graph, hence the term "scatter plot." The closer the points are to lying on a straight line, the higher the degree of correlation. So the procedure is to make a scatter plot and then try to draw a straight line that best fits the points in the plot. If all the points are close to or on this *line of best fit*, then the correlation is high. If the points are widely scattered and not close to any line you could draw, then the correlation is zero or close to it. Finally, if the line of best fit slopes downward to the right, then the correlation is negative, as in Figure A–6. If the line slopes upward to the right, the correlation is positive. Figure A–7 shows three scatter plots. In panel A the two variables in question are highly negatively correlated: the points are all pretty close to the straight line, which slopes downward to the right. In panel B we have the case of a high positive correlation; the points are again all pretty close to the line, but this time the line slopes upward to the right. In panel C there is no correlation; the points are scattered all over, and there is no line that fits them very well.

The *Pearson product moment correlation coefficient* (symbolized r_{XY}) is the most often used of several measures of correlation. It can take on any numerical value from -1.0 through 0.0 up to $+1.0$. A perfect negative product moment correlation, as in Table A–7, is -1.0, and a perfect positive or direct correlation is $+1.0$. Correlations close to zero mean there is little or no relationship between the two variables,

TABLE A–7 The Correlation between Anxiety and Happiness

Name	Anxiety (X)	Happiness (Y)
Joan	1	10
Larry	2	9
Ralph	3	8
Clint	4	7
Sue	5	6
Sharon	6	5
Sam	7	4
Bonnie	8	3
Marsha	9	2
Harry	10	1

Here we have arranged the anxiety scores in order and we see that this results in the happiness scores being arranged in *perfect reverse order*. This is a perfect negative correlation. The coefficient of correlation would be -1.0.

FIGURE A–6 "Scatter plot" of the data from Table A–7, relating anxiety to happiness

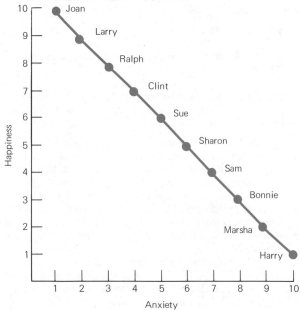

FIGURE A-7 **Scatter plots of three correlations**

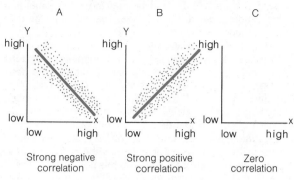

A

Strong negative
correlation

B

Strong positive
correlation

C

Zero
correlation

X and Y. The value of the correlation between 0.0 and 1 (ignoring the sign) represents the degree of relationship. The sign of the correlation (positive or negative) does not tell you the degree of the correlation, only the direction. Thus a negative correlation of −.77 is just as strong a correlation as is a positive correlation of +.77; the only difference is the direction. Table A–8 shows the steps for calculating the Pearson product moment correlation coefficient in case you want to see exactly how it is done.

In all the examples so far, we have been correlating the scores of a person on two different tests. It does not have to be that way. We might correlate the scores of a person on the same test taken at two different times. Then we would be asking if the test is reliable — that is, does a person tend to score about the same on the test if he takes it on two different occasions? If it is a good test, it should be reliable (see Chapter 1 and Appendix C). Another common use of correlation is to determine the validity of a test — does the test measure what it is supposed to measure? If we make up a test of intelligence, we would hope that it would correlate

positively with performance in school. If it did, it would help us argue that our test really did measure intelligence. (See Chapter 1 and Appendix C for a discussion of validity.)

Regression

One important use of the correlational statistics is in a procedure called **regression.** A correlation coefficient tells us the degree to which a person's score on both of two tests are related. Suppose we try to predict your weight. We have no idea what to guess, because about all we know about you is that you are reading this book. If we knew that the average person reading this book weighs 142 pounds, then that is what we would have to guess, and we would make the same guess for every reader. But if we knew your height, and we also knew the correlation between weight and height, then we could make a much more accurate guess about your weight. For example, if we knew that you were 6 feet, 6 inches tall, we would hardly guess 142 pounds. Likewise, if we knew you were 4 feet, 2 inches, 142 pounds would also be an inappropriate guess. We would adjust our weight guess according to what we know about your height. Regression is a fancy, complex, but accurate way of making this adjustment.

Finally, a moment's thought should convince you that the higher the correlation (in either the positive or negative direction), the better job we can do at predicting your weight — the closer we will come to your true weight. If the correlation between the two variables is perfect (+1.0 or −1.0), we can predict perfectly the value of one of the variables if we know the value of the other. But because correlations are almost never perfect, our predictions are somewhat off, and the lower the correlation, the greater the likely error.

Regression is used in many different settings. Most of you probably took the College Board examinations for getting into college. From past research we know there is a positive correlation between your score on the College Boards and your success in college. Therefore, the College Board

TABLE A–8 **Calculating the Pearson Product Moment Correlation Coefficient**

Name	Anxiety (X)	X^2	Happiness (Y)	Y^2	XY (X times Y)
John	2	4	9	81	18
Ralph	5	25	6	36	30
Mary	9	81	4	16	36
Sue	1	1	3	9	3
Jan	3	9	2	4	6
Harvey	7	49	2	4	14
Jane	8	64	4	16	32
Joanne	6	36	5	25	30
N = 8 people	$\Sigma X = 41$	$\Sigma X^2 = 269$	$\Sigma Y = 35$	$\Sigma Y^2 = 191$	$\Sigma XY = 169$

$$r_{XY} \text{ (the correlation between X and Y)} = \frac{N\Sigma XY - (\Sigma X)(\Sigma Y)}{\sqrt{[N\Sigma X^2 - (\Sigma X)^2][N\Sigma Y^2 - (\Sigma Y)^2]}}$$

For these data: $r_{\text{ANXIETY}\cdot\text{HAPPINESS}} = \dfrac{(8)(169) - (41)(35)}{\sqrt{[(8)(269) - (41)^2][(8)(191) - (35)^2]}} = \dfrac{1352 - 1435}{\sqrt{(2152 - 1681)(1528 - 1225)}}$

$$= \frac{-83}{\sqrt{(471)(303)}} = \frac{-83}{\sqrt{142713}} = \frac{-83}{377.77} = -.219$$

tests can now be given to college applicants, and on the basis of their scores, we can predict approximately how a person will do in college. These predictions are used to help decide whom to admit.

Similar procedures are used to process applications for law school, medical school, graduate school, or a job. Using regression techniques, the psychologist predicts the applicant's success on the job or in school, and these predictions are used to determine whether or not to hire or admit the applicant. It is a serious business, and the decisions made on this basis are extremely important to the people involved.

The simplest type of regression (technically known as *linear regression*) involves solving a mathematical equation for a straight line (hence the term "linear"), a line that "fits" the data. What we are looking for is the line that comes closest to the most points on a scatter diagram (see Figure A-8). Figure A-8 shows two different scatter plots relating scores on the College Boards (SAT scores) to grade-point average in college (GPA). Each point in the diagram represents one student; by drawing a line straight down to the

FIGURE A-8 Scatter plots for high (A) and low (B) degrees of relationship between college GPAs and SAT scores. In the regression procedure, we try to predict what a person's score on one test will be using his or her score on another test as a basis.

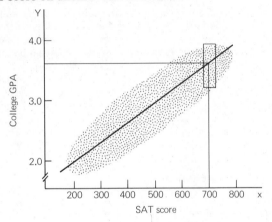

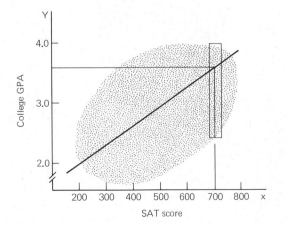

X axis from any point (any particular student), we can tell the student's SAT score, and by drawing a horizontal line from the point over to the Y axis we can tell the student's GPA in college.

Once we have data relating SAT scores and college GPAs we can proceed to use regression to make predictions for future students. First we solve the equation for the best-fitting straight line (known as the *regression line*), a complex procedure we won't describe here. Then we draw the line on the scatter plot. Now we can use the line as a way to predict GPA given a student's SAT score. For example, consider a student who scores 700 on the SAT; we draw a vertical line up from 700 until it intersects the regression line, then we draw a horizontal line from this point over to the Y axis and read off the predicted GPA at the point of intersection. In this case we come up with a prediction of 3.6 for the student's GPA.

This procedure will not give us perfect predictions, as you should be able to see from Figure A-8. Not all students scoring 700 had 3.6 averages in college; some were higher than 3.6 and some lower. As we have said, the major factor in determining the accuracy of our predictions will be the degree of correlation between the two variables. If the variables are highly correlated, as depicted in panel (A), all the points will cluster close to the regression line, and none of the predictions are likely to be far off. In fact, if the correlation were perfect, all the points would be right on the line, and there would be no error. (All students with 700 SATs would get 3.6 GPAs). On the other hand, with low correlations the points will be widely scattered, and many of them will be a long way from the regression line, as depicted in panel (B) of Figure A-8. In such a case our predictions can be way off. Take a look at the students who scored around 700 on the SATs in the two panels; these points are boxed in on the graphs. In the upper panel, which depicts a high correlation, you can see that all the students ended up with high college GPAs, and all were fairly close to 3.6, the average we would predict using the regression line. In contrast, in the lower panel the students with 700 on the SATs varied widely in their GPAs, with some as low as 2.2 and others as high as 3.95. Regression would have predicted 3.6 for all of them, and it would have been way off on many of the predictions. The lower the correlation between the two variables, the less precision we have in predicting using regression. In fact, if the correlation drops to zero, regression is useless—we might as well just guess. Given some degree of correlation, however, we can do better using regression than by simply guessing, and the higher the correlation, the better our guesses will be.

Inferential Statistics

Inferential statistics are used to make inferences from data, to draw conclusions, and to test our hypotheses. Two of the basic concepts in inferential statistics are *estimation* and *hypothesis testing*.

Estimation

One use of inferential statistics is to make estimates of the actual value of some population characteristic. Suppose, for example, we wanted to know how intelligent Americans are on the average. We *could* test all 220 million Americans and compute a mean. But it would be handy to have a shortcut method, even though it is just an estimate.

In order to estimate the mean and standard deviation of a population, we take a *sample* of the population and test the members of the sample. We then compute the statistics on the sample scores and use these statistics to estimate what the mean and standard deviation would be if we *could* test every member of the population. We might sample 200 Americans and use their scores to estimate what the whole population is like. Obviously, this is what public opinion polls and the TV rating services do.

It is important to make sure that the sample is *representative* of the population. This is usually done by making the sample a random selection from all possible members of the population. **Random sampling** means that everyone in the specified population has the same chance of being in the sample. It would not be a fair sample for estimating American intelligence if we measured only white female citizens of La Mirada, California. The second factor in sampling is sample size. The larger the sample, the more accurate the estimates. If you randomly chose one person from the phone book, scheduled him or her for an IQ test, got a score, and then estimated that this IQ score was the mean IQ for all Americans, you would almost certainly be off the mark. More than one score is needed. But how many should there be in the sample? The amazing thing about sampling is that the size of the sample necessary to get a pretty accurate idea of the population is much smaller than you might guess. A sample of 30 or 40 Americans out of the 220 million, if properly drawn, would give a very accurate estimate of the entire population. There are ways of estimating how big a sample you need for a given level of accuracy. Of course, if the sample is not properly drawn, so that it is not representative, then increasing the sample size would not help our estimation much at all.

Hypothesis Testing

When we set out to do an experiment in psychology we always begin with a hypothesis. For our brief discussion we will use the example of a psychologist who wants to know if Zappo cereal increases intelligence in people who eat it. The working hypothesis is: "People who eat Zappo will show an increase in IQ compared with people who eat Brand X." The psychologist gets 20 subjects to volunteer for the experiment and randomly assigns them to one of two groups, 10 per group. The random assignment is designed to create two groups that are equal in average IQ at the start of the experiment, scoring 100 points on the average. The Zappo group eats Zappo for one year and the Brand X group eats Brand X for one year. At the end of this time the psychologist tests all 20 subjects on intelligence and finds that the mean IQ of Zappo eaters is 105 and the mean IQ of Brand X eaters is 100. What can the psychologist conclude or infer about the initial hypothesis? If the Zappo group and the Brand X group were very close—say 99.5 and 100.1 were the means—he or she would probably conclude that Zappo does not increase intelligence. If they were very far apart— say 125 for Zappo eaters and 75 for Brand X eaters—the conclusion is that eating Zappo increases intelligence. But

what do we conclude about results that fall between these extremes?

There has to be an objective way to decide whether the psychologist's hypothesis can be accepted or not. We cannot leave it up to intuition, especially not the intuition of the owner of Zappo Cereal Company. This is where hypothesis-testing statistics come into play. There are many different kinds of these statistics. Here we will consider only one, the *t test,* which is probably the most common statistical technique for hypothesis testing.

We want to decide if the difference between 100 (the mean of the Brand X eaters) and 105 (the mean of the Zappo eaters) is a real difference. Is it a *significant difference?* A difference is said to be significant if it is very unlikely that it would happen by chance, that is, if the chance probability is small for a difference this large. The difference between Zappo and Brand X means is 5.0 IQ points. We say the *mean difference* is 5.0 (105 − 100 = 5.0). For a moment, let's assume that Zappo has no effect on intelligence. This is called the null hypothesis (remember that the psychologist's working hypothesis was that Zappo increases IQ). What we need to know is *if the null hypothesis is true* (Zappo does not affect IQ), what is the probability that the two samples would differ by 5 IQ points or more? If Zappo is not different from Brand X, then any difference we find between our two groups is just a chance difference. After all, we would not expect two random groups of 10 people to have exactly the same means either. Sample means will differ, and every once in a while there will be a difference of 5 or more IQ points just by chance alone, with no help from Zappo. The question is: How often will we get a difference this large? Or what is the probability of the difference occurring by chance alone?

In order to answer this question we must know not only the mean values but also the standard deviations in the two samples. We have to know how much variability there is in the IQ scores. To understand this, look at the three panels in Figure A–9. Each panel shows two frequency distributions, one for a Zappo group and one for a Brand X group. Note that in each panel the mean of the Zappo group is 105 and the mean of the Brand X group is 100. But the three panels display quite different pictures when it comes to IQ variability. In the top panel the variability is very small (all Zappo eaters score about the same, near 105, and Brand X eaters are all close to 100), and the two distributions do not overlap at all (all Zappo eaters have higher IQs than all Brand X eaters). In this case, it looks as though the 5-point difference between the means is a significant one.

In the middle panel the IQ scores are highly variable (Zappo eaters do not all score near the mean of 105, and Brand X scores do not cluster close to 100). This means that there is a lot of overlap in the two distributions. Some Zappo eaters are lower in IQ than some Brand X eaters, and some Brand X eaters are higher in IQ than some Zappo eaters. In fact, there is so much overlap in the two distributions that we would tend to bet that the difference between 100 and 105 (the two means) is just a chance difference. The two distributions look almost identical. In neither the top nor the middle panel would we need a statistical test to help us decide whether or not to accept the null hypothesis.

FIGURE A-9 Three experimental outcomes differing in variability and overlap, but each with the same mean (100 and 105) and the same mean difference (105–100)

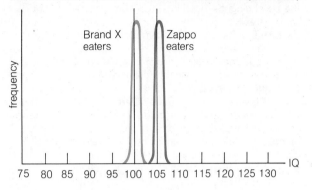

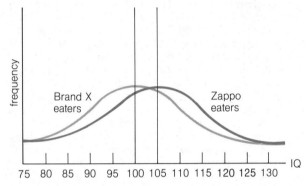

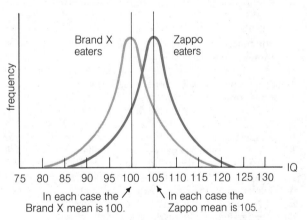

In each case the ↗ ↖ In each case the
Brand X mean is 100.   Zappo mean is 105.

difference. In the top panel the difference is 5 units, but the variability is very small. So if we take 5 and divide it by this very small variability number, we will get a large number for an answer. The t ratio will be large, and we will declare the difference to be significant. In the middle panel the same difference between means, 5, will be divided by a very large variability number to give us a t ratio that will be very small. We declare the difference insignificant. In the bottom panel we have the borderline case, where we will divide 5 by a moderate variability estimate, meaning the t value obtained will be moderately large. What do we conclude? Fortunately for us, statisticians have prepared tables of the probability of

---

Scientists Only 95% Sure Cyclamate Safe

WASHINGTON — The best brains in science cannot answer the question of whether the artificial sweetener cyclamate is totally free of cancer risk, says a blue-ribbon panel that spent six months studying the problem for the government.

The committee concluded . . . that it could say with only 95 per cent probability that cyclamate, 30 to 50 times sweeter than sugar, doesn't cause cancer. The panel said there remains a nagging doubt over whether it may be a weak carcinogen.

The small degree of uncertainty seems certain to touch off a debate over what degree of safety should be required by government regulators.

The scientific panel said that not even a proposed five-year experiment costing $8 million to $10 million and using 52,000 rats and hamsters could establish, with absolute certainty, that the government was wrong in 1969 when it banned the chemical from foods and drugs.

"Science today is just not good enough to answer this question to everyone's satisfaction," said the chairman, Dr. Arnold L. Brown of Mayo Medical School. . . .

One Could Get By

Noting the relatively limited sensitivity of current scientific methods, the committee concluded, "Although no chemical can be proven unequivocally to lack carcinogenicity with these techniques, ones with a significant carcinogenic hazard for humans could escape detection" . . . .

The Denver Post
January 14, 1976

Contrary to Dr. Brown's statement, it may be more a matter of statistics than of scientific methods. As long as there is variability in the data and some overlap in the distribution of scores from an experimental group which used cyclamates and a control group (no cyclamates), there will be some degree of uncertainty about the effects of the experimental manipulation. Just as in the Zappo example, we need a way to measure the probability of an effect. In most experiments, being 95 percent sure of the hypothesis is an acceptable probability level. Where human health is concerned, we demand higher standards.

Situations like those depicted in the top panel are very rare indeed. Unfortunately, the middle panel is a more frequent outcome of an experiment—the experiment is a flop! The bottom panel represents the most common outcome of all, and the only one of the three in which the conclusion is unclear. The two distributions overlap somewhat, much more than in the top panel but much less than in the middle panel. There is a moderate amount of variability. Do we conclude that the 105 to 100 mean difference is a real one or not? Is there a significant difference between the means?

The t test is basically a ratio. It is the *ratio* of the *mean difference to an estimate* of the *variability* involved in this

various values of t happening by chance. We compute the t ratio in our experiment and then look it up in the statistical tables to find the chance probability of a t as large as the one we found. If the table tells us that our t ratio is unlikely to happen by chance, we conclude that what we have is not a chance effect but a real difference. Conventionally, this probability is .05. This means that if our obtained t ratio is likely to happen only 5 percent of the time or less by chance, then the odds are that this is *not* one of those times. The odds are that it is not a chance effect but a real one, which is called a significant effect.

The null hypothesis says, "There is no difference between Zappo and Brand X," and if we obtain a significant t ratio we infer or conclude that the null hypothesis is wrong. Statistical inference is basically a procedure for drawing conclusions about the null hypothesis. What the t test procedure allows us to do is to reject the null hypothesis when we get a t ratio that is very unlikely to occur by chance. If we set up the null hypothesis such that it is the opposite of our working hypothesis (Zappo improves IQ), then rejection of the null hypothesis will be evidence in support of our working hypothesis.

We will not go into the details of actually calculating a t ratio. You can find the information in any elementary statistics book (for example, Wike, 1971). Simply remember

"I'm sorry, but you've been rejected at the .05 level."

APA Monitor, September–October 1973. Copyright 1973 by the American Psychological Association. Reprinted by permission.

Principles of statistical decision theory have wide application.

that when an experiment is done, the results will always indicate some differences between the conditions in the study. The t test as well as many other types of inferential statistics are used to help the experimenter decide if the differences are large enough, relative to the variability, to allow rejection of the null hypothesis and support for the working hypothesis.

This reasoning applies to the correlation coefficient as well as to the difference between two means. If we get two sets of numbers by randomly drawing them out of a hat and correlate them, the correlation will almost never be exactly zero, even though the numbers are clearly unrelated (we drew them by chance from a hat). Suppose the correlation is very high, say, .80. We would probably conclude that the correlation is significant. Suppose it is very low or close to zero, say −.07; obviously we would say there is no significant relationship or correlation. But what if it is .30 or −.42 or −.28? Where do we draw the line and say that it is highly unlikely that a correlation this high would happen by chance? At what point can we infer a real relationship between the two variables? Again, there are procedures in inferential statistics that decide objectively whether the correlation is significant or not. The null hypothesis would be that the correlation is zero, and we would then test this hypothesis to see whether it can be rejected.

Analysis of Quasi-Experiments

As you will remember from Chapter 1, it is often not possible for a researcher to control all variables that might influence his or her data. In many cases, for example, we can't assign subjects randomly to experimental conditions. In other cases, it will not be possible to manipulate, in the usual sense, one or more independent variables. When this is the case, we won't be able to make absolute cause-effect conclusions from the data. There will always be some plausible alternative explanations based on factors we were unable to control. Quasi-experimentation tries to set a study up so that *most major* alternative explanations (but unfortunately, not all) can be ruled out. But quasi-experiments sometimes present some special problems for statistical analysis.

A good example of a design for a quasi-experiment is what is known as the interrupted time-series design. Time-series means that the experimenter takes multiple measurements of target behavior over time. Interrupted means that at some point a treatment or a variable is introduced. The experimenter usually has no control of the variable or when it is introduced. The idea of the study is to find out if the treatment has any effect on the target behavior. If you did expect an effect, the after-treatment measures should look different from the before-treatment measures.

An example of this kind of design might be to determine if the government's ban on television and radio commercials for tobacco companies in 1976 have any effect on the purchase of cigarettes. You go to the sales records of major tobacco companies and make measurements yearly before and after the introduction of this ban and plot the series as a function of time. By plotting the data for cigarette consumption over an extended period of time, you can get a better understanding of what might be going on during any specific period of time. Look at Figure A–10 where

FIGURE A-10 Extended time-series data plotted in four hypothetical situations

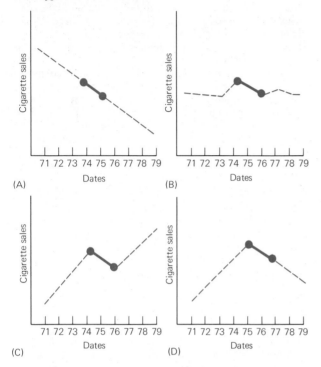

extended time-series data are plotted in four hypothetical outcomes. Note that in each case, there is a significant drop in consumption between 1975 and 1976. Taken out of the time context, this drop between 1975 and 1976 might be misperceived as being caused by the ban on TV advertising of cigarettes. But put into the extended time context, a totally different conclusion might be reached. Figure A–10 shows four different possibilities. In panel A, for example, the extended time-series data points show clearly that consumption was steadily dropping for several years, so the drop between 1975 and 1976 is just a continuation of an ongoing trend and is hardly likely a result of the TV ban. Of the four possibilities shown in Figure A–10, only panel D offers any support for the conclusion that a reduction in sales is attributable to the change in advertising policy.

The extended time series is important in ruling out other factors that might contribute to the trend in the data. It is still not perfect, of course, for we don't have good control over all variables that might operate in the situation. Nonetheless, the data presented in this way are definitely more convincingly in favor of our hypotheses than a simple pre- and post-test comparison.

Advanced Statistical Techniques Commonly Used in Psychology

Analysis of Variance
The t test is used when testing the difference between two groups and only two groups. But most experiments have more than two groups, and the t test is not used in such cases. A complex statistical procedure called the *analysis of variance* is used instead. As the name implies, the variance in the data is analyzed and compared to the mean differences in much the same way as in a t test. In fact, the analysis of variance procedure reduces to a t test when there are only two groups. The test in analysis of variance is known as the *F test*, named after the famous English statistician R. A. Fisher. Basically, the procedure is just like that for the t test. It allows the experimenter to make inferences or conclusions about the differences among a set of means. It is a very common technique now, so you are likely to encounter the F test if you read any modern psychology journal.

Factor Analysis
Factor analysis is a highly sophisticated correlational procedure that is used to identify the basic factors underlying a psychological phenomenon. The technique boils down to finding clusters of tests that correlate with one another. Suppose we administer the following six tests to 100 young men: (1) vocabulary, (2) ability to play basketball, (3) ability to write an essay on philosophy, (4) speed at running the 100-yard dash, (5) ability to understand statistics, and (6) ability to climb trees. Each man takes all six tests, and then we intercorrelate the tests. We correlate test 1 with 2, 1 with 3, 1 with 4, and so on. Suppose we find that tests 1, 3, and 5 correlate highly with one another and that 2, 4, and 6 correlate highly with one another, but 1, 3, and 5 do not correlate at all with 2, 4, and 6. Why would this be the case? Look at the tests; it is easy to see that 1, 3, and 5 all involve thinking or knowledge—they all involve "mental ability." On the other hand, 2, 4, and 6 all involve physical skill. So it probably is the case that 1, 3, and 5 are all measuring something in common, which we might call Factor A. Wouldn't you guess that Factor A has something to do with intelligence? Tests 2, 4, and 6 also seem to be measuring something in common. We call it Factor B. Because 1, 3, and 5 do not correlate with 2, 4, and 6, we conclude that Factor A, which we now have decided to call intelligence, is not the same thing as Factor B. Looking at tests 2, 4, and 6, we decide to call Factor B "athletic ability."

In short, we have isolated two factors that are involved in performance on our 6 tests; one we call "intelligence" and one we call "athletic ability." Factor analysis is basically a correlational technique that allows us to analyze performance on a large number of tests into factors by isolating clusters of tests (where the clustering is not as obvious as it is in the foregoing example). Correlations are high within a cluster but low between clusters. We assume that the clusters then "represent" and measure psychological factors.

This technique has been used extensively in two areas of psychology, intelligence testing and personality assessment (see Appendix C). Intelligence consists of many factors, and so does personality. With factor analysis we can identify these factors and hope to learn from them what intelligence and personality are.

Another example of the application of factor analysis which may be of more direct relevance to you concerns the use of questionnaires to evaluate college teachers. In the typical case you as the student are asked to answer a large number of questions about your reactions to the class and the instructor. Questions such as "Was the professor well organized?" and "Was the grading system fair?" are typical of teacher-evaluation questionnaires. What comes out of such evaluations is an enormous amount of "raw" data — lots of answers by lots of students to lots of questions. It may be difficult to measure teacher effectiveness from this array of answers. In fact, it is often difficult to tell what, if anything, the questionnaire is measuring. Factor analysis can help by reducing the data to factors, cutting down on the number of scores and helping to clarify what is being measured. For example, many of the questions may all be getting at the same general factor, so we can use factor analysis to pool the answers from similar questions and come out with a score for the professor on the overall factor.

Professor Peter Frey of Northwestern University has done factor analysis on students' ratings of their professors and concludes, as many had suspected, that the typical questionnaire is really measuring only two factors: (1) the skill of the professor in teaching and (2) the rapport the professor establishes with the class. Think about your own professors and you will probably agree that these are two fundamental and relatively independent factors in teaching. You probably have had professors with high skill but very low class rapport, high rapport and low skill, and variations in between. Thus factor analysis can help greatly in the analysis of complex situations, reducing massive amounts of data down to a small set of basic factors.

This example points up another very important use of the factor analysis technique, namely, in test construction. Investigators attempting to construct a psychological test to measure some aspect of behavior can begin by building a test containing a very large number of items designed "by intuition" to get at the desired behavior. After administering the large test to a large group of subjects, the results are factor analyzed, the factors are identified, and then the correlation between each item on the test and the factor (this is called *the factor loading* of the item) is determined. In this way the investigator can (1) identify the factor and (2) determine which of the items are the best measures of the factors. Those items with low factor loadings can be eliminated from the test, and the investigator ends up with a short, efficient test consisting of only those items that are the best measures of the factors. In the case of the test designed by Peter Frey to measure teacher effectiveness by student ratings, Frey was able to develop a test consisting of only seven questions which measured the teacher on the two factors he identified — skill and rapport. Factor analytic techniques are crucial tools in the field of test construction, a topic we take up in Appendix C.

B Neurons: The Building Blocks of the Nervous System

The human nervous system is by far the most complex component in the body. Nobody knows for sure, but it is estimated that the brain consists of at least 10 billion nerve cells, or **neurons,** each of which is directly connected, on the average, to some 200 to 1000 other nerve cells. Most nerve cells are present at birth, although many of the connections between individual neurons are formed later during development. Until late in the nineteenth century it was believed that all of the nerve cells formed one continuous network; later it became clear that the nervous system consists of individual nerves that are functionally connected by so-called synaptic junctions. The complex functions of the nervous system depend on the structure and physiology of individual nerve cells and their interconnections; these functions—receiving and transmitting information— are the subject matter of this Appendix.

Structural Properties of the Neuron

Neurons, like all other cells, must carry on all of those processes involved in the utilization of oxygen and the production of energy. In addition, however, nerve cells are specialized in the sense that they are excitable and that they transmit information. Excitability and the transmission of information involve two processes which are called *axonal conduction* and *synaptic transmission.* The means by which these processes take place depend on the special structural features of the neuron, as well as on the neuron's ability to alter its physical characteristics when given appropriate stimulation.

The Nerve Cell

Neurons contain most of the components found in other animal cells (see Figure B–1). The *nucleus* controls all aspects of cellular activity, and many other organelles ("little organs") maintain the structural and functional properties of the cells. For example, energy synthesis occurs in organelles that are known as *mitochondria,* and protein synthesis occurs on structures known as *ribosomes.* In addition, the neurons possess unique features; the most predominant of these are fiber extensions from the cell body. These include **dendrites,** which are generally quite short and numerous, and a single **axon.** The axon may divide into one or more branches, which are referred to as axon *collaterals.* The so-called nerves, which run throughout your body, are bundles of axons from many individual neurons. Cell division, a feature common to most other kinds of cells, does not occur in most adult nerve cells. Nerve cells lost for whatever reason are not replaced. Speculation has it that an average of 10,000 neurons die each day.

Axonal conduction originates at the *axon hillock,* the point at which the axon is connected to the nerve cell body. In some neurons the axon is covered by a sheath made of fatty material called *myelin.* This insulating myelin sheath is broken at short intervals, and the gaps are referred to as *nodes of Ranvier.* In some neurons the dendrites look virtually identical to axons and are difficult to distinguish. The most important difference between axons and dendrites is functional: axons conduct information away from the cell body, while dendrites conduct information toward the cell body. In a manner of speaking, one can think of dendrites as receiving stations and axons as transmitting stations.

As axons approach their destination—most typically these destinations are dendrites and cell bodies of other nerve cells or muscle cells or gland cells—they divide into many small branches called *telodendria.* These telodendria terminate in small swellings which are variously referred to as *synaptic boutons, axon terminals,* or *synaptic terminals.*

The Synapse

The **synapse** is a specialized region where one nerve cell makes "contact" with another nerve cell or with a muscle or gland. It is also that region where one nerve cell transmits information to another cell. A more or less typical synapse is illustrated in Figure B–2. In this figure you should note three features. First, the synapse includes a physical space that separates two cells (the two neurons do not actually touch each other). This space is referred to as the *synaptic space* or *synaptic cleft.* Second, the synaptic region includes many small organelles referred to as *synaptic vesicles.* Third, the synaptic region is rich in mitochondria.

The portion of the axon's synaptic membrane that lines the synaptic space on the side of the axon terminal is called the *presynaptic membrane,* because it is located before the synaptic cleft. Correspondingly, the neuron that contains this membrane is referred to as the *presynaptic neuron.* That portion of the cellular membrane of the neuron lining the opposite side of the synaptic space is termed the *postsynaptic* (after the synapse) *membrane,* and this neuron is called the *postsynaptic neuron.* Information transfer across the synaptic space, *synaptic transmission,* is a chemical process. It involves the release of chemical neurotransmitter molecules by the presynaptic membrane, molecules that then produce an effect on the postsynaptic membrane. The chemical neurotransmitter molecules are believed to be stored in the *synaptic vesicles.* Synaptic transmission is a process that requires energy, and for this reason the area of the synapse is richly supplied with mitochondria, the sites of energy metabolism in all cells.

Functional Properties of the Neuron

The Resting Membrane Potential

The neuron, like all living cells, possesses across its membrane an electrical potential called the *resting membrane potential.* This potential indicates that the cell is alive and functioning normally. It can be measured by means of a voltage measuring device such as a voltmeter. In making such a measurement, one lead from the voltmeter is placed outside the cell and the other lead, a fine wire called a microelectrode, is placed inside the cell. Such an arrangement is

FIGURE B-1   **The neuron**

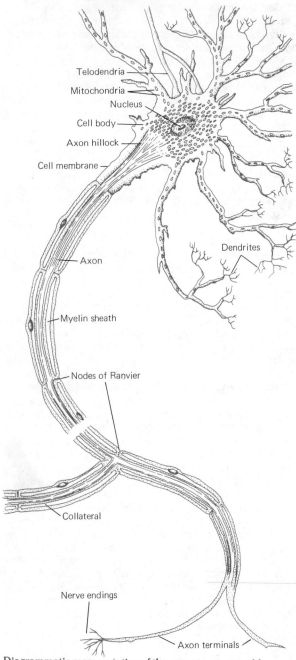

Diagrammatic representation of the common structural features of a neuron. The telodendria and axon terminals shown at the left of the cell body are extended from another neuron, not the one shown.

FIGURE B-2   **The synapse**

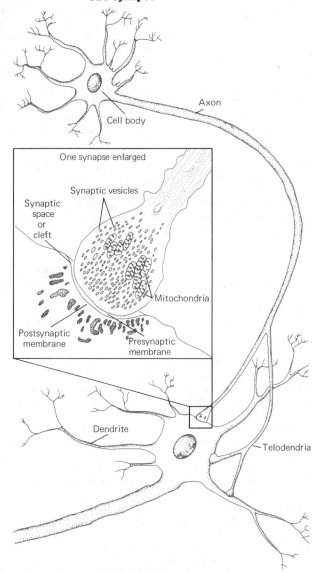

A single synaptic connection is enlarged to illustrate the structural details. The presynaptic neuron contains synaptic vesicles, which are the storage sites of neurotransmitter molecules.

illustrated diagrammatically in Figure B–3. When this is done a voltage difference between the inside and the outside of the cell is detected. In most nerve cells this voltage difference is of the order of 70 millivolts (thousandths of a volt), the inside of the nerve cell being electrically negative with respect to the outside. This potential difference exists only across the membrane of the cell, and this separation of charge, with relatively more negative charge inside the cell, is referred to as a state of *polarization*. In this respect the neuron can be compared to a battery cell. In this analogy the inside of the nerve cell would represent the negative pole, and the outside of the cell would represent the positive pole of the battery, with the voltage across the battery being approximately 70 millivolts. It is important to consider the mechanisms that generate and maintain the resting membrane potential before we consider perturbations in this potential, which occur when the cell becomes active. The

FIGURE B-3 Ion distribution

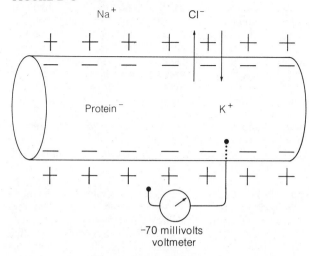

Na⁺ Cl[−]

Protein[−]   K⁺

−70 millivolts
voltmeter

The relative distribution of ions across the cell membrane of a neuron. The membrane is almost completely permeable to potassium (K⁺) and chloride (Cl⁻), but impermeable to sodium (Na⁺) and the large protein molecules. The result of the electrical and diffusional forces acting on these ions is a −70 millivolt resting membrane potential, negative inside relative to outside.

reasons for this are that the electrical activity that characterizes neuronal functioning can be understood in terms of alterations in the resting membrane potential.

In order to understand the details of the resting membrane potential it is first necessary to deal with several physical and chemical principles. A consideration of salt water will serve to illustrate several of these important concepts. When salt, a molecule consisting of two atoms—sodium (Na) and chloride (Cl)—is dissolved in water, it breaks up into two ions, one negative the other positive. An ion is any molecular fragment that possesses an electrical charge. Thus, when salt (NaCl) is dissolved in water it breaks up into sodium (Na⁺) and chloride (Cl⁻) ions. The positive and negative signs associated with the chemical symbols indicate that in a dissolved state these ions carry an electrical charge—positive in the case of sodium and negative in the case of chloride. Salt water contains many sodium and chloride ions.

Nerve cells are bathed in a fluid medium that resembles seawater rather closely. The fluid that surrounds nerve cells contains sodium (Na⁺), chloride (Cl⁻), potassium (K⁺), calcium (Ca⁺⁺), and magnesium (Mg⁺⁺) ions, as well as more complicated molecules such as negatively charged proteins. Simply stated, the resting membrane potential results from an unequal distribution of these charged particles across the cell membrane. The net effect of this unequal distribution of charged ions across the nerve membrane is a 70-millivolt potential difference.

This unequal distribution of charged ions across the nerve cell membrane results from the fact that the membrane itself is *semipermeable*, which means that it allows certain ions, for example, potassium and chloride, to pass

through it; other ions, for example, sodium, cannot pass through the membrane readily. Given a semipermeable membrane, the unequal distribution of ions across the membrane can be understood in terms of two physical-chemical principles called *diffusion* and the *attraction of charged particles*, respectively. The first of these principles, diffusion, states that substances in solution will tend to move from a region of higher concentration to one of lower concentration. The second principle determining the distribution of ions across the membrane is their electrical charge, unlike-charged particles attracting each other and like-charged particles repelling each other.

Let us now consider the situation with respect to each of the ions important in establishing the resting membrane potential. The membrane is totally impermeable to the large, negatively charged proteins; consequently, these are trapped inside the nerve cell (see Figure B-3). Similarly, the nerve cell membrane, when at rest, is impermeable to positively charged sodium (Na⁺) ions, which are therefore concentrated outside the cell. However, the membrane is almost completely permeable to potassium (K⁺) ions; these ions pass into the cell attracted by the negatively charged protein molecules, a movement assisted by their repulsion by the positively charged sodium (Na⁺) ions on the outside of the membrane. Chloride ions are also free to move across the membrane; however, they tend to migrate out of the nerve cell because they are attracted by the positively charged Na⁺ ions outside and repulsed by the negatively charged proteins inside. In keeping with the principle of diffusion, however, some chloride ions move into the cell where chloride is less concentrated, and some potassium moves out of the cell where it is less concentrated. The net effect is a slight excess of negatively charged particles inside the cell, which produces a −70-millivolt resting membrane potential, negative inside relative to outside.

The Action Potential

The **action potential** is the means by which the neuron conducts information along the axon to some destination within, or outside, the central nervous system. The action potential is a brief reversal of the resting membrane potential. It originates at the axon hillock, and it is a response to stimulus inputs to the neuron. The action potential travels down the length of the axon, finally invading the region of the telodendria and axon terminals. Here the action potential initiates those processes that result in synaptic transmission—specifically, it triggers the release of chemical neurotransmitter substances. Thus, action potentials are means of conducting information along the length of a single neuron; the action potentials do not cross the synaptic cleft.

An action potential is characterized by an initial *depolarization*, that is, a movement toward zero of the resting membrane potential. This so-called rising phase of the action potential continues past zero until a value of +40 millivolts is reached, positive inside relative to the outside of the nerve cell. Thus, the action potential is a clear reversal of the resting membrane potential. An action potential is initiated when some stimulus changes the characteristics of the nerve membrane, rendering it permeable to positively charged ions. Specifically, an action potential is initiated when the membrane becomes permeable to sodium; Na⁺ now rushes into the cell.

Following this +40-millivolt peak, the voltage across the membrane begins to fall. This is brought about because potassium ions rush out of the cell. The voltage across the membrane begins to fall until it reaches a value slightly greater than its original resting value, approximately −75 millivolts, negative inside relative to outside. After a brief period the membrane returns to its normal value. The period immediately following the firing of the action potential is known as the **refractory period** because it is difficult to fire the neuron again during this period of time.

Once an action potential has been initiated in the region of the axon hillock it will continue to travel down the length of the nerve fiber. One can think of this somewhat as a wave that travels across water. However—and this is important—unlike a wave, the action potential maintains its original amplitude, shape, and speed for the entire length of the axon, because the action potential is generated anew at each stage of the process. This is referred to as the *all-or-none principle* of axonal conduction. The action potential travels down the entire length of the axon without changing any of its characteristics, somewhat like a burning fuse.

The mechanisms thought to be involved in the propagation or spread of an action potential are really quite simple; they are illustrated diagrammatically in Figure B–4. The initial rising phase of the action potential, during which the membrane potential moves from approximately −70 to +40 millivolts, occurs because the permeability of the membrane to sodium ions suddenly increases. The temporary breakdown of the membrane barrier to sodium results in a sudden inward movement (influx) of Na⁺ into the interior of the neuron because of the electrical and diffusional forces acting in that direction.

This alteration of Na⁺ permeability is quite brief, lasting only 1 millisecond, and then the membrane permeability to sodium is restored. The sodium ions inside the neuron are "pumped out," and the resting membrane potential begins to return to −70 millivolts. This event begins the falling phase of the action potential. This phase is caused by a temporary breakdown in the permeability of the membrane to potassium. You will recall that the membrane is usually quite permeable to K⁺ ions; now, however, the barrier is broken completely. The resulting outward movement (efflux) of K⁺ ions causes the membrane potential to fall from approximately +40 to −75 millivolts, which characterizes the refractory period during which the membrane is slightly more negative than is normally the case. When the permeability to potassium is restored, the normal resting membrane potential is reestablished. All of these events are illustrated schematically in Figure B–4.

Once an action potential is initiated, it is propagated down the axon in a nondecremental fashion. This means that the action potential as it travels the length of the axon retains its original amplitude. The rate of conduction of nerve impulses varies as a function of the diameter of the axon—the thicker the nerve, the greater the rate of conduction. Conduction of nerve impulses is also much faster in myelinated nerves, as we will explain shortly. The rate of conduction of nerve impulses varies between approximately 0.5 meters per second in small unmyelinated fibers to approximately 130 meters per second in large-diameter myelinated fibers.

The propagation of the nerve impulse down the axon can be explained as follows: During the action potential Na⁺ rushes into the neuron. Sodium ions from adjacent regions rush to the excited area, resulting in a partial depolarization of this adjacent region. This, in turn, results in a local action potential in the adjacent region; sodium ions from the next region rush down, another action potential is initiated, and the nerve impulse is propagated down the axon.

In myelinated nerves the propagation of action potentials is slightly different. The action potentials occur only at the nodes of Ranvier, the gaps in the myelin sheath. Thus, the action potentials, instead of moving down the axon, "jump" from one node of Ranvier to another. This kind of propagation of action potential is referred to as *saltatory conduction,* and it is relatively fast. Myelination is a recent evolutionary development; its importance is that it provides large organisms, such as human beings, with

FIGURE B–4   **The action potential**

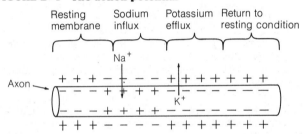

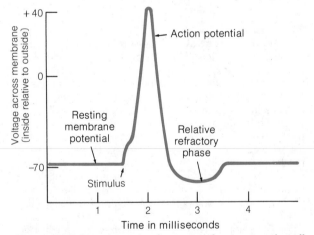

The graph (below) shows the change in voltage across the cell membrane during the rise and fall of the action potential. The voltage changes are produced by the events occurring across the membrane (illustrated above). Thus the rising phase of the action potential is caused by a brief influx of positive sodium ions, and the *hyperpolarization* (movement of the membrane potential away from zero) is produced by the efflux of positive potassium ions. Note that the entire action potential is of relatively short duration.

rapid conduction of nerve impulses from one place to another. This, of course, is adaptive because in large animals the axons can become quite long. For example, some of your neurons extend all the way from the cortex to the lower spinal cord, a distance of several feet. Conduction of nerve impulses over such large distances would take a long time if the individual axons were not myelinated.

Synaptic Transmission

Axonal conduction, the all-or-none propagation of action potentials down the length of the axon, is the mechanism by which neurons conduct information from the region of the axon hillock to the distant reaches of the axon terminals. The transfer of information across the synaptic space is by the process of *synaptic transmission*. The sequence of events that occurs during synaptic transmission can be characterized as follows (see Figure B–5):

1. The action potential traveling down the axon invades the telodendria and axon terminals.
2. This event produces a release of a chemical transmitter, previously stored within the synaptic vesicles.
3. The neurotransmitter diffuses across the synaptic cleft in accordance with the principle of diffusion, discussed previously.
4. The transmitter substances come into contact with the postsynaptic membrane, altering its permeability to certain classes of ions. Specifically, transmitter molecules, after they interact with receptors located on the postsynaptic membrane, alter the permeability of this membrane to either Na^+ or K^+ ions. It is commonly thought that transmitter molecules produce their effects by opening so-called sodium or potassium pores in the postsynaptic membrane.

FIGURE B–5   Diagram of the basic steps involved in chemical neurotransmission

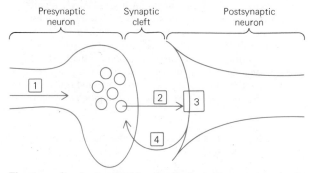

Presynaptic neuron   Synaptic cleft   Postsynaptic neuron

There are five basic steps in chemical neurotransmission: (1) the action potential invades the region of the axon terminal, causing (2) the release of the transmitter from the vesicles; (3) the transmitter diffuses across the synaptic cleft; (4) it interacts with a receptor molecule located on the membrane of the postsynaptic neuron; and (5) the transmitter is removed from the region of the synapse either by chemical degradation or by a reuptake mechanism which returns it to the presynaptic neuron vesicles. Drugs can interfere with chemical neurotransmission by acting on any of these steps.

5. Finally, the transmitter substance is neutralized or reabsorbed by the presynaptic neuron, thus terminating its effect.

These events are essentially the same in all nerves. However, the nature of the transmitter molecules may vary from neuron to neuron. Different kinds of nerves release different kinds of transmitter molecules, and neurons are classified on the basis of the kinds of transmitters they secrete. For example, neurons that release norepinephrine as the transmitter are called *adrenergic neurons;* those that release acetylcholine are referred to as *cholinergic neurons.* From a functional point of view there are essentially two types of synapses in the nervous system. These are the so-called *excitatory synapses,* activity in which results in excitation of the next neuron, and *inhibitory synapses,* activity in which results in inhibition of the next neuron in the circuit. In excitatory synapses the next neuron tends to become depolarized largely as a result of the influx of sodium ions into the neuron, whereas in inhibitory synapses the next neuron tends to become hyperpolarized largely because of the efflux of potassium ions out of the neuron. We will discuss the chemical aspects of neural transmission in greater detail after a brief consideration of electrical excitation or inhibition of neurons.

Excitation   Although we have discussed the mechanisms that generate and carry action potentials down the length of the axon, we have not yet discussed how an action potential is initiated. In some cases the action potentials are generated by external stimuli. The eye, for example, has specialized cells (rods and cones) that convert *(transduce)* light energy into electrical energy, giving rise to action potentials in optic nerve fibers. Within the central nervous system, however, action potentials are generated by a process referred to as *excitatory synaptic transmission.* By this process one nerve cell, the presynaptic neuron, increases the probability of an action potential in another nerve cell, the postsynaptic cell.

When an action potential reaches the region of the telodendria, synaptic transmitter molecules, previously stored in the synaptic vesicles, are released into the synaptic space and diffuse across the cleft toward the postsynaptic membrane. Here the transmitter molecules change the characteristics of the postsynaptic membrane, rendering it more permeable to sodium, potassium, and chloride ions. The ions that have the most potent effect in excitatory synaptic transmission are the sodium ions, because they are characterized by the most unequal distribution across the cell membrane when it is in the resting state. It is common to speak of excitatory synaptic transmission in terms of an opening of so-called sodium pores in the postsynaptic membrane. The result of increasing the permeability of the postsynaptic membrane to sodium ions results in depolarization, a movement of the resting membrane potential toward zero.

Unlike the depolarization that characterizes the rising phase of the action potential, the depolarization produced by excitatory synaptic transmission is graded, the extent of the depolarization depending on the strength of the stimulus, rather than being all or none, which is characteristic of action potentials. This graded change in the membrane potential is referred to as an *excitatory postsynaptic potential (EPSP)*. The relation between an EPSP and the production of an action potential is illustrated diagrammatically in Figure B–6.

An analogy is sometimes made between excitatory synaptic activation and the act of pulling the trigger of a rifle. The trigger can be pulled gently and returned to its original position without causing the rifle to discharge. The pull of the trigger represents the EPSP. If the trigger is pulled to some critical level, representing the firing threshold, the rifle will fire a single shot, which is analogous to the all-or-none discharge, or the action potential. Action potentials are initiated in the region of the axon hillock because this segment of the neural membrane has the lowest firing threshold. In the case of neurons, the firing threshold can be reached by summation of EPSPs that occur close together on the dendrites and cell body, or close together in time. In the former instance one speaks of *spatial summation,* and in the latter case of *temporal summation.* Both types of summation contribute to the triggering of action potentials.

Inhibition Many neurons in the central nervous system perform inhibitory functions. The processes that result in inhibitory synaptic transmission are essentially similar to those outlined above with respect to excitation, except that the changes produced in the postsynaptic membrane are different. Inhibitory synaptic transmission is probably caused by a change in the membrane permeability to potassium and chloride ions. The net effect of inhibition is an outward flow of K^+ ions and an inward flow of Cl^- ions, making the inside of the membrane more negative relative to the outside. Thus, the membrane potential becomes hyperpolarized, moving farther away from zero and farther away from the firing threshold. By analogy, one can say that the trigger is now harder to pull; more precisely, one can say that a stronger stimulus (more EPSP activity) is now required to produce an action potential in the postsynaptic neuron.

The potential changes resulting from inhibitory synaptic activity are referred to as *inhibitory postsynaptic potentials (IPSPs)*. Examples of IPSPs are illustrated diagrammatically in Figure B–6.

Neurotransmitter Substances

Neurotransmitter substances are molecules that are stored in presynaptic vesicles and that produce either EPSPs or IPSPs when they come into contact with receptor molecules located on the postsynaptic membrane. Many different kinds of molecules have been identified that possess a neurotransmitter function. Some types of molecules always produce EPSPs (are always excitatory), others always produce IPSPs (are always inhibitory), whereas yet others produce both EPSPs and IPSPs depending on their site of action. Table B–1 gives a list of chemical substances that are presumed to be neurotransmitter molecules, together with their anatomical site and some of their major effects. In this section we shall describe first some of the general characteristics of neurotransmission and then in some greater

FIGURE B–6 Excitation and inhibition

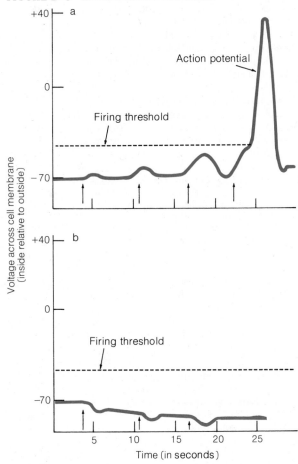

Activation of excitatory synapses results in excitatory postsynaptic potentials, shown in the top graph. Each arrow indicates activation at the synapse. Each successive activation is by a stronger stimulus. The last stimulus produces an EPSP large enough to reach the firing threshold and fire an action potential. Inhibitory postsynaptic potentials are illustrated in the bottom graph. Each arrow represents activation of an inhibitory synapse. Each activation is stronger than the preceding one. Notice that the resting membrane potential is pulled away from the firing threshold by inhibitory synaptic activation.

detail two molecules that are believed to act as major synaptic transmitters.

General Properties of the Neurotransmitter Process Some of the major features of chemical neurotransmission may be presented in summary form as follows:

The molecules from which chemical neurotransmitters are manufactured, the precursor molecules, must first be transported into the neurons. These processes are not passive, in the sense that they require energy and specialized transport mechanisms. Different neurons possess different kinds of transport mechanisms, and this is one

TABLE B-1 Major Neurotransmitters and
Their Hypothesized Effects

Neurotransmitter Molecule	Effect
Acetylcholine (ACh)	Excitatory at the neuromuscular junction; excitatory in autonomic ganglia and in the brain; both excitatory and inhibitory in the end organs of the parasympathetic nervous system.
Norepinephrine (NE)	Inhibitory in the brain; both excitatory and inhibitory in the autonomic nervous system.
Dopamine (DA)	Inhibitory in the brain.
Serotonin (5-HT)	Inhibitory in the brain.
Gamma-aminobutyric acid (GABA)	Inhibitory in the brain.
Glycine	Inhibitory in spinal cord interneurons.
Glutamic acid	Excitatory in the brain and spinal sensory neurons.

way in which nerve cells acquire their chemical specificity.

Once the precursor molecules have been transported into a nerve cell they must be assembled into the chemical that possesses transmitter properties. The manufacture of transmitters—their synthesis—requires special enzymes or organic catalysts. In some instances the synthesis of the transmitter molecule requires but a single enzymatically catalyzed reaction; in other instances many synthetic steps are required, each catalyzed by a specific enzyme. Different nerve cells contain different enzymes, and this is another way in which neurons acquire the characteristic of chemical specificity.

When the transmitter molecule has been manufactured it must be packaged and stored in vesicles, the presynaptic vesicles seen in Figure B-2. This packaging is also an active process requiring specialized mechanisms and energy. Neurotransmitter molecules are packaged to prevent their degradation in the presynaptic neuron.

The transmitter molecule must be released from its presynaptic storage site in response to the arrival of the action potential at the axon terminal. Very little is known about how this process works, except that it is believed that the arrival of the action potential at the terminal increases the influx of Ca^{++} ions, which somehow triggers the release of the transmitter substance.

The transmitter must next diffuse across the synaptic cleft, and it must interact with specialized receptor molecules located at places called receptor sites on the postsynaptic membrane. Different postsynaptic neurons contain different receptor molecules, and this also contributes to chemical specificity of synaptic units.

These receptor molecules are proteins that are embedded in the outer surface of a layer of fatty molecules called lipids, the lipids constituting the bulk of the neuron membrane. The protein receptors are the molecules that the neurotransmitters become attached to, if the chemical

match is just right—it is as if the receptor protein "recognizes" the transmitter, allowing only certain transmitters to hook on. The receptor proteins can be fooled, however, by chemicals similar to the real transmitters. Such substances can then fill up the receptor sites without themselves stimulating the neuron, and in doing so they can prevent much of the action of the real transmitters. Some of the body's naturally occurring hormonelike substances such as the endorphins apparently interact with the neurotransmitters in this way. These were discussed in Chapter 2 and were called the neuromodulators, because they modulate the effects of the regular transmitters.

Finally, the neurotransmitter molecule must be removed from the synaptic cleft after it has produced its effect. Two different mechanisms have been identified that serve this function. These are (1) enzymatic degradation of the transmitter molecule and (2) reabsorption of the transmitter molecule into the presynaptic nerve.

As we shall discuss, different kinds of drugs produce their effects on nervous activity and, therefore, on behavior by potentiating or interfering with the various steps described above.

Acetylcholine Scientists have discovered that *acetylcholine* (ACh) is the synaptic transmitter at the synapse between peripheral motor neurons, that is, those neurons that connect with muscles and muscle tissue. It is by the release of ACh that muscular activity is generated and maintained. It can safely be assumed that ACh serves as an excitatory transmitter in this instance. ACh generates EPSPs and action potentials to produce muscular contractions. There is abundant evidence that ACh is also found in the vesicles of presynaptic neurons in the central nervous system. However, it is not clear whether ACh serves as an excitatory or an inhibitory transmitter in these cases. The most probable answer is that it performs both functions in different parts of the brain, depending on the structure of the postsynaptic receptors.

ACh is produced in nerve cells from acetate and choline, a reaction catalyzed by the enzyme *choline acetylase*. Once it has produced an effect on the postsynaptic neuron it is enzymatically degraded; the destruction is catalyzed by the enzyme *acetylcholinesterase*.

ACh is often considered inhibitory with regard to *behavioral excitability* or reactivity to sensory stimulation measured, for example, as the overall activity level of an animal. Drugs that increase levels of ACh in the brain often produce a reduction in activity, while drugs that destroy or inactivate this transmitter often lead to hyperexcitability. This inhibition of activity could be entirely indirect, however. ACh might be excitatory at synapses in the central nervous system, but subsequent neurons on which it acts might be inhibitory, resulting in indirect behavioral inhibition.

Norepinephrine The second major transmitter substance, *norepinephrine* (NE) was first identified as acting in peripheral nerves. More recently, NE has been identified in the brain and is believed to be a synaptic transmitter there as well. The evidence suggests that NE, and several related chemicals, may play a role in behavioral excitability and

"Brain Food" May Turn Out Not To Be a Myth
By MARY FLACHSENHAAR

As though life weren't bad enough for poor Johnny, his mother may soon have a new weapon for making him learn his abc's and mind his p's and q's. Certain foods, scientists are discovering, have an effect on how the brain works, and, consequently, on how a person behaves.

The research is still in the embryonic stages, but there's a good chance that, more than we ever imagined, we are what we eat. In the future, perhaps, we'll know enough about how diet affects brain chemistry to control our appetites for certain foods, lessen pain, stay alert, induce drowsiness, memorize and concentrate better. Right now, researchers are examining how a change in diet may be able to help patients with mental disorders.

Some food for thought:

Johnny would be well-advised to eat eggs for breakfast if he's about to do some heavy memory work at school. Lecithin, which occurs naturally in protein-rich foods such as eggs, cheese, meat and soybeans, can raise the amount of choline in the blood, which in turn gives the amount of acetylcholine in the brain a boost. That chemical has the power to sharpen short-term learning capabilities, and affect sleeping patterns and motor coordination.

If Johnny's mother wants him wide-eyed and on key for his piano lesson, likely she'll feed him steak or another high-protein food. Low levels of brain serotonin, which occur with a high-protein diet, have been shown to cause insomnia in laboratory cats.

Also, in lab testing, a reduction in brain serotonin made rats less sensitive to pain and increased anxiety in male and female rats. Low levels are also thought to blunt the effect of some drugs on the human system.

And if mother wants to calm rambunctious Johnny at bedtime, she'd be wise to serve him spaghetti for dinner. A high-carbohydrate, protein-poor meal will increase brain serotonin, a condition associated with inducing sleep. High levels of serotonin also can reduce pain, reduce the appetite for more carbohydrates and boost the effect of some antidepressant drugs.

This is how "brain food" chemistry works: Certain chemicals in foods raise the levels of brain neurotransmitters, which carry messages between brain cells.

There are some 10 billion brain cells (called neurons) and maybe as many as 50 different kinds of neurotransmitters zapping messages from neuron to neuron, although scientists have identified only about 30 so far. (When they know about them all, they will know much more about how the brain works.) Certain food chemicals raise the number of neurotransmitters while other chemicals reduce that number.

Is your brain at work right now wondering why scientists haven't come up with this theory until recently?

Richard Wurtman, a professor at MIT in Cambridge, Mass., says scientists, until recently, thought the blood-brain barrier, a layer of tightly packed cells in the brain's capillaries, kept most compounds from entering the brain. The levels of neurotransmitters were unaffected by short-term fluctuations in blood-borne substances, they thought. The only excepted substances seemed to be certain drugs, glucose, water and caffeine.

But scientists have since discovered that some food compounds have indeed been sneaking through the blood-brain barrier all the time. Although most of the neurotransmitters (or brain messengers) aren't influenced by nutrients, some of the most crucial ones are.

One encouraging finding of the brain-food research, much of which has been conducted by MIT's Wurtman, is that diet may be helpful in controlling certain mental and physical disorders. Already the theory has had impressive test results in the treatment of tardive dyskinesia, a disease associated with uncontrollable movements of the lips, tongue and head.

Boulder *(Colo.)* Daily Camera
Summer 1979

Here is a provocative but highly speculative article. The body needs the raw materials to manufacture the neurotransmitters which are stored in the synaptic vesicles. Obviously, it ultimately gets these materials from the food and drink we consume. Some vitamins, for example, are critical to our well-being for this reason. It is clear that the nervous system, like other systems of the body, will benefit if you eat a nutritious diet. It may also be the case that special therapeutic diets can be developed for certain disorders of the nervous system. For now, there is not sufficient evidence to make any particular dietary recommendations.

reactivity increase, suggesting that it may function antagonistically to ACh.

NE is produced in nerve cells from the amino acid tyrosine. A series of enzymatically catalyzed reactions is required. Tyrosine is first metabolized to *dopa*, then to *dopamine* (DA), and then to NE. Each of these steps requires a specific enzyme. DA itself has been shown to function as a neurotransmitter molecule. Nerve cells that utilize DA as a neurotransmitter, so-called *dopaminergic neurons*, lack the enzyme that catalyzes the conversion of DA to NE. Both NE and DA seem to be inactivated by a *reuptake mechanism* rather than by enzymatic degradation. They are reabsorbed into the presynaptic terminal and probably stored again in the vesicles.

A particularly interesting theory of certain forms of behavioral pathology has arisen through work on the so-called *biogenic amines*, as NE and related compounds are called. The theory—the biogenic amine theory of mood—suggests that the biogenic amines may control or produce changes in a person's mood, even to the extreme levels of mania and depression. Although preliminary, the theory is exciting because it relates human behavior pathology to naturally occurring substances in the brain.

Dopamine In this regard *dopamine* itself has attracted more attention and is now considered a major neurotransmitter, particularly in the central nervous system. It has received a great deal of attention because it has been implicated in the cause of certain diseases, such as Huntington's chorea, where it appears that overproduction of dopamine in the basal ganglia of the brain is a factor, and schizophrenia. The dopamine hypothesis about schizophrenia is based on evidence of abnormally high dopamine levels in the brains of schizophrenics. Even more interesting is the fact that the excess dopamine levels seemed to be mainly in those parts of the brain that make up the limbic system,

---

The Brain's "Memory Chemicals"

The brain's catecholamine system has been implicated in many forms of behavior, including certain emotional disturbances. Now, animal study results indicate that catecholamines play a major role in memory functioning.

In a study done at the New York University School of Medicine, mice learned to obtain water from spigots attached to the walls of their cages; in the next stage of the experiment, the mice received an electric shock when they came in contact with the spigots. The animals were then injected with a drug known to produce amnesia, and subsequently continued to attempt to drink from the spigots — forgetting, in effect, their previous shock experiences.

This was followed by the direct injection of one of three substances of the catecholamine family — d-amphetamine, norepinephrine or dopamine — into the brain ventricles, or cavities. Researcher Harvey J. Altman reports that all three chemicals were effective "at certain levels" in reversing the drug-induced amnesia and in motivating the mice to keep away from the spigots. The results, he says, "suggest that the central [catecholamine] receptors are mediators" in memory.

However, Altman concedes he cannot explain that while 70 percent of the mice appeared to recover their memories, the other 30 percent did not. Possible factors, he hypothesizes, are possible side effects of the amnesia-inducing drug or the dissipation of the catecholamine injection somewhere in the brain before it had a chance to enhance memory.

Science News
April 26, 1980

Dopamine has been reported to improve motor (muscle) performance in old animals. Now it's being touted as a memory chemical. Perhaps it will help in the treatment of memory loss in senility. Dopamine cannot get to the brain through the bloodstream but must be injected directly into the brain cavities or ventricles. In pill form, one takes dopa (say for Parkinson's disease) that does go through the bloodstream to the brain, where it is turned into dopamine.

the emotional control system of the brain. Critics of this hypothesis have pointed out that most schizophrenics have been taking potent antipsychotic drugs and that the elevated dopamine is not a cause of schizophrenia but a result of the drug treatment. In any case, dopamine is still high on everyone's list of the most interesting neurotransmitters.

Dopamine also appears to be a major culprit in Parkinson's disease, but this time because of a shortage, not an excess. Now, a common and successful treatment for Parkinson's disease is to inject dopa, which is turned into dopamine when it gets to the brain. Finally, dopamine has been implicated recently in some aspects of senility, particularly the loss of muscle control that often comes with old age. There is some evidence in animal studies that injections of dopa improved the ability of very old rats or mice to move or swim. Some day we may all be taking dopa to stave off the effects of time.

Drugs and Neural Transmission Many important behavioral effects of drugs are believed to take place at the level of synaptic events. We can divide these effects into four categories.

1. Drugs may mimic the effects of transmitters. In many instances this is because the drug is similar in chemical composition to the naturally occurring transmitter molecule, so that it can "impersonate" the transmitter and produce the same effect, excitation or inhibition.
2. Second, the drug may affect the mechanisms that destroy the transmitter, thus impersonating its effects. For example, some drugs inhibit the enzyme acetylcholinesterase, the enzyme that degrades the transmitter acetylcholine, thus allowing the transmitter to have a greater effect. Other drugs prevent the reuptake of norepinephrine and dopamine, resulting in a greater effect.
3. A third way in which drugs can affect neural transmission and ultimately behavior is by directly interfering with the transmitter either by chemically inactivating the transmitter or by filling up its receptor sites on the postsynaptic membrane. Of course, the effect will be the opposite of the effect of the transmitter. Such drugs are called *blocking agents* because they block the action of the transmitter. If the transmitter is excitatory, the blocking agent will produce inhibition, and if it is inhibitory, the blocking agent will produce excitation. Thus, blocking agents are like substitutes for the inactivators of the transmitters.
4. A fourth way for drugs to affect neural transmission would be by influencing the level and/or activity of the neural modulators, the hormonelike proteins that have a slower but longer-lasting effect on neural excitability than the transmitters. The drug *naloxone,* for example, is thought to work by counteracting the effects of naturally occurring endorphin, the body's "morphine." Such drugs, again, could work in either of two ways: chemically inactivating the modulator or filling up the receptor sites on the postsynaptic membrane that the modulator interacts with.

With at least four different means of action, and many different kinds of transmitters, it is no wonder that many different drugs can have profound effects on the nervous system and behavior.

C Psychological Tests and Assessment Techniques

Test Construction

One of the things psychologists are most famous (or is it infamous?) for is their tests. How are psychological tests constructed? Where do personality and behavioral assessment techniques come from? Do psychologists just sit at their desks and decide arbitrarily on what will work? How can psychologists be sure that what they make up will measure what they say it measures? Are test scores meaningful? These questions may have crossed your mind as we discussed such psychological measures as tests of intelligence, creativity, learning, perception, motivation, and personality. We consider the topics of test construction and test evaluation in this Appendix.

Selecting Test Items

A psychological test is made up of a set of individual items — questions, requests, or stimuli — to which the test subject must respond. The particular form of the items depends on the purpose of the test. For example, to measure verbal fluency subjects may be asked for the definitions of words; to measure short-term memory they may be asked to repeat five digits in reverse order; and to measure creativity they may be asked to name as many unusual uses for a brick as they can.

But how do psychologists decide on all the specific items to be used in a test? This is a fair question that is often asked by puzzled people after taking a test ("Why did they want to know if I ever stay up late at night?"). There are actually two ways in which test items are initially selected and evaluated. The first of these is called the *rational* approach and the second the *empirical* approach.

In the rational approach, the test constructor begins by asking a very simple question: What kinds of items make sense for testing what I want to test? The answer is guided to a certain extent by common sense (for example, if you want to test hostility, the items used should have something to do with hostility), but the tester may also depend heavily on a psychological *theory* to help pick good test items. For this reason, the rational approach is also sometimes called the *theoretical* approach to test construction. (Items that appear to make common sense or to follow logically from some theory are said to have *face validity*.)

A psychologist interested in measuring anxiety using the rational approach would first develop or adopt an anxiety theory that is based on past research and other already known factors, and then proceed to design a test that will measure anxiety as defined or characterized by that theory. Suppose the theory says that anxiety is a drive, a motivating force which impels people to act. The implication is that people high in anxiety should show evidence of a high level of motivation. This might be called the drive theory of anxiety. Alternatively, the psychologist might theorize that anxiety has little to do with motivation level but instead is a personality trait which has to do with a person's ability to cope with or deal with stress in an adequate fashion. High-anxiety people have trouble dealing with stressful situations and low-anxiety people do not. This might be called the stress theory of anxiety. Note that the stress theory says that anxiety is independent of drive level or motivation. People can be highly anxious and still have low motivation, or they can be low in anxiety and still have high motivation.

One's theoretical conception of what anxiety really is will determine the kind of test used to measure anxiety. A person who believes in the drive theory of anxiety will obviously develop a different kind of anxiety test than one who believes in the stress theory. The stress theorist is likely to develop a test designed to measure how people handle stressful situations. It might include an item like: "Suppose you are chewed out by your boss in front of several other employees — which of the following things would you most likely do: (a) break down and start crying, (b) tell the boss off, (c) explain to the boss that you have not been feeling well lately, or (d) say nothing to the boss, but, after he leaves, tell him off behind his back." The drive theorist, on the other hand, might have a test item that aims at assessing level of motivation, such as: "Which of the following statements fits you best: (a) I am constantly on the go — I can't sit still, (b) I always take my time, (c) I work hard and I play hard, (d) I am basically a lazy person."

The empirical approach to test construction follows a quite different set of initial procedures. The psychologist who wishes to build a new test for something (again suppose it is anxiety) using the empirical approach would begin by identifying a set of *reference groups,* which are *already known* to be, say, high or low in anxiety. These groups might be created on the basis of existing anxiety tests, self-reports, peer ratings, psychiatric diagnoses, physiological responses to stress, performance on relevant laboratory tasks, or other data.

Then, the psychologist would collect a very large pool of test items (from other tests, from suggestions made by people who are familiar with anxiety, and from other sources) and administer all of them to the high- and low-anxiety groups. All the items that are answered differently by members of the two groups would be kept in the test because they seem to *discriminate* between high and low anxiety. Items that tend to be answered in the same way by all subjects are said not to discriminate and are dropped from future versions of the test. If all goes well, this process results in a set of items that can tell us whether a newly tested person (about whom we have no prior information) is likely to be high or low in anxiety.

As another example, suppose that our psychologist wants to develop an age scale for intelligence. He or she wants items that discriminate ages. A perfect item would be one that is failed by all up to a certain age and passed by all beyond that age. An item that is passed by roughly the same percentage of subjects at every age is a poor item and must be rejected. For example, an item that no 3-year-old passes

FIGURE C-1   Usable and unusable test items

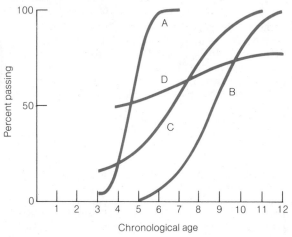

Functions showing percentage of subjects who pass four different test items at each chronological age. Items A and B would be usable in a test to develop an age scale for intelligence. Item C could be used, although it does not discriminate as well. Item D should not be used.

and no 5-year-old fails would be kept and used in the 4-year-old scale (Item A in Figure C-1). Item B in Figure C-1 is likewise very good, although at an older age level. It too would be kept. Item C is marginal and would be rejected if the psychologist had enough other items to replace it. Item D is an unusable item and must be eliminated under any circumstances.

Many tests have been developed in this way. The MMPI was developed by using many groups of people with different psychiatric diagnoses as the reference groups. Rorschach used a similar method in developing the inkblot test. In the most famous test of vocational interest, the Strong Vocational Interest Blank, successful doctors, lawyers, businesspersons, and so on, served as reference groups. If you take the vocational interest test, your answers are scored to see how they correlate with the answers given by various occupational reference subjects. If you answer the items in a manner similar to that of a group of successful lawyers but different from that of successful doctors, the prediction is that you would do better as a lawyer than as a doctor. The reference group approach in various forms is probably the rationale underlying most psychological tests.

Another empirical approach would be to use the statistical tool known as factor analysis (see Appendix A). This is the procedure used by Cattell to develop the 16 PF test. In this approach the psychologist who wished to develop a measure of anxiety would select a large number of existing tests, administer them to a large group of people, and then factor analyze to identify the basic underlying factors. Say, for example, that there are two clusters of tests, one more indicative of arousal and another related to compulsive movement. The last step is to select the two individual tests that best measure these factors. In this case a statistical procedure rather than a set of reference groups is used to decide on the eventual measure.

Although we have divided this rationale section into two parts, empirical and theoretical, in actual practice the two approaches are almost always combined. Sometimes the psychologist does not have a formal, completely specified theory as a guide, and we say that he or she is using the empirical approach. But everyone always has personal hunches, guesses, and ideas, which serve as a theory to guide research. In the case of the theoretical approach, psychologists may have a very formal theory to go by, but they will also make great use of the empirical approaches of reference groups and factor analysis to refine their test procedures, establish construct validity, and modify their theory to account for the new facts brought out by their research.

Evaluating Tests and Test Items

Indeed, whether a test is *constructed* rationally or empirically, it must ultimately be refined and *evaluated* empirically. Usually this process begins with *standardization*, which involves administering the test to large samples of subjects.

One purpose of test *standardization* is to work out the final details of the test procedure. To be fair to every individual, the test must be administered under comparable conditions and in a reasonably constant way. For example, test scores might not be comparable if the test were given under favorable conditions—good lighting, quiet room, period of alertness—to some individuals and unfavorable conditions—dark and noisy room, period of fatigue—to others. In intelligence testing particularly, even minor and seemingly unimportant variations, such as the time between items, can have significant effects. The aim is to identify the test conditions that maximize performance and then make sure that all subjects are tested under these conditions.

A second function of the standardization phase of test construction is to provide *test norms*. This is a complex issue and not easily described in general terms. The norms for a personality test are fundamentally different from the norms for an intelligence test. Establishing norms involves determining the *average* or *typical level of performance* on the test and devising a measure of score variability. Therefore, the relevant statistics are measures of central tendency, such as the mean, and measures of variability in the frequency distribution of test scores, such as the standard deviation.

Consider, for example, a point-scale IQ test. Each item passed in each subscale is awarded a certain number of points, and the total score is the sum of all earned points. In order to understand the score of any particular subject, the tester needs to know how it compares with the scores of similar people. Knowing that 16-year-old Billy earned a score of 75 points on the test is not particularly informative. To make sense of that score the tester needs to know the average score for people like him. It makes considerable difference whether that mean is 100 or 70. Likewise, it is helpful to have an idea of the variation in scores. A score of 75 in a distribution with a mean of 70 and a standard deviation of 2 is indicative of much better performance than a score of 75 in a distribution with a mean of 70 and a standard deviation of 15 (see Appendix A).

The norms of a test usually consist of means and standard deviations for all relevant subgroupings of subjects. Indeed, the better-developed tests provide this infor-

"We had intelligence tests today. Boy! Were they HARD!"

The Family Circus by Bil Keane, reprinted courtesy The Register and Tribune Syndicate, Inc.

In constructing tests we must remember that a test item which everyone gets correct is not worth very much if the goal is to discriminate among people in terms of the amount of knowledge or ability or intelligence they possess. Likewise, an item that is failed by everybody taking the test is not very helpful. Try to remember this important feature of test construction the next time you have a test in your psychology class.

mation for various classifications, such as different ages, different subscales, and so on. To simplify interpretations, many norms are converted to some standard scoring across subclassification. For example, it has become conventional to transform intelligence test scores in such a way that, regardless of age of subject or subscale of test, the mean score is 100. For all subclassifications of the Wechsler test, the standard deviation in IQ points is 15.

Reliability

Standard test conditions and normative data are important in psychological testing, but the primary objective signs of a good test are **reliability** and **validity.** Reliability has to do with the degree to which a test is likely to yield consistent results—do you get about the same score each time you give the test to a particular subject? A rigorous check on reliability can be made in any of three ways, and occasionally all three are used. In the *test-retest method,* the same test is administered twice within a short time span to the same subjects. When there are two comparable forms of the test, which is especially desirable if there is the possibility of some transfer with repeated administrations of the same test, the *alternate forms method* can be used. In this method reliability is indexed by the correlation between the sets of scores obtained by subgroups of subjects who took the different forms of the same test. The *split-half method* is the easiest and most economical check. Here the items of the

test are divided into two comparable groups or halves, and the resulting two sets of scores are correlated.

In any case, the higher the correlation between the two sets of scores, the more reliable is the test and, by implication, all items within it. The best-known tests of intelligence have reliability coefficients of .90 and above, which are extraordinarily high correlations. Such a high correlation indicates that a person is very likely to score approximately the same every time he or she takes the test.

Validity

Validity is the degree to which a test correlates with some accepted criterion of the behavior being measured. We shall consider briefly three kinds of validity. A test of *concurrent validity* is made when the new test is compared with existing tests designed to accomplish the same purpose. A psychologist might, for example, correlate scores on his or her IQ test with scores obtained by the same subjects on the familiar Wechsler-Bellevue test. If the correlation is high, the psychologist can conclude that the test measures what the Wechsler test measures, presumably intelligence.

Predictive validity is based on somewhat less circular reasoning. Here the tester asks if the test can predict later performance. Using subsequent school achievement to validate an IQ test is an example. If a psychologist has designed a test to select students with high engineering aptitude, later grade-point average in engineering school would be the criterion. Again, validity is measured by the magnitude of the correlation between test and the criterion it is used to predict.

Finally, when the test is designed to measure a theoretical idea, its validity is judged by the extent to which it conforms to the requirements of the theory. *Construct validity* is a matter of logical analysis, not correlation.

To determine if a test has construct validity, the psychologist would use the theory to deduce predictions about how people who score high and low on this test behave differently in some situations. He or she would then get a group of people who score high and another group who score low and test them in the situation to see if the prediction is supported. If it is, the test has construct validity. The idea is to make many such predictions and tests and have them heavily supported before a final conclusion about construct validity of the test is reached; establishing construct validity is a long, detailed research process.

Let us illustrate with predictions based on the two different theories of anxiety described earlier. The stress theorist might use the following situation to make predictions about the behavior of people who score high and low on a test of anxiety: The two groups of subjects are put in a learning situation, say memorizing a list of words. At some point in the learning process a stressful event is introduced, such as telling the subjects that they are doing so poorly that they will begin to receive shocks when they make errors. The theory of anxiety as inability to cope with stress predicts that the learning rate of the high-anxiety group will go down, whereas the low-anxiety group will be unaffected or will actually improve. If the experiment confirms the prediction, the stress theorist gains a bit of construct validity for his or her test.

Recruit Evaluation Flaw Admitted

WASHINGTON (AP) — The Pentagon says it has vastly underestimated the percentage of low-mentality recruits accepted into military service.

The Pentagon, in a report to Congress, said it now believes that 30 percent of 1979 recruits belong in the lowest of four mental categories—not 5 percent as previously stated officially.

Although the Pentagon studies focused on 1979 recruits, officials indicated such problems probably have existed over at least four years.

It was in 1976 that the Pentagon put into effect a standard qualification test for all the armed services, which previously had used separate examinations.

The defense manpower official denied that the 1976 tests were designed to "make the all-volunteer force look better than it is."

They said that technical work was flawed in introducing those tests, and that it dawned on them earlier this year that there might be something wrong with the way the results have been

evaluated. The Pentagon reported this to Congress last winter.

After the problem surfaced, three separate studies were conducted by analytical and research groups. Their work was reviewed by what the Pentagon called "wise men" from several universities.

"They indicated that the norms in use were inaccurate and had inflated the armed forces qualification test scores of individuals in the lower end of the test score range," the Pentagon

Without appropriate test norms, it is not possible to interpret test scores.

Tests: How Good? How Fair?

. . . More than 100 million standardized achievement and intelligence tests are administered annually in the U.S. They rank the mental talents of youths from nursery to graduate school. But an eclectic assortment of critics now charge that tests are academically invalid or biased against minorities. Consumer activist Ralph Nader released a vitriolic study of the Educational Testing Service last month, calling it a "private regulator of the human mind" that "served as a formidable barrier to millions of students." The 1.8 million-member National Education Association is campaigning to abolish standardized testing in public schools. After passage of New York's pioneering "truth-in-testing" law, fourteen states and the Federal government are considering similar bills requiring test-makers to offer the contents of exams for public inspection.

To the test-makers, the harsh—often ill-informed—criticism mistakes both their purpose and their influence. "We are both shocked and dismayed by the power critics ascribe to us," says ETS vice president Robert Solomon. Standardized tests—more than 2,000 varieties of which are in current use—merely try to chart different levels of mental achievement and aptitude scientifically and objectively, the creators contend. Test-makers loathe the use of exams to brand children. They deny the perfection of tests, and, well aware of the

magic of numbers, stress the limits of testing as a scholastic tool. "The people who consider tests a panacea make us very nervous," says Thomas Fitzgibbon, president of the New York-based Psychological Corp. Says Solomon, "Tests don't measure attitudes such as persistence and motivation."

Still, children face intelligence tests almost from the day that they step into school. Usually, pupils first come across the Stanford-Binet or Wechsler IQ tests, given to more than 2 million youngsters each year. IQ tests try to forecast intellectual potential. "These aptitude tests are not as much tests of information as devices that measure the facility with which a youngster handles a wide variety of skills," explains Jerome Doppelt, a Psychological Corp. psychometrician. The Wechsler test, for example, is divided into a dozen categories. It includes specific questions in vocabulary and arithmetic and contains items to test general memory, such as asking children to repeat increasingly long series of numbers.

Mastery

Students also encounter separate achievement tests beginning in elementary school. To monitor past academic performance and development, schools routinely give reading and math exams starting in first grade. At this level, achievement tests are usually diagnos-

tic: they can reveal problem areas where children need tutoring or remedial classes. Critics claim that often the tests are misused to track black and Hispanic youngsters, who have not been well prepared at home for school, into inferior programs for slow learners. For high-school and college seniors, achievement tests serve another purpose: admissions deans use exams to evaluate mastery of specific subjects—and to decide which candidates will be admitted or rejected by universities and graduate schools. . . .

For ambitious students who do brilliantly on the SAT or ACT, the testing sweepstakes may not be over. Graduate schools place a higher premium on standardized exams than do colleges and the most selective use rough "cut-off" scores. At first glance, tests such as the Law School Admission Test or the Graduate Record Examinations resemble complicated SAT's. In fact, test-makers often tailor these exams to measure ability and skills that professions especially value. The LSAT, for instance, stresses the analysis of legal principles and situations; it has abandoned sections that tested general knowledge in the arts and humanities.

Bench Marks

One of the largest questions in testing is how much standardized exams affect admissions. Some admissions officers insist that they must rely on dependable

The ETS has recently been "embarrassed" by two incidents where more than one answer was correct.

Recruit Evaluation Flaw Admitted (continued)

report said in describing conclusions submitted last month by the "wise men."

Pentagon officials are particularly sensitive about the new findings because congressional critics have contended the all-volunteer force is suffering from poor quality in the ranks.

Noting this, the Pentagon report to Congress said "millions of low-scoring soldiers, sailors, airmen and Marines served their nation well in the past, both in war and in peace, and they continue to do so today."

Nonetheless, the Pentagon said it is analyzing the relationship between entrance test scores and job performance of Army enlistees with inflated scores.

"The first findings from this analysis suggest that most of the low-scoring people are performing adequately," the Pentagon said. Final results were promised when they are ready.

Statistics in the report show the most dramatic overscoring occurred in the Army among 1979 recruits. The percentage of lower-mental-category

recruits was revised from 9 percent to 46 percent of the year's total.

The Marine Corps' went from 4 percent to 26 percent, the Navy from 4 percent to 18 percent and the Air Force from zero to 9 percent.

A new battery of tests is being prepared for introduction in October, and officials say care is being taken to prevent repetition of errors that have skewed past test results.

The Denver Post
July 31, 1980

Tests: How Good? How Fair? (continued)

bench marks because grade inflation and easily gotten recommendations water down candidate files. "Achievement tests can help to validate or refute high-school grades," says William Elliott, a vice-provost at Carnegie-Mellon University in Pittsburgh. Most admissions committees pay close attention to SAT's only when they conflict sharply with over-all school performance—and high test scores don't always help. "We're skeptical of students with dazzling scores and lackluster academic records," says admissions officer Dwight Hatcher of Kenyon College in Gambier, Ohio. "It often signifies they are troublesome students who are not motivated."

Much of the current controversy centers on the power of ETS, the largest of the nation's test-makers. Located on a 400-acre estate in Princeton, N.J., the nonprofit company designs tests for 375 clients, including major admissions associations and the State Department. ETS spends about $14 million a year on research, carrying its measurements down to learning rates among three-month-old infants. By common agreement, few people land high-prestige positions in the U.S. today without encountering—and doing well on—at least one ETS test. The company's IBM computers—the world's largest educational and psychological data bank—tabulate and store information 24 hours

a day and hold exam scores for at least 15 million citizens. What's more, the tests have always been held in strictest secrecy.

Review

ETS and other test companies construct their tests meticulously. To build the SAT, for example, ETS hires college students, high-school teachers and professors to assist its staff in writing questions. About fifteen people separately review each new test question—about 3,000 each year—for style, content or racial bias. Each multiple-choice option must be plausible; at the same time, four out of five answers must be indisputably wrong. ETS "pretests" its questions by including them in regular SAT's to see how applicants respond (without counting the practice question scores). ETS wants each new question to rank in difficulty with the one it replaces, so that results will compare equally with tests given in previous years. Creating a whole new SAT can take as long as two years and cost more than $60,000.

These efforts to ensure fairness mean little to anti-test crusaders. The new Nader report complained that ETS exams chiefly perpetuate divisions of social class. A Nader study team's six-year investigation concluded that the SAT successfully predicts a student's first-year college performance in only one out of ten cases. SAT scores cor-

respond more readily to family income, it says. In addition, the report claims that cram coaching for tests, which affluent students can afford, and "cultural bias" in questions exclude a disproportionate number of capable minority students from college. ETS official John Fremer immediately dismissed the Nader report as "deliberately fraudulent," arguing that Nader's research distorted data to convict the company on faulty evidence.

Penalized

More serious test critics call all standardized tests biased against minorities. A black or Hispanic youngster who has grown up in a city slum, they argue, encounters references and vocabulary on a test that penalize him in competition with middle-class whites. For example, a question on forests or "Romeo and Juliet" may favor white children who have grown up with both. Test-makers concede that no test is entirely culture-free. "We cannot create tests in a vacuum," says the Psychological Corp.'s Doppelt. "Background influences scores." Adds ETS test-developer Richard Adams, "Tests are biased toward the environment that most people will work in." . . .

Newsweek
February 18, 1980

The anxiety-as-drive theorist might instead make the following experimental prediction: Take two groups, one high and one low in "drive-anxiety," and put them to work sorting different-colored and different-shaped objects into compartments. Because of their higher drive, high-anxiety people will get more objects sorted than low-anxiety people. If this prediction is confirmed, then the test gains in construct validity.

What Do Tests Test?

There are literally thousands of tests in print today, and although each has a specific title, all of them are actually aimed at measuring one of four basic things: (1) intelligence, (2) personality, (3) ability, and (4) attitudes, interests, preferences, and values. Psychologists are actively involved in the development, administration, and evaluation of all four types of tests, but for illustrative purposes we shall focus upon personality tests. As we saw in Chapter 9, personality testing provides one of the main ways through which personality can be assessed.

Uses of Personality Tests

Personality tests are used for two basic purposes: to make a diagnostic decision or to further understanding of the concept of personality. There are two distinct types of diagnostic decisions made on the basis of test results: (1) mental health decisions, that is, whether or not the person is sane, what kind of therapy to use, what aspects of the individual's personality are abnormal, and the like; and (2) prediction decisions, that is, predictions about whether or not a person will be successful in some area, say school or on the job.

The most important and most frequent use of psychological tests is to diagnose mental disorders. You probably know that psychologists and psychiatrists are often called upon by the courts to determine if someone is "legally" sane or not. But not every person with a behavior disorder is involved with the courts. Usually it is the therapist who administers psychological testing in order to understand the client's problem and develop rational ways of proceeding in therapy. For many clinical psychologists behavior or mental disorder means personality disorder, and personality measurement is the first step in diagnosis and therapy. Therapists must be able to measure personality if they are going to base treatment on the notion that something is abnormal about the personality of the clients. The decisions made on the basis of these assessment procedures have incredibly important implications for the client. The results may determine whether or not he or she is committed to a hospital, sentenced to a prison, allowed to continue on a job, keep his or her children, and so on. Thus, the measures of personality and the procedures used to make these judgments must be the best that psychologists can devise. It may be fun to read handwriting or tea leaves or palms or the stars, but these assessment techniques because they have no demonstrated validity are not acceptable means for making decisions about someone's personality.

Assessment procedures are also used to make nonclinical decisions and predictions about future behavior. In education, psychologists use the principles of psychological assessment to develop ability, aptitude, and achievement tests. Intelligence testing is used to diagnose mental retardation, reading difficulties, discipline problems, grade level, who gets into college, medical school, law school, and so on. In industry, personality assessment has become an important aspect of executive hiring. There are also tests of manual ability that determine who gets hired at a factory. The military uses psychological tests in planning the training programs of new recruits and in deciding who is qualified for what service. The government uses psychological tests to make hiring decisions. Just about every area of our lives has been invaded by people using psychological tests to make decisions about us, decisions that have great impact on us.

Despite the importance of the topic, psychologists do not agree completely on what personality is or how it is to be measured. There is a lack of understanding of the con-

---

Psychologists Play Bigger Corporate Role in Placing of Personnel . . .
By JOHN KOTEN

Seated at student desks in a small room, prospective Delta Air Lines pilots pore over a battery of psychological tests.

"This is ridiculous," mutters one of the four applicants. "What do these tests have to do with whether I'll make a good pilot? What the hell does it matter whether I like to sing in the shower?"

It may matter a great deal.

"I tell the company, 'go or no go,'" declares Sidney Janus, a private Atlanta psychologist who gives rigorous tests to Delta's flight and management job candidates. He exaggerates somewhat, of course, but the company says his veto would jeopardize a person's chances of becoming a Delta pilot, stewardess or executive.

Many Seek Guidance
Delta is among hundreds of U.S. concerns that are turning more to psychologists for guidance in deciding who gets what job. . . .

Through testing and interviews, psychologists help screen prospective employees and select promotion candidates—occasionally all the way up the corporate ladder. Some executive-search firms have staff psychologists who advise concerns about presidential prospects.

The trend isn't new; for instance, Sears, Roebuck & Co. began its psychological-assessment program in the early 1940s. But more corporations use psychologists nowadays, partly because testing has become more sophisticated, comprehensive and objective. Increasingly, businesses believe that "promotion and hiring decisions are too important to be made solely on the basis of such things as office politics, tenure and highly subjective performance evaluations" by bosses, says Jon Bentz, Sears's director of psychological research.

The Wall Street Journal
July 11, 1978

cept of personality, and therefore a great deal of research effort is being devoted to the topic. In order to do research on personality it is necessary to have personality tests that can be used to test hypotheses about what personality is. For example, psychologists who believe that personality is made up of a set of traits need ways to demonstrate this in a rigorous fashion. New conceptions of personality mean developing new ways of assessing personality; thus personality tests play a crucial role in the development and refinement of the concept of personality.

Types of Personality Tests

Personality tests are of two basic types: *objective* and *projective*. In objective tests (also known as inventories or self-report measures) the person is asked to answer, usually in writing, a number of objective questions about himself or herself. It is assumed that the person will report the true facts, or perhaps the test might be developed in such a way as to determine if he or she is being truthful. As you might suspect, this is an area of great debate—can an *accurate* measure of personality be arrived at from self-report measures?

Projective tests are much less objective procedures in the sense that they present the subject not with clear questions but with rather vague stimuli (such as inkblots, ambiguous drawings, incomplete sentences, or requests to draw some vaguely specified thing such as "a person"). The "projective hypothesis" suggests that the subject's responses to these stimuli (that is, what is "seen" in them) will reflect unconscious aspects of personality. However, there is considerable room for disagreement about the actual meaning of these responses. Those who use and defend these tests argue that their value lies in the vagueness that others criticize. The situation is so unstructured that there is no way that subjects can fake responses. For example, subjects would have no way of knowing how "sane" as opposed to "insane" persons would answer.

Critics point out that a basic problem with these tests is the difficulty involved in reliable, valid, and widely accepted ways of analyzing the idiosyncratic and often highly unusual responses of subjects who take projective tests.

Objective Tests

A personality inventory generally consists of a large number of objective questions about one's behavior. Test takers are asked about their attitudes, hobbies, personal habits, friends and family, and so on. Usually the inventory is designed to measure personality on several different scales. The test might have 10 subscales, each one presumably measuring a different aspect of personality, and for each subscale there might be 10 to 20 questions designed to get at that factor or subscale.

The MMPI The best-known and most widely used objective personality instrument is the *Minnesota Multiphasic Personality Inventory,* known simply as the MMPI. It consists of 550 statements that subjects must judge as being either "true" of themselves, "false," or "cannot say." The items were selected originally because they tended to be answered differently by normal people and various subgroups of psychiatric patients. The MMPI was developed by

testing people with known behavior disorders and is used mainly as a diagnostic instrument for detecting psychiatric problems, although it can be used to assess individual differences in normal personality as well.

Statements on the MMPI are of this variety:

1. I have trouble making new friends.
2. I am seldom troubled by nightmares.
3. At times, my mind is very confused.
4. My parents often punished me physically.
5. I seldom get headaches.

The 550 items are usually analyzed into 10 basic "clinical" scales and 4 "validity" scales (to determine whether the subject has answered the test validly and truthfully). The 10 clinical scales are:

1. Hypochondriasis (HS)—a scale of how often the subject complains about his or her physical health.
2. Depression (D)—a scale of how depressed and pessimistic the subject is.
3. Hysteria (Hy)—a measure of neurotic reaction to stress by denial of problems with accompanying medical complaints.
4. Psychopathic deviation (Pd)—a measure of the subject's feelings about rules, laws, moral conduct, ethics, and so on.
5. Masculinity-femininity (MF)—a measure of the orientation of the subject toward the traditional masculine or feminine behavior roles.
6. Paranoia (Pa)—a measure of how suspicious the subject is, particularly in the area of interpersonal relations.
7. Psychasthenia (Pt)—a measure of how obsessed the person is with certain thoughts and how compulsive (rigid) he or she is.
8. Schizophrenia (Sc)—a measure of how withdrawn the subject is from the real world and the degree to which his or her thinking could be described as bizarre.
9. Hypomania (Ma)—a measure of how excited and active the subject is, particularly the tendency to show unusual elation and excitement.
10. Social introversion (Si)—a measure of introversion-extroversion.

As an example of how the MMPI differentiates between specified groups of individuals, consider the results of a study in which the test was administered to delinquent and nondelinquent adolescents. As you might guess, the largest difference between the two groups was on the psychopathic deviation (Pd) scale (see Figure C–2). The MMPI has proved to be a very useful clinical tool and has also contributed notably to research on behavior disorders. However, its use as a screening device, say for job applicants, has been severely criticized. Would you think it appropriate for a large company to require all its workers to take the MMPI?

The 16 PF (16 Personality Factors) Another major inventory, the *16 PF,* was developed by using only normal subjects. This is the test devised by Raymond Cattell in order to assess the basic factors of normal personality. Recall that Cattell's factor analytic studies indicated that human personality could be adequately characterized by 16 source traits. The test is called the 16 PF (16 personality factors)

FIGURE C-2 **Differentiating groups with the MMPI**

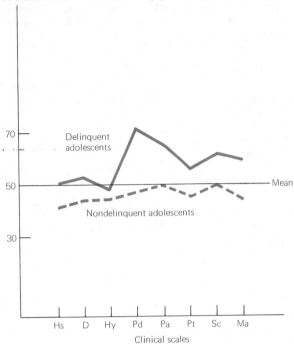

Scores for a group of delinquent adolescents and a group of nondelinquent adolescents on 8 of the 10 clinical scales of the MMPI. The largest difference between the two groups appears on the Pd (psychopathic deviation) scale.

because it consists of separate scales for each of these traits. A sample test profile describing the 16 scales developed by Cattell is shown in Figure C–3.

Suppose a psychologist felt that something was missing from these scales, perhaps that they failed to measure how introverted or extroverted someone's personality was. He or she might devise another test of introversion-extroversion and give it along with the 16 PF to a group of subjects. Factor analysis would involve correlating the new test with each of the existing 16 tests (the 16 factors). If the new test did not correlate with any of the 16 factors, then presumably it measures something that the 16 factors had missed. Chances are, however, that the new test will correlate highly with one of the existing factors, probably factor H (Threctia-Parmia), meaning that it does not measure anything new. Through extended application of this process the personality theorist can narrow the field down to a minimal number of scales necessary to describe personality. Each of the scales would measure something different, meaning that no two scales would correlate highly with each other.

No new scales are needed unless they measure something new, that is, something the 16 existing factors fail to describe. In other words, new scales are not useful unless they fail to correlate with any of the 16 existing ones. The psychologist's description of personality would not be enriched by adding an introversion-extroversion test as a seventeenth factor if that test correlated highly with factor H

or any other factor. Thus factor analysis helps to minimize the number of scales; it allows the psychologist to describe personality adequately with the fewest possible tests.

The 16 PF test (which is actually 16 tests rolled into one) consists of multiple-choice items. Four sample items are:

1. I like to watch team games:
   a. yes   b. occasionally   c. no
2. I prefer people who:
   a. are reserved   b. are in between   c. make friends quickly
3. Money cannot bring happiness:
   a. yes (true)   b. in between   c. no (false)
4. Woman is to child as cat is to:
   a. kitten   b. dog   c. boy

Projective Tests

Rorschach Inkblot Test The most famous projective test, the *Rorschach Inkblot Test*, was developed in 1921 by Hermann Rorschach. The test consists of 10 inkblots similar to the one shown in Figure C–4. Five of the blots are printed in shades of black and 5 contain varying degrees of color. The final set of 10 blots was derived from a large group of blots that was administered to psychiatric patients who had already been classified by type of disorder. Normal people were also tested. The final 10 blots were the ones that best discriminated the reactions of normal people from the reactions of patients and, further, showed some evidence of discriminating among the various disorders within the patient population.

The subject is shown the Rorschach cards one at a time in a specified order and is asked to describe what he or she sees. Instructions are simple in order to keep the situation as unstructured as possible and not restrict the kind of response the subject might give. In addition to recording what the subject says, the interviewer notes other features of the subject's behavior, such as the length of time it takes

"According to your inkblots you're a compulsive thief, Mrs. Barstow."

© Punch (Rothco)

FIGURE C–3 A 16 PF test profile

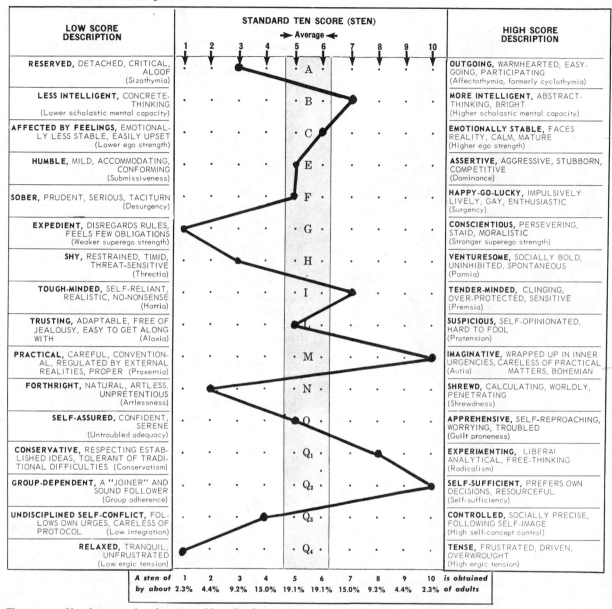

LOW SCORE DESCRIPTION	STANDARD TEN SCORE (STEN) → Average ←										HIGH SCORE DESCRIPTION
	1	2	3	4	5	6	7	8	9	10	
RESERVED, DETACHED, CRITICAL, ALOOF (Sizothymia)					A						**OUTGOING,** WARMHEARTED, EASY-GOING, PARTICIPATING (Affectothymia, formerly cyclothymia)
LESS INTELLIGENT, CONCRETE-THINKING (Lower scholastic mental capacity)					B						**MORE INTELLIGENT,** ABSTRACT-THINKING, BRIGHT (Higher scholastic mental capacity)
AFFECTED BY FEELINGS, EMOTIONAL-LY LESS STABLE, EASILY UPSET (Lower ego strength)					C						**EMOTIONALLY STABLE,** FACES REALITY, CALM, MATURE (Higher ego strength)
HUMBLE, MILD, ACCOMMODATING, CONFORMING (Submissiveness)					E						**ASSERTIVE,** AGGRESSIVE, STUBBORN, COMPETITIVE (Dominance)
SOBER, PRUDENT, SERIOUS, TACITURN (Desurgency)					F						**HAPPY-GO-LUCKY,** IMPULSIVELY LIVELY, GAY, ENTHUSIASTIC (Surgency)
EXPEDIENT, DISREGARDS RULES, FEELS FEW OBLIGATIONS (Weaker superego strength)					G						**CONSCIENTIOUS,** PERSEVERING, STAID, MORALISTIC (Stronger superego strength)
SHY, RESTRAINED, TIMID, THREAT-SENSITIVE (Threctia)					H						**VENTURESOME,** SOCIALLY BOLD, UNINHIBITED, SPONTANEOUS (Parmia)
TOUGH-MINDED, SELF-RELIANT, REALISTIC, NO-NONSENSE (Harria)					I						**TENDER-MINDED,** CLINGING, OVER-PROTECTED, SENSITIVE (Premsia)
TRUSTING, ADAPTABLE, FREE OF JEALOUSY, EASY TO GET ALONG WITH (Alaxia)					L						**SUSPICIOUS,** SELF-OPINIONATED, HARD TO FOOL (Protension)
PRACTICAL, CAREFUL, CONVENTION-AL, REGULATED BY EXTERNAL REALITIES, PROPER (Praxernia)					M						**IMAGINATIVE,** WRAPPED UP IN INNER URGENCIES, CARELESS OF PRACTICAL MATTERS, BOHEMIAN (Autia)
FORTHRIGHT, NATURAL, ARTLESS, UNPRETENTIOUS (Artlessness)					N						**SHREWD,** CALCULATING, WORLDLY, PENETRATING (Shrewdness)
SELF-ASSURED, CONFIDENT, SERENE (Untroubled adequacy)					O						**APPREHENSIVE,** SELF-REPROACHING, WORRYING, TROUBLED (Guilt proneness)
CONSERVATIVE, RESPECTING ESTAB-LISHED IDEAS, TOLERANT OF TRADI-TIONAL DIFFICULTIES (Conservatism)					Q_1						**EXPERIMENTING,** LIBERAL ANALYTICAL, FREE-THINKING (Radicalism)
GROUP-DEPENDENT, A "JOINER" AND SOUND FOLLOWER (Group adherence)					Q_2						**SELF-SUFFICIENT,** PREFERS OWN DECISIONS, RESOURCEFUL (Self-sufficiency)
UNDISCIPLINED SELF-CONFLICT, FOL-LOWS OWN URGES, CARELESS OF PROTOCOL (Low integration)					Q_3						**CONTROLLED,** SOCIALLY PRECISE, FOLLOWING SELF-IMAGE (High self-concept control)
RELAXED, TRANQUIL, UNFRUSTRATED (Low ergic tension)					Q_4						**TENSE,** FRUSTRATED, DRIVEN, OVERWROUGHT (High ergic tension)

	1	2	3	4	5	6	7	8	9	10	
A sten of	1	2	3	4	5	6	7	8	9	10	is obtained
by about	2.3%	4.4%	9.2%	15.0%	19.1%	19.1%	15.0%	9.2%	4.4%	2.3%	of adults

This is a profile of an actual male subject. Note that he is quite high on scales M and Q_2, fairly high on Q_1, fairly low on A and H, and very low on G, N, and Q_4. On the remaining scales his scores are all about average. From the verbal descriptions labeling the endpoints of the 16 scales, try writing a personality sketch of this person. What kind of a person do you think he is? Do you think this test allows you to know a lot about him? For starters, he is a 21-year-old college student at the University of Colorado.

to respond, facial expressions, the way the subject holds the card, and so on. All descriptions are then scored on such dimensions as the form of the description, color responses, perceived movement, the figures seen, and the details of the blots that the subject responds to. Scoring is obviously a problem because it depends so much on the opinion of the psychologist, who must decide whether a response really signifies movement, animal reference, color, or whatever. Clearly, in such an ambiguous situation the psychologist's personality as well as the subject's may influence the outcome.

TAT The other most commonly used projective test is the *Thematic Apperception Test*, the TAT. We encountered this

FIGURE C-4 The Rorschach Inkblot Test

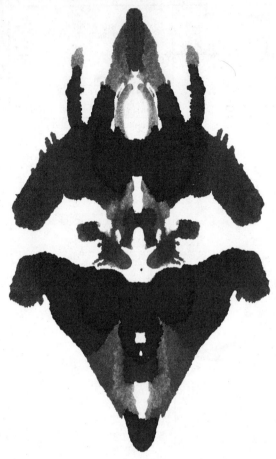

The inkblot is similar to those used in the Rorschach test. Typical responses would involve seeing animals or human beings, whereas a psychotic might respond with a bizarre comment of little relevance to the shape of the blot, such as "pools of blood pouring out of a tree."

test in Chapter 7 because it has been used successfully to measure achievement motivation. In the TAT the subject is shown a picture and is asked to tell a story about it. The story is supposed to tell what is happening in the picture, what led up to the scene in the picture, and what will happen in the future. There are 18 black and white pictures and one blank card (the subject must imagine a picture on the card and then tell the story). A popular shortened version of the test contains only 10 cards.

The stories are scored along several dimensions. A critical one is the person in the picture whom the subject identifies as the central character. Other considerations are how the story reflects certain needs and concerns of the subject and what factors seem to be aiding or hindering the satisfaction of personal needs. There are "norms" of typical responses that may serve as guidelines for the psychologist, but the test is basically *interpreted* and not quantified. This means that the scoring procedure is highly subjective and is perhaps easily affected by extraneous variables, just like the Rorschach test.

Other Projective Techniques   Other basically projective assessment techniques include dream analysis or interpretation, word association tests, analysis of subjects' drawings or other artwork, and the sentence completion test. In a sentence completion test the subject is given a stem of a sentence such as "The main trouble with people is . . ." and is asked to complete the sentence in a way that indicates how he or she really feels. This test is the most objective of the projective tests, because the subject's response is structured in advance by the stem of the sentence. Subjects are also much more aware of the implications of what they say than they are when they respond to an inkblot or TAT card. As a consequence, attitudes and beliefs rather than unconscious processes (which are presumably best revealed by the Rorschach or TAT) are the focus of measurement in sentence completion. Nevertheless, as with the TAT, distortions, themes, and unusual responses can give clues to a person's thought processes.

Projective tests represent a compromise between the free-floating character of some therapeutic interviews and the rigid structure of an inventory. The stimulus materials provide some guidelines and determinants of the client's behavior, but the therapist is free to pursue, with leading questions, the various potential trouble spots as the client may reveal them. Indeed, many diagnosticians do not rely at all on standard scoring methods that have been developed for projective tests but rather use them simply as a way to get a person to speak freely about various issues that he or she might otherwise repress or disguise. Nonetheless, there are ways of scoring a person's performance and of comparing him or her with others with known psychopathology. These comparisons are then used to make a classificatory diagnosis.

The Popularity of Tests

Though psychological testing is not as popular among psychologists today as it was 25 years ago, there is no sign that tests are disappearing from the scene. Recent surveys indicate that testing is still considered by many psychologists to be a major part of their professional activity.

Which tests are the most popular? Surveys of clinical psychologists and others regularly involved in testing resulted in the ranking shown in Table C–1. This table is also useful as an indicator of the wide range of psychological tests in use today.

Critique

In this final section we wish to raise two hotly debated issues about psychological testing. No simple answers are possible, but it is important that you be aware of the issues.

Behavior as Sign or Sample?

Is the behavior of a person taking a test (his or her score or answers to the test) a *sign* telling the psychologist what the

Diagnosis by Drawing

"Draw a picture of everyone in your family *doing* something." Those are the simple instructions that Psychiatrist S. Harvard Kaufman and Psychologist Robert C. Burns give to children sent to them for treatment. In their new book, *Kinetic Family Drawings* (Brunner/Mazel; $8.95), the two therapists show some of the kinetic, or action, pictures drawn by their young patients and explain how the crude art reveals more fully than thousands of words what is troubling the children.

The idea of evaluating the intellectual and emotional makeup of a child by analyzing his drawings did not originate with Kaufman and Burns. Ever since the 1920s, psychologists have been measuring intelligence by asking children to draw a person (the D-A-P test). For the past two decades, clues to children's emotional problems have been found in their drawings of a house, a tree and a person (the H-T-P technique). By requiring children to draw their families in action, however, Kaufman and Burns believe they have opened new avenues of investigation. In fact, they say, kinetic family drawings "tell us more than we can decipher."

Isolated Children

What the therapists find most intriguing are some of the recurring themes that reveal how children feel about their families. Kids who feel neglected will time and again draw their mothers cleaning house and their fathers driving off to work, while "tough or castrating" fathers are often pictured mowing the lawn or chopping wood. The cat, soft and furry but armed with claws—a creature symbolizing ambivalence—turns up frequently in pictures by girls who both love and hate their mothers.

Youngsters who feel isolated, like Mike, 17, frequently draw family members doing things alone in separate rooms instead of together. Mike also showed his mother at work in the kitchen with her back turned, and he drew himself " 'stealing' food (love) from the cold refrigerator." When they first took him to Psychiatrist Kaufman, Mike's parents insisted that the family was close. But they finally admitted to Kaufman what their son's drawings made painfully clear—that they "didn't give a damn what happened to Mike."

Sometimes children leave out of their pictures the very things that bother them most. Mary, 12, who had been raped by her brother, drew him sitting in a chair that concealed his body below the waist. Tim, 16, who suffered severe asthma attacks because he felt utterly unloved by

Assessing intelligence, personality, and emotional disorders in children is difficult. A common technique is to analyze art work they have done.

his alcoholic mother, showed himself running after an elusive butterfly. On his picture he wrote: "Can't draw mother." . . .

In another drawing, Billy, 14, revealed how he felt when his mother remarried. Her new husband had children of his own, and the family was polarized into two camps. Write Kaufman and Burns: "The boy must be aware of the sexual relationship between the stepfather and the mother, as the sword between the stepfather's legs is the largest weapon in the drawing." Billy, obviously jealous, drew himself throwing darts at his stepfather. The darts were very small and could do no harm; the boy must therefore have realized how powerless he was. That feeling of impotence, the authors say, may have accounted for Billy's "bad" behavior at home and at school. . . .

Time
February 1, 1971

person really is (really is sane or really is anxious or really is mentally retarded), or are responses on the test just a small sample of that person's behavior? We can all be anxious, crazy, or stupid at times. If a psychologist catches us at the wrong moment, we might appear worse (or better) than we really are. In fact, are we *really* anything for all time? Or does our behavior change radically with the situation such that sometimes, in some situations, we act silly or stupid, in others we are anxious, and so on? When psychologists say that a person is anxious, they are using the test as a sign that

TABLE C–1 A Ranking of Psychological Tests in Common Use Today

Test	Rank	Test	Rank
WAIS	1	Revised Beta	36
Rorschach	2	Sixteen Personality Factors Questionnaire	37
Visual-Motor Test (Bender-Gestalt)	3.5	Holtzman Inkblot	38.5
TAT	3.5	Make-A-Picture Test	38.5
Draw-A-Person Test (Machover)	5	Leiter International Performance Scale	40.5
MMPI	6	Purdue Pegboard	40.5
WISC	7	Minnesota Clerical Test	42.5
Stanford-Binet	8	Rosenzweig P-F Study	42.5
Sentence Completion Test (all kinds)	(8–9)	Metropolitan Achievement Tests	42.5
House-Tree-Person	9	Stanford Achievement Tests	42.5
Rotter Incomplete Sentences	10	Study of Values (Allport)	42.5
Vineland Social Maturity Scale	11	IPAT Anxiety Quotient	44
Memory for Designs (Graham-Kendall)	12	Revised Minnesota Paper Formboard	45.5
Peabody Picture Vocabulary Test	13	Army General Classification Test	45.5
Children's Apperception Test	14	California Achievement Tests	47.5
Kuder Preference Record	15	Concept Formation	47.5
Kuder Vocational	16	Kent Emergency Scale	47.5
Wechsler Memory Scale	17	Gilford-Zimmerman Temperament Survey	49
Edwards Personal Preference Schedule	18.5	California Test of Mental Maturity	50.5
Strong Vocational Interest Blank (Men)	18.5	Test for Color Blindness (Ishihara)	50.5
Benton Visual Retention Test	20	Arthur Point Scale	52
Gray Oral Reading Test	21	Gesell Developmental Schedule	53.5
Progressive Matrices	22	Block Design (KOHS)	53.5
Cattell Infant Intelligence Scale	23	Merrill-Palmer Scales	55
Goldstein Scheerer	24	The Adjustment Inventory (Bell)	56.5
Blacky Pictures	25.5	IMPS	56.5
Strong Vocational Interest Blank (Women)	25.5	Interpersonal Check List	56.5
Differential Aptitude Tests	27	Kent-Rosanoff Word Association Test	56.5
Porteus Maze Test	28.5	General Aptitude Test Battery	56.5
Wechsler-Bellevue Intelligence Scale	28.5	Tests of Mechanical Comprehension	56.5
Full Range Picture Vocabulary Test	28.5	Maier Art Tests	58
Columbia Mental Maturity Scale	30.5	Cooperative School & College Ability Tests	59.5
Illinois Test of Psycholinguistic Abilities	30.5	Calif. Short Form Test of Mental Maturity	59.5
Mooney Problem Check List	32	California Test of Personality	61.5
Wide Range Achievement Test	33	Kahn Symbol Arrangement Test	61.5
California Psychological Inventory	34	Diagnostic Reading Test	63
Shipley-Institute for Living Scales	35		

the person is or has something (trait anxiety), rather than as just a sample of the way the person behaves in a particular test situation (state anxiety). "Diagnosing" a person attaches a label to him or her, and this label seems to dominate the thinking about this person in such a way that the unique features of behavior are obscured. Just because a person was anxious when he or she took the test, does this mean he or she is always and forever *an anxious person?* Who would not be "anxious" if he or she desperately needed a job and had to face a psychologist who would *determine* his or her qualifications? The tradition in psychology has been to use tests as signs, but there is a growing awareness of the sampling aspect of psychological testing and the situational determinants of test behavior, which can only lead to fairer and more appropriate test use and interpretation.

Projective versus Self-Report Measures

The final issue deals with whether or not it is better to use projective or self-report measures of personality. Projective tests usually receive the most criticism because there is a great deal of subjective judgment and interpretation involved on the part of the psychologist. The projective tests therefore have lower reliability and validity measures, which suggests that these kinds of tests are dangerous to use when crucial decisions are to be made. Self-report, inventory-type tests are objective by comparison. They can be more easily validated (although this does not mean they are necessarily more valid), more impersonally administered, and more objectively scored.

"Well, frankly, no, Miss Kramer, I didn't answer all the questions honestly at the computer-mate office."

Playboy, June 1974. Reproduced by special permission of PLAYBOY Magazine. Copyright © 1974 by Playboy.

One obvious problem with self-report measures is that the person being tested can distort his or her answers in order to appear to be different than he or she actually is.

On the other hand, the self-report measures rely heavily on subjects being honest when they respond. Many of the items in some self-report measures suggest to the subject what the "best" response is, and therefore these tests can easily be faked. An honest person might be penalized by not faking. A less intelligent person might be discriminated against because he or she cannot deceive the psychologists as well as a smarter person. For this reason testers have added to many self-report tests special test items to detect faking.

Finally, even if the subject is honest and clearly understands the questions, is the person likely to be aware of all the aspects of his or her personality that are important? This is the issue of unconscious motivation—are there aspects to personality that a person is unaware of, and if so, how can that person be expected to report adequately in these areas? Projective tests presumably allow these features of personality to manifest themselves in a way that is supposed to be impossible in a self-report test. In response to this criticism, some self-report, objectively scored tests of unconscious processes have been developed. It is unfortunately too early to judge their adequacy.

We hope that you now have a better appreciation of why psychological testing is a controversial issue. It represents one area in which psychology intrudes into the lives of just about everyone in one way or another. When testing is used to decide who gets hired, who gets into a particular school, who goes to jail or to a mental hospital, then emotions are bound to run high. People who are affected by these intrusions in negative ways are bound to question the right of anybody to assess their personalities. All that psychologists can do in such cases is to develop fair tests, administer them under fair conditions, and interpret them with extreme caution. As long as decisions like these must be made by someone, then it is probably best to proceed in the light of as many facts as possible. We expect that many of these facts will come from continuing research in personality.

Altered States of Consciousness

The human organism is an information-processing system. It accepts information from its environment, retrieves other information from memory, processes that information, and reacts. Human beings attend to and are aware of only a portion of the total information flow at any one time. The state of awareness is called *consciousness,* and its contents consist of what is attended to in the overall information flow. At the same time, much of the flow passes through the system without being attended to, that is, without awareness. Information processed without awareness provides the contents of the unconscious.

"Consciousness is the primary reality," the Nobel prize-winning physicist Eugene Wigner put it. Indeed, psychology was defined as the study of consciousness earlier in its history, and many psychologists think it will again be defined that way in another decade. But to study consciousness we must use consciousness: How can consciousness understand itself?

Science tries to arrive at knowledge that is *objective,* so we would like to develop a scientific understanding of consciousness that is independent of the peculiarities and subjectivity of any particular observer. The difficulty with understanding consciousness from a purely introspective position is the obvious capacity of our minds to imagine things vividly and so make them come true.

In spite of problems that may prevent us from ever having a completely objective and comprehensive knowledge of consciousness, we can learn a great deal from observing our own consciousness and behavior and from studying the behavior of others and their reports about their consciousness. Since our consciousness is the ultimate reference point of our individual existence, anything we can learn about it may be of great value.

One of the most obvious things we experience about consciousness is that our experience shows great variations. We find that the totality of these variations, however, usually stays within a certain range which we have come to call *ordinary* or *normal.* Thus, you may wake up with a mild headache one morning, but you are still yourself; you can carry out your ordinary activities and experience things in pretty much the ordinary way, even though the small headache may stay with you all day. It is the experience of the many aspects of your consciousness staying within a customary range that gives you the common sense concept of your *ordinary state of consciousness.*

But some other morning you may wake up with a high fever. Your thoughts wander about in a very strange way—you are *delirious.* Your body is not only painful but seems the wrong shape; you feel like a little child instead of your ordinary adult self. The condition or state of your consciousness has gone far beyond the usual range you call your ordinary state.

It is the experience of *radical* alterations in consciousness, of mental functioning taking on a quite different pattern than it ordinarily does, that leads to the concept of *altered states of consciousness* (altered SoCs). When you awaken suddenly from a dream, for example, there is an abrupt transition to a radically different style of experience and functioning. While you can find elements of commonality, such as speaking English in both the dream and in your ordinary waking state, the overall change between dream and waking is so great that it is not adequate to think of dreaming as just an extreme of the ordinary range; there was a temporary reorganization of many aspects of consciousness leading to what we call the dream. An interesting exercise is to make a list of those aspects of your experience which allow you to say, with certainty, that right now you are not dreaming but awake. Some of these will be specific elements or qualities of consciousness, such as, for some people, continuity of memory, but there is also an overall grasp of the pattern of experience such that you know instantly that you are not dreaming. Altered SoCs, then, are radical alterations of both individual elements and the overall pattern of our consciousness. Altered states that practically everyone has experienced include such things as dreaming, high sexual arousal and orgasm, alcohol intoxication, and intense emotional states such as rage or terror.

Sleep and Dreams

Different stages of sleep are associated with brain waves of different frequency and amplitude, which produce distinctive electroencephalogram (EEG) patterns for each stage (see Figure D–1). The subject who is awake but resting with the eyes closed shows predominantly **alpha brain waves** (a regular rhythm of about 10 cycles per second). As sleep comes on the alpha rhythm is replaced by slower, irregular waves in what is called Initial Stage 1 EEG. With the appearance of bursts of activity of about 14 cycles per second, called *spindles,* the EEG is classified as Stage 2 sleep. When larger, slower **delta waves** (1 to 2 cycles per second) are added to the irregular activity and spindles, the pattern is called Stage 3; and when delta waves predominate, the pattern is Stage 4. The cycle through the stages is repeated four to six times a night.

Eugene Aserinsky found that during Stage I EEG periods (after the initial Stage 1), an electrooculogram (EOG) recorded rapid eye movements (REMs) in sleeping subjects, and if he awakened the subjects during these periods, they recalled a dream about 80 percent of the time. It is now generally accepted that ordinary dreaming occurs in REM sleep, although dreamlike activity is sometimes reported to occur during other stages of sleep. In fact, there appears to be cognitive activity of some kind during all the sleep stages. Dreamlike cognitions predominate in REM sleep, while the cognition in the other stages is typically described as more like the normal thinking of wakefulness. If the REM periods are plotted, the first one occurs about 90 minutes after going to sleep and lasts 5 to 10 minutes. At the second 90-minute mark, a somewhat longer REM period occurs, and this stage of sleep recurs and gets somewhat longer at each 90-minute cycle (see Figure D–2). The last

FIGURE D–1   Brain waves, sleep, and dreaming

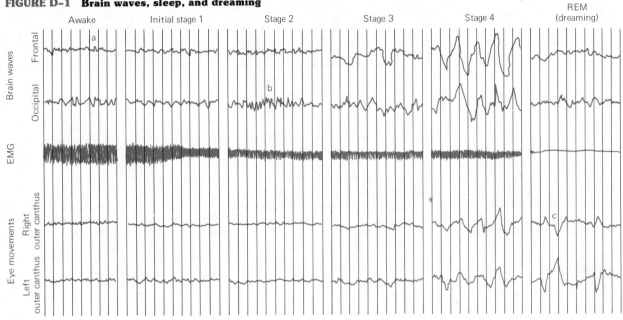

Recordings of brain waves from three cortical areas (frontal is on the forehead, parietal is over the ear, occipital is back of the head) and eye movements as a person goes to sleep. The regular alpha rhythm (a) in the awake subject is replaced by slower, irregular activity in Initial Stage 1. Spindles (b) appear in Stage 2, and delta waves are added to the irregular activity and spindles in Stage 3. The large, slow delta waves predominate in Stage 4. Rapid eye movements (REMs), measured by the electrooculogram (EOG), are associated with dreaming and occur in later Stage 1 periods of the night. They are indicated by synchronous but opposite deflections (c) on the eye-movement channels.

REM dream of the night may be from half an hour to an hour long, and awakening from it is common. This last dream, of course, is the one you are most likely to remember in the morning. As a result of this shifting pattern, REM sleep tends to occur primarily in the latter half of the night, while Stage 4 sleep occurs primarily in the first half of the night. Also, it is worth noting that the need for sleep and its various stages changes with age (see Figure D–3).

Hypnagogic and Hypnopompic States

The SoC that one passes through in going from waking to sleeping is called the **hypnagogic state.** It is similar, and possibly identical to, the SoC that one passes through in going from sleeping to waking, the **hypnopompic state.** The laboratory studies that have been carried out have concentrated on the hypnagogic state, which varies tremendously from individual to individual. For some people the period of falling asleep is filled with experiences as rich as the best nocturnal dreams. For others it is very dull and usually forgotten almost immediately.

Much hypnagogic experience may be identical to later dreaming, although not enough investigation of similarities and differences has been carried out to make this comparison complete. Even for the best hypnagogic "dreamers," the experiences of the hypnagogic state are usually forgotten more rapidly than ordinary dreams, especially if the dreamer continues on into sleep.

You can observe your own hypnagogic state in detail by doing the following: When lying down to sleep, balance one arm vertically, with the elbow resting on the bed. You can go fairly far into a hypnagogic state and maintain your arm in a balanced, comfortable position with little effort. When you are deep in the hypnagogic state your arm will start to fall. The action will usually startle you into wakeful-

FIGURE D–2   A night of sleep and dreams

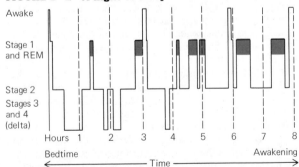

As the night progresses, the typical sleeper cycles through the various sleep stages, periodically dreaming (REM sleep, indicated by the colored bars). The REM periods are characterized by a stage-1 EEG pattern, but in addition there are rapid eye movements present, and the muscle tone in the head region is dramatically decreased. Note that each succeeding dream period is longer, and that most of the "deep" sleep, signaled by the presence of delta waves (stages 3 and 4) occurs in the first half of the night. Correspondingly note that most of the dreaming takes place in the second half of the night.

FIGURE D-3 Age changes in sleep and dreaming

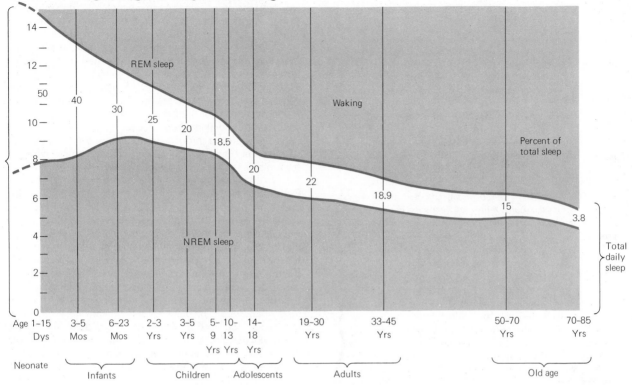

One of the most interesting aspects of sleep is the way our need for it changes with age, especially our need for REM sleep, which declines dramatically. REM sleep, expressed as a percentage of total sleep declines from around 50 percent to less than 10 percent by the time a person reaches age 70. The very high percentage of REM sleep during early infancy is especially intriguing. Is this when the brain is being programmed?

ness, and you can try to fix the memory of the hypnagogic experience in your mind before it fades. With the balanced arm technique the hypnagogic state can be greatly prolonged.

Ordinary Dreaming

Ordinary dreaming refers to the experience almost all of us have had of waking up and recalling scenes and events that seemed to take place in a world that often resembles the physical world, but a world we retrospectively consider to be purely imaginary. Although there have been many laboratory and home studies of dreams, most people in our culture have not learned to be good observers of their dreams. Thus much of what is known about dreams has come from piecing together the reports of poor observers. Interestingly, the kind of "psychological mindedness" that makes people good dream recallers may be helpful when people undergo brief psychotherapy. Psychologist Rosalind Cartwright took a group of nonpsychologically minded students, those who usually drop out of therapy without completing it, and had them awakened from nocturnal dream periods that were monitored in the laboratory. Compared to a control group who were awakened from non-REM periods, the REM-awakened group stayed in therapy longer and showed more appropriate behaviors in therapy sessions.

To illustrate the flavor of ordinary dreaming, consider this beginning of a dream, told by a young woman.

> Someone had brought a tremendous amount of LSD into town and had been dispensing it freely. The cops were frustrated because they couldn't arrest everyone and they didn't know who to pin it on. In dispensing this there seemed to be a spirit of free giving and there were no strangers. Someone said to me that if you took the LSD with fish the way the Indians (American) do, it wouldn't make you sick, but if you took it medically, it might. I took some by itself, but I knew it wouldn't make me sick anyway. I continued walking, and noticed that I wasn't wearing my clothes. The other people in town were dressed, but my unclothed state didn't seem to bother them. I went into a room where there were a lot of young people and also a man I know who is associated with young people as a teacher and counselor. (Tart, 1969, p. 173)

This dream is typical of dreams. Yet from its content we can be sure this was a dream and not a description of a real event—if you walk down a street naked people usually do get bothered! The unreality of dreams is usually a waking state judgment; dreams are real enough at the time they occur.

Sleep Is Crucial for Survival

PHILADELPHIA — No one knows why we sleep. But we must. Experts say we can live weeks without food. But only 10 days without sleep.

"It's not just for rest and relaxation," says noted sleep researcher Dr. Eugene Aserinsky. "That's too neat, too simple an answer.

"It may be a time when the brain circuits are organized or cause consolidation of memory," says the Jefferson Hospital doctor. "It may be like making jello—with all the activity in the day, you may need a time to allow it to solidify into memory."

"My guess is that temperature control would be a stronger reason than the others," Dr. Aserinsky said. During sleep, the body temperature drops as does the basal metabolic rate, which adds credence to the jello theory.

In animals, the amount of sleep is related to their basal metabolic rate—the higher the metabolic rate, the more sleep animals get. A mouse needs 12.8 hours compared to an elephant's 3.9 hours in a 24-hour period.

The most humans can sleep in a 24-hour period is an average of 16 hours, even though they may have been up the night before. However, they usually average between six and eight hours a night, though 10 may be more agreeable to some, according to Aserinsky.

People sleep in 90-minute cycles with 20 minutes of each cycle devoted to rapid eye movements (REM), the period when people dream, says Aserinsky, who discovered the phenomena more than two decades ago. And by counting the REM, he says, researchers can tell when a person has had enough sleep.

If a person doesn't get enough REM sleep one night, he'll make up for it the next, he says. But alcohol and sleeping pills won't help REM sleep—they depress it, which is why a person—under the influence—won't feel as refreshed. . . .

The Sunday Camera (Boulder, Colo.)
March 21, 1976

In general, if you are deprived of sleep or any particular sleep stage such as REM, you will recapture *some, but not all,* of the time lost in subsequent nights. The amount of recapture varies from one person to another—in fact, some people do not recapture lost REM sleep. Do you think personality might have anything to do with REM recapture?

Psychological Effects

Perception   Ordinary dreaming represents one of the most radical changes in perception of any altered SoC, because the external world is almost completely eliminated and replaced by an internal world. There are tremendous individual differences in how "real" the dream world is. At one extreme some people report experiencing every sensory quality that they experience in a wakeful state. They see dream scenes clearly and in color, they hear and speak with dream char-

acters, and they may taste, touch, and smell in the dream world. At the other extreme some people report their dreams to be little more than rather hazy black and white images. The dream reported earlier was one of the more vivid types.

Occasionally stimuli from the external world make their way into the dream world, where they are usually distorted in some fashion to fit in with the action of the dream. The ringing of the alarm clock, for example, may be perceived as a church bell in the dream. There is also selectivity in the perception of the external world during dreaming, as well as during waking (see Chapter 3). An example is the parent who sleeps through the rumble of traffic outside the window, but snaps wide awake at the slightest whimper from his or her child three rooms away.

Performance   Motor output is virtually eliminated during dreaming. Laboratory studies have shown that there is an active inhibition in the spinal cord of nerve impulses to the muscles. Impulses corresponding to the imagery experienced during dreaming may arrive at the muscles, but the inhibitory signal keeps the muscles from reacting. Occasionally the muscles of the limbs or face may twitch slightly, and occasionally there is some vocalization during ordinary dreaming. But for the most part the dreaming person is almost totally paralyzed. The paralysis of the dream state is adaptive in a sense, because if people acted out their dreams the world would be a rather dangerous place at night, for both the dreamers and anyone near them. On occasion the paralysis may last into the waking state for a few seconds.

Cognitive Processes   Cognitive processes in dreams are unusual in several ways. Not only do dreamers fool themselves as to whether they are awake or asleep, but they also accept all sorts of incongruities and absurdities in the dream situation without the slightest question, like walking down the street naked without attracting attention. In the ordinary SoC the person would be immediately alerted by such incongruities and consider them in detail, but the dreamer ignores errors in his or her cognitive processes until afterward, during the waking state. Freud theorized that this was because subconscious desires and emotions were actually responsible for the particular content of the dream, and not enough psychological energy was available to the "secondary processes," the intellectual functions, to allow observation of dream content. Other theorists view dream "stupidity" as a simple consequence of inadequate activation of higher brain centers during sleep.

Emotion   Emotional processes can have a greater effect on the dream experience than cognitive processes. The range of emotional experience is as great as in ordinary waking consciousness, although the emotions may be evoked by rather different stimuli than would evoke them in the waking state. Emotions may also become extremely intense, possibly because the lowered level of critical processes no longer acts to inhibit the emotional systems. Even the amount of sleep and dreaming a person does has been partially tied to emotional factors.

Memory   Memory systems obviously function at a very high level during ordinary dreaming. Almost the entire dream world is constructed from memory images of things the dreamer has seen or otherwise sensed or from new combinations of past memories. In the example of a dream given earlier, the dreamer had to construct the experience of walking down a street naked without attracting attention from memory elements, because she had never experienced this situation in real life. The memory quality of an experience is often missing during ordinary dreaming, and the dreamer almost always mistakes an intense scene constructed from memory for a real world of experience. As is typical in altered SoCs, visual memory seems particularly strong in dreams, much stronger than a person's ability to produce a visual image from memory in the normal state. Vision is usually the dominant sense modality in dreaming, as in ordinary consciousness.

Recall that memory *for* dreams varies tremendously from person to person. Some people almost never remember a dream after waking. Other people remember many dreams practically every morning. With those who do recall their dreams on awakening, the rate at which the dream fades from memory in the normal state also varies. Some people lose the memory of the dream within a few seconds, unless they make a conscious effort to rehearse it; others may remember a dream vividly for months or years. Sometimes a dream will be forgotten, but an incident later in the day will trigger a complete memory of it. Many people who claim they never remember their dreams begin to do so in great detail if they practice taking notes on their dreams as soon as they wake up. If you are interested in your dreams, you might start keeping a "dream diary."

Identity A person's sense of identity is highly variable in a dream. The dreamer can be his or her normal self, can completely identify with an entirely different character in the dream, or can identify with a version of himself or herself that is changed in a number of important ways. At times a person may have no identity at all in a dream, simply perceiving the dream as an "outside" observer might. This is a striking example of the arbitrariness of our belief in a fixed personal identity. Unique combinations of characteristics and personality elements can be grouped as "the ego" quite readily during dreams. Note too that much of the cognitive activity and emotional reaction of a dream takes place with respect to *who* the dreamer is. If he or she becomes a *different* person in a dream, then events that might be important or evoke specific plans or emotions for the individual's ordinary identity might not do so within the dream.

Time Sense Time in dreams generally seems to flow at about the same rate as normal waking activity. This has been established in the laboratory by timing the length of the brain-wave state associated with dreaming and then waking the person and having him or her estimate, in various ways, how long the dream lasted. Generally the subject's estimate is quite close to the actual amount of time elapsed. There still seem to be some dreams, however, in which the perceived time correlates very poorly with clock time. Thus, one might have a dream that seems to take a week, when the sleep stage associated with dreaming could not have lasted more than an hour or so. This may not mean that a week's worth of events actually occurred in the dream, but only that the *feeling* of time was of a week passing.

Physiological Correlates

As we mentioned, nearly all motor functioning is inhibited during dreaming, with two major exceptions. The first is the REMs that are characteristic of dreaming sleep. REMs have been related in some experiments (but not all) to what the dreamer reports he or she is seeing. Thus, if the dreamer reported watching objects fall from airplanes to the ground, his or her electrooculogram might register large vertical REMs. Dreams of watching a ping-pong match would probably produce large horizontal REMs. The other exception to the complete lack of motor functioning in the dream state seems to be the autonomic nervous system. Heart rate, blood pressure, and respiration show great variability and can undergo large, sudden changes during dreaming. It is not yet clear whether this reflects the emotions of the dream or not.

In males the penis is partially erect throughout most of REM dreaming. In females there is increased vaginal blood flow. This does not necessarily represent specific, overt sexual content of the dreams so much as some sort of physiological release phenomenon. The "morning erection," previously attributed to a full bladder, is now seen to result from the last dream of the night, which frequently occurs just before awakening.

In the last two decades many drugs have been administered to subjects just before they go to bed to see what effects they have on the sleep and dream cycle. This research is particularly important because of the enormous use of sleeping medication (sedatives) in our society. Practically all drugs tested, especially the commonly used sedatives, decrease the amount of time sleepers spend in REM sleep. This deficit of REM time often carries over through a period of continuous drug use, such that when the drug is no longer taken there is a temporary increase (over normal) of REM sleep time for a few nights, although the total deficit is not made up. This has been called the *REM rebound effect.* Stimulants such as amphetamines decrease REM sleep time. There is some evidence that psychedelics, like low doses of LSD, or marijuana cause REM time to shift to earlier in the night without having much effect on total REM time.

Such disruptions of the sleep cycle are generally bad for physical health. A positive result has been the finding of a few sedatives, such as chloral hydrate, that promote sleep but do not disturb the sleep cycle.

Very little research has been done on the effects of various drugs on the content of dreams or on the quality of the altered SoC, although these psychological questions are important.

Non-REM Sleep (Dreamless Sleep?)

Dreamless sleep is a term commonly used to refer to Stages 1 (without REM), 2, 3, and 4 of the EEG sleep pattern. They are not accompanied by REMs and are therefore commonly referred to as non-REM stages or non-REM sleep. The term "dreamless sleep" should be used with caution. While there are *seldom* reports of intense, emotional episodes of dreaming from stages other than REM periods, they do occur occasionally. Researchers have not yet been able to decide whether these vivid reports are dreams recalled from an earlier REM period or whether they actually happened in non-REM sleep.

Without My Eight Hours, I'm a Type A
By LINDA ASHER

Sleeping less than other people, and particularly getting less REM (rapid eye movement) sleep, may contribute to the hard-driving, heart attack-prone personality that psychologists call "Type A." A group of researchers at San José State University in California began investigating connections between the two when they noted the similarity between Type A characteristics and the character sketch of short sleepers drawn up by Boston psychiatrist Ernest Hartmann. Hartmann found short sleepers to be "efficient, energetic, ambitious persons who work hard and keep busy . . . [who are] sure of themselves, decisive, [self-] satisfied."

Was that Type A? Psychologists Robert A. Hicks, Robert J. Pellegrini, and James Hawkins gave more than 500 college students a sleep questionnaire and administered a form of the Jenkins Activity Survey, the measure generally used to define Type A personalities. They found that the less the students said they habitually slept, the more likely they were to report Type A behavior.

According to earlier Hartmann counts, short sleepers form a clearly definable category of people who sleep about 20 percent less than normal subjects, and get about 25 percent less REM sleep. Short sleep thus constitutes a kind of spontaneous REM deprivation. More deliberate forms of REM deprivation are under investigation in several psychiatric centers for such therapeutic effects as bestirring deeply depressive patients. In several forthcoming papers, the researchers contend that REM deprivation may lead to Type A behavior by causing increased susceptibility to stress factors: REM-deprived laboratory animals show heightened sensitivity to pain.

Both REM-deprived animals and humans tend to respond to stress with aggression, even when relaxation would be more effective. In one set of experiments, rats that would normally relax and float in a water tank swam frantically if they were short on REM sleep. Moreover, "sleep-deprived animals become fearless, taking chances and abandoning their usual self-protective behaviors," Hicks told *Psychology Today*. In experimental situations, sleep-deprived humans also lose what Hicks calls "fluid intelligence and flexibility," choosing unthinking aggressive responses to stress over more reflective alternatives.

It is unclear at this point whether short-sleeping Type A's could or should try to stretch out their REM time: the pattern that may contribute to their drive and effectiveness may also be implicated in shortening their lives.

Psychology Today
June 1979

Could there be a relationship between your sleeping habits and your personality? If so, which causes which? This article implies that short sleep and perhaps REM deprivation causes you to behave like a Type A person (see Chapter 9). Can you think of an alternative interpretation of this correlation?

If subjects are awakened in the laboratory from non-REM sleep and asked what was going through their minds just before awakening, the usual answer is "nothing." Either there is no mental activity during this kind of sleep or memory of it is extremely poor. On rare occasions something is described by the subject that he or she labels a "dream." More frequently reports from non-REM sleep are labeled by the subject as "thinking." The impression of experiences during dreamless sleep is that they are often a sort of sporadic thinking — brief, relatively logical, and pedestrian thoughts. Perception of the external world is generally nonexistent; either stimuli are not well incorporated into the ongoing experience or the ongoing experience is forgotten. Self-awareness also seems to be nonexistent.

The major exception to the notion that only occasional vague and dull thoughts occur during dreamless sleep is the finding that most *sleep talking, sleep walking,* and what are called *night terrors* (as opposed to nightmares, which occur during REM sleep) occur during non-REM sleep. Since the person is not in a state of peripheral motor paralysis as in REM sleep, mental experiences may be expressed in physical action. The fact that most night terrors occur in non-REM sleep indicates that occasionally exceptionally intense dream-like processes may occur, with maximal emotional arousal. Thus another altered SoC develops from non-REM sleep on these occasions.

Hypnosis

Hypnosis has been one of the most widely investigated SoCs in our society. We can define hypnosis as an SoC characterized by a kind of mental quiet, a lack of the on-going thought processes usually associated with ordinary consciousness, and hypersuggestibility. In hypnosis a wide variety of specific phenomena and experiences can be brought about by suggesting them to the subject.

Hypnosis is usually induced while the subject is sitting or lying in a relaxed position. The hypnotist asks the subject to relax, to be calm and quiet, and not to worry about anything. It is usually suggested that the subject is getting drowsy or sleepy, but the subject implicitly knows that this is merely a way to let his or her mind drift and become completely relaxed. Suggestions that are responded to positively by most people are given early in the induction procedure, and the skillful hypnotist uses positive responses to these to build confidence on the subject's part that the person can go into an even deeper hypnotic state. Various types of "gadgetry" are sometimes used to induce hypnosis, such as fancy machines or crystal balls. These have no real function other than increasing the credibility of the hypnotist. The hypnotist using a machine to hypnotize a subject appears to be very "scientific," and so the subject has that much more confidence in the hypnotist.

Psychologist Aims
at Keeping Ex-Mates
Out of Divorcees' Dreams
By ED LION

CHICAGO (UP) — Happy-ending dreams with the husband returning can be devastating emotionally for newly divorced women, psychologist Rosalind D. Cartwright says.

So she is trying to help them change their dreams while they sleep and thus speed emotional adjustment to their new lifestyle.

The dream specialist at Chicago's Rush-Presbyterian-St. Luke's Hospital is working with 60 divorced women at the hospital's sleep disorder laboratory in a study funded by the National Institute of Mental Health.

"They will dream they are in bed alone," she said in an interview. "Then they hear the husband coming up the stairs toward their room. They think 'Oh, good, he's back.' They dream he sits on the side of the bed, gets under the covers and then they feel that everything's okay again.

"Of course, when they wake up and he's not beside them it hurts them. It can send them deeper and deeper into depression."

Cartwright is attacking this cycle of depression, partially perpetuated by repetitive dreams of the husband returning, by trying to help divorced women "rescript" their dream endings beforehand and then change them on cue in midsleep.

"If it works it could be an effective therapy," she said. "It might be used for other problems too, like nightmares."

Cartwright said she believes one of the functions served by dreaming is to reconcile events of the day with the sleeper's own self-image.

But with certain jarring problems, including divorce, she said, people may spend months — even years — with repetitive dreams that only perpetuate depression and hamper emotional adjustment. People in depression generally dream 10 percent more than others, she said.

"Women who are traditional and always thought of themselves as Mrs. So and So and the wife of So and So can be hit really hard. After the divorce, they are asking, 'Who the heck am I?'"

Thus, she said, their dreams can be caught in repetitive cycles because their "sense of self" is severely disoriented.

In the hospital's sleep lab, brain waves, chin muscles and eye movement are monitored all night.

During dreaming, eyes move rapidly under the lids and the brain is more active. Technicians then know when the women are having heavy dreaming periods.

Cartwright plans to instruct the women to press a microswitch put on their hand when they are aware of their repetitive dream. . . .

The Denver Post
May 18, 1979

The impact of the psychological content of dreams is not well known, although there is strong belief among psychologists that it is important. Here is an interesting possibility. If people could learn to control or modify dream content, perhaps they could become healthier and happier.

The hypnotist's long repetition of suggestions of sleep and drowsiness may lead to a state generally termed *neutral hypnosis,* the hypnotic state without specific suggestions that anything *in particular* will happen. Subjects describe this as a state of detachment and mental quiet. They feel totally relaxed. If asked what they are thinking about, they usually answer "nothing." They describe their minds as blank, although they are alert and attentive to the hypnotist. This state contrasts markedly with our normal SoC, in which, as we discussed in Chapter 6, we are always thinking about something.

There are immense individual differences in response to hypnosis. About 5 to 10 percent of people do not respond at all, while another 10 to 20 percent can achieve very deep hypnotic states and experience almost all hypnotic phenomena. Most people fall on a normal distribution of susceptibility between these two extremes. In spite of an immense amount of research on personality characteristics of responsive and unresponsive hypnotic subjects, no solid findings have come to light. We have little knowledge of why one person is readily susceptible to hypnotic suggestion and another is not. Similarly, there has been a great deal of research on possible physiological changes during hypnosis, but no distinct changes have been identified other than those that can be attributed to physical relaxation.

There is a great deal of controversy about the nature of hypnosis. If one defines hypnosis simply in terms of hypersuggestibility, for example, some subjects will be suggestible and otherwise will behave as a hypnotized person is expected to, but will report little or no changes in their conscious experiences. Indeed, one type of hypnosis research design pioneered by psychologist Martin Orne uses *simulator control groups* — people picked because they are unresponsive to repeated attempts to hypnotize them, and then coached to *act* like hypnotized subjects. Often simulators cannot be distinguished from genuinely hypnotized subjects *on the basis of external behavior:* It is only the later, honest reports of internal experience that distinguish them.

Here we shall take the traditional view of hypnosis as an altered SoC, which is probably basically true for some subjects, but remember that some authorities do not believe that hypnosis is an altered SoC at all, only a case of involved acting or role playing.

Psychological Effects

Perception   Under hypnosis many aspects of perception can be totally restructured from the subject's point of view. Perception in specific sensory modalities can be reduced to various degrees, a state called *hypoesthesia.* Subjects may be told, for example, that they cannot see clearly, and they will report that their vision is blurred or dim. Hypoesthesia can be carried to the point of total blocking of a sensory modality. Subjects may be told that they cannot smell at all, after which some will be able to take a sniff of a bottle of household ammonia, show practically no reaction to it, and report that they smelled nothing. Since the sensation of pain can be completely blocked by hypnotic suggestion, hypnosis has been used as an analgesic (pain killer) in medical and surgical treatment.

On the other hand, *hyperesthesias* may be created by telling subjects that one sense is exceptionally keen. Most

Hypnotism Moves into Mainstream of Therapy
By JANE E. BRODY

In an age of costly medical equipment, complicated research and powerful drugs, a growing number of health practitioners are discovering that one of the most potent therapeutic tools is a basic mental talent exploited by the ancients: hypnosis.

Though once denigrated as a mere parlor game and stage trick, hypnosis is fast gaining professional respectability. In recent years, hypnosis has been endorsed as an effective treatment technique by medical, dental, psychiatric and psychological associations here and abroad. In a 1978 survey, a third of American dental and medical schools were offering courses in hypnosis, twice as many as in 1974.

Patients in therapists' offices and medical facilities throughout the country are undergoing hypnosis to help treat such diverse problems as dental anxiety, phobias, obesity, cigarette smoking, mental depression, neuroses, high blood pressure, seizures, abnormal heart rhythms, excessive bleeding, asthma, and the pain of headache, backache, arthritis, childbirth, surgery, burns and cancer. Hypnotherapy is now used in more than half of patients treated at the pain clinic at Walter Reed Army Medical Center.

At the same time, the newly recognized power and versatility of hypnosis has spawned a host of potentially dangerous self-styled hypnotists and self-help advocates who are inadequately trained to cope with the forces that a hypnotic trance may unleash or to take full advantage of the therapeutic potential of the technique.

Experts emphasize that hypnosis is not appropriate for all persons and all kinds of problems; it takes a well-trained specialist to know when and how to use it properly.

"Anyone can learn to induce hypnosis in about 10 minutes, but that doesn't make you a hypnotherapist," said Dr. Milton V. Kline, director of the Institute for Research in Hypnosis in New York. "Hypnosis is not a magical phenomenon—not a matter of simply making suggestions to change someone's behavior. Rather, it's a complex way of getting into a person's ego functions, perceptions and physiological reactions. It requires careful evaluation of patients, their problems and their total life situations. It is most effectively used by someone well trained in psychological and physiological processes."

Most patients can readily learn to hypnotize themselves, and thus to supplement and reinforce the therapist's efforts. This gives patients a sense of self-control over their problems and often shortens the time and expense involved in professional treatment.

Hypnosis has also become a popular tool of law-enforcement officials, who are using it to jog the memories of witnesses and crime victims, to explore the mental state of defendants and to unearth clues that have led to the capture and conviction of many suspects. However, abuse of the technique abounds, and the uncritical use of hypnosis by detectives unschooled in its potential pitfalls has tainted the testimony of crucial witnesses and led to false arrests.

Despite its burgeoning popularity, hypnosis remains a myth-ridden entity that frightens many physicians and prospective patients. Though practitioners of hypnosis do not yet agree on a single explanation for the hypnotic phenomenon and do not know exactly how it works, they have pointed out that many medical weapons, including penicillin, were widely used long before they were fully understood.

It is known that hypnosis is an altered state of consciousness — not sleep, but rather an intense alertness in which the mind can screen out extraneous matters and focus on particular details. The hypnotic trance is characterized by extreme relaxation and heightened susceptibility to suggestion. It allows people to suspend logical reasoning and to draw on psychological strengths they do not normally command voluntarily.

But contrary to what many persons think, hypnosis does not involve relinquishing one's will or being controlled by someone else. Nor is it an exclusive state applicable only to a few.

The hypnotic trance is now recognized as a fundamental capacity of the human mind attainable to one degree or another by the vast majority of people. Whether they realize it or not, most people often lapse into light trances, for example, while reading or daydreaming. Several simple tests for hypnotizability have been devised, and characteristics of good hypnotic subjects have been defined. These include a high level of imagination, intelligence and intense powers of concentration, with a tendency to daydream.

In its simplest form, treatment with hypnosis involves inducing a trance, then directing the patient's attention to a particular "strategy" for coping with the problem at hand. The focused concentration and heightened suggestibility of the trance state helps the patient accept the therapist's directions and more rapidly solve the problem, according to Dr. Robert T. London, director of the short-term psychotherapy unit at New York University-Bellevue Medical Center.

Link Between Event and Symptom
The trance state also enables the patient to tap information, such as a link between a particular event and the development of an unwanted symptom, that might not otherwise reach the conscious mind, Dr. Kline noted. He told, for example, of a healthy 28-year-old man who developed an unexplained cardiac neurosis. The man had become convinced that he had heart disease and developed palpitations and a dangerously high blood pressure. Under hypnosis, the man recalled an aspect of a routine medical examination that his mind had misinterpreted, provoking the neurosis. Once he understood its origins, the neurosis disappeared and

Hypnosis is one of the most intriguing, mystifying, and versatile tools used by psychologists. Research on hypnosis is beginning to dispel many of the misconceptions people have about hypnosis.

Hypnotism Moves into Mainstream of Therapy *(continued)*

his blood pressure returned to normal.

Recent research has shown that it is not necessary to go into a deep trance to reap the potential benefits of the hypnotic state. Often, in fact, the greatest therapeutic gains are made by those in only a light or moderate trance.

For example, in using hypnosis to treat the pain of advanced cancer, therapists at the University of California, Los Angeles, School of Medicine found that even persons with a "low hypnotic susceptibility" could get significant relief.

Dr. Joseph Barber and Jean Gitelson of U.C.L.A. found that hypnosis can relieve pain in a cancer patient when medication or surgery no longer help. Hypnosis lacks the unpleasant side effects of potent pain-killing drugs and allows the patient to remain alert even during the terminal phases of illness, they noted in the cancer journal, Ca.

Further, they say, cancer patients' self-esteem and outlook on life are enhanced and their anxiety reduced by their ability to participate in their own treatment through self-hypnosis. The

Los Angeles therapists told of a 42-year-old man with intense pain from advanced testicular cancer, who through hypnotherapy, could control his pain without drugs, relax, accept his prognosis, cooperate better with doctors and nurses and make peace with his family before he died.

The hypnotic strategies used by the Los Angeles therapists and others to control pain include suggesting numbness of the painful area; substituting another feeling, such as pressure, for the pain, and shifting the pain to a smaller and less vulnerable area of the body, such as a fingertip.

Pain relief obtained while in a trance continues for a time — and sometimes indefinitely — after the person returns to a normal wakeful state. For many kinds of chronic or recurring pain, such as back pain or tension headaches, permanent relief may eventually be obtained through repeated self-hypnosis.

Perhaps the best testimony to the power of hypnotic suggestion to block pain is its occasional use as the sole means of anesthesia during surgery,

such as Caesarean sections and leg amputations. A Michigan obstetrician performed 93 percent of vaginal deliveries with hypnosis providing the only pain relief.

Hypnosis Only Masks Pain

Experiments by Dr. Ernest R. Hilgard of Stanford University have shown that pain is only masked by hypnosis; the patient still "feels" it at some level though conscious awareness is blocked. Others have shown that the physiological earmarks of pain are still present although the patient is unaware of the discomfort. Just how the trance state enables a patient to "disconnect" pain from awareness of it is not known.

Since pain is a signal that something may be wrong with the body, before treating pain with hypnosis, the therapist must determine its cause. "This is why hypnosis should not be used by a lay hypnotist who lacks proper medical training or backup," Dr. London said.

The New York Times
October 7, 1980

Around the middle of the nineteenth century, hypnosis became a focus of scientific attention. Jean Charcot, a French professor of anatomy, believed that hysterical persons made the best subjects for hypnosis because they were more open to the suggestions of others.

subjects will report "feeling" an increase in sensitivity, although there is little evidence that actual sensitivity changes. Suggestion can be carried to the point of illusion, or even hallucination, in which case the subject will see things that do not really exist. A very responsive subject can be told, for example, to see a friendly polar bear walking around the room, and the person will "see" it. Note that the careful hypnotist is sure to specify a *friendly* polar bear to avoid frightening the subject.

Self-awareness Awareness in hypnosis may readily be focused on various external or internal processes. For example, subjects may feel able to become hyper-aware of their internal bodily processes. Even more interesting, many processes that are ordinarily in the subject's awareness may become dissociated. Thus a subject may be told that his arm will keep moving around in circles without his awareness, and it will do so. A subject may be told that she is going completely blind, but that when the hypnotist makes a certain hand gesture the blindness will cease. The subject will report being completely blind and act appropriately, yet when the hypnotist makes a certain hand gesture the "blindness" disappears. "Seeing" the gesture takes place outside of conscious awareness.

Awareness can be curiously split in hypnosis, as is demonstrated in a technique called the *hidden observer,* developed by Ernest Hilgard at Stanford University. A deeply hypnotized subject is told that there is some part of the mind that is always fully aware of exactly what is happening in the situation and of what he, the subject, is experiencing, and this hidden observer can report by talking in response to special cues. A subject might then be told, for example, that his arm is numb and have it placed in ice water for several minutes. This *cold pressor* test is very painful, especially if the ice water is kept circulating. The hypnotized subject will report that he feels little or no pain, and he will behave like a relaxed, pain-free person. The hidden observer, on the other hand, will report that the pain is agonizing!

Emotion In neutral hypnosis there are generally no emotional feelings at all. Emotions can be totally structured by suggestion; any particular emotion can be elicited at any intensity and in conjunction with any stimulus object. The stimuli can be entirely inappropriate. For example, the subject may be told, "You are about to hear an extremely funny joke"; the hypnotist then tells the person, "Pine needles are green," and the subject laughs uproariously.

The hypnotic state may allow a psychotherapist access to processes that are normally unconscious. By suggesting emotional dulling, for example, the hypnotherapist might then be able to have the patient recall and work with memories that are ordinarily too painful to deal with. Thus, hypnosis can be a useful adjunct to psychotherapy. Often when a subject is told to have a dream while in hypnosis, he or she reports material similar to that experienced in ordinary nocturnal dreams, and thus the subject's subconscious processes can be detected.

Memory Memory function can be drastically altered in hypnosis. If told they cannot remember certain things, responsive subjects cannot consciously do so. They may

be told that after awakening from the hypnotic state they will not be able to remember anything that went on. Or they may be told that they can remember certain parts of the hypnotic experience and not other parts. Alternatively, subjects may be told that their memory is exceptionally good for some sorts of events, and they may sometimes exhibit better memory than usual. The exact nature and size of these effects on memory are still under study. But we can say that, unfortunately, the popular myth that a student could be hypnotized and then learn exam material with little work is not true!

Identity and Regression A subject's sense of identity can be radically altered in hypnosis. It may be suggested that he or she will act like a different person, and the individual will do so. Secondary personalities, completely different from the subject's ordinary personality, have been created experimentally in the laboratory. Such secondary personalities may or may not be aware of the activities of the primary personality. Little research has been done on the creation of secondary personalities, however, because of very real dangers to the normal personality.

One interesting phenomenon of hypnosis is a talented subject's ability to **regress** to an earlier period in life. If a young man is told that he is only 5 years old, he will feel and act, in many cases, as he recalls himself to have been when he was 5. All memories of events subsequent to that age will be temporarily unavailable to consciousness. Experts are still undecided whether a regressed subject can generally recall events of that time which are normally inaccessible to consciousness, but this seems to be possible at times. Experientially, the regressed subject *feels* as if he is 5.

Sometimes hypnotized subjects have been told to regress back to before they were conceived, to a past life or previous incarnation. A fair number of responsive hypnotic subjects will then claim to recall a past life and will tell the hypnotist all about it. This may often be a psychologically meaningful experience to the subject, but its objective truthfulness is not determined by how much the subject is impressed. In most cases of past life regression the subject gives no verifiable details of the past life that he or she could not ordinarily have known. Because reincarnation is not a generally accepted belief in Western society, it is reasonable to treat such past life recall as an interesting fantasy. In a very few cases the subject has given evidential detail. Even in these cases, however, it is not always possible to rule out normal channels of information—for example, the subject may have read a book about some historical personality but be unable` consciously to recall having read it. Thus there is currently no strong scientific proof for reincarnation, although the topic deserves further research.

Performance The popular notion that a hypnotized subject looks rather like a zombie is partially correct; many hypnotized subjects *do* act like zombies at first because they think that is how they are *supposed* to act. What the subject expects to happen is crucial in determining what does happen. A hypnotized subject can act perfectly normal when it is suggested he or she do so, and it is frequently impossible for even an experienced hypnotist to tell whether a subject is hypnotized or not under these conditions. Thus motor functioning can be perfectly normal under hypnosis. There is some evidence that a subject may be somewhat stronger or more skillful in the hypnotic state. We have already mentioned that various kinds of motor acts can be done without conscious awareness of them, a phenomenon called *automatism*. One example is *automatic writing*. The hypnotized subject is given a pencil and paper and told that the hand will begin to write messages of one sort or another, without his or her having any idea of what the hand is doing. A talented subject may converse with someone else during this procedure and be greatly surprised by what he or she reads later.

It should be noted, however, that laboratory studies of hypnosis, done chiefly by T. X. Barber, have shown that many phenomena, which when elicited under hypnosis appear to be quite astounding, can actually be elicited readily *without* inducing hypnosis. This evidence has led Barber and others to attribute all hypnotic phenomena to motivational and social-psychological variables and to conclude that there is no unique state called hypnosis that is qualitatively different from wakefulness.

The typical experiment by Barber involves two basic groups of subjects. One group is administered a hypnotic-induction treatment, and the second group is highly motivated by the experimenter's instructions but is not hypnotized, as defined operationally by the fact that the subjects are not read the hypnotic-induction procedure. The basic finding is that many of the acts accomplished by the hypnosis group can also be accomplished by subjects in the motivated control group, such as lying stretched between two chairs, supported only by the head and ankles. Barber uses such experiments to argue that hypnosis is not a real phenomenon. Therefore, he always puts quotation marks around the word "hypnosis."

Critics have countered that Barber's results are misleading, particularly to those who have never worked with hypnosis and do not understand hypnotic behavior. They feel that defining hypnosis as reading a set of hypnotic instructions is misleading, because many subjects in the hypnosis group do not respond and thus cannot be fairly described as being hypnotized. In the control group some highly suggestible subjects might actually become hypnotized by the instructions for performing—they are so highly motivated that self-hypnosis might be induced. Furthermore, control subjects are often led to believe that everyone can perform these feats, and they might feel so compelled to perform that they would fake some of their responses.

Barber has responded to his critics' arguments, and the debate continues. It does seem clear, however, that the human mind and body are capable of doing some very strange things, with and without hypnosis, and that explanations of hypnotic phenomena will not require the invocation of mystical or magical powers on the part of the hypnotist or the subject.

Posthypnotic Effects

A particularly interesting aspect of hypnosis is what are called *posthypnotic effects*. During hypnosis the subject is told that such and such a hypnotic phenomenon will happen later, after he or she is back in normal waking consciousness. For example, the subject may be told that 15 minutes after awakening he or she will become extremely thirsty and need to get a glass of water. About 15 minutes later the subject does become thirsty, but does not remember that the thirst is the result of posthypnotic suggestion. Subjects will often rationalize posthypnotic behavior even when it is very bizarre.

Uses and Dangers

Hypnosis can serve many important functions if properly used. In addition to being an experimental tool in psychology, hypnosis has important medical and psychiatric uses. As we mentioned, hypnosis was widely used as an analgesic in surgery before chemical anesthetics were available, and it is still used frequently today when chemical anesthetics are inadvisable. Hypnotic suggestions can also relieve tensions and sometimes speed the healing processes of wounds. Many special uses of hypnosis have also been developed in psychotherapy, most recently combining it with behavior modification. Indeed, practically every branch of medicine has found applications of hypnosis.

On the other hand, hypnosis can be dangerous if misused. The dangers stem from two main factors. First, many mentally ill people expect hypnotists to provide them with a magic cure, and, because of the power of hypnosis to restructure experience, they can accidentally be led into experiences that could make them worse. The second factor is that hypnosis techniques are easy to learn. People who do not have training in psychology or medicine can easily begin to practice hypnosis out of a desire to control others (sometimes rationalized as a desire to help others). A combination of these two factors can seriously upset some people. You should, of course, avoid offering yourself as a subject to improperly trained hypnotists.

Drugs

Alcohol Intoxication

Alcohol, in the form of wine, beer, or distilled liquors, is probably the most widely known and used drug in the world. Records of its use go back to the dawn of civilization. Attitudes toward it in various cultures have ranged from acceptance to glorification to total rejection. Cultural attitudes can apparently also affect what we think of as the basic "physiological" effects of drinking alcohol. In some cultures, for example, hangovers are almost unknown in spite of heavy drinking.

Given the extent of use, alcohol intoxication is rather under-researched. There is a large literature on the effects of alcohol, but much of it seems intended to prove that "demon rum" is the devil's tool or that "a few drinks never hurt anybody." Given the ambivalent attitude toward alcohol in our own culture, this is understandable.

Not all drinking, of course, leads to an altered SoC. Degree of intoxication and the effects on behavior and functioning correlate with the concentration of alcohol in the blood (see Table D–1). With low levels of alcohol in the blood we can pretty much talk about effects on ordinary consciousness, but once the level rises to 0.10 percent or higher, we may begin to speak of drunkenness as a distinct SoC.

TABLE D–1 Effects of Alcohol Intoxication

Alcohol Concentration in Blood	Experiential and Behavioral Effects	Amounts of Common Beverages*
.50%	Death likely.	
.30%	Stupor likely.	1 pint whiskey
.15%	Intoxication noticeable to observers: clumsiness, unsteadiness in walking. Reduction of anxiety, fears. Impairment of mental functioning. Feelings of personal power. State-dependent memory (see Chapter 5).	5 cocktails, or 28 ounces wine or 10 bottles beer
.12%	Impairment of fine coordination, some unsteadiness in walking or standing. Feelings of social and personal power.	4 cocktails or 22 ounces wine or 8 bottles beer
.10%	Legally defined as impaired driving in California.	
.09%	Amplified emotions, lowering of inhibitions.	3 cocktails or 1 pint wine or 6 bottles beer
.06%	Relaxation, warmth, feeling "high," some impairment of motor acts that require a high degree of skill.	2 cocktails or 11 ounces wine or 4 bottles beer
.03%	No obvious behavioral effects.	1 cocktail or 5½ ounces wine or 2 bottles beer

* The alcohol concentrations in the blood for the shown quantities of beverages are based on 150 pounds of body weight. Concentrations would be higher for the same amount of beverage consumed by a lighter person and vice versa. A cocktail is specified as containing 1½ ounces of distilled liquor (whiskey, etc.). Wine refers to ordinary table wine, not fortified (dessert) wine.

Psychological Effects

Perception and Self-awareness At low levels of intoxication there actually may be a slight increase in auditory acuity. Pleasant feelings, such as warmth, may dominate perception of the body. At higher levels of intoxication sensory impairment occurs, such that a drunk person may not be able to read or otherwise perform fine visual discriminations. At very high levels the intoxicated person begins to see double. Nausea and vomiting may occur at very high levels, with a hangover the following day.

The primary effect of alcohol on self-awareness is extremely unfortunate; it tends to produce feelings of increased competence and ability rather than a realistic perception of the impairments of mental and motor functioning that occur. Such an effect is responsible for the difficulty one has in convincing a drunk that he or she is incapable of driving and for the death and destruction that the drunk driver produces.

Emotions Alcohol intoxication has long been known for its effects on emotions. The relaxation and lowering of inhibitions that accompany drinking have often been cited as a plus for successful parties, allowing people to feel sociable and intereact more freely. It has been found that reduction of existing anxiety does not occur until rather high levels of intoxication are reached and that a major effect of alcohol is to induce fantasies of *power* in users. At lower levels of intoxication these tend to be feelings of "socialized power," that is, being able to do things to save the world and the like, but at higher levels they become fantasies of purely personal power. Thus a good deal of the aggressiveness that can result from drunkenness is understandable.

Alcohol is also widely touted as reducing sexual inhibitions, but there is some question as to how much of this (as well as other behaviors characteristic of alcohol intoxication) is actually a direct effect or simply a culturally mediated effect. That is, looser standards of conduct are applied to people defined as "drunk," and they are allowed to do things that normally they would be censured for.

Dangers

Drunken persons' feelings of confidence and ability along with their serious loss of competence make them particularly dangerous when driving. They feel they are *better* drivers than usual and so may drive faster and more recklessly than they ordinarily would. As with other SoCs, there are very wide individual differences. Highly overlearned motor actions are somewhat less vulnerable to the effects of alcohol than recently learned ones. Some people have learned to distrust feelings of increased competence and thus handle their alcohol more adequately, but most do not. Curiously, many studies of driving performance during marijuana intoxication have failed to find clearly significant impairment, even though it seems reasonable to expect some impairment.

Despite its wide social use, it is clear that alcohol and the state produced by it can be very dangerous, even if we disregard the danger of the drinker becoming an alcoholic. The effects of alcohol in small quantities are not of great consequence. But when large quantities of alcohol are consumed and/or when alcoholism has developed, the effects constitute one of society's greatest problems (see Chapter 11 for a discussion of alcoholism).

Marijuana Intoxication

Marijuana is the name given to preparations of the flowering tops or leaves of the Indian hemp plant, *Cannabis sativa.* Slang terms for marijuana include pot, grass, shit, dope, maryjane, and hemp. Marijuana has been known as an intoxicant for thousands of years, but research into its effects has only recently begun. For example, the major active ingredient of marijuana, tetrahydrocannabinol (THC), was identified and subsequently synthesized only in the last decade. Despite the sometimes severe legal penalties for possession or sale of marijuana, which still exist in many states, a 1977 Gallup poll estimated that at least 36 million Americans have tried marijuana, and about 15 million Americans were regular users of it. About 50 percent of college students have tried the drug.

In looking at marijuana intoxication as an SoC, we must remember that the particular effects achieved at any time are greatly determined by psychological factors in addition to the pharmacological effects of the drug itself. Indeed, aside from quality and quantity of the drug ingested, almost all other factors influencing the quality of the induced SoC — the "trip" — are psychological. These include the user's personality, expectations, mood, and desires (see Table D-2). Other nondrug factors include the physical setting and the user's physical state. We can think of marijuana intoxication or psychedelic experiences as producing two kinds of effects. The first might be called a *pure drug effect,* almost inevitably resulting from the chemical action of the drug on the human nervous system. The second is what we might call *potential effects.* The chemical action of the drug on the human nervous system creates the potential for certain kinds of experiences *if* various nondrug, psychological factors take on the appropriate values. Indeed, some research suggests that merely paying close attention to subjective experience, something not ordinarily done, produces some of the "psychedelic" effects usually attributed to drug action. The potential effects immensely outnumber the pure drug effects for marijuana. Taking these factors into account, we will describe the most common *experiential* characteristics of marijuana intoxication as it occurs in present-day college-educated users under ordinary social circumstances.

Psychological Effects

Perception Marijuana intoxication has a marked effect on perceptual processes such that intoxicated persons generally feel that their perception is enhanced, that they are closer to the real, true qualities of perceptions they receive. The effects are usually very pleasing. The person may perceive new qualities in sound, taste, and touch; may get more enjoyment from eating; understand the words of songs better; find the sense of touch becoming more sensual; find new and pleasurable qualities in sexual orgasm; and be able to see patterns in visual material that is ordinarily ambiguous. New internal bodily sensations are also frequently available, and generally the intoxicated user's awareness is captivated and pleased by these interesting and pleasurable sensory enhancements. There is no evidence to date indicating an actual lowering of the threshold for any sense receptors, so these effects may be primarily a matter of how incoming stimuli are processed. The marijuana user feels that there is *less* processing; he or she feels in touch with the raw sensory data rather than with an abstract representation of it.

Emotions Experienced users of marijuana almost invariably feel good when intoxicated, but they usually find both pleasant and unpleasant emotions considerably amplified. Naive users trying marijuana may find the experience stressful and have very unpleasant emotions. Although no exact figures can be obtained, given the illegality of marijuana, rough estimates indicate that somewhere between 5 and 10 percent of people trying it have an initial bad reaction and do not go on. Even experienced users occasionally have a bad emotional reaction, particularly if they are trying to escape from unpleasant emotions by using marijuana.

Cognitive Processes Cognitive processes can change radically during intoxication. The user may feel that his or her thoughts are more intuitive, less bound by ordinary logic. Usually the person feels in very good control of his or her thought processes, except at very high levels of intoxication. Characteristic experiences include the ability to turn off the effects of intoxication at will if necessary, feeling more childlike and open to experience, finding it difficult to read, having feelings of psychological insights about others and about oneself, giving little thought to the future and feeling more in the here and now, appreciating very subtle humor, and being more accepting of contradictions.

Memory Marijuana intoxication produces both state-dependent memory and some overall loss of memory functioning. A characteristic effect is that the span of memory may be shortened, so the user forgets the start of a conversation, although he or she may feel able to compensate for this with special effort. Memories may come back as images in various sensory modalities rather than as abstract thought. At very high levels of intoxication even the start of a sentence may be forgotten. This shortened memory span probably explains why performance on difficult tasks that require one to remember previous steps is impaired by marijuana intoxication.

Identity One's sense of identity can change radically with marijuana. Being more childlike and open to experience has already been mentioned; this may be described as perceiving stimuli more as they are instead of as they are *valued* by the ordinary ego. Other characteristic effects are being more accepting of events, feeling less need to control them, finding it hard to play ordinary social games, and having spontaneous insights about oneself.

Time Sense Time usually seems to pass more slowly for the intoxicated, although occasionally the user feels that time passes more rapidly. A sense of being more in the present, more in the here and now, is also characteristic.

Performance Marijuana intoxication makes experienced users feel relaxed and disinclined to move about. They also

How Safe Is Pot?
By MATT CLARK with MARY HAGER
and DAN SHAPIRO

If marijuana were an antibiotic or some less controversial drug, medical researchers would have long ago decided just how hazardous it is. But pot doesn't lend itself to dispassionate study: even the scientists have taken sides on the marijuana issue, and their studies sometimes seem to confirm their own attitudes. For virtually every piece of research showing that marijuana poses a risk there is at least one that shows it's safe. . . .

Some of the research links marijuana to many potentially serious health problems. They include lung damage and possibly cancer, mental and neurological disturbances, defects in the body's ability to fight disease, impaired sexual performance and the threat of chromosome damage and birth defects. Until more research has been done even the most broad-minded scientists agree there is no reason to regard marijuana as innocuous. "The situation is like what followed the popularization of cigarettes," says Dr. William Pollin, head of the National Institute on Drug Abuse. "It took 50 years of research for the truly serious implications of cig-arette smoking to become apparent."

The rapidly increasing use of pot by young people adds to the concern. "The teens is a period of ego growth, of acquiring skills in coping and achieving independence, and I am concerned whether this drug has any effect on the development of these skills," says Harvard psychiatrist Dr. Lester Grinspoon. Grinspoon and some of his colleagues believe the marijuana menace has been somewhat exaggerated. "There's no question that if you smoke enough marijuana it will do some harm," says Dr. Norman Zinberg of Harvard. "But it needs to be put into perspective: there has never been a death attributed to marijuana, but 1,000 deaths a year can be blamed on aspirin." . . .

Marijuana cigarettes are made from the dried flowers and leaves of the cannabis plant. The plant contains more than 400 substances, many of which scientists have not analyzed completely. The main active ingredient is delta-9-tetrahydro-cannabinol, or THC. The substance has several immediate physiologic effects. It increases the heart rate to peaks as high as 120 to 130 beats per minute, and it makes the whites of the eyes redden because it dilates the small blood vessels. Mentally, marijuana produces euphoria, a sense of relaxed well-being and a slowed perception of the passage of time.

The controversy over pot centers around the long-term results of frequent use. That's what most researchers have been trying to pin down during the past decade, with largely conflicting results. Some highlights of their findings:

Cells and Immunity
Several years ago, Dr. Morton Stenchever of the University of Utah found that blood cells from marijuana smokers showed an unusually high number of chromosome breaks, which suggests that pot causes genetic damage. Other studies demonstrated that rats fed THC gave birth to offspring with birth defects. . . .

Alarming as all of these findings were, other scientists have dismissed them. Many chemicals, including caffeine, cause chromosome breakage, and even sunlight impairs DNA function.

Only two things seem clear about marijuana: (1) the experts do not agree on the dangers of long-term use, and (2) a lot of people are smoking it.

report being quieter than they are in their normal state or in a state of alcohol intoxication. If they do move about, though, they usually feel very coordinated and smooth. Laboratory studies have generally found that most motor tasks are not affected by marijuana intoxication in *experienced* users, although the probability of some impairment increases with the complexity of the skill required. Naive users sometimes experience great difficulty in performing simple tasks.

Uses and Dangers
Proponents of marijuana use claim many benefits: relaxation, relief of tension, greatly enhanced sense of beauty, important psychological insights into oneself, and, sometimes, important spiritual or religious experiences. Some data collected suggest that marijuana may have value in the treatment of certain medical conditions such as high blood pressure, glaucoma, and migraine headaches. The primary proven dangers of marijuana intoxication are the adverse effects of being in jail.

The long-term effects of marijuana are still largely unknown. There is, however, no evidence that the psychological or physical effects of marijuana lead users to try more dangerous drugs, nor does any kind of addiction develop. Whether from ignorance or a desire to curb marijuana use, authorities in the past called marijuana "addicting" and today refer to it as producing "psychological dependence." Actually, the term *psychological dependence* refers to the fact that drug withdrawal produces psychological discomfort, mainly anxiety, as opposed to the real physical illness in physical addiction. Other authorities believe that psychological dependence is a meaningless concept, because in operation it simply means that people repeat behavior they find enjoyable.

It is important to distinguish marijuana *use* from marijuana *abuse*. Problems associated with the small percentage of users who become abusers include physiological and psychological effects like blackouts, panics, brief psychotic symptoms, chronic bronchitis, and nausea; control of use problems like early morning use, going on binges, or an

How Safe is Pot? (continued)

"The fact that an agent does these things is not good, but it may not be bad either," says Dr. Jack Mendelson of Harvard. Some studies actually contradict the earlier findings. At UCLA, volunteers who smoked marijuana showed no significant chromosome abnormalities, nor has an increase in the incidence of birth defects been documented among the children of pot users. . . .

Hormones

Dr. Robert Kolodny of the Masters & Johnson Institute in St. Louis reported that male heavy marijuana users had lowered levels of the male hormone testosterone as well as reduced sperm production. Women who smoked marijuana heavily, he found, had slightly shorter fertile cycles, or even failed to ovulate in some cases. On the other hand, Harvard's Mendelson found no effect of pot on testosterone levels. Even Kolodny points out that the levels in most of his subjects were still in the normal range. But he warns that testosterone is important in growth and sexual development, so that even a small change could be harmful for youthful smokers.

Lungs

Because marijuana smokers typically inhale deeply and hold the smoke for some time, pulmonary damage wouldn't be a surprising outcome. Dr. Donald P. Tashkin of UCLA found that 28 young men who smoked an average of five joints a day had impaired respiratory capacity. . . .

Brain and Behavior

Contrary to the long-held doctrine of the anti pot forces, marijuana doesn't cause addiction in the sense that narcotics do, nor does its use lead inevitably to a craving for hard drugs. Marijuana induces tolerance so that its users can smoke massive amounts without ill-effects. Rarely do they go into classic withdrawal, with sweats, chills and nausea, when deprived of their quota of marijuana.

But heavy pot use has been blamed for serious psychological problems, including psychosis, criminal behavior and impaired intellectual function. Dr. Robert Heath of Tulane University, New Orleans, gave monkeys cannabis and produced abnormal brain-wave patterns and pathological changes in brain cells. . . .

Coordination and Judgment

Most investigators now agree that marijuana does share with alcohol the danger of impairing coordination and judgment among its users. Harry Klonoff of the University of British Columbia tested 64 men and women and found that in most cases marijuana interfered with their ability to drive.

The full dangers posed by marijuana probably will not be known for years. But the present implication that the drug is no worse—and perhaps even better—than alcohol hardly justifies approving its use with abandon. "One of the major costs of alcohol to society has been psychological," says Dr. Reese Jones of the University of California in San Francisco. "Marriages are destroyed, kids are messed up, jobs are lost. The psychological costs of marijuana are also going to be great."

Newsweek
January 7, 1980

inability to stop use; and social problems such as job problems, losing friends, and fights. Much research will be required to see which of these sorts of effects is related to the chemical nature of marijuana and which are consequences of a personality defect that would lead to abuse of any drug.

Although any drug can be abused, the evidence does not suggest that marijuana is particularly dangerous in this respect. A recent national commission on marijuana use has concluded that there is a great deal of misinformation about the alleged dangers of marijuana and recommended that private use of the drug should not be considered a crime. Certainly marijuana is no *more* dangerous than alcohol. The fact that alcohol is legally available in most places, while there are often *severe* penalties for marijuana use and sale, makes it appear as if we have drastically overestimated the potential dangers of pot.

The Psychedelic Experience

The term *psychedelic* is now generally applied to any drug whose primary effect is to induce an altered SoC, including LSD (lysergic acid diethylamide), mescaline (the active ingredient of peyote cactus), psilocybin, and a large number of other drugs occurring naturally in plants. Knowledge of the effects of LSD and similar psychedelics comes from several sources: the personal experiences of at least a million Americans, a large number of artistic creations (popularly known as psychedelic art) that attempt to express aspects of the experience in a nonverbal way, and finally the more than one thousand laboratory studies of this class of drugs.

Psychological factors are even more significant in the experience of psychedelics such as LSD than in marijuana intoxication. Indeed, such an immense range of variability is seen in psychedelic states that we may be dealing with many transient SoCs triggered by the drug rather than with any single uniform state. Unfortunately, many laboratory studies have been conducted under the set of psychological conditions indicated in Table D–2 that tend to maximize the probability of a "bad trip." Thus LSD was considered a *psychotomimetic* (mimicking a psychosis) drug when it was first studied. It is now clear, however, that an exceptionally wide range of experiences can be produced depending on the personality factors and the setting. Just about every effect reported for other states of consciousness has been reported at one time or another for LSD experiences.

TABLE D–2   Factors Involved in Maximizing the Probability of a Pleasant or Unpleasant Drug Experience

	Variables	Good Trip Likely	Bad Trip Likely
Drug	Quality	Pure, known	Unknown drug or unknown degree of (harmful) adulterants
	Quantity	Known accurately, adjusted to individual's desire	Unknown, beyond individual's control
Long-term factors	Culture	Acceptance, belief in benefits	Rejection, belief in detrimental effects
	Personality	Stable, open, secure	Unstable, rigid, neurotic or psychotic
	Physiology	Healthy	Specific adverse vulnerability to drug
	Learned drug skills	Wide experience gained under supportive conditions	Little or no experience, preparation; unpleasant past experience
Immediate user factors	Mood	Happy, calm, relaxed, or euphoric	Depressed, overexcited, repressing significant emotions
	Expectations	Pleasure, insight, known factors and eventualities	Danger, harm, manipulation, unknown eventualities
	Desires	General pleasure, specific user-accepted goals	Aimlessness (repressed), desires to harm or degrade self for secondary gains
Environmental situation	Physical setting	Pleasant and esthetically interesting by user's standards	Cold, impersonal, "medical," "psychiatric," "hospital," "scientific"
	Social events	Friendly, nonmanipulative interactions overall	Depersonalization or manipulation of user, hostility overall
	Formal instructions	Clear, understandable, creating trust and purpose	Ambiguous, deliberate lies, creation of mistrust
	Implicit demands	Congruent with explicit communications, supportive	Contradict explicit communications and/or reinforce other negative variables

Profundity of Experience

Certain regularities in what we might consider the profundity of the psychedelic experience have been noted by two of the leading investigators in this area, R. E. L. Masters and Jean Houston. They distinguish four levels of psychedelic experience. The first they call the *Sensory* level, in which the subject's primary experience is that of marvelous and beautiful sensory changes. Colors take on vibrant new values, rainbows may form in the air, commonplace objects become magnificent works of art, and so forth. The second and more profound level is called the *Recollective-Analytic*. Here the subject experiences very strong emotions related to his or her own personal history and, with proper guidance, may have very important therapeutic experiences, resolving personal conflicts. Without competent guidance, most subjects' experiences stay at the Sensory or Recollective-Analytic levels.

The third level of profundity is called the *Symbolic*, and here the images and hallucinations the subject experiences deal with the general history of human beings, animal evolution, rituals of passage, and so forth. If dealt with successfully, usually after successful resolution of problems at the Recollective-Analytic level, the person working at the Symbolic level can have important insights and experiences dealing with the nature of being human.

The most profound level, seldom reached, is called the *Integral* level. Experiences at this level are religious and mystical, often dealing with a confrontation with God. The individual may experience the death of his or her own ego,

a union with God, and being reborn. The feeling is profoundly religious and cannot be adequately dealt with in verbal terms. Because of the experiences at the Integral level, some people have proposed that LSD be made legal for supervised religious use.

Uses and Dangers

A number of research studies have shown that LSD and other psychedelics can be used profitably in psychotherapy, and two major psychotherapeutic applications have been developed. The first, called *psycholytic therapy,* uses small doses of LSD in the course of regular psychotherapeutic work. The drug loosens associations, bypasses some defenses, and puportedly helps the analysis proceed much faster. With prolonged therapy some clients begin to deal with material on the Symbolic or Integral level.

The second major therapeutic use of LSD is called *psychedelic therapy,* in which very large doses and single guided sessions are used to give the patient an overwhelming experience at the Symbolic or Integral level. The theory is that by contacting these extremely deep sources within oneself, a new sense of strength can develop, and many ordinary neurotic problems can be successfully transcended or overcome. Psychedelic therapy has also been successfully used with people suffering "existential neurosis" (that is, suffering from a sense of loss of meaning of life) even though they are otherwise successful members of society.

Considering the immense psychological power of psychedelic drugs, there are real dangers in the SoC produced. Subjects with neurotic or psychotic personality structures, or ordinary subjects who are not prepared for the drug experience, may have extremely bad reactions — sometimes, although rarely, leading to a psychosis. People who buy LSD through black market sources today also risk being poisoned by the many impurities that analyses have shown to be in black market drugs. For example, a wide variety of street drugs sold as mescaline, psilocybin, or THC (the active ingredient in marijuana) actually contain none of these substances. Often they consist either of inert ingredients or LSD, with various degrees of adulteration by highly dangerous substances like strychnine or amphetamines.

Another danger is the amateur therapist, a person who has only a little psychological knowledge and wants to cure people's hangups by giving them LSD. It is quite possible to get people into experiences that they are unprepared for and that contribute to further psychopathology instead of curing. The situation in which psychedelic drugs are taken is important too; unexpected interruptions, ugly surroundings, or being arrested can lead the user into extremely unpleasant, sometimes hellish experiences.

Although controlled studies of therapy have shown that the proper use of LSD (at *infrequent* intervals, under *trained* guidance, with lots of time devoted to *assimilating* the insights) can be valuable for personal and therapeutic growth, the frequent use of LSD generally seems to nullify any actual growth benefits and, instead, is likely to produce someone who talks about his or her great experiences but is otherwise a poorly adjusted, ineffective individual.

A good deal of propaganda about the dangers of LSD is false. First, LSD does not automatically make people go crazy. Indeed, experts have been surprised at the infrequency of psychotic breaks, given not only the impurities of the drugs generally used by individuals on their own, but even more important the uncontrolled and often poor psychological condition associated with illegal drug use. Second, experience with a psychedelic drug does not automatically lead to people "dropping out." In spite of their illegality, psychedelic drugs are used (not openly, of course) by many professional people occupying high-status positions in society. Third, there is no solid evidence that LSD causes chromosomal damage. It should be noted, however, that this statement applies to the use of pure LSD; it is not known what effects the impurities in "street" drugs might have. Finally, although the belief that using LSD during pregnancy causes birth defects has not been clearly substantiated, most physicians suggest that it is probably not a good idea for a pregnant woman to take the drug because of its exceptionally powerful psychological effects.

Drug Use and Drug Abuse
The use of some drugs is automatically assumed to be detrimental to the user or society, while the use of others is casually tolerated. Indeed the topic of drug use is surrounded by much emotion and prejudice. From a "neutral" point of view we might define acceptable drug *use* as a level of use that does not significantly impair the user's functioning or cause his or her actions to be harmful to others. Drug *abuse,* on the other hand, occurs when the user's functioning or health is significantly impaired or his or her actions harm others. Occasional social drinking, in small quantities, might then be considered drug use, while alcoholism or drunken driving would be abuse.

Some individuals can abuse any drug (or anything else, for that matter). Nevertheless, there exist important differences between various drugs in their *potential* for abuse. Almost no one, for example, can experiment with injections of amphetamines ("speed") without significant damage to his or her health and drastic impairment of functioning. Many people, on the other hand, can safely use alcohol or marijuana because the abuse potential of these two drugs is less than that of injected amphetamines.

Although too much emotional bias exists to allow an "objective" ranking of the danger of various drugs, experts would probably agree that the following drugs have a dangerous potential for abuse (because of immediate impairment of body functioning or neural damage, or the possibility of addiction): alcohol, amphetamines, barbiturates, cocaine, and hard narcotics like morphine, opium, and heroin (see Table D–3). Major psychedelics, such as LSD or mescaline, might or might not be added to the list by various experts, but all would agree that the impurities frequently found in black market psychedelics are dangerous.

Alcohol is probably the most dangerous drug in our society in terms of actual frequency of abuse, but tranquilizers (Valium or Librium, for example) are now frequently abused. In 1980 the Food and Drug Administration estimated that five *billion* doses of tranquilizers were being prescribed annually by doctors in the USA. The FDA warns that tranquilizers should not be prescribed simply for the stress of everyday life, and too many Americans have become dependent on them. Sleeping medications, such as barbiturates, are also abused, with more than 750 million pills prescribed annually.

Another important source of danger from drug use comes from taking more than one drug at a time. Many drugs *potentiate* each other's action in ways that are sometimes hard to predict. Amphetamines, for example, potentiate the effects of LSD. Thus an apparently innocuous mixture may be like a far larger dose of one of the drugs than a person would want to take.

Techniques of Mind Control

Meditation
Meditation is a group of mental and physical exercises designed to produce relaxation, tranquility of thought and body, and profound insight into oneself and the meaning of worldly things. Little scientific research has been done on the wide variety of known meditative techniques and their associated SoCs. Most of our knowledge comes from religious sources, particularly Oriental. The best Western psychological approach to these techniques has been made by Ornstein and Naranjo (1971), and much of this section is drawn from their excellent analysis. We shall consider some general principles concerning meditation but will not be able to treat it in any detail.

Why do people practice meditation? A common theory underlying almost all schools of meditation is that people, because of the highly selective perception induced in the course of seeking pleasure and avoiding pain, have come to live in a world of *illusion,* called *maya* (Hindu) or *samsara* (Buddhist).

The Eastern concept that we live in a world of illusion does not mean, as is often supposed, that the world is not

TABLE D–3 Controlled Substances: Uses and Effects

	Drugs	Trade or Other Names	Medical Uses	Physical Dependence	Psychological Dependence
NARCOTICS	Opium	Dover's Powder, Paregoric, Parepectolin	Analgesic, antidiarrheal	High	High
	Morphine	Morphine, Pectoral Syrup	Analgesic, antitussive		
	Codeine	Codeine, Empirin Compound with Codeine, Robitussin A-C	Analgesic, antitussive	Moderate	Moderate
	Heroin	Diacetylmorphine, Horse, Smack	Under investigation	High	High
	Hydromorphone	Dilaudid	Analgesic		
	Meperidine (Pethidine)	Demerol, Pethadol	Analgesic		
	Methadone	Dolophine, Methadone, Methodose	Analgesic, heroin substitute		
	Other Narcotics	LAAM, Leritine, Levo-Dromoran, Percodan, Tussionex, Fentanyl, Darvon*, Talwin*, Lomotil	Analgesic, anti-diarrheal, antitussive	High-Low	High-Low
DEPRESSANTS	Chloral Hydrate	Noctec, Somnos	Hypnotic	Moderate	Moderate
	Barbiturates	Amobarbital, Phenobarbital, Butisol, Phenoxbarbital, Secobarbital, Tuinal	Anesthetic, anticonvulsant sedative, hypnotic	High-Moderate	High Moderate
	Glutethimide	Doriden	Sedative, hypnotic	High	High
	Methaqualone	Optimil, Parest, Quaalude, Somnafac, Sopor			
	Benzodiazepines	Ativan, Azene, Clonopin, Dalmane, Diazepam, Librium, Serax, Tranxene, Valium, Verstran	Anti-anxiety, anti-convulsant, sedative, hypnotic	Low	Low
	Other Depressants	Equanil, Miltown, Noludar, Placidyl, Valmid	Anti-anxiety, sedative, hypnotic	Moderate	Moderate
STIMULANTS	Cocaine†	Coke, Flake, Snow	Local anesthetic	Possible	High
	Amphetamines	Biphetamine, Delcobese, Desoxyn, Dexedrine, Mediatric	Hyperkinesis, narcolepsy, weight control		
	Phenmetrazine	Preludin			
	Methylphenidate	Ritalin			
	Other Stimulants	Adipex, Bacarate, Cylert, Didrex, Ionamin, Plegine, Pre-Sate, Sanorex, Tenuate, Tepanil, Voranil			
HALLUCINOGENS	LSD	Acid, Microdot	None	None	Degree unknown
	Mescaline and Peyote	Mesc, Buttons, Cactus			
	Amphetamine Variants	2,5-DMA, PMA, STP, MDA, MMDA, TMA, DOM, DOB		Unknown	
	Phencyclidine	PCP, Angel Dust, Hog	Veterinary anesthetic	Degree unknown	High
	Phencyclidine Analogs	PCE, PCPy, TCP	None		Degree unknown
	Other Hallucinogens	Bufotenine, Ibogaine, DMT, DET, Psilocybin, Psilocyn		None	
CANNABIS	Marihuana	Pot, Acapulco Gold, Grass, Reefer, Sinsemilla, Thai Sticks	Under investigation	Degree unknown	Moderate
	Tetrahydrocannabinol	THC			
	Hashish	Hash	None		
	Hashish Oil	Hash Oil			

Tolerance	Duration of Effects (in hours)	Usual Methods of Administration	Possible Effects	Effects of Overdose	Withdrawal Syndrome	
Yes	3–6	Oral, smoked	Euphoria, drowsiness, respiratory depression, constricted pupils, nausea	Slow and shallow breathing, clammy skin, convulsions, coma, possible death	Watery eyes, runny nose, yawning, loss of appetite, irritability, tremors, panic, chills and sweating, cramps, nausea	NARCOTICS
		Oral, injected, smoked				
		Oral, injected				
		Injected, sniffed, smoked				
	12–24	Oral, injected				
	Variable					
Possible	5–8	Oral	Slurred speech, disorientation, drunken behavior without odor of alcohol	Shallow respiration, cold and clammy skin, dilated pupils and weak and rapid pulse, coma, possible death	Anxiety, insomnia, tremors, delirium, convulsions, possible death	DEPRESSANTS
	1–16					
Yes	4–8	Oral, injected				
Possible	1–2	Sniffed, injected	Increased alertness, excitation, euphoria, increased pulse rate and blood pressure, insomnia, loss of appetite	Agitation, increase in body temperature, hallucinations, convulsions, possible death	Apathy, long periods of sleep, irritability, depression, disorientation	STIMULANTS
Yes	2–4	Oral, injected				
		Oral				
Yes	8–12	Oral	Illusions and hallucinations, poor perception of time and distance	Longer, more intense "trip" episodes, psychosis, possible death	Withdrawal syndrome not reported	HALLUCINOGENS
	Up to days	Oral, injected				
	Variable	Smoked, oral, injected				
Possible		Oral, injected, smoked, sniffed				
Yes	2–4	Smoked, oral	Euphoria, relaxed inhibitions, increased appetite, disoriented behavior	Fatigue, paronoia, possible psychosis	Insomnia, hyperactivity, and decreased appetite occasionally reported	CANNABIS

*Not designated a narcotic under the CSA
†Designated a narcotic under the CSA

real. The basic idea is that our perceptions of the world are grossly distorted by our personal desires and our cultural conditioning. Our sensory receptors work well, but the final percepts, the interpretations and *meanings* of what we see, are way off. The kinds of pathologies Westerners associate with obvious neuroses and psychoses are, in the Eastern view, much more widespread, and many of them are accepted as normal in a particular culture and so are seen as realistic perceptions rather than as the distortions they are.

Persons cannot attain truth or real happiness in this view because they are out of touch with the real world and themselves. Their actions, being based on distorted information, inevitably produce undesired and pathological consequences. Thus human beings are ordinarily subject to suffering. Meditation techniques are designed ultimately to put the practitioners in a more real relationship with themselves and the world. Meditation techniques are designed to eliminate the illusions constantly being produced by the human mind and, by a nonintellectual process, allowing the person to *directly* perceive truth.

We might define meditation, then, as *a special action and/or deployment of attention designed to (1) purify the ordinary SoC by removing illusions and/or (2) facilitate the eventual production of SoCs in which truth is more directly perceived.*

Techniques of Meditation

The variety of techniques that can be used for meditation is enormous. One may, for example, sit up straight in one of the classical meditation postures and simply concentrate on being aware of the natural movements of the belly in breathing. Or, as in Yoga, the meditator may focus on complex, artificial breathing exercises (*pranayama*). *Mantras* are sound patterns that one may meditate on; some of these are considered to have special qualities in terms of their effect on the mind, and others are regarded primarily as convenient focal points. The sound pattern may be audibly uttered, or it may be imagined in one's own mind. The ancient Indian mantra "Om mani padme hum" is well known. *Yantras* are visual patterns to meditate on. They may be as simple as a burning candle or a religious object, or as complex as diagrams symbolizing the nature of the cosmos, called *mandalas*.

Two major classes of meditation can be distinguished. One might be called *concentrative* or *restrictive meditation,* the other *opening-up* or *widening meditation.*

Concentrative Meditation

The essence of concentrative meditation is "one-pointedness" of the mind, restricting attention to one designated object for long periods. In basic Zen meditation, for example, the meditator focuses on the movement of the belly in breathing. When attention wanders away from the sensation of breathing, the meditator is to gently bring it back. He or she is not to *force* attention back or strain to keep it there, since forcing shifts attention to distractions.

Concentrative meditation is extraordinarily difficult. The meditator often finds that he or she has become lost in flights of fancy or "important" thoughts for long periods of time and has forgotten all about meditating. Some people achieve great success with concentrative meditation in weeks or months; others spend years before they become very good at it.

TM in the Pen

"The vilest deeds like poison weeds bloom well in prison air," wrote Oscar Wilde. In the California prison system, for years one of the most violent in the U.S., something quite different has taken root: Transcendental Meditation. At Folsom Prison, a state-run storehouse for repeat offenders, more than 250 inmates over the past three years have stopped hating and hitting each other to sit quietly and think their mantras. Encouraged by Folsom's example, authorities at San Quentin ("the Q") and Deuel Vocational Institution have opened their doors to TM programs. The state parole board has asked for $42,500 in federal funds to support them.

Says Pat Corum, a three-time loser serving a double life sentence at San Quentin for murder and kidnaping: "The walls in my head were thicker than prison walls. With TM, those walls have come down." Other converts include members of the Mexican Mafia, Aryan Brotherhood and Black Guerrilla Family, groups well known for making mayhem in California prisons. "It don't sound right to say I enjoy being here, but it don't bother me like it did before," says Felix Padia, a Folsom inmate who has been meditating for 17 months. Says Convicted Dope Peddler Willie Castaneda, 55: "I am even beginning to like myself."

To back up these testimonials, Psychologist Alan Abrams, a ten-year practitioner of TM, tested the emotions and psyches of 120 Folsom inmates, half of whom were meditators. Using a battery of psychological and personality tests, he found that neuroticism among the meditators decreased 50% on the average, hostility 22%, anxiety 60% and suspicion 27%. No significant changes were recorded for the non-meditators. Perhaps the most convincing statistic of all is that out of 58 meditators who have been released from Folsom over the past two years, only two have returned. Folsom's average recidivism rate is 15% for prisoners released one to two years, rising eventually to 50%.

Such results may not justify the millennial euphoria of the TM faithful who now predict that meditation may eliminate prison violence, and ultimately prisons, entirely. But any results are encouraging in a field where rehabilitation has been an almost total failure. Says State Department of Corrections Chief of Research Robert Dickover: "I think I have seen enough results from prison studies to justify my opinion that positive effects are emerging. . . ."

The cost of TM training is about $250 a prisoner for a one-year program that includes weekly meetings and videotaped lectures. So far, TM volunteers have picked up almost all of the tab. . . .

Time
November 13, 1978

Many people have reported benefits from the practice of one form or another of meditation, TM being the one to receive the most publicity. Meditation can be self-taught, so you can probably get the same benefits and save yourself $250 by reading a good book on the topic such as, "The Relaxation Response" by Herbert Benson, M.D. (see "What Does It Mean?" in Chapter 7). There is no good evidence that paying a "master" to select a mantra just for you is superior to making up your own.

What does concentrative meditation lead to? Successful practitioners insist that only part of the experience can be expressed in words, but it seems to lead to an SoC that can be characterized by words like *emptiness, clearness,* or *voidness.* All sensory input, all perception of the world, eventually ceases temporarily. Similarly, there is no internal mental activity (fantasizing, thinking, and so on) to replace it. Yet awareness remains—pure awareness, without any particular content. This state may or may not lead to other states in which the meditator feels that he or she has a direct perception of truth.

The aftereffect of reaching a state of voidness through concentrative meditation is a feeling of greatly freshened and enhanced perception of oneself and the world, a feeling that one is perceiving things directly rather than through all the selective filters affecting normal perception. Desire for objects or personal attachments is temporarily transcended following successful concentrative meditation. This transcendence and its effect on perception has been described by a Zen master, Suzuki Roshi, in the following words: "The perfect man employs his mind as a mirror, it grasps nothing, it refuses nothing, it receives but does not keep." One is supposed to perceive with absolute clarity, in much the same way a mirror reflects everything perfectly, without distortion. Some studies of the brain waves of meditating Zen monks may be interpreted as supporting this. The monks did not show the adaptation to repeated stimuli that is considered normal, and so they may have been responding to the actual stimulus *every time* instead of "classifying" it automatically as unimportant and no longer perceiving it fully.

Opening-up Meditation

The second major style of meditation, opening-up meditation, consists basically of paying *full* attention to everything that happens to one *continuously.* Usually this is found to be rather exhausting at first, and so is done only for periods of a few minutes to a half hour. No daydreaming or drifting off into comfortable thoughts is permitted. Unpleasant thoughts and experiences must also be given full attention: It is just this tendency of our ordinary SoC to drift off into fantasies about pleasing things and avoiding full awareness of unpleasant things that is the basis of the state of illusion that meditators believe characterizes ordinary consciousness. Meditators must pay complete attention to *everything* that happens to them and to their own reactions. Opening-up meditation supposedly results in greatly clarified perception of the world and oneself immediately, rather than as an aftereffect, as in concentrative meditation.

Self-remembering

A process similar to opening-up meditation has been described by other writers as *self-remembering.* The rationale for self-remembering is the belief that ordinary persons are so *identified* with events that happen to them, including their own feelings, that they are slaves to them. They exist in a kind of "waking sleep," in which events mechanically catch them up and sweep them away. Their own needs and desires have so distorted their perceptions, even of themselves, that they live in a kind of waking dream. The only freedom they have is an ability to direct a small portion of their attention. If this small amount of

attention is directed toward *being aware of being aware,* it is believed that one can enter an SoC in which one is *not identified* with the events that happen, and thus one can eventually develop genuine freedom.

The technique for dissociating oneself from events requires that one split one's attention. While part of it is observing ordinary events and thoughts, another part is aware of being aware of these events. It is as if one divided oneself into an actor and an observer. The observer is not the same thing we ordinarily think of as *conscience,* which is simply another aspect of oneself that has been mechanically programmed to approve of certain acts and disapprove of others. The observer has no characteristics other than the ability to observe. It does not approve or condemn, initiate or stop, action.

The practice of self-remembering is long and arduous, and few people succeed in it. If successful, the practice is supposed to lead to such total awareness of what is actually happening in the here and now that a person ultimately develops the genuine ability to overcome the deterministic nature of his or her behavior based on upbringing and cultural biases. One develops the freedom to choose how one will react.

Physiological Correlates

The increasing number of physiological studies that have been done on meditation suggest that there may be important brain wave and other physiological changes in experienced practitioners. Studies of Zen monks, practitioners of Yoga in India, and American practitioners of Transcendental Meditation have all found increased amounts of alpha brain waves, occasional slowing of alpha waves, and occasional appearance of theta waves (4 to 7 cycles per second) in some practitioners. There are also reports of lowered metabolism and heart rate, lessened physiological

"Nothing happens next. This is it."

The New Yorker, August 28, 1980. Drawing by Gahan Wilson; © 1980 The New Yorker Magazine, Inc.

One thing seems clear from the psychological research on the experiencing of altered states of consciousness—what the person expects to experience determines a significant part of what is actually experienced. Expectations, however, are not the whole story, and if you expect miracles, you will be disappointed.

responsiveness to stressful stimuli, increased blood flow to the brain, and more left-right hemisphere coherence in brain waves. While "greater brain coherence" sounds very impressive, it is still not clear as to what, if any, significance such changes have. At least some of the physiological changes associated with meditation procedures, however, are probably not unique to meditation but result from the physical relaxation associated with meditating. A noted cardiologist, for example, has claimed that a relaxation procedure of simply mentally repeating the word "one" over and over to oneself is as effective as Transcendental Meditation (a mantra meditation) in producing physical relaxation. Other researchers have found that frequent, brief periods of sleep occur during meditation in many people who practice Transcendental Meditation; some of the relaxing and beneficial effects of this meditation may partially reflect the benefits of napping!

Uses and Dangers

In addition to the use of meditation in seeking valued altered SoCs and a clearer perception of truth within various philosophical and religious contexts, there is increasing evidence that meditation, properly used, may be therapeutic or an aid to development in ordinary people. Many people practice simplified forms of meditation and report that it calms them after a long day at work and generally keeps tension from building up. Meditation as a device for erasing tension may assume increased importance as the steadily accelerating pace of our urban society imposes increasing pressures on each person. Weekend workshops for executives, designed to help them to relax and to be more effective under stress, are now a part of American life. A number of meditative techniques have been incorporated as adjuncts to psychotherapy by various investigators. As a result of an 18-month study, for example, the New York Telephone Company now offers training in meditation to all employees as a stress reducer. The study of 154 employees showed that practice of a simple concentrative meditation exercise for five months significantly lowered the meditators' hostility, as well as lowering symptoms of moderate depression.

There is some danger in meditative technique. For mentally ill or poorly balanced people, various forms of meditation may put them in contact with unacceptable parts of their mind and thus precipitate emotional crises or, in some cases, a psychotic break. Also, some techniques of meditation are extremely strenuous and may cause adverse reactions in people who are otherwise in good mental and physical health. Those who use the strenuous techniques usually point out that they are quite dangerous. They are designed for people who desire higher SoCs so much that they are willing to take severe mental and physical risks.

Biofeedback: Electronic Zen?

There have been reports of specially trained people, such as yogis, who have shown large degrees of control over their "involuntary" bodily functions. For example, there is a yogic practice of sitting in water and voluntarily drawing water up into the lower intestine to cleanse it. Another example is the Indian yogi, Swami Rama, who thought he could stop his heart from beating. In a laboratory at the Menninger Foundation, it was shown that what he actually did was to throw his heart into *fibrillation* for 17 seconds;

that is, he made it beat about 300 beats per minute for that time. At this rate the heart will not pump any blood, and so his pulse disappeared. Reports of such unusual actions have been largely ignored in Western scientific literature but are now being looked at more intensely because of the rapidly developing field of biofeedback research.

Biofeedback research centers on the finding that if instruments are used to inform a person of exactly what some part of his or her body (normally inaccessible to consciousness) is doing, the individual may find various ways of affecting it. If the electrical activity of a single muscle fiber is electronically amplified and displayed to subjects—for example, in the form of a sound whose pitch varies with the intensity of the muscle activity—many subjects can learn to totally relax that single muscle fiber or activate it even more. Similarly, if a sound or light is used to indicate when the alpha rhythm of the brain is present, many subjects can learn to increase or decrease the amount of alpha rhythm in their brain-wave pattern. The essence of biofeedback techniques is that they make available to consciousness information that ordinarily is not present; and, having the information, people can try various strategies to see what affects the involuntary process.

There are two major links of research with biofeedback to SoC. The first link is that when subjects learn an *extreme* degree of control over some things, such as producing profound muscle relaxation throughout their bodies or being able to produce very high levels of alpha or theta waves, they report strong alterations in their states of mind, over and above that necessary for control *per se,* which suggests they may be in an altered SoC. Thus biofeedback techniques may be useful for some people in *inducing* altered SoCs, although much work remains to be done before we can adequately describe what sorts of SoCs can be induced.

The second link to altered SoCs comes from the studies of physiological changes during traditional meditation practices, such as increases in the amount of alpha rhythm and some slowing of its frequency. It would be naive to assume that the SoC Zen monks get into is *simply* a matter of increased amount and slowed frequency of the alpha rhythm. Still, if these physiological changes are one of the components of the state Zen monks get into, perhaps that component could be taught by biofeedback techniques, and thus be learned much more rapidly and efficiently than it is ordinarily learned in Zen meditation. Conceivably, biofeedback techniques can serve as technological aids to developing certain SoCs.

Although little more than a decade old, biofeedback research is an important area in psychology. Popular accounts, however, have frequently exaggerated the effects of biofeedback and often made it seem that if you learned to produce lots of alpha waves you would automatically have health, wealth, and mystical power—a kind of electronic Zen. Many nonscientific groups sprang up to sell biofeedback equipment (at high prices) to the general public with the implication of such fantastic benefits. Other groups offered expensive courses in "alpha mind control" and the like and gave training of questionable value. Some of these training programs still operate, and the old rule of "Let the buyer beware" still applies. In spite of its promise, in the actual application of biofeedback we are still a long way from electronic Zen.

GLOSSARY

Accommodation In vision, a process of changing lens shape or curvature so as to focus the optic array on the retina. In Piaget's theory, a change of mental structure so as to accept new information from the environment.

Action potential Nerve signal in the form of an electrical impulse that travels through the axon of a neuron.

Adrenal cortex Outer layer of the adrenal glands; during emotional arousal it releases hormones called corticosteroids into the circulatory system.

Adrenal medulla Inner core of the adrenal gland, which secretes the hormones epinephrine and norepinephrine into the circulatory system.

Algorithm Method of problem solving in which one performs a single repetitive operation until a solution is reached. Some problems can be solved only by an algorithm procedure.

Alpha waves Particular brain wave pattern that occurs when the subject is in a state of "relaxed wakefulness." People can be taught to control the presence of alpha waves through biofeedback training.

Androgyny A perspective which asserts that, biologically, all human beings have both masculine and feminine characteristics. An androgynous person can adopt either typically feminine or typically masculine behavior patterns depending on which is most adaptive at a given time.

Angiotensin A hormone secreted by the kidneys to signal the hypothalamus of a slowing of blood flow.

Antabuse Drug that causes intense nausea if a person drinks alcohol while the chemical is in the bloodstream.

Antidepressants Drugs that elevate moods and counteract depression.

Antidiuretic hormone (ADH) A hormone secreted by the pituitary gland that inhibits urine formation in the kidneys.

Antipsychotics Drugs that calm and increase the lucidity of psychotics.

Aphagia Condition in which an animal refuses to eat, ignores food, and starves to death unless treated. Aphagia has been produced experimentally by surgical removal of the lateral hypothalamic nucleus.

Artificial intelligence A branch of computer science, concerned with simulating intelligent human behavior.

Attribution In social behavior, the act of assigning causal status to someone or something.

Authoritarian Personality type characterized by, among other traits, high ethnocentrism, conservatism, anti-democratism, and prejudice.

Autonomic nervous system Part of the peripheral nervous system, it contains neurons that connect to glands, smooth muscles, and the heart, and it is central to emotional behavior.

Axon A relatively long structure extending from the cell body of a neuron, it sends messages to other cells.

Basilar membrane A flexible membrane within the inner ear or cochlea that vibrates in response to sounds in the environment.

Behaviorism Strong American school of psychology that viewed psychology as the study of observable, objectively measurable behavior and the way in which stimulus-response relationships are formed; the objective of psychology is to predict what responses will be evoked by what stimuli.

Behavior modification Applying the principles of learning to achieve changes in behavior.

Behavioral viewpoint A model that views pathological behavior as caused by maladaptive learning and not a symptom of any underlying process.

Brightness Psychological sensation corresponding to the physical property of intensity of light stimulation. See **Intensity.**

Brightness constancy Observation that objects maintain their brightness even though the amount of light reflected from them changes.

Bystander apathy A bystander's failure to help someone in need.

Catatonic schizophrenia Subtype of schizophrenia characterized by a waxy flexibility of body and limbs, loss of motion, and a tendency to remain motionless for hours or days. See **Schizophrenia.**

Central nervous system (CNS) Includes the brain and the spinal cord and is contained within the skull and spinal column. It is the integrating center for all bodily functions and behavior.

Chemical transmitter substances Chemicals that are released from the terminals of a neuron when that cell has carried a nerve impulse. The chemicals then travel to the soma or dendrites of a second, connecting neuron and may excite or inhibit activity in the second cell.

Chemotherapy Use of drugs as treatment for psychopathology.

Chromosome A structure composed of many genes found in the nucleus of cells, it contains the hereditary information of organisms. The normal human being has 23 pairs of chromosomes.

Chronological age Actual age, in years and months, of a person; used in computation of IQ.

Chunk A unit of immediate memory that may contain many bits of information.

Classical conditioning Learning of a new response to a stimulus caused by pairing this stimulus with another stimulus that already elicits the response.

Cochlea Structure in the inner ear containing fluid that vibrates with sound stimulation and auditory receptor cells that are stimulated by vibrations in the fluid.

Cognitive balance theory The theory that social behavior is directed by a tendency for cognitions to be in balance, that is, consistent.

Cognitive dissonance theory Leon Festinger's consistency theory, which states that a person act to reduce the inconsistency between two or more ideas or beliefs.

Community mental health Approach to mental health that emphasizes the prevention of mental illness and the need for broader and more effective mental health services based within communities.

Concept Unit of knowledge; principle for systematically responding to the objects and events that make up one's circumstances. Concepts can be classes or categories of things, sequential principles, or relational principles that specify a particular arrangement of things.

Concordance rate Probability that one of a pair of twins will show a given characteristic, given that the other twin has the characteristic.

Conditioned response (CR) In classical conditioning, the response that occurs after training has been completed, upon presentation of the conditioned stimulus.

Conditioned stimulus (CS) In classical conditioning, the neutral stimulus that does not elicit the desired response prior to training.

Congruence Rogerian term meaning that what is experienced inside and what is expressed outwardly are consistent.

Conjunctive concept Concept in which two or more relevant attributes must be present in a stimulus for it to be a positive instance.

Connotation Characteristic of a word; how one reacts emotionally to or feels about the word.

Conscious In Freudian theory, the ideas, thoughts, and images that a person is aware of at any given moment.

Consolidation theory Theory that every experience sets up a circuit in the brain that must be allowed to consolidate or strengthen in order for the experience to be stored permanently in long-term memory.

Conversion disorder A type of somatoform disorder involving the inactivation of part of the body.

Correlation coefficient Numerical value or statistic that represents the degree of relationship between two or more values; can vary from -1 to $+1$, with 0 meaning no relationship and $+$ or -1 indicating a perfect relationship.

Counterconditioning Eliminating unwanted behaviors using extinction, or punishment, while simultaneously replacing them with desirable behaviors.

Crisis Point in a person's life that is unusually stressful and could be handled in a maladaptive way.

Cue-dependent forgetting Inability to remember learned information due to retrieval failure; cues present during learning are not present during recall, see "trace-dependent forgetting."

Dark adaptation Increase in sensitivity to light resulting from the reduction or complete absence of light energy reaching the eye, attributable to changes in the level of light-sensitive pigments in receptor cells.

Decay theory Theory that we forget things because the memory trace for them wears out over time.

Decibels A measure of sound amplitude that underlies the sensation of loudness.

Defense mechanisms Unconscious tactics employed by the ego in order to prevent anxiety, according to Freud.

Deindividuation Loss of one's identity in a crowd so that a person feels he cannot be singled out by others as being personally responsible for the acts of the crowd.

Delta waves A brain wave pattern in the EEG consisting of large amplitude but slow (1 to 2 cycles per second) waves; characteristic of deeper stages of sleep.

Delusion Unshakable idea or belief that is held in the face of contradictory evidence, simple logic, or common experience.

Dendrites Short structures that extend from the cell body of a neuron and pick up signals from other cells.

Denial Removal from consciousness of an external threat; a defense mechanism.

Denotation Characteristic of a word: the specific object, concept, or "event" to which the word refers.

Dependent variable In psychological research, the variable that the psychologist measures—some characteristic of behavior or performance.

Depth perception The ability to construct an internal representation of distance and depth.

Differentiation Learning to discriminate those responses that will be reinforced from those that will not.

Discrimination A learned distinction between two stimuli or two responses.

Discriminative stimulus A cue. A stimulus that, by learning, has come to control a response.

Disjunctive concept An item must have one or more relevant attributes in order to belong to the concept. If it lacks all relevant attributes, the stimulus is a negative instance.

Displacement Rechanneling instinctual energy from an unacceptable object to one that is of neutral value to society. Also, a dream process by which material is disguised. It involves changing the affective emphasis of something in a dream so that if it is very important in real life it is seemingly unimportant in the dream, or vice versa.

Displacement activity. In ethology, a term used to describe a substitute activity brought on by blocking of or competition between other activities.

Double-blind experiment An experiment in which neither the subjects nor the experimenter know which treatment is being applied until the experiment is over.

Drive Energy available for behavior; psychological correlate of a physical need (for example, the hunger drive results from the need for food).

Dynamic viewpoint A model that views pathological behavior as a symptom of underlying unconscious conflicts.

Ego One of the basic structures of the personality as proposed by Freud. The ego maintains a balance between biological impulses and society's demands; it attempts to maintain a realistic approach to life.

Electroconvulsive therapy (ECT) Delivering an electric shock that produces a brief coma in a patient; sometimes used to treat depression.

Electroencephalogram (EEG) Instrument used to sense and record electrical activity originating in the brain.

Empathic understanding Rogerian concept referring to the importance of a therapist actively understanding the immediate feelings of his client.

Encoding Process by which input stimulation is represented in memory.

Encounter group Group experience aimed at increasing an awareness of emotions and an ability to communicate them accurately and effectively. Generally aimed at improving interpersonal relations.

Endocrine gland Gland that secretes its hormone directly into the blood of the circulatory system.

Endocrine system Composed of glands which produce hormones, it is central in the control and regulation of behavior. It interacts closely with the nervous system.

Enuresis Bedwetting.

Equity theory A theory that says interpersonal attraction depends upon the equity of each person's costs and benefits in the relationship.

Ethical viewpoint A model that views psychopathic behavior as reflecting irresponsibility.

Ethology Study of animal behavior in the natural environment.

Experience Learning, or the effects of the environment on development.

Extinction In classical conditioning, presenting a conditioned stimulus repeatedly without the unconditioned stimulus; gradually, the conditioned response disappears.

Instrumental conditioning, eliminating a learned behavior by withholding all reinforcement of it.

Factor analysis A statistical procedure based on correlations between tests that is used to identify the components or factors which make up or contribute to a general form of behavior such as intelligence or personality.

Fixation Stopping one's development at a particular stage and remaining there; a defense mechanism.

Fovea The central region of the retina, containing cones but no rods. It is the area of greatest visual acuity.

Frustration-aggression hypothesis States that all aggressive acts are caused by frustration.

Functional disorder Emotional or behavioral problem resulting from psychological variables rather than biological ones.

Functional fixedness Type of mental set occurring during problem solving in which an object critical to a solution is perceived as having one and only one function different from that required by the solution.

Functionalism Early school of psychological thought that emphasized how behavior helps one adapt to his environment and the role learning plays in this adaptive process.

Generalization The tendency to respond in the same way to a stimulus similar to but different from the CS or the tendency to make a similar response to the one originally learned in the presence of the CS.

Gestalt psychology German school of psychology that opposed reductionistic psychologies such as Structuralism and Behaviorism and emphasized the completeness, continuity, and meaningfulness of behavior as a whole.

Gestalt theory In thinking, the theory that problem solving depends on achieving the correct perspective on problem elements, thereby gaining insight into the solution (as a whole, or Gestalt).

Gestalt therapy A type of psychotherapy developed by Fritz Perls, it focuses on the immediate present and helps the client increase awareness of his experiences in their totality.

Gradient of stimulus generalization Mathematical curve that illustrates the degree of generalization between various stimuli.

Grapheme The basic unit of written language. The written equivalent of a phoneme.

Hair cells Auditory receptor cells located in a membrane in the cochlea that are stimulated by vibrations in the cochlea fluid.

Hedonic bias The tendency to attribute the cause of pleasant states to oneself and to attribute unpleasant states to other causes.

Heuristic Principle of strategy used in problem solving that serves as a device for shortening the solution process; often used when there are many different ways to solve a problem.

Homeostasis Tendency of the body to react in such a way as to maintain a particular, perhaps optimal, state; process of maintaining equilibrium.

Hormone Chemical manufactured and secreted into the bloodstream by an endocrine gland, which may then activate another gland or help to regulate bodily function and behavior.

Hue Color; property of light stimulation (wavelength) corresponding to the sensation of color.

Hypermnesia Enhancement of memory typically due to increased or repeated efforts at recall.

Hypnagogic state State of consciousness experienced when passing from sleep to wakefulness.

Hypochondriasis Neurotic preoccupation with one's health.

Hypothalamus Group of nuclei in the forebrain. The hypothalamus is involved in many behavioral functions, especially the emotional and motivational aspects of behavior. It controls much of the endocrine system's activities through connections with the pituitary gland.

Hypothesis theory In thinking, a theory that describes problem solving in terms of formulating, testing, and revising tentative hypotheses.

Id One of the basic structures of personality as proposed by Freud. The id pushes the individual to seek pleasure and avoid pain; it is the seat of human instincts.

Incentive Circumstance or stimulus situation that one attempts to obtain or avoid.

Inclusive fitness In sociobiology, relating an individual's fitness to survive to his or her genes and to the genes of his or her relatives.

Independent variable In psychological research, the variable which the psychologist manipulates.

Individual differences Refers to the uniqueness of organisms, the fact that all individuals vary and are different from other individuals even though they may have some things in common.

Information-processing theory Theory of problem solving that refers to the way a person receives information from his environment, operates on it, integrates it with other information available in memory, and uses it as a basis for deciding how to act.

Inoculation effect People are more difficult to persuade if they have previously been exposed to small amounts of progaganda.

Insight In Gestalt psychology, the sudden achievement of understanding that arises from a change in perspective. Insight is viewed as the most appropriate description of human problem solving.

Instrumental conditioning Type of learning that uses reinforcers to change the frequency of a behavior. Also called operant conditioning.

Intelligence quotient (IQ) An index of intelligence allowing for comparison of subjects across all chronological ages. IQ is calculated by dividing mental age by chronological age and multiplying by 100.

Intervening variable Factor that stands between and provides a relationship between some stimulus in the environment and some response on the part of an organism.

Introspection Observing one's own private, internal state of being, including one's thoughts and feelings.

Latent content (of dreams) Unconscious wishes or impulses that seek expression through dreams; symbolic aspect of dreaming.

Law of effect The forerunner of the contemporary principle of reinforcement. Responses are learned or extinguished as a consequence of their effect on the organism.

Learned helplessness effect The consequence of exposure to aversive events that cannot be controlled leading to a failure to respond appropriately in a new situation.

Learning Relatively permanent change in behavior traceable to experience and practice.

Levels of processing A theory that relates memory to the nature of the processes used to encode information, their breadth and depth.

Libido According to Freudian theory, the source of instinctual motivating energy.

Lobes The four divisions of the cerebral cortex of the brain.

Long-term memory Memory for learned material over a relatively long retention interval (generally an hour or more). A hypothetical memory system for permanent storage of learning.

Loudness The psychological attribute corresponding to amplitude of a sound wave.

Manifest content (of dreams) Aspects of a dream that are recalled by the dreamer; concrete objects and events of the dream.

Maturation Process involving growth or change over time, with heredity being the main determinant of the change.

Mean Arithmetic average; the sum of all scores divided by number of scores.

Means-end analysis Problem-solving process in which one tests for difference between the present situation and a solution situation and continues to perform operations until no difference is detected. Applicable whenever there is a clearly specifiable problem situation and a clearly specifiable solution.

Median An average, defined as the middle-most score in a set of scores; an equal number of scores are higher and lower than the median.

Mediational theory of thinking A theory which holds that as a consequence of external stimulus-response associations, the individual may form internal miniaturized versions of these stimuli (mediational stimuli) and responses (mediational responses) that serve as the connecting link between the environment and the way one responds to it.

Medical viewpoint A model that views pathological behavior as a symptom of an underlying disease.

Mental age (MA) In the Binet intelligence test the age level at which a child can successfully pass subtests. Computed by adding basal age plus the number of age units corresponding to items the subject passes at successively higher levels. Independent of chronological age.

Mental set Tendency to respond in a given way irrespective of the requirements of the situation. Sets sometimes facilitate performance and sometimes impair it.

Methadone Drug used in treatment of heroin addiction that prevents withdrawal symptoms and blocks the heroin "high" but still is addictive.

Mnemonics Techniques for aiding memory.

Mode A measure of central tendency in a set of scores; the mode is the score that occurs most frequently.

Monocular cues for depth Cues for depth perception derived from information in the optic array that is available to either eye alone — interposition, size perspective, linear perspective, shading, aerial perspective, texture gradients.

Morpheme The smallest meaningful unit of analysis in language; usually a syllable.

Motion parallax A cue to depth based on the relative motion of objects at near and far locations as the head moves.

Motor theory Early stimulus-response theory of thinking espoused by behaviorists and proposing that thinking always involves muscular or glandular activity of some kind. According to this theory, most human thought is basically subvocal speech activity.

Need A basic concept in motivation referring to a state of deficit in an organism.

Neuron Nerve cell. The most elementary unit of the nervous system, its function is to send and receive messages.

Neurosis Special pattern of behavior that is instigated and maintained for the purpose of contending with stress and avoiding anxiety; diagnostic category of psychopathology characterized by anxiety, rigid and unsuccessful attempts to reduce it, and an inability to totally satisfy the need being served by the behavior.

Neurotic paradox Refers to the fact that the neurotic person persists in maladaptive behavior even in the face of unpleasant consequences.

Nondirective therapy Developed by Carl Rogers, this type of psychotherapy is insight oriented and focuses on the present. Emphasis is on regaining the ability to experiencing all feelings fully.

Null hypothesis Prediction that the variable being manipulated will have no effect on the behavior being measured.

Obsessive compulsive disorder A subtype of anxiety disorder category on Axis I of the DSM–III involving persistent thoughts and repetitive behaviors.

Oedipus complex In psychoanalysis, pathological behavior stemming from unresolved conflict between a son and his father over the affections of his mother.

Operant conditioning See **Instrumental conditioning.**

Organic disorder Emotional or behavioral problem resulting from biological causes, usually from impairment of brain functioning.

Ovaries Reproductive organs in females; they are also endocrine glands that secrete many hormones, regulating sexual cycles and behavior and supporting pregnancy.

Paranoid schizophrenia Subtype of schizophrenia characterized by delusions of persecution, suspicion of others, and delusions of grandeur.

Parasympathetic nervous system One part of the autonomic nervous system involved in controlling involuntary behavior, such as digestion; it works in opposition to the sympathetic system and conserves body energy.

Partial reinforcement A reinforcement schedule in which less than 100 percent of all correct responses are rewarded.

Performance One's observable responses or behavior in a given task.

Peripheral nervous system Contains all the nerves which are the communication lines connecting muscles, glands, and sensory receptors with the central nervous system.

Personal space An area with no visible boundaries that surrounds and moves with a person in his or her environment.

Personality disorder Diagnostic category of psychopathology marked by failure to behave in socially appropriate ways due to lack of motivation or lack of skill (competence) in coping with normal stresses of everyday life; such individuals are pathological by society's definition, not in terms of their own personal discomfort.

Pheromones Biochemicals produced by many animals which provide a means of communication, typically about territories and sexual availability.

Phenomenological viewpoint A model that views pathological behavior as an inability to see meaning in the world and as an insensitivity to feelings. The emphasis is on how one sees one's world.

Phobia Neurosis characterized by an intense, irrational fear of something; according to analytic theory, it involves displacement of anxiety onto a situation that is not dangerous or only mildly dangerous.

Phonemes General classes of sounds common to a given language (basic sounds of a language); considered to be the conjunctive combination of several distinctive features associated with a particular language. In English, features include voiced versus voiceless and stopped (air flow interrupted) versus fricative (air flow sliding over articulator.)

Pitch Psychological attribute corresponding to frequency of a sound wave.

Pituitary gland The "master gland," it is activated by the hypothalamus and releases hormones that are responsible for activating many of the other glands, in addition to regulating bodily growth, water loss, and many other functions.

Placebo control group The group of subjects in any experiment that receives a fake treatment—as, for example, a drug that contains no active ingredients.

Pleasure principle A concept originated by Freud, it is the idea that human beings strive to avoid pain and seek pleasure.

Prägnanz A Gestalt principle of perceptual organization that corresponds to a "goodness of figure."

Preconscious In Freudian theory, the ideas, thoughts, and images that a person is not aware of at a given moment but that can be brought into awareness with little or no difficulty.

Prepared learning A built-in conditioning system, genetically based, that quickly associates certain kinds of stimuli. For example, the special system that relates food stimuli, through taste perception, with feeling sick.

Primacy effect Items learned early are better recalled.

Primary gain For neurotic behavior, the immediate reduction of anxiety.

Primary reinforcer Stimulus or event that is innately reinforcing.

Proactive interference Interference with memory for a certain set of items attributable to other items learned at an earlier time.

Probability The proportion of cases in a population that fit a particular description; the probability of an A is equal to the number of A's divided by the total number of cases in the population.

Process schizophrenia Schizophrenic reaction in which there is a slow onset of symptoms over a period of years, with progressive withdrawal from others, increasing deterioration of thought processes, and slow onset of hallucinations and delusions; sometimes called *chronic schizophrenia*.

Prognosis Probability of recovery.

Projection Process of denying the presence of unacceptable impulses or characteristics and then seeing these qualities in another person (who may or may not actually have them); a defense mechanism.

Projective test A test that encourages the subject to project his or her personalities and responses to ambiguous and neutral stimuli such as inkblots.

Psychoanalysis Insight-oriented therapy developed by Freud and based upon his psychoanalytic theory.

Psychogenic pain disorder A somatoform disorder involving pain in the absence of any physical injury.

Psychopathology Inability to behave in a socially appropriate way such that the consequences of one's behavior are maladaptive for oneself or society.

Psychosexual stages The stages of development that, according to Freud, all human beings pass through during early life. Each stage centers around a specific pleasurable area of the body. Each stage presents the opportunity for fixation.

Psychosexual disorders In DSM–III, a major category of pathological behavior on Axis I encompassing various forms of sexual deviance.

Psychosis Diagnostic category of psychopathology characterized by gross distortion of reality or by loss of reality testing, inability to distinguish between reality and fantasy, hallucinations, and/or delusions.

Random sampling Selecting a sample in such a manner that each person in the population has an equal chance of being chosen for the sample.

Range A statistical measure of the variability in a set of scores; the range is the highest score minus the lowest score.

Rationalization A Freudian defense mechanism that involves attempts by a person who is not conscious of the real reasons for his or her inappropriate or unacceptable behavior to justify or explain the behavior by reference to socially acceptable motives.

Reaction formation Denial or masking of one's own unacceptable impulses by stating or emphasizing qualities that are the opposite to one's true feelings; a defense mechanism.

Reactive schizophrenias Schizophrenic reactions in which the onset of symptoms is relatively sudden; sometimes called *acute schizophrenias.*

Reality principle A concept originated by Freud, it involves the idea that in order to exist, people must behave in ways that are consistent with the real world. The ego is the part of the personality that oversees and carries out this need.

Recency effect The fact that items near the end of a list are remembered unusually well.

Receptive field An area of the retina which, when stimulated by light, influences the activity of a cell further along the visual pathway to the brain. The receptive field of a ganglion cell consists of concentric "on" and "off" areas. Cortical cells often are tuned so as to respond only to certain stimuli, for example, a horizontal line in their respective fields.

Receptor Specialized nerve cell which converts physical stimulation into electrical information.

Reconstruction model A theory of memory that is based on the use of fragmentary representations to reconstruct the original event.

Refractory period Time interval, usually following a response, during which almost no stimulus will produce another response.

Regress In relation to hypnosis it involves taking a subject back in time, until he psychologically experiences the past. It may even be possible to take a person back to a past life.

Regression In statistics, a procedure for predicting a person's score on one variable when the person's score on another variable and the correlation between the two variables is already known.

Reinforcer Event or stimulus that increases the frequency of a response with which it is associated.

Relaxation training Learning to relax the body by becoming aware of and controlling the muscles of the body; one part of systematic desensitization.

Releasers See **Sign stimuli.**

Reliability The degree to which a person's score on some variable does not change on repeated testings; it is a critical characteristic of every measuring device.

Repression Act of keeping highly threatening impulses or memories in the unconscious far away from awareness, because they are very likely to produce much anxiety or other negative consequences; a defense mechanism.

Response discrimination Learning to give one, and only one, particular response in a given situation.

Retention interval The time between initial learning of something and its recall.

Retina Photosensitive surface at the back of the eye upon which the optic array is focused; it contains visual receptor cells.

Retinal disparity See **Binocular disparity.**

Retrieval Accessing information available in long-term memory.

Retrograde amnesia Loss of memory for events just prior to the event that caused the memory loss. Long-term memory remains intact.

Saturation The dimension of color experience that corresponds to how much or how deep the hue of a light is.

Schema Theoretically, a knowledge unit; the representation of knowledge in memory; used to organize and interpret new information about the world and to make inferences.

Schizophrenia Group of psychotic disorders in which there are disturbances in thought processes as well as emotions and a marked distortion of reality; often characterized by emotional blunting, disturbances in interpersonal relationships, depersonalization, and preoccupation with inner fantasies.

Secondary gain For neurotic behavior, other positive consequences in addition to the relief from tension or anxiety.

Secondary reinforcer Stimulus or event that becomes a reinforcer only after being paired with a primary reinforcer.

Sedative Drug that reduces anxiety by inducing muscle relaxation, sleep, and inhibition of the cognitive centers of the brain.

Self-concept Fairly consistent and enduring framework of self-regarding attitudes.

Self-fulfilling prophecy In research, an experimenter may have expectations about how the subjects should behave, and may inadvertently or otherwise get subjects to behave that way. By making a prediction one acts to insure that the prediction comes true.

Self theory Approach to personality that focuses on the individual as a whole, unified self. It takes a fairly positive view of human beings and is a part of the humanistic approach to psychology.

Semantic differential Procedure developed by Charles Osgood that uses the ratings that people give to words to derive the basic dimensions of meaning and the location of any given word on those dimensions. Measures word connotation.

Semantics The meaning or message contained in a grammatical or linguistic utterance.

Sensory deprivation Prolonged reduction of external stimulation, either in intensity or variety; produces boredom, restlessness, and disturbances of thought processes.

Shape constancy The fact that objects appear to maintain a constant shape regardless of the angle from which we observe them.

Shaping Process that uses instrumental conditioning in gradual steps to develop an uncommon or difficult behavior.

Short-term memory Memory for learned material over a very brief retention interval. Hypothetical memory system for transient information.

Sign stimuli Environmental cues that trigger instinctual behavior.

Size constancy The observation that heights of objects do not appear to shrink as we move from them even though the size of the image on the retina does become smaller.

Social facilitation Phenomenon in which the mere presence of other persons, as an audience or as coworkers, without any verbal exchange, affects individual performance.

Social interference Decrease in the effectiveness of a person's behavior caused by the presence of other people.

Sociobiology A biological explanation for a social behavior based on the assumption that the primary function of behavior is to insure the survival of an organism's genes.

Sociopath Antisocial personality.

Soma The main cell body of a neuron, containing the nucleus of the nerve cell, which controls all cellular activities such as oxygen utilization and energy production.

Somatic division One of two divisions of the peripheral nervous system, consisting of the nerves that serve the voluntary muscles.

Somatoform disorder In DSM–III, a major category of psychopathology on Axis I encompassing all disorders with physical symptoms for which there is no demonstrable physical cause.

Spinal cord One of two major parts of the central nervous system. A major collection of nerve structures in cable form, carrying information into and out of the brain.

Spontaneous recovery Following extinction training, the return of a learned behavior even though it has not been practiced.

Standard deviation In statistics a measure of the variability or spread of a set of scores around the mean.

State-dependent learning Ability of the learner's internal physiological state to affect learning; the more similar this state is during learning and recall, the better recall will be.

Stereopsis A perceptual process that extracts information from the environment about depth and which operates on the fact that the two eyes are separated horizontally in the head.

Stimulus control Instrumental learning process whereby a cue in the environment comes to control the behavior of an organism.

Stimulus discrimination Learning to respond differently to various stimuli that may have some similarities.

Storage Maintenance of encoded information in memory over time.

Structuralism Early school of psychological thought that held that the subject matter of psychology was conscious experience, that the object of study was to analyze experience into its component parts, and that the primary method of analysis was introspection.

Sublimation Rechanneling instinctual energy from an unacceptable object to one that is highly valued by society.

Substance-use disorder A major category of psychopathology on Axis I of DSM–III encompassing abuse of chemicals.

Superego One of the basic structures of the personality, as proposed by Freud. The superego contains people's values, morals, and basic attitudes as learned from their parents and society.

Syllogism A deductive reasoning problem based on two given premises and a conclusion which can be either correct or incorrect.

Sympathetic nervous system Part of the autonomic nervous system, it prepares the organism for emergencies, making much bodily energy available for use.

Synapse Areas where the end of one neuron connects to the next neuron in a communication chain. Specifically, the axon terminals of the first cell come close to (but do not touch) the dendrites or soma of the second cell.

Syntax Linguistic rules for constructing grammatical utterances.

Systematic desensitization Type of behavior therapy developed by Wolpe to help people overcome fears and anxiety.

Testes Reproductive organs in males; endocrine glands that secrete many hormones that regulate sexual behaviors and characteristics.

Thalamus Portion of the brain that receives information about most of the senses and relays it to the cortex. It also is involved in sleep and attention.

Theory Set of principles and statements that represent, organize and summarize facts and suggest an explanation of what lies behind them.

Threshold The amount of physical stimulus required to achieve a certain level of correctness in a sensory-detection task.

Thyroid gland Produces the hormone thyroxin and thus regulates metabolism and growth.

Timbre A characteristic of sounds which depends on the overtone structure of the vibrating object.

Trace-dependent forgetting Loss of learned information due to the loss of memory. See **Cue-dependent forgetting.**

Trait Relatively permanent characteristic of an individual that he tends to show in most situations.

Transactional analysis A model developed by Eric Berne that recasts Freud's basic concepts of superego, ego, and id into ego states called Parent, Adult and Child.

Tranquilizer A drug that reduces anxiety without inducing sleep.

Transfer In psychoanalysis, the patient confers on the therapeutic relationship those conflicts from earlier life that caused the psychopathological behavior.

Two-process theory A theory of avoidance learning that involves classical conditioning of a negative emotional state and operant or instrumental conditioning of responses that will terminate that state.

Unconditional positive regard Rogerian concept involving the idea that a therapist must care about his client without any conditions put on the caring, even when the client reveals things that the therapist is uncomfortable about.

Unconditioned response (UCR) In classical conditioning, the response that automatically occurs whenever the unconditioned stimulus is presented, without any training.

Unconditioned stimulus (UCS) In classical conditioning, the stimulus that automatically elicits the desired response, without any training.

Unconscious In Freudian theory, that part of a person's mental process that he resists being aware of; unacceptable drives and impulses and material that were once conscious but were removed from awareness because they were anxiety provoking.

Vacuum activity Occurrence of an instinctual behavior in the absence of any releasing stimulus.

Validity Degree to which a measuring device measures what it is supposed to measure.

Variable Any characteristic of an object, event, or person that can take two or more values.

Variance A measure of the variability in a set of scores; it is equal to the square of the standard deviation.

Visual acuity Ability to notice fine detail in a patterned stimulus.

Yerkes-Dodson Law The fact that increased motivation will improve performance up to a point, beyond which there is deterioration. The easier a task is to perform, the higher the drive level for optimal performance.

Bibliography

Adelson, J., Green, B., & O'Neil, R. Growth of the idea of law in adolescence. *Developmental Psychology, 1969, 1,* 327–332.

Adorno, T. W., Frenkel-Brunswik, E., Levinson, D. J., & Sanford, R. N. *The authoritarian personality.* New York: Harper & Row, 1950.

Ainsworth, M. D., Blehar, M. C., Waters, E., & Wall, S. *Patterns of attachment.* Hillsdale, N.J.: Lawrence Erlbaum Associates, 1978.

Alexander, F. Individual psychotherapy. *Psychosomatic Medicine, 1946, 8,* 110–115.

Allbrook, R. C. How to spot executives early. *Fortune, 1968, 78,* 106–111.

Anastasi, A. Heredity, environment, and the question "how"? *Psychological Review, 1958, 65*(4), 197–208.

Anderson, J. *Language, memory, and thought.* Hillsdale, N.J.: Lawrence Erlbaum Associates, 1976.

Apter, M. J. *The computer simulation of behavior.* New York: Harper & Row, 1970.

Aronson, E., & Mills, J. The effect of severity of initiation on liking for a group. *Journal of Abnormal and Social Psychology, 1959, 59,* 177–181.

Asch, S. E. Studies of independence and conformity: I. A minority of one against a unanimous majority. *Psychological Monographs, 1956, 70* (9, whole no. 416).

Aserinsky, E., & Kleitman, N. Regularly occurring periods of eye mobility and concomitant phenomena during sleep. *Science, 1953, 118,* 273–274.

Atkinson, J. W., & McClelland, D. C. The projective expressions of needs. II. The effect of different intensities of the hunger drive on thematic apperception. *Journal of Experimental Psychology, 1948, 38,* 643–658.

Atwood, M. E., & Polson, P. G. A process model for water jug problems. *Cognitive Psychology, 1976, 8,* 191–216.

Ax, A. F. The physiological differentiation between fear and anger in humans. *Psychosomatic Medicine, 1953, 15,* 443–452.

Azrin, N. H., Hutchinson, R. R., & Hake, D. H. Extinction-induced aggression. *Journal of the Experimental Analysis of Behavior, 1966, 9,* 191–204.

Bach-y-rita, P. *Brain mechanisms in sensory substitution.* New York: Academic Press, 1972.

Baltes, P. B. Longitudinal and cross-sectional sequences in the study of age and generation effects. *Human Development, 1968, 11,* 145–171.

Bandura, A. Self-efficacy: Toward a unifying theory of behavior change. *Psychological Review, 1977, 84,* 191–215.

Bandura, A. The self and mechanisms of agency. In Suls, J. (Ed.), *Social psychological perspectives on the self.* Hillsdale, N.J.: Lawrence Erlbaum Associates, 1980.

Bandura, A. The self-system in reciprocal determinism. *American Psychologist, 1978, 33,* 344–358.

Bandura, A. A social learning interpretation of psychological dysfunctions. In London, P., & Rosenhan, D. (Eds.), *Foundations of abnormal psychology.* New York: Holt, Rinehart and Winston, 1968.

Bandura, A. *Social learning theory.* Englewood Cliffs, N.J.: Prentice-Hall, 1977.

Bandura, A. *Social learning theory.* New York: General Learning Press, 1971.

Bandura, A., & Walters, R. H. *Social learning and personality development.* New York: Holt, Rinehart and Winston, 1965.

Barber, T. X. *Hypnosis: A scientific approach.* New York: Van Nostrand Reinhold, 1969.

Bard, P., & Mountcastle, V. B. Some forebrain mechanisms involved in expression of rage with special reference to suppression of angry behavior. *Research Publication Association Nervous and Mental Disorders, 1948, 27,* 362–404.

Baron, R. M., Mandel, D. R., Adams, C. A., & Griffin, L. M. Effects of social density in university residential environments. *Journal of Personality and Social Psychology, 1976, 34,* 434–446.

Barrett, R. S. Guide to using psychological tests. *Harvard Business Review, 1963, 41,* 139.

Bartlett, F. C. *Remembering.* Cambridge, England: Cambridge University Press, 1932.

Bateson, G., Jackson, D. D., Haley, J., & Weakland, J. H. Toward a theory of schizophrenia. *Behavioral Science, 1956, 1,* 251–264.

Baum, A., & Valins, S. Architectural mediation of residential density and control: Crowding and the regulation of social contact. In Berkowitz, L. (Ed.), *Advances in experimental social psychology,* Vol. 12. New York: Academic Press, 1979.

Beck, A. T., Ward, O. H., Mendelson, M., Mock, J. E., & Erbaugh, J. K. Reliability of psychiatric diagnosis: II. A study of consistency of clinical judgments and ratings. *American Journal of Psychiatry, 1962, 119,* 351–357.

Bem, D. J. Self-perception: An alternative interpretation of cognitive dissonance phenomena. *Psychological Review, 1967, 74,* 183–200.

Bem, D. J. Self perception theory. In Berkowitz, L. (Ed.), *Advances in experimental social psychology,* Vol. 6. New York: Academic Press, 1972.

Bem, S. L. The measurement of psychological androgyny.

Journal of Consulting and Clinical Psychology, 1974, *42,* 155–162.

Bengston, V. L. *The social psychology of aging.* Indianapolis: Bobbs-Merrill, 1973.

Bexton, W. H., Heron, W., & Scott, T. H. Effects of decreased variation in the environment. *Canadian Journal of Psychology,* 1954, *8,* 70–76.

Bonime, W. *The clinical use of dreams.* New York: Basic Books, 1962.

Boring, E. G., Langfeld, H. S., & Weld, H. P. *Foundations of psychology.* New York: Wiley, 1948.

Bourne, M. T. The nature of hypnosis: Artifact and essence. *Journal of Abnormal and Social Psychology,* 1959, *58,* 277–299.

Bower, G. H. The influence of graded reductions in reward and prior frustrating events upon the magnitude of the frustration effect. *Journal of Comparative and Physiological Psychology,* 1962, *55,* 582–587.

Bowlby, J. *Attachment and loss.* New York: Basic Books, 1969.

Brady, J. V. Ulcers in "executive" monkeys. *Scientific American,* 1958, *199,* 95–100.

Braine, M. D. S. The ontogeny of English phrase structure: The first phrase. *Language,* 1963, *39,* 1–13.

Bransford, J. D., & Franks, J. J. The abstraction of linguistic ideas. *Cognitive Psychology,* 1971, *2,* 331–350.

Bransford, J. D., & Johnson, M. K. Considerations of some problems of comprehension. In Chase, W. G. (Ed.), *Visual information processing.* New York: Academic Press, 1973.

Breuer, J., & Freud, S. Studies on hysteria. In Strachey, J. (Trans.), *Standard edition of the complete works of Sigmund Freud.* New York: Basic Books, 1957.

Brown, R. *A first language: The early stages.* Cambridge, Mass.: Harvard University Press, 1973.

Bruner, J. S., Goodnow, J. J., & Austin, G. A. *A study of thinking.* New York: Wiley, 1956.

Butler, R. A. Incentive conditions which influence visual exploration. *Journal of Experimental Psychology,* 1954, *48,* 19–23.

Byrne, D. Attitudes and attraction. In Berkowitz, L. (Ed.), *Advances in experimental social psychology,* Vol. 4. New York: Academic Press, 1969.

Byrne, D., & Clore, G. L., Jr. Predicting interpersonal attraction toward strangers presented in three different stimulus modes. *Psychonomic Science,* 1966, *4,* 239–240.

Cameron, N. *Personal development in psychopathology.* Boston: Houghton Mifflin, 1963.

Campbell, D. T. Ethnocentric and other altruistic motives. In Levine, D. (Ed.), *Nebraska symposium on motivation.* Lincoln, Neb.: University of Nebraska Press, 1965.

Cannon, W. B. *Bodily changes in pain, hunger, fear and rage.* New York: Appleton-Century-Crofts, 1929.

Caracena, P. F. Elicitation of dependency expressions in the initial stage of psychotherapy. *Journal of Counseling Psychology,* 1962, *9,* 329–334.

Carlston, D. E. The recall and use of traits and events in social inference processes. *Journal of Experimental Social Psychology,* 1980, *16,* 303–329.

Casebook on ethical standards of psychologists. Washington, D.C.: American Psychological Association, 1967.

Cattell, R. B. *Abilities: Their structure, growth, and action.* Boston: Houghton Mifflin, 1971.

Cattell, R. B. Concepts of personality growing from multivariate experiments. In Wepman, J. M., & Heine, R. W. (Eds.), *Concepts of personality.* Chicago: Aldine, 1963.

Cattell, R. B., & Ebel, H. W. *Handbook for the sixteen personality factor questionnaire.* Champaign, Ill.: Institute for Personality and Ability Testing, 1964.

Cautela, J. R. Covert sensitization. *Psychological Reports,* 1967, *20,* 459–468.

Cautela, J. R. The treatment of alcoholism by covert sensitization. *Psychotherapy: Theory, research and practice,* 1970, *7,* 86–90.

Cautela, J. R. Treatment of compulsive behavior by covert sensitization. *Psychological Record,* 1966, *16,* 33–41.

Cautela, J. R., & Kastenbaum, R. A reinforcement survey schedule for use in therapy, training, and research. *Psychological Reports,* 1967, *20,* 1115–1130.

Clopton, J. R., Pallis, D. J., & Birtchnell, J. Minnesota Multiphasic Personality Inventory profile patterns of suicide attempters. *Journal of Consulting and Clinical Psychology,* 1979, *47,* 135–139.

Collins, A. M., & Loftus, E. F. A spreading activation theory of semantic processing. *Psychological Review,* 1975, *82,* 407–428.

Collins, A. M., & Quillian, M. R. Retrieval from semantic memory. *Journal of Verbal Learning and Verbal Behavior,* 1969, *8,* 240–247.

Cooper, J. Reducing fears and increasing assertiveness: The role of dissonance reduction. *Journal of Experimental Social Psychology,* 1980, *16,* 199–214.

Craik, F. I. M., & Lockhart, R. S. Levels of processing: A framework for memory research. *Journal of Verbal Learning and Verbal Behavior,* 1972, *11,* 671–684.

Crowne, D. P., & Marlowe, D. *The approval motive: Studies in evaluative dependence.* New York: Wiley, 1964.

Damon, W. *The social world of the child.* San Francisco: Jossey-Bass, 1977.

Dattore, P. J., Shontz, F. D., & Coyne, L. Premorbid personality differentiation of cancer and noncancer groups: A test of the hypothesis of cancer proneness. *Journal of Consulting and Clinical Psychology,* 1980, *48,* 388–394.

Davis, H., & Silverman, S. R. *Hearing and deafness.* New York: Holt, Rinehart and Winston, 1961.

Davis, J. H. Group decisions and procedural justice. In Fishbein, M. (Ed.), *Progress in social psychology,* Vol. 1. Hillsdale, N.J.: Lawrence Erlbaum Associates, 1980.

Deci, E. L. Work: Who does not like it and why. *Psychology Today,* 1972, *6,* 56–92.

Delgado, J. M. R. *Physical control of the mind.* New York: Harper & Row, 1969.

Dermer, M., & Thiel, D. L. When beauty may fail. *Journal of Personality and Social Psychology,* 1975, *31,* 1168–1176.

DeValois, R. L., Abromov, I., & Jacobs, G. H. Analysis of response patterns of LGN cells. *Journal of the Optical Society of America,* 1966, *56,* 966–977.

Dion, K. L., Berscheid, E., & Walster, E. What is beautiful is good. *Journal of Personality and Social Psychology,* 1972, *24,* 285–290.

Dollard, J., Doob, L., Miller, N., Mowrer, O., & Sears, R. *Frustration and aggression.* New Haven, Conn: Yale University Press, 1939.

Dollard, J., & Miller, N. E. *Personality and psychotherapy.* New York: McGraw-Hill, 1950.

Dweck, C. S. The role of expectations and attributions in the alleviation of learned helplessness. *Journal of Personality and Social Psychology,* 1975, *31,* 674–685.

Eimas, P. D., Siqueland, E. R., Jusczyk, P., & Vigorito, J. Speech perception in infants. *Science,* 1971, *171,* 303–306.

Ekman, P. Facial signs: Facts, fantasies, and possibilities. In Sebeck, T. (Ed.), *Sight, sound, and sense.* Bloomington, Ind.: Indiana University Press, 1978.

Ekman, P., & Oster, H. Facial expressions of emotion. *Annual Review of Psychology,* 1979, *30,* 527–554.

Ellis, A. *Reason and emotion in psychotherapy.* New York: Lyle Stuart, 1970.

Engberg, L. A., Hansen, G., Welker, R. L., & Thomas, D. R. Acquisition of key-pecking via autoshaping as a function of prior experience: "Learned laziness"? *Science,* 1972, *178,* 1002–1004.

Epstein, S. Toward a unified theory of anxiety. *Progress in Experimental Personality Research,* 1967, *4,* 1–89.

Ericsson, K. A., Chase, W. G., & Saloon, F. Acquisition of a memory skill. *Science,* 1980, *208,* 1181–1182.

Erikson, E. *Childhood and society.* New York: Norton, 1950.

Erikson, E. *Identity: Youth and crisis.* New York: Norton, 1968.

Essen-Moller, E. Psychiatrische untersuchgen an einer Serie von Zwillingen. *Acta Psychiatrica et Neurologica Scandinavica,* 1941, suppl. 23.

Evans, R. M. *An introduction to color.* New York: Wiley, 1948.

Ewald, W. *Street graphics.* Washington, D.C.: American Landscape Architects Association, 1971.

Eysenck, H. J. The effects of psychotherapy: An evaluation. *Journal of Consulting Psychology,* 1952, *16,* 319–324.

Fantz, R. L. The origin of form perception. *Scientific American,* 1961, *204,* 66–72.

Fantz, R. L. Visual perception and experience in early infancy: A look at the hidden side of behavior development. In Stevenson, H. W., Hess, E. H., & Rheingold, H. L. (Eds.), *Early behavior: Comparative and developmental approaches.* New York: Wiley, 1967.

Festinger, L. *A theory of cognitive dissonance.* Stanford, Calif.: Stanford University Press, 1957.

Festinger, L., Riecken, H. W., & Schachter, S. *When prophecy fails; A social and psychological study of a modern group that predicted the destruction of the world.* New York: Harper & Row, 1956.

Fiedler, F. A contingency model of leadership effectiveness. In Berkowitz, L. (Ed.), *Advances in experimental social psychology,* Vol. 1. New York: Academic Press, 1964.

Fitts, W. H. *The experience of psychotherapy.* Princeton, N.J.: Van Nostrand, 1965.

Ford, C. S., & Beach, R. A. *Patterns of sexual behavior.* New York: Harper & Row, 1951.

Foulkes, D. *The psychology of sleep.* New York: Scribner's, 1966.

Fraiberg, S. *Every child's birthright.* New York: Basic Books, 1978.

Freedman, J., & Haber, R. N. One reason why we rarely forget a face. *The Bulletin of the Psychonomic Society,* 1974, *3,* 107–109.

French, E. G. Effects of the interaction of motivation and feedback on task performance. In Atkinson, J. W. (Ed.), *Motives in fantasy, action, and society.* New York: Litton Educational Publishing Company, 1958.

Freud, S. *An outline of psychoanalysis.* New York: Norton, 1949.

Freud, S. *The interpretation of dreams.* New York: Random House, 1950.

Freud, S. Some problems in the treatment of homosexuality. In Eysenck, H. J. (Ed.), *Behavior therapy and the neuroses.* Oxford, England: Pergamon, 1960.

Freud, S. *The interpretation of dreams.* New York: Science Editions, 1961.

Freud, S. Introductory lectures on psychoanalysis (1917). In *The complete introductory lectures on psychoanalysis.* New York: Norton, 1966.

Freud, S. New introductory lectures on psychoanalysis (1932). In *The complete introductory lectures on psychoanalysis.* New York: Norton, 1966.

Frey, D. The effect of negative feedback about oneself and cost of information on preferences for information about the source of this feedback. *Journal of Experimental Social Psychology,* 1980, *16,* 466–471.

Garcia, J., & Koelling, A. Relation of cue to consequence in avoidance learning. *Psychonomic Science,* 1966, *4,* 123–124.

Gardner, R. A., & Gardner, B. T. Teaching sign language to a chimpanzee. *Science,* 1969, *165,* 664–672.

Geller, A. M., & Atkins, A. Cognitive and personality factors in suicidal behavior. *Journal of Consulting and Clinical Psychology,* 1978, *46,* 860–868.

Gibson, E. J. The ontogeny of reading. *American Psychologist,* 1970, *25,* 136–143.

Gibson, E. J., Gibson, J. J., Pick, A. D., & Osser, H. A. A developmental study of the discrimination of letter-like forms. *Journal of Comparative and Physiological Psychology,* 1962, *55,* 897–906.

Gibson, E. J., & Walk, R. D. The "visual cliff." *Scientific American,* 1960, *202,* 67–71.

Gibson, J. J. *The perception of the visual world.* Boston: Houghton Mifflin, 1950.

Gibson, J. J. *The senses considered as perceptual systems.* Boston: Houghton Mifflin, 1966.

Glass, D. C. *Behavior patterns, stress, and coronary disease.* Hillsdale, N.J.: Lawrence Erlbaum Associates, 1977.

Glasser, W. *Reality therapy.* New York: Harper & Row, 1965.

Goldstein, K. *The organism.* New York: American Book, 1939.

Gottesman, I. I., & Shields, J. Contributions of twin studies to perspectives on schizophrenia. In Maher, B. A. (Ed.), *Progress in experimental personality research,* Vol. 3. New York: Academic Press, 1966.

Gottlieb, A. A., Gleser, G. C., & Gottschalk, L. A. Verbal and physiological responses to hypnotic suggestion of attitudes. *Psychosomatic Medicine,* 1967, *29,* 172–183.

Graham, D. T. Psychosomatic medicine. In Greenfield, N. S., & Sternbach, R. A. (Eds.), *Handbook of psychophysiology.* New York: Holt, 1972.

Graham, D. T., Stern, J. A., & Winokur, G. Experimental investigation of the specificity of attitude hypothesis in psychosomatic disease. *Psychosomatic Medicine,* 1958, *20,* 446–457.

Green, R. F. Age-intelligence relationship between 16 and 64: A rising trend. *Developmental Psychology,* 1969, *1,* 618–627.

Gregory, R. L. *Eye and brain,* 2d ed. New York: McGraw-Hill, 1972.

Griffith, R. M., Miyago, O., & Tago, A. The universality of typical dreams: Japanese vs. Americans. *American Anthropologist,* 1958, *60,* 1173–1179.

Gruber, H., & Vonnech, J. *The essential Piaget.* New York: Basic Books, 1977.

Guilford, J. P. Fluid and crystallized intelligences: Two fanciful concepts. *Psychological Bulletin,* 1980, *88,* 406–412.

Guilford, J. P. *The nature of human intelligence.* New York: McGraw-Hill, 1967.

Gulick, W. L. *Hearing: Physiology and psychophysics.* New York: Oxford, 1971.

Gurin, G., Veroff, J., & Feld, S. *Americans view their mental health.* New York: Basic Books, 1960.

Gustavson, C. R., Garcia, J., Hankins, W. G., & Rusiniak, K. W. Coyote predation control by aversive conditioning. *Science,* 1974, *184,* 581–584.

Haber, R. N., & Hershenson, M. *The psychology of visual perception,* 2d ed. New York: Holt, Rinehart and Winston, 1980.

Hanawalt, N. G., & Demarest, I. H. The effect of verbal suggestion in the recall period upon the reproduction of visually perceived forms. *Journal of Experimental Psychology,* 1939, *25,* 159–174.

Hardy, K. R. An appetitional theory of sexual motivation. *Psychological Review,* 1964, *71*(1), 1–18.

Harkins, S. G., Latané, B., & Williams, K. Social loafing: Allocating effort or taking it easy? *Journal of Experimental Social Psychology,* 1980, *16,* 457–465.

Harlow, H. F. The nature of love. *American Psychologist,* 1958, *13,* 673–685.

Harlow, H., & Harlow, M. Learning to think. *Scientific American,* 1949, *181,* 36–39.

Harlow, H., Harlow, M. K., & Meyer, D. R. Learning motivated by a manipulation drive. *Journal of Experimental Psychology,* 1950, *40,* 228–234.

Harlow, H. F., & Suomi, S. J. Nature of love—simplified. *American Psychologist,* 1970, *25,* 161–168.

Harrell, J. P. Psychological factors and hypertension. *Psychological Bulletin,* 1980, *87,* 482–501.

Harris, B. Whatever happened to Little Albert? *American Psychologist,* 1979, *34,* 151–160.

Harris, T. A. *I'm ok—you're ok.* New York: Harper & Row, 1967.

Hebb, D. O. *The organization of behavior.* New York: Wiley, 1949.

Heider, F. *The psychology of interpersonal relations.* New York: Wiley, 1958.

Held, R., & Hein, A. Movement-produced stimulation in the development of visually guided behavior. *Journal of Comparative and Physiological Psychology,* 1963, *56,* 872–876.

Held, R., & Richards, W. (Eds.). *Recent progress in perception.* San Francisco: Freeman, 1976.

Helson, H. Adaptation level theory. In Koch, S. (Ed.), *Psychology: A study of a science* (Vol. 1). New York: McGraw-Hill, 1959.

Hess, E. Ethology: An approach toward the complete analysis of behavior. In Brown, R., Galanter, E., Hess, E., & Mandler, G. (Eds.), *New directions in psychology.* New York: Holt, Rinehart and Winston, 1962.

Heston, L. L. The genetics of schizophrenia and schizoid disease. *Science,* 1970, *167,* 249–256.

Higgins, E. T., Herman, C. P., & Zanna, M. P. *Social cognition: The Ontario Symposium on personality and social psychology.* Hillsdale, N.J.: Lawrence Erlbaum Associates, 1980.

Higgins, E. T., & King, G. Accessibility of social constructs: Information processing consequences of individual and contextual variability. In Cantor, N., & Kihlstrom, J. F. (Eds.), *Personality, cognition and social interaction.* Hillsdale, N.J.: Lawrence Erlbaum Associates, in press.

Hilgard, E. R. Toward a neodissociation theory: Multiple cognitive control in human functioning. *Perspectives in Biology and Medicine,* 1974, *17,* 301–316.

Holmes, T. H., & Masuda, M. Psychosomatic syndrome. *Psychology Today,* 1972, *6,* 106.

Holt, J. *How children fail.* New York: Pitman, 1964.

Horney, K. *Neurotic personality of our times.* New York: Norton, 1937.

Hraba, J. G., & Grant, G. Black is beautiful: A reexamination of racial preference and identification. *Journal of Personality and Social Psychology,* 1970, *16,* 398–402.

Hubel, D. H., & Wiesel, T. N. Receptive fields of single neurons in the cat's striate cortex. *Journal of Physiology,* 1959, *148,* 574–591.

Hunt, E., Lunneborg, C., & Lewis, J. What does it mean to be high verbal? *Cognitive Psychology,* 1975, 7. 194–227.

James, W. *The principles of psychology.* New York: Dover, 1950. (Originally published in 1890)

Janov, A. *The primal scream.* New York: Dell, 1970.

Jellinek, E. M. Phases of alcohol addiction. *Quarterly Journal of Studies on Alcohol,* 1952, *13,* 673–684.

Jenkins, C. D. Behavior that triggers heart attacks. *Science News,* 1974, *105,* 402.

Jensen, A. R. How much can we boost IQ and scholastic achievement? *Harvard Educational Review,* 1969, *39,* 1–123.

Johnson, M. K., Bransford, J. D., & Solomon, S. Memory for tacit implications of sentences. *Journal of Experimental Psychology,* 1973, *98,* 203–205.

Jones, E. E., & Davis, K. E. From acts to dispositions: The attribution process in person perception. In Berkowitz, L. (Ed.), *Advances in experimental social psychology,* Vol. 2. New York: Academic Press, 1965, pp. 219–266.

Jones, E. E., Kanouse, D. E., Kelley, H. H., Nisbett, R. E., Valiens, S., & Weiner, B. *Attribution: Perceiving the causes of behavior.* New York: General Learning Press, 1971.

Jones, E. E., & Nisbett, R. E. *The actor and the observer: Divergent perceptions of the causes of behavior.* New York: General Learning Press, 1971.

Jones, M. C. Psychological correlates of somatic development. *Child Development,* 1965, *36,* 899–911.

Jung, C. G. *Analytical psychology.* New York: Moffat, 1916.

Jung, C. G. *Psychology of the unconscious.* New York: Dodd, 1925.

Just, M. A., & Carpenter, P. A. Personal communication, 1980.

Kagan, J., Kearsley, R., & Zelazo, P. *Infancy.* Cambridge, Mass.: Harvard University Press, 1978.

Kallman, F. J. *Heredity in mental health and disorder.* New York: Norton, 1953.

Kallman, F. J. The use of genetics in psychiatry. *Journal of Mental Science,* 1958, *104,* 542–549.

Kamin, L. J. *The science and politics of I.Q.* Potomac, Md.: Erlbaum, 1974.

Katahn, M. Systematic desensitization and counseling for anxiety in a college basketball player. *Journal of Special Education,* 1967, *1,* 309–314.

Kaye, H. Infant sucking behavior and its modification. In Lipsitt, L. P., & Spiker, C. C. (Eds.), *Advances in child development and behavior,* Vol. 3. New York: Academic Press, 1967.

Kelley, H. H. Interpersonal accommodation. *American Psychiatrist,* 1968, *23,* 399–441.

Kelley, H. H. Attribution theory in social psychology. In Levine, D. (Ed.), *Nebraska symposium on motivation.* Lincoln, Neb.: University of Nebraska Press, 1967.

Kelly, G. A. *The psychology of personal constructs.* New York: Norton, 1955.

Kelly, G. A. *A theory of personality: The psychology of personal constructs.* New York: Norton, 1963.

Kempler, W. Gestalt therapy. In Corsini, R. (Ed.), *Current psychotherapies.* Itasca, Ill.: Peacock Publishers, 1973.

Kleinmuntz, B. The computer as clinician. *American Psychologist,* 1975, *30,* 379–387.

Kleinmuntz, B. Sign and seer: Another example. *Journal of Abnormal Psychology,* 1967, *72,* 163–165.

Kolhberg, L. The development of moral character and moral ideology. In Hoffman, M. L., & Hoffman, L. W. (Eds.), *Review of child development research,* Vol. 1. New York: Russell Sage, 1964.

Köhler, W. *The mentality of apes.* New York: Harcourt, Brace, 1925.

Kolers, P. A. Bilingualism and information processing. *Scientific American,* 1968, *218,* 78–86.

Kopp, S. B. The character structure of sex offenders. *American Journal of Psychotherapy,* 1962, *16,* 64–70.

Labov, W. The logic of nonstandard English. In Alatis, J. E. (Ed.), *20th annual round table meeting on linguistics and language studies.* Washington, D.C.: Georgetown University Press, 1970.

Laing, R. D. *The divided self.* New York: Pantheon, 1969.

Laing, R. D. *The politics of experience.* New York: Pantheon, 1967.

Latané, B., & Darley, J. M. Group inhibition of bystander intervention in emergencies. *Journal of Personality and Social Psychology,* 1968, *10,* 215–221.

Latané, B., & Nida, S. Ten years of research on group size and helping. *Psychological Bulletin,* 1981, *89,* 308–324.

Laughlin, P. Social combination processes of cooperative problem-solving groups on verbal intellective tasks. In Fishbein, M. (Ed.), *Progress in social psychology,* Vol. 1. Hillsdale, N.J.: Lawrence Erlbaum Associates, 1980.

Laurendeau, M., & Pinard, A. *Causal thinking in the child.* New York: International Universities Press, 1962.

Lazarus, R. S., Opton, E. M., Nomikos, M. S., & Rankin, N. O. The principles of short-circuiting of threat: Further evidence. *Journal of Personality,* 1965, *33,* 622–635.

Lehman, H. C. *Age and achievement.* Princeton, N.J.; Princeton University Press, 1953.

Leventhal, H. Findings and theory in the study of fear communications. In Berkowitz, L. (Ed.), *Advances in experimental social psychology,* Vol. 5. New York: Academic Press, 1970.

Lewis, M., & Brooks-Gunn, J. *Social cognition and the acquisition of self.* New York: Plenum, 1979.

Lidz, T., Alanen, Y., & Cornelison, A. Schizophrenic patients and their siblings. *Psychiatry,* 1963, *26,* 1–18.

Liebert, R. M., & Spiegler, M. D. *Personality: Strategies for the study of man,* rev. ed. Homewood, Ill.: Dorsey Press, 1974.

Liebert, R. M., & Spiegler, M. D. *Personality,* 3d ed. Homewood, Ill.: Dorsey Press, 1978.

Lilly, J. C. *Lilly on dolphins.* Garden City, N.Y.: Anchor Books, 1975.

Lindsay, P. H., & Norman, D. A. *Human information processing,* 2d ed. New York: Academic Press, 1977.

Loehlin, J. C., Lindzey, G., & Spuhler, J. N. *Race differences in intelligence.* San Francisco: Freeman, 1975.

Loftus, E. F., & Loftus, G. R. On the permanence of stored information in the human brain. *American Psychologist,* 1980, *35,* 409–420.

Loftus, E. F., & Monahan, J. Trial by data: Psychological research as legal evidence. *American Psychologist,* 1980, *35,* 270–283.

Loftus, E. F., & Palmer, J. C. Reconstruction of automobile destruction. *Journal of Verbal Learning and Verbal Behavior,* 1974, *13,* 585–589.

Loftus, E. F., & Zanni, G. R. Eyewitness identification: Linguistically caused misreflections. Unpublished paper, 1973.

Logan, F. *Fundamentals of learning and motivation.* Dubuque, Iowa: Brown, 1970.

Lorenz, K. Der Kumpan in der Umwelt des Vogels. *Jour. Ornith.,* 1935, *83,* 137–213, 324–331.

Lorenz, K. Vergleichende Verhaltensforschung. *Zool. Anz. Suppl.,* 1939, *12,* 69–102.

Louis Harris and Associates, Inc. *The myth and reality of aging in America.* Washington, D.C.: National Council on the Aging, 1975.

Lubin, B., Wallis, R. R., & Paine, C. Patterns of psychological test usage in the United States: 1935–1969. *Professional Psychology,* 1971, *2,* 70–74.

Luchins, A. S. Mechanization in problem-solving: The effect of *Einstellung. Psychological Monographs,* 1942, *54* (whole no. 248).

Mackintosh, N. J., Bygrave, D. J., & Picton, B. M. B. Locus of the effect of a surprising reinforcer in the attenuation of blocking. *Quarterly Journal of Experimental Psychology,* 1977, *29,* 327–336.

Maher, B. A. *Principles of psychopathology.* New York: McGraw-Hill, 1966.

Maier, N. R. F. Reasoning in humans. II. The solution of a problem and its appearance in consciousness. *Journal of Comparative Psychology,* 1931, *12,* 181–194.

Maslow, A. H. A theory of human motivation. *Psychological Review,* 1943, *50,* 370–396.

Maslow, A. H. *Motivation and personality.* New York: Harper & Row, 1970.

Maslow, A. H. Some basic propositions of a growth and

self-actualization psychology. In *Perceiving, behaving, becoming: A new force for education.* Washington, D.C.: Yearbook of the Association for Supervision and Curriculum Development, 1962.

Masters, R., & Houston, J. *The varieties of psychedelic experience.* New York: Holt, Rinehart and Winston, 1966.

Mathews, K. E., Jr., & Canon, L. K. Environmental noise level as a determinant of helping behavior. *Journal of Personality and Social Psychology,* 1975, *32,* 571–577.

Mayer, R. E., & Greeno, J. G. Structural differences between learning outcomes produced by different instructional methods. *Journal of Educational Psychology,* 1972, *63,* 165–173.

McClelland, D. C. Testing for competence rather than for "intelligence." *American Psychologist,* 1973, *28,* 1–14.

McClelland, D. C., Atkinson, J. W., Clark, R. A., & Lowell, E. L. *The achievement motive.* New York: Appleton-Century-Crofts, 1953.

McClelland, D. C., & Burnham, D. H. Power is the great motivator. *Harvard Business Review,* 1976, 54–71.

McClelland, D. C., & Friedman, G. A. A cross-cultural study of the relationship between child-training practices and achievement motivation appearing in folk tales. In Swanson, G. E., et al. (Eds.), *Readings in social psychology.* New York: Holt, 1952.

McClelland, D. C., & Winter, D. G. *Motivating economic achievement.* New York: Free Press, 1969.

McGuire, W. J. Inducing resistance to persuasion: Some contemporary approaches. In Berkowitz, L. (Ed.), *Advances in experimental social psychology,* Vol. 1. New York: Academic Press, 1964.

McGuire, W. J. Personality and susceptibility to social influence. In Borgatta, E., & Lambert, W. (Eds.), *Handbook of personality theory and research.* Chicago: Rand-McNally, 1968.

McIntire, R. *For love of children.* Del Mar, Calif.: CRM Books, 1970.

Meehl, P. E. Wanted—A good cookbook. *American Psychologist,* 1956, *11,* 262–272.

Megargee, E. I. The prediction of violence with psychological tests. In C. D. Spielberger (Ed.), *Current topics in clinical and community psychology,* Vol. 2. New York: Academic Press, 1970.

Meredith, H. V. A synopsis of puberal changes in youth. *Journal of School of Health,* 1967, *37,* 171–176.

Merton, R. K. *On the shoulders of giants.* New York: Free Press, 1965.

Merton, R. K. *Social theory and social structure.* Glencoe. Ill.: Free Press, 1957.

Milgram, S. Some conditions of obedience and disobedience to authority. *Human Relations,* 1965, *18,* 57–76.

Miller, G. A., Galanter, E., & Pribram, K. L. *Plans and the structure of behavior.* New York: Holt, Rinehart and Winston, 1960.

Miller, N. E. Learning of visceral and glandular responses. *Science,* 1969, *163,* 434–445.

Milner, B. Neuropsychological evidence for differing memory processes. Abstract for the symposium on short-term and long-term memory. *Proceedings of the 18th International Congress of Psychology,* Moscow, 1966.

Mischel, W. On the interface of cognition and personality: Beyond the person-situation debate. *American Psychologist,* 1979, *34,* 740–754.

Mischel, W. Toward a cognitive social learning theory reconceptualization of personality. *Psychological Review,* 1973, *80,* 252–283.

Money, J., & Ehrhardt, A. A. Fetal hormones and the brain: Effect on sexual dimorphism of behavior. A review. *Archives of Sexual Behavior,* 1971, *32,* 241–262.

Moore, O. K. Autotelic responsive environments and exceptional children. In Harvey, O. J. (Ed.), *Experience, structure, and adaptability.* New York: Springer, 1966.

Mosak, H. H. Adlerian psychotherapy. In Corsini, R. J. (Ed.), *Current psychotherapies,* 2d ed. Itasca, Ill.: Peacock, 1979.

Murray, H. A. *Explorations in personality.* New York: Oxford University Press, 1938.

Murray, H. A. Techniques for a systematic investigation of fantasy. *Journal of Psychology,* 1936, *3,* 115–143.

Nation, J. R., & Woods, D. J. Persistence: The role of partial reinforcement in psychotherapy. *Journal of Experimental Psychology: General,* 1980, *109,* 175–207.

Neisser, U., & Hupcey, J. A Sherlockian experiment. *Cognition,* 1975, *3,* 307–311.

Newcomb, T. M. *The acquaintance process.* New York: Holt, Rinehart and Winston, 1961.

Newell, A., & Simon, H. A. *Human problem solving.* Englewood Cliffs, N.J.: Prentice-Hall, 1972.

Nisbett, R. E. Determinants of food intake in human obesity. *Science,* 1968, *59,* 1254–1255.

Nisbett, R. E., Borgida, E., Crandall, R., & Reed, H. Popular induction: Information is not necessarily informative. In Carroll, J., & Payne, J. (Eds.), *Cognition and social behavior.* Hillsdale, N.J.: Lawrence Erlbaum Associates, 1976.

Nisbett, R. E., & Ross, L. D. *Human inference.* Prentice-Hall, 1980.

Nisbett, R. E., & Wilson, T. D. Telling more than we can know: Verbal reports on mental processes. *Psychological Review,* 1977, *84,* 231–259.

Ogden, C. K., & Richards, I. A. *The meaning of meaning.* New York: Harcourt, Brace, 1923.

Olds, J., & Milner, P. M. Positive reinforcement produced by electrical stimulation of septal area and other regions of rat brains. *Journal of Comparative and Physiological Psychology,* 1954, *47,* 419–427.

Ornstein, R., & Naranjo, C. *On the psychology of meditation.* New York: Viking, 1971.

Osgood, C. E. The nature and measurement of meaning. *Psychological Bulletin,* 1952, *49,* 197–237.

Palermo, D. S. Language acquisition. In Reese, H. W., & Lipsitt, L. P. (Eds.), *Experimental child psychology.* New York: Academic Press, 1970.

Palmore, E. Facts on aging. *Gerontologist,* 1977, *17,* 315–320.

Paul, G. L. *Insight vs. desensitization in psychotherapy.* Stanford, Calif.: Stanford University Press, 1966.

Paul, G. L., & Lentz, R. L. *Psychosocial treatment of chronic mental patients: Milieu versus social-learning programs.* Cambridge, Mass. Harvard University Press, 1977.

Pavlov, I. P. *Conditioned reflexes.* New York: Oxford University Press, 1927.

Perls, F. S. *Gestalt therapy verbatim.* Lafayette, Calif.: Real People Press, 1969.

Pervin, L. A. *Personality: Theory, assessment, and research.* New York: Wiley, 1970.

Peterson, L. R., & Peterson, M. J. Short-term retention of individual verbal items. *Journal of Experimental Psychology,* 1959, *58,* 193–198.

Piaget, J. *The language and thought of the child.* New York: Harcourt, Brace, 1926.

Pirenne, M. H. *Optics, painting and photography.* Cambridge, England: Cambridge University Press, 1970.

Posner, M. I. *Cognition: An introduction.* Glenview, Ill.: Scott, Foresman, 1973.

Premack, D. Language in chimpanzee? *Science,* 1971, *172,* 808–822.

Premack, D. Reinforcement theory. In Levine, D. (Ed.), *Nebraska symposium on motivation.* Lincoln, Neb.: University of Nebraska Press, 1965.

Premack, D., & Woodruff, G. Chimpanzee problem-solving: A test for comprehension. *Science,* 1978, *202,* 532–535.

Raimy, V. *Misunderstandings of the self.* San Francisco: Jossey-Bass, 1975.

Raphael, B. *The thinking computer: Mind inside matter.* San Francisco: Freeman, 1976.

Rebelsky, F., & Hanks, C. Father's verbal interaction with infants in the first three months of life. In Rebelsky, F., & Dorman, L. (Eds.), *Child development and behavior.* New York: Knopf, 1973, pp. 145–148.

Rescorla, R. A. Effect of inflation of the unconditioned stimulus value following conditioning. *Journal of Comparative and Physiological Psychology,* 1974, *86,* 101–107.

Revusky, S. H. Aversion to sucrose produced by contingent x-irradiation: Temporal and dosage parameters. *Journal of Comparative and Physiological Psychology,* 1968, *65,* 17–22.

Rodin, J. Current status of the internal-external hypothesis for obesity. What went wrong? *American Psychologist,* 1981, *36,* 361–372.

Rodin, J., & Slochower, J. Externality in the nonobese: Effects of environmental responsiveness on weight. *Journal of Personality and Social Psychology,* 1976, *33,* 338–344.

Rogers, C. R. *Client-centered therapy.* Boston: Houghton Mifflin, 1951.

Rogers, C. R. *On becoming a person: A therapist's view of psychotherapy.* Boston: Houghton Mifflin, 1961.

Rokeach, M. *The open and closed mind.* New York: Basic Books, 1960.

Rosch, E. Cognitive representations of semantic categories. *Journal of Experimental Psychology: General,* 1975, *104,* 192–233.

Rosch, E., & Mervis, C. B. Family resemblances: Studies in the internal structure of categories. *Cognitive Psychology,* 1975, *7,* 573–605.

Rosenman, R. H., Friedman, M., Straus, R., *et al.* A predictive study of coronary heart disease: The Western collaborative group study. *Journal of the American Medical Association,* 1964, *189,* 15–22.

Rosenman, R. H., Brand, R. J., Jenkins, C. D., *et al.* Coronary heart disease in the Western collaborative group study: Final follow-up experience of 8 1/2 years. *Journal of the American Medical Association,* 1975, *233,* 872–877.

Rosenthal, R. *Experimenter effects in behavioral research.* New York: Appleton-Century-Crofts, 1966.

Rosenthal, R. The Pygmalion effect lives. *Psychology Today,* 1973, *7,* 56–62.

Rotter, J. B. Generalized expectancies for internal versus external control of reinforcement. *Psychological Monographs,* 1966, *80* (whole no. 609).

Runyon, R. P., & Haber, A. *Fundamentals of behavioral statistics,* 3d ed. Reading, Mass.: Addison-Wesley, 1976.

Samuels, S. J., Dahl, P., & Archwamety, T. Effect of hypothesis/test training on reading skill. *Journal of Educational Psychology,* 1974, *66,* 835–844.

Schachter, S. Some extraordinary facts about obese humans and rats. *American Psychologist,* 1971, *26,* 129–144.

Schachter, S. *The psychology of affiliation: Experimental studies of the sources of gregariousness.* Stanford, Calif.: Stanford University Press, 1959.

Schachter, S., & Gross, L. P. Manipulated time and eating behavior. *Journal of Personality and Social Psychology,* 1968, *10,* 98–106.

Schachter, S., & Singer, J. E. Cognitive, social and physiological determinants of emotional state. *Psychological Review,* 1962, *69,* 379–399.

Schaie, K. W. A general model of the study of developmental problems. *Psychological Bulletin,* 1965, *64,* 92–107.

Schank, R., & Abelson, R. *Scripts, plans, goals, and understanding.* Hillsdale, N.J.: Lawrence Erlbaum Associates, 1977.

Schiffman, H. R. *Sensation and perception: An integrated approach.* New York: Wiley, 1976.

Schooler, C. Birth order effects: Not here, not now! *Psychological Bulletin,* 1972, *78,* 161–175.

Schwartz, G. E., Fair, P. L., Salt, P., Mandel, M. R. & Klerman, G. I. Facial muscle patterning to affective imagery in depressed and nondepressed subjects. *Signs,* 1976, *192,* 489–491.

Secord, P. F. Facial features and inference processes in interpersonal perception. In Taguiri, R, & Petrullo, L. (Eds.), *Personal perception and interpersonal behavior.* Stanford University Press, 1958.

Seeman, J. Self-exploration in client-centered therapy. In Wolman, B. B. (Ed.), *Handbook of clinical psychology.* New York: McGraw-Hill, 1965.

Seligman, M. E. P. Can we immunize the weak? *Psychology Today,* June 1969, pp. 42–44.

Seligman, M. E. P. Depression and learned helplessness. In Friedman, R. J., & Katz, M. M. (Eds.), *The psychology of depression: Contemporary theory and research.* Washington, D.C.: Winston-Wiley, 1974.

Seligman, M. E. P. *Helplessness.* San Francisco: Freeman, 1975.

Selye, H. *The stress of life.* New York: McGraw-Hill, 1956.

Shannab, M. E., & Yahya, K. A. A behavioral study of obedience in children. *Journal of Personality and Social Psychology,* 1977, *35,* 530–536.

Sherif, M., Harvey, O. J., White, B. J., Hood, W. R., & Sherif, C. W. *Intergroup conflict and cooperation: The*

Robbers Cave experiment. Norman, Okla.: Institute of Group Relations, University of Oklahoma, 1961.

Shoemaker, D. J., South, D. R., & Lowe, J. Facial stereotypes of deviants and judgments of guilt or innocence. *Social Forces,* 1973, *51,* 427–433.

Shostrom, E. L. *Personal orientation inventory.* San Diego: Educational and Industrial Testing Service, 1963.

Sigall, H., & Ostrove, N. Beautiful but dangerous: Effects of offenders' attractiveness and nature of the crime on juridic judgment. *Journal of Personality and Social Psychology,* 1975, *31,* 410–414.

Siqueland, E. R., & Lipsitt, L. P. Conditioned head-turning in newborns. *Journal of Experimental Child Psychology,* 1966, *3,* 356–376.

Skinner, B. F. *The behavior of organisms.* New York: Appleton-Century-Crofts, 1938.

Slobin, D. I. *Psycholinguistics.* Glenview, Ill.: Scott, Foresman, 1971.

Smith, M. When psychology grows up. *New Scientist,* 1976, *64,* 90–93.

Snyder, M., Tanke, E. D., & Berscheid, E. Social perception and interpersonal behavior: On the self-fulfilling nature of social stereotypes. *Journal of Personality and Social Psychology,* 1977, *35,* 656–666.

Solomon, R. L., & Corbit, J. D. An opponent-process theory of motivation: II. Cigarette addiction. *Journal of Abnormal Psychology,* 1973, *83,* 158–171.

Sperling, G. The information available in brief visual presentations. *Psychological Monographs,* 1960 (74, whole no. 498).

Sperry, R. W. Hemisphere deconnection and unity in conscious experience. *American Psychologist,* 1968, *23,* 723–733.

Spock, B. *Baby and child care.* New York: Simon & Schuster, 1957.

Standing, L. G., Conezio, J., & Haber, R. N. Perception and memory for pictures: Single trial learning of 2500 visual stimuli. *Psychonomic Science,* 1970, *19,* 73–74.

Sternberg, S. Memory-scanning: Mental processes revealed by reaction time experiments. *Acta Psychologica,* 1969, *30,* 276–315.

Stewart, K. Dream theory in Malaya. In Tart, C. (Ed.), *Altered states of consciousness: A book of readings.* New York: Wiley, 1969.

Stone, L. J., & Church, J. *Childhood and adolescence.* New York: Random House, 1968.

Storms, M. D., & Nisbett, R. E. Insomnia and the attribution process. *Journal of Personality and Social Psychology,* 1970, *2,* 319–328.

Strupp, H. H. *Psychotherapy and the modification of abnormal behavior.* New York: McGraw-Hill, 1971.

Strupp, H. H., Fox, R. W., & Lessler, K. *Patients view their psychotherapy.* Baltimore: Johns Hopkins University Press, 1969.

Strupp, H. H., Wallach, M. S., Wogan, M., & Jenkins, J. W. Psychotherapists' assessment of former patients. *Journal of Nervous and Mental Disease,* 1963, *137,* 222–230.

Suggs, D., & Sales, B. D. The art and science of conducting *voir dire. Professional Psychology,* 1978, *9,* 367–388.

Sullivan, H. S. *The interpersonal theory of psychiatry.* New York: Norton, 1953.

Szasz, T. S. *Law, liberty, and psychiatry.* New York: Macmillan, 1963.

Szasz, T. S. *The myth of mental illness.* New York: Harper & Row, 1961.

Tart, C. *On being stoned: A psychological study of marijuana intoxication.* Palo Alto, Calif.: Science and Behavior Books, 1971.

Tart, C. The "high" dream: A new state of consciousness. In Tart, C. (Ed.), *Altered states of consciousness: A book of readings.* New York: Wiley, 1969.

Terman, L. M., & Merrill, M. A. *Stanford-Binet intelligence scale: Manual for the third revision form L-M.* Boston: Houghton Mifflin, 1960.

Thibaut, J. W., & Kelley, H. H. *The social psychology of groups.* New York: Wiley, 1959.

Thigpen, C. H., & Cleckley, H. M. *The three faces of Eve.* New York: McGraw-Hill, 1957.

Thorndyke, P. W. Cognitive structures in comprehension and memory of narrative discourse. *Cognitive Psychology,* 1977, *9,* 77–110.

Thurstone, L. L. *Primary mental abilities.* Chicago: University of Chicago Press, 1938.

Tinbergen, N. *The study of instinct.* London: Oxford University Press, 1951.

Tobin, S. A. Saying goodbye in Gestalt therapy. *Psychotherapy: Theory, research, and practice,* 1971, *8,* 150–155.

Trivers, R. L. The evaluation of reciprocal altruism. *The Quarterly Review of Biology,* 1971, *46,* 35–57.

Truax, C. B., Wargo, D. G., Frank, J. D., Imber, S. D., Battle, C., Hoehn-Sarie, R., Wash, E. H., & Stone, A. R. Therapist empathy, genuineness, warmth and patient therapeutic outcome. *Journal of Consulting Psychology,* 1966, *30,* 395–401.

Tryon, R. C. Genetic differences in maze-learning ability in rats. In *39th Yearbook, National Society for the Study of Education.* Chicago: University of Chicago Press, 1940.

Tversky, A., & Kahneman, D. Availability: A heuristic for judging frequency and probability. *Cognitive Psychology,* 1973, *5,* 207–232.

Valenti, A. C., & Downing, L. L. Differential effects of jury size on verdicts following deliberations as a function of the apparent guilt of a defendant. *Journal of Personality and Social Psychology,* 1975, *32,* 655–663.

Valins, S. Cognitive effects of false heart rate feedback. *Journal of Personality and Social Psychology,* 1966, *4,* 400–408.

Wagner, A. R., Rudy, J. W., & Whitlow, J. W. Rehearsal in animal conditioning. *Journal of Experimental Psychology,* 1973, *97,* 407–426.

Wallace, W. P. Review of the historical, empirical, and theoretical status of the von Restorff phenomenon. *Psychological Bulletin,* 1965, *63,* 410–424.

Wallach, M. A., & Kogan, N. *Modes of thinking in young children.* New York: Holt, Rinehart and Winston, 1965.

Walster, E. The effect of self-esteem on romantic liking. *Journal of Experimental Social Psychology,* 1965, *1,* 184–197.

Walster, E., Berscheid, E., & Walster, G. W. New directions in equity research. *Journal of Personality and Social Psychology*, 1973, *25,* 151–176.

Wason, P. C., & Johnson-Laird P. N. (Eds.), *Thinking and reasoning.* Middlesex, England: Penguin, 1968.

Watson, J. B., & Raynor, R. Conditioned emotional reactions. *Journal of Experimental Psychology,* 1920, *3,* 1–14.

Wechsler, D. *Wechsler adult intelligence scale, manual.* New York: Psychological Corporation, 1955.

Wegner, D. M., & Vallacher, R. R. *Implicit psychology: An introduction to social cognition.* New York: Oxford, 1977.

Weiss, J. Psychological factors in stress and disease. *Scientific American,* 1972, *226,* 104–113.

Weiss, J. M., Glazer, H. I., & Pohorecky, L. A. Coping behavior and neurochemical changes: An alternative explanation for the original learned helplessness experiments. In *Relevance of the psychopathological animal model to the human.* New York: Plenum, 1975.

White, R. W. Motivation reconsidered: The concept of competence. *Psychological Review,* 1959, *66,* 297–333.

Whorf, B. L. *Language, thought, and reality.* New York: MIT Press–Wiley, 1956.

Wicklund, R. A. Objective self-awareness. In Berkowitz, L. (Ed.), *Advances in experimental social psychology,* Vol. 8. New York: Academic Press, 1975.

Wilson, E. O. *Sociobiology: The new synthesis.* Cambridge, Mass.: Belknap Press of Harvard University Press, 1975.

Winterbottom, M. R. The relation of need for achievement to learning experiences in independence and mastery. In Atkinson, J. W. (Ed.), *Motives in fantasy action and society.* Princeton, N.J.: Van Nostrand, 1958.

Wolf, M., Birnbrauer, J., Lawler, J., & Williams, T. The operant extinction, reinstatement, and re-extinction of vomiting behavior in a retarded child. In Ulrich, R., Stachnik, T., & Mabry, J. *Control of human behavior: From cure to prevention.* Glenview, Ill.: Scott, Foresman, 1970.

Wolpe, J., & Lang, P. J. A fear survey schedule for use in behavior therapy. *Behavior Research and Therapy,* 1964, *2,* 27.

Wyer, R. S., & Srull, T. K. Category accessibility: Some theoretical and empirical issues concerning the processing of social stimulus information. In Higgins, E. T., Herman, C. P., & Zanna, M. P. (Eds.), *Social cognition: The Ontario symposium on personality and social psychology.* Hillsdale, N.J.: Lawrence Erlbaum Associates, 1980.

Yalom, I. D., & Liebermann, M. A. A study of encounter group casualties. *Archives of General Psychiatry,* 1971, *25,* 16–30.

Yarrow, M. R., Campbell, J. D., & Burton, R. V. Recollections of childhood: A study of the retrospective method. *Monographs of the Society for Research in Child Development,* 1970, *35* (5, whole no. 138).

Youniss, J. *Parents and peers in social development.* Chicago: University of Chicago Press, 1980.

Zajonc, R. B. Social facilitation. *Science,* 1965, *149,* 269–274.

Zajonc, R. B. Family configuration and intelligence. *Science,* 1976, *160,* 227–236.

Zajonc, R. B., & Bargh, J. Birth order, family size, and decline of SAT scores. *American Psychologist,* 1980, *35,* 662–668.

Zajonc, R. B., & Markus, G. B. Birth order and intellectual development. *Psychological Review,* 1975, *82,* 74–88.

Zajonc, R. B., & Sales, S. Social facilitation of dominant and subordinate responses. *Journal of Experimental Social Psychology,* 1966, *2,* 160–168.

Zanna, M. P., & Cooper, J. Dissonance and the pill: An attribution approach to studying the arousal properties of dissonance. *Journal of Personality and Social Psychology,* 1974, *29,* 703–709.

Zimbardo, P. G. The human choice: Individuation, reason, and order versus deindividuation, impulse, and chaos. In *Nebraska symposium on motivation.* Lincoln, Neb.: University of Nebraska Press, 1969.

Zimbardo, P. G. *Shyness: What is it, what to do about it.* New York: Addison-Wesley, 1977.

Zimbardo, P. G., Pilkonis, P. A., & Norwood, R. M. The social disease called shyness. *Psychology Today,* 1975, *9,* 69–72.

Zimbardo, P. G., & Ruch, F. L. *Psychology and life,* 9th ed. Glenview, Ill.: Scott, Foresman, 1977.

Zuckerman, M. Sensation seeking. In London, H., & Exner, J. E. Jr. (Eds.), *Dimensions of personality.* New York: Wiley, 1978.

Zuckerman, M. *Sensation seeking: Beyond the optimal level of arousal.* Hillsdale, N.J.: Lawrence Erlbaum Associates, 1979.

Zuckerman, M., Buchsbaum, M. S., & Murphy, D. L. Sensation seeking and its biological correlates. *Psychological Bulletin,* 1980, *88,* 187–214.

(Continued from p. iv)

Figure 1-1, p. 14, photo courtesy of The Bettmann Archive, Inc.
Figure 1-2, p. 15, photo courtesy of The Bettmann Archive, Inc.
Figure 1-3, p. 16, photo courtesy of James B. Watson.
Figure 1-4, p. 17, photo courtesy of United Press International.
Figure 1-5, p. 18, from *Elements of Psychology*, 2d edition, by David Krech, Richard S. Crutchfield, and Norman Livson. Copyright © 1969 by Alfred A. Knopf, Inc. Reprinted by permission of Alfred A. Knopf, Inc.
Photo, p. 20, by Bob Adelman, courtesy of Magnum Photos.
Highlight 1-6, p. 23, from APA pamphlet, *Careers in Psychology*, 1978, p. 17. Copyright 1978 by the American Psychological Association. Reprinted by permission.
Figure 1-6, p. 24, adapted by permission from *American Psychological Association Human Resources Survey, 1976*.
Figure 1-7, p. 25, adapted by permission from *American Psychological Human Resources Survey, 1976*.

Chapter 2

Photo, p. 28, by Michael Hayman, courtesy of Stock, Boston.
News story, p. 30, copyright 1976 by Newsweek, Inc. All rights reserved. Reprinted by permission.
News story, p. 31, reprinted by permission of Associated Press.
News story, p. 38, reprinted with permission from *Science News,* the weekly newsmagazine of science, copyright 1980 by Science Service, Inc. Originally appeared in "Sexual Dimorphism in Extent of Axonal Sprouting in Rat Hippocampus," Loy, R., and Milner, T. A., *Science*, Vol. 208, pp. 1282, 1283, 13 June 1980. Copyright 1980 by the American Association for the Advancement of Science. Reprinted by permission of the publisher and of the authors, R. Loy and T. A. Milner.
Figure 2-4, p. 38, reprinted courtesy of Hilda Sidney Krech.
Figure 2-5, p. 39, adapted from Fig. 3.2 (p. 63) in *A Primer of Physiological Psychology* by Robert L. Isaacson, Robert J. Douglas, Joel F. Lubar, and Leonard W. Schmaltz. Copyright © 1971 by Harper & Row, Publishers, Inc. Reprinted by permission of the publisher.
Figure 2-6, p. 40, adapted from Fig. 4.6 (p. 88) in *Foundations of Physiological Psychology* by Richard F. Thompson. Copyright © 1967 by Richard F. Thompson. Reprinted by permission of Harper & Row, Publishers, Inc.
Figure 2-7, p. 41, after Figure 14.15 (p. 345) in *A Biology of Human Concern* by William Etkin, Robert M. Devlin, and Thomas G. Bouffard (J. B. Lippincott Company). Copyright © 1972 by J. B. Lippincott Company. Reprinted by permission of Harper & Row, Publishers, Inc.
Figure 2-9, p. 43, adapted from H. F. Harlow, et al., *Psychology* (San Francisco: Albion, 1971). Reprinted by permission.
Figure 2-10, p. 44, adapted from *Physiological Psychology* by Peter Milner. Copyright © 1970 by Holt, Rinehart and Winston. Reprinted by permission of Holt, Rinehart and Winston.
Drawing, p. 45, by Roy Doty, *Newsweek*.
Figure 2-11, p. 46, after Figure 15.1 (p. 353) in *A Biology of Human Concern* by William Etkin, Robert M. Devlin, and Thomas G. Bouffard (J. B. Lippincott Company). Copyright © 1972 by J. B. Lippincott Company. Reprinted by permission of Harper & Row, Publishers, Inc.
News story, p. 48, reprinted by permission of *Science 81* Magazine, copyright the American Association for the Advancement of Science.
News story, p. 50, © The New York Times Company. Reprinted by permission.
Figure 2-13, p. 51, reprinted by permission of Dr. Margery Shaw, University of Texas Health Sciences Center at Houston.

News story, p. 53, copyright 1979 by Newsweek, Inc. All rights reserved. Reprinted by permission.
Photos, p. 53 (parts A and B) by Denise Hunter. Reprinted by permission.
Figure 2-14, p. 54, from *Psychology in the Making* by Leo Postman. Copyright © 1962 by Alfred A. Knopf, Inc. Reprinted by permission of Alfred A. Knopf, Inc. From data provided through courtesy of R. C. Tryon.
Photo, p. 56, courtesy of C. P. Hodge, Montreal Neurological Institute.
Figure 2-15, p. 57, photos courtesy of Dr. José M. R. Delgado, Autonomous Medical School, Madrid, Spain.
News story, p. 58, reprinted with permission from *Science News,* the weekly newsmagazine of science, copyright 1979 by Science Service, Inc.
Figure 2-16, p. 59, from David Foulkes, *The Psychology of Sleep*. Copyright © 1966 by David Foulkes (New York: Charles Scribner's Sons, 1966). Reprinted by permission of Charles Scribner's Sons.
News story, p. 60, reprinted with permission from *Science News,* the weekly newsmagazine of science, copyright 1978 by Science Service, Inc.

Chapter 3

Photo, p. 62, by Nick Sapieha, courtesy of Stock, Boston.
Highlight 3-1, p. 63, drawings from "Multistability in Perception," by F. Attneave, *Scientific American,* December 1971, p. 67. Drawings by Gerald H. Fisher. © 1967 by Gerald H. Fisher. Reprinted by permission.
Figure 3-5, p. 67, from S. R. Detwiler, "Some Biological Aspects of Vision," *American Scientist*, 1941, *29*, p. 114. Reprinted by permission.
Figure 3-7, p. 69, from *Sensation and Perception* E. Bruce Goldstein. © 1980 by Wadsworth, Inc. Reprinted by permission of Wadsworth Publishing Company, Belmont, California 94002.
News story, p. 70, reprinted by permission of *TIME*, The Weekly Newsmagazine; Copyright Time Inc. 1972.
Highlight 3-3, p. 71, data from E. G. Boring, H. S. Langfield, and H. P. Weld, *Foundations of Psychology* (New York: Wiley, 1948). Reprinted by permission of Mrs. Lucy D. Boring.
Table 3-2, p. 71, based on R. Teghtsoonian, "On the Exponent in Stevens' Law and the Constant in Ekman's Law," *Psychological Review*, 1971, *78*, 71–80. Copyright 1971 by the American Psychological Association. Reprinted by permission.
Figure 3-9, p. 72, adapted from S. Hecht, "Vision, II: The Nature of the Photoreceptor Process," in C. Murchison (Ed.), *A Handbook of General Experimental Psychology* (Worcester, Mass.: Clark University Press, 1934). Reprint edition by Russell and Russell, 1969. Reprinted by permission of Clark University Press.
Figure 3-17, p. 77, photo from H. L. Teuber, W. S. Battersby, and M. B. Bender, *Visual Field Defects after Penetrating Missile Wounds of the Brain* (Cambridge, Mass.: Harvard University Press, 1960), p. 36. Reprinted by permission of Harvard University Press. Photo courtesy of Massachusetts Institute of Technology.
Figure 3-18, p. 78, Part A: Adapted from Julian E. Hochberg, *Perception*, © 1964, pp. 64, 84, 88. Adapted by permission of Prentice-Hall, Inc., Englewood Cliffs, N.J. Part B: Adapted from D. H. Huble and W. Torstenn, "Receptive Fields, Binocular Interaction, and Functional Architecture in the Cat's Visual Cortex," *Journal of Physiology* (Cambridge University Press), 1963, *160*, 106–154.
Figure 3-20, p. 79, adapted from Julian E. Hochberg, *Perception*, © 1964, pp. 64, 84, 88. Adapted by permission of Prentice-Hall, Inc., Englewood Cliffs, N.J.
Figure 3-21, p. 79, adapted from *Perception*, by D. J. Weintraub and E. L. Walker. Copyright © 1966 by Wadsworth, Inc. Reprinted

by permission of the publisher, Brooks/Cole Publishing Company, Monterey, California.

Figure 3-23, p. 81, adapted from *Perception,* by D. J. Weintraub and E. L. Walker. Copyright © 1966 by Wadsworth, Inc. Reprinted by permission of the publisher, Brooks/Cole Publishing Company, Monterey, California.

Photo, p. 81, courtesy of FMC Corporation.

Figure 3-24, p. 82, photos courtesy of Lou Harvey.

Photo, p. 84, reprinted by permission of the Pulitzer Publishing Company.

Photo, p. 85, courtesy of Sam Teicher.

Figure 3-31, p. 88, adapted from *Man-Machine Engineering* by A. Chapanis. Copyright © 1965 by Wadsworth, Inc. Reprinted by permission of the publisher, Brooks/Cole Publishing Company, Monterey, California. Also adapted from A. Chapanis, W. R. Garner, and C. T. Morgan, *Applied Experimental Psychology—Human Factors in Engineering Design* (New York: Wiley, 1949). Reprinted by permission of the authors.

Figure 3-33, p. 88, adapted from O. Stuhlman, Jr., *An Introduction to Biophysics* (New York: Wiley, 1943). Reprinted by permission of Mrs. William T. Couch.

Figure 3-34, p. 89, adapted from *Hearing and Deafness,* revised edition, edited by Hallowell Davis and S. Richard Silverman. Copyright 1947, © 1960 by Holt, Rinehart and Winston, Inc. Reprinted by permission of Holt, Rinehart and Winston.

Photo, p. 89, by Jeff Albertson, courtesy of Stock, Boston.

Figure 3-35, p. 92, from *Psychology Today: An Introduction,* 4th ed., p. 281. Copyright © 1979 by Random House, Inc. Reprinted by permission of CRM Books, a Division of Random House, Inc.

Figure 3-36, p. 93, from *Psychology,* 4th ed., by Robert S. Woodworth. Copyright 1921, 1929, 1934, 1940 by Henry Holt and Company, Inc.

News story, p. 93, reprinted with permission from *Science News,* the weekly newsmagazine of science, copyright 1980 by Science Service, Inc.

Figure 3-37, p. 94, from "The Stereochemical Theory of Odor," by J. E. Amoore, J. W. Johnston, Jr., and M. Rubin, *Scientific American,* February 1964, *210* (2), 42–49. Copyright © 1964 by Scientific American, Inc. All rights reserved.

Figure 3-38, p. 94, from "The Stereochemical Theory of Odor," by J. E. Amoore, J. W. Johnston, Jr., and M. Rubin, *Scientific American,* February 1964, *210* (2), 44–45. Copyright © 1964 by Scientific American, Inc. All rights reserved.

News story, p. 95, reprinted by permission of Knight-Ridder Newspapers.

News story, p. 96, reprinted with permission from *Science News,* the weekly newsmagazine of science, copyright 1978 by Science Service, Inc.

News story, p. 100, reprinted by permission of United Press International.

News story, p. 101, reprinted by permission of Associated Press.

Photo, p. 101, courtesy of Wide World Photos. Caption from *Boulder Sunday Camera,* September 30, 1979. Reprinted by permission.

Figure 3-41, p. 101, adapted from *Hearing and Deafness,* revised edition, edited by Hallowell Davis and S. Richard Silverman, p. 102. Copyright 1947, © 1960 by Holt, Rinehart and Winston, Inc. Reprinted by permission of Holt, Rinehart and Winston and C. C. Bunch.

Figure 3-42, p. 102, adapted from *Hearing and Deafness,* revised edition, edited by Hallowell Davis and S. Richard Silverman, p. 107. Copyright 1974, © 1960 by Holt, Rinehart and Winston, Inc. Reprinted by permission of Holt, Rinehart and Winston and *Journal of Acoustic Society of America.* Data from "1954 Wisconsin State Fair Hearing Survey," by A. Glorig et al., American Academy of Ophthalmology and Autolaryngology, 1937, and from Glorig, Quiggle, Wheeler, and Grings, *Journal of the Acoustic Society of America, 28* 1110–1113 (1956). Reprinted by permission of the authors.

News story, p. 102, copyright 1975 by Newsweek, Inc. All rights reserved. Reprinted by permission.

News story, p. 103, © Field Enterprises, Inc., 1977. Article by Michael Dixon reprinted with permission.

Chapter 3 Color Plates

Plate 2, from *Fundamentals of Child Development* by Harry Munsinger. Copyright © 1971 by Holt, Rinehart and Winston, Inc. Reprinted by permission of Holt, Rinehart and Winston.

Plate 3, left portion, standard chromaticity diagram, adapted from *Sight and Mind: An Introduction to Visual Perception,* by Lloyd Kaufman. Copyright © 1974 by Oxford University Press, Inc. Reprinted by permission.

Plate 4, from R. M. Evans, *An Introduction to Color* (New York: Wiley, 1948). Reprinted by permission.

Plate 5, by permission of Inmont Corporation.

Plate 6, by permission of Inmont Corporation.

Plate 7, from AO Pseudo-Isochromatic Color Tests by American Optical Corporation. Reprinted by permission.

Plate 8, reprinted by permission of The Museum of Modern Art.

Plate 10, © copyright 1953, 1972 CIBA Pharmaceutical Company, Division of CIBA-GEIGY Corporation. Reproduced, with permission, from *The Ciba Collection of Medical Illustrations* by Frank H. Netter, M.D. All rights reserved.

Plate 11, © copyright 1953, 1972 CIBA Pharmaceutical Company, Division of CIBA-GEIGY Corporation. Reproduced, with permission, from *The Ciba Collection of Medical Illustrations* by Frank H. Netter, M.D. All rights reserved.

Plate 12, © copyright 1953, 1972 CIBA Pharmaceutical Company, Division of CIBA-GEIGY Corporation. Reproduced, with permission, from *The Ciba Collection of Medical Illustrations* by Frank H. Netter, M.D. All rights reserved.

Plate 13, © copyright 1953, 1972 CIBA Pharmaceutical Company, Division of CIBA-GEIGY Corporation. Reproduced, with permission, from *The Ciba Collection of Medical Illustrations* by Frank H. Netter, M.D. All rights reserved.

Chapter 4

Photo, p. 104, by Jeff Albertson, courtesy of Stock, Boston.

Figure 4-1, p. 106, adapted from C. T. Morgan and R. A. King, *Introduction to Psychology* (New York: McGraw-Hill, 1966). Reprinted by permission. Also adapted from Pavlov, 1928.

News story, p. 107, reprinted by permission of *TIME,* The Weekly Newsmagazine; Copyright Time Inc. 1956.

Figure 4-6, p. 111, photo by Nina Leen. *Life* Magazine, © Time Inc.

Figure 4-7, p. 113, photo courtesy of Yerkes Regional Primate Research Center, Emory University.

News story, p. 116, reprinted with permission of author and publisher from: Blue, Richard, "Use of Punishment in Treatment of Anorexia Nervosa," *Psychological Reports,* 1979, *44,* 743–746.

Photo, p. 120, by Charles Moore, courtesy of Black Star.

Table 4-3, p. 122, adapted from Logan, Frank A., and William C. Gordon, *Fundamentals of Learning and Motivation,* 3rd ed. © 1969, 1970, 1976, 1981 Wm. C. Brown Company Publishers, Dubuque, Iowa. Reprinted by permission.

Figure 4-8, p. 123, reprinted with permission of author and publisher from Guttman, N., "The Pigeon and the Spectrum and Other Perplexities," *Psychological Reports,* 1956, *2,* 449–460.

News story, p. 133, reprinted by permission of the *Denver Post.*

Highlight 4-4, p. 133, text courtesy of Sears, Roebuck and Co.

Figure 4-11, p. 133, photo courtesy of Sears, Roebuck and Co.

News story, p. 134, reprinted by permission of United Press International.

Photo, p. 135, courtesy of Carl R. Gustavson.

Photo, p. 136, by Owen Franken, courtesy of Stock, Boston.

News story, p. 138, © 1976, The Washington Post Company. Reprinted with permission.

News story, p. 139, reprinted by permission from *TIME,* The Weekly Newsmagazine; Copyright Time Inc. 1972.

News story, p. 140, reprinted by permission of the *Denver Post.*

Chapter 5

Photo, p. 142, by Christopher Morrow, courtesy of Stock, Boston.

Photo, p. 145, courtesy of Sam Teicher.

Figure 5–1, p. 146, adapted from J. D. Bransford and J. J. Franks, "The Abstraction of Linguistic Ideas," *Cognitive Psychology,* 1971, 2, 331–350. Reprinted by permission of Academic Press.

News story, p. 149, © 1981 by The New York Times Company. Reprinted by permission.

News story, p. 158, reprinted by permission of *Pittsburgh Post-Gazette.*

Figure 5–6, p. 160, adapted from A. M. Collins and M. R. Quillian, "Retrieval Time from Semantic Memory," *Journal of Verbal Learning and Verbal Behavior,* 1969, 8, 240–247. Copyright 1969 by Academic Press. Reprinted by permission of Academic Press and the authors.

News story, pp. 164–165, copyright 1981 by Newsweek, Inc. All rights reserved. Reprinted by permission.

Figure 5–7, p. 167, from L. Carmichael, H. P. Hogan, and A. Walter, "An Experimental Study of the Effect of Language on the Reproduction of Visually Perceived Form," *Journal of Experimental Psychology,* 1932, 15, pp. 75, 80. Copyright 1932 by the American Psychological Association. Reprinted by permission of the publisher.

Photo, p. 168, by Jean-Claude Lejeune, courtesy of Stock, Boston.

Highlight 5–8, p. 170, based on P. A. Kolers, "Bilingualism and Information Processing," *Scientific American,* March 1968, pp. 78–86. Copyright © 1968 by Scientific American Inc. All rights reserved. Reprinted by permission.

Drawing, p. 173, from J. D. Bransford and M. K. Johnson, "Considerations of Some Problems of Comprehension," in W. G. Chase (ed.), *Visual Information Processing* (New York: Academic Press, 1973). Reprinted by permission.

News story, p. 175, reprinted from *Psychology Today Magazine.* Copyright © 1980 Ziff-Davis Publishing Co.

News story, p. 178, copyright 1979, by Newsweek, Inc. All rights reserved. Reprinted by permission.

Chapter 6

Photo, p. 180, by Bohdan Hrynewych, courtesy of Stock, Boston.

News story, p. 182, reprinted from *Discover* Magazine © 1981 Time Inc. All rights reserved.

Figure 6–1, p. 186, after W. J. McKeachie and C. L. Doyle, *Psychology,* second edition, © 1970, Addison-Wesley, Reading, Massachusetts. Reprinted with permission.

Table 6–1, p. 187, adapted from p. 109 of Abraham S. Luchins and Edith H. Luchins, *Rigidity of Behavior* (Eugene: University of Oregon Press, 1959), which describes experiments that minimized and maximized Einstelling effects and recovery in arithmetic problems, anagrams, and mazes, as well as other material. Reprinted by permission of the authors.

News story, p. 192, © 1980 by The New York Times Company. Reprinted by permission.

Figure 6–9, p. 200, illustration from *The Mind of a Dolphin* by John Cunningham Lilly. Copyright © 1967 by John Cunningham Lilly. Reprinted by permission of Doubleday & Company, Inc.

Photo, p. 201, courtesy of Wide World Photos.

News story, p. 202, reprinted by permission from *TIME,* The Weekly Newsmagazine; Copyright Time Inc. 1980.

Figure 6–10, p. 203, reprinted by permission from "Chimpanzee Problem Solving: A Test for Comprehension," by Premack, D., and Woodruff, G., *Science,* Vol. 202, pp. 532–535, Fig. 1, 3 November 1978. Copyright 1978 by the American Association for the Advancement of Science. Photos courtesy of D. Premack.

Figure 6–11, p. 204, reprinted by permission from *The Thinking Computer, Mind inside Matter,* by Bertram Raphael. W. H. Freeman and Company. Copyright © 1976.

Figure 6–12, p. 204, reprinted by permission from T. Winograd, *Understanding Natural Language* (New York: Academic Press, 1972), fig. 3, p. 8.

Figure 6–13, p. 204, reprinted by permission from T. Winograd, *Understanding Natural Language* (New York: Academic Press, 1972), pp. 8–10.

Highlight 6–3, p. 206, based on C. Loehlin et al., *Race Differences in Intelligence* (San Francisco: W. H. Freeman, 1975). Used by permission.

News story, p. 207, reprinted by permission of United Press International.

Table 6–4, p. 209, adapted from D. Wechsler, *The Measurement and Appraisal of Adult Intelligence,* 4th ed., © 1958 the Williams & Wilkins Co., Baltimore. Reprinted by permission.

Table 6–5, p. 209, after a report of the President's Commission on Mental Retardation, 1963, by F. H. Sanford and L. S. Wrightsman, in *Psychology: A Scientific Study of Man,* 3rd ed. (Monterey, Calif.: Brooks/Cole Publishing, 1970).

Figure 6–14, p. 211, from Joy Paul Guilford, *The Nature of Human Intelligence* (New York: McGraw-Hill, 1967), end paper and front fly leaf.

Boxes, pp. 211 and 213, adapted from F. Barron, "The Psychology of Imagination," *Scientific American,* September 1958. Reprinted by permission of the author.

Photo, p. 217, by Frank Siteman, courtesy of Stock, Boston.

Figure 6–16, p. 218, adapted by permission from R. C. Schank and R. Abelson, *Scripts, Plans, Goals and Understanding* (Hillsdale, N.J.: Erlbaum, 1977), pp. 227 ff.

News story, p. 218, reprinted by permission of *Rocky Mountain News.*

Text excerpt, p. 219, from Brendan Maher, *Principles of Psychotherapy* (New York: McGraw-Hill, 1966).

News story, p. 220, reprinted by permission of *Science 81* Magazine, copyright the American Association for the Advancement of Science.

News story, p. 221, reprinted by permission of United Press International.

News story, pp. 222–223, copyright 1977 by Editorial Projects for Education, 1977. Reprinted by permission.

Chapter 7

Photo, p. 225, by Michael Hayman, courtesy of Stock, Boston.

News story, p. 229, reprinted by permission of United Press International.

Figure 7–1, p. 230, photo from R. A. Butler, "Incentive Conditions Which Influence Visual Exploration," *Journal of Experimental Psychology,* 1954, 48, 19–23. Copyright 1954 by the American Psychological Association. Reprinted by permission. Photo courtesy of Harry F. Harlow, University of Wisconsin Primate Laboratory.

Figure 7–2, p. 232, photo courtesy of Neal E. Miller.

News story, p. 233, copyright © 1978 by the Chicago Daily News.

News story, p. 235, © 1978 by The New York Times Company. Reprinted by permission.

Photo, p. 235, by Barbara Alper, courtesy of Stock, Boston.

Figure 7–3, p. 237, photo courtesy of Dr. Peter Milner, Psychology Department, McGill University, Montreal, Quebec, Canada.

Figure 7–5, p. 238, reprinted by permission from D. L. Hebb, *Textbook of Psychology,* 3rd ed. (Philadelphia: W. B. Saunders, 1972), p. 199.

Figure 7–7, p. 240, from *A Biology of Human Concern* by William Etkin, Robert M. Devlin, and Thomas G. Bouffard. Reprinted by permission of the publisher, J. P. Lippincott Company. Copyright © 1972.

Figure 7–8, p. 242, from *Ethology: The Biology of Behavior,* Second Edition, by Irenäus Eibl-Eibesfeldt. Copyright © 1970, 1975 by Holt, Rinehart and Winston, Inc. Reprinted by permission of Holt, Rinehart and Winston, Inc. After N. Tinbergen, *The Study of Instinct* (New York and London: Oxford University Press, 1951). Used by permission.

Figure 7–9, p. 244, photo by Lyn Gardiner, courtesy of Stock, Boston.

Table 7–2, p. 245, from *Explorations in Personality: A Clinical and Experimental Study of Fifty Men of College Age.* By the Workers at the Harvard Psychological Clinic. Edited by Henry A. Murray. Copyright © 1938 by Oxford University Press, Inc. Renewed 1966 by Henry A. Murray. Reprinted by permission of the publisher. Also from C. S. Hall and G. Lindzey, *Theories of Personality* (New York: Wiley, 1957). Reprinted by permission.

Figure 7–10, p. 246, adapted from Abraham H. Maslow, "A Theory of Human Motivation," *Psychological Review,* 1943, *50,* 370–396.

Photo, p. 249, by Abigail Heyman, Magnum Photos.

News story, p. 252, reprinted by permission from *Psychology Today Magazine.* Copyright © 1980 Ziff-Davis Publishing Company.

News story, p. 254, reprinted with permission from *Science News,* the weekly newsmagazine of science, copyright 1978 by Science Service, Inc.

News stories, p. 255: Left, reprinted by permission from *Psychology Today Magazine.* Copyright © 1979 Ziff-Davis Publishing Company. Right, reprinted by permission from *TIME,* The Weekly Newsmagazine; Copyright Time Inc. 1980.

News story, p. 257, reprinted by permission of United Press International.

Figure 7–12, p. 260, photos from Neal Miller, "Theory and Experiment Relating Psycho-analytic Displacement to Stimulus-Response Generalization," *Journal of Abnormal and Social Psychology,* 1948, *43,* 155–178. Photos courtesy of Neal Miller.

Figure 7–13, p. 261, from Hans Selye, *The Physiology and Pathology of Exposure to Stress,* 1950, ACTA, Montreal. Reprinted by permission of the International Institute of Stress.

News story, p. 263, reprinted by permission of Associated Press.

News story, p. 264, reprinted by permission from *TIME,* The Weekly Newsmagazine; Copyright Time Inc. 1980.

News story, p. 267, reprinted by permission from *Psychology Today Magazine.* Copyright © 1980 Ziff-Davis Publishing Company.

News story, p. 270, reprinted by permission from *TIME,* The Weekly Newsmagazine; Copyright Time Inc. 1977.

News story, p. 272, © 1979 by The New York Times Company. Reprinted by permission.

News story, p. 273, reprinted with permission from *Science News,* the weekly newsmagazine of science, copyright 1979 by Science Service, Inc.

Chapter 8

Photo, p. 275, by Abigail Heyman, courtesy of Magnum Photos.

News story, p. 280, reprinted with permission from *Science News,* the weekly newsmagazine of science, copyright 1979 by Science Service, Inc.

News story, p. 281, from *Chicago Tribune,* March 21, 1976.

Figure 8–2, p. 282, adapted from J. H. Flavell, "Stage-Related Properties of Cognitive Development," in *Cognitive Psychology,* 1971, Vol. 2. Reprinted by permission of Academic Press.

Photo, p. 283, courtesy of Wide World Photos.

News story, p. 284, copyrighted ©, Chicago Tribune. Used with permission.

Figure 8–3, p. 284, adapted from R. L. Fantz, "Visual Perception and Experience in Early Infancy: A Look at the Hidden Side of Behavior Development," in H. W. Stevenson, E. H. Hess, and H. L. Rheingold (Eds.), *Early Behavior: Comparative and Developmental Approaches* (New York: Wiley, 1967). Reprinted by permission.

Figure 8–4, p. 285, from "The Origin of Form Perception" by R. L. Fantz. Copyright © 1961 by Scientific American Inc. All rights reserved. Reprinted by permission.

Figure 8–5, p. 285, photos from E. J. Gibson and R. D. Walk, "The Visual Cliff," *Scientific American,* April 1960. Photos courtesy of William Vandivert.

Figure 8–6, p. 286, adapted from E. J. Gibson, "The Ontogeny of Reading," *American Psychologist,* 1970, *25,* 136–143. Copyright 1970 by the American Psychological Association. Reprinted by permission. Taken from research by Linda Lavine.

News story, p. 287, reprinted by permission of United Press International.

News story, p. 288, copyright 1980 by Newsweek, Inc. All rights reserved. Reprinted by permission.

News story, p. 289, reprinted with permission from *Science News,* the weekly newsmagazine of science, copyright 1979 by Science Service, Inc. Based on Suzanne Chevalier-Skolnikoff, "Kids: Zoo Research Reveals Remarkable Similarities in the Development of Human and Orang-utan Babies . . . and One Very Special Difference," *Animal Kingdom,* June–July 1979, pp. 11–18.

Figure 8–7, p. 290, photos from A. T. Jersild, *Child Psychology,* 6th ed. (Englewood Cliffs, N.J.: Prentice-Hall, 1968). Photos by George Zimbel of Monkmeyer Press.

Figure 8–9, p. 293, adapted from Figure 6 from *The Growth of Logical Thinking: From Childhood to Adolescence* by Barbel Inhelder and Jean Piaget, translated by Anne Parsons and Stanley Milgran. © 1958 by Basic Books, Inc., Publishers, New York. Reprinted by permission.

Table 8–2, p. 294, from Roger Brown and Ursula Bellugi, "Three Processes in the Child's Acquisition of Syntax," *Harvard Educational Review,* 34, Spring 1964, 133–151. Copyright © 1964 by the President and Fellows of Harvard College. Reprinted by permission.

News story, p. 295, reprinted by permission from *TIME,* The Weekly Newsmagazine; Copyright Time Inc. 1976.

News story, p. 296, reprinted with permission from *Science News,* the weekly newsmagazine of science, copyright 1977 by Science Service, Inc.

Figure 8–10, p. 297, photos courtesy of Harry F. Harlow, University of Wisconsin Primate Laboratory.

News story, p. 298, copyright 1981 by Newsweek, Inc. All rights reserved. Reprinted by permission.

News story, p. 299, reprinted by permission from *TIME,* The Weekly Newsmagazine; Copyright Time Inc. 1978.

News story, p. 303, reprinted by permission from *Psychology Today Magazine.* Copyright © 1980 Ziff-Davis Publishing Company.

News story, p. 304, reprinted by permission from *Psychology Today Magazine.* Copyright © 1980 Ziff-Davis Publishing Company.

Figure 8–12, p. 305, adapted from F. K. Shuttleworth, "The Adolescent Period," *Monographs of the Society for Research in Child Development,* 3 (3), 1938. © The Society for Research in Child Development, Inc. Reprinted by permission.

Table 8–3, p. 306, from "The Development of Moral Character

Name Index

Subject Index